HARPER COLLINS
PORTUGUESE
DICTIONARY

PORTUGUESE•ENGLISH ENGLISH•PORTUGUESE

HarperResource
An Imprint of HarperCollins*Publishers*

ISBN 0-06-273748-1

The HarperCollins website address is
www.harpercollins.com

The HarperCollins UK website address is
www.fireandwater.com

Harper*Resource*   A Division of HarperCollins*Publishers*
10 East 53rd Street, New York, N.Y. 10022

first published 1990
second edition 2000

© William Collins Sons & Co. Ltd. 1990
© HarperCollins Publishers 2000

First Harper*Resource* printing: 2000

Typeset by Morton Word Processing Ltd, Scarborough
Printed in the United States of America

10 9 8

Harper*Resource* and colophons are trademarks of
HarperCollins*Publishers*

ÍNDICE

CONTENTS

INTRODUÇÃO

O mini-dicionário de Português da Collins foi concebido para dar a você um vocabulário abrangente e atual num formato compacto e de fácil manuseio. Entre suas características se destacam:

–cobertura completa das palavras mais atuais

–verbetes discriminados com indicadores dos diversos significados dos vocábulos para ajudá-lo a encontrar a exata tradução que você precisa (assim como aquelas que você deveria evitar)

–numerosas expressões idiomáticas e exemplos de frases para lhe dar confiança em se expressar com clareza, precisão e naturalidade

–as principais formas irregulares de verbos e substantivos inseridas alfabetimamente no texto para ajudar você a encontrá-las com rapidez e facilidade

–e todas as mais comuns abreviaturas, siglas e topônimos

Então, se você quiser ler, entender ou comunicar-se em Inglês, você encontrará todo o vocabulário que você precisa minuciosamente tratado neste dicionário. Na casa ou na escola, no trabalho ou nas férias, o minidicionário de Português Collins será uma obra de consulta com valor inestimável.

ABREVIATURAS

ABBREVIATIONS

abreviatura	**ab(b)r**	abbreviation
adjetivo	**adj**	adjective
administração	**ADMIN**	administration
advérbio, locução adverbial	**adv**	adverb, adverbial phrase
aeronáutica	**AER**	flying, air travel
agricultura	**AGR**	agriculture
anatomia	**ANAT**	anatomy
arquitetura	**ARQ, ARCH**	architecture
artigo definido	**art def**	definite article
artigo indefinido	**art indef**	indefinite article
uso atributivo do substantivo	**atr**	compound element
automobilismo	**AUT(O)**	the motor car and motoring
auxiliar	**aux**	auxiliary
aeronáutica	**AVIAT**	flying, air travel
biologia	**BIO**	biology
botânica, flores	**BOT**	botany
português do Brasil	**BR**	Brazilian
inglês britânico	**BRIT**	British English
química	**CHEM**	chemistry
linguagem coloquial (!chulo)	**col(!)**	colloquial (!offensive)
comércio, finanças, bancos	**COM(M)**	commerce, finance, banking
comparativo	**compar**	comparative
computação	**COMPUT**	computing
conjunção	**conj**	conjunction
construção	**CONSTR**	building
uso atributivo do substantivo	**cpd**	compound element
cozinha	**CULIN**	cookery
artigo definido	**def art**	definite article
economia	**ECON**	economics
educação, escola e universidade	**EDUC**	schooling, schools and universities
eletricidade, eletrônica	**ELET, ELEC**	electricity, electronics
especialmente	**esp**	especially
exclamação	**excl**	exclamation
feminino	**f**	feminine
ferrovia	**FERRO**	railways
uso figurado	**fig**	figurative use
física	**FÍS**	physics
fotografia	**FOTO**	photography
(verbo inglês) do qual a partícula é inseparável	**fus**	(phrasal verb) where the particle is inseparable
geralmente	**gen**	generally
geografia, geologia	**GEO**	geography, geology
geralmente	**ger**	generally
impessoal	**impess, impers**	impersonal
artigo indefinido	**indef art**	indefinite article
linguagem coloquial (! chulo)	**inf (!)**	informal (! offensive)
infinitivo	**infin**	infinitive
invariável	**inv**	invariable
irregular	**irreg**	irregular

ABREVIATURAS

ABBREVIATIONS

jurídico	JUR	law
gramática, lingüística	LING	grammar, linguistics
masculino	m	masculine
matemática	MAT(H)	mathematics, calculus
medicina	MED	medicine
ou masculino ou feminino, dependendo do sexo da pessoa	m/f	masculine/feminine
militar, exército	MIL	military matters
música	MÚS, MUS	music
substantivo	n	noun
navegação, náutica	NÁUT, NAUT	sailing, navigation
adjetivo ou substantivo numérico	num	numeral adjective or noun
	o.s.	oneself
pejorativo	pej	pejorative
fotografia	PHOT	photography
física	PHYS	physics
fisiologia	PHYSIO	physiology
plural	pl	plural
política	POL	politics
particípio passado	pp	past participle
preposição	prep	preposition
pronome	pron	pronoun
português de Portugal	PT	European Portuguese
pretérito	pt	past tense
química	QUÍM	chemistry
religião e cultos	REL	religion, church services
	sb	somebody
educação, escola e universidade	SCH	schooling, schools and universities
singular	sg	singular
	sth	something
sujeito (gramatical)	su(b)j	(grammatical) subject
subjuntivo, conjuntivo	sub(jun)	subjunctive
superlativo	superl	superlative
também	tb	also
técnica, tecnologia	TEC(H)	technical term, technology
telecomunicações	TEL	telecommunications
tipografia, imprensa	TIP	typography, printing
televisão	TV	television
tipografia, imprensa	TYP	typography, printing
inglês americano	US	American English
ver	V	see
verbo	vb	verb
verbo intransitivo	vi	intransitive verb
verbo reflexivo	vr	reflexive verb
verbo transitivo	vt	transitive verb
zoologia	ZOOL	zoology
marca registrada	®	registered trademark
indica um equivalente cultural	≈	introduces a cultural equivalent

PRONÚNCIA INGLESA

Vogais e ditongos

	Exemplo Inglês	Explicação
[aː]	father	Entre o *a* de p*a*dre e o *o* de n*ó*; como en f*a*da
[ʌ]	b*u*t, c*o*me	Aproximadamente como o primeiro *a* de c*a*ma
[æ]	m*a*n, c*a*t	Som entre o *a* de l*á* e o *e* de p*é*
[ə]	fath*er*, *a*go	Som parecido com o *e* final pronunciado em Portugal
[əː]	b*i*rd, h*ea*rd	Entre o *e* aberto e o *o* fechado
[ɛ]	g*e*t, b*e*d	Como em p*é*
[ɪ]	*i*t, b*i*g	Mais breve do que em s*i*
[iː]	t*ea*, s*ee*	Como em f*i*no
[ɔ]	h*o*t, w*a*sh	Como em p*ó*
[ɔː]	s*a*w, *a*ll	Como o *o* de p*o*rte
[u]	p*u*t, b*oo*k	Som breve e mais fechado do que em b*u*rro
[uː]	t*oo*, y*ou*	Som aberto como em j*u*ro
[aɪ]	fl*y*, h*i*gh	Como em b*ai*le
[au]	h*o*w, h*ou*se	Como em c*au*sa
[ɛə]	th*ere*, b*ear*	Como o *e* de a*e*roporto
[eɪ]	d*ay*, ob*ey*	Como o *ei* de l*ei*
[ɪə]	h*ere*, h*ear*	Como *ia* de companh*ia*
[əu]	g*o*, n*o*te	[ə] seguido de um *u* breve
[ɔɪ]	b*oy*, *oi*l	Como em b*ói*a
[uə]	p*oor*, s*ure*	Como *ua* em s*ua*

Consoantes

	Exemplo Inglês	*Explicação*
[d]	men*d*ed	Como em *d*a*d*o, an*d*ar
[g]	*g*et, bi*g*	Como em *g*rande
[dʒ]	*g*in, ju*dg*e	Como em ida*d*e
[ŋ]	si*ng*	Como em ci*n*co
[h]	*h*ouse, *h*e	*h* aspirado
[j]	*y*oung, *y*es	Como em *i*ogurte
[k]	*c*ome, mo*ck*	Como em *c*ama
[r]	*r*ed, t*r*ead	*r* como em pa*r*a, mas pronunciado no céu da boca
[s]	*s*and, ye*s*	Como em *s*ala
[z]	ro*s*e, *z*ebra	Como em *z*ebra
[ʃ]	*sh*e, ma*ch*ine	Como em *ch*apéu
[tʃ]	*ch*in, ri*ch*	Como *t* em *t*imbre
[w]	*w*ater, *wh*ich	Como o *u* em á*gu*a
[ʒ]	vi*s*ion	Como em *j*á
[θ]	*th*ink, my*th*	Sem equivalente, aproximadamente como um *s* pronunciado entre os dentes
[ð]	*th*is, *th*e	Sem equivalente, aproximadamente como um *z* pronunciado entre os dentes

b, f, l, m, n, p, t, v pronunciam-se como em português.

O signo [*] indica que o *r* final escrito pronuncia-se apenas em inglês britânico, excepto quando a palavra seguinte começa por uma vogal. O signo ['] indica a sílaba acentuada.

A

PALAVRA CHAVE
---

a [a] *(a + o(s) = ao(s); a + a(s) = à(s); a + aquele/a(s) = àquele/a(s))* art def the; V tb **o**

♦ *pron (ela)* her; *(você)* you; *(coisa)* it; V tb **o**

♦ *prep* **1** *(direção)* to; **à direita/esquerda** to *ou* on the right/left **2** *(distância)*: **está ~ 15 km daqui** it's 15 km from here **3** *(posição)*: **ao lado de** beside, at the side of **4** *(tempo)* at; **~ que horas?** at what time?; **às 5 horas** at 5 o'clock; **à noite** at night; **aos 15 anos** at 15 years of age **5** *(maneira)*: **à francesa** in the French way; **~ cavalo/pé** on horseback/foot **6** *(meio, instrumento)*: **à força** by force; **~ mão** by hand; **~ lápis** in pencil; **fogão ~ gás** gas stove **7** *(razão)*: **~ Cr$300 o quilo** at Cr$300 a kilo; **~ mais de 100 km/h** at over 100 km/h **8** *(depois de certos verbos)*: **começou ~ nevar** it started snowing *ou* to snow; **passar ~ fazer** to become **9** *(+ infin)*: **ao vê-lo, o reconheci imediatamente** when I saw him, I recognized him immediately; **ele ficou muito nervoso ao falar com o professor** he became very nervous while he was talking to the teacher **10** *(PT: + infin: gerúndio)*: **~ correr** running; **estou ~ trabalhar** I'm working

à [a] = **a + a**

(a) *abr (= assinado)* signed

aba [ˈaba] *f (de chapéu)* brim; *(de casaco)* tail; *(de montanha)* foot

abacate [abaˈkatʃi] *m* avocado (pear)

abacaxi [abakaˈʃi] *(BR) m* pineapple

abade(ssa) [aˈbadʒi/abaˈdesa] *m/f* abbot/abbess; **abadia** [abaˈdʒia] *f* abbey

abafado/a [abaˈfadu/a] *adj (ar)* stuffy; *(tempo)* humid, close; *(ocupado)* (extremely) busy; *(angustiado)* anxious

abafar [abaˈfa*] *vt* to suffocate; *(ocultar)* to suppress; *(col)* to pinch

abagunçado/a [abagũˈsadu/a] *adj* messy

abagunçar [abagũˈsa*] *vt* to mess up

abaixar [abajˈʃa*] *vt* to lower; *(luz, som)* to turn down; **~-se** *vr* to stoop

abaixo [aˈbajʃu] *adv* down ♦ *prep*: **~ de**

below; **~ o governo!** down with the government!; **morro ~** downhill; **rio ~** downstream; **mais ~** further down; **~ e acima** up and down; **~ assinado** undersigned; **~-assinado** [-asiˈnadu] *(pl ~-assinados)* *m* petition

abajur [abaˈʒu*] *(BR) m (cúpula)* lampshade; *(luminária)* table lamp

abalado/a [abaˈladu/a] *adj (objeto)* unstable, unsteady; *(fig: pessoa)* shaken

abalar [abaˈla*] *vt* to shake; *(fig: comover)* to affect ♦ *vi* to shake; **~-se** *vr* to be moved

abalizado/a [abaliˈzadu/a] *adj* eminent, distinguished; *(opinião)* reliable

abalo [aˈbalu] *m (comoção)* shock; *(ação)* shaking; **~ sísmico** earth tremor

abanar [abaˈna*] *vt* to shake; *(rabo)* to wag; *(com leque)* to fan

abandonar [abãdoˈna*] *vt* to leave; *(idéia)* to reject; *(esperança)* to give up; *(descuidar)* to neglect; **~-se** *vr*: **~-se a** to abandon o.s. to; **abandono** [abãˈdonu] *m (ato)* desertion; *(estado)* neglect

abarcar [abaxˈka*] *vt (abranger: assunto, país)* to cover; *(: suj: vista)* to take in

abarrotado/a [abaxoˈtadu/a] *adj (gaveta)* crammed full; *(lugar)* packed

abarrotar [abaxoˈta*] *vt*: **~ de** to cram with

abastado/a [abaʃˈtadu/a] *adj* wealthy

abastança [abaʃˈtãsa] *f* abundance

abastardar [abaʃtaxˈda*] *vt* to corrupt

abastecer [abaʃteˈse*] *vt* to supply; *(motor)* to fuel; *(AUTO)* to fill up; *(AER)* to refuel; **~-se** *vr*: **~-se de** to stock up with

abastecimento [abaʃtesiˈmẽtu] *m* supply; *(comestíveis)* provisions *pl*; *(ato)* supplying; **~s** *mpl (suprimentos)* supplies

abater [abaˈte*] *vt (gado)* to slaughter; *(preço)* to reduce; *(desalentar)* to upset; **abatido/a** [abaˈtʃidu/a] *adj (fig)* depressed, downcast; **abatimento** [abatʃiˈmẽtu] *m (fraqueza)* weakness; *(de preço)* reduction; *(prostração)* depression; **fazer um abatimento em** to give a discount on

abaulado/a [abawˈladu/a] *adj* convex; *(estrada)* cambered

abaular-se [abawˈlaxsi] *vr* to bulge

abcesso [abˈsɛsu] *m* = **abscesso**

abdicação [abdʒikaˈsãw] *(pl –ões)* *f* abdication

abdicar [abdʒiˈka*] *vt, vi* to abdicate

abdômen [abˈdomẽ] *m* abdomen

á-bê-cê [abeˈse] *m* alphabet

abecedário [abeseˈdarju] *m* alphabet,

ABC

abeirar [abej'ra*] vt to bring near; ~-se vr: ~-se de to draw near to

abelha [a'beʎa] f bee; ~-**mestra** (pl ~s-mestras) f queen bee

abelhudo/a [abe'ʎudu/a] adj nosy

abençoar [abẽ'swa*] vt to bless

aberração [abexa'sãw] (pl ~ões) f aberration

aberto/a [a'bɛxtu/a] pp de abrir ♦ adj open; (céu) clear; (sinal) green; (torneira) running; **a torneira estava aberta** the tap was on

abertura [abex'tura] f opening; (FOTO) aperture; (ranhura) gap, crevice; (POL) liberalization

abestalhado/a [abeʃta'ʎadu/a] adj stupid

abilolado/a [abilo'ladu/a] adj crazy

abismado/a [abiʒ'madu/a] adj astonished

abismo [a'biʒmu] m abyss, chasm; (fig) depths pl

abjeção [abʒe'sãw] (PT -cç-) f baseness

abjeto/a [ab'ʒɛtu/a] (PT -ct-) adj abject, contemptible

abnegação [abnega'sãw] f self-denial

abnegado/a [abne'gadu/a] adj self-sacrificing

abnegar [abne'ga*] vt to renounce

abóbada [a'bɔbada] f vault; (telhado) arched roof

abobalhado/a [aboba'ʎadu/a] adj (criança) simple

abóbora [a'bɔbora] f pumpkin

abobrinha [abo'briɲa] f courgette (BRIT), zucchini (US)

abolição [aboli'sãw] f abolition

abolir [abo'li*] vt to abolish

abominação [abomina'sãw] (pl ~ões) f abomination

abominar [abomi'na*] vt to loathe, detest

abonar [abo'na*] vt to guarantee

abono [a'bonu] m guarantee; (JUR) bail; (louvor) praise; ~ **de família** child benefit

abordagem [abox'daʒẽ] (pl ~ns) f approach

abordar [abox'da*] vt (NÁUT) to board; (pessoa) to approach; (assunto) to broach, tackle

aborígene [abo'riʒeni] m/f aborigine

aborrecer [aboxe'se*] vt (chatear) to annoy; (maçar) to bore; ~-se vr to get upset; to get bored; **aborrecido/a** [aboxe'sidu/a] adj annoyed; boring; **aborrecimento** [aboxesi'mẽtu] m annoyance; boredom

abortar [abox'ta*] vi (MED) to have a miscarriage; (: de propósito) to have an abortion; **aborto** [a'boxtu] m miscarriage; abortion; **fazer/ter um aborto** to have an abortion/a miscarriage

abotoadura [abotwa'dura] f cufflink

abotoar [abo'twa*] vt to button up ♦ vi (BOT) to bud

abraçar [abra'sa*] vt to hug; (causa) to

embrace; ~-**se** vr to embrace; **ele abraçou-se a mim** he embraced me; **abraço** [a'brasu] m embrace, hug; **com um abraço** (em carta) with best wishes

abrandar [abrã'da*] vt to reduce; (suavizar) to soften ♦ vi to diminish; (acalmar) to calm down

abranger [abrã'ʒe*] vt (assunto) to cover; (alcançar) to reach

abrasar [abra'za*] vt to burn; (desbastar) to erode ♦ vi to be on fire

abre-garrafas ['abri-] (PT) m inv bottle opener

abre-latas ʃ'abri-] (PT) m inv tin (BRIT) ou can opener

abreugrafia [abrewgra'fia] f X-ray

abreviar [abre'vja*] vt to abbreviate; (texto) to abridge; **abreviatura** [abrevja'tura] f abbreviation

abridor [abri'do*] (BR) m: ~ **(de lata)** tin (BRIT) ou can opener; ~ **de garrafa** bottle opener

abrigar [abri'ga*] vt to shelter; (proteger) to protect; ~-**se** vr to take shelter

abrigo [a'brigu] m shelter, cover; ~ **anti-aéreo** air-raid shelter; ~ **anti-nuclear** fall-out shelter

abril [a'briw] (PT A~) m April

abrir [a'bri*] vt to open; (fechadura) to unlock; (vestuário) to unfasten; (torneira) to turn on; (exceção) to make ♦ vi to open; (sinal) to turn green; ~-**se** vr: ~-**se com alguém** to confide in sb

abrolho [a'broʎu] m thorn

abrupto/a [a'bruptu/a] adj abrupt; (repentino) sudden

abscesso [ab'sɛsu] n abscess

abside [ab'sidʒi] f apse; (relicário) shrine

absolutamente [absoluta'mẽtʃi] adv absolutely; (em resposta) absolutely not, not at all

absoluto/a [abso'lutu/a] adj absolute; **em** ~ absolutely not, not at all

absolver [absow've*] vt to absolve; (JUR) to acquit; **absolvição** [absowvi'sãw] (pl ~ões) f absolution; acquittal

absorção [absox'sãw] f absorption

absorto/a [ab'soxtu/a] pp de absorver ♦ adj absorbed, engrossed

absorvente [absox'vẽtʃi] adj (papel etc) absorbent; (livro etc) absorbing

absorver [absox've*] vt to absorb; ~-**se** vr: ~-**se em** to concentrate on

abstêmio/a [abʃ'temju/a] adj abstemious; (álcool) teetotal ♦ m/f abstainer; teetotaller (BRIT), teetotaler (US)

abstenção [abʃtẽ'sãw] (pl ~ões) f abstention

abster-se [ab'ʃtexsi] (irreg: como ter) vr: ~ **de** to abstain ou refrain from

abstracto/a [abʃ'tratu/a] (PT) adj = abstrato

abstrair [abʃtra'i*] vt to abstract; (omitir) to omit; (separar) to separate

abstrato/a [abʃ'tratu/a] adj abstract

absurdo/a [abi'suxdu/a] *adj* absurd ♦ *m* nonsense

abulia [abu'lia] *f* apathy

abundância [abũ'dãsja] *f* abundance; **abundante** [abũ'dãtʃi] *adj* abundant; **abundar** [abũ'da*] *vi* to abound

aburguesado/a [abuxge'zadu/a] *adj* middle-class

abusar [abu'za*] *vi* to go too far; ~ **de** to abuse

abuso [a'buzu] *m* abuse; (*JUR*) indecent assault

abutre [a'butri] *m* vulture

a.C. *abr* (= *antes de Cristo*) B.C.

a/c *abr* (= *aos cuidados de*) c/o

acabado/a [aka'badu/a] *adj* finished; (*esgotado*) worn out

acabamento [akaba'mẽtu] *m* finish

acabar [aka'ba*] *vt* to finish, complete; (*consumir*) to use up; (*rematar*) to finish off ♦ *vi* to finish, end; ~**-se** *vr* to be over; (*prazo*) to expire; (*esgotar-se*) to run out; ~ **com** to put an end to; ~ **de chegar** to have just arrived; ~ **por fazer** to end up (by) doing; **acabou-se!** it's all over!; (*basta!*) that's enough!

acabrunhado/a [akabru'ɲadu/a] *adj* depressed; (*perturbado*) distressed; (*envergonhado*) embarrassed

acabrunhar [akabru'ɲa*] *vt* to depress; (*entristecer*) to distress; (*envergonhar*) to embarrass

academia [akade'mia] *f* academy; **acadêmico/a** [aka'demiku/a] *adj, m/f* academic

açafrão [asa'frãw] *m* saffron

acalentar [akalẽ'ta*] *vt* to rock to sleep; (*esperanças*) to cherish

acalmar [akaw'ma*] *vt* to calm ♦ *vi* (*vento etc*) to abate; ~**-se** *vr* to calm down

acalorado/a [akalo'radu/a] *adj* heated

acalorar [akalo'ra*] *vt* to heat; (*fig*) to inflame; ~**-se** *vr* (*fig*) to get heated

acamado/a [aka'madu/a] *adj* bedridden

acampamento [akãpa'mẽtu] *m* camping; (*MIL*) camp, encampment

acampar [akã'pa*] *vi* to camp

acanhado/a [aka'ɲadu/a] *adj* shy

acanhamento [akaɲa'mẽtu] *m* shyness

acanhar-se [aka'ɲaxsi] *vr* to be shy

ação [a'sãw] (*pl* –**ões**) *f* action; (*ato*) act, deed; (*MIL*) battle; (*enredo*) plot; (*JUR*) lawsuit; (*COM*) share; ~ **ordinária/ preferencial** (*COM*) ordinary/preference share

acarajé [akara'ʒɛ] *m* (*CULIN*) beans fried in palm oil

acarear [aka'rja*] *vt* to confront

acariciar [akari'sja*] *vt* to caress; (*fig*) to cherish

acarretar [akaxe'ta*] *vt* to result in, bring about

acaso [a'kazu] *m* chance; **ao** ~ at random; **por** ~ by chance

acastanhado/a [akaʃta'ɲadu/a] *adj* brownish; (*cabelo*) auburn

acatamento [akata'mẽtu] *m* respect, deference; (*de lei*) observance

acatar [aka'ta*] *vt* to respect; (*lei*) to obey

acautelar [akawte'la*] *vt* to warn; ~**-se** *vr* to be cautious; ~**-se contra** to guard against

acção [a'sãw] (*PT*) *f* = **ação**

accionar *etc* [asjo'na*] (*PT*) = **acionar** *etc*

aceder [ase'de*] *vi*: ~ **a** to agree to, accede to

aceitação [asejta'sãw] *f* acceptance; (*aprovação*) approval

aceitar [asej'ta*] *vt* to accept; (*aprovar*) to approve; **aceitável** [asej'tavew] (*pl* –**eis**) *adj* acceptable; **aceite** [a'sejtʃi] (*PT*) *pp de* **aceitar** ♦ *adj* accepted ♦ *m* acceptance; **aceito** [a'sejtu] *pp de* **aceitar**

acelerado/a [asele'radu/a] *adj* (*rápido*) quick; (*apressado*) hasty

acelerador [aselera'do*] *m* accelerator

acelerar [asele'ra*] *vt* (*AUTO*): ~ **o carro** to accelerate; (*ritmo, negociações*) to speed up ♦ *vi* to accelerate; ~ **o passo** to go faster

acenar [ase'na*] *vi* (*com a mão*) to wave; (*com a cabeça: afirmativo*) to nod; (: *negativo*) to shake one's head

acendedor [asẽde'do*] *m* lighter

acender [asẽ'de*] *vt* (*cigarro, fogo*) to light; (*luz*) to switch on; (*fig*) to excite, inflame

aceno [a'sɛnu] *m* sign, gesture; (*com a mão*) wave; (*com a cabeça: afirmativo*) nod; (: *negativo*) shake

acento [a'sẽtu] *m* accent; (*de intensidade*) stress; **acentuar** [asẽ'twa*] *vt* to accent; (*salientar*) to stress, emphasize

acepção [asep'sãw] (*pl* –**ões**) *f* (*de uma palavra*) sense

acepipe [ase'pipi] *m* titbit (*BRIT*), tidbit (*US*), delicacy; ~**s** *mpl* (*PT*) hors d'oeuvres

acerca [a'sexka]: ~ **de** *prep* about, concerning

acercar-se [asex'kaxsi] *vr*: ~ **de** to approach, draw near to

acérrimo/a [a'seximu/a] *adj* (*acre*) (very) bitter; (*defensor*) staunch

acertado/a [asex'tadu/a] *adj* right, correct; (*sensato*) sensible

acertar [asex'ta*] *vt* (*ajustar*) to put right; (*relógio*) to set; (*alvo*) to hit; (*acordo*) to reach; (*pergunta*) to get right ♦ *vi* to get it right, be right; ~ **o caminho** to find the right way; ~ **com** to hit upon

acervo [a'sexvu] *m* (*de museu etc*) collection; (*JUR*) estate; (*montão*) **um** ~ **de** a pile of

aceso/a [a'sezu/a] *pp de* **acender** ♦ *adj*: **a luz estava acesa/o fogo estava** ~ the light was on/the fire was alight; (*excitado*) excited; (*furioso*) furious

acessar [ase'sa*] *vt* (*COMPUT*) to access

acessível [ase'sivew] (pl -eis) adj accessible; (pessoa) approachable

acesso [a'sɛsu] m access; (MED) fit, attack

acessório/a [ase'sɔrju/a] adj (máquina, equipamento) backup; (EDUC): **matéria acessória** subsidiary subject ♦ m accessory

achado/a [a'ʃadu/a] m find, discovery; (pechincha) bargain; (sorte) godsend

achaque [a'ʃaki] m ailment

achar [a'ʃaɪ] vt (descobrir) to find; (pensar) to think; **~-se** vr to think (that) one is; (encontrar-se) to be; **~ de fazer** (resolver) to decide to do; **o que é que você acha disso?** what do you think of that?; **acho que sim** I think so

achatar [aʃa'taɪ] vt to squash, flatten

achegar-se [aʃe'gaxsi] vr: **~ a** ou **de** to approach, get closer to

acidentado/a [aside'tadu/a] adj (terreno) rough; (estrada) bumpy; (viagem) eventful; (vida) difficult ♦ m/f injured person

acidental [aside'taw] (pl -ais) adj accidental

acidente [asi'dẽtʃi] m accident; **por ~** by accident

acidez [asi'deʒ] f acidity

ácido/a [a'sidu/a] adj acid; (azedo) sour ♦ m acid

acima [a'sima] adv above; (para cima) up ♦ prep: **~ de** above; (além de) beyond; **mais ~** higher up; **rio ~** up river; **passar rua ~** to go up the street; **~ de 1000** more than 1000

acinte [a'sĩtʃi] m provocation ♦ adv on purpose; **acintosamente** [asĩtoza'mẽtʃi] adv on purpose

acionado/a [asjo'nadu/a] m/f (JUR) defendant

acionar [asjo'naɪ] vt to set in motion; (máquina) to operate; (JUR) to sue

acionista [asjo'niʃta] m/f shareholder

acirrado/a [asi'xadu/a] adj (luta, competição) tough

acirrar [asi'xaɪ] vt to incite, stir up

aclamação [aklama'sãw] f acclamation; (ovação) applause

aclamar [akla'maɪ] vt to acclaim; (aplaudir) to applaud

aço ['asu] m steel

acocorar-se [akoko'raxsi] vr to squat, crouch

acode etc [a'kɔdʒi] vb V **acudir**

ações [a'sõjʃ] fpl de **ação**

acoitar [akoj'taɪ] vt to shelter, give refuge to

açoitar [asoj'taɪ] vt to whip, lash; **açoite** [a'sojtʃi] m whip, lash

acolá [ako'la] adv over there

acolchoado [akow'ʃwadu] m quilt

acolchoar [akow'ʃwaɪ] vt to quilt; (forrar) to pad

acolhedor(a) [akoʎe'do'(a)] adj welcoming; (hospitaleiro) hospitable

acolher [ako'ʎeɪ] vt to welcome; (abrigar) to shelter; (aceitar) to accept; **~-se** vr to shelter; **acolhida** [ako'ʎida] f (recepção) reception, welcome; (refúgio) refuge; **acolhimento** [akoʎi'mẽtu] m = **acolhida**

acometer [akome'teɪ] vt to attack

acomodação [akomoda'sãw] (pl -ões) f accommodation; (arranjo) arrangement; (adaptação) adaptation

acomodar [akomo'daɪ] vt to accommodate; (arrumar) to arrange; (adaptar) to adapt

acompanhamento [akõpaɲa'mẽtu] m attendance; (cortejo) procession; (MÚS) accompaniment; (CULIN) side dish

acompanhante [akõpa'ɲãtʃi] m/f companion; (MÚS) accompanist

acompanhar [akõpa'ɲaɪ] vt to accompany

aconchegante [akõʃe'gãtʃi] adj cosy (BRIT), cozy (US)

aconchegar [akõʃe'gaɪ] vt to bring near; **~-se** vr to make o.s. comfortable; **~-se com** to snuggle up to

aconchego [akõ'ʃegu] m cuddle

acondicionar [akõdʒisjo'naɪ] vt to condition; (empacotar) to pack, wrap (up)

aconselhar [akõse'ʎaɪ] vt to advise; **~-se** vr: **~-se com** to consult

acontecer [akõte'seɪ] vi to happen; **acontecimento** [akõtesi'mẽtu] m event

acordar [akox'daɪ] vt to wake (up); (concordar) to agree (on) ♦ vi to wake up

acorde [a'kɔɪdʒi] m chord

acordeão [akox'dʒjãw] (pl -ões) m accordion

acordo [a'koxdu] m agreement; **"de ~!"** "agreed!"; **de ~ com** (pessoa) in agreement with; (conforme) in accordance with; **estar de ~** to agree

Açores [a'sorif] mpl: **os ~** the Azores; **açoriano/a** [aso'rjanu/a] adj, m/f Azorean

acorrentar [akoxẽ'taɪ] vt to chain (up)

acorrer [ako'xeɪ] vi: **~ a alguém** to come to sb's aid

acossar [ako'saɪ] vt (perseguir) to pursue; (atormentar) to harass

acostamento [akoʃta'mẽtu] m hard shoulder (BRIT), berm (US)

acostar [akoʃ'taɪ] vt to lean against; (NÁUT) to bring alongside; **~-se** vr to lean back

acostumado/a [akoʃtu'madu/a] adj usual, customary; **estar ~ a algo** to be used to sth

acostumar [akoʃtu'maɪ] vt to accustom; **~-se** vr: **~-se a** to get used to

acotovelar [akotove'laɪ] vt to jostle; **~-se** vr to jostle

açougue [a'sogi] m butcher's (shop); **~iro** [aso'gejru] m butcher

acovardar-se [akovax'daxsi] vr (desanimar) to lose courage; (amedrontar-se) to flinch, cower

acre ['akri] *adj* (*gosto*) bitter; (*cheiro*) acrid; (*fig*) harsh

acreditado/a [akredʒi'tadu/a] *adj* accredited

acreditar [akredʒi'ta*] *vt* to believe; (*COM*) to credit; (*afiançar*) to guarantee ♦ *vi*: ~ **em** to believe in; **acreditável** [akredʒi'tavew] (*pl* -**eis**) *adj* credible

acre-doce *adj* (*CULIN*) sweet and sour

acrescentar [akresẽ'ta*] *vt* to add

acrescer [akre'se*] *vt* to increase; (*juntar*) to add ♦ *vi* to increase; **acréscimo** [a'kresimu] *m* increase; addition; (*elevação*) rise

acrílico [a'kriliku] *m* acrylic

acrobata [akro'bata] *m/f* acrobat

activo/a [a'tivu/a] (*PT*) = **ativo** *etc*

acto ['atu] (*PT*) *m* = **ato**

actor [a'to*] (*PT*) *m* = **ator**

actriz [a'triʒ] (*PT*) *f* = **atriz**

actual *etc* [a'twaw] (*PT*) = **atual** *etc*

actuar *etc* [a'twa*] (*PT*) = **atuar** *etc*

açúcar [a'suka*] *m* sugar; **açucarado/a** [asuka'radu/a] *adj* sugary; **açucareiro** [asuka'rejru] *m* sugar bowl

açude [a'sudʒi] *m* dam

acudir [aku'dʒi*] *vt* (*ir em socorro*) to help, assist ♦ *vi* (*responder*) to reply, respond; ~ **a** to come to the aid of

açular [asu'la*] *vt* (*incitar*) to incite; ~ **um cachorro contra alguém** to set a dog on sb

acumular [akumu'la*] *vt* to accumulate; (*reunir*) to collect; (*funções*) to combine

acusação [akuza'sãw] (*pl* -**ões**) *f* accusation, charge; (*JUR*) prosecution

acusar [aku'za*] *vt* to accuse; (*revelar*) to reveal; (*culpar*) to blame; ~ **o recebimento de** to acknowledge receipt of

acústica [a'kuʃtʃika] *f* (*ciência*) acoustics *sg*; (*de uma sala*) acoustics *pl*

acústico/a [a'kuʃtʃiku/a] *adj* acoustic

adaga [a'daga] *f* dagger

adaptação [adapta'sãw] (*pl* -**ões**) *f* adaptation

adaptar [adap'ta*] *vt* to adapt; (*acomodar*) to fit; ~-**se** *vr*: ~-**se a** to adapt to

adega [a'dεga] *f* cellar

adelgaçado/a [adewga'sadu/a] *adj* thin; (*aguçado*) pointed

ademais [adʒi'majʃ] *adv* besides, moreover

adentro [a'dẽtru] *adv* inside, in; **mata** ~ into the woods

adepto/a [a'deptu/a] *m/f* follower; (*de time*) supporter

adequado/a [ade'kwadu/a] *adj* appropriate

adequar [ade'kwa*] *vt* to adapt, make suitable

aderecar [adere'sa*] *vt* to adorn, decorate; ~-**se** *vr* to dress up; **adereço** [ade'resu] *m* adornment; **adereços** *mpl* (*TEATRO*) stage props

aderente [ade'rẽtʃi] *adj* adhesive, sticky ♦ *m/f* supporter

aderir [ade'ri*] *vi* to adhere

adesão [ade'zãw] *f* adhesion; (*patrocínio*) support

adesivo/a [ade'zivu/a] *adj* adhesive, sticky ♦ *m* adhesive tape; (*MED*) sticking plaster

adestrado/a [adeʃ'tradu/a] *adj* skilled

adestrador(a) [adeʃtra'do*(a)] *m/f* trainer

adestrar [adeʃ'tra*] *vt* to train; (*cavalo*) to break in

adeus [a'dewʃ] *excl* goodbye!

adiamento [adʒia'mẽtu] *m* postponement; (*de uma sessão*) adjournment

adiantado/a [adʒiã'tadu/a] *adj* advanced; (*relógio*) fast; **chegar** ~ to arrive ahead of time; **pagar** ~ to pay in advance

adiantamento [adʒiãta'mẽtu] *m* progress; (*dinheiro*) advance (payment)

adiantar [adʒiã'ta*] *vt* (*dinheiro, trabalho*) to advance; (*relógio*) to put forward; **não adianta reclamar** there's no point *ou* it's no use complaining

adiante [a'dʒiãtʃi] *adv* (*na frente*) in front; (*para a frente*) forward; **mais** ~ further on; (*no futuro*) later on

adiar [a'dʒia*] *vt* to postpone, put off; (*sessão*) to adjourn

adição [adʒi'sãw] (*pl* -**ões**) *f* addition; (*MAT*) sum; **adicionar** [adʒisjo'na*] *vt* to add

adido/a [a'dʒidu/a] *m/f* attaché

adiro *etc* [a'diru] *vb* V **aderir**

adivinhação [adʒiviɲa'sãw] *f* (*destino*) fortune-telling; (*conjectura*) guessing, guesswork

adivinhar [adʒivi'ɲa*] *vt* to guess; (*ler a sorte*) to foretell ♦ *vi* to guess; ~ **o pensamento de alguém** to read sb's mind; **adivinho/a** [adʒi'viɲu/a] *m/f* fortuneteller

adjetivo [adʒe'tʃivu] *m* adjective

adjudicação [adʒudʒika'sãw] (*pl* -**ões**) *f* grant; (*de contratos*) award; (*JUR*) decision

adjudicar [adʒudʒi'ka*] *vt* to award, grant

adjunto/a [ad'ʒũtu/a] *adj* joined, attached ♦ *m/f* assistant

administração [adʒminiʃtra'sãw] (*pl* -**ões**) *f* administration; (*direção*) management; (*comissão*) board

administrador(a) [adʒminiʃtra'do*(a)] *m/f* administrator; (*diretor*) director; (*gerente*) manager

administrar [adʒminiʃ'tra*] *vt* to administer, manage; (*governar*) to govern

admiração [adʒmira'sãw] *f* wonder; (*estima*) admiration; **ponto de** ~ (*PT*) exclamation mark

admirado/a [adʒimi'radu/a] *adj* astonished, surprised

admirar [adʒimi'ra*] *vt* to admire; ~-**se**

vr: ~**-se de** to be surprised at; **admirável** [adʒimi'ravew] (pl **-eis**) adj amazing

admissão [adʒimi'sãw] (pl **-ões**) f admission; (consentimento para entrar) admittance; (de escola) intake

admitir [adʒimi'tʃiʳ] vt to admit; (permitir) to allow; (funcionário) to take on

admoestação [admweʃta'sãw] (pl **-ões**) f admonition; (repreensão) reprimand

adoção [ado'sãw] f adoption

adoçar [ado'saʳ] vt to sweeten

adoecer [adoe'seʳ] vi: ~ **(de ou com)** to fall ill (with) ♦ vt to make ill

adoidado/a [adoj'dadu/a] adj crazy

adolescente [adole'sẽtʃi] adj, m/f adolescent

adoptar etc [ado'taʳ] (PT) = **adotar** etc

adorar [ado'raʳ] vt to adore; (venerar) to worship

adormecer [adoxme'seʳ] vi to fall asleep; (entorpecer-se) to go numb; **adormecido/a** [adoxme'sidu/a] adj sleeping ♦ m/f sleeper

adornar [adox'naʳ] vt to adorn; **adorno** [a'doxnu] m adornment

adotar [ado'taʳ] vt to adopt; **adotivo/a** [ado'tʃivu/a] adj (filho) adopted

adquirir [adʒiki'riʳ] vt to acquire

adrede [a'dredʒi] adv on purpose

Adriático/a [a'drjatʃiku/a] adj: **o (mar)** ~ the Adriatic

adro ['adru] m (church) forecourt; (em volta da igreja) churchyard

aduana [a'dwana] f customs pl; **aduaneiro/a** [adwa'nejru/a] adj customs atr ♦ m customs officer

adubar [adu'baʳ] vt to manure; (fertilizar) to fertilize; **adubo** [a'dubu] m fertilizer

adulação [adula'sãw] f flattery

adular [adu'laʳ] vt to flatter

adulterar [aduwte'raʳ] vt to adulterate; (contas) to falsify ♦ vi to commit adultery

adultério [aduw'tɛrju] m adultery

adulto/a [a'duwtu/a] adj, m/f adult

adventício/a [advẽ'tʃisju/a] adj (casual) accidental; (estrangeiro) foreign ♦ m/f foreigner

advento [ad'vẽtu] m advent; **o A~** Advent

advérbio [ad'vɛxbju] m adverb

adversário [adʒivex'sarju/a] m adversary

adversidade [adʒivexsi'dadʒi] f adversity

adverso/a [adʒi'vɛxsu/a] adj adverse; (oposto): ~ **a** opposed to

advertência [adʒivex'tẽsja] f warning

advertido/a [adʒivex'tʃidu/a] adj prudent; (informado) well-advised

advertir [adʒivex'tʃiʳ] vt to warn; (repreender) to reprimand; (chamar a atenção a) to draw attention to

advir [ad'viʳ] (irreg: como **vir**) vi: ~ **de** to result from

advogado/a [adʒivo'gadu/a] m/f lawyer

advogar [adʒivo'gaʳ] vt to advocate; (JUR) to plead ♦ vi to practise (BRIT) ou practice (US) law

aéreo/a [a'ɛrju/a] adj air atr

aerobarco [aero'baxku] m hovercraft

aeródromo [aero'drɔmu] m airfield

aeromoço/a [aero'mosu/a] (BR) m/f steward/air hostess

aeronáutica [aero'nawtʃika] f air force; (ciência) aeronautics sg

aeronave [aero'navi] f aircraft

aeroporto [aero'poxtu] m airport

aerossol [aero'sɔw] (pl **-óis**) m aerosol

afã [a'fã] m (entusiasmo) enthusiasm; (diligência) diligence; (ânsia) eagerness; (esforço) effort

afabilidade [afabili'dadʒi] f friendliness

afagar [afa'gaʳ] vt to caress; (cabelo) to stroke

afamado/a [afa'madu/a] adj renowned

afanar [afa'naʳ] (col) vt to nick, pinch

afastado/a [afaʃ'tadu/a] adj (distante) remote; (isolado) secluded; **manter-se** ~ to keep to o.s.

afastamento [afaʃta'mẽtu] m removal; (distância) distance; (de pessoal) lay-off

afastar [afaʃ'taʳ] vt to remove; (separar) to separate; (idéia) to put out of one's mind; (pessoal) to lay off; ~**-se** vr to move away

afável [a'favew] (pl **-eis**) adj friendly

afazer [afa'zeʳ] (irreg: como **fazer**) vt to accustom; ~**-se** vr: ~**-se a** to get used to

afazeres [afa'zerif] mpl business sg; (deveres) duties, tasks; ~ **domésticos** household chores

afectar etc [afek'taʳ] (PT) = **afetar** etc

afeição [afej'sãw] f affection, fondness; (dedicação) devotion; **afeiçoado/a** [afej'swadu/a] adj: **afeiçoado a** (amoroso) fond of; (devotado) devoted to; **afeiçoar-se** [afej'swaxsi] vr: **afeiçoar-se a** to take a liking to

afeito/a [a'fejtu/a] pp de **afazer** ♦ adj: ~ **a** accustomed to, used to

aferir [afe'riʳ] vt (verificar) to check, inspect; (comparar) to compare; (conhecimentos, resultados) to assess

aferrado/a [afe'xadu/a] adj obstinate, stubborn

aferrar [afe'xaʳ] vt to secure; (NÁUT) to anchor; (atirar) to grasp; ~**-se** vr: ~**-se a** to cling to

afetado/a [afe'tadu/a] adj affected

afetar [afe'taʳ] vt to affect; (fingir) to feign

afetivo/a [afe'tʃivu/a] adj affectionate; (problema) emotional

afeto [a'fɛtu] m affection; **afetuoso/a** [afe'twozu/oza] adj affectionate

afiado/a [a'fjadu/a] adj sharp; (pessoa) well-trained

afiançar [afjã'saʳ] vt (JUR) to stand bail for; (garantir) to guarantee

afiar [a'fja⁺] *vt* to sharpen

aficionado/a [afisjo'nadu/a] *m/f* enthusiast

afigurar-se [afigu'raxsi] *vr* to seem, appear; **afigura-se-me que ...** it seems to me that ...

afilhado/a [afi'ʎadu/a] *m/f* godson/goddaughter

afiliar [afi'lja⁺] *vt* to affiliate; **~-se** *vr*: **~-se a** to join

afim [a'fĩ] (*pl* **-ns**) *adj* (*semelhante*) similar; (*consangüíneo*) related ♦ *m/f* relative, relation

afinado/a [afi'nadu/a] *adj* in tune

afinal [afi'naw] *adv* at last, finally; **~** (**de contas**) after all

afinar [afi'na⁺] *vt* (*MÚS*) to tune

afinco [a'fĩku] *m* tenacity, persistence

afinidade [afini'dadʒi] *f* affinity

afins [a'fĩʃ] *pl de* **afim**

afirmação [afixma'sãw] (*pl* **-ões**) *f* affirmation; (*declaração*) statement

afirmar [afix'ma⁺] *vt*, *vi* to affirm, assert; (*declarar*) to declare

afirmativo/a [afixma'tʃivu/a] *adj* affirmative

afiro *etc* [a'firu] *vb* V **aferir**

afivelar [afive'la⁺] *vt* to buckle

afixar [afik'sa⁺] *vt* (*cartazes*) to stick, post

aflição [afli'sãw] *f* affliction; (*ansiedade*) anxiety; (*angústia*) anguish

afligir [afli'ʒi⁺] *vt* to distress; (*atormentar*) to torment; (*inquietar*) to worry; **~-se** *vr*: **~-se com** to worry about; **aflito/a** [a'flitu/a] *pp de* **afligir** ♦ *adj* distressed, anxious

aflorar [aflo'ra⁺] *vi* to emerge, appear

afluência [a'flwẽsja] *f* affluence; (*corrente copiosa*) flow; (*de pessoas*) stream; **afluente** [a'flwẽtʃi] *adj* copious; (*rico*) affluent ♦ *m* tributary

afluir [a'flwi⁺] *vi* to flow; (*pessoas*) to congregate

afobação [afoba'sãw] *f* fluster; (*ansiedade*) panic

afobado/a [afo'badu/a] *adj* flustered; (*ansioso*) panicky, nervous

afobar [afo'ba⁺] *vt* to fluster; (*deixar ansioso*) to make nervous *ou* panicky ♦ *vi* to get flustered; to panic, get nervous; **~-se** *vr* to get flustered

afogador [afoga'do⁺] (*BR*) *m* (*AUTO*) choke

afogar [afo'ga⁺] *vt* to drown ♦ *vi* (*AUTO*) to flood; **~-se** *vr* to drown

afoito/a [a'fojtu/a] *adj* bold, daring

afônico/a [a'foniku/a] *adj*: **estou ~** I've lost my voice

afora [a'fɔra] *prep* except for, apart from ♦ *adv*: **rua ~** down the street

aforrar [afo'xa⁺] *vt* (*roupa*) to line; (*poupar*) to save; (*liberar*) to free

afortunado/a [afoxtu'nadu/a] *adj* fortunate, lucky

afresco [a'freʃku] *m* fresco

África ['afrika] *f*: **a ~** Africa; **a ~ do Sul**

South Africa; **africano/a** [afri'kanu/a] *adj, m/f* African

afro-brasileiro/a ['afru-] (*pl* **~s**) *adj* Afro-Brazilian

afronta [a'frõta] *f* insult, affront; **~r** [afrõ'ta⁺] *vt* to insult; (*ofender*) to offend

afrouxar [afro'ʃa⁺] *vt* (*desapertar*) to slacken; (*soltar*) to loosen ♦ *vi* to come loose

afta ['afta] *f* (mouth) ulcer

afugentar [afuʒẽ'ta⁺] *vt* to drive away, put to flight

afundar [afũ'da⁺] *vt* to sink; (*cavidade*) to deepen; **~-se** *vr* to sink

agachar-se [aga'ʃaxsi] *vr* (*acaçapar-se*) to crouch, squat; (*curvar-se*) to stoop

agarrar [aga'xa⁺] *vt* to seize, grasp; **~-se** *vr*: **~-se a** to cling to, hold on to

agasalhar [agaza'ʎa⁺] *vt* to dress warmly, wrap up; **~-se** *vr* to wrap o.s. up

agasalho [aga'zaʎu] *m* (*casaco*) coat; (*suéter*) sweater

ágeis ['aʒejʃ] *pl de* **ágil**

agência [a'ʒẽsja] *f* agency; (*escritório*) office; **~ de correio** (*BR*) post office; **~ de viagens** travel agency

agenciar [aʒẽ'sja⁺] *vt* (*negociar*) to negotiate; (*obter*) to procure

agenda [a'ʒẽda] *f* diary

agente [a'ʒẽtʃi] *m/f* agent; (*de polícia*) policeman/woman

ágil ['aʒiw] (*pl* **-eis**) *adj* agile

agiota [a'ʒjɔta] *m/f* moneylender

agir [a'ʒi⁺] *vi* to act; **~ bem/mal** to do right/wrong

agitação [aʒita'sãw] (*pl* **-ões**) *f* agitation; (*perturbação*) disturbance; (*inquietação*) restlessness

agitado/a [aʒi'tadu/a] *adj* agitated, disturbed; (*inquieto*) restless

agitar [aʒi'ta⁺] *vt* to agitate, disturb; (*sacudir*) to shake; (*cauda*) to wag; (*mexer*) to stir; **~-se** *vr* to get upset; (*mar*) to get rough

aglomeração [aglomera'sãw] (*pl* **-ões**) *f* gathering; (*multidão*) crowd

aglomerado [aglome'radu] *m*: **~ urbano** city

aglomerar [aglome'ra⁺] *vt* to heap up, pile up; **~-se** *vr* (*multidão*) to crowd together

agonia [ago'nia] *f* agony, anguish; (*ânsia da morte*) death throes *pl*; **agonizante** [agoni'zãtʃi] *adj* dying ♦ *m/f* dying person; **agonizar** [agoni'za⁺] *vi* to be dying; (*afligir-se*) to agonize

agora [a'gɔra] *adv* now; **~ mesmo** right now; (*há pouco*) a moment ago; **até ~** so far, up to now; **por ~** for now

agosto [a'goʃtu] (*PT* **A~**) *m* August

agourar [ago'ra⁺] *vt* to predict, foretell

agouro [a'goru] *m* omen

agraciar [agra'sja⁺] *vt* to decorate

agradar [agra'da⁺] *vt* to please; (*fazer*

agrados a) to be nice to ♦ *vi* to be pleasing: (*satisfazer*) to go down well

agradável [agra'davew] (*pl* -**eis**) *adj* pleasant

agradecer [agrade'se°] *vt*: ~ **algo a alguém**, ~ **a alguém por algo** to thank sb for sth; **mal agradecido/a** [agrade'sidu/a] *adj* grateful; **mal agradecido** ungrateful; **agradecimento** [agradesi'mẽtu] *m* gratitude; **agradecimentos** *mpl* (*gratidão*) thanks

agrado [a'gradu] *m*: **fazer um** ~ **a alguém** (*afagar*) to be affectionate with sb; (*ser agradável*) to be nice to sb

agrário/a [a'grarju/a] *adj* agrarian; **reforma agrária** land reform

agravação [agrava'sãw] (*PT*) *f* aggravation

agravamento [agrava'mẽtu] (*BR*) *m* aggravation

agravante [agra'vãtʃi] *adj* aggravating ♦ *f* aggravating circumstance

agravar [agra'va°] *vt* to aggravate, make worse; ~**se** *vr* (*piorar*) to get worse

agravo [a'gravu] *m* (*JUR*) appeal

agredir [agre'dʒi°] *vt* to attack; (*insultar*) to insult

agregado/a [agre'gadu/a] *m/f* (*lavrador*) tenant farmer; (*BR*) lodger ♦ *m* aggregate, sum total

agregar [agre'ga°] *vt* (*juntar*) to collect; (*acrescentar*) to add

agressão [agre'sãw] (*pl* -**ões**) *f* aggression; (*ataque*) attack; (*assalto*) assault

agressivo/a [agre'sivu/a] *adj* aggressive

agressões [agre'sõjʃ] *fpl de* **agressão**

agreste [a'grɛʃtʃi] *adj* rural, rustic; (*terreno*) wild

agrião [a'grjãw] *m* watercress

agrícola [a'grikola] *adj* agricultural

agricultor [agrikuw'to°] *m* farmer

agricultura [agrikuw'tura] *f* agriculture, farming

agrido *etc* [a'gridu] *vb* V **agredir**

agridoce [agri'dosi] *adj* bittersweet

agronomia [agrono'mia] *f* agronomy

agropecuária [agrope'kwarja] *f* farming, agriculture

agrupar [agru'pa°] *vt* to group; ~**se** *vr* to group together

agrura [a'grura] *f* bitterness

água ['agwa] *f* water; ~**s** *fpl* (*mar*) waters; (*chuvas*) rain *sg*; (*maré*) tides; ~ **abaixo/acima** downstream/upstream; **dar** ~ **na boca** (*comida*) to be mouthwatering; **estar na** ~ (*bêbado*) to be drunk; **fazer** ~ (*NÁUT*) to leak; ~ **benta/ corrente/doce** holy/running/ fresh water; ~ **dura/leve** hard/soft water; ~ **mineral** mineral water; ~ **oxigenada** peroxide; ~ **salgada** salt water; ~ **sanitária** household bleach

aguaceiro [agwa'sejru] *m* (*chuva*) (heavy) shower, downpour

água-de-coco *f* coconut milk

água-de-colônia (*pl* **águas-de-colônia**) *f* eau-de-cologne

aguado/a [a'gwadu/a] *adj* watery

água-furtada [-fux'tada] (*pl* **águas-furtadas**) *f* garret, attic

aguar [a'gwa°] *vt* to water

aguardar [agwax'da°] *vt* to wait for; (*contar com*) to expect ♦ *vi* to wait

aguardente [agwax'dẽtʃi] *m kind of brandy*

aguarrás [agwa'xajʃ] *f* turpentine

água-viva (*pl* **águas-vivas**) *f* jellyfish

aguçado/a [agu'sadu/a] *adj* pointed; (*espírito, sentidos*) acute

agudeza [agu'deza] *f* sharpness; (*perspicácia*) perspicacity; (*de som*) shrillness

agudo/a [a'gudu/a] *adj* sharp, shrill; (*intenso*) acute

agüentar [agwẽ'ta°] *vt* (*muro etc*) to hold up; (*dor, injustiças*) to stand, put up with; (*peso*) to withstand ♦ *vi* to last; ~**se** *vr* to remain, hold on; ~ **fazer algo** to manage to do sth; **não** ~ **de** not to be able to stand

águia ['agja] *f* eagle; (*fig*) genius

agulha [a'guʎa] *f* (*de coser, tricô*) needle; (*NÁUT*) compass; (*FERRO*) points *pl* (*BRIT*), switch (*US*); **trabalho de** ~ needlework

agulheta [agu'ʎeta] *f* nozzle

ai [aj] *excl* (*suspiro*) oh!; (*de dor*) ouch! ♦ *m* (*suspiro*) sigh; (*gemido*) groan; ~ **de mim** poor me!

aí [a'i] *adv* there; (*então*) then; **por** ~ (*em lugar indeterminado*) somewhere over there, thereabouts; **espera** ~! wait!, hang on a minute!; **está** ~! (*col*) right!; **e** ~? and then what?

AIDS ['ajdʒs] *abr f* AIDS

ainda [a'ĩda] *adv* still; (*mesmo*) even; ~ **agora** just now; ~ **assim** even so, nevertheless; ~ **bem** just as well; ~ **por cima** on top of all that, in addition; ~ **não** not yet; ~ **que** even if; **maior** ~ even bigger

aipo ['ajpu] *m* celery

airado/a [aj'radu/a] *adj* (*frívolo*) frivolous; (*leviano*) dissolute

airoso/a [aj'rozu/ɔza] *adj* graceful, elegant

ajeitar [aʒej'ta°] *vt* (*roupa, cabelo*) to adjust; (*emprego*) to arrange; ~**se** *vr* to adapt

ajo *etc* ['aʒu] *vb* V **agir**

ajoelhado/a [aʒwe'ʎadu/a] *adj* kneeling

ajoelhar [aʒwe'ʎa°] *vi* to kneel (down); ~**se** *vr* to kneel down

ajuda [a'ʒuda] *f* help; (*subsídio*) grant, subsidy; **dar** ~ **a alguém** to lend *ou* give sb a hand; ~ **de custo** allowance; ~**nte** [aʒu'dãtʃi] *m/f* assistant, helper; (*MIL*) adjutant

ajudar [aʒu'da°] *vt* to help

ajuizado/a [aʒwi'zadu/a] *adj* (*sensato*) sensible; (*sábio*) wise; (*prudente*) discreet

ajuizar [aʒwi'za*] *vt* to judge; (*calcular*) to calculate

ajuntamento [aʒũta'mẽtu] *m* gathering

ajuntar [aʒũ'ta*] *vt* (*unir*) to join; (*documentos*) to attach; (*reunir*) to gather

ajustagem [aʒuʃ'taʒẽ] (*BR*: *pl* –ns) *f* (*TEC*) adjustment

ajustamento [aʒuʃta'mẽtu] *m* adjustment; (*de contas*) settlement

ajustagens [aʒuʃ'taʒẽʃ] *fpl de* **ajustagem**

ajustar [aʒuʃ'ta*] *vt* to adjust; (*conta, disputa*) to settle; (*acomodar*) to fit; (*roupa*) to take in; (*preço*) to agree on; ~-se *vr*: ~-se a to conform to; (*adaptar-se*) to adapt to

ajuste [a'ʒuʃtʃi] *m* (*acordo*) agreement; (*de contas*) settlement; (*adaptação*) adjustment

ala ['ala] *f* wing; (*fileira*) row; (*passagem*) aisle

alagar [ala'ga*] *vt, vi* to flood

alambique [alã'biki] *m* still

alameda [ala'meda] *f* (*avenida*) avenue; (*arvoredo*) grove

álamo ['alamu] *m* poplar

alar [a'la*] *vt* to haul, heave

alarde [a'laxdʒi] *m* ostentation; (*jactância*) boasting; **fazer** ~ **de** to boast about; **~ar** [alax'dʒa*] *vt* to show off; (*gabar-se de*) to show off ♦ *vi* to show off; to boast; **~ar-se** *vr* to boast

alargar [alax'ga*] *vt* to extend; (*fazer mais largo*) to widen, broaden; (*afrouxar*) to loosen, slacken

alarido [ala'ridu] *m* (*clamor*) outcry; (*tumulto*) uproar

alarma [a'laxma] *f* alarm; (*susto*) panic; (*tumulto*) tumult; (*vozearia*) outcry; **dar o sinal de** ~ to raise the alarm; ~ **de roubo** burglar alarm; **~nte** [alax'mãtʃi] *adj* alarming; **~r** [alax'ma*] *vt* to alarm; **~r-se** *vr* to be alarmed

alarme [a'laxmi] *m* = **alarma**

alastrado/a [alaʃ'tradu/a] *adj*: ~ **de** strewn with

alastrar [alaʃ'tra*] *vt* to scatter; (*disseminar*) to spread; **~-se** *vr* (*epidemia, rumor*) to spread

alavanca [ala'vãka] *f* lever; (*pé-de-cabra*) crowbar; ~ **de mudanças** gear lever

albergue [aw'bɛxgi] *m* (*estalagem*) inn; (*refúgio*) hospice, shelter; ~ **noturno** hotel; ~ **para jovens** youth hostel

albufeira [awbu'fejra] *f* lagoon

álbum ['awbũ] (*pl* –ns) *m* album; ~ **de recortes** scrapbook

alça ['awsa] *f* strap; (*asa*) handle; (*de fusil*) sight

alcácer [aw'kase*] *m* fortress

alcachofra [awka'ʃofra] *f* artichoke

alcaçuz [awka'suʒ] *m* liquorice

alcançar [awkã'sa*] *vt* to reach; (*estender*) to hand, pass; (*obter*) to obtain, get; (*atingir*) to attain; (*compreender*) to un-

derstand; (*desfalcar*): ~ **uma firma em $1 milhão** to embezzle $1 million from a firm

alcance [aw'kãsi] *m* reach; (*competência*) power; (*compreensão*) understanding; (*de tiro, visão*) range; **ao** ~ **de** within reach ou range of; **ao** ~ **da voz** within earshot; **de grande** ~ far-reaching; **fora do** ~ **da mão** out of reach; **fora do** ~ **de alguém** beyond sb's grasp

alçapão [awsa'pãw] (*pl* –ões) *m* trapdoor; (*arapuca*) trap

alcaparra [awka'paxa] *f* caper

alçapões [awsa'põjʃ] *mpl de* **alçapão**

alçaprema [awsa'prɛma] *f* (*alavanca*) crowbar

alçar [aw'sa*] *vt* to lift (up); (*voz*) to raise

alcatéia [awka'tɛja] *f* (*de lobos*) pack; (*de ladrões*) gang

alcatrão [awka'trãw] *m* tar

álcool ['awkɔw] *m* alcohol; **alcoólatra** [aw'kɔlatra] *m/f* alcoholic; **alcoólico/a** [aw'kɔliku/a] *adj, m/f* alcoholic

Alcorão [awko'rãw] *m* Koran

alcova [aw'kova] *f* bedroom

alcunha [aw'kuɲa] *f* nickname

aldeão/eã [aw'dʒjãw/jã] (*pl* –ões/~s) *m/f* villager

aldeia [aw'deja] *f* village

aldeões [aw'dʒjõjʃ] *mpl de* **aldeão**

aleatório/a [alea'tɔrju/a] *adj* random

alecrim [ale'krĩ] *m* rosemary

alegação [alega'sãw] (*pl* –ões) *f* allegation

alegar [ale'ga*] *vt* to allege; (*JUR*) to plead

alegoria [alego'ria] *f* allegory

alegórico/a [ale'gɔriku/a] *adj* allegorical; **carro alegórico** float

alegrar [ale'gra*] *vt* to cheer (up), gladden; (*ambiente*) to brighten up; (*animar*) to liven up); **~-se** *vr* to cheer up

alegre [a'lɛgri] *adj* cheerful; (*contente*) happy, glad; (*cores*) bright; (*embriagado*) merry, tight; **alegria** [ale'gria] *f* joy, happiness

aleijado/a [alej'ʒadu/a] *adj* crippled ♦ *m/f* cripple

aleijar [alej'ʒa*] *vt* to maim

aleitar [alej'ta*] *vt, vi* to breast-feed

além [a'lẽj] *adv* (*lá ou longe*) over there; (*mais adiante*) further on ♦ *m*: **o** ~ the hereafter ♦ *prep*: ~ **de** beyond; (*no outro lado de*) on the other side of; (*para mais de*) over; (*ademais de*) apart from, besides; ~ **disso** moreover; **mais** ~ further

alemã [ale'mã] *f de* **alemão**

alemães [ale'mãjʃ] *mpl de* **alemão**

Alemanha [ale'maɲa] *f*: **a** ~ Germany

alemão/mã [ale'mãw/mã] (*pl* –ães/~s) *adj, m/f* German ♦ *m* (*LING*) German

alentado/a [alẽ'tadu/a] *adj* (*valente*) valiant; (*grande*) great; (*volumoso*) substantial

alentador(a) [alēta'do*(a)] adj encouraging

alentar [alē'ta*] vt to encourage; ~-se vr to cheer up

alento [a'lētu] m (fôlego) breath; (ânimo) courage; **dar** ~ to encourage; **tomar** ~ to draw breath

alergia [alex'ʒia] f: ~ **(a)** allergy (to); (fig) aversion (to); **alérgico/a** [a'lexʒiku/a] adj: **alérgico (a)** allergic (to); **ele é alérgico a João/à política** he can't stand João/politics

alerta [a'lɛxta] adj alert ♦ adv on the alert ♦ m alert

alfabetizar [awfabetʃi'za*] vt to teach to read and write; ~-se vr to learn to read and write

alfabeto [awfa'bɛtu] m alphabet

alface [aw'fasi] f lettuce

alfaia [aw'faja] f (móveis) furniture; (utensílio) utensil; (enfeite) ornament

alfaiate [awfa'jatʃi] m tailor

alfândega [aw'fādʒiga] f customs pl, customs house; **alfandegário/a** [awfāde'garju/a] m/f customs officer

alfavaca [awfa'vaka] f basil

alfazema [awfa'zɛma] f lavender

alfinete [awfi'netʃi] m pin; ~ **de segurança** safety pin

alga ['awga] f seaweed

algarismo [awga'riʒmu] m numeral, digit

Algarve [aw'gaxvi] m: o ~ the Algarve

algazarra [awga'zaxa] f uproar, racket

álgebra ['awʒebra] f algebra

algemas [aw'ʒcmaʃ] fpl handcuffs

algo ['awgu] adv somewhat, rather ♦ pron something; (qualquer coisa) anything

algodão [awgo'dāw] m cotton; ~ **(hidrófilo)** cotton wool (BRIT), absorbent cotton (US); **algodoeiro/a** [awgo'dwejru/a] adj (indústria) cotton atr ♦ m cotton plant

alguém [aw'gēj] pron someone, somebody; (em frases interrogativas ou negativas) anyone, anybody

algum(a) [aw'gũ/'guma] (pl –ns/~s) adj some; (em frases interrogativas ou negativas) any ♦ pron one; (no plural) some; (negativa): **de modo** ~ in no way; **coisa** ~a nothing; ~ **dia** one day; ~ **tempo** for a while; ~**a coisa** something; ~**a vez** sometime

algures [aw'guriʃ] adv somewhere

alheio/a [a'ʎeju/a] adj (de outrem) someone else's; (estranho) alien; (estrangeiro) foreign; (impróprio) irrelevant

alho ['aʎu] m garlic; ~-**poró** [-po'rɔ] (pl ~s-porós) m leek

ali [a'li] adv there; **até** ~ up to there; **por** ~ around there; (direção) that way; ~ **por** (tempo) round about; **de** ~ **por diante** from then on; ~ **dentro** in there

aliado/a [a'ljadu/a] adj allied ♦ m/f ally

aliança [a'ljāsa] f alliance; (anel) wedding ring

aliar [a'lja*] vt to ally; ~-se vr to form an alliance

aliás [a'ljajʃ] adv (a propósito) as a matter of fact; (ou seja) rather, that is; (contudo) nevertheless; (diga-se de passagem) incidentally

álibi ['alibi] m alibi

alicate [ali'katʃi] m pliers pl; ~ **de unhas** nail clippers pl

alicerce [ali'sɛxsi] m (de edifício) foundation; (fig: base) basis

alienação [aljena'sāw] f alienation; (de bens) transfer (of property); ~ **mental** insanity

alienado/a [alje'nadu/a] adj alienated; (demente) insane; (bens) transferred ♦ m/f lunatic

alienar [alje'na*] vt (afastar) to alienate; (bens) to transfer

alijar [ali'ʒa*] vt to jettison; (livrar-se de) to get rid of

alimentação [alimēta'sāw] f (alimentos) food; (ação) feeding; (nutrição) nourishment; (ELET) supply

alimentar [alimē'ta*] vt to feed; (fig) to nurture ♦ adj (produto) food atr; (hábitos) eating atr; ~-se vr: ~-se **de** to feed on

alimentício/a [alimē'tʃisju/a] adj food atr; (nutritivo) nourishing

alimento [ali'mētu] m food; (nutrição) nourishment

alinhado/a [ali'ɲadu/a] adj (elegante) elegant; (texto): ~ **à esquerda/direita** ranged left/right

alinhar [ali'ɲa*] vt to align; ~-se vr to form a line

alinhavar [aliɲa'va*] vt (COSTURA) to tack

alinho [a'liɲu] m (alinhamento) alignment; (elegância) neatness

alíquota [a'likwota] f bracket, percentage

alisar [ali'za*] vt to smooth; (cabelo) to straighten; (acariciar) to stroke

alistar [aliʃ'ta*] vt (MIL) to recruit; ~-se vr to enlist

aliviar [ali'vja*] vt to relieve; (carga etc) to lighten

alívio [a'livju] m relief

alma ['awma] f soul; (entusiasmo) enthusiasm; (caráter) character

almejar [awme'ʒa*] vt to long for, yearn for

almirantado [awmirā'tadu] m admiralty

almirante [awmi'rātʃi] m admiral

almoçar [awmo'sa*] vi to have lunch ♦ vt: ~ **peixe** to have fish for lunch

almoço [aw'mosu] m lunch; **pequeno** ~ (PT) breakfast

almofada [awmo'fada] f cushion; (PT: travesseiro) pillow

almôndega [aw'mõdega] f meat ball

almoxarifado [awmoʃari'fadu] m storeroom

alô [a'lo] (BR) excl (TEL) hullo

alocar [alo'ka*] vt to allocate

alojamento [aloʒa'mētu] m accommodation (BRIT), accommodations pl (US); (habitação) housing

alojar [alo'ʒa*] vt (hóspede: numa pensão) to accommodate; (: numa casa) to put up; (sem teto, refugiado) to house; (MIL) to billet; **~-se** vr to stay

alongar [alõ'ga*] vt to lengthen; (braço) to stretch out; (prazo, contrato) to extend; (reunião, sofrimento) to prolong; **~-se** vr (sobre um assunto) to dwell

aloprado/a [alo'pradu/a] (col) adj nutty

alpendre [aw'pēdri] m (telheiro) shed; (pórtico) porch

alpercata [awpex'kata] f sandal

Alpes ['awpiʃ] mpl: **os ~** the Alps

alpinismo [awpi'niʒmu] m mountaineering, climbing; **alpinista** [awpi'niʃta] m/f mountaineer, climber

alquebrar [awke'bra*] vt to bend; (enfraquecer) to weaken ♦ vi (curvar) to stoop, be bent double

alquimia [awki'mia] f alchemy

alta ['awta] f (de preços) rise; (de hospital) discharge

altaneiro/a [awta'nejru/a] adj (soberbo) proud

altar [aw'ta*] m altar

altear [aw'tʃja*] vt to raise; (reputação) to enhance ♦ vi to spread out

alteração [awtera'sāw] (pl -ões) f alteration; (desordem) disturbance; (falsificação) falsification

alterado/a [awte'radu/a] adj bad-tempered, irritated

alterar [awte'ra*] vt to alter; (falsificar) to falsify; **~-se** vr to change; (enfurecer-se) to get angry, lose one's temper

alternar [awtex'na*] vt, vi to alternate; **~-se** vr to alternate; (por turnos) to take turns

alternativa [awtexna'tʃiva] f alternative

alternativo/a [awtexna'tʃivu/a] adj alternative; (ELET) alternating

alteza [aw'teza] f highness

altissonante [awtʃiso'nātʃi] adj high-sounding

altitude [awtʃi'tudʒi] f altitude

altivez [awtʃi'veʒ] f (arrogância) haughtiness; (nobreza) loftiness; **altivo/a** [aw'tʃivu/a] adj haughty; lofty

alto/a ['awtu/a] adj high; (pessoa) tall; (som) high, sharp; (voz) loud; (GEO) upper ♦ adv (falar) loudly, loud; (voar) high ♦ excl halt! ♦ m top, summit; **do ~** from above; **por ~** superficially; **alta fidelidade** high fidelity, hi-fi; **na alta noite** at dead of night

alto-falante (pl -s) m loudspeaker

altura [aw'tura] f height; (momento) point, juncture; (altitude) altitude; (de um som) pitch; **em que ~ do Rio Branco fica a**

livraria? whereabouts in Rio Branco is the bookshop?; **nesta ~** at this juncture; **estar à ~ de** (ser capaz de) to be up to; **ter 1.80 metros de ~** to be 1.80 metres (BRIT) ou meters (US) tall

alucinação [alusina'sāw] (pl -ões) f hallucination

alucinado/a [alusi'nadu/a] adj crazy

alucinante [alusi'nātʃi] adj crazy

aludir [alu'dʒi*] vi: **~ a** to allude to

alugar [alu'ga*] vt (tomar de aluguel) to rent, hire; (dar de aluguel) to let, rent out; **~-se** vr to let; **aluguel** [alu'gɛw] (pl -éis) (BR) m rent; (ação) renting; **aluguel de carro** car hire (BRIT) ou rental (US); **aluguer** [alu'gɛ*] (PT) m = **aluguel**

aluir [a'lwi*] vt (abalar) to shake; (derrubar) to demolish; (arruinar) to ruin ♦ vi to collapse; (ameaçar ruína) to crumble

alumiar [alu'mja*] vt to light (up) ♦ vi to give light

alumínio [alu'minju] m aluminium (BRIT), aluminum (US)

alunissar [aluni'sa*] vi to land on the moon

aluno/a [a'lunu/a] m/f pupil, student

alusão [alu'zāw] (pl -ões) f allusion

alvejante [awve'ʒātʃi] m bleach

alvejar [awve'ʒa*] vt (tomar como alvo) to aim at; (branquear) to bleach

alvenaria [awvena'ria] f masonry; **de ~** brick atr, brick-built

alvéolo [aw'vɛolu] m cavity

alvitrar [awvi'tra*] vt to propose, suggest; **alvitre** [aw'vitri] m opinion

alvo/a ['awvu/a] adj white ♦ m target

alvorada [awvo'rada] f dawn

alvorecer [awvore'se*] vi to dawn

alvoroçar [awvoro'sa*] vt (agitar) to stir up; (entusiasmar) to excite; **~-se** vr to get agitated

alvoroço [awvo'rosu] m commotion; (entusiasmo) enthusiasm

alvura [aw'vura] f whiteness; (pureza) purity

amabilidade [amabili'dadʒi] f kindness; (simpatia) friendliness

amaciante [ama'sjātʃi] m: **~ (de roupa)** fabric conditioner

amaciar [ama'sja*] vt (tornar macio) to soften; (carro) to run in

ama-de-leite ['ama-] (pl amas-de-leite) f wet-nurse

amado/a [a'madu/a] m/f beloved, sweetheart

amador(a) [ama'do*(a)] adj, m/f amateur

amadurecer [amadure'se*] vt, vi (frutos) to ripen; (fig) to mature

âmago ['amagu] m (centro) heart, core; (medula) pith; (essência) essence

amainar [amaj'na*] vi (tempestade) to abate; (cólera) to calm down

amaldiçoar [amawdʒi'swa*] vt to curse, swear at

amálgama [a'mawgama] *f* amalgam

amalgamar [amawga'ma*] *vt* to amalgamate; (*combinar*) to fuse (*BRIT*), fuze (*US*), blend

amalucado/a [amalu'kadu/a] *adj* crazy, whacky

amamentar [amamē'ta*] *vt, vi* to breastfeed

amanhã [ama'ɲã] *adv, m* tomorrow

amanhecer [amaɲe'se*] *vi* (*alvorecer*) to dawn; (*encontrar-se pela manhã*): **amanhecemos em Paris** we were in Paris at daybreak ♦ *m* dawn; **ao ~** at daybreak

amansar [amã'sa*] *vt* (*animais*) to tame; (*cavalos*) to break in; (*aplacar*) to placate

amante [a'mãtʃi] *m/f* lover

amar [a'ma*] *vt* to love

amarelado/a [amare'ladu/a] *adj* yellowish; (*pele*) sallow

amarelo/a [ama'rɛlu/a] *adj* yellow ♦ *m* yellow

amarfanhar [amaxfa'ɲa*] *vt* to screw up

amargar [amax'ga*] *vt* to make bitter; (*fig*) to embitter

amargo/a [a'maxgu/a] *adj* bitter; **amargura** [amax'gura] *f* bitterness

amarrar [ama'xa*] *vt* to tie (up); (*NÁUT*) to moor; **~ a cara** to frown, scowl

amarrotar [amaxo'ta*] *vt* to crease

amassar [ama'sa*] *vt* (*pão*) to knead; (*misturar*) to mix; (*papel*) to screw up; (*roupa*) to crease; (*carro*) to dent

amável [a'mavew] (*pl* -**eis**) *adj* kind

amazona [ama'zona] *f* horsewoman

Amazonas [ama'zɔnaʃ] *m*: **o ~** the Amazon

Amazônia [ama'zonja] *f*: **a ~** the Amazon region

ambição [ambi'sãw] (*pl* -**ões**) *f* ambition; **ambicionar** [ãbisjo'na*] *vt* to aspire to; **ambicioso/a** [ãbi'sjozu/ɔza] *adj* ambitious

ambidestro/a [ãbi'deʃtru/a] *adj* ambidextrous

ambientar [ãbjẽ'ta*] *vt* (*filme etc*) to set; (*adaptar*): **~ alguém a algo** to get sb used to sth; **~-se** *vr* to fit in

ambiente [a'bjẽtʃi] *m* atmosphere; (*meio, COMPUT*) environment; **meio ~** environment; **temperatura ~** room temperature

ambigüidade [ambigwi'dadʃi] *f* ambiguity

ambíguo/a [ã'bigwu/a] *adj* ambiguous

âmbito [ã'bitu] *m* extent; (*campo de ação*) scope, range

ambos/as ['ãbuʃ/aʃ] *adj pl* both

ambrosia [ãbro'zia] *f* egg custard

ambulância [ãbu'lãsja] *f* ambulance

ambulante [ãbu'lãtʃi] *adj* walking; (*errante*) wandering; (*biblioteca*) mobile

ambulatório [ãbula'tɔrju] *m* outpatient department

ameaça [ame'asa] *f* threat; **~r** [amea'sa*] *vt* to threaten

ameba [a'mɛba] *f* amoeba (*BRIT*), ameba (*US*)

amedrontar [amedrõ'ta*] *vt* to scare, intimidate; **~-se** *vr* to be frightened

ameixa [a'mejʃa] *f* plum; (*passa*) prune

amém [a'mẽj] *excl* amen

amêndoa [a'mẽdwa] *f* almond; **amendoeira** [amẽ'dwejra] *f* almond tree

amendoim [amẽdo'ĩ] (*pl* -**ns**) *m* peanut

amenidade [ameni'dadʒi] *f* wellbeing; **~s** *fpl* (*assuntos superficiais*) small talk *sg*

amenizar [ameni'za*] *vt* (*abrandar*) to soften; (*tornar agradável*) to make pleasant; (*facilitar*) to ease

ameno/a [a'mɛnu/a] *adj* pleasant; (*clima*) mild

América [a'mɛrika] *f*: **a ~** America; **a ~ do Norte/do Sul** North/South America; **a ~ Central/Latina** Central/Latin America; **americano/a** [ameri'kanu/a] *adj, m/f* American

amesquinhar [ameʃki'ɲa*] *vt* to belittle

amestrar [ameʃ'tra*] *vt* to train

ametista [ame'tʃiʃta] *f* amethyst

amianto [a'mjãtu] *m* asbestos

amido [a'midu] *m* starch

amigável [ami'gavew] (*pl* -**eis**) *adj* amicable, friendly

amígdala [a'migdala] *f* tonsil; **amigdalite** [amigda'litʃi] *f* tonsillitis

amigo/a [a'migu/a] *adj* friendly ♦ *m/f* friend; **ser ~ de** to be friends with

amistoso/a [amiʃ'tozu/ɔza] *adj* friendly, cordial ♦ *m* (*jogo*) friendly

amiudar [amju'da*] *vt, vi* to repeat; **~ as visitas** to make frequent visits; **amiúde** [a'mjudʒi] *adv* often, frequently

amizade [ami'zadʒi] *f* (*relação*) friendship; (*simpatia*) friendliness

amnésia [am'nɛzja] *f* amnesia

amnistia [amniʃ'tia] (*PT*) *f* = **anistia**

amofinar [amofi'na*] *vt* to trouble; **~-se (com)** *vr* to fret (over)

amolação [amola'sãw] (*pl* -**ões**) *f* bother, annoyance

amolante [amo'lãtʃi] (*BR*) *adj* bothersome

amolar [amo'la*] *vt* to sharpen; (*aborrecer*) to annoy, bother ♦ *vi* to be annoying

amoldar [amow'da*] *vt* to mould (*BRIT*), mold (*US*); **~-se** *vr*: **~-se a** (*conformar-se*) to conform to; (*acostumar-se*) to get used to

amolecer [amole'se*] *vt* to soften ♦ *vi* to soften; (*abrandar-se*) to relent

amônia [a'monja] *f* ammonia

amoníaco [amo'niaku] *m* ammonia

amontoar [amõ'twa*] *vt* to pile up, accumulate; **~ riquezas** to amass a fortune

amor [a'mo*] *m* love; **por ~ de** for the sake of; **fazer ~** to make love

amora [a'mɔra] *f*: **~ silvestre** blackberry; **~-preta** (*pl* **~s-pretas**) *f* bramble

amordaçar [amoxda'sa*] *vt* to gag

amornar [amox'na*] *vt* to warm

amoroso/a [amo'rozu/ɔza] *adj* loving, affectionate

amor-perfeito (*pl* **amores-perfeitos**) *m* pansy

amortecedor [amoxtese'do*] *m* shock absorber

amortecido/a [amoxte'sidu/a] *adj* deadened; (*enfraquecido*) weak

amortização [amoxtʃiza'sãw] *f* payment in instalments (*BRIT*) *ou* installments (*US*)

amortizar [amoxtʃi'za*] *vt* to pay in instalments (*BRIT*) *ou* installments (*US*)

amostra [a'mɔʃtra] *f* sample

amotinar [amotʃi'na*] *vi* to rebel, mutiny

amparar [ãpa'ra*] *vt* to support; (*ajudar*) to help, assist; **~-se** *vr*: **~-se em** to lean on

amparo [ã'paru] *m* support; help, assistance

ampère [ã'pɛri] (*BR*) *m* ampere, amp

ampliação [amplja'sãw] (*pl* **-ões**) *f* enlargement; (*extensão*) extension

ampliar [ã'plja*] *vt* to enlarge; (*conhecimento*) to broaden

amplificação [amplifika'sãw] (*pl* **-ões**) *f* enlargement; (*de som*) amplification

amplificador [ãplifika'do*] *m* amplifier

amplificar [ãplifi'ka*] *vt* to amplify

amplitude [ãpli'tudʒi] *f* (*espaço*) spaciousness; (*fig: extensão*) extent

amplo/a ['ãplu/a] *adj* (*sala*) spacious; (*conhecimento, sentido*) broad; (*possibilidade*) ample

amputar [ãpu'ta*] *vt* to amputate

Amsterdã [amiʃtex'dã] (*BR*) *n* Amsterdam

Amsterdão [amiʃtex'dãw] (*PT*) *n* = Amsterdã

amuado/a [a'mwadu/a] *adj* sulky

amuar [a'mwa*] *vi* to sulk ♦ *vt* to bore; **~-se** *vr* to get bored

anã [a'nã] *f de* **anão**

anacronismo [anakro'niʒmu] *m* anachronism

anagrama [ana'grama] *m* anagram

anágua [a'nagwa] *f* petticoat

anais [a'najʃ] *mpl* annals

analfabeto/a [anawfa'bɛtu/a] *adj, m/f* illiterate

analgésico [anaw'ʒɛziku] *m* painkiller, analgesic

analisar [anali'za*] *vt* to analyse; **análise** [a'nalizi] *f* analysis; **analista** [ana'liʃta] *m/f* analyst

analogia [analo'ʒia] *f* analogy; **análogo/a** [a'nalogu/a] *adj* analogous

ananás [ana'naʃ] (*pl* **ananases**) *m* (*BR*) variety of pineapple; (*PT*) pineapple

anão/anã [a'nãw/a'nã] (*pl* **-ões/~s**) *m/f* dwarf

anarquia [anax'kia] *f* anarchy; **anarquista** [anax'kiʃta] *m/f* anarchist

anatomia [anato'mia] *f* anatomy

anca ['ãka] *f* (*de pessoa*) hip; (*de animal*) rump

anchova [ã'ʃova] *f* anchovy

ancião/anciã [ã'sjãw/ã'sjã] (*pl* **-ões/~s**) *adj* old ♦ *m/f* old man/woman; (*de uma tribo*) elder

ancinho [ã'siɲu] *m* rake

anciões [a'sjõjʃ] *mpl de* **ancião**

âncora ['ãkora] *f* anchor; **ancoradouro** [ãkora'doru] *m* anchorage; **ancorar** [ãko'ra*] *vt, vi* to anchor

andaime [ã'dajmi] *m* (*ARQ*) scaffolding

andamento [ãda'mẽtu] *m* (*progresso*) progress; (*rumo*) course; (*MÚS*) tempo; **em ~** in progress

andar [ã'da*] *vi* to walk; (*máquina*) to work; (*progredir*) to progress; (*estar*): **ela anda triste** she's been sad lately ♦ *m* gait; (*pavimento*) floor, storey (*BRIT*), story (*US*); **anda!** hurry up!; **~ a cavalo** to ride; **~ de trem/avião/bicicleta** to travel by train/fly/ride a bike

Andes ['ãdʒiʃ] *mpl*: **os ~** the Andes

andorinha [ãdo'riɲa] *f* (*pássaro*) swallow

anedota [ane'dɔta] *f* anecdote

anel [a'nɛw] (*pl* **-éis**) *m* ring; (*elo*) link; (*de cabelo*) curl; **~ de casamento** wedding ring; **~ado/a** [ane'ladu/a] *adj* curly

anemia [ane'mia] *f* anaemia (*BRIT*), anemia (*US*)

anestesia [aneʃte'zia] *f* anaesthesia (*BRIT*), anesthesia (*US*); (*anestésico*) anaesthetic (*BRIT*), anesthetic (*US*)

anexar [anek'sa*] *vt* to annex; (*juntar*) to attach; (*documento*) to enclose; **anexo/a** [a'nɛksu/a] *adj* attached ♦ *m* annexe; (*em carta*) enclosure; **segue em anexo** please find enclosed

anfíbio/a [ã'fibju/a] *adj* amphibious

anfiteatro [ãfi'tʃjatru] *m* amphitheatre (*BRIT*), amphitheater (*US*); (*no teatro*) dress circle

anfitrião/triã [ãfi'trjãw/'trjã] (*pl* **-ões/~s**) *m/f* host/hostess

angariar [ãga'rja*] *vt* (*fundos*) to raise; (*adeptos*) to attract; (*reputação, simpatia*) to gain; **~ votos** to canvass (for votes)

angina [ã'ʒina] *f*: **~ do peito** angina (pectoris)

anglicano/a [ãgli'kanu/a] *adj, m/f* Anglican

Angola [ã'gɔla] *f* Angola

angra ['ãgra] *f* inlet, cove

angu [ã'gu] *m* corn-meal purée

ângulo ['ãgulu] *m* angle; (*canto*) corner

angústia [ã'guʃtʃia] *f* anguish, distress; **angustiante** [ãguʃ'tʃjãtʃi] *adj* distressing; (*momentos*) anxious, nerve-racking; **angustiar** [ãguʃ'tʃja*] *vt* to distress

anil [a'niw] *m* (*cor*) indigo

animação [anima'sãw] *f* (*vivacidade*) liveliness; (*movimento*) bustle; (*entusiasmo*) enthusiasm

animado/a [ani'madu/a] *adj* lively;

(*alegre*) cheerful; ~ **com** enthusiastic about

animador(a) [anima'do*(a)] *adj* encouraging ♦ *m/f* (*BR*: *TV*) presenter

animal [ani'maw] (*pl* –ais) *adj*, *m* animal; ~ **de estimação** pet (animal)

animar [ani'ma*] *vt* to liven up; (*encorajar*) to encourage; ~-**se** *vr* to cheer up; (*festa etc*) to liven up; ~-**se a** to bring o.s. to

ânimo ['animu] *m* (*coragem*) courage; ~! cheer up!; **perder o** ~ to lose heart; **recobrar o** ~ to pluck up courage; (*alegrar-se*) to cheer up

animosidade [animozi'dadʒi] *f* animosity

aninhar [ani'ɲa*] *vt* to nestle; ~-**se** *vr* to nestle

aniquilar [aniki'la*] *vt* to annihilate; (*destruir*) to destroy

anis [a'niʃ] *m* aniseed

anistia [aniʃ'tʃia] *f* amnesty

aniversário [anivex'sarju] *m* anniversary; (*de nascimento*) birthday; (: *festa*) birthday party

anjo ['ãʒu] *m* angel; ~ **da guarda** guardian angel

ano ['anu] *m* year; **Feliz A~ Novo!** Happy New Year!; **o** ~ **que vem** next year; **por per annum**; **fazer** ~**s** to have a birthday; **ter dez** ~ to be ten (years old); **dia de** ~**s** (*PT*) birthday; ~ **letivo** academic year; (*da escola*) school year

anões [a'nõjʃ] *mpl de* **anão**

anoitecer [anojte'se*] *vi* to grow dark ♦ *m* nightfall

anomalia [anoma'lia] *f* anomaly

anônimo/a [a'nonimu/a] *adj* anonymous

anoraque [ano'raki] *m* anorak

anorexia [ano'rɛksja] *f* anorexia

anormal [anox'maw] (*pl* –ais) *adj* abnormal; (*excepcional*) handicapped; ~**idade** [anoxmali'dadʒi] *f* abnormality

anotação [anota'sãw] (*pl* –ões) *f* annotation; (*nota*) note

anotar [ano'ta*] *vt* to annotate; (*tomar nota*) to note down

anseio *etc* [ã'seju] *vb* V **ansiar**

ânsia ['ãsja] *f* anxiety; (*desejo*): ~ (**de**) longing (for); **ter** ~**s de** (*de vômito*) to feel sick

ansiar [ã'sja*] *vi*: ~ **por** (*desejar*) to yearn for; ~ **por fazer** to long to do

ansiedade [ãsje'dadʒi] *f* anxiety; (*desejo*) eagerness

ansioso/a [ã'sjozu/ɔza] *adj* anxious; (*desejoso*) eager

antagonista [ãtago'niʃta] *m/f* antagonist; (*adversário*) opponent

Antártico [ã'taxtʃiku] *m*: **o** ~ the Antarctic

ante [ã'tʃi] *prep* (*na presença de*) before; (*em vista de*) in view of, faced with

antebraço [ãtʃi'brasu] *m* forearm

antecedência [ãtese'dẽsja] *f*: **com** ~ in advance; **3 dias de** ~ three days' notice

antecedente [ãtese'dẽtʃi] *adj* preceding ♦ *m* antecedent; ~**s** *mpl* (*registro*) record *sg*; (*passado*) background *sg*

anteceder [ãtese'de*] *vt* to precede

antecipação [ãtesipa'sãw] *f* anticipation; **com um mês de** ~ a month in advance; ~ **de pagamento** advance (payment)

antecipadamente [ãtesipada'mẽtʃi] *adv* in advance, beforehand

antecipado/a [ãtesi'padu/a] *adj* (*pagamento*) (in) advance

antecipar [ãtesi'pa*] *vt* to anticipate, forestall; (*adiantar*) to bring forward

antemão [ante'mãw]: **de** ~ *adv* beforehand

antena [ã'tɛna] *f* (*BIO*) antenna, feeler; (*RADIO*, *TV*) aerial

anteontem [ãtʃi'õtẽ] *adv* the day before yesterday

antepassado [ãtʃipa'sadu] *m* ancestor

antepor [ãte'po*] (*irreg: como* **pôr**) *vt* to put before; ~-**se a** to anticipate

anteprojeto [ãtepro'ʒɛtu] (*PT* -ect-) *m* outline, draft

anterior [ãte'rjo*] *adj* previous; (*antigo*) former; (*de posição*) front

antes ['ãtʃiʃ] *adv* before; (*antigamente*) formerly; (*ao contrário*) rather ♦ *prep*: ~ **de** before; **o quanto** ~ as soon as possible; ~ **de partir** before leaving; ~ **de tudo** above all; ~ **que** before

antever [ãte've*] (*irreg: como* **ver**) *vt* to anticipate, foresee

anti- [ãtʃi] *prefixo* anti-

antiácido/a [ã'tʃjasidu/a] *adj* antacid ♦ *m* antacid

antiaéreo/a [ãtʃja'ɛrju/a] *adj* anti-aircraft

antibiótico/a [ãtʃi'bjɔtʃiku/a] *adj* antibiotic ♦ *m* antibiotic

anticaspa [ãtʃi'kaʃpa] *adj inv*: **xampu** ~ dandruff shampoo

anticlímax [ãtʃi'klimaks] *m* anticlimax

anticoncepcional [ãtʃikõsepsjo'naw] (*pl* –ais) *adj*, *m* contraceptive

anticongelante [ãtʃikõʒe'lãtʃi] *m* antifreeze

anticorpo [ãtʃi'koxpu] *m* antibody

antídoto [ã'tʃidotu] *m* antidote

antigamente [ãtʃiga'mẽtʃi] *adv* formerly; (*no passado*) in the past

antigo/a [ã'tʃigu/a] *adj* old; (*histórico*) ancient; (*de estilo*) antique; (*chefe etc*) former

antiguidade [ãtʃigi'dadʒi] *f* antiquity, ancient times *pl*; (*de emprego*) seniority; ~**s** *fpl* (*monumentos*) ancient monuments; (*artigos*) antiques

anti-higiênico/a *adj* unhygienic

anti-horário/a *adj* anticlockwise

antilhano/a [ãtʃi'ʎanu/a] *adj*, *m/f* West Indian

Antilhas [ã'tʃiʎaʃ] *fpl*: **as** ~ the West Indies

antílope [ã'tʃilopi] *m* antelope

antipatia [ãtʃipa'tʃia] *f* dislike; **antipático/a** [ãtʃi'patʃiku/a] *adj* unpleasant, unfriendly

antipatizar [ãtʃipatʃi'za*] *vi*: ~ **com alguém** to dislike sb

antiquado/a [ãtʃi'kwadu/a] *adj* antiquated; *(fora de moda)* out of date, old-fashioned

antiquário/a [ãtʃi'kwarju/a] *m/f* antique dealer ♦ *m (loja)* antique shop

anti-semita *adj* anti-Semitic

anti-séptico/a *adj* antiseptic ♦ *m* antiseptic

anti-social *(pl –ais) adj* antisocial

antolhos [ã'tɔʎuʃ] *mpl (pala)* eye-shade *sg*; *(de cavalo)* blinkers

antologia [ãtolo'ʒia] *f* anthology

antropófago/a [ãtro'pɔfagu/a] *m/f* cannibal

anual [a'nwaw] *(pl –ais) adj* annual, yearly

anuário [a'nwarju] *m* yearbook

anulação [anula'sãw] *(pl –ões) f* cancellation; *(de contrato, casamento)* annulment

anular [anu'la*] *vt* to cancel; *(contrato, casamento)* to annul; *(efeito)* to cancel out ♦ *m* ring finger

anunciante [anũ'sjãtʃi] *m (COM)* advertiser

anunciar [anũ'sja*] *vt* to announce; *(COM)* to advertise

anúncio [a'nũsju] *m* announcement; *(COM)* advertisement; *(cartaz)* notice; ~s **classificados** small *ou* classified ads

ânus [ˈanuʃ] *m inv* anus

anzol [ã'zɔw] *(pl –óis) m* fish-hook

ao [aw] = **a** + **o**

aonde [a'õdʒi] *adv* where; ~ **quer que** wherever

aos [awʃ] = **a** + **os**

Ap. *abr* = **apartamento**

apagado/a [apa'gadu/a] *adj*: **o fogo estava** ~/**a luz estava apagada** the fire was out/the light was off

apagar [apa'ga*] *vt* to put out; *(luz elétrica)* to switch off; *(vela)* to blow out; *(com borracha)* to rub out, erase; ~**-se** *vr* to go out

apaixonado/a [apajʃo'nadu/a] *adj (discurso)* impassioned; *(pessoa):* **ele está** ~ **por ela** he is in love with her; **ele é** ~ **por tênis** he's mad about tennis

apaixonar-se [apajʃo'naxsi] *vr*: ~ **por** to fall in love with

apalermado/a [apalex'madu/a] *adj* silly

apalpar [apaw'pa*] *vt* to touch, feel; *(MED)* to examine

apanhado [apa'ɲadu] *m (de flores)* bunch; *(resumo)* summary

apanhar [apa'ɲa*] *vt* to catch; *(algo à mão, do chão)* to pick up; *(surra, táxi)* to get; *(flores, frutas)* to pick; *(agarrar)* to grab ♦ *vi* to get a beating; ~ **sol/chuva** to sunbathe/get soaked

apara [a'para] *f (de madeira)* shaving; *(de*

papel) clipping

aparador [apara'do*] *m* sideboard

apara-lápis [apara'lapiʃ] *(PT) m inv* pencil sharpener

aparar [apa'ra*] *vt (cabelo)* to trim; *(lápis)* to sharpen; *(algo arremessado)* to catch

aparato [apa'ratu] *m* pomp; *(coleção)* array; ~**so/a** [apara'tozu/ɔza] *adj* grand

aparecer [apare'se*] *vi* to appear; *(apresentar-se)* to turn up; *(ser publicado)* to be published; ~ **em casa de alguém** to call on sb; **aparecimento** [aparesi'mẽtu] *m* appearance; *(publicação)* publication

aparelhado/a [apare'ʎadu/a] *adj* ready, prepared

aparelhar [apare'ʎa*] *vt* to prepare, get ready; *(NÁUT)* to rig; ~**-se** *vr* to get ready

aparelho [apa'reʎu] *m* apparatus; *(equipamento)* equipment; *(PESCA)* tackle; *(máquina)* machine; *(BR: fone)* telephone; ~ **de barbear** electric shaver; ~ **de chá** tea set; ~ **de rádio/TV** radio/TV set; ~ **doméstico** domestic appliance

aparência [apa'rẽsja] *f* appearance; **na** ~ apparently; **sob a** ~ **de** under the guise of; **ter** ~ **de** to look like, seem

aparentar [aparẽ'ta*] *vt (fingir)* to feign; *(parecer)* to look; **não aparenta a sua idade** he doesn't look his age

aparente [apa'rẽtʃi] *adj* apparent

aparição [apari'sãw] *(pl –ões) f (visão)* apparition; *(fantasma)* ghost

apartamento [apaxta'mẽtu] *m* apartment, flat *(BRIT)*

apartar [apax'ta*] *vt* to separate; ~**-se** *vr* to separate

aparte [a'paxtʃi] *m (TEATRO)* aside

apartheid [apax'tajdʒi] *m* apartheid

apatetado/a [apate'tadu/a] *adj* thick, stupid

apatia [apa'tʃia] *f* apathy

apático/a [a'patʃiku/a] *adj* apathetic

apavorado/a [apavo'radu/a] *adj* terrified

apavorante [apavo'rãtʃi] *adj* terrifying

apavorar [apavo'ra*] *vt* to terrify ♦ *vi* to be terrifying; ~**-se** *vr* to be terrified

apaziguar [apazi'gwa*] *vt* to appease; ~**-se** *vr* to calm down

apear-se [a'pjaxsi] *vr*: ~ **de** *(cavalo)* to dismount from

apegado/a [ape'gadu/a] *adj*: **ser** ~ **a** *(gostar de)* to be attached to

apegar-se [ape'gaxsi] *vr*: ~ **a** *(afeiçoar-se)* to become attached to

apego [a'pegu] *m (afeição)* attachment

apelação [apela'sãw] *(pl –ões) f* appeal

apelar [ape'la*] *vi* to appeal; ~ **da sentença** *(JUR)* to appeal against the sentence; ~ **para** to appeal to; ~ **para a ignorância/violência** to resort to abuse/violence

apelido [ape'lidu] *m (BR: alcunha)* nickname; *(PT: nome de família)* surname

apelo [a'pelu] *m* appeal

apenas [a'penaʃ] *adv* only

apêndice [a'pẽdʒisi] *m* appendix; (*anexo*) supplement; **apendicite** [apẽdʒi'sitʃi] *f* appendicitis

apequenar [apekє'na*] *vt* to belittle

aperceber-se [apexse'bexsi] *vr*: ~ **de** to notice, see

aperfeiçoamento [apexfejswa'mẽtu] *m* (*perfeição*) perfection; (*melhoramento*) improvement

aperfeiçoar [apexfej'swa*] *vt* to perfect; (*melhorar*) to improve; ~**-se** *vr* to improve o.s.

aperreado/a [ape'xjadu/a] *adj* fed up

apertado/a [apex'tadu/a] *adj* tight; (*estreito*) narrow; (*sem dinheiro*) hard-up; (*vida*) hard

apertar [apex'ta*] *vt* (*agarrar*) to hold tight; (*roupa*) to take in; (*esponja*) to squeeze; (*botão*) to press; (*despesas*) to limit; (*vigilância*) to step up; (*coração*) to break; (*fig*: *pessoa*) to put pressure on ♦ *vi* (*sapatos*) to pinch; (*chuva, frio*) to get worse; (*estrada*) to narrow; ~ **em** (*insistir*) to insist on; ~ **a mão de alguém** to shake hands with sb

aperto [a'pextu] *m* pressure; (*situação difícil*) spot of bother, jam; **um** ~ **de mãos** a handshake

apesar [ape'za*]: ~ **de** *prep* in spite of, despite; ~ **disso** nevertheless; ~ **de que** even though

apetecer [apete'se*] *vi* (*comida*) to be appetizing

apetecível [apete'sivew] (*pl* **-eis**) *adj* tempting

apetite [ape'tʃitʃi] *m* appetite; (*desejo*) desire; **bom** ~**!** enjoy your meal!; **apetitoso/a** [apeti'tozu/ɔza] *adj* appetizing

apetrechos [ape'treʃuʃ] *mpl* gear *sg*; (*PESCA*) tackle *sg*

ápice ['apisi] *m* (*cume*) summit, top; (*vértice*) apex

apiedar-se [apje'daxsi] *vr*: ~ **de** to pity; (*compadecer-se*) to take pity on

apimentado/a [apimẽ'tadu/a] *adj* peppery

apinhado/a [api'ɲadu/a] *adj* crowded

apinhar [api'ɲa*] *vt* to crowd, pack; ~**-se** *vr* to crowd together; ~**-se de** (*gente*) to be filled *ou* packed with

apitar [api'ta*] *vi* to whistle; **apito** [a'pitu] *m* whistle

aplacar [apla'ka*] *vt* to placate ♦ *vi* to calm down; ~**-se** *vr* to calm down

aplainar [aplaj'na*] *vt* to plane; (*nivelar*) to level out

aplanar [apla'na*] *vt* (*alisar*) to smooth; (*nivelar*) to level; (*dificuldades*) to smooth over

aplaudir [aplaw'dʒi*] *vt* to applaud

aplauso [a'plawzu] *m* applause; (*apoio*) support; (*elogio*) praise; (*aprovação*) approval; ~**s** applause *sg*

aplicação [aplika'sãw] (*pl* **-ões**) *f* application; (*esforço*) effort; (*da lei*) enforcement; (*de dinheiro*) investment

aplicado/a [apli'kadu/a] *adj* hard-working

aplicar [apli'ka*] *vt* to apply; (*lei*) to enforce; (*dinheiro*) to invest; ~**-se** *vr*: ~**-se a** to devote o.s. to

apoderar-se [apode'raxsi] *vr*: ~ **de** to seize, take possession of

apodrecer [apodre'se*] *vt* to rot; (*dente*) to decay ♦ *vi* to rot; to decay; **apodrecimento** [apodresi'mẽtu] *m* rottenness; decay

apogeu [apo'ʒew] *m* (*fig*) height, peak

apoiar [apo'ja*] *vt* to support; (*basear*) to base; (*moção*) to second; ~**-se** *vr*: ~**-se em** to rest on

apoio [a'poju] *m* support; (*financeiro*) backing

apólice [a'pɔlisi] *f* (*certificado*) policy, certificate; (*ação*) share, bond; ~ **de seguro** insurance policy

apologia [apolo'ʒia] *f* (*elogio*) eulogy; (*defesa*) defence (*BRIT*), defense (*US*)

apontador [apõta'do*] *m* pencil sharpener

apontamento [apõta'mẽtu] *m* (*nota*) note

apontar [apõ'ta*] *vt* (*fusil*) to aim; (*erro*) to point out; (*com o dedo*) to point at *ou* to; (*razão*) to put forward ♦ *vi* to begin to appear; (*brotar*) to sprout; (*com o dedo*) to point; ~ **para** to point to; (*com arma*) to aim at

apoquentar [apokẽ'ta*] *vt* to annoy, pester; ~**-se** *vr* to get annoyed

após [a'pɔjʃ] *prep* after

aposentado/a [apozẽ'tadu/a] *adj* retired ♦ *m/f* retired person, pensioner; **ser** ~ to be retired; ~**ria** [apozẽtado'ria] *f* retirement; (*dinheiro*) pension

aposentar [apozẽ'ta*] *vt* to retire; ~**-se** *vr* to retire

aposento [apo'zẽtu] *m* room

após-guerra *m*: **a Alemanha do** ~ post-war Germany

apossar-se [apo'saxsi] *vr*: ~ **de** to take possession of, seize

aposta [a'pɔʃta] *f* bet

apostar [apoʃ'ta*] *vt* to bet ♦ *vi*: ~ **em** to bet on

apóstolo [a'pɔʃtolu] *m* apostle

apóstrofo [a'pɔʃtrofu] *m* apostrophe

aprazível [apra'zivew] (*pl* **-eis**) *adj* pleasant

apreçar [apre'sa*] *vt* to value, price

apreciação [apresja'sãw] *f* appreciation

apreciar [apre'sja*] *vt* to appreciate; (*gostar de*) to enjoy

apreciativo/a [apresja'tʃivu/a] *adj* appreciative

apreço [a'presu] *m* esteem, regard; (*consideração*) consideration; **em** ~ in question

apreender [aprjẽ'de*] *vt* to apprehend;

(*tomar*) to seize; (*entender*) to grasp

apreensão [aprjĕ'sãw] (*pl* –ões) *f* (*percepção*) perception; (*tomada*) seizure; (*receio*) apprehension

apreensivo/a [aprjĕ'sivu/a] *adj* apprehensive

apreensões [aprjĕ'sõjʃ] *fpl de* **apreensão**

apregoar [apre'gwa*] *vt* to proclaim, announce; (*mercadorias*) to cry

aprender [aprĕ'de*] *vt, vi* to learn; ~ **a ler** to learn to read; ~ **de cor** to learn by heart

aprendiz [aprĕ'dʒiʒ] *m* apprentice; (*condutor*) learner

aprendizagem [aprĕdʒi'zaʒē] *f* (*num ofício*) apprenticeship; (*numa profissão*) training; (*escolar*) learning

apresentação [aprezĕta'sãw] (*pl* –ões) *f* presentation; (*de peça, filme*) performance; (*de pessoas*) introduction; (*porte pessoal*) appearance

apresentador(a) [aprezĕta'do*(a)] *m/f* presenter

apresentar [aprezĕ'ta*] *vt* to present; (*pessoas*) to introduce; ~**-se** *vr* to introduce o.s.; (*problema*) to present itself; (*à policia etc*) to report; **quero** ~**-lhe** may I introduce you to

apressado/a [apre'sadu/a] *adj* hurried, hasty; **estar** ~ to be in a hurry

apressar [apre'sa*] *vt* to hurry; ~**-se** *vr* to hurry (up)

aprestar [apreʃ'ta*] *vt* to equip, fit out; (*aprontar*) to get ready; ~**-se** *vr* to get ready; **aprestos** [a'prɛʃtuʃ] *mpl* preparations

aprisionamento [aprizjona'mẽtu] *m* imprisonment

aprisionar [aprizjo'na*] *vt* (*cativar*) to capture; (*encarcerar*) to imprison

aprofundar [aprofũ'da*] *vt* to deepen, make deeper; ~**-se** *vr*: ~**-se em** to go deeper into

aprontar [aprõ'ta*] *vt* to get ready, prepare; ~**-se** *vr* to get ready

apropriação [aproprja'sãw] (*pl* –ões) *f* appropriation; (*tomada*) seizure

apropriado/a [apro'prjadu/a] *adj* appropriate, suitable

apropriar [apro'prja*] *vt* to appropriate; ~**-se** *vr*: ~**-se de** to seize, take possession of

aprovação [aprova'sãw] *f* approval; (*louvor*) praise; (*num exame*) pass

aprovado/a [apro'vadu/a] *adj* approved; **ser** ~ **num exame** to pass an exam

aprovar [apro'va*] *vt* to approve of; (*exame*) to pass ♦ *vi* to make the grade

aproveitador(a) [aprovejta'do*(a)] *m/f* opportunist

aproveitamento [aprovejta'mẽtu] *m* use, utilization; (*nos estudos*) progress

aproveitar [aprovej'ta*] *vt* to take advantage of; (*utilizar*) to use; (*oportunidade*) to take ♦ *vi* to make the most of

it; (*PT*) to be of use; **aproveite!** enjoy yourself!

aprovisionar [aprovizjo'na*] *vt* to supply; (*estocar*) to stock

aproximação [aprosima'sãw] (*pl* –ões) *f* approximation; (*chegada*) approach; (*proximidade*) nearness

aproximado/a [aprosi'madu/a] *adj* approximate; (*perto*) nearby

aproximar [aprosi'ma*] *vt* to bring near; (*aliar*) to bring together; ~**-se** *vr*: ~**-se de** to approach

aptidão [aptʃi'dãw] *f* aptitude; (*jeito*) knack; ~ **física** physical fitness

apto/a [a'ptu/a] *adj* apt; (*capaz*) capable

apto. *abr* = **apartamento**

apunhalar [apuɲa'la*] *vt* to stab

apurado/a [apu'radu/a] *adj* refined

apurar [apu'ra*] *vt* to perfect; (*averiguar*) to investigate; (*dinheiro*) to raise, get; (*votos*) to count; ~**-se** *vr* to dress up

apuro [a'puru] *m* refinement, elegance; (*dificuldade*) difficulty; **estar em** ~**s** to be in trouble

aquarela [akwa'rɛla] *f* watercolour (*BRIT*), watercolor (*US*)

aquário [a'kwarju] *m* aquarium; **A**~ (*ASTROLOGIA*) Aquarius

aquartelar [akwaxte'la*] *vt* (*MIL*) to billet, quarter

aquático/a [a'kwatʃiku/a] *adj* aquatic, water *atr*

aquecer [ake'se*] *vt* to heat ♦ *vi* to heat up; ~**-se** *vr* to heat up; **aquecido/a** [ake'sidu/a] *adj* heated; **aquecimento** [akesi'mẽtu] *m* heating; **aquecimento central** central heating

aqueduto [ake'dutu] *m* aqueduct

aquele/ela [a'keli/ɛla] *adj* (*sg*) that; (*pl*) those ♦ *pron* (*sg*) that one; (*pl*) those

àquele/ela [a'keli/ɛla] = **a** + **aquele/ela**

aquém [a'kẽj] *adv* on this side; ~ **de** on this side of

aqui [a'ki] *adv* here; **eis** ~ here is/are; ~ **mesmo** right here; **até** ~ up to here; **por** ~ hereabouts; (*nesta direção*) this way

aquietar [akje'ta*] *vt* to calm, quieten; ~**-se** *vr* to calm down

aquilo [a'kilu] *pron* that; ~ **que** what

àquilo [a'kilu] = **a** + **aquilo**

aquisição [akizi'sãw] (*pl* –ões) *f* acquisition

ar [a*] *m* air; (*aspecto*) look; (*brisa*) breeze; (*PT: AUTO*) choke; ~**es** *mpl* (*atitude*) airs; (*clima*) climate *sg*; **ao** ~ **livre** in the open air; **no** ~ (*TV, RÁDIO*) on air; (*fig: planos*) up in the air; **dar-se** ~**es** to put on airs; ~ **condicionado** (*aparelho*) air conditioner; (*sistema*) air conditioning

árabe ['arabi] *adj*, *m/f* Arab ♦ *m* (*LING*) Arabic

Arábia [a'rabja] *f*: **a** ~ **Saudita** Saudi

Arabia

arado [a'radu] *m* plough (BRIT), plow (US)

aragem [a'raʒẽ] (*pl* –ns) *f* breeze

arame [a'rami] *m* wire

aranha [a'raɲa] *f* spider

arar [a'ra*] *vt* to plough (BRIT), plow (US)

arara [a'rara] *f* macaw

arbitragem [axbi'traʒẽ] *f* arbitration

arbitrar [axbi'tra*] *vt* to arbitrate; (ESPOR-TE) to referee

arbitrário/a [axbi'trarju/a] *adj* arbitrary

arbítrio [ax'bitrju] *m* decision; **ao ~ de** at the discretion of

árbitro ['axbitru] *m* (*juiz*) arbiter; (JUR) arbitrator; (FUTEBOL) referee; (TÊNIS *etc*) umpire

arbusto [ax'buʃtu] *m* shrub, bush

arca ['axka] *f* chest, trunk; **~ de Noé** Noah's Ark

arcada [ax'kada] *f* arcade; (*arco*) arch

arcaico/a [ax'kajku/a] *adj* archaic

arcar [ax'ka*] *vt*: **~ com** (*responsabili-dades*) to shoulder; (*despesas*) to handle; (*consequências*) to take

arcebispo [arse'biʃpu] *m* archbishop

arco ['axku] *m* (ARQ) arch; (MIL, MÚS) bow; (ELET, MAT) arc

arco-íris *m inv* rainbow

ardente [ax'dẽtʃi] *adj* burning; (*intenso*) fervent; (*apaixonado*) ardent

arder [ax'de*] *vi* to burn; (*pele*, *olhos*) to sting; **~ de raiva** to seethe (with rage)

ardido/a [ax'dʒidu/a] *adj* (*picante*) hot

ardil [ax'dʒiw] (*pl* –is) *m* trick, * ruse; **~oso/a** [axdʒi'lozu/ɔza] *adj* cunning

ardor [ax'do*] *m* ardour (BRIT), ardor (US); **~oso/a** [axdo'rozu/ɔza] *adj* ardent

ardósia [ax'dɔzja] *f* slate

árduo/a ['axdwu/a] *adj* arduous; (*difícil*) hard, difficult

área ['arja] *f* area; (ESPORTE) penalty area; (*fig*) field; **~ de serviço** balcony (*for hanging washing etc*)

areia [a'reja] *f* sand; **~ movediça** quick-sand

arejar [are'ʒa*] *vt* to air ♦ *vi* to get some air; (*descansar*) to have a breather; **~-se** *vr* to get some air; to have a break

arena [a'rɛna] *f* arena; (*de circo*) ring

arenito [are'nitu] *m* sandstone

arenoso/a [are'nozu/ɔza] *adj* sandy

arenque [a'rẽki] *m* herring

argamassa [axga'masa] *f* mortar

Argélia [ax'ʒɛlja] *f*: **a ~** Algeria

Argentina [axʒẽ'tʃina] *f*: **a ~** Argentina

argila [ax'ʒila] *f* clay

argola [ax'gɔla] *f* ring; **~s** *fpl* (*brincos*) hooped earrings; **~ (de porta)** door-knocker

argumentação [axgumẽta'sãw] *f* line of argument

argumentador(a) [axgumẽta'do*(a)] *adj* argumentative

argumentar [axgumẽ'ta*] *vt*, *vi* to argue

argumento [axgu'mẽtu] *m* argument; (*de obra*) theme

arguto/a [ax'gutu/a] *adj* subtle; (*astuto*) shrewd

aridez [ari'deʒ] *f* dryness; (*esterilidade*) barrenness; (*falta de interesse*) dullness

árido/a ['aridu/a] *adj* arid, dry; (*estéril*) barren; (*maçante*) dull

Áries ['arif] *f* Aries

aristocrata [ariʃto'krata] *m/f* aristocrat; **aristocrático/a** [ariʃto'kratʃiku/a] *adj* ar-istocratic

aritmética [aritʃ'mɛtʃika] *f* arithmetic

arma ['axma] *f* weapon; **~s** *fpl* (*nucleares etc*) arms; (*brasão*) coat *sg* of arms; **pas-sar pelas ~s** to shoot, execute; **~ convencional/nuclear** conventional/nuclear weapon; **~ de fogo** firearm

armação [axma'sãw] (*pl* –ões) *f* (*arm-adura*) frame; (PESCA) tackle; (NÁUT) rig-ging; (*de óculos*) frames *pl*

armada [ax'mada] *f* navy

armadilha [axma'dʒiʎa] *f* trap

armado/a [ax'madu/a] *adj* armed

armador [axma'do*] *m* (NÁUT) shipowner

armadura [axma'dura] *f* armour (BRIT), armor (US)

armamento [axma'mẽtu] *m* (*armas*) arm-aments *pl*, weapons *pl*; (NÁUT) equip-ment; (*ato*) arming

armar [ax'ma*] *vt* to arm; (*montar*) to as-semble; (*barraca*) to pitch; (*um aparel-ho*) to set up; (*armadilha*) to set; (NÁUT) to fit out; **~-se** *vr* to arm o.s.; **~ uma briga com** to pick a quarrel with

armarinho [axma'riɲu] *m* haberdashery (BRIT), notions *pl* (US)

armário [ax'marju] *m* cupboard; (*de rou-pa*) wardrobe

armazém [axma'zẽj] (*pl* –ns) *m* (*depósito*) warehouse; (*loja*) grocery store; **armaze-nar** [axmaze'na*] *vt* to store; (*provisões*) to stock

armeiro [ax'mejru] *m* gunsmith

arminho [ax'miɲu] *m* ermine

aro ['aru] *m* (*argola*) ring; (*de óculos*, *roda*) rim; (*de porta*) frame

aroma [a'roma] *m* aroma; **aromático/a** [aro'matʃiku/a] *adj* (*comida*) aromatic; (*perfume*) fragrant

arpão [ax'pãw] (*pl* –ões) *m* harpoon

arquear [ax'kja*] *vt* to arch; **~-se** *vr* to bend, arch; (*entortar-se*) to warp

arqueiro/a [ax'kejru/a] *m/f* archer; (*go-leiro*) goalkeeper

arquejar [axke'ʒa*] *vi* to pant, wheeze

arquejo [ax'keʒu] *m* panting, gasping

arqueologia [axkjolo'ʒia] *f* archaeology (BRIT), archeology (US); **arqueólogo/a** [ax'kjɔlogu/a] *m/f* archaeologist (BRIT), archeologist (US)

arquiteto/a [axki'tɛtu/a] (PT **-ect-**) *m/f* architect; **arquitetônico/a** [axkite'toniku/a] (PT **-ectó-**) *adj* architectural; **arquite-tura** [axkite'tura] (PT **-ect-**) *f* architecture

arquivar [axki'va*] *vt* to file; *(projeto)* to shelve

arquivo [ax'kivu] *m* *(ger, COMPUT)* file; *(lugar)* archive; *(de empresa)* files *pl*; *(móvel)* filing cabinet

arraia [a'xaja] *f (peixe)* ray

arraial [axa'jaw] *(pl* –ais) *(PT) m (festa)* fair

arraigado/a [axaj'gadu/a] *adj* deep-rooted; *(fig)* ingrained

arraigar [axaj'ga*] *vi* to root; ~-se *vr* to take root; *(estabelecer-se)* to settle

arrancada [axã'kada] *f (movimento, puxão)* jerk; **dar uma ~ em** *(puxar)* to jerk; **dar uma ~** *(em carro)* to pull away (suddenly)

arrancar [axã'ka*] *vt* to pull out; *(botão etc)* to pull off; *(arrebatar)* to snatch (away); *(fig: confissão)* to extract ♦ *vi* to start (off); ~-se *vr* to leave; *(fugir)* to run off

arranco [a'xãku] *m (puxão)* jerk; *(partida)* sudden start

arranha-céu [a'xaɲa-] *(pl* ~s) *m* skyscraper

arranhadura [axaɲa'dura] *f* scratch

arranhão [axa'ɲãw] *(pl* –ões) *m* scratch

arranhar [axa'ɲa*] *vt* to scratch

arranjar [axã'ʒa*] *vt* to arrange; *(emprego etc: emprego, namorado)* to get, find, to find; *(doença)* to get, catch; *(questão)* to settle; ~-se *vr* to manage; *(conseguir emprego)* to get a job; ~-se sem to do without

arranjo [a'xãʒu] *m* arrangement

arranque [a'xãki] *m:* **motor de ~** starter (motor)

arrasar [axa'za*] *vt* to devastate; *(demolir)* to demolish; *(estragar)* to ruin; ~-se *vr* to be devastated; *(destruir-se)* to destroy o.s.; *(arruinar-se)* to lose everything

arrastão [axaʃ'tãw] *(pl* –ões) *m* tug; *(rede)* dragnet

arrastar [axaʃ'ta*] *vt* to drag; *(atrair)* to draw ♦ *vi* to trail; ~-se *vr* to crawl; *(tempo, processo)* to drag (on)

arrear [a'xja*] *vt (cavalo etc)* to bridle

arrebatado/a [axeba'tadu/a] *adj* rash, impetuous

arrebatar [axeba'ta*] *vt* to snatch (away); *(levar)* to carry off; *(enlevar)* to entrance; *(enfurecer)* to enrage; ~-se *vr* to be entranced

arrebentado/a [axebẽ'tadu/a] *adj* broken; *(estafado)* worn out

arrebentar [axebẽ'ta*] *vt* to break; *(porta)* to break down; *(corda)* to snap ♦ *vi* to break; *(corda)* to snap; *(guerra)* to break out

arrebitado/a [axebi'tadu/a] *adj* turned-up; *(nariz)* snub

arrebitar [axebi'ta*] *vt* to turn up

arrecadar [axeka'da*] *vt (impostos etc)* to collect

arrecife [axe'sifi] *m* reef

arredar [axe'da*] *vt* to move away, move back; ~-se *vr* to move away; **não ~ pé** to stand one's ground

arredio/a [axe'dʒiu/a] *adj (pessoa)* withdrawn

arredondado/a [axedõ'dadu/a] *adj* round, rounded

arredondar [axedõ'da*] *vt* to round (off); *(conta)* to round up

arredores [axe'dɔriʃ] *mpl* suburbs; *(cercanias)* outskirts

arrefecer [axefe'se*] *vt* to cool; *(febre)* to lower; *(desanimar)* to discourage ♦ *vi* to cool (off); to get discouraged

ar-refrigerado [-xefriʒe'radu] *m* air conditioning

arregaçar [axega'sa*] *vt* to roll up

arregalado/a [axega'ladu/a] *adj (olhos)* wide

arregalar [axega'la*] *vt:* ~ **os olhos** to stare in amazement

arreios [a'xejuʃ] *mpl* harness *sg*

arrematar [axema'ta*] *vt (dizer concluindo)* to conclude; *(comprar)* to buy by auction; *(vender)* to sell by auction; *(COSTURA)* to finish off

arremedar [axeme'da*] *vt* to mimic

arremessar [axeme'sa*] *vt* to throw, hurl; **arremesso** [axe'mesu] *m* throw

arremeter [axeme'te*] *vi* to lunge; ~ **contra** *(acometer)* to attack, assail

arrendador(a) [axẽda'do*(a)] *m/f* landlord/landlady

arrendamento [axẽda'mẽtu] *m (ação)* leasing; *(contrato)* lease

arrendar [axẽ'da*] *vt* to lease

arrendatário/a [axẽda'tarju/a] *m/f* tenant

arrepender-se [axepẽ'dexsi] *vr* to repent; *(mudar de opinião)* to change one's mind; ~ **de** to regret, be sorry for; **arrependido/a** [axepẽ'dʒidu/a] *adj (pessoa)* sorry; **arrependimento** [axepẽdʒi'mẽtu] *m* regret; *(REL, de crime)* repentance

arrepiar [axe'pja*] *vt (amedrontar)* to horrify; *(cabelo)* to cause to stand on end; ~-se *vr* to shiver; *(cabelo)* to stand on end; **(ser) de ~ os cabelos** (to be) hair-raising

arrepio [axe'piu] *m* shiver; *(de frio)* chill; **isso me dá ~s** it gives me the creeps

arresto [a'xɛʃtu] *m (JUR)* seizure

arriar [a'xja*] *vt* to lower; *(depor)* to lay down ♦ *vi* to drop; *(vergar)* to sag; *(desistir)* to give up; *(fig)* to collapse

arribar [axi'ba*] *vi (recuperar-se)* to recuperate

arriscado/a [axiʃ'kadu/a] *adj* risky; *(audacioso)* daring

arriscar [axiʃ'ka*] *vt* to risk; *(pôr em perigo)* to endanger, jeopardize; ~-se *vr* to take a risk; ~-se **a fazer** to risk doing

arrivista [axi'viʃta] *m/f* upstart; *(oportu-

nista) opportunist

arrogância [axo'gãsja] *f* arrogance; **arrogante** [axo'gãtʃi] *adj* arrogant

arroio [a'xoju] *m* stream

arrojado/a [axo'ʒadu/a] *adj* (*design*) bold; (*temerário*) rash; (*ousado*) daring

arrojar [axo'ʒa*] *vt* to hurl

arrojo [a'xoʒu] *m* boldness

arrolamento [axola'mẽtu] *m* list

arrolar [axo'la*] *vt* to list

arrombar [axõ'ba*] *vt* (*porta*) to break down; (*cofre*) to crack

arrotar [axo'ta*] *vi* to belch ♦ *vt* (*alardear*) to boast of

arroz [a'xoʒ] *m* rice; ~ **doce** rice pudding

arruela [a'xwɛla] *f* (*TEC*) washer

arruinar [axwi'na*] *vt* to ruin; (*destruir*) to destroy; ~-**se** *vr* to be ruined; (*perder a saúde*) to ruin one's health

arrulhar [axu'ʎa*] *vi* (*pombos*) to coo

arrumação [axuma'sãw] *f* arrangement; (*de um quarto etc*) tidying up; (*de malas*) packing

arrumadeira [axuma'dejra] *f* cleaning lady; (*num hotel*) chambermaid

arrumar [axu'ma*] *vt* to put in order, arrange; (*quarto etc*) to tidy up; (*malas*) to pack; (*emprego*) to get; (*vestir*) to dress up; (*desculpa*) to make up, find; (*vida*) to sort out; ~-**se** *vr* (*aprontar-se*) to get dressed, get ready; (*na vida*) to sort o.s. out; (*virar-se*) to manage

arsenal [axse'naw] (*pl* –**ais**) *m* (*MIL*) arsenal

arsênio [ax'senju] *m* arsenic

arte ['axtʃi] *f* art; (*habilidade*) skill; (*ofício*) trade, craft

artefato [axtʃi'fatu] (*PT* -**act**-) *m* (*manufactured*) article

artéria [ax'tɛrja] *f* (*ANAT*) artery

arterial [axte'rjaw] (*pl* –**ais**) *adj*: **pressão ~** blood pressure

artesão/sã [axte'zãw/zã] (*pl* ~**s**/~**s**) *m/f* artisan, craftsman/woman

ártico/a ['axtʃiku/a] *adj* Arctic ♦ *m*: **o A~** the Arctic

artífice [ax'tʃifisi] *m/f* craftsman/woman; (*inventor*) inventor

artificial [axtʃifi'sjaw] (*pl* –**ais**) *adj* artificial

artifício [axtʃi'fisju] *m* stratagem, trick; **artificioso/a** [axtʃifi'sjozu/ɔza] *adj* (*hábil*) skilful (*BRIT*), skillful (*US*); (*astucioso*) artful

artigo [ax'tʃigu] *m* article; (*COM*) item; ~**s** *mpl* (*produtos*) goods

artilharia [axtʃiʎa'ria] *f* artillery

artista [ax'tʃista] *m/f* artist; **artístico/a** [ax'tʃistʃiku/a] *adj* artistic

artrite [ax'tritʃi] *f* (*MED*) arthritis

árvore ['axvori] *f* tree; (*TEC*) shaft; ~ **de Natal** Christmas tree

arvoredo [axvo'redu] *m* grove

as [aʃ] *art def V* a

ás [ajʃ] *m* ace

às [ajʃ] = **a** + **as**

asa ['aza] *f* wing; (*de xícara etc*) handle

asbesto [aʒ'bɛʃtu] *m* asbestos

ascendência [asẽ'dẽsja] *f* (*antepassados*) ancestry; (*domínio*) ascendancy, sway; **ascendente** [asẽ'dẽtʃi] *adj* rising, upward

ascender [asẽ'de*] *vi* to rise, ascend

ascensão [asẽ'sãw] (*pl* –**ões**) *f* ascent; (*REL*): **dia da A~** Ascension Day

ascensor [asẽ'so*] *m* lift (*BRIT*), elevator (*US*)

asco ['aʃku] *m* loathing, revulsion; **dar ~ a** to revolt, disgust

asfalto [aʃ'fawtu] *m* asphalt

asfixia [aʃfik'sia] *f* asphyxia, suffocation

Ásia ['azja] *f*: **a ~** Asia

asiático/a [a'zjatʃiku/a] *adj*, *m/f* Asian

asilo [a'zilu] *m* (*refúgio*) refuge; (*estabelecimento*) home; ~ **político** political asylum

asma ['aʒma] *f* asthma

asneira [aʒ'nejra] *f* (*tolice*) stupidity; (*ato*, *dito*) stupid thing

asno ['aʒnu] *m* donkey; (*fig*) ass

aspargo [aʃ'paxgu] *m* asparagus

aspas ['aʃpaʃ] *fpl* inverted commas

aspecto [aʃ'pɛktu] *m* aspect; (*aparência*) look, appearance; (*característica*) feature; (*ponto de vista*) point of view

aspereza [aʃpe'reza] *f* roughness; (*severidade*) harshness; (*rudeza*) rudeness

aspergir [aʃpex'ʒi*] *vt* to sprinkle

áspero/a ['aʃperu/a] *adj* rough; (*severo*) harsh; (*rude*) rude

asperso/a [aʃ'pɛxsu/a] *pp de* **aspergir** ♦ *adj* scattered

aspiração [aʃpira'sãw] (*pl* –**ões**) *f* aspiration; (*inalação*) inhalation

aspirador [aʃpira'do*] *m*: ~ (**de pó**) vacuum cleaner; **passar o ~** (**em**) to vacuum

aspirante [aʃpi'rãtʃi] *adj* aspiring ♦ *m/f* candidate

aspirar [aʃpi'ra*] *vt* to breathe in; (*bombear*) to suck up ♦ *vi* to breathe; (*soprar*) to blow; (*desejar*): ~ **a algo** to aspire to sth

aspirina [aʃpi'rina] *f* aspirin

aspirjo *etc* [aʃ'pixʒu] *vb V* **aspergir**

asqueroso/a [aʃke'rozu/ɔza] *adj* disgusting, revolting

assado/a [a'sadu/a] *adj* roasted; (*CULIN*) roast ♦ *m* roast; **carne assada** roast beef

assadura [asa'dura] *f* rash

assaltante [asaw'tãtʃi] *m/f* assailant; (*de banco*) robber; (*de casa*) burglar; (*na rua*) mugger

assaltar [asaw'ta*] *vt* to attack; (*casa*) to break into; (*banco*) to rob; (*pessoa na rua*) to mug; **assalto** [a'sawtu] *m* attack; raid, robbery; burglary, break-in; mugging; (*BOXE*) round

assanhar [asaˈɲaⁿ] vt to excite; ~-se vr to get excited

assar [aˈsaⁿ] vt to roast; (na grelha) to grill

assassinar [asasiˈnaⁿ] vt to murder, kill; (POL) to assassinate; **assassinato** [asasiˈnatu] m murder, killing; assassination; **assassino/a** [asaˈsinu/a] m/f murderer; assassin

assaz [aˈsaʒ] adv (suficientemente) sufficiently; (muito) rather

assediar [aseˈdʒjaⁿ] vt (sitiar) to besiege; (importunar) to pester; **assédio** [aˈsɛdʒu] m siege; (insistência) insistence

assegurar [aseguˈraⁿ] vt to secure; (garantir) to ensure; (afirmar) to assure; ~-se vr: ~-se de to make sure of

asseio [aˈseju] m cleanliness

assembléia [asẽˈblɛja] f assembly; (reunião) meeting; ~ **geral (ordinária)** annual general meeting

assemelhar [asemeˈʎaⁿ] vt to liken; ~-se vr to be alike; ~-se a to resemble, look like

assentado/a [asẽˈtadu/a] adj fixed, secure; (combinado) agreed; (ajuizado) sensible

assentar [asẽˈtaⁿ] vt (fazer sentar) to seat; (colocar) to place; (estabelecer) to establish; (decidir) to decide upon ♦ vi (pó etc) to settle; ~-se vr to sit down; ~ em ou a (roupa) to suit

assente [aˈsẽtʃi] pp de **assentar** ♦ adj agreed, decided

assentimento [asẽtʃiˈmẽtu] m assent, agreement

assentir [asẽˈtʃiⁿ] vi: ~ (em) to agree (to)

assento [aˈsẽtu] m seat; (base) base

assíduo/a [aˈsidwu/a] adj (aluno) who attends regularly; (diligente) assiduous; (constante) constant; **ser ~ num lugar** to be a regular visitor to a place

assim [aˈsĩ] adv (deste modo) like this, in this way, thus; (portanto) therefore; (igualmente) likewise; ~ ~ so-so; ~ **mesmo** in any case; **e ~ por diante** and so on; ~ **como** as well as; **como ~?** how do you mean?; ~ **que** (logo que) as soon as

assimilar [asimiˈlaⁿ] vt to assimilate; (apreender) to take in; (assemelhar) to compare

assinante [asiˈnãtʃi] m/f (de jornal etc) subscriber

assinar [asiˈnaⁿ] vt to sign

assinatura [asinaˈtura] f (nome) signature; (de jornal etc) subscription; (TEATRO) season ticket

assinto etc [aˈsĩtu] vb V **assentir**

assistência [asiʃˈtẽsja] f (presença) presence; (público) audience; (auxílio) aid; ~ **social** social work

assistente [asiʃˈtẽtʃi] adj assistant ♦ m/f spectator, onlooker; (ajudante) assistant;

~ **social** social worker

assistir [asiʃˈtʃiⁿ] vt, vi: ~ (a) (MED) to attend (to); ~ **a** to assist; (TV, filme, jogo) to watch; (reunião) to attend

assoar [asoˈaⁿ] vt: ~ **o nariz** to blow one's nose; ~-se vr (PT) to blow one's nose

assobiar [asoˈbjaⁿ] vi to whistle

assobio [asoˈbiu] m whistle

associação [asosjaˈsãw] (pl -ões) f association; (organização) society; (parceria) partnership

associado/a [asoˈsjadu/a] adj associate ♦ m/f associate, member; (COM) associate; (sócio) partner

associar [asoˈsjaⁿ] vt to associate; ~-se vr: ~-se a to associate with

assomar [asoˈmaⁿ] vi (aparecer) to appear

assombração [asõbraˈsãw] (pl -ões) f ghost

assombrado/a [asõˈbradu/a] adj astonished, amazed

assombrar [asõˈbraⁿ] vt to astonish, amaze; ~-se vr to be amazed

assombro [aˈsõbru] m amazement, astonishment; (maravilha) marvel; ~**so/a** [asõˈbrozu/ɔza] adj astonishing, amazing

assoviar [asoˈvjaⁿ] vt = **assobiar**

assovio [asoˈviu] m = **assobio**

assumir [asuˈmiⁿ] vt to assume, take on; (reconhecer) to accept

assunto [aˈsũtu] m subject, matter; (enredo) plot

assustador(a) [asuʃtaˈdo*(a)] adj (alarmante) startling; (amedrontador) frightening

assustar [asuʃˈtaⁿ] vt to frighten; (alarmar) to startle; ~-se vr to be frightened

asteca [aʃˈtɛka] adj, m/f Aztec

asterisco [aʃteˈriʃku] m asterisk

astrologia [aʃtroloˈʒia] f astrology; **astrólogo/a** [aʃˈtrɔlogu/a] m/f astrologer

astronauta [aʃtroˈnawta] m/f astronaut

astronave [aʃtroˈnavi] f spaceship

astronomia [aʃtronoˈmia] f astronomy; **astrônomo/a** [aʃˈtronomu/a] m/f astronomer

astúcia [aʃˈtusja] f cunning; **astuto/a** [aʃˈtutu/a] adj astute; (esperto) cunning

ata [ˈata] f (de reunião) minutes pl

atacadista [atakaˈdʒiʃta] adj wholesale ♦ m/f wholesaler

atacado [ataˈkadu] m: **por ~** wholesale

atacante [ataˈkãtʃi] adj attacking ♦ m/f attacker, assailant ♦ m (FUTEBOL) forward

atacar [ataˈkaⁿ] vt to attack; (problema etc) to tackle

atado/a [aˈtadu/a] adj (desajeitado) clumsy, awkward; (perplexo) puzzled

atadura [ataˈdura] f bandage

atalhar [ataˈʎaⁿ] vt (impedir) to prevent; (abreviar) to shorten ♦ vi to take a short cut

atalho [a'taʎu] *m* (*caminho*) short cut

atapetar [atape'ta*] *vt* to carpet

ataque [a'taki] *m* attack; ~ **aéreo** air raid

atar [a'ta*] *vt* to tie (up), fasten; **não ~ nem desatar** (*pessoa*) to waver; (*negócio*) to be in the air

atarefado/a [atare'fadu/a] *adj* busy

atarracado/a [ataxa'kadu/a] *adj* stocky

ataúde [ata'udʒi] *m* coffin

ataviar [ata'vja*] *vt* to adorn, decorate; **~-se** *vr* to get dressed up; **atavio** [ata'viu] *m* adornment

até [a'tɛ] *prep* (*PT*: + *a*: *lugar*) up to, as far as; (*tempo etc*) until, till ♦ *adv* (*tb*: ~ **mesmo**) even; ~ **certo ponto** to a certain extent; ~ **em cima** to the top; **já see you soon**; ~ **logo** bye!; ~ **onde** as far as; ~ **que** until; ~ **que enfim!** at last!

atear [ate'a*] *vt* (*fogo*) to kindle; (*fig*) to incite, inflame; **~-se** *vr* to blaze; (*paixões*) to flare up

atéia [a'tɛja] *f de* **ateu**

ateliê [ate'lje] *m* studio

atemorizador(a) [atemoriza'do*(a)] *adj* frightening

atemorizar [atemori'za*] *vt* to frighten; (*intimidar*) to intimidate

Atenas [a'tenaʃ] *n* Athens

atenção [atẽ'sãw] (*pl* **-ões**) *f* attention; (*cortesia*) courtesy; (*bondade*) kindness; **~!** be careful!; **chamar a ~** to attract attention; **atencioso/a** [atẽ'sjozu/ɔza] *adj* considerate

atender [atẽ'de*] *vt*: ~ **(a)** to attend to; (*receber*) to receive; (*deferir*) to grant; (*telefone etc*) to answer; (*paciente*) to see ♦ *vi* to answer; (*dar atenção*) to pay attention; **atendimento** [atẽdʒi'mẽtu] *m* service; (*recepção*) reception; **horário de atendimento** opening hours; (*em consultório*) surgery (*BRIT*) *ou* office (*US*) hours

atentado [atẽ'tadu] *m* attack; (*crime*) crime; (*contra a vida de alguém*) attempt on sb's life

atentar [atẽ'ta*] *vt* (*empreender*) to undertake ♦ *vi* to make an attempt; ~ **a** *ou* **em** *ou* **para** to pay attention to; ~ **contra a vida de alguém** to make an attempt on sb's life; ~ **contra a moral** to offend against morality

atento/a [a'tẽtu/a] *adj* attentive; **estar ~ a** to be aware *ou* mindful of

atenuante [ate'nwãtʃi] *adj* extenuating ♦ *m* extenuating circumstance

atenuar [ate'nwa*] *vt* to reduce, lessen

aterragem [ate'xaʒẽj] (*PT*: *pl* **-ns**) *f* (*AER*) landing

aterrar [ate'xa*] (*PT*) *vi* (*AER*) to land

aterrissagem [atexi'saʒẽ] (*BR*: *pl* **-ns**) *f* (*AER*) landing

aterrissar [atexi'sa*] (*BR*) *vi* (*AER*) to land

aterrizar [atexi'za*] *vi* = **aterrissar**

aterrorizante [atexori'zãtʃi] *adj* terrifying

aterrorizar [atexori'za*] *vt* to terrorize

atestado [ateʃ'tadu] *m* certificate; (*prova*) proof; (*JUR*) testimony

atestar [ateʃ'ta*] *vt* to certify; (*provar*) to prove; (*testemunhar*) to bear witness to

ateu/atéia [a'tew/a'tɛja] *adj*, *m/f* atheist

atiçar [atʃi'sa*] *vt* (*fogo*) to poke; (*incitar*) to incite; (*provocar*) to provoke; (*sentimento*) to induce

atinar [atʃi'na*] *vt* (*acertar*) to guess correctly ♦ *vi*: ~ **com** (*solução*) to find; ~ **em** to notice; ~ **a fazer algo** to succeed in doing sth

atingir [atʃĩ'ʒi*] *vt* to reach; (*acertar*) to hit; (*afetar*) to affect; (*objetivo*) to achieve; (*compreender*) to grasp

atirador(a) [atʃira'do*(a)] *m/f* marksman/woman; ~ **de tocaia** sniper

atirar [atʃi'ra*] *vt* to throw, fling ♦ *vi* (*arma*) to shoot; **~-se** *vr*: **~-se a** to hurl o.s. at

atitude [atʃi'tudʒi] *f* attitude; (*postura*) posture

atividade [atʃivi'dadʒi] *f* activity

ativo/a [a'tʃivu/a] *adj* active ♦ *m* (*COM*) assets *pl*

atlântico/a [at'lãtʃiku/a] *adj* Atlantic ♦ *m*: **o** (**Oceano**) **A~** the Atlantic (Ocean)

atlas ['atlaʃ] *m inv* atlas

atleta [at'lɛta] *m/f* athlete; **atlético/a** [at'lɛtʃiku/a] *adj* athletic; **atletismo** [atle'tʃiʒmu] *m* athletics *sg*

atmosfera [atmoʃ'fera] *f* atmosphere

ato ['atu] *m* act, action; (*cerimônia*) ceremony; (*TEATRO*) act; **em ~ contínuo** straight after; **no ~** on the spot; **no mesmo ~** at the same time

à-toa *adj* (*insignificante*) insignificant; (*simples*) simple, easy ♦ *adv* V **toa**

atoalhado/a [atoa'ʎadu/a] *adj*: (*tecido*) ~ towelling

atoleiro [ato'lejru] *m* bog, quagmire; (*fig*) quandary

atômico/a [a'tomiku/a] *adj* atomic

atomizador [atomiza'do*] *m* atomizer

átomo ['atomu] *m* atom

atônito/a [a'tonitu/a] *adj* astonished, amazed

ator [a'to*] *m* actor

atordoado/a [atox'dwadu/a] *adj* dazed

atordoamento [atoxdwa'mẽtu] *m* daze

atordoar [atox'dwa*] *vt* to daze, stun

atormentar [atoxmẽ'ta*] *vt* to torment

atração [atra'sãw] (*pl* **-ões**) *f* attraction

atracar [atra'ka*] *vt*, *vi* (*NÁUT*) to moor; **~-se** *vr* to grapple

atrações [atra'sõjʃ] *fpl de* **atração**

atractivo/a [atra'tivu/a] (*PT*) *adj* = **atrativo**

atraente [atra'ẽtʃi] *adj* attractive

atraiçoar [atraj'swa*] *vt* to betray

atrair [atra'i*] *vt* to attract; (*fascinar*) to

fascinate

atrapalhar [atrapa'ʎa*] *vt* to confuse; (*perturbar*) to disturb; (*dificultar*) to hinder ♦ *vi* to be a nuisance

atrás [a'trajʃ] *adv* behind; (*no fundo*) at the back ♦ *prep*: ~ **de** behind; (*no tempo*) after; **dois meses** ~ two months ago

atrasado/a [atra'zadu/a] *adj* late; (*país etc*) backward; (*relógio etc*) slow; (*pagamento*) overdue; ~**s** [atra'zaduʃ] *mpl* (*COM*) arrears

atrasar [atra'za*] *vt* to delay; (*progresso, desenvolvimento: progresso*) to hold back; (*relógio*) to put back; (*pagamento*) to be late with ♦ *vi* (*relógio etc*) to be slow; (*avião, pessoa*) to be late; ~**-se** *vr* to be late; (*num trabalho*) to fall behind; (*num pagamento*) to get into arrears

atraso [a'trazu] *m* delay; (*de país etc*) backwardness; ~**s** *mpl* (*COM*) arrears; **com 20 minutos de** ~ 20 minutes late

atrativo/a [atra'tʃivu/a] *adj* attractive ♦ *m* attraction; (*incentivo*) incentive; ~**s** *mpl* (*encantos*) charms

atravancar [atravã'ka*] *vt* to block, obstruct; (*encher*) to fill up

através [atra'vɛʃ] *adv* across; ~ **de** across; (*pelo centro de*) through

atravessar [atrave'sa*] *vt* to cross; (*pôr ao través*) to put *ou* lay across; (*traspassar*) to pass through

atrever-se [atre'vexsi] *vr*: ~ **a** to dare to; **atrevido/a** [atre'vidu/a] *adj* cheeky; (*corajoso*) bold; **atrevimento** [atrevi'mẽtu] *m* cheek; boldness

atribuir [atri'bwi*] *vt*: ~ **algo a** to attribute sth to; (*prêmios, regalias*) to confer sth on

atributo [atri'butu] *m* attribute

átrio ['atrju] *m* hall; (*pátio*) courtyard

atrito [a'tritu] *m* (*fricção*) friction; (*desentendimento*) disagreement

atriz [a'triʒ] *f* actress

atropelamento [atropela'mẽtu] *m* (*de pedestre*) road accident

atropelar [atrope'la*] *vt* to knock down, run over; (*empurrar*) to jostle

atroz [a'trɔʒ] *adj* (*cruel*) merciless; (*crime*) heinous; (*dor, lembrança*) terrible, awful

atuação [atwa'sãw] (*pl* –ões) *f* acting; (*de ator etc*) performance

atual [a'twaw] (*pl* –ais) *adj* current; (*pessoa, carro*) modern; ~**idade** [atwali'dadʒi] *f* present (time); ~**idades** *fpl* (*notícias*) news *sg*; ~**izar** [atwali'za*] *vt* to update; ~**mente** [atwaw'mẽtʃi] *adv* at present, currently; (*hoje em dia*) nowadays

atuante [a'twãtʃi] *adj* active

atuar [a'twa*] *vi* to act; ~ **para** to contribute to; ~ **sobre** to influence

atulhar [atu'ʎa*] *vt* to cram full

atum [a'tũ] (*pl* –ns) *m* tuna (fish)

aturdido/a [atux'dʒidu/a] *adj* stunned; (*com barulho*) deafened; (*com confusão, movimento*) bewildered

aturdimento [atuxdʒi'mẽtu] *m* bewilderment

aturdir [atux'dʒi*] *vt* to stun; (*suj: barulho*) to deafen; (: *confusão, movimento*) to bewilder

audácia [aw'dasja] *f* boldness; (*insolência*) insolence; **audacioso/a** [awda'sjozu/ɔza] *adj* daring; insolent

audição [awdʒi'sãw] (*pl* –ões) *f* audition

audiência [aw'dʒjẽsja] *f* audience; (*de tribunal*) session, hearing

audiovisual [awdʒjovi'zwaw] (*pl* –ais) *adj* audiovisual

auditar [awdʒi'ta*] *vt* to audit

auditor(a) [awdʒi'to*(a)] *m/f* auditor; (*juiz*) judge; (*ouvinte*) listener

auditoria [awdʒito'ria] *f*: **fazer a** ~ **de** to audit

auditório [awdʒi'tɔrju] *m* audience; (*recinto*) auditorium

auge ['awʒi] *m* height, peak

augurar [awgu'ra*] *vt* to augur; (*felicidades*) to wish; **augúrio** [aw'gurju] *m* omen

aula ['awla] *f* (*PT: sala*) classroom; (*lição*) lesson, class; **dar** ~ to teach

aumentar [awmẽ'ta*] *vt* to increase; (*salários, preços: salários*) to raise; (*sala, casa*) to expand, extend; (*suj: lente*) to magnify; (*acrescentar*) to add ♦ *vi* to increase; (*preço, salário: preço*) to rise, go up

aumento [aw'mẽtu] *m* increase; rise; (*ampliação*) enlargement; (*crescimento*) growth

auréola [aw'rɛola] *f* halo

aurora [aw'rɔra] *f* dawn

ausência [aw'zẽsja] *f* absence

ausentar-se [awzẽ'taxsi] *vr* (*ir-se*) to go away; (*afastar-se*) to stay away

ausente [aw'zẽtʃi] *adj* absent

auspício [aw'ʃpisju] *m*: **sob os** ~**s de** under the auspices of

austeridade [awʃteri'dadʒi] *f* austerity

austral [awʃ'traw] (*pl* –ais) *adj* southern

Austrália [awʃ'tralja] *f*: **a** ~ Australia; **australiano/a** [awʃtra'ljanu/a] *adj*, *m/f* Australian

Áustria ['awʃtrja] *f*: **a** ~ Austria; **austríaco/a** [awʃ'triaku/a] *adj*, *m/f* Austrian

autêntico/a [aw'tẽtʃiku/a] *adj* authentic; (*pessoa*) genuine; (*verdadeiro*) true, real

auto ['awtu] *m* car; ~**s** *mpl* (*JUR: processo*) legal proceedings; (*documentos*) legal papers

auto-adesivo/a *adj* self-adhesive

autobiografia [awtobjogra'fia] *f* autobiography

autocarro [awto'kaxu] (*PT*) *m* bus

autodefesa [awtode'feza] *f* self-defence (*BRIT*), self-defense (*US*)

autodidata [awtodʒi'data] *adj* self-taught
autodisciplina [awtodʒisi'plina] *f* self-discipline
autodominio [awtodo'minju] *m* self-control
autódromo [aw'tɔdromu] *m* race track
auto-escola *f* driving school
auto-estrada *f* motorway (*BRIT*), expressway (*US*)
autografar [awtogra'fa*] *vt* to autograph
autógrafo [aw'tɔgrafu] *m* autograph
automação [awtoma'sãw] *f* automation
automático/a [awto'matʃiku/a] *adj* automatic
automatização [awtomatʃiza'sãw] *f* = automação
automobilismo [awtomobi'liʒmu] *m* motoring, (*ESPORTE*) motor car racing
automóvel [awto'mɔvew] (*pl* –eis) *m* motor car (*BRIT*), automobile (*US*)
autonomia [awtono'mia] *f* autonomy; **autônomo/a** [aw'tonomu/a] *adj* autonomous
autópsia [aw'tɔpsja] *f* post-mortem, autopsy
autor(a) [aw'to*(a)] *m/f* author; (*de um crime*) perpetrator; (*JUR*) plaintiff
autoral [awto'raw] (*pl* –ais) *adj*: **direitos autorais** copyright *sg*
autoridade [awtori'dadʒi] *f* authority
autorização [awtoriza'sãw] (*pl* –ões) *f* permission, authorization; **dar ~ a alguém para** to authorize sb to
autorizar [awtori'za*] *vt* to authorize
auto-serviço *m* self-service
auto-suficiente *adj* self-sufficient
auxiliar [awsi'lja*] *adj* auxiliary ♦ *m/f* assistant ♦ *vt* to help; **auxílio** [aw'silju] *m* help, assistance
Av *abr* (= *avenida*) Ave
aval [a'vaw] (*pl* –ais) *m* guarantee
avalancha [ava'lãʃa] *f* avalanche
avalanche [ava'lãʃi] *f* = avalancha
avaliação [avalja'sãw] (*pl* –ões) *f* valuation; (*apreciação*) assessment
avaliar [ava'lja*] *vt* to value; (*apreciar*) to assess
avançada [avã'sada] *f* advance
avançado/a [avã'sadu/a] *adj* advanced; (*idéias, pessoa*) progressive
avançar [avã'sa*] *vi* to move forward ♦ *vi* to advance; **avanço** [a'vãsu] *m* advancement; (*progresso*) progress
avante [a'vãtʃi] *adv* forward
avarento/a [ava'rẽtu/a] *adj* mean ♦ *m/f* miser
avaria [ava'ria] *f* (*TEC*) breakdown; **~do/a** [ava'rjadu/a] *adj* (*máquina*) out of order; (*carro*) broken down; **~r** [ava'rja*] *vt* to damage ♦ *vi* to suffer damage; (*TEC*) to break down
ave [a'vi] *f* bird
aveia [a'veja] *f* oats *pl*
avelã [ave'lã] *f* hazelnut
avenida [ave'nida] *f* avenue

avental [avẽ'taw] (*pl* –ais) *m* apron; (*vestido*) pinafore dress (*BRIT*), jumper (*US*)
aventura [avẽ'tura] *f* adventure; **~r** [avẽtu'ra*] *vt* to risk, venture; **aventureiro/a** [avẽtu'rejru/a] *adj* adventurous
averiguação [averigwa'sãw] (*pl* –ões) *f* investigation, inquiry; (*verificação*) verification
averiguar [averi'gwa*] *vt* to investigate; (*verificar*) to verify
avermelhado/a [avexme'ʎadu/a] *adj* reddish
averso/a [a'vɛxsu/a] *adj*: ~ **a** averse to
avesso/a [a'vesu/a] *adj* (*lado*) opposite, reverse ♦ *m* wrong side, reverse; **ao ~** inside out; **às avessas** (*inverso*) upside down; (*oposto*) the wrong way round
avestruz [aveʃ'truʒ] *m* ostrich
aviação [avja'sãw] *f* aviation, flying
aviador(a) [avja'do*(a)] *m/f* aviator, airman/woman
aviamento [avja'mẽtu] *m* haberdashery (*BRIT*), notions *pl* (*US*)
avião [a'vjãw] (*pl* –ões) *m* aeroplane; ~ **a jato** jet
avidez [avi'deʒ] *f* greed; (*desejo*) eagerness; **ávido/a** ['avidu/a] *adj* greedy; eager
aviltar [aviw'ta*] *vt* to debase; **~-se** *vr* to demean o.s.
aviões [a'vjõjʃ] *mpl de* avião
avisar [avi'za*] *vt* to warn; (*informar*) to tell, let know; **aviso** [a'vizu] *m* (*comunicação*) notice
avistar [aviʃ'ta*] *vt* to catch sight of
avo [a'vu] *m*: **um doze ~s** one twelfth
avô/avó [a'vo/a'vɔ] *m/f* grandfather/mother; **avós** [a'vɔʃ] *mpl* grandparents
avulso/a [a'vuwsu/a] *adj* separate, detached
axila [ak'sila] *f* armpit
azar [a'za*] *m* bad luck; **~!** too bad, bad luck!; **estar com ~**, **ter ~** to be unlucky; **~ento/a** [aza'rẽtu/a] *adj* unlucky
azedar [aze'da*] *vt* to turn sour ♦ *vi* to turn sour; (*leite*) to go off; **azedo/a** [a'zedu/a] *adj* sour; off; (*fig*) grumpy
azeitar [azej'ta*] *vt* (*untar*) to grease; (*lubrificar*) to oil
azeite [a'zejtʃi] *m* oil; (*de oliva*) olive oil
azeitona [azej'tona] *f* olive
azeviche [aze'viʃi] *m* (*cor*) jet black
azevinho [aze'viɲu] *m* holly
azia [a'zia] *f* heartburn
aziago/a [a'zjagu/a] *adj* ominous
azo ['azu] *m* (*oportunidade*) opportunity; (*pretexto*) pretext
azougue [a'zogi] *m* (*QUÍM*) mercury
azul [a'zuw] (*pl* –uis) *adj* blue
azulejo [azu'leʒu] *m* (glazed) tile
azul-marinho *adj inv* navy blue
azul-turquesa *adj inv* turquoise

B

baba ['baba] *f* dribble

babá [ba'ba] *f* nanny

babaca [ba'baka] (*col*) *adj* stupid ♦ *m/f* idiot

baba-de-moça (*pl* **babas-de-moça**) *f* sweet made with sugar, coconut milk and eggs

babado [ba'badu] *m* frill; (*col*) piece of gossip

babador [baba'do*] *m* bib

babar [ba'ba*] *vi* to dribble; **~-se** *vr* to dribble; **babeiro** [ba'bejru] (*PT*) *m* bib

baby-sitter ['bejbisite*] (*pl* ~s) *m/f* baby-sitter

bacalhau [baka'ʎaw] *m* (dried) cod

bacana [ba'kana] (*col*) *adj* great

bacharel [baʃa'rɛw] (*pl* -**éis**) *m* graduate; **~-ar-se** [baʃare'laxsi] *vr* to graduate

bacia [ba'sia] *f* basin; (*ANAT*) pelvis

backup [ba'kapi] (*pl* ~s) *m* (*COMPUT*) back-up; **tirar um ~ de** to back up

baço/a ['basu/a] *adj* dull; (*metal*) tarnished ♦ *m* (*ANAT*) spleen

bactéria [bak'tɛrja] *f* germ, bacterium; **~s** bacteria *pl*

badalar [bada'la*] *vt*, *vi* to ring

baderna [ba'dɛxna] *f* commotion

badulaque [badu'laki] *m* trinket; **~s** *mpl* (*coisas sem valor*) junk *sg*

bafejar [bafe'ʒa*] *vt* (*aquecer com o bafo*) to blow; (*fortuna*) to smile upon; **bafejo** [ba'feʒu] *m* whiff; **bafejo da sorte** stroke of luck

bafo ['bafu] *m* (bad) breath

bafômetro [ba'fometru] *m* Breathalyser ®

baforada [bafo'rada] *f* puff

bagaço [ba'gasu] *m* (*de frutos*) pulp; (*PT: cachaça*) brandy; **estar/ficar um ~** (*fig: pessoa*) to be/get run down

bagageiro [baga'ʒejru] *m* (*AUTO*) roofrack; (*PT*) porter

bagagem [ba'gaʒẽ] *f* luggage; (*fig*) baggage; **recebimento de ~** (*AER*) baggage reclaim

bagatela [baga'tɛla] *f* trinket; (*fig*) trifle

bago ['bagu] *m* (*fruto*) berry; (*uva*) grape; (*de chumbo*) pellet

bagulho [ba'guʎu] *m* (*objeto*) piece of junk

bagunça [ba'gũsa] *f* mess, shambles *sg*; **~-do/a** [bagũ'sadu/a] *adj* in a mess; **~r** [bagũ'sa*] *vt* to mess up; **bagunceiro/a** [bagũ'sejru/a] *adj* messy

baía [ba'ia] *f* bay

bailado [baj'ladu] *m* dance; (*balé*) ballet

bailar [baj'la*] *vt*, *vi* to dance; **~-ino/a** [bajla'rinu/a] *m/f* ballet dancer

baile ['bajli] *m* dance; (*formal*) ball; **~ à fantasia** fancy-dress ball

bainha [ba'ina] *f* (*de arma*) sheath; (*de costura*) hem

bairro ['bajxu] *m* district

baixa ['bajʃa] *f* decrease; (*de preço: redução*) reduction; (: *queda*) fall; (*em vendas*) drop; (*em combate*) casualty; (*do serviço*) discharge

baixar [baj'ʃa*] *vt* to lower; (*ordem*) to issue; (*lei*) to pass; (*COMPUT*) to download ♦ *vi* to go (*ou* come) down; (*temperatura, preço*) to drop, fall

baixinho [baj'ʃinu] *adv* (*falar*) softly, quietly; (*em segredo*) secretly

baixo/a ['bajʃu/a] *adj* low; (*pessoa*) short, small; (*rio*) shallow; (*linguagem*) common; (*olhos, cabeça*) lowered; (*atitude*) mean; (*metal*) base ♦ *adv* low; (*em posição baixa*) low down; (*falar*) softly ♦ *m* (*MÚS*) bass; **em ~** below; (*em casa*) downstairs; **em voz baixa** in a quiet voice; **para ~** down, downwards; (*em casa*) downstairs; **por ~ de** under, underneath; **~-astral** (*col*) *m*: **estar num ~-astral** to be on a downer

bala ['bala] *f* bullet; (*BR: doce*) sweet

balada [ba'lada] *f* ballad

balaio [ba'laju] *m* straw basket

balança [ba'lãsa] *f* scales *pl*; **B~** (*ASTROLOGIA*) Libra; **~ comercial** balance of trade; **~ de pagamentos** balance of payments

balançar [balã'sa*] *vt* to swing; (*pesar*) to weigh (up) ♦ *vi* to swing; (*carro, avião*) to shake; (*em cadeira*) to rock; **~-se** *vr* to swing; **balanço** [ba'lãsu] *m* (*movimento*) swaying; (*brinquedo*) swing; (*de carro, avião*) shaking; (*COM: registro*) balance (sheet); (: *verificação*) audit; **fazer um balanço de** (*fig*) to take stock of

balão [ba'lãw] (*pl* -**ões**) *m* balloon

balar [ba'la*] *vi* to bleat

balaústre [bala'uʃtri] *m* ban(n)ister

balbuciar [bawbu'sja*] *vt*, *vi* to babble; **balbucio** [bawbu'siu] *m* babbling

balbúrdia [baw'buxdʒia] *f* uproar, bedlam

balcão [baw'kãw] (*pl* -**ões**) *m* balcony; (*de loja*) counter; (*TEATRO*) circle; **balconista** [bawko'niʃta] *m/f* shop assistant

balde ['bawdʒi] *m* bucket, pail

baldeação [bawdʒia'sãw] (*pl* -**ões**) *f* transfer

baldio/a [baw'dʒiu/a] *adj* fallow, uncultivated

balé [ba'lɛ] *m* ballet

baleia [ba'leja] *f* whale

baleiro/a [ba'lejru/a] *m/f* confectioner

balística [ba'liʃtʃika] *f* ballistics *sg*

baliza [ba'liza] *f* (*estaca*) post; (*bóia*) buoy; (*luminosa*) beacon; (*ESPORTE*) goal

balneário [baw'njarju] *m* bathing resort

balões [ba'lõjʃ] *mpl de* **balão**

balofo/a [ba'lofu/a] *adj* (*fofo*) fluffy; (*gordo*) plump

baloiço [ba'lojsu] (*PT*) *m* (*de criança*) swing; (*ação*) swinging

balouçar [balo'sa*] (*PT*) *vt*, *vi* to swing

balouço [ba'losu] *(PT) m* = **baloiço**
balsa ['bawsa] *f* raft; *(barca)* ferry
bálsamo ['bawsamu] *m* balm
baluarte [ba'lwaxtʃi] *m* rampart, bulwark; *(fig)* supporter
bamba ['bãba] *adj, m/f* expert
bambo/a ['bãbu/a] *adj* slack, loose
bambolear [bãbo'lja*] *vt* to swing ♦ *vi* to wobble
bambu [bã'bu] *m* bamboo
banal [ba'naw] *(pl* –**ais**) *adj* banal
banana [ba'nana] *f* banana; **bananeira** [bana'nejra] *f* banana tree
banca ['bãka] *f* bench; *(escritório)* office; *(em jogo)* bank; ~ **(de jornais)** newsstand; ~**da** [bã'kada] *f (banco, POL)* bench; *(de cozinha)* worktop
bancar [bã'ka*] *vt* to finance ♦ *vi (fingir)*: ~ **que** to pretend that; **bancário/a** [bã'karju/a] *adj* bank *atr* ♦ *m/f* bank employee
bancarrota [bãka'xota] *f* bankruptcy; **ir à** ~ to go bankrupt
banco ['bãku] *m (assento)* bench; *(COM)* bank; ~ **de areia** sandbank; ~ **de dados** *(COMPUT)* database
banda ['bãda] *f* band; *(lado)* side; *(cinto)* sash; **de** ~ sideways; **pôr de** ~ to put aside; ~ **desenhada** *(PT)* cartoon
bandeira [bã'dejra] *f* flag; *(estandarte)* banner; ~**nte** [bãdej'rãtʃi] *m* pioneer ♦ *f* girl guide; **bandeirinha** [bãdej'riɲa] *m (ESPORTE)* linesman
bandeja [bã'deʒa] *f* tray
bandido [bã'dʒidu/a] *m* bandit
bando ['bãdu] *m* band; *(grupo)* group; *(de malfeitores)* gang; *(de ovelhas)* flock; *(de gado)* herd; *(de livros etc)* pile
bandô [bã'do] *m* pelmet
bandoleiro [bãdo'lejru] *m* bandit
bangalô [bãga'lo] *m* bungalow
banha ['baɲa] *f* fat; *(de porco)* lard
banhar [ba'ɲa*] *vt* to wet; *(mergulhar)* to dip; *(lavar)* to wash; ~**-se** *vr* to bathe
banheira [ba'ɲejra] *f* bath
banheiro [ba'ɲejru] *m* bathroom
banho ['baɲu] *m* bath; *(mergulho)* dip; **tomar** ~ to have a bath; *(de chuveiro)* to have a shower; ~ **de chuveiro** shower; ~ **de sol** sunbathing
banir [ba'ni*] *vt* to banish
banqueiro/a [bã'kejru/a] *m/f* banker
banqueta [bã'keta] *f* stool
banquete [bã'ketʃi] *m* banquet
baptismo *etc* [ba'tiʒmu] *(PT)* = **batismo** *etc*
baque ['baki] *m* thud, thump; *(contratempo)* setback; *(queda)* fall
bar [ba*] *m* bar
barafunda [bara'fũda] *f* confusion
baralhar [bara'ʎa*] *vt (fig)* to mix up, confuse
baralho [ba'raʎu] *m* pack of cards
barão [ba'rãw] *(pl* –**ões**) *m* baron
barata [ba'rata] *f* cockroach

barateiro/a [bara'tejru/a] *adj* cheap
barato/a [ba'ratu/a] *adj* cheap ♦ *adv* cheaply
barba ['baxba] *f* beard; **fazer a** ~ to shave
barbante [bax'bãtʃi] *(BR) m* string
barbaridade [baxbari'dadʒi] *f* barbarity, cruelty; *(disparate)* nonsense; **que** ~! good heavens!
bárbaro/a ['baxbaru/a] *adj* barbaric; *(dor, calor)* terrible; *(maravilhoso)* great
barbatana [baxba'tana] *f* fin
barbeador [baxbja'do*] *m* razor; *(tb:* ~ **elétrico)** shaver
barbear [bax'bja*] *vt* to shave; ~**-se** *vr* to shave; ~**ia** [baxbja'ria] *f* barber's (shop)
barbeiro [bax'bejru] *m* barber; *(loja)* barber's
barca ['baxka] *f* barge; *(de travessia)* ferry; ~**ça** [bax'kasa] *f* barge
barco ['baxku] *m* boat; ~ **a motor** motorboat; ~ **a remo** rowing boat; ~ **a vela** sailing boat
barganha [bax'gaɲa] *f* bargain; ~**r** [baxga'ɲa*] *vt, vi* to negotiate
barman [bax'mã] *(pl* –**men**) *m* barman
barões [ba'rõjʃ] *mpl de* **barão**
barômetro [ba'rometru] *m* barometer
barqueiro [bax'kejru] *m* boatman
barra ['baxa] *f* bar; *(faixa)* strip; *(traço)* stroke; *(alavanca)* lever
barraca [ba'xaka] *f (tenda)* tent; *(de feira)* stall; *(de madeira)* hut; *(de praia)* sunshade; **barracão** [baxa'kãw] *(pl* –**ões**) *m* shed; **barraco** [ba'xaku] *m* shack, shanty
barragem [ba'xaʒẽ] *(pl* –**ns**) *f* dam; *(impedimento)* barrier
barranco [ba'xãku] *m* ravine, gully; *(de rio)* bank
barrar [ba'xa*] *vt* to bar
barreira [ba'xejra] *f* barrier; *(cerca)* fence; *(ESPORTE)* hurdle
barrento/a [ba'xẽtu/a] *adj* muddy
barricada [baxi'kada] *f* barricade
barriga [ba'xiga] *f* belly; **estar de** ~ to be pregnant; ~ **da perna** calf; **barrigudo/a** [baxi'gudu/a] *adj* paunchy, pot-bellied
barril [ba'xiw] *(pl* –**is**) *m* barrel, cask
barro ['baxu] *m* clay; *(lama)* mud
barulhento/a [baru'ʎẽtu/a] *adj* noisy
barulho [ba'ruʎu] *m (ruído)* noise; *(tumulto)* din
base ['bazi] *f* base; *(fig)* basis; **sem** ~ groundless; **com** ~ **em** based on; **na** ~ **de** by means of
basear [ba'zja*] *vt* to base; ~**-se** *vr*: ~**-se em** to be based on
básico/a ['baziku/a] *adj* basic
basquete [baʃ'ketʃi] *m* = **basquetebol**
basquetebol [baʃkete'bɔw] *m* basketball
basta ['baʃta] *m*: **dar um** ~ **em** to call a halt to
bastante [baʃ'tãtʃi] *adj (suficiente)* en-

ough; (*muito*) quite a lot (of) ♦ *adv* enough; a lot

bastão [baʃˈtãw] (*pl* –ões) *m* stick

bastar [baʃˈtaⁿ] *vi* to be enough, be sufficient; **~-se** *vr* to be self-sufficient; **basta!** (that's) enough!; **~ para** to be enough to

bastardo/a [baʃˈtaxdu/a] *adj, m/f* bastard

bastidor [baʃtʃiˈdoⁿ] *m* frame; **~es** *mpl* (*TEATRO*) wings; **nos ~es** (*fig*) behind the scenes

basto/a [ˈbaʃtu/a] *adj* (*espesso*) thick; (*denso*) dense

bastões [baʃˈtõjʃ] *mpl de* **bastão**

bata [ˈbata] *f* (*de mulher*) smock; (*de médico*) overall

batalha [baˈtaʎa] *f* battle; **~dor(a)** [bataʎaˈdo⁎(a)] *adj* struggling ♦ *m/f* fighter; **batalhão** [bataˈʎãw] (*pl* –ões) *m* battalion; **~r** [bataˈʎa⁎] *vi* to battle, fight; (*esforçar-se*) to make an effort, try hard ♦ *vt* (*emprego*) to go after

batata [baˈtata] *f* potato; **~ doce** sweet potato; **~s fritas** chips *pl* (*BRIT*), French fries *pl* (*US*); (*de pacote*) crisps *pl* (*BRIT*), (potato) chips *pl* (*US*)

bate-boca [ˈbatʃi-] (*pl* –s) *m* row, quarrel

batedeira [bateˈdejra] *f* beater; (*de manteiga*) churn; **~ elétrica** mixer

batedor [bateˈdoⁿ] *m* beater; (*polícia*) escort; **~ de carteiras** pickpocket

bátega [ˈbatega] *f* downpour

batente [baˈtẽtʃi] *m* doorpost

bate-papo [ˈbatʃi-] (*pl* –s) (*BR*) *m* chat

bater [baˈteⁿ] *vt* to beat, strike; (*pé*) to stamp; (*foto*) to take; (*porta*) to slam; (*asas*) to flap; (*recorde*) to break; (*roupa*) to wear all the time ♦ *vi* to slam; (*sino*) to ring; (*janela*) to bang; (*coração*) to beat; (*sol*) to beat down; **~-se** *vr*: **~-se para fazer/por** to fight to do/for; **~ (à porta)** to knock (at the door); **~ à máquina** to type; **~ em** to hit; **~ com o carro** to crash one's car; **~ com a cabeça** to bang one's head; **~ com o pé (em)** to kick

bateria [bateˈria] *f* battery; (*MÚS*) drums *pl*; **~ de cozinha** kitchen utensils *pl*; **baterista** [bateˈriʃta] *m/f* drummer

batida [baˈtʃida] *f* beat; (*da porta*) slam; (*à porta*) knock; (*da polícia*) raid; (*AUTO*) crash; (*bebida*) cocktail of *cachaça, fruit and sugar*

batido/a [baˈtʃidu/a] *adj* beaten; (*roupa*) worn ♦ *m*: **~ de leite** (*PT*) milkshake

batina [baˈtʃina] *f* (*REL*) cassock

batismo [baˈtʃiʒmu] *m* baptism, christening

batizar [batʃiˈza⁎] *vt* to baptize, christen

batom [baˈtõ] (*pl* –ns) *m* lipstick

batucada [batuˈkada] *f* dance percussion group

batucar [batuˈka⁎] *vt, vi* to drum

batuta [baˈtuta] *f* baton

baú [baˈu] *m* trunk

baunilha [bawˈniʎa] *f* vanilla

bazar [baˈza⁎] *m* bazaar; (*loja*) shop

bazófia [baˈzɔfja] *f* boasting, bragging

beato/a [beˈatu/a] *adj* blessed; (*devoto*) over-pious

bêbado/a [ˈbebadu/a] *adj, m/f* drunk

bebê [beˈbe] *m* baby

bebedeira [bebeˈdejra] *f* drunkenness; **tomar uma ~** to get drunk

bêbedo/a [ˈbebedu/a] *adj, m/f* = **bêbado**

bebedor(a) [bebeˈdo⁎(a)] *m/f* drinker

bebedouro [bebeˈdouru] *m* drinking fountain

beber [beˈbe⁎] *vt* to drink; (*absorver*) to soak up ♦ *vi* to drink; **bebida** [beˈbida] *f* drink

beça [ˈbɛsa] (*col*) *f*: **à ~** (*com vb*): **ele comeu à ~** he ate a lot; (*com n*): **ela tinha livros à ~** she had a lot of books

beco [ˈbeku] *m* alley, lane; **~ sem saída** cul-de-sac

bege [ˈbɛʒi] *adj inv* beige

beiço [ˈbejsu] *m* lip; **fazer ~** to pout

beija-flor [bejʒa-ˈflɔ⁎] (*pl* –es) *m* hummingbird

beijar [bejˈʒa⁎] *vt* to kiss; **~-se** *vr* to kiss (one another); **beijo** [ˈbejʒu] *m* kiss; **dar beijos em alguém** to kiss sb

beira [ˈbejra] *f* edge; (*de rio*) bank; (*orla*) border; **à ~ de** on the edge of; (*ao lado de*) beside, by; (*fig*) on the verge of; **~ do telhado** eaves *pl*; **~-mar** *f* seaside

beirar [bejˈra⁎] *vt* to be at the edge of; (*caminhar à beira de*) to skirt; (*desespero*) to be on the verge of; (*idade*) to approach ♦ *vi*: **~ com** to border on

beisebol [bejsiˈbɔw] *m* baseball

belas-artes *fpl* fine arts

beldade [bewˈdadʒi] *f* beauty

beleza [beˈleza] *f* beauty; **que ~!** how lovely!

belga [ˈbɛwga] *adj, m/f* Belgian

Bélgica [ˈbɛwʒika] *f*: **a ~** Belgium

beliche [beˈliʃi] *m* bunk

beliscão [beliʃˈkãw] (*pl* –ões) *m* pinch; **beliscar** [beliʃˈka⁎] *vt* to pinch, nip; (*comida*) to nibble

Belize [beˈlizi] *m* Belize

belo/a [ˈbɛlu/a] *adj* beautiful

PALAVRA CHAVE

bem [bẽj] *adv* **1** (*de maneira satisfatória, correta etc*) well; **trabalha/come ~** she works/eats well; **respondeu ~** he answered correctly; **me sinto/não me sinto ~** I feel fine/I don't feel very well; **tudo ~?** – **tudo ~** how's it going? – fine

2 (*valor intensivo*) very; **um quarto ~ quente** a nice warm room; **~ se vê que ...** it's clear that ...

3 (*bastante*) quite, fairly; **a casa é ~ grande** the house is quite big

4 (*exatamente*): ~ **ali** right there; **não é ~ assim** it's not quite like that
5 (*estar* ~): **estou muito ~ aqui** I feel very happy here; **está ~! vou fazê-lo** oh all right, I'll do it!
6 (*de bom grado*): **eu ~ que iria mas ...** I'd gladly go but ...
7 (*cheirar*) good, nice
♦ *m* **1** (*bem-estar*) good; **estou dizendo isso para o seu ~** I'm telling you for your own good; **o ~ e o mal** good and evil
2 (*posses*): **bens** goods, property *sg*; **bens de consumo** consumer goods; **bens de família** family possessions; **bens móveis/imóveis** moveable property *sg*/real estate *sg*
♦ *excl* **1** (*aprovação*): **~!** OK!; **muito ~!** well done!
2 (*desaprovação*): **~ feito!** it serves you right!
♦ *adj inv* (*tom depreciativo*): **gente ~** posh people
♦ *conj* **1**: **nem ~** as soon as, no sooner than; **nem ~ ela chegou começou a dar ordens** as soon as she arrived she started to give orders, no sooner had she arrived than she started to give orders
2: **se ~** que though; **gostaria de ir se ~ que não tenho dinheiro** I'd like to go even though I've got no money
3: **~ como** as well as; **o livro ~ como a peça foram escritos por ele** the book as well as the play was written by him

bem-conceituado/a [bējkōsej'twadu/a] *adj* highly regarded
bem-disposto/a [bějdʒiʃ'poʃtu/'poʃta] *adj* well, in good health
bem-estar *m* well-being
bem-me-quer (*pl* ~**es**) *m* daisy
bem-vindo/a *adj* welcome
bênção ['bēsãw] (*pl* ~**s**) *f* blessing
bendito/a [bē'dʒitu/a] *pp de* **bendizer** ♦ *adj* blessed
bendizer [bēdʒi'ze*] (*irreg: como* **dizer**) *vt* to praise; (*abençoar*) to bless
beneficência [benefi'sēsja] *f* kindness; (*caridade*) charity
beneficiado/a [benefi'sjadu/a] *m/f* beneficiary
beneficiar [benefi'sja*] *vt* to benefit; (*melhorar*) to improve; **~-se** *vr* to benefit
benefício [bene'fisju] *m* benefit; (*vantagem*) profit; (*favor*) favour (*BRIT*), favor (*US*); **em ~ de** in aid of; **benéfico/a** [be'nɛfiku/a] *adj* beneficial; (*generoso*) generous
benemérito/a [bene'mɛritu/a] *adj* worthy; **benévolo/a** [be'nɛvolu/a] *adj* benevolent, kind
benfeitor(a) [bēfej'to*(a)] *m/f* benefactor/benefactress

bengala [bē'gala] *f* walking stick
benigno/a [be'nignu/a] *adj* kind; (*agradável*) pleasant; (*MED*) benign
bens [bējʃ] *mpl de* **bem**
bento/a ['bētu/a] *pp de* **benzer** ♦ *adj* blessed; (*água*) holy
benzer [bē'ze*] *vt* to bless; **~-se** *vr* to cross o.s.
berço ['bexsu] *m* cradle; (*cama*) cot; (*origem*) birthplace
berinjela [berĩ'ʒɛla] *f* aubergine (*BRIT*), eggplant (*US*)
Berlim [bex'lĩ] *n* Berlin
berma ['bɛxma] (*PT*) *f* hard shoulder (*BRIT*), berm (*US*)
berrante [be'xãtʃi] *adj* flashy, gaudy
berrar [be'xa*] *vi* to bellow; (*criança*) to bawl; **berreiro** [be'xejru] *m*: **abrir o berreiro** to burst out crying; **berro** ['bexu] *m* yell
besouro [be'zoru] *m* beetle
besta ['beʃta] *adj* stupid; (*convencido*) full of oneself; **~ de carga** beast of burden; **besteira** [beʃ'tejra] *f* foolishness; **dizer besteiras** to talk nonsense; **fazer uma besteira** to do something silly; **bestial** [beʃ'tʃjaw] (*pl* -**ais**) *adj* bestial; (*repugnante*) repulsive
best-seller ['bɛst'sɛle*] (*pl* ~**s**) *m* best seller
besuntar [bezũ'ta*] *vt* to smear, daub
betão [be'tãw] (*PT*) *m* concrete
beterraba [bete'xaba] *f* beetroot
betoneira [beto'nejra] *f* cement mixer
betume [be'tumi] *m* asphalt
bexiga [be'ʃiga] *f* bladder
bezerro/a [be'zexu/a] *m/f* calf
bibelô [bibe'lo] *m* ornament
Bíblia ['biblja] *f* Bible
bíblico/a ['bibliku/a] *adj* biblical
bibliografia [bibljogra'fia] *f* bibliography
biblioteca [bibljo'tɛka] *f* library; (*estante*) bookcase; **bibliotecário/a** [bibljote'karju/a] *m/f* librarian
bica ['bika] *f* tap; (*PT*) black coffee, expresso
bicar [bi'ka*] *vt* to peck
bicha ['biʃa] *f* (*lombriga*) worm; (*BR: col, pej: homossexual*) queer; (*PT: fila*) queue
bicho ['biʃu] *m* animal; (*inseto*) insect, bug
bicicleta [bisi'klɛta] *f* bicycle; (*col*) bike; **andar de ~** to cycle; **~ do exército** exercise bike
bico ['biku] *m* (*de ave*) beak; (*ponta*) point; (*de chaleira*) spout; (*boca*) mouth; (*de pena*) nib; (*do peito*) nipple; (*de gás*) jet; (*col: emprego*) casual job; (*chupeta*) dummy; **calar o ~** to shut up
bidê [bi'de] *m* bidet
bife ['bifi] *m* (*beef*) steak; **~ a cavalo** steak with fried eggs; **~ à milanesa** beef escalope; **~ de panela** beef stew
bifocal [bifo'kaw] (*pl* -**ais**) *adj*: **óculos bifocais** bifocals

bifurcação [bifuxka'sãw] (*pl* –**ões**) *f* fork
bifurcar-se [bifux'kaxsi] *vr* to fork, divide
bígamo/a ['bigamu/a] *m/f* bigamist
bigode [bi'gɔdʒi] *m* moustache
bigorna [bi'gɔxna] *f* anvil
bijuteria [biʒute'ria] *f* (*costume*) jewellery (*BRIT*) *ou* jewelry (*US*)
bilhão [bi'ʎãw] (*pl* –**ões**) *m* billion
bilhar [bi'ʎa*] *m* (*jogo*) billiards *sg*
bilhete [bi'ʎetʃi] *m* ticket; (*cartinha*) note; ~ **de ida** single (*BRIT*) *ou* one-way ticket; ~ **de ida e volta** return (*BRIT*) *ou* round-trip (*US*) ticket; ~**ira** [biʎe'tejra] (*PT*) *f* = ~**ria**; ~**iro/a** [biʎe'tejru/a] *m/f* ticket seller; ~**ria** [biʎete'ria] *f* ticket office
bilhões [bi'ʎõjʃ] *mpl* **de bilhão**
bilíngüe [bi'lĩgwi] *adj* bilingual
bilioso/a [bi'ljozu/ɔza] *adj* bilious; (*fig*) bad-tempered
bílis [biliʃ] *m* bile
bimotor [bimo'to*] *adj* twin-engined
binário/a [bi'narju/a] *adj* binary
bingo ['bĩgu] *m* bingo
binóculo [bi'nɔkulu] *m* binoculars *pl*; (*para teatro*) opera glasses *pl*
biografia [bjogra'fia] *f* biography
biologia [bjolo'ʒia] *f* biology
biombo ['bjõbu] *m* screen
bip [bip] *m* pager, paging device
biquíni [bi'kini] *m* bikini
birita [bi'rita] (*col*) *f* drink
Birmânia [bix'manja] *f*: **a** ~ Burma
birra ['bixa] *f* wilfulness (*BRIT*), willfulness (*US*), obstinacy; (*aversão*) aversion; **ter** ~ **com** to dislike
biruta [bi'ruta] *adj* crazy ♦ *f* windsock
bis [biʃ] *excl* encore!
bisavô/ó [biza'vo/ɔ] *m/f* great-grandfather/great-grandmother; **bisavós** [biza'vɔʃ] *mpl* great-grandparents
biscate [biʃ'katʃi] *m* odd job
biscoito [biʃ'kojtu] *m* biscuit (*BRIT*), cookie (*US*)
bisnaga [biʒ'naga] *f* (*tubo*) tube; (*pão*) French stick
bisonho/a [bi'zɔɲu/a] *adj* inexperienced ♦ *m/f* newcomer
bispo ['biʃpu] *m* bishop
bissexto/a [bi'seʃtu/a] *adj*: **ano** ~ leap year
bisturi [biʃtu'ri] *m* scalpel
bit ['bitʃi] *m* (*COMPUT*) bit
bitola [bi'tɔla] *f* gauge (*BRIT*), gage (*US*); (*padrão*) pattern; (*estalão*) standard
bizarro/a [bi'zaxu/a] *adj* bizarre
blasfemar [blaʃfe'ma*] *vt* to curse ♦ *vi* to blaspheme; **blasfêmia** [blaʃ'femja] *f* blasphemy; (*ultraje*) curse
blazer ['blejze*] (*pl* ~**s**) *m* blazer
blecaute [ble'kawtʃi] *m* power cut
blindado/a [blĩ'dadu/a] *adj* armoured (*BRIT*), armored (*US*)
blindagem [blĩ'daʒẽ] *f* armour(-plating)

(*BRIT*), armor(-plating) (*US*)
blitz [blits] *f* police raid; (*na estrada*) police road block
bloco ['blɔku] *m* block; (*POL*) bloc; (*de escrever*) writing pad; ~ **de carnaval** carnival troupe
bloquear [blo'kja*] *vt* to blockade; (*obstruir*) to block; **bloqueio** [blo'keju] *m* blockade; blockage
blusa ['bluza] *f* (*de mulher*) blouse; (*de homem*) shirt; ~ **de lã** jumper; **blusão** [blu'zãw] (*pl* –**ões**) *m* jacket
boa ['boa] *adj f de* **bom** ♦ *f* boa constrictor
boate ['bwatʃi] *f* nightclub
boato ['bwatu] *m* rumour (*BRIT*), rumor (*US*)
bobagem [bo'baʒẽ] (*pl* –**ns**) *f* silliness, nonsense; (*dito, ato*) silly thing
bobina [bo'bina] *f* reel, bobbin; (*ELET*) coil; (*FOTO*) spool; (*de papel*) roll
bobo/a ['bobu/a] *adj* silly, daft ♦ *m/f* fool ♦ *m* (*de corte*) jester; **fazer-se de** ~ to act the fool
bobó [bo'bɔ] *m* beans, palm oil and manioc
boca ['boka] *f* mouth; (*entrada*) entrance; (*de fogão*) ring; **de** ~ **aberta** amazed; **bater** ~ to argue
bocadinho [boka'dʒiɲu] *m*: **um** ~ (*pouco tempo*) a little while; (*pouquinho*) a little bit
bocado [bo'kadu] *m* mouthful, bite; (*pedaço*) piece, bit; **um** ~ **de tempo** quite some time
bocal [bo'kaw] (*pl* –**ais**) *m* (*de vaso*) mouth; (*MÚS, de aparelho*) mouthpiece; (*de cano*) nozzle
boçal [bo'saw] (*pl* –**ais**) *adj* ignorant; (*grosseiro*) uncouth
bocejar [bose'ʒa*] *vi* to yawn; **bocejo** [bo'seʒu] *m* yawn
bochecha [bo'ʃeʃa] *f* cheek; **bochecho** [bo'ʃeʃu] *m* mouthwash
boda ['boda] *f* wedding; ~**s** *fpl* (*aniversário de casamento*) wedding anniversary *sg*
bode ['bɔdʒi] *m* goat; ~ **expiatório** scapegoat
bodum [bo'dũ] *m* stink
bofetada [bofe'tada] *f* slap
bofetão [bofe'tãw] (*pl* –**ões**) *m* punch
boi [boj] *m* ox
bóia ['bɔja] *f* buoy; (*col*) grub; (*de braço*) armband, water wing
boiada [bo'jada] *f* herd of cattle
boiar [bo'ja*] *vt, vi* to float
boicotar [bojko'ta*] *vt* to boycott; **boicote** [boj'kɔtʃi] *m* boycott
boiler ['bojla*] (*pl* ~**s**) *m* boiler
boina ['bojna] *f* beret
bojo ['boʒu] *m* bulge; **bojudo/a** [bo'ʒudu/a] *adj* bulging; (*arredondado*) rounded
bola ['bɔla] *f* ball; **dar** ~ **para** (*flertar*) to flirt with; **ela não dá a menor** ~ (*pa-*

ra isso) she couldn't care less (about it); **não ser certo da ~** (col) not to be right in the head

bolacha [bo'laʃa] f biscuit (BRIT), cookie (US); (col: bofetada) wallop; (para chope) beermat

bole etc ['bɔli] vb V **bulir**

boleia [bo'leja] f driver's seat; **dar uma ~ a alguém** (PT) to give sb a lift

boletim [bole'tʃĩ] (pl -ns) m report; (publicação) newsletter; **~ meteorológico** weather forecast

bolha ['boʎa] f (na pele) blister; (de ar, sabão) bubble

boliche [bo'liʃi] m bowling, skittles sg

bolinho [bo'liɲu] m: **~ de carne** meat ball; **~ de arroz/bacalhau** rice/dry cod cake

Bolívia [bo'livja] f: **a ~** Bolivia

bolo ['bolu] m cake; (monte: de gente) bunch; (: de papéis) bundle; **dar o ~ em alguém** to stand sb up; **vai dar ~** (col) there's going to be trouble

bolor [bo'lo*] m mould (BRIT), mold (US); (nas plantas) mildew; (bafio) mustiness

bolota [bo'lɔta] f acorn

bolsa ['bowsa] f bag; (COM: tb: **~ de valores**) stock exchange; **~ (de estudos)** scholarship

bolso ['bowsu] m pocket; **de ~** pocket atr

---

bom/boa [bõ/'boa] (pl bons/boas) adj **1** (ótimo) good; **é um livro ~ ou um ~ livro** it's a good book; **a comida está boa** the food is delicious; **o tempo está ~** the weather's fine; **ele foi muito ~ comigo** he was very nice ou kind to me

2 (apropriado): **ser ~ para** to be good for; **acho ~ você não ir** I think it's better if you don't go

3 (irônico): **um ~ quarto de hora** a good quarter of an hour; **que ~ motorista você é!** a fine ou some driver you are!; **seria ~ que ...!** a fine thing it would be if ...!; **essa é boa!** what a cheek!

4 (saudação): **~ dia!** good morning!; **boa tarde!** good afternoon!; **boa noite!** good evening!; (ao deitar-se) good night!; **tudo ~?** how's it going?

5 (outras frases): **está ~?** OK?

♦ excl: **~!** all right!; **~, ... right, ...**

---

bomba ['bõba] f bomb; (TEC) pump; (fig) bombshell; **~ atômica/relógio/de fumaça** atomic/time/smoke bomb; **~ de gasolina** petrol (BRIT) ou gas (US) pump; **~ de incêndio** fire extinguisher

bombardear [bõbax'dʒja*] vt to bomb; (fig) to bombard; **bombardeio** [bõbax'deju] m bombing, bombardment

bombear [bõ'bja*] vt to pump

bombeiro [bõ'bejru] m fireman; (BR: encanador) plumber; **o corpo de ~s** fire brigade

bombom [bõ'bõ] (pl -ns) m chocolate

bondade [bõ'dadʒi] f goodness, kindness; **tenha a ~ de vir** would you please come

bonde ['bõdʒi] (BR) m tram

bondoso/a [bõ'dozu/ɔza] adj kind, good

boné [bo'nɛ] m cap

boneca [bo'nɛka] f doll

boneco [bo'nɛku] m dummy

bonito/a [bo'nitu/a] adj pretty; (gesto, dia) nice ♦ m (peixe) tuna (fish), tunny

bônus ['bonuʃ] m inv bonus

boquiaberto/a [bokja'bextu/a] adj dumbfounded, astonished

borboleta [boxbo'leta] f butterfly; (BR: roleta) turnstile; **borboletear** [boxbole'tʃja*] vi to flutter

borbotão [boxbo'tãw] (pl -ões) m gush, spurt; **sair aos borbotões** to gush out

borbulhar [boxbu'ʎa*] vi to bubble

borda ['boxda] f edge; (do rio) bank; **à ~ de** on the edge of

bordado [box'dadu] m embroidery

bordão [box'dãw] (pl -ões) m staff

bordar [box'da*] vt to embroider

bordejar [boxde'ʒa*] vi (NÁUT) to tack

bordo ['boxdu] m (embarcação) side; **a ~** on board

bordões [box'dõjʃ] mpl de **bordão**

borla ['boxla] f tassel

borra ['boxa] f dregs pl

borracha [bo'xaʃa] f rubber; **borracheiro** [boxa'ʃejru] m tyre (BRIT) ou tire (US) specialist

borrador [boxa'do*] m (COM) day book

borrão [bo'xãw] (pl -ões) m (rascunho) rough draft; (mancha) blot

borrar [bo'xa*] vt to blot; (riscar) to cross out

borrasca [bo'xaʃka] f storm; (no mar) squall

borrifar [boxi'fa*] vt to sprinkle; **borrifo** [bo'xifu] m spray

borrões [bo'xõjʃ] mpl de **borrão**

bosque ['bɔʃki] m wood, forest

bossa ['bɔsa] f charm; (inchaço) swelling

bota ['bɔta] f boot; **~s de borracha** wellingtons

botânica [bo'tanika] f botany

botão [bo'tãw] (pl -ões) m button; (flor) bud

botar [bo'ta*] vt to put; (roupa, sapatos) to put on; (mesa) to set; (defeito) to find; (ovos) to lay

bote ['bɔtʃi] m boat; (com arma) thrust; (salto) spring

botequim [botʃi'kĩ] (pl -ns) m bar

boticário/a [botʃi'karju/a] m/f pharmacist, chemist (BRIT)

botija [bo'tʃiʒa] f (earthenware) jug

botões [bo'tõjʃ] mpl de **botão**

boxe ['bɔksi] *m* boxing; **~ador** [boks-ja'do*] *m* boxer

brabo/a ['brabu/a] *adj* fierce; (*zangado*) angry; (*ruim*) bad; (*calor*) unbearable

braça ['brasa] *f* (*NÁUT*) fathom

braçada [bra'sada] *f* armful; (*NATAÇÃO*) stroke

braçadeira [brasa'dejra] *f* armband

bracejar [brase'ʒa*] *vi* to wave one's arms about

bracelete [brase'letʃi] *m* bracelet

braço ['brasu] *m* arm; **de ~s cruzados** with arms folded; (*fig*) without lifting a finger; **de ~ dado** arm-in-arm

bradar [bra'da*] *vt*, *vi* to shout, yell; **brado** ['bradu] *m* shout, yell

braguilha [bra'giʎa] *f* flies *pl*

bramido [bra'midu] *m* roar

bramir [bra'mi*] *vi* to roar

branco/a ['brãku/a] *adj* white ♦ *m/f* white man/woman ♦ *m* (*espaço*) blank; **em ~** blank; **noite em ~** sleepless night; **brancura** [brã'kura] *f* whiteness

brandir [brã'dʒi*] *vt* to brandish

brando/a ['brãdu/a] *adj* gentle; (*mole*) soft; **brandura** [brã'dura] *f* gentleness; softness

branquear [brã'kja*] *vt* to whiten; (*alvejar*) to bleach ♦ *vi* to turn white

brasa ['braza] *f* hot coal; **em ~** red-hot; **pisar em ~** to be on tenterhooks

brasão [bra'zãw] (*pl* **-ões**) *m* coat of arms

braseiro [bra'zejru] *m* brazier

Brasil [bra'ziw] *m*: **o ~** Brazil; **b~eiro/a** [brazi'lejru/a] *adj*, *m/f* Brazilian

Brasília [bra'zilja] *n* Brasília

brasões [bra'zõjʃ] *mpl de* **brasão**

bravata [bra'vata] *f* bravado, boasting; **bravatear** [brava'tʃja*] *vi* to boast, brag

bravio/a [bra'viu/a] *adj* (*selvagem*) wild; (*feroz*) ferocious

bravo/a ['bravu/a] *adj* brave; (*furioso*) angry; (*mar*) rough ♦ *m* brave man; **~!** bravo!; **bravura** [bra'vura] *f* courage, bravery

brecar [bre'ka*] *vt* (*carro*) to stop; (*reprimir*) to curb ♦ *vi* to brake

brecha ['brɛʃa] *f* breach; (*abertura*) opening; (*dano*) damage; (*col*) chance

brejo ['breʒu] *m* marsh, swamp

breque ['brɛki] *m* brake

breu [brew] *m* tar, pitch

breve ['brɛvi] *adj* short; (*conciso, rápido*) brief ♦ *adv* soon; **em ~** soon, shortly; **até ~** see you soon; **brevidade** [brevi'dadʒi] *f* brevity, shortness

bridge ['bridʒi] *m* bridge

briga ['briga] *f* fight; (*verbal*) quarrel

brigada [bri'gada] *f* brigade

brigão/ona [bri'gãw/ona] (*pl* **-ões/~s**) *adj* quarrelsome ♦ *m/f* troublemaker

brigar [bri'ga*] *vi* to fight; (*altercar*) to quarrel

brigões [bri'gõjʃ] *mpl de* **brigão**

brigona [bri'gona] *f de* **brigão**

brilhante [bri'ʎãtʃi] *adj* brilliant ♦ *m* diamond

brilhar [bri'ʎa*] *vi* to shine

brilho ['briʎu] *m* (*luz viva*) brilliance; (*esplendor*) splendour (*BRIT*), splendor (*US*); (*nos sapatos*) shine; (*de metais, olhos*) gleam

brincadeira [brĩka'dejra] *f* fun; (*gracejo*) joke; (*de criança*) game; **deixe de ~s!** stop fooling!; **de ~** for fun

brincalhão/ona [brĩka'ʎãw/ona] (*pl* **-ões/~s**) *adj* playful ♦ *m/f* joker, teaser

brincar [brĩ'ka*] *vi* to play; (*gracejar*) to joke; **estou brincando** I'm only kidding; **~ de soldados** to play (at) soldiers; **~ com alguém** to tease sb

brinco ['brĩku] *m* (*jóia*) earring

brindar [brĩ'da*] *vt* to drink to; (*presentear*) to give a present to; **brinde** ['brĩdʒi] *m* toast; free gift

brinquedo [brĩ'kedu] *m* toy

brio ['briu] *m* self-respect, dignity; **~so/a** ['brjozu/ɔza] *adj* self-respecting

brisa ['briza] *f* breeze

britânico/a [bri'taniku/a] *adj* British ♦ *m/f* Briton

broca ['brɔka] *f* drill

broche ['brɔʃi] *m* brooch

brochura [bro'ʃura] *f* (*livro*) paperback; (*folheto*) brochure, pamphlet

brócolis ['brɔkoliʃ] *mpl* broccoli *sg*

bronca ['brõka] (*col*) *f* telling off; **dar uma ~ em** to tell off; **levar uma ~** to get told off

bronco/a ['brõku/a] *adj* (*rude*) coarse; (*burro*) thick

bronquear [brõ'kja*] (*col*) *vi* to get angry; **~ com** to tell off

bronquite [brõ'kitʃi] *f* bronchitis

bronze ['brõzi] *m* bronze; **~ado/a** [brõ'zjadu/a] *adj* (*cor*) bronze; (*pelo sol*) suntanned ♦ *m* suntan; **~ar** [brõ'zja*] *vt* to tan; **~ar-se** *vr* to get a tan

brotar [bro'ta*] *vt* to produce ♦ *vi* (*manar*) to flow; (*BOT*) to sprout; (*nascer*) to spring up

broto ['brotu] *m* bud; (*fig*) youngster

broxa ['brɔʃa] *f* (large) paint brush

bruços ['brusuʃ]: **de ~** *adv* face down

bruma ['bruma] *f* mist, haze; **brumoso/a** [bru'mozu/ɔza] *adj* misty, hazy

brunir [bru'ni*] *vt* to polish

brusco/a ['bruʃku/a] *adj* brusque; (*súbito*) sudden

brutal [bru'taw] (*pl* **-ais**) *adj* brutal; **~idade** [brutali'dadʒi] *f* brutality

bruto/a ['brutu/a] *adj* brutish; (*grosseiro*) coarse; (*móvel*) heavy; (*petróleo*) crude; (*peso, COM*) gross ♦ *m* brute; **em ~** raw, unworked

bruxa ['bruʃa] *f* witch; **~ria** [bruʃa'ria] *f* witchcraft

Bruxelas [bru'ʃɛlaʃ] *n* Brussels

bruxo ['bruʃu] *m* wizard

bruxulear [bruʃu'lja*] *vi* to flicker
buço ['busu] *m* down
budismo [bu'dʒiʒmu] *m* Buddhism
búfalo ['bufalu] *m* buffalo
bufar [bu'fa*] *vi* to puff, pant; (*com raiva*) to snort; (*reclamar*) to moan, grumble
bufê [bu'fe] *m* sideboard; (*comida*) buffet
buffer ['bafe*] (*pl ~s*) *m* (*COMPUT*) buffer
bugiganga [buʒi'gãga] *f* trinket; **~s** *fpl* (*coisas sem valor*) knickknacks
bujão [bu'ʒãw] (*pl -ões*) *m* (*TEC*) cap; **~ de gás** gas cylinder
bula ['bula] *f* (*MED*) directions *pl* for use
bulbo ['buwbu] *m* bulb
buldôzer [buw'doze*] (*pl -es*) *m* bulldozer
bule ['buli] *m* (*de chá*) teapot; (*de café*) coffeepot
Bulgária [buw'garja] *f*: **a ~** Bulgaria; **búlgaro/a** ['buwgaru/a] *adj, m/f* Bulgarian ♦ *m* (*LING*) Bulgarian
bulício [bu'lisju] *m* bustle; (*sussurro*) rustling; **buliçoso/a** [buli'sozu/ɔza] *adj* lively; (*agitado*) restless
bulir [bu'li*] *vt* to move ♦ *vi* to move, stir; **~ com** to tease; **~ em** to touch, meddle with
bunda ['bũda] (*col*) *f* bottom, backside
buquê [bu'ke] *m* bouquet
buraco [bu'raku] *m* hole; (*de agulha*) eye; **ser um ~** to be tough; **~ da fechadura** keyhole
burguês/guesa [bux'geʃ/'geza] *adj* middle-class, bourgeois; **burguesia** [buxge'zia] *f* middle class, bourgeoisie
buril [bu'riw] (*pl -is*) *m* chisel
burla ['buxla] *f* trick, fraud; (*zombaria*) mockery; **~r** [bux'la*] *vt* (*enganar*) to cheat; (*defraudar*) to swindle; (*a lei, impostos*) to evade
burocracia [burokra'sia] *f* bureaucracy; **burocrata** [buro'krata] *m/f* bureaucrat
burro/a ['buxu/a] *adj* stupid ♦ *m/f* (*ZOOL*) donkey; (*pessoa*) fool, idiot; **pra ~** (*col*) a lot; (*com adj*) really; **~ de carga** (*fig*) hard worker
busca ['buʃka] *f* search; **em ~ de** in search of; **dar ~ a** to search for
buscar [buʃ'ka*] *vt* to fetch; (*procurar*) to look *ou* search for; **ir ~** to fetch, go for; **mandar ~** to send for
bússola ['busola] *f* compass
busto ['buʃtu] *m* bust
buzina [bu'zina] *f* horn; **~r** [buzi'na*] *vi* to sound one's horn, toot the horn ♦ *vt* to hoot
búzio ['buzju] *m* conch

C

c/ *abr* = com
Ca *abr* (= *companhia*) Co
cá [ka] *adv* here; **de ~** on this side;

para ~ here, over here; **para lá e para ~** back and forth; **de lá para ~** since then
caatinga [ka'tʃĩga] (*BR*) *f* scrub(-land)
cabal [ka'baw] (*pl -ais*) *adj* complete; (*exato*) exact
cabalar [kaba'la*] *vt* (*votos etc*) to canvass (for) ♦ *vi* to canvass
cabana [ka'bana] *f* hut
cabeça [ka'besa] *f* head; (*inteligência*) brains *pl*; (*de uma lista*) top ♦ *m/f* leader; **de ~** off the top of one's head; (*calcular*) in one's head; **de ~ para baixo** upside down; **por ~** per person, per head; **~da** [kabe'sada] *f* (*pancada com cabeça*) butt; (*FUTEBOL*) header; (*asneira*) blunder; **~lho** [kabe'saʎu] *m* (*de livro*) title page; (*de página, capítulo*) heading
cabeceira [kabe'sejra] *f* (*de cama*) head
cabeçudo/a [kabe'sudu/a] *adj* bigheaded; (*teimoso*) pigheaded
cabeleira [kabe'lejra] *f* head of hair; (*postiça*) wig; **cabeleireiro/a** [kabelej'rejru/a] *m/f* hairdresser
cabelo [ka'belu] *m* hair; **cortar/fazer o ~** to have one's hair cut/done; **cabeludo/a** [kabe'ludu/a] *adj* hairy
caber [ka'be*] *vi*: **~ (em)** to fit; (*ser compatível*) to be appropriate (in); **~ a** (*em partilha*) to fall to; **cabe a alguém fazer** it is up to sb to do; **não cabe aqui fazer comentários** this is not the time or place to comment
cabide [ka'bidʒi] *m* (*coat*) hanger; (*móvel*) hat stand; (*fixo à parede*) coat rack
cabine [ka'bini] *f* cabin; (*em loja*) fitting room; **~ do piloto** (*AER*) cockpit; **~ telefônica** telephone box (*BRIT*) *ou* booth
cabisbaixo/a [kabiʒ'bajʃu/a] *adj* dispirited, crestfallen
cabo ['kabu] *m* (*extremidade*) end; (*de faca, vassoura etc*) handle; (*corda*) rope; (*elétrico etc*) cable; (*GEO*) cape; (*MIL*) corporal; **ao ~ de** at the end of; **de ~ a rabo** from beginning to end; **levar a ~** to carry out; **dar ~ de** to do away with
caboclo/a [ka'boklu/a] (*BR*) *m/f* mestizo
cabra ['kabra] *f* goat
cabreiro/a [ka'brejru/a] (*col*) *adj* suspicious
cabresto [kab'reʃtu] *m* halter
cabrito [ka'britu] *m* kid
caça ['kasa] *f* hunting; (*busca*) hunt; (*animal*) quarry, game ♦ *m* (*AER*) fighter (plane); **~dor(a)** [kasa'do*(a)] *m/f* hunter
caça-níqueis *m inv* slot machine
cação [ka'sãw] (*pl -ões*) *m* shark
caçar [ka'sa*] *vt* to hunt; (*com espingarda*) to shoot; (*procurar*) to seek ♦ *vi* to hunt, go hunting
cacarejar [kakare'ʒa*] *vi* (*galinhas etc*) to cluck

caçarola [kasa'rɔla] f (sauce)pan

cacau [ka'kaw] m cocoa; (BOT) cacao; **~eiro** [kaka'wejru] m cocoa tree

cacetada [kase'tada] f blow (with a stick)

cachaça [ka'ʃasa] f (white) rum

cachaceiro/a [kaʃa'sejru/a] adj drunk ♦ m/f drunkard

cachê [ka'ʃe] m fee

cachecol [kaʃe'kɔw] (pl -óis) m scarf

cachepô [kaʃe'po] m plant pot

cachimbo [ka'ʃibu] m pipe

cacho ['kaʃu] m bunch; (de cabelo) curl; (: longo) ringlet

cachoeira [kaʃ'wejra] f waterfall

cachorra [ka'ʃoxa] f bitch; (cadela) (female) puppy

cachorrinho/a [kaʃo'xiɲu/a] m/f puppy

cachorro [ka'ʃoxu] m dog; (cãozinho) puppy; **~-quente** (pl **~s-quentes**) m hot dog

cacique [ka'siki] m (Indian) chief; (mandachuva) local boss

caco ['kaku] m bit, fragment; (pessoa velha) old relic

caçoada [ka'swada] f jibe

caçoar [ka'swa*] vt, vi to mock

cações [ka'sõjʃ] mpl de cação

cacoete [ka'kwetʃi] m twitch, tic

cacto ['kaktu] m cactus

cada ['kada] adj inv each; (todo) every; **~ um** each one; **~ semana** each week; **~ 3 horas** every 3 hours; **~ vez mais** more and more

cadafalso [kada'fawsu] m gallows sg

cadarço [ka'daxsu] m shoelace

cadastro [ka'daʃtru] m register; (ato) registration; (de criminosos) criminal record

cadáver [ka'dave*] m corpse, (dead) body

cadê [ka'de] (col) adv: **~ ...?** where's/ where are ...?, what's happened to ...?

cadeado [ka'dʒjadu] m padlock

cadeia [ka'deja] f chain; (prisão) prison; (rede) network

cadeira [ka'dejra] f chair; (disciplina) subject; (TEATRO) stall; (função) post; **~s** fpl (ANAT) hips; **~ de balanço/rodas** rocking chair/wheelchair

cadela [ka'dɛla] f (cão) bitch

cadência [ka'dẽsja] f cadence; (ritmo) rhythm

caderneta [kadex'neta] f notebook; **~ de poupança** savings account

caderno [ka'dexnu] m exercise book; (de notas) notebook; (de jornal) section

cadete [ka'detʃi] m cadet

caducar [kadu'ka*] vi to lapse, expire; **caduco/a** [ka'duku/a] adj invalid, expired; (senil) senile; (BOT) deciduous

cães [kãjʃ] mpl de cão

cafajeste [kafa'ʒɛʃtʃi] (col) adj roguish; (vulgar) vulgar, coarse ♦ m/f rogue; rough customer

café [ka'fɛ] m coffee; (estabelecimento) café; **~ com leite** white coffee (BRIT), coffee with cream (US); **~ preto** black coffee; **~ da manhã** (BR) breakfast; **cafeeiro/a** [kafe'ejru/a] adj coffee atr ♦ m coffee plant; **cafeicultor** [kafejkuw'to*] m coffee-grower; **cafeicultura** [kafejkuw'tura] f coffee-growing

cafeína [kafe'ina] f caffein(e)

cafeteira [kafe'tejra] f coffee pot; (máquina) percolator; **cafezal** [kafe'zaw] (pl -ais) m coffee plantation; **cafezinho** [kafe'ziɲu] m small black coffee

cagada [ka'gada] (col!) f shit (!)

cágado ['kagadu] m turtle

cagar [ka'ga*] (col!) vi to (have a) shit (!)

cagüetar [kagwe'ta*] vt to inform on; **cagüete** [ka'gwetʃi] m informer

caiar [kaj'a*] vt to whitewash

caiba etc ['kajba] vb V caber

cãibra ['kãjbra] f (MED) cramp

caída [ka'ida] f = queda

caído/a [ka'idu/a] adj dejected; (derrubado) fallen; (pendente) droopy; **~ por** (apaixonado) in love with

cãimbra ['kãjbra] f = cãibra

caipirinha [kajpi'riɲa] f cocktail of cachaça, lemon and sugar

cair [ka'i*] vi to fall; **~ bem/mal** (roupa) to fit well/badly; (col: pessoa) to look good/bad; **~ em si** to come to one's senses; **ao ~ da noite** at nightfall; **essa comida me caiu mal** that food did not agree with me

Cairo ['kajru] m: **o ~** Cairo

cais [kajʃ] m (NÁUT) quay; (PT: FERRO) platform

caixa ['kajʃa] f box; (cofre) safe; (de uma loja) cashdesk ♦ m/f (pessoa) cashier; **pequena ~** petty cash; **~ de correio** letter box; **~ de mudanças** (BR) ou **de velocidades** (PT) gearbox; **~ econômica** savings bank; **~ postal** P.O. box; **~ registradora** cash register; **~-forte** (pl **~s-fortes**) f vault

caixão [kaj'ʃãw] (pl -ões) m (ataúde) coffin; (caixa grande) large box

caixeiro/a [kaj'ʃejru/a] m/f shop assistant; (entregador) delivery man/woman

caixeiro/a-viajante (pl **caixeiros/as-viajantes**) m/f commercial traveller (BRIT) ou traveler (US)

caixilho [kaj'ʃiʎu] m (moldura) frame

caixões [kaj'ʃõjʃ] mpl de caixão

caixote [kaj'ʃɔtʃi] m packing case; **~ do lixo** (PT) dustbin (BRIT), garbage can (US)

caju [ka'ʒu] m cashew fruit; **~eiro** [ka'ʒwejru] m cashew tree

cal [kaw] f lime; (na água) chalk; (para caiar) whitewash

calabouço [kala'bosu] m dungeon

calado/a [ka'ladu/a] adj quiet

calafrio [kala'friu] m shiver; ter **~s** to

shiver

calamar [kala'ma*] *m* squid

calamidade [kalami'dadʒi] *f* calamity, disaster

calão [ka'lãw] (*PT*) *m*: (**baixo**) ~ slang

calar [ka'la*] *vt* to keep quiet about; (*impor silêncio a*) to silence ♦ *vi* to go quiet; (*manter-se calado*) to keep quiet; ~-**se** *vr* to go quiet; to keep quiet; **cala a boca!** shut up!

calça ['kawsa] *f* (*tb*: ~**s**) trousers *pl* (*BRIT*), pants *pl* (*US*)

calçada [kaw'sada] *f* (*BR*: *passeio*) pavement (*BRIT*), sidewalk (*US*); (*PT*: *rua*) roadway

calçadão [kawsa'dãw] (*pl* -**ões**) *m* pedestrian precinct (*BRIT*)

calçadeira [kawsa'dejra] *f* shoe-horn

calçado/a [kaw'sadu/a] *adj* (*rua*) paved ♦ *m* shoe; ~**s** *mpl* (*para os pés*) footwear *sg*

calçadões [kawsa'dõjʃ] *mpl de* **calçadão**

calçamento [kawsa'mẽtu] *m* paving

calcanhar [kawka'ɲa*] *m* (*ANAT*) heel

calção [kaw'sãw] (*pl* -**ões**) *m* shorts *pl*; ~ **de banho** swimming trunks *pl*

calcar [kaw'ka*] *vt* to tread on; (*espezinhar*) to trample (on)

calçar [kaw'sa*] *vt* (*sapatos, luvas*) to put on; (*pavimentar*) to pave; ~-**se** *vr* to put on one's shoes; **ela calça (número) 28** she takes size 28 (in shoes)

calcário [kaw'karju] *m* limestone

calceiro/a [kaw'sejru/a] *m/f* shoe-maker

calcinha [kaw'siɲa] *f* panties *pl*

calço ['kawsu] *m* wedge

calções [kaw'sõjʃ] *mpl de* **calção**

calculador [kawkula'do*] *m* = **calculadora**

calculadora [kawkula'dora] *f* calculator

calcular [kawku'la*] *vt* to calculate; (*imaginar*) to imagine; ~ **que** to reckon that

cálculo ['kawkulu] *m* calculation; (*MAT*) calculus; (*MED*) stone

calda ['kawda] *f* (*de doce*) syrup; ~**s** *fpl* (*águas termais*) hot springs

caldeira [kaw'dejra] *f* (*TEC*) boiler

caldeirada [kawdej'rada] (*PT*) *f* (*guisado*) fish stew

caldo ['kawdu] *m* broth; (*de fruta*) juice; ~ **de carne/galinha** beef/chicken stock; ~ **verde** potato and cabbage broth

calendário [kalẽ'darju] *m* calendar

calha ['kaʎa] *f* channel; (*para água*) gutter

calhamaço [kaʎa'masu] *m* tome

calhar [ka'ʎa*] *vi*: **calhou viajarmos no mesmo avião** we happened to travel on the same plane; **calhou que** it so happened that; ~ **a** (*cair bem*) to suit; **se** ~ (*PT*) perhaps, maybe

calhau [ka'ʎaw] *m* stone, pebble

calibre [ka'libri] *m* calibre (*BRIT*), caliber (*US*)

cálice ['kalisi] *m* wine glass; (*REL*) chalice

calidez [kali'deʒ] *f* warmth

cálido/a ['kalidu/a] *adj* warm

calista [ka'liʃta] *m/f* chiropodist (*BRIT*), podiatrist (*US*)

calma ['kawma] *f* calm

calmante [kaw'mãtʃi] *adj* soothing ♦ *m* (*MED*) tranquillizer

calmo/a [kaw'mu/a] *adj* calm

calo ['kalu] *m* callus; (*no pé*) corn

calor [ka'lo*] *m* heat; (*agradável, fig*) warmth; **está** *ou* **faz** ~ it is hot; **estar com** ~ to be hot

calorento/a [kalo'rẽtu/a] *adj* (*pessoa*) sensitive to heat; (*lugar*) hot

caloria [calo'ria] *f* calorie

caloroso/a [kalo'rozu/ɔza] *adj* warm; (*entusiástico*) enthusiastic

calota [ka'lɔta] *f* (*AUTO*) hubcap

calouro/a [ka'loru/a] *m/f* (*EDUC*) fresher (*BRIT*), freshman (*US*)

calúnia [ka'lunja] *f* slander

calunioso/a [kalu'njozu/ɔza] *adj* slanderous

calvo/a ['kawvu/a] *adj* bald

cama ['kama] *f* bed; ~ **de casal** double bed; ~ **de solteiro** single bed; **de** ~ (*doente*) ill (in bed); ~**-beliche** (*pl* ~**s-beliches**) *f* bunk bed

camada [ka'mada] *f* layer; (*de tinta*) coat

camafeu [kama'few] *m* cameo

câmara ['kamara] *f* chamber; (*FOTO*) camera; ~ **municipal** (*BR*) town council; (*PT*) town hall; **em** ~ **lenta** in slow motion

camarada [kama'rada] *adj* friendly, nice; (*preço*) good ♦ *m/f* comrade; (*sujeito*) guy/woman

câmara-de-ar (*pl* **câmaras-de-ar**) *f* inner tube

camarão [kama'rãw] (*pl* -**ões**) *m* shrimp; (*graúdo*) prawn

camareiro/a [kama'rejru/a] *m/f* cleaner/ chambermaid

camarim [kama'rĩ] (*pl* -**ns**) *m* (*TEATRO*) dressing room

camarões [kama'rõjʃ] *mpl de* **camarão**

camarote [kama'rɔtʃi] *m* (*NÁUT*) cabin; (*TEATRO*) box

cambaleante [kãba'ljãtʃi] *adj* unsteady (on one's feet)

cambalear [kãba'lja*] *vi* to stagger, reel

cambalhota [kãba'ʎɔta] *f* somersault

câmbio ['kãbju] *m* (*dinheiro etc*) exchange; (*preço de câmbio*) rate of exchange; ~ **livre** free trade; ~ **paralelo** black market

cambista [kã'biʃta] *m* money changer

Camboja [kã'bɔʒa] *m*: **o** ~ Cambodia

camelo [ka'melu] *m* camel

camião [ka'mjãw] (*pl* -**ões**) (*PT*) *m* lorry (*BRIT*), truck (*US*)

caminhada [kami'ɲada] *f* walk

caminhante [kami'ɲãtʃi] *m/f* walker

caminhão [kami'ɲãw] (*pl* -**ões**) (*BR*) *m*

lorry (BRIT), truck (US)

caminhar [kami'ɲa*] vi to walk; (processo) to get under way; (negócios) to progress

caminho [ka'miɲu] m way; (vereda) road, path; ~ **de ferro** (PT) railway (BRIT), railroad (US); **a** ~ on the way, en route; **cortar** ~ to take a short cut; **pôr-se a** ~ to set off

caminhões [kami'ɲõjʃ] mpl de **caminhão**

caminhoneiro/a [kamiɲo'nejru/a] m/f lorry driver (BRIT), truck driver (US)

caminhonete [kamiɲo'nɛtʃi] m (AUTO) van

camiões [ka'mjõjʃ] mpl de **camião**

camioneta [kamjo'neta] (PT) f (para passageiros) coach; (comercial) van

camionista [kamjo'niʃta] (PT) m/f lorry driver (BRIT), truck driver (US)

camisa [ka'miza] f shirt; ~ **de dormir** nightshirt; ~ **esporte/pólo/social** sports/polo/dress shirt; **mudar de** ~ (ESPORTE) to change sides; ~**-de-força** (pl ~**s-de-força**) f straitjacket

camiseta [kami'zɛta] (BR) f T-shirt; (interior) vest

camisinha [kami'ziɲa] (col) f condom

camisola [kami'zɔla] f (BR) nightdress; (PT: pulôver) sweater; ~ **interior** (PT) vest

campainha [kampa'iɲa] f bell

campanário [kãpa'narju] m church tower, steeple

campanha [kã'paɲa] f (MIL etc) campaign; (planície) plain

campeão/peã [kã'pjãw/'pjã] (pl ~ões/ ~s) m/f champion; **campeonato** [kãpjo'natu] m championship

campestre [kã'pɛʃtri] adj rural, rustic

camping ['kãpĩ] (BR: pl ~s) m camping; (lugar) campsite

campismo [kã'piʒmu] m camping; **parque de** ~ campsite

campista [kã'piʃta] m/f camper

campo ['kãpu] m field; (fora da cidade) countryside; (ESPORTE) ground; (acampamento) camp; (TÉNIS) court

camponês/esa [kãpo'neʃ/eza] m/f countryman/woman; (agricultor) farmer

campus ['kãpuʃ] m inv campus

camuflagem [kamu'flaʒẽ] f camouflage

camuflar [kamu'fla*] vt to camouflage

camundongo [kamũ'dõgu] (BR) m mouse

camurça [ka'muxsa] f suede

cana ['kana] f cane; (col: cadeia) nick; (de açúcar) sugar cane

Canadá [kana'da] m: **o** ~ Canada; **canadense** [kana'dẽsi] adj, m/f Canadian

canal [ka'naw] (pl -ais) m channel; (de navegação) canal; (ANAT) duct

canalha [ka'naʎa] f rabble, mob ♦ m/f wretch, scoundrel

canalização [kanaliza'sãw] f plumbing

canalizador(a) [kanaliza'do*(a)] (PT) m/f plumber

canalizar [kanali'za*] vt (água, esforços) to channel

canapé [kana'pɛ] m sofa

canário [ka'narju] m canary

canastra [ka'naʃtra] f (big) basket

canavial [kana'vjaw] (pl -ais) m cane field; **canavieiro/a** [kana'vjejru/a] adj sugar cane atr

canção [kã'sãw] (pl -ões) f song; ~ **de ninar** lullaby

cancela [kã'sɛla] f gate

cancelamento [kãsela'mẽtu] m cancellation

cancelar [kãse'la*] vt to cancel; (riscar) to cross out

câncer ['kãse*] m cancer; **C**~ (ASTROLOGIA) Cancer

canções [kã'sõjʃ] fpl de **canção**

cancro ['kãkru] (PT) m cancer

candelabro [kãde'labru] m candlestick; (lustre) chandelier

candente [kã'dẽtʃi] adj white hot; (fig) inflamed

candidato/a [kãdʒi'datu/a] m/f candidate; (a cargo) applicant; **candidatura** [kãdʒida'tura] f candidature; application

cândido/a ['kãdʒidu/a] adj naive; (inocente) innocent; **candura** [kã'dura] f simplicity; innocence

caneca [ka'nɛka] f mug

canela [ka'nɛla] f cinnamon; (ANAT) shin

caneta [ka'neta] f pen; ~ **esferográfica/ pilot** ballpoint/felt-tip pen; ~ **seletora** (COMPUT) light pen; ~**-tinteiro** (pl ~**s-tinteiro**) f fountain pen

cangaceiro [kãga'sejru] (BR) m bandit

canguru [kãgu'ru] m kangaroo

cânhamo ['kaɲamu] m hemp

canhão [ka'ɲãw] (pl -ões) m cannon; (GEO) canyon

canhoto/a [ka'ɲotu/a] adj left-handed ♦ m/f left-handed person ♦ m (de cheque) stub

canibal [kani'baw] (pl -ais) m/f cannibal

caniço/a [ka'nisu/a] adj (col) skinny ♦ m reed

canil [ka'niw] (pl -is) m kennel

canino/a [ka'ninu/a] adj canine

canivete [kani'vɛtʃi] m penknife

canja ['kãʒa] f chicken broth; (col) cinch, pushover

canjica [kã'ʒika] f maize porridge

cano ['kanu] m pipe; (tubo) tube; (de arma de fogo) barrel; (de bota) top; ~ **de esgoto** sewer

canoa [ka'noa] f canoe

cansaço [kã'sasu] m tiredness

cansado/a [kã'sadu/a] adj tired

cansar [kã'sa*] vt to tire; (entediar) to bore ♦ vi to get tired; ~**-se** vr to get tired; **cansativo/a** [kãsa'tʃivu/a] adj tiring; (tedioso) tedious

cantar [kã'ta*] vt, vi to sing ♦ m song

cantarolar [kãtaro'la*] vt to hum

canteiro [kã'tejru] *m* stonemason; *(de flores)* flower bed

cantiga [kã'tʃiga] *f* ballad; **~ de ninar** lullaby

cantil [kã'tʃiw] *(pl* -is) *m* canteen

cantina [kã'tʃina] *f* canteen

cantis [kã'tʃiʃ] *mpl de* cantil

canto ['kãtu] *m* corner; *(lugar)* place; *(canção)* song

cantor(a) [kã'to*(a)] *m/f* singer

canudo [ka'nudu] *m* tube; *(para beber)* straw

cão [kãw] *(pl* cães) *m* dog

caolho/a [ka'oʎu/a] *adj* cross-eyed

caos ['kaoʃ] *m* chaos

capa ['kapa] *f* cape; *(cobertura)* cover; **livro de ~ dura/mole** hardback/paperback (book)

capacete [kapa'setʃi] *m* helmet

capacho [ka'paʃu] *m* door mat

capacidade [kapasi'dadʒi] *f* capacity; *(aptidão)* ability, competence

capar [ka'pa*] *vt* to castrate, geld

capataz [kapa'taʒ] *m* foreman

capaz [ka'paʒ] *adj* able, capable; **ser ~ de** to be able to *(ou* capable of); **sou ~ de ...** *(talvez)* I might ...; **é ~ de chover hoje** it might rain today

capcioso/a [kap'sjozu/ɔza] *adj (pergunta, pessoa)* tricky

capela [ka'pɛla] *f* chapel

capelão [kape'lãw] *(pl* -ães) *m* (REL) chaplain

capim [ka'pĩ] *m* grass

capinar [kapi'na*] *vt, vi* to weed

capitães [kapi'tãjʃ] *mpl de* capitão

capital [kapi'taw] *(pl* -ais) *adj, m* capital ♦ *f (cidade)* capital; **~ (em) ações** (COM) share capital

capitalismo [kapita'liʒmu] *m* capitalism; **capitalista** [kapita'liʃta] *m/f* capitalist

capitalizar [kapitali'za*] *vt* to capitalize on; (COM) to capitalize

capitanear [kapita'nja*] *vt* to command, head

capitão [kapi'tãw] *(pl* -ães) *m* captain

capítulo [ka'pitulu] *m* chapter

capô [ka'po] *m* (AUTO) bonnet (BRIT), hood (US)

capota [ka'pɔta] *f* (AUTO) hood, top

capotar [kapo'ta*] *vi* to overturn

capote [ka'pɔtʃi] *m* overcoat

capricho [ka'priʃu] *m* whim, caprice; *(teimosia)* obstinacy; *(apuro)* care; **~so/a** [kapri'fozu/ɔza] *adj* capricious; *(com apuro)* meticulous

Capricórnio [kapri'kɔxnju] *m* Capricorn

cápsula ['kapsula] *f* capsule

captar [kap'ta*] *vt (atrair)* to win; (RÁDIO) to pick up

captura [kap'tura] *f* capture; **~r** [kaptu'ra*] *vt* to capture

capuz [ka'puʒ] *m* hood

cáqui ['kaki] *adj* khaki

cara ['kara] *f* face; *(aspecto)* appearance ♦ *m (col)* guy; **~ ou coroa?** heads or tails?; **de ~** straightaway; **dar de ~ com** to bump into; **ser a ~ de** *(col)* to be the spitting image of; **ter ~ de** to look (like)

carabina [kara'bina] *f* rifle

caracol [kara'kɔw] *(pl* -óis) *m* snail; *(de cabelo)* curl; **escada em ~** spiral staircase

caracteres [karak'tɛriʃ] *mpl de* caráter

característica [karakte'riʃtʃika] *f* characteristic, feature

característico/a [karakte'riʃtʃiku/a] *adj* characteristic

cara-de-pau *(pl* caras-de-pau) *adj* brazen ♦ *m/f*: **ele é ~** he's very forward

caramelo [kara'mɛlu] *m* caramel; *(bala)* toffee

caranguejo [karã'geʒu] *m* crab

caratê [kara'te] *m* karate

caráter [ka'rate*] *(pl* caracteres) *m* character

caravana [kara'vana] *f* caravan

carboidrato [kaxboi'dratu] *m* carbohydrate

carbonizar [kaxboni'za*] *vt* to carbonize; *(queimar)* to char

carbono [kax'bɔnu] *m* carbon

carburador [kaxbura'do*] *m* carburettor (BRIT), carburetor (US)

carcaça [kax'kasa] *f* carcass; *(armação)* frame; *(de navio)* hull

cárcere ['kaxseri] *m* prison; **carcereiro/a** [kaxse'rejru/a] *m/f* jailer, warder

carcomido/a [kaxko'midu/a] *adj* worm-eaten

cardápio [kax'dapju] (BR) *m* menu

cardeal [kax'dʒjaw] *(pl* -ais) *adj, m* cardinal

cardíaco/a [kax'dʒiaku/a] *adj* cardiac; **ataque/parada ~** heart attack/cardiac arrest

cardigã [kaxdʒi'gã] *m* cardigan

cardinal [kaxdʒi'naw] *(pl* -ais) *adj* cardinal

cardume [kax'dumi] *m (peixes)* shoal

careca [ka'rɛka] *adj* bald

carecer [kare'se*] *vi*: **~ de** to lack; *(precisar)* to need

carência [ka'rẽsja] *f* lack; *(necessidade)* need; *(privação)* deprivation; **carente** [ka'rẽtʃi] *adj* wanting; *(pessoa)* needy, deprived

carestia [kareʃ'tʃia] *f* high cost; *(preços altos)* high prices *pl*; *(escassez)* scarcity

careta [ka'reta] *adj (col)* straight, square ♦ *f* grimace; **fazer uma ~** to pull a face

carga ['kaxga] *f* load; *(de navio, avião)* cargo; *(ato de carregar)* loading; (ELET) charge; *(fig: peso)* burden; (MIL) attack, charge; **dar ~ em** (COMPUT) to boot (up)

cargo ['kaxgu] *m* responsibility; *(função)* post; **a ~ de** in charge of; **ter a ~ to**

be in charge of; **tomar a ~** to take charge of

cargueiro [kax'gejru] *m* cargo ship

Caribe [ka'ribi] *m*: **o ~** the Caribbean (Sea)

carícia [ka'risja] *f* caress

caridade [kari'dadʒi] *f* charity; **obra de ~** charity

cárie [ˈkari] *f* tooth decay

carimbar [karĩ'ba*] *vt* to stamp; (*no correio*) to postmark

carimbo [ka'rĩbu] *m* stamp; (*postal*) postmark

carinho [ka'riɲu] *m* affection, fondness; (*carícia*) caress; **fazer ~** to caress; (*com ~* affectionately; (*com cuidado*) with care; **~so/a** [kari'ɲozu/ɔza] *adj* affectionate

carioca [ka'rjɔka] *adj* of Rio de Janeiro ♦ *m/f* native of Rio de Janeiro ♦ *m* (*PT: café*) type of weak coffee

carisma [ka'riʒma] *m* charisma

caritativo/a [karita'tʃivu/a] *adj* charitable

carnal [kax'naw] (*pl* –ais) *adj* carnal; **primo ~** first cousin

carnaval [kaxna'vaw] (*pl* –ais) *m* carnival; (*fig*) mess

carne [ˈkaxni] *f* flesh; (*CULIN*) meat; **em ~ e osso** in the flesh

carnê [kax'ne] *m* (*para compras*) payment book

carneiro [kax'nejru] *m* sheep; (*macho*) ram; **perna/costeleta de ~** leg of lamb/lamb chop

carniça [kax'nisa] *f* carrion; **pular ~** to play leapfrog

carnificina [kaxnifi'sina] *f* slaughter

carnudo/a [kax'nudu/a] *adj* plump, fleshy; (*lábios*) thick

caro/a [ˈkaru/a] *adj* dear; **cobrar/pagar ~** to charge a lot/pay dearly

carochinha [karo'ʃina] *f*: **conto** *ou* **história da ~** fairy tale *ou* story

caroço [ka'rosu] *m* (*de frutos*) stone; (*endurecimento*) lump

carona [ka'rɔna] *f* lift; **viajar de ~** to hitchhike; **pegar uma ~** to get a lift

carpete [kax'pɛtʃi] *m* (fitted) carpet

carpintaria [kaxpĩta'ria] *f* carpentry

carpinteiro [kaxpĩ'tejru] *m* carpenter

carranca [ka'xãka] *f* frown, scowl

carrapato [kaxa'patu] *m* (*inseto*) tick

carrasco [ka'xaʃku] *m* executioner; (*fig*) tyrant

carregado/a [kaxe'gadu/a] *adj* loaded; (*semblante*) sullen; (*céu*) dark; (*ambiente*) tense

carregador [kaxega'do*] *m* porter

carregamento [kaxega'mẽtu] *m* (*ação*) loading; (*carga*) load, cargo

carregar [kaxe'ga*] *vt* to load; (*levar*) to carry; (*bateria*) to charge; (*PT: apertar*) to press; (*levar para longe*) to take away ♦ *vi*: **~ em** overdo; (*pôr ênfase*) to bring out

carreira [ka'xejra] *f* run, running; (*profissão*) career; (*TURFE*) race; (*NÁUT*) slipway; (*fileira*) row; **às ~s** in a hurry

carreta [ka'xeta] *f* cart

carretel [kaxe'tɛw] (*pl* –éis) *m* spool, reel

carreto [ka'xetu] *m* freight

carrilhão [kaxi'ʎãw] (*pl* –ões) *m* chime

carrinho [ka'xiɲu] *m* trolley; (*brinquedo*) toy car; **~ (de criança)** pram; **~ de mão** wheelbarrow

carro [ˈkaxo] *m* car; (*de bois*) cart; (*de mão*) barrow; (*de máquina de escrever*) carriage; **~ de corrida/passeio/esporte** racing/saloon/sports car; **~ de praça** cab; **~ de bombeiro** fire engine

carroça [ka'xɔsa] *f* cart, waggon

carroçeria [kaxose'ria] *f* (*AUTO*) bodywork

carro-chefe (*pl* **carros-chefes**) *m* (*de desfile*) main float; (*fig*) flagship, centrepiece (*BRIT*), centerpiece (*US*)

carrocinha [kaxo'siɲa] *f* wagon

carrossel [kaxo'sɛw] (*pl* –éis) *m* merry-go-round

carruagem [ka'xwaʒẽ] (*pl* –ns) *f* carriage, coach

carta [ˈkaxta] *f* letter; (*de jogar*) card; (*mapa*) chart; **~ aérea/registrada** airmail/registered letter; **~ de condução** (*PT*) driving licence (*BRIT*), driver's license (*US*); **dar as ~s** to deal; **~-bomba** (*pl* **~s-bomba**) *f* letter bomb

cartão [kax'tãw] (*pl* –ões) *m* card; (*PT: material*) cardboard; **~ de crédito** credit card; **~-postal** (*pl* **cartões-postais**) *m* postcard

cartaz [kax'taʒ] *m* poster, bill (*US*); (**estar**) **em ~** (*TEATRO, CINEMA*) (to be) showing

cartear [kax'tʃja*] *vi* to play cards ♦ *vt* to play

carteira [kax'tejra] *f* desk; (*para dinheiro*) wallet; (*de ações*) portfolio; **~ de identidade** identity card; **~ de motorista** driving licence (*BRIT*), driver's license (*US*)

carteiro [kax'tejru] *m* postman (*BRIT*), mailman (*US*)

cartões [kax'tõjʃ] *mpl de* **cartão**

cartola [kax'tɔla] *f* top hat

cartolina [kaxto'lina] *f* card

cartomante [kaxto'mãtʃi] *m/f* fortune-teller

cartório [kax'tɔrju] *m* registry office

cartucho [kax'tuʃu] *m* cartridge; (*saco de papel*) packet

cartum [kax'tũ] (*pl* –ns) *m* cartoon

carvalho [kax'vaʎu] *m* oak

carvão [kax'vãw] (*pl* –ões) *m* coal; (*de madeira*) charcoal; **carvoeiro** [kaxvo'ejru] *m* coal merchant

casa [ˈkaza] *f* house; (*lar*) home; (*COM*) firm; (*MAT: decimal*) place; **em/para ~** (at) home/home; **~ de saúde** hospital; **~ da moeda** mint; **~ de banho** (*PT*) bathroom; **~ e comida** board and lodging; ~ **de cômodos** tenement; ~ **popular** ≈ council house

casacão [kaza'kãw] (pl **-ões**) m overcoat

casaco [ka'zaku] m coat; (paletó) jacket

casacões [kaza'kõjʃ] mpl de casacão

casa-forte (pl **casas-fortes**) f vault

casal [ka'zaw] (pl **-ais**) m couple

casamento [kaza'mẽtu] m marriage; (boda) wedding

casar [ka'za*] vt to marry; (combinar) to match (up); ~**-se** vr to get married; to combine well

casarão [kaza'rãw] (pl **-ões**) m mansion

casca ['kaʃka] f (de árvore) bark; (de banana) skin; (de ferida) scab; (de laranja) peel; (de nozes, ovos) shell; (de milho etc) husk; (de pão) crust

cascalho [kaʃ'kaʎu] m gravel; (na praia) shingle

cascão [kaʃ'kãw] m crust; (sujeira) grime

cascata [kaʃ'kata] f waterfall

cascavel [kaʃka'vɛw] (pl **-éis**) m rattlesnake

casco ['kaʃku] m skull; (de animal) hoof; (de navio) hull; (para bebidas) empty bottle; (de tartaruga) shell

casebre [ka'zɛbri] m hovel, shack

caseiro/a [ka'zejru/a] adj home-made; (pessoa, vida) domestic ♦ m/f housekeeper

caserna [ka'zɛxna] f barracks pl

caso ['kazu] m case; (tb: ~ **amoroso**) affair; (estória) story ♦ conj in case, if; no ~ **de** in case (of); **em todo** ~ in any case; **neste** ~ in that case; ~ **necessário** if necessary; **criar** ~ to cause trouble; **não fazer** ~ **de** to ignore; ~ **de emergência** emergency

caspa ['kaʃpa] f dandruff

casquinha [kaʃ'kiɲa] f (de sorvete) cone; (pele) skin

cassar [ka'sa*] vt (direitos, licença) to cancel, withhold; (políticos) to ban

cassete [ka'sɛtʃi] m cassette

cassetete [kase'tɛtʃi] m truncheon (BRIT), nightstick (US) ·

cassino [ka'sinu] m casino

casta ['kaʃta] f caste

castanha [kaʃ'taɲa] f chestnut; ~ **de caju** cashew nut; ~**-do-pará** [-pa'ra] (pl ~**s-do-pará**) f Brazil nut

castanho/a [kaʃ'taɲu/a] adj brown

castanheiro [kaʃta'ɲejru] m chestnut tree

castanholas [kaʃta'ɲɔlaʃ] fpl castanets

castelo [kaʃ'tɛlu] m castle

castiçal [kaʃtʃi'saw] (pl **-ais**) m candlestick

castiço/a [kaʃ'tʃisu/a] adj pure

castidade [kaʃtʃi'dadʒi] f chastity

castigar [kaʃtʃi'ga*] vt to punish; **castigo** [kaʃ'tʃigu] m punishment; (fig: mortificação) pain

casto/a ['kaʃtu/a] adj chaste

castor [kaʃ'to*] m beaver

casual [ka'zwaw] (pl **-ais**) adj chance atr, accidental; (fortuito) fortuitous; ~**idade** [kazwali'dadʒi] f chance; (acidente) accident

casulo [ka'zulu] m (de sementes) pod; (de insetos) cocoon

cata ['kata] f: à ~ **de** in search of

catalizador [kataliza'do*] m catalyst

catalogar [katalo'ga*] vt to catalogue (BRIT), catalog (US)

catálogo [ka'talogu] m catalogue (BRIT), catalog (US); ~ (**telefônico**) telephone directory

catapora [kata'pɔra] (BR) f chickenpox

catar [ka'ta*] vt to pick (up); (procurar) to look for, search for; (recolher) to collect, gather

catarata [kata'rata] f waterfall; (MED) cataract

catarro [ka'taxu] m catarrh

catástrofe [ka'taʃtrofi] f catastrophe

cata-vento m weathercock

cátedra ['katedra] f chair

catedral [kate'draw] (pl **-ais**) f cathedral

catedrático/a [kate'dratʃiku/a] m/f professor

categoria [katego'ria] f category; (social) rank; (qualidade) quality; **de alta** ~ first-rate

cativar [katʃi'va*] vt to enslave; (fascinar) to captivate; (atrair) to charm

cativeiro [katʃi'vejru] m captivity; (escravidão) slavery; (cadeia) prison

cativo/a [ka'tʃivu/a] m/f slave; (prisioneiro) prisoner

católico/a [ka'tɔliku/a] adj, m/f catholic

catorze [ka'toxzi] num fourteen

caução [kaw'sãw] (pl **-ões**) f security, guarantee; (JUR) bail; **sob** ~ on bail; **caucionar** [kawsjo'na*] vt to guarantee, stand surety for; to stand bail for

caudal [kaw'daw] (pl **-ais**) m torrent

caudilho [kaw'dʒiʎu] m leader, chief

caule ['kauli] m stalk, stem

causa ['kawza] f cause; (motivo) motive, reason; (JUR) lawsuit, case; **por** ~ **de** because of; ~**dor(a)** [kawza'do*(a)] adj which caused ♦ m cause; ~**r** [kaw'za*] vt to cause, bring about

cautela [kaw'tɛla] f caution; (senha) ticket; ~ (**de penhor**) pawn ticket; **cauteloso/a** [kawte'lozu/ɔza] adj cautious, wary

cavado/a [ka'vadu/a] adj (olhos) sunken; (roupa) low-cut

cavala [ka'vala] f mackerel

cavalaria [kavala'ria] f cavalry

cavaleiro [kava'lejru] m rider, horseman; (medieval) knight

cavalete [kava'letʃi] m stand; (FOTO) tripod; (de pintor) easel; (de mesa) trestle

cavalgar [kavaw'ga*] vt to ride ♦ vi: ~ **em** to ride on; ~ (**sobre**) to jump over

cavalheiro/a [kava'ʎejru/a] adj courteous, gallant ♦ m gentleman

cavalinho-de-pau [kava'liɲu-] (*pl* **cavalinhos-de-pau**) *m* rocking horse

cavalo [ka'valu] *m* horse; (*XADREZ*) knight; **a ~ on** horseback; **50 ~s(-vapor)** *ou* **(de força)** 50 horsepower; **~ de corrida** racehorse

cavaquinho [kava'kiɲu] *m* small guitar

cavar [ka'va*] *vt* to dig; (*esforçar-se para obter*) to try to get ♦ *vi* to dig; (*fig*) to delve; (*animal*) to burrow

cave ['kavi] (*PT*) *f* wine-cellar

caveira [ka'vejra] *f* skull

caverna [ka'vɛxna] *f* cavern

caviar [ka'vja*] *m* caviar

cavidade [kavi'dadʒi] *f* cavity

cavilha [ka'viʎa] *f* (*de madeira*) peg, dowel; (*de metal*) bolt

cavo/a ['kavu/a] *adj* concave

caxumba [ka'ʃũba] *f* mumps *sg*

CD *abr m* CD

cê [se] (*col*) *pron* = **você**

cear [sja*] *vt* to have for supper ♦ *vi* to dine

cebola [se'bola] *f* onion; **cebolinha** [sebo'liɲa] *f* spring onion

cecear [se'sja*] *vi* to lisp; **ceceio** [se'seju] *m* lisp

ceder [se'de*] *vt* to give up; (*dar*) to hand over; (*emprestar*) to lend ♦ *vi* to give in, yield

cedilha [se'dʒiʎa] *f* cedilla

cedo ['sedu] *adv* early; (*em breve*) soon

cedro ['sɛdru] *m* cedar

cédula ['sɛdula] *f* banknote; (*eleitoral*) ballot paper

CEE *abr f* (= *Comunidade Econômica Européia*) EEC

cegar [se'ga*] *vt* to blind; (*ofuscar*) to dazzle ♦ *vi* to be dazzling

cego/a ['sɛgu/a] *adj* blind; (*total*) complete, total; (*tesoura*) blunt ♦ *m/f* blind man/woman; **às cegas** blindly

cegonha [se'goɲa] *f* stork

cegueira [se'gejra] *f* blindness

CEI *abr f* (= *Comunidade de Estados Independentes*) CIS

ceia ['seja] *f* supper

ceifa ['sejfa] *f* harvest; (*fig*) destruction

cela ['sɛla] *f* cell

celebração [selebra'sãw] (*pl* **–ões**) *f* celebration

celebrar [sele'bra*] *vt* to celebrate; (*exaltar*) to praise; (*acordo*) to seal

célebre ['sɛlebri] *adj* famous, well-known

celebridade [selebri'dadʒi] *f* celebrity

celeiro [se'lejru] *m* granary; (*depósito*) barn

celeste [se'lɛʃtʃi] *adj* celestial, heavenly

celibatário/a [seliba'tarju/a] *adj* unmarried, single ♦ *m/f* bachelor/spinster

celofane [selo'fani] *m* cellophane; **papel ~** cling film

celta ['sɛwta] *adj* Celtic ♦ *m/f* Celt

célula ['sɛlula] *f* (*BIO, ELET*) cell

cem [sẽ] *num* hundred

cemitério [semi'tɛrju] *m* cemetery, graveyard

cena ['sɛna] *f* scene; (*palco*) stage

cenário [se'narju] *m* scenery; (*CINEMA*) scenario; (*de um acontecimento*) setting

cenoura [se'nora] *f* carrot

censo ['sẽsu] *m* census

censor(a) [sẽ'so*(a)] *m/f* censor

censura [sẽ'sura] *f* censorship; (*reprovação*) censure, criticism; **~r** [sẽsu'ra*] *vt* to censure; (*filme, livro etc*) to censor

centavo [sẽ'tavu] *m* cent; **estar sem um ~** to be penniless

centeio [sẽ'teju] *m* rye

centelha [sẽ'tɛʎa] *f* spark

centena [sẽ'tɛna] *f* hundred; **às ~s in** hundreds

centenário/a [sẽte'narju/a] *m* centenary

centígrado [sẽ'tʃigradu] *m* centigrade

centímetro [sẽ'tʃimetru] *m* centimetre (*BRIT*), centimeter (*US*)

cento ['sẽtu] *m*: **~ e um** one hundred and one; **por ~** per cent

centopeia [sẽto'peja] *f* centipede

central [sẽ'traw] (*pl* **–ais**) *adj* central ♦ *f* (*de polícia etc*) head office; **~ elétrica** (electric) power station; **~ telefônica** telephone exchange; **~izar** [sẽtrali'za*] *vt* to centralize

centrar [sẽ'tra*] *vt* to centre (*BRIT*), center (*US*)

centro ['sẽtru] *m* centre (*BRIT*), center (*US*); (*de uma cidade*) town centre; **~avante** [sẽtroa'vãtʃi] *m* (*FUTEBOL*) centre forward

CEP ['sɛpi] (*BR*) *abr m* (= *Código de Endereçamento Postal*) postcode (*BRIT*), zip code (*US*)

céptico/a *etc* ['sɛptiku/a] (*PT*) = **cético** *etc*

ceptro ['sɛtru] (*PT*) *m* = **cetro**

cera ['sera] *f* wax

cerâmica [se'ramika] *f* pottery

cerâmico/a [se'ramiku/a] *adj* ceramic

ceramista [sera'miʃta] *m/f* potter

cerca ['sexka] *f* fence ♦ *prep*: **~ de** (*aproximadamente*) around, about; **~ viva** hedge

cercado [sex'kadu] *m* enclosure; (*para animais*) pen; (*para crianças*) playpen

cercanias [sexka'niaʃ] *fpl* outskirts; (*vizinhança*) neighbourhood *sg* (*BRIT*), neighborhood *sg* (*US*)

cercar [sex'ka*] *vt* to enclose; (*rodear*) to surround; (*assediar*) to besiege

cerco ['sexku] *m* siege; **pôr ~ a** to besiege

cereal [se'rjaw] (*pl* **–ais**) *m* cereal

cérebro ['sɛrebru] *m* brain; (*fig*) brains *pl*

cereja [se'reʒa] *f* cherry

cerimônia [seri'monja] *f* ceremony

cerne ['sɛxni] *m* kernel

cerração [sexa'sãw] *f* fog

cerrado/a [se'xadu/a] *adj* shut, closed; (*denso*) thick ♦ *m* scrub(land)

cerrar [se'xa*] *vt* to close, shut; **~-se** *vr* to close, shut

certeza [sex'teza] *f* certainty; **com ~** certainly, surely; (*provavelmente*) probably; **ter ~ de/de que** to be certain *ou* sure of/to be sure that

certidão [sextʃi'dãw] (*pl* **-ões**) *f* certificate

certificado [sextʃifi'kadu] *m* certificate

certificar [sextʃifi'ka*] *vt* to certify; (*assegurar*) to assure; **~-se** *vr*: **~-se de** to make sure of

certo/a ['sɛxtu/a] *adj* certain, sure; (*exato, direito*) right; (*um, algum*) a certain ♦ *adv* correctly; **na certa** certainly; **ao ~** for certain; **está ~** okay, all right

cerveja [sex'veʒa] *f* beer; **~ria** [sexveʒa'ria] *f* (*fábrica*) brewery; (*bar*) bar, public house

cervical [sexvi'kaw] (*pl* **-ais**) *adj* cervical

cérvice ['sɛxvisi] *f* cervix

cervo ['sɛxvu] *m* deer

cerzir [sex'zi*] *vt* to darn

cessão [se'sãw] (*pl* **-ões**) *f* surrender

cessação [sesa'sãw] *f* halting, ceasing

cessar [se'sa*] *vi* to cease, stop; **sem ~** continually; **~-fogo** *m inv* cease-fire

cessões [se'sõjʃ] *fpl de* cessão

cesta ['sɛʃta] *f* basket

cesto ['sɛʃtu] *m* basket; (*com tampa*) hamper

cético/a ['sɛtʃiku/a] *m/f* sceptic (*BRIT*), skeptic (*US*)

cetim [se'tʃĩ] *m* satin

cetro ['sɛtru] *m* sceptre (*BRIT*), scepter (*US*)

céu [sɛw] *m* sky; (*REL*) heaven; (*da boca*) roof

cevada [se'vada] *f* barley

cevar [se'va*] *vt* (*engordar*) to fatten; (*alimentar*) to feed; (*engodar*) to bait

CFC *abr m* (= *clorofluorcarbono*) CFC

chá [ʃa] *m* tea

chacal [ʃa'kaw] (*pl* **-ais**) *m* jackal

chácara ['ʃakara] *f* farm; (*casa de campo*) country house

chacina [ʃa'sina] *f* slaughter; **~r** [ʃasi'na*] *vt* (*matar*) to slaughter

chacota [ʃa'kɔta] *f* mockery

chafariz [ʃafa'riʒ] *m* fountain

chafurdar [ʃafux'da*] *vi*: **~ em** to wallow in; **~-se** *vr*: **~-se em** to wallow in

chaga ['ʃaga] *f* (*MED*) wound; (*fig*) disease

chalé [ʃa'lɛ] *m* chalet

chaleira [ʃa'lejra] *f* kettle; (*bajulador*) crawler, toady

chama ['ʃama] *f* flame

chamada [ʃa'mada] *f* call; (*MIL*) roll call; (*EDUC*) register; (*no jornal*) headline; **dar uma ~ em alguém** to tell sb off

chamar [ʃa'ma*] *vt* to call; (*convidar*) to invite; (*atenção*) to attract ♦ *vi* to call; (*telefone*) to ring; **~-se** *vr* to be called; **chamo-me João** my name is John; **~ alguém de idiota/Dudu** to call sb an

idiot/Dudu; **mandar ~** to summon, send for

chamariz [ʃama'riʒ] *m* decoy

chamativo/a [ʃama'tʃivu/a] *adj* showy, flashy

chaminé [ʃami'nɛ] *f* chimney; (*de navio*) funnel

champanha [ʃã'paɲa] *m ou f* champagne

champanhe [ʃã'paɲi] *m ou f* = **champanha**

champu [ʃã'pu] (*PT*) *m* shampoo

chamuscar [ʃamuʃ'ka*] *vt* to scorch, singe

chance ['ʃãsi] *f* chance

chanceler [ʃãse'lɛ*] *m* chancellor

chantagear [ʃãta'ʒja*] *vt* to blackmail

chantagem [ʃã'taʒẽ] *f* blackmail

chão [ʃãw] (*pl* **~s**) *m* ground; (*terra*) soil; (*piso*) floor

chapa ['ʃapa] *f* (*placa*) plate; (*eleitoral*) list; **~ de matrícula** (*PT: AUTO*) number (*BRIT*) *ou* license (*US*) plate; **oi, meu ~!** hi, mate!

chapéu [ʃa'pɛw] *m* hat; **~-coco** (*pl* **~s-cocos**) *m* bowler (hat) (*BRIT*), derby (*US*)

chapinha [ʃa'piɲa] *f*: **~ (de garrafa)** (bottle) top

charco ['ʃaxku] *m* marsh, bog

charme ['ʃaxmi] *m* charm; **fazer ~** to be nice, use one's charm; **charmoso/a** [ʃax'mozu/ɔza] *adj* charming

charneca [ʃax'nɛka] *f* moor, heath

charrete [ʃa'xetʃi] *f* cart

charter ['tʃaxte*] (*pl* **~s**) *m* charter flight

charuto [ʃa'rutu] *m* cigar

chassi [ʃa'si] *m* (*AUTO, ELET*) chassis

chata ['ʃata] *f* barge; *V tb* **chato**

chateação [ʃatʃja'sãw] (*pl* **-ões**) *f* bother, upset; (*maçada*) bore

chatear [ʃa'tʃja*] *vt* to bother, upset; (*importunar*) to pester; (*entediar*) to bore; (*irritar*) to annoy ♦ *vi* to be upsetting; to be boring; to be annoying; **~-se** *vr* to get upset; to get bored; to get annoyed

chatice [ʃa'tʃisi] *f* nuisance

chato/a ['ʃatu/a] *adj* flat; (*tedioso*) boring; (*irritante*) annoying; (*que fica mal*) rude ♦ *m/f* bore; (*quem irrita*) pain

chauvinista [ʃawvi'niʃta] *adj* chauvinistic ♦ *m/f* chauvinist

chavão [ʃa'vãw] (*pl* **-ões**) *m* cliché

chave ['ʃavi] *f* key; (*ELET*) switch; **~ de porcas** spanner; **~ inglesa** (monkey) wrench; **~ de fenda** screwdriver

chaveiro [ʃa'vejru] *m* key ring; (*pessoa*) locksmith

chávena ['ʃavena] (*PT*) *f* cup

checar [ʃe'ka*] *vt* to check

check-up [ʃe'kapi] (*pl* **~s**) *m* check-up

chefatura [ʃefa'tura] *f*: **~ de polícia** police headquarters *sg*

chefe ['ʃɛfi] *m/f* head, chief; (*patrão*)

boss; ~ **de estação** stationmaster; **chefia** [ʃe'fia] *f* leadership; (*direção*) management; (*repartição*) headquarters *sg*; **chefiar** [ʃe'fjaʳ] *vt* to lead

chega ['ʃega] (*col*) *m*: **dar um ~ em alguém** to tell sb off

chegada [ʃe'gada] *f* arrival

chegado/a [ʃe'gadu/a] *adj* near; (*íntimo*) close

chegar [ʃe'gaʳ] *vt* to bring near ♦ *vi* to arrive; (*ser suficiente*) to be enough; ~**se** *vr*: ~**se a** to approach; **chega!** that's enough!; ~ **a** (*atingir*) to reach; (*conseguir*) to manage to

cheio/a ['ʃeju/a] *adj* full; (*repleto*) full up; (*col: farto*) fed up

cheirar [ʃej'raʳ] *vt, vi* to smell; ~ **a** to smell of; **cheiro** ['ʃejru] *m* smell; **ter ~ de** to smell of; **cheiroso/a** [ʃej'rozu/ɔza] *adj*: **ser** *ou* **estar cheiroso/a** to smell nice

cheque ['ʃɛki] *m* cheque (*BRIT*), check (*US*); ~ **de viagem** traveller's cheque (*BRIT*), traveler's check (*US*)

chiado [ʃi'jadu] *m* squeak(ing); (*de vapor*) hiss(ing)

chiar [ʃjaʳ] *vi* to squeak; (*porta*) to creak; (*vapor*) to hiss; (*col: eclamar*) to grumble

chiclete [ʃi'klɛtʃi] *m* chewing gum

chicória [ʃi'kɔrja] *f* chicory

chicote [ʃi'kɔtʃi] *m* whip; ~**r** [ʃiko'tʃjaʳ] *vt* to whip

chifrada [ʃi'frada] *f* butt

chifre ['ʃifri] *m* horn

Chile ['ʃili] *m*: **o ~** Chile

chimarrão [ʃima'xãw] (*pl -ões*) *m* mate tea without sugar taken from a pipe-like cup

chimpanzé [ʃĩpã'zɛ] *m* chimpanzee

China ['ʃina] *f*: **a ~** China

chinelo [ʃi'nɛlu] *m* slipper

chinês/esa [ʃi'neʃ/eza] *adj, m/f* Chinese ♦ *m* (*LING*) Chinese

chino/a ['ʃinu/a] *m/f* Chinese

chip ['ʃipi] *m* (*COMPUT*) chip

Chipre ['ʃipri] *f* Cyprus

chique ['ʃiki] *adj* stylish, chic

chiqueiro [ʃi'kejru] *m* pigsty

chispa ['ʃiʃpa] *f* spark

chispar [ʃiʃ'paʳ] *vi* (*correr*) to dash

chocalhar [ʃoka'ʎaʳ] *vt, vi* to rattle

chocalho [ʃo'kaʎu] *m* (*MÚS, brinquedo*) rattle; (*para animais*) bell

chocante [ʃo'kãtʃi] *adj* shocking; (*col*) amazing

chocar [ʃo'kaʳ] *vt* to hatch, incubate; (*ofender*) to offend ♦ *vi* to shock; ~**se** *vr* to crash, collide; to be shocked

chocho/a ['ʃoʃu/a] *adj* hollow, empty; (*fraco*) weak; (*sem graça*) dull

chocolate [ʃoko'latʃi] *m* chocolate

chofer [ʃo'fɛʳ] *m* driver

chope ['ʃopi] *m* draught beer

choque¹ ['ʃɔki] *m* shock; (*colisão*) colli-

sion; (*impacto*) impact; (*conflito*) clash

choque² *etc vb V* **chocar**

choramingar [ʃorami'gaʳ] *vi* to whine, whimper; **choramingo** [ʃora'mĩgu] *m* whine, whimper

chorão/rona [ʃo'rãw/rɔna] (*pl -ões/~s*) *adj* tearful ♦ *m/f* crybaby ♦ *m* (*BOT*) weeping willow

chorar [ʃo'raʳ] *vt, vi* to weep, cry

chorinho [ʃo'riɲu] *m* type of Brazilian music

choro ['ʃoru] *m* crying; (*MÚS*) type of Brazilian music; ~**so/a** [ʃo'rozu/ɔza] *adj* tearful

choupana [ʃo'pana] *f* shack, hut

chouriço [ʃo'risu] *m* (*BR*) black pudding; (*PT*) spicy sausage

chover [ʃo'veʳ] *vi* to rain; ~ **a cântaros** to rain cats and dogs

chuchu [ʃu'ʃu] *m* chayote (*vegetable*)

chulé [ʃu'lɛ] *m* foot odour (*BRIT*) *ou* odor (*US*)

chulear [ʃu'ljaʳ] *vt* to hem

chulo/a ['ʃulu/a] *adj* vulgar

chumaço [ʃu'masu] *m* (*de papel, notas*) wad

chumbar [ʃũ'baʳ] *vt* to fill with lead; (*soldar*) to solder; (*atirar em*) to fire at ♦ *vi* (*PT: reprovar*) to fail

chumbo ['ʃũbu] *m* lead; (*de caça*) gunshot; (*PT: de dente*) filling; **sem ~** (*gasolina*) unleaded

chupar [ʃu'paʳ] *vt* to suck

chupeta [ʃu'peta] *f* dummy (*BRIT*), pacifier (*US*)

churrasco [ʃu'xaʃku] *m*, **churrasqueira** [ʃuxaʃ'kejra] *f* barbecue

churrasquinho [ʃuxaʃ'kiɲu] *m* kebab

chutar [ʃu'taʳ] *vt* to kick; (*col: adivinhar*) to guess at; (: *dar o fora em*) to dump ♦ *vi* to kick; to guess; (: *mentir*) to lie

chute ['ʃutʃi] *m* kick; (*col: mentira*) fib; **dar o ~ em alguém** (*col*) to give sb the boot

chuteira [ʃu'tejra] *f* football boot

chuva ['ʃuva] *f* rain; **chuveiro** [ʃu'vejru] *m* shower

chuviscar [ʃuviʃ'kaʳ] *vi* to drizzle; **chuvisco** [ʃu'viʃku] *m* drizzle

chuvoso/a [ʃu'vozu/ɔza] *adj* rainy

Cia. *abr* (= *companhia*) Co

cibercafé [sibexka'fɛ] *m* cybercafé

ciberespaço [sibexiʃ'pasu] *m* cyberspace

cicatriz [sika'triʒ] *f* scar; ~**ar** [sikatri'zaʳ] *vi* to heal; (*rosto*) to scar

cicerone [sise'rɔni] *m* tourist guide

ciclismo [si'kliʒmu] *m* cycling

ciclista [si'kliʃta] *m/f* cyclist

ciclo ['siklu] *m* cycle

ciclone [si'klɔni] *m* cyclone

cidadã [sida'dã] *f de* **cidadão**

cidadania [sidada'nia] *f* citizenship

cidadão/cidadã [sida'dãw/sida'dã] (*pl ~s/~s*) *m/f* citizen

cidade [si'dadʒi] *f* town; (*grande*) city

ciência ['sjẽsja] f science
ciente ['sjẽtʃi] adj aware
científico/a [sjẽ'tʃifiku/a] adj scientific
cientista [sjẽ'tʃiʃta] m/f scientist
cifra ['sifra] f cipher; (algarismo) number, figure; (total) sum
cifrar [si'fra*] vt to write in code
cigano/a [si'ganu/a] adj, m/f gypsy
cigarra [si'gaxa] f cicada; (ELET) buzzer
cigarrilha [siga'xiʎa] f cheroot
cigarro [si'gaxu] m cigarette
cilada [si'lada] f ambush; (armadilha) trap; (embuste) trick
cilindro [si'lĩdru] m cylinder; (rolo) roller
cílio ['silju] m eyelash
cima ['sima] f: **de ~ para baixo** from top to bottom; **para ~** up; **em ~ de** on, on top of; **por ~ de** over; **de ~** from above; **lá em ~** up there; (em casa) upstairs; **ainda por ~** on top of that
cimeira [si'mejra] (PT) f summit
cimentar [simẽ'ta*] vt to cement
cimento [si'mẽtu] m cement; (fig) foundation
cimo ['simu] m top, summit
cinco ['sĩku] num five
cineasta [sine'aʃta] m/f film maker
cinema [si'nɛma] m cinema
Cingapura [sĩga'pura] f Singapore
cínico/a ['siniku/a] adj cynical ♦ m/f cynic; **cinismo** [si'niʒmu] m cynicism
cinquenta [sĩ'kwẽta] num fifty
cinta ['sĩta] f sash; (de mulher) girdle
cintilar [sĩtʃi'la*] vi to sparkle, glitter
cinto ['sĩtu] m belt; **~ de segurança** safety belt; (AUTO) seatbelt
cintura [sĩ'tura] f waist; (linha) waistline
cinturão [sĩtu'rãw] (pl -ões) m belt; **~ verde** green belt
cinza ['sĩza] adj inv grey (BRIT), gray (US) ♦ f ash, ashes pl
cinzeiro [sĩ'zejru] m ashtray
cinzel [sĩ'zɛw] (pl -éis) m chisel
cinzento/a [sĩ'zẽtu/a] adj grey (BRIT), gray (US)
cio [siu] m: **no ~** on heat, in season
cipreste [si'prɛʃtʃi] m cypress (tree)
cipriota [si'prjɔta] adj, m/f Cypriot
circo ['sixku] m circus
circuito [six'kwitu] m circuit
circulação [sixkula'sãw] f circulation
circular [sixku'la*] adj circular ♦ vi to circulate; (girar, andar) to go round ♦ vt to circulate; (estar em volta de) to surround; (percorrer em roda) to go round
círculo ['sixkulu] m circle
circuncidar [sixkũsi'da*] vt to circumcise
circundar [sixkũ'da*] vt to surround
circunferência [sixkũfe'rẽsja] f circumference
circunflexo [sixkũ'flɛksu] m circumflex (accent)
circunscrição [sixkũʃkri'sãw] (pl -ões) f district; **~ eleitoral** constituency

circunstância [sixkũ'ʃtãsja] f circumstance; **~s atenuantes** mitigating circumstances
cirurgia [sirux'ʒia] f surgery; **~ plástica/estética** plastic/cosmetic surgery
cirurgião/giã [sirux'ʒjãw/'ʒjã] (pl -ões/~s) m/f surgeon
cirúrgico/a [si'ruxʒiku/a] adj surgical
cirurgiões [sirux'ʒjõjʃ] mpl de **cirurgião**
cirzo etc ['sixzu] vb V **cerzir**
cisco ['siʃku] m speck
cisma ['siʒma] f (mania) silly idea; (suspeita) suspicion; (antipatia) dislike; (devaneio) dream; **~do/a** [siʒ'madu/a] adj with fixed ideas
cismar [siʒ'ma*] vi (pensar): **~ em** to brood over; (antipatizar): **~ com** to take a dislike to ♦ vt: **~ que** to be convinced that; **~ de** ou **em fazer** (meter na cabeça) to get into one's head to do; (insistir) to insist on doing
cisne ['siʒni] m swan
cisterna [siʃ'tɛxna] f cistern, tank
citação [sita'sãw] (pl -ões) f quotation; (JUR) summons sg
citar [si'ta*] vt to quote; (JUR) to summon
cítrico/a ['sitriku/a] adj (fruta) citrus; (ácido) citric
ciúme ['sjumi] m jealousy; **ter ~s de** to be jealous of; **ciumento/a** [sju'mẽtu/a] adj jealous
cívico/a ['siviku/a] adj civic
civil [si'viw] (pl -is) adj civil ♦ m/f civilian; **~idade** [sivili'dadʒi] f politeness
civilização [siviliza'sãw] (pl -ões) f civilization
civilizar [sivili'za*] vt to civilize
civis [si'viʃ] pl de **civil**
clamar [kla'ma*] vt to clamour (BRIT) ou clamor (US) for ♦ vi to cry out, clamo(u)r
clamor [kla'mo*] m outcry, uproar; **~oso/a** [klamo'rozo/zza] adj noisy
clandestino/a [klãdeʃ'tʃinu/a] adj clandestine; (ilegal) underground
clara ['klara] f egg white
clarabóia [klara'bɔja] f skylight
clarão [kla'rãw] (pl -ões) m (cintilação) flash; (claridade) gleam
clarear [kla'rja*] vi (dia) to dawn; (tempo) to clear up, brighten up ♦ vt to clarify
clareira [kla'rejra] f (na mata) clearing
clareza [kla'reza] f clarity
claridade [klari'dadʒi] f brightness
clarim [kla'rĩ] (pl -ns) m bugle
clarinete [klari'netʃi] m clarinet
clarins [kla'rĩʃ] mpl de **clarim**
clarividente [klarivi'dẽtʃi] adj farsighted, prudent
claro/a ['klaru/a] adj clear; (luminoso) bright; (cor) light; (evidente) clear, evident ♦ m (na escrita) space; (clareira) clearing ♦ adv clearly; **~!** of course!; **~ que sim!/não!** of course!/of course not!;

às claras openly

clarões [kla'rõjʃ] *mpl de* **clarão**

classe ['klasi] *f* class

clássico/a ['klasiku/a] *adj* classical; *(fig)* classic; *(habitual)* usual ♦ *m* classic

classificação [klasifika'sãw] *(pl -ões) f* classification; *(ESPORTE)* place, placing

classificado/a [klasifi'kadu/a] *adj (em exame)* successful; *(anúncio)* classified; *(ESPORTE)* placed ♦ *m* classified ad

classificar [klasifi'ka*] *vt* to classify; **~-se** *vr*: **~-se de algo** to call o.s. sth, describe o.s. as sth

claustro ['klawʃtru] *m* cloister

cláusula ['klawzula] *f* clause

clausura [klaw'zura] *f* enclosure

clave ['klavi] *f (MÚS)* clef

clavícula [kla'vikula] *f* collar bone

clemência [kle'mẽsja] *f* mercy; **clemente** [kle'mẽtʃi] *adj* merciful

clérigo ['klɛrigu] *m* clergyman

clero ['klɛru] *m* clergy

cliché [kli'ʃe] *m (FOTO)* plate; *(chavão)* cliché

cliente ['kljẽtʃi] *m* client, customer; *(de médico)* patient; **~la** [kljẽ'tɛla] *f* clientele; *(de loja)* customers *pl*

clima ['klima] *m* climate

clímax ['klimaks] *m inv* climax

clínica ['klinika] *f* clinic; *V tb* **clínico**

clínico/a ['kliniku/a] *adj* clinical ♦ *m/f* doctor; **~ geral** general practitioner, GP

clipe ['klipi] *m* clip; *(para papéis)* paper clip

cloro ['kloru] *m* chlorine

close ['klɔzi] *m* close-up

clube ['klubi] *m* club

coadjuvante [koadʒu'vãtʃi] *adj* supporting ♦ *m/f (num crime)* accomplice; *(TEATRO, CINEMA)* co-star

coador [koa'do*] *m* strainer; *(de café)* filter bag; *(para legumes)* colander

coagir [koa'ʒi*] *vt* to coerce, compel

coagular [koagu'la*] *vt, vi* to coagulate; *(sangue)* to clot; **~-se** *vr* to congeal

coágulo [ko'agulu] *m* clot

coajo *etc* [ko'aʒu] *vb V* **coagir**

coalhada [koa'ʎada] *f* curd

coalhar [koa'ʎa*] *vi (leite)* to curdle; **~-se** *vr* to curdle

coalizão [koali'zãw] *(pl -ões) f* coalition

coar [ko'a*] *vt (líquido)* to strain

cobaia [ko'baja] *f* guinea pig

coberta [ko'bɛxta] *f* cover, covering; *(NÁUT)* deck

coberto/a [ko'bɛxtu/a] *pp de* **cobrir** ♦ *adj* covered

cobertor [kobex'to*] *m* blanket

cobertura [kobex'tura] *f* covering; *(telhado)* roof; *(apartamento)* penthouse; *(TV, RÁDIO, JORNALISMO)* coverage; *(SEGUROS)* cover

cobiça [ko'bisa] *f* greed

cobiçar [kobi'sa*] *vt* to covet

cobra ['kɔbra] *f* snake

cobrador(a) [kobra'do*(a)] *m/f* collector; *(em transporte)* conductor

cobrança [ko'brãsa] *f* collection; *(ato de cobrar)* charging

cobrar [ko'bra*] *vt* to collect; *(preço)* to charge

cobre ['kɔbri] *m* copper; **~s** *mpl (dinheiro)* money *sg*

cobrir [ko'bri*] *vt* to cover

cocada [ko'kada] *f* coconut sweet

cocaína [koka'ina] *f* cocaine

coçar [ko'sa*] *vt* to scratch ♦ *vi* to itch; **~-se** *vr* to scratch o.s.

cócegas ['kɔsegaʃ] *fpl*: **fazer ~ em** to tickle; **tenho ~ nos pés** my feet tickle; **sentir ~** to be ticklish

coceira [ko'sejra] *f* itch; *(qualidade)* itchiness

cochichar [koʃi'ʃa*] *vi* to whisper; **cochicho** [ko'ʃiʃu] *m* whispering

cochilada [koʃi'lada] *f* snooze; **dar uma ~** to have a snooze

cochilar [koʃi'la*] *vi* to snooze, doze; **cochilo** [ko'ʃilu] *m* nap

coco ['koku] *m* coconut

cócoras ['kɔkoraʃ] *fpl*: **de ~** squatting; **ficar de ~** to squat (down)

código ['kɔdʒigu] *m* code; **~ de barras** bar code

codorna [ko'dɔxna] *f* quail

coelho [ko'eʎu] *m* rabbit

coerção [koex'sãw] *f* coercion

coerente [koe'rẽtʃi] *adj* coherent; *(conseqüente)* consistent

cofre ['kɔfri] *m* safe; *(caixa)* strongbox; **os ~s públicos** public funds

cogitação [koʒita'sãw] *f*: **estar fora de ~** to be out of the question

cogitar [koʒi'ta*] *vt, vi* to contemplate

cogumelo [kogu'mɛlu] *m* mushroom; **~ venenoso** toadstool

coibição [koibi'sãw] *(pl -ões) f* restraint, restriction

coice ['kojsi] *m* kick; *(de arma)* recoil; **dar ~s em** to kick

coincidência [koĩsi'dẽsja] *f* coincidence

coincidir [koĩsi'dʒi*] *vi* to coincide; *(concordar)* to agree

coisa ['kojza] *f* thing; *(assunto)* matter; **~ de** about

coitado/a [koj'tadu/a] *adj* poor, wretched

cola ['kɔla] *f* glue

colaborador(a) [kolabora'do*(a)] *m/f* collaborator; *(em jornal)* contributor

colaborar [kolabo'ra*] *vi* to collaborate; *(ajudar)* to help; *(escrever artigos etc)* to contribute

colante [ko'lãtʃi] *adj (roupa)* skin-tight

colapso [ko'lapsu] *m* collapse; **~ cardíaco** heart failure

colar [ko'la*] *vt* to stick, glue; *(BR: copiar)* to crib ♦ *vi* to stick; to cheat ♦ *m* necklace

colarinho [kola'riɲu] *m* collar

colarinho-branco *(pl* **colarinhos-**

brancos) *m* white-collar worker

colateral [kolate'raw] (*pl* –ais) *adj*: efeito ~ side effect

colcha ['kowʃa] *f* bedspread

colchão [kow'ʃãw] (*pl* –ões) *m* mattress

colcheia [kow'ʃeja] *f* (*MÚS*) quaver

colchete [kow'ʃetʃi] *m* clasp, fastening; (*parêntese*) square bracket; ~ de gancho hook and eye; ~ de pressão press stud, popper

colchões [kow'ʃõjʃ] *mpl de* colchão

coleção [kole'sãw] (*PT* -cç-; *pl* ~ões) *f* collection; **colecionador(a)** [kolesjona'do'(a)] (*PT* -cc-) *m/f* collector; **colecionar** [kolesjo'na'] (*PT* -cc-) *vt* to collect

colectar *etc* [kolek'ta'] (*PT*) = **coletar** *etc*

colega [ko'lɛga] *m/f* colleague; (*de escola*) classmate

colegial [kole'ʒjaw] (*pl* –ais) *m/f* schoolboy/girl

colégio [ko'lɛʒu] *m* school

coleira [ko'lejra] *f* collar

cólera ['kɔlera] *f* anger ♦ *m ou f* (*MED*) cholera; **colérico/a** [ko'lɛriku/a] *adj* angry

colesterol [kolɛʃte'rɔw] *m* cholesterol

coleta [ko'lɛta] *f* collection; ~r [kole'ta'] *vt* to tax; (*arrecadar*) to collect

colete [ko'letʃi] *m* waistcoat (*BRIT*), vest (*US*); ~ salva-vidas life jacket (*BRIT*), life preserver (*US*)

coletivo/a [kole'tʃivu/a] *adj* collective; (*transportes*) public ♦ *m* bus

coletor(a) [kole'to'(a)] *m/f* collector

colheita [ko'ʎejta] *f* harvest

colher [ko'ʎe'] *vt* to gather, pick; (*dados*) to gather ♦ *f* spoon; ~ de chá/sopa teaspoon/tablespoon; ~ada [koʎe'rada] *f* spoonful

colibri [koli'bri] *m* hummingbird

cólica ['kɔlika] *f* colic

colidir [koli'dʒi'] *vi*: ~ com to collide with, crash into

coligação [koliga'sãw] (*pl* –ões) *f* coalition

coligir [koli'ʒi'] *vt* to collect

colina [ko'lina] *f* hill

colisão [koli'zãw] (*pl* –ões) *f* collision

collant [ko'lã] (*pl* ~s) *m* tights *pl* (*BRIT*), pantihose (*US*); (*blusa*) leotard

colmeia [kow'meja] *f* beehive

colo ['kɔlu] *m* neck; (*regaço*) lap

colocação [koloka'sãw] (*pl* –ões) *f* placing; (*emprego*) job, position

colocar [kolo'ka'] *vt* to put, place; (*empregar*) to find a job for, place; (*COM*) to market; (*pneus, tapetes*) to fit; (*questão, idéia*) to put forward; (*COMPUT*: *dados*) to key (in)

Colômbia [ko'lõbja] *f*: a ~ Colombia

cólon ['kɔlõ] *m* colon

colônia [ko'lonja] *f* colony; (*perfume*) cologne; **colonial** [kolo'njaw] (*pl* –ais) *adj* colonial

colonizador(a) [koloniza'do'(a)] *m/f* co-

lonist, settler

colono [ko'lɔnu/a] *m/f* settler; (*cultivador*) tenant farmer

coloquial [kolo'kjaw] (*pl* –ais) *adj* colloquial

colóquio [ko'lɔkju] *m* conversation; (*congresso*) conference

colorido/a [kolo'ridu/a] *adj* colourful (*BRIT*), colorful (*US*) ♦ *m* colouring (*BRIT*), coloring (*US*)

colorir [kolo'ri'] *vt* to colour (*BRIT*), color (*US*)

coluna [ko'luna] *f* column; (*pilar*) pillar; ~ dorsal *ou* vertebral spine; **colunável** [kolu'navew] (*pl* –eis) *adj* famous ♦ *m/f* celebrity; **colunista** [kolu'niʃta] *m/f* columnist

com [kõ] *prep* with; ~ cuidado carefully; estar ~ câncer to have cancer; estar ~ dinheiro to have some money on one; estar ~ fome to be hungry

coma ['kɔma] *f* coma

comandante [komã'dãtʃi] *m* commander; (*MIL*) commandant; (*NÁUT*) captain

comandar [komã'da'] *vt* to command

comando [ko'mãdu] *m* command

combate [kõ'batʃi] *m* combat; ~r [kõba'te'] *vt* (*opor-se a*) to oppose ♦ *vi* to fight; ~r-se *vr* to fight

combinação [kõbina'sãw] (*pl* –ões) *f* combination; (*QUÍM*) compound; (*acordo*) arrangement; (*plano*) scheme; (*roupa*) slip

combinar [kõbi'na'] *vt* to combine; (*jantar etc*) to arrange; (*fuga etc*) to plan ♦ *vi* (*roupas etc*) to go together; ~-se *vr* to combine; (*pessoas*) to get on well together; ~ com (*harmonizar-se*) to go with; ~ de fazer to arrange to do; combinado! agreed!

comboio [kõ'boju] *m* (*PT*) train; (*de navios, carros*) convoy

combustível [kõbuʃ'tʃivew] *m* fuel

começar [kome'sa'] *vt, vi* to begin, start; ~ a fazer to begin *ou* start to do

começo [ko'mesu] *m* beginning, start

começo *etc vb V* comedir-se

comédia [ko'mɛdʒja] *f* comedy

comedido/a [kome'dʒidu/a] *adj* moderate; (*prudente*) prudent

comemorar [komemo'ra'] *vt* to commemorate

comentar [komẽ'ta'] *vt* to comment on; (*maliciosamente*) to make comments about

comentário [komẽ'tarju] *m* comment, remark; (*análise*) commentary

comentarista [komẽta'riʃta] *m/f* commentator

comer [ko'me'] *vt* to eat; (*DAMAS, XADREZ*) to take, capture ♦ *vi* to eat; dar de ~ a to feed

comercial [komex'sjaw] (*pl* –ais) *adj* commercial; (*relativo ao negócio*) business *atr* ♦ *m* commercial

comercialização [komexsjaliza'sãw] *f* marketing

comercializar [komexsjali'za*] *vt* to market

comerciante [komex'sjãt∫i] *m/f* trader

comerciar [komex'sja*] *vi* to trade, do business

comércio [ko'mɛxsju] *m* commerce; (*tráfico*) trade; (*negócio*) business; (*lojas*) shops *pl*

comes ['kɔmiʃ] *mpl*: ~ **e bebes** food and drink

comestíveis [komeʃ'tʃiveis] *mpl* foodstuffs, food *sg*

comestível [komeʃ'tʃivew] (*pl* -**eis**) *adj* edible

cometer [kome'te*] *vt* to commit

comichão [komi'ʃãw] *f* itch, itching

comichar [komi'ʃa*] *vt, vi* to itch

comício [ko'misju] *m* (POL) rally, meeting; (*assembléia*) assembly

cômico/a ['komiku/a] *adj* comic(al) ♦ *m* comedian; (*de teatro*) actor

comida [ko'mida] *f* (*alimento*) food; (*refeição*) meal

comigo [ko'migu] *pron* with me

comilão/lona [komi'lãw/lona] (*pl* -**ões**/~**s**) *adj* greedy ♦ *m/f* glutton

comiserar-se [komize'raxsi] *vr*: ~-**se** (**de**) to sympathize (with)

comissão [komi'sãw] (*pl* -**ões**) *f* commission; (*comitê*) committee

comissário [komi'sarju] *m* commissioner; (*COM*) agent; ~ **de bordo** (*AER*) steward; (*NÁUT*) purser

comissionar [komisjo'na*] *vt* to commission

comissões [komi'sõjʃ] *fpl de* **comissão**

comitê [komi'te] *m* committee

---

como ['kɔmu] *adv* **1** (*modo*) as; **ela fez ~ eu pedi** she did as I asked; ~ **se** as if; ~ **quiser** as you wish; **seja** ~ **for** be that as it may

2 (*assim* ~) like; **ela tem olhos azuis** ~ **o pai** she has blue eyes like her father's; **ela trabalha numa loja,** ~ **a mãe** she works in a shop, as does her mother

3 (*de que maneira*) how; ~? pardon?; ~! what!; ~ **assim?** what do you mean?; ~ **não!** of course!

♦ *conj* (*porque*) as, since; **como estava tarde ele dormiu aqui** since it was late he slept here

comoção [komo'sãw] (*pl* -**ões**) *f* distress; (*revolta*) commotion

cômoda ['komoda] *f* chest of drawers (*BRIT*), bureau (*US*)

comodidade [komodʒi'dadʒi] *f* comfort; (*conveniência*) convenience

comodismo [komo'dʒiʒmu] *m* complacency; **comodista** [komo'dʒiʃta] *adj* com-

placent

cômodo/a ['komodu/a] *adj* comfortable; (*conveniente*) convenient ♦ *m* room

comovedor(a) [komove'do*(a)] *adj* moving, touching

comovente [komo'vẽt∫i] *adj* moving, touching

comover [komo've*] *vt* to move ♦ *vi* to be moving; ~-**se** *vr* to be moved; **comovido/a** [komo'vidu/a] *adj* moved

compacto/a [kõ'paktu/a] *adj* compact; (*espesso*) thick; (*sólido*) solid ♦ *m* (*disco*) single

compadecer-se [kõpade'sexsi] *vr*: ~-**se de** to be sorry for, pity

compadecido/a [kõpade'sidu/a] *adj* sympathetic

compadre [kõ'padri] *m* (*col*: *companheiro*) buddy, pal

compaixão [kõpaj'ʃãw] *f* compassion; (*misericórdia*) mercy

companheirismo [kõpaɲej'riʒmu] *m* companionship

companheiro/a [kõpa'ɲejru/a] *m/f* companion; (*colega*) friend; (*col*) buddy, mate

companhia [kõpa'ɲia] *f* (*COM*) company, firm; (*convivência*) company

comparação [kõpara'sãw] (*pl* -**ões**) *f* comparison

comparar [kõpa'ra*] *vt* to compare; ~ **a** to liken to; ~ **com** to compare with

comparativo/a [kõpara'tʃivu/a] *adj* comparative

comparecer [kõpare'se*] *vi* to appear, make an appearance; ~ **a uma reunião** to attend a meeting

comparecimento [kõparesi'mẽtu] *m* (*presença*) attendance

comparsa [kõ'paxsa] *m/f* (*TEATRO*) extra; (*cúmplice*) accomplice

compartilhar [kõpaxtʃi'ʎa*] *vt* to share ♦ *vi*: ~ **de** to share in, participate in

compartimento [kõpaxtʃi'mẽtu] *m* compartment; (*aposento*) room

compassado/a [kõpa'sadu/a] *adj* (*medido*) measured; (*moderado*) moderate; (*cadenciado*) regular; (*pausado*) slow

compassivo/a [kõpa'sivu/a] *adj* compassionate

compasso [kõ'pasu] *m* (*instrumento*) pair of compasses; (*MÚS*) time; (*ritmo*) beat

compatível [kõpa'tʃivew] (*pl* -**eis**) *adj* compatible

compatriota [kõpa'trjɔta] *m/f* fellow countryman/woman

compelir [kõpe'li*] *vt* to force, compel

compêndio [kõ'pẽdʒiu] *m* compendium; (*livro de texto*) textbook

compensação [kõpẽsa'sãw] (*pl* -**ões**) *f* compensation; **em** ~ on the other hand

compensar [kõpẽ'sa*] *vt* to make up for, compensate for; (*equilibrar*) to offset; (*cheque*) to clear

competência [kõpe'tẽsja] *f* competence, ability; (*responsabilidade*) responsibility;

competente [kõpe'tẽtʃi] *adj* competent; (*apropriado*) appropriate; (*responsável*) responsible

competição [kõpetʃi'sãw] (*pl* –ões) *f* competition

competidor(a) [kõpetʃi'do*(a)] *m/f* competitor

competir [kõpe'tʃi*] *vi* to compete; ~ **a alguém** (*ser da competência de*) to be sb's responsibility; (*caber*) to be up to sb

competitivo/a [kõpetʃi'tʃivu/a] *adj* competitive

compilar [kõpi'la*] *vt* to compile

compilo *etc* [kõ'pilu] *vb* V **compelir**

compito *etc* [kõ'pitu] *vb* V **competir**

complacente [kõpla'sẽtʃi] *adj* obliging

complementar [kõplemẽ'ta*] *adj* complementary ♦ *vt* to supplement

complemento [kõple'mẽtu] *m* complement

completamente [kõpleta'mẽtʃi] *adv* completely, quite

completar [kõple'ta*] *vt* to complete; (*tanque, carro*) to fill up; ~ **dez anos** to be ten

completo/a [kõ'pletu/a] *adj* complete; (*cheio*) full (up); **por** ~ completely

complexo/a [kõ'plɛksu/a] *adj* complex ♦ *m* complex

complicação [kõplika'sãw] (*pl* –ões) *f* complication

complicado/a [kõpli'kadu/a] *adj* complicated

complicar [kõpli'ka*] *vt* to complicate

complô [kõ'plo] *m* plot, conspiracy

componente [kõpo'nẽtʃi] *adj, m* component

compor [kõ'po*] (*irreg: como* **pôr**) *vt* to compose; (*discurso, livro*) to write; (*arranjar*) to arrange ♦ *vi* to compose; ~-**se** *vr* (*controlar-se*) to compose o.s.; ~-**se de** to consist of

comporta [kõ'pɔxta] *f* (*de canal*) lock

comportamento [kõpoxta'mẽtu] *m* behaviour (*BRIT*), behavior (*US*)

comportar-se [kõpox'taxsi] *vt, vr* to behave; ~ **mal** to misbehave, behave badly

composição [kõpozi'sãw] (*pl* –ões) *f* composition; (*TIP*) typesetting

compositor(a) [kõpozi'to*(a)] *m/f* composer; (*TIP*) typesetter

composto/a [kõ'poʃtu/'pɔʃta] *adj*: ~ **de** made up of, composed of ♦ *m* compound

compostura [kõpoʃ'tura] *f* composure

compota [kõ'pɔta] *f* fruit in syrup

compra ['kõpra] *f* purchase; **fazer** ~**s** to go shopping; ~**dor(a)** [kõpra'do*(a)] *m/f* buyer, purchaser

comprar [kõ'pra*] *vt* to buy

compreender [kõprjen'de*] *vt* to understand; (*constar de*) to be comprised of, consist of; (*abranger*) to cover

compreensão [kõprjẽ'sãw] *f* understanding, comprehension; **compreensivo/a** [kõprjẽ'sivu/a] *adj* understanding

compressa [kõ'prɛsa] *f* compress

comprido/a [kõ'pridu/a] *adj* long; (*alto*) tall; **ao** ~ lengthways

comprimento [kõpri'mẽtu] *m* length

comprimido [kõpri'midu] *m* pill, tablet

comprimir [kõpri'mi*] *vt* to compress

comprometer [kõprome'te*] *vt* to compromise; (*envolver*) to involve; (*arriscar*) to jeopardize; (*empenhar*) to pledge; ~-**se** *vr*: ~-**se a** to undertake to, promise to

compromisso [kõpro'misu] *m* promise; (*obrigação*) commitment; (*hora marcada*) appointment; (*acordo*) agreement

comprovação [kõprova'sãw] (*pl* –ões) *f* proof, evidence

comprovante [kõpro'vãtʃi] *m* receipt

comprovar [kõpro'va*] *vt* to prove; (*confirmar*) to confirm

compulsão [kõpuw'sãw] (*pl* –ões) *f* compulsion; **compulsivo/a** [kõpuw'sivu/a] *adj* compulsive; **compulsório/a** [kõpuw'sɔrju/a] *adj* compulsory

computação [kõputa'sãw] *f* computer science, computing

computador [kõputa'do*] *m* computer

computadorizar [kõputadori'za*] *vt* to computerize

computar [kõpu'ta*] *vt* (*calcular*) to calculate; (*contar*) to count

comum [ko'mũ] (*pl* –**ns**) *adj* ordinary, common; (*habitual*) usual; **em** ~ in common

comungar [komũ'ga*] *vi* to take communion

comunhão [komu'ɲãw] (*pl* –ões) *f* (*ger, REL*) communion

comunicação [komunika'sãw] (*pl* –ões) *f* communication; (*mensagem*) message; (*acesso*) access

comunicado [komuni'kadu] *m* notice

comunicar [komuni'ka*] *vt, vi* to communicate; ~-**se** *vr* to communicate; ~-**se com** (*entrar em contato*) to get in touch with

comunidade [komuni'dadʒi] *f* community; **C~ dos Estados Independentes** Commonwealth of Independent States

comunismo [komu'niʒmu] *m* communism; **comunista** [komu'niʃta] *adj, m/f* communist

comuns [ko'mũʃ] *pl de* **comum**

comutador [komuta'do*] *m* switch

comutar [komu'ta*] *vt* (*JUR*) to commute; (*trocar*) to exchange

côncavo/a ['kõkavu/a] *adj* concave; (*cavado*) hollow ♦ *m* hollow

conceber [kõse'be*] *vt, vi* to conceive

conceder [kõse'de*] *vt* to allow; (*outorgar*) to grant; (*dar*) to give ♦ *vi*: ~ **em** to agree to

conceito [kõ'sejtu] *m* concept, idea; (*fama*) reputation; (*opinião*) opinion;

conceituado/a [kõsej'twadu/a] *adj* well thought of, highly regarded

concentração [kõsẽtra'sãw] (*pl* –ões) *f* concentration

concentrar [kõsẽ'tra*] *vt* to concentrate; (*reunir*) to bring together; ~-se *vr*: ~-se (**em**) to concentrate (on)

concepção [kõsep'sãw] (*pl* –ões) *f* (*geração*) conception; (*noção*) idea, concept; (*opinião*) opinion

concernente [kõsex'nẽtʃi] *adj*: ~ **a** concerning

concernir [kõsex'ni*] *vi*: ~ **a** to concern

concerto [kõ'sextu] *m* concert

concessão [kõse'sãw] (*pl* –ões) *f* concession; (*permissão*) permission

concha ['kõʃa] *f* shell; (*para líquidos*) ladle

conchavo [kõ'ʃavu] *m* conspiracy

conciliação [kõsilja'sãw] (*pl* –ões) *f* reconciliation

conciliar [kõsi'lja*] *vt* to reconcile

concílio [kõ'silju] *m* (*REL*) council

conclamar [kõkla'ma*] *vt* to shout; (*aclamar*) to acclaim; (*convocar*) to call together

concluir [kõ'klwi*] *vt, vi* to conclude

conclusão [kõklu'zãw] (*pl* –ões) *f* end; (*dedução*) conclusion; **conclusivo/a** [kõklu'zivu/a] *adj* conclusive

conclusões [kõklu'zõjʃ] *fpl de* conclusão

concordância [kõkox'dãsja] *f* agreement

concordar [kõkox'da*] *vi, vt* to agree

concorrência [kõko'xẽsja] *f* competition; (*a um cargo*) application

concorrente [kõko'xẽtʃi] *m/f* contestant; (*candidato*) candidate

concorrer [kõko'xe*] *vi* to compete; ~ **a** to apply for

concretizar [kõkretʃi'za*] *vt* to make real; ~-se *vr* (*sonho*) to come true; (*ambições*) to be realized

concreto/a [kõ'kretu/a] *adj* concrete ♦ *m* concrete

concurso [kõ'kuxsu] *m* contest; (*exame*) competition

condado [kõ'dadu] *m* county

conde ['kõdʒi] *m* count

condecorar [kõdeko'ra*] *vt* to decorate

condenação [kõdena'sãw] (*pl* –ões) *f* (*JUR*) conviction

condenar [kõde'na*] *vt* to condemn; (*JUR: sentenciar*) to sentence; (: *declarar culpado*) to convict

condensação [kõdẽsa'sãw] *f* condensation

condensar [kõdẽ'sa*] *vt* to condense; ~-se *vr* to condense

condescendência [kõdesẽ'dẽsja] *f* acquiescence

condescendente [kõdesẽ'dẽtʃi] *adj* condescending

condescender [kõdesẽ'de*] *vi* to acquiesce; ~ **a** *ou* **em** to condescend to, deign to

condessa [kõ'desa] *f* countess

condição [kõdʒi'sãw] (*pl* –ões) *f* condition; (*social*) status; (*qualidade*) capacity; **com a ~ de que** on condition that, provided that; **em condições de fazer** (*pessoa*) able to do; (*carro etc*) in condition to do

condicional [kõdʒisjo'naw] (*pl* –ais) *adj* conditional

condimento [kõdʒi'mẽtu] *m* seasoning

condomínio [kõdo'minju] *m* condominium

condução [kõdu'sãw] *f* driving; (*transporte*) transport; (*ônibus*) bus

conducente [kõdu'sẽtʃi] *adj*: ~ **a** conducive to

conduta [kõ'duta] *f* conduct, behaviour (*BRIT*), behavior (*US*)

conduto [kõ'dutu] *m* (*tubo*) tube; (*cano*) pipe; (*canal*) channel

condutor(a) [kõdu'to*(a)] *m/f* (*de veículo*) driver ♦ *m* (*ELET*) conductor

conduzir [kõdu'zi*] *vt* (*levar*) to lead; (*FIS*) to conduct; ~-se *vr* to behave; ~ **a** to lead to

cone ['kɔni] *m* cone

conectar [konek'ta*] *vt* to connect

cônego ['konegu] *m* (*REL*) canon

conexão [konek'sãw] (*pl* –ões) *f* connection

confecção [kõfek'sãw] (*pl* –ões) *f* making; (*de um boletim*) production; (*roupa*) ready-to-wear clothes *pl*; (*negócio*) business selling ready-to-wear clothes

confeccionar [kõfeksjo'na*] *vt* to make; (*fabricar*) to manufacture

confecções [kõfek'sõjʃ] *fpl de* confecção

confeitar [kõfej'ta*] *vt* (*bolo*) to ice

confeitaria [kõfejta'ria] *f* patisserie

confeiteiro/a [kõfej'tejru/a] *m/f* confectioner

conferência [kõfe'rẽsja] *f* conference; (*discurso*) lecture

conferir [kõfe'ri*] *vt* to check; (*comparar*) to compare; (*outorgar*) to grant ♦ *vi* to tally

confessar [kõfe'sa*] *vt, vi* to confess; ~-se *vr* to confess

confete [kõ'fetʃi] *m* confetti

confiado/a [kõ'fjadu/a] (*col*) *adj* cheeky

confiança [kõ'fjãsa] *f* confidence; (*fé*) trust; **de ~** reliable; **ter ~ em alguém** to trust sb

confiante [kõ'fjãtʃi] *adj*: ~ (**em**) confident (of)

confiar [kõ'fja*] *vt* to entrust; (*segredo*) to confide ♦ *vi*: ~ **em** to trust; (*ter fé*) to have faith in

confiável [kõ'fjavew] (*pl* –eis) *adj* reliable

confidência [kõfi'dẽsja] *f* secret; **em ~** in confidence; **confidencial** [kõfidẽ'sjaw] (*pl* –ais) *adj* confidential

confinamento [kõfina'mẽtu] *m* confinement

confinar [kõfi'na*] *vt* to limit; (*enclausurar*) to confine ♦ *vi*: ~ **com** to border on

confins [kõ'fiʃ] *mpl* limits, boundaries

confirmação [kõfixma'sãw] (*pl* –ões) *f* confirmation

confirmar [kõfix'ma*] *vt* to confirm

confiro *etc* [kõ'firu] *vb* V **conferir**

confiscar [kõfiʃ'ka*] *vt* to confiscate, seize

confissão [kõfi'sãw] (*pl* –ões) *f* confession

conflito [kõ'flitu] *m* conflict

confluente [kõ'flwẽtʃi] *m* tributary

conformação [kõfoxma'sãw] (*pl* –ões) *f* resignation; (*forma*) form

conformar [kõfox'ma*] *vt* to form ♦ *vi*: ~ **com** to conform to; ~-**se** *vr*: ~-**se com** to resign o.s. to; (*acomodar-se*) to conform to

conforme [kõ'fɔxmi] *prep* according to; (*dependendo de*) depending on ♦ *conj* (*logo que*) as soon as; (*como*) as, according to what; (*à medida que*) as; **você vai?** — ~ are you going? — it depends

conformidade [kõfoxmi'dadʒi] *f* agreement; **em** ~ **com** in accordance with

confortar [kõfox'ta*] *vt* to comfort, console

confortável [kõfox'tavew] (*pl* –eis) *f* comfortable

conforto [kõ'foxtu] *m* comfort

confraria [kõfra'ria] *f* fraternity

confrontar [kõfrõ'ta*] *vt* to confront; (*comparar*) to compare

confronto [kõ'frõtu] *m* confrontation; (*comparação*) comparison

confundir [kõfũ'dʒi*] *vt* to confuse; ~-**se** *vr* to get mixed up

confusão [kõfu'zãw] (*pl* –ões) *f* confusion; (*tumulto*) uproar; (*problemas*) trouble

confuso/a [kõ'fuzu/a] *adj* confused; (*problema*) confusing

confusões [kõfu'zõjʃ] *fpl de* confusão

congelado/a [kõʒe'ladu/a] *adj* frozen

congelador [kõʒela'do*] *m* freezer, deep freeze

congelamento [kõʒela'mẽtu] *m* freezing; (*ECON*) freeze

congelar [kõʒe'la*] *vt* to freeze; ~-**se** *vr* to freeze

congestão [kõʒeʃ'tãw] *f* congestion; **congestionado/a** [kõʒeʃtʃjo'nadu/a] *adj* congested; (*olhos*) bloodshot; (*rosto*) flushed; **congestionamento** [kõʒeʃtʃjona'mẽtu] *m* congestion; **um congestionamento (de tráfego)** a traffic jam

congestionar [kõʒeʃtʃjo'na*] *vt* to congest; ~-**se** *vr* (*rosto*) to go red

congratular [kõgratu'la*] *vt*: ~ **alguém por** to congratulate sb on

congregação [kõgrega'sãw] (*pl* –ões) *f* congregation; (*reunião*) gathering

congregar [kõgre'ga*] *vt* to bring to-

gether; ~-**se** *vr* to congregate

congressista [kõgre'siʃta] *m/f* congressman/woman

congresso [kõ'grɛsu] *m* congress, conference

conhaque [ko'naki] *m* cognac, brandy

conhecedor(a) [koɲese'do*(a)] *adj* knowing ♦ *m/f* connoisseur, expert

conhecer [koɲe'se*] *vt* to know; (*travar conhecimento com*) to meet; (*descobrir*) to discover; ~-**se** *vr* to meet; (*ter conhecimento*) to know each other

conhecido/a [koɲe'sidu/a] *adj* known; (*célebre*) well-known ♦ *m/f* acquaintance

conhecimento [koɲesi'mẽtu] *m* (~s) knowledge; (*idéia*) idea; (*conhecido*) acquaintance; (*COM*) bill of lading; **levar ao** ~ **de alguém** to bring to sb's notice

conivente [koni'vẽtʃi] *adj*: **ser** ~ **em** to connive in

conjugado [kõʒu'gadu] *m* studio

cônjuge ['kõʒuʒi] *m* spouse

conjunção [kõʒũ'sãw] (*pl* –ões) *f* union; (*LING*) conjunction

conjuntivite [kõʒũtʃi'vitʃi] *f* conjunctivitis

conjuntivo [kõʒũ'tʃivu] (*PT*) *m* (*LING*) subjunctive

conjunto/a [kõ'ʒũtu/a] *adj* joint ♦ *m* whole; (*coleção*) collection; (*músicos*) group; (*roupa*) outfit

conjuntura [kõʒũ'tura] *f* situation

conosco [ko'noʃku] *pron* with us

conquanto [kõ'kwãtu] *conj* although, though

conquista [kõ'kiʃta] *f* conquest; ~**dor(a)** [kõkiʃta'do*(a)] *adj* conquering ♦ *m* conqueror

conquistar [kõkiʃ'ta*] *vt* to conquer; (*alcançar*) to achieve; (*ganhar*) to win

consagrado/a [kõsa'gradu/a] *adj* established

consagrar [kõsa'gra*] *vt* (*REL*) to consecrate; (*aclamar*) to acclaim; (*dedicar*) to dedicate; (*tempo*) to devote

consangüíneo/a [kõsã'gwĩnju/a] *m/f* blood relation

consciência [kõ'sjẽsja] *f* conscience; (*percepção*) awareness; (*senso de responsabilidade*) conscientiousness; **consciencioso/a** [kõsjẽ'sjozu/ɔza] *adj* conscientious

consciente [kõ'sjẽtʃi] *adj* conscious

conseguinte [kõse'gĩtʃi] *adj*: **por** ~ consequently

conseguir [kõse'gi*] *vt* to get, obtain; ~ **fazer** to manage to do, succeed in doing

conselheiro/a [kõse'ʎejru/a] *m/f* counsellor (*BRIT*), counselor (*US*); (*POL*) councillor

conselho [kõ'seʎu] *m* piece of advice; (*corporação*) council; ~**s** *mpl* (*advertência*) advice *sg*; ~ **de guerra** court martial; **C~ de ministros** (*POL*) Cabinet

consenso [kõ'sẽsu] *m* consensus

consentimento [kõsẽtʃi'mẽtu] *m* consent

consentir [kõsẽ'tʃi*] *vt* to allow, permit; (*aprovar*) to agree to ♦ *vi*: ~ em to agree to

conseqüência [kõse'kwẽsja] *f* consequence; por ~ consequently

consertar [kõsex'ta*] *vt* to mend, repair; (*remediar*) to put right; **conserto** [kõ'sextu] *m* repair

conserva [kõ'sexva] *f* pickle; em ~ pickled

conservação [kõsexva'sãw] *f* conservation; (*de vida, alimentos*) preservation

conservador(a) [kõsexva'do*(a)] *adj* conservative ♦ *m/f* (POL) conservative

conservante [kõsex'vãtʃi] *m* preservative

conservar [kõsex'va*] *vt* to preserve, maintain; (*reter, manter*) to keep, retain; ~-se *vr* to keep

conservatório [kõsexva'tɔrju] *m* conservatory

consideração [kõsidera'sãw] (*pl* -ões) *f* consideration; (*estima*) respect, esteem; levar em ~ to take into account

considerar [kõside'ra*] *vt* to consider; (*prezar*) to respect ♦ *vi* to consider

considerável [kõside'ravew] (*pl* -eis) *adj* considerable

consignação [kõsigna'sãw] (*pl* -ões) *f* consignment

consignar [kõsig'na*] *vt* (*mercadorias*) to send, dispatch; (*registrar*) to record

consigo¹ [kõ'sigu] *pron* (*m*) with him; (*f*) with her; (*pl*) with them; (*com você*) with you

consigo² *etc vb* V **conseguir**

consinto *etc* [kõ'sĩtu] *vb* V **consentir**

consistência [kõsiʃ'tẽsja] *f* consistency

consistente [kõsiʃ'tẽtʃi] *adj* solid; (*espesso*) thick

consistir [kõsiʃ'tʃi*] *vi*: ~ em to be made up of, consist of

consoante [kõso'ãtʃi] *f* consonant ♦ *prep* according to ♦ *conj*: ~ prometera as he had promised

consolação [kõsola'sãw] (*pl* -ões) *f* consolation

consolar [kõso'la*] *vt* to console

console [kõ'sɔli] *f* (COMPUT) console

consolidar [kõsoli'da*] *vt* to consolidate; (*fratura*) to knit ♦ *vi* to become solid; to knit together

consolo [kõ'solu] *m* consolation

consome *etc* [kõ'somi] *vb* V **consumir**

consomê [kõso'me] *m* consommé

consórcio [kõ'sɔxsju] *m* (*união*) partnership; (COM) consortium

conspícuo/a [kõ'ʃpikwu/a] *adj* conspicuous

conspiração [kõʃpira'sãw] (*pl* -ões) *f* plot, conspiracy

conspirar [kõʃpi'ra*] *vt*, *vi* to plot

constante [kõʃ'tãtʃi] *adj* constant

constar [kõʃ'ta*] *vi* to be in; ao que me consta as far as I know

constatar [kõʃta'ta*] *vt* to establish; (*notar*) to notice; (*evidenciar*) to show up

consternado/a [kõʃtex'nadu/a] *adj* depressed; (*desolado*) distressed

consternar [kõʃtex'na*] *vt* to distress; (*desalentar*) to depress

constipação [kõʃtʃipa'sãw] (*pl* -ões) *f* constipation; (PT) cold; apanhar uma ~ (PT) to catch a cold

constipado/a [kõʃtʃi'padu/a] *adj*: estar ~ to be constipated; (PT) to have a cold

constitucional [kõʃtʃitusjo'naw] (*pl* -ais) *adj* constitutional

constituição [kõʃtʃitwi'sãw] (*pl* -ões) *f* constitution

constituinte [kõʃtʃi'twĩtʃi] *m/f* (*deputado*) member ♦ *f* (BR): a C~ the Constituent Assembly, ≈ Parliament

constituir [kõʃtʃi'twi*] *vt* to constitute; (*formar*) to form; (*estabelecer*) to establish; (*nomear*) to appoint

constranger [kõʃtrã'ʒe*] *vt* to constrain; (*acanhar*) to embarrass; ~-se *vr* to feel embarrassed; **constrangimento** [kõʃtrãʒi'mẽtu] *m* constraint; embarrassment

construção [kõʃtru'sãw] (*pl* -ões) *f* building, construction

construir [kõʃ'trwi*] *vt* to build, construct

construtivo/a [kõʃtru'tʃivu/a] *adj* constructive

construtor(a) [kõʃtru'to*(a)] *m/f* builder

cônsul ['kõsuw] (*pl* -es) *m* consul; **consulado** [kõsu'ladu] *m* consulate; **consulesa** [kõsu'leza] *f* (woman) consul

consulta [kõ'suwta] *f* consultation; livro de ~ reference book; horário de ~ surgery hours *pl* (BRIT), office hours *pl* (US); ~r [kõsuw'ta*] *vt* to consult; **consultor(a)** [kõsuw'to*(a)] *m/f* consultant

consultório [kõsuw'tɔrju] *m* surgery

consumar [kõsu'ma*] *vt* to consummate

consumidor(a) [kõsumi'do*(a)] *adj* consumer *atr* ♦ *m/f* consumer

consumir [kõsu'mi*] *vt* to consume; (*gastar*) to use up; ~-se *vr* to waste away

consumo [kõ'sumu] *m* consumption; artigos de ~ consumer goods

conta ['kõta] *f* count; (*em restaurante*) bill; (*fatura*) invoice; (*bancária*) account; (*de colar*) bead; ~s *fpl* (COM) accounts; levar *ou* ter em ~ to take into account; tomar ~ de to take care of; (*dominar*) to take hold of; afinal de ~s after all; dar-se ~ de to realize; (*notar*) to notice; ~ corrente current account

contabilidade [kõtabili'dadʒi] *f* bookkeeping, accountancy

contabilista [kõtabi'liʃta] (PT) *m/f* accountant

contabilizar [kõtabili'za*] *vt* to write up, book

contacto *etc* [kõ'tatu] (*PT*) = **contato** *etc*

contado/a [kõ'tadu/a] (*PT*) *adj*: **pagar de ~ to** pay cash

contador(a) [kõta'do*(a)] *m/f* (*COM*) accountant ♦ *m* (*TEC*: *medidor*) meter

contagem [kõ'taʒẽ] (*pl* **-ns**) *f* (*de números*) counting; (*escore*) score

contagiante [kõta'ʒjãtʃi] *adj* (*alegria*) contagious

contagiar [kõta'ʒja*] *vt* to infect

contágio [kõ'taʒju] *m* infection

contagioso/a [kõta'ʒjozu/ɔza] *adj* (*doença*) contagious

contaminação [kõtamina'sãw] *f* contamination

contaminar [kõtami'na*] *vt* to contaminate

contanto que [kõ'tãtu ki] *conj* provided that

conta-quilómetros (*PT*) *m inv* speedometer

contar [kõ'ta*] *vt* to count; (*narrar*) to tell; (*pretender*) to intend ♦ *vi* to count; ~ **com** to count on; (*esperar*) to expect; ~ **em fazer** to count on doing, expect to do

contatar [kõta'ta*] *vt* to contact; **contato** [kõ'tatu] *m* contact; **entrar em ~ com** to get in touch with, contact

contemplar [kõtẽ'pla*] *vt* to contemplate; (*olhar*) to gaze at

contemplativo/a [kõtẽpla'tʃivu/a] *adj* (*pessoa*) thoughtful

contemporâneo/a [kõtẽpo'ranju/a] *adj*, *m/f* contemporary

contenção [kõtẽ'sãw] (*pl* **-ões**) *f* restriction, containment; ~ **de despesas** cutbacks *pl*

contenda [kõ'tẽda] *f* quarrel, dispute

contentamento [kõtẽta'mẽtu] *m* (*felicidade*) happiness; (*satisfação*) contentment

contentar [kõtẽ'ta*] *vt* to please; (*dar satisfação*) to satisfy; ~-**se** *vr* to be satisfied

contente [kõ'tẽtʃi] *adj* happy; (*satisfeito*) pleased, satisfied

contento [kõ'tẽtu] *m*: **a ~** satisfactorily

conter [kõ'te*] (*irreg: como* **ter**) *vt* to contain, hold; (*refrear*) to restrain, hold back; (*gastos*) to curb

conterrâneo/a [kõte'xanju/a] *adj* fellow ♦ *m/f* compatriot, fellow countryman/woman

contestação [kõteʃta'sãw] (*pl* **-ões**) *f* challenge; (*negação*) denial

contestar [kõteʃ'ta*] *vt* to dispute, contest; (*impugnar*) to challenge

conteúdo [kõte'udu] *m* contents *pl*; (*de um texto*) content

contexto [kõ'teʃtu] *m* context

contigo [kõ'tʃigu] *pron* with you

contíguo/a [kõ'tʃigwu/a] *adj*: ~ **a** next to

continência [kõtʃi'nẽsja] *f* salute

continental [kõtʃinẽ'taw] (*pl* **-ais**) *adj* continental

continente [kõtʃi'nẽtʃi] *m* continent

contingência [kõtʃĩ'ʒẽsja] *f* contingency

contingente [kõtʃĩ'ʒẽtʃi] *adj* uncertain ♦ *m* (*MIL*) contingent; (*COM*) contingency, reserve

continuação [kõtʃinwa'sãw] *f* continuation

continuar [kõtʃi'nwa*] *vt*, *vi* to continue; ~ **falando** *ou* **a falar** to go on talking; **ela continua doente** she is still sick

continuidade [kõtʃinwi'dadʒi] *f* continuity

contínuo/a [kõ'tʃinwu/a] *adj* (*persistente*) continual; (*sem interrupção*) continuous ♦ *m* office boy

conto ['kõtu] *m* story, tale; (*PT*: *dinheiro*) *1000 escudos*

contorção [kõtox'sãw] (*pl* **-ões**) *f* contortion

contorcer [kõtox'se*] *vt* to twist; ~-**se** *vr* to writhe

contorções [kõtox'sõjʃ] *fpl de* **contorção**

contornar [kõtox'na*] *vt* (*rodear*) to go round; (*ladear*) to skirt; (*fig*: *problema*) to get round

contorno [kõ'toxnu] *m* outline; (*da terra*) contour; (*do rosto*) profile

contra ['kõtra] *prep* against ♦ *m*: **os prós e os ~s** the pros and cons; **dar o ~ (a)** to be opposed (to)

contra-ataque *m* counterattack

contrabaixo [kõtra'bajʃu] *m* double bass

contrabandear [kõtrabã'dʒja*] *vt* to smuggle; **contrabandista** [kõtrabã'dʒiʃta] *m/f* smuggler; **contrabando** [kõtra'bãdu] *m* smuggling; (*artigos*) contraband

contração [kõtra'sãw] (*pl* **-ões**) *f* contraction

contraceptivo/a [kõtrasep'tʃivu/a] *adj* contraceptive ♦ *m* contraceptive

contracheque [kõtra'ʃɛki] *m* pay slip (*BRIT*), check stub (*US*)

contrações [kõtra'sõjʃ] *fpl de* **contração**

contradição [kõtradʒi'sãw] (*pl* **-ões**) *f* contradiction

contraditório/a [kõtradʒi'tɔrju/a] *adj* contradictory

contradizer [kõtradʒi'ze*] (*irreg: como* **dizer**) *vt* to contradict

contrafilé [kõtrafi'lɛ] *m* rump steak

contragosto [kõtra'goʃtu] *m*: **a ~** against one's will, unwillingly

contrair [kõtra'i*] *vt* to contract; (*hábito*) to form

contramão [kõtra'mãw] *adj* one-way ♦ *f*: **na ~** the wrong way down a one-way street

contramestre/tra [kõtra'mɛʃtri/tra] *m/f* (*em fábrica*) supervisor ♦ *m* (*NÁUT*) boatswain

contrapesar [kõtrape'za*] *vt* to counterbalance; (*fig*) to offset; **contrapeso**

[kõtra'pezu] *m* counterbalance
contraproducente [kõtraprodu'sẽtʃi] *adj* counterproductive
contra-regra (*pl* ~s) *m/f* stage manager
contrariar [kõtra'rja*] *vt* to contradict; (*aborrecer*) to annoy
contrário/a [kõ'trarju/a] *adj* (*oposto*) opposite; (*pessoa*) opposed; (*desfavorável*) unfavorable (*BRIT*), unfavorable (*US*), adverse ♦ *m* opposite; **do** ~ otherwise; **pelo** *ou* **ao** ~ on the contrary; **ao** ~ the other way round
contra-senso *m* nonsense
contrastante [kõtraʃ'tãtʃi] *adj* contrasting
contrastar [kõtraʃ'ta*] *vt* to contrast; **contraste** [kõ'traʃtʃi] *m* contrast
contratação [kõtrata'sãw] *f* (*de pessoal*) employment
contratante [kõtra'tãtʃi] *m/f* contractor
contratar [kõtra'ta*] *vt* (*serviços*) to contract; (*pessoa*) to employ, take on
contratempo [kõtra'tẽpu] *m* setback; (*aborrecimento*) upset; (*dificuldade*) difficulty
contrato [kõ'tratu] *m* contract; (*acordo*) agreement
contribuição [kõtribwi'sãw] (*pl* –ões) *f* contribution; (*imposto*) tax
contribuinte [kõtri'bwĩtʃi] *m/f* contributor; (*que paga impostos*) taxpayer
contribuir [kõtri'bwi*] *vt* to contribute ♦ *vi* to contribute; (*pagar impostos*) to pay taxes
controlar [kõtro'la*] *vt* to control
controle [kõ'trɔli] *m* control; ~ **remoto** remote control; ~ **de crédito** (*COM*) credit control; ~ **de qualidade** (*COM*) quality control
controvérsia [kõtro'vɛxsja] *f* controversy; (*discussão*) debate; **controverso/a** [kõtro'vɛxsu/a] *adj* controversial
contudo [kõ'tudu] *conj* nevertheless, however
contumaz [kõtu'majʒ] *adj* obstinate, stubborn
contundir [kõtũ'dʒi*] *vt* to bruise
contusão [kõtu'zãw] (*pl* –ões) *f* bruise
convalescença [kõvale'sẽsa] *f* convalescence
convalescer [kõvale'se*] *vi* to convalesce
convenção [kõvẽ'sãw] (*pl* –ões) *f* convention; (*acordo*) agreement
convencer [kõvẽ'se*] *vt* to convince; (*persuadir*) to persuade; ~**-se** *vr*: ~**-se de** to be convinced about; **convencido/a** [kõvẽ'sidu/a] *adj* convinced; (*col: imodesto*) conceited, smug; **convencimento** [kõvẽsi'mẽtu] *m* conviction; (*col: imodéstia*) conceit, smugness
convencional [kõvẽsjo'naw] (*pl* –ais) *adj* conventional
convenções [kõvẽ'sõjʃ] *fpl de* **convenção**
conveniência [kõve'njẽsja] *f* convenience

conveniente [kõve'njẽtʃi] *adj* convenient, suitable; (*vantajoso*) advantageous
convênio [kõ'venju] *m* (*reunião*) convention; (*acordo*) agreement
convento [kõ'vẽtu] *m* convent
convergir [kõvex'ʒi*] *vi* to converge
conversa [kõ'vexsa] *f* conversation; ~-**fiada** idle chat; (*promessa falsa*) hot air
conversação [kõvexsa'sãw] (*pl* –ões) *f* conversation
conversão [kõvex'sãw] (*pl* –ões) *f* conversion
conversar [kõvex'sa*] *vi* to talk
conversível [kõvex'sivew] (*pl* –eis) *adj* convertible ♦ *m* (*AUTO*) convertible
conversões [kõvex'sõjʃ] *fpl de* **conversão**
conversor [kõvex'so*] *m*: ~ **catalítico** catalytic convertor
converter [kõvex'te*] *vt* to convert
convertido/a [kõvex'tʃidu/a] *m/f* convert
convés [kõ'vɛʃ] (*pl* –eses) *m* (*NÁUT*) deck
convexo/a [kõ'vɛksu/a] *adj* convex
convicção [kõvik'sãw] (*pl* –ões) *f* conviction
convicto/a [kõ'viktu/a] *adj* convinced; (*réu*) convicted
convidado/a [kõvi'dadu/a] *m/f* guest
convidar [kõvi'da*] *vt* to invite
convincente [kõvĩ'sẽtʃi] *adj* convincing
convir [kõ'vi*] (*irreg: como* **vir**) *vi* to suit, be convenient; (*ficar bem*) to be appropriate; (*concordar*) to agree; **convém fazer isso o mais rápido possível** we must do this as soon as possible
convirjo *etc* [kõ'vixʒu] *vb V* **convergir**
convite [kõ'vitʃi] *m* invitation
convivência [kõvi'vẽsja] *f* living together; (*familiaridade*) familiarity, intimacy
conviver [kõvi've*] *vi*: ~ **com** (*viver em comum*) to live with; (*ter familiaridade*) to get on with; **convívio** [kõ'vivju] *m* living together; (*familiaridade*) familiarity
convocar [kõvo'ka*] *vt* to summon, call upon; (*reunião, eleições*) to call; (*para o serviço militar*) to call up
convosco [kõ'voʃku] *adv* with you
convulsão [kõvuw'sãw] (*pl* –ões) *f* convulsion
cooper ['kupe*] *m* jogging; **fazer** ~ to go jogging
cooperação [koopera'sãw] *f* cooperation
cooperante [koope'rãtʃi] *adj* cooperative, helpful
cooperar [koope'ra*] *vi* to cooperate
cooperativa [koopera'tʃiva] *f* (*COM*) cooperative
cooperativo/a [koopera'tʃivu/a] *adj* cooperative
coordenada [kooxde'nada] *f* coordinate
coordenar [kooxde'na*] *vt* to co-ordinate
copa ['kɔpa] *f* (*de árvore*) top; (*torneio*) cup; ~**s** *fpl* (*CARTAS*) hearts

cópia [ˈkɔpja] f copy; **tirar ~ de** to copy; **copiadora** [kopjaˈdora] f duplicating machine

copiar [koˈpja*] vt to copy

copioso/a [koˈpjozu/ɔza] adj abundant

copirraite [kopiˈxajtʃi] m copyright

copo [ˈkɔpu] m glass

copyright [kopiˈxajtʃi] m = **copirraite**

coque [ˈkɔki] m (penteado) bun

coqueiro [koˈkejru] m (BOT) coconut palm

coqueluche [kokeˈluʃi] f (MED) whooping cough

coquetel [kokeˈtɛw] (pl -éis) m cocktail; (festa) cocktail party

cor¹ [kɔ*] m: **de ~** by heart

cor² [ko*] f colour (BRIT), color (US); **de ~ colo(u)red**

coração [koraˈsãw] (pl -ões) m heart; **de bom ~** kind-hearted; **de todo o ~** wholeheartedly

corado/a [koˈradu/a] adj ruddy

coragem [koˈraʒē] f courage; (atrevimento) nerve

corais [koˈrajʃ] mpl de **coral**

corajoso/a [koraˈʒozu/ɔza] adj courageous

coral [koˈraw] (pl -ais) m (MÚS) choir; (ZOOL) coral

corante [koˈrãtʃi] adj, m colouring (BRIT), coloring (US)

corar [koˈra*] vt (roupa) to bleach (in the sun) ♦ vi to blush; (tornar-se branco) to bleach

corbelha [kɔxˈbeʎa] f basket

corcova [koxˈkɔva] f hump; **corcunda** [koxˈkũda] adj hunchbacked ♦ f hump ♦ m/f (pessoa) hunchback

corda [ˈkɔxda] f rope, line; (MÚS) string; (varal) clothes line; (de relógio) spring; **dar ~ em** to wind up; **~s vocais** vocal chords

cordão [koxˈdãw] (pl -ões) m string, twine; (jóia) chain; (no carnaval) group; (ELET) lead; (fileira) row

cordeiro [koxˈdejru] m lamb

cordel [koxˈdɛw] (pl -éis) m (PT) string; **literatura de ~** pamphlet literature

cor-de-rosa adj inv pink

cordial [koxˈdʒjaw] (pl -ais) adj cordial ♦ m (bebida) cordial

cordilheira [koxdʒiˈʎejra] f mountain range

cordões [koxˈdõjʃ] mpl de **cordão**

coreano/a [koˈrjanu/a] adj Korean ♦ m/f Korean ♦ m (LING) Korean

Coréia [koˈrɛja] f: **a ~** Korea

coreto [koˈretu] m bandstand

coriza [koˈriza] f runny nose

corja [ˈkɔxʒa] f (canalha) rabble; (bando) gang

córner [ˈkɔxne*] m (FUTEBOL) corner

corneta [koxˈneta] f cornet; (MIL) bugle

cornetim [koxneˈtʃĩ] (pl -ns) m French horn

coro [ˈkoru] m chorus; (conjunto de cantores) choir

coroa [koˈroa] f crown; (de flores) garland ♦ m/f (BR: col) old timer

coroação [korwaˈsãw] (pl -ões) f coronation

coroar [koroˈa*] vt to crown; (premiar) to reward

coronel [koroˈnɛw] (pl -éis) m colonel; (político) local political boss

coronha [koˈrɔɲa] f (de um fuzil) butt

corpete [koxˈpetʃi] m bodice

corpo [ˈkoxpu] m body; (aparência física) figure; (: de homem) build; (de vestido) bodice; (MIL) corps sg; **de ~ e alma** (fig) wholeheartedly; **~ diplomático** diplomatic corps sg

corporal [koxpoˈraw] (pl -ais) adj physical

corpulento/a [koxpuˈlētu/a] adj stout

correção [koxeˈsãw] (PT -cç-; pl -ões) f correction; (exatidão) correctness; **casa de ~** reformatory

corre-corre [ˈkɔxiˈkɔxi] (pl ~s) m rush

correcto/a etc [koˈxɛktu/a] (PT) = **correto** etc

corredor(a) [koxeˈdo*(a)] m/f runner ♦ m corridor; (em avião etc) aisle; (cavalo) racehorse

córrego [ˈkɔxegu] m stream, brook

correia [koˈxeja] f strap; (de máquina) belt; (para cachorro) leash

correio [koˈxeju] m mail, post; (local) post office; (carteiro) postman (BRIT), mailman (US); **~ aéreo** air mail; **pôr no ~** to post; **~ eletrônico** electronic mail; **~ de voz** voice mail

corrente [koˈxẽtʃi] adj (atual) current; (águas) running; (comum) usual, common ♦ f current; (cadeia, jóia) chain; **~ de ar** draught (BRIT), draft (US); **~za** [koxɛˈteza] f (de ar) draught (BRIT), draft (US); (de rio) current

correr [koˈxe*] vt to run; (viajar por) to travel across ♦ vi to run; (o tempo) to elapse; (boato) to go round; (atuar com rapidez) to rush; **~ia** [koxeˈria] f rush

correspondência [koxeʃpõˈdẽsja] f correspondence; **correspondente** [koxeʃpõˈdẽtʃi] adj corresponding ♦ m correspondent

corresponder [koxeʃpõˈde*] vi: **~ a** to correspond to; (ser igual) to match (up to); **~-se** vr: **~-se com** to correspond with

correto/a [koˈxɛtu/a] adj correct; (conduta) right; (pessoa) straight, honest

corretor(a) [koxeˈto*(a)] m/f broker; **~ de fundos** ou **de bolsa** stockbroker; **~ de imóveis** estate agent (BRIT), realtor (US)

corrida [koˈxida] f running; (certame) race; (de táxi) fare; **~ de cavalos** horse race

corrido/a [koˈxidu/a] adj quick; (expulso)

driven out ♦ *adv* quickly

corrigir [koxi'ʒi*] *vt* to correct

corrimão [koxi'mãw] (*pl* ~s) *m* handrail

corriqueiro/a [koxi'kejru/a] *adj* common; (*problema*) trivial

corroborar [koxobo'ra*] *vt* to corroborate, confirm

corroer [koxo'e*] *vt* to corrode; (*fig*) to eat away; **~-se** *vr* to corrode; to be eaten away

corromper [koxõ'pe*] *vt* to corrupt; (*subornar*) to bribe; **~-se** *vr* to be corrupted

corrosão [koxo'zãw] *f* corrosion; (*fig*) erosion

corrosivo/a [koxo'zivu/a] *adj* corrosive

corrupção [koxup'sãw] *f* corruption

corrupto/a [ko'xuptu/a] *adj* corrupt

Córsega ['kɔxsega] *f*: **a ~** Corsica

cortada [kox'tada] *f*: **dar uma ~ em alguém** (*fig*) to cut sb short

cortadura [koxta'dura] *f* cut; (*entre montes*) gap

cortante [kox'tãtʃi] *adj* cutting

cortar [kox'ta*] *vt* to cut; (*eliminar*) to cut out; (*água, telefone etc*) to cut off; (*efeito*) to stop ♦ *vi* to cut; (*encurtar caminho*) to take a short cut; **~ o cabelo** (*no cabeleireiro*) to have one's hair cut; **~ a palavra de alguém** to interrupt sb

corte¹ ['kɔxtʃi] *m* cut; (*de luz*) power cut; **sem ~** (*tesoura etc*) blunt; **~ de cabelo** haircut

corte² ['kɔxtʃi] *f* court; **~s** *fpl* (*PT*) parliament *sg*

cortejar [koxte'ʒa*] *vt* to court

cortejo [kox'teʒu] *m* procession

cortês [kox'teʃ] (*pl* **-eses**) *adj* polite

cortesão/tesã [koxte'zãw/te'zã] (*pl* ~s/ ~s) *m/f* courtier ♦ *f* courtesan

cortesia [koxte'zia] *f* politeness; (*de empresa*) free offer

cortiça [kox'tʃisa] *f* cork

cortiço [kox'tʃisu] *m* slum tenement

cortina [kox'tʃina] *f* curtain

coruja [ko'ruʒa] *f* owl

coruscar [koruʃ'ka*] *vi* to sparkle, glitter

corvo ['koxvu] *m* crow

cós [kɔʃ] *m inv* waistband; (*cintura*) waist

cosca ['kɔʃka] *f*: **fazer ~** to tickle

coser [ko'ze*] *vt, vi* to sew

cosmético/a [koʒ'mɛtʃiku/a] *adj* cosmetic ♦ *m* cosmetic

cosmopolita [koʒmopo'lita] *adj* cosmopolitan

cospe *etc* ['kɔʃpi] *vb* V **cuspir**

costa ['kɔʃta] *f* coast; **~s** *fpl* (*dorso*) back *sg*; **dar as ~s a** to turn one's back on

costado [koʃ'tadu] *m* back

Costa Rica *f*: **a ~** Costa Rica

costear [koʃ'tʃja*] *vt* (*rodear*) to go round

costela [koʃ'tɛla] *f* rib

costeleta [koʃte'leta] *f* chop, cutlet; **~s** *fpl* (*suíças*) side-whiskers

costumar [koʃtu'ma*] *vt* (*habituar*) to accustom ♦ *vi*: **ele costuma chegar às 6.00** he usually arrives at 6.00; **costumava dizer ...** he used to say ...

costume [koʃ'tumi] *m* custom, habit; (*traje*) costume; **~s** *mpl* (*comportamento*) behaviour *sg* (*BRIT*), behavior *sg* (*US*); (*conduta*) conduct *sg*; (*de um povo*) customs; **de ~** usual; **como de ~** as usual

costumeiro/a [koʃtu'mejru/a] *adj* usual, habitual

costura [koʃ'tura] *f* sewing; (*sutura*) seam; **~r** [koʃtu'ra*] *vt, vi* to sew; **costureira** [koʃtu'rejra] *f* dressmaker

cota ['kɔta] *f* quota, share

cotação [kota'sãw] (*pl* **-ões**) *f* (*de preços*) list, quotation; (*BOLSA*) price; (*consideração*) esteem; **~ bancária** bank rate

cotado/a [ko'tadu/a] *adj* (*COM*: *ação*) quoted; (*bem-conceituado*) well thought of; (*num concurso*) fancied

cotar [ko'ta*] *vt* (*ações*) to quote; **~ algo em** to value sth at

cotejar [kote'ʒa*] *vt* to compare; **cotejo** [ko'teʒu] *m* comparison

cotidiano/a [kotʃi'dʒianu/a] *adj* daily, everyday ♦ *m*: **o ~** daily life

cotoco [ko'toku] *m* (*do corpo*) stump; (*de uma vela etc*) stub

cotonete [koto'nɛtʃi] *m* cotton bud

cotovelada [kotove'lada] *f* shove; (*cutucada*) nudge

cotovelo [koto'velu] *m* (*ANAT*) elbow; (*curva*) bend; **falar pelos ~s** to talk non-stop

coube *etc* ['kobi] *vb* V **caber**

couraça [ko'rasa] *f* (*de animal*) shell; **~do** [kora'sadu] (*PT*) *m* battleship

couro ['koru] *m* leather; (*de um animal*) hide

couve ['kovi] *f* spring greens *pl*; **~-bruxelas** (*pl* **~s-de-bruxelas**) *f* Brussels sprout; **~-flor** (*pl* **~s-flores**) *f* cauliflower

couvert [ku'vɛx] *m* cover charge

cova ['kɔva] *f* pit; (*caverna*) cavern; (*sepultura*) grave

covarde [ko'vaxdʒi] *adj* cowardly ♦ *m/f* coward; **covardia** [kovax'dʒia] *f* cowardice

covil [ko'viw] (*pl* **-is**) *m* den, lair

covinha [ko'viɲa] *f* dimple

covis [ko'viʃ] *mpl* de **covil**

coxa ['kɔʃa] *f* thigh

coxear [ko'ʃja*] *vi* to limp

coxia [ko'ʃia] *f* aisle, gangway

coxo/a ['koʃu/a] *adj* lame

cozer [ko'ze*] *vt, vi* to cook

cozido [ko'zidu] *m* stew

cozinha [ko'ziɲa] *f* kitchen; (*arte*) cookery

cozinhar [kozi'ɲa*] *vt, vi* to cook

cozinheiro/a [kozi'ɲejru/a] *m/f* cook

CP *abr* = **Caminhos de Ferro Portugueses**

CPF (*BR*) *abr m* (= *Cadastro de Pessoa Fí-*

sica) identification number

Cr$ *abr* = **cruzeiro**

crachá [kra'ʃa] *m* badge

crânio ['kranju] *m* skull

craque ['kraki] *m/f* ace, expert

crasso/a ['krasu/a] *adj* crass

cratera [kra'tɛra] *f* crater

cravar [kra'va*] *vt* (*prego etc*) to drive (in); (*com os olhos*) to stare at; **~-se** *vr* to penetrate

cravejar [krave'ʒa*] *vt* to nail

cravo ['kravu] *m* carnation; (*MÚS*) harpsichord; (*especiaria*) clove; (*na pele*) blackhead; (*prego*) nail

creche ['krɛʃi] *f* crèche

credenciais [kredẽ'sjajʃ] *fpl* credentials

creditar [kredʒi'ta*] *vt* to guarantee; (*COM*) to credit; **~ algo a alguém** to credit sb with sth; (*garantir*) to assure sb of sth

crédito ['krɛdʒitu] *m* credit; **digno de ~** reliable

credo ['krɛdu] *m* creed; **~!** heavens!

credor(a) [kre'do*(a)] *adj* worthy, deserving; (*COM: saldo*) credit *atr* ♦ *m/f* creditor

cremar [kre'ma*] *vt* to cremate

crematório [krema'tɔrju] *m* crematorium

creme ['krɛmi] *adj inv* cream ♦ *m* cream; (*CULIN: doce*) custard; **~ dental** toothpaste; **cremoso/a** [kre'mozu/ɔza] *adj* creamy

crença ['krẽsa] *f* belief

crendice [krẽ'dʒisi] *f* superstition

crente ['krẽtʃi] *m/f* believer

crepitante [krepi'tãtʃi] *adj* crackling

crepúsculo [kre'puʃkulu] *m* dusk, twilight

crer [kre*] *vt, vi* to believe; **~-se** *vr* to believe o.s. to be; **~ em** to believe in; **creio que sim** I think so

crescente [kre'sẽtʃi] *adj* growing ♦ *m* crescent

crescer [kre'se*] *vi* to grow; **crescimento** [kresi'mẽtu] *m* growth

crespo/a ['kreʃpu/a] *adj* (*cabelo*) curly

cretinice [kretʃi'nisi] *f* stupidity; (*ato, dito*) stupid thing

cretino [kre'tʃinu] *m* cretin, imbecile

cria ['kria] *f* (*animal: sg*) baby animal; (: *pl*) young *pl*

criação [krja'sãw] (*pl* -**ões**) *f* creation; (*de animais*) raising, breeding; (*educação*) upbringing; (*animais domésticos*) livestock *pl*; **filho de ~** adopted child

criado/a ['krjadu/a] *m/f* servant

criado-mudo (*pl* **criados-mudos**) *m* bedside table

criador(a) [krja'do*(a)] *m/f* creator; **~ de gado** cattle breeder

criança ['krjãsa] *adj* childish ♦ *f* child; **~da** [krjã'sada] *f*: **a ~da** the kids

criar [krja*] *vt* to create; (*crianças*) to bring up; (*animais*) to raise; (*amamentar*) to suckle, nurse; (*planta*) to grow;

~-se *vr*: **~-se (com)** to grow up (with); **~ caso** to make trouble

criativo/a [krja'tʃivu/a] *adj* creative

criatura [krja'tura] *f* creature; (*indivíduo*) individual

crime ['krimi] *m* crime; **criminal** [krimi'naw] (*pl* -**ais**) *adj* criminal; **criminalidade** [kriminali'dadʒi] *f* crime; **criminoso/a** [krimi'nozu/ɔza] *adj, m/f* criminal

crina ['krina] *f* mane

crioulo/a [kri'jolu/a] *adj* creole ♦ *m/f* creole; (*BR: negro*) Black (person)

crise ['krizi] *f* crisis; (*escassez*) shortage; (*MED*) attack, fit

crisma ['kriʒma] *f* (*REL*) confirmation; **~r** [kriʒ'ma*] *vt* to confirm; **~r-se** *vr* to be confirmed

crista ['kriʃta] *f* (*de serra, onda*) crest; (*de galo*) cock's comb

cristal [kriʃ'taw] (*pl* -**ais**) *m* crystal; (*vidro*) glass; **cristais** *mpl* (*copos*) glassware *sg*; **~ino/a** [kriʃta'linu/a] *adj* crystal-clear

cristandade [kriʃtã'dadʒi] *f* Christianity

cristão/tã [kriʃ'tãw/tã] (*pl* **~s/~s**) *adj, m/f* Christian

cristianismo [kriʃtʃja'niʒmu] *m* Christianity

Cristo ['kriʃtu] *m* Christ

critério [kri'tɛrju] *m* criterion; (*juízo*) discretion, judgement; **criterioso/a** [krite'rjozu/ɔza] *adj* thoughtful, careful

crítica ['kritʃika] *f* criticism; *V tb* **crítico**

criticar [kritʃi'ka*] *vt* to criticize; (*um livro*) to review

crítico/a ['kritʃiku/a] *adj* critical ♦ *m/f* critic

crivar [kri'va*] *vt* (*com balas etc*) to riddle

crível ['krivew] (*pl* -**eis**) *adj* credible

crivo ['krivu] *m* sieve

crocante [kro'kãtʃi] *adj* crunchy

crochê [kro'ʃe] *m* crochet

crocodilo [kroko'dʒilu] *m* crocodile

cromo ['krɔmu] *m* chrome

cromossomo [kromo'sɔmu] *m* chromosome

crônica ['kronika] *f* chronicle; (*coluna de jornal*) newspaper column; (*texto jornalístico*) feature; (*conto*) short story

crônico/a ['kroniku/a] *adj* chronic

cronista [kro'niʃta] *m/f* (*de jornal*) columnist; (*contista*) short story writer

cronológico/a [krono'lɔʒiku/a] *adj* chronological

cronometrar [kronome'tra*] *vt* to time; **cronômetro** [kro'nometru] *m* stopwatch

croquete [kro'kɛtʃi] *m* croquette

crosta ['krɔʃta] *f* crust; (*MED*) scab

cru(a) [kru/'krua] *adj* raw; (*não refinado*) crude

crucial [kru'sjaw] (*pl* -**ais**) *adj* crucial

crucificação [krusifika'sãw] (*pl* -**ões**) *f* crucifixion

crucificar [krusifi'ka*] *vt* to crucify

crucifixo [krusiˈfiksu] *m* crucifix
cruel [kruˈɛw] (*pl* -**éis**) *adj* cruel; ~**dade** [kruewˈdadʒi] *f* cruelty
cruz [kruʒ] *f* cross; **C~ Vermelha** Red Cross
cruzada [kruˈzada] *f* crusade
cruzado/a [kruˈzadu/a] *adj* crossed ♦ *m* (*moeda*) cruzado
cruzador [kruzaˈdoˑ] *m* cruiser
cruzamento [kruzaˈmẽtu] *m* crossroads
cruzar [kruˈzaˑ] *vt* to cross ♦ *vi* (NÁUT) to cruise; (*pessoas*) to pass each other by; ~ **com** to meet
cruzeiro [kruˈzejru] *m* (*cruz*) (monumental) cross; (*moeda*) cruzeiro; (*viagem de navio*) cruise
cu [ku] (*col!*) *m* arse (!); **vai tomar no ~** fuck off (!)
Cuba [ˈkuba] *f* Cuba
cubículo [kuˈbikulu] *m* cubicle
cubo [ˈkubu] *m* cube; (*de roda*) hub
cubro *etc* [ˈkubru] *vb* V **cobrir**
cuca [ˈkuka] (*col*) *f* head; **fundir a ~** (*quebrar a cabeça*) to rack one's brain; (*baratinar*) to boggle the mind; (*perturbar*) to drive crazy
cuco [ˈkuku] *m* cuckoo
cueca [ˈkwɛka] *f* (BR: tb: ~**s**: *para homens*) underpants *pl*; ~**s** *fpl* (PT) underpants *pl*; (: *para mulheres*) panties *pl*
cuíca [ˈkwika] *f* kind of musical instrument
cuidado [kwiˈdadu] *m* care; **aos** ~**s de** in the care of; **ter ~** to be careful; ~**!** watch out!, be careful!; **tomar ~ (de)** to be careful (of); ~**so/a** [kwidaˈdozu/ɔza] *adj* careful
cuidar [kwiˈdaˑ] *vi*: ~ **de** to take care of, look after; ~-**se** *vr* to look after o.s.
cujo/a [ˈkuʒu/a] *pron* (*de quem*) whose; (*de que*) of which
culinária [kuliˈnarja] *f* cookery
culminar [kuwmiˈnaˑ] *vi*: ~ **(com)** to culminate (in)
culote [kuˈlɔtʃi] *m* (*calça*) jodhpurs *pl*
culpa [ˈkuwpa] *f* fault; (JUR) guilt; **ter ~ de** to be to blame for; **por ~ de** because of; ~**bilidade** [kuwpabiliˈdadʒi] *f* guilt; ~**do/a** [kuwˈpadu/a] *adj* guilty ♦ *m/f* culprit; ~**r** [kuwˈpaˑ] *vt* to blame; (*acusar*) to accuse; ~**r-se** *vr* to take the blame; **culpável** [kuwˈpavew] (*pl* -**éis**) *adj* guilty
cultivar [kuwtʃiˈvaˑ] *vt* to cultivate; (*plantas*) to grow; **cultivo** [kuwˈtʃivu] *m* cultivation
culto/a [ˈkuwtu/a] *adj* cultured ♦ *m* (*homenagem*) worship; (*religião*) cult
cultura [kuwˈtura] *f* culture; (*da terra*) cultivation; ~**l** [kuwtuˈraw] (*pl* **culturais**) *adj* cultural
cume [ˈkumi] *m* top, summit; (*fig*) climax
cúmplice [ˈkũplisi] *m/f* accomplice
cumplicidade [kũplisiˈdadʒi] *f* complicity
cumprimentar [kũprimẽˈtaˑ] *vt* to greet;

(*dar parabéns*) to congratulate
cumprimento [kũpriˈmẽtu] *m* fulfilment; (*saudação*) greeting; (*elogio*) compliment; ~**s** *mpl* (*saudações*) best wishes; ~ **de uma lei/ordem** compliance with a law/an order
cumprir [kũˈpriˑ] *vt* (*desempenhar*) to carry out; (*promessa*) to keep; (*lei*) to obey; (*pena*) to serve ♦ *vi* to be necessary; ~ **a palavra** to keep one's word; **fazer ~** to enforce
cúmulo [ˈkumulu] *m* height; **é o ~!** that's the limit!
cunha [ˈkuɲa] *f* wedge
cunhado/a [kuˈɲadu/a] *m/f* brother-in-law/sister-in-law
cunhar [kuˈɲaˑ] *vt* (*moedas*) to mint; (*palavras*) to coin
cunho [ˈkuɲu] *m* (*marca*) hallmark; (*caráter*) nature
cupê [kuˈpe] *m* coupé
cupim [kuˈpĩ] (*pl* -**ns**) *m* termite
cupincha [kuˈpĩʃa] *m/f* mate, pal
cupins [kuˈpĩʃ] *mpl de* **cupim**
cupom [kuˈpõ] (*pl* -**ns**) *m* coupon
cúpula [ˈkupula] *f* dome; (*de abajur*) shade; (*de partido etc*) leadership; (**reunião de**) ~ summit (meeting)
cura [ˈkura] *f* cure; (*tratamento*) treatment; (*de carnes etc*) curing, preservation ♦ *m* priest
curador(a) [kuraˈdoˑ(a)] *m/f* (*de menores, órfãos*) guardian; (*de instituição*) trustee
curandeiro [kurãˈdejru] *m* healer, medicine man; (*charlatão*) quack
curar [kuˈraˑ] *vt* (*doença, carne*) to cure; (*ferida*) to treat; ~-**se** *vr* to get well
curativo [kuraˈtʃivu] *m* dressing
curiosidade [kurjoziˈdadʒi] *f* curiosity; (*objeto raro*) curio
curioso/a [kuˈrjozu/ɔza] *adj* curious ♦ *m/f* snooper, inquisitive person; ~**s** *mpl* (*espectadores*) onlookers
curral [kuˈxaw] (*pl* -**ais**) *m* pen, enclosure
currar [kuˈxaˑ] (*col*) *vt* to rape
currículo [kuˈxikulu] *m* (*curriculum*) curriculum vitae
cursar [kuxˈsaˑ] *vt* (*aulas, escola*) to attend; (*cursos*) to follow; **ele está cursando História** he's studying *ou* doing history
curso [ˈkuxsu] *m* course; (*direção*) direction; **em ~** (*ano etc*) current; (*processo*) in progress
cursor [kuxˈsoˑ] *m* (COMPUT) cursor
curtição [kuxtʃiˈsãw] (*col*) *f* fun
curtido/a [kuxˈtʃidu/a] *adj* hardened
curtir [kuxˈtʃiˑ] *vt* (*couro*) to tan; (*tornar rijo*) to toughen up; (*padecer*) to suffer, endure; (*col*) to enjoy
curto/a [ˈkuxtu/a] *adj* short ♦ *m* (ELET) short (circuit); ~-**circuito** (*pl* ~-**s-circuitos**) *m* short circuit
curva [ˈkuxva] *f* curve; (*de estrada, rio*) bend; ~ **fechada** hairpin bend

curvar [kux'va*] *vt* to bend, curve; **~-se** *vr* to stoop; **curvo/a** ['kuxvu/a] *adj* curved; *(estrada)* winding

cuscuz [kuʃ'kuʒ] *m* couscous

cusparada [kuʃpa'rada] *f:* **dar uma ~** to spit

cuspe ['kuʃpi] *m* spit, spittle

cuspido/a [kuʃ'pidu/a] *adj:* **ele é o pai ~ e escarrado** *(col)* he's the spitting image of his father

cuspir [kuʃ'pi*] *vt, vi* to spit

custa ['kuʃta] *f:* **à ~ de** at the expense of; **~s** *fpl* *(JUR)* costs

custar [kuʃ'ta*] *vi* to cost; *(ser difícil):* **~ a fazer** to have trouble doing; *(demorar):* **~ a fazer** to take a long time to do; **~ caro** to be expensive

custo ['kuʃtu] *m* cost; **a ~** with difficulty; **a todo ~** at all costs

custódia [kuʃ'tɔdʒja] *f* custody

cutelo [ku'tɛlu] *m* cleaver

cutícula [ku'tʃikula] *f* cuticle

cútis ['kutʃiʃ] *f inv* *(pele)* skin; *(tez)* complexion

cutucar [kutu'ka*] *vt (com o dedo)* to prod, poke; *(com o cotovelo)* to nudge

Cz$ *abr* = **cruzado**

czar [kza*] *m* czar

D

D *abr* = **Dom; Dona;** (= *direito*) r; (= *deve*) d

d/ *abr* = **dia**

da [da] = **de + a**

dá [da] *vb V* **dar**

dactilografar *etc* [datilografa'fa*] *(PT)* = **datilografar** *etc*

dádiva ['dadʒiva] *f* donation; *(oferta)* gift

dado/a ['dadu/a] *adj* given; *(sociável)* sociable **♦ m** *(em jogo)* die; *(fato)* fact; **~s** *mpl* dice; *(fatos, COMPUT)* data *sg*; **~ que** supposing that; *(uma vez que)* given that

daí [da'ji] *adv* = **de + aí**; *(desse lugar)* from there; *(desse momento)* from then; **~ a um mês** a month later

dali [da'li] *adv* = **de + ali**; *(desse lugar)* from there

daltônico/a [daw'toniku/a] *adj* colour-blind *(BRIT)*, color-blind *(US)*

dama ['dama] *f* lady; *(XADREZ, CARTAS)* queen; **~s** *fpl* *(jogo)* draughts *(BRIT)*, checkers *(US)*; **~ de honra** bridesmaid

damasco [da'maʃku] *m* apricot

danado/a [da'nadu/a] *adj* damned; *(zangado)* furious; *(menino)* mischievous

dança ['dãsa] *f* dance; **~r** [dã'sa*] *vi* to dance; **~rino/a** [dãsa'rinu/a] *m/f* dancer; **danceteria** [dãsɛte'ria] *f* disco(theque)

danificar [danifi'ka*] *vt* to damage

dano ['danu] *m (tb.* **~s**) damage, harm; *(a uma pessoa)* injury

dantes ['dãtʃiʃ] *adv* before, formerly

daquele/a [da'kɛli/a] = **de + aquele/a**

daqui [da'ki] *adv* = **de + aqui**; *(deste lugar)* from here; **~ a pouco** soon, in a little while; **~ a uma semana** a week from now; **~ em diante** from now on

daquilo [da'kilu] = **de + aquilo**

dar [da*] *vt* **1** *(ger)* to give; *(festa)* to hold; *(problemas)* to cause; **~ algo a alguém** to give sb sth, give sth to sb; **~ de beber a alguém** to give sb a drink; **~ aula de francês** to teach French

2 *(produzir: fruta etc)* to produce

3 *(notícias no jornal)* to publish

4 *(cartas)* to deal

5 *(+ n: perífrase de vb):* **me dá medo/pena** it frightens/upsets me

♦ vi 1: ~ com *(coisa)* to find; *(pessoa)* to meet

2: ~ em *(bater)* to hit; *(resultar)* to lead to; *(lugar)* to come to

3: dá no mesmo it's all the same

4: ~ de si *(sapatos etc)* to stretch, give

5: ~ para *(impess: ser possível):* **dá para trocar dinheiro aqui?** can I change money here?; **vai ~ para eu ir amanhã** I'll be able to go tomorrow; **dá para você vir amanhã – não, amanhã não vai ~** can you come tomorrow? – no, I can't

6: ~ para *(ser suficiente):* **~ para/para fazer** to be enough for/to do; **dá para todo mundo?** is there enough for everyone?

♦ ~-se *vr* **1** *(sair-se):* **~-se bem/mal** to do well/badly

2: ~-se (com alguém) to be acquainted (with sb); **~-se bem (com alguém)** to get on well (with sb)

3: ~-se por vencido to give up

dardo ['daxdu] *m* dart; *(grande)* spear

das [daʃ] = **de + as**

data ['data] *f* date; *(época)* time; **~r** [da'ta*] *vt* to date **♦ vi: ~r de** to date from

datilografar [datʃilogra'fa*] *vt* to type; **datilografia** [datʃilogra'fia] *f* typing; **datilógrafo/a** [datʃi'lɔgrafu/a] *m/f* typist *(BRIT)*, stenographer *(US)*

d.C. *abr* (= *depois de Cristo*) A.D.

de [dʒi] *(de + o(s)/a(s) = do(s)/da(s); + ele(s)/a(s) = dele(s)/a(s); + esse(s)/a(s) = desse(s)/a(s); + isso = disso; + este(s)/a(s) = deste(s)/a(s); + isto = disto; + aquele(s)/a(s) = daquele(s)/a(s); + aquilo = daquilo) prep* **1** *(posse)* of; **a casa ~ João/da irmã** João's/my sister's house; **é dele** it's his; **um romance ~** a novel by

2 *(origem, distância, com números)* from; **sou ~ São Paulo** I'm from São Paulo;

~ 8 a 20 from 8 to 20; **sair do cinema** to leave the cinema; ~ **dois em dois** two by two, two at a time

3 (*valor descritivo*): **um copo** ~ **vinho** a glass of wine; **um homem** ~ **cabelo comprido** a man with long hair; **o infeliz do homem** (*col*) the poor man; **um bilhete** ~ **avião** an air ticket; **uma criança** ~ **três anos** a three-year-old (child); **uma máquina** ~ **costurar** a sewing machine; **aulas** ~ **inglês** English lessons; **feito** ~ **madeira** made of wood; **vestido** ~ **branco** dressed in white

4 (*modo*): ~ **trem/avião** by train/plane; ~ **lado** sideways

5 (*hora, tempo*): **às 8 da manhã** at 8 o'clock in the morning; ~ **dia/noite** by day/night; ~ **hoje a oito dias** a week from now; ~ **dois em dois dias** every other day

6 (*comparações*): **mais/menos** ~ **cem pessoas** more/less than a hundred people; **é o mais caro da loja** it's the most expensive in the shop; **ela é mais bonita do que sua irmã** she's prettier than her sister; **gastei mais do que pretendia** I spent more than I intended

7 (*causa*): **estou morto** ~ **calor** I'm boiling hot; **ela morreu** ~ **câncer** she died of cancer

8 (*adj* + ~ + *infin*): **fácil** ~ **entender** easy to understand

dê *etc* [de] *vb* V **dar**

debaixo [de'bajʃu] *adv* below, underneath ♦ *prep*: ~ **de** under, beneath

debate [de'batʃi] *m* discussion, debate; (*disputa*) argument; ~**r** [deba'te*] *vt* to debate; (*discutir*) to discuss; ~**r-se** *vr* to struggle

débeis ['dɛbejʃ] *pl de* **débil**

debelar [debe'la*] *vt* to put down, suppress; (*crise*) to overcome

débil ['dɛbiw] (*pl* **–eis**) *adj* weak, feeble ♦ *m*: ~ **mental** mentally handicapped person; **debilidade** [debili'dadʒi] *f* weakness; **debilidade mental** mental handicap; **debilitar** [debili'ta*] *vt* to weaken; **debilitar-se** *vr* to become weak, weaken; **debilóide** [debi'lɔjdʒi] (*col*) *adj* idiotic ♦ *m/f* idiot

debitar [debi'ta*] *vt*: ~ **$40 a** *ou* **na conta de alguém** to debit $40 to sb's account; **débito** *m* debit

debochado/a [debo'ʃadu/a] *adj* (*pessoa*) sardonic; (*jeito, tom*) mocking

debochar [debo'ʃa*] *vt* to mock ♦ *vi*: ~ **de** to mock

debruçar [debru'sa*] *vt* (*coisa*) to bend over; (*pessoa*) to turn over; ~**-se** *vr* to bend over; (*inclinar-se*) to lean over; ~**-se na janela** to lean out of the window

debutar [debu'ta*] *vi* to make one's début

década ['dɛkada] *f* decade

decadência [deka'dẽsja] *f* decadence

decair [deka'i*] *vi* to decline

decapitar [dekapi'ta*] *vt* to behead, decapitate

decência [de'sẽsja] *f* decency

decente [de'sẽtʃi] *adj* decent; (*apropriado*) proper; (*honrado*) honourable (*BRIT*), honorable (*US*); (*trabalho*) neat; ~**mente** [desẽtʃi'mẽtʃi] *adv* decently; properly; hono(u)rably

decepar [dese'pa*] *vt* to cut off, chop off

decepção [desep'sãw] (*pl* **–ões**) *f* disappointment; **decepcionar** [desepsjo'na*] *vt* to disappoint; (*desiludir*) to disillusion; **decepcionar-se** *vr* to be disappointed; to be disillusioned

decerto [dʒi'sɛxtu] *adv* certainly

decidido/a [desi'dʒidu/a] *adj* (*pessoa*) determined; (*questão*) resolved

decidir [desi'dʒi*] *vt* to decide; (*solucionar*) to resolve; ~**-se** *vr*: ~**-se a** to make up one's mind to; ~**-se por** to decide on, go for

decíduo/a [de'sidwu/a] *adj* (*BOT*) deciduous

decifrar [desi'fra*] *vt* to decipher; (*futuro*) to foretell; (*compreender*) to understand

decimal [desi'maw] (*pl* **–ais**) *adj*, *m* decimal

décimo/a ['dɛsimu/a] *adj* tenth ♦ *m* tenth

decisão [desi'zãw] (*pl* **–ões**) *f* decision; **decisivo/a** [desi'zivu/a] *adj* (*fator*) decisive; (*jogo*) deciding

declamar [dekla'ma*] *vt* (*poemas*) to recite ♦ *vi* (*pej*) to rant

declaração [deklara'sãw] (*pl* **–ões**) *f* declaration; (*depoimento*) statement

declarado/a [dekla'radu/a] *adj* (*intenção*) declared; (*opinião*) professed; (*inimigo*) sworn; (*alcoólatra*) self-confessed; (*cristão etc*) avowed

declarante [dekla'rãtʃi] *m/f* (*JUR*) witness

declarar [dekla'ra*] *vt* to declare; (*confessar*) to confess

declinar [dekli'na*] *vt* (*ger*) to decline ♦ *vi* (*sol*) to go down; (*terreno*) to slope down; **declínio** [de'klinju] *m* decline

declive [de'klivi] *m* slope, incline

decodificador [dekodʒifika'do*] *m* (*TV*) decoder

decolagem [deko'laʒẽ] (*pl* **–ns**) *f* (*AER*) take-off

decolar [deko'la*] *vi* (*AER*) to take off

decompor [dekõ'po*] (*irreg*: *como* **pôr**) *vt* to analyse; (*apodrecer*) to rot; ~**-se** *vr* to rot, decompose

decomposição [dekõpozi'sãw] (*pl* **–ões**) *f* decomposition; (*análise*) dissection

decoração [dekora'sãw] *f* decoration; (*TEATRO*) scenery

decorar [deko'ra*] *vt* to decorate; (*aprender*) to learn by heart; **decorativo/a** [dekora'tʃivu/a] *adj* decorative

decoro [de'koru] *m* decency; *(dignidade)* decorum; **~so/a** [deko'rozu/ɔza] *adj* decent, respectable

decorrência [deko'xẽsja] *f* consequence; **em ~ de** as a result of

decorrente [deko'xẽtʃi] *adj*: **~ de** resulting from

decorrer [deko'xe*] *vi* *(tempo)* to pass; *(acontecer)* to take place, happen ♦ *m*: **no ~ de** in the course of; **~ de** to result from

decrépito/a [de'krɛpitu/a] *adj* decrepit

decrescer [dekre'se*] *vi* to decrease, diminish

decretar [dekre'ta*] *vt* to decree, order; **decreto** [de'krɛtu] *m* decree, order; **decreto-lei** *(pl* decretos-leis) *m* act, law

decurso [de'kuxsu] *m*: **no ~ de** in the course of, during

dedal [de'daw] *(pl* -ais) *m* thimble

dedão [de'dãw] *(pl* -ões) *m* thumb; *(do pé)* big toe

dedetizar [dedetʃi'za*] *vt* to spray with insecticide

dedicação [dedʒika'sãw] *f* dedication; *(devotamento)* devotion

dedicado/a [dedʒi'kadu/a] *adj* dedicated

dedicar [dedʒi'ka*] *vt* to dedicate; *(tempo, atenção)* to devote; **~-se** *vr*: **~-se a** to devote o.s. to; **dedicatória** [dedʒika'tɔrja] *f* *(de obra)* dedication

dedo [de'dedu] *m* finger; *(do pé)* toe; **~ anular/indicador/mínimo** *ou* **mindinho** ring/index/little finger; **~ polegar** thumb

dedões [de'dõjʃ] *mpl de* **dedão**

dedução [dedu'sãw] *(pl* -ões) *f* deduction

deduzir [dedu'zi*] *vt* to deduct; *(concluir)* to deduce, infer

defasado/a [defa'zadu/a] *adj*: **~ (de)** out of step (with)

defasagem [defa'zaʒẽ] *(pl* -ns) *f* discrepancy

defeito [de'fejtu] *m* defect, flaw; **pôr ~s em** to find fault with; **com ~** broken, out of order; **para ninguém botar ~** *(col)* perfect; **defeituoso/a** [defej'twozu/ɔza] *adj* defective, faulty

defender [defẽ'de*] *vt* to defend; **~-se** *vr* to stand up for o.s.; *(numa língua)* to get by

defensiva [defẽ'siva] *f*: **estar** *ou* **ficar na ~** to be on the defensive

defensor(a) [defẽ'so*(a)] *m/f* defender; *(JUR)* defending counsel

deferimento [deferi'mẽtu] *m* *(de dinheiro, pedido, petição)* granting; *(de prêmio, condecoração)* awarding; *(aceitação)* acceptance

deferir [defe'ri*] *vt* *(pedido, petição)* to grant; *(prêmio, condecoração)* to award ♦ *vi*: **~ a** to concede to; *(sugestão)* to accept

defesa [de'feza] *f* defence *(BRIT)*, defense *(US)*; *(JUR)* counsel for the defence ♦ *m*

(FUTEBOL) back

deficiente [defi'sjẽtʃi] *adj* *(imperfeito)* defective; *(carente)*: **~ (em)** deficient (in)

déficit ['dɛfisitʃi] *(pl* -s) *m* deficit

definhar [defi'ɲa*] *vt* to debilitate ♦ *vi* to waste away; *(BOT)* to wither

definição [defini'sãw] *(pl* -ões) *f* definition

definir [defi'ni*] *vt* to define; **~-se** *vr* to make a decision; *(explicar-se)* to make one's position clear; **~-se a favor de/contra algo** to come out in favo(u)r of/against sth

definitivamente [definitʃiva'mẽtʃi] *adv* definitively; *(permanentemente)* for good; *(sem dúvida)* definitely

definitivo/a [defini'tʃivu/a] *adj* final, definitive; *(permanente)* permanent; *(resposta, data)* definite

defiro *etc* [de'firu] *vb V* **deferir**

deformação [defoxma'sãw] *(pl* -ões) *f* loss of shape; *(de corpo)* deformation; *(de imagem, pensamento)* distortion

deformar [defox'ma*] *vt* to put out of shape; *(corpo)* to deform; *(imagem, pensamento)* to distort; **~-se** *vr* to lose shape; to be deformed; to become distorted

defraudação [defrawda'sãw] *(pl* -ões) *f* fraud; *(de dinheiro)* embezzlement

defraudar [defraw'da*] *vt* to embezzle; *(uma pessoa)* to defraud

defrontar [defrõ'ta*] *vt* to face ♦ *vi*: **~ com** to face; *(dar com)* to come face to face with; **~-se** *vr* to face each other

defronte [de'frõtʃi] *adv* opposite ♦ *prep*: **~ de** opposite

defumar [defu'ma*] *vt* *(presunto)* to smoke; *(perfumar)* to perfume

defunto/a [de'fũtu/a] *adj* dead ♦ *m/f* dead person

degelar [deʒe'la*] *vt* to thaw; *(geladeira)* to defrost ♦ *vi* to thaw out; to defrost; **degelo** [de'ʒelu] *m* thaw

degenerar [deʒene'ra*] *vi*: **~ (em)** to degenerate (into)

deglutir [deglu'tʃi*] *vt*, *vi* to swallow

degolar [dego'la*] *vt* to decapitate

degradante [degra'dãtʃi] *adj* degrading

degradar [degra'da*] *vt* to degrade, debase; **~-se** *vr* to demean o.s.

degrau [de'graw] *m* step; *(de escada de mão)* rung

degringolar [degrĩgo'la*] *vi* *(cair)* to tumble down; *(fig)* to collapse; (: *deteriorar-se)* to deteriorate; (: *desorganizar-se)* to get messed up

degustação [deguʃta'sãw] *(pl* -ões) *f* tasting, sampling; *(saborear)* savouring *(BRIT)*, savoring *(US)*

degustar [deguʃ'ta*] *vt* *(provar)* to taste; *(saborear)* to savour *(BRIT)*, savor *(US)*

dei *etc* [dej] *vb V* **dar**

deitada [dej'tada] *(col)* *f*: **dar uma ~** to have a lie-down

deitado/a [dej'tadu/a] *adj* (*estendido*) lying down; (*na cama*) in bed

deitar [dej'ta*] *vt* to lay down; (*na cama*) to put to bed; (*colocar*) to put, place; (*lançar*) to cast; (*PT: líquido*) to pour; ~-**se** *vr* to lie down; to go to bed; ~ **sangue** (*PT*) to bleed; ~ **abaixo** to knock down, flatten; ~ **a fazer algo** to start doing sth; ~ **uma carta** (*PT*) to post a letter; ~ **fora** (*PT*) to throw away *ou* out; ~ **e rolar** (*col*) to do as one likes

deixa ['dejʃa] *f* clue, hint; (*TEATRO*) cue; (*chance*) chance

deixar [dej'ʃa*] *vt* to leave; (*abandonar*) to abandon; (*permitir*) to let, allow ♦ *vi*: ~ **de** (*parar*) to stop; (*não fazer*) to fail to; **não posso ~ de ir** I must go; ~ **cair** to drop; ~ **alguém louco** to drive sb crazy *ou* mad; ~ **alguém cansado/nervoso** *etc* to make sb tired/nervous *etc*; **deixa disso!** (*col*) come off it!; **deixa para lá!** (*col*) forget it!

dela ['dɛla] = **de + ela**

delação [dela'sãw] (*pl* –ões) *f* (*de pessoa*: *denúncia*) accusation; (: *traição*) betrayal; (*de abusos*) disclosure; **delatar** [dela'ta*] *vt* (*pessoa*) to inform on; (*abusos*) to reveal; (*à polícia*) to report; **delator(a)** [dela'to*(a)] *m/f* informer

dele ['deli] = **de + ele**

delegação [delega'sãw] (*pl* –ões) *f* delegation

delegacia [delega'sia] *f* office; ~ **de polícia** police station

delegado/a [dele'gadu/a] *m/f* delegate, representative; ~ **de polícia** police chief

delegar [dele'ga*] *vt* to delegate

deleitar [delej'ta*] *vt* to delight; ~-**se** *vr*: ~-**se com** to delight in

deleite [de'lejtʃi] *m* delight; **deleitoso/a** [delej'tozu/ɔza] *adj* delightful

delgado/a [dew'gadu/a] *adj* thin; (*esbelto*) slim; (*fino*) fine

deliberação [delibera'sãw] (*pl* –ões) *f* deliberation; (*decisão*) decision

deliberar [delibe'ra*] *vt* to decide, resolve ♦ *vi* to deliberate

delicadeza [delika'deza] *f* delicacy; (*cortesia*) kindness

delicado/a [deli'kadu/a] *adj* delicate; (*frágil*) fragile; (*cortês*) polite; (*sensível*) sensitive

delícia [de'lisja] *f* delight; (*prazer*) pleasure; **que ~!** how lovely!; **deliciar** [deli'sja*] *vt* to delight; **deliciar-se** *vr*: **deliciar-se com algo** to take delight in sth

delicioso/a [deli'sjozu/ɔza] *adj* lovely; (*comida, bebida*) delicious

delineador [delinja'do*] *m* (*de olhos*) eyeliner

delinear [deli'nja*] *vt* to outline

delinqüência [deli'kwẽsja] *f* delinquency;

delinqüente [deli'kwẽtʃi] *adj, m/f* delinquent, criminal; **delinqüir** [deli'kwi*] *vi* to commit an offence (*BRIT*) *ou* offense (*US*)

delirante [deli'rãtʃi] *adj* delirious; (*show, atuação*) thrilling

delirar [deli'ra*] *vi* (*com febre*) to be delirious; (*de ódio, prazer*) to go mad, go wild

delírio [de'lirju] *m* (*MED*) delirium; (*êxtase*) ecstasy; (*excitação*) excitement

delito [de'litu] *m* (*crime*) crime; (*falta*) offence (*BRIT*), offense (*US*)

delonga [de'lõga] *f* delay; **sem mais ~s** without more ado; ~**r** [delõ'ga*] *vt* to delay; ~**r-se** *vr* (*conversa*) to wear on; ~**r-se em** to dwell on

demais [dʒi'majʃ] *adv* (*em demasia*) too much; (*muitíssimo*) a lot, very much ♦ *pron*: **os/as** ~ the rest (of them); **já é** ~! this is too much!; **é bom** ~ it's really good; **foi** ~ (*col*: *bacana*) it was great

demanda [de'mãda] *f* lawsuit; (*disputa*) claim; (*requisição*) request; (*ECON*) demand; **em** ~ **de** in search of; ~**r** [demã'da*] *vt* (*JUR*) to sue; (*exigir, reclamar*) to demand

demão [de'mãw] (*pl* ~**s**) *f* (*de tinta*) coat, layer

demarcação [demaxka'sãw] *f* demarcation

demasia [dema'zia] *f* excess, surplus; (*imoderação*) lack of moderation; **em** ~ (*dinheiro, comida etc*) too much; (*cartas, problemas etc*) too many

demasiadamente [demazjada'mẽtʃi] *adv* too much; (*com adj*) too

demasiado/a [dema'zjadu/a] *adj* too much; (*pl*) too many ♦ *adv* too much; (*com adj*) too

demente [de'mẽtʃi] *adj* insane, demented

demissão [demi'sãw] (*pl* –ões) *f* dismissal; **pedir** ~ to resign

demitir [demi'tʃi*] *vt* to dismiss; (*col*) to sack, fire; ~-**se** *vr* to resign

democracia [demokra'sia] *f* democracy

democrata [demo'krata] *m/f* democrat; **democrático/a** [demo'kratʃiku/a] *adj* democratic

demolição [demoli'sãw] (*pl* –ões) *f* demolition

demolir [demo'li*] *vt* to demolish, knock down; (*fig*) to destroy

demônio [de'monju] *m* devil, demon; (*col*: *criança*) brat

demonstração [demõʃtra'sãw] (*pl* –ões) *f* demonstration; (*de amizade*) show, display; (*prova*) proof

demonstrar [demõʃ'tra*] *vt* to demonstrate; (*provar*) to prove; (*amizade etc*) to show

demora [de'mɔra] *f* delay; (*parada*) stop; **sem** ~ at once, without delay; **qual é a** ~ **disso?** how long will this take?;

~do/a [demo'radu/a] *adj* slow; **~r** [demo'ra*] *vt* to delay, slow down ♦ *vi* (*permanecer*) to stay; (*tardar a vir*) to be late; (*consertar*) to take (a long) time; **~r-se** *vr* to stay for a long time, linger; **~r a chegar** to be a long time coming; **vai ~r muito?** will it take long?; **não vou ~r** I won't be long

dendê [dẽ'de] *m* (*CULIN*: *óleo*) palm oil; (*BOT*) oil palm

denegrir [dene'gri*] *vt* to blacken; (*difamar*) to denigrate

dengoso/a [dẽ'gozu/ɔza] *adj* coy; (*criança*: *choraminguento*): **ser ~** to be a cry-baby

dengue ['dẽgi] *m* (*MED*) dengue

denigro *etc* [de'nigru] *vb* V **denegrir**

denominação [denomina'sãw] (*pl* **–ões**) *f* (*REL*) denomination; (*título*) name

denominar [denomi'na*] *vt*: **~ algo/alguém ...** to call sth/sb ...; **~se** *vr* to be called; (*a si mesmo*) to call o.s.

denotar [deno'ta*] *vt* (*indicar*) to show, indicate; (*significar*) to signify

densidade [dẽsi'dadʒi] *f* density; **disco de ~ simples/dupla** (*COMPUT*) single-/double-density disk

denso/a [dẽsu/a] *adj* dense; (*espesso*) thick; (*compacto*) compact

dentada [dẽ'tada] *f* bite

dentadura [dẽta'dura] *f* teeth *pl*, set of teeth; (*artificial*) dentures *pl*

dente ['dẽtʃi] *m* tooth; (*de animal*) fang; (*de elefante*) tusk; (*de alho*) clove; **falar entre os ~s** to mutter, mumble; **~ de leite/do siso** milk/wisdom tooth; **~s postiços** false teeth

dentifrício [dẽtʃi'frisju] *m* toothpaste

dentista [dẽ'tʃiʃta] *m/f* dentist

dentre ['dẽtri] *prep* (from) among

dentro ['dẽtru] *adv* inside ♦ *prep*: **~ de** inside; (*tempo*) (with)in; **~ em pouco** *ou* **em breve** soon, before long; **de ~ para fora** inside out; **dar uma ~** (*col*) to get it right; **aí ~** in there; **por ~** on the inside; **estar por ~** (*col*: *fig*) to be in the know

dentuço/a [dẽ'tusu/a]: **ser ~** to have buck teeth

denúncia [de'nũsja] *f* denunciation; (*acusação*) accusation; (*de roubo*) report; **denunciar** [denũ'sja*] *vt* (*acusar*) to denounce; (*delatar*) to inform on; (*revelar*) to reveal

deparar [depa'ra*] *vt* to reveal; (*fazer aparecer*) to present ♦ *vi*: **~ com** to come across, meet; **~se** *vr*: **~se com** to come across, meet

departamento [depaxta'mẽtu] *m* department

dependência [depẽ'dẽsja] *f* dependence; (*edificação*) annexe (*BRIT*), annex (*US*); (*colonial*) dependency; (*cômodo*) room

dependente [depẽ'dẽtʃi] *m/f* dependant

depender [depẽ'de*] *vi*: **~ de** to depend on

depilador(a) [depila'do*(a)] *m/f* beauty therapist

depilar [depi'la*] *vt* (*pernas*) to wax; **depilatório** [depila'tɔrju] *m* hair-remover

deplorar [deplo'ra*] *vt* (*lamentar*) to regret; (*morte, perda*) to lament; **deplorável** [deplo'ravew] (*pl* **–eis**) *adj* deplorable; (*lamentável*) regrettable

depoimento [depoj'mẽtu] *m* testimony, evidence; (*na polícia*) statement

depois [de'pojʃ] *adv* afterwards ♦ *prep*: **~ de** after; **~ de comer** after eating; **~ que** after

depor [de'po*] (*irreg*: *como* **pôr**) *vt* (*pôr*) to place; (*indicar*) to indicate; (*rei*) to depose; (*governo*) to overthrow ♦ *vi* (*JUR*) to testify, give evidence; (*na polícia*) to give a statement

deportar [depox'ta*] *vt* to deport

depositar [depozi'ta*] *vt* to deposit; (*voto*) to cast; (*colocar*) to place

depósito [de'pozitu] *m* deposit; (*armazém*) warehouse, depot; (*de lixo*) dump; (*reservatório*) tank; **~ de bagagens** left-luggage office (*BRIT*), checkroom (*US*)

depravar [depra'va*] *vt* to deprave, corrupt; (*estragar*) to ruin; **~se** *vr* to become depraved

depreciação [depresja'sãw] *f* depreciation

depreciar [depre'sja*] *vt* (*desvalorizar*) to devalue; (*COM*) to write down; (*menosprezar*) to belittle; **~se** *vr* to depreciate, lose value

depredar [depre'da*] *vt* to wreck

depressa [dʒi'prɛsa] *adv* fast, quickly; **vamos ~** let's get a move on!

depressão [depre'sãw] (*pl* **–ões**) *f* depression

deprimente [depri'mẽtʃi] *adj* depressing

deprimido/a [depri'midu/a] *adj* depressed

deprimir [depri'mi*] *vt* to depress; **~se** *vr* to get depressed

depurar [depu'ra*] *vt* to purify

deputado/a [depu'tadu/a] *m/f* deputy; (*agente*) agent; (*POL*) ≈ Member of Parliament (*BRIT*), ≈ Representative (*US*)

deputar [depu'ta*] *vt* to delegate

deque ['dɛki] *m* deck

der *etc* [de*] *vb* V **dar**

deriva [de'riva] *f* drift; **ir à ~** to drift; **ficar à ~** to be adrift

derivar [deri'va*] *vt* to divert; (*LING*) to derive ♦ *vi* to drift; **~se** *vr* to be derived; (*ir à deriva*) to drift; (*provir*): **~(se) (de)** to derive *ou* be derived (from)

derradeiro/a [dexa'dejru/a] *adj* last, final

derramamento [dexama'mẽtu] *m* spilling; (*de sangue, lágrimas*) shedding

derramar [dexa'ma*] *vt* to spill; (*entornar*) to pour; (*sangue, lágrimas*) to shed; **~se** *vr* to pour out

derrame [de'xami] *m* haemorrhage (*BRIT*), hemorrhage (*US*)

derrapagem [dexa'paʒẽ] (*pl* **–ns**) *f* skid;

(*ação*) skidding

derrapar [dexa'pa*] *vi* to skid

derredor [dexe'do*] *adv, prep*: em ~ (de) around

derreter [dexe'te*] *vt* to melt; ~-se *vr* to melt; (*coisa congelada*) to thaw; (*enternecer-se*) to be touched

derrota [de'xɔta] *f* defeat, rout; (*NÁUT*) route; ~**r** [dexo'ta*] *vt* (*vencer*) to defeat; (*em jogo*) to beat

derrubar [dexu'ba*] *vt* to knock down; (*governo*) to bring down; (*suj: doença*) to lay low; (*col: prejudicar*) to put down

desabafar [dʒizaba'fa*] *vt* (*sentimentos*) to give vent to ♦ *vi*: ~ (com) to unburden o.s. (to); ~-se *vr*: ~-se (com) to unburden o.s. (to); **desabafo** [dʒiza'bafu] *m* confession

desabalado/a [dʒizaba'ladu/a] *adj*: sair/ correr ~ to rush out/run headlong

desabamento [dʒizaba'mẽtu] *m* collapse

desabar [dʒiza'ba*] *vi* (*edifício, ponte*) to collapse; (*chuva*) to pour down; (*tempestade*) to break

desabitado/a [dʒizabi'tadu/a] *adj* uninhabited

desabotoar [dʒizabo'twa*] *vt* to unbutton

desabrigado/a [dʒizabri'gadu/a] *adj* (*sem casa*) homeless; (*exposto*) exposed

desabrochar [dʒizabro'ʃa*] *vi* (*flores, fig*) to blossom

desabusado/a [dʒizabu'zadu/a] *adj* unprejudiced; (*atrevido*) impudent

desacatar [dʒizaka'ta*] *vt* (*desrespeitar*) to have ou show no respect for; (*afrontar*) to defy; (*desprezar*) to scorn; **desacato** [dʒiza'katu] *m* disrespect; (*desprezo*) disregard

desacerto [dʒiza'sextu] *m* mistake, blunder

desacompanhado/a [dʒizakõpa'ɲadu/a] *adj* on one's own, alone

desaconselhar [dʒizakõse'ʎa*] *vt*: ~ algo (a alguém) to advise (sb) against sth

desacordado/a [dʒizakox'dadu/a] *adj* unconscious

desacordo [dʒiza'koxdu] *m* disagreement; (*desarmonia*) discord

desacostumado/a [dʒizakoʃtumadu/a] *adj*: ~ (a) unaccustomed (to)

desacreditar [dʒizakredʒi'ta*] *vt* to discredit; ~-se *vr* to lose one's reputation

desafiador(a) [dʒizafja'do*(a)] *adj* challenging; (*pessoa*) defiant ♦ *m/f* challenger

desafiar [dʒiza'fja*] *vt* to challenge; (*afrontar*) to defy

desafinado/a [dʒizafi'nadu/a] *adj* out of tune

desafio [dʒiza'fiu] *m* challenge; (*PT: ESPORTE*) match, game

desafogado/a [dʒizafo'gadu/a] *adj* (*desimpedido*) clear; (*desembaraçado*) free

desafogar [dʒizafo'ga*] *vt* (*libertar*) to free; (*desapertar*) to relieve; (*desabafar*) to give vent to; ~-se *vr* to free o.s.; (*desabafar-se*) to unburden o.s.

desafogo [dʒiza'fogu] *m* relief; (*folga*) leisure

desaforado/a [dʒizafo'radu/a] *adj* rude, insolent

desaforo [dʒiza'foru] *m* insolence, abuse

desafortunado/a [dʒizafoxtu'nadu/a] *adj* unfortunate, unlucky

desagradar [dʒizagra'da*] *vt* to displease ♦ *vi*: ~ a alguém to displease sb; **desagradável** [dʒizagra'davew] (*pl* -eis) *adj* unpleasant; **desagrado** [dʒiza'gradu] *m* displeasure

desagravo [dʒiza'gravu] *m* amends *pl*

desaguar [dʒiza'gwa*] *vt* to drain ♦ *vi*: ~ (em) to flow ou empty (into)

desajeitado/a [dʒizaʒej'tadu/a] *adj* clumsy, awkward

desajuste [dʒiza'ʒuʃtʃi] *m* (*mecânico*) problem

desalentado/a [dʒizalẽ'tadu/a] *adj* disheartened

desalentar [dʒizalẽ'ta*] *vt* to discourage; (*deprimir*) to depress; **desalento** [dʒiza'lẽtu] *m* discouragement

desalinhado/a [dʒizali'ɲadu/a] *adj* untidy

desalinho [dʒiza'liɲu] *m* untidiness

desalmado/a [dʒizaw'madu/a] *adj* cruel, inhuman

desalojar [dʒizalo'ʒa*] *vt* (*expulsar*) to oust; ~-se *vr* to move out

desamarrar [dʒizama'xa*] *vt* to untie ♦ *vi* (*NÁUT*) to cast off

desamassar [dʒizama'sa*] *vt* (*papel*) to smooth out; (*chapéu etc*) to straighten out; (*carro*) to beat out

desambientado/a [dʒizãbjẽ'tadu/a] *adj* unsettled

desamor [dʒiza'mo*] *m* dislike

desamparado/a [dʒizãpa'radu/a] *adj* abandoned; (*sem apoio*) helpless

desamparar [dʒizãpa'ra*] *vt* to abandon

desanimação [dʒizanima'sãw] *f* dejection

desanimado/a [dʒizani'madu/a] *adj* (*pessoa*) fed up, dispirited; (*festa*) dull; ser ~ (*pessoa*) to be apathetic

desanimar [dʒizani'ma*] *vt* to dishearten; (*desencorajar*): ~ (de fazer) to discourage (from doing) ♦ *vi* to lose heart; to be discouraging; ~ de fazer algo to lose the will to do sth; (*desistir*) to give up doing sth

desanuviar [dʒizanu'vja*] *vt* (*céu*) to clear; ~-se *vr* to clear; (*fig*) to stop; ~ alguém to put sb's mind at rest

desapaixonado/a [dʒizapajʃo'nadu/a] *adj* dispassionate

desaparafusar [dʒizaparafu'za*] *vt* to unscrew

desaparecer [dʒizapare'se*] *vi* to disappear, vanish; **desaparecido/a**

[dʒizapare'sidu/a] adj lost, missing ♦ m/f missing person; **desaparecimento** [dʒizaparesi'mẽtu] m disappearance; (falecimento) death

desapegado/a [dʒizape'gadu/a] adj indifferent, detached

desapego [dʒiza'pegu] m indifference, detachment

desapercebido/a [dʒizapexse'bidu/a] adj unnoticed

desapertar [dʒizapex'ta*] vt to loosen; (livrar) to free

desapiedado/a [dʒizapje'dadu/a] adj pitiless, ruthless

desapontador(a) [dʒizapõta'do*(a)] adj disappointing

desapontamento [dʒizapõta'mẽtu] m disappointment

desapontar [dʒizapõ'ta*] vt to disappoint

desapropriar [dʒizapro'prja*] vt (bens) to expropriate; (pessoa) to dispossess

desaprovação [dʒizaprova'sãw] f disapproval

desaprovar [dʒizapro'va*] vt to disapprove of; (censurar) to object to

desarmamento [dʒizaxma'mẽtu] m disarmament

desarmar [dʒizax'ma*] vt to disarm; (desmontar) to dismantle; (bomba) to defuse

desarmonia [dʒizaxmo'nia] f discord

desarranjado/a [dʒizaxã'ʒadu/a] adj (intestino) upset; (TEC) out of order; **estar ~** (pessoa) to have diarrhoea (BRIT) ou diarrhea (US)

desarranjar [dʒizaxã'ʒa*] vt to upset, disturb; (desordenar) to mess up; **desarranjo** [dʒiza'xãʒu] m disorder; (enguiço) breakdown; (diarréia) diarrhoea (BRIT), diarrhea (US)

desarrumado/a [dʒizaxu'madu/a] adj untidy, messy

desarrumar [dʒizaxu'ma*] vt to mess up; (mala) to unpack

desarticular [dʒizaxtʃiku'la*] vt (articulação) to dislocate

desassociar [dʒizaso'sja*] vt to disassociate

desassossego [dʒizaso'segu] m (inquietação) disquiet; (perturbação) restlessness

desastrado/a [dʒizaʃ'tradu/a] adj clumsy

desastre [dʒi'zaʃtri] m disaster; (acidente) accident; (de avião) crash; **desastroso/a** [dʒizaʃ'trozu/ɔza] adj disastrous

desatar [dʒiza'ta*] vt (nó) to undo, untie ♦ vi: **~ a fazer** to begin to do; **~ a chorar** to burst into tears; **~ a rir** to burst out laughing

desatencioso/a [dʒizatẽ'sjozu/ɔza] adj inattentive; (descortês) impolite

desatento/a [dʒiza'tẽtu/a] adj inattentive

desatinado/a [dʒizatʃi'nadu/a] adj crazy, wild ♦ m/f lunatic

desatino [dʒiza'tʃinu] m madness; (ato) folly

desativar [dʒizatʃi'va*] vt (firma, usina) to shut down; (veículos) to withdraw from service; (bomba) to deactivate, defuse

desatualizado/a [dʒizatwali'zadu/a] adj out of date; (pessoa) out of touch

desavença [dʒiza'vẽsa] f (briga) quarrel; (discórdia) disagreement; **em ~** at loggerheads

desavergonhado/a [dʒizavexgo'ɲadu/a] adj shameless

desavisado/a [dʒizavi'zadu/a] adj careless

desbancar [dʒiʒbã'ka*] vt: **~ alguém (em algo)** to outdo sb (in sth)

desbaratar [dʒiʒbara'ta*] vt to ruin; (desperdiçar) to waste, squander; (vencer) to crush; (pôr em desordem) to mess up

desbastar [dʒiʒbaʃ'ta*] vt (cabelo, plantas) to thin (out); (vegetação) to trim

desbocado/a [dʒiʒbo'kadu/a] adj foulmouthed

desbotar [dʒiʒbo'ta*] vt to discolour (BRIT), discolor (US) ♦ vi to fade

desbragadamente [dʒiʒbragada'mẽtʃi] adv (beber) to excess; (mentir) blatantly

desbravador(a) [dʒiʒbrava'do*(a)] m/f explorer

desbravar [dʒiʒbra'va*] vt (terras desconhecidas) to explore

descabelar [dʒiʃkabe'la*] vt: **~ alguém** to mess up sb's hair; **~-se** vr to get one's hair messed up

descabido/a [dʒiʃka'bidu/a] adj improper; (inoportuno) inappropriate

descalçar [dʒiʃkaw'sa*] vt (sapatos) to take off; **~-se** vr to take off one's shoes

descalço/a [dʒiʃ'kawsu/a] adj barefoot

descampado [dʒiʃkã'padu] m open country

descansado/a [dʒiʃkã'sadu/a] adj calm, quiet; (vagaroso) slow; **fique ~** don't worry; **pode ficar ~ que ...** you can rest assured that ...

descansar [dʒiʃkã'sa*] vt to rest; (apoiar) to lean ♦ vi to rest; to lean; **descanso** [dʒiʃ'kãsu] m rest; (folga) break; (para prato) mat

descarado/a [dʒiʃka'radu/a] adj cheeky, impudent

descaramento [dʒiʃkara'mẽtu] m cheek, impudence

descarga [dʒiʃ'kaxga] f unloading; (MIL) volley; (ELET) discharge; (de vaso sanitário) **dar a ~** to flush the toilet

descarnado/a [dʒiʃkax'nadu/a] adj scrawny, skinny

descarregadouro [dʒiʃkaxega'doru] m wharf

descarregamento [dʒiʃkaxega'mẽtu] m (de carga) unloading; (ELET) discharge

descarregar [dʒiʃkaxe'ga*] vt (carga) to unload; (ELET) to discharge; (aliviar) to relieve; (raiva) to vent, give vent to; (arma) to fire ♦ vi to unload; (bateria)

to run out; ~ **a raiva em alguém** to
take it out on sb

descarrilhamento [dʒiʃkaxiʎa'mẽtu] *m*
derailment

descarrilhar [dʒiʃkaxi'ʎa*] *vt* to derail ♦
vi to run off the rails; (*fig*) to go off the
rails

descartar [dʒiʃkax'ta*] *vt* to discard; ~-
se *vr*: ~-**se de** to get rid of; **descartável** [dʒiʃkax'tavew] (*pl* ~**eis**) disposable

descascador [dʒiʃkaʃka'do*] *m* peeler

descascar [dʒiʃkaʃ'ka*] *vt* (*fruta*) to peel;
(*ervilhas*) to shell ♦ *vi* (*depois do sol*) to
peel; (*cobra*) to shed its skin

descaso [dʒiʃ'kazu] *m* disregard

descendência [desẽ'dẽsja] *f* descendants
pl, offspring *pl*

descendente [desẽ'dẽtʃi] *adj* descending,
going down ♦ *m/f* descendant

descender [desẽ'de*] *vi*: ~ **de** to descend from

descer [de'se*] *vt* (*escada*) to go (*ou*
come) down; (*bagagem*) to take down ♦
vi (*saltar*) to get off; (*baixar*) to go (*ou*
come) down; **descida** [de'sida] *f* descent;
(*declive*) slope; (*abaixamento*) fall, drop

desclassificar [dʒisklasifi'ka*] *vt* to disqualify; (*desacreditar*) to discredit

descoberta [dʒiʃko'bexta] *f* discovery;
(*invenção*) invention

descoberto/a [dʒiʃko'bextu/a] *pp de* **descobrir** ♦ *adj* bare, naked; (*exposto*) exposed ♦ *m* overdraft; **a ~** openly; **conta
a ~** overdrawn account; **pôr** *ou* **sacar
a ~** (*conta*) to overdraw

descobridor(a) [dʒiʃkobri'do*(a)] *m/f*
discoverer; (*explorador*) explorer

descobrimento [dʒiʃkobri'mẽtu] *m* discovery

descobrir [dʒiʃko'bri*] *vt* to discover;
(*tirar a cobertura de*) to uncover; (*panela*) to take the lid off; (*averiguar*) to
find out; (*enigma*) to solve

descolar [dʒiʃko'la*] *vt* to unstick ♦ *vi*:
a criança não descola da mãe the
child won't leave his (*ou* her) mother's
side

descolorante [dʒiʃkolo'rãtʃi] *m* bleach

descolorar [dʒiʃkolo'ra*] *vt*, *vi* = **descorar**

descolorir [dʒiʃkolo'ri*] *vt* to discolour
(*BRIT*), discolor (*US*); (*cabelo*) to bleach
♦ *vi* to fade

descompor (*irreg: como* **pôr**) *vt* to dis-
arrange; (*insultar*) to abuse; (*repreender*)
to scold, tell off; (*fisionomia*) to distort,
twist

descomposto/a [dʒiʃkõ'poʃtu/'poʃta] *adj*
(*desalinhado*) dishevelled; (*fisionomia*)
twisted

descompostura [dʒiʃkõpoʃ'tura] *f* (*repreensão*) dressing-down; (*insulto*) abuse;
passar uma ~ em alguém to give sb a
dressing-down; to hurl abuse at sb

descomunal [dʒiʃkomu'naw] (*pl* ~**ais**) *adj*

extraordinary; (*colossal*) huge, enormous

desconcentrar [dʒiʃkõsẽ'tra*] *vt* to distract; ~-**se** *vr* to lose one's concentration

desconcertar [dʒiʃkõsex'ta*] *vt* to confuse, baffle; ~-**se** *vr* to get upset

desconexo/a [dʒiʃko'nɛksu/a] *adj* (*desu-
nido*) disconnected, unrelated; (*incoerente*) incoherent

desconfiado/a [dʒiʃkõ'fjadu/a] *adj* suspicious, distrustful ♦ *m/f* suspicious person

desconfiança [dʒiʃkõ'fjãsa] *f* suspicion,
distrust

desconfiar [dʒiʃkõ'fja*] *vi* to be suspicious; ~ **de alguém** (*não ter confiança
em*) to distrust sb; (*suspeitar*) to suspect
sb; ~ **que ...** to have the feeling that ...

desconforme [dʒiʃkõ'fɔxmi] *adj* in disagreement, at variance

desconfortável [dʒiʃkõfox'tavew] (*pl*
~**eis**) *adj* uncomfortable

desconforto [dʒiʃkõ'foxtu] *m* discomfort

descongelar [dʒiʃkõʒe'la*] *vt* to thaw
out; ~-**se** *vr* to melt

descongestionar [dʒiʃkõʒeʃtʃjo'na*] *vt*
(*cabeça, trânsito*) to clear

desconhecer [dʒiʃkoɲe'se*] *vt* (*ignorar*)
not to know; (*não reconhecer*) not to recognize; (*um benefício*) not to acknowledge; (*não admitir*) not to accept;
desconhecido/a [dʒiʃkoɲe'sidu/a] *adj*
unknown ♦ *m/f* stranger; **desconheci-
mento** [dʒiʃkoɲesi'mẽtu] *m* ignorance

desconjuntado/a [dʒiʃkõʒũ'tadu/a] *adj*
disjointed; (*articulação*) dislocated

desconjuntar [dʒiʃkõʒũ'ta*] *vt* (*articulação*) to dislocate; ~-**se** *vr* to come apart

desconsolado/a [dʒiʃkõso'ladu/a] *adj*
miserable, disconsolate

desconsolar [dʒiʃkõso'la*] *vt* to sadden,
depress; ~-**se** *vr* to despair

descontar [dʒiʃkõ'ta*] *vt* to deduct; (*não
levar em conta*) to discount; (*não fazer
caso de*) to make light of

descontentamento [dʒiʃkõtẽta'mẽtu] *m*
discontent; (*desprazer*) displeasure

descontentar [dʒiʃkõtẽ'ta*] *vt* to displease; **descontente** [dʒiʃkõ'tẽtʃi]* *adj*
discontented, dissatisfied

descontínuo/a [dʒiʃkõ'tʃinwu/a] *adj* broken

desconto [dʒiʃ'kõtu] *m* discount; **com** ~
at a discount; **dar um** ~ **(para)** (*fig*) to
make allowances (for)

descontraído/a [dʒiʃkõtra'idu/a] *adj* casual, relaxed

descontrair [dʒiʃkõtra'i*] *vt* to relax; ~-
se *vr* to relax

descontrolar-se [dʒiʃkõtro'laxsi] *vr* (*situação*) to get out of control; (*pessoa*) to
lose one's self-control

desconversar [dʒiʃkõvex'sa*] *vi* to
change the subject

descorar [dʒiʃko'ra*] *vt* to discolour

(BRIT), discolor (US) ♦ vi to pale, fade

descortês/esa [dʒiʃkox'teʃ/teza] adj rude, impolite; **descortesia** [dʒiʃkoxte'zia] f rudeness, impoliteness

descortinar [dʒiʃkoxtʃi'na*] vt (retrato) to unveil; (avistar) to catch sight of; (notar) to notice

descoser [dʒiʃko'ze*] vt (descosturar) to unstitch; (rasgar) to rip apart; ~-se to come apart at the seams

descrença [dʒiʃ'krẽsa] f disbelief, incredulity

descrente [dʒiʃ'krẽtʃi] adj sceptical (BRIT), skeptical (US) ♦ m/f sceptic (BRIT), skeptic (US)

descrer [dʒiʃ'kre*] (irreg: como crer) vt to disbelieve ♦ vi: ~ de not to believe in

descrever [dʒiʃkre've*] vt to describe

descrição [dʒiʃkri'sãw] (pl –ões) f description; **descritivo/a** [dʒiʃkri'tʃivu/a] adj descriptive

descrito/a [dʒiʃ'kritu/a] pp de descrever

descubro etc [dʒiʃ'kubru] vb V descobrir

descuidado/a [dʒiʃkwi'dadu/a] adj careless

descuidar [dʒiʃkwi'da*] vt to neglect ♦ vi: ~ de to neglect, disregard; **descuido** [dʒiʃ'kwidu] m carelessness; (negligência) neglect; (erro) oversight, slip; **por descuido** inadvertently

desculpa [dʒiʃ'kuwpa] f excuse; (perdão) pardon; **pedir ~s a alguém por ou de algo** to apologise to sb for sth; ~r [dʒiʃkuw'pa*] vt to excuse; (perdoar) to pardon, forgive; ~r-se vr to apologize; ~r algo a alguém to forgive sb for sth; **desculpe!** (I'm) sorry, I beg your pardon; **desculpável** [dʒiʃkuw'pavew] (pl –eis) adj forgivable

---
PALAVRA CHAVE
---

desde ['deʒdʒi] prep 1 (lugar): ~ ... até ... from ... to ...; **andamos ~ a praia até o restaurante** we walked from the beach to the restaurant

2 (tempo: + adv, n): ~ **então** from then on, ever since; ~ **já** (de agora) from now on; (imediatamente) at once, right now; ~ **o casamento** since the wedding

3 (tempo: + vb) since; for; **conhecemo-nos ~ 1978/há 20 anos** we've known each other since 1978/for 20 years; **não o vejo ~ 1983** I haven't seen him since 1983

4 (variedade): ~ **os mais baratos até os mais luxuosos** from the cheapest to the most luxurious

♦ conj: ~ **que** since; ~ **que comecei a trabalhar não o vi mais** I haven't seen him since I started work; **não saiu de casa ~ que chegou** he hasn't been out since he arrived

---

desdém [deʒ'dẽ] m scorn, disdain

desdenhar [deʒde'ɲa*] vt to scorn, disdain

desdenhoso/a [deʒdeɲozu/ɔza] adj disdainful, scornful

desdita [deʒ'dʒita] f misfortune; (infelicidade) unhappiness

desdizer [dʒiʒdʒi'ze*] (irreg: como dizer) vt to contradict; ~-se vr to go back on one's word

desdobrar [dʒiʒdo'bra*] vt (abrir) to unfold; (esforços) to increase, redouble; (tropas) to deploy; (bandeira) to unfurl; (dividir em grupos) to split up; ~-se vr to unfold; (empenhar-se) to work hard, make a big effort

desejar [dese'ʒa*] vt to want, desire; ~ **ardentemente** to long for; **que deseja?** what would you like?; **desejável** [dese'ʒavew] (pl –eis) adj desirable

desejo [de'zeʒu] m wish, desire; ~so/a [deze'ʒozu/ɔza] adj: ~so de algo wishing for sth; ~so de fazer keen to do

desemaranhar [dʒizimara'ɲa*] vt to disentangle

desembaraçado/a [dʒizẽbara'sadu/a] adj (livre) free, clear; (desinibido) uninhibited, free and easy; (expedito) efficient; (cabelo) untangled

desembaraçar [dʒizẽbara'sa*] vt (livrar) to free; (cabelo) to untangle; ~-se vr (desinibir-se) to lose one's inhibitions; ~-se de to get rid of

desembaraço [dʒizẽba'rasu] m liveliness; (facilidade) ease; (confiança) self-assurance

desembarcar [dʒizẽbax'ka*] vt (carga) to unload; (passageiros) to let off ♦ vi to disembark; **desembarque** [dʒizẽ'baxki] m landing, disembarkation; **"desembarque"** (no aeroporto) "arrivals"

desembocadura [dʒizẽboka'dura] f mouth

desembocar [dʒizẽbo'ka*] vi: ~ **em** (rio) to flow into; (rua) to lead into

desembolsar [dʒizẽbow'sa*] vt to spend; **desembolso** [dʒizẽ'bowsu] m expenditure

desembrulhar [dʒizẽbru'ʎa*] vt to unwrap

desempacotar [dʒizẽpako'ta*] vt to unpack

desempatar [dʒizẽpa'ta*] vt to decide ♦ vi to decide the match (ou race etc); **desempate** [dʒizẽ'patʃi] m: **partida de desempate** (jogo) play-off, decider

desempenhar [dʒizẽpe'ɲa*] vt (cumprir) to carry out, fulfil (BRIT), fulfill (US); (papel) to play; **desempenho** [dʒizẽ'peɲu] m performance; (de obrigações etc) fulfilment (BRIT), fulfillment (US)

desemperrar [dʒizẽpe'xa*] vt, vi to loosen

desempregado/a [dʒizẽ'pre'gadu/a] *adj*
unemployed ♦ *m/f* unemployed person

desempregar-se [dʒizẽpre'gaxsi] *vr* to
lose one's job

desemprego [dʒizẽ'pregu] *m* unemployment

desencadear [dʒizẽka'dʒia*] *vt* to unleash; (*despertar*) to provoke, trigger off
♦ *vi* (*chuva*) to pour; ~**-se** *vr* to break
loose; (*tempestade*) to break

desencaixar [dʒizẽkaj'ʃa*] *vt* to put out
of joint; (*deslocar*) to dislodge; ~**-se** *vr*
to become dislodged

desencaixotar [dʒizẽkajʃo'ta*] *vt* to unpack

desencantar [dʒizẽkã'ta*] *vt* to dis-
enchant; (*desiludir*) to disillusion

desencargo [dʒizẽ'kaxgu] *m* fulfilment
(*BRIT*), fulfillment (*US*)

desencarregar-se [dʒizẽkaxe'gaxsi] *vr*
(*de obrigação*) to discharge o.s.

desencontrar-se [dʒizẽkõ'traxsi] *vr* (*não
se encontrar*) to miss each other;
(*perder-se um do outro*: *perder-se*) to lose
each other; ~ **de** to miss; to get se-
parated from

desencorajar [dʒizẽkora'ʒa*] *vt* to discourage

desencostar [dʒizẽkoʃ'ta*] *vt* to move
away; ~**-se** *vr*: ~**-se de** to move away
from

desenferrujar [dʒizẽfexu'ʒa*] *vt* (*pernas*)
to stretch; (*língua*) to brush up

desenfreado/a [dʒizẽ'frjadu/a] *adj* wild

desenganado/a [dʒizẽga'nadu/a] *adj* incurable; (*desiludido*) disillusioned

desenganar [dʒizẽga'na*] *vt*: ~ **alguém**
to disillusion sb; (*de falsas crenças*) to
open sb's eyes; (*doente*) to give up hope
of curing; ~**-se** *vr* to become disillusioned; (*sair de erro*) to realize the
truth; **desengano** [dʒizẽ'ganu] *m* disillu-
sionment; (*desapontamento*) disappointment

desengonçado/a [dʒizẽgõ'sadu/a] *adj*
(*mal-seguro*) rickety; (*pessoa*) ungainly

desengrenado/a [dʒizẽgre'nadu/a] *adj*
(*AUTO*) out of gear, in neutral

desengrossar [dʒizẽgro'sa*] *vt* to thin

desenhar [deze'na*] *vt* to draw; (*TEC*) to
design; ~**-se** *vr* (*destacar-se*) to stand
out; (*figurar-se*) to take shape; **desenhista** [deze'niʃta] *m/f* (*TEC*) designer

desenho [de'zɛɲu] *m* drawing; (*modelo*)
design; (*esboço*) sketch; (*plano*) plan; ~
animado cartoon

desenlace [dʒizẽ'lasi] *m* outcome

desenredar [dʒizẽxe'da*] *vt* to disentangle; (*mistério*) to unravel; (*questão*) to
sort out, resolve; (*dúvida*) to clear up;
(*explicação*) to clarify; ~**-se** *vr*: ~**-se de
algo** to extricate o.s. from sth; ~ **alguém de algo** to extricate sb from sth

desenrolar [dʒizẽxo'la*] *vt* to unroll;
(*narrativa*) to develop; ~**-se** *vr* to unfold

desentender [dʒizẽtẽ'de*] *vt* to misunderstand; ~**-se** *vr*: ~**-se com** to have a
disagreement with; **desentendido/a**
[dʒizẽtẽ'dʒidu/a] *adj*: **fazer-se de desentendido** to pretend not to understand;
desentendimento [dʒizẽtẽdʒi'mẽtu] *m*
misunderstanding

desenterrar [dʒizẽte'xa*] *vt* (*cadáver*) to
exhume; (*tesouro*) to dig up; (*descobrir*)
to bring to light

desentoado/a [dʒizẽ'twadu/a] *adj* out of
tune

desentupir [dʒizẽtu'pi*] *vt* to unblock

desenvolto/a [dʒizẽ'vowtu/a] *adj* self-
assured, confident; (*desinibido*) uninhibited; **desenvoltura** [dʒizẽvow'tura] *f*
self-confidence

desenvolver [dʒizẽvow've*] *vt* to develop; ~**-se** *vr* to develop; **desenvolvimento** [dʒizẽvowvi'mẽtu] *m* development; (*crescimento*) growth; **país em desenvolvimento** developing country

desequilibrado/a [dʒizekili'bradu/a] *adj*
unbalanced

desequilibrar [dʒizekili'bra*] *vt* (*pessoa*)
to throw off balance; (*objeto*) to tip
over; (*fig*) to unbalance; ~**-se** *vr* to lose
one's balance; to tip over

deserção [dezex'sãw] *f* desertion

desertar [desex'ta*] *vt* to desert, abandon
♦ *vi* to desert; **deserto/a** [de'zextu/a] *adj*
deserted ♦ *m* desert; **desertor(a)** [de-
zex'to*(a)] *m/f* deserter

desesperado/a [dʒizeʃpe'radu/a] *adj* desperate; (*furioso*) furious

desesperador(a) [dʒizeʃpera'do*(a)] *adj*
desperate; (*enfurecedor*) maddening

desesperança [dʒizeʃpe'rãsa] *f* despair

desesperar [dʒizeʃpe'ra*] *vt* to drive to
despair; (*enfurecer*) to infuriate; ~**-se** *vr*
to despair; (*enfurecer-se*) to become in-
furiated; **desespero** [dʒizeʃ'peru] *m* despair, desperation; (*raiva*) fury

desestimular [dʒizeʃtʃimu'la*] *vt* to discourage

desfalcar [dʒiʃfaw'ka*] *vt* (*dinheiro*) to
embezzle; (*reduzir*) ~ **(de)** to reduce
(by); **a jogo está desfalcado** the game
is incomplete

desfalecer [dʒiʃfale'se*] *vt* (*enfraquecer*)
to weaken ♦ *vi* (*enfraquecer*) to weaken;
(*desmaiar*) to faint

desfalque [dʒiʃ'fawki] *m* (*de dinheiro*)
embezzlement; (*diminuição*) reduction

desfavorável [dʒiʃfavo'ravew] (*pl* –**eis**)
adj unfavourable (*BRIT*), unfavorable
(*US*)

desfazer [dʒiʃfa'ze*] (*irreg*: *como* **fazer**)
vt (*costura*) to undo; (*dúvidas*) to dispel;
(*agravo*) to redress; (*grupo*) to break up;
(*contrato*) to dissolve; (*noivado*) to break
off ♦ *vi*: ~ **de alguém** to belittle sb;
~**-se** *vr* to vanish; (*tecido*) to come to
pieces; (*grupo*) to break up; (*vaso*) to
break; ~**-se de** (*livrar-se*) to get rid of

~**-se em lágrimas/gentilezas** to burst into tears/go out of one's way to please

desfechar [dʒiʃfe'ʃaˈ] vt (disparar) to fire; (setas) to shoot; (golpe) to deal; (insultos) to hurl

desfecho [dʒiʃ'feʃu] m ending, outcome

desfeita [dʒiʃ'fejta] f affront, insult

desfeito/a [dʒiʃ'fejtu/a] adj undone; (cama) unmade; (contrato) broken

desfiar [dʒiʃ'fjaˈ] vt (tecido) to unravel; (CULIN: galinha) to tear into thin shreds; ~**-se** vr to become frayed; ~ **o rosário** to say one's rosary

desfigurar [dʒiʃfigu'raˈ] vt (pessoa, cidade) to disfigure; (texto) to mutilate; ~**-se** vr to be disfigured

desfiladeiro [dʒiʃfila'dejru] m (de montanha) pass

desfilar [dʒiʃfi'laˈ] vi to parade; **desfile** [dʒiʃ'fili] m parade, procession

desforra [dʒiʃ'fɔxa] f revenge; (reparação) redress; **tirar** ~ to get even

desfrutar [dʒiʃfru'taˈ] vt to enjoy ♦ vi: ~ **de** to enjoy

desgarrado/a [dʒiʒga'xadu/a] adj stray; (navio) off course

desgarrar-se [dʒiʒga'xaxsi] vr: ~ **de** to stray from

desgastante [dʒiʒgaʃ'tãtʃi] adj (fig) stressful

desgastar [dʒiʒgaʃ'taˈ] vt to wear away, erode; (pessoa) to wear out, get down; ~**-se** vr to be worn away; (pessoa) to get worn out; **desgaste** [dʒiʒ'gaʃtʃi] m wear and tear; (mental) stress

desgostar [dʒiʒgoʃ'taˈ] vt to upset ♦ vi: ~ **de** to dislike; ~**-se** vr: ~**-se de** to go off; ~**-se com** to take offence at; **desgosto** [dʒiʒ'goʃtu] m displeasure; (pesar) sorrow, unhappiness

desgraça [dʒiʒ'grasa] f misfortune; (miséria) misery; (desfavor) disgrace; ~**do/a** [dʒiʒgra'sadu/a] adj poor ♦ m/f wretch; **estou com uma gripe desgraçada** (col) I've got a hell of a cold; ~**r** [dʒiʒgra'saˈ] vt to disgrace

desgrenhado/a [dʒiʒgre'ɲadu/a] adj dishevelled, tousled

desgrudar [dʒiʒgru'daˈ] vt to unstick ♦ vi: ~ **de** to tear o.s. away from; ~ **algo de algo** to take sth off sth

desidratar [dʒizidra'taˈ] vt to dehydrate

design [dʒi'zãjn] m design

designação [dezigna'sãw] (pl -ões) f designation; (nomeação) appointment

designar [dezig'naˈ] vt to designate; (nomear) to name, appoint; (dia, data) to fix

designer [dʒi'zajne] (pl ~s) m/f designer

desigual [dezi'gwaw] (pl -ais) adj unequal; (terreno) uneven; ~**dade** [dʒizigwaw'dadʒi] f inequality

desiludir [dʒizilu'dʒiˈ] vt to disillusion; (causar decepção a) to disappoint; ~**-se** vr to lose one's illusions

desimpedido/a [dʒizĩpe'dʒidu/a] adj free

desimpedir [dʒizĩpe'dʒiˈ] vt to unblock; (trânsito) to ease

desinfetante [dʒizĩfe'tãtʃi] (PT -ct-) adj, m disinfectant

desinfetar [dʒizĩfe'taˈ] (PT -ct-) vt to disinfect

desintegração [dʒizĩtegra'sãw] f disintegration, break-up

desintegrar [dʒizĩte'graˈ] vt to separate; ~**-se** vr to disintegrate, fall to pieces

desinteressado/a [dʒizĩtere'sadu/a] adj disinterested

desinteressar [dʒizĩtere'saˈ] vt: ~ **alguém de algo** to make sb lose interest in sth; ~**-se** vr to lose interest; **desinteresse** [dʒizĩte'resi] m lack of interest

desistir [deziʃ'tʃiˈ] vi to give up; ~ **de fumar** to stop smoking; **ele ia, mas no final desistiu** he was going, but in the end he gave up the idea ou he decided not to

desjejum [dʒiʒe'ʒũ] m breakfast

deslavado/a [dʒiʒla'vadu/a] adj (pessoa, atitude) shameless; (mentira) blatant

desleal [dʒiʒle'aw] (pl -ais) adj disloyal

desleixado/a [dʒiʒlej'ʃadu/a] adj sloppy

desleixo [dʒiʒ'lejʃu] m sloppiness

desligado/a [dʒiʒli'gadu/a] adj (eletricidade) off; (pessoa) absent-minded; **estar** ~ to be miles away

desligar [dʒiʒli'gaˈ] vt (TEC) to disconnect; (luz, TV, motor) to switch off; (telefone) to hang up; ~**-se** vr: ~**-se de algo** (afastar-se) to leave sth; (problemas etc) to turn one's back on sth; **não desligue** (TEL) hold the line

deslizar [dʒiʒli'zaˈ] vi to slide; (por acidente) to slip; (passar de leve) to glide; **deslize** [dʒiʒ'lizi] m lapse; (escorregadela) slip

deslocado/a [dʒiʒlo'kadu/a] adj (membro) dislocated; (desambientado) out of place

deslocar [dʒiʒlo'kaˈ] vt to move; (articulação) to dislocate; (funcionário) to transfer; ~**-se** vr to move; to be dislocated

deslumbramento [dʒiʒlũbra'mẽtu] m dazzle; (fascinação) fascination

deslumbrante [dʒiʒlũ'brãtʃi] adj dazzling; (casa, festa) amazing

deslumbrar [dʒiʒlũ'braˈ] vt to dazzle; (maravilhar) to amaze; (fascinar) to fascinate ♦ vi to be dazzling; to be amazing; ~**-se** vr: ~**-se com** to be fascinated by

desmaiado/a [dʒiʒma'jadu/a] adj unconscious; (cor) pale

desmaiar [dʒiʒma'jaˈ] vi to faint; **desmaio** [dʒiʒ'maju] m faint

desmamar [dʒiʒma'maˈ] vt to wean

desmancha-prazeres [dʒiʒ'manʃa-] m/f inv kill-joy, spoilsport

desmanchar [dʒiʒman'ʃaˈ] vt (costura) to

undo; (*contrato*) to break; (*noivado*) to break off; (*penteado*) to mess up; **~-se** *vr* (*costura*) to come undone

desmarcar [dʒiʒmaxˈkaˣ] *vt* (*compromisso*) to cancel

desmascarar [dʒiʒmaʃkaˈraˣ] *vt* to unmask

desmazelado/a [dʒiʒmazeˈladu/a] *adj* slovenly, untidy

desmedido/a [dʒiʒmeˈdʒidu/a] *adj* excessive

desmentido [dʒiʒmẽˈtʃidu] *m* (*negação*) denial; (*contradição*) contradiction

desmentir [dʒiʒmẽˈtʃiˣ] *vt* (*contradizer*) to contradict; (*negar*) to deny

desmerecer [dʒiʒmereˈseˣ] *vt* (*não merecer*) not to deserve; (*desfazer de*) to belittle

desmesurado/a [dʒiʒmezuˈradu/a] *adj* immense, enormous

desmiolado/a [dʒiʒmjoˈladu/a] *adj* brainless; (*esquecido*) forgetful

desmontar [dʒiʒmõˈtaˣ] *vt* (*máquina*) to take to pieces ♦ *vi* (*do cavalo*) to dismount, get off

desmoronamento [dʒiʒmoronaˈmẽtu] *m* collapse

desmoronar [dʒiʒmoroˈnaˣ] *vt* to knock down ♦ *vi* to collapse

desnatado/a [dʒiʒnaˈtadu/a] *adj* (*leite*) skimmed

desnaturado/a [dʒiʒnatuˈradu/a] *adj* inhumane ♦ *m/f* monster

desnecessário/a [dʒiʒneseˈsarju/a] *adj* unnecessary

desnível [dʒiʒˈnivew] *m* unevenness; (*fig*) difference

desnudar [dʒiʒnuˈdaˣ] *vt* to strip; (*revelar*) to expose; **~-se** *vr* to undress

desnutrição [dʒiʒnutriˈsãw] *f* malnutrition

desobedecer [dʒiʒobedeˈseˣ] *vt* to disobey; **desobediência** [dʒiʒobeˈdʒjẽsja] *f* disobedience; **desobediente** [dʒiʒobeˈdʒjẽtʃi] *adj* disobedient

desobrigar [dʒiʒobriˈgaˣ] *vt*: ~ (**de**) to free (from); ~ **de fazer algo** to free from doing sth

desobstruir [dʒiʒobiʃˈtrwiˣ] *vt* to unblock

desocupado/a [dʒiʒokuˈpadu/a] *adj* (*casa*) empty, vacant; (*disponível*) free; (*sem trabalho*) unemployed

desocupar [dʒiʒokuˈpaˣ] *vt* (*casa*) to vacate; (*liberar*) to free

desodorante [dʒizodoˈrãtʃi] (*PT - dorizante*) *m* deodorant

desolação [dʒizolaˈsãw] *f* (*consternação*) grief; (*de um lugar*) desolation; **desolado/a** [dʒezoˈladu/a] *adj* distressed, desolate

desolar [dezoˈlaˣ] *vt* to distress; (*lugar*) to devastate

desonesto/a [dezoˈnɛʃtu/a] *adj* dishonest

desonra [dʒiˈzõxa] *f* dishonour (*BRIT*), dishonor (*US*); (*descrédito*) disgrace; **~r**

[dʒizõˈxaˣ] *vt* (*infamar*) to disgrace; (*mulher*) to seduce; **~r-se** *vr* to disgrace o.s.

desordem [dʒiˈzoxdẽ] *f* disorder, confusion; **em ~** (*casa*) untidy

desorganizar [dʒizoxganiˈzaˣ] *vt* to disorganize; (*dissolver*) to break up; **~-se** *vr* to become disorganized; to break up

desorientação [dʒizorjẽtaˈsãw] *f* bewilderment, confusion

desorientar [dʒizorjẽˈtaˣ] *vt* (*desnortear*) to throw off course; (*perturbar*) to confuse; (*desvairar*) to unhinge; **~-se** *vr* to lose one's way; to get confused; to go mad

desossar [dʒizoˈsaˣ] *vt* (*galinha*) to bone

desovar [dʒizoˈvaˣ] *vt* to lay; (*peixe*) to spawn

despachado/a [dʒiʃpaˈʃadu/a] *adj* (*pessoa*) efficient

despachar [dʒiʃpaˈʃaˣ] *vt* to dispatch, send off; (*atender, resolver*) to deal with; (*despedir*) to sack; **~-se** *vr* to hurry (up); **despacho** [dʒiʃˈpaʃu] *m* dispatch; (*de negócios*) handling; (*nota em requerimento*) ruling; (*reunião*) consultation; (*macumba*) witchcraft

desparafusar [dʒiʃparafuˈsaˣ] *vt* to unscrew

despeço *etc* [dʒiʃˈpesu] *vb* V **despedir**

despedaçar [dʒiʃpedaˈsaˣ] *vt* (*quebrar*) to smash; (*rasgar*) to tear apart; **~-se** *vr* to smash; to tear

despedida [dʒiʃpeˈdʒida] *f* farewell; (*de trabalhador*) dismissal

despedir [dʒiʃpeˈdʒiˣ] *vt* (*de emprego*) to dismiss, sack; **~-se** *vr*: **~-se** (**de**) to say goodbye (to)

despeitado/a [dʒiʃpejˈtadu/a] *adj* spiteful; (*ressentido*) resentful

despeito [dʒiʃˈpejtu] *m* spite; **a ~ de** in spite of, despite

despejar [dʒiʃpeˈʒaˣ] *vt* (*água*) to pour; (*esvaziar*) to empty; (*inquilino*) to evict; **despejo** [dʒiʃˈpeʒu] *m* eviction; **quarto de despejo** junk room

despencar [dʒiʃpẽˈkaˣ] *vi* to fall down, tumble down

despender [dʒiʃpẽˈdeˣ] *vt* (*dinheiro*) to spend; (*energia*) to expend

despensa [dʒiʃˈpẽsa] *f* larder

despentear [dʒiʃpẽˈtʃjaˣ] *vt* (*cabelo: sem querer*) to mess up; (: *de propósito*) to let down; **~-se** *vr* to mess one's hair up; to let one's hair down

despercebido/a [dʒiʃpexseˈbidu/a] *adj* unnoticed

desperdiçar [dʒiʃpexdʒiˈsaˣ] *vt* to waste; (*dinheiro*) to squander; **desperdício** [dʒiʃpexˈdʒisju] *m* waste

despertador [dʒiʃpextaˈdoˣ] *m* (*tb*: **relógio ~**) alarm clock

despertar [dʒiʃpexˈtaˣ] *vt* to wake; (*suspeitas, interesse*) to arouse; (*reminiscências*) to revive; (*apetite*) to whet ♦ *vi* to wake up ♦ *m* awakening; **desperto/a**

[dʒiʃ'pɛxtu/a] *adj* awake

despesa [dʒiʃ'peza] *f* expense; **~s** *fpl (de uma empresa)* expenses, costs; **~s gerais** (*COM*) overheads

despido/a [dʒiʃ'pidu/a] *adj* naked, bare; (*livre*) free

despir [dʒiʃ'pi*] *vt (roupa)* to take off; (*pessoa*) to undress; (*despojar*) to strip; **~-se** *vr* to undress

despojar [dʒiʃpo'ʒa*] *vt (casas)* to loot, sack; (*pessoas*) to rob; **despojo** [dʒiʃ'poʒu] *m* loot, booty; **despojos** *mpl* (*restos*): **despojos mortais** mortal remains

despontar [dʒiʃpõ'ta*] *vi* to emerge; (*sol*) to come out; (: *ao amanhecer*) to come up; **ao ~ do dia** at daybreak

desporto [dʒiʃ'poxtu] (*esp PT*) *m* sport

déspota ['dɛʃpota] *m/f* despot

despovoado/a [dʒiʃpo'vwadu/a] *adj* uninhabited ♦ *m* wilderness

desprazer [dʒiʃpra'ze*] *m* displeasure

despregar [dʒiʃpre'ga*] *vt* to take off, detach; **~-se** *vr* to come off

desprender [dʒiʃprẽ'de*] *vt* to loosen; (*desatar*) to unfasten; (*emitir*) to emit; **~-se** *vr (botão)* to come off; (*cheiro*) to be given off

despreocupado/a [dʒiʃpreoku'pado/a] *adj* carefree, unconcerned

desprestigiar [dʒiʃpreʃtʃi'ʒja*] *vt* to discredit

desprevenido/a [dʒiʃpreve'nidu/a] *adj* unprepared, unready; **apanhar ~** to catch unawares

desprezar [dʒiʃpre'za*] *vt* to despise, disdain; (*não dar importância a*) to disregard, ignore; **desprezível** [dʒiʃpre'zivew] (*pl* -**eis**) *adj* despicable; **desprezo** [dʒiʃ'prezu] *m* scorn, contempt; **dar ao desprezo** to ignore

desproporcional [dʒiʃpropoxsjo'naw] *adj* disproportionate

despropositado/a [dʒiʃpropozi'tadu/a] *adj* (*absurdo*) preposterous

despropósito [dʒiʃpro'pɔzitu] *m* nonsense

desprover [dʒiʃpro've*] *vt*: **~ alguém (de algo)** to deprive sb (of sth); **desprovido/a** [dʒiʃpro'vidu/a] *adj* deprived; **desprovido de** without

desqualificar [dʒiʃkwalifi'ka*] *vt* (*ESPORTE etc*) to disqualify; (*tornar indiguo*) to disgrace, lower

desregrado/a [dʒiʒxe'gradu/a] *adj* disorderly, unruly; (*devasso*) immoderate

desrespeito [dʒiʒxe'ʃpeitu] *m* disrespect

desse *etc* ['desi] *vb* V **dar**

desse/a ['desi/a] = **de** + **esse/a**

destacado/a [dʒiʃta'kadu/a] *adj* outstanding; (*separado*) detached

destacar [dʒiʃta'ka*] *vt* (*MIL*) to detail; (*separar*) to detach; (*enfatizar*) to emphasize ♦ *vi* to stand out; **~-se** *vr* to stand out; (*pessoa*) to be outstanding

destampar [dʒiʃtã'pa*] *vt* to take the lid off

destapar [dʒiʃta'pa*] *vt* to uncover

destaque [dʒiʃ'taki] *m* distinction; (*pessoa, coisa*) highlight

deste/a ['deʃtʃi/a] = **de** + **este/a**

destemido/a [deʃte'midu/a] *adj* fearless, intrepid

destemperar [dʒiʃtẽpe'ra*] *vt* to dilute, weaken

desterrar [dʒiʃte'xa*] *vt* to exile; **desterro** [dʒiʃ'texu] *m* exile

destilar [deʃtʃi'la*] *vt* to distil (*BRIT*), distill (*US*); **~ia** [deʃtʃila'ria] *f* distillery

destinação [deʃtʃina'sãw] (*pl* -**ões**) *f* destination

destinar [deʃ'tʃina*] *vt* to destine; (*dinheiro*): **~ (para)** to set aside (for); **~-se** *vr*: **~-se a** to be intended for; (*carta*) to be addressed to

destinatário/a [deʃtʃina'tarju/a] *m/f* addressee

destino [deʃ'tʃinu] *m* destiny, fate; (*lugar*) destination; **com ~ a** bound for

destituição [deʃtʃitwi'sãw] (*pl* -**ões**) *f* (*demissão*) dismissal

destituir [deʃtʃi'twi*] *vt* to dismiss; **~ de** (*privar de*) to deprive of

destrancar [dʒiʃtrã'ka*] *vt* to unlock

destratar [dʒiʃtra'ta*] *vt* to abuse, insult

destreza [deʃ'treza] *f* skill; (*agilidade*) dexterity

destro/a ['dɛʃtru/a] *adj* skilful (*BRIT*), skillful (*US*); (*ágil*) agile; (*não canhoto*) right-handed

destrocar [dʒiʃtro'ka*] *vt* to give back, return

destroçar [dʒiʃtro'sa*] *vt* to destroy; (*quebrar*) to smash, break; **destroços** [dʒiʃ'trɔsuʃ] *mpl* wreckage *sg*

destróier [dʒiʃ'trɔje*] *m* destroyer

destronar [dʒiʃtro'na*] *vt* to depose

destroncar [dʒiʃtrõ'ka*] *vt* to dislocate

destruição [dʒiʃtrwi'sãw] *f* destruction

destruidor(a) [dʒiʃtrwi'do*(a)] *adj* destructive

destruir [dʒiʃ'trwi*] *vt* to destroy

desuso [dʒi'zuzu] *m* disuse; **em ~** outdated

desvairado/a [dʒiʒvaj'radu/a] *adj* (*louco*) crazy, demented; (*desorientado*) bewildered

desvalorizar [dʒiʒvalori'za*] *vt* to devalue

desvantagem [dʒiʒvã'taʒẽ] (*pl* -**ns**) *f* disadvantage

desvão [dʒiʒ'vãw] (*pl* -**s**) *m* loft

desvario [dʒiʒva'riu] *m* madness, folly

desvelo [dʒiʒ'velu] *m* care; (*dedicação*) devotion

desventura [dʒiʒvẽ'tura] *f* misfortune; (*infelicidade*) unhappiness; **~do/a** [dʒiʒvẽtu'radu/a] *adj* unfortunate; unhappy ♦ *m/f* wretch

desviar [dʒiʒ'vja*] *vt* to divert; (*golpe*) to

deflect; (*dinheiro*) to embezzle; ~**-se** *vr* to turn away; ~**-se de** to avoid; ~ **os olhos** to look away

desvio [dʒiʒ'viu] *m* diversion, detour; (*curva*) bend; (*fig*) deviation; (*de dinheiro*) embezzlement

detalhadamente [detaʎada'mẽtʃi] *adv* in detail •

detalhado/a [deta'ʎadu/a] *adj* detailed

detalhar [deta'ʎa*] *vt* to (give in) detail

detalhe [de'taʎi] *m* detail; **detalhista** [deta'ʎiʃta] *adj* painstaking, meticulous

detectar [detek'ta*] *vt* to detect

detective [detek'tivɛ] (*PT*) *m/f* = **detetive**

detector [detek'to*] *m* detector

detenção [detẽ'sãw] (*pl* -**ões**) *f* detention

détente [de'tãtʃi] *f* détente

deter [de'te*] (*irreg: como* **ter**) *vt* to stop; (*prender*) to arrest; (*manter preso*) to detain; (*reter*) to keep; (*conter: riso*) to contain; ~**-se** *vr* to stop; (*ficar*) to stay; (*conter-se*) to restrain o.s.

detergente [detex'ʒẽtʃi] *m* detergent

deterioração [deterjora'sãw] *f* deterioration

deteriorar [deterjo'ra*] *vt* to spoil, damage; ~**-se** *vr* to deteriorate; (*relações*) to worsen

determinação [detexmina'sãw] *f* determination; (*decisão*) decision; (*ordem*) order

determinado/a [detexmi'nadu/a] *adj* determined; (*certo*) certain, given

determinar [detexmi'na*] *vt* to determine; (*decretar*) to order; (*resolver*) to decide (on); (*causar*) to cause

detestar [deteʃ'ta*] *vt* to hate; **detestável** [deteʃ'tavew] (*pl* -**eis**) *adj* horrible, hateful

detetive [dete'tʃivi] *m/f* detective

detido/a [de'tʃidu/a] *adj* (*preso*) under arrest; (*minucioso*) thorough • *m/f* person under arrest, prisoner

detonação [detona'sãw] (*pl* -**ões**) *f* explosion

detonar [deto'na*] *vt, vi* to detonate

detrás [de'trajʃ] *adv* behind • *prep*: ~ **de** behind

detrimento [detri'mẽtu] *m*: **em ~ de** to the detriment of

detrito [de'tritu] *m* debris *sg*; (*de comida*) remains *pl*; (*resíduo*) dregs *pl*

deturpação [detuxpa'sãw] *f* corruption; (*de palavras*) distortion

deturpar [detux'pa*] *vt* to corrupt; (*desfigurar*) to disfigure; (*palavras*) to twist

deu [dew] *vb* V **dar**

deus(a) [dewʃ(sa)] *m/f* god/goddess; **D~ me livre!** God forbid!; **graças a D~** thank goodness; **meu D~!** good Lord!

devagar [dʒiva'ga*] *adv* slowly

devaneio [deva'neju] *m* daydream

devassa [de'vasa] *f* investigation, inquiry

devassidão [devasi'dãw] *f* debauchery

devasso/a [de'vasu/a] *adj* dissolute

devastar [devaʃ'ta*] *vt* to devastate; (*arruinar*) to ruin

deve ['dɛvi] *m* debit

devedor(a) [deve'do*(a)] *adj* (*pessoa*) in debt • *m/f* debtor

dever [de've*] *m* duty • *vt* to owe • *vi* (*suposição*): **deve (de) estar doente he** must be ill; (*obrigação*): **devo partir às oito** I must go at eight; **você devia ir ao médico** you should go to the doctor; **que devo fazer?** what shall I do?

deveras [dʒi'vɛraʃ] *adv* really, truly

devidamente [devida'mẽtʃi] *adv* properly; (*preencher formulário etc*) duly

devido/a [de'vidu/a] *adj* (*maneira*) proper; (*respeito*) due; ~ **a** due to, owing to; **no ~ tempo** in due course

devoção [devo'sãw] *f* devotion

devolução [devolu'sãw] *f* devolution; (*restituição*) return; (*reembolso*) refund; ~ **de impostos** tax rebate

devolver [devow've*] *vt* to give back, return; (*COM*) to refund

devorar [devo'ra*] *vt* to devour; (*destruir*) to destroy

devotar [devo'ta*] *vt* to devote

devoto/a [de'vɔtu/a] *adj* devout • *m/f* devotee

dez [dɛʒ] *num* ten

dezanove [deza'nɔvə] (*PT*) *num* = **dezenove**

dezasseis [deza'sejʃ] (*PT*) *num* = **dezesseis**

dezassete [deza'sɛtə] (*PT*) *num* = **dezessete**

dezembro [de'zẽbru] (*PT* **D~**) *m* December

dezena [de'zena] *f*: **uma ~ de ...** ten ...

dezenove [deze'nɔvi] *num* nineteen

dezesseis [deze'sejʃ] *num* sixteen

dezessete [deze'sɛtʃi] *num* seventeen

dezoito [dʒi'zojtu] *num* eighteen

dia ['dʒia] *m* day; (*claridade*) daylight; ~ **a** ~ day by day; ~ **santo** holy day; ~ **útil** weekday; **estar** *ou* **andar em** ~ **(com)** to be up to date (with); **de** ~ in the daytime, by day; **mais** ~ **menos** ~ sooner or later; ~ **sim**, ~ **não** every other day; **no ~ seguinte** the next day; **bom** ~ good morning; ~**-a-** ~ *m* daily life, everyday life

diabete(s) [dʒja'bɛtʃi(ʃ)] *f* diabetes *sg*; **diabético/a** [dʒja'bɛtʃiku/a] *adj, m/f* diabetic

diabo ['dʒjabu] *m* devil; **que ~!** (*col*) damn it!

diabrura [dʒja'brura] *f* prank; ~**s** *fpl* (*travessura*) mischief *sg*

diafragma [dʒja'fragma] *m* diaphragm

diagnóstico [dʒjag'nɔʃtʃiku] *m* diagnosis

diagonal [dʒjago'naw] (*pl* -**ais**) *adj*, *f* diagonal

diagrama [dʒja'grama] *m* diagram

dialeto [dʒja'lɛtu] (*PT* -**ect**-) *m* dialect

dialogar [dʒjalo'ga*] *vi*: ~ **(com al-**

guém) to talk (to sb); (POL) to have ou hold talks (with sb)

diálogo ['dʒjalogu] *m* dialogue; (conversa) talk, conversation

diamante [dʒja'mãtʃi] *m* diamond

diâmetro ['dʒjametru] *m* diameter

diante ['dʒjãtʃi] *prep*: ~ **de** before; (na frente de) in front of; (problemas etc) in the face of; **e assim por** ~ and so on; **para** ~ forward

dianteira [dʒjã'tejra] *f* front, vanguard; **tomar a** ~ to get ahead

dianteiro/a [dʒjã'tejru/a] *adj* front

diapositivo [dʒjapozi'tʃivu] *m* (FOTO) slide

diária ['dʒjarja] *f* (de hotel) daily rate

diário/a ['dʒjarju/a] *adj* daily ♦ *m* diary; (jornal) (daily) newspaper; ~ **de bordo** (AER) logbook; **diarista** [dʒja'riʃta] *m/f* casual worker, worker paid by the day; (em casa) cleaner

diarréia [dʒja'xeja] *f* diarrhoea (BRIT), diarrhea (US)

dica ['dʒika] (col) *f* hint

dicionário [dʒisjo'narju] *m* dictionary

didático/a [dʒi'datʃiku/a] (PT -ct-) *adj* (livro) educational; (método) teaching atr; (modo) didactic

diesel ['dʒizew] *m*: **motor a** ~ diesel engine

dieta ['dʒjɛta] *f* diet; **fazer** ~ to be on a diet; (começar) to go on a diet

difamar [dʒifa'ma*] *vt* to slander; (por escrito) to libel

diferença [dʒife'rẽsa] *f* difference; **ela tem uma** ~ **comigo** she's got something against me

diferenciar [dʒiferẽ'sja*] *vt* to differentiate

diferente [dʒife'rẽtʃi] *adj* different; **estar** ~ **com alguém** to be at odds with sb

diferir [dʒife'ri*] *vi*: ~ **(de)** to differ (from) ♦ *vt* to defer

difícil [dʒi'fisiw] (pl -eis) *adj* difficult; (improvável) unlikely; **o** ~ **é** ... the difficult thing is ...; **acho** ~ **ela aceitar nossa proposta** I think it's unlikely she will accept our proposal; **dificilmente** [dʒifisiw'mẽtʃi] *adv* with difficulty; (mal) hardly; (raramente) hardly ever

dificuldade [dʒifikuw'dadʒi] *f* difficulty; (aperto): **em** ~**s** in trouble

dificultar [dʒifikuw'ta*] *vt* to make difficult; (complicar) to complicate

difundir [dʒifũ'dʒi*] *vt* to diffuse; (boato, rumor) to spread

difuso/a [dʒi'fuzu/a] *adj* diffuse

digerir [dʒiʒe'ri*] *vt*, *vi* to digest

digestão [dʒiʒeʃ'tãw] *f* digestion

digital [dʒiʒi'taw] (pl -ais) *adj*: **impressão** ~ fingerprint

digitar [dʒiʒi'ta*] *vt* (COMPUT: dados) to key (in)

dígito ['dʒiʒitu] *m* digit

dignidade [dʒigni'dadʒi] *f* dignity

digno/a ['dʒignu/a] *adj* (merecedor) worthy; (nobre) dignified

digo etc ['dʒigu] *vb* V **dizer**

dilapidar [dʒilapi'da*] *vt* (fortuna) to squander; (casa) to demolish

dilatar [dʒila'ta*] *vt* to dilate, expand; (prolongar) to prolong; (retardar) to delay

dilema [dʒi'lɛma] *m* dilemma

diligência [dʒili'ʒẽsja] *f* diligence; **diligente** [dʒili'ʒẽtʃi] *adj* hardworking, industrious

diluir [dʒi'lwi*] *vt* to dilute

dilúvio [dʒi'luvju] *m* flood

dimensão [dʒimẽ'sãw] (pl -ões) *f* dimension; **dimensões** *fpl* (medidas) measurements

diminuição [dʒiminwi'sãw] *f* reduction

diminuir [dʒimi'nwi*] *vt* to reduce; (som) to turn down; (interesse) to lessen ♦ *vi* to lessen, diminish; (preço) to go down; (dor) to wear off; (barulho) to die down

diminutivo/a [dʒiminu'tʃivu/a] *adj* diminutive ♦ *m* (LING) diminutive

diminuto/a [dʒimi'nutu/a] *adj* minute, tiny

Dinamarca [dʒina'maxka] *f* Denmark; **dinamarquês/quesa** [dʒinamax'keʃ/'keza] *adj* Danish ♦ *m/f* Dane ♦ *m* (LING) Danish

dinâmico/a [dʒi'namiku/a] *adj* dynamic

dinamismo [dʒina'miʒmu] *m* (fig) energy, drive

dinamite [dʒina'mitʃi] *f* dynamite

dínamo ['dʒinamu] *m* dynamo

dinastia [dʒinaʃ'tʃia] *f* dynasty

dinheirão [dʒiɲej'rãw] *m*: **um** ~ loads *pl* of money

dinheiro [dʒi'ɲejru] *m* money; ~ **à vista** cash for paying in cash; ~ **em caixa** money in the till; ~ **em espécie** cash

dinossauro [dʒino'sawru] *m* dinosaur

diocese [dʒjo'sɛzi] *f* diocese

diploma [dʒip'lɔma] *m* diploma

diplomacia [dʒiploma'sia] *f* diplomacy; (fig) tact

diplomata [dʒiplo'mata] *m/f* diplomat; **diplomático/a** [dʒiplo'matʃiku/a] *adj* diplomatic

dique ['dʒiki] *m* dam; (GEO) dyke

direção [dʒire'sãw] (PT -cç-; pl -ões) *f* direction; (endereço) address; (AUTO) steering; (administração) management; (comando) leadership; (diretoria) board of directors; **em** ~ **a** towards

directo/a etc [dʒi'rɛktu/a] (PT) = **direto** etc

direi etc [dʒi'rej] *vb* V **dizer**

direita [dʒi'rejta] *f* (mão) right hand; (lado) right-hand side; (POL) right wing; **à** ~ on the right

direito/a [dʒi'rejtu/a] *adj* (lado) right-hand; (mão) right; (honesto) honest; (devido) proper; (justo) right, just ♦ *m* right; (JUR) law ♦ *adv* straight; (bem)

right; (*de maneira certa*) properly; ~s
mpl (*humanos*) rights; (*alfandegários*)
duty *sg*

direto/a [dʒi'rɛtu/a] *adj* direct ♦ *adv*
straight; **transmissão direta** (*TV*) live
broadcast

diretor(a) [dʒire'to*(a)] *adj* directing,
guiding ♦ *m/f* director; (*de jornal*) editor; (*de escola*) head teacher; ~**ia**
[dʒireto'ria] *f* (*COM*) management

dirigente [dʒiri'ʒẽtʃi] *m/f* (*de país, partido*) leader; (*diretor*) director; (*gerente*)
manager

dirigir [dʒiri'ʒi*] *vt* to direct; (*COM*) to
manage; (*veículo*) to drive ♦ *vi* to drive;
~**-se** *vr*: ~**-se a** (*falar com*) to speak to;
(*ir, recorrer*) to go to; (*esforços*) to be
directed towards

discagem [dʒiʃ'kaʒẽ] *f* (*TEL*) dialling

discar [dʒiʃ'ka*] *vt* to dial

disciplina [dʒisi'plina] *f* discipline; ~**r**
[dʒisipli'na*] *vt* to discipline

discípulo/a [dʒi'sipulu/a] *m/f* disciple;
(*aluno*) pupil

disc-jóquei [dʒiʃk-] *m/f* disc jockey, DJ

disco [dʒiʃku] *m* disc; (*COMPUT*) disk;
(*MÚS*) record; (*de telefone*) dial; ~ **laser**
(*máquina*) compact disc player, CD player; (*disco*) compact disc, CD; ~
flexível/rígido (*COMPUT*) floppy/hard
disk; ~ **do sistema** system disk; ~
voador flying saucer

discordar [dʒiʃkox'da*] *vi*: ~ **de alguém
em algo** to disagree with sb on sth

discórdia [dʒiʃ'kɔxdʒia] *f* discord, strife

discoteca [dʒiʃko'tɛka] *f* discotheque,
disco

discotecário/a [dʒiʃkote'karju/a] *m/f*
disc jockey, DJ

discrepância [dʒiʃkre'pãsja] *f* discrepancy; (*desacordo*) disagreement; **discre-
pante** [dʒiʃkre'pãtʃi] *adj* conflicting

discreto/a [dʒiʃ'krɛtu/a] *adj* discreet;
(*modesto*) modest; (*prudente*) shrewd;
(*roupa*) plain; **discrição** [dʒiʃkri'sãw] *f*
discretion

discriminação [dʒiʃkrimina'sãw] *f* discrimination

discriminar [dʒiʃkrimi'na*] *vt* to distinguish ♦ *vi*: ~ **entre** to discriminate between

discurso [dʒiʃ'kuxsu] *m* speech

discussão [dʒiʃku'sãw] (*pl* –ões) *f* discussion; (*contenda*) argument

discutir [dʒiʃku'tʃi*] *vt* to discuss ♦ *vi*: ~
(**sobre algo**) to talk (about sth); (*conten-
der*) to argue (about sth)

disenteria [dʒizẽte'ria] *f* dysentery

disfarçar [dʒiʃfax'sa*] *vt* to disguise ♦ *vi*
to pretend; ~**-se** *vr*: ~**-se em** ou **de
algo** to disguise o.s. as sth; **disfarce**
[dʒiʃ'faxsi] *m* disguise; (*máscara*) mask

díspar ['dʒiʃpa] *adj* dissimilar

disparado/a [dʒiʃpa'radu/a] *adj* very fast
♦ *adv* by a long way

disparar [dʒiʃpa'ra*] *vt* to shoot, fire ♦ *vi*
to fire; (*arma*) to go off; (*correr*) to
shoot off, bolt

disparatado/a [dʒiʃpara'tadu/a] *adj* silly,
absurd

disparate [dʒiʃpa'ratʃi] *m* nonsense, rubbish

disparidade [dʒiʃpari'dadʒi] *f* disparity

dispensar [dʒiʃpẽ'sa*] *vt* to excuse; (*prescindir de*) to do without; (*conferir*) to
grant; **dispensável** [dʒiʃpẽ'savew] (*pl*
-eis) *adj* expendable

dispersar [dʒiʃpex'sa*] *vt, vi* to disperse;
disperso/a [dʒiʃ'pexsu/a] *adj* scattered

displicência [dʒiʃpli'sensja] (*BR*) *f* negligence, carelessness; **displicente**
[dʒiʃpli'sẽtʃi] *adj* careless

dispo *etc* ['dʒiʃpu] *vb* V **despir**

disponível [dʒiʃpo'nivew] (*pl* -**eis**) *adj*
available

dispor [dʒiʃ'po*] (*irreg: como* **pôr**) *vt* to
arrange ♦ *vi*: ~ **de** to have the use of;
(*ter*) to have, own; (*pessoas*) to have at
one's disposal; ~**-se** *vr*: ~**-se a** (*estar
pronto a*) to be prepared to, be willing
to; (*decidir*) to decide to; ~ **sobre** to
talk about; **disponha!** feel free!

disposição [dʒiʃpozi'sãw] (*pl* –ões) *f* arrangement; (*humor*) disposition; (*inclinação*) inclination; **à sua ~** at your disposal

dispositivo [dʒiʃpozi'tʃivu] *m* gadget, device; (*determinação de lei*) provision

disposto/a [dʒiʃ'poʃtu/poʃta] *adj*: **estar
~ a** to be willing to; **estar bem ~** to
look well

disputa [dʒiʃ'puta] *f* dispute, argument;
(*competição*) contest; ~**r** [dʒiʃpu'ta*] *vt* to
dispute; (*concorrer a*) to compete for;
(*lutar por*) to fight over ♦ *vi* to quarrel,
argue; to compete; ~**r uma corrida** to
run a race

disquete [dʒiʃ'ketʃi] *m* (*COMPUT*) floppy
disk, diskette

disse *etc* ['dʒisi] *vb* V **dizer**

dissecar [dʒise'ka*] *vt* to dissect

disseminar [dʒisemi'na*] *vt* to disseminate; (*espalhar*) to spread

dissertação [dʒisexta'sãw] (*pl* –ões) *f* dissertation; (*discurso*) lecture

dissertar [dʒisex'ta*] *vi* to speak

dissidência [dʒisi'dẽsja] *f* (*cisão*) difference of opinion; **dissidente** [dʒisi'dẽtʃi]
adj, m/f dissident

dissimular [dʒisimu'la*] *vt* to hide;
(*fingir*) to feign

dissipar [dʒisi'pa*] *vt* to disperse, dispel;
(*malgastar*) to squander, waste; ~**-se** *vr*
to vanish

disso ['dʒisu] = **de** + **isso**

dissociar [dʒiso'sja*] *vt*: ~ **algo (de/em
algo)** to separate sth (from sth)/break
sth up (into sth); ~**-se** *vr*: ~**-se de algo**
to dissociate o.s. from sth

dissolução [dʒisolu'sãw] *f* (*libertinagem*)

debauchery; *(de casamento)* dissolution

dissoluto/a [dʒiso'lutu/a] *adj* dissolute

dissolver [dʒisow've°] *vt* to dissolve; *(dispersar)* to disperse; *(motim)* to break up

dissuadir [dʒiswa'dʒi°] *vt* to dissuade; ~ **alguém de fazer algo** to talk sb out of doing sth, dissuade sb from doing sth

distância [dʒiʃ'tãsja] *f* distance; **a 3 quilômetros de** ~ 3 kilometres *(BRIT)* ou kilometers *(US)* away

distanciar [dʒiʃtã'sja°] *vt* to distance, set apart; *(colocar por intervalos)* to space out; ~**-se** *vr* to move away; *(fig)* to distance o.s.

distante [dʒiʃ'tãtʃi] *adj* distant

distender [dʒiʃtẽ'de°] *vt* to expand; *(estirar)* to stretch; *(dilatar)* to distend; *(músculo)* to pull; ~**-se** *vr* to expand; to distend

distinção [dʒiʃtʃĩ'sãw] *(pl* –**ões)** *f* distinction; **fazer** ~ to make a distinction

distinguir [dʒiʃtʃĩ'gi°] *vt* to distinguish; *(avistar, ouvir)* to make out; ~**-se** *vr* to stand out

distintivo/a [dʒiʃtʃĩ'tʃivu/a] *adj* distinctive ♦ *m (insígnia)* badge; *(emblema)* emblem

distinto/a [dʒiʃ'tʃĩtu/a] *adj* different; *(eminente)* distinguished; *(claro)* distinct; *(refinado)* refined

disto [dʒiʃtu] = **de + isto**

distorcer [dʒiʃtox'se°] *vt* to distort

distração [dʒiʃtra'sãw] *(PT* –**çç-;** *pl* –**ões)** *f (alheamento)* absent-mindedness; *(divertimento)* pastime; *(descuido)* oversight

distraído/a [dʒiʃtra'idu/a] *adj* absent-minded; *(não atento)* inattentive

distrair [dʒiʃtra'i°] *vt* to distract; *(divertir)* to amuse

distribuição [dʒiʃtribwi'sãw] *f* distribution; *(de cartas)* delivery

distribuidor(a) [dʒiʃtribwi'do°(a)] *m/f* distributor ♦ *m (AUTO)* distributor ♦ *f (COM)* distribution company, distributor

distribuir [dʒiʃtri'bwi°] *vt* to distribute; *(repartir)* to share out; *(cartas)* to deliver

distrito [dʒiʃ'tritu] *m* district; *(delegacia)* police station; ~ **eleitoral** constituency; ~ **federal** federal area

distúrbio [dʒiʃ'tuxbju] *m* disturbance

ditado [dʒi'tadu] *m* dictation; *(provérbio)* saying

ditador [dʒita'do°] *m* dictator; **ditadura** [dʒita'dura] *f* dictatorship

ditar [dʒi'ta°] *vt* to dictate; *(impor)* to impose

dito/a ['dʒitu/a] *pp de* **dizer** ~ **e feito** no sooner said than done

ditongo [dʒi'tõgu] *m* diphthong

ditoso/a [dʒi'tozu/zza] *adj (feliz)* happy; *(venturoso)* lucky

DIU *abr m* (= *dispositivo intra-uterino*) IUD

diurno/a ['dʒiuxnu/a] *adj* daytime *atr*

divã [dʒi'vã] *m* couch, divan

divagar [dʒiva'ga°] *vi* to wander; *(falar sem nexo)* to ramble (on)

divergir [dʒivex'ʒi°] *vi* to diverge; *(discordar)* ~ **(de alguém)** to disagree (with sb)

diversão [dʒivex'sãw] *(pl* –**ões)** *f* amusement; *(passatempo)* pastime

diverso/a [dʒi'vɛxsu/a] *adj* different; ~**s** various, several

diversões [divex'sõjʃ] *fpl de* **diversão**

diversos [dʒi'vɛxsuʃ] *mpl (COM)* sundries

divertido/a [dʒivex'tʃidu/a] *adj* amusing, funny

divertimento [dʒivextʃi'mẽtu] *m* amusement, entertainment

divertir [dʒivex'tʃi°] *vt* to amuse, entertain; ~**-se** *vr* to enjoy o.s., have a good time

dívida ['dʒivida] *f* debt; **contrair** ~**s** to run into debt; ~ **externa** foreign debt

dividendo [dʒivi'dẽdu] *m* dividend

dividir [dʒivi'dʒi°] *vt* to divide; *(despesas, lucro, comida etc)* to share; *(separar)* to separate ♦ *vi (MAT)* to divide; ~**-se** *vr* to divide, split up

divindade [dʒivĩ'dadʒi] *f* divinity

divino/a [dʒi'vinu/a] *adj* divine ♦ *m* Holy Ghost

divirjo *etc* [dʒi'vixʒu] *vb* V **divergir**

divisa [dʒi'viza] *f* emblem; *(frase)* slogan; *(fronteira)* border; *(MIL)* stripe; ~**s** *fpl (câmbio)* foreign exchange *sg*

divisão [dʒivi'zãw] *(pl* –**ões)** *f* division; *(discórdia)* split; *(partilha)* sharing

divisar [dʒivi'za°] *vt* to see, make out

divisões [dʒivi'zõjʃ] *fpl de* **divisão**

divisória [dʒivi'zɔrja] *f* partition

divisório/a [dʒivi'zɔrju/a] *adj (linha)* dividing

divorciado/a [dʒivox'sjadu/a] *adj* divorced ♦ *m/f* divorcé(e)

divorciar [dʒivox'sja°] *vt* to divorce; ~**-se** *vr* to get divorced; **divórcio** [dʒi'vɔxsju] *m* divorce

divulgar [dʒivuw'ga°] *vt (notícias)* to spread; *(segredo)* to divulge; *(produto)* to market; *(livro)* to publish; ~**-se** *vr* to leak out

dizer [dʒi'ze°] *vt* to say ♦ *m* saying; ~**-se** *vr* to claim to be; **diz-se** *ou* **dizem que ...** it is said that ...; ~ **algo a alguém** to tell sb sth; *(falar)* to say sth to sb; ~ **a alguém que ...** to tell sb that ...; **o que você diz da minha gestão?** what do you think of my suggestion?; **querer** ~ to mean; **quer** ~ that is to say; **digo** *(ou seja)* I mean; **não diga!** you don't say!; **por assim** ~ so to speak; **até** ~ **chega** as much as possible

dizimar [dʒizi'ma°] *vt* to decimate

do [du] = **de +o**

doação [doa'sãw] *(pl* –**ões)** *f* donation

doador(a) [doa'do°(a)] *m/f* donor

doar [do'a*] vt to donate, give

dobra ['dɔbra] f fold; (prega) pleat; (de calças) turn-up

dobradiça [dobra'dʒisa] f hinge

dobradiço/a [dobra'dʒisu/a] adj flexible

dobradinha [dobra'dʒiɲa] f (CULIN) tripe stew

dobrar [do'bra*] vt to double; (papel) to fold; (joelho) to bend; (esquina) to turn, go round; (fazer ceder): ~ alguém to talk sb round ♦ vi to double; (sino) to toll; (vergar) to bend; ~-se vr to double (up)

dobro ['dobru] m double

doca ['dɔka] f (NÁUT) dock

doce ['dosi] adj sweet; (terno) gentle ♦ m sweet

dóceis ['dɔsejʃ] adj pl de **dócil**

docente [do'sẽtʃi] adj: **o corpo ~** the teaching staff

dócil ['dɔsiw] (pl -eis) adj docile

documentação [dokumẽta'sãw] f documentation; (documentos) papers pl

documentário/a [dokumẽ'tarju/a] adj documentary ♦ m documentary

documento [doku'mẽtu] m document

doçura [do'sura] f sweetness; (brandura) gentleness

doença [do'ẽsa] f illness

doente [do'ẽtʃi] adj ill, sick ♦ m/f sick person; (cliente) patient

doentio/a [doẽ'tʃiu/a] adj (pessoa) sickly; (clima) unhealthy; (curiosidade) morbid

doer [do'e*] vi to hurt, ache; ~ a alguém (pesar) to grieve sb

doido/a ['dojdu/a] adj mad, crazy ♦ m/f madman/woman

doído/a [do'idu/a] adj painful; (moralmente) hurt; (que causa dor) painful

dois/duas [dojʃ/'duaʃ] num two; **conversa a ~** tête-à-tête

dólar ['dɔla*] m dollar; ~ **oficial/paralelo** dollar at the official/black-market rate; ~-**turismo** dollar at the special tourist rate; **doleiro/a** [do'lejru/a] m/f (black market) dollar dealer

dolo ['dɔlu] m fraud

dolorido/a [dolo'ridu/a] adj painful, sore

doloroso/a [dolo'rozu/ɔza] adj painful

dom [dõ] m gift; (aptidão) knack

domar [do'ma*] vt to tame

doméstica [do'mɛʃtʃika] f maid

domesticado/a [domeʃtʃi'kadu/a] adj domesticated; (manso) tame

domesticar [domeʃtʃi'ka*] vt to domesticate; (povo) to tame

doméstico/a [do'mɛʃtʃiku/a] adj domestic; (vida) home atr

domiciliar [domisi'lja*] adj home atr

domicílio [domi'silju] m home, residence; **"entregamos a ~"** "we deliver"

dominador(a) [domina'do*(a)] adj (pessoa) domineering; (olhar) imposing ♦ m/f ruler

dominante [domi'nãtʃi] adj dominant; (predominante) predominant

dominar [domi'na*] vt to dominate; (reprimir) to overcome ♦ vi to dominate; ~-**se** vr to control o.s.

domingo [do'mĩgu] m Sunday

domínio [do'minju] m power; (dominação) control; (território) domain; (esfera) sphere; ~ **próprio** self-control

domo ['dɔmu] m dome

dona ['dɔna] f owner; (col: mulher) lady; ~ **de casa** housewife; **D~ Ligia** Ligia; **D~ Luísa Souza** Mrs Luísa Souza

donatário/a [dona'tarju/a] m/f recipient

donde ['dõdə] (PT) adv from where; (daí) thus

dono ['donu] m owner

donzela [dõ'zɛla] f maiden

dopar [do'pa*] vt to drug

dor [do*] f ache; (aguda) pain; (fig) grief, sorrow; ~ **de cabeça/dentes/estômago** headache/toothache/stomachache

dormente [dox'mẽtʃi] adj numb ♦ m (FERRO) sleeper

dormir [dox'mi*] vi to sleep; ~ **fora** to spend the night away

dormitar [doxmi'ta*] vi to doze

dormitório [doxmi'tɔrju] m bedroom; (coletivo) dormitory

dorso ['doxsu] m back

dos [duʃ] = de + os

dosagem [do'zaʒẽ] m dosage

dose ['dɔzi] f dose

dossiê [do'sje] m dossier, file

dotado/a [do'tadu/a] adj gifted; ~ **de** endowed with

dotar [do'ta*] vt to endow

dote ['dɔtʃi] m dowry; (fig) gift

dou [do] vb V dar

dourado/a [do'radu/a] adj golden; (com camada de ouro) gilt ♦ m gilt

douto/a ['dotu/a] adj learned

doutor(a) [do'to*(a)] m/f doctor; **D~** (forma de tratamento) Sir; **D~ Eduardo Souza** Mr Eduardo Souza

doutrina [do'trina] f doctrine

doze ['dozi] num twelve

Dr(a). abr (= Doutor(a)) Dr

dragão [dra'gãw] (pl -ões) m dragon

dragar [dra'ga*] vt to dredge

drágea ['draʒia] f tablet

dragões [dra'gõjʃ] mpl de **dragão**

drama ['drama] m drama; **dramático/a** [dra'matʃiku/a] adj dramatic; ~**tizar** [dramatʃi'za*] vt, vi to dramatize; ~**turgo/a** [drama'tuxgu/a] m/f playwright, dramatist

drástico/a ['draʃtʃiku/a] adj drastic

drenar [dre'na*] vt to drain

dreno ['drɛnu] m drain

driblar [dri'bla*] vt, vi (FUTEBOL) to dribble

drinque ['drĩki] m drink

droga ['drɔga] f drug; (fig) rubbish; ~**do/a** [dro'gadu/a] m/f drug addict; ~**r** [dro'ga*] vt to drug; ~**r-se** vr to take drugs

drogaria [droga'ria] *f* chemist's shop (*BRIT*), drugstore (*US*)
duas ['duaʃ] *f de* **dois**
dublar [du'bla*] *vt* to dub
dublê [du'ble] *m/f* double
ducha ['duʃa] *f* shower
duelo ['dwɛlu] *m* duel
dueto ['dwetu] *m* duet
duna ['duna] *f* dune
duodécimo/a [dwo'dɛsimu/a] *num* twelfth
dupla ['dupla] *f* pair; (*ESPORTE*): ~ **masculina/feminina/mista** men's/ women's/mixed doubles
duplicar [dupli'ka*] *vt* to duplicate ♦ *vi* to double; **duplicata** [dupli'kata] *f* duplicate; (*título*) trade note, bill
duplo/a ['duplu/a] *adj* double ♦ *m* double
duque ['duki] *m* duke; ~**sa** [du'keza] *f* duchess
duração [dura'sãw] *f* duration; **de pouca** ~ short-lived
duradouro/a [dura'doru/a] *adj* lasting
durante [du'rãtʃi] *prep* during; ~ **uma hora** for an hour
durar [du'ra*] *vi* to last
durável [du'ravew] (*pl* **-eis**) *adj* lasting
durex [du'rɛks] ® *adj*: **fita** ~ adhesive tape, sellotape ® (*BRIT*), scotchtape ® (*US*)
dureza [du'reza] *f* hardness
durmo *etc* ['duxmu] *vb* V **dormir**
duro/a ['duru/a] *adj* hard; (*severo*) harsh; (*resistente, fig*) tough; **estar** ~ (*col*) to be broke
dúvida ['duvida] *f* doubt; **sem** ~ undoubtedly, without a doubt; **duvidar** [duvi'da*] *vt* to doubt ♦ *vi* to have one's doubts; **duvidar de alguém/algo** to doubt sb/sth; **duvidar que ...** to doubt that ...; **duvido!** I doubt it!; **duvidoso/a** [duvi'dozu/ɔza] *adj* doubtful; (*suspeito*) dubious
duzentos/as [du'zẽtuʃ/aʃ] *num* two hundred
dúzia ['duzja] *f* dozen; **meia** ~ half a dozen
DVD *abr m* (= *digital versatile disc*) DVD
dz. *abr* = **dúzia**

E

e [i] *conj* and; ~ **a bagagem?** what about the luggage?
é [ɛ] *vb* V **ser**
ébano ['ɛbanu] *m* ebony
ébrio/a ['ɛbrju/a] *adj* drunk ♦ *m/f* drunkard
ebulição [ebuli'sãw] *f* boiling; (*fig*) ferment
eclesiástico/a [ekle'zjastʃiku/a] *adj* ecclesiastical, church *atr*
eclipse [e'klipsi] *m* eclipse
eclusa [e'kluza] *f* (*de canal*) lock; (*com-*

porta) floodgate
eco ['ɛku] *m* echo; **ter** ~ to catch on; ~**ar** [e'kwa*] *vt* to echo ♦ *vi* (*ressoar*) to echo
ecologia [ekolo'ʒia] *f* ecology
economia [ekono'mia] *f* economy; (*ciência*) economics *sg*; ~**s** *fpl* (*poupanças*) savings; **fazer** ~ (**de**) to economize (with)
econômico/a [eko'nomiku/a] *adj* económical; (*pessoa*) thrifty; (*COM*) economic
economista [ekono'miʃta] *m/f* economist
economizar [ekonomi'za*] *vt* (*gastar com economia*) to economize on; (*poupar*) to save (up) ♦ *vi* to economize; to save up
écran ['ɛkrã] (*PT*) *m* screen
ECU *abr m* ECU
edição [edʒi'sãw] (*pl* **-ões**) *f* publication; (*conjunto de exemplares*) edition; (*TV, CINEMA*) editing
edicto [e'ditu] (*PT*) *m* = **edito**
edifício [edʒi'fisju] *m* building; ~ **garagem** multistorey car park (*BRIT*), multi-story parking lot (*US*)
Edimburgo [edʒī'buxgu] *n* Edinburgh
editar [edʒi'ta*] *vt* to publish; (*COMPUT etc*) to edit
edito [e'dʒitu] *m* edict, decree
editor(a) [edʒi'to*(a)] *adj* publishing *atr* ♦ *m/f* publisher; (*redator*) editor ♦ *f* publishing company; **casa** ~**a** publishing house; **editorial** [edʒitor'jaw] (*pl* **-ais**) *adj* publishing *atr* ♦ *m* editorial
edredão [ɘdrɘ'dãw] (*pl* **-ões**) (*PT*) *m* = **edredom**
edredom [ɘdre'dõ] (*pl* **-ns**) *m* eiderdown
educação [eduka'sãw] *f* education; (*criação*) upbringing; (*de animais*) training; (*maneiras*) good manners *pl*; **educacional** [edukasjo'naw] (*pl* **-ais**) *adj* education *atr*
educar [edu'ka*] *vt* to educate; (*criar*) to bring up; (*animal*) to train
efectivo/a *etc* [efek'tivu/a] (*PT*) *adj* = **efetivo** *etc*
efectuar [efek'twa*] (*PT*) *vt* = **efetuar**
efeito [e'fejtu] *m* effect; **fazer** ~ to work; **levar a** ~ to put into effect; **com** ~ indeed
efervescente [efexve'sẽtʃi] *adj* fizzy
efetivamente [efetʃiva'mẽtʃi] *adv* effectively; (*realmente*) really, in fact
efetivar [efetʃi'va*] *vt* (*mudanças, cortes*) to carry out
efetividade [efetʃivi'dadʒi] *f* effectiveness; (*realidade*) reality
efetivo/a [efe'tʃivu/a] *adj* effective; (*real*) actual, real; (*cargo, funcionário*) permanent
efetuar [efe'twa*] *vt* to carry out; (*soma*) to do, perform
eficácia [efi'kasja] *f* (*de pessoa*) efficiency; (*de tratamento*) effectiveness
eficaz [efi'kaʒ] *adj* (*pessoa*) efficient; (*tratamento*) effective

eficiência [efi'sjɛsja] f efficiency; **eficien‐te** [efi'sjɛtʃi] adj efficient

efusivo/a [efu'zivu/a] adj effusive; (cumprimentos) warmest

egípcio/a [e'ʒipsju/a] adj, m/f Egyptian

Egito [e'ʒitu] (PT -**pt**-) m: o ~ Egypt

egoísmo [ego'iʒmu] m selfishness, egoism; **egoísta** [ego'ifta] adj selfish, egoistic ♦ m/f egoist

égua ['ɛgwa] f mare

ei [ej] excl hey!

ei-lo etc = eis + o

eis [ejʃ] adv (sg) here is; (pl) here are; ~ aí there is; there are

eixo ['ejʃu] m (de rodas) axle; (MAT) axis; (de máquina) shaft; ~ **de transmissão** drive shaft

ejacular [eʒaku'la*] vt (sêmen) to ejaculate; (líquido) to spurt ♦ vi to ejaculate

ela ['ɛla] pron (pessoa) she; (coisa) it; (com prep) her; it; ~s fpl they; (com prep) them; ~s por ~s (col) tit for tat

elaboração [elabora'sãw] (pl -ões) f (de uma teoria) working out; (preparo) preparation

elaborar [elabo'ra*] vt (preparar); (fazer) to make; (teoria) to work out

elástico/a [e'laʃtʃiku/a] adj elastic; (flexível) flexible; (colchão) springy ♦ m elastic band

ele ['eli] pron he; (coisa) it; (com prep) him; it; ~s mpl they; (com prep) them

electri... etc [elektri] (PT) = **eletri...** etc

eléctrico/a [e'lɛktriku/a] (PT) adj = **elétrico** ♦ m tram (BRIT), streetcar (US)

electro... etc [elektru] (PT) = **eletro...** etc

eléctrodo [e'lɛktrodu] (PT) m = **eletrodo**

elefante/ta [ele'fãtʃi/ta] m/f elephant

elegância [ele'gãsja] f elegance

elegante [ele'gãtʃi] adj elegant; (da moda) fashionable

eleger [ele'ʒe*] vt to elect; (escolher) to choose

elegível [ele'ʒivɛw] (pl -**eis**) adj eligible

eleição [elej'sãw] (pl -ões) f election; (escolha) choice

eleito/a [e'lejtu/a] pp de **eleger** ♦ adj elected; chosen

eleitor(a) [elej'to*(a)] m/f voter; ~**do** [elejto'radu] m electorate

elejo etc [ele'ʒu] vb V **eleger**

elementar [elemẽ'ta*] adj elementary; (fundamental) basic, fundamental

elemento [ele'mẽtu] m element; (parte) component; (recurso) means; (informação) grounds pl; ~**s** mpl (rudimentos) rudiments

elenco [e'lẽku] m list; (de atores) cast

elepê [eli'pe] m LP, album

eletricidade [eletrisi'dadʒi] f electricity

eletricista [eletri'sifta] m/f electrician

elétrico/a [e'lɛtriku/a] adj electric; (fig: agitado) worked up

eletrificar [eletrifi'ka*] vt to electrify

eletrizar [eletri'za*] vt to electrify; (fig) to thrill

eletro... [eletru] prefixo electro...; ~**cutar** [eletroku'ta*] vt to electrocute; ~**do** [ele'trodu] m electrode; ~**domésticos** [eletrodo'mɛʃtʃikuʃ] (BR) mpl (electrical) household appliances

eletrônica [ele'tronika] f electronics sg

eletrônico/a [ele'troniku/a] adj electronic

elevação [eleva'sãw] (pl -ões) f (ARQ) elevation; (aumento) rise; (ato) raising; (altura) height; (promoção) promotion; (ponto elevado) bump

elevador [eleva'do*] m lift (BRIT), elevator (US)

elevar [ele'va*] vt to lift up; (voz, preço) to raise; (exaltar) to exalt; (promover) to promote; ~**-se** vr to rise

eliminar [elimi'na*] vt to remove; (suprimir) to delete; (possibilidade) to rule out; (MED, banir) to expel; (ESPORTE) to eliminate; **eliminatória** [elimina'tɔrja] f (ESPORTE) heat, preliminary round; (exame) test

elite [e'litʃi] f elite

elo ['elu] m link

elogiar [elo'ʒja*] vt to praise; **elogio** [elo'ʒiu] m praise; (cumprimento) compliment

eloquência [elo'kwẽsja] f eloquence

eloquente [elo'kwẽtʃi] adj eloquent; (persuasivo) persuasive

El Salvador [ew-] n El Salvador

PALAVRA CHAVE

em [ẽ] (em + o(s)/a(s) = no(s)/na(s); + ele(s)/a(s) = nele(s)/a(s); + esse(s)/a(s) = nesse(s)/a(s); + isso = nisso; + este(s)/a(s) = neste(s)/a(s); + isto = nisto; + aquele(s)/a(s) = naquele(s)/a(s); + aquilo = naquilo) prep **1** (posição) in; (: sobre) on; **está na gaveta/no bolso** it's in the drawer/pocket; **está na mesa/no chão** it's on the table/floor

2 (lugar) in; (: casa, escritório etc) at; (: andar, meio de transporte) on; **no Brasil/em São Paulo** in Brazil/São Paulo; ~ **casa/no dentista** at home/the dentist; **no avião** on the plane; **no quinto andar** on the fifth floor

3 (ação) into; **ela entrou na sala de aula** she went into the classroom; **colocar algo na bolso** to put sth into one's bag

4 (tempo) in; on; ~ **1962/3 semanas** in 1962/3 weeks; **no inverno** in the winter; ~ **janeiro, no mês de janeiro** in January; **nessa ocasião/altura** on that occasion/at that time; ~ **breve** soon

5 (diferença): **reduzir/aumentar** ~ **um** 20% to reduce/increase by 20%

6 (modo): **escrito** ~ **inglês** written in English

7 (após vb que indica gastar etc) on; a **metade do seu salário vai** ~ **comida**

he spends half his salary on food **8** (*tema, ocupação*): **especialista no assunto** expert on the subject; **ele trabalha na construção civil** he works in the building industry

emagrecer [imagre'se*] *vt* to make thin
♦ *vi* to grow thin; (*mediante regime*) to slim; **emagrecimento** [imagresi'mẽtu] *m* (*mediante regime*) slimming

emanar [ema'na*] *vi*: ~ **de** to come from, emanate from

emancipar [imãsi'pa*] *vt* to emancipate; **~-se** *vr* to come of age

emaranhado/a [imara'ɲadu/a] *adj* tangled ♦ *m* tangle

emaranhar [imara'ɲa*] *vt* to tangle (up); **~-se** *vr* to get entangled

emassar [ema'sa*] *vt* to plaster

embaçado/a [ẽba'sadu/a] *adj* (*vidro*) steamed up

embaixada [ẽbaj'ʃada] *f* embassy

embaixador(a) [ẽbajʃa'do*(a)] *m/f* ambassador

embaixatriz [ẽbajʃa'triʒ] *f* ambassador; (*mulher de embaixador*) ambassador's wife

embaixo [ẽ'bajʃu] *adv* below, underneath ♦ *prep*: ~ **de** under, underneath; **(lá)** ~ (*em andar inferior*) downstairs

embalado/a [ẽba'ladu/a] *adj* (*acelerado*) fast; **ir** ~ to race (along)

embalagem [ẽba'laʒẽ] *f* packing; (*de produto: caixa etc*) packaging

embalar [ẽba'la*] *vt* to pack; (*balançar*) to rock

embaraçar [ẽbara'sa*] *vt* to hinder; (*complicar*) to complicate; (*encabular*) to embarrass; (*confundir*) to confuse; (*obstruir*) to block; **~-se** *vr* to become embarrassed

embaraço [ẽba'rasu] *m* hindrance; (*cábula*) embarrassment; **~so/a** [ẽbara'sozu/ɔza] *adj* embarrassing

embarcação [ẽbaxka'sãw] (*pl* –ões) *f* vessel

embarcadouro [ẽbaxka'doru] *m* wharf

embarcar [ẽbax'ka*] *vt* to embark, put on board; (*mercadorias*) to ship, stow ♦ *vi* to go on board, embark

embargar [ẽbax'ga*] *vt* (*JUR*) to seize; (*pôr obstáculos a*) to hinder; (*reprimir: voz*) to keep down; (*impedir*) to forbid; **embargo** [ẽ'baxgu] *m* seizure; (*impedimento*) impediment; **sem embargo** nevertheless

embarque [ẽ'baxki] *m* (*de pessoas*) boarding, embarkation; (*de mercadorias*) shipment

embasamento [ẽbaza'mẽtu] *m* (*ARQ*) foundation

embebedar [ẽbebe'da*] *vt* to make drunk ♦ *vi*: **o vinho embebeda** wine makes you drunk; **~-se** *vr* to get drunk

embelezar [ẽbele'za*] *vt* to make beauti-

ful; (*casa*) to brighten up; **~-se** *vr* to make o.s. beautiful

embicar [ẽbi'ka*] *vi* (*NÁUT*) to enter port; (*fig*): ~ **para** to head for; ~ **com alguém** to quarrel with sb

emblema [ẽ'blɛma] *m* emblem; (*na roupa*) badge

embocadura [ẽboka'dura] *f* (*de rio*) mouth; (*MÚS*) mouthpiece; (*de freio*) bit

êmbolo [ẽ'bolu] *m* piston

embolsar [ẽbow'sa*] *vt* to pocket; (*herança*) to come into; (*indenizar*) to refund

embora [ẽ'bɔra] *conj* though, although ♦ *excl* even so; **ir(-se)** ~ to go away

emboscada [ẽboʃ'kada] *f* ambush

embreagem [ẽb'rjaʒẽ] (*pl* –ns) *f* (*AUTO*) clutch

embrenhar [ẽbre'ɲa*] *vt* to penetrate; **~-se** *vr*: **~-se (em/por)** to make one's way (into/through)

embriagar [ẽbrja'ga*] *vt* to make drunk, intoxicate; **~-se** *vr* to get drunk; **embriaguez** [ẽbrja'geʒ] *f* drunkenness; (*fig*) rapture

embrião [e'brjãw] (*pl* –ões) *m* embryo

embromar [ẽbro'ma*] *vt* (*adiar*) to put off; (*enganar*) to cheat ♦ *vi* (*prometer e não cumprir*) to make empty promises, be all talk (and no action); (*protelar*) to stall; (*falar em rodeios*) to beat about the bush

embrulhada [ẽbru'ʎada] *f* muddle, mess

embrulhar [ẽbru'ʎa*] *vt* (*pacote*) to wrap; (*enrolar*) to roll up; (*confundir*) to muddle up; (*enganar*) to cheat; (*estômago*) to upset; **~-se** *vr* to get into a muddle

embrulho [ẽ'bruʎu] *m* package, parcel; (*confusão*) mix-up

embrutecer [ẽbrute'se*] *vt* to brutalize; **~-se** *vr* to be brutalized

emburrar [ẽbu'xa*] *vi* to sulk

embuste [ẽ'buʃtʃi] *m* (*engano*) deception; (*ardil*) trick; **~iro/a** [ẽbuʃ'tejru/a] *adj* deceitful ♦ *m/f* cheat; (*mentiroso*) liar; (*impostor*) impostor

embutido/a [ẽbu'tʃidu/a] *adj* (*armário*) built-in, fitted

emenda [e'mẽda] *f* correction; (*de lei*) amendment; (*de uma pessoa*) improvement; (*ligação*) join; (*sambladura*) joint; (*COSTURA*) seam

emendar [emẽ'da*] *vt* to correct; (*reparar*) to mend; (*injustiças*) to make amends for; (*lei*) to amend; (*ajuntar*) to put together; **~-se** *vr* to mend one's ways

ementa [e'mẽta] (*PT*) *f* menu

emergência [imex'ʒẽsja] *f* emergence; (*crise*) emergency

emergir [imex'ʒi*] *vi* to emerge, appear; (*submarino*) to surface

emigração [emigra'sãw] (*pl* –ões) *f* emigration; (*de aves*) migration

emigrado/a [emi'gradu/a] *adj* emigrant

emigrante [emi'grãtʃi] *m/f* emigrant

emigrar [emi'gra*] *vi* to emigrate; *(aves)* to migrate

eminência [emi'nèsja] *f* eminence; *(altura)* height; **eminente** [emi'nètʃi] *adj* eminent, distinguished; *(GEO)* high

emirjo *etc* [e'mixʒu] *vb* V **emergir**

emissão [emi'sãw] *(pl* **-ões)** *f* emission; *(RÁDIO)* broadcast; *(de moeda, ações)* issue

emissário/a [emi'sarju/a] *m/f* emissary ♦ *m* outlet

emissões [emi'sõjʃ] *fpl de* **emissão**

emissor(a) [emi'so*(a)] *adj (de moeda-papel)* issuing ♦ *m (RÁDIO)* transmitter ♦ *f (estação)* broadcasting station; *(empresa)* broadcasting company

emitir [emi'tʃi*] *vt (som)* to give out; *(cheiro)* to give off; *(moeda, ações)* to issue; *(RÁDIO)* to broadcast; *(opinião)* to express ♦ *vi (emitir moeda)* to print money

emoção [emo'sãw] *(pl* **-ões)** *f* emotion; *(excitação)* excitement; **emocional** [imosjo'naw] *(pl* **-ais)** *adj* emotional; **emocionante** [imosjo'nãtʃi] *adj* moving; exciting; **emocionar** [imosjo'na*] *vt* to move; *(perturbar)* to upset; *(excitar)* to excite, thrill ♦ *vi* to be exciting; *(comover)* to be moving; **emocionar-se** *vr* to get emotional

emoldurar [emowdu'ra*] *vt* to frame

emotivo/a [emo'tʃivu/a] *adj* emotional

empacotar [ẽpako'ta*] *vt* to pack, wrap up

empada [ẽ'pada] *f* pie

empadão [ẽpa'dãw] *(pl* **-ões)** *m* pie

empalhar [ẽpa'ʎa*] *vt (animal)* to stuff

empalidecer [ẽpalide'se*] *vi* to turn pale

empanturrar [ẽpãtu'xa*] *vt:* ~ **alguém de algo** to stuff sb full of sth

emparelhar [ẽpare'ʎa*] *vt* to pair; *(equiparar)* to match ♦ *vi:* ~ **com** to be equal to

empatar [ẽpa'ta*] *vt* to hinder; *(dinheiro)* to tie up; *(no jogo)* to draw; *(tempo)* to take up ♦ *vi (no jogo):* ~ **(com)** to draw (with); **empate** [ẽ'patʃi] *m* draw; tie; *(XADREZ)* stalemate; *(em negociações)* deadlock

empecilho [ẽpe'siʎu] *m* obstacle; *(col)* snag

empedernido/a [ẽpedex'nidu/a] *adj* hard-hearted

empedrar [ẽpe'dra*] *vt* to pave

empenar [ẽpe'na*] *vt, vi (curvar)* to warp

empenhar [ẽpe'ɲa*] *vt (objeto)* to pawn; *(palavra)* to pledge; *(empregar)* to exert; *(compelir)* to oblige; **~-se** *vr:* **~-se em fazer** to strive to do, do one's utmost to do; **empenho** [ẽ'peɲu] *m* pawning; pledge; *(insistência):* **empenho (em)** commitment (to)

empestar [ẽpeʃ'ta*] *vt* to infect

empilhar [ẽpi'ʎa*] *vt* to pile up

empinado/a [ẽpi'nadu/a] *adj* upright;

(cavalo) rearing; *(colina)* steep

empinar [ẽpi'na*] *vt* to raise, uplift

emplastro [ẽ'plaʃtru] *m (MED)* plaster

empobrecer [ẽpobre'se*] *vt* to impoverish ♦ *vi* to become poor; **empobrecimento** [ẽpobresi'mẽtu] *m* impoverishment

empola [ẽ'pola] *f (na pele)* blister; *(de água)* bubble; **~-do/a** [ẽpo'ladu/a] *adj* covered with blisters; *(estilo)* pompous, bombastic

empolgação [ẽpowga'sãw] *f* excitement; *(entusiasmo)* enthusiasm

empolgante [ẽpow'gãtʃi] *adj* exciting

empolgar [ẽpow'ga*] *vt* to stimulate, fill with enthusiasm; *(prender a atenção de):* ~ **alguém** to keep sb riveted

empório [ẽ'porju] *m (mercado)* market; *(armazém)* department store

empossar [ẽpo'sa*] *vt* to appoint

empreendedor(a) [ẽprjẽde'do*(a)] *adj* enterprising ♦ *m/f* entrepreneur

empreender [ẽprjẽ'de*] *vt* to undertake; **empreendimento** [ẽprjẽdʒi'mẽtu] *m* undertaking

empregada [ẽpre'gada] *f (BR: doméstica)* maid; *(PT: de restaurante)* waitress; V *tb* **empregado**

empregado/a [ẽpre'gadu/a] *m/f* employee; *(em escritório)* clerk ♦ *m (PT: de restaurante)* waiter

empregador(a) [ẽprega'do*(a)] *m/f* employer

empregar [ẽpre'ga*] *vt (pessoa)* to employ; *(coisa)* to use; **~-se** *vr* to get a job

emprego [ẽ'pregu] *m* job; *(uso)* use

empreiteira [ẽprej'tejra] *f (firma)* contractor

empreiteiro [ẽprej'tejru] *m* contractor

empresa [ẽ'preza] *f* undertaking; *(COM)* enterprise, firm; **empresário/a** [ẽpre'zarju/a] *m/f* businessman/woman; *(de cantor, boxeador etc)* manager

emprestado/a [ẽpreʃ'tadu/a] *adj* on loan; **pedir** ~ to borrow; **tomar algo** ~ to borrow sth

emprestar [ẽpreʃ'ta*] *vt* to lend; **empréstimo** [ẽ'preʃtʃimu] *m* loan

empunhar [ẽpu'ɲa*] *vt* to grasp, seize

empurrão [ẽpu'xãw] *(pl* **-ões)** *m* push, shove; **aos empurrões** jostling

empurrar [ẽpu'xa*] *vt* to push

empurrões [ẽpu'xõjʃ] *mpl de* **empurrão**

emudecer [emude'se*] *vt* to silence ♦ *vi* to fall silent, go quiet

enamorado/a [enamo'radu/a] *adj* enchanted; *(apaixonado)* in love

encabeçar [ẽkabe'sa*] *vt* to head

encabulado/a [ẽkabu'ladu/a] *adj* shy

encabular [ẽkabu'la*] *vt* to embarrass ♦ *vi (fato, situação)* to be embarrassing; *(pessoa)* to get embarrassed

encadernação [ẽkadexna'sãw] *(pl* **-ões)** *f (de livro)* binding

encadernado/a [ẽkadex'nadu/a] *adj*

bound; (*de capa dura*) hardback

encadernar [ēkadex'na*] *vt* to bind

encaixar [ēkaj'ʃa*] *vt* (*colocar*) to fit in; (*inserir*) to insert ♦ *vi* to fit; **encaixe** [ē'kajʃi] *m* (*ato*) fitting; (*ranhura*) groove; (*buraco*) socket

encalço [ē'kawsu] *m* pursuit; **ir no ~ de** to pursue

encalhado/a [ēka'ʎadu/a] *adj* stranded; (*mercadoria*) unsaleable; (*col: solteiro*) on the shelf

encalhar [ēka'ʎa*] *vi* (*embarcação*) to run aground; (*fig: processo*) to grind to a halt; (: *mercadoria*) to be returned, not to sell; (*col: ficar solteiro*) to be left on the shelf

encalorado/a [ēkalo'radu/a] *adj* hot

encaminhar [ēkami'ɲa*] *vt* to direct; (*no bom caminho*) to put on the right path; (*processo*) to set in motion; **~-se *vr*: ~-se para/a** to set out for/to

encanador [ēkana'do*] (*BR*) *m* plumber

encanamento [ēkana'mētu] (*BR*) *m* plumbing

encanar [ēka'na*] *vt* to channel

encantado/a [ēkā'tadu/a] *adj* delighted; (*castelo etc*) enchanted; (*fascinado*): ~ **(por)** smitten (with)

encantador(a) [ēkāta'do*(a)] *adj* delightful, charming

encantamento [ēkāta'mētu] *m* (*magia*) spell; (*fascinação*) charm

encantar [ēkā'ta*] *vt* to bewitch; to charm; (*deliciar*) to delight

encanto [ē'kātu] *m* delight; charm

encapar [ēka'pa*] *vt* (*livro, sofá*) to cover; (*envolver*) to wrap

encapotar [ēkapo'ta*] *vt* to wrap up; **~-se *vr*** to wrap o.s. up

encarar [ēka'ra*] *vt* to face; (*olhar*) to look at; (*considerar*) to consider

encarcerar [ēkaxse'ra*] *vt* to imprison

encardido/a [ēkax'dʒidu/a] *adj* (*roupa, casa*) grimy; (*pele*) sallow

encarecer [ēkare'se*] *vt* to raise the price of; (*louvar*) to praise; (*exagerar*) to exaggerate ♦ *vi* to go up in price, get dearer

encargo [ē'kaxgu] *m* responsibility; (*ocupação*) job, assignment; (*fardo*) burden

encarnação [ēkaxna'sāw] (*pl* –ões) *f* incarnation

encarnado/a [ēkax'nadu/a] *adj* red, scarlet

encarnar [ēkax'na*] *vt* to embody, personify; (*TEATRO*) to play

encarquilhado/a [ēkaxki'ʎadu/a] *adj* (*fruta*) wizened; (*rosto*) wrinkled

encarregado/a [ēkaxe'gadu/a] *adj*: ~ **de** in charge of ♦ *m/f* person in charge ♦ *m* (*de operários*) foreman

encarregar [ēkaxe'ga*] *vt*: ~ **alguém de algo** to put sb in charge of sth; **~-se *vr*: ~-se de fazer** to undertake to do

encenação [ēsena'sāw] (*pl* –ões) *f* (*de peça*) staging, putting on; (*produção*) production; (*fingimento*) playacting; (*atitude fingida*) put-on

encenar [ēse'na*] *vt* (*TEATRO*): *pôr em cena* to stage, put on; (: *produzir*) to produce; (*fingir*) to put on

encerar [ēse'ra*] *vt* to wax

encerramento [ēsexa'mētu] *m* close, end

encerrar [ēse'xa*] *vt* to shut in, lock up; (*conter*) to contain; (*concluir*) to close

encharcar [ēʃax'ka*] *vt* to flood; (*ensopar*) to soak, drench; **~-se *vr*** to get soaked *ou* drenched

enchente [ē'ʃētʃi] *f* flood

encher [ē'ʃe*] *vt* to fill (up); (*balão*) to blow up; (*tempo*) to fill, take up ♦ *vi* (*col*) to be annoying; **~-se *vr*** to fill up; **~-se (de)** (*col*) to get fed up (with); **enchimento** [ēʃi'mētu] *m* filling

enchova [ē'ʃova] *f* anchovy

enciclopédia [ēsiklo'pɛdʒja] *f* encyclopedia, encyclopaedia (*BRIT*)

encoberto/a [ēko'bɛxtu/a] *pp de* **encobrir** ♦ *adj* concealed; (*tempo*) overcast

encobrir [ēko'bri*] *vt* to conceal, hide

encolher [ēko'ʎe*] *vt* (*pernas*) to draw up; (*os ombros*) to shrug; (*roupa*) to shrink ♦ *vi* to shrink; **~-se *vr*** (*de frio*) to huddle

encomenda [ēko'mēda] *f* order; **feito de ~** made to order, custom-made; **~r** [ēkome'da*] *vt*: **~r algo a alguém** to order sth from sb

encontrar [ēkō'tra*] *vt* to find; (*pessoa*) to meet; (*inesperadamente*) to come across; (*dar com*) to bump into ♦ *vi*: ~ **com** to bump into; **~-se *vr*** (*achar-se*) to be; (*ter encontro*): **~-se (com alguém)** to meet (sb)

encontro [ē'kōtru] *m* (*de pessoas*) meeting; (*MIL*) encounter; ~ **marcado** appointment; **ir/vir ao ~ de** to go/come and meet

encontrões [ēkō'trōjʃ] *mpl de* **encontrão**

encorajar [ēkora'ʒa*] *vt* to encourage

encorpado/a [ēkox'padu/a] *adj* stout; (*vinho*) full-bodied; (*tecido*) closely-woven; (*papel*) thick

encosta [ē'kɔʃta] *f* slope

encostar [ēkoʃ'ta*] *vt* (*cabeça*) to put down; (*carro*) to park; (*pôr de lado*) to put to one side; (*pôr junto*) to put side by side; (*porta*) to leave ajar ♦ *vi* to pull in; **~-se *vr*: ~-se em** to lean against; (*deitar-se*) to lie down on; ~ **em** to lean against; ~ **a mão em** (*bater*) to hit

encosto [ē'koʃtu] *m* (*arrimo*) support; (*de cadeira*) back

encrencar [ēkrē'ka*] (*col*) *vt* (*situação*) to complicate; (*pessoa*) to get into trouble ♦ *vi* to get complicated; (*carro*) to break down; **~-se *vr*** to get complicated; to get into trouble

encrespar [ēkreʃ'pa*] *vt* (*o cabelo*) to

curl; ~-**se** vr (o cabelo) to curl

encruzilhada [ẽkruzi'ʎada] f crossroads sg

encurtar [ẽkux'ta*] vt to shorten

endereçamento [ẽderesa'mẽtu] m (endereço) address

endereçar [ẽdere'sa*] vt (carta) to address; (encaminhar) to direct

endereço [ẽde'resu] m address

endiabrado/a [ẽdʒja'bradu/a] adj devilish; (travesso) mischievous

endinheirado/a [ẽdʒiɲej'radu/a] adj rich, wealthy

endireitar [ẽdʒirej'ta*] vt (objeto) to straighten; (fig: retificar) to put right; ~-**se** vr to straighten up

endividar-se [ẽdʒivi'daxsi] vr to run into debt

endoidecer [ẽdojde'se*] vt to madden ♦ vi to go mad

endossar [ẽdo'sa*] vt to endorse; **endosso** [ẽ'dosu] m endorsement

endurecer [ẽdure'se*] vt, vi to harden

energia [enex'ʒia] f energy, drive; (TEC) power, energy; **enérgico/a** [e'nɛxʒiku/a] adj energetic, vigorous

enervante [enex'vãtʃi] adj annoying

enevoado/a [ene'vwadu/a] adj misty, hazy

enfado [ẽ'fadu] m annoyance; ~**nho/a** [ẽfa'doɲu/a] adj tiresome; (aborrecido) boring

enfaixar [ẽfaj'ʃa*] vt (perna) to bandage, bind

enfarte [ẽ'faxtʃi] m (MED) coronary

ênfase [ẽ'fazi] f emphasis, stress

enfastiado/a [ẽfaʃ'tʃjadu/a] adj bored

enfastiar [ẽfaʃ'tʃja*] vt to weary; (aborrecer) to bore; ~-**se** vr: ~-**se de** ou **com** to get tired of; to get bored with

enfático/a [ẽ'fatʃiku/a] adj emphatic

enfatizar [ẽfatʃi'za*] vt to emphasize

enfeitar [ẽfej'ta*] vt to decorate; ~-**se** vr to dress up; **enfeite** [ẽ'fejtʃi] m decoration

enfeitiçar [ẽfejtʃi'sa*] vt to bewitch, cast a spell on

enfermagem [ẽfex'maʒẽ] f nursing

enfermaria [ẽfexma'ria] f ward

enfermeiro/a [ẽfex'mejru/a] m/f nurse

enfermidade [ẽfexmi'dadʒi] f illness

enfermo/a [ẽ'fexmu/a] adj ill, sick ♦ m/f sick person, patient

enferrujar [ẽfexu'ʒa*] vt to rust, corrode ♦ vi to go rusty

enfiada [ẽ'fjada] f row

enfiar [ẽ'fja*] vt (meter) to put; (agulha) to thread; (vestir) to slip on; ~-**se** vr: ~-**se em** to slip into

enfim [ẽ'fĩ] adv finally, at last; (em suma) in short; **até que** ~! at last!

enfoque [ẽ'fɔki] m approach

enforcar [ẽfox'ka*] vt to hang; (trabalho, aulas) to skip; ~-**se** vr to hang o.s.

enfraquecer [ẽfrake'se*] vt to weaken ♦

vi to grow weak

enfrentar [ẽfrẽ'ta*] vt to face; (confrontar) to confront; (problemas) to face up to

enfurecer [ẽfure'se*] vt to infuriate; ~-**se** vr to get furious

engajar [ẽga'ʒa*] vt (trabalhadores) to take on, hire; ~-**se** vr to take up employment; (MIL) to enlist; ~-**se em algo** to get involved in sth; (POL) to be committed to sth

enganado/a [ẽga'nadu/a] adj mistaken; (traído) deceived

enganar [ẽga'na*] vt to deceive; (desonrar) to seduce; (cônjuge) to be unfaithful to; (fome) to stave off; ~-**se** vr to be wrong, be mistaken; (iludir-se) to deceive o.s.

enganchar [ẽgã'ʃa*] vt: ~ **algo (em algo)** to hook sth up (to sth)

engano [ẽ'gãnu] m mistake; (ilusão) deception; (logro) trick; **é** ~ (TEL) I've (ou you've) got the wrong number

engarrafamento [ẽgaxafa'mẽtu] m bottling; (de trânsito) traffic jam

engarrafar [ẽgaxa'fa*] vt to bottle; (trânsito) to block

engasgar [ẽgaʒ'ga*] vt to choke ♦ vi to choke; (máquina) to splutter; ~-**se** vr to choke

engastar [ẽgaʃ'ta*] vt (jóias) to set, mount

engatinhar [ẽgatʃi'ɲa*] vi to crawl

engendrar [ẽʒẽ'dra*] vt to dream up

engenharia [ẽʒeɲa'ria] f engineering; **engenheiro/a** [ẽʒe'nejru/a] m/f engineer

engenho [ẽ'ʒeɲu] m talent; (destreza) skill; (máquina) machine; (moenda) mill; (fazenda) sugar plantation; ~**so/a** [ẽʒe'ɲozu/ɔza] adj clever, ingenious

engessar [ẽʒe'sa*] vt (perna) to put in plaster; (parede) to plaster

englobar [ẽglo'ba*] vt to include

engodar [ẽgo'da*] vt to lure, entice

engodo [ẽ'godu] m bait

engolir [ẽgo'li*] vt to swallow

engomar [ẽgo'ma*] vt to starch; (passar) to iron

engonço [ẽ'gõsu] m hinge

engordar [ẽgox'da*] vt to fatten ♦ vi to put on weight

engraçado/a [ẽgra'sadu/a] adj funny, amusing

engradado [ẽgra'dadu] m crate

engrandecer [ẽgrãde'se*] vt to elevate ♦ vi to grow; ~-**se** vr to become great

engraxador [ẽgrafa'do*] (PT) m shoe shiner

engraxar [ẽgra'ʃa*] vt to polish

engraxate [ẽgra'ʃatʃi] m shoe shiner

engrenagem [ẽgre'naʒẽ] (pl ~**ns**) f (AUTO) gear

engrenar [ẽgre'na*] vt to put into gear; (fig: conversa) to strike up ♦ vi: ~ **com alguém** to get on with sb

engrossar [ēgro'sa*] vt (sopa) to thicken; (aumentar) to swell; (voz) to raise ♦ vi to thicken; to swell; to rise; (col: pessoa, conversa) to turn nasty

enguia [ē'gia] f eel

enguiçar [ēgi'sa*] vi (máquina) to break down ♦ vt to cause to break down; **enguiço** [ē'gisu] m snag; (desarranjo) breakdown

enigma [e'nigma] m enigma; (mistério) mystery

enjaular [ēʒaw'la*] vt (fera) to cage, cage up; (pessoa) to imprison

enjeitado/a [ēʒej'tadu/a] m/f foundling, waif

enjeitar [ēʒej'ta*] vt to reject; (abandonar) to abandon; (condenar) to condemn

enjoado/a [ē'ʒwadu/a] adj sick; (enfastiado) bored; (enfadonho) boring; (malhumorado) in a bad mood

enjoar [ē'ʒwa*] vt to make sick; to bore ♦ vi (pessoa) to be sick; (comida) to cause nausea; ~-se vr: ~-se de to get sick of

enjôo [ē'ʒou] m sickness; (em carro) travel sickness; (em navio) seasickness; boredom

enlaçar [ēla'sa*] vt to tie, bind; (abraçar) to hug; (unir) to link, join; (bois) to hitch; (cingir) to wind around; ~-se vr to be linked

enlatado/a [ēla'tadu/a] adj tinned (BRIT), canned ♦ m (pej: filme) foreign import; ~s mpl (comida) tinned (BRIT) ou canned foods

enlatar [ēla'ta*] vt (comida) to can

enlouquecer [ēloke'se*] vt to drive mad ♦ vi to go mad

enlutado/a [ēlu'tadu/a] adj in mourning

enojar [eno'ʒa*] vt to disgust, sicken

enorme [e'nɔxmi] adj enormous, huge; **enormidade** [enoxmi'dadʒi] f enormity; **uma enormidade (de)** (col) a hell of a lot (of)

enquadrar [ēkwa'dra*] vt to fit; (gravura) to frame ♦ vi: ~ com (condizer) to fit ou tie in with

enquanto [ē'kwãtu] conj while; (considerado como) as; ~ isso meanwhile; por ~ for the time being; ~ ele não vem until he comes; ~ que whereas

enquête [ē'kɛtʒi] f survey

enraivecer [ēxajve'se*] vt to enrage

enredar [ēxe'da*] vt to entangle; (complicar) to complicate; ~-se vr to get entangled

enredo [ē'xedu] m (de uma obra) plot; (intriga) intrigue

enriquecer [ēxike'se*] vt to make rich; (fig) to enrich ♦ vi to get rich; ~-se vr to get rich

enrolar [ēxo'la*] vt to roll up; (agasalhar) to wrap up; (col: enganar) to con ♦ vi (col) to waffle; ~-se vr to roll up; to wrap up; (col: confundir-se) to get mixed ou muddled up

enroscar [ēxoʃ'ka*] vt (torcer) to twist, wind (round); ~-se vr to coil up

enrubescer [ēxube'se*] vt to redden, colour (BRIT), color (US) ♦ vi (por vergonha) to blush, go red

enrugar [ēxu'ga*] vt (pele) to wrinkle; (testa) to furrow; (tecido) to crease ♦ vi (pele, mãos) to go wrinkly; (pessoa) to get wrinkles

ensaiar [ēsa'ja*] vt to test, try out; (treinar) to practise (BRIT), practice (US); (TEATRO) to rehearse

ensaio [ē'saju] m test; (tentativa) attempt; (treino) practice; (TEATRO) rehearsal; (literário) essay

ensangüentar [ēsãgwē'ta*] vt to stain with blood

enseada [ē'sjada] f inlet, cove; (baía) bay

ensejo [ē'seʒu] m chance, opportunity

ensinamento [ēsina'mētu] m teaching; (exemplo) lesson

ensinar [ēsi'na*] vt, vi to teach

ensino [ē'sinu] m teaching, tuition; (educação) education

ensolarado/a [ēsola'radu/a] adj sunny

ensopado/a [ēso'padu/a] adj soaked ♦ m stew

ensopar [ēso'pa*] vt to soak, drench

ensurdecer [ēsuxde'se*] vt to deafen ♦ vi to go deaf

entalar [ēta'la*] vt to wedge, jam; (encher): **ela me entalou de comida** she stuffed me full of food

entalhar [ēta'ʎa*] vt to carve; **entalhe** [ē'taʎi] m groove, notch; **entalho** [ē'taʎu] m woodcarving

entanto [ē'tãtu]: **no ~** adv yet, however

então [ē'tãw] adv then; **até ~** up to that time; **desde ~** ever since; **e ~?** well then?; **para ~** so that; **pois ~** in that case; **~, você vai ou não?** so, are you going or not?

entardecer [ētaxde'se*] vi to get late ♦ m sunset

ente ['ētʃi] m being

enteado/a [ē'tʃjadu/a] m/f stepson/stepdaughter

entediar [ēte'dʒja*] vt to bore; ~-se vr to get bored

entender [ētē'de*] vt to understand; (pensar) to think; (ouvir) to hear; ~-se vr to understand one another; **dar a ~** to imply; **no meu ~** in my opinion; ~ **de música** to know about music; ~ **de fazer** to decide to do; ~-se **por** to be meant by; ~-se **com alguém** to get along with sb; (dialogar) to sort things out with sb

entendido/a [ētē'dʒidu/a] adj (col) gay; (conhecedor) ~ **em** good at ♦ m/f expert; (col) homosexual, gay; **bem ~** that is

entendimento [ētēdʒi'mētu] m understanding; (opinião) opinion; (combinação) agreement

enternecer [ẽtexne'se*] vt to move, touch; ~-se vr to be moved

enterrar [ẽte'xa*] vt to bury; (faca) to plunge; (lever à ruina) to ruin; (assunto) to close

enterro [ẽ'texu] m burial; (funeral) funeral

entidade [ẽtʃi'dadʒi] f (ser) being; (corporação) body; (coisa que existe) entity

entoar [ẽ'twa*] vt to chant

entonação [ẽtona'sãw] (pl –ões) f intonation

entornar [ẽtox'na*] vt to spill; (fig: copo) to drink ♦ vi to drink a lot

entorpecente [ẽtoxpe'sẽtʃi] m narcotic

entorpecer [ẽtoxpe'se*] vt to numb, stupefy; (retardar) to slow down; **entorpecimento** [ẽtoxpesi'mẽtu] m numbness; (torpor) lethargy

entorse [ẽ'toxsi] f sprain

entortar [ẽtox'ta*] vt (curvar) to bend; (empenar) to warp; ~ os olhos to squint

entrada [ẽ'trada] f (ato) entry; (lugar) entrance; (TEC) inlet; (de casa) doorway; (começo) beginning; (bilhete) ticket; (CULIN) starter, entrée; (COMPUT) input; (pagamento inicial) down payment; (corredor de casa) hall; ~s fpl (no cabelo) receding hairline sg; ~ gratuita admission free; "~ proibida" "no entry", "no admittance"; meia ~ half-price ticket

entra-e-sai [ẽtrai'saj] m comings and goings pl

entranhado/a [ẽtra'ɲadu/a] adj deep-rooted

entranhas [ẽ'traɲaʃ] fpl bowels, entrails; (sentimentos) feelings; (centro) heart sg

entrar [ẽ'tra*] vi to go (ou come) in, enter; ~ com (COMPUT: dados etc) to enter; **eu entrei com £10** I contributed £10; ~ **de férias/licença** to start one's holiday (BRIT) ou vacation (US)/leave; ~ **em** to go (ou come) into, enter; (assunto) to get onto; (comida, bebida) to start in on

entravar [ẽtra'va*] vt to obstruct, impede; **entrave** [ẽ'travi] m (fig) impediment

entre [ˈẽtri] prep (dois) between; (mais de dois) among(st); ~ **si** amongst themselves

entreaberto/a [ẽtrja'bɛxtu/a] pp de entreabrir ♦ adj half-open; (porta) ajar

entreabrir [ẽtrja'bri*] vt to half open; ~-se vr (flores) to open up

entrega [ẽ'trɛga] f (de mercadorias) delivery; (a alguém) handing over; (rendição) surrender; ~ **rápida** special delivery

entregar [ẽtre'ga*] vt to hand over; (mercadorias) to deliver; (confiar) to entrust; (devolver) to return; ~-se vr (render-se) to give o.s. up; (dedicar-se) to devote o.s.

entregue [ẽ'trɛgi] pp de entregar

entrelaçar [ẽtrila'sa*] vt to entwine

entrelinha [ẽtre'liɲa] f line space; **ler nas ~s** to read between the lines

entremear [ẽtri'mja*] vt to intermingle

entreolhar-se [ẽtrio'ʎaxsi] vr to exchange glances

entrepor [ẽtripo*] (irreg: como pôr) vt to insert; ~-se vr: ~-se entre to come between

entretanto [ẽtri'tãtu] conj however

entretenimento [ẽtriteni'mẽtu] m entertainment; (distração) pastime

entreter [ẽtri'te*] (irreg: como ter) vt to entertain, amuse; (ocupar) to occupy; (manter) to keep up; (esperanças) to cherish; ~-se vr to amuse o.s.; to occupy o.s.

entrevista [ẽtre'viʃta] f interview; ~ **coletiva (à imprensa)** press conference; ~**r** [ẽtreviʃ'ta*] vt to interview; ~-**r-se** vr to have an interview

entristecer [ẽtriʃte'se*] vt to sadden, grieve ♦ vi to feel sad; ~-se vr to feel sad

entroncamento [ẽtrõka'mẽtu] m junction

entrudo [ẽ'trudu] (PT) m carnival; (REL) Shrovetide

entulhar [ẽtu'ʎa*] vt to cram full; (suj: multidão) to pack

entulho [ẽ'tuʎu] m rubble, debris sg

entupido/a [ẽtu'pidu/a] adj blocked; **estar ~** (col: congestionado) to have a blocked-up nose; (de comida) to be fit to burst, be full up

entupimento [ẽtupi'mẽtu] m blockage

entupir [ẽtu'pi*] vt to block, clog; ~-se vr to become blocked; (de comida) to stuff o.s.

entusiasmar [ẽtuzjaʒ'ma*] vt to fill with enthusiasm; (animar) to excite; ~-se vr to get excited

entusiasmo [ẽtu'zjaʒmu] m enthusiasm; (júbilo) excitement

entusiasta [ẽtu'zjaʃta] adj enthusiastic ♦ m/f enthusiast

enumerar [enume'ra*] vt to enumerate; (com números) to number

enunciar [enũ'sja*] vt to express, state

envelhecer [ẽveʎe'se*] vt to age ♦ vi to grow old, age

envelope [ẽve'lɔpi] m envelope

envenenamento [ẽvenena'mẽtu] m poisoning; ~ **do sangue** blood poisoning

envenenar [ẽvene'na*] vt to poison; (fig) to corrupt; (: declaração, palavras) to distort, twist; (tornar amargo) to sour ♦ vi to be poisonous; ~-se vr to poison o.s.

enveredar [ẽvere'da*] vi: ~ **por um caminho** to follow a road; ~ **para** to head for

envergadura [ẽvexga'dura] f (de asas, velas) spread; (de avião) wingspan; (fig) scope; **de grande ~** large-scale

envergonhado/a [ēvexgoˈɲadu/a] *adj* ashamed; (*tímido*) shy

envergonhar [ēvexgoˈɲaˈ] *vt* to shame; (*degradar*) to disgrace; **~se** *vr* to be ashamed

envernizar [ēvexniˈzaˈ] *vt* to varnish

enviado/a [ēˈvjadu/a] *m/f* envoy, messenger

enviar [ēˈvjaˈ] *vt* to send

envidraçar [ēvidraˈsaˈ] *vt* to glaze

envio [ēˈviu] *m* sending; (*expedição*) dispatch; (*remessa*) remittance; (*de mercadorias*) consignment

enviuvar [ēvjuˈvaˈ] *vi* to be widowed

envolto/a [ēˈvowtu/a] *pp de* envolver

envoltório [ēvowˈtɔrju] *m* cover

envolver [ēvowˈveˈ] *vt* to wrap (up); (*cobrir*) to cover; (*comprometer, acarretar*) to involve; (*nos braços*) to embrace; **~se** *vr* (*intrometer-se*) to become involved; (*cobrir-se*) to wrap o.s. up; **envolvimento** [ēvowviˈmētu] *m* involvement

enxada [ēˈʃada] *f* hoe

enxaguar [ēʃaˈgwaˈ] *vt* to rinse

enxame [ēˈʃami] *m* swarm

enxaqueca [ēʃaˈkeka] *f* migraine

enxergar [ēʃexˈgaˈ] *vt* (*avistar*) to catch sight of; (*divisar*) to make out; (*notar*) to observe, see

enxofre [ēˈʃofri] *m* sulphur (*BRIT*), sulfur (*US*)

enxotar [ēʃoˈtaˈ] *vt* to drive out

enxoval [ēʃoˈvaw] (*pl* **-ais**) *m* (*de noiva*) trousseau; (*de recém-nascido*) layette

enxugador [ēʃugaˈdoˈ] *m* clothes drier

enxugar [ēʃuˈgaˈ] *vt* to dry; (*fig: texto*) to tidy up

enxurrada [ēʃuˈxada] *f* (*de água*) torrent; (*fig*) spate

enxuto/a [ēˈʃutu/a] *adj* dry; (*corpo*) shapely; (*bonito*) good-looking

épico/a [ˈɛpiku/a] *adj* epic ♦ *m* epic poet

epidemia [epideˈmia] *f* epidemic

epilepsia [epileˈpsia] *f* epilepsy; **epiléptico/a** [epiˈlɛptʃiku/a] *adj, m/f* epileptic

episódio [epiˈzɔdʒu] *m* episode

epístola [eˈpiʃtola] *f* epistle; (*carta*) letter

epitáfio [epiˈtafju] *m* epitaph

epítome [eˈpitomi] *m* summary; (*fig*) epitome

época [ˈɛpoka] *f* time, period; (*da história*) age, epoch; **naquela ~** at that time; **fazer ~** to be epoch-making

epopéia [epoˈpɛja] *f* epic

equação [ekwaˈsāw] (*pl* **-ões**) *f* equation

equador [ekwaˈdoˈ] *m* equator; **o E~** Ecuador

equânime [eˈkwanimi] *adj* fair; (*caráter*) unbiassed, neutral

equilibrar [ekiliˈbraˈ] *vt* to balance; **~se** *vr* to balance; **equilíbrio** [ekiˈlibrju] *m* balance

equipa [eˈkipa] (*PT*) *f* team

equipamento [ekipaˈmētu] *m* equipment, kit

equipar [ekiˈpaˈ] *vt*: **~ (com)** (*navio*) to fit out (with); (*prover*) to equip (with)

equiparar [ekipaˈraˈ] *vt* (*comparar*) to equate; **~se** *vr*: **~se a** to equal

equipe [eˈkipi] (*BR*) *f* team

equitação [ekitaˈsāw] *f* (*ato*) riding; (*arte*) horsemanship

eqüitativo/a [ekwitaˈtʃivu/a] *adj* fair, equitable

equivalente [ekivaˈlētʃi] *adj, m* equivalent

equivaler [ekivaˈleˈ] *vi*: **~ a** to be the same as, equal

equivocado/a [ekivoˈkadu/a] *adj* mistaken, wrong

equivocar-se [ekivoˈkaxsi] *vr* to make a mistake, be wrong

equívoco/a [eˈkivoku/a] *adj* ambiguous ♦ *m* (*engano*) mistake

era[1] [ˈɛra] *f* era, age

era[2] *etc vb V* ser

erário [eˈrarju] *m* exchequer

erecto/a [eˈrɛktu/a] (*PT*) *adj* = ereto

eremita [ereˈmita] *m/f* hermit

ereto/a [eˈrɛtu/a] *adj* upright, erect

erguer [exˈgeˈ] *vt* to raise, lift; (*edificar*) to build, erect; **~se** *vr* to rise; (*pessoa*) to stand up

eriçado/a [eriˈsadu/a] *adj* bristling; (*cabelos*) (standing) on end

eriçar [eriˈsaˈ] *vt*: **~ o cabelo de alguém** to make sb's hair stand on end; **~se** *vr* to bristle; (*cabelos*) to stand on end

erigir [eriˈʒiˈ] *vt* to erect

ermo/a [ˈexmu/a] *adj* lonely; (*desabitado*) uninhabited ♦ *m* wilderness

erosão [eroˈzāw] *f* erosion

erótico/a [eˈrɔtʃiku/a] *adj* erotic; **erotismo** [eroˈtʃiʒmu] *m* eroticism

erradicar [exadʒiˈkaˈ] *vt* to eradicate

errado/a [eˈxadu/a] *adj* wrong; **dar ~** to go wrong

errante [eˈxātʃi] *adj* wandering

errar [eˈxaˈ] *vt* (*alvo*) to miss; (*conta*) to get wrong ♦ *vi* to wander, roam; (*enganar-se*) to be wrong, make a mistake; **~ o caminho** to lose one's way

erro [ˈexu] *m* mistake; **salvo ~** unless I am mistaken; **~ de imprensa** misprint

errôneo/a [eˈxonju/a] *adj* wrong, mistaken; (*falso*) false, untrue

erudição [erudʒiˈsāw] *f* erudition, learning; **erudito/a** [eruˈdʒitu/a] *adj* learned, scholarly ♦ *m* scholar

erupção [erupˈsāw] (*pl* **-ões**) *f* eruption; (*na pele*) rash; (*fig*) outbreak

erva [ˈexva] *f* herb; (*col: dinheiro*) dosh; (: *maconha*) dope; **~ daninha** weed

erva-mate (*pl* **ervas-mates**) *f* mate

ervilha [exˈviʎa] *f* pea

esbaforido/a [iʒbafoˈridu/a] *adj* breathless, panting

esbanjar [iʒbāˈʒaˈ] *vt* to squander, waste

esbarrar [iʒbaˈxaˈ] *vi*: **~ em** to bump

into; (*obstáculo, problema*) to come up against

esbelto/a [iʒ'bɛwtu/a] *adj* slim, slender

esboçar [iʒbo'sa*] *vt* to sketch; (*delinear*) to outline; (*traçar*) to draw up; **esboço** [iʒ'bosu] *m* sketch; (*primeira versão*) draft; (*fig: resumo*) outline

esbofetear [iʒbofe'tʃja*] *vt* to slap, hit

esbugalhado/a [iʒbuga'ʎadu/a] *adj*: **olhos ~s** goggle eyes

esburacar [iʒbura'ka*] *vt* to make holes (*ou* a hole) in

esc (*PT*) *abr* = **escudo**

escabroso/a [iʃka'brozu/ɔza] *adj* (*difícil*) tough; (*indecoroso*) indecent

escada [iʃ'kada] *f* (*dentro da casa*) staircase, stairs *pl*; (*fora da casa*) steps *pl*; (*de mão*) ladder; **~ de incêndio** fire escape; **~ rolante** escalator; **~ria** [iʃkada'ria] *f* staircase

escafandrista [iʃkafã'driʃta] *m/f* deep-sea diver

escala [iʃ'kala] *f* scale; (*NÁUT*) port of call; (*parada*) stop; **fazer ~ em** to call at; **sem ~** non-stop

escalada [iʃka'lada] *f* (*de guerra*) escalation

escalão [eʃka'lãw] (*pl* -ões) *m* step; (*MIL*) echelon

escalar [iʃka'la*] *vt* (*montanha*) to climb; (*muro*) to scale; (*designar*) to select

escaldar [iʃkaw'da*] *vt* to scald; **~-se** *vr* to scald o.s.

escalfar [iʃkaw'fa*] (*PT*) *vt* (*ovos*) to poach

escalões [eʃka'lõjʃ] *mpl de* **escalão**

escama [iʃ'kama] *f* (*de peixe*) scale; (*de pele*) flake

escamar [iʃka'ma*] *vt* to scale

escamotear [iʃkamo'tʃja*] *vt* to pilfer, pinch (*BRIT*); (*empalmar*) to make disappear (by sleight of hand)

escancarado/a [iʃkãka'radu/a] *adj* wide open

escandalizar [iʃkãdali'za*] *vt* to shock; **~-se** *vr* to be shocked; (*ofender-se*) to be offended

escândalo [iʃ'kãdalu] *m* scandal; (*indignação*) outrage; **fazer ou dar um ~** to make a scene; **escandaloso/a** [iʃkãda'lozu/ɔza] *adj* shocking, scandalous

Escandinávia [iʃkãdʒi'navja] *f*: **a ~** Scandinavia; **escandinavo/a** [iʃkãdʒi'navu/a] *adj, m/f* Scandinavian

escangalhar [iʃkãga'ʎa*] *vt* to break, smash (up); (*a própria saúde*) to ruin; **~-se** *vr*: **~-se de rir** to split one's sides laughing

escaninho [iʃka'niɲu] *m* (*na secretária*) pigeonhole

escapar [iʃka'pa*] *vi*: **~ a ou de** to escape from; (*fugir*) to run away from; **~-se** *vr* to run away, flee; **deixar ~** (*uma oportunidade*) to miss; (*palavras*) to blurt out; **~ de boa** (*col*) to have a close shave

escapatória [iʃkapa'tɔrja] *f* way out; (*desculpa*) excuse

escape [iʃ'kapi] *m* (*de gás*) leak; (*AUTO*) exhaust

escapulir [iʃkapu'li*] *vi*: **~ (de)** to get away (from); (*suj: coisa*) to slip (from)

escaravelho [iʃkara'veʎu] *m* beetle

escarlate [iʃkax'latʃi] *adj* scarlet; **escarlatina** [iʃkaxla'tʃina] *f* scarlet fever

escárnio [iʃ'kaxnju] *m* mockery; (*desprezo*) derision

escarpado/a [iʃkax'padu/a] *adj* steep

escarrar [iʃka'xa*] *vt* to spit, cough up ♦ *vi* to spit

escarro [iʃ'kaxu] *m* phlegm, spit

escassear [iʃka'sja*] *vt* to skimp on ♦ *vi* to become scarce

escassez [iʃka'seʒ] *f* (*falta*) shortage

escasso/a [iʃ'kasu/a] *adj* scarce

escavação [iʃkava'sãw] (*pl* -ões) *f* excavation

escavar [iʃka'va*] *vt* to excavate

esclarecer [iʃklare'se*] *vt* (*situação*) to explain; (*mistério*) to clear up, explain; **~-se** *vr*: **~-se (sobre algo)** to find out (about sth); **esclarecimento** [iʃklaresi'mẽtu] *m* explanation; (*informação*) information

escoadouro [iʃkoa'doru] *m* drain; (*cano*) drainpipe

escoar [iʃko'a*] *vt* to drain off ♦ *vi* to drain away; **~-se** *vr* to seep out

escocês/esa [iʃko'seʃ/seza] *adj* Scottish, Scots ♦ *m/f* Scot, Scotsman/woman

Escócia [iʃ'kɔsja] *f* Scotland

escola [iʃ'kɔla] *f* school; **~ naval** naval college; **~ primária** primary (*BRIT*) ou elementary (*US*) school; **~ secundária** secondary (*BRIT*) ou high (*US*) school; **~ particular/pública** private/state (*BRIT*) ou public (*US*) school; **~ superior** college

escolar [iʃko'la*] *adj* school *atr* ♦ *m/f* schoolboy/girl

escolha [iʃ'kɔʎa] *f* choice

escolher [iʃko'ʎe*] *vt* to choose, select

escolho [iʃ'koʎu] *m* (*recife*) reef; (*rocha*) rock

escolta [iʃ'kɔwta] *f* escort; **~r** [iʃkow'ta*] *vt* to escort

escombros [iʃ'kõbruʃ] *mpl* ruins, debris *sg*

esconde-esconde [iʃkõdʃiʃ'kõdʒi] *m* hide-and-seek

esconder [iʃkõ'de*] *vt* to hide, conceal; **~-se** *vr* to hide

esconderijo [iʃkõde'riʒu] *m* hiding place; (*de bandidos*) hideout

escondidas [iʃkõ'dʒidaʃ] *fpl*: **às ~** secretly

esconjurar [iʃkõʒu'ra*] *vt* to exorcize; (*afastar*) to keep off; (*amaldiçoar*) to curse; **~-se** *vr* (*lamentar-se*) to complain

escopo [iʃ'kopu] *m* aim, purpose

escora [iʃ'kɔra] *f* prop, support; (*cilada*)

ambush

escorar [iʃko'ra*] *vt* to prop (up); (*amparar*) to support; (*esperar de espreita*) to lie in wait for ♦ *vi* to lie in wait; ~-**se** *vr*: ~-**se em** (*fundamentar-se*) to go by; (*amparar-se*) to live off

escore [iʃ'kɔri] *m* score

escoriação [iʃkorja'sãw] (*pl* -ões) *f* abrasion, scratch

escorpião [iʃkopi'ãw] (*pl* -ões) *m* scorpion; **E~** (*ASTROLOGIA*) Scorpio

escorrega [iʃko'xega] *f* slide; ~**dela** [iʃkoxega'dɛla] *f* slip; ~**diço/a** [iʃkoxega'dʒi(s)u/a] *adj* slippery; ~**dor** [iʃkoxega'do*] *m* slide; **escorregão** [iʃkoxe'gãw] (*pl* -ões) *m* slip; (*fig*) slip(-up); ~**r** [iʃkoxe'ga*] *vi* to slip; (*errar*) to slip up

escorrer [iʃko'xe*] *vt* to drain (off); (*verter*) to pour out ♦ *vi* (*pingar*) to drip; (*correr em fio*) to trickle

escoteiro [iʃko'tejru] *m* scout

escotilha [iʃko'tʃiʎa] *f* hatch, hatchway

escova [iʃ'kova] *f* brush; (*penteado*) blow-dry; ~ **de dentes** toothbrush; ~**r** [iʃko'va*] *vt* to brush

escovinha [iʃko'viɲa] *f*: **cabelo à** ~ crew cut

escravatura [iʃkrava'tura] *f* (*tráfico*) slave trade; (*escravidão*) slavery

escravidão [iʃkravi'dãw] *f* slavery

escravizar [iʃkravi'za*] *vt* to enslave; (*cativar*) to captivate

escravo/a [iʃ'kravu/a] *adj* captive ♦ *m/f* slave

escrevente [iʃkre'vẽtʃi] *m/f* clerk

escrever [iʃkre've*] *vt*, *vi* to write; ~-**se** *vr* to write to each other; ~ **à máquina** to type

escrevinhar [iʃkrevi'ɲa*] *vt* to scribble

escrita [eʃ'krita] *f* writing; (*letra*) handwriting

escrito/a [eʃ'kritu/a] *pp* **de escrever** ♦ *adj* written ♦ *m* piece of writing; ~ **à mão** handwritten; **dar por** ~ to put in writing

escritor(a) [iʃkri'to*(a)] *m/f* writer; (*autor*) author

escritório [iʃkri'tɔrju] *m* office; (*em casa*) study

escritura [iʃkri'tura] *f* (*JUR*) deed; (*na compra de imóveis*) ≈ exchange of contracts; **as Sagradas E~s** the Scriptures

escrituração [iʃkritura'sãw] *f* book-keeping; (*de transações, quantias*) entering, recording

escriturar [iʃkritu'ra*] *vt* (*contas*) to register; (*documento*) to draw up

escriturário/a [iʃkritu'rarju/a] *m/f* clerk

escrivã [iʃkri'vã] *f* **de escrivão**

escrivaninha [iʃkriva'niɲa] *f* writing desk

escrivão/vã [iʃkri'vãw/vã] (*pl* -ões/~s) *m/f* registrar, recorder

escrúpulo [iʃ'krupulu] *m* scruple; (*cuidado*) care; **sem** ~ unscrupulous;

escrupuloso/a [iʃkrupu'lozu/ɔza] *adj* scrupulous; careful

escrutínio [iʃkru'tʃinju] *m* (*votação*) poll; (*apuração de votos*) counting; (*exame atento*) scrutiny; ~ **secreto** secret ballot

escudo [iʃ'kudu] *m* shield; (*moeda*) escudo

esculhambado/a [iʃkuʎã'badu/a] (*col!*) *adj* shabby, slovenly; (*estragado*) knackered

esculhambar [iʃkuʎã'ba*] (*col!*) *vt* to mess up, fuck up (*!*); ~ **alguém** (*criticar*) to give sb stick; (*descompor*) to give sb a bollocking (*!*)

esculpir [iʃkuw'pi*] *vt* to carve, sculpt; (*gravar*) to engrave

escultor(a) [iʃkuw'to*(a)] *m/f* sculptor

escultura [iʃkuw'tura] *f* sculpture

escuna [iʃ'kuna] *f* (*NÁUT*) schooner

escuras [iʃ'kuraʃ] *fpl*: **às** ~ in the dark

escurecer [iʃkure'se*] *vt* to darken ♦ *vi* to get dark; **ao** ~ at dusk

escuridão [iʃkuri'dãw] *f* (*trevas*) dark

escuro/a [iʃ'kuru/a] *adj* dark; (*dia*) overcast; (*pessoa*) swarthy; (*negócios*) shady ♦ *m* darkness

escusa [iʃ'kuza] *f* excuse

escusar [iʃku'za*] *vt* to excuse, forgive; (*justificar*) to justify; (*dispensar*) to exempt; (*não precisar de*) not to need; ~-**se** *vr* to apologize; ~-**se de fazer** to refuse to do

escuta [iʃ'kuta] *f* listening; **à** ~ listening out; **ficar na** ~ to stand by

escutar [iʃku'ta*] *vt* to listen to; (*sem prestar atenção*) to hear ♦ *vi* to listen; to hear

esfacelar [iʃfase'la*] *vt* to destroy

esfaquear [iʃfaki'a*] *vt* to stab

esfarelar [iʃfare'la*] *vt* to crumble; ~-**se** *vr* to crumble

esfarrapado/a [iʃfaxa'padu/a] *adj* ragged, tattered

esfarrapar [iʃfaxa'pa*] *vt* to tear to pieces

esfera [iʃ'fɛra] *f* sphere; (*globo*) globe; (*TIP, COMPUT*) golfball; **esférico/a** [iʃ'fɛriku/a] *adj* spherical

esferográfico/a [iʃfero'grafiku/a] *adj*: **caneta esferográfica** ballpoint pen

esfolar [iʃfo'la*] *vt* to skin; (*arranhar*) to graze; (*cobrar demais a*) to overcharge, fleece

esfomeado/a [iʃfo'mjadu/a] *adj* famished, starving

esforçado/a [iʃfox'sadu/a] *adj* committed, dedicated

esforçar-se [iʃfox'saxsi] *vr*: ~ **para** to try hard to, strive to

esforço [iʃ'foxsu] *m* effort

esfregar [iʃfre'ga*] *vt* to rub; (*com água*) to scrub

esfriar [iʃ'frja*] *vt* to cool, chill ♦ *vi* to get cold; (*fig*) to cool off

esfuziante [iʃfuˈzjãtʃi] adj (pessoa) bubbly; (alegria) irrepressible

esganado/a [iʒgaˈnadu/a] adj choked; (voraz) greedy; (avaro) grasping

esganar [iʒgaˈna*] vt to strangle, choke

esganiçado/a [iʒganiˈsadu/a] adj (voz) shrill

esgotado/a [iʒgoˈtadu/a] adj exhausted; (consumido) used up; (livros) out of print; (ingressos) sold out

esgotamento [iʒgotaˈmẽtu] m exhaustion

esgotar [iʒgoˈta*] vt to drain, empty; (recursos) to use up; (pessoa, assunto) to exhaust; ~-se vr to become exhausted; (mercadorias, edição) to be sold out; (recursos) to run out

esgoto [iʒˈgotu] m drain; (público) sewer

esgrima [iʒˈgrima] f (esporte) fencing; **esgrimir** [iʒgriˈmi*] vi to fence

esgueirar-se [iʒgejˈraxsi] vr to slip away, sneak off

esguelha [iʒˈgeʎa] f slant; **olhar alguém de ~** to look at sb out of the corner of one's eye

esguichar [iʒgiˈʃa*] vt to squirt ♦ vi to squirt out

esguicho [iʒˈgiʃu] m (jacto) jet; (de mangueira etc) spout

esguio/a [eʒˈgiu/a] adj slender

esmaecer [iʒmajeˈse*] vi to fade

esmagador(a) [iʒmagadoˈ*(a)] adj crushing; (provas) irrefutable; (maioria) overwhelming

esmagar [iʒmaˈga*] vt to crush

esmalte [iʒˈmawtʃi] m enamel; (de unhas) nail polish

esmerado/a [iʒmeˈradu/a] adj careful, neat; (bem acabado) polished

esmeralda [iʒmeˈrawda] f emerald

esmerar-se [iʒmeˈraxsi] vr: ~ **em fazer algo** to take great care in doing sth

esmigalhar [iʒmigaˈʎa*] vt to crumble; (despedaçar) to shatter; (esmagar) to crush; ~-se vr to crumble; to smash, shatter

esmiuçar [iʒmjuˈsa*] vt to crumble; (examinar) to examine in detail

esmo [ˈeʒmu] m: **a ~** at random; **falar a ~** to prattle

esmola [iʒˈmɔla] f alms pl; **pedir ~s** to beg

esmurrar [iʒmuˈxa*] vt to punch

esnobe [iʒˈnɔbi] adj snobbish ♦ m/f snob; **esnobismo** [iʒnoˈbiʒmu] m snobbery

espaçar [iʃpaˈsa*] vt to space out; ~ **visitas/saídas** etc to visit/go out etc less often

espacial [iʃpaˈsjaw] (pl -ais) adj space atr; **nave ~** spaceship

espaço [iʃˈpasu] m space; (tempo) period; ~ **para 3 pessoas** room for 3 people; **a ~s** from time to time; **~so/a** [iʃpaˈsozu/ɔza] adj spacious, roomy

espada [iʃˈpada] f sword; **~s** fpl (CARTAS) spades

espadarte [iʃpaˈdaxtʃi] m swordfish

espádua [iʃˈpadwa] f shoulder blade

espairecer [iʃpajreˈse*] vt to amuse, entertain ♦ vi to relax; **~-se** vr to relax

espaldar [iʃpawˈda*] m (chair) back

espalhafato [iʃpaʎaˈfatu] m din, commotion

espalhar [iʃpaˈʎa*] vt to scatter; (boato, medo) to spread; (luz) to shed; **~-se** vr to spread; (refestelar-se) to lounge

espanador [iʃpanaˈdo*] m duster

espanar [iʃpaˈna*] vt to dust

espancar [iʃpãˈka*] vt to beat up

Espanha [iʃˈpaɲa] f: **a ~** Spain; **espanhol/a** [iʃpaˈɲow/ɔla] (pl -óis/~s) adj Spanish ♦ m/f Spaniard ♦ m (LING) Spanish; **os espanhóis** mpl the Spanish

espantado/a [iʃpãˈtadu/a] adj astonished, amazed; (assustado) frightened

espantalho [iʃpãˈtaʎu] m scarecrow

espantar [iʃpãˈta*] vt to frighten; (admirar) to amaze, astonish; (afugentar) to frighten away ♦ vi to be amazing; **~-se** vr to be astonished ou amazed; to be frightened

espanto [iʃˈpãtu] m fright, fear; (admiração) astonishment, amazement; **~so/a** [iʃpãˈtozu/ɔza] adj amazing

esparadrapo [iʃparaˈdrapu] m (sticking) plaster (BRIT), bandaid ® (US)

esparramar [iʃpaxaˈma*] vt to splash; (espalhar) to scatter

esparso/a [iʃˈpaxsu/a] adj scattered; (solto) loose

espartilho [iʃpaxˈtʃiʎu] m corset

espasmo [iʃˈpaʒmu] m spasm, convulsion

espatifar [iʃpatʃiˈfa*] vt to smash; **~-se** vr to smash; (avião) to crash

especial [iʃpeˈsjaw] (pl -ais) adj special; **em ~** especially; **~idade** [iʃpesjaliˈdadʒi] f speciality (BRIT), specialty (US); (ramo de atividades) specialization; **~ista** [iʃpesjaˈliʃta] m/f specialist; (perito) expert; **~izar-se** [iʃpesjaliˈzaxsi] vr: **~izar-se (em)** to specialize (in)

especiaria [iʃpesjaˈria] f spice

espécie [iʃˈpɛsi] f (BIO) species; (tipo) sort, kind; **causar ~** to be surprising; **pagar em ~** to pay in cash

especificar [iʃpesifiˈka*] vt to specify; **específico/a** [iʃpeˈsifiku/a] adj specific

espécime [iʃˈpɛsimi] m specimen

espécimen [iʃˈpɛsimẽ] (pl ~s) m = espécime

espectáculo etc [iʃpekˈtakulu] (PT) m = espetáculo etc

espectador(a) [iʃpektaˈdo*(a)] m/f onlooker; (TV) viewer; (ESPORTE) spectator; (TEATRO) member of the audience; **~es** mpl (TV, TEATRO) audience sg

espectro [iʃˈpektru] m spectre (BRIT), specter (US); (FÍS) spectrum

especulação [iʃpekula'sãw] (pl -ões) f speculation

especular [iʃpeku'la*] vi: ~ **(sobre)** to speculate (on)

espelho [iʃ'peʌu] m mirror; (fig) model; ~ **retrovisor** (AUTO) rearview mirror

espera [iʃ'pεra] f (demora) wait; (expectativa) expectation; **à ~ de** waiting for; **à minha ~** waiting for me

esperança [iʃpe'rãsa] f hope; (expectativa) expectation; **dar ~s a alguém** to raise sb's hopes; **esperançoso/a** [iʃperã'sozu/ɔza] adj hopeful

esperar [iʃpe'ra*] vt to wait for; (contar com: bebê) to expect; (desejar) to hope for ♦ vi to wait; to hope; to expect

esperma [iʃ'pεxma] f sperm

espertalhão/lhona [iʃpεxta'ʌãw/ʎona] (pl -ões/~s) adj crafty, shrewd

esperteza [iʃpex'teza] f cleverness; (astúcia) cunning

esperto/a [iʃ'pεxtu/a] adj clever; (espertalhão) crafty

espesso/a [iʃ'pesu/a] adj thick; **espessura** [iʃpe'sura] f thickness

espetacular [iʃpetaku'la*] adj spectacular

espetáculo [iʃpe'takulu] m (TEATRO) show; (vista) sight; (cena ridícula) spectacle; **dar ~** to make a spectacle of o.s.

espetar [iʃpe'ta*] vt (carne) to put on a spit; (cravar) to stick; **~-se** vr to prick o.s.; ~ **algo em algo** to pin sth to sth

espetinho [iʃpe'tʃiɲu] m skewer

espeto [iʃ'petu] m spit; (pau) pointed stick; **ser um ~** (ser difícil) to be awkward

espevitado/a [iʃpevi'tadu/a] adj (fig: vivo) lively

espezinhar [iʃpezi'ɲa*] vt to trample (on); (humilhar) to treat like dirt

espia [iʃ'pia] m/f spy

espiã [iʃ'pjã] f de **espião**

espiada [iʃ'pjada] f: **dar uma ~** to have a look

espião/piã [iʃ'pjãw/'pjã] (pl -ões/~s) m/f spy

espiar [iʃ'pja*] vt to spy on; (uma ocasião) to watch out for; (olhar) to watch ♦ vi to spy; (olhar) to peer

espichar [iʃpi'ʃa*] vt (couro) to stretch out; (pescoço, pernas) to stretch ♦ vi (col: crescer) to shoot up; **~-se** vr to stretch out

espiga [iʃ'piga] f (de milho) ear

espinafre [iʃpi'nafri] m spinach

espingarda [iʃpĩ'gaxda] f shotgun, rifle

espinha [iʃ'piɲa] f (de peixe) bone; (na pele) spot, pimple; (coluna vertebral) spine

espinhar [iʃpi'ɲa*] vt to prick; (irritar) to irritate, annoy

espinheiro [iʃpi'ɲejro] m bramble bush

espinhento/a [iʃpi'ɲẽtu/a] adj spotty, pimply

espinho [iʃ'piɲu] m thorn; (de animal)

spine; (fig: dificuldade) snag; **~so/a** [iʃpi'ɲozu/ɔza] adj (planta) prickly, thorny; (fig: difícil) difficult; (: problema) thorny

espiões [iʃ'pjõjʃ] mpl de **espião**

espionagem [iʃpio'naʒẽ] f spying, espionage

espionar [iʃpjo'na*] vt to spy on ♦ vi to spy, snoop

espiral [iʃpi'raw] (pl -ais) adj, f spiral

espírito [iʃ'piritu] m spirit; (pensamento) mind; ~ **esportivo** sense of humo(u)r; **E~ Santo** Holy Spirit

espiritual [iʃpiri'twaw] (pl -ais) adj spiritual ♦

espirituoso/a [iʃpiri'twozu/ɔza] adj witty

espirrar [iʃpi'xa*] vi to sneeze; (jorrar) to spurt out ♦ vt (água) to spurt; **espirro** [iʃ'pixu] m sneeze

esplêndido/a [iʃ'plẽʒidu/a] adj splendid

esplendor [iʃplẽ'do*] m splendour (BRIT), splendor (US)

espoleta [iʃpo'leta] f (de arma) fuse

espólio [iʃ'pɔlju] m (herança) estate, property; (roubado) booty, spoils pl

esponja [iʃ'põʒa] f sponge

espontâneo/a [iʃpõ'tanju/a] adj spontaneous; (pessoa) straightforward

espora [iʃ'pɔra] f spur

esporádico/a [iʃpo'radʒiku/a] adj sporadic

esporte [iʃ'pɔxtʃi] (BR) m sport; **esportista** [iʃpox'tʃiʃta] adj sporting ♦ m/f sportsman/woman; **esportivo/a** [iʃpox'tʃivu/a] adj sporting

esposa [iʃ'poza] f wife

esposar [iʃpo'za*] vt to marry; (causa) to defend

esposo [iʃ'pozu] m husband

espreguiçadeira [iʃpregisa'dejra] f deck chair; (com lugar para as pernas) lounger

espreguiçar-se [iʃpregi'saxsi] vr to stretch

espreita [iʃ'prejta] f: **ficar à ~** to keep watch

espreitar [iʃprej'ta*] vt to spy on; (observar) to observe, watch

espremer [iʃpre'me*] vt (fruta) to squeeze; (roupa molhada) to wring out; (pessoas) to squash; **~-se** vr (multidão) to be squashed together; (uma pessoa) to squash up

espuma [iʃ'puma] f foam; (de cerveja) froth, head; (de sabão) lather; (de ondas) surf; ~ **de borracha** foam rubber; **~nte** [iʃpu'mãtʃi] adj frothy, foamy; (vinho) sparkling; **~r** [iʃpu'ma*] vi to foam; (fera, cachorro) to foam at the mouth

espúrio/a [iʃ'purju/a] adj spurious, bogus

esq. abr (= esquerdo/a)

esquadra [iʃ'kwadra] f (NÁUT) fleet; (PT: da polícia) police station

esquadrão [iʃkwa'drãw] (pl -ões) m

squadron

esquadrilha [iʃkwa'driʎa] *f* squadron

esquadrinhar [iʃkwadri'na*] *vt* (*casa, área*) to search, scour; (*fatos*) to scrutinize

esquadrões [iʃkwa'drõjʃ] *mpl de* **esquadrão**

esqualidez [iʃkwali'deʃ] *f* squalor; **esquálido/a** [iʃ'kwalidu/a] *adj* squalid, filthy

esquartejar [iʃkwaxte'ʒa*] *vt* to quarter

esquecer [iʃke'se*] *vt, vi* to forget; ~**-se** *vr*: ~**-se de** to forget; **esquecido/a** [iʃke'sidu/a] *adj* forgotten; (*pessoa*) forgetful

esqueleto [iʃke'letu] *m* skeleton; (*arcabouço*) framework

esquema [iʃ'kɛma] *m* outline; (*plano*) scheme; (*diagrama*) diagram, plan

esquentar [iʃkẽ'ta*] *vt* to heat (up), warm (up); (*fig: irritar*) to annoy ♦ *vi* to warm up; (*casaco*) to be warm; ~**-se** *vr* to get annoyed

esquerda [iʃ'kexda] *f* (*tb: POL*) left; à ~ on the left

esquerdista [iʃkex'dʒiʃta] *adj* left-wing ♦ *m/f* left-winger

esquerdo/a [iʃ'kexdu/a] *adj* left

esquete [iʃ'kɛtʃi] *m* (*TEATRO, TV*) sketch

esqui [iʃ'ki] *m* (*patim*) ski; (*esporte*) skiing; ~ **aquático** water skiing; **fazer** ~ to go skiing; ~**ador/a** [iʃkja'do*(a)] *m/f* skier; ~**ar** [iʃ'kja*] *vi* to ski

esquilo [iʃ'kilu] *m* squirrel

esquina [iʃ'kina] *f* corner

esquisito/a [iʃki'zitu/a] *adj* strange, odd

esquivar-se [iʃki'vaxsi] *vr*: ~ **de** to escape from, get away from; (*deveres*) to get out of

esquivo/a [iʃ'kivu/a] *adj* aloof, standoffish

esq. *abr* = **esquerdo**

essa ['ɛsa] *pron*: ~ **é/foi boa** that is/was a good one; ~ **não, sem** ~ come off it!; **vamos nessa** let's go!; **ainda mais** ~! that's all I need!; **corta** ~! cut it out!; **por** ~**s e outras** for these and other reasons; ~ **de fazer ...** this business of doing ...

esse ['esi] *adj* (*sg*) that; (*pl*) those; (*BR: este: sg*) this; (: *pl*) these ♦ *pron* (*sg*) that one; (*pl*) those; (*BR: este: sg*) this one; (: *pl*) these

essência [e'sẽsja] *f* essence; **essencial** [esẽ'sjaw] (*pl* –**ais**) *adj* essential; (*principal*) main ♦ *m*: **o essencial** the main thing

esta ['ɛʃta] *f de* **este**

estabelecer [iʃtabele'se*] *vt* to establish; (*fundar*) to set up

estabelecimento [iʃtabelesi'mẽtu] *m* establishment; (*casa comercial*) business

estábulo [iʃ'tabulu] *m* cow-shed

estaca [iʃ'taka] *f* post, stake; (*de barraca*) peg

estação [iʃta'sãw] (*pl* –**ões**) *f* station; (*do ano*) season; ~ **de águas** spa; ~ **balneária** seaside resort; ~ **emissora** broadcasting station

estacionamento [iʃtasjona'mẽtu] *m* (*ato*) parking; (*lugar*) car park (*BRIT*), parking lot (*US*)

estacionar [iʃtasjo'na*] *vt* to park ♦ *vi* to park; (*não mover*) to remain stationary

estacionário/a [iʃtasjo'narju/a] *adj* (*veículo*) stationary; (*COM*) slack

estações [iʃta'sõjʃ] *fpl de* **estação**

estada [iʃ'tada] *f* stay

estadia [iʃta'dʒia] *f* = **estada**

estádio [iʃ'tadʒu] *m* stadium

estadista [iʃta'dʒiʃta] *m/f* statesman/woman

estado [iʃ'tadu] *m* state; **E~s Unidos (da América)** United States (of America); ~ **civil** marital status; ~ **de espírito** state of mind; ~ **maior** staff; **estadual** [iʃta'dwaw] (*pl* –**ais**) *adj* state *atr*

estadunidense [iʃtaduni'dẽsi] *adj* (North) American, US *atr*

estafa [iʃ'tafa] *f* fatigue; (*esgotamento*) nervous exhaustion

estagiário/a [iʃta'ʒjarju/a] *m/f* probationer, trainee; (*professor*) student teacher; (*médico*) junior doctor

estágio [iʃ'taʒu] *m* (*aprendizado*) traineeship; (*fase*) stage

estagnação [iʃtagna'sãw] *f* stagnation

estagnado/a [iʃtag'nadu/a] *adj* stagnant

estagnar [iʃtag'na*] *vt* to make stagnant; (*país*) to bring to a standstill ♦ *vi* to stagnate; ~**-se** *vr* to stagnate

estalagem [iʃta'laʒẽ] (*pl* –**ns**) *f* inn

estalar [iʃta'la*] *vt* to break; (*os dedos*) to snap ♦ *vi* to split, crack; (*crepitar*) to crackle

estaleiro [iʃta'lejru] *m* shipyard

estalido [iʃta'lidu] *m* pop

estalo [iʃ'talu] *m* (*do chicote*) crack; (*dos dedos*) snap; (*dos lábios*) smack; (*de foguete*) bang; ~ **de trovão** thunderclap; **de** ~ suddenly

estampa [iʃ'tãpa] *f* (*figura impressa*) print; (*ilustração*) picture

estampado/a [iʃtã'padu/a] *adj* printed ♦ *m* (*tecido*) print; (*num tecido*) pattern

estampar [iʃtã'pa*] *vt* to print; (*marcar*) to stamp; ~**ia** [iʃtãpa'ria] *f* (*oficina*) printshop; (*tecido, figura*) print

estampido [iʃtã'pidu] *m* bang

estancar [iʃtã'ka*] *vt* to staunch; (*fazer cessar*) to stop; ~**-se** *vr* to stop

estância [iʃ'tãsja] *f* ranch, farm

estandarte [iʃtã'daxtʃi] *m* standard, banner

estanho [iʃ'taɲu] *m* (*metal*) tin

estante [iʃ'tãtʃi] *f* bookcase; (*suporte*) stand

estapafúrdio/a [iʃtapa'fuxdʒu/a] *adj* outlandish, odd

PALAVRA CHAVE

---

estar [iʃˈtaˣ] vi **1** (lugar) to be; (em casa) to be in; (no telefone): **a Lúcia está? –** **não, ela não está** is Lúcia there? – no, she's not here

2 (estado) to be; **~ doente** to be ill; **~** **bem** (de saúde) to be well; (financeiramente) to be well off; **~ calor/frio** to be hot/cold; **~ com fome/sede/medo** to be hungry/thirsty/afraid

3 (ação contínua): **~ fazendo** (BR) ou **a** **fazer** (PT) to be doing

4 (+ pp: = adj): **~ sentado/cansado** to be sitting down/tired

5 (+ pp: uso passivo): **está condenado** **à morte** he's been condemned to death; **o livro está emprestado** the book's been borrowed

6: **~ de: ~ de férias/licença** to be on holiday (BRIT) ou vacation (US)/leave; **ela estava de chapéu** she had a hat on, she was wearing a hat

7: **~ para: ~ para fazer** to be about to do; **ele está para chegar a qualquer momento** he'll be here any minute; **não ~ para conversas** not to be in the mood for talking

8: **~ por fazer** to be still to be done

9: **~ sem: ~ sem dinheiro** to have no money; **~ sem dormir** not to have slept; **estou sem dormir há três dias** I haven't slept for three days; **está sem** **terminar** it isn't finished yet

10 (frases): **está bem, tá (bem)** (col) OK; **~ bem com** to be on good terms with

---

estardalhaço [iʃtaxdaˈʎasu] m fuss; (ostentação) ostentation

estarrecer [iʃtaxeˈseˣ] vt to petrify ♦ vi to be petrified

estas [ˈeʃtaʃ] fpl de **este**

estatal [iʃtaˈtaw] (pl **-ais**) adj nationalized, state-owned ♦ f state-owned company

estático/a [iʃˈtatʃiku/a] adj static

estatística [iʃtaˈtʃiʃtʃika] f statistic; (ciência) statistics sg

estatizar [iʃtatʃiˈza] vt to nationalize

estátua [iʃˈtatwa] f statue

estatura [iʃtaˈtura] f stature

estatuto [iʃtaˈtutu] m statute; (de cidade) bye-law; (de associação) rule

estável [iʃˈtavew] (pl **-eis**) adj stable

este [ˈeʃtʃi] m east ♦ adj inv (região) eastern; (vento, direção) easterly

este/ta [ˈeʃtʃi/ˈeʃta] adj (sg) this; (pl) these ♦ pron this one; (pl) these; (a quem/que se referiu por último) the latter; **esta noite** (noite passada) last night; (noite de hoje) tonight

esteio [iʃˈteju] m prop, support; (NÁUT) stay

esteira [iʃˈtejra] f mat; (de navio) wake;

(rumo) path

esteja etc [iʃˈteʒa] vb V **estar**

estelionato [iʃteljoˈnatu] m fraud

estêncil [iʃˈtẽsiw] (pl **-eis**) m stencil

estender [iʃtẽˈdeˣ] vt to extend; (mapa) to spread out; (pernas) to stretch; (massa) to roll out; (conversa) to draw out; (corda) to pull tight; (roupa molhada) to hang out; **~-se** vr to lie down; (fila, terreno) to stretch, extend; **~ a mão** to hold out one's hand; **~-se sobre algo** to dwell on sth, expand on sth

estenodatilógrafo/a [iʃtenodatʃiˈlɔgrafu/a] m/f shorthand typist (BRIT), stenographer (US)

estenografia [iʃtenograˈfia] f shorthand

estepe [iʃˈtɛpi] m spare wheel

esterco [iʃˈtexku] m dung

estéreis [iʃˈtɛrejʃ] adj pl de **estéril**

estereo... [iʃˈtɛrju] prefixo stereo...; **~fônico/a** [iʃterjoˈfoniku/a] adj stereo(phonic); **estereótipo** [iʃteˈrjɔtʃipu] m stereotype

estéril [iʃˈtɛriw] (pl **-eis**) adj sterile; (terra) infertile; (fig) futile; **esterilizar** [iʃteriliˈzaˣ] vt to sterilize

esterlino/a [iʃtexˈlinu/a] adj: **libra esterlina** pound sterling

estético/a [iʃˈtɛtʃiku/a] adj aesthetic (BRIT), esthetic (US)

estetoscópio [iʃtetoˈskɔpju] m stethoscope

esteve [iʃˈtevi] vb V **estar**

estiagem [iʃˈtʃjaʒẽ] (pl **-ns**) f (depois da chuva) calm after the storm; (falta de chuva) dry spell

estiar [iʃˈtʃja] vi (não chover) to stop raining; (o tempo) to clear up

estibordo [iʃtʃiˈbɔxdu] m starboard

esticar [iʃtʃiˈka] vt to stretch; **~-se** vr to stretch out

estigma [iʃˈtʃigima] m mark, scar; (fig) stigma

estigmatizar [iʃtʃigimatʃiˈza] vt: **~ alguém de algo** to brand sb (as) sth

estilhaçar [iʃtʃiʎaˈsa] vt to splinter; (despedaçar) to shatter; **~-se** vr to shatter; **estilhaço** [iʃtʃiˈʎasu] m fragment; (de pedra) chip; (de madeira, metal) splinter

estilo [iʃˈtʃilu] m style; (TEC) stylus; **~** **de vida** way of life

estima [iʃˈtʃima] f esteem; (afeto) affection; **ter ~ a** to have a high regard for

estimação [iʃtʃimaˈsãw] f: **E~ de ~** favourite (BRIT), favorite (US) ...

estimado/a [iʃtʃiˈmadu/a] adj respected; (em cartas): **E~ Senhor** Dear Sir

estimar [iʃtʃiˈma] vt to appreciate; (avaliar) to value; (ter estima a) to have a high regard for; (calcular aproximadamente) to estimate

estimativa [iʃtʃimaˈtʃiva] f estimate

estimulante [iʃtʃimuˈlãtʃi] adj stimulating ♦ m stimulant

estimular [iʃtʃimuˈla] vt to stimulate;

(*incentivar*) to encourage; **estímulo** [iʃˈtʃimulu] *m* stimulus; (*ânimo*) encouragement

estipular [iʃtʃipuˈlaʳ] *vt* to stipulate

estirar [iʃtʃiˈraʳ] *vt* to stretch (out); **~-se** *vr* to stretch

estivador(a) [iʃtʃivaˈdo*(a)] *m/f* docker

estive *etc* [iʃˈtʃivi] *vb* V estar

estocada [iʃtoˈkada] *f* stab, thrust

estocar [iʃtoˈkaʳ] *vt* to stock

estofar [iʃtoˈfaʳ] *vt* to upholster; (*acolchoar*) to pad, stuff; **estofo** [iʃˈtofu] *m* (*tecido*) material; (*para acolchoar*) padding, stuffing

estóico/a [iʃˈtɔjku/a] *adj* stoical

estojo [iʃˈtoʒu] *m* case; **~ de ferramentas** tool kit; **~ de unhas** manicure set

estola [iʃˈtɔla] *f* stole

estólido/a [iʃˈtolidu/a] *adj* stupid

estômago [iʃˈtomagu] *m* stomach; **ter ~ para (fazer) algo** to be up to (doing) sth

estontear [iʃtõˈtʃjaʳ] *vt* to stun, daze

estoque [iʃˈtɔki] *m* (*COM*) stock

estória [iʃˈtɔrja] *f* story

estorvo [iʃˈtoxvu] *m* hindrance, obstacle; (*amolação*) bother, nuisance

estourado/a [iʃtoˈradu/a] *adj* (*temperamental*) explosive; (*col: cansado*) shattered, worn out

estourar [iʃtoˈraʳ] *vi* to explode; (*pneu*) to burst; (*escândalo*) to blow up; (*guerra*) to break out; (*BR: chegar*) to turn up, arrive; **~ (com alguém)** (*zangar-se*) to blow up (at sb)

estouro [iʃˈtoru] *m* explosion; **dar o ~** (*fig: zangar-se*) to blow up, blow one's top

estrábico/a [iʃˈtrabiku/a] *adj* cross-eyed

estrabismo [iʃtraˈbiʒmu] *m* squint

estraçalhar [iʃtrasaˈʎaʳ] *vt* (*livro, objeto*) to pull to pieces; (*pessoa*) to tear to pieces

estrada [iʃˈtrada] *f* road; **~ de ferro** (*BR*) railway (*BRIT*), railroad (*US*); **~ principal** main road (*BRIT*), state highway (*US*)

estrado [iʃˈtradu] *m* (*tablado*) platform; (*de cama*) base

estragado/a [iʃtraˈgadu/a] *adj* ruined; (*fruta*) rotten; (*muito mimado*) spoiled, spoilt (*BRIT*)

estragão [iʃtraˈgãw] *m* tarragon

estraga-prazeres [iʃtraga-] *m/f inv* spoilsport

estragar [iʃtraˈgaʳ] *vt* to spoil; (*arruinar*) to ruin, wreck; (*desperdiçar*) to waste; (*saúde*) to damage; (*mimar*) to spoil; **estrago** [iʃˈtragu] *m* destruction; waste; damage; **os estragos da guerra** the ravages of war

estrangeiro/a [iʃtrãˈʒejru/a] *adj* foreign ♦ *m/f* foreigner; **no ~** abroad

estrangular [iʃtrãguˈlaʳ] *vt* to strangle

estranhar [iʃtraˈɲaʳ] *vt* to be surprised

at; (*achar estranho*): **~ algo** to find sth strange; **estranhei o clima** the climate did not agree with me; **não é de se ~** it's not surprising

estranho/a [iʃˈtraɲu/a] *adj* strange, odd; (*influências*) outside ♦ *m/f* (*desconhecido*) stranger; (*de fora*) outsider

estratagema [iʃtrataˈʒema] *m* (*MIL*) stratagem; (*ardil*) trick

estratégia [iʃtraˈtɛʒa] *f* strategy; **estratégico/a** [iʃtraˈtɛʒiku/a] *adj* strategic

estrato [iʃˈtratu] *m* layer, stratum

estrear [iʃˈtrjaʳ] *vt* (*vestido*) to wear for the first time; (*peça de teatro*) to perform for the first time; (*veículo*) to use for the first time; (*filme*) to show for the first time, première; (*iniciar*): **~ uma carreira** to embark on *ou* begin a career ♦ *vi* (*ator, jogador*) to make one's first appearance; (*filme, peça*) to open

estrebaria [iʃtrebaˈria] *f* stable

estréia [iʃˈtreja] *f* (*de artista*) debut; (*de uma peça*) first night; (*de um filme*) première, opening

estreitar [iʃtrejˈtaʳ] *vt* to narrow; (*roupa*) to take in; (*abraçar*) to hug; (*laços de amizade*) to strengthen ♦ *vi* (*estrada*) to narrow

estreito/a [iʃˈtrejtu/a] *adj* narrow; (*saia*) straight; (*vínculo, relação*) close; (*medida*) strict ♦ *m* strait

estrela [iʃˈtrela] *f* star; **~ cadente** falling star; **~do/a** [iʃtreˈladu/a] *adj* (*céu*) starry; (*ovo*) fried; **~-do-mar** (*pl* **~s-do-mar**) *f* starfish

estremecer [iʃtremeˈseʳ] *vt* to shake; (*amizade*) to strain; (*fazer tremer*): **~ alguém** to make sb shudder ♦ *vi* to shake; (*tremer*) to tremble; (*horrorizar-se*) to shudder; (*amizade*) to be strained

estremecimento [iʃtremesiˈmẽtu] *m* shaking, trembling; (*tremor*) tremor; (*numa amizade*) tension

estresse [iʃˈtresi] *m* stress

estria [iʃˈtria] *f* groove

estribeira [iʃtriˈbejra] *f*: **perder as ~s** (*col*) to fly off the handle, lose one's temper

estribo [iʃˈtribu] *m* (*de cavalo*) stirrup; (*degrau*) step; (*fig: apoio*) support

estridente [iʃtriˈdẽtʃi] *adj* shrill, piercing

estrito/a [iʃˈtritu/a] *adj* strict; (*restrito*) restricted

estrofe [iʃˈtrɔfi] *f* stanza

estrondo [iʃˈtrõdu] *m* (*de trovão*) rumble; (*de armas*) din; **~so/a** [iʃtrõˈdozu/ɔza] *adj* (*ovação*) tumultuous, thunderous; (*sucesso*) resounding; (*notícia*) sensational

estropiar [iʃtroˈpjaʳ] *vt* to maim, cripple; (*fatigar*) to wear out, exhaust

estrume [iʃˈtrumi] *m* manure

estrutura [iʃtruˈtura] *f* structure; (*arm-*

ação) framework; (*de edifício*) fabric

estuário [iʃtu'arju] *m* estuary

estudante [iʃtu'dãtʃi] *m/f* student; **estudantil** [iʃtudã'tʃiw] (*pl* **-is**) *adj* student *atr*

estudar [iʃtu'da*] *vt, vi* to study

estúdio [iʃ'tudʒu] *m* studio

estudioso/a [iʃtu'dʒozu/ɔza] *adj* studious ♦ *m/f* student

estudo [iʃ'tudu] *m* study

estufa [iʃ'tufa] *f* (*fogão*) stove; (*de plantas*) greenhouse; (*de fogão*) plate warmer; **efeito ~** greenhouse effect

estufado [iʃtu'fadu] (*PT*) *m* stew

estulto/a [iʃ'tuwtu/a] *adj* foolish, silly

estupefação [iʃtupefa'sãw] (*PT* **-cç-**) *f* amazement, astonishment

estupefato/a [iʃtupe'fatu/a] (*PT* **-ct-**) *adj* dumbfounded

estupendo/a [iʃtu'pẽdu/a] *adj* wonderful, terrific

estupidez [iʃtupi'deʒ] *f* stupidity; (*ato, dito*) stupid thing; (*grosseria*) rudeness

estúpido/a [iʃ'tupidu/a] *adj* stupid; (*grosseiro*) rude, churlish ♦ *m/f* idiot; oaf

estuprar [iʃtu'pra*] *vt* to rape; **estupro** [iʃ'tupru] *m* rape

estuque [iʃ'tuki] *m* stucco; (*massa*) plaster

esvair-se [iʒva'jixsi] *vr* to vanish, disappear; **~ em sangue** to lose a lot of blood

esvaziar [iʒva'zja*] *vt* to empty; **~-se** *vr* to empty

esvoaçar [iʒvoa'sa*] *vi* to flutter

etapa [e'tapa] *f* stage

etc. *abr* (= et cetera) etc

eternidade [etexni'dadʒi] *f* eternity

eterno/a [e'texnu/a] *adj* eternal

ética ['ɛtʃika] *f* ethics *pl*

ético/a ['ɛtʃiku/a] *adj* ethical

Etiópia [e'tʃjɔpja] *f*: **a ~** Ethiopia

etiqueta [etʃi'keta] *f* etiquette; (*rótulo, em roupa*) label; (*que se amarra*) tag

étnico/a ['ɛtʃniku/a] *adj* ethnic

etos ['ɛtuʃ] *m inv* ethos

eu [ew] *pron* I ♦ *m* self; **sou ~** it's me

EUA *abr mpl* (= *Estados Unidos da América*) USA

eucaristia [ewkariʃ'tʃia] *f* Holy Communion

eufemismo [ewfe'miʒmu] *m* euphemism

euro ['ewru] *m* (*moeda*) euro

Europa [ew'rɔpa] *f*: **a ~** Europe; **europeu/péia** [ewro'peu/'pɛja] *adj, m/f* European

evacuação [evakwa'sãw] (*pl* **-ões**) *f* evacuation

evacuar [eva'kwa*] *vt* to evacuate; (*sair de*) to leave; (*MED*) to discharge ♦ *vi* to defecate

evadir [eva'dʒi*] *vt* to evade; **~-se** *vr* to escape

evangelho [evã'ʒeʎu] *m* gospel

evaporar [evapo'ra*] *vt, vi* to evaporate;

~-se *vr* to evaporate; (*desaparecer*) to vanish

evasão [eva'zãw] (*pl* **-ões**) *f* escape, flight; (*fig*) evasion

evasiva [eva'ziva] *f* excuse

evasivo/a [eva'zivu/a] *adj* evasive

evasões [eva'zõjʃ] *fpl de* **evasão**

evento [e'vẽtu] *m* event; (*eventualidade*) eventuality

eventual [evẽ'tuaw] (*pl* **-ais**) *adj* fortuitous, accidental; **~idade** [evẽtwali'dadʒi] *f* eventuality

evidência [evi'dẽsja] *f* evidence, proof; **evidenciar** [evidẽ'sja*] *vt* to prove; (*mostrar*) to show; **evidenciar-se** *vr* to be evident, be obvious

evidente [evi'dẽtʃi] *adj* obvious, evident

evitar [evi'ta*] *vt* to avoid; **~ de fazer algo** to avoid doing sth

evocar [evo'ka*] *vt* to evoke; (*espíritos*) to invoke

evolução [evolu'sãw] (*pl* **-ões**) *f* development; (*MIL*) manoeuvre (*BRIT*), maneuver (*US*); (*movimento*) movement; (*BIO*) evolution

evoluir [evo'lwi*] *vi* to evolve; **~ para** to evolve into

ex- [ɛʃ-, eʒ-] *prefixo* ex-, former

Ex.ª *abr* = **Excelência**

exacerbar [ezasex'ba*] *vt* to irritate, annoy; (*agravar*) to aggravate, worsen; (*revolta, indignação*) to deepen

exacto/a [e'zatu/a] (*PT*) = **exato** *etc*

exagerar [ezaʒe'ra*] *vt* to exaggerate ♦ *vi* to exaggerate; (*agir com exagero*) to overdo it; **exagero** [eza'ʒeru] *m* exaggeration

exalar [eza'la*] *vt* (*odor*) to give off

exaltado/a [ezaw'tadu/a] *adj* fanatical; (*apaixonado*) overexcited

exaltar [ezaw'ta*] *vt* (*elevar: pessoa, virtude*) to exalt; (*louvar*) to praise; (*excitar*) to excite; (*irritar*) to annoy; **~-se** *vr* (*irritar-se*) to get worked up; (*arrebatar-se*) to get carried away

exame [e'zami] *m* (*EDUC*) examination, exam; (*MED etc*) examination; **fazer um ~** (*EDUC*) to take an exam; (*MED*) to have an examination

examinar [ezami'na*] *vt* to examine

exasperar [ezaʃpe'ra*] *vt* to exasperate; **~-se** *vr* to get exasperated

exatidão [ezatʃi'dãw] *f* accuracy; (*perfeição*) correctness

exato/a [e'zatu/a] *adj* right, correct; (*preciso*) exact; **~!** exactly!

exaurir [ezaw'ri*] *vt* to exhaust, drain; **~-se** *vr* to become exhausted

exaustão [ezaw'ʃtãw] *f* exhaustion; **exausto/a** [e'zawʃtu/a] *pp de* **exaurir** ♦ *adj* exhausted

exaustor [ezaw'ʃto*] *m* extractor fan

exceção [ese'sãw] (*pl* **-ões**) *f* exception; **com ~ de** with the exception of; **abrir ~** to make an exception

excedente [eseˈdẽtʃi] *adj* excess; (*COM*) surplus ♦ *m* (*COM*) surplus

exceder [eseˈde*] *vt* to exceed; (*superar*) to surpass; **~-se** *vr* (*cometer excessos*) to go too far; (*cansar-se*) to overdo things

excelência [eseˈlẽsja] *f* excellence; **por ~** par excellence; **Vossa E~** Your Excellency; **excelente** [eseˈlẽtʃi] *adj* excellent

excêntrico/a [eˈsẽtriku/a] *adj, m/f* eccentric

excepção [eseˈsãw] (*PT*) *f* = **exceção**

excepcional [esepsjoˈnaw] (*pl* **-ais**) *adj* exceptional; (*especial*) special; (*MED*) handicapped

excepto *etc* [eˈsɛtu] (*PT*) = **exceto** *etc*

excerto [eˈsɛxtu] *m* fragment, excerpt

excessivo/a [eseˈsivu/a] *adj* excessive

excesso [eˈsɛsu] *m* excess; (*COM*) surplus

exceto [eˈsɛtu] *prep* except (for), apart from

excetuar [eseˈtwa*] *vt* to except, make an exception of

excitação [esitaˈsãw] *f* excitement

excitado/a [esiˈtadu/a] *adj* excited; (*estimulado*) aroused

excitante [esiˈtãtʃi] *adj* exciting

excitar [esiˈta*] *vt* to excite; (*estimular*) to arouse; **~-se** *vr* to get excited

exclamação [iʃklamaˈsãw] (*pl* **-ões**) *f* exclamation

exclamar [iʃklaˈma*] *vi* to exclaim

excluir [iʃkluˈi*] *vt* to exclude, leave out; (*eliminar*) to rule out; (*ser incompatível com*) to preclude; **exclusão** [iʃkluˈzãw] *f* exclusion; **exclusivo/a** [iʃkluˈzivu/a] *adj* exclusive

excomungar [iʃkomũˈga*] *vt* to excommunicate

excursão [iʃkuxˈsãw] (*pl* **-ões**) *f* outing, excursion; **~ a pé** hike; **excursionista** [iʃkuxsjoˈniʃta] *m/f* tourist; (*para o dia*) day-tripper; (*a pé*) hiker

execução [ezekuˈsãw] (*pl* **-ões**) *f* execution; (*de música*) performance

executar [ezekuˈta*] *vt* to execute; (*MÚS*) to perform; (*plano*) to carry out; (*papel teatral*) to play

executivo/a [ezekuˈtʃivu/a] *adj, m/f* executive

executor(a) [ezekuˈto*(a)] *m/f* executor

exemplar [ezẽˈpla*] *adj* exemplary ♦ *m* model, example; (*BIO*) specimen; (*livro*) copy; (*peça*) piece

exemplo [eˈzẽplu] *m* example; **por ~** for example

exéquias [eˈzɛkjaʃ] *fpl* funeral rites

exercer [ezexˈse*] *vt* to exercise; (*influência, pressão*) to exert; (*função*) to perform; (*profissão*) to practise (*BRIT*), practice (*US*); (*obrigações*) to carry out

exercício [ezexˈsisju] *m* exercise; (*de medicina*) practice; (*MIL*) drill; (*COM*) financial year

exercitar [ezexsiˈta*] *vt* (*profissão*) to practise (*BRIT*), practice (*US*); (*direitos,*

músculos) to exercise; (*adestrar*) to train

exército [eˈzɛxsito] *m* army

exibição [ezibiˈsãw] (*pl* **-ões**) *f* show, display; (*de filme*) showing

exibir [eziˈbi*] *vt* to show, display; (*alardear*) to show off; (*filme*) to show, screen; **~-se** *vr* to show off; (*indecentemente*) to expose o.s.

exigência [eziˈʒẽsja] *f* demand; (*o necessário*) requirement; **exigente** [eziˈʒẽtʃi] *adj* demanding

exigir [eziˈʒi*] *vt* to demand

exíguo/a [eˈzigwu/a] *adj* (*diminuto*) small; (*escasso*) scanty

exilado/a [eziˈladu/a] *m/f* exile

exilar [eziˈla*] *vt* to exile; **~-se** *vr* to go into exile; **exílio** [eˈzilju] *m* exile; (*forçado*) deportation

exímio/a [eˈzimju/a] *adj* famous, distinguished; (*excelente*) excellent

eximir [eziˈmi*] *vt*: **~ de** to exempt from; (*obrigação*) to free from; (*culpa*) to clear of; **~-se** *vr*: **~-se de** to avoid, shun

existência [eziʃˈtẽsja] *f* existence; (*vida*) life

existir [eziʃˈtʃi*] *vi* to exist; **existe/existem ...** (*há*) there is/are ...

êxito [ˈezitu] *m* result; (*sucesso*) success; (*música, filme etc*) hit; **ter ~ (em)** to succeed (in), be successful (in)

Exmo(s)/a(s) *abr* (= *Excelentíssimo(s)/a(s)*) Dear

êxodo [ˈezodu] *m* exodus

exonerar [ezoneˈra*] *vt* (*demitir*) to dismiss; **~ de uma obrigação** to free from an obligation; **exorcista** [ezoxˈsiʃta] *m/f* exorcist

exortar [ezoxˈta*] *vt*: **~ alguém a fazer algo** to urge sb to do sth

exótico/a [eˈzɔtʃiku/a] *adj* exotic

expandir [iʃpãˈdʒi*] *vt* to expand; (*espalhar*) to spread; **~-se** *vr* to expand; **~-se com alguém** to be frank with sb

expansão [iʃpãˈsãw] *f* expansion, spread; (*de alegria*) effusiveness

expansivo/a [iʃpãˈsivu/a] *adj* (*pessoa*) outgoing

expeça *etc* [iʃˈpɛsa] *vb* V **expedir**

expectativa [iʃpektaˈtʃivaj] *f* expectation

expedição [iʃpedʒiˈsãw] (*pl* **-ões**) *f* (*viagem*) expedition; (*de mercadorias*) despatch; (*por navio*) shipment; (*de passaporte etc*) issue

expediente [iʃpeˈdʒẽtʃi] *m* means; (*serviço*) working day; (*correspondência*) correspondence ♦ *adj* expedient; **~ bancário** banking hours *pl*; **~ do escritório** office hours *pl*

expedir [iʃpeˈdʒi*] *vt* to send, despatch; (*bilhete, passaporte, decreto*) to issue

expedito/a [iʃpeˈdʒitu/a] *adj* prompt, speedy; (*pessoa*) efficient

expelir [iʃpeˈli*] *vt* to expel; (*sangue*) to spit

experiência [iʃpeˈrjẽsja] f experience; (prova) experiment, test; em ~ on trial

experiente [iʃpeˈrjẽtʃi] adj experienced

experimentar [iʃperimẽˈta*] vt (comida) to taste; (vestido) to try on; (pôr à prova) to try out, test; (conhecer pela experiência) to experience; (sofrer) to suffer, undergo; **experimento** [iʃperiˈmẽtu] m experiment

expilo etc [iʃˈpilu] vb V **expelir**

expirar [iʃpiˈra*] vt to exhale, breathe out ♦ vi to die; (terminar) to end

explicação [iʃplikaˈsãw] (pl -ões) f explanation

explicar [iʃpliˈka*] vt, vi to explain; ~-se vr to explain o.s.

explícito/a [iʃˈplisitu/a] adj explicit, clear

explodir [iʃploˈdʒi*] vt, vi to explode

exploração [iʃploraˈsãw] f exploration; (abuso) exploitation; (de uma mina) working

explorador(a) [iʃploraˈdo*(a)] m/f explorer; (de outros) exploiter

explorar [iʃploˈra*] vt (região) to explore; (mina) to work, run; (ferida) to probe; (trabalhadores etc) to exploit

explosão [iʃploˈzãw] (pl -ões) f explosion; (fig) outburst; **explosivo/a** [iʃploˈzivu/a] adj explosive; (pessoa) hotheaded ♦ m explosive

expor [iʃˈpo*] (irreg: como **pôr**) vt to expose; (a vida) to risk; (teoria) to explain; (revelar) to reveal; (mercadorias) to display; (quadros) to exhibit; ~-se vr to expose o.s.

exportação [iʃpoxtaˈsãw] f (ato) export(ing); (mercadorias) exports pl

exportador(a) [iʃpoxtaˈdo*(a)] adj exporting ♦ m/f exporter

exportar [iʃpoxˈta*] vt to export

exposição [iʃposiˈsãw] (pl -ões) f exhibition; (explicação) explanation; (declaração) statement; (narração) account; (FOTO) exposure

exposto/a [iʃˈpoʃtu/pɔʃta] adj (lugar) exposed; (quadro, mercadoria) on show ou display ♦ m: o acima ~ the above

expressão [iʃpreˈsãw] (pl -ões) f expression

expressar [iʃpreˈsa*] vt to express; **expressivo/a** [iʃpreˈsivu/a] adj expressive; (pessoa) demonstrative

expresso/a [iʃˈpresu/a] pp de **exprimir** ♦ adj definite, clear; (trem, ordem, carta) express ♦ m express

expressões [iʃpreˈsõjʃ] fpl de **expressão**

exprimir [iʃpriˈmi*] vt to express

expulsão [iʃpulˈsãw] (pl -ões) f expulsion; (ESPORTE) sending off

expulsar [iʃpuwˈsa*] vt to expel; (de uma festa, clube etc) to throw out; (inimigo) to drive out; (estrangeiro) to expel, deport; (jogador) to send off

expulso/a [iʃˈpuwsu/a] pp de **expulsar**

expulsões [iʃpulˈsõjʃ] fpl de **expulsão**

expurgar [iʃpuxˈga*] vt to expurgate

êxtase [ˈeʃtazi] m ecstasy

extensão [iʃtẽˈsãw] (pl -ões) f (ger, TEL) extension; (de uma empresa) expansion; (terreno) expanse; (tempo) length, duration; (de conhecimentos) extent

extensivo/a [iʃteˈsivu/a] adj extensive; ser ~ a to extend to

extenso/a [iʃˈtẽsu/a] adj extensive; (comprido) long; (artigo) full, comprehensive; por ~ in full

extensões [iʃteˈsõjʃ] fpl de **extensão**

extenuado/a [iʃteˈnwadu/a] adj (esgotado) worn out

extenuante [iʃteˈnwãtʃi] adj exhausting; (debilitante) debilitating

extenuar [iʃteˈnwa*] vt to exhaust; (debilitar) to weaken

exterior [iʃteˈrjo*] adj (de fora) outside, exterior; (aparência) outward; (comércio) foreign ♦ m (da casa) outside; (aspecto) outward appearance; do ~ (do estrangeiro) from abroad; no ~ abroad

exterminar [iʃtexmiˈna*] vt (inimigo) to wipe out, exterminate; (acabar com) to do away with

externato [iʃtexˈnatu] m day school

externo/a [iʃˈtexnu/a] adj external; (aparente) outward; aluno ~ day pupil

extinguir [iʃtʃĩˈgi*] vt (fogo) to put out, extinguish; (um povo) to wipe out; ~-se vr (fogo, luz) to go out; (BIO) to become extinct

extinto/a [iʃˈtʃĩtu/a] adj (fogo) extinguished; (língua, pessoa) dead; (animal, vulcão) extinct; (associação etc) defunct; ~r [iʃtʃĩˈto*] m (fire) extinguisher

extirpar [iʃtʃixˈpa*] vt to uproot; (corrupção) to eradicate; (tumor) to remove

extorquir [iʃtoxˈki*] vt to extort

extorsão [iʃtoxˈsãw] f extortion

extra [ˈeʃtra] adj extra ♦ m/f extra person; (TEATRO) extra

extração [iʃtraˈsãw] (PT -cç-) (pl -ões) f extraction; (de loteria) draw

extracto [iʃˈtratu] (PT) m = **extrato**

extraditar [eʃtradʒiˈta*] vt to extradite

extrair [iʃtraˈji*] vt to extract, take out

extraordinário/a [iʃtraoxdʒiˈnarju/a] adj extraordinary; (despesa) extra; (reunião) special

extrato [iʃˈtratu] m extract; (resumo) summary; ~ (bancário) (bank) statement

extravagância [iʃtravaˈgãsja] f extravagance; **extravagante** [iʃtravaˈgãtʃi] adj extravagant; (roupa) outlandish; (conduta) wild

extravasar [iʃtravaˈza*] vi to overflow

extraviado/a [iʃtraˈvjadu/a] adj lost, missing

extraviar [iʃtraˈvja*] vt to mislay; (pessoa) to lead astray; (dinheiro) to embezzle; ~-se vr to get lost; **extravio**

[iʃtra'viu] *m* loss; embezzlement; (*fig*) deviation

extremado/a [iʃtre'madu/a] *adj* extreme

extremidade [iʃtremi'dadʒi] *f* extremity; (*do dedo*) tip; (*ponta*) end; (*beira*) edge

extremo/a [iʃ'trɛmu/a] *adj* extreme ♦ *m* extreme; ao ~ extremely

extrovertido/a [eʃtrovex'tʃidu/a] *adj* extrovert, outgoing ♦ *m/f* extrovert

exuberante [ezube'rãtʃi] *adj* exuberant

exultante [ezuw'tãtʃi] *adj* jubilant, exultant

exultar [ezuw'ta*] *vi* to rejoice

exumar [ezu'ma*] *vt* (*corpo*) to exhume; (*fig*) to dig up

F

fã [fã] (*col*) *m/f* fan

fábrica ['fabrika] *f* factory; ~ **de cerveja** brewery; **a preço de** ~ wholesale

fabricação [fabrika'sãw] *f* manufacture; ~ **em série** mass production

fabricar ['fabri'ka*] *vt* to manufacture, make

fábula ['fabula] *f* fable; (*conto*) tale

fabuloso/a [fabu'lozu/ɔza] *adj* fabulous

faca ['faka] *f* knife; **~da** [fa'kada] *f* stab, cut

façanha [fa'saɲa] *f* exploit, deed

facão [fa'kãw] (*pl* –ões) *m* carving knife; (*para cortar o mato*) machete

facção [fak'sãw] (*pl* –ões) *f* faction

face ['fasi] *f* face; (*bochecha*) cheek; em ~ **de** in view of; **fazer** ~ **a** to face up to; **disquete de** ~ **simples/dupla** (*COMPUT*) single-/double-sided disk

fáceis ['fasejʃ] *adj pl* de **fácil**

faceta [fa'seta] *f* facet

fachada [fa'ʃada] *f* façade, front

fácil ['fasiw] (*pl* –eis) *adj* easy; (*temperamento, pessoa*) easy-going ♦ *adv* easily; **facilidade** [fasili'dadʒi] *f* ease; (*jeito*) facility; ~s *fpl* (*recursos*) facilities; **ter facilidade para algo** to have a talent for sth

facilitar [fasili'ta*] *vt* to facilitate, make easy; (*fornecer*): ~ **algo a alguém** to provide sb with sth

faço *etc* ['fasu] *vb* V **fazer**

facões [fa'kõjʃ] *fpl* de **facão**

fac-símile [fak'simili] (*pl* ~s) *m* (*cópia*) facsimile; (*carta*) fax; (*máquina*) fax (machine); **enviar por** ~ to fax

factício/a [fak'tʃisju/a] *adj* unnatural

facto ['faktu] (*PT*) *m* = **fato**

factor [fak'to*] (*PT*) *m* = **fator**

factual [fak'twaw] (*pl* –ais) *adj* factual

factura *etc* [fak'tura] (*PT*) = **fatura** *etc*

faculdade [fakuw'dadʒi] *f* (*ger, EDUC*) faculty; (*poder*) power

facultativo/a [fakuwta'tʃivu/a] *adj* optional ♦ *m/f* doctor

fada ['fada] *f* fairy; **conto de ~s** fairy tale

fadado/a [fa'dadu/a] *adj* destined

fadiga [fa'dʒiga] *f* fatigue

fadista [fa'dʒiʃta] *m/f* fado singer ♦ *m* (*PT*) ruffian

fado ['fadu] *m* fate; (*canção*) fado (*traditional Portuguese folk song*)

fagulha [fa'guʎa] *f* spark

faia ['faja] *f* beech (tree)

faisão [faj'zãw] (*pl* –ães *ou* –ões) *m* pheasant

faísca [fa'iʃka] *f* spark; (*brilho*) flash

faiscar [fajʃ'ka*] *vi* to sparkle; (*brilhar*) to flash

faisões [faj'zõjʃ] *mpl* de **faisão**

faixa ['fajʃa] *f* (*cinto, JUDÔ*) belt; (*tira*) strip; (*área*) zone; (*AUTO: pista*) lane; (*BR: para pedestres*) zebra crossing (*BRIT*), crosswalk (*US*); (*MED*) bandage; (*num disco*) track

fala ['fala] *f* speech; **chamar às ~s** to call to account; **sem** ~ speechless

falácia [fa'lasja] *f* fallacy

falador/deira [fala'do*/dejra] *adj* talkative ♦ *m/f* chatterbox

falante [fa'lãtʃi] *adj* talkative

falar [fa'la*] *vt* (*língua*) to speak; (*besteira etc*) to talk; (*dizer*) to say; (*verdade, mentira*) to tell ♦ *vi* to speak; ~ **algo a alguém** to tell sb sth; ~ **de** *ou* **em algo** to talk about sth; ~ **com alguém** to talk to sb; **por** ~ **em** speaking of; **sem** ~ **em** not to mention; **falou!**, **'tá falado!** (*col*) OK!

falatório [fala'tɔrju] *m* (*ruído de vozes*) voices *pl*, talking; (*maledicência*) rumour (*BRIT*), rumor (*US*)

falcão [faw'kãw] (*pl* –ões) *m* falcon

falecer [fale'se*] *vi* to die; **falecimento** [falesi'mẽtu] *m* death

falência [fa'lẽsja] *f* bankruptcy; **abrir** ~ to declare o.s. bankrupt; **ir à** ~ to go bankrupt; **levar à** ~ to bankrupt

falésia [fa'lɛzja] *f* cliff

falha ['faʎa] *f* fault; (*lacuna*) omission; (*de caráter*) flaw

falhar [fa'ʎa*] *vi* to fail; (*não acertar*) to miss; (*errar*) to be wrong

falho/a [fa'ʎu/a] *adj* faulty; (*deficiente*) wanting

falido/a [fa'lidu/a] *adj*, *m/f* bankrupt

falir [fa'li*] *vi* to fail; (*COM*) to go bankrupt

falsário/a [faw'sarju/a] *m/f* forger

falsidade [fawsi'dadʒi] *f* falsehood; (*fingimento*) pretence (*BRIT*), pretense (*US*)

falsificar [fawsifi'ka*] *vt* (*forjar*) to forge; (*falsear*) to falsify; (*adulterar*) to adulterate; (*desvirtuar*) to misrepresent

falso/a ['fawsu/a] *adj* false; (*fraudulento*) dishonest; (*errôneo*) wrong; (*jóia, moeda, quadro*) fake; **pisar em** ~ to blunder

falta ['fawta] *f* (*carência*) lack; (*ausência*) absence; (*defeito, culpa*) fault; (*FUTEBOL*) foul; **por** *ou* **na** ~ **de** for lack of; **sem**

~ **without fail; fazer** ~ **to** be lacking, be needed; **sentir** ~ **de alguém/algo** to miss sb/sth; **ter** ~ **de** to lack, be in need of

faltar [faw'ta*] vi to be lacking, be wanting; (pessoa) to be absent; (falhar) to fail; ~ **ao trabalho** to be absent from work; ~ **à palavra** to break one's word; **falta pouco para ...** it won't be long until ...

fama ['fama] f (renome) fame; (reputação) reputation

família [fa'milja] f family

familiar [fami'lja*] adj (da família) family atr; (conhecido) familiar ♦ m/f relation, relative; ~**idade** [familjari'dadʒi] f familiarity; (sem-cerimônia) informality; ~**izar** [familjari'za*] vt to familiarize; ~**izar-se** vr: ~**izar-se com algo** to familiarize o.s. with sth

faminto/a [fa'mĩtu/a] adj hungry; (fig): ~ **de** eager for

famoso/a [fa'mozu/ɔza] adj famous

fanático/a [fa'natʃiku/a] adj fanatical ♦ m/f fanatic

fantasia [fãta'zia] f fantasy; (imaginação) imagination; (capricho) fancy; (traje) fancy dress

fantasiar [fãta'zja*] vt to imagine ♦ vi to daydream; ~**-se** vr to dress up (in fancy dress)

fantasma [fã'taʒma] m ghost; (alucinação) illusion

fantástico/a [fã'taʃtʃiku/a] adj fantastic; (ilusório) imaginary; (incrível) unbelievable

fantoche [fã'tɔʃi] m puppet

farda ['faxda] f uniform

fardo ['faxdu] m bundle; (carga) load; (fig) burden

farei etc [fa'rej] vb V **fazer**

farelo [fa'rɛlu] m (de pão) crumb; (de madeira) sawdust; ~ **de trigo** bran

farfalhar [faxfa'ʎa*] vi to rustle

farinha [fa'riɲa] f: ~ **(de mesa)** (manioc) flour; ~ **de rosca** breadcrumbs pl; ~ **de trigo** plain flour

farmacêutico/a [faxma'sewtʃiku/a] adj pharmaceutical ♦ m/f pharmacist, chemist (BRIT)

farmácia [fax'masja] f pharmacy, chemist's (shop) (BRIT)

faro ['faru] m sense of smell; (fig) flair

farofa [fa'rɔfa] f (CULIN) side dish based on manioc flour

farol [fa'rɔw] (pl -óis) m lighthouse; (AUTO) headlight; **com** ~ **alto** (AUTO) on full (BRIT) ou high (US) beam; **com** ~ **baixo** dipped headlights pl (BRIT), dimmed beam (US); ~**ete** [faro'letʃi] m (AUTO: dianteiro) sidelight; (tb: ~ete traseiro) tail-light

farpado/a [fax'padu/a] adj: **arame** ~ barbed wire

farra ['faxa] f binge, spree

farrapo [fa'xapu] m rag

farsa ['faxsa] f farce; ~**nte** [fax'sãtʃi] m/f joker

farta ['faxta] f: **comer à** ~ to eat one's fill

fartar [fax'ta*] vt to satiate; (encher) to fill up; ~**-se** vr to gorge o.s.

farto/a ['faxtu/a] adj full, satiated; (abundante) plentiful; (aborrecido) fed up

fartura [fax'tura] f abundance

fascinante [fasi'nãtʃi] adj fascinating

fascinar [fasi'na*] vt to fascinate; (encantar) to charm; **fascínio** [fa'sinju] m fascination

fascismo [fa'siʒmu] m fascism

fase ['fazi] f phase

fastidioso/a [faʃtʃi'dʒjozu/ɔza] adj tedious; (enfadonho) annoying

fatal [fa'taw] (pl -ais) adj (mortal) fatal; (inevitável) inevitable; ~**idade** [fatali'dadʒi] f fate; (desgraça) disaster

fatia [fa'tʃia] f slice

fatigante [fatʃi'gãtʃi] adj tiring; (aborrecido) tiresome

fatigar [fatʃi'ga*] vt to tire; (aborrecer) to bore; ~**-se** vr to get tired

fato ['fatu] m fact; (acontecimento) event; (PT: traje) suit; **de banho** (PT) swimming costume (BRIT), bathing suit (US); **de** ~ in fact, really

fator [fa'to*] m factor

fatura [fa'tura] f bill, invoice; ~**r** [fatu'ra*] vt to invoice; (dinheiro) to make ♦ vi (col: ganhar dinheiro): ~**r (alto)** to rake it in

fava ['fava] f broad bean; **mandar alguém às** ~**s** to send sb packing

favela [fa'vela] f slum

favor [fa'vo*] m favour (BRIT), favor (US); **a** ~ **de** in favo(u)r of; **por** ~ please; **faça** ou **faz o** ~ **de ...** would you be so good as to ...; kindly ...; ~**ável** [favo'ravew] (pl -eis) adj: ~**ável (a)** favo(u)rable (to); ~**ecer** [favore'se*] vt to favo(u)r; (beneficiar) to benefit; (suj: vestido) to suit; (: retrato) to flatter; ~**ito** [favo'ritu/a] adj, m/f favo(u)rite

faxina [fa'ʃina] f: **fazer** ~ to clean up; **faxineiro/a** [faʃi'nejru/a] m/f cleaner

fazenda [fa'zẽda] f farm; (de café) plantation; (de gado) ranch; (pano) cloth, fabric; (ECON) treasury; **fazendeiro** [fazẽ'dejru] m farmer; (de café) plantation-owner; (de gado) rancher, ranch-owner

PALAVRA CHAVE

fazer [fa'ze*] vt **1** (fabricar, produzir) to make; (construir) to build; (pergunta) to ask; (poema, música) to write; ~ **um filme/ruído** to make a film/noise; **eu fiz o vestido** I made the dress

2 (executar) to do; **o que você está fazendo?** what are you doing? ~ **a comida** to do the cooking; ~ **o papel de**

(*TEATRO*) to play

3 (*estudos, alguns esportes*) to do; ~ **medicina/direito** to do *ou* study medicine/law; ~ **ioga/ginástica** to do yoga/keep-fit

4 (*transformar, tornar*): **sair o fará sentir melhor** going out will make him feel better; **sua partida fará o trabalho mais difícil** his departure will make work more difficult

5 (*como substituto de vb*): **ele bebeu e eu fiz o mesmo** he drank and I did likewise

6: ~ **anos**: **ele faz anos hoje** it's his birthday today; **fiz 30 anos ontem** I was 30 yesterday

♦ *vi* **1** (*portar-se*) to act, behave; ~ **bem/mal** to do the right/wrong thing; **não fiz por mal** I didn't mean it; **faz como quem não sabe** act as if you don't know anything

2: ~ **com que alguém faça algo** to make sb do sth

♦ *vb impess* **1**: **faz calor/frio** it's hot/cold

2 (*tempo*): **faz um ano** a year ago; **faz dois anos que ele se formou** it's two years since he graduated; **faz três meses que ele está aqui** he's been here for three months

3: **não faz mal** never mind; **tanto faz** it's all the same

♦ ~**se** *vr* **1**: ~**se de desentendido** to pretend not to understand

2: **faz-se com ovos e leite** it's made with eggs and milk; **isso não se faz** that's not done

fé [fɛ] *f* faith; (*crença*) belief; (*confiança*) trust; **de boa/má** ~ in good/bad faith

febre ['fɛbri] *f* fever; (*fig*) excitement; ~ **do feno** hay fever; **febril** [fe'briw] (*pl* -**is**) *adj* feverish

fechado/a [fe'ʃadu/a] *adj* shut, closed; (*pessoa*) reserved; (*sinal*) red; (*luz, torneira*) off; (*tempo*) overcast; (*cara*) stern

fechadura [feʃa'dura] *f* (*de porta*) lock

fechar [fe'ʃa*] *vt* to close, shut; (*concluir*) to finish, conclude; (*luz, torneira*) to turn off; (*rua*) to close off; (*ferida*) to close up; (*bar, loja*) to close down ♦ *vi* to close (up), shut; to close down; (*tempo*) to cloud over; ~**se** *vr* to close, shut; (*pessoa*) to withdraw; ~ **à chave** to lock

fecho ['feʃu] *m* fastening; (*trinco*) latch; (*término*) close; ~ **ecler** zip fastener (*BRIT*), zipper (*US*)

fécula ['fɛkula] *f* starch

fecundar [fekũ'da*] *vt* to fertilize

feder [fe'de*] *vi* to stink

federação [federa'sãw] (*pl* -**ões**) *f* federation

federal [fede'raw] (*pl* -**ais**) *adj* federal; (*col: grande*) huge

fedor [fe'do*] *m* stench

feição [fej'sãw] (*pl* -**ões**) *f* form, shape; (*caráter*) nature; (*modo*) manner; **feições** *fpl* (*face*) features; **à** ~ **de** in the manner of

feijão [fej'ʒãw] (*pl* -**ões**) *m* bean(s) (*pl*); (*preto*) black bean(s) (*pl*); **feijoada** [fej'ʒwada] *f* (*CULIN*) meat, rice and black beans

feio/a ['feju/a] *adj* ugly; (*situação*) grim; (*atitude*) bad; (*tempo*) horrible ♦ *adv* (*perder*) badly

feira ['fejra] *f* fair; (*mercado*) market

feiticeira [fejtʃi'sejra] *f* witch

feiticeiro/a [fejtʃi'sejru/a] *adj* bewitching, enchanting ♦ *m* wizard

feitiço [fej'tʃisu] *m* charm, spell

feitio [fej'tʃiu] *m* shape, pattern; (*caráter*) nature, manner; (*TEC*) workmanship

feito/a ['fejtu/a] *pp de* **fazer** ♦ *adj* finished, ready ♦ *m* act, deed; (*façanha*) feat ♦ *conj* like; ~ **a mão** hand-made; **homem** ~ grown man

feiúra [fe'jura] *f* ugliness

feixe ['fejʃi] *m* bundle, bunch; (*TEC*) beam

fel [fɛw] *m* bile, gall; (*fig*) bitterness

felicidade [felisi'dadʒi] *f* happiness; (*sorte*) good luck; (*êxito*) success; ~**s** *fpl* (*congratulações*) congratulations

felicitações [felisita'sõjʃ] *fpl* congratulations, best wishes

feliz [fe'liʒ] *adj* happy; (*afortunado*) lucky; ~**mente** [feliʒ'mẽtʃi] *adv* fortunately

felpudo/a [few'pudu/a] *adj* (*penujento*) fuzzy; (*peludo*) downy

feltro ['fewtru] *m* felt

fêmea ['femja] *f* female

feminino/a [femi'ninu/a] *adj* feminine; (*sexo*) female; (*equipe, roupa*) women's ♦ *m* (*LING*) feminine

feminista [femi'niʃta] *adj, m/f* feminist

fenda ['fẽda] *f* slit, crack; (*GEO*) fissure

fender [fẽ'de*] *vt, vi* to split, crack

fenecer [fene'se*] *vi* to die; (*terminar*) to come to an end

feno ['fenu] *m* hay

fenomenal [fenome'naw] (*pl* -**ais**) *adj* phenomenal; (*espantoso*) amazing; (*pessoa*) brilliant

fenômeno [fe'nomenu] *m* phenomenon

fera ['fɛra] *f* wild animal

féretro ['fɛretru] *m* coffin

feriado [fe'rjadu] *m* holiday (*BRIT*), vacation (*US*)

férias ['fɛrjaʃ] *fpl* holidays, vacation *sg*; **de** ~ on holiday; **tirar** ~ to have *ou* take a holiday

ferida [fe'rida] *f* wound, injury; *V tb* **ferido**

ferido/a [fe'ridu/a] *adj* injured; (*em batalha*) wounded; (*magoado*) hurt ♦ *m/f* casualty

ferimento [feri'mẽtu] *m* injury; (*em ba-*

talha) wound

ferir [fe'ri*] *vt* to injure; (*tb fig*) to hurt; (*em batalha*) to wound; (*ofender*) to offend

fermentar [fexmẽ'ta*] *vi* to ferment

fermento [fex'mẽtu] *m* yeast; ~ **em pó** baking powder

ferocidade [ferosi'dadʒi] *f* fierceness, ferocity

feroz [fe'roʒ] *adj* fierce, ferocious; (*cruel*) cruel

ferradura [fexa'dura] *f* horseshoe

ferragem [fe'xaʒẽ] (*pl* –**ns**) *f* (*peças*) hardware; (*guarnição*) metalwork; **loja de ferragens** ironmonger's (*BRIT*), hardware store

ferramenta [fexa'mẽta] *f* tool; (*caixa de ~s*) tool kit

ferrão [fe'xãw] (*pl* –**ões**) *m* goad; (*de inseto*) sting

ferreiro [fe'xejru] *m* blacksmith

ferrenho/a [fe'xeɲu/a] *adj* (*vontade*) iron

férreo/a ['fɛxju/a] *adj* iron *atr*; (*disciplina*) strict; **via férrea** railway (*BRIT*), railroad (*US*)

ferro ['fɛxu] *m* iron; ~**s** *mpl* (*algemas*) shackles, chains; ~ **batido** wrought iron; ~ **de passar** iron; ~ **fundido** cast iron; ~ **ondulado** corrugated iron

ferrões [fe'xõjʃ] *mpl de* **ferrão**

ferrolho [fe'xoʎu] *m* (*trinco*) bolt

ferrovia [fexo'via] *f* railway (*BRIT*), railroad (*US*); **ferroviário/a** [fexo'vjarju/a] *adj* railway *atr* (*BRIT*), railroad *atr* (*US*) ♦ *m/f* railway *ou* railroad worker

ferrugem [fe'xuʒẽ] *f* rust

fértil ['fɛxtʃiw] (*pl* –**eis**) *adj* fertile; **fertilidade** [fextʃili'dadʒi] *f* fertility; **fertilizante** [fextʃili'zãtʃi] *m* fertilizer; **fertilizar** [fextʃili'za*] *vt* to fertilize

fervente [fex'vẽtʃi] *adj* boiling

ferver [fex've*] *vt*, *vi* to boil; ~ **de raiva/indignação** to seethe with rage/indignation; ~ **em fogo baixo** (*CULIN*) to simmer

fervilhar [fexvi'ʎa*] *vi* to simmer; (*com atividade*) to hum; (*pulular*): ~ **de** to swarm with

fervor [fex'vo*] *m* fervour (*BRIT*), fervor (*US*)

fervoroso/a [fexvo'rozu/ɔza] *adj* fervent

festa ['fɛʃta] *f* (*reunião*) party; (*conjunto de ceremônias*) festival; ~**s** *fpl* (*carícia*) embrace *sg*; **boas ~s** Merry Christmas and a Happy New Year; **dia de ~** public holiday

festejar [feʃte'ʒa*] *vt* to celebrate; (*acolher*) to welcome, greet; **festejo** [feʃ'teʒu] *m* festivity; (*ato*) celebration

festim [feʃ'tʃĩ] (*pl* –**ns**) *m* feast

festival [feʃtʃi'vaw] (*pl* –**ais**) *m* festival

festividade [feʃtʃivi'dadʒi] *f* festivity

festivo/a [feʃ'tʃivu/a] *adj* festive

fetiche [fe'tʃiʃi] *m* fetish

fétido/a ['fɛtʃidu/a] *adj* foul

feto ['fɛtu] *m* (*MED*) foetus (*BRIT*), fetus (*US*)

fevereiro [feve'rejru] (*PT* **F-**) *m* February

fez [feʒ] *vb V* **fazer**

fezes ['fɛziʃ] *fpl* faeces (*BRIT*), feces (*US*)

fiada ['fjada] *f* (*fileira*) row, line

fiado/a ['fjadu/a] *adv*: **comprar/vender** ~ to buy/sell on credit

fiador(a) [fja'do*(a)] *m/f* (*JUR*) guarantor; (*COM*) backer

fiambre ['fjãbri] *m* cold meat; (*presunto*) ham

fiança ['fjãsa] *f* guarantee; (*JUR*) bail; **prestar** ~ **por** to stand bail for; **sob** ~ on bail

fiar ['fja*] *vt* (*algodão etc*) to spin; (*confiar*) to entrust; (*vender a crédito*) to sell on credit; ~**-se** *vr*: ~**-se em** to trust

fiasco ['fjaʃku] *m* fiasco

fibra ['fibra] *f* fibre (*BRIT*), fiber (*US*)

PALAVRA CHAVE

ficar [fi'ka*] *vi* **1** (*permanecer*) to stay; (*sobrar*) to be left; ~ **perguntando/olhando** *etc* to keep asking/looking *etc*; ~ **por fazer** to have still to be done; ~ **para trás** to be left behind

2 (*tornar-se*) to become; ~ **cego/surdo/louco** to go blind/deaf/mad; **fiquei contente ao saber da notícia** I was happy when I heard the news; ~ **com raiva/medo** to get angry/frightened; ~ **de bem/mal com alguém** (*col*) to make up/fall out with sb

3 (*posição*) to be; **a casa fica ao lado da igreja** the house is next to the church; ~ **sentado/deitado** to be sitting down/lying down

4 (*tempo: durar*): **ele ficou duas horas para resolver** he took two hours to decide; (*: ser adiado*): **a reunião ficou para amanhã** the meeting was postponed until the following day

5: ~ **bem** (*comportamento*): **sua atitude não ficou bem** his (*ou* her *etc*) behaviour was inappropriate; (*cor*): **você fica bem em azul** blue suits you, you look good in blue; (*roupa*): ~ **bem para** to suit

6: ~ **bom** (*de saúde*) to be cured; (*trabalho, foto etc*) to turn out well

7: ~ **de fazer algo** (*combinar*) to arrange to do sth; (*prometer*) to promise to do sth

8: ~ **de pé** to stand up

---

ficção [fik'sãw] *f* fiction

ficha ['fiʃa] *f* (*tb*: ~ **de telefone**) token; (*tb*: ~ **de jogo**) chip; (*de fichário*) (index) card; (*POLÍCIA*) record; (*PT: ELET*) plug; (*em loja, lanchonete*) ticket; ~**r** [fi'ʃa*] *vt* to file, index

fichário [fi'ʃarju] *m* filing cabinet; (*caixa*) card index; (*caderno*) file

ficheiro [fi'ʃejru] (*PT*) *m* = **fichário**

fictício/a [fik'tʃisju/a] *adj* fictitious
fidalgo [fi'dawgu] *m* nobleman
fidelidade [fideli'dadʒi] *f* fidelity, loyalty; (*exatidão*) accuracy
fiel [fjɛw] (*pl* **-éis**) *adj* (*leal*) faithful, loyal; (*acurado*) accurate; (*que não falha*) reliable
figa ['figa] *f* talisman; **fazer uma ~** to make a *figa*, ≈ cross one's fingers; **de uma ~** (*col*) damned
fígado ['figadu] *m* liver
figo ['figu] *m* fig; **figueira** [fi'gejra] *f* fig tree
figura [fi'gura] *f* figure; (*forma*) form, shape; (*LING*) figure of speech; (*aspecto*) appearance
figurante [figu'rãtʃi] *m/f* (*CINEMA*) extra
figurar [figu'ra*] *vi* (*ator*) to appear; (*fazer parte*): **~ (entre/em)** to figure *ou* appear (among/in) ♦ *vt* (*imaginar*) to imagine
figurino [figu'rinu] *m* model; (*revista*) fashion magazine
figurões [figu'rõjʃ] *mpl de* **figurão**
fila ['fila] *f* row, line; (*BR*: *fileira de pessoas*) queue (*BRIT*), line (*US*); (*num teatro, cinema*) row; **em ~** in a row; **fazer ~** to form a line, queue; **~ indiana** single file
filamento [fila'mẽtu] *m* filament
filantropo [filã'tropu] *m* philanthropist
filatelia [filate'lia] *f* stamp collecting
filé [fi'lɛ] *m* (*bife*) steak; (*peixe*) fillet
fileira [fi'lejra] *f* row, line; **~s** *fpl* (*serviço militar*) military service sg
filho/a ['fiʎu/a] *m/f* son/daughter; **~s** *mpl* children; (*de animais*) young; **~ da mãe, ~ da puta** (*col!*) bastard(!)
filhote [fi'ʎɔtʃi] *m* (*de leão, urso etc*) cub; (*cachorro*) pup(py)
filial [fi'ljaw] (*pl* **-ais**) *f* (*sucursal*) branch
Filipinas [fili'pinaʃ] *fpl*: **as ~** the Philippines
filmadora [fiwma'dora] *f* camcorder
filmar [fiw'ma*] *vt, vi* to film
filme ['fiwmi] *m* film (*BRIT*), movie (*US*)
filologia [filolo'ʒia] *f* philology
filosofia [filozo'fia] *f* philosophy; **filósofo/a** [fi'lɔzofu/a] *m/f* philosopher
filtrar [fiw'tra*] *vt* to filter; **~-se** *vr* to filter; (*infiltrar-se*) to infiltrate
filtro ['fiwtru] *m* (*TEC*) filter
fim [fĩ] (*pl* **-ns**) *m* end; (*motivo*) aim, purpose; (*de história, filme*) ending; **a ~ de** in order to; **no ~ das contas** after all; **por ~** finally; **sem ~** endless; **levar ao ~** to carry through; **pôr** *ou* **dar ~ a** to put an end to; **ter ~** to come to an end; **~ de semana** weekend
final [fi'naw] (*pl* **-ais**) *adj* final, last ♦ *m* end; (*MÚS*) finale ♦ *f* (*ESPORTE*) final; **~ista** [fina'liʃta] *m/f* finalist; **~izar** [finali'za*] *vt* to finish, conclude
finanças [fi'nãsaʃ] *fpl* finance sg; **financeiro/a** [finã'sejru/a] *adj* financial ♦

m/f financier; **financiar** [finã'sja*] *vt* to finance
finar-se [fi'naxsi] *vr* to waste away; (*morrer*) to die
fincar [fĩ'ka*] *vt* (*cravar*) to drive in; (*fixar*) to fix; (*apoiar*) to lean
fineza [fi'neza] *f* fineness; (*gentileza*) kindness
fingimento [fĩʒi'mẽtu] *m* pretence (*BRIT*), pretense (*US*)
fingir [fĩ'ʒi*] *vt* to feign ♦ *vi* to pretend; **~-se** *vr*: **~-se de** to pretend to be
finito/a [fi'nitu/a] *adj* finite
finlandês/esa [fĩlã'deʃ/eza] *adj* Finnish ♦ *m/f* Finn ♦ *m* (*LING*) Finnish
Finlândia [fĩ'lãdʒia] *f*: **a ~** Finland
fino/a ['finu/a] *adj* fine; (*delgado*) slender; (*educado*) polite; (*som, voz*) shrill; (*elegante*) refined ♦ *adv*: **falar ~** to talk in a high voice
fins [fĩʃ] *mpl de* **fim**
finura [fi'nura] *f* fineness; (*elegância*) finesse
fio ['fiu] *m* thread; (*BOT*) fibre (*BRIT*), fiber (*US*); (*ELET*) wire; (*TEL*) line; (*de líquido*) trickle; (*gume*) edge; (*encadeamento*) series; **horas/dias a ~** hours/ days on end
fiorde ['fjɔxdʒi] *m* fjord
firma ['fixma] *f* signature; (*COM*) firm, company
firmar [fix'ma*] *vt* to secure, make firm; (*assinar*) to sign; (*estabelecer*) to establish; (*basear*) to base ♦ *vi* (*tempo*) to settle; **~-se** *vr*: **~-se em** (*basear-se*) to rest on, be based on
firme ['fixmi] *adj* firm; (*estável*) stable; (*sólido*) solid; (*tempo*) settled ♦ *adv* firmly; **~za** [fix'meza] *f* firmness; stability; solidity
fiscal [fiʃ'kaw] (*pl* **-ais**) *m/f* supervisor; (*aduaneiro*) customs officer; (*de impostos*) tax inspector; (*de...*) **~izar** [fiʃkali'za*] *vt* to supervise; (*examinar*) to inspect, check
fisco ['fiʃku] *m*: **o ~** ≈ the Inland Revenue (*BRIT*), ≈ the Internal Revenue Service (*US*)
física ['fizika] *f* physics sg; *V tb* **físico**
físico/a ['fiziku/a] *adj* physical ♦ *m/f* (*cientista*) physicist ♦ *m* (*corpo*) physique
fisionomia [fizjono'mia] *f* (*rosto*) face; (*ar*) expression, look; (*aspecto de algo*) appearance
fisioterapia [fizjotera'pia] *f* physiotherapy
fissura [fi'sura] *f* crack
fita ['fita] *f* tape; (*tira*) strip, band; (*filme*) film; (*para máquina de escrever*) ribbon; **~ durex** ® adhesive tape, sellotape ® (*BRIT*), scotchtape ® (*US*); **~ métrica** tape measure
fitar [fi'ta*] *vt* to stare at, gaze at
fivela [fi'vɛla] *f* buckle
fixador [fiksa'do*] *m* (*de cabelo*) hair gel; (: *líquido*) setting lotion

fixar [fik'sa*] vt to fix; (colar, prender) to stick; (data, prazo, regras) to set; (atenção) to concentrate; **~-se** vr: **~-se em** (assunto) to concentrate on; (detalhe) to fix on; (apegar-se a) to be attached to; **~ os olhos em** to stare at; **~ residência** to set up house

fixo/a ['fiksu/a] adj fixed; (firme) firm; (permanente) permanent; (cor) fast

fiz etc [fiʒ] vb V **fazer**

flagelado/a [flaʒe'ladu/a] m/f: **os ~s** the afflicted, the victims

flagrante [fla'grātʃi] adj flagrant; **apanhar em ~ (delito)** to catch redhanded ou in the act

flagrar [fla'gra*] vt to catch

flamejar [flame'ʒa*] vi to blaze

flâmula ['flamula] f pennant

flanco ['flãku] m flank

flanela [fla'nɛla] f flannel

flash [flaʃ] m (FOTO) flash

flauta ['flawta] f flute

flecha ['flɛʃa] f arrow

fleu(g)ma ['flewma] f phlegm

flexível [flek'sivew] (pl -eis) adj flexible

fliperama [flipe'rama] m (jogo) pinball machine; (local) amusement arcade

floco ['flɔku] m flake; **~ de milho** cornflake; **~ de neve** snowflake

flor [flo*] f flower; (o melhor): **a ~ de** the cream of, the pick of; **em ~** in bloom; **à ~ de** on the surface of; **floreado/a** [flo'rjadu/a] adj (jardim) full of flowers

florescente [flore'sētʃi] adj (BOT) in flower; (próspero) flourishing

florescer [flore'se*] vi (BOT) to flower; (prosperar) to flourish

floresta [flo'rɛʃta] f forest; **~ tropical** rainforest; **~l** [floreʃ'taw] (pl **florestais**) adj forest atr

florido/a [flo'ridu/a] adj (jardim) in flower

fluente [flu'ētʃi] adj fluent

fluido/a ['flwidu/a] adj fluid ♦ m fluid

fluir [flwi*] vi to flow

fluminense [flumi'nēsi] adj from the state of Rio de Janeiro ♦ m/f native ou inhabitant of the state of Rio de Janeiro

flutuar [flu'twa*] vi to float; (bandeira) to flutter; (fig: vacilar) to waver

fluvial [flu'vjaw] (pl **-ais**) adj river atr

fluxo ['fluksu] m (corrente) flow; (ELET) flux; **~ de caixa** (COM) cash flow; **~grama** [flukso'grama] m flow chart

fobia [fo'bia] f phobia

foca ['fɔka] f seal

focalizar [fokali'za*] vt to focus (on)

focinho [fo'siɲu] m snout, (col: cara) face, mug (col)

foco ['fɔku] m focus; (MED, fig) seat, centre (BRIT), center (US); **fora de ~ em/fora de ~** out of focus, in/out of focus

fofo/a ['fofu/a] adj soft; (col: pessoa) cute

fofoca [fo'fɔka] f piece of gossip; **~s** fpl (mexericos) gossip sg; **fofocar** [fofo'ka*] vi to gossip

fogão [fo'gãw] (pl **-ões**) m stove, cooker

fogareiro [foga'rejru] m stove

foge etc ['fɔʒi] vb V **fugir**

fogo ['fogu] m fire; (fig) ardour (BRIT), ardor (US); **você tem ~?** have you got a light?; **~s de artifício** fireworks; **pôr ~ a** to set fire to

fogões [fo'gõjʃ] mpl de **fogão**

fogueira [fo'gejra] f bonfire

foguete [fo'getʃi] m rocket

foi [foj] vb V **ir**; **ser**

foice ['fɔjsi] f scythe

folclore [fowk'lɔri] m folklore

folclórico/a [fowk'lɔriku/a] adj (música etc) folk; (comida, roupa) ethnic

fole ['fɔli] m bellows sg

fôlego ['folegu] m breath; (folga) breathing space; **perder o ~** to get out of breath

folga ['fowga] f rest, break; (espaço livre) clearance; (ócio) inactivity; (col: atrevimento) cheek; **dia de ~** day off; **~do/a** [fow'gadu/a] adj (roupa) loose; (vida) leisurely; (col: atrevido) cheeky; **~r** [fow'ga*] vt to loosen ♦ vi (descansar) to rest; (divertir-se) to have fun

folha ['foʎa] f leaf; (de papel, de metal) sheet; (página) page; (de faca) blade; (jornal) paper; **novo em ~** brand new; **~ de estanho** tinfoil (BRIT), aluminum foil (US)

folhagem [fo'ʎaʒẽ] f foliage

folhear [fo'ʎja*] vt to leaf through

folheto [fo'ʎetu] m booklet, pamphlet

fome ['fɔmi] f hunger; (escassez) famine; (fig: avidez) longing; **passar ~** to go hungry; **estar com** ou **ter ~** to be hungry

fomentar [fomẽ'ta*] vt to instigate, incite; **fomento** [fo'mẽtu] m (estímulo) incitement

fone ['fɔni] m telephone, phone; (peça do telefone) receiver

fonética [fo'nɛtʃika] f phonetics sg

fonte ['fõtʃi] f (nascente) spring; (chafariz) fountain; (origem) source; (ANAT) temple

footing ['futʃiŋ] m jogging

for etc [fo*] vb V **ir**; **ser**

fora¹ ['fɔra] adv out, outside ♦ prep (além de) apart from ♦ m: **dar o ~** (bateria, radio) to give out; (pessoa) to leave, be off; **dar um ~** to blow; **dar um ~ em/levar um ~** (namorado) to chuck ou dump/be given the boot; (esnobar) to snub sb/get the brush-off; **~ de** outside; **~ de si** beside o.s.; **estar ~** (viajando) to be away; **estar ~ (de casa)** (de casa) to be out; **lá ~** outside; (no exterior) abroad; **jantar ~** to eat out; **com os braços de ~** with bare arms; **ser de ~**

to be from out of town; **ficar de** ~ not to join in; **lá para** ~ outside; **ir para** ~ *(viajar)* to go out of town; **com a cabeça para** ~ **da janela** with one's head sticking out of the window; **costurar/cozinhar para** ~ to do sewing/cooking for other people; **por** ~ on the outside; **cobrar por** ~ *(cobrar)* to charge extra, extra; ~ **de dúvida** beyond doubt; ~ **de propósito** irrelevant

fora² *etc vb V* **ir; ser**

foragido/a [fora'ʒidu/a] *adj, m/f (fugitivo)* fugitive

forasteiro/a [foraʃ'tejru/a] *m/f* outsider, stranger; *(de outro país)* foreigner

forca ['foxka] *f* gallows *sg*

força ['foxsa] *f* strength; *(TEC, ELET)* power; *(esforço)* effort; *(coerção)* force; **à** ~ by force; **à** ~ **de** by dint of; **com** ~ hard; **por** ~ of necessity; **fazer** ~ to try (hard); ~ **de trabalho** workforce

forçado/a [fox'sadu/a] *adj* forced; *(afetado)* false

forçar [fox'sa*] *vt* to force; *(olhos, voz)* to strain

forçoso/a [fox'sozu/ɔza] *adj* necessary; *(obrigatório)* obligatory

forjar [fox'ʒa*] *vt* to forge; *(pretexto)* to invent

forma ['foxma] *f* form; *(de um objeto)* shape; *(físico)* figure; *(maneira)* way; *(MED)* fitness; **desta** ~ in this way; **de qualquer** ~ anyway; **manter a** ~ to keep fit

fôrma ['foxma] *f (CULIN)* cake tin; *(molde)* mould *(BRIT)*, mold *(US)*

formação [foxma'sãw] *(pl* -ões*) f* formation; *(antecedentes)* background; *(caráter)* make-up; *(profissional)* training

formado/a [fox'madu/a] *adj (modelado)*: **ser** ~ **de** to consist of ♦ *m/f* graduate

formal [fox'maw] *(pl* -ais*) adj* formal; ~**idade** [foxmali'dadʒi] *f* formality

formão [fox'mãw] *(pl* -ões*) m* chisel

formar [fox'ma*] *vt* to form; *(constituir)* to constitute, make up; *(educar)* to train; ~**-se** *vr* to form; *(EDUC)* to graduate

formatar [foxma'ta*] *vt (COMPUT)* to format

formidável [foxmi'davew] *(pl* -eis*) adj* tremendous, great

formiga [fox'miga] *f* ant

formigar [foxmi'ga*] *vi* to abound; *(sentir comichão)* to itch

formões [fox'mõjʃ] *mpl de* **formão**

formoso/a [fox'mozu/ɔza] *adj* beautiful; *(esplêndido)* superb

fórmula ['fɔxmula] *f* formula

formular [foxmu'la*] *vt* to formulate; *(queixas)* to voice

formulário [foxmu'larju] *m* form; ~**s** *mpl*: ~**s contínuos** *(COMPUT)* continuous stationery *sg*

fornecedor(a) [foxnɛse'do*(a)] *m/f* supplier ♦ *f (empresa)* supplier

fornecer [foxne'se*] *vt* to supply, provide; **fornecimento** [foxnesi'mẽtu] *m* supply

forno ['foxnu] *m (CULIN)* oven; *(TEC)* furnace; *(para cerâmica)* kiln; **alto** ~ blast furnace

foro ['foru] *m* forum; *(JUR)* Court of Justice; ~**s** *mpl (privilégios)* privileges

forrar [fo'xa*] *vt (cobrir)* to cover; (*: interior)* to line; *(de papel)* to paper; **forro** ['foxu] *m* covering; lining

fortalecer [foxtale'se*] *vt* to strengthen

fortaleza [foxta'leza] *f* fortress; *(força)* strength; *(moral)* fortitude

forte ['fɔxtʃi] *adj* strong; *(pancada)* hard; *(chuva)* heavy; *(tocar)* loud; *(dor)* sharp ♦ *adv* strongly; *(tocar)* loud(ly) ♦ *m* fort; *(talento)* strength; **ser** ~ **em algo** *(versado)* to be good at sth *ou* strong in sth

fortuito/a [fox'twitu/a] *adj* accidental

fortuna [fox'tuna] *f* fortune, (good) luck; *(riqueza)* fortune, wealth

fosco/a ['foʃku/a] *adj* dull; *(opaco)* opaque

fósforo ['fɔʃforu] *m* match

fossa ['fɔsa] *f* pit

fosse *etc* ['fosi] *vb V* **ir; ser**

fóssil ['fɔsiw] *(pl* -eis*) m* fossil

fosso ['fosu] *m* trench, ditch

foto ['fɔtu] *f* photo

fotocópia [foto'kɔpja] *f* photocopy; **fotocopiadora** [fotokopja'dora] *f* photocopier; **fotocopiar** [fotoko'pja*] *vt* to photocopy

fotografar [fotogra'fa*] *vt* to photograph

fotografia [fotogra'fia] *f* photography; *(uma* ~*)* photograph

fotógrafo/a [fo'tɔgrafu/a] *m/f* photographer

fotonovela [fotono'vɛla] *f* photo story

foz [fɔʒ] *f* mouth of river

fração [fra'sãw] *(pl* -ões*) f* fraction

fracassar [fraka'sa*] *vi* to fail; **fracasso** [fra'kasu] *m* failure

fracção [fra'sãw] *(PT) f* = **fração**

fraco/a ['fraku/a] *adj* weak; *(sol, som)* faint

frações [fra'sõjf] *fpl de* **fração**

fractura *etc* [fra'tura] *(PT) f* = **fratura** *etc*

frade ['fradʒi] *m (REL)* friar; (*: monge)* monk

fraga ['fraga] *f* crag, rock

fragata [fra'gata] *f (NÁUT)* frigate

frágil ['fraʒiw] *(pl* -eis*) adj (débil)* fragile; *(COM)* breakable; *(pessoa)* frail; *(saúde)* delicate, poor

fragmento [frag'mẽtu] *m* fragment

fragrância [fra'grãsja] *f* fragrance, perfume; **fragrante** [fra'grãtʃi] *adj* fragrant

fralda ['frawda] *f (da camisa)* shirt tail; *(para bebê)* nappy *(BRIT)*, diaper *(US)*; *(de montanha)* foot

framboesa [frã'beza] *f* raspberry

França ['frãsa] *f* France

francamente [frãka'mẽtʃi] *adv (aberta-*

mente) frankly; (*realmente*) really

francês/esa [frã'seʃ/eza] *adj* French ♦ *m/f* Frenchman/woman ♦ *m* (*LING*) French

franco/a ['frãku/a] *adj* frank; (*isento de pagamento*) free; (*óbvio*) clear ♦ *m* franc; **entrada franca** free admission

frango ['frãgu] *m* chicken

franja ['frãʒa] *f* fringe (*BRIT*), bangs *pl* (*US*)

franquear [frã'kja*] *vt* (*caminho*) to clear; (*isentar de imposto*) to exempt from duties; (*carta*) to frank

franqueza [frã'keza] *f* frankness

franquia [frã'kia] *f* (*COM*) franchise; (*isenção*) exemption

franzido [frã'zidu] *m* pleat

franzino/a [frã'zinu/a] *adj* skinny

franzir [frã'zi*] *vt* (*preguear*) to pleat; (*enrugar*) to wrinkle, crease; ~ **as sobrancelhas** to frown

fraqueza [fra'keza] *f* weakness

frasco ['fraʃku] *m* bottle

frase ['frazi] *f* sentence; ~ **feita** set phrase

fratura [fra'tura] *f* fracture, break; **~r** [fratu'ra*] *vt* to fracture

fraude [ˈfrawdʒi] *f* fraud

freada [fre'ada] (*BR*) *f*: **dar uma ~** to slam on the brakes

frear [fre'a*] (*BR*) *vt* to curb, restrain; (*veículo*) to stop ♦ *vi* (*veículo*) to brake

freezer [ˈfrize*] *m* freezer

freguês/guesa [fre'geʃ/geza] *m/f* customer; (*PT*) parishioner; **freguesia** [frege'zia] *f* customers *pl*; parish

frei [frej] *m* friar, monk

freio ['freju] *m* (*BR*: *de veículo*) brake; (*de cavalo*) bridle; (*bocado do ~*) bit; ~ **de mão** handbrake

freira ['frejra] *f* nun

frenesi [frene'zi] *m* frenzy; **frenético/a** [fre'nɛtʃiku/a] *adj* frantic, frenzied

frente [ˈfrẽtʃi] *f* front; (*rosto*) face; (*fachada*) façade; ~ **a** ~ face to face; **de ~ para** facing; **em** ~ **de** in front of; (*de fronte a*) opposite; **para a** ~ ahead, forward; **porta da** ~ front door; **seguir em** ~ to go straight on; **na minha** (*ou* **sua** *etc*) ~ in front of me (*ou* you *etc*); **sair da** ~ to get out of the way; **pra** ~ (*col*) fashionable, trendy

freqüência [fre'kwẽsja] *f* frequency; **com** ~ often, frequently

freqüentar [frekwẽ'ta*] *vt* to frequent

freqüente [fre'kwẽtʃi] *adj* frequent

fresco/a ['freʃku/a] *adj* fresh; (*vento, tempo*) cool; (*col*: *efeminado*) camp; (: *afetado*) pretentious; (: *cheio de luxo*) fussy ♦ *m* (*ar*) fresh air

frescobol [freʃko'bɔw] *m* (kind of) racketball (*played mainly on the beach*)

frescura [freʃ'kura] *f* freshness; (*frialdade*) coolness; (*col*: *luxo*) fussiness; (: *afetação*) pretentiousness

fretar [fre'ta*] *vt* (*avião, navio*) to charter; (*caminhão*) to hire

frete ['frɛtʃi] *m* (*carregamento*) freight, cargo; (*tarifa*) freightage

frevo ['frevu] *m* improvised Carnival dance

fria ['fria] *f*: **dar uma ~ em alguém** to give sb the cold shoulder; **estar/entrar numa** ~ (*col*) to be in/get into a mess

fricção [frik'sãw] *f* friction; (*ato*) rubbing; (*MED*) massage; **friccionar** [friksjo'na*] *vt* to rub

frieza ['frjeza] *f* coldness; (*indiferença*) coolness

frigideira [friʒi'dejra] *f* frying pan

frígido/a ['friʒidu/a] *adj* frigid

frigir [fri'ʒi*] *vt* to fry

frigorífico [frigo'rifiku] *m* refrigerator; (*congelador*) freezer

frio/a ['friu/a] *adj* cold ♦ *m* cold; ~**s** *mpl* (*CULIN*) cold meats; **estou com** ~ I'm cold; **faz** *ou* **está** ~ it's cold

frisar [fri'za*] *vt* (*encrespar*) to curl; (*salientar*) to emphasize

fritar [fri'ta*] *vt* to fry

fritas ['fritas] *fpl* chips (*BRIT*), French fries (*US*)

frito/a ['fritu/a] *adj* fried; (*col*): **estar** ~ to be done for

frívolo/a ['frivolu/a] *adj* frivolous

fronha ['frona] *f* pillowcase

fronte ['frõtʃi] *f* (*ANAT*) forehead, brow

fronteira [frõ'tejra] *f* frontier, border

frota ['frɔta] *f* fleet

frouxo/a ['froʃu/a] *adj* loose; (*corda, fig*: *pessoa*) slack; (*fraco*) weak; (*col*: *condescendente*) soft

frustrar [fruʃ'tra*] *vt* to frustrate

fruta ['fruta] *f* fruit; ~-**de-conde** (*pl* ~**s-de-conde**) *f* sweetsop; **fruteira** [fru'tejra] *f* fruit bowl; **frutífero/a** [fru'tʃiferu/a] *adj* (*proveitoso*) fruitful; (*árvore*) fruit-bearing

fruto ['frutu] *m* (*BOT*) fruit; (*resultado*) result, product; **dar** ~ (*fig*) to bear fruit

fubá [fu'ba] *m* corn meal

fuga ['fuga] *f* flight, escape; (*de gás etc*) leak

fugaz [fu'gaʒ] *adj* fleeting

fugir [fu'ʒi*] *vi* to flee, escape; (*prisioneiro*) to escape

fugitivo/a [fuʒi'tʃivu/a] *adj, m/f* fugitive

fui [fuj] *vb* V ir; ser

fulano/a [fu'lanu/a] *m/f* so-and-so

fulgor [fuw'go*] *m* brilliance

fuligem [fu'liʒẽ] *f* soot

fulminante [fuwmi'nãtʃi] *adj* devastating; (*palavras*) scathing

fulminar [fuwmi'na*] *vt* (*ferir, matar*) to strike down; (*aniquilar*) to annihilate ♦ *vi* to flash with lightning; **fulminado por um raio** struck by lightning

fulo/a ['fulu/a] *adj*: **estar** *ou* **ficar** ~ **de raiva** to be furious

fumaça [fu'masa] (*BR*) *f* (*de fogo*) smoke;

(*de gás*) fumes *pl*

fumador(a) [fuma'do*(a)] (*PT*) *m/f* smoker

fumante [fu'mãtʃi] *m/f* smoker

fumar [fu'ma*] *vt, vi* to smoke

fumo ['fumu] *m* (*PT: de fogo*) smoke; (: *de gás*) fumes *pl*; (*BR: tabaco*) tobacco; (*fumar*) smoking

função [fũ'sãw] (*pl* –ões) *f* function; (*ofício*) duty; (*papel*) role; (*espetáculo*) performance

funcionalismo [fũsjona'liʒmu] *m*: ~ público civil service

funcionamento [fũsjona'mẽtu] *m* functioning, working; **pôr em** ~ to set going, start

funcionar [fũsjo'na*] *vi* to function; (*máquina*) to work, run; (*dar bom resultado*) to work

funcionário/a [fũsjo'narju/a] *m/f* official; ~ (**público**) civil servant

funções [fũ'sõjʃ] *fpl de* função

fundação [fũda'sãw] (*pl* –ões) *f* foundation

fundamental [fũdamẽ'taw] (*pl* –ais) *adj* fundamental, basic

fundamento [fũda'mẽtu] *m* (*fig*) foundation, basis; (*motivo*) motive

fundar [fũ'da*] *vt* to establish, found; (*basear*) to base; ~-se *vr*: ~-se em to be based on

fundição [fũdʒi'sãw] (*pl* –ões) *f* fusing; (*fábrica*) foundry

fundir [fũ'dʒi*] *vt* to fuse; (*metal*) to smelt, melt down; (*COM: empresas*) to merge; (*em molde*) to cast; ~-se *vr* to melt; (*juntar-se*) to merge

fundo/a ['fũdu/a] *adj* deep; (*fig*) profound ♦ *m* (*do mar, jardim*) bottom; (*profundidade*) depth; (*base*) basis; (*da loja, casa, do papel*) back; (*de quadro*) background; (*de dinheiro*) fund ♦ *adv* deeply; ~s *mpl* (*COM*) funds; (*da casa etc*) back *sg*; **a** ~ thoroughly; **no** ~ at the bottom; (*da casa etc*) at the back; (*fig*) basically

fúnebre ['funebri] *adj* funeral *atr*, funereal; (*fig*) gloomy

funeral [fune'raw] (*pl* –ais) *m* funeral

funesto/a [fu'nɛʃtu/a] *adj* fatal; (*infausto*) disastrous

fungo ['fũgu] *m* fungus

funil [fu'niw] (*pl* –is) *m* funnel

furacão [fura'kãw] (*pl* –ões) *m* hurricane

furado/a [fu'radu/a] *adj* perforated; (*pneu*) flat; (*orelha*) pierced

furão/rona [fu'rãw/'rona] (*pl* –ões/~s) *m* ferret ♦ *m/f* (*col*) go-getter ♦ *adj* (*col*) hard-working, dynamic

furar [fu'ra*] *vt* to perforate; (*orelha*) to pierce; (*penetrar*) to penetrate; (*frustrar*) to foil; (*fila*) to jump ♦ *vi* (*col: programa*) to fall through

furgoneta [fuxgo'neta] (*PT*) *f* van

fúria ['furja] *f* fury, rage; **furioso/a** [fu'rjozu/ɔza] *adj* furious

furo ['furu] *m* hole; (*num pneu*) puncture

furões [fu'rõjʃ] *mpl de* furão

furona [fu'rona] *f de* furão

furor [fu'ro*] *m* fury, rage; **fazer** ~ to be all the rage

furtar [fux'ta*] *vt, vi* to steal; ~-se *vr*: ~-se a to avoid

furtivo/a [fux'tʃivu/a] *adj* furtive, stealthy

furto ['fuxtu] *m* theft

furúnculo [fu'rũkulu] *m* (*MED*) boil

fusão [fu'zãw] (*pl* –ões) *f* fusion; (*COM*) merger; (*derretimento*) melting; (*união*) union

fusível [fu'zivew] (*pl* –eis) *m* (*ELET*) fuse

fuso ['fuzu] *m* (*TEC*) spindle; ~ **horário** time zone

fusões [fu'zõjʃ] *fpl de* fusão

fustigar [fuʃtʃi'ga*] *vt* (*açoitar*) to flog, whip; (*suj: vento*) to lash; (*maltratar*) to lash out at

futebol [futʃi'bɔw] *m* football; ~ **de salão** five-a-side football

fútil ['futʃiw] (*pl* –eis) *adj* (*pessoa*) shallow; (*insignificante*) trivial

futilidade [futʃili'dadʒi] *f* (*de pessoa*) shallowness; (*insignificância*) triviality; (*coisa*) trivial thing

futuro/a [fu'turu/a] *adj* future ♦ *m* future; **no** ~ in the future

fuzil [fu'ziw] (*pl* –is) *m* rifle; ~**ar** [fuzi'la*] *vt* to shoot

fuzileiro/a [fuzi'lejru/a] *m/f*: ~ **naval** (*MIL*) marine

fuzis [fu'ziʃ] *mpl de* fuzil

G

g. *abr* (= *grama*) gr

G7 *abr* (= *Grupo dos Sete*) G7

gabar [ga'ba*] *vt* to praise; ~-se *vr*: ~-se de to boast about

gabinete [gabi'netʃi] *m* (*COM*) office; (*escritório*) study; (*POL*) cabinet

gado ['gadu] *m* livestock; (*bovino*) cattle; ~ **leiteiro** dairy cattle; ~ **suíno** pigs *pl*

gaélico/a [ga'ɛliku/a] *adj* Gaelic ♦ *m* (*LING*) Gaelic

gafanhoto [gafa'ɲotu] *m* grasshopper

gafe ['gafi] *f* gaffe, faux pas

gagueira [ga'gejra] *f* stutter

gaguejar [gage'ʒa*] *vi* to stammer, stutter

gaiato/a [ga'jatu/a] *adj* funny

gaiola [ga'jɔla] *f* cage; (*cadeia*) jail ♦ *m* (*barco*) riverboat

gaita ['gajta] *f* harmonica; ~ **de foles** bagpipes *pl*

gaivota [gaj'vota] *f* seagull

gajo ['gaʒu] (*PT: col*) *m* guy, fellow

gala ['gala] *f*: **traje de** ~ evening dress; **festa de** ~ gala

galante [ga'lãtʃi] *adj* graceful; (*gentil*) gallant

galão [ga'lãw] (pl ~ões) m (MIL) stripe; (medida) gallon; (PT: café) white coffee; (passamanaria) braid

Galápagos [ga'lapaguʃ]: **(as) Ilhas ~** fpl (the) Galapagos Islands

galáxia [ga'laksja] m galaxy

galego/a [ga'legu/a] adj Galician ♦ m/f Galician; (col: pej) Portuguese ♦ m (LING) Galician

galera [ga'lɛra] f (NÁUT) galley; (col: pessoas, público) crowd

galeria [gale'ria] f gallery; (TEATRO) circle

Gales ['galiʃ] m: **País de ~** Wales; **galês/esa** [ga'leʃ/eza] adj Welsh ♦ m/f Welshman/woman ♦ m (LING) Welsh

galgo ['gawgu] m greyhound

galho ['gaʎu] m (de árvore) branch

galinha [ga'liɲa] f hen; (CULIN) chicken; **galinheiro** [gali'ɲejru] m hen-house

galo ['galu] m cock, rooster; (inchação) bump; **missa do ~** midnight mass

galocha [ga'lɔʃa] f Wellington (boot)

galões [ga'lõjʃ] mpl de **galão**

galopar [galo'pa*] vi to gallop; **galope** [ga'lɔpi] m gallop

galpão [gaw'pãw] (pl ~ões) m shed

gama ['gama] f (MÚS) scale; (fig) range; (ZOOL) doe

gambá [gã'ba] m (ZOOL) opossum

Gana ['gana] m Ghana

gana ['gana] f craving, desire; (ódio) hate; **ter ~s de (fazer) algo** to feel like (doing) sth; **ter ~ de alguém** to hate sb

ganância [ga'nãsja] f greed; **ganancioso/a** [ganã'sjozu/ɔza] adj greedy

gancho ['gãʃu] m hook; (de calça) crotch

gangorra [gã'goxa] f seesaw

gângster ['gãŋʃte*] m gangster

gangue ['gãgi] (col) f gang

ganhador(a) [gaɲa'do*(a)] adj winning ♦ m/f winner

ganha-pão ['gaɲa-] (pl ~ães) m living, livelihood

ganhar [ga'ɲa*] vt to win; (salário) to earn; (adquirir) to get; (lugar) to reach; (lucrar) to gain ♦ vi to win; **~ de alguém** (num jogo) to beat sb; **ganho/a** ['gaɲu/a] pp de **ganhar** ♦ m profit, gain; **ganhos** mpl (ao jogo) winnings

ganir [ga'ni*] vi (cão) to yelp; (pessoa) to squeal

ganso/a ['gãsu/a] m/f gander/goose

garagem [ga'raʒẽ] (pl ~ns) f garage

garanhão [gara'ɲãw] (pl ~ões) m stallion

garantia [garã'tʃia] f guarantee; (de dívida) surety

garantir [garã'tʃi*] vt to guarantee; **~-se vr: ~-se contra algo** to defend o.s. against sth; **~ que ...** to maintain that ...

garbo ['gaxbu] m elegance; (distinção) distinction; **~so/a** [gax'bozu/ɔza] adj elegant; distinguished

garça ['gaxsa] f heron

garçom [gax'sõ] (BR: pl ~ns) m waiter

garçonete [gaxso'netʃi] (BR) f waitress

garçons [gax'sõʃ] mpl de **garçom**

garfo ['gaxfu] m fork

gargalhada [gaxga'ʎada] f burst of laughter; **rir às ~s** to roar with laughter; **dar** ou **soltar uma ~** to burst out laughing

gargalo [gax'galu] m (tb fig) bottleneck

garganta [gax'gãta] f throat; (GEO) gorge, ravine

gargarejar [gaxgare'ʒa*] vi to gargle; **gargarejo** [gaxga'reʒu] m (ato) gargling; (líquido) gargle

gari ['gari] m/f (na rua) roadsweeper (BRIT), streetsweeper (US); (lixeiro) dustman (BRIT), garbage man (US)

garoa [ga'roa] f drizzle; **~r** [ga'rwa*] vi to drizzle

garotada [garo'tada] f: **a ~** the kids pl

garoto/a [ga'rotu/a] m/f boy/girl; (namorado) boyfriend/girlfriend ♦ m (PT: café) coffee with milk

garoupa [ga'ropa] f (peixe) grouper

garra ['gaxa] f claw; (de ave) talon; (fig: entusiasmo) enthusiasm, drive; **~s** fpl (fig) clutches

garrafa [ga'xafa] f bottle

garrote [ga'xɔtʃi] m (MED) tourniquet; (tortura) garrote

garupa [ga'rupa] f (de cavalo) hindquarters pl; (de moto) back seat; **andar na ~ (de moto)** to ride pillion

gás [gajʃ] m gas; **gases** mpl (do intestino) wind sg; **~ natural** natural gas

gasóleo [ga'zɔlju] m diesel oil

gasolina [gazo'lina] f petrol (BRIT), gas(oline) (US)

gasosa [ga'zɔza] f fizzy drink

gasoso/a [ga'zozu/ɔza] adj (água) sparkling; (bebida) fizzy

gastador/deira [gaʃta'do*/'dejra] adj, m/f spendthrift

gastar [gaʃ'ta*] vt to spend; (gasolina, eletricidade) to use; (roupa, sapato) to wear out; (salto, piso etc) to wear down; (saúde) to damage; (desperdiçar) to waste ♦ vi to spend; **~-se** vr to wear out; to wear down; **~-se** vr to wear out; to wear down

gasto/a ['gaʃtu/a] pp de **gastar** ♦ adj spent; (frase) trite; (sapato etc, fig: pessoa) worn out; (salto, piso) worn down ♦ m (despesa) expense; **~s** mpl (COM) expenses, expenditure sg

gástrico/a ['gaʃtriku/a] adj gastric

gata ['gata] f (she-)cat

gatilho [ga'tʃiʎu] m trigger

gato ['gatu] m cat; **~ montês** wild cat

gatuno/a [ga'tunu/a] adj thieving ♦ m/f thief

gaveta [ga'veta] f drawer

gavião [ga'vjãw] (pl ~ões) m hawk

gaze ['gazi] f gauze

gazela [ga'zɛla] f gazelle

gazeta [ga'zeta] f (jornal) newspaper, gazette; **fazer** ~ (PT) to play truant

geada ['ʒjada] f frost

geladeira [ʒela'dejra] (BR) f refrigerator, icebox (US)

gelado/a [ʒe'ladu/a] adj frozen ♦ m (PT: sorvete) ice cream

gelar [ʒe'la*] vt to freeze; (vinho etc) to chill ♦ vi to freeze

gelatina [ʒela'tʃina] f gelatine; (sobremesa) jelly (BRIT), jello (US)

geléia [ʒe'lɛja] f jam

geleira [ʒe'lejra] f (GEO) glacier

gélido/a ['ʒɛlidu/a] adj chill, icy

gelo ['ʒɛlu] adj inv light grey (BRIT) ou gray (US) ♦ m ice; (cor) light grey (BRIT) ou gray (US)

gema ['ʒɛma] f yolk; (pedra preciosa) gem; ~**da** [ʒe'mada] f eggnog

gêmeo/a ['ʒemju/a] adj, m/f twin; **G~s** mpl (ASTROLOGIA) Gemini sg

gemer [ʒe'me*] vi (de dor) to groan, moan; (lamentar-se) to wail; (animal) to whine; (vento) to howl; **gemido** [ʒe'midu] m groan, moan; wail; whine

gene ['ʒeni] m gene

genealógico/a [ʒenja'lɔʒiku/a] adj: árvore genealógica family tree

Genebra [ʒe'nɛbra] f Geneva

genebra [ʒe'nɛbra] (PT) f gin

general [ʒene'raw] (pl -ais) m general

generalizar [ʒenerali'za*] vt to propagate ♦ vi to generalize; ~-se vr to become general, spread

gênero ['ʒeneru] m type, kind; (BIO) genus; (LING) gender; ~**s** mpl (produtos) goods; ~**s alimentícios** foodstuffs; ~ **humano** humankind, human race

generosidade [ʒenerozi'dadʒi] f generosity

generoso/a [ʒene'rozu/ɔza] adj generous

genética [ʒe'nɛtʃika] f genetics sg

gengibre [ʒe'ʒibri] m ginger

gengiva [ʒẽ'ʒiva] f (ANAT) gum

genial [ʒe'njaw] (pl -ais) adj inspired, brilliant; (col) terrific, fantastic

gênio ['ʒenju] m (temperamento) nature; (irascibilidade) temper; (talento, pessoa) genius; **de bom/mau** ~ good-natured/bad-tempered

genital [ʒeni'taw] (pl -ais) adj: **órgãos genitais** genitals pl

genro ['ʒẽxu] m son-in-law

gente ['ʒẽtʃi] f people pl; (col) folks pl, family; (: alguém): **tem** ~ **batendo à porta** there's somebody knocking at the door; **a** ~ (nós: suj) we; (: objeto) us; **a casa da** ~ our house; **toda a** ~ everybody; ~ **grande** grown-ups pl

gentil [ʒẽ'tʃiw] (pl -is) adj kind; ~**eza** [ʒẽtʃi'leza] f kindness; **por** ~**eza** if you please; **tenha a** ~**eza de fazer ...?** would you be so kind as to do ...?

genuíno/a [ʒe'nwinu/a] adj genuine

geografia [ʒeogra'fia] f geography

geologia [ʒeolo'ʒia] f geology

geometria [ʒeome'tria] f geometry

geração [ʒera'sãw] (pl -ões) f generation

gerador(a) [ʒera'do*(a)] m/f (produtor) creator ♦ m (TEC) generator

geral [ʒe'raw] (pl -ais) adj general ♦ f (TEATRO) gallery; **em** ~ in general, generally; **de um modo** ~ on the whole; ~**mente** [ʒeraw'mẽtʃi] adv generally, usually

gerânio [ʒe'ranju] m geranium

gerar [ʒe'ra*] vt to produce; (eletricidade) to generate

gerência [ʒe'rẽsja] f management; **gerenciar** [ʒerẽ'sja*] vt, vi to manage

gerente [ʒe'rẽtʃi] adj managing ♦ m/f manager

gergelim [ʒexʒe'lĩ] m (BOT) sesame

geriátrico/a [ʒi'rjatriku/a] adj geriatric

gerir [ʒe'ri*] vt to manage, run

germe ['ʒexmi] m (embrião) embryo; (micróbio) germ

gesso ['ʒesu] m plaster (of Paris)

gestante [ʒeʃ'tãtʃi] f pregnant woman

gesticular [ʒeʃtʃiku'la*] vi to make gestures, gesture

gesto ['ʒeʃtu] m gesture

Gibraltar [ʒibraw'ta*] f Gibraltar

gigante/ta [ʒi'gãtʃi/ta] adj gigantic, huge ♦ m giant; ~**sco/a** [ʒigã'teʃku/a] adj gigantic

gim [ʒĩ] (pl -ns) m gin

ginásio [ʒi'nazju] m gymnasium; (escola) secondary (BRIT) ou high (US) school

ginástica [ʒi'naʃtʃika] f gymnastics sg; (para fortalecer o corpo) keep-fit

ginecologia [ʒinekolo'ʒia] f gynaecology (BRIT), gynecology (US)

ginecologista [ʒinekolo'ʒiʃta] m/f gynaecologist (BRIT), gynecologist (US)

ginjinha [ʒĩ'ʒiɲa] (PT) f cherry brandy

gins [ʒĩʃ] mpl de gim

gira-discos ['ʒira-] (PT) m inv record-player

girafa [ʒi'rafa] f giraffe

girar [ʒi'ra*] vt to turn, rotate; (como pião) to spin ♦ vi to go round; to spin; (vaguear) to wander

girassol [ʒira'sɔw] (pl -óis) m sunflower

giratório/a [ʒira'tɔrju/a] adj revolving

gíria ['ʒirja] f (calão) slang; (jargão) jargon

giro¹ ['ʒiru] m turn; **dar um** ~ to go for a wander; (em veículo) to go for a spin; **que** ~! (PT) terrific!

giro² etc vb V **gerir**

giz [ʒiʒ] m chalk

glacê [gla'se] m icing

glacial [gla'sjaw] (pl -ais) adj icy

glamouroso/a [glamu'rozu/ɔza] adj glamorous

glândula ['glãdula] f gland

glicerina [glise'rina] f glycerine

glicose [gli'kɔzi] f glucose

global [glo'baw] (*pl* –ais) *adj* global; (*total*) overall; **quantia** ~ lump sum

globo ['globu] *m* globe; ~ **ocular** eyeball

glória ['glɔrja] *f* glory; **glorificar** [glorifi'ka*] *vt* to glorify; **glorioso/a** [glo'rjozu/ɔza] *adj* glorious

glossário [glo'sarju] *m* glossary

glutão/tona [glu'tãw/tɔna] (*pl* –ões/~s) *adj* greedy ♦ *m/f* glutton

gnomo ['gnomu] *m* gnome

Goa ['goa] *n* Goa

godê [go'de] *adj* (*saia*) flared

goiaba [go'jaba] *f* guava; ~**da** [goja'bada] *f* guava jelly

gol [gow] (*pl* ~s) *m* goal

gola ['gɔla] *f* collar

gole ['gɔli] *m* gulp, swallow; (*pequeno*) sip; **tomar um** ~ **de** to sip

goleiro [go'lejru] (*BR*) *m* goalkeeper

golfe ['gowfi] *m* golf; **campo de** ~ golf course

golfinho [gow'fiɲu] *m* (*ZOOL*) dolphin

golfista [gow'fiʃta] *m/f* golfer

golfo ['gowfu] *m* gulf

golinho [go'liɲu] *m* sip; **beber algo aos** ~s to sip sth

golo ['golu] (*PT*) *m* = gol

golpe ['gowpi] *m* (*tb fig*) blow; (*de mão*) smack; (*de punho*) punch; (*manobra*) ploy; (*de vento*) gust; **de um só** ~ at a stroke; **dar um** ~ **em alguém** to hit sb; (*fig: trapacear*) to trick sb; ~ **(de estado)** coup (d'état); ~ **de mestre** masterstroke; ~**ar** [gow'pja*] *vt* to hit; (*com navalha*) to stab; (*com o punho*) to punch

golquíper [gow'kipe*] *m* goalkeeper

goma ['gɔma] *f* gum, glue; (*de roupa*) starch; ~ **de mascar** chewing gum

gomo ['gomu] *m* (*de laranja*) slice

gongo ['gõgu] *m* gong; (*sineta*) bell

gorar [go'ra*] *vt* to frustrate, thwart ♦ *vi* (*plano*) to fail, go wrong

gordo/a ['goxdu/a] *adj* fat; (*gordurento*) greasy; (*carne*) fatty; (*fig: quantia*) considerable, ample ♦ *m/f* fat man/woman

gordura [gox'dura] *f* fat; (*derretida*) grease; (*obesidade*) fatness; **gorduroso/a** [goxdu'rozu/ɔza] *adj* (*pele*) greasy; (*comida*) fatty

gorila [go'rila] *m* gorilla

gorjeta [gox'ʒeta] *f* tip, gratuity

gorro ['goxu] *m* cap; (*de lã*) hat

gosma ['gɔʒma] *f* spittle; (*fig*) slime

gostar [goʃ'ta*] *vi*: ~ **de** to like; (*férias, viagem etc*) to enjoy; ~**se** *vr* to like each other; ~ **mais de** ... to prefer ..., like ... better

gosto ['goʃtu] *m* taste; (*prazer*) pleasure; **a seu** ~ to your liking; **com** ~ willingly; (*vestir-se*) tastefully; (*comer*) heartily; **de bom/mau** ~ in good/bad taste; **ter** ~ **de** to taste of; ~**so/a** [goʃ'tozu/ɔza] *adj* tasty; (*agradável*) pleasant; (*cheiro*) lovely; (*risada*) good; (*col: pessoa*) gorgeous

gota ['gota] *f* drop; (*de suor*) bead; (*MED*) gout; ~ **a** ~ drop by drop

goteira [go'tejra] *f* (*cano*) gutter; (*buraco*) leak

gotejar [gote'ʒa*] *vt* to drip ♦ *vi* to drip; (*telhado*) to leak

gourmet [gux'me] (*pl* ~s) *m/f* gourmet

governador(a) [govexnado*(a)] *m/f* governor

governamental [govexnamẽ'taw] (*pl* –ais) *adj* government *atr*

governanta [govex'nãta] *f* (*de casa*) housekeeper; (*de criança*) governess

governante [govex'nãtʃi] *adj* ruling ♦ *m/f* ruler ♦ *f* governess

governar [govex'na*] *vt* to govern, rule; (*barco*) to steer

governo [go'vexnu] *m* government; (*controle*) control

gozação [goza'sãw] (*pl* –ões) *f* enjoyment; (*zombaria*) teasing; (*uma* ~) joke

gozado/a [go'zadu/a] *adj* funny; (*estranho*) strange, odd

gozar [go'za*] *vt* to enjoy; (*col: rir de*) to make fun of ♦ *vi* to enjoy o.s.; ~ **de** to enjoy; to make fun of; **gozo** ['gozu] *m* (*prazer*) pleasure; (*uso*) enjoyment, use; (*orgasmo*) orgasm

Grã-Bretanha [grã-bre'taɲa] *f* Great Britain

graça ['grasa] *f* (*REL*) grace; (*charme*) charm; (*gracejo*) joke; (*JUR*) pardon; **de** ~ (*grátis*) for nothing; (*sem motivo*) for no reason; **sem** ~ dull, boring; **fazer ou ter** ~ to be funny; **ficar sem** ~ to be embarrassed; ~**s a** thanks to

gracejar [grase'ʒa*] *vi* to joke; **gracejo** [gra'seʒu] *m* joke

gracioso/a [gra'sjozu/ɔza] *adj* (*pessoa*) charming; (*gestos*) gracious

gradativo/a [grada'tʃivu/a] *adj* gradual

grade ['gradʒi] *f* (*no chão*) grating; (*grelha*) grill; (*na janela*) bars *pl*; (*col: cadeia*) nick, clink

gradear [gra'dʒja*] *vt* (*janela*) to put bars up at; (*jardim*) to fence off

graduação [gradwa'sãw] (*pl* –ões) *f* (*classificação*) grading; (*EDUC*) graduation; (*MIL*) rank

gradual [gra'dwaw] (*pl* –ais) *adj* gradual

graduar [gra'dwa*] *vt* (*classificar*) to grade; (*luz, fogo*) to regulate; ~**se** *vr* to graduate

grafia [gra'fia] *f* (*escrita*) writing; (*ortografia*) spelling

gráfica ['grafika] *f* graphics *sg*; *V tb* gráfico

gráfico/a ['grafiku/a] *adj* graphic ♦ *m/f* printer ♦ *m* (*MAT*) graph; (*diagrama*) diagram, chart; ~**s** *mpl* (*COMPUT*) graphics; ~ **de barras** bar chart

grã-fino/a [grã'finu/a] (*col*) *adj* posh ♦ *m/f* nob, toff

grama ['grama] *m* gramme ♦ *f* (*BR: ca-*

pim) grass

gramado [gra'madu] (*BR*) *m* lawn; (*FUTE-BOL*) pitch

gramar [gra'ma*] *vt* to plant *ou* sow with grass

gramática [gra'matʃika] *f* grammar; **gramatical** [gramatʃi'kaw] (*pl* **-ais**) *adj* grammatical

gramofone [gramo'fɔni] *m* gramophone

grampeador [grãpja'do*] *m* stapler

grampear [grã'pja*] *vt* to staple

grampo [ˈgrãpu] *m* staple; (*no cabelo*) hairgrip; (*de carpinteiro*) clamp; (*de chapéu*) hatpin

granada [gra'nada] *f* (*MIL*) shell; **~ de mão** hand grenade

grande [ˈgrãdʒi] *adj* big, large; (*alto*) tall; (*notável, intenso*) great; (*longo*) long; (*adulto*) grown-up; **mulher ~** big woman; **~ mulher** great woman; **~za** [grã'deza] *f* size; (*fig*) greatness; (*ostentação*) grandeur

grandioso/a [grã'dʒjozu/ɔza] *adj* magnificent, grand

granel [gra'nɛw] *m*: **a ~** (*COM*) in bulk

granito [gra'nitu] *m* granite

granizo [gra'nizu] *m* hailstone; **chover ~** to hail; **chuva de ~** hailstorm

granja [ˈgrãʒa] *f* farm; (*de galinhas*) chicken farm

granulado/a [granu'ladu/a] *adj* grainy; (*açúcar*) granulated

grânulo [ˈgranulu] *m* granule

grão [ˈgrãw] (*pl* **~s**) *m* grain; (*semente*) seed; (*de café*) bean; **~-de-bico** (*pl* **~s-de-bico**) *m* chickpea

grapefruit [greip'frutʃi] (*pl* **~s**) *m* grapefruit

grasnar [graʒ'na*] *vi* (*corvo*) to caw; (*pato*) to quack; (*rã*) to croak

gratidão [gratʃi'dãw] *f* gratitude

gratificação [gratʃifika'sãw] (*pl* **-ões**) *f* gratuity, tip; (*bônus*) bonus; (*recompensa*) reward

gratificante [gratʃifi'kãtʃi] *adj* gratifying

gratificar [gratʃifi'ka*] *vt* to tip; (*dar bônus a*) to give a bonus to; (*recompensar*) to reward

grátis [ˈgratʃiʃ] *adj* free

grato/a [ˈgratu/a] *adj* grateful; (*agradável*) pleasant

gratuito/a [gra'twitu/a] *adj* (*grátis*) free; (*infundado*) gratuitous

grau [graw] *m* degree; (*nível*) level; (*EDUC*) class; **em alto ~** to a high degree; **ensino de primeiro/segundo ~** primary (*BRIT*) *ou* elementary (*US*)/secondary education

gravação [grava'sãw] *f* (*em madeira*) carving; (*em disco, fita*) recording

gravador [grava'do*] *m* tape recorder

gravar [gra'va*] *vt* to carve; (*metal, pedra*) to engrave; (*na memória*) to fix; (*disco, fita*) to record

gravata [gra'vata] *f* tie; **~ borboleta** bow tie

grave [ˈgravi] *adj* serious; (*tom*) deep; **~mente** [grave'mẽtʃi] *adv* (*doente, ferido*) seriously

grávida [ˈgravida] *adj* pregnant

gravidade [gravi'dadʒi] *f* gravity

gravidez [gravi'deʒ] *f* pregnancy

gravura [gra'vura] *f* (*em madeira*) engraving; (*estampa*) print

graxa [ˈgraʃa] *f* (*para sapatos*) polish; (*lubrificante*) grease

Grécia [ˈgrɛsja] *f*: **a ~** Greece; **grego/a** [ˈgregu/a] *adj*, *m/f* Greek ♦ *m* (*LING*) Greek

grei [grej] *f* flock

grelha [ˈgrɛʎa] *f* grill; (*de fornalha*) grate; **bife na ~** grilled steak; **~do** [grɛ'ʎadu] *m* (*prato*) grill; **~r** [gre'ʎa*] *vt* to grill

grêmio [ˈgremju] *m* (*associação*) guild; (*clube*) club

grená [gre'na] *adj*, *m* dark red

greta [ˈgreta] *f* crack

greve [ˈgrɛvi] *f* strike; **fazer ~** to go on strike; **~ branca** go-slow; **grevista** [gre'viʃta] *m/f* striker

grifar [gri'fa*] *vt* to italicize; (*sublinhar*) to underline; (*fig*) to emphasize

grifo [ˈgrifu] *m* italics *pl*

grilo [ˈgrilu] *m* cricket; (*AUTO*) squeak; (*col: de pessoa*) hang-up; **qual é o ~?** what's the matter?; **não tem ~!** (*col*) (there's) no problem!

grinalda [gri'nawda] *f* garland

gringo/a [ˈgrĩgu/a] (*col: pej*) *m/f* foreigner

gripado/a [gri'padu/a] *adj*: **estar/ficar ~** to have/get a cold

gripe [ˈgripi] *f* flu, influenza

grisalho/a [gri'zaʎu/a] *adj* (*cabelo*) grey (*BRIT*), gray (*US*)

gritante [gri'tãtʃi] *adj* (*hipocrisia*) glaring; (*desigualdade*) gross; (*mentira*) blatant; (*cor*) loud, garish

gritar [gri'ta*] *vt* to shout, yell ♦ *vi* to shout; (*de dor, medo*) to scream; **~ com alguém** to shout at sb; **~ia** [grita'ria] *f* shouting, din; **grito** [ˈgritu] *m* shout; (*de medo*) scream; (*de dor*) cry; (*de animal*) call; **dar um grito** to cry out; **falar/protestar aos gritos** to shout/shout protests

Groenlândia [grwẽ'lãdʒja] *f*: **a ~** Greenland

grosa [ˈgrɔza] *f* gross

grosseiro/a [gro'sejru/a] *adj* rude; (*piada*) crude; (*modos, tecido*) coarse; **grosseria** [grose'ria] *f* rudeness; (*ato*) **fazer uma grosseria** to be rude; (*dito*) **dizer uma grosseria** to be rude, say something rude

grosso/a [ˈgrosu/ˈgrɔsa] *adj* thick; (*áspero*) rough; (*voz*) deep; (*col: pessoa, piada*) rude ♦ *m*: **o ~ de** the bulk of;

grossura [gro'sura] *f* thickness

grotesco/a [gro'teʃku/a] adj grotesque
grudar [gru'da*] vt to glue, stick ♦ vi to stick
grude ['grudʒi] f glue; **~nto/a** [gru'dẽtu/a] adj sticky
grunhido [gru'ɲidu] m grunt
grunhir [gru'ɲi*] vi (porco) to grunt; (tigre) to growl; (resmungar) to grumble
grupo ['grupu] m group
gruta ['gruta] f grotto
guarda ['gwaxda] m/f policeman/woman ♦ f (vigilância) guarding; (de objeto) safekeeping ♦ m (MIL) guard; **estar de ~** to be on guard; **pôr-se em ~** to be on one's guard; **a G~ Civil** the Civil Guard; **~-chuva** (pl **~-chuvas**) m umbrella; **~-civil** (pl **~s-civis**) m civil guard; **~-costas** m inv (NÁUT) coastguard boat; (capanga) bodyguard; **~-dos** [gwax'daduʃ] mpl keepsakes, valuables; **~-fogo** (pl **~-fogos**) m fireguard; **~-louça** [gwaxda'losa] (pl **~-louças**) m sideboard; **~-napo** [gwaxda'napu] m napkin; **~-noturno** (pl **~s-noturnos**) m night watchman; **~r** [gwax'da*] vt to put away; (zelar por) to guard; (lembrança, segredo) to keep; **~r-se** vr (defender-se) to protect o.s.; **~r-se de** (acautelar-se) to guard against; **~-redes** (PT) m inv goalkeeper; **~-roupa** (pl **~-roupas**) m wardrobe; **~-sol** (pl **~-sóis**) m sunshade, parasol
guardião/diã [gwax'dʒjãw/d'ʒjã] (pl **-ães** ou **-ões/~s**) m/f guardian
guarnecer [gwaxne'se*] vt to garnish
guarnição [gwaxni'sãw] (pl **-ões**) f (MIL) garrison; (NÁUT) crew; (CULIN) garnish
Guatemala [gwate'mala] f: **a ~** Guatemala
gude ['gudʒi] m: **bola de ~** marble; (jogo) marbles pl
guelra ['gɛwxa] f (de peixe) gill
guerra ['gɛxa] f war; **em ~** at war; **fazer ~** to wage war; **~ civil** civil war; **~ mundial** world war; **guerreiro/a** [ge'xejru/a] adj (espírito) fighting; (belicoso) warlike ♦ m warrior
guerrilha [ge'xiʎa] f (luta) guerrilla warfare; (tropa) guerrilla band; **guerrilheiro/a** [gexi'ʎejru/a] m/f guerrilla
gueto ['getu] m ghetto
guia ['gia] f guidance; (COM) permit, bill of lading; (formulário) advice slip ♦ m (livro) guide(book) ♦ m/f (pessoa) guide
Guiana ['gjana] f: **a ~** Guyana
guiar [gja*] vt to guide; (AUTO) to drive ♦ vi to drive; **~-se** vr: **~-se por** to go by
guichê [gi'ʃe] m ticket window; (em banco, repartição) window, counter
guidom [gi'dõ] (pl **-ns**) m handlebar
guilhotina [giʎo'tʃina] f guillotine
guinada [gi'nada] f: **dar uma ~** (com o carro) to swerve
guincho ['gĩʃu] m (de animal, rodas) squeal; (de pessoa) shriek
guindaste [gĩ'daʃtʃi] m hoist, crane
guisado [gi'zadu] m stew
guisar [gi'za*] vt to stew
guitarra [gi'taxa] f (electric) guitar
gula ['gula] f gluttony, greed
gulodice [gulo'dʒisi] f greed
guloseima [gulo'zejma] f delicacy, titbit
guloso/a [gu'lozu/ɔza] adj greedy

H

há [a] vb V haver
hábil ['abiw] (pl **-eis**) adj competent, capable; (astucioso, esperto) clever; (sutil) diplomatic; **em tempo ~** in reasonable time; **habilidade** [abili'dadʒi] f skill, ability; (astúcia, esperteza) shrewdness; (tato) discretion; **habilidoso/a** [abili'dozu/ɔza] adj skilled, clever
habilitação [abilita'sãw] (pl **-ões**) f competence; (ato) qualification; **habilitações** fpl (conhecimentos) qualifications
habilitado/a [abili'tadu/a] adj qualified; (manualmente) skilled
habilitar [abili'ta*] vt to enable; (dar direito a) to qualify, entitle; (preparar) to prepare
habitação [abita'sãw] (pl **-ões**) f dwelling, residence; (alojamento) housing
habitante [abi'tãtʃi] m/f inhabitant
habitar [abi'ta*] vt to live in; (povoar) to inhabit ♦ vi to live
hábitat ['abitatʃi] m habitat
hábito ['abitu] m habit; (social) custom; (REL: traje) habit
habituado/a [abi'twadu/a] adj: **~ a** (fazer) algo used to (doing) sth
habitual [abi'twaw] (pl **-ais**) adj usual
habituar [abi'twa*] vt: **~ alguém a** to get sb used to, accustom sb to; **~-se** vr: **~-se a** to get used to
hacker ['ake*] (pl **~s**) m (COMPUT) hacker
hadoque [a'dɔki] m haddock
Haia ['aja] n the Hague
haja etc ['aʒa] vb V haver
hálito ['alitu] m breath
hall [xɔw] (pl **~s**) m hall; (de teatro, hotel) foyer; **~ de entrada** entrance hall
halo ['alu] m halo
halterofilista [awterofi'liʃta] m/f weightlifter
hambúrguer [ã'buxge*] m hamburger
handicap [ãdʒi'kapi] m handicap
hangar [ã'ga*] m hangar
hão [ãw] vb V haver
hardware ['xadwe*] m (COMPUT) hardware
harmonia [axmo'nia] f harmony
harmônica [ax'monika] f concertina
harmonioso/a [axmo'njozu/ɔza] adj harmonious
harmonizar [axmoni'za*] vt (MÚS) to harmonize; (conciliar): **~ algo (com algo)**

to reconcile sth (with sth); **~-se** *vr*: **~(-se)** to coincide; (*pessoas*) to be in agreement

harpa ['axpa] *f* harp

haste ['aʃtʃi] *f* flagpole; (*TEC*) shaft, rod; (*BOT*) stem

Havaí [ava'i] *m*: **o ~** Hawaii

havana [a'vana] *adj inv* light brown

PALAVRA CHAVE
---

haver [a've'] *vb aux* **1** (*ter*) to have; ele havia saído/comido he had left/eaten **2**: **~ de**: quem ~ia de dizer que ... who would have thought that ...
♦ *vb impess* **1** (*existência*): **há** (*sg*) there is; (*pl*) there are; **o que é que há?** what's the matter?; **o que é que houve?** what happened?, what was that?; **não há de quê** don't mention it, you're welcome; **haja o que houver** come what may
2 (*tempo*): **há séculos/cinco dias que não o vejo** I haven't seen him for ages/five days; **há um ano que ela chegou** it's a year since she arrived; **há cinco dias (atrás)** five days ago
♦ **~-se** *vr*: **~-se com alguém** to sort things out with sb
♦ *m* (*COM*) credit; **~es** *mpl* (*pertences*) property *sg*, possessions; (*riqueza*) wealth *sg*

---

haxixe [a'ʃiʃi] *m* hashish

hebraico/a [e'brajku/a] *adj* Hebrew ♦ *m* (*LING*) Hebrew

Hébridas [ɛ'bridaʃ] *fpl*: **as (ilhas) ~** the Hebrides

hectare [ek'tari] *m* hectare

hediondo/a [e'dʒjõdu/a] *adj* vile, revolting; (*crime*) heinous

hei [ej] *vb V* haver

hélice ['ɛlisi] *f* propeller

helicóptero [eli'kɔpteru] *m* helicopter

hélio ['ɛlju] *m* helium

hematoma [ema'tɔma] *m* bruise

hemorragia [emoxa'ʒia] *f* haemorrhage (*BRIT*), hemorrhage (*US*); **~ nasal** nosebleed

hemorróidas [emo'xɔjdaʃ] *fpl* haemorrhoids (*BRIT*), hemorrhoids (*US*), piles

hepatite [epa'tʃitʃi] *f* hepatitis

hera ['ɛra] *f* ivy

heráldica [e'rawdʒika] *f* heraldry

herança [e'rãsa] *f* inheritance; (*fig*) heritage

herbicida [exbi'sida] *m* weedkiller

herdar [ex'da'] *vt*: **~ algo (de)** to inherit sth (from); **~ a** to bequeath to

herdeiro/a [ex'dejru/a] *m/f* heir(ess)

hérnia ['ɛxnja] *f* hernia

herói [e'rɔj] *m* hero; **~co/a** [e'rɔjku/a] *adj* heroic

heroína [ero'ina] *f* heroine; (*droga*) heroin

herpes-zoster [ɛxpiʃ'zɔʃte'] *m* (*MED*)

shingles *sg*

hesitação [ezita'sãw] *f* (*pl* **-ões**) hesitation

hesitante [ezi'tãtʃi] *adj* hesitant

hesitar [ezi'ta'] *vi* to hesitate

heterossexual [eterosek'swaw] (*pl* **-ais**) *adj*, *m/f* heterosexual

hibernar [ibex'na'] *vi* to hibernate

híbrido/a ['ibridu/a] *adj* hybrid

hidratante [idra'tãtʃi] *m* moisturizer

hidrato [i'dratu] *m*: **~ de carbono** carbohydrate

hidráulico/a [i'drawliku/a] *adj* hydraulic

hidrelétrico/a [idre'lɛtriku/a] (*PT* **-ct-**) *adj* hydroelectric

hidro... [idru] *prefixo* hydro..., water..., atr

hidrofobia [idrofo'bia] *f* rabies *sg*

hidrogênio [idro'ʒenju] *m* hydrogen

hierarquia [jerax'kia] *f* hierarchy; **hierárquico/a** [je'raxkiku/a] *adj* hierarchical

hífen ['ifẽ] (*pl* **~s**) *m* hyphen

higiene [i'ʒjeni] *f* hygiene; **higiênico/a** [i'ʒjeniku/a] *adj* hygienic; (*pessoa*) clean; **papel higiênico** toilet paper

hilariante [ila'rjãtʃi] *adj* hilarious

hindu [ĩ'du] *adj*, *m/f* Hindu

hino ['inu] *m* hymn; **~ nacional** national anthem

hipermercado [ipexmex'kadu] *m* hypermarket

hipertensão [ipextẽ'sãw] *f* high blood pressure

hípico/a ['ipiku/a] *adj*: **clube ~** riding club

hipismo [i'piʒmu] *m* (*turfe*) horse racing; (*equitação*) (horse) riding

hipnotismo [ipno'tʃiʒmu] *m* hypnotism; **hipnotizar** [ipnotʃi'za'] *vt* to hypnotize

hipocondríaco/a [ipokõ'driaku/a] *adj*, *m/f* hypochondriac

hipocrisia [ipokri'sia] *f* hypocrisy; **hipócrita** [i'pɔkrita] *adj* hypocritical ♦ *m/f* hypocrite

hipódromo [i'pɔdromu] *m* racecourse

hipopótamo [ipo'pɔtamu] *m* hippopotamus

hipoteca [ipo'tɛka] *f* mortgage; **~r** [ipote'ka'] *vt* to mortgage

hipótese [i'pɔtezi] *f* hypothesis; **na ~ de** in the event of; **em ~ alguma** under no circumstances; **na melhor/pior das ~s** at best/worst

hispânico/a [iʃ'paniku/a] *adj* Hispanic

histeria [iʃte'ria] *f* hysteria; **histérico/a** [iʃ'tɛriku/a] *adj* hysterical; **histerismo** [iʃte'riʒmu] *m* hysteria

história [iʃ'tɔrja] *f* history; (*conto*) story; **~s** *fpl* (*chateação*) bother *sg*, fuss *sg*; **isso é outra ~** that's a different matter; **que ~ é essa?** what's going on?; **historiador(a)** [iʃtorja'do'(a)] *m/f* historian; **histórico/a** [iʃ'tɔriku/a] *adj* historical; (*fig*: *notável*) historic ♦ *m* history

hobby ['xɔbi] (pl –bies) m hobby

hoje ['oʒi] adv today; (tb: ~ **em dia**) now(adays); ~ **à noite** tonight

Holanda [o'lãda] f: **a ~** Holland; **holandês/esa** [olã'deʃ/eza] adj Dutch ♦ m/f Dutchman/woman ♦ m (LING) Dutch

holocausto [olo'kawʃtu] m holocaust

holofote [olo'fɔtʃi] m searchlight; (em campo de futebol etc) floodlight

homem ['omẽ] (pl –ns) m man; (a humanidade) mankind; ~ **de empresa** ou **negócios** businessman; ~ **de estado** statesman; **~-rã** (pl **homens-rã(s)**) m frogman

homenagear [omena'ʒjaˣ] vt (pessoa) to pay tribute to, honour (BRIT), honor (US)

homenagem [ome'naʒẽ] f tribute; (REL) homage; **prestar ~ a alguém** to pay tribute to sb

homens ['omẽʃ] mpl de homem

homicida [omi'sida] adj homicidal ♦ m/f murderer; **homicídio** [omi'sidʒju] m murder; **homicídio involuntário** manslaughter

homologar [omolo'gaˣ] vt to ratify

homólogo/a [o'mɔlogu/a] adj homologous; (fig) equivalent ♦ m/f opposite number

homossexual [omosek'swal] (pl –ais) adj, m/f homosexual

Honduras [õ'duraʃ] f Honduras

honestidade [oneʃtʃi'dadʒi] f honesty; (decência) decency; (justeza) fairness

honesto/a [o'nɛʃtu/a] adj honest; (decente) decent; (justo) fair, just

honorário/a [ono'rarju/a] adj honorary; **~s** [ono'rarjuʃ] mpl fees

honra ['õxa] f honour (BRIT), honor (US); **em ~ de** in hono(u)r of

honradez [õxa'deʒ] f honesty; (de pessoa) integrity

honrado/a [õ'xadu/a] adj honest; (respeitado) honourable (BRIT), honorable (US)

honrar [õ'xaˣ] vt to honour (BRIT), honor (US)

honroso/a [õ'xozu/ɔza] adj hono(u)rable

hóquei ['ɔkej] m hockey; ~ **sobre gelo** ice hockey

hora ['ɔra] f (60 minutos) hour; (momento) time; **a que ~s?** (at) what time?; **que ~s são?** what time is it?; **são duas ~s** it's two o'clock; **você tem as ~s?** have you got the time?; **fazer ~** to kill time; **de ~ em ~** every hour; **na ~** on the spot; **chegar na ~** to be on time; **de última ~** adj last-minute ♦ adv at the last minute; **meia ~** half an hour; **~s extras** overtime sg; **horário/a** [o'rarju/a] adj: **100 km horários** 100 km an hour ♦ m timetable; (hora) time; **horário de expediente** working hours pl; (de um escritório) office hours pl

horda ['ɔxda] f horde

horizontal [orizõ'taw] (pl –ais) adj horizontal

horizonte [ori'zõtʃi] m horizon

hormônio [ox'monju] m hormone

horóscopo [o'rɔʃkopu] m horoscope

horrendo/a [o'xẽdu/a] adj horrendous, frightful

horripilante [oxipi'lãtʃi] adj horrifying, hair-raising

horrível [o'xivew] (pl –eis) adj awful, horrible

horror [o'xoˣ] m horror; **que ~!** how awful!; **ter ~ a algo** to hate sth; **~izar** [oxori'zaˣ] vt to horrify, frighten; **~oso/a** [oxo'rozu/ɔza] adj horrible, ghastly

horta ['ɔxta] f vegetable garden

hortaliças [oxta'lisaʃ] fpl vegetables

hortelã [oxte'lã] f mint; ~ **pimenta** peppermint

hortênsia [ox'tẽsja] f hydrangea

horticultor(a) [oxtʃikuw'to(ˣa)] m/f market gardener (BRIT), truck farmer (US)

hortifrutigranjeiros [oxtʃifrutʃigrã'ʒejruʃ] mpl fruit and vegetables

horto ['ɔxtu] m market garden (BRIT), truck farm (US)

hospedagem [oʃpe'daʒẽ] f guest house

hospedar [oʃpe'daˣ] vt to put up; **~-se** vr to stay, lodge; **~ia** [oʃpeda'ria] f guest house

hóspede ['ɔʃpedʒi] m (amigo) guest; (estranho) lodger

hospedeira [oʃpe'dejra] f landlady; (PT: de bordo) stewardess, air hostess (BRIT)

hospedeiro [oʃpe'dejru] m (dono) landlord

hospício [oʃ'pisju] m mental hospital

hospital [oʃpi'taw] (pl –ais) m hospital

hospitalidade [oʃpitali'dadʒi] f hospitality

hostess ['ɔʃtes] (pl –es) f hostess

hostil [oʃ'tʃiw] (pl –is) adj hostile; **~izar** [oʃtʃili'zaˣ] vt to antagonize; (MIL) to wage war on

hotel [o'tɛw] (pl –éis) m hotel; **~eiro/a** [ote'lejru/a] m/f hotelier

houve etc ['ovi] vb V haver

humanidade [umani'dadʒi] f (os homens) man(kind); (compaixão) humanity

humanitário/a [umani'tarju/a] adj humane

humano/a [u'manu/a] adj human; (bondoso) humane

húmido/a (PT) adj = úmido

humildade [umiw'dadʒi] f humility; (pobreza) poverty

humilde [u'miwdʒi] adj humble; (pobre) poor

humilhar [umi'ʎaˣ] vt to humiliate

humor [u'moˣ] m mood, temper; (graça) humour (BRIT), humor (US); **de bom/mau ~** in a good/bad mood; **~ista** [umo'riʃta] m/f comedian; **~ístico/a** [umo'riʃtʃiku/a] adj humorous

húngaro/a ['ūgaru/a] *adj, m/f* Hungarian

Hungria [ũ'gria] *f:* **a ~** Hungary

hurra ['uxa] *m* cheer ♦ *excl* hurrah!

I

ia *etc* ['ia] *vb* V **ir**

iate ['jatʃi] *m* yacht; **~ clube** yacht club; **iatismo** [ja'tʃiʒmu] *m* yachting; **iatista** [ja'tʃiʃta] *m/f* yachtsman/woman

ibérico/a [i'bεriku/a] *adj, m/f* Iberian

ibero-americano/a [iberu-] *adj, m/f* Ibero-American

içar [i'sa*] *vt* to hoist, raise

iceberg [ajs'bεxgi] (*pl* **~s**) *m* iceberg

ICM (*BR*) *abr m* (= *Imposto sobre Circulação de Mercadorias*) ≈ VAT

ícone ['ikoni] *m* icon

icterícia [ikte'risja] *f* jaundice

ida ['ida] *f* going, departure; **~ e volta** round trip, return; **a (viagem de) ~** the outward journey; **na ~** on the way there

idade [i'dadʒi] *f* age; **ter cinco anos de ~** to be five (years old); **de meia ~** middle-aged; **qual é a ~ dele?** how old is he?; **na minha ~** at my age; **ser menor/maior de ~** to be under/of age; **pessoa de ~** elderly person; **I~ Média** Middle Ages *pl*

ideal [ide'jaw] (*pl* **-ais**) *adj, m* ideal; **~ista** [idea'liʃta] *adj* idealistic ♦ *m/f* idealist

idéia [i'dεja] *f* idea; (*mente*) mind; **mudar de ~** to change one's mind; **não ter a mínima ~** to have no idea; **não faço ~** I can't imagine; **estar com ~ de fazer** to plan to do

idem ['idē] *pron* ditto

idêntico/a [i'dētʃiku/a] *adj* identical

identidade [idētʃi'dadʒi] *f* identity

identificação [idētʃifika'sāw] *f* identification

identificar [idētʃifi'ka*] *vt* to identify; **~-se** *vr*: **~-se com** to identify with

ideologia [ideolo'ʒia] *f* ideology

idílico/a [i'dʒiliku/a] *adj* idyllic

idioma [i'dʒoma] *m* language; **idiomático/a** [idʒo'matʃiku/a] *adj* idiomatic

idiota [i'dʒɔta] *adj* idiotic ♦ *m/f* idiot

ido/a ['idu/a] *adj* past

idolatrar [idola'tra*] *vt* to idolize

ídolo ['idolu] *m* idol

idôneo/a [i'donju/a] *adj* suitable, fit; (*pessoa*) able, capable

idoso/a [i'dozu/za] *adj* elderly, old

ignição [igni'sãw] (*pl* **-ões**) *f* ignition

ignomínia [igno'minja] *f* disgrace, ignominy

ignorado/a [igno'radu/a] *adj* unknown

ignorância [igno'rãsja] *f* ignorance; **ignorante** [igno'rãtʃi] *adj* ignorant, uneducated ♦ *m/f* ignoramus

ignorar [igno'ra*] *vt* not to know; (*não dar atenção a*) to ignore

igreja [i'greʒa] *f* church

igual [i'gwaw] (*pl* **-ais**) *adj* equal; (*superfície*) even ♦ *m/f* equal

igualar [igwa'la*] *vt* to equal; (*fazer igual*) to make equal; (*nivelar*) to level ♦ *vi*: **~ a** *ou* **com** to be equal to, be the same as; (*ficar no mesmo nível*) to be level with; **~-se** *vr*: **~-se a alguém** to be sb's equal

igualdade [igwaw'dadʒi] *f* equality; (*uniformidade*) uniformity

igualmente [igwaw'mētʃi] *adv* equally; (*também*) likewise, also; **~!** (*saudação*) the same to you!

ilegal [ile'gaw] (*pl* **-ais**) *adj* illegal

ilegítimo/a [ile'ʒitʃimu/a] *adj* illegitimate; (*ilegal*) unlawful

ilegível [ile'ʒivew] (*pl* **-eis**) *adj* illegible

ileso/a [i'lεzu/a] *adj* unhurt

iletrado/a [ile'tradu/a] *adj* illiterate

ilha ['iʎa] *f* island; **ilhéu/ilhoa** [i'ʎεw/i'ʎoa] *m/f* islander

ilícito/a [i'lisitu/a] *adj* illicit

ilimitado/a [ilimi'tadu/a] *adj* unlimited

ilógico/a [i'lɔʒiku/a] *adj* illogical

iludir [ilu'dʒi*] *vt* to delude; (*enganar*) to deceive; (*a lei*) to evade

iluminação [ilumina'sãw] (*pl* **-ões**) *f* lighting; (*fig*) enlightenment

iluminar [ilumi'na*] *vt* to light up; (*estádio etc*) to floodlight; (*fig*) to enlighten

ilusão [ilu'zãw] (*pl* **-ões**) *f* illusion; (*quimera*) delusion; **ilusionista** [iluzjo'niʃta] *m/f* conjurer; **ilusório/a** [ilu'zɔrju/a] *adj* deceptive

ilustração [iluʃtra'sãw] (*pl* **-ões**) *f* illustration

ilustrado/a [iluʃ'tradu/a] *adj* illustrated; (*erudito*) learned

ilustrar [iluʃ'tra*] *vt* to illustrate; (*instruir*) to instruct

ilustre [i'luʃtri] *adj* illustrious; **um ~ desconhecido** a complete stranger

ilustríssimo/a [iluʃ'trisimu/a] *adj* (*tratamento*): **~ senhor** dear Sir

ímã ['imã] *m* magnet

imaculado/a [imaku'ladu/a] *adj* immaculate

imagem [i'maʒē] (*pl* **-ns**) *f* image; (*semelhança*) likeness; (*TV*) picture; **imagens** *fpl* (*LITERATURA*) imagery *sg*

imaginação [imaʒina'sãw] (*pl* **-ões**) *f* imagination

imaginar [imaʒi'na*] *vt* to imagine; (*supor*) to suppose; **~-se** *vr* to imagine o.s.; **imagine só!** just imagine!; **imaginário/a** [imaʒi'narju/a] *adj* imaginary; **imaginativo/a** [imaʒina'tʃivu/a] *adj* imaginative

imaturo/a [ima'turu/a] *adj* immature

imbatível [ĩba'tʃivew] (*pl* **-eis**) *adj* invincible

imbecil [ĩbe'siw] (*pl* **-is**) *adj* stupid ♦ *m/f*

imbecile; ~**idade** [ībesili'dadʒi] f stupidity

imediações [imedʒa'sojʃ] fpl vicinity sg, neighbourhood sg (BRIT), neighborhood sg (US)

imediatamente [imedʒata'mētʃi] adv immediately, right away

imediato/a [ime'dʒatu/a] adj immediate; (seguinte) next; ~ **a** next to; **de** ~ straight away

imenso/a [i'mēsu/a] adj immense, huge; (ódio, amor) great

imerecido/a [imere'sidu/a] adj undeserved

imergir [imex'ʒi*] vt to immerse; (fig) to plunge ♦ vi to be immersed; to plunge

imigração [imigra'sãw] (pl –ões) f immigration

imigrante [imi'grãtʃi] adj, m/f immigrant

iminente [imi'nētʃi] adj imminent

imitação [imita'sãw] (pl –ões) f imitation

imitar [imi'ta*] vt to imitate; (assinatura) to copy

imobiliária [imobi'ljarja] f estate agent's (BRIT), real estate broker's (US)

imobiliário/a [imobi'ljarju/a] adj property atr

imobilizar [imobili'za*] vt to immobilize; (fig) to bring to a standstill

imoral [imo'raw] (pl –ais) adj immoral

imortal [imox'taw] (pl –ais) adj immortal

imóvel [i'mɔvew] (pl –eis) adj motionless, still; (não movediço) immovable ♦ m property; (edifício) building; **imóveis** mpl (propriedade) real estate sg, property sg

impaciência [ĩpa'sjēsja] f impatience; **impacientar-se** [ĩpasjē'taxsi] vr to lose one's patience; **impaciente** [ĩpa'sjētʃi] adj impatient

impacto [ĩ'paktu] (PT -cte) m impact

impaludismo [ĩpalu'dʒiʒmu] m malaria

impar [ˈĩpa*] adj (número) odd; (sem igual) unique, unequalled

imparcial [ĩpax'sjaw] (pl –ais) adj fair, impartial

impasse [ĩ'pasi] m impasse

impassível [ĩpa'sivew] (pl –eis) adj impassive

impecável [ĩpe'kavew] (pl –eis) adj perfect, impeccable

impeço etc [ĩ'pɛsu] vb V **impedir**

impedido/a [ĩpe'dʒidu/a] adj (FUTEBOL) offside; (PT: TEL) engaged (BRIT), busy (US)

impedimento [ĩpedʒi'mētu] m impediment

impedir [ĩpe'dʒi*] vt to obstruct; (estrada, tráfego) to block; (movimento, progresso) to impede; ~ **alguém de fazer algo** to prevent sb from doing sth; (proibir) to forbid sb to do sth; ~ **(que aconteça) algo** to prevent sth (happening)

impelir [ĩpe'li*] vt (tb fig) to drive (on); (obrigar) to force

impenetrável [ĩpene'travew] (pl –eis) adj impenetrable

impensado/a [ĩpē'sadu/a] adj thoughtless; (não calculado) unpremeditated; (imprevisto) unforeseen

impensável [ĩpē'savew] (pl –eis) adj unthinkable

imperador [ĩpera'do*] m emperor

imperativo/a [ĩpera'tʃivu/a] adj imperative ♦ m imperative

imperatriz [ĩpera'triʒ] f empress

imperdoável [ĩpex'dwavew] (pl –eis) adj unforgivable, inexcusable

imperfeição [ĩpexfej'sãw] (pl –ões) f imperfection

imperfeito/a [ĩpex'fejtu/a] adj imperfect ♦ m (LING) imperfect (tense)

imperial [ĩpe'rjaw] (pl –ais) adj imperial; ~**ismo** [ĩperja'liʒmu] m imperialism

imperícia [ĩpe'risja] f inability; (inexperiência) inexperience

império [ĩ'pɛrju] m empire

impermeável [ĩpex'mjavew] (pl –eis) adj: ~ **a** (tb fig) impervious to; (à água) waterproof ♦ m raincoat

impertinente [ĩpextʃi'nētʃi] adj irrelevant; (insolente) impertinent

imperturbável [ĩpextux'bavew] (pl –eis) adj imperturbable; (impassível) impassive

impessoal [ĩpe'swaw] (pl –ais) adj impersonal

ímpeto [ˈĩpetu] m (TEC) impetus; (movimento súbito) start; (de cólera) fit; (de emoção) surge; (de chamas) fury; **agir com** ~ to act on impulse; **levantar-se num** ~ to get up with a start

impetuoso/a [ĩpe'twozu/ɔza] adj (pessoa) headstrong, impetuous; (ato) rash, hasty

impiedade [ĩpje'dadʒi] f irreverence; (crueldade) cruelty; **impiedoso/a** [ĩpje'dozu/ɔza] adj merciless, cruel

impilo etc [ĩ'pilu] vb V **impelir**

implacável [ĩpla'kavew] (pl –eis) adj relentless; (pessoa) unforgiving

implantação [ĩplãta'sãw] (pl –ões) f introduction; (MED) implant

implementar [ĩpleme'ta*] vt to implement

implemento [ĩple'mētu] m implement

implicação [ĩplika'sãw] (pl –ões) f implication; (envolvimento) involvement

implicar [ĩpli'ka*] vt (envolver) to implicate; (pressupor) to imply ♦ vi: ~ **com alguém** (chatear) to tease sb, pick on sb; ~**-se** vr to get involved; ~ **(em) algo** to involve sth

implícito/a [ĩ'plisitu/a] adj implicit

implorar [ĩplo'ra*] vt: ~ **(algo a alguém)** to beg ou implore (sb for sth)

imponente [ĩpo'nētʃi] adj impressive, imposing

impopular [ĩpopu'la*] adj unpopular; ~**idade** [ĩpopulari'dadʒi] f unpopularity

impor [ĩ'po*] (irreg: como **pôr**) vt to impose; (respeito) to command; **~-se** vr to assert o.s.; **~ algo a alguém** to impose sth on sb

importação [ĩpoxta'sãw] (pl **-ões**) f (ato) importing; (mercadoria) import

importador(a) [ĩpoxta'do*(a)] adj import atr ♦ m/f importer

importância [ĩpox'tãsja] f importance; (de dinheiro) sum, amount; **não tem ~** it doesn't matter, never mind; **ter ~** to be important; **sem ~** unimportant; **importante** [ĩpox'tãtʃi] adj important ♦ m: **o (mais) importante** the (most) important thing

importar [ĩpox'ta*] vt (COM) to import; (trazer) to bring in; (causar: prejuízos etc) to cause; (implicar) to imply, involve ♦ vi to matter, be important; **~-se** vr: **~-se com algo** to mind sth; **não me importo** I don't care

importunar [ĩpoxtu'na*] vt to bother, annoy

importuno/a [ĩpox'tunu/a] adj annoying; (inoportuno) inopportune ♦ m/f nuisance

imposição [ĩpozi'sãw] (pl **-ões**) f imposition

impossibilitado/a [ĩposibili'tadu/a] adj: **~ de fazer** unable to do

impossibilitar [ĩposibili'ta*] vt: **~ algo** to make sth impossible; **~ alguém de fazer, ~ a alguém fazer** to prevent sb doing; **~ algo a alguém, ~ alguém para algo** to make sth impossible for sb

impossível [ĩpo'sivew] (pl **-eis**) adj impossible; (insuportável: pessoa) insufferable; (incrível) incredible

imposto [ĩ'poʃtu] m tax; **antes/depois de ~s** before/after tax; **~ de renda** (BR) income tax; **~ predial** rates pl; **I~ sobre Circulação de Mercadorias (e Serviços)** (BR), **~ sobre valor acrescentado** (PT) value added tax (BRIT), sales tax (US)

impostor(a) [ĩpoʃ'to*(a)] m/f impostor

impotente [ĩpo'tẽtʃi] adj powerless; (MED) impotent

impraticável [ĩpratʃi'kavew] (pl **-eis**) adj impracticable; (rua, rio etc) impassable

impreciso/a [ĩpre'sizu/a] adj vague; (falto de rigor) inaccurate

impregnar [ĩpreg'na*] vt to impregnate

imprensa [ĩ'prẽsa] f printing; (máquina, jornais) press

imprescindível [ĩpresĩ'dʒivew] (pl **-eis**) adj essential, indispensable

impressão [ĩpre'sãw] (pl **-ões**) f impression; (de livros) printing; (marca) imprint; **causar boa ~** to make a good impression; **ficar com/ter a ~ (de) que** to get/have the impression that

impressionante [ĩpresjo'nãtʃi] adj impressive

impressionar [ĩpresjo'na*] vt to affect ♦

vi to be impressive; (pessoa) to make an impression; **~-se** vr: **~-se (com algo)** to be moved (by sth)

impressionista [ĩpresjo'niʃta] adj, m/f impressionist

impresso/a [ĩ'prɛsu/a] pp de **imprimir** ♦ adj printed ♦ m (para preencher) form; (folheto) leaflet; **~s** mpl (formulário) printed matter sg

impressões [ĩpre'sõjʃ] fpl de **impressão**

impressor [ĩpre'so*] m printer

impressora [ĩpre'sora] f printing machine; (COMPUT) printer; **~ matricial/a laser** dot-matrix/laser printer

imprestável [ĩpreʃ'tavew] (pl **-eis**) adj (inútil) useless; (pessoa) unhelpful

imprevisível [ĩprevi'zivew] (pl **-eis**) adj unforeseeable

imprevisto/a [ĩpre'viʃtu/a] adj unexpected, unforeseen ♦ m: **um ~** something unexpected

imprimir [ĩpri'mi*] vt to print; (marca) to stamp; (infundir) to instil (BRIT), instill (US); (COMPUT) to print out

improcedente [ĩprose'dẽtʃi] adj groundless, unjustified

impróprio/a [ĩ'prɔprju/a] adj inappropriate; (indecente) improper

improvável [ĩpro'vavew] (pl **-eis**) adj unlikely

improvisar [ĩprovi'za*] vt, vi to improvise; (TEATRO) to ad-lib

improviso [ĩpro'vizu] m: **de ~** adv (de repente) suddenly; (sem preparação) without preparation

imprudente [ĩpru'dẽtʃi] adj (irrefletido) rash; (motorista) careless

impulsionar [ĩpuwsjo'na*] vt to drive, impel; (fig) to urge

impulsivo/a [ĩpuw'sivu/a] adj impulsive

impulso [ĩ'puwsu] m impulse; (fig: estímulo) urge

impune [ĩ'puni] adj unpunished; **impunidade** [ĩpuni'dadʒi] f impunity

impureza [ĩpu'reza] f impurity

impuro/a [ĩ'puru/a] adj impure

imundície [imũ'dʒisji] f filth; **imundo/a** [i'mũdu/a] adj filthy; (obsceno) dirty

imune [i'muni] adj: **~ a** immune to; **imunidade** [imuni'dadʒi] f immunity; **imunizar** [imuni'za*] vt: **imunizar alguém (contra algo)** to immunize sb (against sth)

inábil [i'nabiw] (pl **-eis**) adj incapable; (desajeitado) clumsy; **inabilidade** [inabili'dadʒi] f (incompetência) incompetence; (falta de destreza) clumsiness; **inabilitar** [inabili'ta*] vt to incapacitate; (em exame) to disqualify

inabitado/a [inabi'tadu/a] adj uninhabited

inacabado/a [inaka'badu/a] adj unfinished

inacessível [inase'sivew] (*pl* –eis) *adj* inaccessible

inacreditável [inakredʒi'tavew] (*pl* –eis) *adj* unbelievable, incredible

inactivo/a *etc* [ina'tivu/a] (*PT*) = **inativo/a** *etc*

inadequado/a [inade'kwadu/a] *adj* inadequate; (*impróprio*) unsuitable

inadiável [ina'dʒjavew] (*pl* –eis) *adj* pressing

inadimplência [inadʒĩ'plẽsja] *f* (*JUR*) breach of contract, default

inadvertido/a [inadʒivex'tʃidu/a] *adj* inadvertent

inalar [ina'la*] *vt* to inhale

inalcançável [inawkã'savew] (*pl* –eis) *adj* out of reach; (*sucesso, ambição*) unattainable

inanimado/a [inani'madu/a] *adj* inanimate

inaptidão [inaptʃi'dãw] (*pl* –ões) *f* inability

inapto/a [i'naptu/a] *adj* unfit, incapable; (*inadequado*) unsuited

inarticulado/a [inaxtʃiku'ladu/a] *adj* inarticulate

inatingível [inatʃi'ʒivew] (*pl* –eis) *adj* unattainable

inatividade [inatʃivi'dadʒi] *f* inactivity

inativo/a [ina'tʃivu/a] *adj* inactive; (*aposentado, reformado*) retired

inato/a [i'natu/a] *adj* innate, inborn

inaudito/a [inaw'dʒitu/a] *adj* unheard-of

inaudível [inaw'dʒjvew] (*pl* –eis) *adj* inaudible

inauguração [inawgura'sãw] (*pl* –ões) *f* inauguration; (*de exposição*) opening; **inaugural** [inawgu'raw] (*pl* –ais) *adj* inaugural; **inaugurar** [inawgu'ra*] *vt* to inaugurate; (*exposição*) to open

incansável [ĩkã'savew] (*pl* –eis) *adj* tireless, untiring

incapacidade [ĩkapasi'dadʒi] *f* incapacity; (*incompetência*) incompetence

incapacitado/a [ĩkapasi'tadu/a] *adj* (*inválido*) disabled, handicapped ♦ *m/f* handicapped person; **estar ~ de fazer** to be unable to do

incapaz [ĩka'pajʒ] *adj*, *m/f* incompetent; **~ de fazer** incapable of doing; **~ para** unfit for

incauto/a [in'kawtu/a] *adj* rash

incendiar [ĩsẽ'dʒja*] *vt* to set fire to; (*fig*) to inflame; **~-se** *vr* to catch fire; **incendiário/a** [ĩsẽ'dʒjarju/a] *adj* incendiary; (*fig*) inflammatory

incêndio [ĩ'sẽdʒju] *m* fire; **~ criminoso** *ou* **premeditado** arson

incenso [ĩ'sẽsu] *m* incense

incentivar [ĩsẽtʃi'va*] *vt* to stimulate, encourage

incentivo [ĩsẽ'tʃivu] *m* incentive; **~ fiscal** tax incentive

incerteza [ĩsex'teza] *f* uncertainty

incerto/a [ĩ'sɛxtu/a] *adj* uncertain

incessante [ĩse'sãtʃi] *adj* incessant

incesto [ĩ'sɛʃtu] *m* incest

inchação [ĩʃa'sãw] (*pl* –ões) *f* swelling

inchado/a [ĩ'ʃadu/a] *adj* swollen; (*fig*) conceited

inchar [ĩ'ʃa*] *vt, vi* to swell

incidência [ĩsi'dẽsja] *f* incidence, occurrence

incidente [ĩsi'dẽtʃi] *m* incident

incisivo/a [ĩsi'zivu/a] *adj* cutting, sharp; (*fig*) incisive

incitar [ĩsi'ta*] *vt* to incite; (*pessoa, animal*) to drive on

inclemente [ĩkle'mẽtʃi] *adj* severe, harsh

inclinação [ĩklina'sãw] (*pl* –ões) *f* inclination; **~ da cabeça** nod

inclinado/a [ĩkli'nadu/a] *adj* (*terreno*) sloping; (*corpo, torre*) leaning

inclinar [ĩkli'na*] *vt* to tilt; (*cabeça*) to nod ♦ *vi* to slope; (*objeto*) to tilt; **~-se** *vr* to tilt; (*dobrar o corpo*) to bow, stoop; **~-se sobre algo** to lean over sth

incluir [ĩ'klwi*] *vt* to include; (*em carta*) to enclose; **~-se** *vr* to be included

inclusão [ĩklu'zãw] *f* inclusion; **inclusive** [ĩklu'zivi] *prep* including ♦ *adv* inclusive; (*até mesmo*) even

incluso/a [ĩ'kluzu/a] *adj* included

incoerente [ĩkoe'rẽtʃi] *adj* incoherent; (*contraditório*) inconsistent

incógnita [ĩ'kɔgnita] *f* (*MAT*) unknown; (*fato incógnito*) mystery; **incógnito/a** [ĩ'kɔgnitu/a] *adj* unknown ♦ *adv* incognito

incolor [ĩko'lo*] *adj* colourless (*BRIT*), colorless (*US*)

incólume [ĩ'kɔlumi] *adj* safe and sound; (*ileso*) unharmed

incomodar [ĩkomo'da*] *vt* to bother, trouble; (*aborrecer*) to annoy ♦ *vi* to be bothersome; **~-se** *vr* to bother, put o.s. out; **~-se com algo** to be bothered by sth, mind sth; **não se incomode!** don't worry!

incômodo/a [ĩ'komodu/a] *adj* uncomfortable; (*incomodativo*) troublesome; (*inoportuno*) inconvenient

incomparável [ĩkõpa'ravew] (*pl* –eis) *adj* incomparable

incompatível [ĩkõpa'tʃivew] (*pl* –eis) *adj* incompatible

incompetente [ĩkõpe'tẽtʃi] *adj*, *m/f* incompetent

incompleto/a [ĩkõ'pletu/a] *adj* incomplete

incompreendido/a [ĩkõprjẽ'dʒidu/a] *adj* misunderstood

incompreensível [ĩkõprjẽ'sivew] (*pl* –eis) *adj* incomprehensible

incomum [ĩko'mũ] *adj* uncommon

incomunicável [ĩkomuni'kavew] (*pl* –eis) *adj* cut off; (*privado de comunicação, fig*) incommunicado; (*preso*) in solitary confinement

inconcebível [ĩkõse'bivew] (pl -eis) adj inconceivable

inconciliável [ĩkõsi'ljavew] (pl -eis) adj irreconcilable

incondicional [ĩkõdʒisjo'naw] (pl -ais) adj unconditional; (apoio): wholehearted; (partidário) staunch; (amizade, fé) loyal

inconformado/a [ĩkõfox'madu/a] adj bitter; ~ com unreconciled to

inconfundível [ĩkõfũ'dʒivew] (pl -eis) adj unmistakeable

inconsciência [ĩkõ'sjẽsja] f (MED) unconsciousness; (irreflexão) thoughtlessness

inconsciente [ĩkõ'sjẽtʃi] adj unconscious ♦ m unconscious

inconseqüente [ĩkõse'kwẽtʃi] adj inconsistent; (contraditório) illogical; (irresponsável) irresponsible

inconsistente [ĩkõsiʃ'tẽtʃi] adj inconsistent; (sem solidez) runny

inconstante [ĩkõʃ'tãtʃi] adj fickle; (tempo) changeable

incontável [ĩkõ'tavew] (pl -eis) adj countless

incontestável [ĩkõteʃ'tavew] (pl -eis) adj undeniable

incontinência [ĩkõtʃi'nẽsja] f (MED) incontinence; (sensual) licentiousness

incontrolável [ĩkõtro'lavew] (pl -eis) adj uncontrollable

inconveniência [ĩkõve'njẽsja] f inconvenience; (impropriedade) inappropriateness

inconveniente [ĩkõve'njẽtʃi] adj inconvenient; (inoportuno) awkward; (grosseiro) rude; (importuno) annoying ♦ m disadvantage; (obstáculo) difficulty, problem

incorporar [ĩkoxpo'ra*] vt to incorporate; (juntar) to add; (COM) to merge; ~-se vr: ~-se a ou em to join

incorreto/a [ĩko'xɛtu/a] (PT -ect-) adj incorrect; (desonesto) dishonest

incorrigível [ĩkoxi'ʒivew] (pl -eis) adj incorrigible

incrédulo/a [ĩ'krɛdulu/a] adj incredulous; (cético) sceptical (BRIT), skeptical (US) ♦ m/f sceptic (BRIT), skeptic (US)

incremento [ĩkre'mẽtu] m (desenvolvimento) growth; (aumento) increase

incrível [ĩ'krivew] (pl -eis) adj incredible

incubadora [ĩkuba'dora] f incubator

inculpar [ĩkuw'pa*] vt: ~ alguém de algo (culpar) to blame sb for sth; (acusar) to accuse sb of sth; ~-se vr: ~-se de algo to blame o.s. for sth

inculto/a [ĩ'kuwtu/a] adj (pessoa) uncultured, uneducated; (terreno) uncultivated

incumbência [ĩkũ'bẽsja] f task, duty

incumbir [ĩkũ'bi*] vt: ~ alguém de algo ou algo a alguém to put sb in charge of sth ♦ vi: ~ a alguém to be sb's duty; ~-se vr: ~-se de to undertake, take charge of

incurável [ĩku'ravew] (pl -eis) adj incurable

incursão [ĩkux'sãw] (pl -ões) f (invasão) raid, attack; (penetração) foray

indagação [ĩdaga'sãw] (pl -ões) f investigation; (pergunta) inquiry, question

indagar [ĩda'ga*] vt to investigate ♦ vi to inquire; ~-se vr: ~-se a si mesmo to ask o.s.; ~ algo de alguém to ask sb about sth

indecente [ĩde'sẽtʃi] adj indecent, improper; (obsceno) rude, vulgar

indeciso/a [ĩde'sizu/a] adj undecided; (indistinto) vague; (hesitante) hesitant, indecisive

indecoroso/a [ĩdeko'rozu/ɔza] adj indecent, improper

indeferir [ĩdefe'ri*] vt (desatender) to reject; (requerimento) to turn down

indefeso/a [ĩde'fezu/a] adj undefended; (população) defenceless (BRIT), defenseless (US)

indefinido/a [ĩdefi'nidu/a] adj indefinite; (vago) vague, undefined; por tempo ~ indefinitely

indefiro etc [ĩde'firu] vb V indeferir

indelével [ĩde'lɛvew] (pl -eis) adj indelible

indelicado/a [ĩdeli'kadu/a] adj impolite, rude

indene [ĩ'dɛni] (PT -mn-) adj (pessoa) unharmed; (objeto) undamaged

indenização [ĩdeniza'sãw] (PT -mn-) (pl -ões) f compensation; (COM) indemnity

indenizar [ĩdeni'za*] (PT -mn-) vt: ~ alguém por ou de algo (compensar) to compensate sb for sth; (por gastos) to reimburse sb for sth

independência [ĩdepẽ'dẽsja] f independence; **independente** [ĩdepẽ'dẽtʃi] adj independent

indesejável [ĩdeze'ʒavew] (pl -eis) adj undesirable

indestrutível [ĩdʒiʃtru'tʃivew] (pl -eis) adj indestructible

indeterminado/a [ĩdetexmi'nadu/a] adj indeterminate

indevassável [ĩdeva'savew] (pl -eis) adj impenetrable

indevido/a [ĩde'vidu/a] adj (imerecido) unjust; (impróprio) inappropriate

índex ['ĩdeks] (pl índices) m = índice

Índia ['ĩdʒa] f: a ~ India; as ~s Ocidentais the West Indies; **indiano/a** [ĩ'dʒanu/a] adj, m/f Indian

indicação [ĩdʒika'sãw] (pl -ões) f indication; (de termômetro) reading; (para um cargo, prêmio) nomination; (recomendação) recommendation; (de um caminho) directions pl

indicado/a [ĩdʒi'kadu/a] adj appropriate

indicador(a) [ĩdʒika'do*(a)] adj: ~ de indicative of ♦ m indicator; (TEC) gauge; (dedo) index finger; (ponteiro) pointer

indicar [ĩdʒi'ka*] vt to indicate; (apontar)

to point to; (*temperatura*) to register;
(*recomendar*) to recommend; (*para um
cargo*) to nominate; (*determinar*) to determine; ~ **o caminho a alguém** to
give sb directions

indicativo/a [idʒika'tʃivu/a] *adj* (*tb:
LING*) indicative

índice ['indʒisi] *m* (*de livro*) index; (*taxa*)
rate

índices ['indʒisiʃ] *mpl de* **índex**

indício [in'dʒisju] *m* (*sinal*) sign; (*vestígio*)
trace; (*JUR*) clue

indiferença [idʒife'rēsa] *f* indifference;
indiferente [idʒife'rētʃi] *adj* indifferent;
isso me é indiferente it's all the same
to me

indígena [i'dʒiʒena] *adj*, *m/f* native; (*ín-
dio: da América*) Indian

indigência [idʒi'ʒēsja] *f* poverty; (*fig*)
lack, need

indigestão [idʒiʒeʃ'tãw] *f* indigestion

indigesto/a [idʒi'ʒɛʃtu/a] *adj* indigestible

indignação [idʒigna'sãw] *f* indignation;
indignado/a [idʒig'nadu/a] *adj* indignant

indignar [idʒig'na*] *vt* to anger, incense;
~-**se** *vr* to get angry

indignidade [idʒigni'dadʒi] *f* indignity

indigno/a [i'dʒignu/a] *adj* unworthy; (*desprezível*) disgraceful, despicable

índio/a [i'dʒju/a] *adj*, *m/f* (*da América*)
Indian; **o Oceano Í~** the Indian Ocean

indireto/a [idʒi'rɛtu/a] (*PT* -ct-) *adj* indirect

indiscreto/a [idʒiʃ'krɛtu/a] *adj* indiscreet

indiscriminado/a [idʒiʃkrimi'nadu/a] *adj*
indiscriminate

indiscutível [idʒiʃku'tʃivew] (*pl* -**eis**) *adj*
indisputable

indispensável [idʒiʃpē'savew] (*pl* -**eis**)
adj essential, vital ♦ *m*: **o** ~ the essentials *pl*

indispor [idʒiʃ'po*] (*irreg: como* **pôr**) *vt*
(*de saúde*) to make ill; (*aborrecer*) to upset; **indisposto/a** [idʒiʃ'poʃtu/poʃta] *adj*
unwell, poorly; upset

indistinto/a [idʒiʃ'tʃitu/a] *adj* indistinct

individual [idʒivi'dwaw] (*pl* -**ais**) *adj* individual

indivíduo [idʒi'vidwu] *m* individual; (*col:
sujeito*) guy

indócil [i'dɔsiw] (*pl* -**eis**) *adj* unruly,
wayward; (*impaciente*) restless

índole ['idoli] *f* (*temperamento*) nature;
(*tipo*) sort, type

indolente [ido'lētʃi] *adj* indolent; (*apático*) apathetic

indolor [ido'lo*] *adj* painless

indomável [ido'mavew] (*pl* -**eis**) *adj* (*animal*) untameable; (*coragem*) indomitable

Indonésia [ido'nɛzja] *f*: **a** ~ Indonesia

indulgência [iduw'ʒēsja] *f* indulgence;
(*tolerância*) leniency; **indulgente**
[iduw'ʒētʃi] *adj* indulgent; (*atitude*) lenient

indulto [i'duwtu] *m* (*JUR*) reprieve

indumentária [idumē'tarja] *f* costume

indústria [i'duʃtrja] *f* industry; **industrial**
[iduʃ'trjaw] (*pl* -**ais**) *adj* industrial ♦ *m/f*
industrialist; **industrializar** [iduʃtrjali'za*]
vt (*país*) to industrialize; (*aproveitar*) to
process; **industrioso/a** [iduʃ'trjozu/ɔza]
adj hard-working, industrious; (*hábil*)
clever, skilful (*BRIT*), skillful (*US*)

induzir [idu'zi*] *vt* to induce; (*persuadir*)
to persuade

inédito/a [i'nɛdʒitu/a] *adj* (*livro*) unpu-
blished; (*incomum*) unheard-of, rare

ineficaz [inefi'kajʒ] *adj* (*remédio, medida*)
ineffective; (*empregado, máquina*) inefficient

ineficiente [inefi'sjētʃi] *adj* inefficient

inegável [ine'gavew] (*pl* -**eis**) *adj* undeniable

inelutável [inelu'tavew] (*pl* -**eis**) *adj* inescapable

inepto/a [i'nɛptu/a] *adj* inept, incompetent

inequívoco/a [ine'kivoku/a] *adj* (*evidente*)
clear; (*inconfundível*) unmistakeable

inércia [i'nɛrsja] *f* lethargy; (*FIS*) inertia

inerente [ine'rētʃi] *adj*: ~ **a** inherent in
ou to

inerte [i'nɛrtʃi] *adj* lethargic; (*FIS*) inert

inescrupuloso/a [ineʃkrupu'lozu/ɔza] *adj*
unscrupulous

inescusável [ineʃku'zavew] (*pl* -**eis**) *adj*
inexcusable; (*indispensável*) essential

inesgotável [ineʒgo'tavew] (*pl* -**eis**) *adj*
inexhaustible; (*superabundante*) boundless

inesperado/a [ineʃpe'radu/a] *adj* unexpected, unforeseen ♦ *m*: **o** ~ the unexpected

inesquecível [ineʃke'sivew] (*pl* -**eis**) *adj*
unforgettable

inestimável [ineʃtʃi'mavew] (*pl* -**eis**) *adj*
invaluable

inevitável [inevi'tavew] (*pl* -**eis**) *adj* inevitable

inexato/a [ine'zatu/a] (*PT* -ct-) *adj* inaccurate

inexeqüível [ineze'kwivew] (*pl* -**eis**) *adj*
impracticable

inexistência [ineziʃ'tēsja] *f* lack

inexistente [ineziʃ'tētʃi] *adj* non-existent

inexperiência [ineʃpe'rjēsja] *f* inexperience; **inexperiente** [ineʃpe'rjētʃi] *adj* inexperienced; (*ingênuo*) naive

inexpressivo/a [ineʃpre'sivu/a] *adj* ex-
pressionless

infalível [ifa'livew] (*pl* -**eis**) *adj* infallible;
(*sucesso*) guaranteed

infâmia [i'famja] *f* (*desonra*) disgrace; (*vi-
leza*) vicious behaviour; (*dito*) nasty
thing

infância [i'fãsja] *f* childhood

infantaria [ifãta'ria] *f* infantry

infantil [ifã'tʃiw] (*pl* -**is**) *adj* (*ingênuo*)
childlike; (*pueril*) childish; (*para crianças*) children's

infarto [ĩ'faxtu] *m* heart attack
infatigável [ĩfatʃi'gavew] (*pl* -**eis**) *adj* untiring
infecção [ĩfek'sãw] (*pl* -**ões**) *f* infection;
infeccionar [ĩfeksjo'na*] *vt* (*ferida*) to infect; **infeccioso/a** [ĩfek'sjozu/ɔza] *adj* infectious
infectar [ĩfek'ta*] (*PT*) *vt* = **infetar**
infelicidade [ĩfelisi'dadʒi] *f* unhappiness; (*desgraça*) misfortune
infeliz [ĩfe'liʒ] *adj* unhappy; (*infausto*) unlucky; (*ação, medida*) unfortunate; (*sugestão, idéia*) inappropriate ♦ *m/f* unhappy person; **~mente** [ĩfeliʒ'mẽtʃi] *adv* unfortunately
inferior [ĩfe'rjo*] *adj*: ~ **(a)** (*em valor, qualidade*) inferior (to); (*mais baixo*) lower (than) ♦ *m/f* inferior, subordinate; **~idade** [ĩferjori'dadʒi] *f* inferiority
infernal [ĩfex'naw] (*pl* -**ais**) *adj* infernal
inferno [ĩ'fɛxnu] *m* hell; **vá pro ~!** (*col*) piss off!
infértil [ĩ'fɛxtʃiw] (*pl* -**eis**) *adj* infertile
infestar [ĩfeʃ'ta*] *vt* to infest
infetar [ĩfe'ta*] *vt* to infect
infidelidade [ĩfideli'dadʒi] *f* infidelity, unfaithfulness
infiel [ĩ'fjɛw] (*pl* -**éis**) *adj* disloyal; (*marido, mulher*) unfaithful; (*texto*) inaccurate ♦ *m/f* (*REL*) non-believer
infiltrar [ĩfiw'tra*] *vt* to permeate; **~-se** *vr* (*água, luz, odor*) to permeate; **~-se em algo** (*pessoas*) to infiltrate sth
ínfimo/a ['ĩfimu/a] *adj* lowest; (*qualidade*) poorest
infindável [ĩfĩ'davew] (*pl* -**eis**) *adj* unending, constant
infinidade [ĩfini'dadʒi] *f* infinity; **uma ~ de** countless
infinitivo [ĩfini'tʃivu] *m* (*LING*) infinitive
infinito/a [ĩfi'nitu/a] *adj* infinite ♦ *m* infinity
inflação [ĩfla'sãw] *f* inflation;
inflacionário/a [ĩflasjo'narju/a] *adj* inflationary
inflamação [ĩflama'sãw] (*pl* -**ões**) *f* inflammation; **inflamado/a** [ĩfla'madu/a] *adj* (*MED*) inflamed; (*discurso*) heated
inflamar [ĩfla'ma*] *vt* (*madeira, pólvora*) to set fire to; (*MED, fig*) to inflame; **~-se** *vr* to catch fire; (*fig*) to get worked up; **~-se de algo** to be consumed with sth
inflamável [ĩfla'mavew] (*pl* -**eis**) *adj* inflammable
inflar [ĩ'fla*] *vt* to inflate, blow up; **~-se** *vr* to swell (up)
inflexível [ĩflek'sivew] (*pl* -**eis**) *adj* stiff, rigid; (*fig*) unyielding
infligir [ĩfli'ʒi*] *vt* to inflict
influência [ĩ'flwẽsja] *f* influence; **sob a ~ de** under the influence of; **influenciar** [ĩflwẽ'sja*] *vt* to influence ♦ *vi*: **influenciar em algo** to influence sth, have an influence on sth; **influenciar-se** *vr*: **influenciar-se por** to be influenced by;

influente [ĩ'flwẽtʃi] *adj* influential; **influir** [ĩ'flwi*] *vi* to matter, be important; **influir em** *ou* **sobre** to influence, have an influence on
influxo [ĩ'fluksu] *m* influx; (*maré-cheia*) high tide
informação [ĩfoxma'sãw] (*pl* -**ões**) *f* (piece of) information; (*notícia*) news *sg*; **informações** *fpl* (*detalhes*) information *sg*; **Informações** (*TEL*) directory enquiries (*BRIT*), information (*US*); **pedir informações sobre** to ask about, inquire about
informal [ĩfox'maw] (*pl* -**ais**) *adj* informal; **~idade** [ĩfoxmali'dadʒi] *f* informality
informante [ĩfox'mãtʃi] *m* informant; (*JUR*) informer
informar [ĩfox'ma*] *vt*: ~ **alguém (de/ sobre algo)** to inform sb (of/about sth) ♦ *vi* to inform, be informative; **~-se** *vr*: **~-se de** to find out about, inquire about; ~ **de** to report on
informática [ĩfox'matʃika] *f* computer science; (*ramo*) computing, computers *pl*
informativo/a [ĩfoxma'tʃivu/a] *adj* informative
informatizar [ĩfoxmatʃi'za*] *vt* to computerize
informe [ĩ'fɔxmi] *m* (piece of) information; **~s** *mpl* (*informações*) information *sg*
infortúnio [ĩfox'tunju] *m* misfortune
infração [ĩfra'sãw] (*PT* -**cç**-; *pl* -**ões**) *f* breach, infringement; (*ESPORTE*) foul
infractor(a) [ĩfra'to*(a)] (*PT*) *m/f* = **infrator(a)**
infra-estrutura [ĩfra-] *f* infrastructure
infrator(a) [ĩfra'to*(a)] *m/f* offender
infravermelho/a [ĩfravex'meʎu/a] *adj* infra-red
infringir [ĩfrĩ'ʒi*] *vt* to infringe, contravene
infrutífero/a [ĩfru'tʃiferu/a] *adj* fruitless
infundado/a [ĩfũ'dadu/a] *adj* groundless, unfounded
ingênuo/a [ĩ'ʒenwu/a] *adj* ingenuous, naïve; (*comentário*) harmless ♦ *m/f* naïve person
ingerir [ĩʒe'ri*] *vt* to ingest; (*engolir*) to swallow
Inglaterra [ĩgla'tɛxa] *f*: **a ~** England; **inglês/esa** [ĩ'gleʃ/eza] *adj* English ♦ *m/f* Englishman/woman ♦ *m* (*LING*) English; **os ingleses** *mpl* the English
ingratidão [ĩgratʃi'dãw] *f* ingratitude
ingrato/a [ĩ'gratu/a] *adj* ungrateful
ingrediente [ĩgre'dʒjẽtʃi] *m* ingredient
íngreme ['ĩgremi] *adj* steep
ingressar [ĩgre'sa*] *vi*: ~ **em** to enter, go into; (*um clube*) to join
ingresso [ĩ'gresu] *m* (*entrada*) entry; (*admissão*) admission; (*bilhete*) ticket
inibição [inibi'sãw] (*pl* -**ões**) *f* inhibition
inibido/a [ini'bidu/a] *adj* inhibited

inibir [ini'bi*] vt to inhibit

iniciação [inisja'sāw] (pl -ões) f initiation

inicial [ini'sjaw] (pl -ais) adj, f initial

iniciar [ini'sja*] vt, vi (começar) to begin, start; ~ **alguém em algo** (arte, seita) to initiate sb into sth

iniciativa [inisja'tʃiva] f initiative; **a ~ privada** (ECON) private enterprise

início [i'nisju] m beginning, start; **no ~** at the start

inimigo/a [ini'migu/a] adj, m/f enemy

inimizade [inimi'zadʒi] f enmity, hatred

ininterrupto/a [inīte'xuptu/a] adj continuous; (esforço) unstinting; (vôo) non-stop; (serviço) 24-hour

injeção [inʒe'sāw] (PT -cç-; pl -ões) f injection

injetar [īʒe'ta*] (PT -ct-) vt to inject

injúria [ī'ʒurja] f insult; **injuriar** [īʒu'rja*] vt to insult

injustiça [īʒuʃ'tʃisa] f injustice

injusto/a [ī'ʒuʃtu/a] adj unfair, unjust

inocência [ino'sēsja] f innocence

inocentar [inosē'ta*] vt: ~ **alguém (de algo)** to clear sb (of sth)

inocente [ino'sētʃi] adj innocent ♦ m/f innocent man/woman

inocular [inoku'la*] vt to inoculate

inócuo/a [i'nɔkwu/a] adj harmless

inodoro/a [ino'dɔru/a] adj odourless (BRIT), odorless (US)

inofensivo/a [inofē'sivu/a] adj harmless, inoffensive

inoportuno/a [inopox'tunu/a] adj inconvenient, inopportune

inovação [inova'sāw] (pl -ões) f innovation

inoxidável [inoksi'davew] (pl -eis) adj: **aço ~** stainless steel

INPS (BR) abr m (= Instituto Nacional de Previdência Social) ≈ DSS (BRIT), ≈ Welfare Dept (US)

inquérito [ī'kɛritu] m inquiry; (JUR) inquest

inquietação [īkjeta'sāw] f anxiety, uneasiness; (agitação) restlessness

inquietante [īkje'tātʃi] adj worrying, disturbing

inquietar [īkje'ta*] vt to worry, disturb; ~-**se** vr to worry, bother; **inquieto/a** [ī'kjɛtu/a] adj anxious, worried; (agitado) restless

inquilino/a [īki'linu/a] m/f tenant

inquisição [īkizi'sāw] (pl -ões) f: **a I~** the Inquisition

insaciável [īsa'sjavew] (pl -eis) adj insatiable

insalubre [īsa'lubri] adj unhealthy

insanidade [īsani'dadʒi] f madness, insanity; **insano/a** [ī'sanu/a] adj insane

insatisfação [īsatʃiʃfa'sāw] f dissatisfaction

insatisfatório/a [īsatʃiʃfa'tɔrju/a] adj unsatisfactory

insatisfeito/a [īsatʃiʃ'fejtu/a] adj dissatisfied, unhappy

inscrever [īʃkre've*] vt to inscribe; (aluno) to enrol (BRIT), enroll (US); (em registro) to register

inscrição [īʃkri'sāw] (pl -ões) f inscription

inscrito/a [ī'ʃkritu/a] pp de **inscrever**

insecto etc [ī'sɛktu] (PT) = **inseto** etc

insegurança [īsegu'rāsa] f insecurity; **inseguro/a** [īse'guru/a] adj insecure

inseminação [īsemina'sāw] f: ~ **artificial** artificial insemination

insensatez [īsēsa'teʒ] f folly, madness; **insensato/a** [īsē'satu/a] adj unreasonable, foolish

insensível [īsē'sivew] (pl -eis) adj insensitive; (dormente) numb

inserir [īse'ri*] vt to insert, put in; (COMPUT: dados) to enter

inseticida [īsetʃi'sida] m insecticide

inseto [ī'setu] m insect

insidioso/a [īsi'dʒiozu/ɔza] adj insidious

insígnia [ī'signia] f (sinal distintivo) badge; (emblema) emblem

insignificante [īsignifi'kātʃi] f insignificant

insincero/a [īsī'sɛru/a] adj insincere

insinuar [īsi'nwa*] vt to insinuate, imply

insípido/a [ī'sipidu/a] adj insipid

insiro etc [ī'siru] vb V **inserir**

insistência [īsiʃ'tēsja] f: ~ **(em)** insistence (on); (obstinação) persistence (in); **insistente** [īsiʃ'tētʃi] adj (pessoa) insistent; (apelo) urgent

insistir [īsiʃ'tʃi*] vi: ~ **(em)** to insist (on); (perseverar) to persist (in); ~ **(em) que** to insist that

insociável [īso'sjavew] (pl -eis) adj unsociable, antisocial

insolação [insola'sāw] f sunstroke; **pegar uma ~** to get sunstroke

insolência [īso'lēsja] f insolence

insolente [īso'lētʃi] adj insolent

insólito/a [ī'sɔlitu/a] adj unusual

insolúvel [īso'luvew] (pl -eis) adj insoluble

insolvente [īsow'vētʃi] adj insolvent

insônia [ī'sonja] f insomnia

insosso/a [ī'sosu/a] adj unsalted; (sem sabor) tasteless; (pessoa) uninteresting, dull

inspeção [īʃpe'sāw] (PT -cç-; pl -ões) f inspection, check; **inspecionar** [īʃpesjo'na*] (PT -cc-) vt to inspect

inspetor(a) [īʃpe'to*(a)] (PT -ct-) m/f inspector

inspiração [īʃpira'sāw] (pl -ões) f inspiration

inspirador(a) [īʃpira'do*(a)] adj inspiring

inspirar [īʃpi'ra*] vt to inspire; (MED) to inhale; ~-**se** vr to be inspired

instabilidade [īʃtabili'dadʒi] f instability

instalação [īʃtala'sāw] (pl -ões) f installation; ~ **elétrica** (de casa) wiring

instalar [ĩʃta'la*] vt to install; (estabele- cer) to set up; ~-se vr (numa cadeira) to settle down

instância [ĩʃ'tãsja] f persistence; (súplica) entreaty; **em última** ~ as a last resort

instantâneo/a [ĩʃtã'tanju/a] adj instant, instantaneous ♦ m (FOTO) snap

instante [ĩʃ'tãtʃi] adj urgent ♦ m moment; **num** ~ in an instant, quickly; **só um** ~! just a moment!

instar [ĩʃ'ta*] vt to urge ♦ vi to insist; ~ **com alguém para que faça algo** to urge sb to do sth

instauração [ĩʃtawra'sãw] f setting-up; (de processo, inquérito) institution

instaurar [ĩʃtaw'ra*] vt to establish, set up

instável [ĩʃ'tavew] (pl -eis) adj unstable; (tempo) unsettled

instigar [ĩʃtʃi'ga*] vt to urge; (provocar) to provoke

instintivo/a [ĩʃtʃĩ'tʃivu/a] adj instinctive

instinto [ĩʃ'tʃĩtu] m instinct; **por** ~ instinctively

instituição [ĩʃtʃitwi'sãw] (pl -ões) f insti- tution

instituto [ĩʃtʃi'tutu] m (escola) institute; (instituição) institution; ~ **de beleza** beauty salon

instrução [ĩʃtru'sãw] (PT -çç-; pl -ões) f education; (erudição) learning; (diretriz) instruction; (MIL) training; **instruções** fpl (para o uso) instructions (for use)

instructor(a) [ĩʃtru'to*(a)] (PT) m/f = **instrutor(a)**

instruído/a [ĩʃ'trwidu/a] adj educated

instruir [ĩʃ'trwi*] vt to instruct; (MIL) to train; ~-se vr: ~-se **em algo** to learn sth; ~ **alguém de** ou **sobre algo** to in- form sb about sth

instrumental [ĩʃtrumẽ'taw] (pl -ais) adj instrumental

instrumento [ĩʃtru'mẽtu] m instrument; (ferramenta) implement; (JUR) deed, do- cument; ~ **de cordas/percussão/sopro** stringed/percussion/wind instrument; ~ **de trabalho** tool

instrutivo/a [ĩʃtru'tʃivu/a] adj instructive

instrutor(a) [ĩʃtru'to*(a)] m/f instructor; (ESPORTE) coach

insubordinação [ĩsuboxdʒina'sãw] f re- bellion; (MIL) insubordination

insubstituível [ĩsubiʃtʃi'twivew] (pl -eis) adj irreplaceable

insuficiência [ĩsufi'sjẽsja] f inadequacy; (carência) shortage; (MED) deficiency; ~ **cardíaca** heart failure; **insuficiente** [ĩsufi'sjẽtʃi] adj insufficient; (EDUC: nota) ~ fail; (pessoa) incompetent

insular [ĩsu'la*] adj insular ♦ vt (TEC) to insulate

insulina [ĩsu'lina] f insulin

insultar [ĩsuw'ta*] vt to insult; **insulto** [ĩ'suwtu] m insult

insuperável [ĩsupe'ravew] (pl -eis) adj

(dificuldade) insuperable; (qualidade) un- surpassable

insuportável [ĩsupox'tavew] (pl -eis) adj unbearable

insurgente [ĩsux'ʒẽtʃi] adj rebellious ♦ m/f rebel

insurgir-se [ĩsux'ʒixsi] vr to rebel, revolt

insurreição [ĩsuxej'sãw] (pl -ões) f rebel- lion, insurrection

insuspeito/a [ĩsuʃ'pejtu/a] adj unsu- spected; (imparcial) impartial

intato/a [ĩ'tatu/a] (PT -act-) adj intact

íntegra ['ĩtegra] f: **na** ~ in full

integral [ĩte'graw] (pl -ais) adj whole ♦ f (MAT) integral; **pão** ~ wholemeal (BRIT) ou wholewheat (US) bread; ~**mente** [ĩtegraw'mẽtʃi] adv in full, fully

integrar [ĩte'gra*] vt to unite, combine; (completar) to form, make up; (MAT, raças) to integrate; ~-se vr to become complete; ~-se **em** ou **a algo** to join sth; (adaptar-se) to integrate into sth

integridade [ĩtegri'dadʒi] f entirety; (fig: de pessoa) integrity

íntegro/a ['ĩtegru/a] adj entire; (honesto) upright, honest

inteiramente [ĩtejra'mẽtʃi] adv comple- tely

inteirar [ĩtej'ra*] vt (completar) to com- plete; ~-se vr: ~-se **de** to find out about; ~ **alguém de** to inform sb of

inteiro/a [ĩ'tejru/a] adj whole, entire; (ile- so) unharmed; (não quebrado) unda- maged

intelecto [ĩte'lɛktu] m intellect; **intelec- tual** [ĩtelek'twaw] (pl -ais) adj, m/f intel- lectual

inteligência [ĩteli'ʒẽsja] f intelligence; **inteligente** [ĩteli'ʒẽtʃi] adj intelligent, clever

inteligível [ĩteli'ʒivew] (pl -eis) adj intel- ligible

intenção [ĩtẽ'sãw] (pl -ões) f intention; **segundas intenções** ulterior motives; **ter a** ~ **de** to intend to; **intencionado/ a** [ĩtẽsjo'nadu/a] adj: **bem intencionado** well-meaning; **mal intencionado** spite- ful; **intencional** [ĩtẽsjo'naw] (pl -ais) adj intentional, deliberate; **intencionar** [ĩtẽsjo'na*] vt to intend

intendência [ĩtẽ'dẽsja] (PT) f manage- ment, administration

intensidade [ĩtẽsi'dadʒi] f intensity

intensificar [ĩtẽsifi'ka*] vt to intensify; ~-se vr to intensify

intensivo/a [ĩtẽ'sivu/a] adj intensive

intenso/a [ĩ'tẽsu/a] adj intense; (emoção) deep; (impressão) vivid; (vida social) full

interação [ĩtera'sãw] (PT -çç-) f interac- tion

interativo/a [ĩtera'tʃivu/a] (PT -ct-) adj (COMPUT) interactive

intercâmbio [ĩtex'kãbju] m exchange

interceptar [ĩtexsep'ta*] vt to intercept; (fazer parar) to stop; (ligação telefônica) to cut off; (*ser obstáculo a*) to hinder

interditar [ĩtɛxdʒi'ta*] *vt* (*importação etc*) to ban; (*estrada, praia*) to close off; (*cinema etc*) to close down

interessado/a [ĩtɛre'sadu/a] *adj* interested; (*amizade*) self-seeking

interessante [ĩtɛre'sãtʃi] *adj* interesting

interessar [ĩtɛre'sa*] *vt* to interest ♦ *vi* to be interesting; ~-se *vr*: ~-se em *ou* por to take an interest in, be interested in; **a quem possa** ~ to whom it may concern

interesse [ĩte'resi] *m* interest; (*próprio*) self-interest; (*proveito*) advantage; **no** ~ **de** for the sake of; **por** ~ (*próprio*) for one's own ends; ~**iro/a** [ĩtɛre'sejru/a] *adj* self-seeking

interface [ĩtɛx'fasi] *f* (*COMPUT*) interface

interferência [ĩtɛxfe'rẽsja] *f* interference

interferir [ĩtɛxfe'ri*] *vi*: ~ **em** to interfere in; (*rádio*) to jam

interfone [ĩtɛx'fɔni] *m* intercom

ínterim ['ĩterĩ] *m* interim; **nesse** ~ in the meantime

interino/a [ĩte'rinu/a] *adj* temporary, interim

interior [ĩte'rjo*] *adj* inner, inside; (*COM*) domestic, internal ♦ *m* inside, interior; (*do país*) **no** ~ inland; **Ministério do I**~ ≈ Home Office (*BRIT*), ≈ Department of the Interior (*US*)

interjeição [ĩtɛxʒej'sãw] (*pl* -ões) *f* interjection

interlocutor(a) [ĩtɛxloku'to*(a)] *m/f* speaker; **meu** ~ the person I was speaking to

interlúdio [ĩtɛx'ludʒu] *m* interlude

intermediário/a [ĩtɛxme'dʒjarju/a] *adj* intermediary ♦ *m/f* (*COM*) middleman; (*mediador*) intermediary, mediator

intermédio [ĩtɛx'mɛdʒu] *m*: **por** ~ **de** through

interminável [ĩtɛxmi'navew] (*pl* -eis) *adj* endless

intermitente [ĩtɛxmi'tẽtʃi] *adj* intermittent

internação [ĩtɛxna'sãw] (*pl* -ões) *f* (*de doente*) admission

internacional [ĩtɛxnasjo'naw] (*pl* -ais) *adj* international

internações [ĩtɛxna'sõjʃ] *fpl de* **internação**

internar [ĩtɛx'na*] *vt* (*aluno*) to put into boarding school; (*doente*) to take into hospital; (*MIL, POL*) to intern

internato [ĩtɛx'natu] *m* boarding school

internauta [ĩtɛx'nawta] *m/f* Internet user

Internet [ĩtɛx'nɛtʃi] *f* Internet

interno/a [ĩ'tɛxnu/a] *adj* internal; (*POL*) domestic ♦ *m/f* (*tb*: **aluno** ~) boarder; (*MED*: *estudante*) houseman (*BRIT*), intern (*US*); **de uso** ~ (*MED*) for internal use

interpretação [ĩtɛxpreta'sãw] (*pl* -ões) *f* interpretation; (*TEATRO*) performance

interpretar [ĩtɛxpre'ta*] *vt* to interpret; (*um papel*) to play; **intérprete** [ĩ'tɛxpretʃi] *m/f* interpreter; (*TEATRO*) performer, artist

interrogação [ĩtɛxoga'sãw] (*pl* -ões) *f* interrogation; **ponto de** ~ question mark

interrogar [ĩtɛxo'ga*] *vt* to question, interrogate; (*JUR*) to cross-examine; **interrogativo/a** [ĩtɛxoga'tʃivu/a] *adj* interrogative

interromper [ĩtɛxõ'pe*] *vt* to interrupt; (*parar*) to stop; (*ELET*) to cut off

interrupção [ĩtɛxup'sãw] (*pl* -ões) *f* interruption; (*intervalo*) break

interruptor [ĩtɛxup'to*] *m* (*ELET*) switch

interseção [ĩtɛxse'sãw] (*PT* -cç-; *pl* -ões) *f* intersection

interurbano/a [ĩtɛrux'banu/a] *adj* (*TEL*) long-distance ♦ *m* long-distance *ou* trunk call

intervalo [ĩtɛx'valu] *m* interval; (*descanso*) break; **a** ~**s** every now and then

intervenção [ĩtɛxvẽ'sãw] (*pl* -ões) *f* intervention; ~ **cirúrgica** (*MED*) operation

interventor(a) [ĩtɛxvẽ'to*(a)] *m/f* inspector

intervir [ĩtɛx'vi*] (*irreg*: *como* **vir**) *vi* to intervene; (*sobrevir*) to come up

intestino [ĩteʃ'tʃinu] *m* intestine

intimação [ĩʃima'sãw] (*pl* -ões) *f* (*ordem*) order; (*JUR*) summons

intimar [ĩʃi'ma*] *vt* (*JUR*) to summon; ~ **alguém a fazer** *ou* **a alguém que faça** to order sb to do

intimidade [ĩʃimi'dadʒi] *f* intimacy; (*vida privada*) private life; (*familiaridade*) familiarity; **ter** ~ **com alguém** to be close to sb

intimidar [ĩʃimi'da*] *vt* to intimidate

íntimo/a ['ĩʃimu/a] *adj* intimate; (*sentimentos*) innermost; (*amigo*) close; (*vida*) private ♦ *m/f* close friend; **no** ~ at heart

intolerância [ĩtole'rãsja] *f* intolerance; **intolerante** [ĩtole'rãtʃi] *adj* intolerant

intolerável [ĩtole'ravew] (*pl* -eis) *adj* intolerable, unbearable

intoxicação [ĩtoksika'sãw] *f* poisoning; ~ **alimentar** food poisoning

intoxicar [ĩtoksi'ka*] *vt* to poison

intranet [ĩtra'nɛtʃi] *f* intranet

intranquilidade [ĩtrãkwili'dadʒi] *f* disquiet; **intranquilo/a** [ĩtrã'kwilu/a] *adj* worried; (*desassossegado*) restless

intransigente [ĩtrãsi'ʒẽtʃi] *adj* uncompromising; (*fig: rígido*) strict

intransitável [ĩtrãsi'tavew] (*pl* -eis) *adj* impassable

intransitivo/a [ĩtrãsi'tʃivu/a] *adj* intransitive

intransponível [ĩtrãʃpo'nivew] (*pl* -eis) *adj* (*rio*) impossible to cross; (*problema*) insurmountable

intratável [ĩtra'tavew] (*pl* -eis) *adj* (*pessoa*) contrary, awkward; (*doença*) untreatable; (*problema*) insurmountable

intravenoso/a [ĩtrave'nozu/ɔza] *adj* intravenous

intrépido/a [ĩ'trɛpidu/a] *adj* intrepid

intriga [ĩ'triga] *f* intrigue; (*enredo*) plot; (*fofoca*) piece of gossip; ~s (*fofocas*) gossip *sg*; ~ **amorosa** (*PT*) love affair; ~**nte** [ĩtri'gãtʃi] *m/f* troublemaker ♦ *adj* intriguing; ~**r** [ĩtri'ga*] *vt* to intrigue ♦ *vi* to be intriguing

introdução [ĩtrodu'sãw] (*pl* -ões) *f* introduction

introduzir [ĩtrodu'zi*] *vt* to introduce

intrometer-se [ĩtrome'texsi] *vr* to interfere, meddle; **intrometido/a** [ĩtrome'tʃidu/a] *adj* interfering; (*col*) nosey ♦ *m/f* busybody

introvertido/a [ĩtrovex'tʃidu/a] *adj* introverted ♦ *m/f* introvert

intruso/a [ĩ'truzu/a] *m/f* intruder

intuição [ĩtwi'sãw] (*pl* -ões) *f* intuition

intuito [ĩ'tuito] *m* intention, aim

inumano/a [inu'manu/a] *adj* inhuman

inúmero/a [i'numeru/a] *adj* countless, innumerable

inundação [inũda'sãw] (*pl* -ões) *f* (*enchente*) flood; (*ato*) flooding

inundar [inũ'da*] *vt* to flood; (*fig*) to inundate ♦ *vi* to flood

inusitado/a [inuzi'tadu/a] *adj* unusual

inútil [i'nutʃiw] (*pl* -eis) *adj* useless; (*esforço*) futile; (*desnecessário*) pointless; **inutilizar** [inutʃili'za*] *vt* to make useless, render useless; (*incapacitar*) to put out of action; (*danificar*) to ruin; (*esforços*) to thwart; **inutilmente** [inutʃiw'mẽtʃi] *adv* in vain

invadir [ĩva'dʒi*] *vt* to invade; (*suj: água*) to overrun; (*: sentimento*) to overcome

inválido/a [ĩ'validu/a] *adj*, *m/f* invalid

invariável [ĩva'rjavew] (*pl* -eis) *adj* invariable

invasão [ĩva'zãw] (*pl* -ões) *f* invasion

invasor(a) [ĩva'zo*(a)] *adj* invading ♦ *m/f* invader

inveja [ĩ'veʒa] *f* envy; ~**r** [ĩve'ʒa*] *vt* to envy; (*cobiçar*) to covet ♦ *vi* to be envious; **invejoso/a** [ĩve'ʒozu/ɔza] *adj* envious

invenção [ĩvẽ'sãw] (*pl* -ões) *f* invention

inventar [ĩvẽ'ta*] *vt* to invent

inventário [ĩvẽ'tarju] *m* inventory

inventiva [ĩvẽ'tʃiva] *f* inventiveness; **inventivo/a** [ĩvẽ'tʃivu/a] *adj* inventive

inventor(a) [ĩvẽ'to*(a)] *m/f* inventor

inverdade [ĩvex'dadʒi] *f* untruth

inverno [ĩ'vɛxnu] *m* winter

inverossímil [ĩvero'simiw] (*PT* -osí-; *pl* -eis) *adj* unlikely, improbable; (*inacreditável*) implausible

inverso/a [ĩ'vɛxsu/a] *adj* inverse; (*oposto*) opposite; (*ordem*) reverse ♦ *m* opposite, reverse; **ao** ~ **de** contrary to

invertebrado [ĩvexte'bradu] *m* inverte-

brate

inverter [ĩvex'te*] *vt* to alter; (*ordem*) to invert, reverse; (*colocar às avessas*) to turn upside down, invert

invés [ĩ'vɛʃ] *m*: **ao** ~ **de** instead of

investida [ĩveʃ'tʃida] *f* attack; (*tentativa*) attempt

investigação [ĩveʃtʃiga'sãw] (*pl* -ões) *f* investigation; (*pesquisa*) research

investigar [ĩveʃtʃi'ga*] *vt* to investigate; (*examinar*) to examine

investimento [ĩveʃtʃi'mẽtu] *m* investment

investir [ĩveʃ'tʃi*] *vt* (*dinheiro*) to invest

inveterado/a [ĩvete'radu/a] *adj* inveterate

inviável [ĩ'vjavew] (*pl* -eis) *adj* impracticable

invicto/a [ĩ'viktu/a] *adj* unconquered

invisível [ĩvi'zivew] (*pl* -eis) *adj* invisible

invisto *etc* [ĩ'viʃtu] *vb V* **investir**

invocar [ĩvo'ka*] *vt* to invoke

invólucro [ĩ'vɔlukru] *m* (*cobertura*) covering; (*envoltório*) wrapping; (*caixa*) box

involuntário/a [ĩvolũ'tarju/a] *adj* involuntary; (*ofensa*) unintentional

iodo [ˈjodu] *m* iodine

ioga [ˈjɔga] *f* yoga

iogurte [jo'guxtʃi] *m* yogurt

íon [ˈiõ] (*pl* ~s) *m* ion

IR (*BR*) *abr m* = **Imposto de Renda**

PALAVRA CHAVE

ir [i*] *vi* **1** to go; (*a pé*) to walk; (*a cavalo*) to ride; (*viajar*) to travel; ~ **caminhando** to walk; **fui de trem I** went *ou* travelled by train; **vamos!, vamos nessa!**, (*col*) **vamos embora!** let's go!; **já vou!** I'm coming!; ~ **atrás de alguém** (*seguir*) to follow sb; (*confiar*) to take sb's word for it

2 (*progredir: pessoa, coisa*) to go; **o trabalho vai muito bem** work is going very well; **como vão as coisas?** how are things going?; **vou muito bem** I'm very well; (*na escola etc*) I'm getting on very well

♦ *vb aux* **1** (+ *infin*): **vou fazer** I will do, I am going to do

2 (+ *gerúndio*): ~ **fazendo** to keep on doing

♦ ~**-se** *vr* to go away, leave

---

ira [ˈira] *f* anger, rage

Irã [i'rã] *m*: **o** ~ Iran

irado/a [i'radu/a] *adj* angry, irate

iraniano/a [ira'njanu/a] *adj*, *m/f* Iranian

Irão [i'rãw] (*PT*) *m* = **Irã**

Iraque [i'raki] *m*: **o** ~ Iraq; **iraquiano/a** [ira'kjanu/a] *adj*, *m/f* Iraqi

irascível [ira'sivew] (*pl* -eis) *adj* irritable, short-tempered

ir-e-vir (*pl* **ires-e-vires**) *m* comings and goings *pl*

íris [ˈiriʃ] *f inv* iris

Irlanda [ix'lɐ̃da] *f*: **a ~** Ireland; **a ~ do Norte** Northern Ireland; **irlandês/esa** [ixlɐ̃'deʃ/eza] *adj* Irish ♦ *m/f* Irishman/woman ♦ *m* (*LING*) Irish

irmã [ix'mɐ̃] *f* sister; **~ de criação** adoptive sister; **~ gêmea** twin sister

irmandade [ixmɐ̃'dadʒi] *f* brotherhood; (*confraternidade*) fraternity

irmão [ix'mɐ̃w] (*pl* **~s**) *m* brother; (*fig*: *similar*) twin; (*col*: *companheiro*) mate; **~ de criação** adoptive brother; **~ gêmeo** twin brother

ironia [iro'nia] *f* irony

irra! ['ixa] (*PT*) *excl* damn!

irracional [ixasjo'naw] (*pl* **-ais**) *adj* irrational

irradiar [ixa'dʒjaˣ] *vt* (*luz*) to radiate; (*espalhar*) to spread; (*RÁDIO*) to broadcast, transmit; (*simpatia*) to exude

irreal [ixe'aw] (*pl* **-ais**) *adj* unreal

irreconciliável [ixekõsi'ljavew] (*pl* **-eis**) *adj* irreconcilable

irregular [ixegu'laˣ] *adj* irregular; (*vida*) unconventional; (*feições*) unusual; (*aluno, gênio*) erratic

irrelevante [ixele'vãtʃi] *adj* irrelevant

irremediável [ixeme'dʒjavew] (*pl* **-eis**) *adj* irremediable; (*sem remédio*) incurable

irreprimível [ixepri'mivew] (*pl* **-eis**) *adj* irrepressible

irrequieto/a [ixe'kjɛtu/a] *adj* restless

irresistível [ixezi'ʃtʃivew] (*pl* **-eis**) *adj* irresistible

irresoluto/a [ixezo'lutu/a] *adj* (*pessoa*) irresolute, indecisive; (*problema*) unresolved

irresponsável [ixeʃpõ'savew] (*pl* **-eis**) *adj* irresponsible

irrigação [ixiga'sãw] *f* irrigation

irrigar [ixi'gaˣ] *vt* to irrigate

irrisório/a [ixi'zɔrju/a] *adj* derisory

irritação [ixita'sãw] (*pl* **-ões**) *f* irritation

irritadiço/a [ixita'dʒisu/a] *adj* irritable

irritante [ixi'tãtʃi] *adj* irritating, annoying

irritar [ixi'taˣ] *vt* to irritate; **~-se** *vr* to get angry, get annoyed

irromper [ixõ'peˣ] *vi* (*entrar subitamente*): **~ (em)** to burst in(to)

isca ['iʃka] *f* (*PESCA*) bait; (*fig*) lure, bait

isenção [izẽ'sãw] (*pl* **-ões**) *f* exemption

isentar [izẽ'taˣ] *vt* to exempt; (*livrar*) to free

isento/a [i'zẽtu/a] *adj* exempt; (*livre*) free; **~ de taxas** duty-free

Islã [iʒ'lã] *m* Islam; **islâmico/a** [iʒ'lamiku/a] *adj* Islamic

Islândia [iʒ'lãdʒa] *f*: **a ~** Iceland

isolado/a [izo'ladu/a] *adj* isolated; (*solitário*) lonely

isolamento [izola'mẽtu] *m* isolation; (*ELET*) insulation

isolar [izo'laˣ] *vt* to isolate; (*ELET*) to insulate

isopor [izo'poˣ] ® *m* polystyrene

isqueiro [iʃ'kejru] *m* (*cigarette*) lighter

Israel [iʒxa'ɛw] *m* Israel; **israelense** [iʒxae'lẽsi] *adj*, *m/f* Israeli

isso ['isu] *pron* that; (*col*: *isto*) this; **~ mesmo** exactly; **por ~** therefore, so; **por ~ mesmo** for that very reason; **só ~?** is that all?

istmo ['iʃtʃimu] *m* isthmus

isto ['iʃtu] *pron* this; **~ é** that is, namely

Itália [i'talja] *f*: **a ~** Italy; **italiano/a** [ita'ljanu/a] *adj*, *m/f* Italian ♦ *m* (*LING*) Italian

itálico [i'taliku] *m* italics *pl*

item ['itẽ] (*pl* **-ns**) *m* item

itinerário [itʃine'rarju] *m* itinerary; (*caminho*) route

Iugoslávia [jugoʒ'lavja] *f*: **a ~** Yugoslavia; **iugoslavo/a** [jugoʒ'lavu/a] *adj*, *m/f* Yugoslav(ian)

J

já [ʒa] *adv* already; (*em perguntas*) yet; (*agora*) now; (*imediatamente*) right away; (*agora mesmo*) right now ♦ *conj* on the other hand; **até ~** bye; **desde ~** from now on; **~ não** no longer; **~ que** as, since; **~ se vê** of course; **~ vou** I'm coming; **~ até** even; **~, ~** right away

jabuti [ʒabu'tʃi] *m* giant tortoise

jabuticaba [ʒabutʃi'kaba] *f* jaboticaba (*type of berry*)

jaca ['ʒaka] *f* jack fruit

jacaré [ʒaka'rɛ] (*BR*) *m* alligator

jacto ['ʒaktu] (*PT*) *m* = **jato**

jaguar [ʒa'gwaˣ] *m* jaguar

jaguatirica [ʒagwatʃi'rika] *f* leopard cat

Jamaica [ʒa'majka] *f*: **a ~** Jamaica

jamais [ʒa'majʃ] *adv* never; (*com palavra negativa*) ever

jamanta [ʒa'mãta] *f* juggernaut (*BRIT*), truck-trailer (*US*)

janeiro [ʒa'nejru] (*PT* **J-**) *m* January

janela [ʒa'nɛla] *f* window

jangada [ʒã'gada] *f* raft

jantar [ʒã'taˣ] *m* dinner ♦ *vt* to have for dinner ♦ *vi* to have dinner

Japão [ʒa'pãw] *m*: **o ~** Japan; **japonês/esa** [ʒapo'neʃ/eza] *adj*, *m/f* Japanese ♦ *m* (*LING*) Japanese

jaqueta [ʒa'keta] *f* jacket

jararaca [ʒara'raka] *f* jararaca (*snake*)

jardim [ʒax'dʒĩ] (*pl* **-ns**) *m* garden; **~ zoológico** zoo; **~-de-infância** (*pl* **jardins-de-infância**) *m* kindergarten; **jardinagem** [ʒaxdʒi'naʒẽ] *f* gardening

jardineira [ʒaxdʒi'nejra] *f* (*caixa*) trough; (*calça*) dungarees *pl*; *V tb* **jardineiro**

jardineiro/a [ʒaxdʒi'nejru/a] *m/f* gardener

jardins [ʒax'dʒĩʃ] *mpl de* **jardim**

jargão [ʒax'gãw] *m* jargon

jarra ['ʒaxa] *f* pot

jarro ['ʒexu] *m* jug

jasmim [ʒaʒ'mĩ] *m* jasmine

jato ['ʒatu] *m* jet; *(de luz)* flash; *(de ar)* blast; **a ~** at top speed

jaula ['ʒawla] *f* cage

javali [ʒava'li] *m* wild boar

jazida [ʒa'zida] *f* deposit

jazigo [ʒa'zigu] *m* grave; *(monumento)* tomb

jazz [dʒɛz] *m* jazz

jeito ['ʒejtu] *m* *(maneira)* way; *(aspecto)* appearance; *(habilidade)* skill, knack; *(modos pessoais)* manner; **ter ~ de** to look like; **não ter ~ (pessoa)** to be awkward; *(situação)* to be hopeless; **dar um ~ em** *(pé)* to twist; *(quarto, casa, papéis)* to tidy up; *(consertar)* to fix; **dar um ~ para** to find a way; **o ~ é ...** the thing to do is ...; **é o ~** it's the best way; **ao ~ de** in the style of; **com ~** tactfully; **daquele ~ (in)** that way; *(col: em desordem, mal)* anyhow; **de qualquer ~** anyway; **de ~ nenhum!** no way!

jeitoso/a [ʒej'tozu/ɔza] *adj* skilful *(BRIT)*, skillful *(US)*; *(apropriado)* suitable

jejuar [ʒe'ʒwa²] *vi* to fast

jejum [ʒe'ʒũ] *(pl* –ns*) m* fast; **em ~** fasting

jérsei ['ʒexsej] *m* jersey

jesuíta [ʒe'zwita] *m* Jesuit

Jesus [ʒe'zuʃ] *m* Jesus ♦ *excl* heavens!

jibóia [ʒi'bɔja] *f* boa (constrictor)

jiló [ʒi'lɔ] *m* kind of vegetable

jingle ['dʒĩgew] *m* jingle

jipe ['ʒipi] *m* jeep ®

joalheiro/a [ʒoa'ʎejru/a] *m/f* jeweller *(BRIT)*, jeweler *(US)*; **joalheria** [ʒoaʎe'ria] *f* jeweller's (shop) *(BRIT)*, jewelry store *(US)*

joanete [ʒwa'netʃi] *m* bunion

joaninha [ʒwa'niɲa] *f* ladybird *(BRIT)*, ladybug *(US)*

joelho [ʒo'eʎu] *m* knee; **de ~s** kneeling; **ficar de ~s** to kneel down

jogada [ʒo'gada] *f* move; *(lanço)* throw; *(negócio)* scheme, move

jogador(a) [ʒoga'do²(a)] *m/f* player; *(de jogo de azar)* gambler

jogar [ʒo'ga²] *vt* to play; *(em jogo de azar)* to gamble; *(atirar)* to throw; *(indiretas)* to drop ♦ *vi* to play; to gamble; *(barco)* to pitch; **~ fora** to throw away

jogging ['ʒɔgĩ] *m* jogging; *(roupa)* track suit; **fazer ~** to go jogging, jog

jogo ['ʒogu] *m* game; *(jogar)* play; *(de azar)* gambling; *(conjunto)* set; *(artimanha)* trick; **J~s Olímpicos** Olympic Games

jóia ['ʒɔja] *f* jewel

jóquei ['ʒɔkej] *m* jockey

Jordânia [ʒox'danja] *f*: **a ~** Jordan; **Jordão** [ʒox'dãw] *m*: **o (rio) Jordão** the Jordan (River)

jornada [ʒox'nada] *f* journey; **~ de trabalho** working day

jornal [ʒox'naw] *(pl* –ais*) m* newspaper; *(TV, RÁDIO)* news *sg*; **~eiro/a** [ʒoxna'lejru/a] *m/f* newsagent *(BRIT)*, newsdealer *(US)*

jornalismo [ʒoxna'liʒmu] *m* journalism; **jornalista** [ʃoxna'liʃta] *m/f* journalist

jorrar [ʒo'xa²] *vi* to gush, spurt out

jovem ['ʒɔvẽ] *(pl* –ns*) adj* young ♦ *m/f* young person

jovial [ʒo'vjaw] *(pl* –ais*) adj* jovial, cheerful

Jr *abr* = **Júnior**

juba ['ʒuba] *f* *(de leão)* mane

jubileu [ʒubi'lew] *m* jubilee

júbilo ['ʒubilu] *m* rejoicing

judaico/a [ʒu'dajku/a] *adj* Jewish

judeu/judia [ʒu'dew/ʒu'dʒia] *adj* Jewish ♦ *m/f* Jew

judiação [ʒudʒja'sãw] *f* ill-treatment

judiar [ʒu'dʒja²] *vi*: **~ de** to ill-treat

judicial [ʒudʒi'sjaw] *(pl* –ais*) adj* judicial

judiciário/a [ʒudʒi'sjarju/a] *adj* judicial; **o (poder) ~** the judiciary

judicioso/a [ʒudʒi'sjozu/ɔza] *adj* judicious

judô [ʒu'do] *m* judo

juiz/íza [ʒwiʒ/'iza] *m/f* judge; *(em jogos)* referee; **~ de paz** justice of the peace; **~ado** [ʒwi'zado] *m* court

juízo ['ʒwizu] *m* judgement; *(parecer)* opinion; *(siso)* common sense; *(foro)* court; **perder o ~** to lose one's mind; **não ter ~** to be foolish; **tomar** *ou* **criar ~** to come to one's senses; **chamar/levar a ~** to summon/take to court; **~!** behave yourself!

julgamento [ʒuwga'mẽtu] *m* judgement; *(audiência)* trial; *(sentença)* sentence

julgar [ʒuw'ga²] *vt* to judge; *(achar)* to think; *(JUR: sentenciar)* to sentence; **~-se** *vr*: **~-se algo** to consider o.s. sth, think of o.s. as sth

julho ['ʒuʎu] *(PT* **J-***) m* July

jumento/a [ʒu'mẽtu/a] *m/f* donkey

junção [ʒũ'sãw] *(pl* –ões*) f* *(ato)* joining; *(junta)* join

junco ['ʒũku] *m* reed, rush

junções [ʒũ'sõjʃ] *fpl de* **junção**

junho ['ʒuɲu] *(PT* **J-***) m* June

júnior ['ʒunjo²] *(pl* **juniores***) adj* younger, junior ♦ *m/f* *(ESPORTE)* junior; **Eduardo Autran J~** Eduardo Autran Junior

junta ['ʒũta] *f* board, committee; *(POL)* junta; *(articulação, juntura)* joint

juntar [ʒũ'ta²] *vt* to join; *(reunir)* to bring together; *(aglomerar)* to gather together; *(recolher)* to collect up; *(acrescentar)* to add; *(dinheiro)* to save up ♦ *vi* to gather; **~-se** *vr* to gather; *(associar-se)* to join up; **~-se a alguém** to join sb

junto/a ['ʒũtu/a] *adj* joined; *(chegado)* near; **ir ~s** to go together; **~ a/de** near/next to; **segue ~** *(COM)* please find enclosed

jura ['ʒura] f vow

jurado/a [ʒu'radu/a] adj sworn ♦ m/f juror

juramento [ʒura'mẽtu] m oath

jurar [ʒu'ra*] vt, vi to swear; **jura?** really?

júri ['ʒuri] m jury

jurídico/a [ʒu'ridʒiku/a] adj legal

jurisdição [ʒurifdʒi'sãw] f jurisdiction

juros ['ʒuruf] mpl (ECON) interest sg; ~ **simples/compostos** simple/compound interest

justamente [ʒufta'mẽtʃi] adv fairly, justly; (precisamente) exactly

justapor [ʒufta'po*] (irreg: como **pôr**) vt to juxtapose

justeza [ʒuf'teza] f fairness; (precisão) precision

justiça [ʒuf'tʃisa] f justice; (poder judiciário) judiciary; (equidade) fairness; (tribunal) court; **com** ~ justly, fairly; **ir à** ~ to go to court; **justiceiro/a** [ʒuftʃi'sejru/a] adj righteous; (inflexível) inflexible

justificação [ʒuftʃifika'sãw] (pl –ões) f justification

justificar [ʒuftʃifi'ka*] vt to justify

justo/a ['ʒuftu/a] adj just, fair; (legítimo: queixa) legitimate, justified; (exato) exact; (apertado) tight ♦ adv just

juvenil [ʒuve'niw] (pl –is) adj youthful; (roupa) young; (livro) for young people; (ESPORTE: equipe, campeonato) youth atr, junior

juventude [ʒuvẽ'tudʒi] f youth; (jovialidade) youthfulness; (jovens) young people pl, youth

K

kg abr (= quilograma) kg

kit ['kitʃi] (pl ~s) m kit

kitchenette [kitʃe'netʃi] f studio flat

km abr (= quilômetro) km

km/h abr (= quilômetros por hora) km/h

L

-la [la] pron her; (você) you; (coisa) it

lá [la] adv there ♦ m (MÚS) A; ~ **fora** outside; ~ **em baixo** down there; **por** ~ (direção) that way; (situação) over there; **até** ~ (no espaço) there; (no tempo) until then

lã [lã] f wool

labareda [laba'reda] f flame; (fig) ardour (BRIT), ardor (US)

labia ['labja] f (astúcia) cunning; **ter** ~ to have the gift of the gab

lábio ['labju] m lip

labirinto [labi'rĩtu] m labyrinth, maze

laboratório [labora'tɔrju] m laboratory

laca ['laka] f lacquer

laçar [la'sa*] vt to bind, tie

laço ['lasu] m bow; (de gravata) knot; (armadilha) snare; (fig) bond, tie; **dar um** ~ to tie a bow

lacônico/a [la'koniku/a] adj laconic

lacrar [la'kra*] vt to seal (with wax); **lacre** ['lakri] m sealing wax

lacrimogêneo/a [lakrimo'ʒenju/a] adj: **gás** ~ tear gas

lácteo/a ['laktju/a] adj milk atr; **Via Láctea** Milky Way

lacuna [la'kuna] f gap; (omissão) omission; (espaço em branco) blank

ladeira [la'dejra] f slope

lado ['ladu] m side; (MIL) flank; (rumo) direction; **ao** ~ (perto) close by; **a casa ao** ~ the house next door; **ao** ~ **de** beside; **deixar de** ~ to set aside; (fig) to leave out; **de um** ~ **para outro** back and forth

ladra ['ladra] f thief, robber; (picareta) crook

ladrão/ona [la'drãw/ɔna] (pl –ões/~s) adj thieving ♦ m/f thief, robber; (picareta) crook

ladrilho [la'driʎu] m tile; (chão) tiled floor, tiles pl

ladrões [la'drõjʃ] mpl de **ladrão**

ladrona [la'drɔna] f de **ladrão**

lagarta [la'gaxta] f caterpillar

lagartixa [lagax'tʃifa] f gecko

lagarto [la'gaxtu] m lizard

lago ['lagu] m lake; (de jardim) pond

lagoa [la'goa] f pool, pond; (lago) lake

lagosta [la'goʃta] f lobster

lagostim [lagoʃ'tʃĩ] (pl –ns) m crayfish

lágrima ['lagrima] f tear

laguna [la'guna] f lagoon

laje ['laʒi] f paving stone, flagstone

lajota [la'ʒɔta] f paving stone

lama ['lama] f mud

lamaçal [lama'saw] (pl –ais) m quagmire; (pântano) bog, marsh

lamacento/a [lama'sẽtu/a] adj muddy

lamaçal [lama'sejru] m = lamaçal

lamber [lã'be*] vt to lick; **lambida** [lã'bida] f: **dar uma lambida em algo** to lick sth

lambiscar [lãbiʃ'ka*] vt, vi to nibble

lambuzar [lãbu'za*] vt to smear

lamentar [lamẽ'ta*] vt to lament; (sentir) to regret; ~**-se** vr: ~**-se (de algo)** to lament (sth); ~ **(que)** to be sorry (that); **lamentável** [lamẽ'tavew] (pl –eis) adj regrettable; (deplorável) deplorable; **lamento** [la'mẽtu] m lament; (gemido) moan

lâmina ['lamina] f (chapa) sheet; (placa) plate; (de faca) blade; (de persiana) slat; **laminar** [lami'na*] vt to laminate

lâmpada ['lãpada] f lamp; (tb: ~ **elétrica**) light bulb; ~ **de mesa** table lamp; **lamparina** [lãpa'rina] f lamp

lança ['lãsa] f lance, spear

lançamento [lãsa'mẽtu] m throwing; (de

navio, produto, campanha) launch; (*de disco, filme*) release; (*COM: em livro*) entry

lançar [lã'sa"] *vt* to throw; (*navio, produto, campanha*) to launch; (*disco, filme*) to release; (*COM: em livro*) to enter; (*em leilão*) to bid

lance ['lãsi] *m* (*arremesso*) throw; (*incidente*) incident; (*história*) story; (*situação*) position; (*fato*) fact; (*ESPORTE: jogada*) shot; (*em leilão*) bid; (*de escada*) flight; (*de casas*) row; (*episódio*) moment; (*de muro, estrada*) stretch

lancha ['lãʃa] *f* launch; ~ **torpedeira** torpedo boat

lanchar [lã'ʃa"] *vi* to have a snack ♦ *vt* to have as a snack; **lanche** ['lãʃi] *m* snack

lanchonete [lãʃo'netʃi] (*BR*) *f* snack bar

languidez [lãgi'deʒ] *f* languor, listlessness

lânguido/a ['lãgidu/a] *adj* languid, listless

lanterna [lã'tɛxna] *f* lantern; (*portátil*) torch (*BRIT*), flashlight (*US*)

lapela [la'pɛla] *f* lapel

lapidar [lapi'da"] *vt* (*jóias*) to cut; (*fig*) to polish, refine ♦ *adj* (*fig*) masterful

lápide ['lapidʒi] *f* (*tumular*) tombstone; (*comemorativa*) memorial stone

lápis ['lapiʃ] *m inv* pencil; ~ **de cor** coloured (*BRIT*) *ou* colored (*US*) pencil, crayon; ~ **de olho** eyebrow pencil; **lapiseira** [lapi'zejra] *f* propelling (*BRIT*) *ou* mechanical (*US*) pencil; (*caixa*) pencil case

Lapônia [la'ponja] *f*: **a** ~ Lapland

lapso ['lapsu] *m* lapse; (*de tempo*) interval; (*erro*) slip

lar [la"] *m* home

laranja [la'rãʒa] *adj inv* orange ♦ *f* orange ♦ *m* (*cor*) orange; ~**da** [larã'ʒada] *f* orangeade; ~**l** [larã'ʒaw] (*pl* ~**is**) *m* orange grove; **laranjeira** [larã'ʒejra] *f* orange tree

lareira [la'rejra] *f* hearth, fireside

larga ['laxga] *f*: **à** ~ lavishly; **dar** ~**s a** to give free rein to; **viver à** ~ to lead a lavish life

largada [lax'gada] *f* start; **dar a** ~ to start; (*fig*) to make a start

largar [lax'ga"] *vt* to let go of, release; (*deixar*) to leave; (*deixar cair*) to drop; (*risada*) to let out; (*velas*) to unfurl; (*piada*) to tell; (*pôr em liberdade*) to let go ♦ *vi* (*NÁUT*) to set sail; ~**-se** *vr* (*desprender-se*) to free o.s.; (*ir-se*) to go off; (*pôr-se*) to proceed

largo/a ['laxgu/a] *adj* wide, broad; (*amplo*) extensive; (*roupa*) loose, baggy; (*conversa*) long ♦ *m* (*praça*) square; (*altomar*) open sea; **ao** ~ at a distance, far off; **passar de** ~ **sobre um assunto** to gloss over a subject; **passar ao** ~ **de algo** (*fig*) to sidestep sth; **largura**

[lax'gura] *f* width, breadth

laringe [la'rĩʒi] *f* larynx; **laringite** [larĩ'ʒitʃi] *f* laryngitis

larva ['laxva] *f* larva, grub

lasanha [la'zaɲa] *f* lasagna

lasca ['laʃka] *f* (*de madeira, metal*) splinter; (*de pedra*) chip; (*fatia*) slice

laser ['lejze"] *m* laser; **raio** ~ laser beam

lástima ['laʃtʃima] *f* pity, compassion; (*infortúnio*) misfortune; **é uma** ~ (**que**) it's a shame (that); **lastimar** [laʃtʃi'ma"] *vt* to lament; **lastimar-se** *vr* to complain, be sorry for o.s.

lata ['lata] *f* tin (*BRIT*), can; (*material*) tin-plate; ~ **de lixo** rubbish bin (*BRIT*), garbage can (*US*); ~ **velha** (*col: carro*) old banger (*BRIT*) *ou* clunker (*US*)

latão [la'tãw] *m* brass

lataria [lata'ria] *f* (*AUTO*) bodywork; (*enlatados*) canned food

latejar [late'ʒa"] *vi* to throb; **latejo** [la'teʒu] *m* throbbing, beat

latente [la'tẽtʃi] *adj* latent

lateral [late'raw] (*pl* ~**ais**) *adj* side, lateral ♦ *f* (*FUTEBOL*) sideline ♦ *m* (*FUTEBOL*) throw-in

latido [la'tʃidu] *m* bark(ing), yelp(ing)

latifundiário/a [latʃifũ'dʒjarju/a] *m/f* landowner

latifúndio [latʃi'fũdʒju] *m* large estate

latim [la'tʃĩ] *m* (*LING*) Latin; **gastar o seu** ~ to waste one's breath

latino/a [la'tʃinu/a] *adj* Latin; ~**americano/a** *adj, m/f* Latin-American

latir [la'tʃi"] *vi* to bark, yelp

latitude [latʃi'tudʒi] *f* latitude; (*largura*) breadth; (*fig*) scope

latrocínio [latro'sinju] *m* armed robbery

laudo ['lawdu] *m* (*JUR*) decision; (*resultados*) findings *pl*; (*peça escrita*) report

lava ['lava] *f* lava

lavabo [la'vabu] *m* toilet

lavadeira [lava'dejra] *f* washerwoman

lavadora [lava'dora] *f* washing machine

lavagem [la'vaʒẽ] *f* washing; ~ **a seco** dry cleaning; ~ **cerebral** brainwashing

lavanda [la'vãda] *f* (*BOT*) lavender; (*colônia*) lavender water; (*para lavar os dedos*) fingerbowl

lavanderia [lavãde'ria] *f* laundry; (*aposento*) laundry room

lavar [la'va"] *vt* to wash; (*culpa*) to wash away; ~ **a seco** to dry clean

lavatório [lava'tɔrju] *m* washbasin; (*aposento*) toilet

lavoura [la'voura] *f* tilling; (*agricultura*) farming; (*terreno*) plantation

lavra ['lavra] *f* ploughing (*BRIT*), plowing (*US*); (*de minerais*) mining; (*mina*) mine; **ser da** ~ **de** to be the work of

lavradio [lavra'dʒiu] *m* farming

lavrador(a) [lavra'do"(a)] *m/f* farmhand

laxativo/a [laʃa'tʃivu/a] *adj* laxative ♦ *m* laxative

lazer [la'ze"] *m* leisure

leal [le'aw] (pl -ais) adj loyal; ~**dade**
[leaw'dadʒi] f loyalty
leão [le'ãw] (pl -ões) m lion; **L~** (ASTRO-
LOGIA) Leo
lebre ['lɛbri] f hare
lecionar [lesjo'na*] (PT -cc-) vt, vi to
teach
lectivo/a [lɛk'tivu/a] (PT) adj = **letivo**
legal [le'gaw] (pl -ais) adj legal, lawful;
(col) fine; (: pessoa) nice ♦ adv (col)
well; (tá) ~! OK!; ~**idade** [legali'dadʒi]
f legality, lawfulness; ~**izar** [legali'za*]
vt to legalize; (documento) to authenti-
cate
legenda [le'ʒẽda] f inscription; (texto explicativo) caption; (CINEMA) subtitle;
legendário/a [leʒẽ'darju/a] adj legendary
legião [le'ʒjãw] (pl -ões) f legion
legislação [leʒiʒla'sãw] f legislation
legislar [leʒiʒ'la*] vi to legislate ♦ vt to
pass
legislativo/a [leʒiʒla'tʃivu/a] adj legisla-
tive ♦ m legislature
legislatura [leʒiʒla'tura] f legislature;
(período) term of office
legitimar [leʒitʃi'ma*] vt to legitimize;
(justificar) to legitimate
legítimo/a [le'ʒitʃimu/a] adj legitimate;
(justo) rightful; (autêntico) genuine; **legítima defesa** self-defence (BRIT), self-
defense (US)
legível [le'ʒivew] (pl -eis) adj legible
légua ['lɛgwa] f league
legume [le'gumi] m vegetable
lei [lej] f law; (regra) rule; (metal) standard
leigo/a ['lejgu/a] adj (REL) lay, secular ♦
m layman; **ser ~ em algo** (fig) to be no
expert at sth, be unversed in sth
leilão [lej'lãw] (pl -ões) m auction; **vender em ~** to sell by auction, auction
off; **leiloar** [lej'lwa*] vt to auction;
leiloeiro/a [lej'lwejru/a] m/f auctioneer
leio etc ['leju] vb V **ler**
leitão/toa [lej'tãw/toa] (pl -ões/~s) m/f
sucking (BRIT) ou suckling (US) pig
leite ['lejtʃi] m milk; ~ **em pó** powdered
milk; ~ **desnatado** ou **magro** skimmed
milk; ~ **de magnésia** milk of magne-
sia; ~**ira** [lej'tejra] f (para ferver) milk
pan; (para servir) milk jug; ~**iro/a**
[lej'tejru/a] adj (vaca, gado) dairy ♦ m/f
milkman/woman; ~**ria** [lejte'ria] f dairy
leito ['lejtu] m bed
leitoa [lej'toa] f de **leitão**
leitões [lej'tõjʃ] mpl de **leitão**
leitor(a) [lej'to*(a)] m/f reader; (professor) lector
leitoso/a [lej'tozu/ɔza] adj milky
leitura [lej'tura] f reading; (livro etc) reading matter
lema ['lɛma] m motto; (POL) slogan
lembrança [lẽ'brãsa] f recollection, memory; (presente) souvenir; ~**s** fpl (recomendações): ~**s a sua mãe!** regards to your

mother!
lembrar [lẽ'bra*] vt, vi to remember; ~-
se vr: ~(-**se**) **de** to remember; ~(-**se**)
(**de**) **que** to remember that; ~ **algo a
alguém**, ~ **alguém de algo** to remind
sb of sth; ~ **alguém de que**, ~ **a alguém que** to remind sb that; **ele me lem-
bra meu irmão** he reminds me of my
brother, he is like my brother; **lembre-
te** [lẽ'bretʃi] m reminder
leme ['lɛmi] m rudder; (NÁUT) helm; (fig)
control
lenço ['lẽsu] m handkerchief; (de pescoço)
scarf; (de cabeça) headscarf; ~ **de papel**
tissue
lençol [lẽ'sɔw] (pl -óis) m sheet; **estar
em maus lençóis** to be in a fix
lenda ['lẽda] f legend; (fig: mentira) lie;
lendário/a [lẽ'darju/a] adj legendary
lenha ['lɛɲa] f firewood; ~**dor** [leɲa'do*]
m woodcutter
lente ['lẽtʃi] f lens sg; ~ **de aumento**
magnifying glass; ~**s de contato** contact lenses
lentidão [lẽtʃi'dãw] f slowness
lentilha [lẽ'tʃiʎa] f lentil
lento/a ['lẽtu/a] adj slow
leoa [le'oa] f lioness
leões [le'õjʃ] mpl de **leão**
leopardo [ljo'paxdu] m leopard
lépido/a ['lɛpidu/a] adj (alegre) sprightly,
bright; (ágil) nimble, agile
lepra ['lɛpra] f leprosy; **leproso/a**
[le'prozu/ɔza] adj leprous ♦ m/f leper
leque ['lɛki] m fan; (fig) array
ler [le*] vt, vi to read
lerdo/a ['lɛxdu/a] adj slow, sluggish
lesão [le'zãw] (pl -ões) f harm, injury;
(JUR) violation; (MED) lesion; ~ **corporal** (JUR) bodily harm
lesar [le'za*] vt to harm, damage; (direitos) to violate
lésbica ['lɛʒbika] f lesbian
lesma ['lɛʒma] f slug; (fig: pessoa) slow-
coach
lesões [le'zõjʃ] fpl de **lesão**
lesse etc ['lesi] vb V **ler**
leste ['lɛʃtʃi] m east
letal [le'taw] (pl -ais) adj lethal
letargia [letax'ʒia] f lethargy; **letárgico/a**
[le'taxʒiku/a] adj lethargic
letivo/a [le'tʃivu/a] adj school atr; **ano
~** academic year
letra ['letra] f letter; (caligrafia) handwriting; (de canção) lyrics pl; **L~s** fpl (curso) language and literature; **à ~** literally; **ao pé da ~** literally, word for
word; ~ **de câmbio** (COM) bill of exchange; ~ **de imprensa** print; ~**do/a**
[le'tradu/a] adj learned, erudite ♦ m/f
scholar; **letreiro** [le'trejru] m sign, notice; (inscrição) inscription; (CINEMA)
subtitle
leu etc [lew] vb V **ler**
léu [lɛw] m: **ao ~** (à toa) aimlessly; (à

mostra) uncovered

leucemia [lewse'mia] *f* leukaemia (*BRIT*), leukemia (*US*)

levado/a [le'vadu/a] *adj* mischievous; (*criança*) naughty

levantador(a) [levãta'do°(a)] *adj* lifting ♦ *m/f*: ~ **de pesos** weightlifter

levantamento [levãta'mẽtu] *m* lifting, raising; (*revolta*) uprising, rebellion; (*arrolamento*) survey

levantar [levã'ta°] *vt* to lift, raise; (*voz, capital*) to raise; (*apanhar*) to pick up; (*suscitar*) to arouse; (*ambiente*) to brighten up ♦ *vi* to stand up; (*da cama*) to get up; (*dar vida*) to brighten; ~**-se** *vr* to stand up; (*da cama*) to get up; (*rebelar-se*) to rebel

levar [le'va°] *vt* to take; (*portar*) to carry; (*tempo*) to pass, spend; (*roupa*) to wear; (*lidar com*) to handle; (*induzir*) to lead; (*filme*) to show; (*peça teatral*) to do, put on; (*vida*) to lead ♦ *vi* to get a beating; ~ **a** to lead to; ~ **a mal** to take amiss

leve ['lɛvi] *adj* light; (*insignificante*) slight; **de** ~ lightly, softly

levedo [le'vedu] *m* yeast

levedura [leve'dura] *f* = **levedo**

leviandade [levjã'dadʒi] *f* frivolity

leviano/a [le'vjanu/a] *adj* frivolous

lha(s) [ʎa(ʃ)] = **lhe + a(s)**

lhama ['ʎama] *m* llama

lhe [ʎi] *pron* (*a ele*) to him; (*a ela*) to her; (*a você*) to you

lhes [ʎiʃ] *pron pl* (*a eles/elas*) to them; (*a vocês*) to you

lho(s) [ʎu(ʃ)] = **lhe + o(s)**

li *etc* [li] *vb* V **ler**

Líbano ['libanu] *m*: **o** ~ (the) Lebanon

libelo [li'bɛlu] *m* satire, lampoon; (*JUR*) formal indictment

libélula [li'bɛlula] *f* dragonfly

liberação [libera'sãw] *f* liberation

liberal [libe'raw] (*pl* -**ais**) *adj, m/f* liberal

liberar [libe'ra°] *vt* to release; (*libertar*) to free

liberdade [libex'dadʒi] *f* freedom; ~**s** *fpl* (*direitos*) liberties; **pôr alguém em** ~ to set sb free; ~ **condicional** probation; ~ **de palavra** freedom of speech; ~ **sob palavra** parole

libertação [libexta'sãw] *f* release

libertar [libex'ta°] *vt* to free, release

libertino/a [libex'tʃinu/a] *adj* loose-living ♦ *m/f* libertine

liberto/a [li'bɛxtu/a] *pp* de **libertar**

Líbia ['libja] *f*: **a** ~ Libya; **líbio/a** ['libju/a] *adj, m/f* Libyan

libidinoso/a [libidʒi'nozu/ɔza] *adj* lecherous, lustful

libra ['libra] *f* pound; **L~** (*ASTROLOGIA*) Libra

libreto [li'bretu] *m* libretto

lição [li'sãw] (*pl* -**ões**) *f* lesson

licença [li'sẽsa] *f* licence (*BRIT*), license (*US*); (*permissão*) permission; (*do trabal-*

ho, MIL) leave; **com** ~ excuse me; **estar de** ~ to be on leave; **dá** ~? may I?

licenciado/a [lisẽ'sjadu/a] *m/f* graduate

licenciar [lisẽ'sja°] *vt* to license; ~**-se** *vr* (*EDUC*) to graduate; (*ficar de licença*) to take leave; **licenciatura** [lisẽsja'tura] *f* (*título*) degree; (*curso*) degree course

liceu [li'sew] (*PT*) *m* secondary (*BRIT*) *ou* high (*US*) school

lições [li'sõjʃ] *fpl* de **lição**

licor [li'ko°] *m* liqueur

lidar [li'da°] *vi*: ~ **com** (*ocupar-se*) to deal with; (*combater*) to struggle against; ~ **em algo** to work in sth

líder ['lidɛ°] *m/f* leader; **liderança** [lide'rãsa] *f* leadership; (*ESPORTE*) lead; **liderar** [lide'ra°] *vt* to lead

liga ['liga] *f* league; (*de meias*) suspender (*BRIT*), garter (*US*); (*metal*) alloy

ligação [liga'sãw] (*pl* -**ões**) *f* connection; (*fig: de amizade*) bond; (*TEL*) call; (*relação amorosa*) liaison; **fazer uma** ~ **para alguém** to call sb; **não consigo completar a** ~ (*TEL*) I can't get through; **caiu a** ~ (*TEL*) I (*ou he etc*) was cut off

ligada [li'gada] *f* (*TEL*) ring, call; **dar uma** ~ **para alguém** (*col*) to give sb a ring

ligado/a [li'gadu/a] *adj* (*TEC*) connected; (*luz, rádio etc*) on; (*metal*) alloy

ligadura [liga'dura] *f* bandage

ligamento [liga'mẽtu] *m* ligament

ligar [li'ga°] *vt* to tie, bind; (*unir*) to join, connect; (*luz, TV*) to switch on; (*afetivamente*) to bind together; (*carro*) to start (up) ♦ *vi* (*telefonar*) to ring; ~**-se** *vr* to join; ~**-se com alguém** to join with sb; ~**-se a algo** to be connected with sth; ~ **para alguém** to ring sb up; ~ **para ou a algo** (*dar atenção*) to take notice of sth; (*dar importância*) to care about sth; **eu nem ligo** it doesn't bother me; **não ligo a mínima (para)** I couldn't care less (about)

ligeireza [liʒej'reza] *f* lightness; (*rapidez*) swiftness; (*agilidade*) nimbleness

ligeiro/a [li'ʒejru/a] *adj* light; (*ferimento*) slight; (*referência*) passing; (*conhecimentos*) scant; (*rápido*) quick, swift; (*ágil*) nimble ♦ *adv* swiftly, nimbly

lilás [li'laʃ] *adj, m* lilac

lima ['lima] *f* (*laranja*) type of (*very sweet*) orange; (*ferramenta*) file; ~ **de unhas** nailfile

limão [li'mãw] (*pl* -**ões**) *m* lime; ~**(-galego)** (*pl* -**es(-galegos)**) *m* lemon

limbo ['libu] *m*: **estar no** ~ to be in limbo

limiar [li'mja°] *m* threshold

limitação [limita'sãw] (*pl* -**ões**) *f* limitation, restriction

limitar [limi'ta°] *vt* to limit, restrict; ~**-se** *vr*: ~**-se a** to limit o.s. to; ~**-se com** to border on; **limite** [li'mitʃi] *m* limit, boundary; (*fig*) limit; **passar dos limites** to go too far

limo ['limu] *m* (*BOT*) water weed; (*lodo*) slime

limoeiro [li'mwejru] *m* lemon tree

limões [li'mõjʃ] *mpl de* **limão**

limonada [limo'nada] *f* lemonade (*BRIT*), lemon soda (*US*)

limpador [lĩpa'do*] *m*: ~ **de pára-brisas** windscreen wiper (*BRIT*), windshield wiper (*US*)

limpar [lĩ'pa*] *vt* to clean; (*lágrimas, suor*) to wipe away; (*polir*) to shine, polish; (*fig*) to clean up; (*roubar*) to rob

limpeza [lĩ'peza] *f* cleanliness; (*esmero*) neatness; (*ato*) cleaning; ~ **pública** rubbish (*BRIT*) *ou* garbage (*US*) collection, sanitation

limpo/a ['lĩpu/a] *pp de* **limpar** ♦ *adj* clean; (*céu, consciência*) clear; (*COM*) net; (*fig*) pure; (*col: pronto*) ready; **passar a ~** to make a fair copy; **tirar a ~** to find out the truth about, clear up; **estar ~ com alguém** (*col*) to be in with sb

lince ['lĩsi] *m* lynx

linchar [lĩ'ʃa*] *vt* to lynch

lindo/a ['lĩdu/a] *adj* lovely

lingerie [lĩʒe'ri] *m* lingerie

lingote [lĩ'gotʃi] *m* ingot

língua ['lĩgwa] *f* tongue; (*linguagem*) language; **botar a ~ para fora** to stick out one's tongue; **dar com a ~ nos dentes** to let the cat out of the bag; **estar na ponta da ~** to be on the tip of one's tongue

linguado [lĩ'gwadu] *m* (*peixe*) sole

linguagem [lĩ'gwaʒẽ] (*pl* **-ns**) *f* (*tb: COMPUT*) language; (*falada*) speech; ~ **de máquina** (*COMPUT*) machine language

linguarudo/a [lĩgwa'rudu/a] *adj* gossiping ♦ *m/f* gossip

lingüeta [lĩ'gweta] *f* (*fechadura*) bolt

lingüiça [lĩ'gwisa] *f* sausage

lingüista [lĩ'gwiʃta] *m/f* linguist; **lingüística** [lĩ'gwiʃtʃika] *f* linguistics *sg*

linha ['lĩɲa] *f* line; (*para costura*) thread; (*barbante*) string, cord; ~**s** *fpl* (*carta*) letter *sg*; **em ~** in line, in a row; (*COMPUT*) on line; **fora de ~** (*COMPUT*) off line; **manter/perder a ~** to keep/lose one's cool; **o telefone não deu ~** the line was dead; ~ **aérea** airline; ~ **de mira** sights *pl*; ~ **de montagem** assembly line; ~ **férrea** railway (*BRIT*), railroad (*US*)

linho ['lĩɲu] *m* linen; (*planta*) flax

linóleo [li'nɔlju] *m* linoleum

liquidação [likida'sãw] (*pl* **-ões**) *f* liquidation; (*em loja*) (clearance) sale; (*de conta*) settlement; **em ~ on sale**

liquidar [liki'da*] *vt* to liquidate; (*conta*) to settle; (*mercadoria*) to sell off; (*assunto*) to lay to rest ♦ *vi* (*loja*) to have a sale; ~**-se** *vr* (*destruir-se*) to be de-

stroyed; ~ **(com) alguém** (*fig: arrasar*) to destroy sb; (: *matar*) to do away with sb

liqüidificador [likwidʒifika'do*] *m* liquidizer

líquido/a ['likidu/a] *adj* liquid, fluid; (*COM*) net ♦ *m* liquid

lira ['lira] *f* lyre; (*moeda*) lira

lírica ['lirika] *f* (*MÚS*) lyrics *pl*; (*poesia*) lyric poetry

lírico/a ['liriku/a] *adj* lyric(al)

lírio ['lirju] *m* lily

Lisboa [liʒ'boa] *n* Lisbon; **lisboeta** [liʒ'bweta] *adj* Lisbon *atr* ♦ *m/f* inhabitant *ou* native of Lisbon

liso/a ['lizu/a] *adj* smooth; (*tecido*) plain; (*cabelo*) straight; (*col: sem dinheiro*) broke

lisonja [li'zõʒa] *f* flattery; **lisonjear** [lizõ'ʒja*] *vt* to flatter; **lisonjeiro/a** [lizõ'ʒejru/a] *adj* flattering

lista ['liʃta] *f* list; (*listra*) stripe; (*PT: menu*) menu; ~ **negra** blacklist; ~ **telefônica** telephone directory; ~**do/a** [liʃ'tadu/a] *adj* striped; ~**r** [liʃ'ta*] *vt* (*COMPUT*) to list

listra ['liʃtra] *f* stripe; ~**do/a** [liʃ'tradu/a] *adj* striped

literal [lite'raw] (*pl* **-ais**) *adj* literal

literário/a [lite'rarju/a] *adj* literary

literatura [litera'tura] *f* literature

litígio [li'tʃiʒju] *m* (*JUR*) lawsuit; (*contenda*) dispute

litoral [lito'raw] (*pl* **-ais**) *adj* coastal ♦ *m* coast, seaboard

litro ['litru] *m* litre (*BRIT*), liter (*US*)

lívido/a ['lividu/a] *adj* livid

livrar [li'vra*] *vt* to release, liberate; (*salvar*) to save; ~**-se** *vr* to escape; ~**-se de** to get rid of; (*compromisso*) to get out of; **Deus me livre!** Heaven forbid!

livraria [livra'ria] *f* bookshop (*BRIT*), bookstore (*US*)

livre ['livri] *adj* free; (*lugar*) unoccupied; (*desimpedido*) clear, open; ~ **de impostos** tax-free; ~-**arbítrio** *m* free will

livreiro/a [liv'rejru/a] *m/f* bookseller

livro ['livru] *m* book; ~ **brochado** paperback; ~ **de bolso** pocket-sized book; ~ **de cheques** cheque book (*BRIT*), check book (*US*); ~ **de consulta** reference book; ~ **encadernado** *ou* **de capa dura** hardback

lixa ['liʃa] *f* sandpaper; (*de unhas*) nailfile; (*peixe*) dogfish; ~**r** [li'ʃa*] *vt* to sand

lixeira [li'ʃejra] *f* dustbin (*BRIT*), garbage can (*US*)

lixeiro [li'ʃejru] *m* dustman (*BRIT*), garbage man (*US*)

lixo ['liʃu] *m* rubbish, garbage (*US*); **ser um ~** (*col*) to be rubbish; ~ **atômico** nuclear waste

-lo [lu] *pron* him; (*você*) you; (*coisa*) it

lóbi ['lɔbi] *m* = **lobby**

lobo ['lobu] *m* wolf; **~-marinho** (*pl* ~s-marinhos) *m* sea lion

lóbulo ['lɔbulu] *m* lobe

locação [loka'sãw] (*pl* -ões) *f* lease; (*de vídeo etc*) rental

locador(a) [loka'do*(a)] *m/f* (*de casa*) landlord; (*de carro, filme*) rental agent ♦ *f* rental company; **~a de vídeo** video rental shop

local [lo'kaw] (*pl* -ais) *adj* local ♦ *m* site, place ♦ *f* (*notícia*) story; **~idade** [lokali'dadʒi] *f* (*lugar*) locality; (*povoação*) town; **~ização** [lokaliza'sãw] (*pl* -ões) *f* location; **~izar** [lokali'za*] *vt* to locate; **~izar-se** *vr* to be located; (*orientar-se*) to get one's bearings

loção [lo'sãw] (*pl* -ões) *f* lotion; **~ após-barba** aftershave (lotion)

locatário/a [loka'tarju/a] *m/f* (*de casa*) tenant; (*de carro, filme*) hirer

loções [lo'sõjf] *fpl* de loção

locomotiva [lokomo'tʃiva] *f* railway (*BRIT*) *ou* railroad (*US*) engine, locomotive

locomover-se [lokomo'vexsi] *vr* to move around

locução [loku'sãw] (*pl* -ões) *f* (*frase*) phrase; (*dicção*) diction

locutor(a) [loku'to*(a)] *m/f* (*TV, RÁDIO*) announcer

lodo ['lodu] *m* (*lama*) mud; (*limo*) slime; **~so/a** [lo'dozu/ɔza] *adj* muddy; slimy

lógica ['lɔʒika] *f* logic; **lógico/a** ['lɔʒiku/a] *adj* logical; **(é) lógico!** of course!

logística [lo'ʒiʃtʃika] *f* logistics *sg*

logo ['lɔgu] *adv* (*imediatamente*) right away, at once; (*em breve*) soon; (*justamente*) just, right; (*mais tarde*) later; **~, ~** straightaway, without delay; **~ mais** later; **~ no começo** right at the start; **~ que, tão ~** as soon as; **até ~!** bye!; **~ antes/depois** just before/shortly afterwards; **~ de saída** *ou* **de cara** straightaway, right away

logopedista [logope'dʒiʃta] *m/f* speech therapist

logotipo [logo'tʃipu] *m* logo

logradouro [logra'doru] *m* public area

lograr [lo'gra*] *vt* (*alcançar*) to achieve; (*obter*) to get, obtain; (*enganar*) to cheat; **~ fazer** to manage to do

logro ['logru] *m* fraud

loiro/a ['lojru/a] *adj* = **louro/a**

loja ['lɔʒa] *f* shop; **lojista** [lo'ʒiʃta] *m/f* shopkeeper

lombada [lõ'bada] *f* (*de animal*) back; (*de livro*) spine; (*na estrada*) ramp

lombar [lõ'ba*] *adj* lumbar

lombo ['lõbu] *m* back; (*carne*) loin

lombriga [lõ'briga] *f* ringworm

lona ['lona] *f* canvas

Londres ['lõdriʃ] *n* London; **londrino/a** [lõ'drinu/a] *adj* London *atr* ♦ *m/f* Londoner

longa-metragem (*pl* longas-metragens) *m*: **(filme de) ~** feature (film)

longe ['lõʒi] *adv* far, far away ♦ *adj* distant; **ao ~** in the distance; **de ~** from far away; (*sem dúvida*) by a long way; **~ de** a long way *ou* far from; **~ disso** far from it; **ir ~ demais** (*fig*) to go too far

longínquo/a [lõ'ʒĩkwu/a] *adj* distant, remote

longitude [lõʒi'tudʒi] *f* (*GEO*) longitude

longo/a ['lõgu/a] *adj* long ♦ *m* (*vestido*) long dress, evening dress; **ao ~ de** along, alongside

lontra ['lõtra] *f* otter

loquaz [lo'kwaʒ] *adj* talkative

losango [lo'zãgu] *m* lozenge, diamond

lotação [lota'sãw] *f* capacity; (*de funcionários*) complement; (*BR: ônibus*) bus; **~ completa** *ou* **esgotada** (*TEATRO*) sold out

lotado/a [lo'tadu/a] *adj* (*TEATRO*) full; (*ônibus*) full up; (*bar, praia*) packed, crowded

lotar [lo'ta*] *vt* to fill, pack; (*funcionário*) to place ♦ *vi* to fill up

lote ['lɔtʃi] *m* portion, share; (*em leilão*) lot; (*terreno*) plot; (*de ações*) parcel, batch

loteria [lote'ria] *f* lottery; **~ esportiva** football pools *pl* (*BRIT*), lottery (*US*)

louça ['losa] *f* china; (*conjunto*) crockery; (*tb*: **~ sanitária**) bathroom suite; **de ~ china** *atr*; **~ de barro** earthenware; **~ de jantar** dinner service; **lavar a ~** to do the washing up (*BRIT*) *ou* the dishes

louco/a ['loku/a] *adj* crazy, mad; (*sucesso*) runaway; (*frio*) freezing ♦ *m/f* lunatic; **~ varrido** raving mad; **~ de fome/raiva** ravenous/hopping mad; **~ por** crazy about; **deixar alguém ~** to drive sb crazy; **loucura** [lo'kura] *f* madness; (*ato*) crazy thing; **ser loucura (fazer)** to be crazy (to do); **ser uma loucura** to be crazy; (*col: ser muito bom*) to be fantastic

louro/a ['loru/a] *adj* blond, fair ♦ *m* laurel; (*CULIN*) bay leaf; (*papagaio*) parrot; **~s** *mpl* (*fig*) laurels

louva-a-deus ['lova-] *m inv* praying mantis

louvar [lo'va*] *vt* to praise ♦ *vi*: **~ a** to praise; **louvável** [lo'vavew] (*pl* -eis) *adj* praiseworthy

louvor [lo'vo*] *m* praise

LP *abr m* LP

Ltda. *abr* (= *Limitada*) Ltd (*BRIT*), Inc. (*US*)

lua ['lua] *f* moon; **estar** *ou* **viver no mundo da ~** to have one's head in the clouds; **estar de ~** (*col*) to be in a mood; **ser de ~** (*col*) to be moody; **~ cheia/nova** full/new moon; **~- de-mel** *f* honeymoon

luar ['lwa*] *m* moonlight

lubrificante [lubrifi'kātʃi] *m* lubricant
lubrificar [lubrifi'ka*] *vt* to lubricate
lúcido/a ['lusidu/a] *adj* lucid
lúcio ['lusju] *m* (*peixe*) pike
lucrar [lu'kra*] *vt* (*tirar proveito*) to profit
from *ou* by; (*dinheiro*) to make; (*gozar*)
to enjoy ♦ *vi* to make a profit; ~ **com**
ou **em** to profit by
lucrativo/a [lukra'tʃivu/a] *adj* lucrative,
profitable
lucro ['lukru] *m* gain; (*COM*) profit; ~**s e**
perdas (*COM*) profit and loss
lúdico/a ['ludʒiku/a] *adj* playful
lugar [lu'ga*] *m* place; (*espaço*) space,
room; (*para sentar*) seat; (*emprego*) job;
(*ocasião*) opportunity; **em ~ de** instead
of; **dar ~ a** (*causar*) to give rise to; ~
comum commonplace; **em primeiro ~**
in the first place; **em algum/nenhum/**
todo ~ somewhere/nowhere/
everywhere; **em outro ~** somewhere
else, elsewhere; **ter ~** (*acontecer*) to take
place; ~ **de nascimento** place of birth;
~**ejo** [luga'reʒu] *m* village
lúgubre ['lugubri] *adj* mournful; (*escuro*)
gloomy
lula ['lula] *f* squid
lume ['lumi] *m* fire; (*luz*) light
luminária [lumi'narja] *f* lamp; ~**s** *fpl* (*ilu-*
minações) illuminations
luminosidade [luminozi'dadʒi] *f* brightness
luminoso/a [lumi'nozu/ɔza] *adj* luminous; (*fig: raciocínio*) clear; (: *idéia, ta-*
lento) brilliant; (*letreiro*) illuminated
lunar [lu'na*] *adj* lunar ♦ *m* (*na pele*)
mole
lunático/a [lu'natʃiku/a] *adj* mad
luneta [lu'neta] *f* eye-glass; (*telescópio*)
telescope
lúpulo ['lupulu] *m* (*BOT*) hop
lusitano/a [luzi'tanu/a] *adj* Portuguese,
Lusitanian
luso/a ['luzu/a] *adj* Portuguese; ~**-**
brasileiro/a (*pl* ~**s-brasileiros/as**) *adj*
Luso-Brazilian
lustrar [luʃ'tra*] *vt* to polish, clean; **lus-**
tre ['luʃtri] *m* gloss, sheen; (*fig*) lustre
(*BRIT*), luster (*US*); (*luminária*) chandelier
luta ['luta] *f* fight, struggle; ~ **de boxe**
boxing; ~ **livre** wrestling; ~**dor(a)**
[luta'do*(a)] *m/f* fighter; (*atleta*) wrestler;
~**r** [lu'ta*] *vi* to fight, struggle; (*luta*
livre) to wrestle ♦ *vt* (*caratê, judô*) to
do; ~**r contra/por algo** to fight
against/for sth; ~**r para fazer algo** to
fight *ou* struggle to do sth; ~**r com**
(*dificuldades*) to struggle against; (*compe-*
tir) to fight with
luto ['lutu] *m* mourning; (*tristeza*) grief;
de ~ in mourning; **pôr** ~ to go into
mourning
luva ['luva] *f* glove; ~**s** *fpl* (*pagamento*)
payment *sg*; (*ao locador*) fee *sg*

Luxemburgo [luʃē'buxgu] *m*: **o** ~ Luxembourg
luxo ['luʃu] *m* luxury; **de** ~ luxury *atr*;
dar-se ao ~ **de** to allow o.s. to;
luxuoso/a [lu'ʃwozu/ɔza] *adj* luxurious
luxúria [lu'ʃurja] *f* lust
luxuriante [luʃu'rjātʃi] *adj* lush
luz [luʒ] *f* light; (*eletricidade*) electricity;
à ~ **de** by the light of; (*fig*) in the light
of; **a meia** ~ with subdued lighting;
dar à ~ (**um filho**) to give birth (to a
son); **deu-me uma** ~ I had an idea
luzir [lu'zi*] *vi* to shine, gleam; (*fig*) to be
successful

M

ma [ma] *pron* = **me** + **a**
má [ma] *f de* **mau**
maca ['maka] *f* stretcher
maçã [ma'sã] *f* apple; ~ **do rosto** cheek-
bone
macabro/a [ma'kabru/a] *adj* macabre
macacão [maka'kãw] (*pl* ~**ões**) *m* (*de tra-*
balhador) overalls *pl* (*BRIT*), coveralls *pl*
(*US*); (*da moda*) jump-suit
macaco/a [ma'kaku/a] *m/f* monkey ♦ *m*
(*MECÂNICA*) jack; (**fato**) ~ (*PT*) overalls
pl (*BRIT*), coveralls *pl* (*US*); ~ **velho**
(*fig*) old hand
macacões [maka'kõjʃ] *mpl de* **macacão**
macadame [maka'dami] *m* asphalt, tarmac (*BRIT*)
maçador(a) [masa'do*(a)] (*PT*) *adj* boring
maçaneta [masa'neta] *f* knob
maçante [ma'sãtʃi] (*BR*) *adj* boring
maçarico [masa'riku] *m* blowpipe
maçaroca [masa'rɔka] *f* wad
macarrão [maka'xãw] *m* pasta; (*em for-*
ma de canudo) spaghetti; **macarronada**
[makaxo'nada] *f* pasta with cheese and
tomato sauce
Macau [ma'kaw] *n* Macao
macete [ma'setʃi] *m* mallet
machado [ma'ʃadu] *m* axe (*BRIT*), ax
(*US*)
machê [ma'ʃe] *adj*: **papel** ~ papier-mâché
machete [ma'ʃetʃi] *m* machete
machista [ma'ʃiʃta] *adj* chauvinistic,
macho ♦ *m* male chauvinist
macho ['maʃu] *adj* male; (*fig*) virile,
manly; (*valentão*) tough ♦ *m* male; (*TEC*)
tap
machucado/a [maʃu'kadu/a] *adj* hurt;
(*pé, braço*) bad ♦ *m* injury; (*área machu-*
cada) sore patch
machucar [maʃu'ka*] *vt* to hurt; (*produ-*
zir contusão) to bruise ♦ *vi* to hurt; ~**-**
se *vr* to hurt o.s.
maciço/a [ma'sisu/a] *adj* solid; (*espesso*)
thick; (*quantidade*) massive
macieira [ma'sjejra] *f* apple tree
macilento/a [masi'lētu/a] *adj* gaunt, hag-

gard

macio/a [ma'siu/a] *adj* soft; (*liso*) smooth

maço ['masu] *m* (*de folhas, notas*) bundle; (*de cigarros*) packet

maçom [ma'sõ] (*pl* **-ns**) *m* (free)mason

maconha [ma'kɔɲa] *f* dope; **cigarro de ~** joint

maçons [ma'sõʃ] *mpl de* **maçom**

má-criação (*pl* **-ões**) *f* rudeness; (*ato, dito*) rude thing

mácula ['makula] *f* stain, blemish

macumba [ma'kũba] *f* ≈ voodoo; (*despacho*) macumba offering; **macumbeiro/a** [makũ'bejru/a] *adj* ≈ voodoo *atr* ♦ *m/f* follower of macumba

madama [ma'dama] *f* = **madame**

madame [ma'dami] *f* (*senhora*) lady; (*col: dona-de-casa*) lady of the house

Madeira [ma'dejra] *f:* **a ~** Madeira

madeira [ma'dejra] *f* wood ♦ *m* Madeira (wine); **de ~** wooden; **bater na ~** (*fig*) to touch (*BRIT*) ou knock on (*US*) wood; **~ compensada** plywood

madeirense [madej'rẽsi] *adj, m/f* Madeiran

madeiro [ma'dejru] *m* (*lenho*) log; (*viga*) beam

madeixa [ma'dejʃa] *f* (*de cabelo*) lock

madrasta [ma'draʃta] *f* stepmother

madre ['madri] *f* nun; (*superiora*) mother superior

madrepérola [madre'pɛrola] *f* mother of pearl

madressilva [madre'siwva] *f* honeysuckle

Madri [ma'dri] *n* Madrid

Madrid [ma'drid] (*PT*) *n* Madrid

madrinha [ma'driɲa] *f* godmother

madrugada [madru'gada] *f* (*early*) morning; (*alvorada*) dawn, daybreak

madrugar [madru'ga*] *vi* to get up early; (*aparecer cedo*) to be early

madureza [madu'reza] *f* (*de pessoa*) maturity

maduro/a [ma'duro/a] *adj* ripe; (*fig*) mature; (*: prudente*) prudent

mãe [mãj] *f* mother; **~ adotiva** ou **de criação** adoptive mother

mãe-benta (*pl* **mães-bentas**) *f* (*CULIN*) coconut cookie

maestro/trina [ma'ɛʃtru/'trina] *m/f* conductor

má-fé *f* malicious intent

máfia ['mafja] *f* mafia

magazine [maga'zini] *m* magazine; (*loja*) department store

magia [ma'ʒia] *f* magic

mágica ['maʒika] *f* magic; (*truque*) magic trick; *V tb* **mágico**

mágico/a ['maʒiku/a] *adj* magic ♦ *m/f* magician

magistério [maʒiʃ'tɛrju] *m* (*ensino*) teaching; (*profissão*) teaching profession; (*professorado*) teachers *pl*

magistrado [maʒiʃ'tradu] *m* magistrate

magnata [mag'nata] *m* magnate, tycoon

magnético/a [mag'nɛtʃiku/a] *adj* magnetic

magnífico/a [mag'nifiku/a] *adj* splendid, magnificent

magnitude [magni'tudʒi] *f* magnitude

mago ['magu] *m* magician; **os reis ~s** the Three Wise Men, the Three Kings

mágoa ['magwa] *f* (*tristeza*) sorrow, grief; (*fig: desagrado*) hurt

magoado/a [ma'gwadu/a] *adj* hurt

magoar [ma'gwa*] *vt, vi* to hurt; **~-se** *vr*: **~-se com algo** to be hurt by sth

magro/a ['magru/a] *adj* (*pessoa*) slim; (*carne*) lean; (*fig: parco*) meagre (*BRIT*), meager (*US*); (*leite*) skimmed

maio ['maju] (*PT* **M-**) *m* May

maiô [ma'jo] (*BR*) *m* swimsuit

maionese [majo'nɛzi] *f* mayonnaise

maior [ma'jɔ*] *adj* (*compar: de tamanho*) bigger; (: *de importância*) greater; (*superl: de tamanho*) biggest; (: *de importância*) greatest ♦ *m/f* adult; **~ de idade** of age, adult; **~ de 21 anos** over 21; **~ia** [majo'ria] *f* majority; **a ~ia de** most of; **~idade** [majori'dadʒi] *f* adulthood

PALAVRA CHAVE

mais [majʃ] *adv* **1** (*compar*): **~ magro/ inteligente (do que)** thinner/more intelligent (than); **ele trabalha ~ (do que eu)** he works more (than me)

2 (*superl*): **o ~ ... o ~ ...**; **o ~ magro/inteligente** the thinnest/most intelligent

3 (*negativo*): **ele não trabalha ~ aqui** he doesn't work here any more; **nunca ~** never again

4 (+ *adj: valor intensivo*): **que livro ~ chato!** what a boring book!

5: **por ~ que** however much; **por ~ que se esforce ...** no matter how hard you try ...; **por ~ que eu quisesse ...** much as I should like to ...

6: **a ~**: **temos um a ~** we've got one extra

7 (*tempo*): **~ cedo ou ~ tarde** sooner or later; **a ~ tempo** sooner; **logo ~** later on; **no ~ tardar** at the latest

8 (*frases*): **~ ou menos** more or less; **uma vez ~** once more; **cada vez ~** more and more; **sem ~ nem menos** out of the blue

♦ *adj* **1** (*compar*): **~ (do que)** more (than); **ele tem ~ dinheiro (do que o irmão)** he's got more money (than his brother)

2 (*superl*): **ele é quem tem ~ dinheiro** he's got most money

3 (+ *números*): **ela tem ~ de dez bolsas** she's got more than ten bags

4 (*negativo*): **não tenho ~ dinheiro** I haven't got any more money

5 (*adicional*) else; **~ alguma coisa?** anything else?; **nada/ninguém**

nothing/no-one else
♦ *prep*: **2 ~ 2 são 4** 2 and 2 *ou* plus 2 are 4
♦ *m*: **o ~** the rest

maisena [maj'zena] *f* cornflower
maiúscula [ma'juʃkula] *f* capital letter
majestade [maʒeʃ'tadʒi] *f* majesty;
majestoso/a [maʒeʃ'tozu/ɔza] *adj* majestic
major [ma'ʒɔʰ] *m* (MIL) major
majoritário/a [maʒori'tarju/a] *adj* majority *atr*
mal [maw] (*pl* **~es**) *m* harm; (MED) illness
♦ *adv* badly; (*quase não*) hardly ♦ *conj* hardly; **~ desliguei o fone, a campainha tocou** I had hardly put the phone down when the doorbell rang; **falar ~ de alguém** to speak ill of sb, run sb down; **não faz ~** never mind; **estar ~** (*doente*) to be ill; **passar ~** to be sick; **estar de ~ com alguém** not to be speaking to sb
mal- [mal-] *prefixo* badly
mala [mala] *f* suitcase; (BR: AUTO) boot, trunk (US); **~s** *fpl* (*bagagem*) luggage *sg*; **fazer as ~s** to pack
malabarismo [malaba'riʒmu] *m* juggling;
malabarista [malaba'riʃta] *m/f* juggler
mal-acabado/a *adj* badly finished; (*pessoa*) deformed
malagueta [mala'geta] *f* chilli (BRIT) *ou* chili (US) pepper
Malaísia [mala'izja] *f*: **a ~** Malaysia
malandragem [malã'draʒẽ] *f* (*patifaria*) double-dealing; (*preguiça*) idleness; (*esperteza*) cunning
malandro/a [ma'lãdru/a] *adj* double-dealing; (*preguiçoso*) idle; (*esperto*) wily, cunning ♦ *m/f* crook; idler, layabout; streetwise person
malária [ma'larja] *f* malaria
mal-arrumado/a [-axu'madu/a] *adj* untidy
malbaratar [mawbara'taʰ] *vt* (*dinheiro*) to squander, waste
malcomportado/a [mawkõpox'tadu/a] *adj* badly behaved
malcriado/a [maw'krjadu/a] *adj* rude ♦ *m/f* slob
maldade [maw'dadʒi] *f* cruelty; (*malícia*) malice
maldição [mawdʒi'sãw] (*pl* **-ões**) *f* curse
maldito/a [maw'dʒitu/a] *adj* damned
maldizer [mawdʒi'zeʰ] (*irreg*: *como* **dizer**) *vt* to curse
maldoso/a [maw'dozu/ɔza] *adj* wicked; (*malicioso*) malicious
maledicência [maledʒi'sẽsja] *f* slander
mal-educado/a *adj* rude ♦ *m/f* slob
malefício [male'fisju] *m* harm;
maléfico/a [ma'lɛfiku/a] *adj* (*pessoa*) malicious; (*prejudicial*: *efeito*) harmful, injurious
mal-entendido/a *adj* misunderstood ♦

m misunderstanding
mal-estar *m* indisposition; (*embaraço*) uneasiness
maleta [ma'leta] *f* small suitcase, grip
malevolência [malevo'lẽsja] *f* malice, spite
malfeito/a [mal'fejtu/a] *adj* (*roupa*) poorly made; (*corpo*) misshapen
malfeitor(a) [mawfej'to*(a)] *m/f* wrongdoer
malgastar [mawgaʃ'ta*] *vt* to waste
malha [ma'ʎa] *f* (*de rede*) mesh; (*tecido*) jersey; (*suéter*) sweater; (*de ginástica*) leotard; **fazer ~** (PT) to knit; **artigos de ~** knitwear
malhado/a [ma'ʎadu/a] *adj* mottled; (*roque*) heavy
malhar [ma'ʎa*] *vt* (*bater*) to beat; (*cereais*) to thresh; (*col*: *criticar*) to knock, run down
malharia [maʎa'ria] *f* (*fábrica*) mill; (*artigos de malha*) knitted goods *pl*
malho [ma'ʎu] *m* mallet; (*grande*) sledgehammer
mal-humorado/a [-umo'radu/a] *adj* grumpy, sullen
malícia [ma'lisja] *f* malice; (*astúcia*) slyness; (*esperteza*) cleverness; **malicioso/a** [mali'sjozu/ɔza] *adj* malicious; sly; clever; (*mente suja*) dirty-minded
maligno/a [ma'lignu/a] *adj* evil, malicious; (*danoso*) harmful; (MED) malignant
malograr [malo'gra*] *vt* (*planos*) to upset; (*frustrar*) to thwart, frustrate ♦ *vi* (*planos*) to fall through; (*fracassar*) to fail; **~-se** *vr* to fall through; to fail; **malogro** [ma'logru] *m* failure
malote [ma'lɔtʃi] *m* pouch; (*serviço*) express courier
mal-passado/a *adj* underdone; (*bife*) rare
malsucedido/a [mawsuse'dʒidu/a] *adj* unsuccessful
Malta [mawta] *f* Malta
malta [mawta] (PT) *f* gang, mob
malte [mawtʃi] *m* malt
maltrapilho/a [mawtra'piʎu/a] *adj* in rags, ragged ♦ *m/f* ragamuffin
maltratar [mawtra'ta*] *vt* to ill-treat; (*com palavras*) to abuse; (*estragar*) to ruin, damage
maluco/a [ma'luku/a] *adj* crazy, daft ♦ *m/f* madman/woman
malvadeza [mawva'deza] *f* wickedness; (*ato*) wicked thing
malvado/a [maw'vadu/a] *adj* wicked
Malvinas [maw'vinaʃ] *fpl*: **as (ilhas) ~** the Falklands, the Falkland Islands
mama [mama] *f* breast
mamadeira [mama'dejra] (BR) *f* feeding bottle
mamãe [ma'mãj] *f* mum, mummy
mamão [ma'mãw] (*pl* **-ões**) *m* papaya
mamar [ma'ma*] *vt* to suck; (*dinheiro*) to

extort ♦ *vi* to be breastfed; **dar de ~ a um bebê** to (breast)feed a baby

mamífero [ma'mifɛru] *m* mammal

mamilo [ma'milu] *m* nipple

mamões [ma'mõjʃ] *mpl de* **mamão**

manada [ma'nada] *f* herd, drove

manancial [manã'sjaw] (*pl* **-ais**) *m* spring; (*fig: fonte*) source; (*: abundância*) wealth

mancada [mã'kada] *f* (*erro*) mistake; (*gafe*) blunder; **dar uma ~** to blunder

mancar [mã'ka*] *vt* to cripple ♦ *vi* to limp; **~-se** *vr* (*col*) to get the message, take the hint

mancebo/a [mã'sebu/a] *m/f* young man/woman

Mancha ['mãʃa] *f*: **o canal da ~** the English Channel

mancha ['mãʃa] *f* (*na pele*) mark, spot; **sem ~s** (*reputação*) spotless; **~do/a** [mã'ʃadu/a] *adj* soiled; (*malhado*) mottled, spotted; **~r** [mã'ʃa*] *vt* to stain, mark; (*reputação*) to soil

manchete [mã'ʃetʃi] *f* headline

manco/a ['mãku/a] *adj* crippled, lame ♦ *m/f* cripple

mandado [mã'dadu] *m* order; (*JUR*) writ; (*: tb:* **~ de segurança**) injunction; **~ de prisão/busca** warrant for sb's arrest/ search warrant; **~ de segurança** injunction

mandamento [mãda'mẽtu] *m* order, command; (*REL*) commandment

mandão/dona [mã'dãw/'dɔna] (*pl* **-ões/~s**) *adj* bossy, domineering

mandar [mã'da*] *vt* (*ordenar*) to order; (*enviar*) to send ♦ *vi* to be in charge; **~-se** *vr* (*col: partir*) to make tracks, get going; (*fugir*) to take off; **~ buscar** *ou* **chamar** to send for; **~ fazer um vestido** to have a dress made; **~ que alguém faça**, **~ alguém fazer** to tell sb to do; **o que é que você manda?** (*col*) what can I do for you?; **~ em alguém** to boss sb around

mandato [mã'datu] *m* mandate; (*ordem*) order; (*POL*) term of office

mandíbula [mã'dʒibula] *f* jaw

mandioca [mã'dʒjɔka] *f* cassava, manioc

mando ['mãdu] *m* (*comando*) command; (*poder*) power; **a ~ de** by order of

mandões [mã'dõjʃ] *mpl de* **mandão**

mandona [mã'dɔna] *f de* **mandão**

mandriar [mã'nejru/a] *vi* to idle, loaf about

maneira [ma'nejra] *f* (*modo*) way; (*estilo*) style, manner; **~s** *fpl* (*modas*) manners; **à ~ de** like; **de ~ que** so that; **de ~ alguma** *ou* **nenhuma** not at all; **desta ~** in this way; **de qualquer ~** anyway; **não houve ~ de convencê-lo** it was impossible to convince him

maneiro/a [ma'nejru/a] *adj* (*ferramenta*) easy to use; (*roupa*) attractive; (*trabalho*) easy; (*pessoa*) capable; (*col: bacana*) great, brilliant

manejar [mane'ʒa*] *vt* (*instrumento*) to handle; (*máquina*) to work; **manejável** [mane'ʒavew] (*pl* **-eis**) *adj* manageable; **manejo** [ma'neʒu] *m* handling

manequim [mane'kĩ] (*pl* **-ns**) *m* (*boneco*) dummy ♦ *m/f* model

maneta [ma'neta] *adj* one-handed

manga ['mãga] *f* sleeve; (*fruta*) mango; **em ~s de camisa** in (one's) shirt sleeves

mangue ['mãgi] *m* mangrove swamp; (*planta*) mangrove

mangueira [mã'gejra] *f* hose(pipe); (*árvore*) mango tree

manha ['maɲa] *f* guile, craftiness; (*destreza*) skill; (*ardil*) trick; (*birra*) tantrum; **fazer ~** to have a tantrum

manhã [ma'ɲã] *f* morning; **de** *ou* **pela ~** in the morning; **amanhã/hoje de ~** tomorrow/this morning

manhoso/a [ma'ɲozu/ɔza] *adj* crafty, sly; (*criança*) whining

mania [ma'nia] *f* (*MED*) mania; (*obsessão*) craze; **estar com ~ de ...** to have a thing about ...; **maníaco/a** [ma'niaku/a] *adj* manic ♦ *m/f* maniac

manicômio [mani'komju] *m* asylum, mental hospital

manicura [mani'kura] *f* manicure

manicure [mani'kuri] *f* = **manicura**

manifestação [manifeʃta'sãw] (*pl* **-ões**) *f* show, display; (*expressão*) expression, declaration; (*política*) demonstration

manifestar [manifeʃ'ta*] *vt* to show, display; (*declarar*) to express, declare

manifesto/a [mani'fɛʃtu/a] *adj* obvious, clear ♦ *m* manifesto

manipulação [manipula'sãw] *f* handling; (*fig*) manipulation

manipular [manipu'la*] *vt* to manipulate; (*manejar*) to handle

manivela [mani'vɛla] *f* crank

manjericão [mãʒeri'kãw] *m* basil

manobra [ma'nɔbra] *f* manoeuvre (*BRIT*), maneuver (*US*); (*de mecanismo*) operation; (*de trens*) shunting; **~r** [mano'bra*] *vt* to manoeuvre *ou* maneuver; (*mecanismo*) to operate, work; (*governar*) to take charge of; (*manipular*) to manipulate ♦ *vi* to manoeuvre *ou* maneuver

mansão [mã'sãw] (*pl* **-ões**) *f* mansion

mansidão [mãsi'dãw] *f* gentleness, meekness

manso/a ['mãsu/a] *adj* gentle; (*mar*) calm; (*animal*) tame

mansões [ma'sõjʃ] *fpl de* **mansão**

manta ['mãta] *f* blanket; (*xale*) shawl; (*agasalho*) cloak

manteiga [mã'tejga] *f* butter; **~ de cacau** cocoa butter

manter [mã'te*] (*irreg: como* **ter**) *vt* to maintain; (*num lugar*) to keep; (*uma família*) to support; (*a palavra*) to keep; (*princípios*) to abide by; **~-se** *vr* to support o.s.; (*permanecer*) to remain; **man-**

timento [mãtʃi'mẽtu] *m* maintenance;
mantimentos *mpl* (*alimentos*) provisions
manto ['mãtu] *m* cloak; (*de cerimônia*)
robe
manual [ma'nwaw] (*pl* -**ais**) *adj* manual
♦ *m* handbook, manual
manufatura [manufa'tura] (*PT* -**ct**-) *f* manufacture; **~r** [manufatu'ra*] (*PT* -**ct**-) *vt* to
manufacture
manuscrito/a [manuʃ'kritu/a] *adj* handwritten ♦ *m* manuscript
manusear [manu'zja*] *vt* to handle; (*livro*) to leaf through
manutenção [manutẽ'sãw] *f* maintenance; (*da casa*) upkeep
mão [mãw] (*pl* ~**s**) *f* hand; (*de animal*)
paw; (*de pintura*) coat; (*de direção*) flow
of traffic; **à ~** by hand; (*perto*) at hand;
de segunda ~ second-hand; **em ~** by
hand; **dar a ~ a alguém** to hold sb's
hand; (*cumprimentar*) to shake hands
with sb; **dar uma ~ a alguém** to give
sb a hand, help sb out; **~ única/dupla**
one-way/two-way traffic; **rua de duas
~s** two-way street; **~-de-obra** *f* (*trabalhadores*) labour (*BRIT*), labor (*US*); (*coisa
difícil*) tricky thing
mapa ['mapa] *m* map; (*gráfico*) chart
maquete [ma'kɛtʃi] *f* model
maquiagem [ma'kjaʒẽ] *f* = **maquilagem**
maquiar [ma'kja*] *vt* to make up; **~-se**
vr to make o.s. up, put on one's make-
up
maquilagem [maki'laʒẽ] (*PT* -**lha**-) *f*
make-up; (*ato*) making up
maquilar [makila*] (*PT* -**lha**-) *vt* = **maquiar**
máquina ['makina] *f* machine; (*de trem*)
engine; (*fig*) machinery; **~ de
calcular/costura/escrever** calculator/
sewing machine/typewriter; **~ fotográfica** camera; **~ de filmar** camera;
(*de vídeo*) camcorder; **~ de lavar
(roupa)/pratos** washing machine/
dishwasher; **escrito à ~** typewritten
maquinar [maki'na*] *vt* to plot ♦ *vi* to
conspire
maquinaria [makina'ria] *f* machinery
maquinismo [maki'niʒmu] *m* mechanism; (*máquinas*) machinery
maquinista [maki'niʃta] *m* (*FERRO*) engine driver; (*NAUT*) engineer
mar [ma*] *m* sea; **por ~** by sea; **fazer-se
ao ~** to set sail; **pleno ~, ~ alto** high
sea; **o ~ Morto/Negro/Vermelho** the
Dead/Black/Red Sea
maracujá [maraku'ʒa] *m* passion fruit;
pé de ~ passion flower
maratona [mara'tona] *f* marathon
maravilha [mara'viʎa] *f* marvel, wonder;
maravilhoso/a [maravi'ʎozu/ɔza] *adj*
marvellous (*BRIT*), marvelous (*US*)
marca ['maxka] *f* mark; (*COM*) make,
brand; (*carimbo*) stamp; **~ de fábrica**
trademark; **~ registrada** registered tra-

demark
marcação [maxka'sãw] (*pl* -**ões**) *f* mark-
ing; (*em jogo*) scoring; (*de instrumento*)
reading; (*TEATRO*) action; (*PT*: *TEL*) dialling
marcador [maxka'do*] *m* marker; (*de livro*) bookmark; (*ESPORTE*: *quadro*) scoreboard; (: *jogador*) scorer
marcapasso [maxka'pasu] *m* (*MED*) pace-
maker
marcar [max'ka*] *vt* to mark; (*hora,
data*) to fix, set; (*PT*: *TEL*) to dial; (*gol,
ponto*) to score ♦ *vi* to make one's
mark; **~ uma consulta, ~ hora** to
make an appointment; **~ um encontro
com alguém** to arrange to meet sb
marcha ['maxʃa] *f* march; (*de acontecimentos*) course; (*passo*) pace; (*AUTO*)
gear; (*progresso*) progress; **~ à ré** (*BR*),
~ atrás (*PT*) reverse (gear); **pôr-se em
~** to set off
marchar [max'ʃa*] *vi* to go; (*andar a pé*)
to walk; (*MIL*) to march
marcial [max'sjaw] (*pl* -**ais**) *adj* martial;
corte ~ court martial
marco ['maxku] *m* landmark; (*de janela*)
frame; (*fig*) frontier; (*moeda*) mark
março ['maxsu] (*PT* **M**-) *m* March
maré [ma'rɛ] *f* tide
marechal [mare'ʃaw] (*pl* -**ais**) *m* marshal
maremoto [mare'mɔtu] *m* tidal wave
marfim [max'fĩ] *m* ivory
margarida [maxga'rida] *f* daisy; (*COMPUT*)
daisy wheel
margarina [maxga'rina] *f* margarine
margem ['maxʒẽ] (*pl* -**ns**) *f* (*borda*) edge;
(*de rio*) bank; (*litoral*) shore; (*de impresso*) margin; (*fig: tempo*) time; (: *lugar*)
space; **à ~ de** alongside
marginal [maxʒi'naw] (*pl* -**ais**) *adj* marginal ♦ *m/f* delinquent
marido [ma'ridu] *m* husband
marimbondo [marĩ'bõdu] *m* hornet
marinha [ma'riɲa] *f* (*tb*: **~ de guerra**)
navy; **~ mercante** merchant navy; **marinheiro** [mari'ɲejru] *m* seaman, sailor
marinho/a [ma'riɲu/a] *adj* sea *atr*, marine
marionete [marjo'netʃi] *f* puppet
mariposa [mari'poza] *f* moth
marisco [ma'riʃku] *m* shellfish
marital [mari'taw] (*pl* -**ais**) *adj* marital
marítimo/a [ma'ritʃimu/a] *adj* sea *atr*
marketing ['maxketʃĩ] *m* marketing
marmelada [maxme'lada] *f* quince jam
marmelo [max'mɛlu] *m* quince
marmita [max'mita] *f* (*vasilha*) pot
mármore ['maxmori] *m* marble
marquês/quesa [max'keʃ/'keza] *m/f*
marquis/marchioness
marquise [max'kizi] *f* awning, canopy
marreco [ma'xɛku] *m* duck
Marrocos [ma'xɔkuʃ] *m*: **o ~** Morocco
marrom [ma'xõ] (*pl* -**ns**) *adj*, *m* brown
martelar [maxte'la*] *vt* to hammer; (*amo-

lar) to bother ♦ *vi* to hammer; (*insistir*): ~ **(em algo)** to keep *ou* harp on (about sth); **martelo** [maxˈtɛlu] *m* hammer

mártir [ˈmaxtʃiˈ] *m/f* martyr; **martírio** [maxˈtʃirju] *m* martyrdom; (*fig*) torment

marxista [maxˈksiʃta] *adj, m/f* Marxist

marzipã [maxziˈpã] *m* marzipan

mas [ma(j)ʃ] *conj* but ♦ *pron* = **me** + **as**

mascar [maʃˈkaˈ] *vt* to chew

máscara [ˈmaʃkara] *f* mask; (*para limpeza de pele*) face pack; **sob a ~ de** under the guise of; **mascarar** [maʃkaˈraˈ] *vt* to mask; (*disfarçar*) to disguise; (*encobrir*) to cover up

mascavo/a [maʃˈkavu/a] *adj*: **açúcar ~** brown sugar

mascote [maʃˈkɔtʃi] *f* mascot

masculino/a [maʃkuˈlinu/a] *adj* masculine; (*BIO*) male

masoquista [mazoˈkiʃta] *m/f* masochist

massa [ˈmasa] *f* (*FIS, fig*) mass; (*de tomate*) paste; (*CULIN: de pão*) dough; (: *macarrão etc*) pasta

massacrar [masaˈkraˈ] *vt* to massacre; **massacre** [maˈsakri] *f* massacre

massagear [masaˈʒjaˈ] *vt* to massage; **massagem** [maˈsaʒẽ] (*pl* -ns) *f* massage

mastigar [maʃtʃiˈgaˈ] *vt* to chew

mastro [ˈmaʃtru] *m* (*NÁUT*) mast; (*para bandeira*) flagpole

masturbar-se [maʃtuxˈbaxsiˈ] *vr* to masturbate

mata [ˈmata] *f* forest, wood

matadouro [mataˈdoru] *m* slaughterhouse

matagal [mataˈgaw] (*pl* -ais) *m* bush; (*brenha*) thicket, undergrowth

matança [maˈtãsa] *f* massacre; (*de reses*) slaughter(ing)

matar [maˈtaˈ] *vt* to kill; (*sede*) to quench; (*fome*) to satisfy; (*aula*) to skip; (*trabalho: não aparecer*) to skive off; (: *fazer rápido*) to dash off; (*adivinhar*) to guess ♦ *vi* to kill; **~se** *vr* to kill o.s.; (*esfalfar-se*) to wear o.s. out; **um calor/ uma dor de** ~ stifling heat/ excruciating pain

mate [ˈmatʃi] *adj* matt ♦ *m* (*chá*) maté tea; (*xeque*~) checkmate

matemática [mateˈmatʃika] *f* mathematics *sg*, maths *sg* (*BRIT*), math (*US*); **matemático/a** [mateˈmatʃiku/a] *adj* mathematical ♦ *m/f* mathematician

matéria [maˈtɛrja] *f* matter; (*TEC*) material; (*EDUC*: *assunto*) subject; (*tema*) topic; (*jornalística*) story, article; **em ~ de** on the subject of

material [mateˈrjaw] (*pl* -ais) *adj* material; (*físico*) physical ♦ *m* material; (*TEC*) equipment; **~ista** [materjaˈliʃta] *adj* materialistic; **~izar** [materjaliˈzaˈ] *vt* to materialize; **~izar-se** *vr* to materialize

matéria-prima (*pl* **matérias-primas**) *f* raw material

maternal [matexˈnaw] (*pl* -ais) *adj*

motherly, maternal; **escola** ~ nursery (school); **maternidade** [matexniˈdadʒi] *f* motherhood, maternity; (*hospital*) maternity hospital

materno/a [maˈtɛxnu/a] *adj* motherly, maternal; (*língua*) native

matinê [matʃiˈne] *f* matinée

matiz [maˈtʃiʒ] *m* (*de cor*) shade; **~ar** [matʃiˈzaˈ] *vt* to colour (*BRIT*), color (*US*); (*combinar cores*) to blend

mato [ˈmatu] *m* scrubland, bush; (*plantas agrestes*) scrub; (*o campo*) country

matraca [maˈtraka] *f* rattle

matrícula [maˈtrikula] *f* (*lista*) register; (*inscrição*) registration; (*pagamento*) enrolment (*BRIT*) *ou* enrollment (*US*) fee; (*PT: AUTO*) registration number (*BRIT*), license number (*US*); **fazer a ~** to enrol (*BRIT*), enroll (*US*); **matricular** [matrikuˈlaˈ] *vt* to enrol (*BRIT*), enroll (*US*), register; **matricular-se** *vr* to enrol(l), register

matrimonial [matrimoˈnjawˈ] (*pl* -ais) *adj* marriage *atr*, matrimonial

matrimônio [matriˈmonju] *m* marriage

matriz [maˈtriʒ] *f* (*MED*) womb; (*fonte*) source; (*molde*) mould (*BRIT*), mold (*US*); (*COM*) head office

matrona [maˈtrɔna] *f* matron

maturidade [maturiˈdadʒi] *f* maturity

mau/má [maw/ma] *adj* bad; (*malvado*) evil, wicked ♦ *m* bad; (*REL*) evil; **os ~s** *mpl* (*pessoas*) bad people; (*num filme*) the baddies

mausoléu [mawzoˈlɛw] *m* mausoleum

maus-tratos [mawsˈtratus] *mpl* ill-treatment *sg*

maxila [makˈsila] *f* jawbone

maxilar [maksiˈlaˈ] *m* jawbone

máxima [ˈmasima] *f* maxim

máximo/a [ˈmasimu/a] *adj* (*maior que todos*) greatest; (*o maior possível*) maximum ♦ *m* maximum; (*o cúmulo*) peak; (*temperature*) high; **no ~** at most; **ao ~** to the utmost

MCE *abr m* = **Mercado Comum Europeu**

me [mi] *pron* (*direto*) me; (*indireto*) (to) me; (*reflexivo*) (to) myself

meado [ˈmjadu] *m* middle; **em ~s** *ou* **no(s)** ~**(s) de julho** in mid-July

Meca [ˈmɛka] *n* Mecca

mecânica [meˈkanika] *f* (*ciência*) mechanics *sg*; (*mecanismo*) mechanism; *V tb* **mecânico**

mecânico/a [meˈkaniku/a] *adj* mechanical ♦ *m/f* mechanic

mecanismo [mekaˈniʒmu] *m* mechanism

mecha [ˈmeʃa] *f* (*de vela*) wick; (*de cabelo*) tuft; (*no cabelo*) highlight; (*MED*) swab; **fazer ~ no cabelo** to put highlights in one's hair, to highlight one's hair

meço *etc* [ˈmɛsu] *vb V* **medir**

medalha [meˈdaʎa] *f* medal; **medalhão** [medaˈʎãw] (*pl* -ões) *m* medallion

média ['mɛdʒja] f average; (café) coffee with milk; **em ~** on average

mediano/a [me'dʒjanu/a] adj medium; (médio) average; (mediocre) mediocre

mediante [me'dʒjãtʃi] prep by (means of), through; (a troco de) in return for

medicação [medʒika'sãw] (pl -ões) f treatment; (medicamentos) medication

medicamento [medʒika'mẽtu] m medicine

medicar [medʒi'ka*] vt to treat; **~-se** vr to take medicine

medicina [medʒi'sina] f medicine

médico/a ['mɛdʒiku/a] adj medical ♦ m/f doctor; **receita médica** prescription

medida [me'dʒida] f measure; (providência) step; (medição) measurement; (moderação) prudence; **à ~ que** while, as; **na ~ em que** in so far as; **feito sob ~** made to measure; **ir além da ~** to go too far; **tirar as ~s de alguém** to take sb's measurements; **tomar ~s** to take steps; **tomar as ~s de** to measure

medieval [medʒje'vaw] (pl -ais) adj medieval

médio/a ['mɛdʒju/a] adj (dedo, classe) middle; (tamanho, estatura) medium; (mediano) average; **ensino ~** secondary education

mediocre [me'dʒiɔkri] adj mediocre

medir [me'dʒi*] vt to measure; (atos, palavras) to weigh; (avaliar: conseqüências, distâncias) to weigh up ♦ vi to measure; **quanto você mede?** — **meço 1.60 m** how tall are you? — I'm 1.60 m (tall)

meditar [medʒi'ta*] vi to meditate; **~ sobre algo** to ponder (on) sth

mediterrâneo/a [medʒite'xanju/a] adj Mediterranean ♦ m: **o M~** the Mediterranean

médium ['mɛdʒjũ] (pl -ns) m (pessoa) medium

medo ['medu] m fear; **com ~** afraid; **meter ~ em alguém** to frighten sb; **ter ~ de** to be afraid of

medonho/a [me'doɲu/a] adj terrible, awful

medroso/a [me'drozu/ɔza] adj (com medo) frightened; (tímido) timid

medula [me'dula] f marrow

megabyte [mega'bajtʃi] m megabyte

meia ['meja] f stocking; (curta) sock; (meia-entrada) half-price ticket ♦ num six; **~-calça** (pl **~s-calças**) f tights pl (BRIT), panty hose (US); **~-idade** f middle age; **pessoa de ~-idade** middle-aged person; **~-noite** f midnight

meigo/a ['mejgu/a] adj sweet

meio/a ['meju/a] adj half ♦ adv a bit, rather ♦ m middle; (social, profissional) milieu; (tb: **~ ambiente**) environment; (maneira) way; (recursos: tb: **~s**) means pl; **~ quilo** half a kilo; **um mês e ~** one and a half months; **cortar ao ~** to cut in half; **dividir algo ~ a ~** to divide sth in half ou fifty-fifty; **em ~ a** amid; **no ~ (de)** in the middle (of); **~s de comunicação (de massa)** (mass) media pl; **por ~ de** through; **~-dia** m midday, noon; **~-fio** m kerb (BRIT), curb (US); **~-termo** (pl **~s-termos**) m (fig) compromise

mel [mɛw] m honey

melaço [me'lasu] m treacle (BRIT), molasses pl (US)

melado/a [me'ladu/a] adj (pegajoso) sticky ♦ m = **melaço**

melancia [melã'sia] f watermelon

melancolia [melãko'lia] f melancholy, sadness; **melancólico/a** [melã'kɔliku/a] adj melancholy, sad

melão [me'lãw] (pl -ões) m melon

melhor [me'ʎɔ*] adj, adv (compar) better; (superl) best; **~ que nunca** better than ever; **quanto mais ~** the more the better; **seria ~ começarmos** we had better begin; **tanto ~** so much the better; **ou ~ ...** (ou antes) or rather ...; **~a** [me'ʎɔra] f improvement; **~as!** get well soon!; **~amento** [me'ʎɔra'mẽtu] m improvement; **~ar** [me'ʎɔ'ra*] vt to improve, make better; (doente) to cure ♦ vi to improve, get better

melindrar [melĩ'dra*] vt to offend, hurt; **~-se** vr to take offence (BRIT) ou offense (US), be hurt

melindroso/a [melĩ'drozu/ɔza] adj sensitive, touchy; (problema, situação) tricky; (operação) delicate

melodia [melo'dʒia] f melody; (composição) tune

melodrama [melo'drama] m melodrama

melões [me'lõjʃ] mpl de **melão**

melro ['mɛwxu] m blackbird

membro ['mẽbru] m member; (ANAT: braço, perna) limb

memorando [memo'rãdu] m (aviso) note; (COM: comunicação) memorandum

memória [me'mɔrja] f memory; **~s** fpl (de autor) memoirs; **de ~** by heart

memorial [memo'rjaw] (pl -ais) m memorial

memorizar [memori'za*] vt to memorize

menção [mẽ'sãw] (pl -ões) f mention, reference; **fazer ~ de algo** to mention sth; **mencionar** [mẽsjo'na*] vt to mention

mendigar [mẽdʒi'ga*] vt to beg for ♦ vi to beg; **mendigo/a** [mẽ'dʒigu/a] m/f beggar

menear [me'nja*] vt (corpo, cabeça) to shake; **~ a cabeça de modo afirmativo** to nod (one's head)

menina [me'nina] f: **~ do olho** pupil; **ser a ~ dos olhos de alguém** (fig) to be the apple of sb's eye; V tb **menino**

meninada [meni'nada] f kids pl

meningite [menĩ'ʒitʃi] f meningitis

menino/a [me'ninu/a] m/f boy/girl

menopausa [menoˈpawza] *f* menopause
menor [meˈnɔʳ] *adj* (*mais pequeno: comparar*) smaller; (: *superl*) smallest; (*mais jovem: comparar*) younger; (: *superl*) youngest; (*o mínimo*) least, slightest; (*tb:* ~ **de idade**) under age ♦ *m/f* juvenile, young person; (*JUR*) minor; **não tenho a ~ idéia** I haven't the slightest idea

PALAVRA CHAVE

menos [ˈmenuʃ] *adj* **1** (*comparar*): ~ (**do que**) (*quantidade*) less (than); (*número*) fewer (than); **com ~ entusiasmo** with less enthusiasm; ~ **gente** fewer people **2** (*superl*) least; **é o que tem ~ culpa** he is the least to blame

♦ *adv* **1** (*comparar*): ~ (**do que**) less (than); **gostei ~ do que do outro** I liked it less than the other one

2 (*superl*): **é o ~ inteligente da classe** he is the least bright in his class; **de todas elas é a que ~ me agrada** out of all of them she's the one I like least; **pelo ~** at (the very) least

3 (*frases*): **temos sete a ~** we are seven; **não é para ~** it's no wonder; **isso é o de ~** that's nothing

♦ *prep* (*exceção*) except; (*números*) minus; **todos ~ eu** everyone except (for) me; **5 ~ 2** 5 minus 2

♦ *conj*: **a ~ que** unless; **a ~ que ele venha amanhã** unless he comes tomorrow

♦ *m*: **o ~** the least

menosprezar [menuʃpreˈzaʳ] *vt* (*subestimar*) to underrate; (*desprezar*) to despise, scorn; **menosprezo** [menuʃˈprezu] *m* contempt, disdain
mensageiro/a [mẽsaˈʒejru/a] *m/f* messenger
mensagem [mẽˈsaʒẽ] (*pl* **-ns**) *f* message
mensal [mẽˈsaw] (*pl* **-ais**) *adj* monthly; **ele ganha £1000 mensais** he earns £1000 a month; **~idade** [mẽsaliˈdadʒi] *f* monthly payment; **~mente** [mẽsawˈmẽtʃi] *adv* monthly
menstruação [mẽʃtrwaˈsãw] *f* period; (*MED*) menstruation
menta [ˈmẽta] *f* mint
mental [mẽˈtaw] (*pl* **-ais**) *adj* mental; **~idade** [mẽtaliˈdadʒi] *f* mentality
mente [ˈmẽtʃi] *f* mind; **de boa ~** willingly; **ter em ~** to bear in mind
mentir [mẽˈtʃiʳ] *vi* to lie
mentira [mẽˈtʃira] *f* lie; (*ato*) lying; **parece ~ que** it seems incredible that; **de ~** not for real; **~!** (*acusação*) that's a lie!, you're lying; (*de surpresa*) you don't say!, no!; **mentiroso/a** [mẽtʃiˈrozu/ɔza] *adj* lying ♦ *m/f* liar
menu [meˈnu] *m* (*tb: COMPUT*) menu
mercado [mexˈkadu] *m* market; **M~ Comum** Common Market; **~ negro** *ou* **paralelo** black market

mercadoria [mexkadoˈria] *f* commodity; **~s** *fpl* (*produtos*) goods
mercearia [mexsjaˈria] *f* grocer's (shop) (*BRIT*), grocery store
mercenário/a [mexseˈnarju/a] *adj* mercenary ♦ *m* mercenary
mercúrio [mexˈkurju] *m* mercury
merda [ˈmexda] (*col!*) *f* shit (!) ♦ *m/f* (*pessoa*) jerk; **a ~ do carro** the bloody (*BRIT!*) *ou* goddamn (*US!*) car
merecer [mereˈseʳ] *vt* to deserve; (*consideração*) to merit; (*valer*) to be worth ♦ *vi* to be worthy; **merecido/a** [mereˈsidu/a] *adj* deserved; (*castigo, prêmio*) just
merenda [meˈrẽda] *f* packed lunch
merengue [meˈrẽgi] *m* meringue
mergulhador(a) [mexguʎaˈdo(a)] *m/f* diver
mergulhar [mexguˈʎaʳ] *vi* to dive; (*penetrar*) to plunge ♦ *vt*: ~ **algo em algo** (*num líquido*) to dip sth into sth; (*na terra etc*) to plunge sth into sth; **mergulho** [mexˈguʎu] *m* dip(ping), immersion; (*em natação*) dive; **dar um mergulho** (*na praia*) to go for a dip
meridional [meridʒjoˈnaw] (*pl* **-ais**) *adj* southern
mérito [ˈmeritu] *m* merit
merluza [mexˈluza] *f* hake
mero/a [ˈmɛru/a] *adj* mere
mês [meʃ] *m* month
mesa [ˈmeza] *f* table; (*de trabalho*) desk; (*comitê*) board; (*numa reunião*) panel; **pôr/tirar a ~** to lay/clear the table; **à ~** at the table; **~ de toalete** dressing table; **~ telefônica** switchboard
mesada [meˈzada] *f* monthly allowance; (*de criança*) pocket money
mesa-de-cabeceira (*pl* **mesas-de-cabeceira**) *f* bedside table
mescla [ˈmeʃkla] *f* mixture, blend; **~r** [meʃˈklaʳ] *vt* to mix (up); (*cores*) to blend
meseta [meˈzeta] *f* plateau, tableland
mesmo/a [ˈmeʒmu/a] *adj* same; (*enfático*) very ♦ *adv* (*exatamente*) right; (*até*) even; (*realmente*) really ♦ *m/f*: **o ~/a** the same (one); **o ~** (*a mesma coisa*) the same (thing); **este ~ homem** this very man; **ele ~ o fez** he did it himself; **dá no ~** *ou* **na mesma** it's all the same; **aqui/agora/hoje ~** right here/right now/this very day; ~ **que** even if; **é ~ ? is it true?**; **é ~?** really?; **(é) isso ~!** exactly!; **por isso ~** that's why; **nem ~** not even; **só ~** only; **por si ~** by oneself
mesquinho/a [meʃˈkiɲu/a] *adj* mean
mesquita [meʃˈkita] *f* mosque
mestiço/a [meʃˈtʃisu/a] *adj* half-caste, of mixed race; (*animal*) crossbred ♦ *m/f* half-caste; crossbreed
mestre/a [ˈmɛʃtri/a] *adj* (*chave, viga*) master; (*linha, estrada*) main ♦ *m/f* master/mistress; (*professor*) teacher;

obra mestra masterpiece; **~-de-cerimônias** (pl **~s-de-cerimônias**) *m* master of ceremonies, MC; **mestria** [meʃ'tria] *f* mastery; (habilidade) expertise; **com mestria** to perfection

mesura [me'zura] *f* (cumprimento) bow; (cortesia) courtesy

meta ['mɛta] *f* (em corrida) finishing post; (gol) goal; (objetivo) aim

metabolismo [metabo'liʒmu] *m* metabolism

metade [me'tadʒi] *f* half; (meio) middle

metáfora [me'tafora] *f* metaphor

metal [me'taw] (pl **-ais**) *m* metal; **metais** *mpl* (MÚS) brass *sg*; **metálico/a** [me'taliku/a] *adj* metallic; (de metal) metal *atr*

metalurgia [metalux'ʒia] *f* metallurgy; **metalúrgica** [meta'luxʒika] *f* metalworks *sg*; **metalúrgico/a** [meta'luxʒiku/a] *m/f* metalworker

meteorito [meteo'ritu] *m* meteorite

meteoro [me'tʒoru] *m* meteor

meteorologia [meteorolo'ʒia] *f* meteorology; **meteorologista** [meteorolo'ʒiʃta] *m/f* meteorologist; (TV, RÁDIO) weather forecaster

meter [me'te*] *vt* (colocar) to put; (envolver) to involve; (introduzir) to introduce; **~-se** *vr* (esconder-se) to hide; **~-se a fazer algo** to decide to have a go at sth; **~-se com** (provocar) to pick a quarrel with; (associar-se) to get involved with; **~-se em** to get involved in; (intrometer-se) to interfere in

meticuloso/a [metʃiku'lozu/ɔza] *adj* meticulous

metido/a [me'tʃidu/a] *adj* (envolvido) involved; (intrometido) meddling; **~ (a besta)** snobbish

metódico/a [me'tɔdʒiku/a] *adj* methodical

metodista [meto'dʒiʃta] *adj, m/f* Methodist

método ['mɛtodu] *m* method

metragem [me'traʒẽ] *f* length (in metres (BRIT) ou meters (US)); (CINEMA) footage, length; **filme de longa/curta** ~ feature ou full-length/short film

metralhadora [metraʎa'dora] *f* submachine gun

métrico/a [me'mɛtriku/a] *adj* metric

metro ['mɛtru] *m* metre (BRIT), meter (US); (PT) = **metrô**

metrô [me'tro] (BR) *m* underground (BRIT), subway (US)

metrópole [me'trɔpoli] *f* metropolis; (capital) capital

meu/minha [mew/'miɲa] *adj* my ♦ *pron* mine; **os** ~**s** *mpl* (minha família) my family ou folks (col); **um amigo** ~ a friend of mine

mexer [me'ʃe*] *vt* to move; (cabeça: dizendo sim) to nod; (: dizendo não) to shake; (misturar) to stir; (ovos) to

scramble ♦ *vi* to move; **~-se** *vr* to move; (apressar-se) to get a move on; **~ em algo** to touch sth; **mexa-se!** get going!, move yourself!

mexerica [meʃe'rika] *f* tangerine

mexerico [meʃe'riku] *m* piece of gossip; **~s** *mpl* (fofocas) gossip *sg*

México ['mɛʃiku] *m*: **o** ~ Mexico

mexido/a [me'ʃidu/a] *adj* (papéis) mixed up; (ovos) scrambled

mexilhão [meʃi'ʎãw] (pl **-ões**) *m* mussel

mi [mi] *m* (MÚS) E

miar [mja*] *vi* to miaow; (vento) to whistle

miau [mjaw] *m* miaow

micro... [mikru] *prefixo* micro...; **~(computador)** [mikro(kõputa'do*)] *m* micro(computer); **~filme** [mikro'fiwmi] *m* microfilm; **~fone** [mikro'fɔni] *m* microphone; **~ondas** [mikro'õdaʃ] *m inv* (tb: **forno de ~ondas**) microwave (oven); **~ônibus** [mikro'onibuʃ] *m inv* minibus; **~plaqueta** [mikropla'keta] *f* microchip; **~plaqueta de silicone** silicon chip; **~processador** [mikroprosesa'do*] *m* microprocessor; **~scópio** [mikro'ʃkopju] *m* microscope

mídia ['midʒia] *f* media *pl*

migalha [mi'gaʎa] *f* crumb; **~s** *fpl* (restos, sobras) scraps

migrar [mi'gra*] *vi* to migrate

mijar [mi'ʒa*] (col) *vi* to pee; **~-se** *vr* to wet o.s.

mil [miw] *num* thousand; **dois** ~ two thousand

milagre [mi'lagri] *m* miracle; **por** ~ miraculously; **milagroso/a** [mila'grozu/ɔza] *adj* miraculous

milha ['miʎa] *f* mile

milhão [mi'ʎãw] (pl **-ões**) *m* million; **um** ~ **de vezes** hundreds of times

milhar [mi'ʎa*] *m* thousand; **turistas aos ~es** tourists in their thousands

milho ['miʎu] *m* maize (BRIT), corn (US)

milhões [mi'ʎõjʃ] *mpl* de **milhão**

milícia [mi'lisja] *f* militia

miligrama [mili'grama] *m* milligram(me)

milionário/a [miljo'narju/a] *m/f* millionaire

militante [mili'tãtʃi] *adj* militant ♦ *m/f* activist; (extremista) militant

militar [mili'ta*] *adj* military ♦ *m* soldier ♦ *vi* to fight; ~ **em** (MIL: regimento) to serve in; (POL: partido) to belong to, be active in; (profissão) to work in

mim [mĩ] *pron* me; (reflexivo) myself; **de** ~ **para** ~ to myself

mimar [mi'ma*] *vt* to pamper, spoil

mímica ['mimika] *f* mime

mimo ['mimu] *m* gift; (pessoa, coisa encantadora) delight; (carinho) tenderness; (gentileza) kindness; **cheio de ~s** (criança) spoiled, spoilt (BRIT); **~so/a** [mi'mozu/ɔza] *adj* (delicado) delicate; (carinhoso) tender, loving; (encantador) delightful

mina ['mina] f mine; **~r** [mi'na*] vt to mine; (fig) to undermine

mindinho [mī'dʒiɲu] m (tb: **dedo ~**) little finger

mineiro/a [mi'nejru/a] adj mining atr ♦ m/f miner

mineração [minera'sãw] f mining

mineral [mine'raw] (pl **-ais**) adj, m mineral

minerar [mine'ra*] vt, vi to mine

minério [mi'nɛrju] m ore

míngua ['mĩgwa] f lack; **à ~ de** for want cf; **viver à ~** to live in poverty; **minguado/a** [mĩ'gwadu/a] adj scant; (criança) stunted; **minguado de algo** short of sth

minguar [mĩ'gwa*] vi (diminuir) to decrease, dwindle; (faltar) to run short

minha ['miɲa] f de **meu**

minhoca [mi'ɲɔka] f (earth)worm

mini... [mini] prefixo mini...

miniatura [minja'tura] adj, f miniature

mínima ['minima] f (temperatura) low; (MÚS) minim

mínimo/a ['minimu/a] adj minimum ♦ m minimum; (tb: **dedo ~**) little finger; **não dou ou ligo a mínima para isso** I couldn't care less about it; **a mínima importância/idéia** the slightest importance/idea; **no ~** at least

minissaia [mini'saja] f miniskirt

ministério [minis'tɛrju] m ministry; **~ da Fazenda** ≈ Treasury (BRIT), ≈ Treasury Department (US); **M~ das Relações Exteriores** ≈ Foreign Office (BRIT), ≈ State Department (US)

ministro/a [mi'nistru/a] m/f minister

minoria [mino'ria] f minority; **minoritário/a** [minori'tarju/a] adj minority atr

minto etc ['mĩtu] vb V **mentir**

minúcia [mi'nusja] f detail; **minucioso/a** [minu'sjozu/ɔza] adj (indivíduo, busca) thorough; (explicação) detailed

minúsculo/a [mi'nuʃkulu/a] adj minute, tiny; **letra minúscula** lower case

minuta [mi'nuta] f rough draft

minuto [mi'nutu] m minute

miolo ['mjolu] m inside; (polpa) pulp; (de maçã) core; **~s** mpl (cérebro, inteligência) brains

míope ['miopi] adj short-sighted

mira ['mira] f (de fuzil) sight; (pontaria) aim; (fig) aim, purpose; **à ~ de** on the lookout for; **ter em ~** to have one's eye on

mirada [mi'rada] f look

miragem [mi'raʒẽ] (pl **-ns**) f mirage

mirar [mi'ra*] vt to look at; (observar) to watch; (apontar para) to aim at ♦ vi: **~ em** to aim at; **~ para** to look onto

miscelânea [mise'lanja] f miscellany; (confusão) muddle

miserável [mize'ravew] (pl **-eis**) adj (dig-

no de compaixão) wretched; (pobre) impoverished; (avaro) stingy, mean; (insignificante) paltry; (lugar) squalid; (infame) despicable ♦ m wretch; (coitado) poor thing; (pessoa infame) rotter

miséria [mi'zɛrja] f misery; (pobreza) poverty; (avareza) stinginess

misericórdia [mizeri'kɔxdʒja] f (compaixão) pity, compassion; (graça) mercy

missa ['misa] f (REL) mass

missão [mi'sãw] (pl **-ões**) f mission; (dever) duty

misse ['misi] f beauty queen

míssil ['misiw] (pl **-eis**) m missile

missionário/a [misjo'narju/a] m/f missionary

missões [mi'sõjʃ] fpl de **missão**

mistério [miʃ'tɛrju] m mystery; **misterioso/a** [miʃte'rjozu/ɔza] adj mysterious

mistificar [miʃtʃifi'ka*] vt, vi to fool

misto/a ['miʃtu/a] adj mixed; (confuso) mixed up ♦ m mixture; **~-quente** (pl **~s-quentes**) m toasted cheese and ham sandwich

mistura [miʃ'tura] f mixture; (ato) mixing; **~da** [miʃu'rada] f jumble; **~r** [miʃtu'ra*] vt to mix; (confundir) to mix up; **~r-se** vr: **~r-se com** to mingle with

mitigar [mitʃi'ga*] vt (raiva) to temper; (dor) to relieve; (sede) to lessen

mito ['mitu] m myth

miudezas [mju'dezaʃ] fpl minutiae; (bugigangas) odds and ends; (objetos pequenos) trinkets

miúdo/a [mi'judu/a] adj tiny, minute ♦ m/f (PT: criança) youngster, kid; **~s** mpl (dinheiro) change sg; (de aves) giblets; **dinheiro ~** small change

mm abr (= milímetro) mm

mo [mu] pron = **me + o**

moa etc ['moa] vb V **moer**

móbil ['mɔbiw] (pl **-eis**) adj = **móvel**; **mobilar** [mobi'la*] (PT) vt to furnish

móbile ['mɔbili] m mobile

mobília [mo'bilja] f furniture; **mobiliar** [mobi'lja*] (BR) vt to furnish; **mobiliário** [mobi'ljarju] m furnishings pl

moça ['mosa] f girl, young woman

Moçambique [mosã'biki] m Mozambique

moção [mo'sãw] (pl **-ões**) f motion

mochila [mo'ʃila] f rucksack

mocidade [mosi'dadʒi] f youth; (os moços) young people pl

moço/a [mo'su/a] adj young ♦ m young man, lad

moções [mo'sõjʃ] fpl de **moção**

moda ['mɔda] f fashion; **estar na ~** to be in fashion, be all the rage; **fora da ~** old-fashioned; **sair da ou cair de ~** to go out of fashion

modalidade [modali'dadʒi] f kind; (ESPORTE) event

modelar [mode'la*] vt to model

modelo [mo'delu] m model; (criação de

estilista) design

moderado/a [mode'radu/a] *adj* moderate; (*clima*) mild

moderar [mode'ra*] *vt* to moderate; (*violência*) to control, restrain; (*velocidade*) to reduce; (*voz*) to lower; (*gastos*) to cut down

modernizar [modexni'za*] *vt* to modernize; ~-se *vr* to modernize

moderno/a [mo'dɛxnu/a] *adj* modern; (*atual*) present-day

modéstia [mo'dɛʃtʃja] *f* modesty

modesto/a [mo'dɛʃtu/a] *adj* modest; (*simples*) simple, plain; (*vida*) frugal

módico/a [ˈmɔdʒiku/a] *adj* moderate; (*preço*) reasonable; (*bens*) scant

modificar [modʒifi'ka*] *vt* to modify, alter

modista [mo'dʒiʃta] *f* dressmaker

modo [ˈmɔdu] *m* (*maneira*) way, manner; (*método*) way; (*MÚS*) mode; ~s *mpl* (*comportamento*) manners; **de (tal) ~ que** so (that); **de ~ nenhum** in no way; **de qualquer ~** anyway, anyhow; **~ de emprego** instructions *pl* for use

modorra [mo'doxa] *f* (*sonolência*) drowsiness; (*letargia*) lethargy

módulo [ˈmɔdulu] *m* module

moeda [ˈmwɛda] *f* (*uma* ~) coin; (*dinheiro*) currency; **uma ~ de 10p a 10p** piece; **~ corrente** currency; **Casa da M~** ≈ the Mint (*BRIT*), ≈ the (*US*) Mint

moedor [moe'do*] *m* (*de café*) grinder; (*de carne*) mincer

moer [mwe*] *vt* (*café*) to grind; (*cana*) to crush

mofado/a [mo'fadu/a] *adj* mouldy (*BRIT*), moldy (*US*)

mofar [mo'fa*] *vi* to go mouldy (*BRIT*) ou moldy (*US*); (*ficar esperando*) to hang around; (*zombar*) to mock, scoff; **mofo** [ˈmofu] *m* (*BOT*) mo(u)ld; **cheiro de mofo** musty smell

mogno [ˈmɔgnu] *m* mahogany

mói *etc* [ˈmɔj] *vb* V **moer**

moía *etc* [mo'ia] *vb* V **moer**

moído/a [mo'idu/a] *adj* (*café*) ground; (*carne*) minced; (*cansado*) tired out; (*corpo*) aching

moinho [ˈmwiɲu] *m* mill; (*de café*) grinder; **~ de vento** windmill

moisés [moj'zɛʃ] *m inv* carry-cot

moita [ˈmɔjta] *f* thicket; **na ~** (*fig*) on the quiet

mola [ˈmɔla] *f* (*TEC*) spring; (*fig*) motive, motivation

molar [mo'la*] *m* molar (tooth)

moldar [mow'da*] *vt* to mould (*BRIT*), mold (*US*); (*metal*) to cast; **molde** [ˈmɔwdʒi] *m* mo(u)ld; (*de papel*) pattern; (*fig*) model; **molde de vestido** dress pattern

moldura [mow'dura] *f* (*de pintura*) frame

mole [ˈmɔli] *adj* soft; (*sem energia*) list-

less; (*carnes*) flabby; (*col: fácil*) easy; (*lento*) slow; (*preguiçoso*) sluggish ♦ *adv* (*lentamente*) slowly

molécula [mo'lɛkula] *f* molecule

moleque [mo'lɛki] *m* (*de rua*) urchin; (*menino*) youngster; (*pessoa sem palavra*) unreliable person; (*canalha*) scoundrel ♦ *adj* (*levado*) mischievous; (*brincalhão*) funny

molestar [moleʃ'ta*] *vt* to upset; (*enfadar*) to annoy; (*importunar*) to bother

moléstia [mo'lɛʃtʃja] *f* illness

moleza [mo'leza] *f* softness; (*falta de energia*) listlessness; (*falta de força*) weakness; **ser (uma) ~** (*col*) to be easy; **na ~** without exerting oneself

molhado/a [mo'ʎadu/a] *adj* wet, damp

molhar [mo'ʎa*] *vt* to wet; (*de leve*) to moisten, dampen; (*mergulhar*) to dip; **~-se** *vr* to get wet

molho¹ [ˈmɔʎu] *m* (*de chaves*) bunch; (*de trigo*) sheaf

molho² [ˈmoʎu] *m* (*CULIN*) sauce; (: *de salada*) dressing; (: *de carne*) gravy; **pôr de ~** to soak; **estar/deixar de ~** (*roupa etc*) to be/leave to soak

molinete [moli'netʃi] *m* reel; (*caniço*) fishing rod

momentâneo/a [momē'tanju/a] *adj* momentary

momento [mo'mētu] *m* moment; (*TEC*) momentum; **a todo ~** constantly; **de um ~ para outro** suddenly; **no ~ em que** just as

Mônaco [ˈmonaku] *m* Monaco

monarca [mo'naxka] *m/f* monarch; **monarquia** [monax'kia] *f* monarchy

monastério [monaʃ'tɛrju] *m* monastery

monção [mõ'sãw] (*pl* -ões) *f* monsoon

monetário/a [mone'tarju/a] *adj* monetary

monge [ˈmõʒi] *m* monk

monitor [moni'to*] *m* monitor

monja [ˈmõʒa] *f* nun

monopólio [mono'pɔlju] *m* monopoly; **monopolizar** [monopoli'za*] *vt* to monopolize

monotonia [monoto'nia] *f* monotony; **monótono/a** [mo'nɔtonu/a] *adj* monotonous

monóxido [mo'nɔksidu] *m*: **~ de carbono** carbon monoxide

monstro/a [ˈmõʃtru/a] *adj inv* giant ♦ *m* (*tb fig*) monster; **monstruoso/a** [mõʃtrwozu/ɔza] *adj* monstrous; (*enorme*) gigantic, huge

montagem [mõ'taʒē] (*pl* -ns) *f* assembly; (*ARQ*) erection; (*CINEMA*) editing; (*TEATRO*) production

montanha [mõ'taɲa] *f* mountain; **~-russa** *f* roller coaster; **montanhismo** [mõta'ɲiʒmu] *m* mountaineering; **montanhoso/a** [mõta'ɲozu/ɔza] *adj* mountainous

montante [mõ'tãtʃi] *m* amount, sum; **a ~** (*nadar*) upstream

montar [mõ'ta*] vt (cavalo) to mount, get on; (colocar em) to put on; (cavalgar) to ride; (peças) to assemble, put together; (loja, máquina) to set up; (casa) to put up; (peça teatral) to put on ♦ vi to ride; ~ a ou em (animal) to get on; (cavalgar) to ride; (despesa) to come to

monte [mõtʃi] m hill; (pilha) heap, pile; um ~ de (muitos) a lot of, lots of; gente aos ~s loads of people

montra ['mõtra] (PT) f shop window

monumental [monumẽ'taw] (pl -ais) adj monumental; (fig) magnificent, splendid

monumento [monu'mẽtu] m monument

moqueca [mo'keka] f fish or seafood simmered in coconut cream and palm oil; ~ de camarão prawn moqueca

morada [mo'rada] f home, residence; (PT: endereço) address; **moradia** [mora'dʒia] f home, dwelling; **morador(a)** [mora'do*(a)] m/f resident; (de casa alugada) tenant

moral [mo'raw] (pl -ais) adj moral ♦ f (ética) ethics pl; (conclusão) moral ♦ m (de pessoa) sense of morality; (ânimo) morale; ~idade [morali'dadʒi] f morality

morango [mo'rãgu] m strawberry

morar [mo'ra*] vi to live, reside

mórbido/a ['mɔxbidu/a] adj morbid

morcego [mox'segu] m (BIO) bat

mordaça [mox'dasa] f (de animal) muzzle; (fig) gag

mordaz [mox'daʒ] adj scathing

morder [mox'de*] vt to bite; (corroer) to corrode; **mordida** [mox'dʒida] f bite

mordomia [moxdo'mia] f (de executivos) perk; (col: regalia) luxury, comfort

mordomo [mox'dɔmu] m butler

moreno/a [mo'renu/a] adj dark(-skinned); (de cabelos) dark(-haired); (de tomar sol) brown ♦ m/f dark person

morfina [mox'fina] f morphine

moribundo/a [mori'būdu/a] adj dying

mormaço [mox'masu] m sultry weather

mórmon ['mɔxmõ] m/f Mormon

morno/a ['mɔxnu/'mɔxna] adj lukewarm, tepid

morrer [mo'xe*] vi to die; (luz, cor) to fade; (fogo) to die down; (AUTO) to stall

morro ['moxu] m hill; (favela) slum

mortadela [moxta'dɛla] f salami

mortal [mox'taw] (pl -ais) adj mortal; (letal, insuportável) deadly ♦ m mortal

mortalha [mox'taʎa] f shroud

mortalidade [moxtali'dadʒi] f mortality

morte ['mɔxtʃi] f death

morteiro [mox'tejru] m mortar

mortífero/a [mox'tʃiferu/a] adj deadly, lethal

morto/a ['mɔxtu/'mɔxta] pp de **matar** ♦ pp de **morrer** ♦ adj dead; (cor) dull; (exausto) exhausted; (inexpressivo) lifeless ♦ m/f dead man/woman; **estar/ser** ~ to be dead/killed; **estar** ~ **de inveja** to be green with envy; **estar** ~ **de vontade**

de to be dying to

mos [muʃ] pron = **me** + **os**

mosca ['moʃka] f fly; **estar às** ~s (bar etc) to be deserted

Moscou [moʃ'ku] (BR) n Moscow

Moscovo [moʃ'kovu] (PT) n Moscow

mosquiteiro [moʃki'tejru] m mosquito net

mosquito [moʃ'kitu] m mosquito

mostarda [moʃ'taxda] f mustard

mosteiro [moʃ'tejru] m monastery; (de monjas) convent

mostra ['mɔʃtra] f (exibição) display; (sinal) sign, indication; **dar** ~s **de** to show signs of

mostrador [moʃtra'do*] m (de relógio) face, dial

mostrar [moʃ'tra*] vt to show; (mercadorias) to display; (provar) to demonstrate, prove; ~-se vr to show o.s. to be; (exibir-se) to show off

mote ['mɔtʃi] m motto

motel [mo'tɛw] (pl -éis) m motel

motim [mo'tʃĩ] (pl -ns) m riot, revolt; (militar) mutiny

motivar [motʃi'va*] vt (causar) to cause, bring about; (estimular) to motivate; **motivo** [mo'tʃivu] m (causa): **motivo** (de ou para) cause (of), reason (for); (fim) motive; (ARTE, MÚS) motif; **por motivo de** because of, owing to

moto ['mɔtu] f motorbike ♦ m (lema) motto

motoca [mo'tɔka] (col) f motorbike, bike

motocicleta [motosi'kleta] f motorcycle, motorbike

motociclista [motosi'kliʃta] m/f motorcyclist

motociclo [moto'siklu] (PT) m = **motocicleta**

motoneta [moto'neta] f (motor-) scooter

motor/motriz [mo'to*/mo'triʒ] adj: **força motriz** driving force ♦ m motor; (de carro, avião) engine; ~ **diesel/de explosão** diesel/internal combustion engine

motorista [moto'riʃta] m/f driver

motriz [mo'triʒ] f de **motor**

movediço/a [move'dʒisu/a] adj easily moved; (instável) unsteady

móvel ['mɔvew] (pl -eis) adj movable ♦ m piece of furniture; **móveis** mpl (mobília) furniture sg

mover [mo've*] vt to move; (cabeça) to shake; (mecanismo) to drive; (campanha) to start (up); ~-se vr to move

movimentado/a [movimẽ'tadu/a] adj (rua, lugar) busy; (pessoa) active; (show, música) up-tempo

movimentar [movimẽ'ta*] vt to move; (animar) to liven up

movimento [movi'mẽtu] m movement; (TEC) motion; (na rua) activity, bustle; **de muito** ~ busy

muamba ['mwãba] (col) f (contrabando) contraband; (objetos roubados) loot

muco ['muku] *m* mucus

muçulmano/a [musuw'manu/a] *adj, m/f* Moslem

muda ['muda] *f* (*planta*) seedling; (*vestuário*) outfit; ~ **de roupa** change of clothes

mudança [mu'dãsa] *f* change; (*de casa*) move; (*AUTO*) gear

mudar [mu'da*] *vt* to change; (*deslocar*) to move ♦ *vi* to change; (*ave*) to moult (*BRIT*), molt (*US*); ~**-se** *vr* (*de casa*) to move (away); ~ **de roupa/de assunto** to change clothes/the subject; ~ **de casa** to move (house); ~ **de idéia** to change one's mind

mudez [mu'deʒ] *f* muteness; (*silêncio*) silence

mudo/a ['mudu/a] *adj* dumb; (*calado, CINEMA*) silent; (*telefone*) dead ♦ *m/f* mute

mugir [mu'ʒi*] *vi* (*vaca*) to moo

PALAVRA CHAVE
---

muito/a ['mwĩtu/a] *adj* (*quantidade*) a lot of; (: *em frase negativa ou interrogativa*) much; (*número*) lots of, a lot of; many; ~ **esforço** a lot of effort; **faz ~ calor** it's very hot; ~ **tempo** a long time; **muitas amigas** lots *ou* a lot of friends; **muitas vezes** often

♦ *pron* a lot; (*em frase negativa ou interrogativa*: *sg*) much; (: *pl*) many; **tenho ~ que fazer** I've got a lot to do; ~**s dizem que ...** a lot of people say that ...

♦ *adv* **1** a lot; (+ *adj*) very; (+ *compar*): ~ **melhor** much *ou* far *ou* a lot better; **gosto ~ disto** I like it a lot; **sinto ~** I'm very sorry; ~ **interessante** very interesting

2 (*resposta*) very; **está cansado? - ~** are you tired? - very

3 (*tempo*): ~ **depois** long after; **há ~** a long time ago; **não demorou ~** it didn't take long

---

mula ['mula] *f* mule

mulato/a [mu'latu/a] *adj, m/f* mulatto

muleta [mu'leta] *f* crutch; (*fig*) support

mulher [mu'ʎe*] *f* woman; (*esposa*) wife

multa ['muwta] *f* fine; **levar uma ~** to be fined; ~**r** [muw'ta*] *vt* to fine; ~**r alguém em $1000** to fine sb $1000

multi... [muwtʃi] *prefixo* multi...

multidão [muwtʃi'dãw] (*pl* -**ões**) *f* crowd; **uma ~ de** (*muitos*) lots of

multinacional [muwtʃinasjo'naw] (*pl* -**ais**) *adj, f* multinational

multiplicar [muwtʃipli'ka*] *vt* to multiply; (*aumentar*) to increase

múltiplo/a ['muwtʃiplu/a] *adj* multiple ♦ *m* multiple

múmia ['mumja] *f* mummy

mundial [mũ'dʒjaw] (*pl* -**ais**) *adj* worldwide; (*guerra, recorde*) world *atr* ♦ *m* world championship

mundo ['mũdu] *m* world; **todo o ~** everybody; **um ~ de** lots of, a great many

munição [muni'sãw] (*pl* -**ões**) *f* (*de armas*) ammunition; (*chumbo*) shot; (*MIL*) munitions *pl*, supplies *pl*

municipal [munisi'paw] (*pl* -**ais**) *adj* municipal

município [muni'sipju] *m* local authority; (*cidade*) town; (*condado*) county

munições [muni'sõjʃ] *fpl de* **munição**

munir [mu'ni*] *vt*: ~ **de** to provide with, supply with; ~**-se** *vr*: ~**-se de** (*provisões*) to equip o.s. with

mural [mu'raw] (*pl* -**ais**) *adj, m* mural

muralha [mu'raʎa] *f* (*de fortaleza*) rampart; (*muro*) wall

murchar [mux'ʃa*] *vt* (*BOT*) to wither; (*sentimentos*) to dull; (*pessoa*) to sadden ♦ *vi* to wither, wilt; (*fig*) to fade

murmurar [muxmu'ra*] *vi* to murmur, whisper; (*queixar-se*) to mutter, grumble; (*água*) to ripple; (*folhagem*) to rustle ♦ *vt* to murmur; **murmúrio** [mux'murju] *m* murmuring, whispering; grumbling; rippling; rustling

muro ['muru] *m* wall

murro ['muxu] *m* punch; **dar um ~ em alguém** to punch sb

musa ['muza] *f* muse

musculação [muʃkula'sãw] *f* bodybuilding

músculo ['muʃkulu] *m* muscle; **musculoso/a** [muʃku'lozu/ɔza] *adj* muscular

museu [mu'zew] *m* museum; (*de pintura*) gallery

musgo ['muʒgu] *m* moss

música ['muzika] *f* music; (*canção*) song; **músico/a** ['muziku/a] *adj* musical ♦ *m/f* musician

musselina [muse'lina] *f* muslin

mutilar [mutʃi'la*] *vt* to mutilate; (*pessoa*) to maim; (*texto*) to cut

mútuo/a ['mutwu/a] *adj* mutual

N

N *abr* (= *norte*) N

na [na] = **em** + **a**

-na [na] *pron* her; (*coisa*) it

nabo ['nabu] *m* turnip

nação [na'sãw] (*pl* -**ões**) *f* nation

nácar ['naka*] *m* mother-of-pearl

nacional [nasjo'naw] (*pl* -**ais**) *adj* national; (*carro, vinho etc*) domestic, home-produced; ~**idade** [nasjonali'dadʒi] *f* nationality; ~**ismo** [nasjona'liʒmu] *m* nationalism; ~**ista** [nasjona'liʃta] *adj, m/f* nationalist; ~**izar** [nasjonali'za*] *vt* to nationalize

nações [na'sõjʃ] *fpl de* **nação**

nada ['nada] *pron* nothing ♦ *adv* at all; **antes de mais ~** first of all; **não é ~**

difícil it's not at all hard, it's not hard at all; ~ **mais** nothing else; ~ **de novo** nothing new; **obrigado — de ~** thank you — not at all *ou* don't mention it
nadadeira [nadaˈdejra] *f (de peixe)* fin; *(de golfinho, foca, mergulhador)* flipper
nadador(a) [nadaˈdo*(a)] *m/f* swimmer
nadar [naˈda*] *vi* to swim
nádegas [ˈnadegaʃ] *fpl* buttocks
nado [ˈnadu] *m*: **atravessar a ~** to swim across; ~ **borboleta/de costas/de peito** butterfly (stroke)/backstroke/breaststroke
náilon [ˈnajlõ] *m* nylon
naipe [ˈnajpi] *m (cartas)* suit
namorado/a [namoˈradu/a] *m/f* boyfriend/girlfriend
namorar [namoˈra*] *vt (ser namorado de)* to be going out with
namoro [naˈmoru] *m* relationship
não [nãw] *adv* not; *(resposta)* no ♦ *m* no; ~ **sei** I don't know; ~ **muito** not much; ~ **só ... mas também** not only ... but also; **agora** ~ not now; ~ **tem de quê** don't mention it; ~ **é?** isn't it?, won't you? *(etc, segundo o verbo precedente)*; **eles são brasileiros,** ~ **é?** they're Brazilian, aren't they?
não- [nãw-] *prefixo* non-
naquele(s)/a(s) [naˈkeli(ʃ)/na'kɛla(ʃ)] = **em + aquele(s)/a(s)**
naquilo [naˈkilu] = **em + aquilo**
narciso [naxˈsizu] *m (BOT)*: ~ **dos prados** daffodil
narcótico/a [naxˈkɔtʃiku/a] *adj* narcotic ♦ *m* narcotic
narina [naˈrina] *f* nostril
nariz [naˈriʒ] *m* nose
narração [naxaˈsãw] *(pl -ões) f* narration; *(relato)* account; **narrador(a)** [naxaˈdo*(a)] *m/f* narrator
narrar [naˈxa*] *vt* to narrate
narrativa [naxaˈtʃiva] *f* narrative; *(história)* story
nas [naʃ] = **em + as**
-nas [naʃ] *pron* them
nascença [naˈsẽsa] *f* birth; **de ~** by birth; **ele é surdo de ~** he was born deaf
nascente [naˈsẽtʃi] *m*: **o ~** the East, the Orient ♦ *f (fonte)* spring
nascer [naˈse*] *vi* to be born; *(plantas)* to sprout; *(o sol)* to rise; *(ave)* to hatch; *(fig: ter origem)* to come into being ♦ *m*: ~ **do sol** sunrise; **ele nasceu para médico** *etc* he's a born doctor *etc*; **nascimento** [nasiˈmẽtu] *m* birth; *(fig)* origin; *(estirpe)* descent
nata [ˈnata] *f* cream
natação [nataˈsãw] *f* swimming
natais [naˈtajʃ] *adj pl de* **natal**
Natal [naˈtaw] *m* Christmas; **Feliz ~!** Merry Christmas!
natal [naˈtaw] *(pl -ais) adj (relativo ao nascimento)* natal; *(país)* native; **cidade**

~ **home town;** ~**idade** [natali'daʒi] *f*: **(índice de)** ~**idade** birth rate
natalino/a [nataˈlinu/a] *adj* Christmas *atr*
nativo/a [naˈtʃivu/a] *adj, m/f* native
natural [natuˈraw] *(pl -ais) adj* natural; *(nativo)* native ♦ *m/f* native; **ao ~** *(CULIN)* fresh, uncooked; ~**idade** [naturali'daʒi] *f* naturalness; **de ~idade paulista** *etc* born in São Paulo *etc*; ~**izar** [naturaliˈza*] *vt* to naturalize; ~**izar-se** *vr* to become naturalized; ~**mente** [naˈturawˈmẽtʃi] *adv* naturally; ~**mente!** of course!
natureza [natuˈreza] *f* nature; *(espécie)* kind, type
nau [naw] *f (literário)* ship
naufragar [nawfraˈga*] *vi (navio)* to be wrecked; *(marinheiro)* to be shipwrecked; **naufrágio** [nawˈfraʒu] *m* shipwreck; **náufrago/a** [ˈnawfragu/a] *m/f* castaway
náusea [ˈnawzea] *f* nausea; **dar ~s a alguém** to make sb feel sick; **sentir ~s** to feel sick; **nausear** [nawˈzja*] *vt* to nauseate, sicken
náutica [ˈnawtʃika] *f* seamanship
náutico/a [ˈnawtʃiku/a] *adj* nautical
naval [naˈvaw] *(pl -ais) adj* naval; **construção** ~ shipbuilding
navalha [naˈvaʎa] *f (de barba)* razor; *(faca)* knife
nave [ˈnavi] *f (de igreja)* nave
navegação [navegaˈsãw] *f* navigation, sailing; ~ **aérea** air traffic; **companhia de** ~ shipping line
navegar [naveˈga*] *vt* to navigate; *(mares)* to sail ♦ *vi* to sail; *(dirigir o rumo)* to navigate
navio [naˈviu] *m* ship; ~ **aeródromo/ cargueiro/petroleiro** aircraft carrier/ cargo ship/oil tanker; ~ **de guerra** *(BR)* battleship
nazi [naˈzi] *(PT) adj, m/f* = **nazista**
nazista [naˈziʃta] *adj, m/f* Nazi
NB *abr* (= *note bem*) NB
neblina [neˈblina] *f* fog, mist
nebuloso/a [nebuˈlozu/za] *adj* foggy, misty; *(céu)* cloudy; *(fig)* vague
necessário/a [neseˈsarju/a] *adj* necessary ♦ *m*: **o** ~ the necessities *pl*
necessidade [nesesiˈdadʒi] *f* need, necessity; *(o que se necessita)* need; *(pobreza)* poverty, need; **ter** ~ **de** to need; **em caso de** ~ if need be
necessitado/a [nesesiˈtadu/a] *adj* needy, poor; ~ **de** in need of
necessitar [nesesiˈta*] *vt* to need, require ♦ *vi*: ~ **de** to need
necrotério [nekroˈtɛrju] *m* mortuary, morgue *(US)*
neerlandês/esa [neexlãˈdeʃ/eza] *adj* Dutch ♦ *m/f* Dutchman/woman
Neerlândia [neexˈlãdʒa] *f* the Netherlands *pl*
nefasto/a [neˈfaʃtu/a] *adj (de mau*

agouro) ominous; (*trágico*) tragic

negar [ne'ga*] *vt* to deny; (*recusar*) to refuse; **~-se** *vr*: **~-se a** to refuse to

negativa [nega'tiiva] *f* negative; (*recusa*) denial

negativo/a [nega'tʃivu/a] *adj* negative ♦ *m* (*TEC, FOTO*) negative ♦ *excl* (*col*) nope!

negligência [negli'ʒẽsja] *f* negligence, carelessness; **negligente** [negli'ʒẽtʃi] *adj* negligent, careless

negociação [negosja'sãw] (*pl* –ões) *f* negotiation

negociante [nego'sjãtʃi] *m/f* businessman/woman

negociar [nego'sja*] *vt* to negotiate; (*COM*) to trade ♦ *vi*: **~ (com)** to trade *ou* deal (in); to negotiate (with); **negociável** [nego'sjavew] (*pl* –eis) *adj* negotiable

negócio [ne'gɔsju] *m* (*COM*) business; (*transação*) deal; (*questão*) matter; (*col*: *troço*) thing; (*assunto*) affair, business; **homem de ~s** businessman; **a ~s** on business; **fechar um ~** to make a deal

negro/a ['negru/a] *adj* black; (*raça*) Black; (*fig*: *lúgubre*) black, gloomy ♦ *m/f* Black man/woman

nele(s)/a(s) ['neli(ʃ)/'nɛla(ʃ)] = **em + ele(s)/a(s)**

nem [nẽj] *conj* nor, neither; **~ (sequer)** not even; **~ que** even if; **~ bem** hardly; **~ um só** not a single one; **~ estuda ~ trabalha** he neither studies nor works; **~ eu** nor me; **sem ~** without even; **~ todos** not all; **~ tanto** not so much; **~ sempre** not always

nenê [ne'ne] *m/f* baby

neném [ne'nẽj] (*pl* –ns) *m/f* = **nenê**

nenhum(a) [ne'nũ/'numa] *adj* no, not any ♦ *pron* (*nem um só*) none, not one; (*de dois*) neither; **~ lugar** nowhere

neozelandês/esa [neozela'deʃ/deza] *adj* New Zealand *atr* ♦ *m/f* New Zealander

nervo ['nexvu] *m* (*ANAT*) nerve; (*fig*) energy, strength; (*em carne*) sinew; **~sismo** [nexvo'ziʒmu] *m* (*nervosidade*) nervousness; (*irritabilidade*) irritability; **~so** [nex'vozu/ɔza] *adj* nervous; (*irritável*) touchy, on edge; (*exaltado*) worked up; **isso/ele me deixa ~so** he gets on my nerves

nervura [nex'vura] *f* rib; (*BOT*) vein

nesse(s)/a(s) ['nesi(ʃ)/'nɛsa(ʃ)] = **em + esse(s)/a(s)**

neste(s)/a(s) ['neʃtʃi(ʃ)/'nɛʃta(ʃ)] = **em + este(s)/a(s)**

neto/a ['nɛtu/a] *m/f* grandson/daughter; **~s** *mpl* grandchildren

neurose [new'rɔzi] *f* neurosis; **neurótico/a** [new'rɔtʃiku/a] *adj*, *m/f* neurotic

neutralizar [newtrali'za*] *vt* to neutralize; (*anular*) to counteract

neutro/a ['newtru/a] *adj* (*LING*) neuter; (*imparcial*) neutral

nevada [ne'vada] *f* snowfall

nevado/a [ne'vadu/a] *adj* snow-covered; (*branco*) snow-white

nevar [ne'va*] *vi* to snow; **nevasca** [ne'vaʃka] *f* snowstorm; **neve** [ˈnɛvi] *f* snow

névoa [ˈnɛvoa] *f* fog; **nevoeiro** [nevo'ejru] *m* thick fog

nexo ['nɛksu] *m* connection, link; **sem ~** disconnected, incoherent

Nicarágua [nika'ragwa] *f*: **a ~** Nicaragua

nicotina [niko'tʃina] *f* nicotine

Nigéria [ni'ʒɛrja] *f*: **a ~** Nigeria

Nilo ['nilu] *m*: **o ~** the Nile

ninguém [nĩ'gẽj] *pron* nobody, no-one

ninho ['niɲu] *m* nest; (*toca*) lair; (*lar*) home

níquel ['nikew] *m* nickel

nisso ['nisu] = **em + isso**

nisto ['niʃtu] = **em + isto**

nitidez [nitʃi'deʒ] *f* (*clareza*) clarity; (*brilho*) brightness; (*imagem*) sharpness

nítido/a ['nitʃidu/a] *adj* clear, distinct; (*brilhante*) bright; (*imagem*) sharp, clear

nitrogênio [nitro'ʒenju] *m* nitrogen

nível ['nivew] (*pl* –eis) *m* level; (*fig*: *padrão*) standard; (: *ponto*) point, pitch; **~ de vida** standard of living; **nivelar** [nive'la*] *vt* (*terreno etc*) to level ♦ *vi*: **nivelar com** to be level with; **nivelar-se** *vr*: **nivelar-se com** to be equal to

no [nu] = **em + o**

-no [nu] *pron* him; (*coisa*) it

nº *abr* (= *número*) no

nó [nɔ] *m* knot; (*de uma questão*) crux; **~s dos dedos** knuckles; **dar um ~** to tie a knot

nobre ['nɔbri] *adj*, *m/f* noble; **horário ~** prime time; **~za** [no'breza] *f* nobility

noção [no'sãw] (*pl* –ões) *f* notion; **noções** *fpl* (*rudimentos*) rudiments, basics; **~ vaga** inkling; **não ter a menor ~ de algo** not to have the slightest idea about sth

nocaute [no'kawtʃi] *m* knockout ♦ *adv*: **pôr alguém ~** to knock sb out

nocivo/a [no'sivu/a] *adj* harmful

noções [no'sõjʃ] *fpl de* **noção**

nocturno/a [no'tuxnu/a] (*PT*) *adj* = **noturno**

nódoa ['nɔdwa] *f* spot; (*mancha*) stain

nogueira [no'gejra] *f* (*árvore*) walnut tree; (*madeira*) walnut

noite ['nojtʃi] *f* night; **à ou de ~** at night, in the evening; **boa ~** good evening; (*despedida*) good night; **da ~ para o dia** overnight; **tarde da ~** late at night

noivado [noj'vadu] *m* engagement

noivo/a ['nojvu/a] *m/f* (*prometido*) fiancé(e); (*no casamento*) bridegroom/bride; **os ~s** *mpl* (*prometidos*) the engaged couple; (*no casamento*) the bride and groom; (*recém-casados*) the newlyweds

nojento/a [no'ʒẽtu/a] *adj* disgusting

nojo ['noʒu] *m* nausea; *(repulsão)* disgust, loathing; **ela é um ~** she's horrible; **este trabalho está um ~** this work is messy

no-la(s) = nos + a(s)

no-lo(s) = nos + o(s)

nômade ['nomadʒi] *m/f* nomad

nome ['nɔmi] *m* name; *(fama)* fame; **de ~ by** name; **escritor de ~** famous writer; **um restaurante de ~** a restaurant with a good reputation; **em ~ de** in the name of; **~ de batismo** Christian name

nomeação [nomja'sãw] *(pl -ões)* *f* nomination; *(para um cargo)* appointment

nomeada [no'mjada] *f* fame

nomear [no'mja*] *vt* to nominate; *(conferir um cargo a)* to appoint; *(dar nome a)* to name

nominal [nomi'naw] *(pl -ais)* *adj* nominal

nono/a ['nɔnu/a] *num* ninth

nora ['nɔra] *f* daughter-in-law

nordeste [nox'dɛʃtʃi] *m, adj* northeast

norma ['nɔxma] *f* standard, norm; *(regra)* rule; **como ~** as a rule

normal [nox'maw] *(pl -ais)* *adj* normal; *(habitual)* usual; **~izar** [noxmali'za*] *vt* to bring back to normal; **~izar-se** *vr* to return to normal

noroeste [nor'wɛʃtʃi] *adj* northwest, northwestern ♦ *m* northwest

norte ['nɔxtʃi] *adj* northern, north; *(vento, direção)* northerly ♦ *m* north; **~americano/a** *adj, m/f* (North) American

Noruega [nor'wega] *f* Norway; **norueguês/esa** [norwe'geʃ/geza] *adj, m/f* Norwegian ♦ *m (LING)* Norwegian

nos [nuʃ] *pron* = em + os *pron (direto)* us; *(indireto)* us, to us, for us; *(reflexivo)* (to) ourselves; *(recíproco)* (to) each other

-nos [nuʃ] *pron* them

nós [nɔʃ] *pron* we; *(depois de prep)* us; **~ mesmos** we ourselves

nosso/a ['nɔsu/a] *adj* our ♦ *pron* ours; **um amigo ~** a friend of ours; **Nossa Senhora** *(REL)* Our Lady

nostalgia [noʃtaw'ʒia] *f* nostalgia; *(saudades da pátria etc)* homesickness; **nostálgico/a** [noʃ'tawʒiku/a] *adj* nostalgic; homesick

nota ['nɔta] *f* note; *(EDUC)* mark; *(conta)* bill; *(cédula)* banknote; **~ de venda** sales receipt; **~ fiscal** receipt

notar [no'ta*] *vt* to notice, note; **~-se** *vr* to be obvious; **fazer ~** to call attention to; **notável** [no'tavew] *(pl -eis)* *adj* notable, remarkable

notícia [no'tʃisja] *f (uma ~)* piece of news; *(TV etc)* news item; **~s** *fpl (informações)* news *sg;* **pedir ~s de** to inquire about; **ter ~s de** to hear from; **noticiário** [notʃi'sjarju] *m (de jornal)* news section; *(CINEMA)* newsreel; *(TV,*

RÁDIO) news bulletin

notificar [notʃifi'ka*] *vt* to notify, inform

notoriedade [notorje'dadʒi] *f* renown, fame

notório/a [no'tɔrju/a] *adj* well-known

noturno/a [no'tuxnu/a] *adj* nocturnal, nightly; *(trabalho)* night *atr* ♦ *m (trem)* night train

nova ['nɔva] *f* piece of news; **~s** *fpl (novidades)* news *sg*

novamente [nova'mẽtʃi] *adv* again

novato/a [no'vatu/a] *adj* inexperienced, raw ♦ *m/f* beginner, novice; *(EDUC)* fresher

nove ['nɔvi] *num* nine

novela [no'vɛla] *f* short novel, novella; *(RÁDIO, TV)* soap opera

novelo [no'velu] *m* ball of thread

novembro [no'vẽbru] *(PT N-)* *m* November

noventa [no'vẽta] *num* ninety

noviço/a [no'visu/a] *m/f* novice

novidade [novi'dadʒi] *f* novelty; *(notícia)* piece of news; **~s** *fpl (notícias)* news *sg;* **~iro/a** [novida'dejru/a] *adj* chatty ♦ *m/f* gossip

novilho/a [no'viʎu/a] *m/f* young bull/heifer

novo/a ['novu/'nɔva] *adj* new; *(jovem)* young; *(adicional)* further; **de ~** again

noz [nɔʒ] *f* nut; *(da nogueira)* walnut; **~ moscada** nutmeg

nu(a) [nu/'nua] *adj* naked; *(arvore, sala, parede)* bare ♦ *m* nude

nublado/a [nu'bladu/a] *adj* cloudy, overcast

nublar [nu'bla*] *vt* to darken; **~-se** *vr* to cloud over

nuca ['nuka] *f* nape (of the neck)

nuclear [nu'klja*] *adj* nuclear

núcleo ['nuklju] *m* nucleus *sg;* *(centro)* centre *(BRIT)*, center *(US)*

nudez [nu'deʒ] *f* nakedness, nudity; *(de paredes etc)* bareness

nudista [nu'dʒiʃta] *adj, m/f* nudist

nulo/a ['nulu/a] *adj (JUR)* null, void; *(nenhum)* non-existent; *(sem valor)* worthless; *(esforço)* vain, useless

num [nũ] = em + um

numa(s) ['numa(ʃ)] = em + uma(s)

numeral [nume'raw] *(pl -ais)* *m* numeral

numerar [nume'ra*] *vt* to number

numérico/a [nu'mɛriku/a] *adj* numerical

número ['numeru] *m* number; *(de jornal)* issue; *(TEATRO etc)* act; *(de sapatos, roupa)* size; **sem ~** countless; **~ de matrícula** registration *(BRIT)* ou license plate *(US)* number; **numeroso/a** [nume'rozu/ɔza] *adj* numerous

nunca ['nũka] *adv* never; **~ mais** never again; **quase ~** hardly ever; **mais que ~** more than ever

nuns [nũʃ] = em + uns

núpcias ['nupsjaʃ] *fpl* nuptials, wedding *sg*

nutrição [nutri'sãw] *f* nutrition
nutrido/a [nu'tridu/a] *adj* well-nourished; (*robusto*) robust
nutrir [nu'tri*] *vt* (*sentimento*) to harbour (*BRIT*), harbor (*US*); (*alimentar-se*): ~ **(de)** to nourish (with), feed (on); (*fig*) to feed (on) ♦ *vi* to be nourishing; **nutritivo/a** [nutri'tʃivu/a] *adj* nourishing
nuvem ['nuvẽj] (*pl* **-ns**) *f* cloud; (*de insetos*) swarm

O

PALAVRA CHAVE

o/a [u/a] *art def* **1** the; **o livro/a mesa/ os estudantes** the book/table/students
2 (*com n abstrato: não se traduz*): **o amor/a juventude** love/youth
3 (*posse: traduz-se muitos vezes por adj possessivo*): **quebrar o braço** to break one's arm; **ele levantou a mão** he put his hand up; **ela colocou o chapéu** she put her hat on
4 (*valor descritivo*): **ter a boca grande/os olhos azuis** to have a big mouth/blue eyes
♦ *pron demonstrativo*: **meu livro e o seu** my book and yours; **as de Pedro são melhores** Pedro's are better; **não a(s) branca(s) mas a(s) cinza(s)** not the white one(s) but the grey one(s)
♦ *pron relativo*: **o que** *etc* **1** (*indef*): **o(s) que quiser(em) pode(m)** sair anyone who wants to can leave; **leve o que mais gustar** take the one you like best
2 (*def*): **o que comprei ontem** the one I bought yesterday; **os que sairam** those who left
3: **o que** what; **o que eu acho/mais gosto** what I think/like most
♦ *pron pessoal* **1** (*pessoa: m*): him; (*: f*) her; (*: pl*) them; **não posso vê-lo(s)** I can't see him/them; **vemo-la todas as semanas** we see her every week
2 (*animal, coisa: sg*) it; (*: pl*) them; **não posso vê-lo(s)** I can't see it/them; **acharam-nos na praia** they found us on the beach

oásis [o'asiʃ] *m inv* oasis
obedecer [obede'se*] *vi*: ~ **a** to obey; **obediência** [obe'dʒẽsja] *f* obedience; **obediente** [obe'dʒẽtʃi] *adj* obedient
óbito ['ɔbitu] *m* death; **atestado de** ~ death certificate
obituário [obi'twarju] *m* obituary
objeção [obʒe'sãw] (*PT* **-cç-**; *pl* **-ões**) *f* objection; **fazer** *ou* **pôr objeções a** to object to
objetivo/a [obʒe'tʃivu/a] (*PT* **-ct-**) *adj* objective ♦ *m* objective
objeto [ob'ʒɛtu] (*PT* **-ct-**) *m* object

oblíqua [o'blikwa] *f* oblique
oblíquo/a [o'blikwu/a] *adj* oblique; (*olhar*) sidelong
oblongo/a [ob'lõgu/a] *adj* oblong
oboé [o'bwɛ] *m* oboe
obra ['ɔbra] *f* work; (*ARQ*) building, construction; (*TEATRO*) play; **em** ~**s** under repair; **ser** ~ **de alguém/algo** to be the work of sb/the result of sth; ~ **de arte** work of art; ~**s públicas** public works; ~**-prima** (*pl* ~**s-primas**) *f* masterpiece
obrigação [obriga'sãw] (*pl* **-ões**) *f* obligation; (*COM*) bond
obrigado/a [obri'gadu/a] *adj* obliged, compelled ♦ *excl* thank you; (*recusa*) no, thank you
obrigar [obri'ga*] *vt* to oblige, compel; ~**-se** *vr*: ~**-se a fazer algo** to undertake to do sth; **obrigatório/a** [obriga'tɔrju/a] *adj* compulsory, obligatory
obsceno/a [obi'sɛnu/a] *adj* obscene
obscurecer [obiʃkure'se*] *vt* to darken; (*entendimento, verdade etc*) to obscure ♦ *vi* to get dark
obscuro/a [obi'ʃkuru/a] *adj* dark; (*fig*) obscure
obséquio [ob'sɛkju] *m* favour (*BRIT*), favor (*US*), kindness
observação [obisexva'sãw] (*pl* **-ões**) *f* observation; (*comentário*) remark, comment; (*de leis, regras*) observance
observador(a) [obisexva'do*(a)] *m/f* observer
observar [obisex'va*] *vt* to observe; (*notar*) to notice; ~ **algo a alguém** to point sth out to sb
observatório [obisexva'tɔrju] *m* observatory
obsessão [obise'sãw] (*pl* **-ões**) *f* obsession; **obsessivo/a** [obise'sivu/a] *adj* obsessive
obsoleto/a [obiso'lɛtu/a] *adj* obsolete
obstáculo [obi'ʃtakulu] *m* obstacle; (*dificuldade*) hindrance, drawback
obstetrícia [obiʃte'trisja] *f* obstetrics *sg*
obstinado/a [obiʃtʃi'nadu/a] *adj* obstinate, stubborn
obstrução [obiʃtru'sãw] (*pl* **-ões**) *f* obstruction; **obstruir** [obi'ʃtrwi*] *vt* to obstruct; (*impedir*) to impede
obter [obi'te*] (*irreg: como* **ter**) *vt* to obtain, get; (*alcançar*) to gain
obturação [obitura'sãw] (*pl* **-ões**) *f* (*de dente*) filling
obturador [obitura'do*] *m* (*FOTO*) shutter
obturar [obitu'ra*] *vt* to stop up, plug; (*dente*) to fill
obtuso/a [obi'tuzu/a] *adj* (*ger*) obtuse; (*fig: pessoa*) thick
óbvio/a ['ɔbvju/a] *adj* obvious; **(é)** ~! of course!
ocasião [oka'zjãw] (*pl* **-ões**) *f* opportunity, chance; (*momento, tempo*) occasion;

ocasionar [okazjo'na*] *vt* to cause, bring about

oceano [o'sjanu] *m* ocean

ocidental [osidē'taw] (*pl* –ais) *adj* western ♦ *m/f* westerner

ocidente [osi'dētʃi] *m* west

ócio ['ɔsju] *m* (*lazer*) leisure; (*inação*) idleness; **ocioso/a** [o'sjozu/ɔza] *adj* idle; (*vaga*) unfilled

oco/a ['oku/a] *adj* hollow, empty

ocorrência [oko'xēsja] *f* incident, event; (*circunstância*) circumstance

ocorrer [oko'xe*] *vi* to happen, occur; (*vir ao pensamento*) to come to mind; ~ **a alguém** to happen to sb; to occur to sb

ocre ['ɔkri] *adj, m* ochre (*BRIT*), ocher (*US*)

ocular [oku'la*] *adj* ocular; **testemunha ~** eye witness

oculista [oku'liʃta] *m/f* optician

óculo ['ɔkulu] *m* spyglass; **~s** *mpl* (*para ver melhor*) glasses, spectacles; **~s de proteção** goggles

ocultar [okuw'ta*] *vt* to hide, conceal; **ocultas** [o'kuwtaʃ] *fpl*: **às ocultas** in secret; **oculto/a** [o'kuwtu/a] *adj* hidden; (*desconhecido*) unknown; (*secreto*) secret; (*sobrenatural*) occult

ocupação [okupa'sãw] (*pl* –ões) *f* occupation

ocupado/a [oku'padu/a] *adj* (*pessoa*) busy; (*lugar*) taken, occupied; (*BR: telefone*) engaged (*BRIT*), busy (*US*); **sinal de ~** (*BR: TEL*) engaged tone (*BRIT*), busy signal (*US*)

ocupar [oku'pa*] *vt* to occupy; (*tempo*) to take up; (*pessoa*) to keep busy; **~-se** *vr*: **~-se com** *ou* **de** *ou* **em algo** (*dedicar-se a*) to deal with sth; (*cuidar de*) to look after sth; (*passar seu tempo com*) to occupy o.s. with sth

odiar [o'dʒja*] *vt* to hate; **ódio** ['ɔdʒju] *m* hate, hatred; **odioso/a** [o'dʒjozu/ɔza] *adj* hateful

odor [o'do*] *m* smell

oeste ['wɛʃtʃi] *m* west ♦ *adj inv* (*região*) western; (*direção, vento*) westerly

ofegante [ofe'gãtʃi] *adj* breathless, panting

ofegar [ofe'ga*] *vi* to pant, puff

ofender [ofē'de*] *vt* to offend; **~-se** *vr*: **~-se (com)** to take offence (*BRIT*) *ou* offense (*US*) (at)

ofensa [o'fēsa] *f* insult; (*à lei, moral*) offence (*BRIT*), offense (*US*); **ofensiva** [ofē'siva] *f* offensive; **ofensivo/a** [ofē'sivu/a] *adj* offensive

oferecer [ofere'se*] *vt* to offer; (*dar*) to give; (*jantar*) to give; (*propor*) to propose; (*dedicar*) to dedicate; **~-se** *vr* (*pessoa*) to offer o.s., volunteer; (*oportunidade*) to present itself, arise; **~-se para fazer** to offer to do; **oferecimento** [oferesi'mētu] *m* offer; **oferta** [o'fɛxta] *f* offer; (*dádiva*) gift; (*COM*) bid; (*em loja*) special offer

oficial [ofi'sjaw] (*pl* –ais) *adj* official ♦ *m/f* official; (*MIL*) officer; **~ de justiça** bailiff

oficina [ofi'sina] *f* workshop; **~ mecânica** garage

ofício [o'fisju] *m* profession, trade; (*REL*) service; (*carta*) official letter; (*função*) function; (*encargo*) job, task

ofuscar [ofuʃ'ka*] *vt* (*obscurecer*) to blot out; (*deslumbrar*) to dazzle; (*suplantar em brilho*) to outshine ♦ *vi* to be dazzling

oitavo/a [oj'tavu/a] *num* eighth

oitenta [oj'tēta] *num* eighty

oito ['ojtu] *num* eight

olá [o'la] *excl* hello!

olaria [ola'ria] *f* (*fábrica: de louças de barro*) pottery; (: *de tijolos*) brickworks *sg*

óleo ['ɔlju] *m* (*lubrificante*) oil; **~ diesel/de bronzear** diesel/suntan oil; **oleoduto** [oljo'dutu] *m* (*oil*) pipeline; **oleoso/a** [o'ljozu/ɔza] *adj* oily; (*gorduroso*) greasy

olfato [ow'fatu] *m* sense of smell

olhada [o'ʎada] *f* glance, look; **dar uma ~** to have a look

olhadela [oʎa'dɛla] *f* peep

olhar [o'ʎa*] *vt* to look at; (*observar*) to watch; (*ponderar*) to consider; (*cuidar de*) to look after ♦ *vi* to look ♦ *m* look; **~-se** *vr* to look at o.s.; (*duas pessoas*) to look at each other; **~ fixamente** to stare at; **~ para** to look at; **~ por** to look after; **~ fixo** stare

olho ['oʎu] *m* (*ANAT: de agulha*) eye; (*vista*) eyesight; **~ nele!** watch him!; **~ vivo!** keep your eyes open!; **a ~** (*medir, calcular etc*) by eye; **~ mágico** (*na porta*) peephole; **~ roxo** black eye; **num abrir e fechar de ~s** in a flash

olimpíada [oli'piada] *f*: **as O~s** the Olympics

oliveira [oli'vejra] *f* olive tree

olmeiro [ow'mejru] *m* = **olmo**

olmo ['owmu] *m* elm

ombro ['ôbru] *m* shoulder; **encolher os ~s , dar de ~s** to shrug one's shoulders

omeleta [ome'leta] (*PT*) *f* = **omelete**

omelete [ome'letʃi] (*BR*) *f* omelette (*BRIT*), omelet (*US*)

omissão [omi'sãw] (*pl* –ões) *f* omission; (*negligência*) negligence

omitir [omi'tʃi*] *vt* to omit

omoplata [omo'plata] *f* shoulder blade

onça ['ôsa] *f* (*peso*) ounce; (*animal*) jaguar; **~-parda** (*pl* **~s-pardas**) *f* puma

onda ['ôda] *f* wave; (*moda*) fashion; **~ curta/média/longa** short/medium/long wave; **~ de calor** heat wave

onde ['ôdʒi] *adv* where ♦ *conj* where, in which; **de ~ você é?** where are you from?; **por ~** through which; **por ~?**

which way?; ~ **quer que** wherever
ondear [õ'dʒja*] vt to wave ♦ vi to wave; (água) to ripple
ondulado/a [õdu'ladu/a] adj wavy
ônibus ['onibuʃ] (BR) m inv bus; **ponto de** ~ bus-stop
onomástico/a [ono'maʃtʃiku/a] adj: **dia** ~ name day
ontem ['õtẽ] adv yesterday; ~ **à noite** last night
ONU ['onu] abr f (= Organização das Nações Unidas) UNO
ônus ['onuʃ] m inv onus; (obrigação) obligation; (COM) charge; (encargo desagradável) burden
onze ['õzi] num eleven
opaco/a [o'paku/a] adj opaque; (obscuro) dark
opala [o'pala] f opal
opção [op'sãw] (pl -ões) f option, choice; (preferência) first claim, right
OPEP [o'pɛpi] abr f (= Organização dos Países Exportadores de Petróleo) OPEC
ópera ['ɔpera] f opera
operação [opera'sãw] (pl -ões) f operation; (COM) transaction
operador(a) [opera'do*(a)] m/f operator; (cirurgião) surgeon; (num cinema) projectionist
operar [ope'ra*] vt to operate; (produzir) to effect, bring about; (MED) to operate on ♦ vi to operate; (agir) to act, function; ~**-se** vr (suceder) to take place; (MED) to have an operation
operariado [opera'rjadu] m: **o** ~ **the** working class
operário/a [ope'rarju/a] adj working ♦ m/f worker; **classe operária** working class
opinar [opi'na*] vt to think ♦ vi to give one's opinion
opinião [opi'njãw] (pl -ões) f opinion; **mudar de** ~ to change one's mind
ópio ['ɔpju] m opium
oponente [opo'nẽtʃi] adj opposing ♦ m/f opponent
opor [o'po*] (irreg: como **pôr**) vt to oppose; (resistência) to put up, offer; (objeção, dificuldade) to raise; ~**-se a** to object to; (resistir) to oppose
oportunidade [opoxtuni'dadʒi] f opportunity
oportunista [opoxtu'niʃta] adj, m/f opportunist
oportuno/a [opox'tunu/a] adj (momento) opportune, right; (oferta de ajuda) well-timed; (conveniente) convenient, suitable
oposição [opozi'sãw] f opposition; **em** ~ **a** against; **fazer** ~ **a** to oppose
oposto/a [o'poʃtu/'pɔʃta] adj opposite; (em frente) facing; (opiniões) opposing ♦ m opposite
opressão [opre'sãw] (pl -ões) f oppression; **opressivo/a** [opre'sivu/a] adj oppressive

oprimir [opri'mi*] vt to oppress; (comprimir) to press
optar [op'ta*] vi to choose; ~ **por** to opt for; ~ **por fazer** to opt to do
óptico/a etc ['ɔtʃiku/a] (PT) = **ótico** etc
óptimo/a etc ['ɔtʃimu/a] (PT) adj = **ótimo** etc
opulento/a [opu'lẽtu/a] adj opulent
ora ['ɔra] adv now ♦ conj well; **por** ~ for the time being; ~ ..., ~ ... one moment ..., the next ...; ~ **bem** now then
oração [ora'sãw] (pl -ões) f prayer; (discurso) speech; (LING) clause
oráculo [o'rakulu] m oracle
orador(a) [ora'do*(a)] m/f speaker
oral [o'raw] (pl -ais) adj oral ♦ f oral (exam)
orar [o'ra*] vi (REL) to pray
órbita ['ɔxbita] f orbit; (do olho) socket
Órcades ['ɔxkadʒiʃ] fpl: **as** ~ **the** Orkneys
orçamento [oxsa'mẽtu] m (do estado etc) budget; (avaliação) estimate
orçar [ox'sa*] vt to value, estimate ♦ vi: ~ **em** (gastos etc) to be valued at, be put at
ordem ['ɔxdẽ] (pl -ns) f order; **até nova** ~ until further notice; **de primeira** ~ first-rate; **estar em** ~ to be tidy; **por** ~ in order, in turn; ~ **do dia** agenda; ~ **pública** public order, law and order
ordenado/a [oxde'nadu/a] adj (posto em ordem) in order; (metódico) orderly ♦ m salary, wages pl
ordenhar [oxde'ɲa*] vt to milk
ordens ['ɔxdẽʃ] fpl de **ordem**
ordinário/a [oxdʒi'narju/a] adj ordinary; (comum) usual; (medíocre) mediocre; (grosseiro) coarse, vulgar; (de má qualidade) inferior; **de** ~ usually
orelha [o'reʎa] f ear; (aba) flap
órfã ['ɔxfã] f de **órfão**
orfanato [oxfa'natu] m orphanage
órfão/fã ['ɔxfãw/fã] (pl -s) adj, m/f orphan
orgânico/a [ox'ganiku/a] adj organic
organismo [oxga'niʒmu] m organism; (entidade) organization
organista [oxga'niʃta] m/f organist
organização [oxganiza'sãw] (pl -ões) f organization; **organizar** [oxgani'za*] vt to organize
órgão ['ɔxgãw] (pl -s) m organ; (governamental) institution, body
orgasmo [ox'gaʒmu] m orgasm
orgia [ox'ʒia] f orgy
orgulho [ox'guʎu] m pride; (arrogância) arrogance; ~**so/a** [oxgu'ʎozu/ɔza] adj proud; haughty
orientação [orjẽta'sãw] f direction; (posição) position; ~ **educacional** training, guidance
oriental [orjẽ'taw] (pl -ais) adj eastern; (do Extremo Oriente) oriental
orientar [orjẽ'ta*] vt to orientate; (indicar)

o rumo) to direct; (*aconselhar*) to guide; ~**-se** *vr* to get one's bearings; ~**-se por algo** to follow sth

oriente [o'rjẽtʃi] *m*: **o O~** the East; **Extremo O~** Far East; **O~ Médio** Middle East

origem [o'riʒẽ] (*pl* -**ns**) *f* origin; (*ascendência*) lineage, descent; **lugar de ~** birthplace

original [oriʒi'naw] (*pl* -**ais**) *adj* original; (*estranho*) strange, odd ♦ *m* original; ~**idade** [oriʒinali'dadʒi] *f* originality; (*excentricidade*) eccentricity

originar [oriʒi'na*] *vt* to give rise to, start; ~**-se** *vr* to arise; ~**-se de** to originate from; **originário/a** [oriʒi'narju/a] *adj* (*natural*) native

oriundo/a [o'rjũdu/a] *adj*: ~ **de** arising from; (*natural*) native of

orla ['ɔxla] *f*.: ~ **marítima** seafront

ornamento [oxna'mẽtu] *m* adornment, decoration

orquestra [ox'kɛʃtra] (*PT* -**esta**) *f* orchestra

orquídea [ox'kidʒia] *f* orchid

ortodoxo/a [oxto'dɔksu/a] *adj* orthodox

ortografia [oxtogra'fia] *f* spelling

ortopédico/a [oxto'pɛdʒiku/a] *adj* orthopaedic (*BRIT*), orthopedic (*US*)

orvalho [ox'vaʎu] *m* dew

os [uʃ] *art def* V **o**

oscilar [osi'la*] *vi* to oscillate; (*balançarse*) to sway, swing; (*variar*) to fluctuate; (*hesitar*) to hesitate

ósseo/a ['ɔsju/a] *adj* bony; (*ANAT*: *medula etc*) bone *atr*

osso ['osu] *m* bone

ostensivo/a [oʃtẽ'sivu/a] *adj* ostensible

ostentar [oʃtẽ'ta*] *vt* to show; (*alardear*) to show off, flaunt

ostentoso/a [oʃtẽ'tozu/ɔza] *adj* ostentatious

ostra ['oʃtra] *f* oyster

OTAN ['otã] *abr f* (= *Organização do Tratado do Atlântico Norte*) NATO

ótica ['ɔtʃika] *f* optics *sg*; (*loja*) optician's; (*fig*: *ponto de vista*) viewpoint; *V tb* **ótico**

ótico/a ['ɔtʃiku/a] *adj* optical ♦ *m/f* optician

otimista [otʃi'miʃta] *adj* optimistic ♦ *m/f* optimist

ótimo/a ['ɔtʃimu/a] *adj* excellent, splendid ♦ *excl* great!, super!

ou [o] *conj* or; ~ **este ~ aquele** either this one or that one; ~ **seja** in other words

ouço *etc* ['osu] *vb* V **ouvir**

ouriço [o'risu] *m* (*europeu*) hedgehog; (*casca*) shell

ouro ['oru] *m* gold; ~**s** *mpl* (*CARTAS*) diamonds

ousadia [oza'dʒia] *f* daring; **ousado/a** [o'zadu/a] *adj* daring, bold

ousar [o'za*] *vt*, *vi* to dare

outono [o'tɔnu] *m* autumn

PALAVRA CHAVE

outro/a ['otru/a] *adj* **1** (*distinto*: *sg*) another; (: *pl*) other; **outra coisa** something else; **de ~ modo, de outra maneira** otherwise; **no ~ dia** the next day; **ela está outra** (*mudada*) she's changed

2 (*adicional*): **traga-me ~ café, por favor** can I have another coffee please?; **outra vez** again

♦ *pron* **1 o ~** the other one; (**os**) ~**s** (the) others; **de ~** somebody else's

2 (*recíproco*): **odeiam-se uns aos ~s** they hate one another *ou* each other

3: ~ **tanto** the same again; **comer ~ tanto** to eat the same *ou* as much again; **ele recebeu uma dezena de telegramas e outras tantas chamadas** he got about ten telegrams and as many calls

outubro [o'tubru] (*PT* **O-**) *m* October

ouvido/a [o'vidu] *m* (*ANAT*) ear; (*sentido*) hearing; **de ~** by ear; **dar ~s a** to listen to

ouvinte [o'vĩtʃi] *m/f* listener; (*estudante*) auditor

ouvir [o'vi*] *vt* to hear; (*com atenção*) to listen to; (*missa*) to attend ♦ *vi* to hear; to listen; ~ **dizer que ...** to hear that ...; ~ **falar de** to hear of

ova ['ɔva] *f* roe

ovação [ova'sãw] (*pl* -**ões**) *f* ovation, acclaim

oval [o'vaw] (*pl* -**ais**) *adj*, *f* oval

ovário [o'varju] *m* ovary

ovelha [o've ʎa] *f* sheep

óvni ['ɔvni] *m* UFO

ovo ['ovu] *m* egg; ~**s de granja** free-range eggs; ~ **pochê** (*BR*) *ou* **escalfado** (*PT*) poached egg; ~ **estrelado** *ou* **frito** fried egg; ~**s mexidos** scrambled eggs; ~ **quente/cozido duro** hard-boiled/soft-boiled egg

oxidado/a [oksi'dadu/a] *adj* rusty

oxidar [oksi'da*] *vt* to rust; ~**-se** *vr* to rust, go rusty

oxigenado/a [oksiʒe'nadu/a] *adj* (*cabelo*) bleached; **água oxigenada** peroxide

oxigenar [oksiʒe'na*] *vt* (*cabelo*) to bleach

oxigênio [oksi'ʒenju] *m* oxygen

ozônio [o'zonju] *m* ozone; **camada de ~** ozone layer

P

P. *abr* (= *Praça*) Sq

p.a. *abr* (= *por ano*) p.a

pá [pa] *f* shovel; (*de remo, hélice*) blade ♦ *m* (*PT*) pal, mate; ~ **de lixo** dustpan

paca ['paka] *f* (*ZOOL*) paca

pacato/a [pa'katu/a] *adj* (*pessoa*) quiet;

(*lugar*) peaceful

pachorrento/a [paʃoˈxẽtu/a] *adj* slow, sluggish

paciência [paˈsjẽsja] *f* patience; **paciente** [paˈsjẽtʃi] *adj, m/f* patient

pacificar [pasifiˈkaˀ] *vt* to pacify, calm (down)

pacífico/a [paˈsifiku/a] *adj* (*pessoa*) peace-loving; (*aceito sem discussão*) undisputed; (*sossegado*) peaceful; **o (Oceano) P~** the Pacific (Ocean)

pacifista [pasiˈfiʃta] *m/f* pacifist

pacote [paˈkɔtʃi] *m* packet; (*embrulho*) parcel; (*ECON, COMPUT, TURISMO*) package

pacto [ˈpaktu] *m* pact; (*ajuste*) agreement

padaria [padaˈria] *f* bakery, baker's (shop)

padecer [padeˈseˀ] *vt* to suffer; (*suportar*) to put up with, endure ♦ *vi*: ~ **de** to suffer from; **padecimento** [padesiˈmẽtu] *m* suffering; (*dor*) pain

padeiro [paˈdejru] *m* baker

padiola [paˈdʒjɔla] *f* stretcher

padrão [paˈdrãw] (*pl* ~**ões**) *m* standard; (*medida*) gauge; (*desenho*) pattern; (*fig: modelo*) model

padrasto [paˈdraʃtu] *m* stepfather

padre [ˈpadri] *m* priest

padrinho [paˈdriɲu] *m* godfather; (*de noivo*) best man; (*patrono*) sponsor

padroeiro/a [paˈdrwejru/a] *m/f* patron; (*santo*) patron saint

padrões [paˈdrõjʃ] *mpl de* **padrão**

padronizar [padroniˈzaˀ] *vt* to standardize

pães [pãjʃ] *mpl de* **pão**

pagã [paˈgã] *f de* **pagão**

pagador(a) [pagaˈdoˀ(a)] *adj* paying ♦ *m/f* payer; (*de salário*) pay clerk; (*de banco*) teller

pagamento [pagaˈmẽtu] *m* payment; ~ **a prazo** *ou* **em prestações** payment in instal(l)ments; ~ **à vista** cash payment; ~ **contra entrega** (*COM*) COD, cash on delivery

pagão/gã [paˈgãw/gã] (*pl* ~**s**/~**s**) *adj, m/f* pagan

pagar [paˈgaˀ] *vt* to pay; (*compras, pecados*) to pay for; (*o que devia*) to pay back; (*retribuir*) to repay ♦ *vi* to pay; ~ **por algo** (*tb fig*) to pay for sth; ~ **a prestações** to pay in instal(l)ments; ~ **de contado** (*PT*) to pay cash

página [ˈpaʒina] *f* page

pago/a [ˈpagu/a] *pp de* **pagar** ♦ *adj* paid; (*fig*) even ♦ *m* pay

pai [paj] *m* father; ~**s** *mpl* parents

painel [pajˈnɛw] (*pl* ~**eis**) *m* panel; (*quadro*) picture; (*AUTO*) dashboard; (*de avião*) instrument panel

paiol [paˈjɔw] (*pl* ~**óis**) *m* storeroom; (*celeiro*) barn; (*de pólvora*) powder magazine

país [paˈjiʃ] *m* country; (*região*) land; ~ **natal** native land

paisagem [pajˈzaʒẽ] (*pl* ~**ns**) *f* scenery, landscape

paisano/a [pajˈzanu/a] *adj* civilian ♦ *m/f* (*não militar*) civilian; (*compatriota*) fellow countryman

Países Baixos *mpl*: **os** ~ the Netherlands

paixão [pajˈʃãw] (*pl* ~**ões**) *f* passion

palácio [paˈlasju] *m* palace; ~ **da justiça** courthouse

paladar [palaˈdaˀ] *m* taste; (*ANAT*) palate

palafita [palaˈfita] *f* (*estacaria*) stilts *pl*; (*habitação*) stilt house

palanque [paˈlãki] *m* (*estrado*) stand

palavra [paˈlavra] *f* word; (*fala*) speech; (*promessa*) promise; (*direito de falar*) right to speak; **dar a** ~ **a alguém** to give sb the chance to speak; **ter** ~ (*pessoa*) to be reliable; ~**s cruzadas** crossword (puzzle) *sg*; **palavrão** [palaˈvrãw] (*pl* ~**ões**) *m* swearword

palco [ˈpawku] *m* (*TEATRO*) stage; (*fig: local*) scene

Palestina [paleʃˈtʃina] *f*: **a** ~ Palestine; **palestino/a** [paleʃˈtʃinu/a] *adj, m/f* Palestinian

palestra [paˈlɛʃtra] *f* chat, talk; (*conferência*) lecture

paleta [paˈleta] *f* palette

paletó [paleˈtɔ] *m* jacket

palha [ˈpaʎa] *f* straw

palhaço [paˈʎasu] *m* clown

palhoça [paˈʎɔsa] *f* thatched hut

pálido/a [ˈpalidu/a] *adj* pale

palito [paˈlitu] *m* stick; (*para os dentes*) toothpick

palma [ˈpawma] *f* (*folha*) palm leaf; (*da mão*) palm; **bater** ~**s** to clap; ~**da** [pawˈmada] *f* slap

palmeira [pawˈmejra] *f* palm tree

palmo [ˈpawmu] *m* span; ~ **a** ~ inch by inch

palpável [pawˈpavew] (*pl* ~**eis**) *adj* tangible; (*fig*) obvious

pálpebra [ˈpawpebra] *f* eyelid

palpitação [pawpitaˈsãw] (*pl* ~**ões**) *f* beating, throbbing; **palpitações** *fpl* (*batimentos cardíacos*) palpitations

palpitante [pawpiˈtãtʃi] *adj* beating, throbbing; (*fig: emocionante*) thrilling; (*de interesse atual*) sensational

palpitar [pawpiˈtaˀ] *vi* (*coração*) to beat

palpite [pawˈpitʃi] *m* (*intuição*) hunch; (*JOGO, TURFE*) tip; (*opinião*) opinion

paludismo [paluˈdʒiʒmu] *m* malaria

pampa [ˈpãpa] *f* pampas

Panamá [panaˈma] *m*: **o** ~ Panama, the Panama Canal

pancada [pãˈkada] *f* (*no corpo*) blow, hit; (*choque*) knock; (*de relógio*) stroke; **dar** ~ **em alguém** to hit sb; ~**ria** [pãkadaˈria] *f* (*surra*) beating; (*tumulto*) fight

panda [ˈpãda] *f* panda

pandeiro [pãˈdejru] *m* tambourine

pandemônio [pãde'monju] *m* pandemonium

pane ['pani] *f* breakdown

panela [pa'nɛla] *f* (*de barro*) pot; (*de metal*) pan; (*de cozinhar*) saucepan; (*no dente*) hole; ~ **de pressão** pressure cooker

panfleto [pã'fletu] *m* pamphlet

pânico ['paniku] *m* panic; **entrar em** ~ to panic

panificação [panifika'sãw] (*pl* –ões) *f* (*fabricação*) bread-making; (*padaria*) bakery

pano ['panu] *m* cloth; (*TEATRO*) curtain; (*vela*) sheet, sail; ~ **de pratos** tea-towel; ~ **de pó** duster; ~ **de fundo** (*tb fig*) backdrop

panorama [pano'rama] *m* view

panqueca [pã'kɛka] *f* pancake

pantanal [pãta'naw] (*pl* –ais) *m* swampland

pântano ['pãtanu] *m* marsh, swamp; **pantanoso/a** [pãta'nozu/ɔza] *adj* marshy, swampy

pantera [pã'tɛra] *f* panther

pantomima [pãto'mima] *f* pantomime

pão [pãw] (*pl* **pães**) *m* bread; **o P~ de Açúcar** (*no Rio*) Sugarloaf Mountain; ~ **torrado** toast; ~-**duro** (*pl* **pães-duros**) (*col*) *adj* mean, stingy ♦ *m/f* miser; ~**zinho** [pãw'ziɲu] *m* roll

papa ['papa] *m* Pope; (*mingau*) porridge

papagaio [papa'gaju] *m* parrot; (*pipa*) kite

papai [pa'paj] *m* dad, daddy; **P~ Noel** Santa Claus, Father Christmas

papel [pa'pɛw] (*pl* –**éis**) *m* paper; (*TEATRO, função*) role; ~ **de embrulho/de escrever/de alumínio** wrapping paper/writing paper/tinfoil; ~ **higiênico/usado** toilet/waste paper; ~ **de parede/de seda/transparente** wallpaper/tissue paper/tracing paper; ~**ada** [pape'lada] *f* pile of papers; (*burocracia*) paperwork, red tape; ~**ão** [pape'lãw] *m* cardboard; (*fig*) fiasco; ~**aria** [papela'ria] *f* stationer's (shop); ~**carbono** *m* carbon paper; ~**eta** [pape'leta] *f* (*cartaz*) notice; (*papel avulso*) piece of paper

papo ['papu] (*col*) *m* (*conversa*) chat; **bater** *ou* **levar um** ~ (*col*) to have a chat; **ficar de** ~ **para o ar** (*fig*) to laze around

papoula [pa'pola] *f* poppy

páprica ['paprika] *f* paprika

paquerar [pake'ra*] (*col*) *vi* to flirt ♦ *vt* to chat up

paquistanês/esa [pakiʃta'neʃ/eza] *adj*, *m/f* Pakistani

Paquistão [pakiʃ'tãw] *m*: **o** ~ Pakistan

par [pa*] *adj* (*igual*) equal; (*número*) even ♦ *m* pair; (*casal*) couple; (*pessoa na dança*) partner; ~ **a** ~ side by side, level; **sem** ~ incomparable

para ['para] *prep* for; (*direção*) to, towards; ~ **que** so that, in order that; ~ **quê?** what for?, why?; **ir** ~ **casa** to go home; ~ **com** (*atitude*) towards; **de lá** ~ **cá** since then; ~ **a semana** next week; **estar** ~ to be about to; **é** ~ **nós ficarmos aqui?** should we stay here?

parabéns [para'bẽjʃ] *mpl* congratulations; (*no aniversário*) happy birthday; **dar** ~ **a** to congratulate

parábola [pa'rabola] *f* parable

pára-brisa ['para-] (*pl* ~s) *m* windscreen (*BRIT*), windshield (*US*)

pára-choque ['para-] (*pl* ~s) *m* (*AUTO*) bumper

parada [pa'rada] *f* stop; (*COM*) stoppage; (*militar, colegial*) parade

paradeiro [para'dejru] *m* whereabouts

parado/a [pa'radu/a] *adj* (*imóvel*) standing still; (*sem vida*) lifeless; (*carro*) stationary; (*máquina*) out of action; (*olhar*) fixed; (*trabalhador, fábrica*) idle

paradoxo [para'dɔksu] *m* paradox

parafina [para'fina] *f* paraffin

parafrasear [parafra'zja*] *vt* to paraphrase

parafuso [para'fuzu] *m* screw

paragem [pa'raʒẽ] (*pl* –**ns**) *f* stop; **paragens** *fpl* (*lugares*) places, parts; ~ **eléctrico** (*PT*) tram (*BRIT*) *ou* streetcar (*US*) stop

parágrafo [pa'ragrafu] *m* paragraph

Paraguai [para'gwaj] *m*: **o** ~ Paraguay; **paraguaio/a** [para'gwaju/a] *adj*, *m/f* Paraguayan

paraíso [para'izu] *m* paradise

pára-lama ['para-] (*pl* ~s) *m* wing (*BRIT*), fender (*US*); (*de bicicleta*) mudguard

paralelepípedo [paralele'pipedu] *m* paving stone

paralelo/a [para'lɛlu/a] *adj* parallel

paralisar [parali'za*] *vt* to paralyse; (*trabalho*) to bring to a standstill; ~-**se** *vr* to become paralysed; (*fig*) to come to a standstill; **paralisia** [parali'zia] *f* paralysis

paranasal [parana'zaw] (*pl* –**ais**) *adj* V seio

paraninfo [para'nĩfu] *m* patron

paranóico/a [para'nɔjku/a] *adj*, *m/f* paranoid

parapeito [para'pejtu] *m* wall, parapet; (*da janela*) windowsill

pára-quedas ['para-] *m inv* parachute; **pára-quedista** [parake'dʒiʃta] *m/f* parachutist ♦ *m* (*MIL*) paratrooper

parar [pa'ra*] *vi* to stop; (*ficar*) to stay ♦ *vt* to stop; **fazer** ~ (*deter*) to stop; ~ **na cadeia** to end up in jail; ~ **de fazer** to stop doing

pára-raios ['para-] *m inv* lightning conductor

parasita [para'zita] *m* parasite

parasito [para'zitu] *m* parasite

parceiro/a [pax'sejru/a] *adj* matching ♦

m/f partner

parcela [pax'sɛla] *f* piece, bit; *(de pagamento)* instalment *(BRIT)*, installment *(US)*; *(de terra)* plot; *(do eleitorado etc)* section; *(MAT)* item

parceria [paxse'ria] *f* partnership

parcial [pax'sjaw] *(pl* –ais*) adj* partial; *(feito por partes)* in parts; *(pessoa)* bias(s)ed; *(POL)* partisan; **~idade** [paxsjali'dadʒi] *f* bias, partiality

parco/a [ˈpaxku/a] *adj (escasso)* scanty; *(econômico)* thrifty; *(refeição)* frugal

pardal [pax'daw] *(pl* –ais*) m* sparrow

pardieiro [pax'dʒjejru] *m* ruin, heap

pardo/a [ˈpaxdu/a] *adj (cinzento)* grey *(BRIT)*, gray *(US)*; *(castanho)* brown; *(mulato)* mulatto

parecer [pare'se*] *m, vi (ter a aparência de)* to look, seem; **~-se** *vr*: **~-se com alguém** to look like sb; **~ (com)** *(ter semelhança com)* to look (like); **ao que parece** apparently; **parece-me que** I think that, it seems to me that; **que lhe parece?** what do you think?; **parece que** it looks as if

parecido/a [pare'sidu/a] *adj* alike, similar; **~ com** like

parede [pa'redʒi] *f* wall

parente/a [paˈrẽtʃi] *m/f* relative, relation; **~sco** [parẽˈteʃku] *m* relationship; *(fig)* connection

parêntese [paˈrẽtezi] *m* parenthesis; *(na escrita)* bracket; *(fig: digressão)* digression

páreo [ˈparju] *m* race; *(fig)* competition

parir [pa'ri*] *vt* to give birth to ♦ *vi* to give birth; *(mulher)* to have a baby

Paris [paˈriʃ] *n* Paris; **p~iense** [pari'zjẽsi] *adj, m/f* Parisian

parlamentar [paxlamẽ'ta*] *adj* parliamentary ♦ *m/f* member of parliament

parlamento [paxla'mẽtu] *m* parliament

pároco [ˈparoku] *m* parish priest

paródia [pa'rɔdʒja] *f* parody

paróquia [pa'rɔkja] *f (REL)* parish

parque [ˈpaxki] *m* park; **~ industrial/infantil** industrial estate/children's playground

parte [ˈpaxtʃi] *f* part; *(quinhão)* share; *(lado)* side; *(ponto)* point; *(JUR)* party; *(papel)* role; **a maior ~ de** most of; **à ~ aside;** *(separado)* separate; *(separadamente)* separately; *(além de)* apart from; **da ~ de alguém** on sb's part; **em alguma/qualquer ~** somewhere/anywhere; **em ~ alguma** nowhere; **por toda (a) ~** everywhere; **pôr de ~** to set aside; **tomar ~ em** to take part in; **dar ~ de alguém à polícia** to report sb to the police

parteira [pax'tejra] *f* midwife

participação [paxtʃisipa'sãw] *f* participation; *(COM)* stake, share; *(comunicação)* announcement, notification

participante [paxtʃisi'pãtʃi] *m/f* partici-

pant

participar [paxtʃisi'pa*] *vt* to announce, notify of ♦ *vi*: **~ de** *ou* **em** to participate in, take part in; *(compartilhar)* to share in

particípio [paxtʃi'sipju] *m* participle

partícula [pax'tʃikula] *f* particle

particular [paxtʃiku'la*] *adj* particular, special; *(privativo, pessoal)* private ♦ *m* particular; *(indivíduo)* individual; **~es** *mpl (pormenores)* details; **em ~** in private; **~idade** [paxtʃikulari'dadʒi] *f* peculiarity; **~izar** [paxtʃikulari'za*] *vt (especificar)* to specify; *(detalhar)* to give details of; **~mente** [paxtʃikulaxˈmẽtʃi] *adv* privately; *(especialmente)* particularly

partida [pax'tʃida] *f (saída)* departure; *(ESPORTE)* game, match

partidário/a [paxtʃi'darju/a] *adj* supporting ♦ *m/f* supporter, follower

partido [pax'tʃidu] *m (POL)* party; **tirar ~ de** to profit from; **tomar o ~ de** to side with

partilha [pax'tʃiʎa] *f* share; **~r** [paxtʃi'ʎa*] *vt* to share; *(distribuir)* to share out

partir [pax'tʃi*] *vt* to break; *(dividir)* to divide, split ♦ *vi (pôr-se a caminho)* to set off, set out; *(ir-se embora)* to leave, depart; **~-se** *vr* to break; **a ~ de** *(starting)* from

parto [ˈpaxtu] *m* (child)birth; **estar em trabalho de ~** to be in labour *(BRIT)* ou labor *(US)*

Páscoa [ˈpaʃkwa] *f* Easter; *(dos judeus)* Passover

pasmado/a [paʒ'madu/a] *adj* amazed, astonished

pasmar [paʒ'ma*] *vt* to amaze, astonish; **~-se** *vr*: **~-se com** to be amazed at

pasmo/a [ˈpaʒmu/a] *adj* astonished ♦ *m* amazement

passa [ˈpasa] *f* raisin

passadeira [pasa'dejra] *f (tapete)* stair carpet; *(mulher)* ironing lady; *(PT: para peões)* zebra crossing *(BRIT)*, crosswalk *(US)*

passado/a [pa'sadu/a] *adj* past; *(antiquado)* old-fashioned; *(fruta)* bad; *(peixe)* off ♦ *m* past; **o ano ~** last year; **bem/mal passado** *(carne)* well done/rare

passageiro/a [pasa'ʒejru/a] *adj* passing ♦ *m/f* passenger

passagem [pa'saʒẽ] *(pl* –ns*) f* passage; *(preço de condução)* fare; *(bilhete)* ticket; **~ de ida e volta** return ticket, round trip ticket *(US)*; **~ de nível level** *(BRIT)* ou **grade** *(US)* crossing; **~ de pedestres** pedestrian crossing *(BRIT)*, crosswalk *(US)*; **~ subterrânea** underpass, subway *(BRIT)*

passaporte [pasaˈpɔxtʃi] *m* passport

passar [pa'sa*] *vt* to pass; *(exceder)* to go beyond, exceed; *(a ferro)* to iron; *(o tempo)* to spend; *(a outra pessoa)* to pass on; (*pomada*) to put on ♦ *vi* to pass; (*na rua*) to go past; (*tempo*) to go by; (*dor*) to wear off; (*terminar*) to be over; ~-se *vr* (*acontecer*) to go on, happen; ~ **bem** (*de saúde*) to be well; **passava das dez horas** it was past ten o' clock; ~ **alguém para trás** to con sb; (*cônjuge*) to cheat on sb; ~ **por algo** (*sofrer*) to go through sth; (*transitar: estrada*) to go along sth; (*ser considerado como*) to be thought of as sth; ~ **sem** to do without

passarela [pasaˈrɛla] *f* footbridge

pássaro [ˈpasaru] *m* bird

passatempo [pasaˈtẽpu] *m* pastime

passe [ˈpasi] *m* pass

passear [paˈsja*] *vt* to take for a walk ♦ *vi* (*a pé*) to go for a walk; (*sair*) to go out; ~ **a cavalo** (*ou de carro*) to go for a ride; **passeata** [paˈsjata] *f* (*marcha coletiva*) protest march; **passeio** [paˈseju] *m* walk; (*de carro*) drive, ride; (*excursão*) outing; (*calçada*) pavement (*BRIT*), sidewalk (*US*); **dar um passeio** to go for a walk; (*de carro*) to go for a drive ou ride

passional [pasjoˈnaw] (*pl* –**ais**) *adj* passionate

passível [paˈsivew] (*pl* –**eis**) *adj*: ~ **de** (*dor etc*) susceptible to; (*pena, multa*) subject to

passivo/a [paˈsivu/a] *adj* passive ♦ *m* (*COM*) liabilities *pl*

passo [ˈpasu] *m* step; (*medida*) pace; (*modo de andar*) walk; (*ruído dos passos*) footstep; (*sinal de pé*) footprint; **ao** ~ **que** while; **ceder o** ~ **a** to give way to

pasta [ˈpaʃta] *f* paste; (*de couro*) briefcase; (*de cartolina*) folder; (*de ministro*) portfolio; ~ **dentifrícia** ou **de dentes** toothpaste

pastagem [paʃˈtaʒẽ] (*pl* –**ns**) *f* pasture

pastar [paʃˈta*] *vt* to graze on ♦ *vi* to graze

pastel [paʃˈtɛw] (*pl* –**éis**) *adj inv* (*cor*) pastel ♦ *m* samosa

pastelão [paʃteˈlãw] *m* slapstick

pastelaria [paʃtelaˈria] *f* cake shop; (*comida*) pastry

pasteurizado/a [paʃtewriˈzadu/a] *adj* pasteurized

pastilha [paʃˈtiʎa] *f* (*MED*) tablet; (*doce*) pastille; (*COMPUT*) chip

pasto [ˈpaʃtu] *m* (*erva*) grass; (*terreno*) pasture; **casa de** ~ (*PT*) cheap restaurant, diner

pastor(a) [paʃˈto*(a)] *m/f* shepherd(ess) ♦ *m* (*REL*) clergyman, pastor

pata [ˈpata] *f* (*pé de animal*) foot, paw; (*ave*) duck; (*col: pé*) foot; ~**da** [paˈtada] *f* kick

patamar [pataˈma*] *m* (*de escada*) landing; (*fig*) level

patê [paˈte] *m* pâté

patente [paˈtẽtʃi] *adj* obvious, evident ♦

f (*COM*) patent

paternal [patexˈnaw] (*pl* –**ais**) *adj* paternal, fatherly; **paternidade** [patexniˈdadʒi] *f* paternity; **paterno/a** [paˈtɛxnu/a] *adj* paternal, fatherly; **casa paterna** family home

pateta [paˈtɛta] *adj* stupid, daft ♦ *m/f* idiot

patético/a [paˈtɛtʃiku/a] *adj* pathetic, moving

patife [paˈtʃifi] *m* scoundrel, rogue

patim [paˈtʃĩ] (*pl* –**ns**) *m* skate; ~ **de rodas** roller skate; **patinação** [patʃinaˈsãw] (*pl* –**ões**) *f* skating; (*lugar*) skating rink; **patinar** [patʃiˈna*] *vi* to skate; (*AUTO: derrapar*) to skid; **patinete** [patʃiˈnɛtʃi] *f* skateboard

patinho [paˈtʃiɲu] *m* duckling; (*carne*) leg of beef

patins [paˈtʃĩʃ] *mpl de* **patim**

pátio [ˈpatʃju] *m* (*de uma casa*) patio, backyard; (*espaço cercado de edifícios*) courtyard; (*ib*: ~ **de recreio**) playground; (*MIL*) parade ground

pato [ˈpatu] *m* duck; (*macho*) drake

patologia [patoloˈʒia] *f* pathology; **patológico/a** [patoˈlɔʒiku/a] *adj* pathological

patrão [paˈtrãw] (*pl* –**ões**) *m* (*COM*) boss; (*dono de casa*) master; (*proprietário*) landlord; (*NÁUT*) skipper

pátria [ˈpatrja] *f* homeland

patrimônio [patriˈmonju] *m* (*herança*) inheritance; (*fig*) heritage; (*bens*) property

patriota [paˈtrjota] *m/f* patriot

patrocinador(a) [patrosinaˈdo*(a)] *m/f* sponsor, backer

patrocinar [patrosiˈna*] *vt* to sponsor; (*proteger*) to support; **patrocínio** [patroˈsinju] *m* sponsorship, backing; support

patrões [paˈtrõjʃ] *mpl de* **patrão**

patrono [paˈtrɔnu] *m* patron

patrulha [paˈtruʎa] *f* patrol; ~**r** [paˈtruʎa*] *vt, vi* to patrol

pau [paw] *m* (*madeira*) wood; (*vara*) stick; ~**s** *mpl* (*CARTAS*) clubs; ~ **a** ~ neck and neck; ~ **de bandeira** flagpole

pausa [ˈpawza] *f* pause; (*intervalo*) break; (*descanso*) rest

pauta [ˈpawta] *f* (*linha*) (guide)line; (*ordem do dia*) agenda; (*indicações*) guidelines *pl*; **sem** ~ (*papel*) plain; **em** ~ on the agenda

pavão/voa [paˈvãw/ˈvoa] (*pl* –**ões**/~**s**) *m/f* peacock/peahen

pavilhão [paviˈʎãw] (*pl* –**ões**) *m* tent; (*de madeira*) hut; (*no jardim*) summerhouse; (*em exposição*) pavilion; (*bandeira*) flag

pavimentar [pavimẽˈta*] *vt* to pave

pavimento [paviˈmẽtu] *m* (*chão, andar*) floor; (*da rua*) road surface

pavio [paˈviu] *m* wick

pavoa [paˈvoa] *f de* **pavão**

pavões [paˈvõjʃ] *mpl de* **pavão**

pavor [pa'vo*] *m* dread, terror; **ter ~ de** to be terrified of; **~oso/a** [pavo'rozu/ɔza] *adj* dreadful, terrible

paz [pajʒ] *f* peace; **fazer as ~es** to make up, be friends again

PC *abr m* = personal computer

Pça. *abr* (= *Praça*) Sq

pé [pɛ] *m* foot; (*da mesa*) leg; (*fig: base*) footing; (*de milho, café*) plant; **ir a ~** to walk, go on foot; **ao ~ de** near, by; **ao ~ da letra** literally; **estar de ~** (*festa etc*) to be on; **em** *ou* **de ~** standing (up); **dar no ~** (*col*) to run away, take off; **não ter ~ nem cabeça** (*fig*) to make no sense

peão [pjãw] (*PT: pl -ões*) *m* pedestrian

peça ['pɛsa] *f* piece; (*AUTO*) part; (*aposento*) room; (*TEATRO*) play; **~ de reposição** spare part; **~ de roupa** garment

pecado [pe'kadu] *m* sin

pecar [pe'ka*] *vi* to sin; **~ por excesso de zelo** to be over-zealous

pechincha [pe'ʃĩʃa] *f* (*vantagem*) godsend; (*coisa barata*) bargain; **~r** [peʃĩ'ʃa*] *vi* to bargain, haggle

peço *etc* ['pɛsu] *vb* V **pedir**

pecuária [pe'kwarja] *f* cattle-raising

peculiar [peku'lja*] *adj* special, peculiar; (*particular*) particular; **~idade** [pekulja-ri'dadʒi] *f* peculiarity

pedaço [pe'dasu] *m* piece; (*fig: trecho*) bit; **aos ~s** in pieces

pedágio [pe'daʒju] (*BR*) *m* (*pagamento*) toll

pedal [pe'daw] (*pl -ais*) *m* pedal; **~ar** [peda'la*] *vt, vi* to pedal

pedante [pe'dãtʃi] *adj* pretentious ♦ *m/f* pseud

pé-de-galinha (*pl* **pés-de-galinha**) *m* crow's foot

pedestre [pe'dɛʃtri] (*BR*) *m* pedestrian

pediatria [pedʒja'tria] *f* paediatrics *sg* (*BRIT*), pediatrics *sg* (*US*)

pedicuro/a [pedʒi'kuru/a] *m/f* chiropodist (*BRIT*), podiatrist (*US*)

pedido [pe'dʒidu] *m* request; (*COM*) order; **~ de demissão** resignation; **~ de desculpa** apology

pedigree [pedʒi'gri] *m* pedigree

pedinte [pe'dʒĩtʃi] *m/f* beggar

pedir [pe'dʒi*] *vt* to ask for; (*COM, comida*) to order; (*exigir*) to demand ♦ *vi* to ask; (*num restaurante*) to order; **~ algo a alguém** to ask sb for sth; **~ a alguém que faça**, **~ para alguém fazer** to ask sb to do

pedra ['pɛdra] *f* stone; (*rochedo*) rock; (*de granizo*) hailstone; (*de açúcar*) lump; (*quadro-negro*) slate; **~ de gelo** ice cube; **pedreira** [pe'drejra] *f* quarry; **pedreiro** [pe'drejru] *m* stonemason

pegada [pe'gada] *f* (*de pé*) footprint; (*FUTEBOL*) save

pegado/a [pe'gadu/a] *adj* stuck; (*unido*) together

pegajoso/a [pega'ʒozu/ɔza] *adj* sticky

pegar [pe'ga*] *vt* to catch; (*selos*) to stick (on); (*segurar*) to take hold of; (*hábito, mania*) to get into; (*compreender*) to take in; (*trabalho*) to take on; (*estação de rádio*) to pick up, get ♦ *vi* to stick; (*planta*) to take; (*moda*) to catch on; (*doença*) to be catching; (*motor*) to start; **~ em** (*segurar*) to grab, pick up; **ir ~** (*buscar*) to go and get; **~ um emprego** to get a job; **~ fogo a algo** to set fire to sth; **~ no sono** to fall asleep

pego/a ['pɛgu/a] *pp de* **pegar**

peito ['pejtu] *m* (*ANAT*) chest; (*de ave, mulher*) breast; (*fig*) courage

peitoril [pejto'riw] (*pl -is*) *m* windowsill

peixada [pej'ʃada] *f* fish cooked in a sea-food sauce

peixaria [pejʃa'ria] *f* fish shop, fishmonger's (*BRIT*)

peixe ['pejʃi] *m* fish; **P~s** *mpl* (*ASTROLOGIA*) Pisces *sg*

pejorativo/a [peʒora'tʃivu/a] *adj* pejorative

pela ['pɛla] = **por** + **a**

pelada [pe'lada] *f* football game

pelado/a [pe'ladu/a] *adj* (*sem pele*) skinned; (*sem pêlo, cabelo*) shorn; (*nu*) naked, in the nude; (*sem dinheiro*) broke

pelar [pe'la*] *vt* (*tirar a pele*) to skin; (*tirar o pêlo*) to shear

pelas ['pɛlaʃ] = **por** + **as**

pele ['pɛli] *f* skin; (*couro*) leather; (*como agasalho*) fur; (*de animal*) hide

pelerine [pele'rini] *f* cape

pelicano [peli'kanu] *m* pelican

película [pe'likula] *f* film

pelo ['pɛlu] = **por** + **o**

pêlo ['pelu] *m* hair; (*de animal*) fur, coat; **nu em ~** stark naked

pelos ['pɛluʃ] = **por** + **os**

peludo/a [pe'ludu/a] *adj* hairy; (*animal*) furry

pena ['pena] *f* feather; (*de caneta*) nib; (*escrita*) writing; (*JUR*) penalty, punishment; (*sofrimento*) suffering; (*piedade*) pity; **que ~!** what a shame!; **dar ~** to be upsetting; **ter ~ de** to feel sorry for; **~ capital** capital punishment

penal [pe'naw] (*pl -ais*) *adj* penal; **~idade** [penali'dadʒi] *f* (*JUR*) penalty; (*castigo*) punishment; **~izar** [penali'za*] *vt* to trouble; (*castigar*) to penalize

pênalti ['penawtʃi] *m* (*FUTEBOL*) penalty (kick)

penar [pe'na*] *vt* to grieve ♦ *vi* to suffer

penca ['pẽka] *f* bunch

pence ['pẽsi] *f* dart

pendência [pẽ'dẽsja] *f* dispute, quarrel

pendente [pẽ'dẽtʃi] *adj* hanging; (*por decidir*) pending; (*inclinado*) sloping; (*dependent*): **~ (de)** dependent (on) ♦ *m* pendant

pender [pẽ'de*] *vt, vi* to hang

pêndulo ['pẽdulu] *m* pendulum

pendurar [pēdu'ra*] vt to hang
penedo [pe'nedu] m rock, boulder
peneira [pe'nejra] f sieve; ~**r** [penej'ra*]
vt to sift, sieve ♦ vi (chover) to drizzle
penetrante [pene'trātʃi] adj (olhar)
searching; (ferida) deep; (frio) biting;
(som, análise) penetrating, piercing;
(dor, arma) sharp; (inteligência, idéias)
incisive
penetrar [penc'tra*] vt to get into, penetrate; (compreender) to understand ♦ vi:
~ **em** ou **por** ou **entre** to penetrate; ~
em (segredo) to find out
penhasco [pe'naʃku] m cliff, crag
penhor [pe'no*] m pledge; **casa de ~es**
pawnshop; **dar em ~** to pawn; ~**ar**
[peɲo'ra*] vt (dar em penhor) to pledge,
pawn
pêni ['peni] m penny
penicilina [penisi'lina] f penicillin
península [pe'nĩsula] f peninsula
pênis ['peniʃ] m inv penis
penitência [peni'tēsja] f penitence; (ex-
piação) penance; **penitenciária** [peni-
tē'sjarja] f prison; **penitenciário/a**
[penitē'sjarju/a] m/f prisoner, inmate
penoso/a [pe'nozu/ɔza] adj (assunto, tratamento) painful; (trabalho) hard
pensamento [pēsa'mētu] m thought;
(mente) mind; (opinião) way of thinking;
(idéia) idea
pensão [pē'sāw] (pl -ões) f (tb: casa de
~) boarding house; (comida) board; ~
completa full board; ~ **de aposentadoria** (retirement) pension
pensar [pē'sa*] vi to think; (imaginar) to
imagine; ~ **em** to think of ou about; ~
fazer to intend to do; **pensativo/a**
[pēsa'tʃivu/a] adj thoughtful, pensive
pensionista [pēsjo'niʃta] m/f pensioner
pensões [pē'sõjʃ] fpl de **pensão**
pente ['pētʃi] m comb; ~**ado/a**
[pē'tʃjadu/a] adj (cabelo) in place; (pessoa) smart ♦ m hairdo, hairstyle; ~**ar**
[pē'tʃja*] vt to comb; (arranjar o cabelo)
to do, style; ~**ar-se** vr to comb one's
hair; to do one's hair
Pentecostes [pētʃi'kɔʃtʃiʃ] m Whitsun
penugem [pe'nuʒē] f (de ave) down;
(pêlo) fluff
penúltimo/a [pe'nuwtʃimu/a] adj last
but one, penultimate
penumbra [pe'nūbra] f twilight, dusk;
(sombra) shadow; (meia-luz) half-light
penúria [pe'nurja] f poverty
peões [pjõjʃ] mpl de **peão**
pepino [pe'pinu] m cucumber
pequeno/a [pe'kenu/a] adj small; (mesquinho) petty ♦ m boy
pequerrucho [peke'xuʃu] m thimble
Pequim [pe'kĩ] n Peking, Beijing
pêra ['pera] f pear
perambular [perābu'la*] vi to wander
perante [pe'rātʃi] prep before, in the presence of

per capita [pex'kapita] adv, adj per capita
perceber [pexse'be*] vt to realize; (por
meio dos sentidos) to perceive; (compreender) to understand; (ver) to see;
(ouvir) to hear; (ver ao longe) to make
out; (dinheiro: receber) to receive
percentagem [pexsē'taʒē] f percentage
percepção [pexsep'sāw] f perception;
perceptível [pexsep'tʃivew] (pl -eis) adj
perceptible, noticeable; (som) audible;
perceptivo/a [pexsep'tʃivu/a] adj perceptive
percevejo [pexse'veʒu] m (inseto) bug;
(prego) drawing pin (BRIT), thumbtack
(US)
perco etc ['pexku] vb V **perder**
percorrer [pexko'xe*] vt (viajar por) to
travel (across ou over); (passar por) to
go through, traverse; (investigar) to
search through
percurso [pex'kuxsu] m (espaço percorri-
do) distance (covered); (trajeto) route;
(viagem) journey
percussão [pexku'sāw] f (MÚS) percussion
perda ['pexda] f loss; (desperdício) waste;
~**s e danos** damages, losses
perdão [pex'dāw] m pardon, forgiveness;
~! sorry!, I beg your pardon!
perder [pex'de*] vt to lose; (tempo) to
waste; (trem, show, oportunidade) to
miss ♦ vi to lose; ~**se** vr to get lost;
(arruinar-se) to be ruined; (desaparecer)
to disappear; ~**se de alguém** to lose
sb
perdição [pexdʒi'sāw] f perdition, ruin;
(desonra) depravity
perdido/a [pex'dʒidu/a] adj lost; ~**s e
achados** lost and found, lost property
perdigão [pexdʒi'gāw] (pl -ões) m
(macho) partridge
perdiz [pex'dʒiʒ] f partridge
perdoar [pex'dwa*] vt to forgive
perdurar [pexdu'ra*] vi to last a long
time; (continuar a existir) to still exist
perecer [pere'se*] vi to perish; (morrer)
to die; (acabar) to come to nothing; **perecível** [pere'sivew] (pl -eis) adj perish-
able
peregrinação [peregrina'sāw] (pl -ões) f
(viagem) travels pl; (REL) pilgrimage
peregrino/a [pere'grinu/a] m/f pilgrim
peremptório/a [perēp'tɔrju/a] adj final;
(decisivo) decisive
perene [pe'rɛni] adj everlasting; (BOT)
perennial
perfeição [pexfej'sāw] f perfection
perfeitamente [pexfejta'mētʃi] adv per-
fectly ♦ excl exactly!
perfeito/a [pex'fejtu/a] adj perfect ♦ m
(LING) perfect
pérfido/a ['pexfidu/a] adj treacherous
perfil [pex'fiw] (pl -is) m profile; (silhueta) silhouette, outline; (ARQ) (cross) sec-

tion

perfume [pex'fumi] *m* perfume, scent

perfurador [pexfura'do*] *m* punch

perfurar [pexfu'ra*] *vt* (*o chão*) to drill a hole in; (*papel*) to punch (a hole in)

pergaminho [pexga'miɲu] *m* parchment; (*diploma*) diploma

pergunta [pex'gũta] *f* question; **fazer uma ~ a alguém** to ask sb a question; **~r** [pexgũ'ta*] *vt* to ask; (*interrogar*) to question ♦ *vi*: **~r por alguém** to ask after sb; **~r-se** *vr* to wonder; **~r algo a alguém** to ask sb sth

perícia [pe'risja] *f* expertise; (*destreza*) skill; (*exame*) investigation

periferia [perife'ria] *f* periphery; (*da cidade*) outskirts *pl*

periférico/a [peri'feriku/a] *adj* peripheral ♦ *m* (*COMPUT*) peripheral; **estrada periférica** ring road

perigo [pe'rigu] *m* danger; **~so/a** [peri'gozu/ɔza] *adj* dangerous; (*arriscado*) risky

perímetro [pe'rimetru] *m* perimeter

periódico/a [pe'rjɔdʒiku/a] *adj* periodic ♦ *m* (*revista*) magazine, periodical; (*jornal*) (news)paper

período [pe'riodu] *m* period; (*estação*) season

peripécia [peri'pɛsja] *f* (*aventura*) adventure; (*incidente*) turn of events

periquito [peri'kitu] *m* parakeet

perito/a [pe'ritu/a] *adj* expert ♦ *m/f* expert; (*quem faz perícia*) investigator

permanecer [pexmane'se*] *vi* to remain; (*num lugar*) to stay; (*continuar a ser*) to remain, keep; **~ parado** to keep still

permanência [pexma'nẽsja] *f* permanence; (*estada*) stay; **permanente** [pexma'nẽtʃi] *adj* (*dor*) constant; (*cor*) fast; (*residência*, *pregas*) permanent ♦ *m* (*cartão*) pass ♦ *f* perm

permissão [pexmi'sãw] *f* permission, consent; **permissível** [pexmi'sivew] (*pl* -eis) *adj* permissible; **permissivo/a** [pexmi'sivu/a] *adj* permissive

permitir [pexmi'tʃi*] *vt* to allow, permit

perna ['pɛxna] *f* leg; **~s tortas** bow legs

pernicioso/a [pexni'sjozu/ɔza] *adj* pernicious; (*MED*) malignant

pernil [pex'niw] (*pl* -is) *m* (*de animal*) haunch; (*CULIN*) leg

pernilongo [pexni'lõgu] *m* mosquito

pernis [pex'nif] *mpl de* **pernil**

pernoitar [pexnoj'ta*] *vi* to spend the night

pérola ['pɛrola] *f* pearl

perpendicular [pexpẽdʒiku'la*] *adj*, *f* perpendicular

perpetrar [pexpe'tra*] *vt* to perpetrate

perpetuar [pexpe'twa*] *vt* to perpetuate; **perpétuo/a** [pex'pɛtwu/a] *adj* perpetual

perplexidade [pexpleksi'dadʒi] *f* confusion, bewilderment

perplexo/a [pex'plɛksu/a] *adj* bewildered,

puzzled; (*indeciso*) uncertain; **ficar ~ to be taken aback**

persa ['pɛxsa] *adj*, *m/f* Persian

perseguição [pexsegi'sãw] *f* pursuit; (*REL*, *POL*) persecution

perseguir [pexse'gi*] *vt* to pursue; (*correr atrás*) to chase (after); (*REL*, *POL*) to persecute; (*importunar*) to harass, pester

perseverante [pexseve'rãtʃi] *adj* persistent

perseverar [pexseve'ra*] *vi*: **~ (em)** to persevere (in), persist (in)

Pérsia ['pɛxsja] *f*: **a ~ Persia**

persiana [pex'sjana] *f* blind

Pérsico/a ['pɛxsiku/a] *adj*: **o golfo ~ the Persian Gulf**

persigo *etc* [pex'sigu] *vb V* **perseguir**

persistente [pexsif'tẽtʃi] *adj* persistent

persistir [pexsif'tʃi*] *vi*: **~ (em)** to persist (in)

personagem [pexso'naʒẽ] (*pl* -ns) *m/f* famous person, celebrity; (*num livro*, *filme*) character

personalidade [pexsonali'dadʒi] *f* personality

perspectiva [pexʃpek'tʃiva] *f* perspective; (*panorama*) view; (*probabilidade*) prospect; (*ponto de vista*) point of view

perspicácia [pexʃpi'kasja] *f* insight, perceptiveness; **perspicaz** [pexʃpi'kajʒ] *adj* observant; (*sagaz*) shrewd

persuadir [pexswa'dʒi*] *vt* to persuade; **~-se** *vr* to convince o.s.; **persuasão** [pexswa'zãw] *f* persuasion; **persuasivo/a** [pexswa'zivu/a] *adj* persuasive

pertencente [pextẽ'sẽtʃi] *adj*: **~ a pertaining to**

pertencer [pextẽ'se*] *vi*: **~ a** to belong to; (*referir-se*) to concern

pertences [pex'tẽsif] *mpl* (*de uma pessoa*) belongings

pertinaz [pextʃi'najʒ] *adj* persistent; (*obstinado*) obstinate

pertinência [pextʃi'nẽsja] *f* relevance; **pertinente** [pextʃi'nẽtʃi] *adj* relevant; (*apropriado*) appropriate

perto/a ['pɛxtu/a] *adj* nearby ♦ *adv* near; **~ de** near to; (*em comparação com*) next to; **de ~** closely; (*ver*) close up; (*conhecer*) very well

perturbar [pextux'ba*] *vt* to disturb; (*abalar*) to upset, trouble; (*atrapalhar*) to put off; (*andamento*, *trânsito*) to disrupt; (*envergonhar*) to embarrass; (*alterar*) to affect

Peru [pe'ru] *m*: **o ~ Peru**

peru(a) [pe'ru(a)] *m/f* turkey

peruca [pe'ruka] *f* wig

perverso/a [pex'vɛxsu/a] *adj* perverse; (*malvado*) wicked

perverter [pexvex'te*] *vt* to corrupt, pervert; **pervertido/a** [pexvex'tʃidu/a] *adj* perverted ♦ *m/f* pervert

pesadelo [peza'delu] *m* nightmare

pesado/a [pe'zadu/a] *adj* heavy; (*am-

biente) tense; (*trabalho*) hard; (*estilo*) dull, boring; (*andar*) slow; (*piada*) coarse; (*comida*) stodgy; (*tempo*) sultry ♦ *adv* heavily

pêsames ['pesamiʃ] *mpl* condolences, sympathy *sg*

pesar [pe'za*] *vt* to weigh; (*fig*) to weigh up ♦ *vi* to weigh; (*ser pesado*) to be heavy; (*influir*) to carry weight; (*causar mágoa*): ~ **a** to hurt, grieve ♦ *m* grief; ~ **sobre** (*recair*) to fall upon

pesaroso/a [peza'rozu/ɔza] *adj* sorrowful, sad; (*arrependido*) regretful, sorry

pesca ['peʃka] *f* fishing; (*os peixes*) catch; **ir à** ~ to go fishing

pescada [peʃ'kada] *f* whiting

pescado [peʃ'kadu] *m* fish

pescador(a) [peʃka'do*(a)] *m/f* fisherman/woman; ~ **à linha** angler

pescar [peʃ'ka*] *vt* (*peixe*) to catch; (*tentar apanhar*) to fish for; (*retirar da água*) to fish out ♦ *vi* to fish

pescoço [peʃ'kosu] *m* neck

peso ['pezu] *m* weight; (*fig*: *ônus*) burden; (*importância*) importance; ~ **bruto/líquido** gross/net weight

pesqueiro/a [peʃ'kejru/a] *adj* fishing *atr*

pesquisa [peʃ'kiza] *f* inquiry, investigation; (*científica, de mercado*) research; **~dor(a)** [peʃkiza'do*(a)] *m/f* investigator; researcher; **~r** [peʃki'za*] *vt, vi* to investigate; to research

pêssego ['pesegu] *m* peach

pessimista [pesi'miʃta] *adj* pessimistic ♦ *m/f* pessimist

péssimo/a ['pɛsimu/a] *adj* very bad, awful

pessoa [pe'soa] *f* person; ~**s** *fpl* (*gente*) people; ~**l** [pe'swaw] (*pl* ~**is**) *adj* personal ♦ *m* personnel *pl*, staff *pl*; (*col*) people *pl*, folks *pl*

pestana [peʃ'tana] *f* eyelash; **pestanejar** [peʃtane'ʒa*] *vi* to blink

peste ['pɛʃtʃi] *f* epidemic; (*bubónica*) plague; (*fig*) pest, nuisance

pesticida [peʃtʃi'sida] *m* pesticide

pétala ['pɛtala] *f* petal

petição [petʃi'sãw] (*pl* ~**ões**) *f* request; (*documento*) petition

petisco [pe'tʃiʃku] *m* savoury (*BRIT*), savory (*US*), titbit (*BRIT*), tidbit (*US*)

petit-pois [petʃi'pwa] *m inv* pea

petrificar [petrifi'ka*] *vt* to petrify

petroleiro/a [petro'lejru/a] *adj* oil *atr*, petroleum *atr* ♦ *m* (*navio*) oil tanker

petróleo [pe'trɔlju] *m* oil, petroleum; ~ **bruto** crude oil; **petrolífero/a** [petro'liferu/a] *adj* oil-producing

petulância [petu'lãsja] *f* impudence; **petulante** [petu'lãtʃi] *adj* impudent

peúga ['pjuga] (*PT*) *f* sock

pevide [pe'vidʒi] (*PT*) *f* (*de melão*) seed; (*de maçã*) pip

p. ex. *abr* (= *por exemplo*) e.g.

pia ['pia] *f* wash basin; (*da cozinha*) sink;

~ **batismal** font

piada ['pjada] *f* joke

pianista [pja'niʃta] *m/f* pianist

piano ['pjanu] *m* piano

pião [pjãw] (*pl* ~**ões**) *m* (*brinquedo*) top

piar [pja*] *vi* (*pinto*) to cheep; (*coruja*) to hoot

picada [pi'kada] *f* (*de agulha etc*) prick; (*de abelha*) sting; (*de mosquito, cobra*) bite; (*de avião*) dive; (*de navalha*) stab; (*atalho*) path, trail

picadinho [pika'dʒiɲu] *m* stew

picante [pi'kãtʃi] *adj* (*tempero*) hot

pica-pau ['pika-] (*pl* ~**s**) *m* woodpecker

picar [pi'ka*] *vt* to prick; (*suj*: *abelha*) to sting; (:*mosquito*) to bite; (:*pássaro*) to peck; (*um animal*) to goad; (*carne*) to mince; (*papel*) to shred; (*fruta*) to chop up ♦ *vi* (*comichar*) to prickle

picareta [pika'reta] *f* pickaxe (*BRIT*), pickax (*US*) ♦ *m/f* crook

pico ['piku] *m* (*cume*) peak; (*ponta aguda*) sharp point; (*PT*: *um pouco*) a bit; **mil e** ~ just over a thousand

picolé [piko'lɛ] *m* lolly

picotar [piko'ta*] *vt* to perforate; (*bilhete*) to punch

piedade [pje'dadʒi] *f* piety; (*compaixão*) pity; **ter** ~ **de** to have pity on; **piedoso/a** [pje'dozu/ɔza] *adj* pious; (*compassivo*) merciful

pier ['pie] *m* pier

pifar [pi'fa*] (*col*) *vi* (*carro*) to break down; (*rádio etc*) to go wrong; (*plano, programa*) to fall through

pigméia [pig'mɛja] *f de* **pigmeu**

pigmento [pig'mẽtu] *m* pigment

pigmeu/méia [pig'mew/'mɛja] *adj*, *m/f* pigmy

pijama [pi'ʒama] *m ou f* pyjamas *pl* (*BRIT*), pajamas *pl* (*US*)

pilantra [pi'lãtra] (*col*) *m/f* crook

pilar [pi'la*] *vt* to pound, crush ♦ *m* pillar

pilha ['piʎa] *f* (*ELET*) battery; (*monte*) pile, heap

pilhagem [pi'ʎaʒẽ] *f* (*ato*) pillage; (*objetos*) plunder, booty

pilhar [pi'ʎa*] *vt* to plunder, pillage; (*roubar*) to rob; (*surpreender*) to catch

pilhéria [pi'ʎɛrja] *f* joke

pilotar [pilo'ta*] *vt* (*avião*) to fly

piloto [pi'lotu] *m* pilot; (*motorista*) (racing) driver; (*bico de gás*) pilot light ♦ *adj* (*usina, plano*) pilot; (*peça*) sample *atr*

pílula ['pilula] *f* pill; **a** ~ (*anticoncepcional*) the pill

pimenta [pi'mẽta] *f* (*CULIN*) pepper; ~ **de Caiena** cayenne pepper; ~**-do-reino** *f* black pepper; ~**-malagueta** (*pl* ~**s-malagueta**) *f* chilli (*BRIT*) ou chili (*US*) pepper; **pimentão** [pimẽ'tãw] (*pl* ~**ões**) *m* (*BOT*) pepper; **pimenteira** [pimẽ'tejra] *f* (*BOT*) pepper plant; (*à mesa*) pepper pot;

(: *moedor*) pepper mill

pinacoteca [pinako'tɛka] *f* art gallery

pinça ['pĩsa] *f* (*de sobrancelhas*) tweezers *pl*; (*de casa*) tongs *pl*; (*MED*) callipers *pl* (*BRIT*), calipers *pl* (*US*)

píncaro ['pĩkaru] *m* summit, peak

pincel [pĩ'sɛw] (*pl* **-éis**) *m* brush; (*para pintar*) paintbrush; **~ar** [pĩse'la*] *vt* to paint

pinga ['pĩga] *f* (*cachaça*) rum; (*PT*: *trago*) drink

pingar [pĩ'ga*] *vi* to drip

pingente [pĩ'ʒẽtʃi] *m* pendant

pingo ['pĩgu] *m* (*gota*) drop

pingue-pongue ® [pĩgi-'põgi] *m* ping-pong ®

pingüim [pĩ'gwĩ] (*pl* **-ns**) *m* penguin

pinheiro [pĩ'ɲejru] *m* pine (tree)

pinho ['pĩɲu] *m* pine

pino ['pinu] *m* (*peça*) pin; (*AUTO*: *na porta*) lock; **a ~** upright

pinta ['pĩta] *f* (*mancha*) spot

pintar [pĩ'ta*] *vt* to paint; (*cabelo*) to dye; (*rosto*) to make up; (*descrever*) to describe; (*imaginar*) to picture ♦ *vi* to paint; **~-se** *vr* to make o.s. up

pintarroxo [pĩta'xoʃu] *m* (*BR*) linnet; (*PT*) robin

pinto ['pĩtu] *m* chick; (*col!*) prick (!)

pintor(a) [pĩ'to*(a)] *m/f* painter

pintura [pĩ'tura] *f* painting; (*maquiagem*) make-up

pio/a ['piu/a] *adj* pious; (*caridoso*) charitable ♦ *m* cheep, chirp

piões [pjõjʃ] *mpl de* **pião**

piolho ['pjoʎu] *m* louse

pioneiro/a [pjo'nejru/a] *m/f* pioneer

pior ['pjɔ*] *adj*, *adv* (*compar*) worse; (*superl*) worst ♦ *m*: **o ~** worst of all; **~ar** [pjo'ra*] *vt* to make worse, worsen ♦ *vi* to get worse

pipa ['pipa] *f* barrel, cask; (*de papel*) kite

pipi [pi'pi] (*col*) *m* pee; **fazer ~** to have a pee

pipoca [pi'pɔka] *f* popcorn

pipocar [pipo'ka*] *vi* to go pop, pop

pique[1] ['piki] *m* (*corte*) nick; (*auge*) peak; **a ~** vertically, steeply

pique[2] *etc vb V* **picar**

piquenique [piki'niki] *m* picnic

pirâmide [pi'ramidʒi] *f* pyramid

piranha [pi'raɲa] *f* piranha (fish)

pirata [pi'rata] *m* pirate

pires ['piriʃ] *m inv* saucer

Pirineus [piri'newʃ] *mpl*: **os ~** the Pyrenees

pirueta [pi'rweta] *f* pirouette

pirulito [piru'litu] (*BR*) *m* lollipop

pisada [pi'zada] *f* (*passo*) footstep; (*rastro*) footprint

pisar [pi'za*] *vt* to tread on; (*esmagar*, *subjugar*) to crush ♦ *vi* to step, tread

pisca-pisca [piʃka-'piʃka] (*pl* **~s**) *m* (*AUTO*) indicator

piscar [piʃ'ka*] *vt* to blink; (*dar sinal*) to wink; (*estrelas*) to twinkle ♦ *m*: **num ~ de olhos** in a flash

piscina [pi'sina] *f* swimming pool

piso ['pizu] *m* floor

pisotear [pizo'tʃja*] *vt* to trample (on)

pista ['piʃta] *f* (*vestígio*) trace; (*indicação*) clue; (*de corridas*) track; (*AVIAT*) runway; (*de estrada*) lane; (*de dança*) (dance) floor

pistola [piʃ'tɔla] *f* pistol; **pistoleiro** [piʃto'lejru] *m* gunman

pistom [piʃ'tõ] (*pl* **-ns**) *m* piston

pitada [pi'tada] *f* (*porção*) pinch

pitoresco/a [pito'reʃku/a] *adj* picturesque

pivete [pi'vɛtʃi] *m* child thief

pivô [pi'vo] *m* pivot; (*fig*) central figure, prime mover

pizza ['pitsa] *f* pizza

placa ['plaka] *f* plate; (*AUTO*) number plate (*BRIT*), license plate (*US*); (*comemorativa*) plaque; (*na pele*) blotch; **~ de sinalização** roadsign

placar [pla'ka*] *m* scoreboard

plácido/a ['plasidu/a] *adj* calm; (*manso*) placid

plágio ['plaʒu] *m* plagiarism

planador [plana'do*] *m* glider

planalto [pla'nawtu] *m* tableland, plateau

planar [pla'na*] *vi* to glide

planear [pla'nja*] (*PT*) *vt* = **planejar**

planejador(a) [planeʒa'do*(a)] *m/f* planner

planejamento [planeʒa'mẽtu] *m* planning; **~ familiar** family planning

planejar [plane'ʒa*] (*BR*) *vt* to plan; (*edifício*) to design

planeta [pla'neta] *m* planet

planície [pla'nisi] *f* plain

planilha [pla'niʎa] *f* (*COMPUT*) spreadsheet

plano/a ['planu/a] *adj* flat, level; (*liso*) smooth ♦ *m* plan; **em primeiro/em último ~** in the foreground/background

planta ['plãta] *f* plant; (*de pé*) sole; (*ARQ*) plan

plantação [plãta'sãw] *f* (*ato*) planting; (*terreno*) planted land; (*plantio*) crops *pl*

plantão [plã'tãw] (*pl* **-ões**) *m* duty; (*noturno*) night duty; (*plantonista*) person on duty; (*MIL*: *serviço*) sentry duty; (: *pessoa*) sentry; **estar de ~** to be on duty

plantar [plã'ta*] *vt* to plant; (*estaca*) to drive in; (*estabelecer*) to set up

plantões [plã'tõjʃ] *mpl de* **plantão**

plaqueta [pla'keta] *f* plaque; (*AUTO*) licensing badge (*attached to number plate*); (*COMPUT*) chip

plástico/a ['plaʃtʃiku/a] *adj* plastic ♦ *m* plastic

plataforma [plata'fɔxma] *f* platform; **~ de exploração de petróleo** oil rig; **~ de lançamento** launch pad

platéia [pla'tɛja] *f* (*TEATRO etc*) stalls *pl* (*BRIT*), orchestra (*US*); (*espectadores*) audience

platina [pla'tʃina] *f* platinum

platinados [platʃi'naduʃ] *mpl* (AUTO) points

plausível [plaw'zivew] (*pl* -**eis**) *adj* credible, plausible

playground [plej'grãwdʒi] (*pl* ~**s**) *m* (children's) playground

pleito ['plejtu] *m* lawsuit, case; (*fig*) dispute; ~ (**eleitoral**) election

plenamente [plena'mētʃi] *adv* fully, completely

pleno/a ['plenu/a] *adj* full; (*completo*) complete; **em** ~ **dia** in broad daylight; **em** ~ **inverno** in the middle *ou* depths of winter

pluma ['pluma] *f* feather

plural [plu'raw] (*pl* -**ais**) *adj, m* plural

plutônio [plu'tonju] *m* plutonium

pneu ['pnew] *m* tyre (BRIT), tire (US)

pneumático/a [pnew'matʃiku/a] *adj* pneumatic ♦ *m* tyre (BRIT), tire (US)

pneumonia [pnewmo'nia] *f* pneumonia

pó [pɔ] *m* powder; (*sujeira*) dust; **sabão em** ~ soap powder; **tirar o** ~ (**de algo**) to dust (sth)

pobre ['pɔbri] *adj* poor ♦ *m/f* poor person; ~**za** [po'breza] *f* poverty

poça ['posa] *f* puddle, pool

poção [po'sãw] (*pl* -**ões**) *f* potion

pocilga [po'siwga] *f* pigsty

poço ['posu] *m* well; (*de mina, elevador*) shaft

poções [po'sõjʃ] *fpl de* **poção**

podar [po'daʰ] *vt* to prune

pôde *etc* ['podʒi] *vb* V **poder**

pó-de-arroz *m* face powder

PALAVRA CHAVE

poder [po'deʰ] *vi* **1** (*capacidade*) can, be able to; **não posso fazê-lo** I can't do it, I'm unable to do it

2 (*ter o direito de*) can, may, be allowed to; **posso fumar aqui?** can I smoke here?; **pode entrar?** (*posso?*) can I come in?

3 (*possibilidade*) may, might, could; **pode ser** maybe; **pode ser que** it may be that; **ele** ~**á vir amanhã** he might come tomorrow

4: não ~ **com: não posso com ele** I cannot cope with him

5 (*col: indignação*): **pudera!** no wonder!; **como é que pode?** you're joking!

♦ *m* power; (*autoridade*) authority; ~ **aquisitivo** purchasing power; **estar no** ~ to be in power; **em** ~ **de alguém** in sb's hands

---

poderio [pode'riu] *m* might, power

poderoso/a [pode'rozu/oza] *adj* mighty, powerful

podre ['podri] *adj* rotten; **podridão** [podri'dãw] *f* decay, rottenness; (*fig*) corruption

põe *etc* [põj] *vb* V **pôr**

poeira ['pwejra] *f* dust; ~ **radioativa** fall-out; **poeirento/a** [pwej'rētu/a] *adj* dusty

poema ['pwɛma] *m* poem

poesia [poe'zia] *f* poetry; (*poema*) poem

poeta ['pwɛta] *m* poet; **poético/a** ['pwetʃiku/a] *adj* poetic; **poetisa** [pwe'tʃiza] *f* (woman) poet

pois [pojʃ] *adv* (*portanto*) so; (PT: *assentimento*) yes ♦ *conj* as, since; (*mas*) but; ~ **bem** well then; ~ **é** that's right; ~ **não!** (BR) of course!; ~ **não?** (BR: *numa loja*) what can I do for you?; (PT) isn't it?, aren't you?, didn't they? *etc*; ~ **sim!** certainly not!; ~ (**então**) then

polaco/a [po'laku/a] *adj* Polish ♦ *m/f* Pole ♦ *m* (LING) Polish

polar [po'laʰ] *adj* polar

polegada [pole'gada] *f* inch

polegar [pole'gaʰ] *m* (*tb: dedo* ~) thumb

polêmica [po'lemika] *f* controversy; **polêmico/a** [po'lemiku/a] *adj* controversial

pólen ['pɔlē] *m* pollen

polia [po'lia] *f* pulley

polícia [po'lisja] *f* police, police force ♦ *m/f* policeman/woman; **policial** [poli'sjaw] (*pl* -**ais**) *adj* police *atr* ♦ *m/f* (BR) policeman/woman; **novela** *ou* **romance policial** detective novel; **policiar** [poli'sjaʰ] *vt* to police; (*instintos, modos*) to control, keep in check

polidez [poli'deʒ] *f* good manners *pl*, politeness

polido/a [po'lidu/a] *adj* polished, shiny; (*cortês*) well-mannered, polite

poliéster [po'ljɛfteʰ] *m* polyester

poliestireno [poljeftʃi'rɛnu] *m* polystyrene

polietileno [poljetʃi'lɛnu] *m* polythene (BRIT), polyethylene (US)

polimento [poli'mētu] *m* polishing; (*finura*) refinement

pólio ['pɔlju] *f* polio

polir [po'liʰ] *vt* to polish

politécnica [poli'tɛknika] *f* polytechnic

política [po'litʃika] *f* politics *sg*; (*programa*) policy; **político/a** [po'litʃiku/a] *adj* political ♦ *m/f* politician

pólo ['pɔlu] *m* pole; (ESPORTE) polo; **P~ Norte/Sul** North/South Pole

polonês/esa [polo'neʃ/eza] *adj* Polish ♦ *m/f* Pole ♦ *m* (LING) Polish

Polônia [po'lonja] *f*: **a** ~ Poland

polpa ['powpa] *f* pulp

poltrona [pow'trona] *f* armchair

poluição [polwi'sãw] *f* pollution; **poluir** [po'lwiʰ] *vt* to pollute

polvilho [pow'viʎu] *m* powder; (*farinha*) manioc flour

polvo ['powvu] *m* octopus

pólvora ['pɔwvora] *f* gunpowder

pomada [po'mada] *f* ointment

pomar [po'maʰ] *m* orchard

pomba ['põba] f dove
pombo ['põbu] m pigeon
pomos ['pomoʃ] vb V **pôr**
pompa ['põpa] f pomp
pompom [põ'põ] (pl -ns) m pompom
pomposo/a [põ'pozu/ɔza] adj pompous
poncho ['põʃu] m poncho
ponderação [põdera'sãw] f consideration, meditation; (prudência) prudence
ponderado/a [põde'radu/a] adj prudent
ponderar [põde'ra*] vt to consider, weigh up ♦ vi to meditate, muse
pônei ['ponej] m pony
ponho etc ['poɲu] vb V **pôr**
ponta ['põta] f (de faca) point; (de sapato) toe; (extremidade) end; (FUTEBOL: posição) wing; (: jogador) winger; **uma ~ de** (um pouco) a touch of; **~ do dedo** fingertip
pontada [põ'tada] f (dor) twinge
pontão [põ'tãw] m pontoon
pontapé [põta'pɛ] m kick; **dar ~s em alguém** to kick sb
pontaria [põta'ria] f aim; **fazer ~** to take aim
ponte ['põtʃi] f bridge; **~ aérea** air shuttle, airlift; **~ de safena** (heart) bypass operation
ponteiro [põ'tejru] m (indicador) pointer; (de relógio) hand
pontiagudo/a [põtʃja'gudu/a] adj sharp, pointed
pontífice [põ'tʃifisi] m pontiff, Pope
ponto ['põtu] m point; (MED, COSTURA, TRICÔ) stitch; (pequeno sinal, do i) dot; (na pontuação) full stop (BRIT), period (US); (na pele) spot; (de ônibus) stop; (de táxi) rank (BRIT), stand (US); (matéria escolar) subject; **estar a ~ de fazer** to be on the point of doing; **às cinco em ~** at five o'clock on the dot; **dois ~s** colon sg; **~ de admiração** (PT) exclamation mark; **~ de exclamação/interrogação** exclamation/question mark; **~ de vista** point of view, viewpoint; **~-e-vírgula** (pl **~-e-vírgulas**) m semicolon
pontuação [põtwa'sãw] f punctuation
pontual [põ'twaw] (pl -ais) adj punctual
pontudo/a [põ'tudu/a] adj pointed
popa ['popa] f stern
população [popula'sãw] (pl -ões) f population
popular [popu'la*] adj popular; **~idade** [populari'dadʒi] f popularity
pôquer ['poke*] m poker

por [po*] (por + o(s)/a(s) = pelo(s)/a(s)) prep **1** (objetivo) for; **lutar pela pátria** to fight for one's country
2 (+ infin): **está ~ acontecer** it is about to happen, it is yet to happen; **está ~ fazer** it is still to be done
3 (causa) out of, because of; **~ falta de** fundos through lack of funds; **~ hábito/natureza** out of habit/by nature; **faço isso ~ ela** I do it for her; **~ isso** therefore; **a razão pela qual ... the reason why ...; pelo amor de Deus!** for Heaven's sake!
4 (tempo): **pela manhã** in the morning; **~ volta das duas horas** at about two o'clock; **ele vai ficar ~ uma semana** he's staying for a week
5 (lugar): **~ aqui** this way; **viemos pelo parque** we came through the park; **passar ~ São Paulo** to pass through São Paulo; **~ fora/dentro** outside/inside
6 (troca, preço) for; **trocar o velho pelo novo** to change old for new; **comprei o livro ~ dez libras** I bought the book for ten pounds
7 (valor proporcional): **~ cento** per cent; **~ hora/dia/semana/mês/ano** hourly/daily/weekly/monthly/yearly; **~ cabeça** a ou per head; **~ mais difícil** etc **que seja** however difficult etc it is
8 (modo, meio) by; **~ correio/avião** by post/air; **~ sí** by o.s.; **~ escrito** in writing; **entrar pela entrada principal** to go in through the main entrance
9: **~ que** (por causa) because why (PT), why (BR); **~ quê?** why?
10: **~ mim tudo bem** as far as I'm concerned that's OK

pôr [po*] vt **1** (colocar) to put; (roupas) to put on; (objeções, dúvidas) to raise; (ovos, mesa) to lay; (defeito) to find; **põe mais forte** turn it up; **você põe açúcar?** do you take sugar?; **~ de lado** to set aside
2 (+ adj) to make; **você está me pondo nervoso** you're making me nervous
♦ **~-se** vr **1** (sol) to set
2 (colocar-se): **~-se de pé** to stand up; **ponha-se no meu lugar** put yourself in my position
3: **~-se a** to start to; **ela pôs-se a chorar** she started crying
♦ m: **o ~ do sol** sunset

porão [po'rãw] (pl -ões) m (de casa) basement; (: armazém) cellar
porca ['pɔxka] f (animal) sow
porção [pox'sãw] (pl -ões) f portion, piece; **uma ~ de** a lot of
porcaria [poxka'ria] f filth; (dito sujo) obscenity; (coisa ruim) piece of junk
porcelana [poxse'lana] f porcelain
porcentagem [poxsẽ'taʒẽ] (pl -ns) f percentage
porco/a ['poxku/'pɔxka] adj filthy ♦ m (animal) pig; (carne) pork
porções [pox'sõjʃ] fpl de **porção**
porco-espinho (pl **porcos-espinhos**) m

porcupine
porém [po'rẽ] *conj* however
pormenor [poxme'no*] *m* detail
pornografia [poxnogra'fia] *f* pornography
poro ['poru] *m* pore
porões [po'rõjs] *mpl de* **porão**
poroso/a [po'rozu/ɔza] *adj* porous
porquanto [pox'kwãtu] *conj* since, seeing
that
porque ['poxke] *conj* because; (*interrogativo: PT*) why
porquê ['pox'ke] *adv* why ♦ *m* reason,
motive; **~?** (*PT*) why?
porquinho-da-índia [pox'kiɲu-] (*pl*
porquinhos-da-índia) *m* guinea pig
porrete [po'xetʃi] *m* club
porta ['pɔxta] *f* door; (*vão da* ~) doorway; (*de um jardim*) gate
porta-aviões *m inv* aircraft carrier
porta-bagagem (*pl* **-ns**) (*PT*) *m* =
porta-malas
portador(a) [poxta'do*(a)] *m/f* bearer
portagem [pox'taʒẽ] (*PT: pl* **-ns**) *f* toll
portal [pox'taw] (*pl* **-ais**) *m* doorway
porta-luvas *m inv* (*AUTO*) glove compartment
porta-malas *m inv* (*AUTO*) boot (*BRIT*),
trunk (*US*)
porta-níqueis *m inv* purse
portanto [pox'tãtu] *conj* so, therefore
portão [pox'tãw] (*pl* **-ões**) *m* gate
portar [pox'ta*] *vt* to carry; **~-se** *vr* to
behave
portaria [poxta'ria] *f* (*de um edifício*) entrance hall; (*recepção*) reception desk;
(*do governo*) edict, decree
portátil [pox'tatʃiw] (*pl* **-eis**) *adj* portable
porta-voz (*pl* **-es**) *m/f* (*pessoa*)
spokesman/woman
porte ['pɔxtʃi] *m* transport; (*custo*)
freight charge, carriage; **~ pago** post
paid; **de grande ~** far-reaching, important
porteiro/a [pox'tejru/a] *m/f* caretaker; **~
eletrônico** entryphone
portentoso/a [poxtẽ'tozu/ɔza] *adj* amazing, marvellous (*BRIT*), marvelous (*US*)
pórtico ['pɔxtʃiku] *m* porch, portico
porto ['poxtu] *m* (*do mar*) port, harbour
(*BRIT*), harbor (*US*); (*vinho*) port; **o P~**
Oporto
portões [pox'tõjʃ] *mpl de* **portão**
Portugal [poxtu'gaw] *m* Portugal;
português/guesa [portu'geʃ/'geza] *adj*
Portuguese ♦ *m/f* Portuguese *inv* ♦ *m*
(*LING*) Portuguese
porventura [poxvẽ'tura] *adj* by chance;
se ~ você ... if you happen to ...
pôs [poʃ] *vb V* **pôr**
posar [po'za*] *vi* (*FOTO*): **~ (para)** to
pose (for)
pós-escrito [pɔjseʃkritu/a] *m* postscript
posição [pozi'sãw] (*pl* **-ões**) *f* position;
(*social*) standing, status; **posicionar** [po-
zisjo'na*] *vt* to position

positivo/a [pozi'tʃivu/a] *adj* positive
possante [po'sãtʃi] *adj* powerful, strong;
(*carro*) flashy
posse ['pɔsi] *f* possession, ownership; **~s**
fpl (*pertences*) possessions, belongings;
tomar ~ de to take possession of
possessão [pose'sãw] *f* possession;
possessivo/a [pose'sivu/a] *adj* possessive
possibilidade [posibili'dadʒi] *f* possibility; **~s** *fpl* (*recursos*) means
possibilitar [posibili'ta*] *vt* to make possible, permit
possível [po'sivew] (*pl* **-eis**) *adj* possible;
fazer todo o ~ to do one's best
posso *etc* ['posu] *vb* V **poder**
possuidor(a) [poswi'do*(a)] *m/f* owner
possuir [po'swi*] *vt* (*casa, livro etc*) to
own; (*dinheiro, talento*) to possess
postal [poʃ'taw] (*pl* **-ais**) *adj* postal ♦ *m*
postcard
poste ['pɔʃtʃi] *m* pole, post
pôster ['poʃte*] *m* poster
posteridade [poʃteri'dadʒi] *f* posterity
posterior [poʃte'rjo*] *adj* (*mais tarde*)
subsequent, later; (*traseiro*) rear, back;
~mente [poʃterjox'mẽtʃi] *adv* later, subsequently
postiço/a [poʃ'tʃisu/a] *adj* false, artificial
postigo [poʃ'tʃigu] *m* (*em porta*) peephole
posto/a ['poʃtu/pɔʃta] *pp de* **pôr** ♦ *m*
post, position; (*emprego*) job; **~ de gasolina** service *ou* petrol station; **~ que**
although; **~ de saúde** health centre *ou*
center
póstumo/a ['pɔʃtumu/a] *adj* posthumous
postura [poʃ'tura] *f* posture; (*aspecto físico*) appearance
potável [po'tavew] (*pl* **-eis**) *adj* drink-
able; **água ~** drinking water
pote ['potʃi] *m* jug, pitcher; (*de geléia*)
jar; (*de creme*) pot; **chover a ~s** (*PT*) to
rain cats and dogs
potência [po'tẽsja] *f* power
potencial [potẽ'sjaw] (*pl* **-ais**) *adj, m* potential
potente [po'tẽtʃi] *adj* powerful, potent
pot-pourri [popu'xi] *m* (*MÚS*) medley
potro/a ['potru/a] *m/f* (*cavalo*) colt/filly;
(: *bem jovem*) foal

PALAVRA CHAVE

pouco/a ['poku/a] *adj* **1** (*sg*) little, not
much; **~ tempo** little *ou* not much
time; **de ~ interesse** of little interest,
not very interesting; **pouca coisa** not
much
2 (*pl*) few, not many; **uns ~s** a few,
some; **poucas vezes** rarely; **poucas
crianças comem o que devem** few
children eat what they should
♦ *adv* **1** little, not much; **custa ~** it
doesn't cost much; **dentro em ~, daqui
a ~** shortly; **~ antes** shortly before
2 (+ *adj*:) = *negativo*): **ela é ~
inteligente/simpática** she's not very

bright/friendly
3: por ~ eu não morri I almost died
4: ~ a ~ little by little
5: aos ~s gradually
♦ *m*: **um ~** a little, a bit; **nem um ~** not at all

poupador(a) [popa'do*(a)] *adj* thrifty
poupança [po'pãsa] *f* thrift; (*economias*) savings *pl*; (*tb*: **caderneta de ~**) savings bank
poupar [po'pa*] *vt* to save; (*vida*) to spare
pouquinho [po'kiɲu] *m*: **um ~ (de)** a little
pousada [po'zada] *f* (*hospedagem*) lodging; (*hospedaria*) inn
pousar [po'za*] *vt* to place; (*mão*) to rest ♦ *vi* (*avião, pássaro*) to land; (*pernoitar*) to spend the night
povo ['povu] *m* people; (*raça*) people *pl*, race; (*plebe*) common people *pl*; (*multidão*) crowd
povoação [povwa'sãw] (*pl* –ões) *f* (*aldeia*) village, settlement; (*habitantes*) population
povoado [po'vwadu] *m* village
povoar [po'vwa*] *vt* (*de habitantes*) to people, populate; (*de animais etc*) to stock
pra [pra] (*col*) *prep* = **para a**
praça ['prasa] *f* (*largo*) square; (*mercado*) marketplace; (*soldado*) soldier; **~ de touros** bullring
prado ['pradu] *m* meadow, grassland
praga ['praga] *f* nuisance; (*maldição*) curse; (*desgraça*) misfortune; (*erva daninha*) weed
pragmático/a [prag'matʃiku/a] *adj* pragmatic
praia ['praja] *f* beach
prancha ['prãʃa] *f* plank; (*de surfe*) board
pranto ['prãtu] *m* weeping
prata ['prata] *f* silver; (*col: cruzeiro*) ≈ quid (*BRIT*), ≈ buck (*US*); **prataria** [prata'ria] *f* silverware; (*pratos*) crockery
prateado/a [pra'tʃjadu/a] *adj* silver-plated; (*brilhante*) silvery; (*cor*) silver ♦ *m* (*cor*) silver; (*de um objeto*) silver-plating; **papel ~** silver paper
prateleira [prate'lejra] *f* shelf
prática ['pratʃika] *f* practice; (*experiência*) experience, know-how; (*costume*) habit, custom; *V tb* **prático**
praticante [pratʃi'kãtʃi] *adj* practising (*BRIT*), practicing (*US*) ♦ *m/f* apprentice; (*de esporte*) practitioner
praticar [pratʃi'ka*] *vt* to practise (*BRIT*), practice (*US*); (*roubo, operação*) to carry out; **praticável** [pratʃi'kavew] (*pl* –eis) *adj* practical, feasible; **prático/a** ['pratʃiku/a] *adj* practical ♦ *m/f* expert
prato ['pratu] *m* plate; (*comida*) dish; (*de uma refeição*) course; (*de toca-discos*) turntable; **~s** *mpl* (*MÚS*) cymbals

praxe ['praksi] *f* custom, usage; **de ~** usually; **ser de ~** to be the norm
prazer [pra'ze*] *m* pleasure; **muito ~ em conhecê-lo** pleased to meet you
prazo ['prazu] *m* term, period; (*vencimento*) expiry date, time limit; **a curto/médio/longo ~** in the short/medium/long term; **comprar a ~** to buy on hire purchase (*BRIT*) *ou* on the installment plan (*US*)
precário/a [pre'karju/a] *adj* precarious; (*escasso*) failing
precaução [prekaw'sãw] (*pl* –ões) *f* precaution
precaver-se [preka'vexsi] *vr*: **~ (contra *ou* de)** to be on one's guard (against); **precavido/a** [preka'vidu/a] *adj* cautious
prece ['presi] *f* prayer; (*súplica*) entreaty
precedência [prese'dẽsja] *f* precedence; **precedente** [prese'dẽtʃi] *adj* preceding ♦ *m* precedent
preceder [prese'de*] *vt, vi* to precede; **~ a algo** to precede sth; (*ter primazia*) to take precedence over sth
preceito [pre'sejtu] *m* precept
precioso/a [pre'sjozu/ɔza] *adj* precious
precipício [presi'pisju] *m* precipice; (*fig*) abyss
precipitação [presipita'sãw] *f* haste; (*imprudência*) rashness
precipitado/a [presipi'tadu/a] *adj* hasty; (*imprudente*) rash
precipitar [presipi'ta*] *vt* to hurl; (*acontecimentos*) to precipitate; **~se** *vr* (*atirar-se*): **~ contra** to hurl o.s. against; (*apressar-se*) to rush; (*agir com precipitação*) to be rash, act rashly
precisamente [presiza'mẽtʃi] *adv* precisely
precisão [presi'zãw] *f* precision, accuracy
precisar [presi'za*] *vt* to need; (*especificar*) to specify; **~-se** *vr*: **"precisa-se"** "needed"; **~ de** to need; (*uso impess*): **não precisa você se preocupar** you needn't worry
preciso/a [pre'sizu/a] *adj* precise, accurate; (*necessário*) necessary; (*claro*) concise; **é ~ você ir** you must go
preço ['presu] *m* price; (*custo*) cost; (*valor*) value; **a ~ de banana** (*BR*) *ou* **de chuva** (*PT*) dirt cheap
precoce [pre'kɔsi] *adj* precocious; (*antecipado*) early
preconcebido/a [prekõse'bidu/a] *adj* preconceived
preconceito [prekõ'sejtu] *m* prejudice
precursor(a) [prekux'so*(a)] *m/f* precursor, forerunner; (*mensageiro*) herald
predador [preda'do*] *m* predator
predecessor [predese'so*] *m* predecessor
predição [predʒi'sãw] (*pl* –ões) *f* prediction, forecast
predileção [predʒile'sãw] (*PT* **-cç-**; *pl* –ões) *f* preference; **predileto/a** [predʒi'lɛtu/a] (*PT* **-ct-**) *adj* favourite

(BRIT), favorite (US)

prédio ['prɛdʒju] m building; **~ de apartamentos** block of flats (BRIT), apartment house (US)

predispor [predʒiʃ'po*] (irreg: como pôr) vt: **~ alguém contra** to prejudice sb against; **~-se** vr: **~-se a/para** to get o.s. in the mood to/for

predizer [predʒi'ze*] (irreg: como dizer) vt to predict, forecast

predominar [predomi'na*] vi to predominate, prevail

preencher [preẽ'ʃe*] vt (formulário) to fill in (BRIT) ou out, complete; (requisitos) to fulfil (BRIT), fulfill (US), meet, to fill

pré-estréia [prɛ-] f preview

prefácio [pre'fasju] m preface

prefeito/a [pre'fejtu/a] m/f mayor; **prefeitura** [prefej'tura] f town hall

preferência [prefe'rẽsja] f preference; (AUTO) priority; **de ~** preferably; **preferencial** [preferẽ'sjaw] (pl -ais) adj (rua) main ♦ f main road (with priority)

preferido/a [prefe'ridu/a] adj favourite (BRIT), favorite (US)

preferir [prefe'ri*] vt to prefer

prefiro etc [pre'firu] vb V **preferir**

prefixo [pre'fiksu] m (LING) prefix; (TEL) code

prega ['prɛga] f pleat, fold

pregador [prega'do*] m preacher; (de roupa) peg

pregão [pre'gãw] (pl -ões) m proclamation, cry

pregar¹ [prɛ'ga*] vt, vi to preach

pregar² [pre'ga*] vt (com prego) to nail; (fixar) to pin, fasten; (cosendo) to sew on; **~ uma peça** to play a trick; **~ um susto em alguém** to give sb a fright

prego ['prɛgu] m nail; (col: casa de penhor) pawn shop

pregões [pre'gõjʃ] mpl de **pregão**

preguiça [pre'gisa] f laziness; (animal) sloth; **estar com ~** to feel lazy; **~r** [pregi'sa*] vi to laze around; **preguiçoso/a** [pregi'sozu/ɔza] adj lazy

pré-histórico/a [prɛ-] adj prehistoric

preia-mar (PT) f high tide

prejudicar [preʒudʒi'ka*] vt to damage; (atrapalhar) to hinder; **prejudicial** [preʒudʒi'sjaw] (pl -ais) adj damaging; (à saúde) harmful

prejuízo [pre'ʒwizu] m damage, harm; (em dinheiro) loss; **em ~ de** to the detriment of

prelúdio [pre'ludʒju] m prelude

prematuro/a [prema'turu/a] adj premature

premiado/a [pre'mjadu/a] adj prize-winning; (bilhete) winning ♦ m/f prize-winner

premiar [pre'mja*] vt to award a prize to; (recompensar) to reward

prêmio ['premju] m prize; (recompensa)

reward; (SEGUROS) premium

premonição [premoni'sãw] (pl -ões) f premonition

pré-natal [prɛ-] (pl -ais) adj antenatal (BRIT), prenatal (US)

prenda ['prẽda] f gift, present; (em jogo) forfeit; **~s domésticas** housework sg

prendado/a [prẽ'dadu/a] adj gifted, talented

prendedor [prẽde'do*] m fastener; (de cabelo, gravata) clip; **~ de roupa** clothes peg; **~ de papéis** paper clip

prender [prẽ'de*] vt to fasten, fix; (roupa) to pin; (cabelo) to put back; (capturar) to arrest; (atar, ligar) to tie; (atenção) to catch; (afetivamente) to tie, bind; (reter: doença, compromisso) to keep; (movimentos) to restrict; **~-se** vr to get caught, stick; **~-se a alguém** (por amizade) to be attached to sb

prenome [pre'nɔmi] m first name, Christian name

prensar [prẽ'sa*] vt to press; (fruta) to squeeze

pronunciar [prenũ'sja*] vt to predict, foretell; **prenúncio** [pre'nũsju] m forewarning, sign

preocupação [preokupa'sãw] (pl -ões) f preoccupation; (inquietação) worry, concern

preocupar [preoku'pa*] vt to preoccupy; (inquietar) to worry; **~-se** vr: **~-se com** to worry about, be worried about

preparação [prepara'sãw] (pl -ões) f preparation

preparar [prepa'ra*] vt to prepare; **~-se** vr to get ready; **preparativos** [prepara'tʃivuʃ] mpl preparations, arrangements

preponderante [prepõde'rãtʃi] adj predominant

preposição [prepozi'sãw] (pl -ões) f preposition

prepotente [prepo'tẽtʃi] adj predominant; (despótico) despotic; (atitude) overbearing

prerrogativa [prexoga'tʃiva] f prerogative

presa ['preza] f (na guerra) spoils pl; (vítima) prey; (dente de animal) fang

presbiteriano/a [preʒbite'rjanu/a] adj, m/f Presbyterian

prescrever [preʃkre've*] vt to prescribe; (prazo) set; **prescrição** [preʃkri'sãw] (pl -ões) f order, rule; (MED) instruction; (: de um remédio) prescription

prescrito/a [preʃ'kritu/a] pp de **prescrever**

presença [pre'zẽsa] f presence; (frequência) attendance; **ter boa ~** to be presentable; **presenciar** [prezẽ'sja*] vt to be present at; (testemunhar) to witness

presente [pre'zẽtʃi] adj present; (fig: interessado) attentive; (: evidente) clear, obvious ♦ m present ♦ f (COM: carta): **a ~**

this letter; **os** ~**s** *mpl* (*pessoas*) those present; ~**ar** [prezē'tʃjaˣ] *vt*: ~**ar alguém (com algo)** to give sb (sth as) a present; ~**mente** [prezētʃe'mētʃi] *adv* at present

preservação [prezexva'sãw] *f* preservation

preservar [prezex'vaˣ] *vt* to preserve, protect; **preservativo** [prezexva'tʃivu] *m* preservative; (*anticoncepcional*) condom

presidente/a [prezi'dētʃi/ta] *m/f* president

presidiário/a [-'dʒjarju/a] *m/f* convict

presídio [pre'zidʒju] *m* prison

presidir [prezi'dʒiˣ] *vt, vi*: ~ **(a)** to preside over; (*reunião*) to chair; (*suj: leis, critérios*) to govern

presilha [pre'ziʎa] *f* fastener; (*para o cabelo*) slide

preso/a ['prezu/a] *adj* imprisoned; (*capturado*) under arrest; (*atado*) tied ♦ *m/f* prisoner; **estar** ~ **a alguém** to be attached to sb

pressa ['prɛsa] *f* haste, hurry; (*rapidez*) speed; (*urgência*) urgency; **às** ~**s** hurriedly; **estar com** ~ to be in a hurry; **ter** ~ **de** *ou* **em fazer** to be in a hurry to do

pressagiar [presa'ʒjaˣ] *vt* to foretell; **presságio** [pre'saʒu] *m* omen, sign; (*pressentimento*) premonition

pressão [pre'sãw] (*pl* –**ões**) *f* pressure; (**colchete de**) ~ press stud, popper

pressentimento [presētʃi'mētu] *m* premonition

pressentir [presē'tʃiˣ] *vt* to foresee; (*suspeitar*) to sense

pressionar [presjo'naˣ] *vt* (*botão*) to press; (*coagir*) to pressure ♦ *vi* to press, put on pressure

pressões [pre'sõjʃ] *fpl de* **pressão**

pressupor [presu'poˣ] (*irreg: como* **pôr**) *vt* to presuppose

prestação [presta'sãw] (*pl* –**ões**) *f* instalment (*BRIT*), installment (*US*); (*por uma casa*) repayment

prestar [preʃ'taˣ] *vt* (*cuidados*) to give; (*favores, serviços*) to do; (*contas*) to render; (*informações*) to supply; (*uma qualidade a algo*) to lend ♦ *vi*: ~ **a alguém para algo** to be of use to sb for sth; ~**se** *vr*: ~**se a** to be suitable for; (*admitir*) to lend o.s. to; (*dispor-se*) to be willing to; ~ **atenção** to pay attention

prestativo/a [preʃta'tʃivu/a] *adj* helpful, obliging

prestes ['prɛʃtʃiʃ] *adj inv* ready; (*a ponto de*): ~ **a partir** about to leave

prestígio [preʃ'tʃiʒju] *m* prestige; **prestigioso/a** [preʃtʃi'ʒozu/ɔza] *adj* prestigious

presumir [prezu'miˣ] *vt* to presume; **presunção** [prezū'sãw] (*pl* –**ões**) *f* presumption; (*vaidade*) conceit, self-importance; **presunçoso/a** [prezū'sozu/ɔza] *adj* vain,

self-important

presunto [pre'zūtu] *m* ham

pretendente [pretē'dētʃi] *m/f* claimant; (*candidato*) candidate, applicant ♦ *m* suitor

pretender [pretē'deˣ] *vt* to claim; (*cargo, emprego*) to go for; ~ **fazer** to intend to do

pretensão [pretē'sãw] (*pl* –**ões**) *f* claim; (*vaidade*) pretension; (*propósito*) aim; (*aspiração*) aspiration; **pretensioso/a** [pretē'sjozu/ɔza] *adj* pretentious

pretérito [pre'tɛritu] *m* (*LING*) preterite

pretexto [pre'tɛʃtu] *m* pretext

preto/a ['pretu/a] *adj* black ♦ *m/f* Black (man/woman)

prevalecer [prevale'seˣ] *vi* to prevail; ~**se** *vr*: ~**se de** (*aproveitar-se*) to take advantage of

prevenção [prevē'sãw] (*pl* –**ões**) *f* prevention; (*preconceito*) prejudice; (*cautela*) caution; **estar de** ~ **com** *ou* **contra alguém** to be bias(s)ed against sb

prevenido/a [preve'nidu/a] *adj* cautious, wary

prevenir [preve'niˣ] *vt* to prevent; (*avisar*) to warn; (*preparar*) to prepare

preventivo/a [prevē'tʃivu/a] *adj* preventive

prever [pre'veˣ] (*irreg: como* **ver**) *vt* to predict, foresee; (*pressupor*) to presuppose

previamente [prevja'mētʃi] *adv* previously

previdência [previ'dēsja] *f* foresight; (*precaução*) precaution

previdente [previ'dētʃi] *adj*: **ser** ~ to show foresight

prévio/a ['prɛvju/a] *adj* prior; (*preliminar*) preliminary

previsão [previ'zãw] (*pl* –**ões**) *f* foresight; (*prognóstico*) prediction, forecast; ~ **do tempo** weather forecast

previsível [previ'zivew] (*pl* –**eis**) *adj* predictable

previsões [previ'zõjʃ] *fpl de* **previsão**

prezado/a [pre'zadu/a] *adj* esteemed; (*numa carta*) dear

prezar [pre'zaˣ] *vt* (*amigos*) to value highly; (*autoridade*) to respect; (*gostar de*) to appreciate

primário/a [pri'marju/a] *adj* primary; (*elementar*) basic, rudimentary; (*primitivo*) primitive ♦ *m* (*curso*) elementary education

primata [pri'mata] *m* (*ZOOL*) primate

primavera [prima'vɛra] *f* spring; (*planta*) primrose

primeira [pri'mejra] *f* (*AUTO*) first (gear)

primeiro/a [pri'mejru/a] *adj, adv* first; **de primeira** first-class

primitivo/a [primi'tʃivu/a] *adj* primitive; (*original*) original

primo/a ['primu/a] *m/f* cousin; ~ **irmão** first cousin

primogênito/a [primo'ʒenitu/a] *adj*, *m/f* first-born

princesa [prĩ'seza] *f* princess

principal [prĩsi'paw] (*pl* -ais) *adj* principal; (*entrada, razão, rua*) main ♦ *m* head, principal; (*essencial, de dívida*) principal

príncipe ['prĩsipi] *m* prince

principiante [prĩsi'pjãtʃi] *m/f* beginner

principiar [prĩsi'pja*] *vt*, *vi* to begin

princípio [prĩ'sipju] *m* beginning, start; (*origem*) origin; (*legal, moral*) principle; ~s *mpl* (*de matéria*) rudiments

prioridade [prjori'dadʒi] *f* priority

prisão [pri'zãw] (*pl* -ões) *f* imprisonment; (*cadeia*) prison, jail; (*detenção*) arrest; ~ de ventre constipation; **prisioneiro/a** [prizjo'nejru/a] *m/f* prisoner

privação [priva'sãw] (*pl* -ões) *f* deprivation; **privações** *fpl* (*penúria*) hardship *sg*

privacidade [privasi'dadʒi] *f* privacy

privações [priva'sõjʃ] *fpl* *de* privação

privada [pri'vada] *f* toilet

privado/a [pri'vadu/a] *adj* private; (*carente*) deprived

privar [pri'va*] *vt* to deprive

privativo/a [priva'tʃivu/a] *adj* (*particular*) private; ~ de peculiar to

privilegiado/a [privile'ʒjadu/a] *adj* privileged; (*excepcional*) unique, exceptional

privilegiar [privile'ʒja*] *vt* to privilege; (*favorecer*) to favour (*BRIT*), favor (*US*)

privilégio [privi'lɛʒu] *m* privilege

pró [prɔ] *adv* for, in favour (*BRIT*) *ou* favor (*US*) ♦ *m* advantage; os ~s e os contras the pros and cons; em ~ de in favo(u)r of

pró- [prɔ] *prefixo* pro-

proa ['proa] *f* prow, bow

probabilidade [probabili'dadʒi] *f* probability; ~s *fpl* (*chances*) odds

problema [prob'lɛma] *m* problem

procedência [prose'dẽsja] *f* origin, source; (*lugar de saída*) point of departure

proceder [prose'de*] *vi* to proceed; (*comportar-se*) to behave; (*agir*) to act ♦ *m* conduct; **procedimento** [prosedʒi'mẽtu] *m* conduct, behaviour (*BRIT*), behavior (*US*); (*processo*) procedure; (*JUR*) proceedings *pl*

processador [prosesa'do*] *m* processor; ~ de texto word processor

processamento [prosesa'mẽtu] *m* processing; (*JUR*) prosecution; (*verificação*) verification; ~ de texto word processing

processar [prose'sa*] *vt* (*JUR*) to take proceedings against, prosecute; (*requerimentos, COMPUT*) to process

processo [pro'sɛsu] *m* process; (*procedimento*) procedure; (*JUR*) lawsuit, legal proceedings *pl*; (: *autos*) record; (*conjunto de documentos*) documents *pl*

procissão [prosi'sãw] (*pl* -ões) *f* procession

proclamação [proklama'sãw] (*pl* -ões) *f* proclamation

proclamar [prokla'ma*] *vt* to proclaim

proclamas [pro'klamaʃ] *mpl* banns

procura [pro'kura] *f* search; (*COM*) demand

procuração [prokura'sãw] *f*: **por ~** by proxy

procurador(a) [prokura'do*(a)] *m/f* attorney; **P~ Geral da República** Attorney General

procurar [proku'ra*] *vt* to look for, seek; (*emprego*) to apply for; (*ir visitar*) to call on; (*contatar*) to get in touch with; ~ fazer to try to do

prodígio [pro'dʒiʒu] *m* prodigy

produção [produ'sãw] (*pl* -ões) *f* production; (*volume de produção*) output; (*produto*) product; ~ em massa, ~ em série mass production

produtivo/a [produ'tʃivu/a] *adj* productive; (*rendoso*) profitable

produto [pro'dutu] *m* product; (*renda*) proceeds *pl*, profit

produtor(a) [produ'to*(a)] *adj* producing ♦ *m/f* producer

produzir [produ'zi*] *vt* to produce; (*ocasionar*) to cause, bring about; (*render*) to bring in

proeminente [proemi'nẽtʃi] *adj* prominent

proeza [pro'eza] *f* achievement, feat

profanar [profa'na*] *vt* to desecrate, profane; **profano/a** [pro'fanu/a] *adj* profane ♦ *m/f* layman/woman

profecia [profe'sia] *f* prophecy

proferir [profe'ri*] *vt* to utter; (*sentença*) to pronounce

professar [profe'sa*] *vt* to profess

professor(a) [profe'so*(a)] *m/f* teacher; (*universitário*) lecturer

profeta/isa [pro'fɛta/profe'tʃiza] *m/f* prophet; **profetizar** [profetʃi'za*] *vt*, *vi* to prophesy, predict

proficiência [profi'sjẽsja] *f* proficiency, competence; **proficiente** [profi'sjẽtʃi] *adj* proficient, competent

profiro *etc* [pro'firu] *vb* V proferir

profissão [profi'sãw] (*pl* -ões) *f* profession; **profissional** [profisjo'naw] (*pl* -ais) *adj*, *m/f* professional; **profissionalizante** [profisjonali'zãtʃi] *adj* (*ensino*) vocational

profundidade [profũdʒi'dadʒi] *f* depth

profundo/a [pro'fũdu/a] *adj* deep; (*fig*) profound

profusão [profu'zãw] *f* profusion, abundance

profuso/a [pro'fuzu/a] *adj* profuse, abundant

prognosticar [prognoʃtʃi'ka*] *vt* to predict, forecast; **prognóstico** [prog'nɔʃtʃiku] *m* prediction, forecast

programa [pro'grama] *m* programme

(*BRIT*), program (*US*); (*COMPUT*) program; (*plano*) plan; (*diversão*) thing to do; (*de um curso*) syllabus; **~ção** [progra'sãw] *f* planning; (*TV, RÁDIO, COMPUT*) programming; **~dor(a)** [programa'do*(a)] *m/f* programmer; **~r** [progra'ma*] *vt* to plan; (*COMPUT*) to program

progredir [progre'dʒi*] *vi* to progress; (*avançar*) to move forward; (*infecção*) to progress

progressista [progre'siʃta] *adj, m/f* progressive

progressivo/a [progre'sivu/a] *adj* progressive; (*gradual*) gradual

progresso [pro'grɛsu] *m* progress

progrido *etc* [pro'gridu] *vb* V **progredir**

proibição [proibi'sãw] (*pl* –ões) *f* prohibition, ban

proibir [proi'bi*] *vt* to prohibit; (*livro, espetáculo*) to ban; **"é proibido fumar"** "no smoking"; **~ alguém de fazer, ~ que alguém faça** to forbid sb to do

projeção [proʒe'sãw] (*PT* -cç-; *pl* –ões) *f* projection

projetar [proʒe'ta*] (*PT* -ct-) *vt* to project

projétil [pro'ʒɛtʃiw] (*PT* -ct-; *pl* –eis) *m* projectile, missile

projeto [pro'ʒɛtu] (*PT* -ct-) *m* project; (*plano, ARQ*) plan; (*TEC*) design; **~ de lei** bill

projetor [proʒe'to*] (*PT* -ct-) *m* (*CINEMA*) projector

proletariado [proleta'rjadu] *m* proletariat; **proletário/a** [prole'tarju/a] *adj, m/f* proletarian

proliferar [prolife'ra*] *vi* to proliferate; **prolífico/a** [pro'lifiku/a] *adj* prolific

prolixo/a [pro'liksu/a] *adj* long-winded, tedious

prólogo ['prɔlogu] *m* prologue

prolongação [prolõga'sãw] *f* extension

prolongado/a [prolõ'gadu/a] *adj* prolonged; (*alongado*) extended

prolongar [prolõ'ga*] *vt* to extend, lengthen; (*decisão etc*) to postpone; (*vida*) to prolong; **~-se** *vr* to extend; (*durar*) to last

promessa [pro'mɛsa] *f* promise

prometer [prome'te*] *vt, vi* to promise

promíscuo/a [pro'miʃkwu/a] *adj* disorderly, mixed up; (*comportamento sexual*) promiscuous

promissor(a) [promi'so*(a)] *adj* promising

promoção [promo'sãw] (*pl* –ões) *f* promotion; **fazer ~ de alguém/algo** to promote sb/sth

promotor(a) [promo'to*(a)] *m/f* promoter; (*JUR*) prosecutor

promover [promo've*] *vt* to promote; (*causar*) to cause, bring about

promulgar [promuw'ga*] *vt* to promulgate; (*tornar público*) to declare publicly

pronome [pro'nɔmi] *m* pronoun

pronto/a [prõtu/a] *adj* ready; (*rápido*)

quick, speedy; (*imediato*) prompt ♦ *adv* promptly; **de ~** promptly; **estar ~ a ...** to be prepared *ou* willing to ...; **~-socorro** (*pl* **~-s-socorros**) (*PT*) *m* tow-truck

prontuário [prõ'twarju] *m* (*manual*) handbook; (*policial*) record

pronúncia [pro'nũsja] *f* pronunciation; (*JUR*) indictment

pronunciar [pronũ'sja*] *vt* to pronounce; (*discurso*) to make, deliver; (*JUR*: *réu*) to indict; (: *sentença*) to pass

propaganda [propa'gãda] *f* (*POL*) propaganda; (*COM*) advertising; (: *uma ~*) advert, advertisement; **fazer ~ de** to advertise

propagar [propa'ga*] *vt* to propagate; (*fig*: *difundir*) to disseminate

propensão [propẽ'sãw] (*pl* –ões) *f* inclination, tendency; **propenso/a** [pro'pẽsu/a] *adj*: **propenso a** inclined to; **ser propenso a** to be inclined to, have a tendency to

propina [pro'pina] *f* (*gorjeta*) tip; (*PT*: *cota*) fee

propor [pro'po*] (*irreg*: *como* **pôr**) *vt* to propose; (*oferecer*) to offer; (*um problema*) to pose; **~-se** *vr*: **~-se (a) fazer** (*pretender*) to intend to do; (*visar*) to aim to do; (*dispor-se*) to decide to do; (*oferecer-se*) to offer to do

proporção [propox'sãw] (*pl* –ões) *f* proportion; **proporções** *fpl* (*dimensões*) dimensions; **proporcionado/a** [propoxsjo'nadu/a] *adj* proportionate; **proporcional** [propoxsjo'naw] (*pl* –ais) *adj* proportional; **proporcionar** [propoxsjo'na*] *vt* to provide, give; (*adaptar*) to adjust, adapt

proposição [propozi'sãw] (*pl* –ões) *f* proposition, proposal

proposital [propozi'taw] (*pl* –ais) *adj* intentional

propósito [pro'pɔzitu] *m* (*intenção*) purpose; (*objetivo*) aim; **a ~** by the way; **a ~ de** with regard to; **de ~** on purpose

proposta [pro'pɔʃta] *f* proposal; (*oferecimento*) offer

propriamente [proprja'mẽtʃi] *adv* properly, exactly; **~ falando** *ou* **dito** strictly speaking

propriedade [proprje'dadʒi] *f* property; (*direito de proprietário*) ownership; (*o que é apropriado*) propriety

proprietário/a [proprje'tarju/a] *m/f* owner, proprietor

próprio/a ['prɔprju/a] *adj* own, of one's own; (*mesmo*) very, selfsame; (*hora, momento*) opportune, right; (*nome*) proper; (*característico*) characteristic; (*sentido*) proper, true; (*depois de pronome*) -self; **~ (para)** suitable (for); **eu ~** I myself; **por si ~** of one's own accord; **ele é o ~ inglês** he's a typical Englishman; **é o ~** it's him himself

propulsor [propuw'so*] m propeller

prorrogação [proxoga'sãw] (pl –ões) f extension

prorrogar [proxo'ga*] vt to extend, prolong

prosa ['prɔza] f prose; (conversa) chatter; (fanfarrice) boasting, bragging

proscrever [proʃkre've*] vt to prohibit, ban

proscrito/a [proʃ'kritu/a] pp de **proscrever** ♦ m/f exile

prospecto [proʃ'pɛktu] m leaflet; (em forma de livro) brochure

prosperar [proʃpe'ra*] vi to prosper, thrive; **prosperidade** [proʃperi'dadʒi] f prosperity; (bom êxito) success; **próspero/a** ['prɔʃperu/a] adj prosperous; (bem sucedido) successful; (favorável) favourable (BRIT), favorable (US)

prosseguir [prose'gi*] vt, vi to continue; ~ **em** to continue (with)

prostíbulo [proʃ'tʃibulu] m brothel

prostituta [proʃtʃi'tuta] f prostitute

prostrado/a [proʃ'tradu/a] adj prostrate

protagonista [protago'niʃta] m/f protagonist

proteção [prote'sãw] (PT -cç-) f protection

protector(a) [protek'to*(a)] (PT) = **protetor(a)**

proteger [prote'ʒe*] vt to protect; **protegido/a** [prote'ʒidu/a] m/f protégé(e)

proteína [prote'ina] f protein

protejo etc [pro'teʒu] vb V **proteger**

protestante [proteʃ'tãtʃi] adj, m/f Protestant

protestar [proteʃ'ta*] vt, vi to protest; **protesto** [pro'tɛʃtu] m protest

protetor(a) [prote'to*(a)] adj protective ♦ m/f protector

protocolo [proto'kɔlu] m protocol

protuberância [protube'rãsja] f bump; **protuberante** [protube'rãtʃi] adj sticking out

prova ['prɔva] f proof; (TEC: teste) test, trial; (EDUC: exame) examination; (sinal) sign; (de comida, bebida) taste; (de roupa) fitting; (ESPORTE) competition; (TIP) proof; ~(s) f(pl) (JUR) evidence sg; à ~ **de bala/fogo/água** bulletproof/fireproof/waterproof; **pôr à** ~ to put to the test

provar [pro'va*] vt to prove; (comida) to taste, try; (roupa) to try on ♦ vi to try

provável [pro'vavew] (pl –eis) adj probable, likely

provedor(a) [prove'do*(a)] m/f supplier; ~ **de acesso à Internet** Internet service provider

proveito [pro'vejtu] m advantage; (ganho) profit; **em** ~ **de** for the benefit of; **fazer** ~ **de** to make use of; ~**so/a** [provej'tozu/ɔza] adj profitable, advantageous; (útil) useful

proveniência [prove'njẽsja] f source, origin; **proveniente** [prove'njẽtʃi] adj: pro-

veniente de originating from; (que resulta de) arising from

prover [pro've*] (irreg: como **ver**) vt to provide, supply; (vaga) to fill ♦ vi: ~ **a** to take care of, see to

provérbio [pro'vɛxbju] m proverb

proveta [pro'veta] f test tube

providência [provi'dẽsja] f providence; ~**s** fpl (medidas) measures, steps; **providencial** [providẽ'sjaw] (pl –ais) adj opportune; **providenciar** [providẽ'sja*] vt to provide; (tomar providências) to arrange ♦ vi to make arrangements; **providenciar para que** to see to it that

provimento [provi'mẽtu] m provision

província [pro'vĩsja] f province; **provinciano/a** [provĩ'sjanu/a] adj provincial

provisão [provi'zãw] (pl –ões) f provision, supply; **provisões** fpl (suprimentos) provisions

provisório/a [provi'zɔrju/a] adj provisional, temporary

provocador(a) [provoka'do*(a)] adj provocative

provocante [provo'kãtʃi] adj provocative

provocar [provo'ka*] vt to provoke; (ocasionar) to cause; (atrair) to tempt, attract; (estimular) to rouse, stimulate

proximidade [prosimi'dadʒi] f proximity, nearness; ~**s** fpl (vizinhança) neighbourhood sg (BRIT), neighborhood sg (US), vicinity sg

próximo/a ['prɔsimu/a] adj (no espaço) near, close; (no tempo) close; (seguinte) next; (amigo, parente) close; (vizinho) neighbouring (BRIT), neighboring (US) ♦ adv near ♦ m fellow man; ~ **a** ou **de** near, close to; **até a próxima!** see you again soon!

prudência [pru'dẽsja] f care, prudence; **prudente** [pru'dẽtʃi] adj prudent

prurido [pru'ridu] m itch

pseudônimo [psew'donimu] m pseudonym

psicanálise [psika'nalizi] f psychoanalysis

psicologia [psikolo'ʒia] f psychology; **psicológico/a** [psiko'lɔʒiku/a] adj psychological; **psicólogo/a** [psi'kɔlogu/a] m/f psychologist

psique ['psiki] f psyche

psiquiatra [psi'kjatra] m/f psychiatrist

psiquiatria [psikja'tria] f psychiatry; **psiquiátrico/a** [psi'kjatriku/a] adj psychiatric

psíquico/a ['psikiku/a] adj psychological

puberdade [pubex'dadʒi] f puberty

publicação [publika'sãw] f publication

publicar [publi'ka*] vt to publish; (divulgar) to divulge; (proclamar) to announce

publicidade [publisi'dadʒi] f publicity; (COM) advertising; **publicitário/a** [publisi'tarju/a] adj publicity atr; advertising atr

público/a ['publiku/a] *adj* public ♦ *m*
public; (*CINEMA, TEATRO etc*) audience
pude *etc* ['pudʒi] *vb V* **poder**
pudera *etc* [pu'dɛra] *vb V* **poder**
pudim [pu'dʒĩ] (*pl* **-ns**) *m* pudding; **~-flã**
[-flã] (*PT*) *m* crème caramel
pudor [pu'do*] *m* bashfulness, modesty;
(*moral*) decency
pugilismo [puʒi'liʒmu] *m* boxing
puído/a ['pwidu/a] *adj* worn
pular [pu'la*] *vi* to jump; (*no Carnaval*)
to celebrate ♦ *vt* to jump (over); (*pági-
nas, trechos*) to skip; **~ Carnaval** to celebrate Carnival; **~ corda** to skip
pulga ['puwga] *f* flea
pulmão [puw'mãw] (*pl* **-ões**) *m* lung
pulo[1] ['pulu] *m* jump; **dar um ~ em** to
stop off at
pulo[2] *etc vb V* **polir**
pulôver [pu'love*] (*BR*) *m* pullover
púlpito ['puwpitu] *m* pulpit
pulsação [puwsa'sãw] *f* pulsation, beating; (*MED*) pulse
pulsar [puw'sa*] *vi* (*palpitar*) to pulsate,
throb
pulseira [puw'sejra] *f* bracelet; (*de sapato*) strap
pulso ['puwsu] *m* (*ANAT*) wrist; (*MED*)
pulse; (*fig*) vigour (*BRIT*), vigor (*US*), energy
pulverizar [puwveri'za*] *vt* to pulverize;
(*líquido*) to spray; (*polvilhar*) to dust
pungente [pũ'ʒẽtʃi] *adj* painful
punha *etc* ['puɲa] *vb V* **pôr**
punhado [pu'ɲadu] *m* handful
punhal [pu'ɲaw] (*pl* **-ais**) *m* dagger; **~-
ada** [puɲa'lada] *f* stab
punho ['puɲu] *m* fist; (*de manga*) cuff;
(*de espada*) hilt
punição [puni'sãw] (*pl* **-ões**) *f* punishment
punir [pu'ni*] *vt* to punish
pupila [pu'pila] *f* (*ANAT*) pupil
purê [pu're] *m* purée; **~ de batatas**
mashed potatoes
pureza [pu'reza] *f* purity
purgante [pux'gãtʃi] *m* purgative; (*col:
pessoa*) bore
purgar [pux'ga*] *vt* to purge
purgatório [puxga'tɔrju] *m* purgatory
purificar [purifi'ka*] *vt* to purify
puritano/a [puri'tanu/a] *adj* puritanical;
(*seita*) puritan ♦ *m/f* puritan
puro/a ['puru/a] *adj* pure; (*uísque etc*)
neat; (*verdade*) plain; (*intenções*) honourable (*BRIT*), honorable (*US*); (*estilo*) clear
púrpura ['puxpura] *f* purple
purpúreo/a [pux'purju/a] *adj* crimson
pus[1] [puʃ] *m* pus
pus[2] *etc* [pujʃ] *vb V* **pôr**
puser *etc* [pu'ze*] *vb V* **pôr**
puta ['puta] (*col!*) *vb tb* **puto**
puto/a ['putu/a] (*col!*) *m/f* (*sem-vergonha*)
bastard ♦ *adj* (*zangado*) furious; (*incrível*): **um ~ ...** a hell of a ...; **o ~ de ...**

the bloody ...
putrefato/a [putre'fatu/a] *adj* rotten
putrefazer [putrefa'ze*] (*irreg: como* **fazer**) *vt, vi* to rot; **~-se** *vr* to putrefy, rot
pútrido/a ['putridu/a] *adj* putrid, rotten
puxador [puʃa'do*] *m* handle, knob
puxão [pu'ʃãw] (*pl* **-ões**) *m* tug, jerk
puxar [pu'ʃa*] *vt* to pull; (*sacar*) to pull
out; (*assunto*) to bring up; (*conversa*) to
strike up; (*briga*) to pick ♦ *vi*: **~ de
uma perna** to limp; **~ a** to take after
puxões [pu'ʃõjʃ] *mpl de* **puxão**

Q

QG *abr m* (= *Quartel-General*) HQ
QI *abr m* (= *Quociente de Inteligência*) IQ
quadra ['kwadra] *f* (*quarteirão*) block; (*de
tênis etc*) court; (*período*) time, period
quadrado/a [kwa'dradu/a] *adj* square ♦
m square ♦ *m/f* (*col*) square
quadril [kwa'driw] (*pl* **-is**) *m* hip
quadrinho [kwa'driɲu] *m*: **história em
~s** (*BR*) cartoon, comic strip
quadris [kwa'driʃ] *mpl de* **quadril**
quadro ['kwadru] *m* painting; (*gravura,
foto*) picture; (*lista*) table; (*tabela*) chart,
table; (*TEC: painel*) panel; (*pessoal*) staff;
(*time*) team; (*TEATRO, fig*) scene; **~-
negro** (*pl* **~s-negros**) *m* blackboard
quadruplicar [kwadrupli'ka*] *vt, vi* to
quadruple
qual [kwaw] (*pl* **-ais**) *pron* which ♦ *conj*
as, like ♦ *excl* what!; **o ~** which; (*pessoa: suj*) who; (*: objeto*) whom; **seja ~**
for for whatever *ou* whichever it may be;
cada ~ each one
qualidade [kwali'dadʒi] *f* quality
qualificação [kwalifika'sãw] (*pl* **-ões**) *f*
qualification
qualificado/a [kwalifi'kadu/a] *adj* qualified
qualificar [kwalifi'ka*] *vt* to qualify; (*avaliar*) to evaluate; **~-se** *vr* to qualify; **~
de** *ou* **como** to classify as
qualquer [kwaw'ke*] (*pl* **quaisquer**) *adj,
pron* any; **~ pessoa** anyone, anybody;
~ um dos dois either; **~ que seja**
whichever it may be; **a ~ momento** at
any moment
quando ['kwãdu] *adv* when ♦ *conj* when;
(*interrogativo*) when?; (*ao passo que*)
whilst; **~ muito** at the most
quantia [kwã'tʃia] *f* sum, amount
quantidade [kwãtʃi'dadʒi] *f* quantity,
amount

PALAVRA CHAVE

quanto/a ['kwãtu/a] *adj* **1** (*interrogativo:
sg*) how much?; (*: pl*) how many?; **~
tempo?** how long?
2 (*o (que for) necessário*) all that, as
much as; **daremos ~s exemplares ele
precisar** we'll give him as many copies

as *ou* all the copies he needs
3: tanto/tantos ... ~ as much/many ... as
♦ *pron* **1** how much?; how many?; ~ **custa?** how much?; **a ~ está o jogo?** what's the score?
2: tudo ~ everything that, as much as
3: tanto/tantos ~ ... as much/as many as ...
4: um tanto ~ somewhat, rather
♦ *adv* **1:** **~ a** as regards; ~ **a mim** as for me
2: ~ antes as soon as possible
3: ~ mais (*principalmente*) especially; (*muito menos*) let alone; **~ mais cedo melhor** the sooner the better
4: tanto ~ possível as much as possible; **tão ... ~ ...** as ... as ...
♦ *conj:* ~ **mais trabalha, mais ele ganha** the more he works, the more he earns; ~ **mais, (tanto) melhor** the more, the better

quarenta [kwa'rẽta] *num* forty
quarentena [kwarẽ'tɛna] *f* quarantine
quaresma [kwa'rɛʒma] *f* Lent
quarta ['kwaxta] *f* (*tb:* ~-**feira**) Wednesday; (*parte*) quarter; (*AUTO*) fourth (gear); ~-**feira** (*pl* ~**s-feiras**) *f* Wednesday; ~-**feira de cinzas** Ash Wednesday
quarteirão [kwaxtej'rãw] (*pl* ~**ões**) *m* (*de casas*) block
quartel [kwax'tɛw] (*pl* ~**éis**) *m* barracks *sg*; ~-**general** *m* headquarters *pl*
quarteto [kwax'tetu] *m* quartet(te)
quarto/a ['kwaxtu/a] *num* fourth ♦ *m* quarter; (*aposento*) room; ~ **de banho/dormir** bathroom/bedroom; **três ~s de hora** three quarters of an hour
quartzo ['kwaxtsu] *m* quartz
quase ['kwazi] *adv* almost, nearly; ~ **nunca** hardly ever
quatorze [kwa'toxzi] *num* fourteen
quatro ['kwatru] *num* four

PALAVRA CHAVE

que [ki] *conj* **1** (*com oração subordinada:* muitas vezes não se traduz*) that; **ele disse ~ viria** he said (that) he would come; **não há nada ~ fazer** there's nothing to be done; **espero ~ sim/não** I hope so/not; **dizer ~ sim/não** to say yes/no
2 (*consecutivo:* muitas vezes não se traduz*) that; **é tão pesado ~ não consigo levantá-lo** it's so heavy (that) I can't lift it
3 (*comparações*): (**do**) ~ than; *V tb* **mais; menos; mesmo**
♦ *pron* **1** (*coisa*) which, that; (+ *prep*) which; **o chapéu ~ você comprou** the hat (that *ou* which) you bought
2 (*pessoa: suj*) who, that; (*: complemento*) whom, that; **o amigo ~ me levou ao museu** the friend who took me to

the museum; **a moça ~ eu convidei** the girl (that *ou* whom) I invited
3 (*interrogativo*) what?; **o ~ você disse?** what did you say?
4 (*exclamação*) what!; ~ **pena!** what a pity!; ~ **lindo!** how lovely!

quê [ke] *m* (*col*) something ♦ *pron* what; ~! what!; **não tem de ~** don't mention it; **para ~?** what for?; **por ~?** why?
quebra ['kɛbra] *f* break, rupture; (*falência*) bankruptcy; (*de energia elétrica*) cut; **de ~** in addition; ~-**cabeça** (*pl* ~-**cabeças**) *m* puzzle, problem; (*jogo*) jigsaw puzzle
quebradiço/a [kebra'dʒisu/a] *adj* fragile, breakable
quebrado/a [ke'bradu/a] *adj* broken; (*cansado*) exhausted; (*falido*) bankrupt; (*carro, máquina*) broken down; (*telefone*) out of order
quebra-nozes *m* *inv* nutcrackers *pl* (*BRIT*), nutcracker (*US*)
quebranto [ke'brãtu] *m* weakness
quebrar [ke'bra*] *vt* to break ♦ *vi* to break; (*carro*) to break down; (*COM*) to go bankrupt; (*ficar sem dinheiro*) to go broke
queda ['kɛda] *f* fall; (*fig*) downfall; **ter ~ para algo** to have a bent for sth; ~ **de barreira** landslide; ~-**d'água** (*pl* ~**s-d'água**) *f* waterfall
queijo ['kejʒu] *m* cheese
queimado/a [kej'madu/a] *adj* burnt; (*de sol: machucado*) sunburnt; (*: bronzeado*) brown, tanned; (*planta, folhas*) dried up
queimadura [kejma'dura] *f* burn; (*de sol*) sunburn
queimar [kej'ma*] *vt* to burn; (*roupa*) to scorch; (*com líquido*) to scald; (*bronzear a pele*) to tan; (*planta, folha*) to wither ♦ *vi* to burn; ~-**se** *vr* (*pessoa*) to burn o.s.; (*de sol*) to tan
queima-roupa *f*: **à ~** point-blank, at point-blank range
queira *etc* ['kejra] *vb V* **querer**
queixa ['kejʃa] *f* complaint; (*lamentação*) lament; **fazer ~ de alguém** to complain about sb
queixar-se [kej'ʃaxsi] *vr* to complain; ~ **de** to complain about; (*dores etc*) to complain of
queixo ['kejʃu] *m* chin; (*maxilar*) jaw; **bater o ~** to shiver
queixoso/a [kej'ʃozu/ɔza] *adj* complaining; (*magoado*) doleful
quem [kẽj] *pron* who; (*como objeto*) who(m); **de ~ é isto?** whose is this?; ~ **diria!** who would have thought (it)!; ~ **sabe** (*talvez*) perhaps
Quênia ['kenja] *m*: **o ~** Kenya
quente ['kẽtʃi] *adj* hot; (*roupa*) warm; **quentura** [kẽ'tura] *f* heat, warmth
quer [ke*] *vb V* **querer** ♦ *conj:* ~ ... ~ ... whether ... or ...; ~ **chova ~ não**

whether it rains or not; **onde/quando/ quem ~ que** wherever/whenever/ whoever; **o que ~ que seja** whatever it is

querela [ke'rɛla] f dispute

PALAVRA CHAVE

querer [ke're°] vt **1** (desejar) to want; **quero mais dinheiro** I want more money; **queria um chá** I'd like a cup of tea; **quero ajudar/que vá** I want to help/you to go; **você vai ~ sair amanhã?** do you want to go out tomorrow?; **eu vou ~ uma cerveja** (num bar etc) I'd like a beer; **por/sem ~** intentionally/unintentionally; **como queira** as you wish
2 (perguntas para pedir algo): **você quer fechar a janela?** will you shut the window?; **quer me dar uma mão?** can you give me a hand?
3 (amar) to love
4 (convite): **quer entrar/sentar** do come in/sit down
5: **~ dizer** (significar) to mean; (pretender dizer) to mean to say; **quero dizer** I mean; **quer dizer** (com outras palavras) in other words
♦ vi: **~ bem a** to be fond of
♦ **~-se** vr to love one another
♦ m (vontade) wish; (afeto) affection

querido/a [ke'ridu/a] adj dear ♦ m/f darling; **Q~ João** Dear John
querosene [kero'zɛni] m kerosene
questão [keʃ'tãw] (pl **-ões**) f question, inquiry; (problema) matter, question; (JUR) case; (contenda) dispute, quarrel; **fazer ~ (de)** to insist (on); **em ~** in question; **há ~ de um ano** about a year ago; **questionar** [keʃtʃjo'na°] vi to question ♦ vt to question, call into question; **questionário** [keʃtʃjo'narju] m questionnaire; **questionável** [keʃtʃjo'navew] (pl **-eis**) adj questionable
quiabo ['kjabu] m okra
quicar [ki'ka°] vt, vi to bounce
quieto/a ['kjɛtu/a] adj quiet; (imóvel) still; **quietude** [kje'tudʒi] f calm, tranquillity
quilate [ki'latʃi] m carat
quilo ['kilu] m kilo; **~byte** [kilo'bajtʃi] m kilobyte; **~grama** [kilo'grama] m kilogram; **~metragem** [kilome'traʒẽ] f number of kilometres ou kilometres travelled, ≈ mileage; **quilômetro** [ki'lometru] m kilometre (BRIT), kilometer (US); **~watt** [kilo'watʃi] m kilowatt
quimérico/a [ki'mɛriku/a] adj fantastic
química ['kimika] f chemistry
químico/a ['kimiku/a] adj chemical ♦ m/f chemist
quina ['kina] f corner; (de mesa etc) edge; **de ~** edgeways (BRIT), edgewise (US)

quindim [ki'dʒĩ] m sweet made of egg yolks, coconut and sugar
quinhão [ki'nãw] (pl **-ões**) m share, portion
quinhentos/as [ki'nẽtuʃ/aʃ] num five hundred
quinhões [ki'nõjʃ] mpl de **quinhão**
quinina [ki'nina] f quinine
quinquilharias [kĩkiʎa'riaʃ] fpl odds and ends; (miudezas) knicknacks, trinkets
quinta ['kĩta] f (tb: **~-feira**) Thursday; (propriedade) estate; (PT) farm; **~-feira** ['kĩta-'fejra] (pl **~s-feiras**) f Thursday
quintal [kĩ'taw] (pl **-ais**) m back yard
quinteto [kĩ'tetu] m quintet(te)
quinto/a ['kĩtu/a] num fifth
quintuplos/as [kĩ'tupluʃ/aʃ] m/fpl quins, quintuplets
quinze ['kĩzi] num fifteen; **duas e ~** a quarter past (BRIT) ou after (US) two; **~ para as sete** a quarter to (BRIT) ou of (US) seven
quinzena [kĩ'zɛna] f two weeks, fortnight (BRIT); **~l** [kĩze'naw] (pl **~is**) adj fortnightly; **~lmente** [kĩzenaw'mẽtʃi] adv fortnightly
quiosque ['kjɔʃki] m kiosk
qüiproquó [kwipro'kwɔ] m misunderstanding, mix-up
quiromante [kiro'mãtʃi] m/f palmist, fortune teller
quis etc [kiʒ] vb V **querer**
quiser etc [ki'ze°] vb V **querer**
quisto ['kiʃtu] m cyst
quitanda [ki'tãda] f grocer's (shop) (BRIT), grocery store (US); **quitandeiro/a** [kitã'dejru/a] m/f grocer; (vendedor de hortaliças) greengrocer (BRIT), produce dealer (US)
quitar [ki'ta°] vt (dívida: pagar) to pay off; (: perdoar) to cancel; (devedor) to release
quite ['kitʃi] adj (livre) free; (com um credor) squared up; (igualado) even; **estar ~ (com alguém)** to be quits (with sb)
quitute [ki'tutʃi] m titbit (BRIT), tidbit (US)
quociente [kwo'sjẽtʃi] m quotient; **~ de inteligência** intelligence quotient
quota ['kwota] f quota; (porção) share, portion
quotidiano/a [kwotʃi'dʒjanu/a] adj everyday

R

R abr (= **rua**) St
rã [xã] f frog
rabanete [xaba'netʃi] m radish
rabicho [xa'biʃu] m ponytail
rabino [xa'binu] m rabbi
rabiscar [xabiʃ'ka°] vt to scribble; (papel) to scribble on ♦ vi to scribble; (desenhar) to doodle; **rabisco** [xa'biʃku] m

scribble

rabo ['xabu] *m* tail; ~-**de-cavalo** (*pl* ~s-de-cavalo) *m* ponytail

rabugento/a [xabu'ʒẽtu/a] *adj* grumpy

raça ['xasa] *f* breed; (*grupo étnico*) race; **cão/cavalo de** ~ pedigree dog/thoroughbred horse

ração [xa'sãw] (*pl* –ões) *f* ration; (*para animal*) food

racha ['xaʃa] *f* (*fenda*) split; (*greta*) crack; ~**dura** [xaʃa'dura] *f* crack; ~**r** [xa'ʃa*] *vt* to crack; (*objeto, despesas*) to split; (*lenha*) to chop ♦ *vi* to split; (*cristal*) to crack; ~**r-se** *vr* to split; to crack

racial [xa'sjaw] (*pl* –ais) *adj* racial

raciocínio [xasjo'sinju] *m* reasoning

racional [xasjo'naw] (*pl* –ais) *adj* rational; ~**izar** [xasjonali'za*] *vt* to rationalize

racionamento [xasjona'mẽtu] *m* rationing

racionar [xasjo'na*] *vt* to ration (out)

racismo [xa'siʒmu] *m* racism; **racista** [xa'siʃta] *adj*, *m/f* racist

raçoes [xa'sõjʃ] *fpl de* **ração**

radar [xa'da*] *m* radar

radiação [xadʒja'sãw] *f* radiation

radiador [xadʒja'do*] *m* radiator

radiante [xa'dʒjãtʃi] *adj* radiant

radical [xadʒi'kaw] (*pl* –ais) *adj* radical

radicar-se [xadʒi'kaxsi] *vr* to take root; (*fixar residência*) to settle

rádio ['xadʒju] *m* radio; (*QUÍM*) radium; **radioativo/a** [xadʒjua'tʃivu/a] (*PT* -act-) *adj* radioactive; **radiodifusão** [xadʒjodʒifu'zãw] *f* broadcasting; **radiografar** [xadʒjogra'fa*] *vt* to X-ray; **radiografia** [xadʒjogra'fia] *f* X-ray; **radiologia** [xadʒjolo'ʒia] *f* radiology; **radiopatrulha** [xadʒjopa'truʎa] *f* patrol car; **radioterapia** [xadʒjotera'pia] *f* radiotherapy

raia [xaja] *f* (*risca*) line; (*fronteira*) boundary; (*limite*) limit; (*de corrida*) lane; (*peixe*) ray

raiado/a [xa'jadu/a] *adj* striped

raiar [xa'ja*] *vi* to shine

rainha [xa'iɲa] *f* queen

raio ['xaju] *m* (*de sol*) ray; (*de luz*) beam; (*de roda*) spoke; (*relâmpago*) flash of lightning; (*alcance*) range; (*MAT*) radius; ~s **X** X-rays

raiva ['xajva] *f* rage, fury; (*MED*) rabies *sg*; **estar/ficar com ~ (de)** to be/get angry (with); **ter ~ de** to hate; **raivoso/a** [xaj'vozu/ɔza] *adj* furious

raiz [xa'iʒ] *f* root; (*origem*) origin, source; ~ **quadrada** square root

rajada [xa'ʒada] *f* (*vento*) gust

ralado/a [xa'ladu/a] *adj* grated; ~**r** [xala'do*] *m* grater

ralar [xa'la*] *vt* to grate

ralhar [xa'ʎa*] *vi* to scold; ~ **com alguém** to tell sb off

rali [xa'li] *m* rally

ralo/a ['xalu/a] *adj* (*cabelo*) thinning; (*tecido*) flimsy; (*vegetação*) sparse; (*sopa*)

thin, watery; (*café*) weak ♦ *m* (*de regador*) rose, nozzle; (*de pia, banheiro*) drain

rama ['xama] *f* branches *pl*, foliage; **pela** ~ superficially; ~**gem** [xa'maʒẽ] *f* branches *pl*, foliage; ~**l** [xa'maw] (*pl* ~**is**) *m* (*FERRO*) branch line; (*TEL*) extension; (*AUTO*) side road

ramalhete [xama'ʎetʃi] *m* bouquet

ramificar-se [xamifi'kaxsi] *vr* to branch out

ramo ['xamu] *m* branch; (*profissão, negócios*) line; (*de flores*) bunch; **Domingo de R~s** Palm Sunday

rampa ['xãpa] *f* ramp; (*ladeira*) slope

rancor [xã'ko*] *m* bitterness; (*ódio*) hatred; ~**oso/a** [xãko'rozu/ɔza] *adj* bitter, resentful; hateful

rançoso/a [xã'sozu/ɔza] *adj* rancid; (*cheiro*) musty

ranger [xã'ʒe*] *vi* to creak ♦ *vt*: ~ **os dentes** to grind one's teeth

ranhura [xa'ɲura] *f* groove; (*para moeda*) slot

ranjo *etc* ['xãju] *vb* V **ranger**

rapar [xa'pa*] *vt* to scrape; (*a barba*) to shave; (*o cabelo*) to crop

rapariga [xapa'riga] *f* girl

rapaz [xa'pajʒ] *m* boy; (*col*) lad

rapé [xa'pɛ] *m* snuff

rapidez [xapi'deʒ] *f* speed

rápido/a ['xapidu/a] *adj* fast, quick ♦ *adv* fast, quickly ♦ *m* (*trem*) express

rapina [xa'pina] *f* robbery; **ave de** ~ bird of prey

raposo/a [xa'pozu/ɔza] *m/f* fox/vixen

rapsódia [xap'sɔdʒja] *f* rhapsody

raptar [xap'ta*] *vt* to kidnap; **rapto** ['xaptu] *m* kidnapping; **raptor** [xap'to*] *m* kidnapper

raqueta [xa'keta] (*PT*) *f* = **raquete**

raquete [xa'ketʃi] *f* racquet

raquítico/a [xa'kitʃiku/a] *adj* (*franzino*) puny; (*vegetação*) poor

raquitismo [xaki'tʃiʒmu] *m* rickets *sg*

raramente [xara'mẽtʃi] *adv* rarely, seldom

rarefeito/a [xare'fejtu/a] *adj* rarefied; (*multidão, população*) sparse

raro/a ['xaru/a] *adj* rare ♦ *adv* rarely, seldom

rascunhar [xaʃku'ɲa*] *vt* to draft, make a rough copy of; **rascunho** [xaʃ'kuɲu] *m* draft, rough copy

rasgado/a [xaʒ'gadu/a] *adj* (*roupa*) torn, ripped

rasgão [xaʒ'gãw] (*pl* –ões) *m* tear, rip

rasgar [xaʒ'ga*] *vt* to tear, rip; (*destruir*) to tear up, rip up; ~**-se** *vr* to split; **rasgo** ['xaʒgu] *m* tear, rip

rasgões [xaʒ'gõjʃ] *mpl de* **rasgão**

raso/a ['xazu/a] *adj* (*liso*) flat, level; (*não fundo*) shallow; (*baixo*) low; **soldado** ~ private

raspa ['xaʃpa] *f* (*de madeira*) shaving; (*de*

metal) filing
raspão [xaʃ'pãw] (*pl* –ões) *m* scratch, graze
raspar [xaʃ'pa*] *vt* to scrape; (*alisar*) to file; (*tocar de raspão*) to graze; (*arranhar*) to scratch; (*pêlos, cabeça*) to shave; (*apagar*) to rub out ♦ *vi*: ~ **em** to scrape
raspões [xaʃ'põjʃ] *mpl de* raspão
rasteira [xaʃ'tejra] *f*: **dar uma** ~ **em alguém** to trip sb up
rasteiro/a [xaʃ'tejru/a] *adj* crawling; (*planta*) creeping
rastejante [xaʃte'ʒãtʃi] *adj* trailing; (*arrastando-se*) creeping
rastejar [xaʃte'ʒa*] *vi* to crawl; (*furtivamente*) to creep; (*fig: rebaixar-se*) to grovel ♦ *vt* (*fugitivo etc*) to track
rasto ['xaʃtu] *m* (*pegada*) track; (*de veículo*) trail; (*fig*) sign, trace; **andar de** ~**s** to crawl
rastro ['xaʃtru] *m* = rasto
rata ['xata] *f* rat; (*pequena*) mouse; **ratão** [xa'tãw] (*pl* –ões) *m* rat
ratear [xa'tʃja*] *vt* to share
ratificar [xatʃifi'ka*] *vt* to ratify
rato ['xatu] *m* rat; (*pequeno*) mouse; ~ **de hotel/praia** hotel/beach thief; ~**eira** [xa'twejra] *f* rat trap; mousetrap
ratões [xa'tõjʃ] *mpl de* ratão
ravina [xa'vina] *f* ravine
razão [xa'zãw] (*pl* –ões) *f* reason; (*argumento*) reasoning; (*MAT*) ratio ♦ *m* (*COM*) ledger; **à** ~ **de** at the rate of; **em** ~ **de** on account of; **dar** ~ **a alguém** to support sb; **ter/não ter** ~ to be right/wrong; **razoável** [xa'zwavew] (*pl* –eis) *adj* reasonable
r/c (*PT*) *abr* = rés-do-chão
ré [xɛ] *f* (*AUTO*) reverse (gear); **dar (marcha à)** ~ to reverse, back up; *V tb* réu
reá [xe'a] *vb V* reaver
reabastecer [xeabaʃte'se*] *vt* (*avião*) to refuel; (*carro*) to fill up; ~**-se** *vr*: ~**-se de** to replenish one's supply of
reação [xea'sãw] (*PT* -**cç**-; *pl* –ões) *f* reaction; **reacionário/a** [xeasjo'narju/a] *adj* reactionary
reactor [xea'to*] (*PT*) *m* = reator
reagir [xea'ʒi*] *vi* to react; (*doente, time perdedor*) to fight back; ~ **a** (*resistir*) to resist; (*protestar*) to rebel against
reais [xe'ajʃ] *adj pl de* real
reaja etc [xe'aʒa] *vb V* reagir; reaver
reajuste [xea'ʒuʃtʃi] *m* adjustment
real [xe'aw] (*pl* –ais) *adj* real; (*relativo à realeza*) royal
realçar [xeaw'sa*] *vt* to highlight; **realce** [xe'awsi] *m* emphasis; (*mais brilho*) highlight; **dar realce a** to enhance
realeza [xea'leza] *f* royalty
realidade [xeali'dadʒi] *f* reality; **na** ~ actually, in fact
realista [xea'liʃta] *adj* realistic ♦ *m/f* realist

realização [xealiza'sãw] *f* fulfilment (*BRIT*), fulfillment (*US*), realization; (*de projeto*) execution, carrying out
realizador(a) [xealiza'do*(a)] *adj* enterprising
realizar [xeali'za*] *vt* to achieve; (*projeto*) to carry out; (*ambições, sonho*) to fulfil (*BRIT*), fulfill (*US*), realize; (*negócios*) to transact; (*perceber*) to realize; ~**-se** *vr* to take place; (*ambições*) to be realized; (*sonhos*) to come true
realmente [xeaw'mẽtʃi] *adv* really; (*de fato*) actually
reanimar [xeani'ma*] *vt* to revive; (*encorajar*) to encourage; ~**-se** *vr* to cheer up
reão [xe'ãw] *vb V* reaver
reatar [xea'ta*] *vt* to resume, take up again
reator [xea'to*] *m* reactor
reaver [xea've*] *vt* to recover, get back
reavivar [xeavi'va*] *vt* (*cor*) to brighten up; (*lembrança*) to revive; (*sofrimento, dor*) to bring back
rebaixar [xebaj'ʃa*] *vt* to lower; (*mercadorias*) to lower the price of; (*humilhar*) to put down, humiliate ♦ *vi* to drop; ~**-se** *vr* to demean o.s.
rebanho [xe'baɲu] *m* (*de carneiros, fig*) flock; (*de gado, elefantes*) herd
rebate [xe'batʃi] *m* (*sinal*) alarm; (*COM*) discount
rebater [xeba'te*] *vt* (*golpe*) to ward off; (*acusações, argumentos*) to refute
rebelar-se [xebe'laxsi] *vr* to rebel; **rebelde** [xe'bewdʒi] *adj* rebellious; (*indisciplinado*) unruly, wild ♦ *m/f* rebel; **rebeldia** [xebew'dʒia] *f* rebelliousness; (*fig: obstinação*) stubbornness; (: *oposição*) defiance
rebelião [xebe'ljãw] (*pl* –ões) *f* rebellion
rebentar [xebẽ'ta*] *vi* (*guerra*) to break out; (*louça*) to smash; (*corda*) to snap; (*represa*) to burst; (*ondas*) to break ♦ *vt* to smash; to snap; (*porta*) to break down
rebocador [xeboka'do*] *m* tug(boat)
rebocar [xebo'ka*] *vt* (*paredes*) to plaster; (*veículo*) to tow; **reboco** [xe'boku] *m* plaster
rebolar [xebo'la*] *vt* to swing ♦ *vi* to sway
reboque¹ [xe'bɔki] *m* tow; (*veículo: tb*: **carro** ~) trailer; (*cabo*) towrope; (*BR: de socorro*) towtruck; **a** ~ on *ou* in (*US*) tow
reboque² *etc vb V* rebocar
rebuçado [xebu'sadu] (*PT*) *m* sweet, candy (*US*)
rebuliço [xebu'lisu] *m* commotion, hubbub
recado [xe'kadu] *m* message; **deixar** ~ to leave a message
recaída [xeka'ida] *f* relapse
recair [xeka'i*] *vi* (*doente*) to relapse
recalcar [xekaw'ka*] *vt* to repress

recalque *etc* [xe'kawki] *vb* V **recalcar**

recanto [xe'kãtu] *m* corner, nook

recapitular [xekapitu'la*] *vt* to sum up, recapitulate; (*fatos*) to review; (*matéria escolar*) to revise

recatado/a [xeka'tadu/a] *adj* (*modesto*) modest; (*reservado*) reserved

recauchutado/a [xekawʃu'tadu/a] *adj:* **pneu ~** (*AUTO*) retread, remould (*BRIT*)

recear [xe'sja*] *vt* to fear ♦ *vi:* **~ por** to fear for; **~ fazer/que** to be afraid to do/that

recebedor(a) [xesebe'do*(a)] *m/f* recipient

receber [xese'be*] *vt* to receive; (*ganhar*) to earn, get; (*hóspedes*) to take in; (*convidados*) to entertain; (*acolher bem*) to welcome ♦ *vi* (*~ convidados*) to entertain; **recebimento** [xesebi'mẽtu] (*BR*) *m* reception; (*de uma carta*) receipt; **acusar o recebimento de** to acknowledge receipt of

receio [xe'seju] *m* fear; **ter ~ de que** to fear that

receita [xe'sejta] *f* income; (*do Estado*) revenue; (*MED*) prescription; (*CULIN*) recipe; **R~ Federal** ≈ Inland Revenue (*BRIT*), ≈ IRS (*US*); **~r** [xesej'ta*] *vt* to prescribe

recém [xe'sẽ] *adv* recently, newly; **~casado/a** *adj:* **os ~casados** the newlyweds; **~chegado/a** *m/f* newcomer; **~nascido/a** *m/f* newborn child

recenseamento [xesẽsja'mẽtu] *m* census

recente [xe'sẽtʃi] *adj* recent; (*novo*) new ♦ *adv* recently; **~mente** [xesẽtʃi'mẽtʃi] *adv* recently

receoso/a [xe'sjozu/ɔza] *adj* frightened, fearful; **estar ~ de (fazer)** to be afraid of (doing)

recepção [xesep'sãw] (*pl* **-ões**) *f* reception; (*PT: de uma carta*) receipt; **acusar a ~ de** (*PT*) to acknowledge receipt of; **recepcionista** [xesepsjo'niʃta] *m/f* receptionist

receptivo/a [xesep'tʃivu/a] *adj* receptive; (*acolhedor*) welcoming

receptor [xesep'to*] *m* receiver

recessão [xese'sãw] (*pl* **-ões**) *f* recession

recesso [xe'sɛsu] *m* recess

recessões [xese'sõjʃ] *fpl* de **recessão**

rechaçar [xeʃa'sa*] *vt* (*ataque*) to repel; (*idéias, argumentos*) to oppose; (*oferta*) to turn down

recheado/a [xe'ʃjadu/a] *adj* (*ave, carne*) stuffed; (*empada, bolo*) filled; (*cheio*) full, crammed

rechear [xe'ʃja*] *vt* to fill; (*ave, carne*) to stuff; **recheio** [xe'ʃeju] *m* stuffing; (*de empada, de bolo*) filling; (*o conteúdo*) contents *pl*

rechonchudo/a [xeʃõ'ʃudu/a] *adj* chubby, plump

recibo [xe'sibu] *m* receipt

reciclar [xesi'kla*] *vt* to recycle

recife [xe'sifi] *m* reef

recinto [xe'sĩtu] *m* enclosure; (*lugar*) area

recipiente [xesi'pjẽtʃi] *m* container, receptacle

recíproco/a [xe'siproku/a] *adj* reciprocal

récita ['xɛsita] *f* (*teatral*) performance

recital [xesi'taw] (*pl* **-ais**) *m* recital

recitar [xesi'ta*] *vt* to recite

reclamação [xeklama'sãw] (*pl* **-ões**) *f* complaint

reclamar [xekla'ma*] *vt* to demand; (*herança*) to claim ♦ *vi* to complain

reclame [xe'klami] *m* advertisement

reclinar [xekli'na*] *vt* to rest, lean; **~-se** *vr* to lie back; (*deitar-se*) to lie down

recobrar [xeko'bra*] *vt* to recover, get back; **~-se** *vr* to recover

recolher [xeko'ʎe*] *vt* to collect; (*coisas dispersas*) to pick up; (*gado, roupa do varal*) to bring in; (*juntar*) to gather together; **recolhido/a** [xeko'ʎidu/a] *adj* (*lugar*) secluded; (*pessoa*) withdrawn; **recolhimento** [xekoʎi'mẽtu] *m* retirement; (*arrecadação*) collection; (*ato de levar*) taking

recomeçar [xekome'sa*] *vt, vi* to restart

recomendação [xekomẽda'sãw] (*pl* **-ões**) *f* recommendation; **recomendações** *fpl* (*cumprimentos*) regards

recomendar [xekomẽ'da*] *vt* to recommend; **recomendável** [xekomẽ'davew] (*pl* **-eis**) *adj* advisable

recompensa [xekõ'pẽsa] *f* reward; **~r** [xekõpẽ'sa*] *vt* to reward

recompor [xekõ'po*] (*irreg: como* **pôr**) *vt* to reorganize; (*restabelecer*) to restore

reconciliação [xekõsilja'sãw] (*pl* **-ões**) *f* reconciliation

reconciliar [xekõsi'lja*] *vt* to reconcile

recondicionar [xekõdʒisjo'na*] *vt* to recondition

reconhecer [xekoɲe'se*] *vt* to recognize; (*MIL*) to reconnoitre (*BRIT*), reconnoiter (*US*); **reconhecido/a** [xekoɲe'sidu/a] *adj* recognized; (*agradecido*) grateful, thankful; **reconhecimento** [xekoɲeci'mẽtu] *m* recognition; (*admissão*) admission; (*gratidão*) gratitude; (*MIL*) reconnaissance; **reconhecível** [xekoɲe'sivew] (*pl* **-eis**) *adj* recognizable

reconstruir [xekõʃ'trwi*] *vt* to rebuild

recontar [xekõ'ta*] *vt* to recount

recordação [xekoxda'sãw] (*pl* **-ões**) *f* (*reminiscência*) memory; (*objeto*) memento

recordar [xekox'da*] *vt* to remember; (*parecer*) to look like; (*recapitular*) to revise; **~-se** *vr:* **~-se de** to remember; **~ algo a alguém** to remind sb of sth

recorde [xe'kɔxdʒi] *adj inv* record *atr* ♦ *m* record

recorrer [xeko'xe*] *vi:* **~ a** to turn to; (*valer-se de*) to resort to

recortar [xekox'ta*] *vt* to cut out; **recorte** [xe'kɔxtʃi] *m* (*ato*) cutting out; (*de* *jornal*) cutting, clipping

recostar [xekoʃ'ta⁺] *vt* to lean, rest; **~-se** *vr* to lean back; (*deitar-se*) to lie down

recreação [xekrja'sãw] *f* recreation

recrear [xe'krja⁺] *vt* to entertain, amuse; **~-se** *vr* to have fun; **recreativo/a** [xekrja'tʃivu/a] *adj* recreational; **recreio** [xe'kreju] *m* recreation

recriminar [xekrimi'na⁺] *vt* to reproach, reprove

recruta [xe'kruta] *m/f* recruit; **~mento** [xekruta'mētu] *m* recruitment; **~r** [xekruta'ta⁺] *vt* to recruit

rectângulo [xek'tãgulu] (*PT*) = **retângulo**

recto/a [xe 'xckto/a] (*PT*) = **reto** *etc*

recuar [xe'kwa⁺] *vt* to move back ♦ *vi* to move back; (*exército*) to retreat

recuperação [xekupera'sãw] *f* recovery

recuperar [xekupe'ra⁺] *vt* to recover; (*tempo perdido*) to make up for; (*reabilitar*) to rehabilitate; **~-se** *vr* to recover

recurso [xe'kuxsu] *m* resource; (*JUR*) appeal; **~s** *mpl* (*financeiros*) resources

recusa [xe'kuza] *f* refusal; (*negação*) denial; **~r** [xeku'za⁺] *vt* to refuse; to deny; **~r-se** *vr*: **~r-se a** to refuse to

redação [xeda'sãw] (*PT* -**çç**-; *pl* -**ões**) *f* (*ato*) writing; (*EDUC*) composition, essay; (*redatores*) editorial staff

redator(a) [xeda'to⁺(a)] (*PT* -**act**-) *m/f* journalist; (*editor*) editor; (*quem redige*) writer

rede ['xedʒi] *f* net; (*de dormir*) hammock; (*cilada*) trap; (*FERRO, TEC, fig*) network; **a R~** (*a Internet*) the Net

rédea ['xedʒja] *f* rein

redentor(a) [xedē'to⁺(a)] *adj* redeeming

redigir [xedʒi'ʒi⁺] *vt, vi* to write

redimir [xedʒi'mi⁺] *vt* (*livrar*) to free; (*REL*) to redeem

redobrar [xedo'bra⁺] *vt* (*aumentar*) to increase; (*esforços*) to redouble

redondamente [xedõda'mētʃi] *adv* (*completamente*) completely

redondezas [xedõ'dezaʃ] *fpl* surroundings

redondo/a [xe'dõdu/a] *adj* round

redor [xe'do⁺] *m*: **ao** *ou* **em ~ (de)** around, round about

redução [xedu'sãw] (*pl* -**ões**) *f* reduction

redundância [xedũ'dãsja] *f* redundancy; **redundante** [xedũ'dãtʃi] *adj* redundant

reduzido/a [xedu'zidu/a] *adj* reduced; (*limitado*) limited; (*pequeno*) small

reduzir [xedu'zi⁺] *vt* to reduce; **~-se** *vr*: **~-se a** to be reduced to; (*fig: resumir-se em*) to come down to

reedificar [xeedʒifi'ka⁺] *vt* to rebuild

reembolsar [xeēbow'sa⁺] *vt* to recover; (*restituir*) to reimburse; (*depósito*) to refund; **reembolso** [xeē'bowsu] *m* (*de depósito*) refund; (*de despesa*) reimbursement

reencontro [xeē'kõtru] *m* reunion

refazer [xefa'ze⁺] (*irreg: como* **fazer**) *vt* to redo; (*consertar*) to repair; **~-se** *vr* (*MED*

etc) to recover

refeição [xefej'sãw] (*pl* -**ões**) *f* meal; **refeitório** [xefej'tɔrju] *m* refectory

refém [xe'fē] (*pl* -**ns**) *m* hostage

referência [xefe'rēsja] *f* reference; **~s** *fpl* (*informações para emprego*) references; **fazer ~ a** to make reference to, refer to

referendum [xefe'rēdũ] *m* (*POL*) referendum

referente [xefe'rētʃi] *adj*: **~ a** concerning, regarding

referir [xefe'ri⁺] *vt* to relate, tell; **~-se** *vr*: **~-se a** to refer to

REFESA *f* (= *Rede Ferroviária SA*) ≈ BR

refinamento [xefina'mētu] *m* refinement

refinar [xefi'na⁺] *vt* to refine; **~ia** [xefina'ria] *f* refinery

refiro *etc* [xe'firu] *vb* V **referir**

refletir [xefle'tʃi⁺] (*PT* -**ct**-) *vt* to reflect ♦ *vi*: **~ em** *ou* **sobre** to consider, think about

reflexão [xeflek'sãw] (*pl* -**ões**) *f* reflection

reflexivo/a [xeflek'sivu/a] *adj* reflexive

reflexo/a [xe'flɛksu/a] *adj* (*luz*) reflected; (*ação*) reflex ♦ *m* reflection; (*ANAT*) reflex; (*no cabelo*) highlight

reflexões [xeflek'sõjʃ] *fpl* de **reflexão**

reflito *etc* [xe'flitu] *vb* V **refletir**

refluxo [xe'fluksu] *m* ebb

reforçado/a [xefox'sadu/a] *adj* reinforced; (*pessoa*) strong; (*café da manhã, jantar*) hearty

reforçar [xefox'sa⁺] *vt* to reinforce; (*revigorar*) to invigorate; **reforço** [xe'foxsu] *m* reinforcement

reforma [xe'fɔxma] *f* reform; (*ARQ*) renovation; **~-do/a** [xefox'madu/a] *adj* reformed; renovated; (*MIL*) retired; **~r** [xefox'ma⁺] *vt* to reform; to renovate; **~-se** *vr* to reform

reformatório [xefoxma'tɔrju] *m* reformatory, approved school (*BRIT*)

refractário/a [xefra'tarju/a] (*PT*) *adj* = **refratário/a**

refrão [xe'frãw] (*pl* -**ãos** *ou* -**ães**) *m* chorus, refrain; (*provérbio*) saying

refratário/a [xefra'tarju/a] *adj* (*TEC*) heat-resistant; (*CULIN*) ovenproof

refrear [xefre'a⁺] *vt* (*cavalo*) to rein in; (*inimigo*) to contain, check; (*paixões, raiva*) to control; **~-se** *vr* to restrain o.s.

refrescante [xefreʃ'kãtʃi] *adj* refreshing

refrescar [xefreʃ'ka⁺] *vt* (*ar, ambiente*) to cool; (*pessoa*) to refresh ♦ *vi* to cool down

refresco [xe'freʃku] *m* cool fruit drink, squash; **~s** *mpl* (*refrigerantes*) refreshments

refrigeração [xefriʒera'sãw] *f* refrigeration; (*de casa*) air conditioning

refrigerador [xefriʒera'do⁺] *m* refrigerator, fridge (*BRIT*)

refrigerante [xefriʒe'rãtʃi] *m* soft drink

refrigerar [xefriʒe'ra⁺] *vt* to keep cool;

(*com geladeira*) to refrigerate; (*casa*) to air-condition

refugiado/a [xefu'ʒjadu/a] *adj, m/f* refugee

refugiar-se [xefu'ʒjaxsi] *vr* to take refuge; **refúgio** [xe'fuʒju] *m* refuge

refugo [xe'fugu] *m* rubbish, garbage (*US*); (*mercadoria*) reject

refutar [xefu'ta*] *vt* to refute

rega ['xɛga] (*PT*) *f* irrigation

regaço [xe'gasu] *m* (*colo*) lap

regador [xega'do*] *m* watering can

regalia [xega'lia] *f* privilege

regalo [xe'galu] *m* present; (*prazer*) pleasure, treat

regar [xe'ga*] *vt* (*plantas, jardim*) to water; (*umedecer*) to sprinkle

regatear [xega'tʃja*] *vt* (*o preço*) to haggle over, bargain for ♦ *vi* to haggle

regenerar [xeʒene'ra*] *vt* to regenerate

regente [xe'ʒẽtʃi] *m* regent; (*de orquestra*) conductor; (*de banda*) leader

reger [xe'ʒe*] *vt* to govern; (*orquestra*) to conduct; (*empresa*) to run ♦ *vi* to rule; (*maestro*) to conduct

região [xe'ʒjãw] (*pl* -ões) *f* region, area

regime [xe'ʒimi] *m* (*POL*) regime; (*dieta*) diet; (*maneira*) way; **estar de ~** to be on a diet

regimento [xeʒi'mẽtu] *m* regiment

régio/a ['xɛʒju/a] *adj* royal; (*digno dos rei*) regal

regiões [xe'ʒjõjʃ] *fpl de* região

regional [xeʒjo'naw] (*pl* -ais) *adj* regional

registrador(a) [xeʒiʃtra'do*(a)] (*PT* -ista-) *m/f* registrar, recorder ♦ *f*: (*caixa*) ~a cash register, till

registrar [xeʒiʃ'tra*] (*PT* -ista-) *vt* to register; (*anotar*) to record

registro [xe'ʒiʃtru] (*PT* -to) *m* registration; (*anotação*) recording; (*livro, LING*) register; (*histórico*) record; ~ **civil** registry office

regra ['xɛgra] *f* rule; ~**s** *fpl* (*MED*) periods

regressar [xegre'sa*] *vi* to come (*ou* go) back, return; **regressivo/a** [xegre'sivu/a] *adj* regressive; **contagem regressiva** countdown; **regresso** [xe'grɛsu] *m* return

régua ['xɛgwa] *f* ruler; ~ **de calcular** slide rule

regulador [xegula'do*] *m* regulator

regulamento [xegula'mẽtu] *m* rules *pl*, regulations *pl*

regular [xegu'la*] *adj* regular; (*estatura*) average, medium; (*tamanho*) normal; (*razoável*) not bad ♦ *vt* to regulate; (*reger*) to govern; (*máquina*) to adjust; (*carro, motor*) to tune ♦ *vi* to work, function; ~**idade** [xegulari'dadʒi] *f* regularity

rei [xej] *m* king; **Dia de R~s** Epiphany; **R~ Momo** carnival king

reinado [xej'nadu] *m* reign

reinar [xej'na*] *vi* to reign

reino ['xejnu] *m* kingdom; (*fig*) realm; **o R~ Unido** the United Kingdom

reiterar [xeite'ra*] *vt* to reiterate

reivindicação [xejvĩdʒika'sãw] (*pl* -ões) *f* claim, demand

reivindicar [xejvĩdʒi'ka*] *vt* to claim; (*aumento salarial, direitos*) to demand

rejeição [xeʒej'sãw] (*pl* -ões) *f* rejection

rejeitar [xeʒej'ta*] *vt* to reject; (*recusar*) to refuse

rejo *etc* ['xeju] *vb* V **reger**

rejuvenescer [xeʒuvene'se*] *vt* to rejuvenate

relação [xela'sãw] (*pl* -ões) *f* relation; (*conexão*) connection; (*relacionamento*) relationship; (*MAT*) ratio; (*lista*) list; **com** *ou* **em ~ a** regarding, with reference to; **relações públicas** public relations; **relacionamento** [xelasjona'mẽtu] *m* relationship; **relacionar** [xelasjo'na*] *vt* to make a list of; (*ligar*): ~ **algo com algo** to connect sth with sth, relate sth to sth; **relacionar-se** *vr* to be connected *ou* related

relâmpago [xe'lãpagu] *m* flash of lightning; ~**s** *mpl* (*clarões*) lightning *sg*

relampejar [xelãpe'ʒa*] *vi* to flash; **relampejou** the lightning flashed

relance [xe'lãsi] *m* glance; **olhar de ~** to glance at

relapso/a [xe'lapsu/a] *adj* (*negligente*) negligent

relatar [xela'ta*] *vt* to give an account of

relativo/a [xela'tʃivu/a] *adj* relative

relato [xe'latu] *m* account

relatório [xela'tɔrju] *m* report

relaxado/a [xela'ʃadu/a] *adj* relaxed; (*desleixado*) slovenly, sloppy; (*relapso*) negligent

relaxante [xela'ʃãtʃi] *adj* relaxing

relaxar [xela'ʃa*] *vt, vi* to relax; **relaxe** [xe'laʃi] *m* relaxation

relegar [xele'ga*] *vt* to relegate

relembrar [xelẽ'bra*] *vt* to recall

relevante [xele'vãtʃi] *adj* relevant

relevo [xe'levu] *m* relief

religião [xeli'ʒãw] (*pl* -ões) *f* religion; **religioso/a** [xeli'ʒozu/ɔza] *adj* religious ♦ *m/f* religious person; (*frade/freira*) monk/nun

relíquia [xe'likja] *f* relic; ~ **de família** family heirloom

relógio [xe'lɔʒu] *m* clock; (*de gás*) meter; ~ **(de pulso)** (wrist)watch; ~ **de sol** sundial; **relojoeiro/a** [xelo'ʒwejru/a] *m/f* watchmaker, clockmaker

relutante [xelu'tãtʃi] *adj* reluctant

reluzente [xelu'zẽtʃi] *adj* brilliant, shining

relva ['xɛwva] *f* grass; (*terreno gramado*) lawn

relvado [xew'vadu] (*PT*) *m* lawn

remar [xe'ma*] *vt, vi* to row

rematar [xema'ta*] *vt* to finish off; **re-**

mate [xe'matʃi] m (fim) end; (acabamento) finishing touch

remediar [xeme'dʒja*] vt to put right, remedy

remédio [xe'mɛdʒju] m (medicamento) medicine; (recurso, solução) remedy; (JUR) recourse; **não tem ~** there's no way

remendar [xemē'da*] vt to mend; (com pano) to patch; **remendo** [xe'mēdu] m repair; patch

remessa [xe'mɛsa] f shipment; (de dinheiro) remittance

remetente [xeme'tētʃi] m/f sender

remeter [xeme'te*] vt to send, dispatch; (dinheiro) to remit

remexer [xeme'ʃe*] vt (papéis) to shuffle; (sacudir: braços) to wave; (folhas) to shake; (revolver: areia, lama) to stir up ♦ vi: ~ **em** to rummage through

reminiscência [xemini'sēsja] f reminiscence

remisso/a [xe'misu/a] adj remiss

remissões [xemi'sōjʃ] fpl de **remissão**

remo ['xemu] m oar; (ESPORTE) rowing

remoção [xemo'sãw] f removal

remorso [xe'mɔxsu] m remorse

remoto/a [xe'mɔtu/a] adj remote

remover [xemo've*] vt to move; (transferir) to transfer; (demitir) to dismiss; (retirar, afastar) to remove; (terra) to churn up

rena ['xɛna] f reindeer

renal [xe'naw] (pl -ais) adj renal, kidney atr

Renascença [xena'sēsa] f: **a ~** the Renaissance

renascer [xena'se*] vi to be reborn; (fig) to revive

renascimento [xenasi'mētu] m rebirth; (fig) revival; **o R~** the Renaissance

renda ['xɛda] f income; (nacional) revenue; (de aplicação, locação) yield; (tecido) lace

render [xē'de*] vt (lucro, dinheiro) to bring in, yield; (preço) to fetch; (homenagem) to pay; (graças) to give; (serviços) to render; (armas) to surrender; (guarda) to relieve; (causar) to bring ♦ vi (dar lucro) to pay; **~-se** vr to surrender; **rendição** [xēdʒi'sãw] f surrender

rendimento [xēdʒi'mētu] m income; (lucro) profit; (juro) yield, interest

renegado/a [xene'gadu/a] adj, m/f renegade

renegar [xene'ga*] vt (crença) to renounce; (detestar) to hate; (trair) to betray; (negar) to deny; (desprezar) to reject

renomado/a [xeno'madu/a] adj renowned

renome [xe'nɔmi] m renown

renovação [xenova'sãw] (pl -ões) f renewal; (ARQ) renovation

renovar [xeno'va*] vt to renew; (ARQ) to renovate

rentabilidade [xētabili'dadʒi] f profitability

rentável [xē'tavew] (pl -eis) adj profitable

renúncia [xe'nūsja] f resignation

renunciar [xenū'sja*] vt to give up, renounce ♦ vi to resign; (abandonar): **~ a algo** to give sth up

reouve etc [xe'ovi] vb V **reaver**

reouver etc [xeo've*] vb V **reaver**

reparação [xepara'sãw] (pl -ões) f mending, repairing; (de mal, erros) remedying; (fig) amends pl, reparation

reparar [xepa'ra*] vt to repair; (forças) to restore; (mal, erros) to remedy; (prejuizo, danos, ofensa) to make amends for; (notar) to notice ♦ vi: **~ em** to notice; **reparo** [xe'paru] m repair; (crítica) criticism; (observação) observation

repartição [xepaxtʃi'sãw] (pl -ões) f distribution

repartir [xepax'tʃi*] vt (distribuir) to distribute; (dividir entre vários) to share out; (dividir em várias porções) to divide up

repassar [xepa'sa*] vt (ponte, fronteira) to go over again; (lição) to revise, go over ♦ vi: **passar e ~** to go back and forth

repelente [xepe'lētʃi] adj, m repellent

repelir [xepe'li*] vt to repel

repente [xe'pētʃi] m outburst; **de ~** suddenly; (col: talvez) maybe

repentino/a [xepē'tʃinu/a] adj sudden

repercussão [xepexku'sãw] (pl -ões) f repercussion

repercutir [xepexku'tʃi*] vt to echo ♦ vi to reverberate, echo; (fig): **~ (em)** to have repercussions (on)

repertório [xepex'tɔrju] m list; (coleção) collection; (MÚS) repertoire

repetidamente [xepetʃida'mētʃi] adv repeatedly

repetido/a [xepe'tʃidu/a] adj: **repetidas vezes** repeatedly, again and again

repetir [xepe'tʃi*] vt to repeat ♦ vi (ao comer) to have seconds; **~-se** vr to happen again; (pessoa) to repeat o.s.; **repetitivo/a** [xepetʃi'tʃivu/a] adj repetitive

repilo etc [xe'pilu] vb V **repelir**

repique¹ [xe'piki] m (de sinos) peal

repique² etc vb V **repicar**

repito etc [xe'pitu] vb V **repetir**

repleto/a [xe'plɛtu/a] adj replete, full up

réplica ['xɛplika] f replica; (contestação) reply, retort

replicar [xepli'ka*] vt to answer, reply to ♦ vi to reply, answer back

repolho [xe'poʎu] m cabbage

repor [xe'po*] (irreg: como **pôr**) vt to put back, replace; (restituir) to return; **~-se** vr to recover

reportagem [xepox'taʒē] (pl -ns) f reporting; (notícia) report

repórter [xe'pɔxte] *m/f* reporter

repousar [xepo'za*] *vi* to rest; **repouso** [xe'pozu] *m* rest

repreender [xeprjě'de*] *vt* to reprimand; **repreensão** [xeprjě'sãw] (*pl* –ões) *f* reprimand; **repreensível** [xeprjě'sivew] (*pl* –eis) *adj* reprehensible

represa [xe'preza] *f* dam

represália [xepre'zalja] *f* reprisal

representação [xeprezěta'sãw] (*pl* –ões) *f* representation; (*TEATRO*) performance; **representante** [xeprezě'tãtʃi] *m/f* representative

representar [xeprezě'ta*] *vt* to represent; (*TEATRO*: *papel*) to play; (: *peça*) to put on ♦ *vi* to act; **representativo/a** [xeprezěta'tʃivu/a] *adj* representative

repressão [xepre'sãw] (*pl* –ões) *f* repression

reprimir [xepri'mi*] *vt* to repress

reprodução [xeprodu'sãw] (*pl* –ões) *f* reproduction; **reprodutor(a)** [xeprodu'to*(a)] *adj* reproductive

reproduzir [xeprodu'zi*] *vt* to reproduce; (*repetir*) to repeat; ~-**se** *vr* to breed

reprovar [xepro'va*] *vt* to disapprove of; (*aluno*) to fail

réptil ['xɛptʃiw] (*pl* –eis) *m* reptile

república [xe'publika] *f* republic; **republicano/a** [xepubli'kanu/a] *adj, m/f* republican

repudiar [xepu'dʒja*] *vt* to repudiate; **repúdio** [xe'pudʒju] *m* repudiation

repugnância [xepug'nãsja] *f* repugnance; **repugnante** [xepug'nãtʃi] *adj* repugnant

repulsa [xe'puwsa] *f* (*ato*) rejection; (*sentimento*) repugnance; (*física*) repulsion; **repulsivo/a** [xepuw'sivu/a] *adj* repulsive

reputação [reputa'sãw] (*pl* –ões) *f* reputation

repuxar [xepu'ʃa*] *vt* to tug

requeijão [xekej'ʒãw] *m* cheese spread

requerer [xeke're*] *vt* (*emprego*) to apply for; (*pedir*) to request; (*exigir*) to require; **requerimento** [xekeri'mětu] *m* application; request; (*petição*) petition

requintado/a [xekĩ'tadu/a] *adj* refined, elegant

requinte [xe'kĩtʃi] *m* refinement, elegance; (*cúmulo*) height

requisito [xeki'zitu] *m* requirement

rescindir [xesĩ'dʒi*] *vt* (*contrato*) to rescind

rés-do-chão [xɛʒ-] (*PT*) *m inv* ground floor (*BRIT*), first floor (*US*)

resenha [xe'zɛɲa] *f* report; (*resumo*) summary; (*de livro*) review

reserva [xe'zɛxva] *f* reserve; (*para hotel, fig*) reservation ♦ *m/f* (*ESPORTE*) reserve

reservado/a [xezex'vadu/a] *adj* reserved

reservar [xezex'va*] *vt* to reserve; (*guardar de reserva*) to keep; (*forças*) to conserve; ~-**se** *vr* to save o.s.

reservatório [xezexva'tɔrju] *m* reservoir

rêses ['xesiʃ] *fpl* (*gado*) cattle, livestock

sg

resfriado/a [xeʃ'frjadu/a] (*BR*) *adj*: **estar/ficar** ~ to have a cold/catch (a) cold ♦ *m* cold, chill

resfriar [xeʃ'frja*] *vt* to cool, chill ♦ *vi* to catch (a) cold; ~-**se** *vr* to catch (a) cold

resgatar [xeʒga'ta*] *vt* (*salvar*) to rescue; (*prisioneiro*) to ransom; (*retomar*) to get back, recover; **resgate** [xeʒ'gatʃi] *m* rescue; ransom; recovery

resguardar [xeʒgwax'da*] *vt* to protect

residência [xezi'děsja] *f* residence; **residencial** [xezidě'sjaw] (*pl* –ais) *adj* residential; (*computador, telefone etc*) home *atr*; **residente** [xezi'dětʃi] *adj, m/f* resident

residir [xezi'dʒi*] *vi* to live, reside

resíduo [xe'zidwu] *m* residue

resignação [xezigna'sãw] (*pl* –ões) *f* resignation

resignar-se [xezig'naxsi] *vr*: ~ **com** to resign o.s. to

resiliente [xezi'ljětʃi] *adj* resilient

resina [xe'zina] *f* resin

resistente [xeziʃ'tětʃi] *adj* resistant; (*material, objeto*) hard-wearing, strong

resistir [xeziʃ'tʃi*] *vi* to hold; (*pessoa*) to hold out; ~ **a** to resist; (*sobreviver*) to survive

resmungar [xeʒmũ'ga*] *vt, vi* to mutter, mumble

resolução [xezolu'sãw] (*pl* –ões) *f* resolution; (*de um problema*) solution; **resoluto/a** [xezo'lutu/a] *adj* decisive

resolver [xezow've*] *vt* to sort out; (*problema*) to solve; (*questão*) to resolve; (*decidir*) to decide; ~-**se** *vr*: ~-**se (a fazer)** to make up one's mind (to do), decide (to do)

respectivo/a [xeʃpek'tʃivu/a] *adj* respective

respeitar [xeʃpej'ta*] *vt* to respect; **respeitável** [xeʃpej'tavew] (*pl* –eis) *adj* respectable; (*considerável*) considerable

respeito [xeʃ'pejtu] *m*: ~ (**a** *ou* **por**) respect (for); ~**s** *mpl* (*cumprimentos*) regards; **a** ~ **de, com** ~ **a** as to, as regards; (*sobre*) about; **dizer** ~ **a** to concern; **em** ~ **a** with respect to

respingar [xeʃpĩ'ga*] *vt, vi* to splash, spatter; **respingo** [xeʃ'pĩgu] *m* splash

respiração [xeʃpira'sãw] *f* breathing

respirar [xeʃpi'ra*] *vt, vi* to breathe

respiro [xeʃ'piru] *m* breath

resplandecente [xeʃplãde'sětʃi] *adj* resplendent

resplandecer [xeʃplãde'se*] *vi* to gleam, shine (out); **resplendor** [xeʃplě'do*] *m* brilliance; (*fig*) glory

responder [xeʃpõ'de*] *vt* to answer ♦ *vi* to answer; (*ser respondão*) to answer back; ~ **por** to be responsible for, answer for

responsabilidade [xeʃpõsabili'dadʒi] *f* responsibility

responsabilizar [xeʃpõsabili'za*] vt: ~ **alguém (por algo)** to hold sb responsible (for sth); **~-se** vr: **~-se por** to take responsibility for

responsável [xeʃpõ'savew] (pl **-eis**) adj: ~ **(por)** responsible (for); ~ **a** answerable to, accountable to

resposta [xeʃ'poʃta] f answer, reply

resquício [xeʃ'kisju] m (vestígio) trace

ressabiado/a [xesa'bjadu/a] adj wary; (ressentido) resentful

ressaca [xe'saka] f undertow; (mar bravo) rough sea; (fig: de quem bebeu) hangover

ressaltar [xesaw'ta*] vt to emphasize ♦ vi to stand out

ressalva [xe'sawva] f safeguard

ressarcir [xesax'si*] vt (pagar) to compensate; (compensar) to compensate for; ~ **alguém de** to compensate sb for

ressecar [xese'ka*] vt, vi to dry up

ressentido/a [xesẽ'tʃidu/a] adj resentful

ressentimento [xesẽtʃi'mẽtu] m resentment

ressentir-se [xesẽ'tʃixsi] vr: ~ **de** (ofender-se) to resent; (magoar-se) to be hurt by; (sofrer) to suffer from, feel the effects of

ressoar [xe'swa*] vi to resound; (ecoar) to echo; **ressonante** [xeso'nãtʃi] adj resonant

ressurgimento [xesuxʒi'mẽtu] m resurgence, revival

ressurreição [xesuxej'sãw] (pl **-ões**) f resurrection

ressuscitar [xesusi'ta*] vt, vi to revive

restabelecer [xeʃtabele'se*] vt to re-establish, restore; **~-se** vr to recover, recuperate; **restabelecimento** [xeʃtabelesi'mẽtu] m re-establishment; restoration; recovery

restante [xeʃ'tãtʃi] adj remaining ♦ m rest

restar [xeʃ'ta*] vi to remain, be left

restauração [xeʃtawra'sãw] (pl **-ões**) f restoration; (de costumes, usos) revival

restaurante [xeʃtaw'rãtʃi] m restaurant

restaurar [xeʃtaw'ra*] vt to restore

réstia ['xɛʃtʃja] f (luz) ray

restituição [xeʃtʃitwi'sãw] (pl **-ões**) f restitution, return; (de dinheiro) repayment

restituir [xeʃtʃi'twi*] vt to return; (dinheiro) to repay; (forças, saúde) to restore; (usos) to revive; (reempossar) to reinstate

resto ['xɛʃtu] m rest; (MAT) remainder; **~s** mpl (sobras) remains; (de comida) scraps

restrição [xeʃtri'sãw] (pl **-ões**) f restriction

restringir [xeʃtrĩ'ʒi*] vt to restrict

resultado [xezuw'tadu] m result

resultante [xezuw'tãtʃi] adj resultant; ~ **de** resulting from

resultar [xezuw'ta*] vi: ~ **(de/em)** to result (from/in) ♦ vi (vir a ser) to turn out to be

resumir [xezu'mi*] vt to summarize; (livro) to abridge; (reduzir) to reduce; (conter em resumo) to sum up; **resumo** [xe'zumu] m summary, résumé; **em resumo** in short, briefly

retaguarda [xeta'gwaxda] f rearguard; (posição) rear

retalho [xe'taʎu] m (de pano) scrap, remnant; **vender a ~** (PT) to sell retail

retaliação [xetalja'sãw] (pl **-ões**) f retaliation

retaliar [xeta'lja*] vt to repay ♦ vi to retaliate

retângulo [xe'tãgulu] m rectangle

retardar [xetax'da*] vt to hold up, delay; (adiar) to postpone

reter [xe'te*] (irreg: como **ter**) vt (guardar, manter) to keep; (deter) to stop; (segurar) to hold; (ladrão, suspeito) to detain; (na memória) to retain; (lágrimas, impulsos) to hold back; (impedir de sair) to keep back

retesar [xete'za*] vt (músculo) to flex

reticente [xetʃi'sẽtʃi] adj reticent

retidão [xetʃi'dãw] f rectitude; (de linha) straightness

retificar [xetʃifi'ka*] vt to rectify

retirada [xetʃi'rada] f (MIL) retreat; (salário, saque) withdrawal

retirar [xetʃi'ra*] vt to withdraw; (afastar) to take away, remove; **~-se** vr to withdraw; (de uma festa etc) to leave; (MIL) to retreat; **retiro** [xe'tʃiru] m retreat

reto/a ['xɛtu/a] adj straight; (fig: justo) fair; (: honesto) honest, upright ♦ m (ANAT) rectum

retoque etc [xe'tɔki] vb V **retocar**

retorcer [xetox'se*] vt to twist; **~-se** vr to wriggle, writhe

retornar [xetox'na*] vi to return, go back; **retorno** [xe'toxnu] m return; **dar retorno** to do a U-turn; **retorno (do carro)** (COMPUT) (carriage) return

retraído/a [xetra'idu/a] adj (tímido) reserved, timid

retraimento [xetraj'mẽtu] m withdrawal; (contração) contraction; (fig: de pessoa) timidity, shyness

retrair [xetra'i*] vt to withdraw; (contrair) to contract; (pessoa) to make reserved

retratar [xetra'ta*] vt to portray, depict; (mostrar) to show; (dito) to retract; **~-se** vr (de algo) to retract (sth)

retrato [xe'tratu] m portrait; (FOTO) photo; (fig: efígie) likeness; (: representação) portrayal; ~ **falado** identikit ® picture

retribuir [xetri'bwi*] vt to reward, recompense; (pagar) to remunerate; (hospitalidade, favor, sentimento, visita) to return

retroceder [xetrose'de*] vi to retreat, fall

back; **retrocesso** [xetro'sɛsu] *m* retreat; (*ao passado*) return

retrógrado/a [xe'trɔgradu/a] *adj* retrograde; (*reacionário*) reactionary

retrospectivo/a [xetroʃpek'tʃivu/a] *adj* retrospective

retrospecto [xetro'ʃpɛktu] *m*: **em ~** in retrospect

retrovisor [xetrovi'zo*] *adj, m*: (**espelho**) **~** (rear-view) mirror

réu/ré [xɛw/xɛ] *m/f* defendant; (*culpado*) culprit, criminal

reumatismo [xewma'tʃiʒmu] *m* rheumatism

reunião [xeu'njãw] (*pl* -ões) *f* meeting; (*ato, reencontro*) reunion; (*festa*) get-together, party; **~ de cúpula** summit (meeting)

reunir [xeu'ni*] *vt* (*pessoas*) to bring together; (*partes*) to join, unite; (*qualidades*) to combine; **~-se** *vr* to meet; **~-se a** to join

revanche [xe'vãʃi] *f* revenge

reveillon [xeve'jõ] *m* New Year's Eve

revelação [xevela'sãw] (*pl* -ões) *f* revelation

revelar [xeve'la*] *vt* to reveal; (*FOTO*) to develop; **~-se** *vr* to turn out to be

revelia [xeve'lia] *f* default; **à ~** by default; **à ~ de** without the knowledge *ou* consent of

revendedor(a) [xevẽde'do*(a)] *m/f* dealer

rever [xe've*] (*irreg: como* **ver**) *vt* to see again; (*examinar*) to check; (*revisar*) to revise

reverência [xeve'rẽsja] *f* reverence, respect; (*ato*) bow; (: *de mulher*) curtsey; **fazer uma ~** to bow; to curtsey

reverenciar [xeverẽ'sja*] *vt* to revere

reverendo/a [xeve'rẽdu/a] *adj* reverend ♦ *m* priest, clergyman

reverso [xe'vɛxsu] *m* reverse

reverter [xevex'te*] *vt* to revert

revés [xe've ʃ] *m* reverse; (*infortúnio*) setback, mishap; **ao ~** (*roupa*) inside out; **de ~** (*olhar*) askance

revestir [xeveʃ'tʃi*] *vt* (*paredes etc*) to cover; (*interior de uma caixa etc*) to line

revezar [xeve'za*] *vt, vi* to alternate; **~-se** *vr* to take turns, alternate

revidar [xevi'da*] *vt* (*soco, insulto*) to return; (*retrucar*) to answer; (*crítica*) to rise to, respond to ♦ *vi* to hit back; (*retrucar*) to respond

revirado/a [xevi'radu/a] *adj* (*casa*) untidy, upside-down

revirar [xevi'ra*] *vt* to turn round; (*gaveta*) to turn out, go through

reviravolta [xevira'vɔwta] *f* about-turn, U-turn; (*mudança da situação*) turn

revisão [xevi'zãw] (*pl* -ões) *f* revision; (*de máquina*) overhaul; (*de carro*) service; (*JUR*) appeal

revisar [xevi'za*] *vt* to revise

revisões [xevi'zõjʃ] *fpl* de **revisão**

revista [xe'viʃta] *f* (*busca*) search; (*MIL. exame*) inspection; (*publicação*) magazine; (: *profissional, erudita*) journal; (*TEATRO*) revue

revistar [xeviʃ'ta*] *vt* to search; (*tropa*) to review; (*examinar*) to examine

revisto *etc* [xe'viʃtu] *vb* V **revestir**

revitalizar [xevitali'za*] *vt* to revitalize

revogação [xevoga'sãw] (*pl* -ões) *f* repeal

revogar [xevo'ga*] *vt* to revoke

revolta [xe'vɔwta] *f* revolt; (*fig: indignação*) disgust; **~-do/a** [xevow'tadu/a] *adj* in revolt; (*indignado*) disgusted; (*amargo*) bitter; **~nte** [xevow'tãtʃi] *adj* disgusting, revolting

revoltar [xevow'ta*] *vt* to disgust; **~-se** *vr* to rebel, revolt; (*indignar-se*) to be disgusted

revolto/a [xe'vowtu/a] *pp de* **revolver** ♦ *adj* (*década*) turbulent; (*mundo*) troubled; (*cabelo*) untidy, unkempt; (*mar*) rough; (*desarrumado*) untidy

revolução [xevolu'sãw] (*pl* -ões) *f* revolution; **revolucionar** [xevolusjo'na*] *vt* to revolutionize; **revolucionário/a** [xevolusjo'narju/a] *adj, m/f* revolutionary

revolver [xevow've*] *vi* to revolve, rotate

revólver [xe'vɔwve*] *m* revolver

reza ['xɛza] *f* prayer; **~r** [xe'za*] *vi* to pray

riacho ['xjaʃu] *m* brook, stream

ribeirão [xibej'rãw] (*BR: pl* -ões) *m* stream; **ribeiro** [xi'bejru] *m* brook, stream

rícino ['xisinu] *m*: **óleo de ~** castor oil

rico/a ['xiku/a] *adj* rich; (*PT: lindo*) beautiful; (: *excelente*) splendid ♦ *m/f* rich man/woman

ricota [xi'kɔta] *f* cream cheese

ridicularizar [xidʒikulari'za*] *vt* to ridicule

ridículo/a [xi'dʒikulu/a] *adj* ridiculous

rifa ['xifa] *f* raffle

rifle ['xifli] *m* rifle

rigidez [xiʒi'deʒ] *f* rigidity, stiffness; (*austeridade*) severity, strictness

rígido/a ['xiʒidu/a] *adj* rigid, stiff; (*fig*) strict

rigor [xi'go*] *m* rigidity; (*meticulosidade*) rigour (*BRIT*), rigor (*US*); (*severidade*) harshness, severity; (*exatidão*) precision; **ser de ~** to be essential *ou* obligatory; **~oso/a** [xigo'rozu/ɔza] *adj* rigorous; (*severo*) strict; (*exigente*) demanding; (*minucioso*) precise, accurate; (*inverno*) hard, harsh

rijo/a ['xiʒu/a] *adj* tough, hard; (*severo*) harsh, severe

rim [xĩ] (*pl* -ns) *m* kidney; **rins** *mpl* (*parte inferior das costas*) small *sg* of the back

rima ['xima] *f* rhyme; (*poema*) verse, poem; **~r** [xi'ma*] *vt, vi* to rhyme

rímel ['ximew] (TM) (pl -eis) m mascara

rinçar [xĩ'sa*] vt to rinse

ringue ['xĩgi] m ring

rinoceronte [xinose'rõtʃi] m rhinoceros

rinque [xĩki] m rink

rins [xĩʃ] mpl de rim

Rio ['xiu] m: o ~ (de Janeiro) Rio (de Janeiro)

rio ['xiu] m river

riqueza [xi'keza] f wealth, riches pl; (qualidade) richness

rir [xi*] vi to laugh; ~ de to laugh at

risada [xi'zada] f laughter

risca ['xiʃka] f stroke; (listra) stripe; (no cabelo) parting

riscar [xiʃ'ka*] vt (marcar) to mark; (apagar) to cross out; (desenhar) to outline

risco ['xiʃku] m (marca) mark, scratch; (traço) stroke; (desenho) drawing, sketch; (perigo) risk; correr o ~ de to run the risk of

riso ['xizu] m laughter; ~nho/a [xi'zoɲu/a] adj smiling; (contente) cheerful

ríspido/a ['xiʃpidu/a] adj brusque; (áspero) harsh

ritmo ['xitʃmu] m rhythm

rito ['xitu] m rite

ritual [xi'twaw] (pl -ais) adj, m ritual

rival [xi'vaw] (pl -ais) adj, m/f rival; ~idade [xivali'dadʒi] f rivalry; ~izar [xivali'za*] vt to rival ♦ vi: ~izar com to compete with, vie with

roa etc ['xoa] vb V roer

robô [xo'bo] m robot

robusto/a [xo'buʃtu/a] adj strong, robust

roça ['xɔsa] f plantation; (no mato) clearing; (campo) country

roçar [xo'sa*] vt (terreno) to clear; (tocar de leve) to brush against ♦ vi: ~ em ou por to brush against

rocha ['xɔʃa] f rock; (penedo) crag

rochedo [xo'ʃedu] m crag, cliff

rock ['xɔki] m = roque

rock-and-roll [-ã'xɔw] m rock and roll

roda ['xɔda] f wheel; (círculo) circle; ~ dentada cog(wheel); em ou à ~ de round, around

rodada [xo'dada] f (de bebidas, ESPORTE) round

rodamoinho [xodamo'iɲu] m (na água) whirlpool; (de vento) whirlwind; (no cabelo) swirl

rodar [xo'da*] vt to turn, spin; (viajar por) to tour, travel round; (quilómetros) to do; (filme) to make; (imprimir) to print; (COMPUT: programa) to run ♦ vi to turn round; (AUTO) to drive around; ~ por (a pé) to wander around; (de carro) to drive around

rodear [xo'dʒja*] vt to go round; (circundar) to surround

rodeio [xo'deju] m (em discurso) circumlocution; (subterfúgio) subterfuge; (de gado) round-up; fazer ~s to beat about the bush; sem ~s plainly, frankly

rodela [xo'dɛla] f (pedaço) slice

rodízio [xo'dʒizju] m rota; em ~ on a rota basis

rodo ['xodu] m rake

rodopiar [xodo'pja*] vi to whirl around, swirl

rodopio [xodo'piu] m spin

rodovia [xodo'via] f highway, ≈ motorway (BRIT), ≈ interstate (US)

rodoviária [xodo'vjarja] f (tb: estação ~) bus station; V tb rodoviário

rodoviário/a [xodo'vjarju/a] adj road atr; (polícia) traffic atr

roedor [xwe'do*] m rodent

roer [xwe*] vt to gnaw, nibble; (enferrujar) to corrode; (afligir) to eat away

rogar [xo'ga*] vi to ask, request; ~ a alguém que faça (algo) to beg sb to do (sth); rogo ['xogu] m request

rói [xɔj] vb V roer

roía etc [xo'ia] vb V roer

róis [xɔjʃ] mpl de rol

rol [xɔw] (pl róis) m roll, list

rolar [xo'la*] vt, vi to roll

roldana [xow'dana] f pulley

roleta [xo'leta] f roulette; (borboleta) turnstile

rolha ['xoʎa] f cork

roliço/a [xo'lisu/a] adj (pessoa) plump, chubby; (objeto) round, cylindrical

rolo ['xolu] m (de papel etc) roll; (para nivelar o solo, para pintura) roller; (para cabelo) curler; (col: briga) brawl, fight; cortina de ~ roller blind; ~ compressor steamroller

Roma ['xoma] n Rome

romã [xo'mã] f pomegranate

romance [xo'mãsi] m novel; (caso amoroso) romance; ~ policial detective story; romancista [xo'mã'siʃta] m/f novelist

romano/a [xo'manu/a] adj, m/f Roman

romântico/a [xo'mãtʃiku/a] adj romantic

rombo ['xõbu] m (buraco) hole; (fig: desfalque) embezzlement; (: prejuízo) loss, shortfall

Romênia [xo'menja] f: a ~ Romania; **romeno/a** [xo'mɛnu/a] adj, m/f Rumanian ♦ m (LING) Rumanian

romper [xõ'pe*] vt to break; (rasgar) to tear; (relações) to break off ♦ vi (sol) to appear, emerge; (: surgir) to break through; (ano, dia) to start, begin; ~ em pranto ou lágrimas to burst into tears; **rompimento** [xõpi'mẽtu] m breakage; (fenda) break; (de relações) breaking off

roncar [xõ'ka*] vi to snore; **ronco** ['xõku] m snore

ronda ['xõda] f patrol, beat; fazer a ~ de to go the rounds of, patrol; ~r [xõ'da*] vt to patrol; (espreitar) to prowl ♦ vi to prowl, lurk; (fazer a ronda) to patrol; a inflação ronda os 30% ao mês inflation is in the region of 30% a month

roque ['xɔkɪ] *m* (*XADREZ*) rook, castle; (*MÚS*) rock

rosa ['xɔza] *adj inv* pink ♦ *f* rose; ~**do/a** [xo'zadu/a] *adj* rosy, pink

rosário [xo'zarju] *m* rosary

rosbife [xoʒ'bifi] *m* roast beef

rosca ['xoʃka] *f* spiral, coil; (*de parafuso*) thread; (*pão*) ring-shaped loaf

roseira [xo'zejra] *f* rosebush

roseta [xo'zeta] *f* rosette

rosnar [xoʒ'na*] *vi* (*cão*) to growl, snarl; (*murmurar*) to mutter, mumble

rossio [xo'siu] (*PT*) *m* large square

rosto ['xoʃtu] *m* face

rota ['xɔta] *f* route, course

rotativo/a [xota'tʃivu/a] *adj* rotary

roteiro [xo'tejru] *m* itinerary; (*ordem*) schedule; (*guia*) guidebook; (*de filme*) script

rotina [xo'tʃina] *f* routine; **rotineiro/a** [xotʃi'nejru/a] *adj* routine

roto/a ['xotu/a] *adj* broken; (*rasgado*) torn

rótula ['xɔtula] *f* kneecap

rotular [xotu'la*] *vt* to label; **rótulo** ['xɔtulu] *m* label

roubar [xo'ba*] *vt* to steal; (*loja, casa, pessoa*) to rob ♦ *vi* to steal; (*em jogo, no preço*) to cheat; ~ **algo a alguém** to steal sth from sb; **roubo** ['xobu] *m* theft, robbery

rouco/a ['roku/a] *adj* hoarse

round ['xãwdʒi] (*pl* ~**s**) *m* (*BOXE*) round

roupa ['xopa] *f* clothes *pl*, clothing; ~ **de baixo** underwear; ~ **de cama** bedclothes *pl*, bed linen

roupão [xo'pãw] (*pl* ~**ões**) *m* dressing gown

rouxinol [xoʃi'nɔw] (*pl* ~**óis**) *m* nightingale

roxo/a ['xoʃu/a] *adj* purple, violet

royalty ['xɔjawtʃi] (*pl* ~**ies**) *m* royalty

rua ['xua] *f* street; ~ **principal** main street; ~ **sem saída** no through road, cul-de-sac

rubéola [xu'bɛola] *f* (*MED*) German measles *sg*

rubi [xu'bi] *m* ruby

rublo ['xublu] *m* rouble (*BRIT*), ruble (*US*)

rubor [xu'bo*] *m* blush; (*fig*) shyness, bashfulness; ~**izar-se** [xubori'axsi] *vr* to blush

rubrica [xu'brika] *f* (signed) initials *pl*; ~**r** [xubri'ka*] *vt* to initial

rubro/a ['xubru/a] *adj* (*faces*) rosy, ruddy

ruço/a ['xusu/a] *adj* grey (*BRIT*), gray (*US*), dun; (*desbotado*) faded

rude ['xudʒi] *adj* (*ingênuo*) simple; (*grosseiro*) rude; ~**za** [xu'deza] *f* simplicity, rudeness

rudimento [xudʒi'mẽtu] *m* rudiment

ruela ['xwɛla] *f* lane, alley

ruga ['xuga] *f* (*na pele*) wrinkle; (*na roupa*) crease

rúgbi ['xugbi] *m* rugby

ruge ['xuʒi] *m* rouge

rugido [xu'ʒidu] *m* roar

rugir [xu'ʒi*] *vi* to roar

ruibarbo [xwi'baxbu] *m* rhubarb

ruído ['xwidu] *m* noise; **ruidoso/a** [xwi'dozu/oza] *adj* noisy

ruim [xu'ĩ] (*pl* ~**ns**) *adj* bad; (*defeituoso*) defective

ruína ['xwina] *f* ruin; (*decadência*) downfall

ruindade [xwĩ'dadʒi] *f* wickedness, evil; (*ação*) bad thing

ruins [xu'ĩʃ] *pl de* **ruim**

ruir ['xwi*] *vi* to collapse, go to ruin

ruivo/a ['xwivu/a] *adj* red-haired ♦ *m/f* redhead

rujo *etc* ['xuju] *vb V* **rugir**

rulê [xu'le] *adj*: **gola** ~ polo neck

rum [xũ] *m* rum

rumar [xu'ma*] *vt* (*barco*) to steer ♦ *vi*: ~ **para** to head for

ruminar [xumi'na*] *vt* to chew; (*fig*) to ponder ♦ *vi* (*tb fig*) to ruminate

rumo ['xumu] *m* course, bearing; (*fig*) course; ~ **a** a bound for; **sem** ~ adrift

rumor [xu'mo*] *m* noise; (*notícia*) rumour (*BRIT*), rumor (*US*), report

rupia [xu'pia] *f* rupee

ruptura [xup'tura] *f* break, rupture

rural [xu'raw] (*pl* ~**ais**) *adj* rural

rush [xʌʃ] *m* rush; (**a hora do**) ~ rush hour

Rússia ['xusja] *f*: **a** ~ Russia; **russo/a** ['xusu/a] *adj, m/f* Russian ♦ *m* (*LING*) Russian

rústico/a ['xuʃtʃiku/a] *adj* rustic; (*pessoa*) simple; (*utensílio, objeto*) crude

S

S. *abr* (= *Santo/a ou São*) St

SA *abr* (= *Sociedade Anônima*) Ltd (*BRIT*), Inc. (*US*)

sã [sã] *f de* **são**

Saara [sa'ara] *m*: **o** ~ the Sahara

sábado ['sabadu] *m* Saturday

sabão [sa'bãw] (*pl* ~**ões**) *m* soap

sabedoria [sabedo'ria] *f* wisdom; (*erudição*) learning

saber [sa'be*] *vt, vi* to know; (*descobrir*) to find out ♦ *m* knowledge; **a** ~ namely; ~ **fazer** to know how to do, be able to do; **que eu saiba** as far as I know

sabiá [sa'bja] *m/f* thrush

sabido/a [sa'bidu/a] *adj* knowledgeable; (*esperto*) shrewd

sábio/a ['sabju/a] *adj* wise; (*erudito*) learned ♦ *m/f* wise person; (*erudito*) scholar

sabões [sa'bõjʃ] *mpl de* **sabão**

sabonete [sabo'netʃi] *m* toilet soap

sabor [sa'bo*] *m* taste, flavour (*BRIT*), flavor (*US*); ~**ear** [sabo'rja*] *vt* to taste,

savour (BRIT), savor (US); ~**oso/a**
[sabo'rozu/ɔza] adj tasty, delicious
sabotagem [sabo'taʒẽ] f sabotage
sabotar [sabo'ta*] vt to sabotage
saca ['saka] f sack
sacada [sa'kada] f balcony
sacar [sa'ka*] vt to take out; (dinheiro) to
withdraw; (arma, cheque) to draw; (ES-
PORTE) to serve; (col: entender) to understand ♦ vi (col: entender) to understand;
~ **sobre um devedor** to borrow money
from sb
sacarina [saka'rina] f saccharine (BRIT),
saccharin (US)
saca-rolhas m inv corkscrew
sacerdote [sasex'dɔtʃi] m priest
saciar [sa'sja*] vt (fome, curiosidade) to
satisfy; (sede) to quench
saco ['saku] m bag; (enseada) inlet; ~ **de**
café coffee filter; ~ **de dormir** sleeping
bag
sacode etc [sa'kɔdʒi] vb V **sacudir**
sacola [sa'kɔla] f bag
sacolejar [sakole'ʒa*] vt, vi to shake
sacramento [sakra'mẽtu] m sacrament
sacrificar [sakrifi'ka*] vt to sacrifice; **sa-**
crifício [sakri'fisju] m sacrifice
sacrilégio [sakri'lɛʒu] m sacrilege
sacro/a ['sakru/a] adj sacred
sacudida [saku'dʒida] f shake
sacudir [saku'dʒi*] vt to shake; ~**-se** vr
to shake
sádico/a ['sadʒiku/a] adj sadistic
sadio/a [sa'dʒiu/a] adj healthy
safado/a [sa'fadu/a] adj shameless; (imoral) dirty; (travesso) mischievous ♦ m rogue
safári [sa'fari] m safari
safira [sa'fira] f sapphire
safra ['safra] f harvest
saga ['saga] f saga
sagaz [sa'gajs] adj sagacious, shrewd
Sagitário [saʒi'tarju] m Sagittarius
sagrado/a [sa'gradu/a] adj sacred, holy
saguão [sa'gwãw] (pl -ões) m yard; (pátio interno) courtyard, patio; (entrada)
foyer, lobby
saia ['saja] f skirt; ~**-calça** (pl ~**s-calças**)
f culottes pl
saiba etc ['sajba] vb V **saber**
saída [sa'ida] f exit, way out; (partida)
departure; (ato: de pessoa) going out;
(fig: solução) way out; (COMPUT: de programa) exit; (: de dados) output; ~ **de**
emergência emergency exit
sair [sa'i*] vi to go (ou come) out; (partir) to leave; (realizar-se) to turn out;
(COMPUT) to exit; ~**-se** vr: ~**-se bem/**
mal de to be successful/unsuccessful in
sal [saw] (pl **sais**) m salt; **sem** ~ (comida)
salt-free; (pessoa) lacklustre (BRIT), lack-
luster (US)
sala ['sala] f room; (num edifício público)
hall; (classe, turma) class; ~ **(de aula)**
classroom; ~ **de espera/(de estar)/de**

jantar waiting/living/dining room; ~
de operação (MED) operating theatre
(BRIT) ou theater (US)
salada [sa'lada] f salad; (fig) confusion,
jumble
sala-e-quarto (pl ~**s** ou **salas-e-quarto**)
m two-room flat (BRIT) ou apartment
(US)
salão [sa'lãw] (pl -ões) m large room,
hall; (exposição) show; ~ **de beleza**
beauty salon
salário [sa'larju] m wages pl, salary
saldar [saw'da*] vt (contas) to settle; (dívida) to pay off; **saldo** ['sawdu] m balance; (sobra) surplus
saleiro [sa'lejru] m salt cellar
salgadinho [sawga'dʒiɲu] m savoury
(BRIT), savory (US), snack
salgado/a [saw'gadu/a] adj salty, salted
salgar [saw'ga*] vt to salt
salgueiro [saw'gejru] m willow; ~ **cho-**
rão weeping willow
salientar [saljẽ'ta*] vt to point out; (acentuar) to stress, emphasize; **saliente**
[sa'ljẽtʃi] adj prominent; (evidente) clear,
conspicuous; (importante) outstanding;
(assanhado) forward
salina [sa'lina] f salt bed; (empresa) salt
company
saliva [sa'liva] f saliva
salmão [saw'mãw] (pl -ões) m salmon
salmo ['sawmu] m psalm
salmões [saw'mõjʃ] mpl de **salmão**
salmoura [saw'mora] f brine
salões [sa'lõjʃ] mpl de **salão**
saloio [sa'lɔju] (PT) m (camponês) country
bumpkin
salpicar [sawpi'ka*] vt to splash; (polvilhar, fig) to sprinkle
salsa ['sawsa] f parsley
salsicha [saw'siʃa] f sausage; **salsichão**
[sawsi'ʃãw] (pl -ões) m sausage
saltar [saw'ta*] vt to jump (over), leap
(over); (omitir) to skip ♦ vi to jump,
leap; (sangue) to spurt out; (de ônibus,
cavalo): ~ **de** to get off
salto ['sawtu] m jump, leap; (de calçado)
heel; ~ **de vara/em altura/em dis-**
tância pole vault/high jump/long jump;
~**-mortal** (pl ~**s-mortais**) m somersault
salubre [sa'lubri] adj healthy, salubrious
salutar [salu'ta*] adj salutary, beneficial
salva ['sawva] f salvo; (bandeja) tray, sal-
ver; (BOT) sage; ~ **de palmas** round of
applause
salvação [sawva'sãw] f salvation
salvador [sawva'do*] m saviour (BRIT),
savior (US)
salvaguardar [sawvagwax'da*] vt to safeguard
salvamento [sawva'mẽtu] m rescue; (de
naufrágio) salvage
salvar [saw'va*] vt to save; (resgatar) to
rescue; (objetos, de ruína) to salvage;
(honra) to defend; ~**-se** vr to escape

salva-vidas *m inv* (*bóia*) lifebuoy ♦ *m/f inv* (*pessoa*) lifeguard; **barco ~** lifeboat
salvo/a ['sawvu/a] *adj* safe ♦ *prep* except, save; **a ~** in safety
samambaia [samã'baja] *f* fern
sanar [sa'na*] *vt* to cure; (*remediar*) to remedy
sanção [sã'sãw] (*pl* –ões) *f* sanction; **sancionar** [sansjo'na*] *vt* to sanction
sandália [sã'dalja] *f* sandal
sandes ['sãdəʃ] (*PT*) *f inv* sandwich
sanduíche [sand'wiʃi] (*BR*) *m* sandwich
saneamento [sanja'mẽtu] *m* sanitation
sanear [sa'nja*] *vt* to clean up
sanfona [sã'fɔna] *f* (*MÚS*) accordion
sangrar [sã'gra*] *vt, vi* to bleed; **sangrento/a** [sã'grẽtu/a] *adj* bloody; (*CULIN: carne*) rare
sangria [sã'gria] *f* bloodshed; (*bebida*) sangria
sangue ['sãgi] *m* blood
sanguessuga [sãgi'suga] *f* leech
sanguinário/a [sãgi'narju/a] *adj* bloodthirsty
sanguíneo/a [sã'ginju/a] *adj*: **grupo ~** blood group; **pressão sanguínea** blood pressure; **vaso ~** blood vessel
sanidade [sani'dadʒi] *f* (*saúde*) health; (*mental*) sanity
sanita [sa'nita] (*PT*) *f* toilet, lavatory
sanitário/a [sani'tarju/a] *adj* sanitary; **vaso ~** toilet, lavatory (bowl); **~s** [sani'tarjuʃ] *mpl* toilets
santidade [sãtʃi'dadʒi] *f* holiness, sanctity
santo/a ['sãtu/a] *adj* holy ♦ *m/f* saint
santuário [sã'twarju] *m* shrine, sanctuary
São [sãw] *m* Saint
são/sã [sãw/sã] (*pl* ~s/~s) *adj* healthy; (*conselho*) sound; (*mentalmente*) sane; **~ e salvo** safe and sound
São Paulo [-'pawlu] *n* São Paulo
sapataria [sapata'ria] *f* shoe shop
sapateado [sapa'tʃjadu] *m* tap dancing
sapateiro [sapa'tejru] *m* shoemaker; (*vendedor*) shoe salesman; (*que conserta*) shoe repairer; (*loja*) shoe repairer's
sapatilha [sapa'tʃiʎa] *f* (*de balé*) shoe; (*sapato*) pump; (*de atleta*) running shoe
sapato [sa'patu] *m* shoe
sapo ['sapu] *m* toad
saque¹ ['saki] *m* (*de dinheiro*) withdrawal; (*COM*) draft, bill; (*ESPORTE*) serve; (*pilhagem*) plunder, pillage; **~ a descoberto** (*COM*) overdraft
saque² *etc vb* V **sacar**
saquear [sa'kja*] *vt* to pillage, plunder
saraivar [sarai'va*] *vi* to hail
sarampo [sa'rãpu] *m* measles *sg*
sarar [sa'ra*] *vt* to cure; (*ferida*) to heal ♦ *vi* to recover
sarcasmo [sax'kaʒmu] *m* sarcasm; **sarcástico/a** [sax'kaʃtʃiku/a] *adj* sarcastic

sarda ['saxda] *f* freckle
Sardenha [sax'dɛɲa] *f*: **a ~** Sardinia
sardinha [sax'dʒiɲa] *f* sardine
sardônico/a [sax'doniku/a] *adj* sardonic, sarcastic
sargento [sax'ʒẽtu] *m* sergeant
sarjeta [sax'ʒeta] *f* gutter
sarna ['saxna] *f* scabies *sg*
Satã [sa'tã] *m* Satan
Satanás [sata'naʃ] *m* Satan
satélite [sa'tɛlitʃi] *m* satellite
sátira ['satʃira] *f* satire
satisfação [satʃiʃfa'sãw] (*pl* –ões) *f* satisfaction; (*recompensa*) reparation; **satisfatório/a** [satʃiʃfa'tɔrju/a] *adj* satisfactory
satisfazer [satʃiʃfa'ze*] (*irreg: como fazer*) *vt* to satisfy ♦ *vi* to be satisfactory; **~-se** *vr* to be satisfied; (*saciar-se*) to fill o.s. up; **~ a** to satisfy; **satisfeito/a** [satʃiʃ'fejtu/a] *adj* satisfied; (*saciado*) full; **dar-se por satisfeito com algo** to be content with sth
saturar [satu'ra*] *vt* to saturate; (*de comida, aborrecimento*) to fill
saudação [sawda'sãw] (*pl* –ões) *f* greeting
saudade [saw'dadʒi] *f* longing, yearning; (*lembrança nostálgica*) nostalgia; **deixar ~s** to be greatly missed; **ter ~(s) de** (*desejar*) to long for; (*sentir falta de*) to miss; **~(s) de casa, ~(s) da pátria** homesickness *sg*
saudar [saw'da*] *vt* to greet; (*dar as boas vindas*) to welcome; (*aclamar*) to acclaim
saudável [saw'davew] (*pl* –eis) *adj* healthy; (*moralmente*) wholesome
saúde [sa'udʒi] *f* health; (*brinde*) toast; **~!** (*brindando*) cheers!; (*quando se espirra*) bless you!; **beber à ~ de** to drink to, toast; **estar bem/mal de ~** to be well/ill
saudosismo [sawdo'ziʒmu] *m* nostalgia
saudoso/a [saw'dozu/ɔza] *adj* (*nostálgico*) nostalgic; (*da família ou terra natal*) homesick; (*de uma pessoa*) longing; (*que causa saudades*) much-missed
sauna ['sawna] *f* sauna
saveiro [sa'vejru] *m* sailing boat
saxofone [sakso'fɔni] *m* saxophone
sazonado/a [sazo'nadu/a] *adj* ripe, mature
sazonal [sazo'naw] (*pl* –ais) *adj* seasonal

PALAVRA CHAVE

se [si] *pron* **1** (*reflexivo: impess*) oneself; (: *m*) himself; (: *f*) herself; (: *coisa*) itself; (: *você*) yourself; (: *pl*) themselves; (: *vocês*) yourselves; **ela está ~ vestindo** she's getting dressed; (*usos léxicos del pron*) V o vb em questão p. ex. **arrepender-se**
2 (*uso recíproco*) each other, one another; **olharam-~** they looked at each

other

3 (*impess*): come-~ bem aqui you can eat well here; sabe-~ que ... it is known that ...; vende(m)-~ jornais naquela loja they sell newspapers in that shop

♦ *conj* if; (*em pergunta indireta*) whether; ~ bem que even though

sê [se] *vb* V **ser**

sebe ['sɛbi] (*PT*) *f* fence; ~ viva hedge

sebento/a [se'bētu/a] *adj* greasy; (*sujo*) dirty, filthy

sebo ['sebu] *m* tallow; ~**so/a** [se'bozu/ɔza] *adj* greasy; (*sujo*) dirty

seca ['sɛka] *f* drought

secador [seka'do*] *m*: ~ de cabelo/ roupa hairdryer/clothes horse

seção [se'sãw] (*pl* -ões) *f* section; (*em loja, repartição*) department

secar [se'ka*] *vt* to dry; (*planta*) to parch ♦ *vi* to dry; to wither; (*fonte*) to dry up

secção [sek'sãw] (*PT*) = **seção**

seco/a ['seku/a] *adj* dry; (*ríspido*) curt, brusque; (*magro*) thin; (*pessoa: frio*) cold; (: *sério*) serious

seções [se'sõjʃ] *fpl de* **seção**

secreção [sekre'sãw] (*pl* -ões) *f* secretion

secretaria [sekreta'ria] *f* general office; (*de secretário*) secretary's office; (*ministério*) ministry

secretária [sekre'tarja] *f* writing desk; ~ eletrônica (*telephone*) answering machine; *V tb* **secretário**

secretário/a [sekre'tarju/a] *m/f* secretary; S~ de Estado de ... Secretary of State for ...

secreto/a [se'krɛtu/a] *adj* secret

sectário/a [sek'tarju/a] *adj* sectarian

sector [sek'to*] (*PT*) *m* = **setor**

secular [seku'la*] *adj* secular, lay

século ['sɛkulu] *m* century; (*época*) age

secundar [sekũ'da*] *vt* to second, support

secundário/a [sekũ'darju/a] *adj* secondary

seda ['seda] *f* silk

sedativo [seda'tʃivu] *m* sedative

sede¹ ['sɛdʒi] *f* (*de empresa, instituição*) headquarters *sg*; (*de governo*) seat; (*REL*) see, diocese

sede² ['sedʒi] *f* thirst; estar com *ou* ter ~ to be thirsty; ~**nto/a** [se'dētu/a] *adj* thirsty

sediar [se'dʒja*] *vt* to base

sedimento [sedʒi'mētu] *m* sediment

sedoso/a [se'dozu/ɔza] *adj* silky

sedução [sedu'sãw] (*pl* -ões) *f* seduction

sedutor(a) [sedu'to*(a)] *adj* seductive; (*oferta etc*) tempting

seduzir [sedu'zi*] *vt* to seduce; (*fascinar*) to fascinate

segmento [seg'mētu] *m* segment

segredo [se'gredu] *m* secret; (*sigilo*) secrecy; (*de fechadura*) combination

segregar [segre'ga*] *vt* to segregate

seguidamente [segida'mētʃi] *adv* (*sem parar*) continuously; (*logo depois*) soon afterwards

seguido/a [se'gidu/a] *adj* following; (*contínuo*) continuous, consecutive; ~ de *ou* por followed by; três dias ~s three days running; horas seguidas for hours on end; em seguida next; (*logo depois*) soon afterwards; (*imediatamente*) immediately, right away

seguidor(a) [segi'do*(a)] *m/f* follower

seguimento [segi'mētu] *m* continuation; dar ~ a to proceed with; em ~ de after

seguinte [se'gĩtʃi] *adj* following, next; eu lhe disse o ~ this is what I said to him

seguir [se'gi*] *vt* to follow; (*continuar*) to continue ♦ *vi* to follow; to continue, carry on; (*ir*) to go; ~-se *vr*: ~-se (a) to follow; logo a ~ next; ~-se (de) to result (from)

segunda [se'gũda] *f* (*tb*: ~-feira) Monday; (*AUTO*) second (gear); de ~ second-rate; ~-feira (*pl* ~s-feiras) *f* Monday

segundo/a [se'gũdu/a] *adj* second ♦ *prep* according to ♦ *conj* as, from what ♦ *adv* secondly ♦ *m* second; de segunda mão second-hand; de segunda (*classe*) second-class; ~ ele disse according to what he said; ~ dizem apparently; ~ me consta as far as I know; segundas intenções ulterior motives

seguramente [segura'mētʃi] *adv* certainly; (*muito provavelmente*) surely

segurança [segu'rãsa] *f* security; (*ausência de perigo*) safety; (*confiança*) confidence ♦ *m/f* security guard; com ~ assuredly

segurar [segu'ra*] *vt* to hold; (*amparar*) to hold up; (*COM: bens*) to insure ♦ *vi*: ~ em to hold; ~-se *vr*: ~-se em to hold on to

seguro/a [se'guru/a] *adj* safe; (*livre de risco, firme*) secure; (*certo*) certain, assured; (*confiável*) reliable; (*de si mesmo*) confident; (*tempo*) settled ♦ *adv* confidently ♦ *m* (*COM*) insurance; estar ~ de/de que to be sure of that; fazer ~ to take out an insurance policy; ~ contra acidentes/incêndio accident/fire insurance; ~-saúde (*pl* ~s-saúde) *m* health insurance

sei [sej] *vb* V **saber**

seio ['seju] *m* breast, bosom; (*âmago*) heart; ~ paranasal sinus

seis [sejʃ] *num* six

seita ['sejta] *f* sect

seiva ['sejva] *f* sap

seixo ['sejʃu] *m* pebble

seja *etc* ['seʒa] *vb* V **ser**

sela ['sɛla] *f* saddle

selar [se'la*] *vt* (*carta*) to stamp; (*docu-*

mento oficial, pacto) to seal; (*cavalo*) to saddle

seleção [sele'sãw] (*PT* -cç-) (*pl* -ões) *f* selection; (*ESPORTE*) team

selecionar [selesjo'na°] (*PT* -cc-) *vt* to select

seleções [sele'sõjʃ] *fpl de* seleção

seleta [se'lcta] (*PT* -ct-) *f* anthology

seleto/a [se'lctu/a] (*PT* -ct-) *adj* select

selim [se'lĩ] (*pl* -ins *m* saddle

selo ['selu] *m* stamp; (*carimbo, sinete*) seal

selva ['sɛwva] *f* jungle

selvagem [sew'vaʒẽ] (*pl* -ns) *adj* wild; (*feroz*) fierce; (*povo*) savage; **selvageria** [sewvaʒe'ria] *f* savagery

sem [sẽ] *prep* without ♦ *conj*: ~ que eu peça without my asking; estar/ficar ~ dinheiro/gasolina to have no/have run out of money/petrol

semáforo [se'maforu] *m* (*AUTO*) traffic lights *pl*; (*FERRO*) signal

semana [se'mana] *f* week; ~l [sema'naw] (*pl* ~is) *adj* weekly; **semanário** [sema'narju] *m* weekly (publication)

semblante [sẽ'blãtʃi] *m* face; (*fig*) appearance, look

semear [se'mja°] *vt* to sow

semelhança [seme'ʎãsa] *f* similarity, resemblance; **semelhante** [seme'ʎãtʃi] *adj* similar; (*tal*) such ♦ *m* fellow creature

sêmen ['semẽ] *m* semen

semente [se'mẽtʃi] *f* seed

semestral [semeʃ'traw] (*pl* -ais) *adj* half-yearly, bi-annual

semestre [se'mɛʃtri] *m* six months; (*EDUC*) semester

semi... [semi] *prefixo* semi..., half...; ~**círculo** [semi'sixkulu] *m* semicircle; ~**condutor** [semikõdu'to°] *m* semiconductor; ~**final** [semi'finaw] (*pl* ~**finais**) *f* semi-final

seminário [semi'narju] *m* seminar; (*REL*) seminary

sem-número *m*: um ~ de coisas loads of things

sem-par *adj inv* unequalled, unique

sempre ['sẽpri] *adv* always; você ~ vai? (*PT*) are you still going?; ~ que whenever; como ~ as usual; a comida/hora etc de ~ the usual food/time *etc*

sem-terra *m/f* landless labourer (*BRIT*) *ou* laborer (*US*)

sem-vergonha *adj inv* shameless ♦ *m/f inv* (*pessoa*) rogue

senado [se'nadu] *m* senate; ~**r(a)** [sena'do°(a)] *m/f* senator

senão [se'nãw] (*pl* -ões) *conj* otherwise; (*mas sim*) but, but rather ♦ *prep* except ♦ *m* flaw, defect

senda ['sẽda] *f* path

senha ['sɛɲa] *f* sign; (*palavra de passe*) password; (*de caixa automática*) PIN number; (*recibo*) receipt; (*passe*) pass

senhor(a) [se'ɲo°(a)] *m* (*homem*) man;

(*formal*) gentleman; (*homem idoso*) elderly man; (*REL*) lord; (*dono*) owner; (*tratamento*) Mr(.); (*tratamento respeitoso*) sir ♦ *f* (*mulher*) lady; (*esposa*) wife; (*mulher idosa*) elderly lady; (*dona*) owner; (*tratamento*) Mrs(.), Ms(.); (*tratamento respeitoso*) madam; o ~/a ~a (*você*) you; nossa ~a! (*col*) gosh; sim, ~(a)! yes indeed; ~ia [se ɲo'ria] *f* landlady; Vossa S~ia (*em cartas*) you

senhorita [seɲo'rita] *f* young lady; (*tratamento*) Miss, Ms(.); a ~ (*você*) you

senil [se'niw] (*pl* -is) *adj* senile

senões [se'nõjʃ] *mpl de* senão

sensação [sẽsa'sãw] (*pl* -ões) *f* sensation; **sensacional** [sẽsasjo'naw] (*pl* -ais) *adj* sensational

sensato/a [sẽ'satu/a] *adj.* sensible

sensível [sẽ'sivew] (*pl* -eis) *adj* sensitive; (*visível*) noticeable; (*considerável*) considerable; (*dolorido*) tender

senso ['sẽsu] *m* sense; (*juízo*) judgement

sensual [sẽ'swaw] (*pl* -ais) *adj* sensual

sentado/a [sẽ'tadu/a] *adj* sitting

sentar [sẽ'ta°] *vt* to seat ♦ *vi* to sit; ~-se *vr* to sit down

sentença [sẽ'tẽsa] *f* (*JUR*) sentence; **sentenciar** [sẽtẽ'sja°] *vt* (*julgar*) to pass judgement on; (*condenar por sentença*) to sentence

sentidamente [sẽtʃida'mẽtʃi] *adv* (*chorar*) bitterly; (*desculpar-se*) abjectly

sentido/a [sẽ'tʃidu/a] *adj* (*magoado*) hurt; (*choro, queixa*) heartfelt ♦ *m* sense; (*direção*) direction; (*atenção*) attention; (*aspecto*) respect; ~! (*MIL*) attention!; em certo ~ in a sense; (não) ter ~ (not) to be acceptable; "~ único" (*PT: sinal*) "one-way"

sentimental [sẽtʃimẽ'taw] (*pl* -ais) *adj* sentimental; vida ~ love life

sentimento [sẽtʃi'mẽtu] *m* feeling; (*senso*) sense; ~s *mpl* (*pésames*) condolences

sentinela [sẽtʃi'nɛla] *f* sentry, guard

sentir [sẽ'tʃi°] *vt* to feel; (*perceber, pressentir*) to sense; (*ser afetado por*) to be affected by; (*magoar-se*) to be upset by ♦ *vi* to feel; (*sofrer*) to suffer; ~-se *vr* to feel; (*julgar-se*) to consider o.s. (to be); ~ (a) falta de to miss; ~ cheiro/gosto (de) to smell/taste; ~ vontade de to feel like; sinto muito I am very sorry

separação [separa'sãw] (*pl* -ões) *f* separation

separado/a [sepa'radu/a] *adj* separate; em ~ separately, apart

separar [sepa'ra°] *vt* to separate; (*dividir*) to divide; (*pôr de lado*) to put aside; ~-se *vr* to separate; to be divided

séptico/a ['sɛptʃiku/a] *adj* septic

sepultamento [sepuwta'mẽtu] *m* burial

sepultar [sepuw'ta°] *vt* to bury; **sepultura** [sepuw'tura] *f* grave, tomb

seqüência [se'kwẽsja] *f* sequence

sequer [se'kɛ°] *adv* at least; (nem) ~

not even

seqüestrador(a) [sekweʃtra'do*(a)] *m/f* kidnapper; *(de avião etc)* hijacker

seqüestrar [sekweʃ'tra*] *vt (bens)* to seize, confiscate; *(raptar)* to kidnap; *(avião etc)* to hijack; **seqüestro** [se'kweʃtru] *m* seizure; abduction, kidnapping; hijack

PALAVRA CHAVE

ser [se*] *vi* **1** *(descrição)* to be; **ela é médica/muito alta** she's a doctor/very tall; **é Ana** *(TEL)* Ana speaking *ou* here; **ela é de uma bondade incrível** she's incredibly kind; **ele está é danado** he's really angry; **~ de mentir/briga** to be the sort to lie/fight

2 *(horas, datas, números)*: **é uma hora** it's one o'clock; **são seis e meia** it's half past six; **é dia 1º de junho** it's the first of June; **somos/são seis** there are six of us/them

3 *(origem, material)*: **~ de** to be *ou* come from; *(feito de)* to be made of; *(pertencer)* to belong to; **sua família é da Bahia** his *(ou her etc)* family is from Bahia; **a mesa é de mármore** the table is made of marble; **é de Pedro** it's Pedro's, it belongs to Pedro

4 *(em orações passivas)*: **já foi descoberto** it had already been discovered

5 *(locuções com subjun)*: **ou seja** that is to say; **seja quem for** whoever it may be; **se eu fosse você** if I were you; **se não fosse você**, ... if it hadn't been for you ...

6 *(locuções)*: **a não ~** except; **a não ~ que** unless; **é** *(resposta afirmativa)* yes; **..., não é?** isn't it?, don't you? *etc*; **ah, é?** really?; **que foi?** *(o que aconteceu?)* what happened?; **qual é o problema?** what's the problem?; **~á que ...?** I wonder if ...?

♦ *m* being; **~es** *mpl (criaturas)* creatures

sereia [se'reja] *f* mermaid

serenar [sere'na*] *vt* to calm

sereno/a [se'rɛnu/a] *adj* calm; *(tempo)* fine, clear

série ['sɛri] *f* series; *(seqüência)* sequence, succession; *(EDUC)* grade; *(categoria)* category; **fora de ~** out of order; *(fig)* extraordinary

seriedade [serje'dadʒi] *f* seriousness; *(honestidade)* honesty

seringa [se'riga] *f* syringe

seringueiro/a [seri'gejru/a] *m/f* rubber tapper

sério/a ['sɛrju/a] *adj* serious; *(honesto)* honest, decent; *(responsável)* responsible; *(confiável)* reliable; *(roupa)* sober ♦ *adv* seriously; **a ~** seriously; **~?** really?

sermão [sex'mãw] *(pl* **-ões**) *m* sermon; *(fig)* telling-off

serões [se'rõjʃ] *mpl de* serão

serpente [sex'pẽtʃi] *f* snake

serpentina [sexpẽ'tʃina] *f* streamer

serra ['sɛxa] *f (montanhas)* mountain range; *(TEC)* saw

serragem [se'xaʒẽ] *f* sawdust

serralheiro/a [sexa'ʎejru/a] *m/f* locksmith

serrano/a [se'xanu/a] *adj* highland *atr* ♦ *m/f* highlander

serrar [se'xa*] *vt* to saw

sertanejo/a [sexta'neʒu/a] *adj* rustic, country ♦ *m/f* inhabitant of the *sertão*

sertão [sex'tãw] *(pl* **-ões**) *m* backwoods *pl*, bush (country)

servente [sex'vẽtʃi] *m/f* servant; *(operário)* labourer *(BRIT)*, laborer *(US)*

serviçal [sexvi'saw] *(pl* **-ais**) *adj* obliging, helpful ♦ *m/f* servant; *(trabalhador)* wage earner

serviço [sex'visu] *m* service; *(de chá etc)* set; **estar de ~** to be on duty; **prestar ~** to help

servidor(a) [sexvi'do*(a)] *m/f* servant; *(funcionário)* employee; **~ público** civil servant

servil [sex'viw] *(pl* **-is**) *adj* servile

servir [sex'vi*] *vt* to serve ♦ *vi* to serve; *(ser útil)* to be useful; *(ajudar)* to help; *(roupa: caber)* to fit; **~-se** *vr*: **~-se (de)** *(comida, café)* to help o.s. (to); *(meios)*: **~-se de** to use, make use of; **~ de** *(prover)* to supply with, provide with; **você está servido?** *(num bar)* are you all right for a drink?; **~ de algo** to serve as sth; **qualquer ônibus serve** any bus will do

servis [sex'viʃ] *adj pl de* servil

sessão [se'sãw] *(pl* **-ões**) *f (do parlamento etc)* session; *(reunião)* meeting; *(de cinema)* showing

sessenta [se'sẽta] *num* sixty

sessões [se'sõjʃ] *fpl de* sessão

sesta ['sɛʃta] *f* siesta, nap

set ['sɛtʃi] *m (TÊNIS)* set

seta ['sɛta] *f* arrow

sete ['sɛtʃi] *num* seven

setembro [se'tẽbru] *(PT* S-) *m* September

setenta [se'tẽta] *num* seventy

sétimo/a ['sɛtʃimu/a] *num* seventh

setor [se'to*] *m* sector

seu/sua [sew/sua] *adj (dele)* his; *(dela)* her; *(de coisa)* its; *(deles, delas)* their; *(de você, vocês)* your ♦ *pron*: **(o) ~/(a) sua** his; hers; its; theirs; yours ♦ *m (senhor)* Mr(.)

severidade [severi'dadʒi] *f* severity

severo/a [se'vɛru/a] *adj* severe

sexo ['sɛksu] *m* sex

sexta ['sɛʃta] *f (tb:* **~-feira**) Friday; **~-feira** *(pl* **~s-feiras**) *f* Friday; **S~-feira Santa** Good Friday

sexto/a ['sɛʃtu/a] *num* sixth

sexual [se'kswaw] *(pl* **-ais**) *adj* sexual; *(vida, ato)* sex *atr*

sexy ['sɛksi] (pl ~s) adj sexy

s.f.f. (PT) abr = **se faz favor**

short ['ʃɔxtʃi] m (pair of) shorts pl

si [si] pron oneself; (ele) himself; (ela) herself; (coisa) itself; (PT: você) yourself, you; (: vocês) yourselves; (eles, elas) themselves

SIDA ['sida] (PT) abr f (= síndrome de deficiência imunológica adquirida) a ~ AIDS

siderúrgica [side'ruxʒika] f steel industry; **siderúrgico/a** [side'ruxʒiku/a] adj: **(usina) siderúrgica** steelworks sg

sidra ['sidra] f cider

sifão [si'fãw] (pl -ões) m syphon

sifões [si'fõjʃ] mpl de **sifão**

sigilo [si'ʒilu] m secrecy

sigla ['sigla] f acronym; (abreviação) abbreviation

significado [signifi'kadu] m meaning

significar [signifi'ka*] vt to mean, signify; **significativo/a** [signifika'tʃivu/a] adj significant

signo ['signu] m sign

sigo etc ['sigu] vb V **seguir**

sílaba ['silaba] f syllable

silenciar [silẽ'sja*] vt to silence

silêncio [si'lẽsju] m silence, quiet; **silencioso/a** [silẽ'sjozu/ɔza] adj silent, quiet ♦ m (AUTO) silencer (BRIT), muffler (US)

silhueta [si'ʎweta] f silhouette

silício [si'lisju] m silicon

silo ['silu] m silo

silvar [siw'va*] vi to hiss; (assobiar) to whistle

silvestre [siw'vɛʃtri] adj wild

sim [sĩ] adv yes; **creio que ~** I think so

símbolo ['sĩbolu] m symbol

simetria [sime'tria] f symmetry

similar [simi'la*] adj similar

símile ['simili] m simile

similitude [simili'tudʒi] f similarity

simpatia [sĩpa'tʃia] f liking; (afeto) affection; (afinidade, solidariedade) sympathy; ~s fpl (inclinações) sympathies; **simpático/a** [sĩ'patʃiku/a] adj (pessoa, decoração etc) nice; (lugar) pleasant, nice; (amável) kind; **simpatizante** [sĩpatʃi'zãtʃi] adj sympathetic ♦ m/f sympathizer; **simpatizar** [sĩpatʃi'za*] vi: **simpatizar com** (pessoa) to like; (causa) to sympathize with

simples ['sĩpliʃ] adj inv simple; (único) single; (fácil) easy; (mero) mere; (ingênuo) naïve ♦ adv simply; **simplicidade** [sĩplisi'dadʒi] f simplicity; **simplificar** [sĩplifi'ka*] vt to simplify

simular [simu'la*] vt to simulate

simultaneamente [simuwtanja'mẽtʃi] adv simultaneously

simultâneo/a [simuw'tanju/a] adj simultaneous

sinagoga [sina'gɔga] f synagogue

sinal [si'naw] (pl -ais) m sign; (gesto,

TEL) signal; (na pele) mole; (: de nascença) birthmark; (depósito) deposit; (tb: ~ de tráfego, ~ luminoso) traffic light; **por ~** (por falar nisso) by the way; (aliás) as a matter of fact; ~ **de chamada** (TEL) ringing tone; ~ **de discar** (BR) ou **de marcar** (PT) dialling tone (BRIT), dial tone (US); ~ **de ocupado** (BR) ou **de impedido** (PT) engaged tone (BRIT), busy signal (US); **sinalização** [sinaliza'sãw] f (ato) signalling; (para motoristas) traffic signs pl; ~**izar** [sinali'za*] vi to signal

sinceridade [sĩseri'dadʒi] f sincerity

sincero/a [sĩ'seru/a] adj sincere

sindical [sĩdʒi'kaw] (pl -ais) adj (trade) union atr; ~**ista** [sĩdʒika'liʃta] m/f trade unionist

sindicato [sĩdʒi'katu] m trade union; (financeiro) syndicate

síndrome ['sĩdromi] f syndrome; ~ **de Down** Down's syndrome

sinfonia [sĩfo'nia] f symphony

singelo/a [sĩ'ʒɛlu/a] adj simple

singular [sĩgu'la*] adj singular; (extraordinário) exceptional; (bizarro) odd

sino ['sinu] m bell

sintaxe [sĩ'tasi] f syntax

síntese ['sĩtezi] f synthesis; **sintético/a** [sĩ'tɛtʃiku/a] adj synthetic; **sintetizar** [sĩtetʃi'za*] vt to synthesize

sinto etc ['sĩtu] vb V **sentir**

sintoma [sĩ'toma] m symptom

sintonizar [sĩtoni'za*] vt (RÁDIO) to tune ♦ vi to tune in

sinuca [si'nuka] f snooker

sinuoso/a [si'nwozu/ɔza] adj (caminho) winding; (linha) wavy

sirena [si'rɛna] f siren

sirene [si'rɛni] f = **sirena**

siri [si'ri] m crab

Síria ['sirja] f: **a** ~ Syria; **sírio/a** ['sirju/a] adj, m/f Syrian

sirvo etc ['sixvu] vb V **servir**

sísmico/a ['siʒmiku/a] adj seismic

siso ['sizu] m good sense; **dente de** ~ wisdom tooth

sistema [siʃ'tɛma] m system; (método) method

sisudo/a [si'zudu/a] adj serious, sober

site ['sajtʃi] m (na Internet) website

sitiar [si'tʃja*] vt to besiege

sítio ['sitʃju] m (MIL) siege; (propriedade rural) small farm; (PT: lugar) place

situação [sitwa'sãw] (pl -ões) f situation; (posição) position

situado/a [si'twadu/a] adj situated

situar [si'twa*] vt to place, put; (edifício) to situate, locate; ~**-se** vr to position o.s.; (estar situado) to be situated

slogan [iʃ'lɔgã] (pl ~s) m slogan

SME abr m (= Sistema Monetário Europeu) ERM

smoking [iʒ'mokiʃ] (pl ~s) m dinner jacket (BRIT), tuxedo (US)

só [sɔ] *adj* alone; *(único)* single; *(solitário)* solitary ♦ *adv* only; **a ~s** alone

soar [swa*] *vi* to sound ♦ *vt (horas)* to strike; *(instrumento)* to play; **~ a** to sound like; **~ bem/mal** *(fig)* to go down well/badly

sob [sob] *prep* under; **~ juramento** on oath; **~ medida** *(roupa)* made to measure

sobe *etc* ['sɔbi] *vb* V **subir**

soberania [sobera'nia] *f* sovereignty

soberano/a [sobe'ranu/a] *adj* sovereign; *(fig: supremo)* supreme ♦ *m/f* sovereign

soberbo/a [so'bexbu/a] *adj* haughty, arrogant; *(magnífico)* magnificent, splendid

sobra ['sɔbra] *f* surplus, remnant; **~s** *fpl (restos)* remains; *(de tecido)* remnants; *(de comida)* leftovers; **ter algo de ~** to have sth extra; *(tempo, comida, motivos)* to have plenty of sth; **ficar de ~** to be left over

sobrado [so'bradu] *m (andar)* floor; *(casa)* house *(of two or more storeys)*

sobrancelha [sobrã'seʎa] *f* eyebrow

sobrar [so'bra*] *vi* to be left; *(dúvidas)* to remain

sobre ['sobri] *prep* on; *(por cima de)* over; *(acima de)* above; *(a respeito de)* about

sobreaviso [sobrja'vizu] *m* warning; **estar de ~** to be alert, be on one's guard

sobrecarregar [sobrikaxe'ga*] *vt* to overload

sobremesa [sobri'meza] *f* dessert

sobrenatural [sobrinatu'raw] *(pl* **-ais***) adj* supernatural

sobrenome [sobri'nɔmi] *(BR) m* surname, family name

sobrepor [sobri'po*] *(irreg: como* **pôr***) vt*: **~ algo a algo** to put sth on top of sth

sobressair [sobrisa'i*] *vi* to stand out; **~-se** *vr* to stand out

sobressalente [sobrisa'lẽtʃi] *adj, m* spare

sobressaltar [sobrisaw'ta*] *vt* to startle, frighten; **sobressalto** [sobri'sawtu] *m* start; *(temor)* trepidation; **de sobressalto** suddenly

sobretaxa [sobri'taʃa] *f* surcharge

sobretudo [sobri'tudu] *m* overcoat ♦ *adv* above all, especially

sobrevivência [sobrivi'vẽsja] *f* survival; **sobrevivente** [sobrivi'vẽtʃi] *adj* surviving ♦ *m/f* survivor

sobreviver [sobrivi've*] *vi*: **~ (a)** to survive

sobriedade [sobrje'dadʒi] *f* soberness; *(comedimento)* moderation, restraint

sobrinho/a [so'briɲu/a] *m/f* nephew/niece

sóbrio/a ['sɔbrju/a] *adj* sober; *(moderado)* moderate, restrained

socar [so'ka*] *vt* to hit, strike; *(calcar)* to crush, pound; *(massa de pão)* to knead

social [so'sjaw] *(pl* **-ais***) adj* social; **~ista** [sosja'liʃta] *adj, m/f* socialist

sociedade [sosje'dadʒi] *f* society; *(COM: empresa)* company; *(associação)* association; **~ anônima** limited company *(BRIT)*, incorporated company *(US)*

sócio/a ['sɔsju/a] *m/f (COM)* partner; *(de clube)* member

sociologia [sosjolo'ʒia] *f* sociology

soco ['soku] *m* punch; **dar um ~ em** to punch

socorrer [soko'xe*] *vt* to help, assist; *(salvar)* to rescue; **~-se** *vr*: **~-se de** to resort to, have recourse to; **socorro** [so'koxu] *m* help, assistance; *(reboque)* breakdown *(BRIT)* ou tow *(US)* truck; **socorro!** help!; **primeiros socorros** first aid *sg*

soda ['sɔda] *f* soda (water)

sofá [so'fa] *m* sofa, settee; **~-cama** *(pl* **~s-camas***)* m sofa-bed

sofisticado/a [sofiʃtʃi'kadu/a] *adj* sophisticated; *(afetado)* pretentious

sôfrego/a ['sofregu/a] *adj* keen; *(impaciente)* impatient; *(no comer, beber)* greedy

sofrer [so'fre*] *vt* to suffer; *(acidente)* to have; *(agüentar)* to bear, put up with; *(experimentar)* to undergo ♦ *vi* to suffer; **sofrido/a** [so'fridu/a] *adj* long-suffering; **sofrimento** [sofri'mẽtu] *m* suffering

software [sof'twɛr] *m (COMPUT)* software

sogro/a ['sogru/'sɔgra] *m/f* father-in-law/mother-in-law

sóis [sɔjʃ] *mpl de* **sol**

soja ['sɔʒa] *f* soya *(BRIT)*, soy *(US)*

sol [sɔw] *(pl* **sóis***) m* sun; *(luz)* sunshine, sunlight; **fazer ~** to be sunny; **tomar ~** to sunbathe

sola ['sɔla] *f* sole

solar [so'la*] *adj* solar; **energia/painel ~** solar energy/panel

solda ['sowda] *f* solder

soldado [sow'dadu] *m* soldier

soldar [sow'da*] *vt* to weld

soleira [so'lejra] *f* doorstep

solene [so'lɛni] *adj* solemn; **solenidade** [soleni'dadʒi] *f* solemnity; *(cerimônia)* ceremony

soletrar [sole'tra*] *vt* to spell

solicitar [solisi'ta*] *vt* to ask for; *(emprego etc)* to apply for; *(amizade, atenção)* to seek; **~ algo a alguém** to ask sb for sth

solícito/a [so'lisitu/a] *adj* helpful

solidão [soli'dãw] *f* solitude; *(sensação)* loneliness

solidariedade [solidarje'dadʒi] *f* solidarity

solidário/a [soli'darju/a] *adj*: **ser ~ a** *ou* **com** *(pessoa)* to stand by; *(causa)* to be sympathetic to, sympathize with

sólido/a ['sɔlidu/a] *adj* solid

solista [so'liʃta] *m/f* soloist

solitária [soli'tarja] *f (verme)* tapeworm; *(cela)* solitary confinement

solitário/a [soli'tarju/a] *adj* lonely; (*isolado*) solitary ♦ *m* hermit

solo ['sɔlu] *m* ground, earth; (*MÚS*) solo

soltar [sow'ta*] *vt* to set free; (*desatar*) to loosen; (*largar*) to let go of; (*emitir*) to emit; (*grito*) to let out; (*cabelo*) to let down; (*freio*) to release; **~-se** *vr* to come loose; (*desinibir-se*) to let o.s. go

solteirão/ona [sowtej'rãw/rɔna] (*pl* **-ões/~s**) *adj* unmarried, single ♦ *m/f* confirmed bachelor/spinster

solteiro/a [sow'tejru/a] *adj* unmarried, single ♦ *m/f* bachelor/single woman

solteirões [sowtej'rõjʃ] *mpl de* **solteirão**

solteirona [sowtej'rɔna] *f de* **solteirão**

solto/a ['sowtu/a] *pp de* **soltar** ♦ *adj* loose; (*livre*) free; (*sozinho*) alone

solução [solu'sãw] (*pl* **-ões**) *f* solution

soluçar [solu'sa*] *vi* (*chorar*) to sob; (*MED*) to hiccup

solucionar [solusjo'na*] *vt* to solve; (*decidir*) to resolve

soluço [so'lusu] *m* sob; (*MED*) hiccup

soluções [solu'sõjʃ] *fpl de* **solução**

solvente [sow'vẽtʃi] *adj* solvent ♦ *m* solvent

som [sõ] (*pl* **-ns**) *m* sound; **~ cd** compact disc player

soma ['sɔma] *f* sum; **~r** [so'ma*] *vt* (*adicionar*) to add (up); (*chegar a*) to add up to, amount to ♦ *vi* to add up; **~tório** [soma'tɔrju] *m* sum

sombra ['sõbra] *f* shadow; (*proteção*) shade; (*indício*) trace, sign

sombrinha [sõ'briɲa] *f* parasol, sunshade

sombrio/a [sõ'briu/a] *adj* shady, dark; (*triste*) gloomy

some *etc* ['sɔmi] *vb* V **sumir**

somente [sɔ'mẽtʃi] *adv* only

somos ['sɔmoʃ] *vb* V **ser**

sonâmbulo/a [so'nãbulu/a] *m/f* sleepwalker

sonda ['sõda] *f* (*MED*) probe; (*de petróleo*) drill; (*de alimentação*) drip; **~ espacial** space probe; **~gem** [sõ'daʒẽ] (*pl* **~gens**) *f* (*NÁUT*) sounding; (*de terreno, opinião*) survey; (*para petróleo*) drilling; (*para minerais*) boring; **~r** [sõ'da*] *vt* to probe; (*opinião etc*) to sound out

soneca [so'nɛka] *f* nap, snooze

sonegar [sone'ga*] *vt* (*dinheiro, valores*) to conceal, withhold; (*furtar*) to steal, pilfer; (*impostos*) to dodge, evade; (*informações, dados*) to withhold

soneto [so'netu] *m* sonnet

sonhador(a) [soɲa'do*(a)] *adj* dreamy ♦ *m/f* dreamer

sonhar [so'ɲa*] *vt, vi* to dream; **~ com** to dream about; **sonho** ['sɔɲu] *m* dream; (*CULIN*) doughnut

sono ['sɔnu] *m* sleep; **estar com** *ou* **ter ~** to be sleepy

sonolento/a [sono'lẽtu/a] *adj* sleepy, drowsy

sonoro/a [so'nɔru/a] *adj* resonant

sons [sõʃ] *mpl de* **som**

sonso/a ['sõsu/a] *adj* sly, artful

sopa ['sopa] *f* soup; **sopeira** [so'pejra] *f* (*CULIN*) soup dish

soporífero [sopo'riferu], **soporífico** [sopo'rifiku] *m* sleeping drug

soprano [so'pranu] *f* soprano

soprar [so'pra*] *vt* to blow; (*balão*) to blow up; (*vela*) to blow out; (*dizer em voz baixa*) to whisper ♦ *vi* to blow; **sopro** ['sopru] *m* blow, puff; (*de vento*) gust

sórdido/a ['sɔxdʒidu/a] *adj* sordid; (*imundo*) squalid

soro ['soru] *m* (*MED*) serum

sorridente [soxi'dẽtʃi] *adj* smiling

sorrir [so'xi*] *vi* to smile; **sorriso** [so'xizu] *m* smile

sorte ['sɔxtʃi] *f* luck; (*casualidade*) chance; (*destino*) fate, destiny; (*condição*) lot; (*espécie*) sort, kind; **de ~ que** so that; **dar ~** (*trazer sorte*) to bring good luck; (*ter sorte*) to be lucky; **estar com** *ou* **ter ~** to be lucky

sortear [sox'tʃja*] *vt* to draw lots for; (*rifar*) to raffle; (*MIL*) to draft; **sorteio** [sox'teju] *m* draw; raffle; draft

sortido/a [sox'tʃidu/a] *adj* (*abastecido*) supplied, stocked; (*variado*) assorted; (*loja*) well-stocked

sortimento [soxtʃi'mẽtu] *m* assortment, stock

sortudo/a [sox'tudu/a] (*col*) *adj* lucky

sorvete [sox'vetʃi] (*BR*) *m* ice cream

SOS *abr* SOS

sósia ['sɔzja] *m/f* double

soslaio [soʒ'laju]: **de ~** *adv* sideways, obliquely

sossegado/a [sose'gadu/a] *adj* peaceful, calm

sossegar [sose'ga*] *vt* to calm, quieten ♦ *vi* to quieten down

sossego [so'segu] *m* peace (and quiet)

sótão ['sɔtãw] (*pl* **~s**) *m* attic, loft

sotaque [so'taki] *m* accent

sotavento [sota'vẽtu] *m* (*NÁUT*) lee

soterrar [sote'xa*] *vt* to bury

sou [so] *vb* V **ser**

soube *etc* ['sobi] *vb* V **saber**

soutien [su'tʃjã] (*PT*) *m* = **sutiã**

sova ['sɔva] *f* beating, thrashing

sovaco [so'vaku] *m* armpit

soviético/a [so'vjetʃiku/a] *adj, m/f* Soviet

sovina [so'vina] *adj* mean, stingy ♦ *m/f* miser

sozinho/a [sɔ'ziɲu/a] *adj* (all) alone, by oneself; (*por si mesmo*) by oneself

spot [iʃ'pɔtʃi] (*pl* **~s**) *m* spotlight

spread [iʃ'prɛdʒi] *m* (*COM*) spread

squash [iʃ'kwɛʃ] *m* squash

Sr. *abr* (= *senhor*) Mr(.)

Sr.ª *abr* (= *senhora*) Mrs(.)

Sr.ta *abr* (= *senhorita*) Miss

status [iʃ'tatus] *m* status

sua ['sua] *f de* seu

suar [swa*] *vt, vi* to sweat

suástica ['swaʃtʃika] *f* swastika

suave ['swavi] *adj* gentle; (*música, voz*) soft; (*sabor, vinho*) smooth; (*cheiro*) delicate; (*dor*) mild; (*trabalho*) light; **suavidade** [suavi'dadʒi] *f* gentleness; softness; **suavizar** [swavi'za*] *vt* to soften; (*dor, sofrimento*) to alleviate

subalimentado/a [subalimē'tadu/a] *adj* undernourished

subalterno/a [subaw'tɛxnu/a] *adj, m/f* subordinate

subalugar [subalu'ga*] *vt* to sublet

subconsciente [subkõ'sjētʃi] *adj, m* subconscious

subdesenvolvido/a [subdʒizẽvow'vidu/a] *adj* underdevel oped

súbdito ['subditu] (*PT*) *m* = **súdito**

subentender [subẽtē'de*] *vt* to understand, assume; **subentendido/a** [subẽtē'dʒidu/a] *adj* implied ♦ *m* implication

subestimar [subeʃtʃi'ma*] *vt* to underestimate

subida [su'bida] *f* ascent, climb; (*ladeira*) slope; (*de preços*) rise

subido/a [su'bidu/a] *adj* high

subir [su'bi*] *vi* to go up; (*preço, de posto etc*) to rise ♦ *vt* to raise; (*ladeira, escada, rio*) to climb, go up; ~ **em** to climb, go up; (*cadeira, palanque*) to climb onto, get up onto; (*ônibus*) to get on

súbito/a ['subitu/a] *adj* sudden ♦ *adv* (*tb:* **de** ~) suddenly

subjetivo/a [subʒe'tʃivu/a] (*PT* **-ct-**) *adj* subjective

subjugar [subʒu'ga*] *vt* to subjugate, subdue; (*inimigo*) to overpower; (*moralmente*) to dominate

subjuntivo/a [subʒũ'tʃivu/a] *adj* subjunctive ♦ *m* subjunctive

sublime [su'blimi] *adj* sublime

sublinhar [subli'ɲa*] *vt* to underline; (*destacar*) to emphasize, stress

sublocar [sublo'ka*] *vt, vi* to sublet

submarino/a [subma'rinu/a] *adj* underwater ♦ *m* submarine

submergir [submex'ʒi*] *vt* to submerge; ~**se** *vr* to submerge

submeter [subme'te*] *vt* to subdue; (*plano*) to submit; (*sujeitar*) ~ **a** to subject to; ~**se** *vr*: ~**se a** to submit to; (*operação*) to undergo

submirjo *etc* [sub'mixju] *vb* V **submergir**

submisso/a [sub'misu/a] *adj* submissive

subnutrição [subnutri'sãw] *f* malnutrition

subornar [subox'na*] *vt* to bribe; **suborno** [su'boxnu] *m* bribery

subscrever [subʃkre've*] *vt* to sign; (*opinião; COM: ações*) to subscribe to ♦ *vi*: ~ **a** to endorse

subscrito/a [sub'ʃkritu/a] *pp de* **sub-**

screver

subseqüente [subse'kwētʃi] *adj* subsequent

subserviente [subsex'vjētʃi] *adj* obsequious, servile

subsidiar [subsi'dʒa*] *vt* to subsidize

subsidiária [subsi'dʒjarja] *f* (*COM*) subsidiary (company)

subsidiário/a [subsi'dʒjarju/a] *adj* subsidiary

subsídio [sub'sidʒu] *m* subsidy; (*ajuda*) aid

subsistência [subsiʃ'tēsja] *f* subsistence

subsistir [subsiʃ'tʃi*] *vi* to exist; (*viver*) to subsist

subsolo [sub'sɔlu] *m* (*de prédio*) basement

substância [subʃ'tãsja] *f* substance; **substancial** [subʃtã'sjaw] (*pl* **-ais**) *adj* substantial

substantivo [subʃtã'tʃivu] *m* noun

substituir [subʃtʃi'twi*] *vt* to substitute; **substituto/a** [subʃti'tutu/a] *adj, m/f* substitute

subterrâneo/a [subite'xanju/a] *adj* subterranean, underground

subtil *etc* [sub'tiw] (*PT*) = **sutil** *etc*

subtítulo [subi'tʃitulu] *m* subtitle

subtrair [subtra'i*] *vt* to steal; (*deduzir*) to subtract ♦ *vi* to subtract

subumano/a [subu'manu/a] *adj* subhuman; (*desumano*) inhuman

suburbano/a [subux'banu/a] *adj* suburban

subúrbio [su'buxbju] *m* suburb

subvenção [subvē'sãw] (*pl* **-ões**) *f* subsidy, grant; **subvencionar** [subvēsjo'na*] *vt* to subsidize

subversivo/a [subvex'sivu/a] *adj, m/f* subversive

sucata [su'kata] *f* scrap metal

succção [suk'sãw] *f* suction

suceder [suse'de*] *vi* to happen ♦ *vt* to succeed; ~ **a** (*num cargo*) to succeed; (*seguir*) to follow; **sucedido** [suse'dʒidu] *m* event, occurrence

sucessão [suse'sãw] (*pl* **-ões**) *f* succession; **sucessivo/a** [suse'sivu/a] *adj* successive

sucesso [su'sɛsu] *m* success; (*música, filme*) hit; **fazer** *ou* **ter** ~ to be successful

sucinto/a [su'sĩtu/a] *adj* succinct

suco ['suku] (*BR*) *m* juice

suculento/a [suku'lẽtu/a] *adj* succulent

sucumbir [sukũ'bi*] *vi* to succumb; (*morrer*) to die, perish

sucursal [sukux'saw] (*pl* **-ais**) *f* (*COM*) branch

Sudão [su'dãw] *m*: **o** ~ (the) Sudan

sudeste [su'dɛʃtʃi] *m* south-east

súdito ['sudʒitu] *m* (*de rei etc*) subject

sudoeste [sud'wɛʃtʃi] *m* south-west

Suécia ['swɛsja] *f*: **a** ~ Sweden; **sueco** ['swɛku/a] *adj* Swedish ♦ *m/f* Swede ♦ *m*

(LING) Swedish

suéter ['swɛtɛ*] *(BR) m ou f* sweater

suficiente [sufi'sjẽtʃi] *adj* sufficient, enough

sufixo [su'fiksu] *m* suffix

suflê [su'fle] *m* soufflé

sufocante [sufo'kãtʃi] *adj* suffocating; *(calor)* sweltering, oppressive

sufocar [sufo'ka*] *vt, vi* to suffocate

sufrágio [su'fraʒu] *m (direito de voto)* suffrage; *(voto)* vote

sugar [su'ga*] *vt* to suck

sugerir [suʒe'ri*] *vt* to suggest

sugestão [suʒeʃ'tãw] *(pl –ões) f* suggestion; **dar uma ~** to make a suggestion; **sugestionar** [suʒeʃtʃjo'na*] *vt* to influence; **sugestivo/a** [suʒeʃ'tʃivu/a] *adj* suggestive

sugiro *etc* [su'ʒiru] *vb V* sugerir

Suíça ['swisa] *f*: **a ~** Switzerland

suíças ['swisaʃ] *fpl* sideburns; *V tb* suíço

suicida [swi'sida] *adj* suicidal ♦ *m/f* suicidal person; *(morto)* suicide; **~r-se** [swisi'daxsi] *vr* to commit suicide; **suicídio** [swi'sidʒu] *m* suicide

suíço/a ['swisu/a] *adj, m/f* Swiss

suíno ['swinu] *m* pig, hog ♦ *adj V* gado

suíte ['switʃi] *f (MÚS, em hotel)* suite

sujar [su'ʒa*] *vt* to dirty ♦ *vi* to make a mess; **~-se** *vr* to get dirty

sujeira [su'ʒejra] *f* dirt; *(estado)* dirtiness; *(col)* dirty trick

sujeitar [suʒej'ta*] *vt* to subject; **~-se** *vr* to submit

sujeito/a [su'ʒejtu/a] *adj*: **~ a** subject to ♦ *m (LING)* subject ♦ *m/f* man/woman

sujo/a ['suʒu/a] *adj* dirty; *(fig: desonesto)* dishonest ♦ *m* dirt

sul [suw] *adj inv* south, southern ♦ *m*: **o ~** the south; **~-africano/a** *adj, m/f* South African; **~-americano/a** *adj, m/f* South American; **sulco** [suw'ku] *m* furrow

sulista [su'liʃta] *adj* Southern ♦ *m/f* Southerner

suma ['suma] *f*: **em ~** in short

sumamente [suma'mẽtʃi] *adv* extremely

sumário/a [su'marju/a] *adj (breve)* brief, concise; *(JUR)* summary; *(biquíni)* skimpy ♦ *m* summary

sumiço [su'misu] *m* disappearance

sumir [su'mi*] *vi* to disappear, vanish

sumo/a ['sumu/a] *adj (importância)* extreme; *(qualidade)* supreme ♦ *m (PT)* juice

sumptuoso/a [sũ'twozu/ɔza] *(PT) adj =* suntuoso/a

sunga ['sũga] *f* swimming trunks *pl*

suntuoso/a [sũ'twozu/ɔza] *adj* sumptuous

suor [swɔ*] *m* sweat

super- [supɛ*-] *prefixo* super-

superado/a [supɛ'radu/a] *adj (idéias)* outmoded

superar [supɛ'ra*] *vt (rival)* to surpass; *(inimigo, dificuldade)* to overcome; *(expectativa)* to exceed

superficial [supɛxfi'sjaw] *(pl –ais) adj* superficial

superfície [supɛx'fisi] *f* surface; *(extensão)* area; *(fig: aparência)* appearance

supérfluo/a [su'pɛxflwu/a] *adj* superfluous

superintendente [superĩtẽ'dẽtʃi] *m* superintendent

superior [supe'rjo*] *adj* superior; *(mais elevado)* higher; *(quantidade)* greater; *(mais acima)* upper ♦ *m* superior; **~idade** [superjori'dadʒi] *f* superiority

superlativo [supɛxla'tʃivu] *m* superlative

superlotado/a [supɛxlo'tadu/a] *adj* crowded; *(excessivamente cheio)* overcrowded

supermercado [supɛxmex'kadu] *m* supermarket

superpotência [supɛxpo'tẽsja] *f* superpower

superpovoado/a [supɛxpo'vwadu/a] *adj* overpopulated

supersônico/a [supɛx'soniku/a] *adj* supersonic

superstição [supɛxʃtʃi'sãw] *(pl –ões) f* superstition; **supersticioso/a** [supɛxʃtʃi'sjozu/ɔza] *adj* superstitious

supervisão [supɛxvi'zãw] *f* supervision; **supervisionar** [supɛxvizjo'na*] *vt* to supervise; **supervisor(a)** [supɛxvi'zo*(a)] *m/f* supervisor

suplantar [suplã'ta*] *vt* to supplant

suplementar [suplemẽ'ta*] *adj* supplementary ♦ *vt* to supplement

suplemento [suple'mẽtu] *m* supplement

súplica ['suplika] *f* supplication, plea; **suplicar** [supli'ka*] *vt, vi* to plead, beg

suplício [su'plisju] *m* torture

supor [su'po*] *(irreg: como* pôr*) vt* to suppose; *(julgar)* to think

suportar [supox'ta*] *vt* to hold up, support; *(tolerar)* to bear, tolerate; **suportável** [supox'tavew] *(pl –eis) adj* bearable; **suporte** [su'pɔxtʃi] *m* support

suposto/a [su'poʃtu/pɔʃta] *adj* supposed ♦ *m* assumption, supposition

supremo/a [su'prɛmu/a] *adj* supreme

supressão [supre'sãw] *(pl –ões) f* suppression

suprimento [supri'mẽtu] *m* supply

suprimir [supri'mi*] *vt* to suppress

suprir [su'pri*] *vt (fazer as vezes de)* to take the place of; **~ alguém de** to provide *ou* supply sb with

surdez [sux'deʒ] *f*: **aparelho para a ~** hearing aid

surdina [sux'dʒina] *f*: **em ~** stealthily, on the quiet

surdo/a ['suxdu/a] *adj* deaf; *(som)* muffled, dull ♦ *m/f* deaf person; **surdo/a-mudo/a** *adj* deaf and dumb ♦ *m/f* deaf-mute

surfe ['suxfi] *m* surfing

surgir [sux'ʒi*] *vi* to appear; (*problema*, *oportunidade*) to arise

surjo *etc* ['suxju] *vb* V **surgir**

surpreendente [suxprjĕ'dětʃi] *adj* surprising

surpreender [suxprjĕ'de*] *vt* to surprise; **~-se** *vr*: **~-se (de)** to be surprised (at); **surpresa** [sux'preza] *f* surprise; **surpreso/a** [sux'prezu/a] *pp de* **surpreender** ♦ *adj* surprised

surra ['suxa] *f* (*ger, ESPORTE*): **dar uma ~ em** to thrash; **levar uma ~ (de)** to get thrashed (by); **~r** [su'xa*] *vt* to beat, thrash

surtir [sux'tʃi*] *vt* to produce, bring about

surto ['suxtu] *m* outbreak

suscetível [suse'tʃivew] (*pl* -**eis**) *adj* susceptible; **~ de** liable to

suscitar [susi'ta*] *vt* to arouse; (*admiração*) to cause; (*dúvidas*) to raise; (*obstáculos*) to throw up

suspeita [suʃ'pejta] *f* suspicion; **~r** [suʃpej'ta*] *vt* to suspect ♦ *vi*: **~r de algo** to suspect sth; **suspeito/a** [suʃ'pejtu/a] *adj, m/f* suspect

suspender [suʃpĕ'de*] *vt* (*levantar*) to lift; (*pendurar*) to hang; (*trabalho, funcionário etc*) to suspend; (*encomenda*) to cancel; (*sessão*) to adjourn, defer; (*viagem*) to put off; **suspensão** [suʃpĕ'sãw] (*pl* -**ões**) *f* (*ger, AUTO*) suspension; (*de trabalho, pagamento*) stoppage; (*de viagem, sessão*) deferment; (*de encomenda*) cancellation; **suspense** [suʃ'pěsi] *m* suspense; **filme de suspense** thriller; **suspenso/a** [suʃ'pěsu/a] *pp de* **suspender**

suspensórios [suʃpĕ'sɔrjuʃ] *mpl* braces (*BRIT*), suspenders (*US*)

suspirar [suʃpi'ra*] *vi* to sigh; **suspiro** [suʃ'piru] *m* sigh; (*doce*) meringue

sussurrar [susu'xa*] *vt, vi* to whisper; **sussurro** [su'suxu] *m* whisper

sustentar [suʃtĕ'ta*] *vt* to sustain; (*prédio*) to hold up; (*padrão*) to maintain; (*financeiramente, acusação*) to support; **sustentável** [suʃtĕ'tavew] *adj* (*pl* -**eis**) sustainable; **sustento** [suʃ'tĕtu] *m* sustenance; (*subsistência*) livelihood; (*amparo*) support

suster [suʃ'te*] (*irreg: como* **ter**) *vt* to support, hold up

susto ['suʃtu] *m* fright, scare

sutiã [su'tʃjã] *m* bra(ssiere)

sutil [su'tʃiw] (*pl* -**is**) *adj* subtle; **~eza** [sutʃi'leza] *f* subtlety

T

ta [ta] = **te** + **a**

tabacaria [tabaka'ria] *f* tobacconist's (shop)

tabaco [ta'baku] *m* tobacco

tabela [ta'bɛla] *f* table, chart; (*lista*) list; **por ~** indirectly

tabelião [tabe'ljãw] (*pl* -**ães**) *m* notary public

taberna [ta'bɛxna] *f* tavern, bar

tabique [ta'biki] *m* partition

tablado [ta'bladu] *m* platform; (*para espectadores*) grandstand

tablete [ta'blɛtʃi] *m* (*de chocolate*) bar

tablóide [ta'blɔjdʒi] *m* tabloid

tabu [ta'bu] *adj, m* taboo

tábua ['tabwa] *f* plank, board; (*MAT*) table; **~ de passar roupa** ironing board

tabuleiro [tabu'lejru] *m* tray; (*XADREZ*) board

tabuleta [tabu'leta] *f* (*letreiro*) sign, signboard

taça ['tasa] *f* cup

tacada [ta'kada] *f* shot; **de uma ~** in one go

tacanho/a [ta'kaɲu/a] *adj* mean; (*de idéias curtas*) narrow-minded; (*baixo*) small

tacha ['tafa] *f* tack

tachinha [ta'fiɲa] *f* drawing pin (*BRIT*), thumb tack (*US*)

tácito/a ['tasitu/a] *adj* tacit

taciturno/a [tasi'tuxnu/a] *adj* taciturn

taco ['taku] *m* (*BILHAR*) cue; (*GOLFE*) club

táctico/a *etc* ['tatiku/a] (*PT*) = **tático** *etc*

tacto ['tatu] (*PT*) *m* = **tato**

tagarela [taga'rɛla] *adj* talkative ♦ *m/f* chatterbox; **~r** [tagare'la*] *vi* to chatter

Tailândia [taj'lãdʒja] *f*: **a ~** Thailand

tal [taw] (*pl* **tais**) *adj* such; **~ e coisa** this and that; **um ~ de Sr. X** a certain Mr. X; **que ~?** what do you think?; (*PT*) how are things?; **que ~ um cafezinho?** what about a coffee?; **que ~ nós irmos ao cinema?** what about (us) going to the cinema?; **~ pai, ~ filho** like father, like son; **~ como** such as; (*da maneira que*) just as; **~ qual** just like; **o ~ professor** that teacher; **a ~ ponto** to such an extent; **de ~ maneira** in such a way; **e ~ e** and so on; **o/a ~** (*col*) the greatest; **o Pedro de ~** Peter what's-his-name; **na rua ~** in such and such a street; **foi um ~ de gente ligar lá para casa** there were people ringing home non-stop

tala ['tala] *f* (*MED*) splint

talão [ta'lãw] (*pl* -**ões**) *m* (*de recibo*) stub; **~ de cheques** cheque book (*BRIT*), check book (*US*)

talco ['tawku] *m* talcum powder; **pó de ~** (*PT*) talcum powder

talento [ta'lĕtu] *m* talent; (*aptidão*) ability

talha ['taʎa] *f* carving; (*vaso*) pitcher; (*NÁUT*) tackle

talhar [ta'ʎa*] *vt* to cut; (*esculpir*) to carve ♦ *vi* (*coalhar*) to curdle

talhe ['taʎi] *m* cut, shape; (*de rosto*) line

talher [ta'ʎe*] *m* set of cutlery; **~es** *mpl*

cutlery *sg*

talho ['taʎu] *m (corte)* cutting, slicing; *(PT: açougue)* butcher's (shop)

talo ['talu] *m* stalk, stem

talões [ta'lõjʃ] *mpl de* talão

talvez [taw'veʒ] *adv* perhaps, maybe

tamanco [ta'mãku] *m* clog, wooden shoe

tamanduá [tamã'dwa] *m* anteater

tamanho/a [ta'maɲu/a] *adj* such (a) great ♦ *m* size

tâmara ['tamara] *f* date

também [tã'bẽj] *adv* also, too, as well; *(além disso)* besides; ~ **não** not ... either, nor

tambor [tã'bo*] *m* drum

tamborim [tãbo'rĩ] *(pl* -ns) *m* tambourine

Tâmisa ['tamiza] *m*: **o** ~ the Thames

tampa ['tãpa] *f* lid; *(de garrafa)* cap

tampão [tã'pãw] *(pl* -ões) *m* tampon; *(de olho)* (eye) patch

tampar [tã'pa*] *vt (lata, garrafa)* to put the lid on; *(cobrir)* to cover

tampinha [tã'piɲa] *f* lid, top

tampo ['tãpu] *m* lid

tampões [tã'põjʃ] *mpl de* tampão

tampouco [tã'poku] *adv* nor, neither

tangente [tã'ʒẽtʃi] *f* tangent

tanger [tã'ʒe*] *vt (MÚS)* to play ♦ *vi*: ~ **a** *(dizer respeito a)* to concern; **no que tange a** as regards, with respect to

tangerina [tãʒe'rina] *f* tangerine

tangível [tã'ʒivew] *(pl* -eis) *adj* tangible

tanjo *etc* ['tãʒu] *vb V* tanger

tanque ['tãki] *m* tank; *(de lavar roupa)* sink

tanto/a ['tãtu/a] *adj, pron (sg)* so much; (: + *interrogativa/negativa)* as much; *(pl)* so many; (: + *interrogativa/negativa)* as many ♦ *adv* so much; ~ ... **como** ... both ... and ...; ~ ... **quanto** ... as much ... as ...; ~ **tempo** so long; **quarenta e ~s anos** forty-odd years; ~ **faz** it's all the same to me, I don't mind; **um** ~ **(quanto)** *(como adv)* rather, somewhat; ~ **(assim) que** so much so that

tão [tãw] *adv* so; ~ **rico quanto** as rich as; ~**-só** *adv* only

tapa ['tapa] *m ou f* slap

tapar [ta'pa*] *vt* to cover; *(garrafa)* to cork; *(caixa)* to put the lid on; *(orifício)* to block up; *(encobrir)* to block out

tapear [ta'pja*] *vt, vi* to cheat

tapeçaria [tapesa'ria] *f* tapestry

tapete [ta'petʃi] *m* carpet, rug

taquigrafia [takigra'fia] *f* shorthand; **taquígrafo/a** [ta'kigrafu/a] *m/f* shorthand typist *(BRIT)*, stenographer *(US)*

tardar [tax'da*] *vi* to delay; *(chegar tarde)* to be late ♦ *vt* to delay; **sem mais** ~ without delay; ~ **a ou em fazer** to take a long time to do; **o mais** ~ at the latest

tarde ['taxdʒi] *f* afternoon ♦ *adv* late;

mais cedo ou mais ~ sooner or later; **antes** ~ **do que nunca** better late than never; **boa** ~! good afternoon!; **à** *ou* **de** ~ in the afternoon

tardio/a [tax'dʒiu/a] *adj* late

tarefa [ta'rɛfa] *f* task, job; *(faina)* chore

tarifa [ta'rifa] *f* tariff; *(para transportes)* fare; *(lista de preços)* price list; ~ **alfandegária** customs duty

tarimbado/a [tarĩ'badu/a] *adj* experienced

tártaro ['taxtaru] *m* tartar

tartaruga [taxta'ruga] *f* turtle

tasca ['taʃka] *(PT)* *f* cheap eating place

tática ['tatʃika] *f* tactics *pl*

tático/a ['tatʃiku/a] *adj* tactical

tato ['tatu] *m* touch; *(fig: diplomacia)* tact

tatu [ta'tu] *m* armadillo

tatuagem [ta'twaʒẽ] *(pl* -ns) *f* tattoo; **tatuar** [ta'twa*] *vt* to tattoo

tauromaquia [tawroma'kia] *f* bullfighting

taxa ['taʃa] *f (imposto)* tax; *(preço)* fee; *(índice)* rate; ~ **de câmbio/juros** exchange/interest rate; ~**ção** [taʃa'sãw] *f* taxation; ~**r** [ta'ʃa*] *vt (fixar o preço de)* to fix the price of; *(lançar impostos sobre)* to tax

taxativo/a [taʃa'tʃivu/a] *adj* categorical, firm

táxi ['taksi] *m* taxi

tchau [tʃaw] *excl* bye!

tcheco/a ['tʃɛku/a] *adj, m/f* Czech

Tcheco-Eslováquia [tʃɛkuiʒlo'vakja] *f* = Tchecoslováquia

Tchecoslováquia [tʃɛkoʒlo'vakja] *f*: **a** ~ Czechoslovakia

te [tʃi] *pron* you; *(para você)* (to) you

té [tɛ] *prep abr de* até

tear [tʃja*] *m* loom

teatral [tʃja'traw] *(pl* -ais) *adj* theatrical; *(grupo)* theatre *atr (BRIT)*, theater *atr (US)*; *(obra, arte)* dramatic

teatro ['tʃjatru] *m* theatre *(BRIT)*, theater *(US)*; *(obras)* plays *pl*, dramatic works *pl*; *(gênero, curso)* drama; **peça de** ~ play; **teatrólogo/a** [tʃja'trɔlogu/a] *m/f* playwright, dramatist

tecelão/lã [tese'lãw/'lã] *(pl* -ões/~s) *m/f* weaver

tecer [te'se*] *vt, vi* to weave; **tecido** [te'sidu] *m* cloth, material; *(ANAT)* tissue

tecla ['tɛkla] *f* key; ~**do** [tek'ladu] *m* keyboard

técnica ['tɛknika] *f* technique; *V tb* **técnico**

técnico/a ['tɛkniku/a] *adj* technical ♦ *m/f* technician; *(especialista)* expert

tecnologia [teknolo'ʒia] *f* technology; **tecnológico/a** [tekno'lɔʒiku/a] *adj* technological

tecto ['tɛktu] *(PT)* *m* = teto

tédio ['tɛdʒju] *m* tedium, boredom; **tedioso/a** [te'dʒjozu/ɔza] *adj* tedious, boring

teia ['teja] *f* web; ~ **de aranha** cobweb

teimar [tej'ma*] *vi* to insist, keep on; ~ **em** to insist on

teimosia [tejmo'zia] *f* stubbornness; ~ **em fazer** insistence on doing

teimoso/a [tej'mozu/ɔza] *adj* obstinate; (*criança*) wilful (*BRIT*), willful (*US*)

teixo ['tejʃu] *m* yew

Tejo ['teʒu] *m*: **o (rio)** ~ the (river) Tagus

tela ['tɛla] *f* fabric, material; (*de pintar*) canvas; (*CINEMA, TV*) screen

tele... ['tɛle] *prefixo* tele...; ~**comunicações** [telekomunika'sõjʃ] *fpl* telecommunications

teleférico [tele'fɛriku] *m* cable car

telefonar [telefo'na*] *vi*: ~ **para alguém** to (tele)phone sb

telefone [tele'fɔni] *m* phone, telephone; (*número*) (tele)phone number; (*telefonema*) phone call; ~ **celular** cellphone, mobile phone; ~ **de carro** car phone; ~**ma** [telefo'nɛma] *m* phone call; **dar um ~ma** to make a phone call; **telefônico/a** [tele'foniku/a] *adj* telephone *atr*; **telefonista** [telefo'niʃta] *m/f* telephonist; (*na companhia telefônica*) operator

telégrafo [te'lɛgrafu] *m* telegraph

telegrama [tele'grama] *m* telegram, cable; **passar um** ~ to send a telegram

tele...: ~**guiado/a** [tele'gjadu/a] *adj* remote-controlled; ~**impressor** [teleĩpre'so*] *m* teleprinter; ~**jornal** [teleʒor'naw] (*pl* ~**jornais**) *m* television news *sg*; ~**novela** [teleno'vɛla] *f* (*TV*) soap opera; ~**objetiva** [teleobʒe'tʃiva] (*PT* -**ct**-) *f* telephoto lens; ~**patia** [telepa'tʃia] *f* telepathy; ~**scópio** [tele'skɔpju] *m* telescope; ~**spectador(a)** [teleʃpekta'do*(a)] *m/f* viewer

televisão [televi'zãw] *f* television; ~ **a cores** colo(u)r television; ~ **digital** digital TV; ~ **via satélite** satellite television; **aparelho de** ~ television set; **televisionar** [televizjo'na*] *vt* to televise; **televisivo/a** [televi'zivu/a] *adj* television *atr*

televisor [televi'zo*] *m* (*aparelho*) television (set), TV (set)

telex [te'lɛks] *m* telex; **enviar por** ~ to telex; ~**ar** [telɛks'a*] *vt* to telex

telha ['teʎa] *f* tile; (*col: cabeça*) head; **ter uma** ~ **de menos** to have a screw loose

telhado [te'ʎadu] *m* roof

tema ['tɛma] *m* theme; (*assunto*) subject; **temática** [te'matʃika] *f* theme

temer [te'me*] *vt* to fear, be afraid of ♦ *vi* to be afraid

temerário/a [teme'rarju/a] *adj* reckless; (*arriscado*) risky; **temeridade** [temeri'dadʒi] *f* recklessness

temeroso/a [teme'rozu/ɔza] *adj* fearful, afraid; (*pavoroso*) dreadful

temido/a [te'midu/a] *adj* fearsome, frightening

temível [te'mivew] (*pl* -**eis**) *adj* = **temido**

temor [te'mo*] *m* fear

temperado/a [tẽpe'radu/a] *adj* (*clima*) temperate; (*comida*) seasoned

temperamento [tẽpera'mẽtu] *m* temperament, nature

temperar [tẽpe'ra*] *vt* to season

temperatura [tẽpera'tura] *f* temperature

tempero [tẽ'peru] *m* seasoning, flavouring (*BRIT*), flavoring (*US*)

tempestade [tẽpeʃ'tadʒi] *f* storm; **tempestuoso/a** [tẽpeʃ'twozu/ɔza] *adj* stormy

templo ['tẽplu] *m* temple; (*igreja*) church

tempo ['tẽpu] *m* time; (*meteorológico*) weather; (*LING*) tense; **o** ~ **todo** the whole time; **a** ~ on time; **ao mesmo** ~ at the same time; **a um** ~ at once; **com** ~ in good time; **de** ~ **em** ~ from time to time; **nesse meio** ~ in the meantime; **quanto** ~? how long?; **mais** ~ longer; **há** ~**s** for ages; (*atrás*) ages ago; **primeiro/segundo** ~ (*ESPORTE*) first/second half

têmpora ['tẽpora] *f* (*ANAT*) temple

temporada [tẽpo'rada] *f* season; (*tempo*) spell

temporal [tẽpo'raw] (*pl* -**ais**) *m* storm, gale

temporário/a [tẽpo'rarju/a] *adj* temporary, provisional

tenacidade [tenasi'dadʒi] *f* tenacity

tenaz [te'najʃ] *adj* tenacious

tencionar [tẽsjo'na*] *vt* to intend, plan

tenda ['tẽda] *f* tent

tendão [tẽ'dãw] (*pl* -**ões**) *m* tendon

tendência [tẽ'dẽsja] *f* tendency; (*da moda etc*) trend; **a** ~ **de** *ou* **em** *ou* **a fazer** the tendency to do; **tendencioso/a** [tẽdẽ'sjozu/ɔza] *adj* tendentious, bias(s)ed

tender [tẽ'de*] *vi*: ~ **para** to tend towards; ~ **a fazer** to tend *ou* have a tendency to do

tendões [tẽ'dõjʃ] *mpl de* **tendão**

tenebroso/a [tene'brozu/ɔza] *adj* dark, gloomy; (*fig*) horrible

tenente [te'nẽtʃi] *m* lieutenant

tenho *etc* ['teɲu] *vb* V **ter**

tênis ['teniʃ] *m inv* tennis; (*sapatos*) training shoes *pl*; (*um sapato*) training shoe; ~ **de mesa** table tennis; **tenista** [te'niʃta] *m/f* tennis player

tenor [te'no*] *m* (*MÚS*) tenor

tenro/a ['tẽxu/a] *adj* tender; (*macio*) soft; (*delicado*) delicate; (*novo*) young

tensão [tẽ'sãw] *f* tension; (*pressão*) pressure, strain; (*rigidez*) tightness; (*ELET: voltagem*) voltage

tenso/a ['tẽsu/a] *adj* tense; (*sob pressão*) under stress, strained

tentação [tẽta'sãw] *f* temptation

tentáculo [tẽ'takulu] *m* tentacle

tentador(a) [tẽta'do*(a)] *adj* tempting

tentar [tẽ'ta*] *vt* to try; (*seduzir*) to tempt

♦ *vi* to try; **tentativa** [tẽta'tʃiva] *f* attempt; **tentiva de homicídio/suicídio/roubo** attempted murder/suicide/robbery; **por tentativas** by trial and error; **tentativo/a** [tẽta'tʃivu/a] *adj* tentative

tênue ['tenwi] *adj* tenuous; (*fino*) thin; (*delicado*) delicate; (*luz, voz*) faint; (*pequeníssimo*) minute

teologia [teolo'ʒia] *f* theology

teor [te'o*] *m* (*conteúdo*) tenor; (*sentido*) meaning, drift

teorema [teo'rɛma] *m* theorem

teoria [teo'ria] *f* theory; **teoricamente** [teorika'mẽtʃi] *adv* theoretically, in theory; **teórico/a** [te'ɔriku/a] *adj* theoretical ♦ *m/f* theoretician

tépido/a ['tɛpidu/a] *adj* tepid

PALAVRA CHAVE

ter [te*] *vt* **1** (*possuir, ger*) to have; (*na mão*) to hold; **você tem uma caneta?** have you got a pen?; **ela vai ~ neném** she is going to have a baby
2 (*idade, medidas, estado*) to be; **ela tem 7 anos** she's 7 (years old); **a mesa tem 1 metro de comprimento** the table is 1 metre long; **~ fome/sorte** to be hungry/lucky; **~ frio/calor** to be cold/hot **3** (*conter*) to hold, contain; **a caixa tem um quilo de chocolates** the box holds one kilo of chocolates
4: **~ que** *ou* **de fazer** to have to do
5: **~ a ver com** to have to do with
6: **ir ~ com** to (go and) meet
♦ *vb impess* **1**: **tem** (*sg*) there is; (*pl*) there are; **tem 3 dias que não saio de casa** I haven't been out for 3 days
2: **não tem de quê** don't mention it

terapeuta [tera'pewta] *m/f* therapist

terapia [tera'pia] *f* therapy

terça ['texsa] *f* (*tb:* **~-feira**) Tuesday; **~-feira** (*pl* **~s-feiras**) *f* Tuesday; **~ gorda** Shrove Tuesday

terceiro/a [tex'sejru/a] *num* third; **~s** *mpl* (*os outros*) outsiders

terço ['texsu] *m* third (part)

terçol [tex'sɔw] (*pl* **-óis**) *m* stye

tergal [tex'gaw] ® *m* Terylene ®

termal [tex'maw] (*pl* **-ais**) *adj* thermal

termas ['texmaʃ] *fpl* bathhouse *sg*

térmico/a ['tɛxmiku/a] *adj* thermal; **garrafa térmica** (Thermos ®) flask

terminal [texmi'naw] (*pl* **-ais**) *adj* terminal ♦ *m* (*de rede, ELET, COMPUT*) terminal ♦ *f* terminal; **~ (de vídeo)** monitor, visual display unit

terminar [texmi'na*] *vt* to finish ♦ *vi* (*pessoa*) to finish; (*coisa*) to end; **~ de fazer** to finish doing; (*ter feito há pouco*) to have just done; **~ por fazer algo** to end up doing sth

término ['tɛxminu] *m* end, termination

termo ['texmu] *m* term; (*fim*) end, termi-

nation; (*limite*) limit, boundary; (*prazo*) period; (*PT: garrafa*) (Thermos ®) flask; **meio ~** compromise; **em ~s (de)** in terms (of)

termômetro [tex'mometru] *m* thermometer

termostato [texmoʃ'tatu] *m* thermostat

terno/a ['tɛxnu/a] *adj* gentle, tender ♦ *m* (*BR: roupa*) suit; **ternura** [tex'nura] *f* gentleness, tenderness

terra ['tɛxa] *f* earth, world; (*AGR. propriedade*) land; (*pátria*) country; (*chão*) ground; (*GEO*) soil; (*pó*) dirt

terraço [te'xasu] *m* terrace

terramoto [texa'mɔtu] (*PT*) *m* = **terremoto**

terreiro [te'xejru] *m* yard, square

terremoto [texe'mɔtu] *m* earthquake

terreno/a [te'xɛnu/a] *m* ground, land; (*porção de terra*) plot of land ♦ *adj* earthly

térreo/a ['tɛxju/a] *adj*: **andar ~** (*BR*) ground floor (*BRIT*), first floor (*US*)

terrestre [te'xɛʃtri] *adj* land *atr*

terrina [te'xina] *f* tureen

território [texi'tɔrju] *m* territory

terrível [te'xivew] (*pl* **-eis**) *adj* terrible, dreadful

terror [te'xo*] *m* terror, dread; **~ista** [texo'riʃta] *adj, m/f* terrorist

tertúlia [tex'tulja] *f* gathering (of friends)

tese ['tɛzi] *f* proposition, theory; (*EDUC*) thesis; **em ~** in theory

teso/a ['tezu/a] *adj* (*cabo*) taut; (*rígido*) stiff

tesoura [te'zora] *f* scissors *pl*; **uma ~ a** pair of scissors

tesouraria [tezora'ria] *f* treasury

tesoureiro/a [tezo'rejru/a] *m/f* treasurer

tesouro [te'zoru] *m* treasure; (*erário*) treasury, exchequer; (*livro*) thesaurus

testa ['tɛʃta] *f* brow, forehead

testamento [teʃta'mẽtu] *m* will, testament; (*REL*): **Velho/Novo T~** Old/New Testament

testar [teʃ'ta*] *vt* to test; (*deixar em testamento*) to bequeath

teste ['tɛʃtʃi] *m* test

testemunha [teʃte'muɲa] *f* witness; **~r** [teʃtemu'ɲa*] *vi* to testify ♦ *vt* to give evidence about; (*presenciar*) to witness; (*confirmar*) to demonstrate; **testemunho** [teʃte'muɲu] *m* evidence

testículo [teʃ'tʃikulu] *m* testicle

teta ['tɛta] *f* teat, nipple

tétano ['tɛtanu] *m* tetanus

teto ['tɛtu] *m* ceiling; (*telhado*) roof; (*habitação*) home

tétrico/a ['tɛtriku/a] *adj* gloomy, dismal; (*horrível*) horrible

teu/tua [tew/'tua] *adj* your ♦ *pron* yours

teve ['tevi] *vb* V **ter**

têxtil ['teʃtʃiw] (*pl* **-eis**) *m* textile

texto ['teʃtu] *m* text

textura [teʃ'tura] *f* texture

texugo [te'ʃugu] *m* badger

tez [teʒ] *f* complexion; (*pele*) skin

thriller ['srila*] (*pl* ~s) *m* thriller

ti [tʃi] *pron* you

tia [tʃia] *f* aunt

Tibete [tʃi'betʃi] *m*: o ~ Tibet

tido/a [tʃidu/a] *pp de* ter ♦ *adj*: ~ como *ou* por considered to be

tifóide [tʃi'ɔidʒi] *adj*: febre ~ typhoid (fever)

tigela [tʃi'ʒεla] *f* bowl

tigre ['tʃigri] *m* tiger

tijolo [tʃi'ʒolu] *m* brick

til [tʃiw] (*pl* **tis**) *m* tilde

timão [tʃi'mãw] (*pl* ~ões) *m* (NÁUT) helm, tiller

timbre ['tʃibri] *m* insignia, emblem; (*selo*) stamp; (MÚS) tone, timbre; (*de voz*) tone; (*em papel de carta*) heading

time ['tʃimi] (BR) *m* team; **de segundo** ~ (*fig*) second-rate

tímido/a ['tʃimidu/a] *adj* shy, timid

timões [tʃi'mõjʃ] *mpl de* timão

timoneiro [tʃimo'nejru] *m* helmsman, coxswain

tímpano ['tʃipanu] *m* eardrum; (MÚS) kettledrum

tina ['tʃina] *f* vat

tingir [tʃi'ʒi*] *vt* to dye; (*fig*) to tinge

tinha *etc* ['tʃiɲa] *vb* V ter

tinhoso/a [tʃi'ɲozu/ɔza] *adj* single-minded

tinir [tʃi'ni*] *vi* to jingle, tinkle; (*ouvidos*) to ring; (*de frio, febre*) to shiver; (*de raiva, fome*) to tremble

tinjo *etc* ['tʃiʒu] *vb* V tingir

tino ['tʃinu] *m* discernment, judgement; (*intuição*) intuition; (*prudência*) prudence

tinta ['tʃita] *f* (*de pintar*) paint; (*de escrever*) ink; (*para tingir*) dye; (*fig*: *vestígio*) shade, tinge; **tinteiro** [tʃi'tejru] *m* inkwell

tinto/a ['tʃitu/a] *adj* dyed; (*fig*) stained; **vinho** ~ red wine

tintura [tʃi'tura] *f* dye; (*ato*) dyeing; (*fig*) tinge, hint

tinturaria [tʃitura'ria] *f* dry-cleaner's

tio ['tʃiu] *m* uncle

típico/a ['tʃipiku/a] *adj* typical

tipo ['tʃipu] *m* type; (*de imprensa*) print; (*de impressora*) typeface; (col: *sujeito*) guy, chap; (*pessoa*) person

tipografia [tʃipogra'fia] *f* printing; (*estabelecimento*) printer's; **tipógrafo/a** [tʃi'pɔgrafu/a] *m/f* printer

tipóia [tʃi'pɔja] *f* (*tira de pano*) sling

tique ['tʃiki] *m* (MED) tic; (*sinal*) tick

tíquete ['tʃiketʃi] *m* ticket

tira ['tʃira] *f* strip ♦ *m* (BR: col) cop

tiragem [tʃi'raʒẽ] *f* (*de livro*) print run; (*de jornal, revista*) circulation

tira-gosto (*pl* ~s) *m* snack, savoury (BRIT); **tirano/a** [tʃi'ranu/a] *adj* tyrannical ♦ *m/f* tyrant

tirar [tʃi'ra*] *vt* to take away; (*de dentro*)

to take out; (*de cima*) to take off; (*roupa, sapatos*) to take off; (*arrancar*) to pull out; (*férias*) to take, have; (*boas notas*) to get; (*salário*) to earn; (*curso*) to do, take; (*mancha*) to remove; (*foto, cópia*) to take; (*mesa*) to clear; ~ **algo a alguém** to take sth from sb

tiritar [tʃiri'ta*] *vi* to shiver

tiro ['tʃiru] *m* shot; (*ato de disparar*) shooting; ~ **ao alvo** target practice; **trocar** ~s to fire at one another

tiroteio [tʃiro'teju] *m* shooting, exchange of shots

tis [tʃiʃ] *mpl de* til

titubear [tʃitu'bja*] *vi* to totter, stagger; (*vacilar*) to hesitate

titular [tʃitu'la*] *adj* titular ♦ *m/f* holder

título ['tʃitulu] *m* title; (COM) bond; (*universitário*) degree; ~ **de propriedade** title deed

tive *etc* ['tʃivi] *vb* V ter

to [tu] = te + o

toa ['toa] *f* towrope; à ~ at random; (*sem motivo*) for no reason; (*inutilmente*) in vain, for nothing

toalete [twa'letʃi] *m* (*banheiro*) toilet; (*traje*) outfit ♦ *f*: **fazer a** ~ to have a wash

toalha [to'aʎa] *f* towel

toca ['tɔka] *f* burrow, hole

toca-discos (BR) *m inv* record-player

toca-fitas *m inv* cassette player

tocaia [to'kaja] *f* ambush

tocante [to'kãtʃi] *adj* moving, touching; **no** ~ **a** regarding, concerning

tocar [to'ka*] *vt* to touch; (MÚS) to play ♦ *vi* to touch; to play; (*campainha, sino, telefone*) to ring; ~-**se** *vr* to touch (each other); ~ **a** (*dizer respeito a*) to concern, affect; ~ **em** to touch; (*assunto*) to touch upon; ~ **para alguém** (*telefonar*) to ring sb (up), call sb (up); **pelo que me toca** as far as I am concerned

tocha ['tɔʃa] *f* torch

toco ['toku] *m* (*de cigarro*) stub; (*de árvore*) stump

todavia [toda'via] *adv* yet, still, however

todo/a ['todu/'tɔda] *adj* **1** (*com artigo sg*) all; **toda a carne** all the meat; **toda a noite** all night, the whole night; ~ **o Brasil** the whole of Brazil; **a toda (velocidade)** at full speed; ~ **o mundo** (BR), **toda a gente** (PT) everybody, everyone; **em toda (a) parte** everywhere

2 (*com artigo pl*) all; (: *cada*) every; ~s **os livros** all the books; ~s **os dias**/**todas as noites** every day/night; ~s **os que querem sair** all those who want to leave; ~s **nós** all of us

♦ *adv*: **ao** ~ altogether; (*no total*) in all; **de** ~ completely

♦ *pron*: ~s
♦ *mpl* everybody *sg*, everyone *sg*

todo-poderoso/a *adj* all-powerful ♦ *m*: o T~ the Almighty
tofe ['tɔfi] *m* toffee
toicinho [toj'siɲu] *m* bacon fat
toldo ['towdu] *m* awning, sun blind
tolerância [tole'rãsja] *f* tolerance; **tolerante** [tole'rãtʃi] *adj* tolerant
tolerar [tole'ra*] *vt* to tolerate; **tolerável** [tole'ravew] *adj* (~ *eis*) *adj* tolerable, bearable; (*satisfatório*) passable; (*falta*) excusable
tolher [to'ʎe*] *vt* to impede, hinder; ~ **alguém de fazer** to stop sb doing
tolice [to'lisi] *f* stupidity, foolishness; (*ato, dito*) stupid thing
tolo/a ['tolu/a] *adj* foolish, silly, stupid ♦ *m/f* fool
tom [tõ] *m* (*pl* ~**ns**) *m* tone; (*MÚS*: *altura*) pitch; (: *escala*) key; (*cor*) shade
tomada [to'mada] *f* capture; (*ELET*) socket
tomar [to'ma*] *vt* to take; (*capturar*) to capture, seize; (*decisão*) to make; (*bebida*) to drink; ~ **café** (*de manhã*) to have breakfast
tomara [to'mara] *excl*: ~! if only!; ~ **que venha hoje** I hope he comes today
tomate [to'matʃi] *m* tomato
tombadilho [tõba'dʒiʎu] *m* deck
tombar [tõ'ba*] *vi* to fall down, tumble down ♦ *vt* to knock down, knock over; **tombo** ['tõbu] *m* tumble, fall
tomilho [to'miʎu] *m* thyme
tona ['tɔna] *f* surface; **vir à** ~ to come to the surface; (*fig*) to emerge; **trazer à** ~ to bring up; (*recordações*) to bring back
tonalidade [tonali'dadʒi] *f* (*de cor*) shade; (*MÚS*: *tom*) key
tonel [to'nɛw] *m* (*pl* ~**éis**) cask, barrel
tonelada [tone'lada] *f* ton; **tonelagem** [tone'laʒẽ] *f* tonnage
tônica ['tonika] *f* (*água*) tonic (water); (*fig*) keynote
tônico ['toniku] *m* tonic; **acento** ~ stress
tonificar [tonifi'ka*] *vt* to tone up
tons [tõʃ] *mpl* **de tom**
tontear [tõ'tʃja*] *vi* (*pessoa*: *com bebida*) to get dizzy; (: *com barulho*) to get a headache; (: *com alvoroço*) to be dazed; (*barulho*) to be wearing; (*alvoroço*) to be upsetting
tonteira [tõ'tejra] *f* dizziness
tonto/a ['tõtu/a] *adj* stupid, silly; (*zonzo*) dizzy, lightheaded; (*atarantado*) flustered
topada [to'pada] *f* trip; **dar uma** ~ **em** to stub one's toe on
topar [to'pa*] *vt* to agree to ♦ *vi*: ~ **com** to come across; ~**se** *vr* (*duas pessoas*) to run into one another; ~ **em** (*tropeçar*) to stub one's toe on; (*esbarrar*) to run into; (*tocar*) to touch
tópico/a ['tɔpiku/a] *adj* topical ♦ *m* topic

topless [tɔp'lɛs] *adj inv* topless
topo ['topu] *m* top; (*extremidade*) end, extremity
toque1 ['tɔki] *m* touch; (*de instrumento musical*) playing; (*de campainha*) ring; (*retoque*) finishing touch
toque2 *etc vb V* **tocar**
Tóquio ['tɔkju] *n* Tokyo
tora ['tɔra] *f* (*pedaço*) piece; (*de madeira*) log; (*sesta*) nap
toranja [to'rãʒa] *f* grapefruit
torção [tox'sãw] (*pl* ~**ões**) *m* twist; (*MED*) sprain
torcedor(a) [toxse'do*(a)] *m/f* supporter, fan
torcedura [toxse'dura] *f* twist; (*MED*) sprain
torcer [tox'se*] *vt* to twist; (*MED*) to sprain; (*desvirtuar*) to distort, misconstrue; (*roupa*: *espremer*) to wring; (: *na máquina*) to spin; (*vergar*) to bend ♦ *vi*: ~ **por** (*time*) to support; ~**se** *vr* to squirm, writhe
torcicolo [toxsi'kɔlu] *m* stiff neck
torcida [tox'sida] *f* (*pavio*) wick; (*ESPORTE*: *ato de torcer*) cheering; (: *torcedores*) supporters *pl*
torções [tox'sõjʃ] *mpl* **de torção**
tormenta [tox'mẽta] *f* storm
tormento [tox'mẽtu] *m* torment; (*angústia*) anguish
tornado [tox'nadu] *m* tornado
tornar [tox'na*] *vi* to return, go back ♦ *vt*: ~ **algo em algo** to turn *ou* make sth into sth; ~**se** *vr* to become; ~ **a fazer algo** to do sth again
torneio [tox'neju] *m* tournament
torneira [tox'nejra] *f* tap (*BRIT*), faucet (*US*)
torno ['tɔxnu] *m* lathe; (*CERÂMICA*) wheel; **em** ~ **de** (*ao redor de*) around; (*sobre*) about
tornozelo [toxno'zelu] *m* ankle
torpe ['tɔxpi] *adj* vile
torpor [tox'po*] *m* torpor; (*MED*) numbness
torrada [to'xada] *f* toast; **uma** ~ a piece of toast; **torradeira** [toxa'dejra] *f* toaster
torrão [to'xãw] (*pl* ~**ões**) *m* turf, sod; (*terra*) soil, land; (*de açúcar*) lump
torrar [to'xa*] *vt* to toast; (*café*) to roast
torre ['tɔxi] *f* tower; (*XADREZ*) castle, rook; (*ELET*) pylon; ~ **de controle** (*AER*) control tower
torrente [to'xẽtʃi] *f* torrent
tórrido/a ['tɔxidu/a] *adj* torrid
torrinha [to'xiɲa] *f* (*TEATRO*) gallery
torrões [to'xõjʃ] *mpl* **de torrão**
torrone [to'xoni] *m* nougat
torso ['tɔxsu] *m* torso
torta ['tɔxta] *f* pie, tart
torto/a ['tɔxtu/'tɔxta] *adj* twisted, crooked; **a** ~ **e a direito** indiscriminately
tortuoso/a [tox'twozu/ɔza] *adj* winding

tortura [tox'tura] f torture; (fig) anguish; ~r [toxtu'ra*] vt to torture, to torment

torvelinho [toxve'liɲu] m (de vento) whirlwind; (de água) whirlpool; (fig: de pensamentos) swirl

tos [tuʃ] = te + os

tosar [to'za*] vt (ovelha) to shear; (cabelo) to crop

tosco/a ['toʃku/a] adj rough, unpolished; (grosseiro) coarse, crude

tosões [to'zõjʃ] mpl de tosão

tosquiar [toʃ'kja*] vt (ovelha) to shear, clip

tosse ['tɔsi] f cough; ~ de cachorro whooping cough; **tossir** [to'si*] vi to cough

tosta ['tɔʃta] (PT) f toast; ~ **mista** toasted cheese and ham sandwich

tostão [toʃ'tãw] m cash

tostar [toʃ'ta*] vt to toast; (pele, pessoa) to tan; ~se vr to get tanned

total [to'taw] (pl -ais) adj, m total

totalitário/a [totali'tarju/a] adj totalitarian

totalmente [totaw'mẽtʃi] adv totally

touca ['toka] f bonnet; ~ de banho bathing cap

toupeira [to'pejra] f mole; (fig) numbskull, idiot

tourada [to'rada] f bullfight; **tourear** [to'rja*] vi to fight bulls; **toureiro** [to'rejru] m bullfighter

touro ['toru] m bull; **T~** (ASTROLOGIA) Taurus

toxemia [tokse'mia] f blood poisoning

tóxico/a ['tɔksiku/a] adj toxic ♦ m poison; (droga) drug; **toxicômano/a** [toksi'komanu/a] m/f drug addict

trabalhadeira [trabaʎa'dejra] f: ela é ~ she's a hard worker

trabalhador(a) [trabaʎa'do*(a)] adj hard-working, industrious; (POL: classe) working ♦ m/f worker

trabalhar [traba'ʎa*] vi to work ♦ vt (terra) to till; (madeira, metal) to work; (texto) to work on; ~ **com** (comerciar) to deal in; ~ **de** ou **como** to work as; **trabalhista** [traba'ʎiʃta] adj labour atr (BRIT), labor atr (US); **trabalho** [tra'baʎu] m work; (emprego, tarefa) job; (ECON) labo(u)r; **trabalho braçal** manual work; **trabalho doméstico** housework; **trabalhoso/a** [traba'ʎozu/ɔza] adj laborious, arduous

traça ['trasa] f moth

traçado [tra'sadu] m sketch, plan

tração [tra'sãw] f traction

traçar [tra'sa*] vt to draw; (determinar) to set out, outline; (planos) to draw up; (escrever) to compose

tracção [tra'sãw] (PT) f = tração

traço ['trasu] m line, dash; (vestígio) trace, vestige; (aspecto) feature, trait; ~s mpl (do rosto) features; ~ (de união) hyphen; (entre frases) dash

tractor [tra'to*] (PT) m = trator

tradição [tradʒi'sãw] (pl -ões) f tradition; **tradicional** [tradʒisjo'naw] (pl -ais) adj traditional

tradução [tradu'sãw] (pl -ões) f translation

tradutor(a) [tradu'to*(a)] m/f translator

traduzir [tradu'zi*] vt to translate

trafegar [trafe'ga*] vi to move, go

tráfego ['trafegu] m traffic

traficante [trafi'kãtʃi] m/f trafficker, dealer

traficar [trafi'ka*] vi: ~ (com) to deal (in)

tráfico ['trafiku] m traffic

tragar [tra'ga*] vt to swallow; (fumaça) to inhale; (suportar) to tolerate ♦ vi to inhale

tragédia [tra'ʒɛdʒja] f tragedy; **trágico/a** ['traʒiku/a] adj tragic

trago¹ ['tragu] m mouthful

trago² etc vb V trazer

traição [traj'sãw] (pl -ões) f treason, treachery; (deslealdade) disloyalty; (infidelidade) infidelity; **traiçoeiro/a** [traj'swejru/a] adj treacherous, disloyal

traidor(a) [traj'do*(a)] m/f traitor

trailer ['trejla] (pl ~s) m trailer; (tipo casa) caravan (BRIT), trailer (US)

traineira [traj'nejra] f trawler

training ['trejnĩŋ] (pl ~s) m track suit

trair [tra'i*] vt to betray; (mulher, marido) to be unfaithful to; (esperanças) not to live up to; ~se vr to give o.s. away

trajar [tra'ʒa*] vt to wear

traje [tra'ʒi] m dress, clothes pl; ~ de banho swimsuit

trajeto [tra'ʒɛtu] (PT -ct-) m course, path

trajetória [traʒe'tɔrja] (PT -ct-) f trajectory, path; (fig) course

tralha ['traʎa] f fishing net

trama ['trama] f (tecido) weft (BRIT), woof (US); (enredo, conspiração) plot

tramar [tra'ma*] vt (tecer) to weave; (maquinar) to plot ♦ vi: ~ **contra** to conspire against

trâmites ['tramitʃiʃ] mpl procedure sg, channels

tramóia [tra'mɔja] f (fraude) swindle, trick; (trama) plot, scheme

trampolim [trãpo'lĩ] (pl -ns) m trampoline; (de piscina) diving board; (fig) springboard

tranca ['trãka] f (de porta) bolt; (de carro) lock

trança ['trãsa] f (cabelo) plait; (galão) braid

trancafiar [trãka'fja*] vt to lock up

trancar [trã'ka*] vt to lock

trançar [trã'sa*] vt to weave; (cabelo) to plait, braid

tranqüilidade [trãkwili'dadʒi] f tranquillity; (paz) peace

tranqüilizante [trãkwili'zãtʃi] m (MED) tranquillizer

tranqüilizar [trãkwili'za*] vt to calm, quieten; (despreocupar): ~ **alguém** to reassure sb, put sb's mind at rest; ~-se vr to calm down

tranqüilo/a [trã'kwilu/a] adj peaceful; (mar, pessoa) calm; (criança) quiet; (consciência) clear; (seguro) sure, certain

transação [trãza'sãw] (PT -cç-; pl -ões) f transaction

transbordar [trãzbox'da*] vi to overflow

transbordo [trãz'boxdu] m (de viajantes) change, transfer

transcorrer [trãʃko'xe*] vi to elapse, go by; (evento) to pass off

transe ['trãzi] m ordeal; (lance) plight; (hipnótico) trance

transeunte [trã'zjutʃi] m/f passer-by

transferência [trãʃfe'rẽsja] f transfer

transferir [trãʃfe'ri*] vt to transfer; (adiar) to postpone

transformação [trãʃfoxma'sãw] (pl -ões) f transformation

transformador [trãʃfoxma'do*] m (ELET) transformer

transformar [trãʃfox'ma*] vt to transform; ~-se vr to turn

trânsfuga ['trãʃfuga] m deserter; (político) turncoat

transfusão [trãʃfu'zãw] (pl -ões) f transfusion

transgênico/a [trõʒ'ʒeniku/a] adj genetically modified

transgredir [trãʒgre'dʒi*] vt to infringe

transição [trãzi'sãw] (pl -ões) f transition

transistor [trãziʃ'to*] m transistor

transitar [trãzi'ta*] vi: ~ **por** to move through; (rua) to go along

transitivo/a [trãzi'tʃivu/a] adj (LING) transitive

trânsito ['trãzitu] m transit, passage; (na rua: veículos) traffic; (: pessoas) flow; **transitório/a** [trãzi'torju/a] adj transitory; (período) transitional

transmissão [trãʒmi'sãw] (pl -ões) f transmission; (transferência) transfer; ~ **ao vivo** live broadcast

transmissor [trãʒmi'so*] m transmitter

transmitir [trãʒmi'tʃi*] vt to transmit; (RÁDIO, TV) to broadcast; (transferir) to transfer; (recado, notícia) to pass on

transparência [trãʃpa'rẽsja] f transparency; (de água) clarity; **transparente** [trãʃpa'rẽtʃi] adj transparent; (roupa) see-through; (água) clear

transpassar [trãʃpa'sa*] vt = **traspassar**

transpirar [trãʃpi'ra*] vi to perspire; (divulgar-se) to become known; (verdade) to come out ♦ vt to exude

transplante [trãʃ'plãtʃi] m transplant

transportar [trãʃpox'ta*] vt to transport; (levar) to carry; (enlevar) to entrance, enrapture

transporte [trãʃ'pɔxtʃi] m transport; (COM) haulage

transtornar [trãʃtox'na*] vt to upset; (ro-

tina, reunião) to disrupt; **transtorno** [trãʃ'toxnu] m upset, disruption

trapaça [tra'pasa] f swindle, fraud; **trapacear** [trapa'sja*] vt, vi to swindle; **trapaceiro/a** [trapa'sejru/a] adj crooked, cheating ♦ m/f swindler, cheat

trapalhão/lhona . [trapa'ʎãw/'ʎɔna] (pl -ões/~s) m/f bungler, blunderer

trapézio [tra'pezju] m trapeze

trapo ['trapu] m rag

traquéia [tra'keja] f windpipe

trarei etc [tra'rej] vb V **trazer**

trás [trajʃ] prep, adv: **para** ~ backwards; **por** ~ **de** behind; **de** ~ from behind

traseira [tra'zejra] f rear; (ANAT) bottom

traseiro/a [tra'zejru/a] adj back, rear ♦ m (ANAT) bottom

traspassar [traʃpa'sa*] vt (rio etc) to cross; (penetrar) to pierce, penetrate; (exceder) to exceed, overstep; (transferir) to transmit, transfer; (PT: sublocar) to sublet

traste ['traʃtʃi] m thing; (coisa sem valor) piece of junk

tratado [tra'tadu] m treaty

tratamento [trata'mẽtu] m treatment

tratar [tra'ta*] vt to treat; (tema) to deal with; (combinar) to agree ♦ vi: ~ **com** to deal with; (combinar) to agree with; ~ **de** to deal with; **de que se trata?** what is it about?

trato ['tratu] m treatment; (contrato) agreement, contract; ~**s** mpl (relações) dealings

trator [tra'to*] m tractor

trauma ['trawma] m trauma

travão [tra'vãw] (PT: pl -ões) m brake

travar [tra'va*] vt (roda) to lock; (iniciar) to engage in; (conversa) to strike up; (luta) to wage; (carro) to stop; (passagem) to block; (movimentos) to hinder ♦ vi (PT) to brake

trave ['travi] f beam; (ESPORTE) crossbar

través [tra'vɛʃ] m slant, incline; **de** ~ across, sideways

travessa [tra'vɛsa] f crossbeam, crossbar; (rua) lane, alley; (prato) dish; (para o cabelo) comb, slide

travessão [trave'sãw] (pl -ões) m (de balança) bar, beam; (pontuação) dash

travesseiro [trave'sejru] m pillow

travessia [trave'sia] f (viagem) journey, crossing

travesso/a [tra'vesu/a] adj mischievous, naughty

travessões [trave'sõjʃ] mpl de **travessão**

travessura [trave'sura] f mischief, prank

travões [tra'võjʃ] mpl de **travão**

trazer [tra'ze*] vt to bring

trecho ['treʃu] m passage; (de rua, caminho) stretch; (espaço) space

trégua ['trɛgwa] f truce; (descanso) respite

treinador(a) [trejna'do*(a)] m/f trainer

treinamento [trejna'mẽtu] m training

treinar [trej'na*] *vt* to train; **~-se** *vr* to train; **treino** ['trejnu] *m* training

trejeito [tre'ʒejtu] *m* gesture; (*careta*) grimace, face

trela ['trɛla] *f* lead, leash

treliça [tre'lisa] *f* trellis

trem [trẽj] (*pl* **-ns**) *m* train; **~ de aterrissagem** (*avião*) landing gear

tremeluzir [tremelu'zi*] *vi* to twinkle, glimmer

tremendo/a [tre'mẽdu/a] *adj* tremendous; (*terrível*) terrible, awful

tremer [tre'me*] *vi* to shudder, quake; (*terra*) to shake; (*de frio, medo*) to shiver

tremor [tre'mo*] *m* tremor; **~ de terra** (earth) tremor

trêmulo/a ['tremulu/a] *adj* shaky, trembling

trenó [tre'nɔ] *m* sledge, sleigh (*BRIT*), sled (*US*)

trens [trẽjʃ] *mpl de* **trem**

trepadeira [trepa'dejra] *f* (*BOT*) creeper

trepar [tre'pa*] *vt* to climb ♦ *vi*: **~ em** to climb

trepidar [trepi'da*] *vi* to tremble, shake

três [treʃ] *num* three; **~-quartos** *m inv* (*apartamento*) three-room flat (*BRIT*) *ou* apartment (*US*)

trespassar [treʃpa'sa*] *vt* = **traspassar**

trespasse [treʃ'pasi] *m* = **traspasse**

trevas ['trɛvaʃ] *fpl* darkness *sg*

trevo ['trevu] *m* clover; (*de vias*) intersection

treze ['trezi] *num* thirteen

triagem ['trjaʒẽ] *f* selection; (*separação*) sorting; **fazer uma ~ de** to make a selection of, sort out

triângulo ['trjãgulu] *m* triangle

tribal [tri'baw] (*pl* **-ais**) *adj* tribal

tribo ['tribu] *f* tribe

tribulação [tribula'sãw] (*pl* **-ões**) *f* tribulation, affliction

tribuna [tri'buna] *f* platform, rostrum; (*REL*) pulpit

tribunal [tribu'naw] (*pl* **-ais**) *m* court; (*comissão*) tribunal

tributar [tribu'ta*] *vt* to tax; (*pagar*) to pay

tributário [tribu'tarju] *m* tributary

tributo [tri'butu] *m* tribute; (*imposto*) tax

tricô [tri'ko] *m* knitting; **tricotar** [triko'ta*] *vt*, *vi* to knit

trigêmeo/a [tri'ʒemju/a] *m/f* triplet

trigo ['trigu] *m* wheat

trilha ['triʎa] *f* (*caminho*) path; (*rasto*) track, trail; **~ sonora** soundtrack

trilhão [tri'ʎãw] (*pl* **-ões**) *m* billion (*BRIT*), trillion (*US*)

trilho ['triʎu] *m* (*BR: FERRO*) rail; (*vereda*) path, track

trilhões [tri'ʎõjʃ] *mpl de* **trilhão**

trimestral [trimeʃ'traw] (*pl* **-ais**) *adj* quarterly; **~mente** [trimeʃtraw'mẽtʃi] *adv* quarterly

trimestre [tri'mɛʃtri] *m* (*EDUC*) term; (*COM*) quarter

trincar [trĩ'ka*] *vt* to crunch; (*morder*) to bite; (*dentes*) to grit ♦ *vi* to crunch

trincheira [trĩ'ʃejra] *f* trench

trinco ['trĩku] *m* latch

trinta ['trĩta] *num* thirty

trio ['triu] *m* trio; **~ elétrico** music float

tripa ['tripa] *f* gut, intestine; **~s** *fpl* (*intestinos*) bowels; (*vísceras*) guts; (*CULIN*) tripe *sg*

tripé [tri'pɛ] *m* tripod

triplicar [tripli'ka*] *vt*, *vi* to treble; **~-se** *vr* to treble

tripulação [tripula'sãw] (*pl* **-ões**) *f* crew

tripulante [tripu'lãtʃi] *m/f* crew member

tripular [tripu'la*] *vt* to man

triste ['triʃtʃi] *adj* sad; (*lugar*) depressing; **~eza** [triʃ'teza] *f* sadness; gloominess

triturar [tritu'ra*] *vt* to grind

triunfar [trjũ'fa*] *vi* to triumph; **triunfo** ['trjũfu] *m* triumph

trivial [tri'vjaw] (*pl* **-ais**) *adj* common(place), ordinary; (*insignificante*) trivial; **~idade** [trivjali'dadʒi] *f* triviality; **~idades** *fpl* (*futilidades*) trivia *sg*

triz [triʒ] *m*: **por um ~** by a hair's breadth

troca ['trɔka] *f* exchange, swap

trocadilho [troka'dʒiʎu] *m* pun, play on words

trocado [tro'kadu] *m*: **~(s)** (small) change

trocador(a) [troka'do*(a)] *m/f* (*em ônibus*) conductor

trocar [tro'ka*] *vt* to exchange, swap; (*mudar*) to change; (*inverter*) to change *ou* swap round; (*confundir*) to mix up; **~-se** *vr* to change; **~ dinheiro** to change money

troco ['trɔku] *m* (*dinheiro*) change; (*revide*) retort, rejoinder

troféu [tro'fɛw] *m* trophy

tromba ['trõba] *f* (*do elefante*) trunk; (*de outro animal*) snout

trombeta [trõ'beta] *f* trumpet

trombone [trõ'bɔni] *m* trombone

trombose [trõ'bɔzi] *f* thrombosis

trompa ['trõpa] *f* horn

tronco ['trõku] *m* trunk; (*ramo*) branch; (*de corpo*) torso, trunk

trono ['trɔnu] *m* throne

tropa ['trɔpa] *f* troop; (*exército*) army; **ir para a ~** (*PT*) to join the army

tropeçar [trope'sa*] *vi* to stumble, trip; (*fig*) to blunder

trôpego/a ['tropegu/a] *adj* shaky, unsteady

tropical [tropi'kaw] (*pl* **-ais**) *adj* tropical

trópico ['trɔpiku] *m* tropic

trotar [tro'ta*] *vi* to trot; **trote** ['trɔtʃi] *m* trot; (*por telefone etc*) hoax call

trouxe *etc* ['trosi] *vb* V **trazer**

trova ['trɔva] *f* ballad, folksong

trovão [tro'vãw] (pl -ões) m clap of thunder; (trovoada) thunder; **trovejar** [trove'ʒa*] vi to thunder; **trovoada** [tro'vwada] f thunderstorm

trucidar [trusi'da*] vt to butcher, slaughter

trufa ['trufa] f (BOT) truffle

truncar [trũ'ka*] vt to chop off, cut off

trunfo ['trũfu] m trump (card)

truque ['truki] m trick; (publicitário) gimmick

truta ['truta] f trout

tu [tu] (PT) pron you

tua ['tua] f de teu

tuba ['tuba] f tuba

tubarão [tuba'rãw] (pl -ões) m shark

tuberculose [tubexku'lɔzi] f tuberculosis

tubo ['tubu] m tube, pipe; ~ de ensaio test tube

tucano [tu'kanu] m toucan

tudo ['tudu] pron everything; ~ quanto everything that; **antes de** ~ first of all; **acima de** ~ above all

tufão [tu'fãw] (pl -ões) m typhoon

tulipa [tu'lipa] f tulip

tumba ['tũba] f tomb; (lápide) tombstone

tumor [tu'mo*] m tumour (BRIT), tumor (US)

túmulo ['tumulu] m tomb; (sepultura) burial

tumulto [tu'muwtu] m uproar, trouble; (grande movimento) bustle; (balbúrdia) hubbub; (motim) riot; **tumultuado/a** [tumuw'twadu/a] adj riotous, heated; **tumultuar** [tumuw'twa*] vt to disrupt; (amotinar) to rouse, incite

túnel ['tunew] (pl -eis) m tunnel

túnica ['tunika] f tunic

Tunísia [tu'nizja] f: **a** ~ Tunisia

tupi [tu'pi] m Tupi (tribe); (LING) Tupi ♦ m/f Tupi Indian

tupiniquim [tupini'kĩ] (pej) (pl -ns) adj Brazilian (Indian)

turbante [tux'bãtʃi] m turban

turbilhão [tuxbi'ʎãw] (pl -ões) m (de vento) whirlwind; (de água) whirlpool

turbina [tux'bina] f turbine

turbulência [tuxbu'lẽsja] f turbulence; **turbulento/a** [tuxbu'lẽtu/a] adj turbulent

turco/a ['tuxku/a] adj Turkish ♦ m/f Turk ♦ m (LING) Turkish

turfe ['tuxfi] m horse-racing

turismo [tu'riʒmu] m tourism; **turista** [tu'riʃta] m/f tourist ♦ adj (classe) tourist atr

turma ['tuxma] f group; (EDUC) class

turno ['tuxnu] m shift; (vez) turn; (ESPORTE, de eleição) round; **por** ~s alternately, by turns, in turn

turquesa [tux'keza] adj inv turquoise

Turquia [tux'kia] f: **a** ~ Turkey

tusso etc ['tusu] vb V tossir

tutano [tu'tanu] m (ANAT) marrow

tutela [tu'tɛla] f protection; (JUR) guardianship

tutor(a) [tu'to*(a)] m/f guardian

tutu [tu'tu] m (CULIN) beans, bacon and manioc flour

TV [te've] abr f (= televisão) TV

U

úbere ['uberi] m udder

ufanar-se [ufa'naxsi] vr: ~ **de** to take pride in, pride o.s. on

Uganda [u'gãda] m Uganda

uísque ['wiʃki] m whisky (BRIT), whiskey (US)

uivar [wi'va*] vi to howl; (berrar) to yell; **uivo** ['wivu] m howl; (fig) yell

úlcera ['uwsera] f ulcer

ulterior [uwte'rjo*] adj (além) further, farther; (depois) later, subsequent; ~**mente** [uwteriox'mẽtʃi] adv later on, subsequently

ultimamente [uwtʃima'mẽtʃi] adv lately

ultimato [uwtʃi'matu] m ultimatum

último/a ['uwtʃimu/a] adj last; (mais recente) latest; (qualidade) lowest; (fig) final; **por** ~ finally; **nos** ~**s anos** in recent years; **a última** (notícia) the latest (news)

ultra- [uwtra-] prefixo ultra-

ultrajar [uwtra'ʒa*] vt to outrage; (insultar) to insult, offend; **ultraje** [uw'traʒi] m outrage; (insulto) insult, offence (BRIT), offense (US)

ultramar [uwtra'ma*] m overseas; ~**ino/a** [uwtrama'rinu/a] adj overseas atr

ultrapassado/a [uwtrapa'sadu/a] adj (idéias etc) outmoded

ultrapassar [uwtrapa'sa*] vt (atravessar) to cross, go beyond; (ir além de) to exceed; (transgredir) to overstep; (AUTO) to overtake (BRIT), pass (US); (ser superior a) to surpass ♦ vi (AUTO) to overtake (BRIT), pass (US)

ultra-som m ultrasound

ultravioleta [uwtravjo'leta] adj ultraviolet

ulular [ulu'la*] vi to howl, wail

PALAVRA CHAVE
---

um(a) [ũ/'uma] (pl **uns**/~**s**) num one; ~ **e outro** both; ~ **a** ~ one by one; **à** ~**a (hora)** at one (o'clock)
♦ adj: **uns cinco** about five; **uns poucos** a few
♦ art indef **1** (sg) a; (: antes de vogal ou 'h' mudo) an; (pl) some; **ela é de** ~**a beleza incrível** she's incredibly beautiful
2 (dando ênfase): **estou com** ~**a fome!** I'm so hungry!
3 ~ **ao outro** one another; (entre dois) each other

---

umbigo [ũ'bigu] m navel

umbilical [ũbili'kaw] (pl -**ais**) adj: **cordão** ~ umbilical cord

umbral [ũ'braw] (pl **-ais**) m (limiar) threshold

umedecer [umede'se*] vt to moisten, wet; **~-se** vr to get wet; **umedecido/a** [umede'sidu/a] adj damp

umidade [umi'dadʒi] f dampness; (clima) humidity

úmido/a ['umidu/a] adj wet, moist; (roupa) damp; (clima) humid

unânime [u'nanimi] adj unanimous

ungir [ũ'ʒi*] vt to rub with ointment; (REL) to anoint

ungüento [ũ'gwẽtu] m ointment

unha ['uɲa] f nail; (garra) claw; **~da** [u'ɲada] f scratch; **~r** [u'ɲa*] vt to scratch

união [u'ɲjãw] (pl **-ões**) f union; (ato) joining; (unidade, solidariedade) unity; (casamento) marriage; (TEC) joint; **a U~ Soviética** the Soviet Union

unicamente [unika'mẽtʃi] adv only

único/a ['uniku/a] adj only; (sem igual) unique; (um só) single

unidade [uni'dadʒi] f unity; (TEC, COM) unit; **~ central de processamento** (COMPUT) central processing unit; **~ de disco** (COMPUT) disk drive

unido/a [u'nidu/a] adj joined, linked; (fig) united

unificar [unifi'ka*] vt to unite; **~-se** vr to join together

uniforme [uni'fɔxmi] adj uniform; (semelhante) alike, similar; (superfície) even ♦ m uniform; **uniformizado/a** [unifoxmi'zadu/a] adj uniform, standardized; (vestido de uniforme) in uniform; **uniformizar** [unifoxmi'za*] vt to standardize

uniões [u'njõjʃ] fpl de **união**

unir [u'ni*] vt to join together; (ligar) to link; (pessoas, fig) to unite; (misturar) to mix together; **~-se** vr to come together; (povos etc) to unite

uníssono [u'nisonu] m: **em ~** in unison

universal [univex'saw] (pl **-ais**) adj universal; (mundial) worldwide

universidade [univexsi'dadʒi] f university; **universitário/a** [univexsi'tarju/a] adj university atr ♦ m/f (professor) lecturer; (aluno) university student

universo [uni'vɛxsu] m universe; (mundo) world

unjo etc ['ũʒu] vb V **ungir**

uns [ũʃ] mpl de **um**

untar [ũ'ta*] vt (esfregar) to rub; (com óleo, manteiga) to grease

urânio [u'ranju] m uranium

urbanidade [uxbani'dadʒi] f courtesy, politeness

urbanismo [uxba'niʒmu] m town planning; **urbanista** [uxba'niʃta] m/f town planner

urbano/a [ux'banu/a] adj (da cidade) urban; (fig) urbane

urgência [ux'ʒẽsja] f urgency; **com toda**

~ as quickly as possible; **urgente** [ux'ʒẽtʃi] adj urgent

urina [u'rina] f urine; **~r** [uri'na*] vi to urinate ♦ vt (sangue) to pass; (cama) to wet; **~-se** vr to wet o.s.; **urinol** [uri'nɔw] (pl **-óis**) m chamber pot

urna ['uxna] f urn; **~ eleitoral** ballot box

urrar [u'xa*] vt, vi to roar; (de dor) to yell; **urro** ['uxu] m roar; yell

urso/a ['uxsu/a] m/f bear; **~-branco** (pl **~s-brancos**) m polar bear

URSS abr f (= União das Repúblicas Socialistas Soviéticas) **a ~** the USSR

urtiga [ux'tʃiga] f nettle

urubu [uru'bu] m vulture

Uruguai [uru'gwaj] m: **o ~** Uruguay

urze ['uxzi] m heather

usado/a [u'zadu/a] adj used; (comum) common; (roupa) worn; (gasto) worn out; (de segunda mão) second-hand

usar [u'za*] vt (servir-se de) to use; (vestir) to wear; (gastar com o uso) to wear out; (barba, cabelo curto) to have, wear ♦ vi: **~ de** to use; **modo de ~** directions pl

usina [u'zina] f (fábrica) factory; (de energia) plant

uso ['uzu] m use; (utilização) usage; (prática) practice

usual [u'zwaw] (pl **-ais**) adj usual; (comum) common

usuário/a [u'zwarju/a] m/f user

usufruir [uzu'frwi*] vt to enjoy ♦ vi: **~ de** to enjoy

usurário/a [uzu'rarju/a] m/f (avaro) miser ♦ adj avaricious

usurpar [uzux'pa*] vt to usurp

úteis ['utejʃ] pl de **útil**

utensílio [utẽ'silju] m utensil

útero ['uteru] m womb, uterus

útil ['utʃiw] (pl **-eis**) adj useful; (vantajoso) profitable, worthwhile; **utilidade** [utʃili'dadʒi] f usefulness; **utilização** [utʃiliza'sãw] f use; **utilizar** [utʃili'za*] vt to use; **utilizar-se** vr: **utilizar-se de** to make use of

uva ['uva] f grape

V

v abr (= volt) v

vá etc [va] vb V **ir**

vã [vã] f de **vão**

vaca ['vaka] f cow; **carne de ~** beef

vacilante [vasi'lãtʃi] adj hesitant

vacilar [vasi'la*] vi to hesitate; (balançar) to sway; (cambalear) to stagger; (luz) to flicker; (col) to slip up

vacina [va'sina] f vaccine; **~r** [vasi'na*] vt to vaccinate

vácuo ['vakwu] m vacuum; (fig) void; (espaço) space

vadiação [vadʒja'sãw] f vagrancy

vadiar [va'dʒja*] *vi* to lounge about; (*não trabalhar*) to idle about; (*perambular*) to wander

vadio/a [va'dʒiu/a] *adj* (*ocioso*) idle, lazy; (*vagabundo*) vagrant ♦ *m/f* idler; vagabond, vagrant

vaga ['vaga] *f* wave; (*em hotel, trabalho*) vacancy

vagabundo/a [vaga'bũdu/a] *adj* vagrant; (*vadio*) lazy, idle; (*de má qualidade*) shoddy ♦ *m/f* tramp

vagão [va'gãw] (*pl* -ões) *m* (*de passageiros*) carriage; (*de cargas*) wagon; **~-leito** (*pl* **vagões-leitos**) (*PT*) *m* sleeping car; **~-restaurante** (*pl* **vagões-restaurantes**) *m* buffet car

vagar [va'ga*] *vi* to wander about; (*barco*) to drift; (*ficar vago*) to be vacant

vagaroso/a [vaga'rozu/ɔza] *adj* slow

vagem ['vaʒē] (*pl* -ns) *f* green bean

vagina [va'ʒina] *f* vagina

vago/a ['vagu/a] *adj* vague; (*desocupado*) vacant, free

vagões [va'gõjʃ] *mpl de* **vagão**

vaguear [va'gja*] *vi* to wander, roam; (*passear*) to ramble

vai *etc* [vaj] *vb* V **ir**

vaia ['vaja] *f* booing; **~r** [va'ja*] *vt, vi* to boo, hiss

vaidade [vaj'dadʒi] *f* vanity; (*futilidade*) futility

vaidoso/a [vaj'dozu/ɔza] *adj* vain

vaivém [vaj'vēj] *m* to-ing and fro-ing

vala ['vala] *f* ditch

vale ['vali] *m* valley; (*escrito*) voucher; **~ postal** postal order

valente [va'lētʃi] *adj* brave; **valentia** [valē'tʃia] *f* courage, bravery; (*proeza*) feat

valer [va'le*] *vi* to be worth; (*ser válido*) to be valid; (*ter influência*) to carry weight; (*servir*) to serve; (*ser proveitoso*) to be useful; **~-se** *vr*: **~-se de** to use, make use of; **~ a pena** to be worthwhile; **~ por** (*equivaler*) to be worth the same as; **para** (*muito*) very much, a lot; (*realmente*) for real, properly; **vale dizer** in other words; **mais vale ... (do que ...)** it would be better to ... (than ...)

valeta [va'leta] *f* gutter

valete [va'letʃi] *m* (*CARTAS*) jack

valha *etc* ['vaʎa] *vb* V **valer**

valia [va'lia] *f* value

validade [vali'dadʒi] *f* validity

validar [vali'da*] *vt* to validate; **válido/a** ['validu/a] *adj* valid

valioso/a [va'ljozu/ɔza] *adj* valuable

valise [va'lizi] *f* case, grip

valor [va'lo*] *m* value; (*mérito*) merit; (*coragem*) courage; (*preço*) price; (*importância*) importance; **~es** *mpl* (*morais*) values; (*num exame*) marks; (*COM*) securities; **dar ~ a** to value; **~izar** [valori'za*] *vt* to value

valsa ['vawsa] *f* waltz

válvula ['vawvula] *f* valve

vampiro/a [vã'piru/a] *m/f* vampire

vandalismo [vãda'liʒmu] *m* vandalism

vândalo/a ['vãdalu/a] *m/f* vandal

vangloriar-se [vãglo'rjaxsi] *vr*: **~ de** to boast of *ou* about

vanguarda [vã'gwaxda] *f* vanguard; (*arte*) avant-garde

vantagem [vã'taʒē] (*pl* -ns) *f* advantage; (*ganho*) profit, benefit; **tirar ~ de** to take advantage of; **vantajoso/a** [vãta'ʒozu/ɔza] *adj* advantageous; (*lucrativo*) profitable; (*proveitoso*) beneficial

vão¹/vã [vãw/vã] (*pl* -s/-s) *adj* vain; (*fútil*) futile ♦ *m* (*intervalo*) space; (*de porta etc*) opening

vão² *vb* V **ir**

vapor [va'po*] *m* steam; (*navio*) steamer; (*de gas*) vapour (*BRIT*), vapor (*US*); **~izador** [vaporiza'do*] *m* (*de perfume*) spray; **~oso/a** [vapo'rozu/ɔza] *adj* steamy, misty

vaqueiro [va'kejru] *m* cowboy

vara ['vara] *f* stick; (*TEC*) rod; (*JUR*) jurisdiction; (*de porcos*) herd; **salto de ~** pole vault; **~ de condão** magic wand

varal [va'raw] (*pl* -ais) *m* clothes line

varanda [va'rãda] *f* verandah; (*balcão*) balcony

varar [va'ra*] *vt* to pierce; (*passar*) to cross

varejeira [vare'ʒejra] *f* bluebottle

varejista [vare'ʒiʃta] (*BR*) *m/f* retailer ♦ *adj* (*mercado*) retail

varejo [va'reʒu] (*BR*) *m* (*COM*) retail trade; **a ~** retail

variação [varja'sãw] (*pl* -ões) *f* variation

variado/a [va'rjadu/a] *adj* varied; (*sortido*) assorted

variar [va'rja*] *vt, vi* to vary; **variável** [va'rjavew] (*pl* -eis) *adj* variable; (*tempo, humor*) changeable

varicela [vari'sɛla] *f* chickenpox

variedade [varje'dadʒi] *f* variety

varinha [va'riɲa] *f* wand; **~ de condão** magic wand

vário/a ['varju/a] *adj* (*diverso*) varied; (*pl*) various, several; (*COM*) sundry

varíola [va'riola] *f* smallpox

varizes [va'riziʃ] *fpl* varicose veins

varrer [va'xe*] *vt* to sweep; (*fig*) to sweep away

várzea ['vaxzja] *f* meadow, field

vasculhar [vaʃku'ʎa*] *vt* (*pesquisar*) to research; (*remexer*) to rummage through

vaselina [vaze'lina] ® *f* vaseline ®

vasilha [va'ziʎa] *f* (*para líquidos*) jug; (*para alimentos*) dish; (*barril*) barrel

vaso ['vazu] *m* pot; (*para flores*) vase

vassoura [va'sora] *f* broom

vasto/a ['vaʃtu/a] *adj* vast

vatapá [vata'pa] *m* fish or chicken with coconut milk, shrimps, peanuts, palm oil and spices

Vaticano [vatʃi'kanu] *m*: **o ~** the Vatican

vau [vaw] *m* ford

vazamento [vaza'mẽtu] *m* leak

vazão [va'zāw] (*pl* –ões) *f* flow; (*venda*) sale; **dar ~ a** (*expressar*) to give vent to; (*atender*) to deal with; (*resolver*) to attend to

vazar [va'za*] *vt* to empty; (*derramar*) to spill; (*verter*) to pour out ♦ *vi* to leak

vazio/a [va'ziu/a] *adj* empty; (*pessoa*) empty-headed, frivolous; (*cidade*) deserted ♦ *m* emptiness; (*deixado por alguém/algo*) void

vazões [va'zōjʃ] *fpl de* **vazão**

vê *etc* [ve] *vb* V **ver**

veado/a ['vjadua] *m* deer; **carne de ~** venison

vedado/a [ve'dadu/a] *adj* (*proibido*) forbidden; (*fechado*) enclosed

vedar [ve'da*] *vt* to ban, prohibit; (*buraco*) to stop up; (*entrada, passagem*) to block; (*terreno*) to close off

vedete [ve'dɛtʃi] *f* star

veemente [vje'mẽtʃi] *adj* vehement

vegetação [veʒeta'sāw] *f* vegetation

vegetal [veʒe'taw] (*pl* –ais) *adj* vegetable *atr*; (*reino, vida*) plant *atr* ♦ *m* vegetable

vegetariano/a [veʒeta'rjanu/a] *adj, m/f* vegetarian

veia ['veja] *f* vein

veículo [ve'ikulu] *m* vehicle; (*fig: meio*) means *sg*

veio ['veju] *vb* V **vir** ♦ *m* (*de rocha*) vein; (*na mina*) seam; (*de madeira*) grain

vejo *etc* ['veʒu] *vb* V **ver**

vela ['vɛla] *f* candle; (*AUTO*) spark plug; (*NÁUT*) sail; **barco à ~** sailing boat

velar [ve'la*] *vt* to veil; (*ocultar*) to hide; (*vigiar*) to keep watch over; (*um doente*) to sit up with ♦ *vi* (*não dormir*) to stay up; (*vigiar*) to keep watch; **~ por** to look after

veleiro [ve'lejru] *m* sailing boat (*BRIT*), sailboat (*US*)

velejar [vele'ʒa*] *vi* to sail

velhaco/a [ve'ʎaku/a] *adj* crooked ♦ *m/f* crook

velhice [ve'ʎisi] *f* old age

velho/a ['vɛʎu/a] *adj* old ♦ *m/f* old man/woman

velocidade [velosi'dadʒi] *f* speed, velocity; (*PT: AUTO*) gear

velocímetro [velo'simetru] *m* speedometer

velório [ve'lɔrju] *m* wake

veloz [ve'lɔʒ] *adj* fast

vem [vẽj] *vb* V **vir**

vêm [vẽj] *vb* V **vir**

vencedor(a) [vẽse'do*(a)] *adj* winning ♦ *m/f* winner

vencer [vẽ'se*] *vt* (*num jogo*) to beat; (*competição*) to win; (*inimigo*) to defeat; (*exceder*) to surpass; (*obstáculos*) to overcome; (*percorrer*) to pass ♦ *vi* (*num jogo*)

to win; **vencido/a** [vẽ'sidu/a] *adj*: **dar-se por vencido** to give in; **vencimento** [vẽsi'mẽtu] *m* (*COM*) expiry; (*data*) expiry date; (*salário*) salary; (*de gêneros alimentícios etc*) sell-by date; **vencimentos** *mpl* (*ganhos*) earnings

venda ['vẽda] *f* sale; (*pano*) blindfold; (*mercearia*) general store; **à ~** on sale, for sale

vendaval [vẽda'vaw] (*pl* –ais) *m* gale

vendedor(a) [vẽde'do*(a)] *m/f* seller; (*em loja*) sales assistant; **~ ambulante** street vendor

vender [vẽ'de*] *vt, vi* to sell; **~ por atacado/a varejo** to sell wholesale/retail

veneno [ve'nɛnu] *m* poison; **~so/a** [vene'nozu/ɔza] *adj* poisonous

venerar [vene'ra*] *vt* to revere; (*REL*) to worship

venéreo/a [ve'nɛrju/a] *adj*: **doença venérea** venereal disease

Venezuela [vene'zwɛla] *f*: **a ~** Venezuela

venha *etc* ['vɛɲa] *vb* V **vir**

ventania [vẽta'nia] *f* gale

ventar [vẽ'ta*] *vi*: **está ventando** it is windy

ventarola [vẽta'rɔla] *f* fan

ventilação [vẽtʃila'sāw] *f* ventilation

ventilador [vẽtʃila'do*] *m* ventilator; (*elétrico*) fan

ventilar [vẽtʃi'la*] *vt* to ventilate; (*roupa, sala*) to air

vento ['vẽtu] *m* wind; (*brisa*) breeze; **~inha** [vẽ'wiɲa] *f* weathercock, weather vane; (*PT: AUTO*) fan; **~so/a** [vẽ'tozu/ɔza] *adj* windy

ventre ['vẽtri] *m* belly

ventríloquo/a [vẽ'trilokwu/a] *m/f* ventriloquist

ventura [vẽ'tura] *f* fortune; (*felicidade*) happiness; **venturoso/a** [vẽtu'rozu/ɔza] *adj* happy

ver [ve*] *vt* to see; (*olhar para, examinar*) to look at; (*televisão*) to watch ♦ *vi* to see ♦ *m*: **a meu ~** in my opinion; **vai ~ que ...** maybe ...; **não tem nada a ~ (com)** it has nothing to do (with)

veracidade [verasi'dadʒi] *f* truthfulness

veranear [vera'nja*] *vi* to spend the summer; **veraneio** [vera'neju] *m* summer holidays *pl* (*BRIT*) *ou* vacation (*US*); **veranista** [vera'niʃta] *m/f* holidaymaker (*BRIT*), (summer) vacationer (*US*)

verão [ve'rãw] (*pl* –ões) *m* summer

verba ['vɛxba] *f* allowance; **~(s)** *f(pl)* (*recursos*) funds *pl*

verbal [vex'baw] (*pl* –ais) *adj* verbal

verbete [vex'betʃi] *m* (*num dicionário*) entry

verbo ['vɛxbu] *m* verb; **~so/a** [vex'bozu/ɔza] *adj* wordy, verbose

verdade [vex'dadʒi] *f* truth; **de ~** (*falar*) truthfully; (*ameaçar etc*) really; **na ~** in fact; **para falar a** ~ to tell the truth; **~iro/a** [vexda'dejru/a] *adj* true; (*genuíno*) real; (*pessoa*) truthful

verde ['vexdʒi] *adj* green; (*fruta*) unripe ♦ *m* green; (*plantas etc*) greenery; **~jar** [vexde'ʒa*] *vi* to turn green; **verdor** [vex'do*] *m* greenness; (*BOT*) greenery

verdura [vex'dura] *f* (*hortaliça*) greens *pl*; (*BOT*) greenery; (*cor verde*) greenness

verdureiro/a [vexdu'rejru/a] *m/f* greengrocer (*BRIT*), produce dealer (*US*)

vereador(a) [verja'do*(a)] *m/f* councillor (*BRIT*), councilor (*US*)

vereda [ve'reda] *f* path

veredicto [vere'dʒiktu] *m* verdict

verga ['vexga] *f* (*vara*) stick; (*de metal*) rod

vergonha [vex'gɔɲa] *f* shame; (*timidez*) embarrassment; (*humilhação*) humiliation; (*ato indecoroso*) indecency; (*brio*) self-respect; **ter** ~ to be ashamed; (*tímido*) to be shy; **vergonhoso/a** [vexgo'nozu/ɔza] *adj* shameful; (*indecoroso*) disgraceful

verídico/a [ve'ridʒiku/a] *adj* true, truthful

verificar [verifi'ka*] *vt* to check; (*confirmar*) to verify

verme ['vexmi] *m* worm

vermelho/a [vex'meʎu/a] *adj* red ♦ *m* red

vermute [vex'mutʃi] *m* vermouth

vernáculo/a [vex'nakulu/a] *adj*: **língua vernácula** vernacular ♦ *m* vernacular

verniz [vex'niʒ] *m* varnish; (*couro*) patent leather

verões [ve'rõjʃ] *mpl de* **verão**

verossímil [vero'simiw] (*PT* -osí-) (*pl* -eis) *adj* likely, probable; (*crível*) credible

verruga [ve'xuga] *f* wart

versado/a [vex'sadu/a] *adj*: ~ **em** clever at, good at

versão [vex'sãw] (*pl* -ões) *f* version; (*tradução*) translation

versátil [vex'satʃiw] (*pl* -eis) *adj* versatile

versículo [vex'sikulu] *m* (*REL*) verse

verso ['vexsu] *m* verse; (*linha*) line of poetry

versões [vex'sõjʃ] *fpl de* **versão**

vertente [vex'tẽtʃi] *f* slope

verter [vex'te*] *vt* to pour; (*por acaso*) to spill; (*traduzir*) to translate; (*lágrimas, sangue*) to shed ♦ *vi*: ~ **de** to spring from; ~ **em** (*rio*) to flow into

vertical [vextʃi'kaw] (*pl* -ais) *adj* vertical; (*de pé*) upright, standing ♦ *f* vertical

vértice ['vextʃisi] *m* apex

vertigem [vex'tʃiʒẽ] *f* (*medo de altura*) vertigo; (*tonteira*) dizziness; **vertiginoso/a** [vextʃiʒi'nozu/ɔza] *adj* dizzy, giddy; (*velocidade*) frenetic

vesgo/a ['veʒgu/a] *adj* cross-eyed

vesícula [ve'zikula] *f*: ~ (**biliar**) gall bladder

vespa ['veʃpa] *f* wasp

véspera ['veʃpera] *f*: **a** ~ **de** the day before; **a** ~ **de Natal** Christmas Eve

veste ['veʃtʃi] *f* garment

vestiário [veʃ'tʃjarju] *m* (*em casa, teatro*) cloakroom; (*ESPORTE*) changing room; (*de ator*) dressing room

vestíbulo [veʃ'tʃibulu] *m* hall(way), vestibule; (*TEATRO*) foyer

vestido/a [veʃ'tʃidu/a] *adj*: ~ **de branco** *etc* dressed in white *etc* ♦ *m* dress

vestígio [veʃ'tʃiʒju] *m* (*rastro*) track; (*fig*) sign, trace

vestimenta [veʃtʃi'mẽta] *f* garment

vestir [veʃ'tʃi*] *vt* (*uma criança*) to dress; (*pôr sobre si*) to put on; (*trajar*) to wear; (*comprar, dar roupa para*) to clothe; (*fazer roupa para*) to make clothes for; **~-se** *vr* to get dressed

vestuário [veʃ'twarju] *m* clothing

vetar [ve'ta*] *vt* to veto

veterano/a [vete'ranu/a] *adj, m/f* veteran

veterinário/a [veteri'narju/a] *m/f* vet (-erinary surgeon)

veto ['vetu] *m* veto

véu [vɛw] *m* veil

vexame [ve'ʃami] *f* shame, disgrace; (*tormento*) affliction; (*humilhação*) humiliation; (*afronta*) insult

vez [veʒ] *f* time; (*turno*) turn; **uma** ~ once; **algumas ~es, às ~es** sometimes; ~ **por outra** sometimes; **cada** ~ **(que)** every time; **de** ~ **em quando** from time to time; **em** ~ **de** instead of; **uma** ~ **que** since; **3 ~es 6** 3 times 6; **de uma** ~ **por todas** once and for all; **muitas ~es** many times; (*freqüentemente*) often; **toda** ~ **que** every time; **um de cada** ~ one at a time; **uma** ~ **ou outra** once in a while

vi [vi] *vb V* **ver**

via¹ ['via] *f* road, route; (*meio*) way; (*documento*) copy; (*conduto*) channel ♦ *prep* via, by way of; **em ~s de** about to; **por** ~ **terrestre/marítima** by land/sea

via² *etc vb V* **ver**

viaduto [vja'dutu] *m* viaduct

viagem ['vjaʒẽ] (*pl* -ns) *f* journey, trip; (*o viajar*) travel; (*NÁUT*) voyage; **viagens** *fpl* (*jornadas*) travels; ~ **de ida e volta** return trip, round trip

viajante [vja'ʒãtʃi] *adj* travelling (*BRIT*), traveling (*US*) ♦ *m* traveller (*BRIT*), traveler (*US*)

viajar [vja'ʒa*] *vi* to travel

viável ['vjavew] (*pl* -eis) *adj* feasible, viable

víbora ['vibora] *f* viper

vibração [vibra'sãw] (*pl* -ões) *f* vibration; (*fig*) thrill

vibrante [vi'brãtʃi] *adj* vibrant; (*discurso*) stirring

vibrar [vi'bra*] *vt* to brandish; (*fazer estremecer*) to vibrate; (*cordas*) to strike ♦ *vi* to vibrate; (*som*) to echo

vice ['visi] *m/f* deputy

vice- [visi-] *prefixo* vice-; **~presidente/a** *m/f* vice president; **~versa** [-'vɛxsa] *adv* vice-versa

viciado/a [vi'sjadu/a] *adj* addicted; *(ar)* foul ♦ *m/f* addict; **~ em algo** addicted to sth

viciar [vi'sja*] *vt (falsificar)* to falsify; **~-se** *vr*: **~-se em algo** to become addicted to sth

vício ['visju] *m* vice; *(defeito)* failing; *(costume)* bad habit; *(em entorpecentes)* addiction

viço ['visu] *m* vigour *(BRIT)*, vigor *(US)*; *(da pele)* freshness; **~so/a** [vi'sozu/ɔza] *adj (plantas)* luxuriant; *(fig)* exuberant

vida ['vida] *f* life; *(duração)* lifetime; *(fig)* vitality; **com ~** alive; **ganhar a ~** to earn one's living; **modo de ~** way of life; **dar a ~ por algo/por fazer algo** to give one's right arm for sth/to do sth; **estar bem de ~** to be well off

vide ['vidʒi] *vt* see; **~ verso** see over

videira [vi'dejra] *f* grapevine

vidente [vi'dẽtʃi] *m/f* clairvoyant

vídeo ['vidʒju] *m* video; **videocassete** [vidʒjuka'sɛtʃi] *m* video cassette *ou* tape; *(aparelho)* video (recorder); **videoteipe** [vidʒju'tejpi] *m* video tape

vidraça [vi'drasa] *f* window pane; **vidraceiro** [vidra'sejru] *m* glazier

vidrado/a [vi'dradu/a] *adj* glazed; *(porta)* glass *atr*; *(olhos)* glassy

vidrar [vi'dra*] *vt* to glaze

vidro ['vidru] *m* glass; *(frasco)* bottle; **fibra de ~** fibreglass *(BRIT)*, fiberglass *(US)*; **~ de aumento** magnifying glass

viela ['vjɛla] *f* alley

vier *etc* [vje*] *vb* V **vir**

viés [vjɛʃ] *m* slant; **ao** *ou* **de ~** diagonally

vieste ['vjeʃtʃi] *vb* V **vir**

Vietnã [vjet'nã] *m*: **o ~** Vietnam; **vietnamita** [vjetna'mita] *adj, m/f* Vietnamese

viga ['viga] *f* beam; *(de ferro)* girder

vigário [vi'garju] *m* vicar

vigência [vi'ʒẽsja] *f* validity; **vigente** [vi'ʒẽtʃi] *adj* in force, valid

viger [vi'ʒe*] *vi* to be in force

vigia [vi'ʒia] *f* watching; *(NÁUT)* porthole ♦ *m* night watchman; **vigiar** [vi'ʒja*] *vt* to watch; *(ocultamente)* to spy on; *(presos, fronteira)* to guard ♦ *vi* to be on the lookout

vigilância [viʒi'lãsja] *f* vigilance; **vigilante** [viʒi'lãtʃi] *adj* vigilant; *(atento)* alert

vigília [vi'ʒilja] *f* wakefulness; *(vigilância)* vigilance

vigor [vi'go*] *m* energy, vigour *(BRIT)*, vigor *(US)*; **em ~** in force; **entrar/pòr em ~** to take effect/put into effect; **~ar** [vigo'ra*] *vi* to be in force; **~oso/a** [vigo'rozu/ɔza] *adj* vigorous

vil [viw] *(pl* **vis)** *adj* vile

vila ['vila] *f* town; *(casa)* villa

vilão/lã [vi'lãw/'lã] *(pl* **~s/~s)** *m/f* villain

vilarejo [vila'reʒu] *m* village

vim [vĩ] *vb* V **vir**

vime ['vimi] *m* wicker

vinagre [vi'nagri] *m* vinegar

vinco ['vĩku] *m* crease; *(sulco)* furrow; *(no rosto)* line

vincular [vĩku'la*] *vt* to link, tie; **vínculo** ['vĩkulu] *m* bond, tie; *(relação)* link

vinda ['vĩda] *f* arrival; *(regresso)* return; **dar as boas ~s a** to welcome

vindicar [vĩdʒi'ka*] *vt* to vindicate

vindouro/a [vĩ'doru/a] *adj* future, coming

vingança [vĩ'gãsa] *f* vengeance, revenge; **vingar** [vĩ'ga*] *vt* to avenge; **vingar-se** *vr*: **vingar-se de** to take revenge on; **vingativo/a** [vĩga'tʃivu/a] *adj* vindictive

vinha¹ *etc* ['viɲa] *vb* V **vir**

vinha² *f* vineyard; *(planta)* vine; **vinhedo** [vi'ɲedu] *m* vineyard

vinho ['viɲu] *m* wine; **~ branco/rosado/tinto** white/rosé/red wine; **~ seco/doce** dry/sweet wine; **~ do Porto** port

vinil [vi'niw] *m* vinyl

vinte ['vĩtʃi] *num* twenty

vintena [vĩ'tɛna] *f*: **uma ~** twenty, a score

viola ['vjɔla] *f* viola

violação [vjola'sãw] *(pl* **-ões)** *f* violation; **~ de domicílio** housebreaking

violão [vjo'lãw] *(pl* **-ões)** *m* guitar

violar [vjo'la*] *vt* to violate; *(a lei)* to break

violência [vjo'lẽsja] *f* violence; **violentar** [vjolẽ'ta*] *vt* to force; *(mulher)* to rape; **violento/a** [vjo'lẽtu/a] *adj* violent

violeta [vjo'leta] *f* violet

violino [vjo'linu] *m* violin

violões [vjo'lõjʃ] *mpl de* **violão**

violoncelo [vjolõ'sɛlu] *m* 'cello

vir¹ [vi*] *vi* to come; **~ a ser** to turn out to be; **a semana que vem** next week

vir² *etc* *vb* V **ver**

viração [vira'sãw] *(pl* **-ões)** *f* breeze

virada [vi'rada] *f* turning; *(guinada)* swerve

vira-lata ['vira-] *(pl* **~s)** *m (cão)* mongrel

virar [vi'ra*] *vt* to turn; *(página, disco, barco)* to turn over; *(copo)* to empty; *(transformar-se em)* to become ♦ *vi* to turn; *(barco)* to capsize; *(mudar)* to change; **~-se** *vr* to turn; *(voltar-se)* to turn round; *(defender-se)* to fend for o.s.

virgem ['vixʒẽ] *(pl* **-ns)** *f* virgin; **V~** *(ASTROLOGIA)* Virgo

vírgula ['vixgula] *f* comma; *(decimal)* point

viril [vi'riw] *(pl* **-is)** *adj* virile

virilha [vi'riʎa] *f* groin

viris [vi'riʃ] *adj pl de* **viril**

virtual [vix'twaw] *(pl* **-ais)** *adj* virtual; *(potencial)* potential; **~mente** [vixtwaw'mẽtʃi] *adv* virtually

virtude [vix'tudʒi] *f* virtue; **em ~ de** owing to, because of; **virtuoso/a** [vix'twozu/ɔza] *adj* virtuous

virulento/a [viru'lẽtu/a] *adj* virulent

vírus ['viruʃ] *m inv* virus

vis [viʃ] *adj* de **vil**

visão [vi'zãw] (*pl* -ões) *f* vision; (*ANAT*) eyesight; (*vista*) sight; (*maneira de perceber*) view

visar [vi'za*] *vt* (*alvo*) to aim at; (*ter em vista*) to have in view; (*ter como objetivo*) to aim for

vísceras ['viseraʃ] *fpl* innards, bowels

viseira [vi'zejra] *f* visor

visita [vi'zita] *f* visit, call; (*pessoa*) visitor; **fazer uma ~ a** to visit; **~nte** [vizi'tãtʃi] *adj* visiting ♦ *m/f* visitor; **~r** [vizi'ta*] *vt* to visit

visível [vi'zivew] (*pl* -eis) *adj* visible

vislumbrar [viʒlũ'bra*] *vt* to glimpse, catch a glimpse of; **vislumbre** [viʒ'lũbri] *m* glimpse

visões [vi'zõjʃ] *fpl de* **visão**

visom [vi'zõ] (*pl* -ns) *m* mink

visor [vi'zo*] *m* (*FOTO*) viewfinder

visse *etc* ['visi] *vb V* **ver**

vista ['viʃta] *f* sight; (*MED*) eyesight; (*panorama*) view; **à** *ou* **em ~ de** in view of; **dar na ~** to attract attention; **dar uma ~ de olhos em** to glance at; **fazer ~ grossa (a)** to turn a blind eye (to); **ter em ~** to have in mind; **à ~** visible, showing; (*COM*) in cash; **até a ~!** see you!

visto/a [viʃtu/a] *pp de* **ver** ♦ *adj* seen ♦ *m* (*em passaporte*) visa; (*em documento*) stamp; **pelo ~** by the looks of things

visto *etc vb V* **vestir**

vistoria [viʃto'ria] *f* inspection; **~r** [viʃto'rja*] *vt* to inspect

vistoso/a [viʃ'tozu/ɔza] *adj* eye-catching

visual [vi'zwaw] (*pl* -ais) *adj* visual; **~izar** [vizwali'za*] *vt* to visualize

vital [vi'taw] (*pl* -ais) *adj* vital; **~ício/a** [vita'lisju/a] *adj* for life

vitamina [vita'mina] *f* vitamin; (*para beber*) fruit crush

vitela [vi'tɛla] *f* calf; (*carne*) veal

vítima ['vitʃima] *f* victim

vitória [vi'tɔrja] *f* victory; **~-régia** (*pl* **~s-régias**) *f* giant water lily; **vitorioso/a** [vito'rjozu/ɔza] *adj* victorious

vítreo/a ['vitrju/a] *adj* (*feito de vidro*) glass *atr*; (*com o aspecto de vidro*) glassy; (*água*) clear

vitrina [vi'trina] *f* = **vitrine**

vitrine [vi'trini] *f* shop window; (*armário*) display case

viúvo/a ['vjuvu/a] *m/f* widower/widow

viva ['viva] *m* cheer; **~!** hurray!

vivamente [viva'mẽtʃi] *adv* animatedly; (*descrever, sentir*) vividly; (*protestar*) loudly

vivaz [vi'vajʒ] *adj* lively

viveiro [vi'vejru] *m* nursery

vivência [vi'vẽsja] *f* existence; (*experiência*) experience

vivenda [vi'vẽda] *f* (*casa*) residence

vivente [vi'vẽtʃi] *adj* living

viver [vi've*] *vt, vi* to live ♦ *m* life; **~ de** to live on

víveres ['vivereʃ] *mpl* provisions

vívido/a ['vividu/a] *adj* vivid

vivissecção [vivisek'sãw] *f* vivisection

vivo/a ['vivu/a] *adj* living; (*esperto*) clever; (*cor*) bright; (*criança, debate*) lively ♦ *m*: **os ~s** the living

vizinhança [vizi'ɲãsa] *f* neighbourhood (*BRIT*), neighborhood (*US*)

vizinho/a [vi'ziɲu/a] *adj* neighbouring (*BRIT*), neighboring (*US*); (*perto*) nearby ♦ *m/f* neighbour (*BRIT*), neighbor (*US*)

voar [vo'a*] *vi* to fly; (*explodir*) to blow up, explode

vocabulário [vokabu'larju] *m* vocabulary

vocábulo [vo'kabulu] *m* word

vocação [voka'sãw] (*pl* -ões) *f* vocation; **vocacional** [vokasjo'naw] (*pl* -ais) *adj* vocational; (*orientação*) careers *atr*

vocal [vo'kaw] (*pl* -ais) *adj* vocal

você(s) [vo'se(ʃ)] *pron* (*pl*) you

vodca ['vɔdʒka] *f* vodka

voga ['vɔga] *f* (*NÁUT*) rowing; (*moda*) fashion

vogal [vo'gaw] (*pl* -ais) *f* (*LING*) vowel

voile ['vwali] *m*: **cortina de ~** net curtain

vol. *abr* (= *volume*) vol

volante [vo'lãtʃi] *m* steering wheel

volátil [vo'latʃiw] (*pl* -eis) *adj* volatile

vôlei ['volej] *m* volleyball

voleibol [volej'bow] *m* = **vôlei**

volt ['vɔwtʃi] (*pl* -s) *m* volt

volta ['vɔwta] *f* turn; (*regresso*) return; (*curva*) bend, curve; (*circuito*) lap; (*resposta*) retort; **dar uma ~** (*a pé*) to go for a walk; (*de carro*) to go for a drive; **estar de ~** to be back; **na ~ do correio** by return (post); **por ~ de** about, around; **à** *ou* **em ~ de** around; **na ~** (*no caminho de ~*) on the way back

voltagem [vow'taʒẽ] *f* voltage

voltar [vow'ta*] *vt* to turn ♦ *vi* to return, go (*ou* come) back; **~-se** *vr* to turn round; **~ a fazer** to do again; **~ a si** to come to; **~-se para** to turn to; **~-se contra** to turn against

volume [vo'lumi] *m* volume; (*pacote*) package; **volumoso/a** [volu'mozu/ɔza] *adj* bulky, big

voluntário/a [volũ'tarju/a] *adj* voluntary ♦ *m/f* volunteer

volúpia [vo'lupja] *f* pleasure, ecstasy

volúvel [vo'luvew] (*pl* -eis) *adj* fickle

volver [vow've*] *vt* to turn ♦ *vi* to go (*ou* come) back

vomitar [vomi'ta*] *vt, vi* to vomit; **vômito** ['vomitu] *m* (*ato*) vomiting; (*efeito*) vomit

vontade [võ'tadʒi] f will; (desejo) wish; **com ~** (com prazer) with pleasure; (com gana) with gusto; **estar com** ou **ter ~ de fazer** to feel like doing

vôo ['vou] (PT **voo**) m flight; **levantar ~** to take off; **~ livre** (ESPORTE) hang-gliding

voraz [vo'rajʒ] adj voracious

vos [vuʃ] pron you; (indireto) to you

vós [vɔʃ] pron you

vosso/a ['vɔsu/a] adj your ♦ pron: **(o) ~** yours

votação [vota'sãw] (pl **-ões**) f vote, ballot; (ato) voting

votante [vo'tãtʃi] m/f voter

votar [vo'ta*] vt (eleger) to vote for; (aprovar) to pass; (submeter a votação) to vote on ♦ vi to vote; **voto** ['vɔtu] m vote; (promessa) vow; **votos** mpl (desejos) wishes

vou [vo] vb V **ir**

vovó [vo'vɔ] f grandma

vovô [vo'vo] m grandad

voz [vɔʒ] f voice; (clamor) cry; **a meia ~** in a whisper; **de viva ~** orally; **ter ~ ativa** to have a say; **em ~ alta/baixa** aloud/in a low voice; **~ de comando** command; **~erio** [voze'riu] m hullabaloo

vulcão [vuw'kãw] (pl **~s** ou **-ões**) m volcano

vulgar [vuw'ga*] adj common; (pej: pessoa etc) vulgar; **~idade** [vuwgari'dadʒi] f commonness; vulgarity; **~izar** [vuwgari'za*] vt to popularize; **~mente** [vuwgax'mẽtʃi] adv commonly, popularly

vulgo ['vuwgu] m common people pl ♦ adv commonly known as

vulnerável [vuwne'ravew] (pl **-eis**) adj vulnerable

vulto ['vuwtu] m figure; (volume) mass; (fig) importance; (pessoa importante) important person; **~so/a** [vuw'tozu/ɔza] adj bulky; (importante) important; (quantia) considerable

W

walkie-talkie [wɔki'tɔki] (pl **~s**) m walkie-talkie

watt ['wɔtʃi] (pl **~s**) m watt

Web ['wɛbi] f: **a ~** the (World Wide) Web

X

xadrez [ʃa'dreʒ] m chess; (tabuleiro) chessboard; (tecido) checked cloth

xale ['ʃali] m shawl

xampu [ʃã'pu] m shampoo

xarope [ʃa'rɔpi] m syrup; (para a tosse) cough syrup

xelim [ʃe'lĩ] (pl **-ns**) m shilling

xeque ['ʃɛki] m (soberano) sheikh; **pôr em ~** (fig) to call into question; **~-mate** (pl **~s-mate**) m checkmate

xerife [ʃe'rifi] m sheriff

xerocar [ʃero'ka*] vt to photocopy, Xerox ®

xerocópia [ʃero'kɔpja] f photocopy

xerocopiar [ʃeroko'pja*] vt = **xerocar**

xerox [ʃe'rɔks] ® m (cópia) photocopy; (máquina) photocopier

xícara ['ʃikara] (BR) f cup

xilofone [ʃilo'fɔni] m xylophone

xilografia [ʃilogra'fia] f woodcut

xingar [ʃĩ'ga*] vt to swear at ♦ vi to swear

xinxim [ʃĩ'ʃĩ] m (tb: **~ de galinha**) chicken ragout

Z

zagueiro [za'gejru] m (FUTEBOL) full-back

Zâmbia ['zãbja] f Zambia

zanga ['zãga] f anger; (irritação) annoyance; **~do/a** [zã'gadu/a] adj angry; annoyed; (irritadiço) bad-tempered

zangão [zã'gãw] (pl **~s** ou **-ões**) m (inseto) drone

zangar [zã'ga*] vt to annoy, irritate ♦ vi to get angry; **~-se** vr (aborrecer-se) to get annoyed; **~-se com** to get cross with

zangões [zã'gõjʃ] mpl de **zangão**

zarpar [zax'pa*] vi (navio) to set sail; (irse) to set off; (fugir) to run away

zebra ['zebra] f zebra

zelador(a) [zela'do*(a)] m/f caretaker

zelar [ze'la*] vt, vi: **~ (por)** to look after

zelo ['zelu] m devotion, zeal; **~so/a** [ze'lozu/ɔza] adj zealous; (diligente) hard-working

zerar [ze'ra*] vt (conta, inflação) to reduce to zero; (déficit) to pay off, wipe out

zero ['zɛru] m zero; (ESPORTE) nil; **~-quilômetro** adj inv brand new

ziguezague [zigi'zagi] m zigzag; **~ar** [zigiza'gja*] vi to zigzag

Zimbábue [zĩ'babwi] m: **o ~** Zimbabwe

zinco ['zĩku] m zinc

-zinho/a [-'ziɲu/a] sufixo little; **florzinha** little flower

zipe ['zipi] m = **zíper**

zíper ['zipe*] m zip (BRIT), zipper (US)

zodíaco [zo'dʒiaku] m zodiac

zoeira ['zwejra] f din

zombar [zõ'ba*] vi to mock; **~ de** to make fun of; **~ia** [zõba'ria] f mockery, ridicule

zona ['zɔna] f area; (de cidade) district; (GEO) zone; (col: local de meretrício) red-light district; (: confusão) mess; (: tumulto) free-for-all; **~ eleitoral** electoral district, constituency

zonzo/a ['zõzu/a] adj dizzy

zôo ['zou] m zoo

zoologia [zolo'ʒia] *f* zoology; **zoológico/a** [zo'lɔʒikʊ/a] *adj* zoological; **jardim zoológico** zoo

zuarte ['zwaxtʃi] *m* denim

zumbido [zũ'bidu] *m* buzz(ing); (*de tráfego*) hum

zumbir [zũ'bi*] *vi* to buzz; (*ouvido*) to ring ♦ *m* buzzing; ringing

zunido [zu'nidu] *m* (*de vento*) whistling; (*de inseto*) buzz

zunzum [zũ'zũ] *m* buzz(ing)

zurrar [zu'xa*] *vi* to bray

A

A [eɪ] *n* (*MUS*) lá *m*

KEYWORD
---

a [eɪ,ə] *indef art* (*before vowel or silent h:* an) **1** um(a); ~ **book/girl** um livro/ uma menina; **an apple** uma maçã; **she's** ~ **doctor** ela é médica
2 (*instead of the number "one"*) um(a); ~ **year ago** há um ano, um ano atrás; ~ **hundred/thousand** *etc* **pounds** cem/ mil *etc* libras
3 (*in expressing ratios, prices etc*): **3** ~ **day/week** 3 por dia/semana; **10 km an hour** 10 km por hora; **30p** ~ **kilo** 30p o quilo

---

AA *n abbr* (= *Alcoholics Anonymous*) AA *m*; (*BRIT* = *Automobile Association*) ≈ TCB *m* (*BR*), ≈ ACP *m* (*PT*)
AAA *n abbr* (= *American Automobile Association*) ≈ TCB *m* (*BR*), ≈ ACP *m* (*PT*)
aback [əˈbæk] *adv*: **to be taken** ~ ficar surpreendido, sobressaltar-se
abandon [əˈbændən] *vt* abandonar ♦ *n*: **with** ~ com desenfreio
abashed [əˈbæʃt] *adj* envergonhado
abate [əˈbeɪt] *vi* acalmar-se
abattoir [ˈæbətwɑː*] (*BRIT*) *n* matadouro
abbey [ˈæbɪ] *n* abadia, mosteiro
abbot [ˈæbət] *n* abade *m*
abbreviate [əˈbriːvɪeɪt] *vt* (*essay*) resumir; (*word*) abreviar; **abbreviation** *n* abreviatura
abdicate [ˈæbdɪkeɪt] *vt* abdicar, renunciar a ♦ *vi* abdicar, renunciar ao trono
abdomen [ˈæbdəmən] *n* abdómen *m*
abduct [æbˈdʌkt] *vt* seqüestrar
abet [əˈbet] *vt see* **aid**
abeyance [əˈbeɪəns] *n*: **in** ~ (*law*) em desuso; (*matter*) suspenso
abhor [əbˈhɔː*] *vt* detestar, odiar
abide [əˈbaɪd] *vt*: **I can't** ~ **him** eu não o suporto; ~ **by** *vt fus* ater-se a
ability [əˈbɪlɪtɪ] *n* habilidade *f*, capacidade *f*; (*talent*) talento; (*skill*) perícia
abject [ˈæbdʒekt] *adj* (*poverty*) miserável; (*apology*) humilde
ablaze [əˈbleɪz] *adj* em chamas
able [ˈeɪbl] *adj* capaz; (*skilled*) hábil, competente; **to be** ~ **to do sth** poder fazer algo; ~**-bodied** *adj* são/sã; **ably** *adv* habilmente
abnormal [æbˈnɔːməl] *adj* anormal
aboard [əˈbɔːd] *adv* a bordo ♦ *prep* a bordo de
abode [əˈbəud] *n* (*LAW*): **of no fixed** ~ sem domicílio fixo

abolish [əˈbɔlɪʃ] *vt* abolir
abominable [əˈbɔmɪnəbl] *adj* abominável, detestável
aborigine [æbəˈrɪdʒɪnɪ] *n* aborígene *m/f*
abort [əˈbɔːt] *vt* (*MED*) abortar; (*plan*) cancelar; ~**ion** *n* aborto; **to have an** ~**ion** fazer um aborto, abortar; ~**ive** *adj* fracassado
abound [əˈbaund] *vi*: **to** ~ (**in** *or* **with**) abundar (em)

KEYWORD
---

about [əˈbaut] *adv* **1** (*approximately*) aproximadamente; **it takes** ~ **10 hours** leva mais ou menos 10 horas; **it's just** ~ **finished** está quase terminado
2 (*referring to place*) por toda parte, por todo lado; **to run/walk** *etc* ~ correr/ andar *etc* por todos os lados
3: **to be** ~ **to do sth** estar a ponto de fazer algo
♦ *prep* **1** (*relating to*) acerca de, sobre; **what is it** ~? do que se trata?, é sobre o quê?; **what** *or* **how** ~ **doing this?** que tal se fizermos isso?
2 (*place*) em redor de, por

---

about face *n* (*MIL*) meia-volta; (*fig*) reviravolta
about turn *n* = **about face**
above [əˈbʌv] *adv* em *or* por cima, acima; (*greater*) acima ♦ *prep* acima de, por cima de; (*greater than:* in rank) acima de; (: *in number*) mais de; ~ **all** sobretudo; ~**board** *adj* legítimo, limpo
abrasive [əˈbreɪzɪv] *adj* abrasivo; (*fig*) cáustico, mordaz
abreast [əˈbrest] *adv* lado a lado; **to keep** ~ **of** (*fig*) estar a par de
abridge [əˈbrɪdʒ] *vt* resumir, abreviar
abroad [əˈbrɔːd] *adv* (*be*) no estrangeiro; (*go*) ao estrangeiro
abrupt [əˈbrʌpt] *adj* (*sudden*) brusco; (*curt*) ríspido; ~**ly** *adv* bruscamente
abscess [ˈæbsɪs] *n* abscesso (*BR*), abcesso (*PT*)
abscond [əbˈskɔnd] *vi*: **to** ~ **with** sumir com; **to** ~ **from** fugir de
absence [ˈæbsəns] *n* ausência
absent [ˈæbsənt] *adj* ausente; ~**ee** *n* ausente *m/f*; ~**-minded** *adj* distraído
absolute [ˈæbsəluːt] *adj* absoluto; ~**ly** *adv* absolutamente
absolve [əbˈzɔlv] *vt*: **to** ~ **sb** (**from**) (*sin etc*) absolver alguém (de); (*blame*)

isentar alguém (de)

absorb [əb'zɔːb] *vt* absorver; (*business*) incorporar; (*changes*) assimilar; (*information*) digerir; **~ent cotton** (*US*) *n* algodão *m* hidrófilo; **~ing** *adj* absorvente

abstain [əb'steɪn] *vi*: **to ~ (from)** abster-se (de)

abstemious [əb'stiːmɪəs] *adj* abstinente

abstract ['æbstrækt] *adj* abstrato

absurd [əb'sɜːd] *adj* absurdo

abuse [*n* ə'bjuːs, *vt* ə'bjuːz] *n* (*insults*) insultos *mpl*; (*ill-treatment*) maus-tratos *mpl*; (*misuse*) abuso ♦ *vt* insultar; maltratar; abusar de; **abusive** *adj* ofensivo

abysmal [ə'bɪzməl] *adj* (*ignorance*) profundo, total; (*failure*) péssimo

abyss [ə'bɪs] *n* abismo

AC *abbr* (= *alternating current*) CA

academic [ækə'demɪk] *adj* acadêmico; (*pej*: *issue*) teórico ♦ *n* universitário/a; **~ year** *n* ano letivo

academy [ə'kædəmɪ] *n* (*learned body*) academia; **~ of music** conservatório

accelerate [æk'seləreɪt] *vt*, *vi* acelerar; **accelerator** *n* acelerador *m*

accent ['æksənt] *n* (*written*) acento; (*pronunciation*) sotaque *m*; (*fig*: *emphasis*) ênfase *f*

accept [ək'sept] *vt* aceitar; (*responsibility*) assumir; **~able** *adj* (*offer*) bem-vindo; (*risk*) aceitável; **~ance** *n* aceitação *f*

access ['ækses] *n* acesso; **~ible** *adj* acessível; (*available*) disponível

accessory [æk'sesərɪ] *n* acessório *m*; (*LAW*): **~ to** cúmplice *m/f* de

accident ['æksɪdənt] *n* acidente *m*; (*chance*) casualidade *f*; **by ~** (*unintentionally*) sem querer; (*by coincidence*) por acaso; **~al** *adj* acidental; **~ally** *adv* sem querer; **~-prone** *adj* com tendência para sofrer *or* causar acidente, desastrado

acclaim [ə'kleɪm] *n* aclamação *f*

accolade ['ækəleɪd] *n* louvor *m*, honra

accommodate [ə'kɔmədeɪt] *vt* alojar; (*subj*: *car*, *hotel*, *etc*) acomodar; (*oblige*, *help*) comprazer a; **accommodating** *adj* serviçal; **accommodation** *n* alojamento; **accommodations** (*US*) *npl* = **accommodation**

accompany [ə'kʌmpənɪ] *vt* acompanhar

accomplice [ə'kʌmplɪs] *n* cúmplice *m/f*

accomplish [ə'kʌmplɪʃ] *vt* (*task*) concluir; (*goal*) alcançar; **~ed** *adj* (*person*) talentoso; (*performance*) brilhante; **~ment** *n* realização *f*

accord [ə'kɔːd] *n* tratado ♦ *vt* conceder; **of his own ~** por sua iniciativa; **~ance** *n*: **in ~ance with** de acordo com; **~ing**: **~ing to** *prep* segundo, conforme; **~ingly** *adv* por conseguinte; (*appropriately*) do modo devido

accordion [ə'kɔːdɪən] *n* acordeão *m*

accost [ə'kɔst] *vt* abordar

account [ə'kaunt] *n* conta; (*report*) relato; **~s** *npl* (*books*, *department*) contabilidade

f; **of no ~** sem importância; **on ~** por conta; **on no ~** de modo nenhum; **on ~ of** por causa de; **to take into ~**, **take ~ of** levar em conta; **~ for** *vt fus* (*explain*) explicar; (*represent*) representar; **~able** *adj*: **~able (to)** responsável (por); **~ancy** *n* contabilidade *f*; **~ant** *n* contador(a) *m/f* (*BR*), contabilista *m/f* (*PT*); **~ number** *n* número de conta

accredited [ə'kredɪtɪd] *adj* autorizado

accrued interest [ə'kruːd-] *n* juros *mpl* acumulados

accumulate [ə'kjuːmjuleɪt] *vt* acumular ♦ *vi* acumular-se

accuracy ['ækjurəsɪ] *n* exatidão *f*, precisão *f*

accurate ['ækjurɪt] *adj* (*description*) correto; (*person*, *device*) preciso; **~ly** *adv* com precisão

accusation [ækjuː'zeɪʃən] *n* (*act*) incriminação *f*; (*instance*) acusação *f*

accuse [ə'kjuːz] *vt* acusar; **~d** *n*: **the ~d** o/a acusado/a

accustom [ə'kʌstəm] *vt* acostumar; **~ed** *adj*: **~ed to** acostumado a

ace [eɪs] *n* ás *m*

ache [eɪk] *n* dor *f* ♦ *vi* (*yearn*): **to ~ to do sth** ansiar por fazer algo; **my head ~s** dói-me a cabeça

achieve [ə'tʃiːv] *vt* alcançar; (*victory*, *success*) obter; **~ment** *n* realização *f*; (*success*) proeza

acid ['æsɪd] *adj* ácido; (*taste*) azedo ♦ *n* ácido; **~ rain** *n* chuva ácida

acknowledge [ək'nɔlɪdʒ] *vt* (*fact*) reconhecer; (*also*: **~ receipt of**) acusar o recebimento de (*BR*) *or* a recepção de (*PT*); **~ment** *n* notificação *f* de recebimento

acne ['æknɪ] *n* acne *f*

acorn ['eɪkɔːn] *n* bolota

acoustic [ə'kuːstɪk] *adj* acústico; **~s** *n*, *npl* acústica

acquaint [ə'kweɪnt] *vt*: **to ~ sb with sth** pôr alguém ao corrente de algo; **to be ~ed with** conhecer; **~ance** *n* conhecimento; (*person*) conhecido/a

acquiesce [ækwɪ'es] *vi*: **to ~ (to)** condescender (a); (*request*) ceder (a)

acquire [ə'kwaɪə*] *vt* adquirir; **acquisition** *n* aquisição *f*

acquit [ə'kwɪt] *vt* absolver; **to ~ o.s. well** desempenhar-se bem; **~tal** *n* absolvição *f*

acre ['eɪkə*] *n* acre *m* (= 4047m²)

acrid ['ækrɪd] *adj* acre

acrimonious [ækrɪ'məunɪəs] *adj* (*remark*) mordaz; (*argument*) acrimonioso

acrobat ['ækrəbæt] *n* acrobata *m/f*

across [ə'krɔs] *prep* (*on the other side of*) no outro lado de; (*crosswise*) através de ♦ *adv*: **to go** (*or* **walk**) **~** atravessar; **the lake is 12km ~** o lago tem 12km de largura; **~ from** em frente de

acrylic [ə'krɪlɪk] *adj* acrílico ♦ *n* acrílico

act [ækt] n ação f; (THEATRE) ato; (in show) número; (LAW) lei f ♦ vi tomar ação; (behave, have effect, THEATRE) agir; (pretend) fingir ♦ vt (part) representar; **in the ~** of no ato de; **to ~ as** servir de; **~ing** adj interino ♦ n: **to do some ~ing** fazer teatro

action ['ækʃən] n ação f; (MIL) batalha, combate m; (LAW) ação judicial; **out of ~** (person) fora de combate; (thing) com defeito; **to take ~** tomar atitude; **~ replay** n (TV) replay m

activate ['æktɪveɪt] vt acionar

active ['æktɪv] adj ativo; (volcano) em atividade; **~ly** adv ativamente; **activist** n ativista m/f, militante m/f; **activity** n atividade f

actor ['æktə*] n ator m

actress ['æktrɪs] n atriz f

actual ['æktjuəl] adj real; (emphatic use) em si; **~ly** adv realmente; (in fact) na verdade; (even) mesmo

acumen ['ækjumən] n perspicácia

acute [ə'kjuːt] adj agudo; (person) perspicaz

ad [æd] n abbr = **advertisement**

A.D. adv abbr (= Anno Domini) d.C.

adamant ['ædəmənt] adj inflexível

adapt [ə'dæpt] vt adaptar ♦ vi: **to ~ (to)** adaptar-se (a); **~able** adj (device) ajustável; (person) adaptável; **~er** n (ELEC) adaptador m; **~or** = **adapter**

add [æd] vt acrescentar; (figures: also: ~ up) somar ♦ vi: **to ~ to** aumentar

adder ['ædə*] n víbora

addict ['ædɪkt] n viciado/a; **drug ~** toxicômano/a; **~ed** adj: **to be ~ed to** ser viciado em; (fig) ser fanático por; **~ion** n dependência; **~ive** adj que causa dependência

addition [ə'dɪʃən] n adição f; (thing added) acréscimo; **in ~** além disso; **in ~ to** além de; **~al** adj adicional

additive ['ædɪtɪv] n aditivo

address [ə'drɛs] n endereço; (speech) discurso ♦ vt (letter) endereçar; (speak to) dirigir-se a, dirigir a palavra a; **to ~ (o.s. to)** enfocar

adept ['ædɛpt] adj: **~ at** hábil or competente em

adequate ['ædɪkwɪt] adj (enough) suficiente; (satisfactory) satisfatório

adhere [əd'hɪə*] vi: **to ~ to** aderir a; (abide by) ater-se a

adhesive [əd'hiːzɪv] n adesivo; **~ tape** n (BRIT) durex ® m, fita adesiva; (US) esparadrapo

adjective ['ædʒɛktɪv] n adjetivo

adjoining [ə'dʒɔɪnɪŋ] adj adjacente

adjourn [ə'dʒəːn] vt (session) suspender ♦ vi ser suspenso

adjust [ə'dʒʌst] vt (change) ajustar; (clothes) arrumar; (machine) regular ♦ vi: **to ~ (to)** adaptar-se (a); **~ment** n ajuste m; (of engine) regulagem f; (of prices, wages) reajuste m; (of person) adaptação f

ad-lib [-lɪb] vi improvisar ♦ adv: **ad lib** à vontade

administer [əd'mɪnɪstə*] vt administrar; (justice) aplicar; (drug) ministrar; **administration** n administração f; (management) gerência; (government) governo; **administrative** adj administrativo

admiral ['ædmərəl] n almirante m; **A~ty** (BRIT) n (also: **A~ty Board**) Ministério da Marinha, Almirantado

admire [əd'maɪə*] vt (respect) respeitar; (appreciate) admirar

admission [əd'mɪʃən] n (admittance) entrada; (fee) ingresso; (confession) confissão f

admit [əd'mɪt] vt admitir; (accept) aceitar; (confess) confessar; **~ to** vt fus confessar; **~tance** n entrada; **~tedly** adv evidentemente

admonish [əd'mɔnɪʃ] vt admoestar

ad nauseam [æd'nɔːsɪæm] adv sem parar

ado [ə'duː] n: **without (any) more ~** sem mais cerimônias

adolescent [ædə'lɛsnt] adj, n adolescente m/f

adopt [ə'dɔpt] vt adotar; **~ed** adj adotivo; **~ion** n adoção f; **~ive** adj adotivo

adore [ə'dɔː*] vt adorar

Adriatic (Sea) [eɪdrɪ'ætɪk-] n (mar m) Adriático

adrift [ə'drɪft] adv à deriva

adult ['ædʌlt] n adulto/a ♦ adj adulto; (literature, education) para adultos

adultery [ə'dʌltərɪ] n adultério

advance [əd'vɑːns] n avanço; (money) adiantamento ♦ adj antecipado ♦ vt (money) adiantar ♦ vi (move forward) avançar; (progress) progredir; **in ~** com antecedência; **to make ~s to sb** (gen) fazer propostas a alguém; **~d** adj (studies, country) adiantado

advantage [əd'vɑːntɪdʒ] n (gen, TENNIS) vantagem f; (supremacy) supremacia; **to take ~ of** aproveitar-se de, levar vantagem de

advent ['ædvənt] n advento; **A~** (REL) Advento

adventure [əd'vɛntʃə*] n façanha; (excitement in life) aventura

adverb ['ædvəːb] n advérbio

adverse ['ædvəːs] adj (effect) contrário; (weather, publicity) desfavorável

advert ['ædvəːt] n abbr = **advertisement**

advertise ['ædvətaɪz] vi anunciar ♦ vt (event, job) anunciar; (product) fazer a propaganda de; **to ~ for** (staff) procurar; **~ment** n (classified) anúncio; (display, TV) propaganda, anúncio; **~r** n anunciante m/f; **advertising** n publicidade f

advice [əd'vaɪs] n conselhos mpl; (notifi-

cation) aviso; **piece of ~** conselho; **to take legal ~** consultar um advogado

advise [əd'vaɪz] *vt* aconselhar; (*inform*): **to ~ sb of sth** avisar alguém de algo; **to ~ sb against sth/doing sth** desaconselhar algo a alguém/ aconselhar alguém a não fazer algo; **~dly** *adv* de propósito; **~r** *or* **advisor** *n* conselheiro/a; (*consultant*) consultor(a) *m/f*; **advisory** *adj* consultivo; **in an advisory capacity** na qualidade de assessor *or* consultor

advocate [*vt* 'ædvəkeɪt, *n* 'ædvəkɪt] *vt* defender; (*recommend*) advogar ♦ *n* advogado/a; (*supporter*) defensor(a) *m/f*

Aegean [iː'dʒiːən] *n*: **the ~ (Sea)** o (mar) Egeu

aerial ['ɛərɪəl] *n* antena ♦ *adj* aéreo

aerobics [ɛə'rəubɪks] *n* ginástica

aeroplane ['ɛərəpleɪn] (*BRIT*) *n* avião *m*

aerosol ['ɛərəsɒl] *n* aerossol *m*

aesthetic [iːs'θɛtɪk] *adj* estético

afar [ə'fɑː'] *adv*: **from ~** de longe

affair [ə'fɛə'] *n* (*matter*) assunto; (*business*) negócio; (*question*) questão *f*; (*also*: **love ~**) caso

affect [ə'fɛkt] *vt* afetar; (*move*) comover; **~ed** *adj* afetado

affection [ə'fɛkʃən] *n* afeto, afeição *f*; **~ate** *adj* afetuoso

affiliated [ə'fɪlɪeɪtd] *adj*: **~ (to)** afiliado (a); **~ company** filial *f*

affix [ə'fɪks] *vt* (*stamp*) colar

afflict [ə'flɪkt] *vt* afligir

affluence ['æfluəns] *n* riqueza; **affluent** *adj* rico; **the affluent society** a sociedade de abundância

afford [ə'fɔːd] *vt* (*provide*) fornecer; (*goods etc*) ter dinheiro suficiente para; (*permit o.s.*): **I can't ~ the time/to take that risk** não tenho tempo/não posso correr esse risco

affront [ə'frʌnt] *n* ofensa

afield [ə'fiːld] *adv*: **far ~** muito longe

afloat [ə'fləut] *adv* flutuando

afoot [ə'fut] *adv*: **there is something ~** está acontecendo algo

afraid [ə'freɪd] *adj* assustado; **to be ~ of/to** ter medo de; **I am ~ that** lamento que; **I'm ~ so/not** receio que sim/não

afresh [ə'frɛʃ] *adv* de novo

Africa ['æfrɪkə] *n* África; **~n** *adj*, *n* africano/a

aft [ɑːft] *adv* a ré

after ['ɑːftə'] *prep* depois de ♦ *adv* depois ♦ *conj* depois que; **a quarter ~ two** (*US*) duas e quinze; **what/ who are you ~?** o que você quer?/ quem procura?; **~ having done** tendo feito; **he was named ~ his grandfather** ele recebeu o nome do avô; **to ask ~ sb** perguntar por alguém; **~ all** afinal (de contas); **~ you!** passe primeiro!; **~-effects** *npl* efeitos *mpl* secundários;

~math *n* conseqüências *fpl*; **~noon** *n* tarde *f*; **~s** (*inf*) *n* sobremesa; **~-sales service** (*BRIT*) *n* serviço pós-vendas; **~-shave (lotion)** *n* loção *f* após-barba; **~thought** *n* reflexão *f* posterior *or* tardia; **~wards** *adv* depois

again [ə'gɛn] *adv* (*once more*) outra vez; (*repeatedly*) de novo; **to do sth ~** voltar a fazer algo; **not ... ~!** ... de novo!; **~ and ~** repetidas vezes

against [ə'gɛnst] *prep* contra; (*compared to*) em contraste com

age [eɪdʒ] *n* idade *f*; (*period*) época ♦ *vt*, *vi* envelhecer; **he's 20 years of ~** ele tem 20 anos de idade; **to come of ~** atingir a maioridade; **it's been ~s since I saw him** faz muito tempo que eu não o vejo; **~d¹** [eɪdʒd] *adj*: **~d 10** de 10 anos de idade; **~d²** ['eɪdʒɪd] *adj* idoso ♦ *npl*: **the ~d** os idosos; **~ group** *n* faixa etária; **~ limit** *n* idade *f* mínima/máxima

agency ['eɪdʒənsɪ] *n* agência; (*government body*) órgão *m*

agenda [ə'dʒɛndə] *n* ordem *f* do dia

agent ['eɪdʒənt] *n* agente *m/f*

aggravate ['ægrəveɪt] *vt* agravar; (*annoy*) irritar

aggregate ['ægrɪgət] *n* conjunto

aggressive [ə'grɛsɪv] *adj* agressivo

aggrieved [ə'griːvd] *adj* aflito

aghast [ə'gɑːst] *adj* horrorizado

agitate ['ædʒɪteɪt] *vt* agitar ♦ *vi*: **to ~ for** fazer agitação a favor de

AGM *n abbr* (= *annual general meeting*) AGO *f*

ago [ə'gəu] *adv*: **2 days ~** há 2 dias (atrás); **not long ~** há pouco tempo; **how long ~?** há quanto tempo?

agog [ə'gɒg] *adj* (*eager*) ávido; (*excited*) entusiasmado

agonizing ['ægənaɪzɪŋ] *adj* (*pain*) agudo; (*wait*) angustiante

agony ['ægənɪ] *n* (*pain*) dor *f*; **to be in ~** sofrer dores terríveis

agree [ə'griː] *vt* combinar ♦ *vi* (*correspond*) corresponder; **to ~ (with)** concordar (com); **to ~ to sth/to do sth** consentir algo/aceitar fazer algo; **to ~ that** concordar *or* admitir que; **~able** *adj* agradável; (*willing*) disposto; **~d** *adj* combinado; **~ment** *n* acordo; (*COMM*) contrato; **in ~ment** de acordo

agricultural [ægrɪ'kʌltʃərəl] *adj* (*of crops*) agrícola; (*of crops and cattle*) agropecuário

agriculture ['ægrɪkʌltʃə'] *n* (*of crops*) agricultura; (*of crops and cattle*) agropecuária

aground [ə'graund] *adv*: **to run ~** encalhar

ahead [ə'hɛd] *adv* adiante; **go right** *or* **straight ~** siga em frente; **go ~!** (*fig*) vá em frente!; **~ of** na frente de

aid [eɪd] *n* ajuda; (*device*) aparelho ♦ *vt*

ajudar; **in ~ of** em beneficio de; **to ~ and abet** (*LAW*) ser cúmplice de

aide [eɪd] *n* assessor(a) *m/f*

AIDS [eɪdz] *n abbr* (= *acquired immune deficiency syndrome*) AIDS *f* (*BR*), SIDA *f* (*PT*)

ailing ['eɪlɪŋ] *adj* enfermo

ailment ['eɪlmənt] *n* achaque *m*

aim [eɪm] *vt*: **to ~ sth (at)** apontar algo (para); (*remark*) dirigir algo (a) ♦ *vi* (*also*: **take ~**) apontar ♦ *n* (*skill*) pontaria; (*objective*) objetivo; **to ~ at** mirar; **to ~ to do** pretender fazer

ain't [eɪnt] (*inf*) = **am not; aren't; isn't**

air [eə*] *n* ar *m*; (*appearance*) aparência, aspeto; (*tune*) melodia ♦ *vt* arejar; (*grievances, ideas*) discutir ♦ *cpd* aéreo; **to throw sth into the ~** jogar algo para cima; **by ~** (*travel*) de avião; **on the ~** (*RADIO, TV*) no ar; **~bed** (*BRIT*) *n* colchão *m* de ar; **~borne** *adj* no ar; **~ conditioning** *n* ar condicionado; **~craft** *n inv* aeronave *f*; **~craft carrier** *n* porta-aviões *m inv*; **~field** *n* campo de aviação; **A~ Force** *n* Força Aérea, Aeronáutica; **~ freshener** *n* perfumador *m* de ar; **~gun** *n* espingarda de ar comprimido; **~ hostess** (*BRIT*) *n* aeromoça (*BR*), hospedeira (*PT*); **~ letter** (*BRIT*) *n* aerograma *m*; **~lift** *n* ponte aérea; **~line** *n* linha aérea; **~liner** *n* avião *m* de passageiros; **~mail** *n*: **by ~mail** por via aérea; **~plane** (*US*) *n* avião *m*; **~port** *n* aeroporto; **~ raid** *n* ataque *m* aéreo; **~sick** *adj*: **to be ~sick** enjoar (no avião); **~ terminal** *n* terminal *m* aéreo; **~tight** *adj* hermético; **~ traffic controller** *n* controlador(a) *m/f* de tráfego aéreo; **~y** *adj* (*room*) arejado; (*manner*) leviano

aisle [aɪl] *n* (*of church*) nave *f*; (*of theatre etc*) corredor *m*

ajar [ə'dʒɑː*] *adj* entreaberto

akin [ə'kɪn] *adj*: **~ to** parecido com

alacrity [ə'lækrɪtɪ] *n* alacridade *f*

alarm [ə'lɑːm] *n* alarme *m*; (*anxiety*) inquietação *f* ♦ *vt* alarmar; **~ call** *n* (*in hotel etc*) chamada para acordar alguém; **~ clock** *n* despertador *m*

alas [ə'læs] *excl* ai, ai de mim

albeit [ɔːl'biːɪt] *conj* embora

album ['ælbəm] *n* (*for stamps etc*) álbum *m*; (*record*) elepê *m*

alcohol ['ælkəhɔl] *n* álcool *m*; **~ic** *adj* alcoólico ♦ *n* alcoólatra *m/f*

ale [eɪl] *n* cerveja

alert [ə'ləːt] *adj* atento; (*to danger, opportunity*) alerta ♦ *n* alerta ♦ *vt* alertar; **to be on the ~** estar alerta; (*MIL*) ficar de prontidão

Algarve [æl'gɑːv] *m*: **the ~** o Algarve

algebra ['ældʒɪbrə] *n* álgebra

Algeria [æl'dʒɪərɪə] *n* Argélia

alias ['eɪlɪəs] *adv* também chamado ♦ *n* (*of criminal*) alcunha; (*of writer*) pseu-

dônimo

alibi ['ælɪbaɪ] *n* álibi *m*

alien ['eɪlɪən] *n* estrangeiro/a; (*from space*) alienígena *m/f* ♦ *adj*: **~ to** alheio a; **~ate** *vt* alienar

alight [ə'laɪt] *adj* em chamas; (*eyes*) aceso; (*expression*) intento ♦ *vi* (*passenger*) descer (de um veículo); (*bird*) pousar

align [ə'laɪn] *vt* alinhar

alike [ə'laɪk] *adj* semelhante ♦ *adv* similarmente, igualmente; **to look ~** parecer-se

alimony ['ælɪmənɪ] *n* (*payment*) pensão *f* alimenticia

alive [ə'laɪv] *adj* vivo; (*lively*) alegre

KEYWORD

all [ɔːl] *adj* (*sg*) todo/a; (*pl*) todos/as; **~ day/night** o dia inteiro/a noite inteira; **~ five came** todos os cinco vieram; **~ the books/food** todos os livros/toda a comida

♦ *pron* **1** tudo; **~ of us/the boys went** todos nós fomos/todos os meninos foram; **is that ~?** é só isso? (*in shop*) mais alguma coisa?

2 (*in phrases*): **above ~** sobretudo; **after ~** afinal (de contas); **at ~: not at ~** (*in answer to question*) em absoluto, absolutamente não; **I'm not at ~ tired** não estou nada cansado; **anything at ~ will do** qualquer coisa serve; **~ in ~** ao todo

♦ *adv* todo, completamente; **~ alone** completamente só; **it's not as hard as ~ that** não é tão dificil assim; **~ the more** ainda mais; **~ the better** tanto melhor, ainda mais; **~ but** quase; **the score is 2 ~** o escore é 2 a 2

allay [ə'leɪ] *vt* (*fears*) acalmar

all clear *n* sinal *m* de tudo limpo; (*after air raid*) sinal de fim de alerta aérea

allege [ə'ledʒ] *vt* alegar; **~dly** *adv* segundo dizem

allegiance [ə'liːdʒəns] *n* lealdade *f*

allergic [ə'ləːdʒɪk] *adj*: **~ (to)** alérgico (a)

alleviate [ə'liːvɪeɪt] *vt* (*pain*) aliviar; (*difficulty*) minorar

alley ['ælɪ] *n* viela

alliance [ə'laɪəns] *n* aliança

all-in (*BRIT*) *adj, adv* (*charge*) tudo incluído; **~ wrestling** (*BRIT*) *n* luta livre

all-night *adj* (*café*) aberto toda a noite; (*party*) dança toda a noite

allocate ['æləkeɪt] *vt* destinar

allot [ə'lɔt] *vt*: **to ~ to** designar para; **~ment** *n* partilha; (*garden*) lote *m*

all-out *adj* (*effort etc*) máximo ♦ *adv*: **all out** com toda a força

allow [ə'lau] *vt* permitir; (*claim, goal*) admitir; (*sum, time*) calcular; (*concede*): **to ~ that** reconhecer que; **to ~ sb to do** permitir a alguém fazer; **~ for** *vt* *fus* levar em conta; **~ance** *n* ajuda de custo; (*welfare payment*) pensão *f*, auxílio; (*TAX*) abatimento; (*pocket money*) mesada; **to make ~ances for** levar em consideração

alloy ['æloɪ] *n* liga

all: ~ right *adv* (*well*) bem; (*correctly*) corretamente; (*as answer*) está bem!; **~- rounder** (*BRIT*) *n*: **to be a good ~- rounder** ser homem/mulher para tudo; **~-time** *adj* de todos os tempos

allude [ə'luːd] *vi*: **to ~ to** aludir a

alluring [ə'ljuərɪŋ] *adj* tentador(a)

ally [*n* 'ælaɪ, *vt* ə'laɪ] *n* aliado ♦ *vt*: **to ~ o.s. with** aliar-se com

almighty [ɔːl'maɪtɪ] *adj* onipotente; (*row etc*) a maior

almond ['ɑːmənd] *n* amêndoa

almost ['ɔːlməust] *adv* quase

alms [ɑːmz] *npl* esmolas *fpl*, esmola

aloft [ə'lɔft] *adv* em cima

alone [ə'ləun] *adj* só, sozinho; (*unaided*) sozinho ♦ *adv* só, somente, sozinho; **to leave sb ~** deixar alguém em paz; **to leave sth ~** não tocar em algo; **let ~** ... sem falar em ...

along [ə'lɔŋ] *prep* por, ao longo de ♦ *adv*: **is he coming ~?** ele vem conosco?; **he was hopping/limping ~** ele ia pulando/coxeando; **~ with** junto com; **all ~** o tempo tudo; **~side** *prep* ao lado de ♦ *adv* encostado

aloof [ə'luːf] *adj* afastado, altivo ♦ *adv*: **to stand ~** afastar-se

aloud [ə'laud] *adv* em voz alta

alphabet ['ælfəbɛt] *n* alfabeto

Alps [ælps] *npl*: **the ~** os Alpes

already [ɔːl'rɛdɪ] *adv* já

alright ['ɔːl'raɪt] (*BRIT*) *adv* = **all right**

Alsatian [æl'seɪʃən] (*BRIT*) *n* (*dog*) pastor *m* alemão

also ['ɔːlsəu] *adv* também; (*moreover*) além disso

altar ['ɔltə*] *n* altar *m*

alter ['ɔltə*] *vt* alterar ♦ *vi* modificar-se

alternate [*adj* ɔl'təːnɪt, *vi* 'ɔltəːneɪt] *adj* alternado; (*US*: *alternative*) alternativo ♦ *vi* alternar-se; **alternating** *adj*: **alternating current** corrente *f* alternada

alternative [ɔl'təːnətɪv] *adj* alternativo ♦ *n* alternativa; **~ly** *adv*: **~ly one could** ... por outro lado se podia ...

alternator ['ɔltəːneɪtə*] *n* (*AUT*) alternador *m*

although [ɔːl'ðəu] *conj* embora; (*given that*) se bem que

altitude ['æltɪtjuːd] *n* altitude *f*

alto ['æltəu] *n* (*female*) contralto *f*; (*male*) alto

altogether [ɔːltə'gɛðə*] *adv* totalmente; (*on the whole*) no total

aluminium [ælju'mɪnɪəm] (*US* **aluminum**) *n* alumínio

always ['ɔːlweɪz] *adv* sempre

Alzheimer's (disease) ['æltshaɪməz] *n*

doença de Alzheimer

am [æm] *vb see* **be**

a.m. *adv abbr* (= *ante meridiem*) da manhã

amalgamate [ə'mælgəmeɪt] *vi* amalgamar-se ♦ *vt* amalgamar

amass [ə'mæs] *vt* acumular

amateur ['æmətə*] *adj*, *n* amador(a) *m/f*; **~ish** *adj* amador(a)

amaze [ə'meɪz] *vt* pasmar; **to be ~d (at)** espantar-se (de *or* com); **~ment** *n* pasmo, espanto; **amazing** *adj* surpreendente; (*fantastic*) fantástico

Amazon ['æməzən] *n* Amazonas *m*

ambassador [æm'bæsədə*] *n* embaixador/embaixatriz *m/f*

amber ['æmbə*] *n* âmbar *m*; **at ~** (*BRIT*: *AUT*) em amarelo

ambiguous [æm'bɪgjuəs] *adj* ambíguo

ambition [æm'bɪʃən] *n* ambição *f*; **ambitious** *adj* ambicioso

amble ['æmbl] *vi* (*also*: **~ along**) andar a furta-passo

ambulance ['æmbjuləns] *n* ambulância

ambush ['æmbuʃ] *n* emboscada ♦ *vt* emboscar

amen ['ɑː'mɛn] *excl* amém

amenable [ə'miːnəbl] *adj*: **~ to** (*advice etc*) receptivo a

amend [ə'mɛnd] *vt* emendar; **to make ~s (for)** compensar; **~ment** *n* (*to text*) correção *f*

amenities [ə'miːnɪtɪz] *npl* atrações *fpl*, comodidades *fpl*

America [ə'mɛrɪkə] *n* (*continent*) América; (*USA*) Estados Unidos *mpl*; **~n** *adj* americano; norte-americano, estadunidense ♦ *n* americano/a; norte-americano/a

amiable ['eɪmɪəbl] *adj* amável

amicable ['æmɪkəbl] *adj* amigável

amid(st) [ə'mɪd(st)] *prep* em meio a

amiss [ə'mɪs] *adv*: **to take sth ~** levar algo a mal; **there's something ~** aí tem coisa

ammonia [ə'məunɪə] *n* amoníaco

ammunition [æmju'nɪʃən] *n* munição *f*

amok [ə'mɔk] *adv*: **to run ~** enlouquecer

among(st) [ə'mʌŋ(st)] *prep* entre, no meio de

amorous ['æmərəs] *adj* amoroso

amount [ə'maunt] *n* quantidade *f*; (*of money etc*) quantia ♦ *vi*: **to ~ to** (*total*) montar a; (*be same as*) equivaler a, significar

amp(ère) ['æmp(ɛə*)] *n* ampère *m*

ample ['æmpl] *adj* amplo; (*abundant*) abundante; (*enough*) suficiente

amplifier ['æmplɪfaɪə*] *n* amplificador *m*

amuck [ə'mʌk] *adv* = **amok**

amuse [ə'mjuːz] *vt* divertir; (*distract*) distrair; **~ment** *n* diversão *f*; (*pleasure*) divertimento; (*pastime*) passatempo; **~ment arcade** *n* fliperama *m*

an [æn, ən, n] *indef art see* **a**
anaemic [ə'niːmɪk] (*US* **anemic**) *adj* anêmico
anaesthetic [ænɪs'θɛtɪk] (*US* **anesthetic**) *n* anestésico
analog(ue) ['ænələg] *adj* analógico
analyse ['ænəlaɪz] (*US* **analyze**) *vt* analizar; **analysis** (*pl* **analyses**) *n* análise *f*; **analyst** *n* analista *m/f*; (*psychoanalyst*) psicanalista *m/f*
analyze ['ænəlaɪz] (*US*) *vt* = **analyse**
anarchist ['ænəkɪst] *n* anarquista *m/f*
anarchy ['ænəkɪ] *n* anarquia
anathema [ə'næθɪmə] *n*: **it is ~ to him** ele tem horror disso
anatomy [ə'nætəmɪ] *n* anatomia
ancestor ['ænsɪstə*] *n* antepassado
anchor ['æŋkə*] *n* âncora ♦ *vi* (*also*: **to drop ~**) ancorar, fundear ♦ *vt* (*fig*): **to ~ sth to** firmar algo em; **to weigh ~** levantar âncoras
anchovy ['æntʃəvɪ] *n* enchova
ancient ['eɪnʃənt] *adj* antigo; (*person, car*) velho
ancillary [æn'sɪlərɪ] *adj* auxiliar
and [ænd] *conj* e; **~ so on** e assim por diante; **try ~ come** tente vir; **he talked ~ talked** ele falou sem parar; **better ~ better** cada vez melhor
Andes ['ændiːz] *npl*: **the ~** os Andes
anemic [ə'niːmɪk] (*US*) *n* = **anaemic**
anesthetic [ænɪs'θɛtɪk] (*US*) *n* = **anaesthetic**
anew [ə'njuː] *adv* de novo
angel ['eɪndʒəl] *n* anjo
anger ['æŋgə*] *n* raiva
angina [æn'dʒaɪnə] *n* angina (de peito)
angle ['æŋgl] *n* ângulo; (*viewpoint*): **from their ~** do ponto de vista deles
Anglican ['æŋglɪkən] *adj, n* anglicano/a
angling ['æŋglɪŋ] *n* pesca à vara (*BR*) *or* à linha (*PT*)
Anglo- ['æŋgləu] *prefix* anglo-
Angola [æŋ'gəulə] *n* Angola (*no article*)
angrily ['æŋgrɪlɪ] *adv* com raiva
angry ['æŋgrɪ] *adj* zangado; **to be ~ with sb/at sth** estar zangado com alguém/algo; **to get ~** zangar-se
anguish ['æŋgwɪʃ] *n* (*physical*) dor *f*, sofrimento; (*mental*) angústia
animal ['ænɪməl] *n* animal *m*, bicho ♦ *adj* animal
animate ['ænɪmɪt] *adj* animado; **~d** *adj* animado
aniseed ['ænɪsiːd] *n* erva-doce *f*, anis *f*
ankle ['æŋkl] *n* tornozelo; **~ sock** *n* (meia) soquete *f*
annex [*n* 'ænɛks, *vt* æ'nɛks] *n* (*also*: *BRIT*: *annexe*: *building*) anexo ♦ *vt* anexar
annihilate [ə'naɪəleɪt] *vt* aniquilar
anniversary [ænɪ'vəːsərɪ] *n* aniversário
announce [ə'nauns] *vt* anunciar; **~ment** *n* anúncio; (*official*) comunicação *f*; (*in letter etc*) aviso; **~r** *n* (*RADIO, TV*) locutor(a) *m/f*

annoy [ə'nɔɪ] *vt* aborrecer; **don't get ~ed!** não se aborreça!; **~ance** *n* aborrecimento; **~ing** *adj* irritante
annual ['ænjuəl] *adj* anual ♦ *n* (*BOT*) anual *m*; (*book*) anuário
annul [ə'nʌl] *vt* anular
annum ['ænəm] *n*: **per ~** por ano
anonymous [ə'nɒnɪməs] *adj* anônimo
anorak ['ænəræk] *n* anoraque *m* (*BR*), anorak *m* (*PT*)
another [ə'nʌðə*] *adj*: **~ book** (*one more*) outro livro, mais um livro; (*a different one*) um outro livro, um livro diferente ♦ *pron* outro; *see also* **one**
answer ['ɑːnsə*] *n* resposta; (*to problem*) solução *f* ♦ *vi* responder ♦ *vt* (*reply to*) responder a; (*problem*) resolver; **in ~ to your letter** em resposta *or* respondendo à sua carta; **to ~ the phone** atender o telefone; **to ~ the bell** *or* **the door** atender à porta; **~ back** *vi* replicar, retrucar; **~ for** *vt fus* responder por, responsabilizar-se por; **~ to** *vt fus* (*description*) corresponder a; **~able** *adj*: **~able (to sb/for sth)** responsável (perante alguém/por algo); **~ing machine** *n* secretária eletrônica
ant [ænt] *n* formiga
antagonism [æn'tægənɪzm] *n* antagonismo
antagonize [æn'tægənaɪz] *vt* contrariar, hostilizar
Antarctic [ænt'ɑːktɪk] *n*: **the ~** o Antártico
antenatal ['æntɪ'neɪtl] *adj* pré-natal; **~ clinic** *n* clínica pré-natal
anthem ['ænθəm] *n*: **national ~** hino nacional
anthology [æn'θɒlədʒɪ] *n* antologia
anti... [æntɪ] *prefix* anti...; **~-aircraft** *adj* antiaéreo; **~biotic** *adj* antibiótico ♦ *n* antibiótico; **~body** *n* anticorpo
anticipate [æn'tɪsɪpeɪt] *vt* prever; (*expect*) esperar; (*look forward to*) aguardar, esperar; **anticipation** *n* expectativa; (*eagerness*) entusiasmo
anticlimax [æntɪ'klaɪmæks] *n* desapontamento
anticlockwise [æntɪ'klɒkwaɪz] (*BRIT*) *adv* em sentido anti-horário
antics ['æntɪks] *npl* bobices *fpl*; (*of child*) travessuras *fpl*
antifreeze ['æntɪfriːz] *n* anticongelante *m*
antihistamine [æntɪ'hɪstəmiːn] *n* anti-histamínico
antiquated ['æntɪkweɪtɪd] *adj* antiquado
antique [æn'tiːk] *n* antiguidade *f* ♦ *adj* antigo; **~ dealer** *n* antiquário/a; **~ shop** *n* loja de antiguidades
antiquity [æn'tɪkwɪtɪ] *n* antiguidade *f*
anti-Semitism [-'sɛmɪtɪzəm] *n* anti-semitismo
antiseptic [æntɪ'sɛptɪk] *n* anti-séptico
antisocial [æntɪ'səuʃəl] *adj* anti-social
antlers ['æntləz] *npl* esgalhos *mpl*, chi-

fres *mpl*

anvil ['ænvɪl] *n* bigorna

anxiety [æŋ'zaɪətɪ] *n* (*worry*) inquietude *f*; (*MED*) ansiedade *f*; (*eagerness*): ~ **to do** ânsia de fazer

anxious ['æŋkʃəs] *adj* (*worried*) preocupado; (*worrying*) angustiante; (*keen*): ~ **to do** ansioso para fazer; **to be** ~ **that** desejar que

KEYWORD

any ['ɛnɪ] *adj* **1** (*in questions etc*) algum(a); **have you** ~ **butter/ children?** você tem manteiga/ filhos?; **if there are** ~ **tickets left** se houver alguns bilhetes sobrando

2 (*with negative*) nenhum(a); **I haven't** ~ **money/books** não tenho dinheiro/ livros

3 (*no matter which*) qualquer; **choose** ~ **book you like** escolha qualquer livro que quiser

4 (*in phrases*): **in** ~ **case** em todo o caso; ~ **day now** qualquer dia desses; **at** ~ **moment** a qualquer momento; **at** ~ **rate** de qualquer modo; ~ **time** a qualquer momento; (*whenever*) quando quer que seja

♦ *pron* **1** (*in questions etc*) algum(a); **have you got** ~? tem algum?

2 (*with negative*) nenhum(a); **I haven't** ~ (**of them**) não tenho nenhum (deles)

3 (*no matter which one(s)*): **take** ~ **of those books (you like)** leve qualquer um desses livros (que você quiser)

♦ *adv* **1** (*in questions etc*) algo; **do you want** ~ **more soup/sandwiches?** quer mais sopa/sanduíches?; **are you feeling** ~ **better?** você está se sentindo melhor?

2 (*with negative*) nada; **I can't hear him** ~ **more** não consigo mais ouvi-lo

anybody ['ɛnɪbɔdɪ] *pron* = **anyone**

anyhow ['ɛnɪhau] *adv* (*at any rate*) de qualquer modo, de qualquer maneira; (*haphazard*) de qualquer jeito; **I shall go** ~ eu irei de qualquer jeito; **do it** ~ **you like** faça do jeito que você quiser; **she leaves things just** ~ ela deixa as coisas de qualquer maneira

anyone ['ɛnɪwʌn] *pron* (*in questions etc*) alguém; (*with negative*) ninguém; (*no matter who*) quem quer que seja; **can you see** ~? você pode ver alguém?; **if** ~ **should phone ...** se alguém telefonar ...; ~ **could do it** qualquer um(a) poderia fazer isso

anything ['ɛnɪθɪŋ] *pron* (*in questions etc*) alguma coisa; (*with negative*) nada; (*no matter what*) qualquer coisa; **can you see** ~? você pode ver alguma coisa?

anyway ['ɛnɪweɪ] *adv* (*at any rate*) de qualquer modo; (*besides*) além disso; **I shall go** ~ eu irei de qualquer jeito

anywhere ['ɛnɪwɛə*] *adv* (*in questions etc*) em algum lugar; (*with negative*) em parte nenhuma; (*no matter where*) não importa onde, onde quer que seja; **can you see him** ~? você pode vê-lo em algum lugar?; **I can't see him** ~ não o vejo em parte nenhuma; ~ **in the world** em qualquer lugar do mundo

apart [ə'pɑːt] *adv* à parte, à distância; (*separately*) separado; (*movement*): **to move** ~ distanciar-se; (*aside*): ... ~, ... de lado, além de ...; **10 miles** ~ separados por 10 milhas; **to take** ~ desmontar; ~ **from** com exceção de; (*in addition to*) além de

apartheid [ə'pɑːteɪt] *n* apartheid *m*

apartment [ə'pɑːtmənt] (*US*) *n* apartamento

apathetic [æpə'θɛtɪk] *adj* apático

ape [eɪp] *n* macaco ♦ *vt* macaquear, imitar

aperitif [ə'pɛrɪtiːv] *n* aperitivo

aperture ['æpətʃjuə*] *n* orifício; (*PHOT*) abertura

apex ['eɪpɛks] *n* ápice *m*

apiece [ə'piːs] *adv* (*for each person*) cada um, por cabeça; (*for each item*) cada

aplomb [ə'plɔm] *n* desenvoltura

apologetic [əpɔlə'dʒɛtɪk] *adj* cheio de desculpas

apologize [ə'pɔlədʒaɪz] *vi*: **to** ~ (**for sth to sb**) desculpar-se *or* pedir desculpas (por *or* de algo a alguém); **apology** *n* desculpas *fpl*

apostle [ə'pɔsl] *n* apóstolo

apostrophe [ə'pɔstrəfɪ] *n* apóstrofo

appal [ə'pɔːl] *vt* horrorizar; ~**ling** *adj* horrível; (*ignorance*) terrível

apparatus [æpə'reɪtəs] *n* aparelho; (*in gym*) aparelhos *mpl*; (*organization*) aparato

apparel [ə'pærəl] (*US*) *n* vestuário, roupa

apparent [ə'pærənt] *adj* aparente; (*obvious*) claro, patente; ~**ly** *adv* aparentemente, pelo(s) visto(s)

apparition [æpə'rɪʃən] *n* (*ghost*) fantasma *m*

appeal [ə'piːl] *vi* (*LAW*) apelar, recorrer ♦ *n* (*LAW*) recurso, apelação *f*; (*request*) pedido; (*plea*) súplica; (*charm*) atração *f*; **to** ~ (**to sb**) **for sth** (*request*) pedir algo (a alguém); (*plead*) suplicar algo (a alguém); **to** ~ **to** atrair; ~**ing** *adj* atraente

appear [ə'pɪə*] *vi* aparecer; (*LAW*) apresentar-se, comparecer; (*publication*) ser publicado; (*seem*) parecer; **to** ~ **in "Hamlet"** trabalhar em "Hamlet"; **to** ~ **on TV** (*person, news item*) sair na televisão; (*programme*) passar na televisão; ~**ance** *n* aparecimento; (*presence*) comparecimento; (*look*) aparência

appease [ə'piːz] *vt* apaziguar

appendices [ə'pɛndɪsiːz] *npl of* **appendix**

appendicitis [əpɛndɪ'saɪtɪs] n apendicite f

appendix [ə'pɛndɪks] (pl **appendices**) n apêndice m

appetite ['æpɪtaɪt] n apetite m; (fig) desejo; **appetizer** n (food) tira-gosto; (drink) aperitivo

applaud [ə'plɔːd] vi aplaudir ♦ vt aplaudir; (praise) admirar; **applause** n aplausos mpl

apple ['æpl] n maçã f; ~ **tree** n macieira

appliance [ə'plaɪəns] n aparelho; **electrical** or **domestic** ~s eletrodomésticos mpl

applicant ['æplɪkənt] n (for post) candidato/a; (for benefit etc) requerente m/f

application [æplɪ'keɪʃən] n aplicação f; (for a job, a grant etc) candidatura, requerimento; (hard work) esforço; ~ **form** n (formulário de) requerimento

applied [ə'plaɪd] adj aplicado

apply [ə'plaɪ] vt (paint etc) usar; (law etc) pôr em prática ♦ vi: **to** ~ **to** (be suitable for) ser aplicável a; (be relevant to) valer para; (ask) pedir; **to** ~ **for** (permit, grant) solicitar, pedir; (job) candidatar-se a; **to** ~ **o.s.** to aplicar-se a, dedicar-se a

appoint [ə'pɔɪnt] vt (to post) nomear; ~**ed: at the ~ed time** na hora marcada; ~**ment** n (engagement) encontro marcado, compromisso; (at doctor's etc) hora marcada; (act) nomeação f; (post) cargo; **to make an ~ment (with sb)** marcar um encontro (com alguém)

appraisal [ə'preɪzl] n avaliação f

appreciate [ə'priːʃɪeɪt] vt (like) apreciar, estimar; (be grateful for) agradecer a; (understand) compreender ♦ vi (COMM) valorizar-se; **appreciation** n apreciação f, estima; (understanding) compreensão f; (gratitude) agradecimento; (COMM) valorização f; **appreciative** adj (person) agradecido; (comment) elogioso

apprehend [æprɪ'hɛnd] vt (arrest) prender; **apprehension** n apreensão f; **apprehensive** adj apreensivo, receoso

apprentice [ə'prɛntɪs] n aprendiz m/f; ~**ship** n aprendizado, aprendizagem f

approach [ə'prəutʃ] vi aproximar-se ♦ vt aproximar-se de; (ask, apply to) dirigir-se a; (subject, passer-by) abordar ♦ n aproximação f; (access) acesso; (to problem, situation) enfoque m; ~**able** adj (person) tratável; (place) acessível

appropriate [adj ə'prəupriːt, vt ə'prəupriːeɪt] adj (apt) apropriado; (relevant) adequado ♦ vt apropriar-se de

approval [ə'pruːvəl] n aprovação f; **on** ~ (COMM) a contento

approve [ə'pruːv] vt (publication, product) autorizar; (motion, decision) aprovar; ~ **of** vt fus aprovar

approximate [ə'prɔksɪmɪt] adj aproximado; ~**ly** adv aproximadamente

apricot ['eɪprɪkɔt] n damasco

April ['eɪprəl] n abril m; ~ **Fool's Day** n Primeiro-de-abril m

apron ['eɪprən] n avental m

apt [æpt] adj (suitable) adequado; (appropriate) apropriado; (likely): ~ **to do** sujeito a fazer

aptitude ['æptɪtjuːd] n aptidão f, talento

aqualung ['ækwəlʌŋ] n aparelho respiratório autônomo

aquarium [ə'kwɛərɪəm] n aquário

Aquarius [ə'kwɛərɪəs] n Aquário

Arab ['ærəb] adj, n árabe m/f

Arabian [ə'reɪbɪən] adj árabe

Arabic ['ærəbɪk] adj árabe ♦ n (LING) árabe m; (numerals) arábico

arbitrary ['aːbɪtrərɪ] adj arbitrário

arbitration [aːbɪ'treɪʃən] n arbitragem f

arcade [aː'keɪd] n arcos mpl; (passage with shops) galeria

arch [aːtʃ] n arco; (of foot) curvatura ♦ vt arquear, curvar

archaeologist [aːkɪ'ɔlədʒɪst] (US **archeologist**) n arqueólogo/a

archaeology [aːkɪ'ɔlədʒɪ] (US **archeology**) n arqueologia

archbishop [aːtʃ'bɪʃəp] n arcebispo

arch-enemy n arquiinimigo/a

archeology etc [aːkɪ'ɔlədʒɪ] (US) = **archaeology** etc

archery ['aːtʃərɪ] n tiro de arco

architect ['aːkɪtɛkt] n arquiteto/a; ~**ural** adj arquitetônico; ~**ure** n arquitetura

archives ['aːkaɪvz] npl arquivo

Arctic ['aːktɪk] adj ártico ♦ n: **the** ~ o Ártico

ardent ['aːdənt] adj (admirer) ardente; (discussion) acalorado

are [aː*] vb see **be**

area ['ɛərɪə] n (zone) zona, região f; (part of place) região; (in room, of knowledge, experience) área; (MAT) superfície f, extensão f

aren't [aːnt] = **are not**

Argentina [aːdʒən'tiːnə] n Argentina

arguably ['aːgjuəblɪ] adv possivelmente

argue ['aːgjuː] vi (quarrel) discutir; (reason) argumentar; **to** ~ **that** sustentar que

argument ['aːgjumənt] n (reasons) argumento; (quarrel) briga, discussão f; ~**ative** adj briguento

Aries ['ɛərɪz] n Aries m

arise [ə'raɪz] (pt **arose**, pp **arisen**) vi (emerge) surgir

arisen [ə'rɪzn] pp of **arise**

aristocrat ['ærɪstəkræt] n aristocrata m/f

arithmetic [ə'rɪθmətɪk] n aritmética

ark [aːk] n: **Noah's A~** arca de Noé

arm [aːm] n braço; (of clothing) manga; (of organization etc) divisão f ♦ vt armar; ~**s** npl (weapons) armas fpl; (HERALDRY) brasão m; ~ **in** ~ de braços da-

dos
armaments [ˈɑːməmənts] *npl* armamento
arm: ~**chair** *n* poltrona; ~**ed** *adj* armado; ~**ed robbery** *n* assalto à mão armada
armour [ˈɑːmə*] (*US* **armor**) *n* armadura; ~**ed car** *n* carro blindado
armpit [ˈɑːmpɪt] *n* sovaco
armrest [ˈɑːmrɛst] *n* braço (de poltrona)
army [ˈɑːmɪ] *n* exército
aroma [əˈrəumə] *n* aroma
arose [əˈrəuz] *pt of* **arise**
around [əˈraund] *adv* em volta; (*in the area*) perto ♦ *prep* em volta de; (*near*) perto de; (*fig: about*) cerca de
arouse [əˈrauz] *vt* despertar; (*anger*) provocar
arrange [əˈreɪndʒ] *vt* (*organize*) organizar; (*put in order*) arrumar; **to ~ to do sth** combinar em *or* ficar de fazer algo; ~**ment** *n* (*agreement*) acordo; (*order, layout*) disposição *f*; ~**ments** *npl* (*plans*) planos *mpl*; (*preparations*) preparativos *mpl*; **home deliveries by** ~**ment** entregas a domicílio por convênio; **I'll make all the necessary** ~**ments** eu vou tomar todas as providências necessárias
array [əˈreɪ] *n*: ~ **of** variedade *f* de
arrears [əˈrɪəz] *npl* atrasos *mpl*; **to be in** ~ **with one's rent** atrasar o aluguel
arrest [əˈrɛst] *vt* prender, deter; (*sb's attention*) chamar, prender ♦ *n* detenção *f*, prisão *f*; **under** ~ preso
arrival [əˈraɪvəl] *n* chegada; **new** ~ recém-chegado; (*baby*) recém-nascido
arrive [əˈraɪv] *vi* chegar
arrogant [ˈærəgənt] *adj* arrogante
arrow [ˈærəu] *n* flecha; (*sign*) seta
arse [ɑːs] (*BRIT: inf!*) *n* cu *m* (!)
arson [ˈɑːsn] *n* incêndio premeditado
art [ɑːt] *n* arte *f*; (*skill*) habilidade *f*, jeito; **A**~**s** *npl* (*SCH*) letras *fpl*
artefact [ˈɑːtɪfækt] *n* artefato
artery [ˈɑːtərɪ] *n* (*MED*) artéria; (*fig*) estrada principal
artful [ˈɑːtful] *adj* ardiloso, esperto
art gallery *n* museu *m* de belas artes; (*small, private*) galeria de arte
arthritis [ɑːˈθraɪtɪs] *n* artrite *f*
artichoke [ˈɑːtɪtʃəuk] *n* (*also*: **globe** ~) alcachofra; (*also*: **Jerusalem** ~) topinambo
article [ˈɑːtɪkl] *n* artigo; ~**s** *npl* (*BRIT*: *LAW*: *training*) contrato de aprendizagem; ~**s of clothing** peças *fpl* de vestuário
articulate [*adj* ɑːˈtɪkjulɪt, *vt* ɑːˈtɪkjuleɪt] *adj* (*speech*) bem articulado; (*writing*) bem escrito; (*person*) eloqüente ♦ *vt* expressar; ~**d lorry** (*BRIT*) *n* caminhão *m* (*BR*) *or* camião *m* (*PT*) articulado, jamanta
artificial [ɑːtɪˈfɪʃəl] *adj* artificial; (*manner*) afetado

artillery [ɑːˈtɪlərɪ] *n* artilharia
artisan [ˈɑːtɪzæn] *n* artesão/sã *m/f*
artist [ˈɑːtɪst] *n* artista *m/f*; (*MUS*) intérprete *m/f*; ~**ic** *adj* artístico; ~**ry** *n* arte *f*, mestria
artless [ˈɑːtlɪs] *adj* natural, simples
art school *n* ≈ escola de artes

KEYWORD
---

as [æz, əz] *conj* **1** (*time*) quando; ~ **the years went by** no decorrer dos anos; **he came in** ~ **I was leaving** ele chegou quando eu estava saindo; ~ **from tomorrow** a partir de amanhã
2 (*in comparisons*) tão ... (como), tanto(s) ... (como); ~ **big** ~ tão grande como; **twice** ~ **big** ~ duas vezes maior que; ~ **much/many** ~ tanto/tantos como; ~ **much money/many books** ~ tanto dinheiro quanto/tantos livros quanto; ~ **soon** ~ logo que, assim que
3 (*since, because*) como
4 (*referring to manner, way*) como; **do** ~ **you wish** faça como quiser
5 (*concerning*): ~ **for** *or* **to that** quanto a isso
6: ~ **if** *or* **though** como se; **he looked** ~ **if he was ill** ele parecia doente
♦ *prep* (*in the capacity of*): **he works** ~ **a driver** ele trabalha como motorista; **he gave it to me** ~ **a present** ele me deu isso de presente; *see also* **long**; **such**; **well**

a.s.a.p. *abbr* = **as soon as possible**
asbestos [æzˈbɛstəs] *n* asbesto, amianto
ascend [əˈsɛnd] *vt* subir; (*throne*) ascender; ~**ancy** *n* predomínio, ascendência
ascent [əˈsɛnt] *n* subida; (*slope*) rampa
ascertain [æsəˈteɪn] *vt* averiguar, verificar
ascribe [əˈskraɪb] *vt*: **to** ~ **sth to** atribuir algo a
ash [æʃ] *n* cinza; (*tree, wood*) freixo
ashamed [əˈʃeɪmd] *adj* envergonhado; **to be** ~ **of** ter vergonha de
ashen [ˈæʃn] *adj* cinzento
ashore [əˈʃɔː*] *adv* em terra; **to go** ~ descer à terra, desembarcar
ashtray [ˈæʃtreɪ] *n* cinzeiro
Ash Wednesday *n* quarta-feira de cinzas
Asia [ˈeɪʃə] *n* Ásia; ~**n** *adj*, *n* asiático/a
aside [əˈsaɪd] *adv* à parte, de lado ♦ *n* aparte *m*
ask [ɑːsk] *vt* perguntar; (*invite*) convidar; **to** ~ **sb sth/to do sth** perguntar algo a alguém/pedir para alguém fazer algo; **to** ~ **(sb) a question** fazer uma pergunta (a alguém); **to** ~ **sb out to dinner** convidar alguém para jantar; ~ **after** *vt fus* perguntar por; ~ **for** *vt fus* pedir; **it's just** ~**ing for trouble** é procurar encrenca
askance [əˈskɑːns] *adv* de soslaio

askew [əˈskjuː] *adv* torto
asleep [əˈsliːp] *adj* dormindo; **to fall ~**
dormir, adormecer
asparagus [əsˈpærəgəs] *n* aspargo (*BR*),
espargo (*PT*)
aspect [ˈæspɛkt] *n* aspecto; (*direction in
which a building etc faces*) direção *f*
aspersions [əsˈpɔːʃənz] *npl*: **to cast ~
on** difamar, caluniar
asphyxiation [æsfɪksɪˈeɪʃən] *n* asfixia
aspire [əsˈpaɪə*] *vi*: **to ~ to** aspirar a
aspirin [ˈæsprɪn] *n* aspirina
ass [æs] *n* jumento, burro; (*inf*) imbecil
m/f; (*US: inf!*) cu *m* (*!*)
assailant [əˈseɪlənt] *n* assaltante *m/f*,
atacante *m/f*
assassinate [əˈsæsɪneɪt] *vt* assassinar;
assassination *n* assassinato, assassínio
assault [əˈsɔːlt] *n* assalto; (*MIL, fig*) ataque *m* ♦ *vt* assaltar, atacar; (*sexually*)
agredir, violar
assemble [əˈsɛmbl] *vt* (*people*) reunir;
(*objects*) juntar; (*TECH*) montar ♦ *vi*
reunir-se
assembly [əˈsɛmblɪ] *n* reunião *f*; (*institution*) assembléia; **~ line** *n* linha de
montagem
assent [əˈsɛnt] *n* aprovação *f*
assert [əˈsɔːt] *vt* afirmar; **~ion** *n* afirmação *f*
assess [əˈsɛs] *vt* avaliar; (*tax, damages*)
calcular; **~ment** *n* avaliação *f*, cálculo
asset [ˈæsɛt] *n* vantagem *f*, trunfo; **~s**
npl (*property, funds*) bens *mpl*
assign [əˈsaɪn] *vt* (*date*) fixar; **to ~ (to)**
(*task*) designar (a); (*resources*) destinar
(a); **~ment** *n* tarefa
assist [əˈsɪst] *vt* ajudar; **~ance** *n* ajuda,
auxílio; **~ant** *n* assistente *m/f*, auxiliar
m/f; (*BRIT: also*: **shop ~ant**) vende-
dor(a) *m/f*
associate [*adj, n* əˈsəʊʃɪɪt, *vt, vi*
əˈsəʊʃɪeɪt] *adj* associado; (*professor etc*)
adjunto ♦ *n* sócio/a ♦ *vi*: **to ~ with**
associar-se com ♦ *vt* associar; **association** *n* associação *f*; (*link*) ligação *f*
assorted [əˈsɔːtɪd] *adj* sortido
assortment [əˈsɔːtmənt] *n* (*of shapes, colours*) sortimento *f*; (*of books, people*) variedade *f*
assume [əˈsjuːm] *vt* (*suppose*) supor, presumir; (*responsibilities etc*) assumir; (*attitude, name*) adotar, tomar; **~d name**
n nome *m* falso; **assumption** *n* suposição *f*, presunção *f*
assurance [əˈʃʊərəns] *n* garantia; (*confidence*) confiança; (*insurance*) seguro
assure [əˈʃʊə*] *vt* assegurar; (*guarantee*)
garantir
asthma [ˈæsmə] *n* asma
astonish [əˈstɒnɪʃ] *vt* assombrar, espantar; **~ment** *n* assombro, espanto
astound [əˈstaʊnd] *vt* pasmar, estarrecer
astray [əˈstreɪ] *adv*: **to go ~** extraviar-
se; **to lead ~** desencaminhar

astride [əˈstraɪd] *prep* montado
astrology [əsˈtrɒlədʒɪ] *n* astrologia
astronaut [ˈæstrənɔːt] *n* astronauta *m/f*
astronomy [əsˈtrɒnəmɪ] *n* astronomia
astute [əsˈtjuːt] *adj* astuto
asylum [əˈsaɪləm] *n* (*refuge*) asilo; (*hospital*) manicômio

KEYWORD

at [æt] *prep* **1** (*referring to position*) em;
(*referring to direction*) a; **~ the top** em
cima; **~ home** em casa; **to look ~ sth**
olhar para algo
2 (*referring to time*): **~ 4 o'clock** às
quatro horas; **~ night** à noite; **~
Christmas** no Natal; **~ times** às vezes
3 (*referring to rates, speed etc*): **~ £1 a
kilo** a uma libra o quilo; **two ~ a
time** de dois em dois
4 (*referring to manner*): **~ a stroke** de
um golpe; **~ peace** em paz
5 (*referring to activity*): **to be ~ work**
estar no trabalho; **to play ~ cowboys**
brincar de mocinho
6 (*referring to cause*): **to be shocked/
surprised/annoyed ~ sth** ficar
chocado/surpreso/chateado com algo; **I
went ~ his suggestion** eu fui por causa da sugestão dele

ate [eɪt] *pt of* **eat**
atheist [ˈeɪθɪɪst] *n* ateu/atéia *m/f*
Athens [ˈæθɪnz] *n* Atenas
athlete [ˈæθliːt] *n* atleta *m/f*; **athletic**
adj atlético; **athletics** *n* atletismo
Atlantic [ətˈlæntɪk] *adj* atlântico ♦ *n*: **the
~ (Ocean)** o (oceano) Atlântico
atlas [ˈætləs] *n* atlas *m inv*
atmosphere [ˈætməsfɪə*] *n* atmosfera;
(*of place*) ambiente *m*
atom [ˈætəm] *n* átomo; **~ic** *adj* atômico;
~(ic) bomb *n* bomba atômica; **~izer** *n*
atomizador *m*, pulverizador *m*
atone [əˈtəʊn] *vi*: **to ~ for** (*sin*) expiar;
(*mistake*) reparar
atrocious [əˈtrəʊʃəs] *adj* péssimo
attach [əˈtætʃ] *vt* prender; (*document*)
juntar, anexar; (*importance etc*) dar; **to
be ~ed to sb/sth** (*like*) ter afeição por
alguém/algo
attaché [əˈtæʃeɪ] *n* adido/a; **~ case** *n*
pasta
attachment [əˈtætʃmənt] *n* (*tool*) acessório; (*love*) *n* afeição *f* (por)
attack [əˈtæk] *vt* atacar; (*subj: criminal*)
assaltar; (*task etc*) empreender ♦ *n* ataque *m*; (*on sb's life*) atentado; **heart ~**
ataque cardíaco *or* de coração; **~er** *n*
agressor(a) *m/f*; (*criminal*) assaltante
m/f
attain [əˈteɪn] *vt* (*also*: **~ to**: *happiness,
results*) alcançar, atingir; (: *knowledge*)
obter; **~ment** *n* feito
attempt [əˈtɛmpt] *n* tentativa ♦ *vt* tentar; **to make an ~ on sb's life** atentar

contra a vida de alguém; **~ed** adj: **~ed theft** tentativa de roubo

attend [ə'tɛnd] vt (lectures) assistir a; (school) cursar; (church) ir a; (course) fazer; (patient) tratar; **~ to** vt fus (matter) encarregar-se de; (needs, customer) atender a; (patient) tratar de; **~ance** n comparecimento; (people present) assistência; **~ant** n servidor(a) m/f ♦ adj concomitante

attention [ə'tɛnʃən] n atenção f; (care) cuidados mpl ♦ excl (MIL) sentido!; **for the ~ of ...** (ADMIN) atenção ...

attentive [ə'tɛntɪv] adj atento; (polite) cortês

attic ['ætɪk] n sótão m

attitude ['ætɪtjuːd] n atitude f

attorney [ə'təːnɪ] n (US: lawyer) advogado/a; **A~ General** n (BRIT) procurador(a) m/f geral da Justiça; (US) Secretário de Justiça

attract [ə'trækt] vt atrair, chamar; **~ion** n atração f; **~ive** adj atraente; (idea, offer) interessante

attribute [n 'ætrɪbjuːt, vt ə'trɪbjuːt] n atributo ♦ vt: to **~ sth to** atribuir algo a

attrition [ə'trɪʃən] n: **war of ~** guerra de atrição

aubergine ['əʊbəʒiːn] n berinjela

auburn ['ɔːbən] adj castanho-avermelhado

auction ['ɔːkʃən] n (also: **sale by ~**) leilão m ♦ vt leiloar; **~eer** n leiloeiro/a

audible ['ɔːdɪbl] adj audível

audience ['ɔːdɪəns] n audiência; (at concert, theatre) platéia; (public) público

audio-typist ['ɔːdɪəʊ-] n datilógrafo/a (de textos ditados em fita)

audio-visual ['ɔːdɪəʊ-] adj audiovisual; **~ aid** n recurso audiovisual

audit ['ɔːdɪt] vt fazer a auditoria de

audition [ɔː'dɪʃən] n audição f

auditor ['ɔːdɪtə*] n auditor(a) m/f

augment [ɔːg'mɛnt] vt aumentar

augur ['ɔːgə*] vi: **it ~s well** é de bom augúrio

August ['ɔːgəst] n agosto

aunt [ɑːnt] n tia; **~ie** n titia; **~y** n titia

au pair ['əʊ'pɛə*] n (also: **~ girl**) au pair f

aura ['ɔːrə] n ar m, aspecto

auspicious [ɔːs'pɪʃəs] adj favorável; (occasion) propício

austerity [ɔs'tɛrɪtɪ] n simplicidade f; (ECON) privação f

Australia [ɔs'treɪlɪə] n Austrália; **~n** adj, n australiano/a

Austria ['ɔstrɪə] n Áustria; **~n** adj, n austríaco/a

authentic [ɔː'θɛntɪk] adj autêntico

author ['ɔːθə*] n autor(a) m/f

authoritarian [ɔːθɔrɪ'tɛərɪən] adj autoritário

authoritative [ɔː'θɔrɪtətɪv] adj (account) autorizado; (manner) autoritário

authority [ɔː'θɔrɪtɪ] n autoridade f; (government body) jurisdição f; (permission) autorização f; **the authorities** npl (ruling body) as autoridades

authorize ['ɔːθəraɪz] vt autorizar

auto ['ɔːtəʊ] (US) n carro, automóvel m

autobiography [ɔːtəbaɪ'ɔɡrəfɪ] n autobiografia

autograph ['ɔːtəɡrɑːf] n autógrafo ♦ vt (photo etc) autografar

automata [ɔː'tɔmətə] npl of **automaton**

automatic [ɔːtə'mætɪk] adj automático ♦ n (gun) pistola automática; (washing machine) máquina de lavar roupa automática; (car) carro automático

automaton [ɔː'tɔmətən] (pl **automata**) n autômato

automobile ['ɔːtəməbiːl] (US) n carro, automóvel m

autonomy [ɔː'tɔnəmɪ] n autonomia

autumn ['ɔːtəm] n outono

auxiliary [ɔːg'zɪlɪərɪ] adj, n auxiliar m/f

avail [ə'veɪl] vt: to **~ o.s. of** aproveitar, valer-se de ♦ n: to **no ~** em vão, inutilmente

available [ə'veɪləbl] adj disponível; (time) livre

avalanche ['ævəlɑːnʃ] n avalanche f

avant-garde ['ævɑŋ'ɡɑːd] adj de vanguarda

Ave. abbr (= avenue) Av., Avda.

avenge [ə'vɛndʒ] vt vingar

avenue ['ævənjuː] n avenida; (drive) caminho; (means) solução f

average ['ævərɪdʒ] n média ♦ adj (mean) médio; (ordinary) regular ♦ vt alcançar uma média de; **on ~** em média; **~ out** vi: to **~ out at** dar uma média de

averse [ə'vəːs] adj averso

avert [ə'vəːt] vt prevenir; (blow, one's eyes) desviar

aviary ['eɪvɪərɪ] n aviário, viveiro de aves

avid ['ævɪd] adj ávido

avocado [ævə'kɑːdəʊ] n (also: BRIT: **~ pear**) abacate m

avoid [ə'vɔɪd] vt evitar

avuncular [ə'vʌŋkjulə*] adj paternal

await [ə'weɪt] vt esperar, aguardar

awake [ə'weɪk] (pt awoke, pp awoken or **~d**) adj acordado ♦ vt, vi despertar, acordar; **~ to** atento a; **~ning** n despertar m

award [ə'wɔːd] n prêmio, condecoração f; (LAW) indenização f ♦ vt outorgar, conceder; indenizar

aware [ə'wɛə*] adj: **~ of** (conscious) consciente de; (informed) informado de or sobre; to **become ~ of** reparar em, saber de; **~ness** n consciência

awash [ə'wɔʃ] adj: **~ with** (also fig) inundado de

away [ə'weɪ] adv fora; (far~) muito longe; **two kilometres ~** a dois quilômetros de distância; **the holiday was**

two weeks ~ faltavam duas semanas
para as férias; he's ~ for a week está
ausente uma semana; to take ~ levar;
to work etc ~ trabalhar etc sem parar;
to fade ~ (colour) desbotar; (enthusiasm,
sound) diminuir; ♦ game n (SPORT)
jogo de fora
awe [ɔ:] n temor m respeitoso; **~-**
inspiring adj imponente; **~some** adj =
~-inspiring
awful ['ɔ:fəl] adj terrível, horrível;
(quantity): **an ~ lot of** um monte de;
~ly adv (very) muito
awhile [ə'waɪl] adv por algum tempo,
um pouco
awkward ['ɔ:kwəd] adj (person, movement) desajeitado; (shape) incômodo;
(problem) difícil; (situation) embaraçoso,
delicado
awning ['ɔ:nɪŋ] n toldo
awoke [ə'wəuk] pt of awake; **~n** pp of
awake
awry [ə'raɪ] adv: **to be ~** estar de viés
or de esguelha; **to go ~** sair mal
axe [æks] (US **ax**) n machado ♦ vt (project
etc) abandonar; (jobs) reduzir
axes ['æksɪz] npl of axis
axis ['æksɪs] (pl **axes**) n eixo
axle ['æksl] n (also: **~ tree**: AUT) eixo
ay(e) [aɪ] excl sim
Azores [ə'zɔ:z] npl: **the ~** os Açores

B

B [bi:] n (MUS) si m
BA n abbr = Bachelor of Arts
babble ['bæbl] vi balbuciar; (brook) mur-
murinhar
baby ['beɪbɪ] n neném m/f, nenê m/f, bebê m/f; (US: inf) querido/a; **~ carriage**
(US) n carrinho de bebê; **~-sit** (irreg) vi
tomar conta da(s) criança(s); **~-sitter** n
baby-sitter m/f
bachelor ['bætʃələ*] n solteiro; **B~ of**
Arts/Science ≈ bacharel m em Letras/
Ciências
back [bæk] n (of person) costas fpl; (of
animal) lombo; (of hand) dorso; (of car,
train) parte f traseira; (of house) fundos
mpl; (of chair) encosto; (of page) verso;
(of book) lombada; (of crowd) fundo;
(FOOTBALL) zagueiro (BR), defesa m (PT)
♦ vt (candidate: also: **~ up**) apoiar; (horse: at races) apostar em; (car) recuar ♦
vi (car etc: also: **~ up**) dar marcha-ré
(BR), fazer marcha atrás (PT) ♦ cpd
(payment) atrasado; (AUT: seats, wheels)
de trás ♦ adv (not forward) para trás;
(returned): **he's ~** ele voltou; (restitution): **throw the ball ~** devolva a bola;
(again): **he called ~** chamou de novo;
he ran ~ recuou correndo; **~ down** vi
desistir; **~ out** vi (of promise) voltar
atrás, recuar; **~ up** vt (support) apoiar;

(COMPUT) tirar um backup de; **~bench-**
er (BRIT) n membro do parlamento sem
pasta; **~bone** n coluna vertebral; (fig)
esteio; **~cloth** (BRIT) n pano de fundo;
~date vt (letter) antedatar; **~dated pay**
rise aumento de vencimento com efeito
retroativo; **~drop** n ~cloth; **~fire** vi
(AUT) engasgar; (plan) sair pela culatra;
~ground n fundo; (of events) antecedentes
mpl; (basic knowledge) bases fpl; (experience) conhecimentos mpl, experiência; **family ~ground** antecedentes
mpl familiares; **~hand** n (TENNIS: also:
~hand stroke) revés m; **~handed** adj
(fig) ambíguo; **~hander** (BRIT) n (bribe)
propina, peita (PT); **~ing** n (fig) apoio;
~lash n reação f; **~log** n: **~log of**
work atrasos mpl; **~ number** n (of magazine etc) número atrasado; **~pack** n
mochila; **~ pay** n salário atrasado;
~side (inf) n traseiro; **~stage** adv nos
bastidores; **~stroke** n nado de costas;
~up adj (train, plane) reserva 'inv;
(COMPUT) de backup ♦ n (support) apoio;
(COMPUT: also: **~up file**) backup m;
~ward adj (movement) para trás; (person, country) atrasado; **~wards** adv
(move, go) para trás; (read a list) às
avessas; (fall) de costas; **~water** n (fig)
lugar m atrasado; **~yard** n quintal m
bacon ['beɪkən] n toucinho, bacon m
bad [bæd] adj mau/má, ruim; (child) levado; (mistake, injury) grave; (meat,
food) estragado; **his ~ leg** sua perna
machucada; **to go ~** estragar-se
bade [bæd] pt of bid
badge [bædʒ] n (of school etc) emblema
m; (policeman's) crachá m
badger ['bædʒə*] n texugo
badly ['bædlɪ] adv mal; **~ wounded** gravemente ferido; **he needs it ~** faz-lhe
grande falta; **to be ~ off (for money)**
estar com pouco dinheiro
badminton ['bædmɪntən] n badminton m
bad-tempered [-'tɛmpəd] adj mal hu-
morado; (temporary) de mau humor
baffle ['bæfl] vt (puzzle) deixar perplexo,
desconcertar
bag [bæg] n saco, bolsa; (handbag) bolsa;
(satchel) sacola; (case) mala; **~s of ...**
(inf: lots of) ... de sobra; **~age** n bagagem f; **~gy** adj folgado, largo; **~pipes**
npl gaita de foles
bail [beɪl] n (payment) fiança; (release) liberdade f sob fiança ♦ vt (prisoner: gen:
grant ~ to) libertar sob fiança; (boat:
also: **~ out**) baldear a água de; **on ~**
sob fiança; see also **bale**; **~ out** vt (prisoner) afiançar
bailiff ['beɪlɪf] n (LAW: BRIT) oficial m/f
de justiça (BR) or de diligências (PT); (:
US) funcionário encarregado de acompanhar presos no tribunal
bait [beɪt] n isca, engodo; (for criminal
etc) atrativo, chamariz m ♦ vt iscar, ce-

var; (*person*) apoquentar

bake [beɪk] *vt* cozinhar ao forno; (*TECH*: *clay etc*) cozer ♦ *vi* assar; ~**d beans** *npl* feijão *m* cozido com molho de tomate; ~**r** *n* padeiro/a; ~**ry** *n* (*for bread*) padaria; (*for cakes*) confeitaria; **baking** *n* (*act*) cozimento; (*batch*) fornada ♦ *adj* (*inf*: *hot*) escaldante; **baking powder** *n* fermento em pó

balance ['bæləns] *n* equilibrio; (*scales*) balança; (*COMM*) balanço; (*remainder*) resto, saldo ♦ *vt* equilibrar; (*budget*) nivelar; (*account*) fazer o balanço de; ~ **of trade/payments** balança comercial/balanço de pagamentos; ~**d** *adj* (*report*) objetivo; (*personality, diet*) equilibrado; ~ **sheet** *n* balanço geral

balcony ['bælkənɪ] *n* varanda; (*closed*) galeria; (*in theatre*) balcão *m*

bald [bɔːld] *adj* calvo, careca; (*tyre*) careca

bale [beɪl] *n* (*AGR*) fardo; ~ **out** *vi* (*of a plane*) atirar-se de pára-quedas

baleful ['beɪlful] *adj* (*look*) triste

ball [bɔːl] *n* bola; (*of wool, string*) novelo; (*dance*) baile *m*; **to play ~ with sb** jogar bola com alguém; (*fig*) fazer o jogo de alguém

ballast ['bæləst] *n* lastro

ball bearings *npl* rolimã *m*

ballerina [bælə'riːnə] *n* bailarina

ballet ['bæleɪ] *n* balé *m*; ~ **dancer** *n* bailarino/a

balloon [bə'luːn] *n* balão *m*

ballot ['bælət] *n* votação *f*; ~ **paper** *n* cédula eleitoral

ballpoint (pen) ['bɔːlpɔɪnt-] *n* (caneta) esferográfica

ballroom ['bɔːlrum] *n* salão *m* de baile

balm [bɑːm] *n* bálsamo

ban [bæn] *n* proibição *f*, interdição *f*; (*suspension*) exclusão *f* ♦ *vt* proibir, interditar; excluir

banana [bə'nɑːnə] *n* banana

band [bænd] *n* (*group*) orquestra; (*MIL*) banda; (*strip*) faixa, cinta; ~ **together** *vi* juntar-se, associar-se

bandage ['bændɪdʒ] *n* atadura (*BR*), ligadura (*PT*) ♦ *vt* enfaixar

bandaid ['bændeɪd] ® (*US*) *n* esparadrapo

bandwagon ['bændwægən] *n*: **to jump on the ~** (*fig*) entrar na roda, ir na onda

bandy ['bændɪ] *vt* trocar; ~-**legged** *adj* cambaio, de pernas tortas

bang [bæŋ] *n* estalo; (*of door*) estrondo; (*of gun, exhaust*) explosão *f*; (*blow*) pancada ♦ *excl* bum!, bumba! ♦ *vt* (*one's head etc*) bater; (*door*) fechar com violência ♦ *vi* produzir estrondo; (*door*) bater; (*fireworks*) soltar

bangle ['bæŋgl] *n* bracelete *m*

bangs [bæŋz] (*US*) *npl* (*fringe*) franja

banish ['bænɪʃ] *vt* banir

banister(s) ['bænɪstə(z)] *n(pl)* corrimão

m

bank [bæŋk] *n* banco; (*of river, lake*) margem *f*; (*of earth*) rampa, ladeira ♦ *vi* (*AVIAT*) ladear-se; ~ **on** *vt fus* contar com, apostar em; ~ **account** *n* conta bancária; ~ **card** *n* cartão *m* de garantia de cheques; ~**er** *n* banqueiro/a; ~**er's card** (*BRIT*) *n* = ~ **card**; **B~ holiday** (*BRIT*) *n* feriado nacional; ~**ing** *n* transações *fpl* bancárias; ~**note** *n* nota (bancária); ~ **rate** *n* taxa bancária

bankrupt ['bæŋkrʌpt] *adj* falido, quebrado; **to go ~** falir; ~**cy** *n* falência

bank statement *n* extrato bancário

banner ['bænə] *n* faixa

banns [bænz] *npl* proclamas *fpl*

baptism ['bæptɪzəm] *n* batismo

bar [bɑː] *n* barra; (*rod*) vara; (*of window etc*) grade *f*; (*fig*: *hindrance*) obstáculo; (*prohibition*) impedimento; (*pub*) bar *m*; (*counter*: *in pub*) balcão *m* ♦ *vt* (*road*) obstruir; (*person*) excluir; (*activity*) proibir ♦ *prep*: ~ **none** sem exceção; **behind ~s** (*prisoner*) atrás das grades; **the B~** (*LAW*) a advocacia

barbaric [bɑː'bærɪk] *adj* bárbaro

barbecue ['bɑːbɪkjuː] *n* churrasco

barbed wire ['bɑːbd-] *n* arame *m* farpado

barber ['bɑːbə] *n* barbeiro, cabeleireiro

bar code *n* código de barras

bare [bɛə] *adj* despido; (*head*) descoberto; (*trees*) sem vegetação; (*minimum*) básico ♦ *vt* mostrar; ~**back** *adv* em pêlo, sem arreios; ~**faced** *adj* descarado; ~**foot** *adj, adv* descalço; ~**ly** *adv* apenas, mal

bargain ['bɑːgɪn] *n* negócio; (*agreement*) acordo; (*good buy*) pechincha ♦ *vi* (*haggle*) regatear; (*negotiate*): **to ~ (with sb)** pechinchar (com alguém); **into the ~** ainda por cima; ~ **for** *vt fus*: **he got more than he ~ed for** ele conseguiu mais do que pediu

barge [bɑːdʒ] *n* barcaça; ~ **in** *vi* irromper

bark [bɑːk] *n* (*of tree*) casca; (*of dog*) latido ♦ *vi* latir

barley ['bɑːlɪ] *n* cevada

barmaid ['bɑːmeɪd] *n* garçonete *f* (*BR*), empregada (de bar) (*PT*)

barman ['bɑːmən] (*irreg*) *n* garçom *m* (*BR*), empregado (de bar) (*PT*)

barn [bɑːn] *n* celeiro

barometer [bə'rɔmɪtə] *n* barômetro

baron ['bærən] *n* barão *m*; (*of press, industry*) magnata *m*; ~**ess** *n* baronesa

barracks ['bærəks] *npl* quartel *m*, caserna

barrage ['bærɑːʒ] *n* (*MIL*) fogo de barragem; (*dam*) barragem *f*; (*fig*): **a ~ of questions** uma saraivada de perguntas

barrel ['bærəl] *n* barril *m*; (*of gun*) cano

barren ['bærən] *adj* (*land*) árido

barricade [bærɪ'keɪd] *n* barricada

barrier ['bærɪə*] n barreira; (fig: to progress etc) obstáculo

barring ['bɑːrɪŋ] prep exceto, salvo

barrister ['bærɪstə*] (BRIT) n advogado/a, causídico/a

barrow ['bærəu] n (wheel~) carrinho (de mão)

bartender ['bɑːtendə*] (US) n garçom m (BR), empregado (de bar) (PT)

barter ['bɑːtə*] vt: **to ~ sth for sth** trocar algo por algo

base [beɪs] n base f ♦ vt (opinion, belief): **to ~ sth on** basear or fundamentar algo em ♦ adj (thoughts) sujo; **~ball** n beisebol m

basement ['beɪsmənt] n porão m

bases¹ ['beɪsɪz] npl of **base**

bases² ['beɪsɪz] npl of **basis**

bash [bæʃ] (inf) vt (with fist) dar soco or murro em; (with object) bater em

bashful ['bæʃful] adj tímido, envergonhado

basic ['beɪsɪk] adj básico; (facilities) mínimo; **~ally** adv basicamente; (really) no fundo; **~s** npl: **the ~s** o essencial

basil ['bæzl] n manjericão m

basin ['beɪsn] n (vessel, GEO) bacia; (also: wash~) pia

basis ['beɪsɪs] (pl **bases**) n base f; **on a part-time ~** num esquema de meio-expediente; **on a trial ~** em experiência

bask [bɑːsk] vi: **to ~ in the sun** tomar sol

basket ['bɑːskɪt] n cesto; (with handle) cesta; **~ball** n basquete(bol) m

bass [beɪs] n (MUS) baixo

bassoon [bə'suːn] n fagote m

bastard ['bɑːstəd] n bastardo/a; (inf!) filho-da-puta m (!)

bat [bæt] n (ZOOL) morcego; (for ball games) bastão m; (BRIT: for table tennis) raquete f ♦ vt: **he didn't ~ an eyelid** ele nem pestanejou

batch [bætʃ] n (of bread) fornada; (of papers) monte m

bated ['beɪtɪd] adj: **with ~ breath** contendo a respiração

bath [bɑːθ, pl bɑːðz] n banho; (bathtub) banheira ♦ vt banhar; **to have a ~** tomar banho (de banheira); see also **baths**

bathe [beɪð] vi banhar-se; (US: have a bath) tomar um banho ♦ vt (wound) lavar; **~r** n banhista m/f; **bathing** n banho; **bathing cap** n touca de banho; **bathing costume** (US **bathing suit**) n (woman's) maiô m (BR), fato de banho (PT)

bathrobe ['bɑːθrəub] n roupão m de banho

bathroom ['bɑːθrum] n banheiro (BR), casa de banho (PT)

baths [bɑːðz] npl banhos mpl públicos

baton ['bætən] n (MUS) batuta; (ATHLE-

TICS) bastão m; (truncheon) cassetete m

batter ['bætə*] vt espancar; (subj: wind, rain) castigar ♦ n massa (mole); **~ed** adj (hat, pan) amassado, surrado

battery ['bætərɪ] n bateria; (of torch) pilha

battle ['bætl] n batalha; (fig) luta ♦ vi lutar; **~field** n campo de batalha; **~ship** n navio de guerra (BR), couraçado (PT)

bawdy ['bɔːdɪ] adj indecente; (joke) imoral

bawl [bɔːl] vi gritar; (child) berrar

bay [beɪ] n (GEO) baía; **to hold sb at ~** manter alguém a distância; **~ leaf** n louro; **~ window** n janela saliente

bazaar [bə'zɑː*] n bazar m

B & B n abbr = **bed and breakfast**

BBC n abbr (= British Broadcasting Corporation) companhia britânica de rádio e televisão

B.C. adv abbr (= before Christ) a.C.

KEYWORD

---

be [biː] (pt **was** or **were**, pp **been**) aux vb **1** (with present participle: forming continuous tense) estar; **what are you doing?** o que você está fazendo (BR) or a fazer (PT)?; **it is raining** está chovendo (BR) or a chover (PT); **I've been waiting for you for hours** há horas que eu espero por você

2 (with pp: forming passives): **to ~ killed** ser morto; **the box had been opened** a caixa tinha sido aberta; **the thief was nowhere to ~ seen** ninguém viu o ladrão

3 (in tag questions): **it was fun, wasn't it?** foi divertido, não foi?; **she's back again, is she?** ela voltou novamente, é?

4 (+ **to** + infin): **the house is to ~ sold** a casa está à venda; **you're to ~ congratulated for all your work** você devia ser cumprimentado pelo seu trabalho; **he's not to open it** ele não pode abrir isso

♦ vb + complement **1** (gen): **I'm English** sou inglês; **I'm tired** estou cansado; **2 and 2 are 4** dois e dois são quatro; **~ careful!** tome cuidado!; **~ quiet!** fique quieto!, fique calado!; **~ good!** seja bonzinho!

2 (of health) estar; **how are you?** como está?

3 (of age): **how old are you?** quantos anos você tem?; **I'm twenty (years old)** tenho vinte anos

4 (cost) ser; **how much was the meal?** quanto foi a refeição?; **that'll ~ £5.75, please** são £5.75, por favor

♦ vi **1** (exist, occur etc) existir, haver; **the best singer that ever was** o maior cantor de todos os tempos; **is there a God?** Deus existe?; **~ that as it may** ... de qualquer forma ...; **so ~ it** que seja assim

2 (*referring to place*) estar; **I won't ~ here tomorrow** eu não estarei aqui amanhã; **Edinburgh is in Scotland** Edinburgo é *or* fica na Escócia
3 (*referring to movement*) ir; **where have you been?** onde você foi?; **I've been in the garden** estava no quintal ♦ *impers vb* **1** (*referring to time*) ser; **it's 8 o'clock** são 8 horas; **it's the 28th of April** é 28 de abril
2 (*referring to distance*) ficar; **it's 10 km to the village** fica a 10 km do lugarejo
3 (*referring to the weather*) estar; **it's too hot/cold** está quente/frio demais
4 (*emphatic*): **it's only me** sou eu!; **it was Maria who paid the bill** foi Maria quem pagou a conta

beach [biːtʃ] *n* praia ♦ *vt* puxar para a terra *or* praia, encalhar
beacon ['biːkən] *n* (*lighthouse*) farol *m*; (*marker*) baliza
bead [biːd] *n* (*of necklace*) conta; (*of sweat*) gota
beak [biːk] *n* bico
beaker ['biːkə*] *n* copo com bico
beam [biːm] *n* (*ARCH*) viga; (*of light*) raio ♦ *vi* (*smile*) sorrir
bean [biːn] *n* feijão *m*; (*of coffee*) grão *m*; **runner/broad ~** vagem *f*/fava
beansprouts ['biːnsprauts] *npl* brotos *mpl* de feijão
bear [bɛə*] (*pt* bore, *pp* borne) *n* urso ♦ *vt* (*carry, support*) arcar com; (*tolerate*) suportar ♦ *vi*: **to ~ right/left** virar à direita/à esquerda; **~ out** *vt* (*theory, suspicion*) confirmar, corroborar; **~ up** *vi* agüentar, resistir
beard [biəd] *n* barba; **~ed** *adj* barbado, barbudo
bearer ['bɛərə*] *n* portador(a) *m/f*; (*of title*) detentor(a) *m/f*
bearing ['bɛərɪŋ] *n* porte *m*, comportamento; (*connection*) relação *f*; **~s** *npl* (*also*: **ball ~s**) rolimã *m*; **to take a ~** fazer marcação
beast [biːst] *n* bicho; (*inf*) fera; **~ly** *adj* horrível
beat [biːt] (*pt* beat, *pp* beaten) *n* (*of heart*) batida; (*MUS*) ritmo, compasso; (*of policeman*) ronda ♦ *vt* (*hit*) bater em; (*eggs*) bater; (*defeat*) vencer, derrotar ♦ *vi* (*heart*) bater; **to ~ it** (*inf*) cair fora; **off the ~en track** fora de mão; **~ off** *vt* repelir; **~ up** *vt* (*inf*: *person*) espancar; (*eggs*) bater; **~ing** *n* (*thrashing*) surra
beautiful ['bjuːtɪful] *adj* belo, lindo, formoso; **~ly** *adv* admiravelmente
beauty ['bjuːtɪ] *n* beleza; (*person*) beldade *f*, beleza; **~ salon** *n* salão *m* de beleza; **~ spot** (*BRIT*) *n* (*TOURISM*) lugar *m* de beleza excepcional
beaver ['biːvə*] *n* castor *m*

became [bɪ'keɪm] *pt of* become
because [bɪ'kɔz] *conj* porque; **~ of** por causa de
beck [bɛk] *n*: **to be at sb's ~ and call** estar às ordens de alguém
beckon ['bɛkən] *vt* (*also*: **~ to**) chamar com sinais, acenar para
become [bɪ'kʌm] (*irreg*: *like* come) *vi* (+ *n*) virar, fazer-se, tornar-se; (+ *adj*) tornar-se, ficar; **becoming** *adj* (*behaviour*) decoroso; (*clothes*) favorecedor(a), elegante
BEd *n abbr* (= *Bachelor of Education*) habilitação ao magistério
bed [bɛd] *n* cama; (*of flowers*) canteiro; (*of coal, clay*) camada, base *f*; (*of sea, lake*) fundo; (*of river*) leito; **to go to ~** ir dormir, deitar(-se); **~ and breakfast** *n* (*place*) pensão *f*; (*terms*) cama e café da manhã (*BR*) *or* pequeno almoço (*PT*); **~clothes** *npl* roupa de cama; **~ding** *n* roupa de cama
bedlam ['bɛdləm] *n* confusão *f*
bedraggled [bɪ'dræɡld] *adj* molhado, ensopado
bed: **~ridden** *adj* acamado; **~room** *n* quarto, dormitório; **~side** *n*: **at sb's ~side** à cabeceira de alguém; **~sit(ter)** (*BRIT*) *n* conjugado; **~spread** *n* colcha; **~time** *n* hora de ir para cama
bee [biː] *n* abelha
beech [biːtʃ] *n* faia
beef [biːf] *n* carne *f* de vaca; **roast ~** rosbife *m*; **~burger** *n* hambúrguer *m*; **~eater** *n* alabardeiro (*da guarda da Torre de Londres*)
beehive ['biːhaɪv] *n* colméia
beeline ['biːlaɪn] *n*: **to make a ~ for** ir direto a
been [biːn] *pp of* be
beer [bɪə*] *n* cerveja
beet [biːt] (*US*) *n* beterraba
beetle ['biːtl] *n* besouro
beetroot ['biːtruːt] (*BRIT*) *n* beterraba
before [bɪ'fɔː*] *prep* (*of time*) antes de; (*of space*) diante de ♦ *conj* antes que ♦ *adv* antes, anteriormente; à frente, na dianteira; **~ going** antes de sair; **the week ~** a semana anterior; **I've never seen it** ~ nunca vi isso antes; **~hand** *adv* antes
beg [bɛɡ] *vi* mendigar, pedir esmola ♦ *vt* (*also*: **~ for**) mendigar; **to ~ sb to do sth** implorar a alguém para fazer algo; *see also* pardon
began [bɪ'ɡæn] *pt of* begin
beggar ['bɛɡə*] *n* mendigo/a
begin [bɪ'ɡɪn] (*pt* began, *pp* begun) *vt, vi* começar, iniciar; **to ~ doing** *or* **to do sth** começar a fazer algo; **~ner** *n* principiante *m/f*; **~ning** *n* início, começo
begun [bɪ'ɡʌn] *pp of* begin
behalf [bɪ'hɑːf] *n*: **on** *or* **in** (*US*) **~ of** (*as representative of*) em nome de; (*for benefit of*) no interesse de

behave [bɪ'heɪv] *vi* comportar-se; (*well: also*: ~ **o.s.**) comportar-se (bem); **behaviour** (*US* **behavior**) *n* comportamento
behead [bɪ'hɛd] *vt* decapitar, degolar
beheld [bɪ'hɛld] *pt, pp of* **behold**
behind [bɪ'haɪnd] *prep* atrás de ♦ *adv* atrás; (*move*) para trás ♦ *n* traseiro; to be ~ (**schedule**) **with** sth estar atrasado *or* com atraso em algo; ~ **the scenes** nos bastidores
behold [bɪ'həʊld] (*irreg*) *vt* contemplar
beige [beɪʒ] *adj* bege
Beijing [beɪ'ʒɪŋ] *m* Pequim
being ['biːɪŋ] *n* (*state*) existência; (*entity*) ser *m*
belated [bɪ'leɪtɪd] *adj* atrasado
belch [bɛltʃ] *vi* arrotar ♦ *vt* (*also*: ~ **out**: *smoke etc*) vomitar
belfry ['bɛlfrɪ] *n* campanário
Belgian ['bɛldʒən] *adj, n* belga *m/f*
Belgium ['bɛldʒəm] *n* Bélgica
belie [bɪ'laɪ] *vt* (*give false impression of*) esconder; (*disprove*) desmentir
belief [bɪ'liːf] *n* (*opinion*) opinião *f*; (*trust, faith*) fé *f*
believe [bɪ'liːv] *vt*: to ~ sth/sb acreditar algo/em alguém ♦ *vi*: to ~ **in** (*God*) crer em; (*method, person*) acreditar em; ~**r** *n* (*REL*) crente *m/f*, fiel *m/f*; (*in idea*) partidário/a
belittle [bɪ'lɪtl] *vt* diminuir, depreciar
Belize [bɛ'liːz] *n* Belize *m* (*no article*)
bell [bɛl] *n* sino; (*small, door~*) campainha
belligerent [bɪ'lɪdʒərənt] *adj* agressivo
bellow ['bɛləʊ] *vi* mugir; (*person*) bramar
bellows ['bɛləʊz] *npl* fole *m*
belly ['bɛlɪ] *n* barriga, ventre *m*
belong [bɪ'lɒŋ] *vi*: to ~ **to** pertencer a; (*club etc*) ser sócio de; **the book** ~**s here** o livro fica guardado aqui; ~**ings** *npl* pertences *mpl*
beloved [bɪ'lʌvɪd] *adj* querido, amado
below [bɪ'ləʊ] *prep* (*beneath*) embaixo de; (*less than*) abaixo de ♦ *adv* em baixo; **see** ~ ver abaixo
belt [bɛlt] *n* cinto; (*of land*) faixa; (*TECH*) correia ♦ *vt* (*thrash*) surrar; ~**way** (*US*) *n* via circular
bemused [bɪ'mjuːzd] *adj* bestificado, estupidificado
bench [bɛntʃ] *n* banco; (*work* ~) bancada (de carpinteiro); (*BRIT: POL*) assento num Parlamento; **the B~** (*LAW: judge*) o magistrado; (: *judges*) os magistrados, o corpo de magistrados
bend [bɛnd] (*pt, pp* **bent**) *vt* (*leg, arm*) dobrar; (*pipe*) curvar ♦ *vi* dobrar-se, inclinar-se ♦ *n* curva; (*in pipe*) curvatura; ~ **down** *vi* abaixar-se; ~ **over** *vi* debruçar-se
beneath [bɪ'niːθ] *prep* abaixo de; (*unworthy of*) indigno de ♦ *adv* em baixo
benefactor ['bɛnɪfæktə*] *n* benfeitor(a)

m/f
beneficial [bɛnɪ'fɪʃəl] *adj*: ~ (**to**) benéfico (a)
benefit ['bɛnɪfɪt] *n* benefício, vantagem *f*; (*money*) subsídio, auxílio ♦ *vt* beneficiar ♦ *vi*: to ~ **from** sth beneficiar-se de algo
benevolent [bɪ'nɛvələnt] *adj* benévolo
benign [bɪ'naɪn] *adj* (*person, smile*) afável, bondoso; (*MED*) benigno
bent [bɛnt] *pt, pp of* **bend** ♦ *n* inclinação *f* ♦ *adj*: to be ~ **on** estar empenhado em
bequest [bɪ'kwɛst] *n* legado
bereaved [bɪ'riːvd] *npl*: **the** ~ os enlutados
beret ['bɛreɪ] *n* boina
Berlin [bəː'lɪn] *n* Berlim
berm [bəːm] (*US*) *n* acostamento (*BR*), berma (*PT*)
berry ['bɛrɪ] *n* baga
berserk [bə'səːk] *adj*: to go ~ perder as estribeiras
berth [bəːθ] *n* (*bed*) beliche *m*; (*cabin*) cabine *f*; (*on train*) leito; (*for ship*) ancoradouro ♦ *vi* (*in harbour*) atracar, encostar-se; (*at anchor*) ancorar
beseech [bɪ'siːtʃ] (*pt, pp* **besought**) *vt* suplicar, implorar
beset [bɪ'sɛt] (*pt, pp* **beset**) *vt* acossar
beside [bɪ'saɪd] *prep* (*next to*) junto de, ao lado de, ao pé de; to be ~ **o.s.** (**with anger**) estar fora de si; **that's** ~ **the point** isso não tem nada a ver
besides [bɪ'saɪdz] *adv* além disso; (*in any case*) de qualquer jeito ♦ *prep* (*as well as*) além de
besiege [bɪ'siːdʒ] *vt* (*town*) sitiar, pôr cerco a; (*fig*) assediar
besought [bɪ'sɔːt] *pt, pp of* **beseech**
best [bɛst] *adj* melhor ♦ *adv* (o) melhor; **the** ~ **part of** (*quantity*) a maior parte de; **at** ~ na melhor das hipóteses; **to make the** ~ **of** sth tirar o maior partido possível de algo; **to do one's** ~ fazer o possível; **to the** ~ **of my knowledge** que eu saiba; **to the** ~ **of my ability** o melhor que eu puder; ~ **man** *n* padrinho de casamento
bestow [bɪ'stəʊ] *vt*: to ~ sth **on** sb outorgar algo a alguém
bet [bɛt] (*pt, pp* **bet** *or* ~**ted**) *n* aposta ♦ *vt, vi* apostar
betray [bɪ'treɪ] *vt* trair; (*denounce*) delatar; ~**al** *n* traição *f*
better ['bɛtə*] *adj, adv* melhor ♦ *vt* melhorar; (*go above*) superar ♦ *n*: to get **the** ~ **of** vencer; **you had** ~ **do it** é melhor você fazer isso; **he thought** ~ **of it** pensou melhor, mudou de opinião; **to get** ~ melhorar; ~ **off** *adj* mais rico; (*fig*): **you'd be** ~ **off this way** seria melhor para você assim
betting ['bɛtɪŋ] *n* jogo; ~ **shop** (*BRIT*) *n* agência de apostas

between [bɪ'twiːn] *prep* no meio de, entre ♦ *adv* no meio

beverage ['bevərɪdʒ] *n* bebida

beware [bɪ'weə*] *vi*: **to ~ (of)** precaver-se (de), ter cuidado (com); **"~ of the dog"** "cuidado com o cachorro"

bewildered [bɪ'wɪldəd] *adj* atordeado; (*confused*) confuso

bewitching [bɪ'wɪtʃɪŋ] *adj* encantador(a), sedutor(a)

beyond [bɪ'jɔnd] *prep* (*in space*) além de; (*exceeding*) acima de, fora de; (*date*) mais tarde que; (*above*) acima de ♦ *adv* além; (*in time*) mais longe, mais adiante; **~ doubt** fora de qualquer dúvida; **to be ~ repair** não ter conserto

bias ['baɪəs] *n* (*prejudice*) preconceito; **~(s)ed** parcial

bib [bɪb] *n* babadouro, babador *m*

Bible ['baɪbl] *n* Bíblia

bicarbonate of soda [baɪ'kɑːbənɪt-] *n* bicarbonato de sódio

bicker ['bɪkə*] *vi* brigar

bicycle ['baɪsɪkl] *n* bicicleta

bid [bɪd] (*pt* **bade** *or* **bid**, *pp* **bidden** *or* **bid**) *n* oferta; (*at auction*) lance *m*; (*attempt*) tentativa ♦ *vi* fazer lance ♦ *vt* oferecer; **to ~ sb good day** dar bom dia a alguém; **~der** *n*: **the highest ~der** quem oferece mais; **~ding** *n* (*at auction*) lances *mpl*

bide [baɪd] *vt*: **to ~ one's time** esperar o momento adequado

bifocals [baɪ'fəʊklz] *npl* óculos *mpl* bifocais

big [bɪg] *adj* grande; (*bulky*) volumoso; **~ brother/sister** irmão/irmã mais velho/a

big dipper [-'dɪpə*] *n* montanha-russa

bigheaded ['bɪg'hedɪd] *adj* convencido

bigot ['bɪgət] *n* fanático/a, intolerante *m/f*

big top *n* tenda de circo

bike [baɪk] *n* bicicleta

bikini [bɪ'kiːnɪ] *n* biquíni *m*

bilingual [baɪ'lɪŋgwəl] *adj* bilíngue

bill [bɪl] *n* conta; (*invoice*) fatura; (*POL*) projeto de lei; (*US*: *banknote*) bilhete *m*, nota; (*in restaurant*) conta, notinha; (*of bird*) bico; (*THEATRE*) cartaz *m*; **to fit** *or* **fill the ~** (*fig*) servir; **~board** *n* quadro para cartazes

billet ['bɪlɪt] *n* alojamento

billfold ['bɪlfəʊld] (*US*) *n* carteira

billiards ['bɪlɪədz] *n* bilhar *m*

billion ['bɪlɪən] *n* (*BRIT*) trilhão *m*; (*US*) bilhão *m*

bin [bɪn] *n* caixa; (*BRIT*: *for rubbish*) lata de lixo

bind [baɪnd] (*pt, pp* **bound**) *vt* atar, amarrar; (*oblige*) obrigar; (*book*) encadernar ♦ *n* (*inf*) saco; (*nuisance*) chatice *f*; **~ing** *adj* (*contract*) sujeitante

binge [bɪndʒ] (*inf*) *n*: **to go on a ~** tomar uma bebedeira

bingo ['bɪŋgəʊ] *n* bingo

binoculars [bɪ'nɔkjʊləz] *npl* binóculo

bio... [baɪəʊ] *prefix* bio...; **~chemistry** *n* bioquímica; **~graphy** *n* biografia; **~logy** *n* biologia

birch [bɜːtʃ] *n* bétula

bird [bɜːd] *n* ave *f*, pássaro; (*BRIT*: *inf*: *girl*) gatinha; **~'s-eye view** *n* vista aérea; (*overview*) vista geral; **~-watcher** *n* ornitófilo/a

Biro ['baɪərəʊ] ® *n* (caneta) esferográfica

birth [bɜːθ] *n* nascimento; **to give ~ to** dar à luz, parir; **~ control** *n* controle *m* da natalidade; (*methods*) métodos *mpl* anticoncepcionais; **~day** *n* aniversário (*BR*), dia *m* de anos (*PT*) ♦ *cpd* de aniversário; *see also* **happy**; **~ rate** *n* (índice *m* de) natalidade *f*

biscuit ['bɪskɪt] *n* (*BRIT*) bolacha, biscoito; (*US*) pão *m* doce

bisect [baɪ'sekt] *vt* dividir ao meio

bishop ['bɪʃəp] *n* bispo; (*CHESS*) peça de jogo de xadrez

bit [bɪt] *pt of* **bite** ♦ *n* pedaço, bocado; (*of horse*) freio; (*COMPUT*) bit *m*; **a ~ of** (*a little*) um pouco de; **~ by ~** pouco a pouco

bitch [bɪtʃ] *n* (*dog*) cadela, cachorra; (*inf!*) cadela (!), vagabunda (!)

bite [baɪt] (*pt* **bit**, *pp* **bitten**) *vt, vi* morder; (*insect etc*) picar ♦ *n* (*insect ~*) picada; (*mouthful*) bocado; **to ~ one's nails** roer as unhas; **let's have a ~ (to eat)** (*inf*) vamos fazer uma boquinha; **bitten** *pp of* **bite**

bitter ['bɪtə*] *adj* amargo; (*wind, criticism*) cortante, penetrante; (*weather*) horrível ♦ *n* (*BRIT*: *beer*) cerveja amarga; **~ness** *n* amargor *m*; (*anger*) rancor *m*

blab [blæb] *vi* dar *or* bater com a língua nos dentes

black [blæk] *adj* preto; (*humour*) negro ♦ *n* (*colour*) cor *f* preta; (*person*): **B~** negro/a, preto/a ♦ *vt* (*BRIT*: *INDUSTRY*) boicotar; **to give sb a ~ eye** esmurrar alguém e deixá-lo de olho roxo; **~ and blue** contuso, contundido; **to be in the ~** (*in credit*) estar com saldo credor; **~berry** *n* amora silvestre; **~bird** *n* melro; **~board** *n* quadro(-negro); **~ coffee** *n* café *m* preto, bica (*PT*); **~currant** *n* groselha negra; **~en** *vt* (*fig*) denegrir; **~leg** (*BRIT*) *n* fura-greve *m/f*; **~list** *n* lista negra; **~mail** *n* chantagem *f* ♦ *vt* fazer chantagem a; **~ market** *n* mercado *or* câmbio negro; **~out** *n* blecaute *m*; (*fainting*) desmaio; (*of radio signal*) desvanecimento; **B~ Sea** *n*: **the B~ Sea** *o* mar Negro; **~ sheep** *n* (*fig*) ovelha negra; **~smith** *n* ferreiro; **~ spot** *n* (*AUT*) lugar *m* perigoso

bladder ['blædə*] *n* bexiga

blade [bleɪd] *n* lâmina; (*of oar*) pá *f*; **a ~ of grass** uma folha de relva

blame [bleɪm] *n* culpa ♦ *vt*: **to ~ sb for**

sth culpar alguém por algo; **to be to ~** ter a culpa; **~less** *adj* inocente

bland [blænd] *adj* (*taste*) brando

blank [blæŋk] *adj* em branco; (*look*) sem expressão ♦ *n* (*of memory*): **to go ~** dar um branco; (*on form*) espaço em branco; (*cartridge*) bala de festim; **~ cheque** (*US* **~ check**) *n* cheque *m* em branco

blanket ['blæŋkɪt] *n* cobertor *m*

blare [blɛə˙] *vi* (*horn, radio*) clangorar

blast [blɑːst] *n* (*of wind*) rajada; (*of explosive*) explosão *f* ♦ *vt* fazer voar; **~-off** *n* (*SPACE*) lançamento

blatant ['bleɪtənt] *adj* descarado

blaze [bleɪz] *n* (*fire*) fogo; (*in building etc*) incêndio; (*fig: of colour*) esplendor *m*; (: *of glory, publicity*) explosão *f* ♦ *vi* (*fire*) arder; (*guns*) descarregar; (*eyes*) brilhar ♦ *vt*: **to ~ a trail** (*fig*) abrir (um) caminho

blazer ['bleɪzə˙] *n* casaco esportivo, blazer *m*

bleach [bliːtʃ] *n* (*also*: **household ~**) água sanitária ♦ *vt* (*linen*) branquear; **~ed** *adj* (*hair*) oxigenado; **~ers** (*US*) *npl* (*SPORT*) arquibancada descoberta

bleak [bliːk] *adj* (*countryside*) desolado; (*prospect*) desanimador(a), sombrio; (*weather*) ruim

bleary-eyed ['blɪərɪ'aɪd] *adj* de olhos injetados

bleat [bliːt] *vi* balir

bled [blɛd] *pt, pp* of **bleed**

bleed [bliːd] (*pt, pp* **bled**) *vi* sangrar

bleeper ['bliːpə˙] *n* (*of doctor*) bip *m*

blemish ['blɛmɪʃ] *n* mancha; (*on reputation*) mácula

blend [blɛnd] *n* mistura ♦ *vt* misturar ♦ *vi* (*colours etc*: *also*: **~ in**) combinar-se, misturar-se

bless [blɛs] (*pt, pp* **~ed** *or* **blest**) *vt* abençoar; **~ you!** (*after sneeze*) saúde!; **~ing** *n* bênção *f*; (*godsend*) graça, dádiva; (*approval*) aprovação *f*

blew [bluː] *pt* of **blow**

blight [blaɪt] *vt* frustrar, gorar

blimey ['blaɪmɪ] (*BRIT: inf*) *excl* nossa!

blind [blaɪnd] *adj* cego ♦ *n* (*for window*) persiana; (: *also*: **Venetian ~**) veneziana ♦ *vt* cegar; (*dazzle*) deslumbrar; **the ~** *npl* (~ *people*) os cegos; **~ alley** *n* beco-sem-saída *m*; **~ corner** (*BRIT*) *n* curva sem visibilidade; **~fold** *n* venda ♦ *adj, adv* com os olhos vendados, às cegas ♦ *vt* vendar os olhos a; **~ly** *adv* às cegas; (*without thinking*) cegamente; **~ness** *n* cegueira; **~ spot** *n* (*AUT*) local *m* pouco visível; (*fig*) ponto fraco

blink [blɪŋk] *vi* piscar; **~ers** *npl* antolhos *mpl*

bliss [blɪs] *n* felicidade *f*

blister ['blɪstə˙] *n* (*on skin*) bolha; (*in paint, rubber*) empola ♦ *vi* empolar-se

blithely ['blaɪðlɪ] *adv* tranqüilamente

blitz [blɪts] *n* bombardeio aéreo

blizzard ['blɪzəd] *n* nevasca

bloated ['bləʊtɪd] *adj* (*swollen*) inchado; (*full*) empanturrado

blob [blɔb] *n* (*drop*) gota; (*indistinct shape*) ponto

bloc [blɔk] *n* (*POL*) bloco

block [blɔk] *n* (*of wood*) bloco; (*of stone*) laje *f*; (*in pipes*) entupimento; (*of buildings*) quarteirão *m* ♦ *vt* obstruir, bloquear; (*progress*) impedir; **~ of flats** (*BRIT*) prédio (de apartamentos); **mental ~** bloqueio; **~ade** *n* bloqueio; **~age** *n* obstrução *f*; **~buster** *n* grande sucesso; **~ letters** *npl* letras *fpl* maiúsculas

bloke [bləʊk] (*BRIT: inf*) *n* cara *m* (*BR*), gajo (*PT*)

blond(e) [blɔnd] *adj, n* louro/a

blood [blʌd] *n* sangue *m*; **~ donor** *n* doador(a) *m/f* de sangue; **~ group** *n* grupo sangüíneo; **~hound** *n* sabujo; **~ poisoning** *n* toxemia; **~ pressure** *n* pressão *f* arterial *or* sangüínea; **~shed** *n* matança, carnificina; **~shot** *adj* (*eyes*) injetado; **~stream** *n* corrente *f* sangüínea; **~ test** *n* exame *m* de sangue; **~thirsty** *adj* sangüinário; **~ vessel** *n* vaso sangüíneo; **~y** *adj* sangrento; (*nose*) ensangüentado; (*BRIT: inf!*): **this ~y ... essa droga de ...**, esse maldito ...; **~y strong/good** forte/bom pra burro; **~y-minded** (*BRIT: inf*) *adj* espírito de porco *inv*

bloom [bluːm] *n* flor *f* ♦ *vi* florescer

blossom ['blɔsəm] *n* flor *f* ♦ *vi* florescer; (*fig*): **to ~ into** (*fig*) tornar-se

blot [blɔt] *n* borrão *m*; (*fig*) mancha ♦ *vt* borrar; **~ out** *vt* (*view*) tapar; (*memory*) apagar

blotchy ['blɔtʃɪ] *adj* (*complexion*) cheio de manchas

blotting paper ['blɔtɪŋ-] *n* mata-borrão *m*

blouse [blauz] *n* blusa

blow [bləʊ] (*pt* **blew**, *pp* **blown**) *n* golpe *m*; (*punch*) soco ♦ *vi* soprar ♦ *vt* (*subj: wind*) soprar; (*instrument*) tocar; (*fuse*) queimar; **to ~ one's nose** assoar o nariz; **~ away** *vt* levar, arrancar ♦ *vi* ser levado pelo vento; **~ down** *vt* derrubar; **~ off** *vt* levar; **~ out** *vi* (*candle*) apagar; **~ over** *vi* (*storm, crisis*) passar; **~ up** *vi* explodir ♦ *vt* explodir; (*tyre*) encher; (*PHOT*) ampliar; **~-dry** *n* escova; **~lamp** (*BRIT*) *n* maçarico; **~-n** *pp* of **blow**; **~-out** *n* (*of tyre*) furo; **~torch** *n* = **~lamp**

blue [bluː] *adj* azul; (*depressed*) deprimido; **~s** *n* (*MUS*): **the ~s** o blues; **~ film/joke** filme/anedota picante; **out of the ~** (*fig*) de estalo, inesperadamente; **~bell** *n* campainha; **~bottle** *n* varejeira azul; **~print** *n* (*fig*): **~ print (for)** esquema *m* (de)

bluff [blʌf] *vi* blefar ♦ *n* blefe *m*; **to call sb's ~** pagar para ver alguém

blunder ['blʌndə*] n gafe f ♦ vi cometer or fazer uma gafe

blunt [blʌnt] adj (knife) cego; (pencil) rombudo; (person) franco, direto

blur [blə:*] n borrão m ♦ vt (vision) embaçar; (distinction) reduzir, diminuir

blurb [blə:b] n dizeres mpl de propaganda

blurt out [blə:t-] vt (say) balbuciar

blush [blʌʃ] vi corar, ruborizar-se ♦ n rubor m, vermelhidão f

blustering ['blʌstəriŋ] adj (person) fanfarrão/rona

blustery ['blʌstəri] adj (weather) borrascoso, tormentoso

boar [bɔ:*] n javali m

board [bɔ:d] n tábua; (card~) quadro; (notice ~) quadro de avisos; (for chess etc) tabuleiro; (committee) junta, conselho; (in firm) diretoria, conselho administrativo; (NAUT, AVIAT): **on ~** a bordo ♦ vt embarcar em; **full ~** (BRIT) pensão f completa; **half ~** (BRIT) meia-pensão f; **~ and lodging** casa e comida; **to go by the ~** ficar abandonado, dançar (inf); **~ up** vt entaburar; **~ er** n interno/a; **~ing card** n = **~ing pass**; **~ing house** n pensão m; **~ing pass** (BRIT) n cartão m de embarque; **~ing school** n internato; **~ room** n sala da diretoria

boast [bəust] vi: **to ~** (about or of) gabar-se (de), jactar-se (de)

boat [bəut] n (small) bote m; (big) navio; **~er** n (hat) chapéu m de palha; **~swain** n contramestre m

bob [bɔb] vi balouçar-se; **~ up** vi aparecer, surgir

bobby ['bɔbi] (BRIT: inf) n policial m/f (BR), polícia m (PT)

bobsleigh ['bɔbslei] n bob m, trenó m duplo

bode [bəud] vi: **to ~ well/ill (for)** ser de bom/mau agouro (para)

bodily ['bɔdili] adj corporal; (needs) material ♦ adv (lift) em peso

body ['bɔdi] n corpo; (corpse) cadáver m; (of car) carroceria; (fig: group) grupo; (: organization) organização f; (quantity) conjunto; (of wine) corpo; **~-building** n musculação f; **~guard** n guarda-costas m inv; **~work** n lataria

bog [bɔg] n pântano, atoleiro ♦ vt: **to get ~ged down** (fig) atolar-se

boggle ['bɔgl] vi: **the mind ~s** (wonder) não dá para imaginar; (innuendo) nem quero pensar

bogus ['bəugəs] adj falso

boil [bɔil] vt ferver; (CULIN) cozer, cozinhar ♦ vi ferver n (MED) furúnculo; **to come to the** (BRIT) **or a** (US) **~** começar a ferver; **~ down to** vt fus (fig) reduzir-se a; **~ over** vi transbordar; **~ed egg** n ovo cozido; **~ed potatoes** npl batatas fpl cozidas; **~er** n caldeira;

(for central heating) boiler m; **~er suit** (BRIT) n macacão m (BR), fato macaco (PT); **~ing point** n ponto de ebulição

boisterous ['bɔistərəs] adj (noisy) barulhento; (excitable) agitado; (crowd) turbulento

bold [bəuld] adj corajoso; (pej) atrevido, insolente; (outline, colour) forte

Bolivia [bə'liviə] n Bolívia

bollard ['bɔləd] (BRIT) n (AUT) poste m de sinalização

bolster ['bəulstə*] n travesseiro; **~ up** vt sustentar

bolt [bəult] n (lock) trinco, ferrolho; (with nut) parafuso, cavilha ♦ adv: **~ upright** direito como um fuso ♦ vt (door) fechar a ferrolho, trancar; (food) engolir às pressas ♦ vi fugir; (horse) disparar

bomb [bɔm] n bomba ♦ vt bombardear

bomber ['bɔmə*] n (AVIAT) bombardeiro

bombshell ['bɔmʃel] n (fig) bomba

bona fide ['bəunə'faidi] adj genuíno, autêntico

bond [bɔnd] n (binding promise) compromisso; (link) vínculo, laço; (FINANCE) obrigação f; (COMM): **in ~** (goods) retido sob caução na alfândega; **~age** n escravidão f

bone [bəun] n osso; (of fish) espinha ♦ vt desossar; tirar as espinhas de; **~ idle** adj preguiçoso

bonfire ['bɔnfaiə*] n fogueira

bonnet ['bɔnit] n toucado; (BRIT: of car) capô m

bonus ['bəunəs] n (payment) bônus m; (fig) gratificação f

bony ['bəuni] adj ossudo; (meat) cheio de ossos; (fish) cheio de espinhas

boo [bu:] vt vaiar ♦ excl ruuh!, bu!

booby trap ['bu:bi-] n armadilha explosiva

book [buk] n livro; (of stamps, tickets) talão m ♦ vt reservar; (driver) autuar; (football player) mostrar o cartão amarelo a; **~s** npl (COMM) contas fpl, contabilidade f; **~case** n estante f (para livros); **~ing office** (BRIT) n (RAIL, THEATRE) bilheteria (BR), bilheteira (PT); **~-keeping** n escrituração f, contabilidade f; **~let** n livrinho, brochura; **~maker** n book(maker) m (BR), agenciador m de apostas (PT); **~seller** n livreiro/a; **~shop**, **~store** n livraria

boom [bu:m] n (noise) barulho, estrondo; (in sales) aumento rápido ♦ vi retumbar; (business) tomar surto

boon [bu:n] n dádiva, benefício

boost [bu:st] n estímulo ♦ vt estimular; **~er** n (MED) revacinação f; **~er cushion** (AUT) almofada para crianças

boot [bu:t] n bota; (for football) chuteira; (BRIT: of car) porta-malas m (BR), porta-bagagem m (PT) ♦ vt (COMPUT) dar carga em; **to ~ ...** (in addition) ainda por cima ...

booth [buːð] *n* (*at fair*) barraca; (*telephone ~, voting ~*) cabine *f*

booty ['buːtɪ] *n* despojos *mpl*, pilhagem *f*

booze [buːz] (*inf*) *n* bebida alcoólica

border ['bɔːdə*] *n* margem *f*; (*for flowers*) borda; (*of a country*) fronteira; (*on cloth etc*) debrum *m*, remate *m* ♦ *vt* (*also: ~ on*) limitar-se com; ~ **on** *vt fus* (*fig*) chegar às raias de; ~**line** *n* fronteira; ~**line case** *n* caso-limite *m*; **B~s** *n*: **the B~s** a região fronteiriça entre a Escócia e a Inglaterra

bore [bɔː*] *pt of* **bear** ♦ *vt* (*hole*) abrir; (*well*) cavar; (*person*) aborrecer ♦ *n* (*person*) chato/a, maçante *m/f*; (*of gun*) calibre *m*; **to be ~d** estar entediado; ~**dom** *n* tédio, aborrecimento; **boring** *adj* chato, maçante

born [bɔːn] *adj*: **to be ~** nascer

borne [bɔːn] *pp of* **bear**

borough ['bʌrə] *n* município

borrow ['bɔrəu] *vt*: **to ~ sth (from sb)** pedir algo emprestado a alguém

Bosnia (and) Herzegovina ['bɔznɪə hɜːtsəgəu'viːnə] *n* Bósnia e Herzegovina

bosom ['buzəm] *n* peito; ~ **friend** *n* amigo/a íntimo/a *or* do peito

boss [bɔs] *n* (*employer*) patrão/troa *m/f* ♦ *vt* (*also: ~ about; ~ around*) mandar em; ~**y** *adj* mandão/dona

bosun ['bəusn] *n* contramestre *m*

botany ['bɔtənɪ] *n* botânica

botch [bɔtʃ] *vt* (*also: ~ up*) estropiar, atamancar

both [bəuθ] *adj, pron* ambos/as, os dois/as duas ♦ *adv*: ~ **A and B** tanto A como B; ~ **of us went, we ~ went** nós dois fomos, ambos fomos

bother ['bɔðə*] *vt* (*worry*) preocupar; (*disturb*) atrapalhar ♦ *vi* (*also: ~ o.s.*) preocupar-se ♦ *n* preocupação *f*; (*nuisance*) amolação *f*, inconveniente *m*

bottle ['bɔtl] *n* garrafa; (*of perfume, medicine*) frasco; (*baby's*) mamadeira (*BR*), biberão *m* (*PT*) ♦ *vt* engarrafar; ~ **up** *vt* conter, refrear; ~**neck** *n* (*traffic*) engarrafamento; (*fig*) obstáculo, problema *m*; ~**opener** *n* abridor *m* (de garrafas) (*BR*), abre-garrafas *m inv* (*PT*)

bottom ['bɔtəm] *n* fundo; (*buttocks*) traseiro; (*of page, list*) pé *m*; (*of class*) nível *m* mais baixo ♦ *adj* (*low*) inferior, mais baixo; (*last*) último; ~**less** *adj* (*funds*) ilimitado

bough [bau] *n* ramo

bought [bɔːt] *pt, pp of* **buy**

boulder ['bəuldə*] *n* pedregulho, matacão *m*

bounce [bauns] *vi* saltar, quicar; (*cheque*) ser devolvido ♦ *vt* fazer saltar ♦ *n* (*rebound*) salto; ~**r** (*inf*) *n* leão-de-chácara *m*

bound [baund] *pt, pp of* **bind** ♦ *n* (*leap*) pulo, salto; (*gen pl: limit*) limite *m* ♦ *vi* (*leap*) pular, saltar ♦ *vt* (*border*) demar-

car ♦ *adj*: ~ **by** limitado por; **to be ~ to do sth** (*obliged*) ter a obrigação de fazer algo; (*likely*) na certa ir fazer algo; ~ **for** com destino a

boundary ['baundrɪ] *n* limite *m*, fronteira

boundless ['baundlɪs] *adj* ilimitado

bouquet ['bukeɪ] *n* (*of flowers*) buquê *m*, ramalhete *m*

bourgeois ['buəʒwɑː] *adj* burguês/guesa

bout [baut] *n* (*of malaria etc*) ataque *m*; (*of activity*) explosão *f*; (*BOXING etc*) combate *m*

bow¹ [bəu] *n* (*knot*) laço; (*weapon, MUS*) arco

bow² [bau] *n* (*of the body*) reverência; (*of the head*) inclinação *f*; (*NAUT: also: ~s*) proa ♦ *vi* curvar-se, fazer uma reverência; (*yield*): **to ~ to** *or* **before** ceder ante, submeter-se a

bowels ['bauəlz] *npl* intestinos *mpl*, tripas *fpl*; (*fig*) entranhas *fpl*

bowl [bəul] *n* tigela; (*ball*) bola ♦ *vi* (*CRICKET*) arremessar a bola

bow-legged *adj* cambaio, de pernas tortas

bowler ['bəulə*] *n* (*CRICKET*) lançador *m* (da bola); (*BRIT: also: ~ hat*) chapéu-coco *m*

bowling ['bəulɪŋ] *n* (*game*) boliche *m*; ~ **alley** *n* boliche *m*; ~ **green** *n* gramado (*BR*) *or* relvado (*PT*) para jogo de bolas

bowls [bəulz] *n* jogo de bolas

bow tie ['bəu-] *n* gravata-borboleta

box [bɔks] *n* caixa; (*THEATRE*) camarote *m* ♦ *vt* encaixotar; (*SPORT*) boxear contra ♦ *vi* (*SPORT*) boxear; ~**er** *n* (*person*) boxeador *m*, pugilista *m*; ~**ing** *n* (*SPORT*) boxe *m*, pugilismo; **B~ing Day** (*BRIT*) *n* Dia de Santo Estêvão (*26 de dezembro*); ~**ing ring** *n* ringue *m* de boxe; ~ **office** *n* bilheteria (*BR*), bilheteira (*PT*); ~**room** *n* quarto pequeno

boy [bɔɪ] *n* (*young*) menino, garoto; (*older*) moço, rapaz *m*; (*son*) filho

boycott ['bɔɪkɔt] *n* boicote *m*, boicotagem *f* ♦ *vt* boicotar

boyfriend ['bɔɪfrɛnd] *n* namorado

boyish ['bɔɪʃ] *adj* (*man*) jovial; (*looks*) pueril; (*woman*) com ares de menino

BR *abbr* = **British Rail**

bra [brɑː] *n* sutiã *m* (*BR*), soutien *m* (*PT*)

brace [breɪs] *n* (*on teeth*) aparelho; (*tool*) arco de pua ♦ *vt* retesar; ~**s** *npl* (*BRIT*) suspensórios *mpl*; **to ~ o.s.** (*also fig*) preparar-se

bracelet ['breɪslɪt] *n* pulseira

bracing ['breɪsɪŋ] *adj* tonificante

bracken ['brækən] *n* samambaia (*BR*), feto (*PT*)

bracket ['brækɪt] *n* (*TECH*) suporte *m*; (*group*) classe *f*, categoria; (*range*) faixa, parêntese *m* ♦ *vt* pôr entre parênteses; (*fig*) agrupar

brag [bræg] *vi* gabar-se, contar vantagem

braid [breɪd] n (trimming) galão m; (of hair) trança

brain [breɪn] n cérebro; ~s npl (CULIN) miolos mpl; (intelligence) inteligência, miolos; ~**child** n idéia original; ~**wash** vt fazer uma lavagem cerebral em; ~**wave** n inspiração f, idéia luminosa or brilhante; ~**y** adj inteligente

braise [breɪz] vt assar na panela

brake [breɪk] n freio (BR), travão m (PT) ♦ vt, vi frear (BR), travar (PT); ~ **fluid** n óleo de freio (BR) or dos travões (PT); ~ **light** n farol m do freio (BR), farolim m de travagem (PT)

bramble [ˈbræmbl] n amora-preta

bran [bræn] n farelo

branch [brɑːntʃ] n ramo, galho; (COMM) sucursal f, filial f; ~ **out** vi (fig) diversificar suas atividades; **to ~ out into** estender suas atividades a

brand [brænd] n marca; (fig: type) tipo ♦ vt (cattle) marcar com ferro quente

brandish [ˈbrændɪʃ] vt brandir

brand-new adj novo em folha, novinho

brandy [ˈbrændɪ] n conhaque m

brash [bræʃ] adj (forward) descarado

Brasilia [brəˈzɪliə] n Brasília

brass [brɑːs] n latão m; **the ~** (MUS) os metais; ~ **band** n banda de música

brassiere [ˈbræsɪə] n sutiã m (BR), soutien m (PT)

brat [bræt] n (pej) pirralho/a, fedelho/a, malcriado/a

bravado [brəˈvɑːdəu] n bravata

brave [breɪv] adj valente, corajoso ♦ vt (face up to) desafiar; ~**ry** n coragem f, bravura

brawl [brɔːl] n briga, pancadaria

brawny [ˈbrɔːnɪ] adj musculoso, carnudo

bray [breɪ] vi zurrar, ornejar

brazen [ˈbreɪzn] adj descarado ♦ vt: **to ~ it out** defender-se descaradamente

brazier [ˈbreɪzɪə] n braseiro

Brazil [brəˈzɪl] n Brasil m; ~**ian** adj, n brasileiro/a

Brazil nut n castanha-do-pará f

breach [briːtʃ] vt abrir brecha em ♦ n (gap) brecha; (breaking): ~ **of contract** inadimplência (BR), inadimplemento (PT); ~ **of the peace** perturbação f da ordem pública

bread [brɛd] n pão m; ~ **and butter** n pão m com manteiga; (fig) ganha-pão m; ~**bin** (US ~ **box**) n caixa de pão; ~**crumbs** npl migalhas fpl; (CULIN) farinha de rosca; ~**line** n: **to be on the** ~**line** viver na miséria

breadth [brɛtθ] n largura; (fig) amplitude f

breadwinner [ˈbrɛdwɪnə] n arrimo de família

break [breɪk] (pt **broke**, pp **broken**) vt quebrar (BR), partir (PT); (promise) quebrar; (law) violar, transgredir; (record) bater ♦ vi quebrar-se, partir-se; (storm) começar subitamente; (weather) mudar; (dawn) amanhecer; (story, news) revelar ♦ n (gap) abertura; (fracture) fratura; (rest) descanso; (interval) intervalo; (at school) recreio; (chance) oportunidade f; **to ~ the news to sb** dar a notícia a alguém; **to ~ even** sair sem ganhar nem perder; **to ~ free** or **loose** soltar-se; **to ~ open** (door etc) arrombar; ~ **down** vt (figures, data) analisar ♦ vi (machine, AUT) enguiçar, pifar (inf); (MED) sofrer uma crise nervosa; (person: cry) desatar a chorar; (talks) fracassar; ~ **in** vt (horse etc) domar ♦ vi (burglar) forçar uma entrada; (interrupt) interromper; ~ **into** vt fus (house) arrombar; ~ **off** vi (speaker) parar-se, deter-se; (branch) partir; ~ **out** vi (war) estourar; (prisoner) libertar-se; **to ~ out in spots/a rash** aparecer coberto de manchas/brotvejas; ~ **up** vi (ship) partir-se; (partnership) acabar; (marriage) desmanchar-se ♦ vt (rocks) partir; (biscuit etc) quebrar; (journey) romper; (fight) intervir em; ~**age** n quebradura; ~**down** n (AUT) enguiço, avaria; (in communications) interrupção f; (of marriage) fracasso, término; (MED: also: **nervous** ~**down**) esgotamento nervoso; (of figures) discriminação f, desdobramento; ~**down van** (BRIT) n reboque m (BR), pronto socorro (PT); ~**er** n onda grande

breakfast [ˈbrɛkfəst] n café m da manhã (BR), pequeno almoço (PT)

break: ~**-in** n roubo com arrombamento; ~**ing and entering** n (LAW) arrombamento; ~**through** n (fig) avanço, novo progresso; ~**water** n quebra-mar m

breast [brɛst] n (of woman) peito, seio; (chest, meat) peito; ~**-feed** (irreg: like **feed**) vt, vi amamentar; ~**-stroke** n nado de peito

breath [brɛθ] n fôlego, respiração f; **out of** ~ ofegante, sem fôlego; **B~alyser** ® n bafômetro

breathe [briːð] vt, vi respirar; ~ **in** vt, vi inspirar; ~ **out** vt, vi expirar; ~**r** n pausa; **breathing** n respiração f; **breathing space** n (fig) descanso, repouso

breathless [ˈbrɛθlɪs] adj sem fôlego

breathtaking [ˈbrɛθteɪkɪŋ] adj comovedor(a), emocionante

bred [brɛd] pt, pp of **breed**

breed [briːd] (pt, pp **bred**) vt (animals) criar; (plants) multiplicar ♦ vi criar, reproduzir ♦ n raça; ~**ing** n (upbringing) educação f

breeze [briːz] n brisa, aragem f; **breezy** adj (person) despreocupado, animado; (weather) ventoso

brew [bruː] vt (tea) fazer; (beer) fermentar ♦ vi (storm, fig) armar-se; ~**ery** n cervejaria

bribe [braɪb] *n* suborno ♦ *vt* subornar;
~**ry** *n* suborno
brick [brɪk] *n* tijolo; ~**layer** *n* pedreiro
bridal ['braɪdl] *adj* nupcial
bride [braɪd] *n* noiva; ~**groom** *n* noivo;
~**smaid** *n* dama de honra
bridge [brɪdʒ] *n* ponte *f*; (NAUT) ponte de
comando; (CARDS) bridge *m*; (of nose) cavalete *m* ♦ *vt* transpor
bridle ['braɪdl] *n* cabeçada, freio; ~ **path**
n senda
brief [briːf] *adj* breve ♦ *n* (LAW) causa;
(task) tarefa ♦ *vt* (inform) informar; ~**s**
npl (for men) cueca, (BR), cuecas *fpl*
(PT); (for women) calcinha (BR), cuecas
fpl (PT); ~**case** *n* pasta; ~**ing** *n* instruções *fpl*; (PRESS) informações *fpl*; ~**ly**
adv (glance) rapidamente; (say) em poucas palavras
bright [braɪt] *adj* claro, brilhante; (weather) resplandecente; (person: clever) inteligente; (: lively) alegre, animado; (colour) vivo; (future) promissor(a), favorável; ~**en** (also: ~**en up**) *vt* (room) tornar
mais alegre; (event) animar, alegrar ♦ *vi*
(weather) clarear; (person) animar-se,
alegrar-se; (face) iluminar-se; (prospects)
tornar-se animado or favorável
brilliance ['brɪljəns] *n* brilho, claridade *f*
brilliant ['brɪljənt] *adj* brilhante; (inf:
great) sensacional
brim [brɪm] *n* borda; (of hat) aba
brine [braɪn] *n* (CULIN) salmoura
bring [brɪŋ] (pt, pp brought) *vt* trazer; ~
about *vt* ocasionar, produzir; ~ **back**
vt restabelecer; (return) devolver; ~
down *vt* (price) abaixar; (government,
plane) derrubar; ~ **forward** *vt* adiantar;
~ **off** *vt* (plan) levar a cabo; ~ **out** *vt*
(object) tirar; (meaning) salientar; (book
etc) lançar; ~ **round** *vt* fazer voltar a
si; ~ **up** *vt* (person) educar, criar;
(carry up) subir; (question) introduzir;
(food) vomitar
brink [brɪŋk] *n* beira
brisk [brɪsk] *adj* vigoroso; (tone, person)
enérgico; (trade) ativo
bristle ['brɪsl] *n* (of animal) pêlo rijo; (of
beard) pêlo de barba curta; (of brush)
cerda ♦ *vi* (in anger) encolerizar-se
Britain ['brɪtən] *n* (also: **Great** ~) Grã-
Bretanha
British ['brɪtɪʃ] *adj* britânico ♦ *npl*: **the**
~ os britânicos; ~ **Isles** *npl* **the** ~
Isles as ilhas Britânicas; ~ **Rail** *n* companhia ferroviária britânica
Briton ['brɪtən] *n* britânico/a
brittle ['brɪtl] *adj* quebradiço, frágil
broach [brəʊtʃ] *vt* abordar, tocar em
broad [brɔːd] *adj* (street, range) amplo;
(shoulders, smile) largo; (distinction) geral; (accent) carregado; **in** ~ **daylight**
em plena luz do dia; ~**cast** (pt, pp
~**cast**) *n* transmissão *f* ♦ *vt, vi* transmitir; ~**en** *vt* alargar ♦ *vi* alargar-se; **to**

~**en one's mind** abrir os horizontes;
~**ly** *adv* em geral; ~-**minded** *adj* tolerante, liberal
broccoli ['brɒkəlɪ] *n* brócolis *mpl*
brochure ['brəʊʃjʊə*] *n* folheto, brochura
broil [brɔɪl] *vt* grelhar
broke [brəʊk] *pt of* **break** ♦ *adj* (inf) sem
um vintém, duro; (: company): **to go** ~
quebrar
broken ['brəʊkən] *pp of* **break** ♦ *adj*
quebrado; **in** ~ **English** num inglês
mascavado; ~-**hearted** *adj* com o coração partido
broker ['brəʊkə*] *n* corretor(a) *m/f*
brolly ['brɒlɪ] (BRIT: inf) *n* guarda-chuva
m
bronchitis [brɒŋ'kaɪtɪs] *n* bronquite *f*
bronze [brɒnz] *n* bronze *m*
brooch [brəʊtʃ] *n* broche *m*
brood [bruːd] *n* ninhada ♦ *vi* (person) cismar, remoer
brook [brʊk] *n* arroio, ribeiro
broom [brum] *n* vassoura; (BOT) giesta-
das-vassouras; ~**stick** *n* cabo de vassoura
Bros. *abbr* (COMM: = brothers) Irmãos
broth [brɒθ] *n* caldo
brothel ['brɒθl] *n* bordel *m*
brother ['brʌðə*] *n* irmão *m*; ~-**in-law** *n*
cunhado
brought [brɔːt] *pt, pp of* **bring**
brow [braʊ] *n* (forehead) fronte *f*, testa;
(rare: gen: eye~) sobrancelha; (of hill)
cimo, cume *m*
brown [braʊn] *adj* marrom (BR), castanho (PT); (hair) castanho; (tanned) bronzeado, moreno ♦ *n* (colour) cor *f* marrom (BR) or castanha (PT) ♦ *vt* (CULIN)
dourar; ~ **bread** *n* pão *m* integral;
B~ie *n* (also: **B~ie Guide**) fadinha de
bandeirante; ~**ie** (US) *n* (cake) docinho
de chocolate com amêndoas; ~ **paper** *n*
papel *m* pardo; ~ **sugar** *n* açúcar *m*
mascavo
browse [braʊz] *vi* (in shop) dar uma
olhada; **to** ~ **through a book** folhear
um livro
browser ['braʊzə*] *n* (COMPUT) browser
m
bruise [bruːz] *n* hematoma *m*, contusão *f*
♦ *vt* machucar
brunette [bruːˈnɛt] *n* morena
brunt [brʌnt] *n*: **the** ~ **of** (greater part) a
maior parte de
brush [brʌʃ] *n* escova; (for painting, shaving) pincel *m*; (quarrel) bate-boca *m* ♦
vt varrer; (groom) escovar; (also:
~ **against**) tocar ao passar, roçar; ~
aside *vt* afastar, não fazer caso de; ~
up *vt* retocar, revisar; ~**wood** *n* lenha,
gravetos *mpl*
brusque [bruːsk] *adj* rispido; (apology)
abrupto
Brussels ['brʌslz] *n* Bruxelas; ~ **sprout**
n couve-de-bruxelas *f*

brutal ['bruːtl] *adj* brutal

brute [bruːt] *n* bruto; *(person)* animal *m*
♦ *adj:* **by ~ force** por força bruta

BSc *n abbr* = **Bachelor of Science**

bubble ['bʌbl] *n* bolha *(BR)*, borbulha
(PT) ♦ *vi* borbulhar; ~ **bath** *n* banho
de espuma; ~ **gum** *n* chiclete *m* (de
bola) *(BR)*, pastilha elástica *(PT)*

buck [bʌk] *n (rabbit)* macho; *(deer)* cervo; *(US: inf)* dólar *m* ♦ *vi* corcovear; **to
pass the** ~ fazer o jogo de empurra; **to
up** *vi (cheer up)* animar-se, cobrar
ânimo

bucket ['bʌkɪt] *n* balde *m*

buckle ['bʌkl] *n* fivela ♦ *vt* afivelar ♦ *vi*
torcer-se, cambar-se

bud [bʌd] *n* broto; *(of flower)* botão *m* ♦
vi brotar, desabrochar

Buddhism ['budɪzəm] *n* budismo

budding ['bʌdɪŋ] *adj* em ascensão

buddy ['bʌdɪ] *(US)* *n* camarada *m*, companheiro

budge [bʌdʒ] *vt* mover ♦ *vi* mexer-se

budgerigar ['bʌdʒərɪgaː] *n* periquito

budget ['bʌdʒɪt] *n* orçamento ♦ *vi:* **to ~
for sth** incluir algo no orçamento

budgie ['bʌdʒɪ] *n* = **budgerigar**

buff [bʌf] *adj (colour)* cor de camurça ♦
n (inf: enthusiast) aficionado/a

buffalo ['bʌfələu] *(pl ~ or ~es) n (BRIT)*
búfalo; *(US: bison)* bisão *m*

buffer ['bʌfəˈ] *n* pára-choque *m*; *(COM-
PUT)* buffer *m*, memória intermediária

buffet1 ['bufeɪ] *(BRIT) n (in station)* bar
m; *(food)* bufê *m*; ~ **car** *(BRIT) n* vagão-
restaurante *m*

buffet2 ['bʌfɪt] *vt* fustigar

bug [bʌg] *n (esp US: insect)* bicho; *(fig:
germ)* micróbio; *(spy device)* microfone
m oculto, escuta clandestina; *(COMPUT:
of program)* erro ♦ *vt (inf: annoy)* apoquentar, incomodar; *(room)* colocar mi-
crofones em; *(phone)* grampear

buggy ['bʌgɪ] *n (for baby)* carrinho (des-
dobrável) de bebê

bugle ['bjuːgl] *n* trompa, corneta

build [bɪld] *(pt, pp* **built***) n (of person)* talhe *m*, estatura ♦ *vt* construir, edificar;
~ **up** *vt* acumular; ~**er** *n* construtor/a
m/f, empreiteiro/a; ~**ing** *n* construção
f; *(a ~)* edifício, prédio; ~**ing society**
(BRIT) *n* sociedade *f* de crédito imobiliário, financiador

built [bɪlt] *pt, pp of* **build** ♦ *adj:* ~-**in**
embutido; ~-**up area** *n* zona urbaniza-
da

bulb [bʌlb] *n (BOT)* bulbo; *(ELEC)* lâmpada

Bulgaria [bʌlˈgɛərɪə] *n* Bulgária; ~**n** *adj*
búlgaro ♦ *n* búlgaro/a

bulge [bʌldʒ] *n* bojo, saliência ♦ *vi*
inchar-se; *(pocket etc)* fazer bojo

bulk *n (of building, object)* volume
(of person) corpanzil *m*; **in** ~ *(COMM)*
~ranel; **the** ~ **of** a maior parte de;
~*adj* volumoso

bull [bul] *n* touro; ~**dog** *n* buldogue *m*

bulldozer ['buldəuzəˈ] *n* buldôzer *m*, es-
cavadora

bullet ['bulɪt] *n* bala

bulletin ['bulɪtɪn] *n* noticiário; *(journal)*
boletim *m*

bulletproof ['bulɪtpruːf] *adj* à prova de
balas

bullfight ['bulfaɪt] *n* tourada; ~**er** *n* toureiro; ~**ing** *n* tauromaquia

bullion ['buljən] *n* ouro *(or* prata) em
barras

bullock ['buləək] *n* boi *m*, novilho

bullring ['bulrɪŋ] *n* praça de touros

bull's-eye *n* centro do alvo, mosca (do
alvo) *(BR)*

bully ['bulɪ] *n* fanfarrão *m*, valentão *m* ♦
vt intimidar, tiranizar

bum [bʌm] *n (inf: backside)* bum-bum *m*;
(esp US: tramp) vagabundo/a, vadio/a

bumblebee ['bʌmblbiː] *n* mamangaba

bump [bʌmp] *n (in car)* batida; *(jolt)* sacudida; *(on head)* galo; *(on road)* elevação *f* ♦ *vt* bater contra, dar encontrão
em ♦ *vi* dar sacudidas; ~ **into** *vt fus*
chocar-se com *or* contra, colidir com;
(inf: person) dar com, topar com; ~**er** *n*
(BRIT) pára-choque *m* ♦ *adj:* ~**er crop**
supersafra; ~**er cars** *npl* carros *mpl* de
trombada

bumptious ['bʌmpʃəs] *adj* presunçoso

bumpy ['bʌmpɪ] *adj (road)* acidentado,
cheio de altos e baixos

bun [bʌn] *n* pão *m* doce *(BR)*, pãozinho
(PT); *(in hair)* coque *m*

bunch [bʌntʃ] *n (of flowers)* ramo; *(of
keys)* molho; *(of bananas)* cacho; *(of people)* grupo; ~**es** *npl (in hair)* cachos *mpl*

bundle ['bʌndl] *n* trouxa, embrulho; *(of
sticks)* feixe *m*; *(of papers)* maço ♦ *vt
(also:* ~ **up)** embrulhar, atar; *(put):* **to ~
sth/sb into** meter *or* enfiar algo/
alguém correndo em

bungalow ['bʌŋgələu] *n* bangalô *m*, chalé *m*

bungle ['bʌŋgl] *vt* estropear, estragar

bunion ['bʌnjən] *n* joanete *m*

bunk [bʌŋk] *n* beliche *m*; ~ **beds** *npl*
beliche *m*, cama-beliche *f*

bunker ['bʌŋkəˈ] *n (coal store)* carvoeira;
(MIL) abrigo, casamata; *(GOLF)* bunker *m*

bunny ['bʌnɪ] *n (also:* ~ **rabbit)** coelhi-
nho

bunting ['bʌntɪŋ] *n* bandeiras *fpl*

buoy [bɔɪ] *n* bóia; ~ **up** *vt (fig)* animar;
~**ant** *adj* flutuante; *(person)* alegre;
(COMM: market) animado

burden ['bəːdn] *n* responsabilidade *f*, fardo; *(load)* carga ♦ *vt* sobrecarregar;
(trouble): **to be a ~ to sb** ser um estorvo para alguém

bureau [bjuəˈrəu] *(pl ~x) n (BRIT: desk)*
secretária, escrivaninha; *(US: chest of
drawers)* cômoda; *(office)* escritório,
agência

bureaucracy [bjuəˈrɔkrəsɪ] n burocracia
bureaux [bjuəˈrəuz] npl of **bureau**
burglar [ˈbɜːglə*] n ladrão/ladrona m/f;
~ **alarm** n alarme de roubo; **~y** n roubo
burial [ˈbɛrɪəl] n enterro
burly [ˈbɜːlɪ] adj robusto, forte
Burma [ˈbɜːmə] n Birmânia
burn [bɜːn] (pt, pp ~**ed** or **burnt**) vt queimar; (house) incendiar ♦ vi queimar-se, arder; (sting) arder, picar ♦ n queimadura; ~ **down** vt incendiar; **~er** n (on cooker, heater) bico de gás, fogo; ~**ing** adj ardente; (hot: sand etc) abrasador(a); (ambition) grande; ~**t** pt, pp of **burn**
burrow [ˈbʌrəu] n toca, lura ♦ vi fazer uma toca, cavar; (rummage) esquadrinhar
bursary [ˈbɜːsərɪ] (BRIT) n (SCH) bolsa
burst [bɜːst] (pt, pp **burst**) vt arrebentar; (banks) romper ♦ vi estourar; (tyre) furar ♦ n rajada; to ~ **into flames** incendiar-se de repente; to ~ **into tears** desatar a chorar; to ~ **out laughing** cair na gargalhada; to be ~**ing** with (subj: room, container) estar abarrotado de; (: person: emotion) estar tomado de; a ~ **of energy** uma explosão de energia; ~ **into** vt fus (room etc) irromper em
bury [ˈbɛrɪ] vt enterrar; (at funeral) sepultar; to ~ **one's head in one's hands** cobrir o rosto com as mãos; to ~ **one's head in the sand** (fig) bancar avestruz; to ~ **the hatchet** (fig) fazer as pazes
bus [bʌs] n ônibus m inv (BR), autocarro (PT)
bush [buʃ] n arbusto, mata; (scrubland) sertão m; to **beat about the** ~ ser evasivo
bushy [ˈbuʃɪ] adj (thick) espesso
busily [ˈbɪzɪlɪ] adv atarefadamente
business [ˈbɪznɪs] n negócio; (trading) comércio, negócios mpl; (firm) empresa; (occupation) profissão f; to be away on ~ estar fora a negócios; it's my ~ to ... encarrego-me de ...; it's none of my ~ eu não tenho nada com isto; he means ~ fala a sério; ~**like** adj eficiente, metódico; ~**man/woman** (irreg) n homem m/mulher f de negócios; ~ **trip** n viagem f de negócios
busker [ˈbʌskə*] (BRIT) n artista m/f de rua
bus-stop n ponto de ônibus (BR), paragem f de autocarro (PT)
bust [bʌst] n (ANAT) busto ♦ adj (inf: broken) quebrado; **to go** ~ falir
bustle [ˈbʌsl] n animação f, movimento ♦ vi apressar-se, andar azafamado; **bustling** adj (town) animado, movimentado
busy [ˈbɪzɪ] adj (person) ocupado, atarefado; (place) movimentado; (US: TEL) ocu-

pado (BR), impedido (PT) ♦ vt: to ~ **o.s. with** ocupar-se em or de; ~**body** n intrometido/a

but [bʌt] conj **1** (yet) mas, porém; **he's tired** ~ **Paul isn't** ele está cansado mas Paul não; **the trip was enjoyable** ~ **tiring** a viagem foi agradável porém cansativa
2 (however) mas; **I'd love to come,** ~ **I'm busy** eu adoraria vir, mas estou ocupado
3 (showing disagreement, surprise etc) mas; ~ **that's far too expensive!** mas isso é caro demais!
♦ prep (apart from, except) exceto, menos; **he was nothing** ~ **trouble** ele só deu problema; **no-one** ~ **him** só ele, ninguém a não ser ele; ~ **for** sem, se não fosse; **(I'll do) anything** ~ **that** (eu faria) qualquer coisa menos isso
♦ adv (just, only) apenas; **had I** ~ **known** se eu soubesse; **I can** ~ **try** a única coisa que eu posso fazer é tentar; **all** ~ quase

butcher [ˈbutʃə*] n açougueiro (BR), homem m do talho (PT) ♦ vt (prisoners etc) chacinar, massacrar; (cattle etc for meat) abater e carnear; ~**'s (shop)** n açougue m (BR), talho (PT)
butler [ˈbʌtlə*] n mordomo
butt [bʌt] n (cask) tonel m; (of gun) coronha; (of cigarette) toco (BR), ponta (PT); (BRIT: fig: target) alvo ♦ vt (subj: goat) marrar; ~ **in** vi (interrupt) interromper
butter [ˈbʌtə*] n manteiga ♦ vt untar com manteiga; ~**cup** n botão-de-ouro m, ranúnculo
butterfly [ˈbʌtəflaɪ] n borboleta; (SWIMMING: also: ~ **stroke**) nado borboleta
buttocks [ˈbʌtəks] npl nádegas fpl
button [ˈbʌtn] n botão m; (US: badge) emblema m ♦ vt (also: ~ **up**) abotoar ♦ vi ter botões
buttress [ˈbʌtrɪs] n contraforte m
buxom [ˈbʌksəm] adj rechonchudo
buy [baɪ] (pt, pp **bought**) vt comprar ♦ n compra; to ~ **sb sth/sth from sb** comprar algo para alguém/algo a alguém; to ~ **sb a drink** pagar um drinque para alguém; ~**er** n comprador(a) m/f
buzz [bʌz] n zumbido; (inf: phone call): **to give sb a** ~ dar uma ligada para alguém ♦ vi zumbir; ~**er** n cigarra, vibrador m
buzz word n modismo

by [baɪ] prep **1** (referring to cause, agent) por, de; **killed** ~ **lightning** morto por um raio; **a painting** ~ **Picasso** um quadro de Picasso

2 (referring to method, manner, means) de, com; ~ **bus/car/train** de ônibus/carro/trem; **to pay** ~ **cheque** pagar com cheque; ~ **moonlight/candlelight** sob o luar/à luz de vela; ~ **saving hard, he** ... economizando muito, ele ...
3 (via, through) por, via; **we came** ~ **Dover** viemos por ou via Dover
4 (close to) perto de, ao pé de; **a holiday** ~ **the sea** férias à beira-mar; **she sat** ~ **his bed** ela sentou-se ao lado de seu leito
5 (past) por; **she rushed** ~ **me** ela passou por mim correndo
6 (not later than): ~ **4 o'clock** antes das quatro; ~ **this time tomorrow** esta mesma hora amanhã; ~ **the time I got here it was too late** quando eu cheguei aqui, já era tarde demais
7 (during): ~ **daylight** durante o dia
8 (amount) por; ~ **the kilometre** por quilômetro
9 (MATH, measure) por; **it's broader** ~ **a metre** tem um metro a mais de largura
10 (according to) segundo, de acordo com; **it's all right** ~ **me** por mim tudo bem
11: **(all)** ~ **oneself** etc (completamente) só, sozinho; **he did it (all)** ~ **himself** ele fêz tudo sozinho
12: ~ **the way** a propósito
♦ adv **1** see **go**; **pass** etc
2: ~ **and** ~ logo, mais tarde; ~ **and large** em geral

bye(-bye) ['baɪ'baɪ] excl até logo (BR), tchau (BR), adeus (PT)
bye(e)-law n lei f de município
by-election (BRIT) n eleição f parlamentar complementar
bygone ['baɪgɔn] adj passado, antigo ♦ n: **let** ~s **be** ~s o que passou passou
bypass ['baɪpɑːs] n via secundária, desvio; (MED) ponte f de safena ♦ vt evitar
by-product n subproduto, produto derivado; (of situation) subproduto
bystander ['baɪstændə*] n circunstante m/f; (observer) espectador(a) m/f
byte [baɪt] n (COMPUT) byte m
byword ['baɪwɜːd] n: **to be a** ~ **for** ser sinônimo de
by-your-leave n: **without so much as a** ~ sem mais aquela

C

C [siː] n (MUS) dó m
C. abbr (= Celsius or centigrade) C.
CA n abbr = **chartered accountant**
cab [kæb] n táxi m; (of truck etc) boléia; (of train) cabina de maquinista
cabaret ['kæbəreɪ] n cabaré m
cabbage ['kæbɪdʒ] n repolho (BR), couve

f (PT)
cabin ['kæbɪn] n cabana; (on ship) camarote m; (on plane) cabina de passageiros; ~ **cruiser** n lancha a motor com cabine
cabinet ['kæbɪnɪt] n (POL) gabinete m; (furniture) armário; (also: **display** ~) armário com vitrina
cable ['keɪbl] n cabo; (telegram) cabograma m ♦ vt enviar cabograma para; ~ **car** n bonde m (BR), teleférico (PT)
cache [kæʃ] n esconderijo; **a** ~ **of arms** etc um depósito secreto de armas etc
cackle ['kækl] vi gargalhar; (hen) cacarejar
cactus ['kæktəs] (pl **cacti**) n cacto
caddie ['kædɪ] n carregador m de tacos
caddy ['kædɪ] n = **caddie**
cadet [kə'dɛt] n (MIL) cadete m
cadge [kædʒ] (inf) vt filar
café ['kæfeɪ] n café m
cafeteria [kæfɪ'tɪərɪə] n lanchonete f
cage [keɪdʒ] n (bird ~) gaiola; (for large animals) jaula; (of lift) cabina
cagey ['keɪdʒɪ] (inf) adj cuidadoso, reservado, desconfiado
cagoule [kə'guːl] n casaco de náilon
Cairo ['kaɪərəu] n o Cairo
cajole [kə'dʒəul] vt lisonjear
cake [keɪk] n (large) bolo; (small) doce m, bolinho; ~ **of soap** sabonete m; ~**d** adj: ~**d with** encrostado de
calculate ['kælkjuleɪt] vt calcular; (estimate) avaliar; **calculation** n cálculo; **calculator** n calculador m, calculadora
calendar ['kæləndə*] n calendário; ~ **month/year** mês m/ano civil
calf [kɑːf] (pl **calves**) n (of cow) bezerro, vitela; (of other animals) cria; (also: ~**skin**) pele f or couro de bezerro; (ANAT) barriga-da-perna
calibre ['kælɪbə*] (US **caliber**) n (of person) capacidade f, calibre m
call [kɔːl] vt chamar; (label) qualificar, descrever; (TEL) telefonar a, ligar para; (witness) citar; (meeting) convocar ♦ vi chamar; (shout) gritar; (TEL) telefonar; (visit: also: ~ **in**; ~ **round**) dar um pulo ♦ n (shout) chamada; (also: **telephone** ~) chamada, telefonema m; (of bird) canto; **to be** ~**ed** chamar-se; **on** ~ de plantão; ~ **back** vi (return) voltar, passar de novo; (TEL) ligar de volta; ~ **for** vt fus (demand) requerer, exigir; (fetch) ir buscar; ~ **off** vt (cancel) cancelar; ~ **on** vt fus (visit) visitar; (appeal to) pedir; ~ **out** vi gritar, bradar; ~ **up** vt (MIL) chamar às fileiras; (TEL) dar uma ligada; ~**box** (BRIT) n cabine f telefônica; ~**er** n visita m/f; (TEL) chamador(a) m/f; ~ **girl** n call girl f, prostituta; ~-**in** (US) n (RADIO) programa com participação dos ouvintes; (TV) programa com participação dos espectadores; ~**ing** n vocação f; (trade) profissão f; ~**ing**

card (US) n cartão m de visita
callous ['kæləs] adj cruel, insensível
calm [kɑːm] adj calmo; (peaceful) tranqüilo; (weather) estável ♦ n calma ♦ vt acalmar; (fears, grief) abrandar; ~ **down** vt acalmar, tranqüilizar ♦ vi acalmar-se
Calor gas ['kælə°-] ® n butano
calorie ['kælərɪ] n caloria
calves [kɑːvz] npl of **calf**
camber ['kæmbə°] n abaulamento
Cambodia [kæm'bəudjə] n Camboja
camcorder ['kæmkɔːdə°] n filmadora, máquina de filmar
came [keɪm] pt of **come**
camel ['kæməl] n camelo
camera ['kæmərə] n máquina fotográfica; (CINEMA, TV) câmera; **in ~** (LAW) em câmara; **~man** (irreg) n cinegrafista m
camouflage ['kæməflɑːʒ] n camuflagem f ♦ vt camuflar
camp [kæmp] n campo, acampamento; (MIL) acampamento; (for prisoners) campo; (faction) facção f ♦ vi acampar ♦ adj afeminado
campaign [kæm'peɪn] n (MIL, POL etc) campanha ♦ vi fazer campanha
camp bed (BRIT) n cama de campanha
camper ['kæmpə°] n campista m/f; (vehicle) reboque m
camping ['kæmpɪŋ] n camping m (BR), campismo (PT); **to go ~** acampar
campsite ['kæmpsaɪt] n camping m (BR), parque m de campismo (PT)
campus ['kæmpəs] n campus m, cidade f universitária
can[1] [kæn] n lata ♦ vt enlatar

KEYWORD

can[2] [kæn] (negative **cannot** or **can't**, pt, conditional **could**) aux vb **1** (be able to) poder; **you ~ do it if you try** se você tentar, você consegue fazê-lo; **I'll help you all I ~** ajudarei você em tudo que eu puder; **she couldn't sleep that night** ela não conseguiu dormir aquela noite; **~ you hear me?** você está me ouvindo?
2 (know how to) saber; **I ~ swim** sei nadar; **~ you speak Portuguese?** você fala português?
3 (may) **could I have a word with you?** será que eu podia falar com você?
4 (expressing disbelief, puzzlement): **it CAN'T be true!** não pode ser verdade!; **what CAN he want?** o que é que ele quer?
5 (expressing possibility, suggestion etc): **he could be in the library** ele talvez esteja na biblioteca; **they could have forgotten** eles podiam ter esquecido

Canada ['kænədə] n Canadá m; **Canadian** adj, n canadense m/f
canary [kə'nɛərɪ] n canário

cancel ['kænsəl] vt cancelar; (contract) anular; (cross out) riscar, invalidar; **~lation** n cancelamento
cancer ['kænsə°] n câncer m (BR), cancro (PT); **C~** (ASTROLOGY) Câncer
candid ['kændɪd] adj franco, sincero
candidate ['kændɪdeɪt] n candidato/a
candle ['kændl] n vela; (in church) círio; **~light: by ~light** à luz de vela; **~stick** n (plain) castiçal m; (bigger, ornate) candelabro, lustre m
candour ['kændə°] n (US **candor**) n franqueza
candy ['kændɪ] n (also: **sugar~**) açúcar m cristalizado; (US) bala (BR), rebuçado (PT); **~floss** (BRIT) n algodão-doce m
cane [keɪn] n (BOT) cana; (stick) bengala ♦ vt (BRIT: SCH) castigar (com bengala)
canister ['kænɪstə°] n lata
cannabis ['kænəbɪs] n maconha
canned [kænd] adj (food) em lata, enlatado
cannon ['kænən] (pl inv or **~s**) n canhão m
cannot ['kænɔt] = **can not**
canny ['kænɪ] adj astuto
canoe [kə'nuː] n canoa
canon ['kænən] n (clergyman) cônego; (standard) cânone m
can opener n abridor m de latas (BR), abre-latas m inv (PT)
canopy ['kænəpɪ] n dossel m
can't [kɑːnt] = **can not**
cantankerous [kæn'tæŋkərəs] adj rabugento, irritável
canteen [kæn'tiːn] n cantina; (BRIT: of cutlery) jogo (de talheres)
canter ['kæntə°] vi ir a meio galope
canvas ['kænvəs] n (material) lona; (for painting) tela; (NAUT) velas fpl
canvass ['kænvəs] vi (POL): **to ~ for** fazer campanha por ♦ vt sondar
canyon ['kænjən] n canhão m, garganta, desfiladeiro
cap [kæp] n gorro; (of pen, bottle) tampa; (contraceptive: also: **Dutch ~**) diafragma m; (for toy gun) cartucho ♦ vt (outdo) superar; (put limit on) limitar
capability [keɪpə'bɪlɪtɪ] n capacidade f
capable ['keɪpəbl] adj (of sth) capaz; (competent) competente, hábil
capacity [kə'pæsɪtɪ] n capacidade f; (of stadium etc) lotação f; (role) condição f, posição f
cape [keɪp] n capa; (GEO) cabo
caper ['keɪpə°] n (CULIN: gen: **~s**) alcaparra; (prank) travessura
capital ['kæpɪtl] n (also: **~ city**) capital f; (money) capital m; (also: **~ letter**) maiúscula; **~ gains tax** n imposto sobre ganhos de capital; **~ism** n capitalismo; **~ist** adj, n capitalista m/f; **~ize** vi: **to ~ize on** aproveitar, explorar; **~ punishment** n pena de morte
Capricorn ['kæprɪkɔːn] n Capricórnio

capsize [kæp'saɪz] *vt*, *vi* emborcar, virar
capsule ['kæpsju:l] *n* cápsula
captain ['kæptɪn] *n* capitão *m*
caption ['kæpʃən] *n* legenda
captivate ['kæptɪveɪt] *vt* cativar
captive ['kæptɪv] *adj*, *n* cativo/a; **captivity** *n* cativeiro
capture ['kæptʃə*] *vt* prender, aprisionar; (*person*) capturar; (*place*) tomar; (*attention*) atrair, chamar ♦ *n* captura; (*of place*) tomada
car [kɑː*] *n* carro, automóvel *m*; (*RAIL*) vagão *m*
carafe [kə'ræf] *n* garrafa de mesa
caramel ['kærəməl] *n* (*sweet*) caramelo; (*burnt sugar*) caramelado
carat ['kærət] *n* quilate *m*
caravan ['kærəvæn] *n* reboque *m* (*BR*), trailer *m* (*BR*), rulote *f* (*PT*); (*in desert*) caravana; ~ **site** (*BRIT*) *n* parque *m* de campismo
carbohydrate [kɑːbəʊ'haɪdreɪt] *n* hidrato de carbono; (*food*) carboidrato
carbon ['kɑːbən] *n* carbono
carburettor [kɑːbju'retə*] (*US* **carburetor**) *n* carburador *m*
card [kɑːd] *n* (*also*: **playing** ~) carta; (*visiting* ~) cartão *m*; (*thin cardboard*) cartolina; ~**board** *n* cartão *m*, papelão *m*
cardiac ['kɑːdɪæk] *adj* cardíaco
cardigan ['kɑːdɪgən] *n* casaco de lã, cardigã *m*
cardinal ['kɑːdɪnl] *adj* cardeal; (*MATH*) cardinal ♦ *n* (*REL*) cardeal *m*
card index *n* index *m* fichário
care [kɛə*] *n* atenção; (*worry*) preocupação *f*; (*charge*) encargo, custódia ♦ *vi*: to ~ **about** (*person, animal*) preocupar-se com; (*thing, idea*) ter interesse em; ~ **of** (*on letter*) aos cuidados de; **in sb's** ~ a cargo de alguém; **to take** ~ (**to do**) ter o cuidado (de fazer); **to take** ~ **of** (*person*) cuidar de; (*situation*) encarregar-se de; **I don't** ~ não me importa; **I couldn't** ~ **less** não dou a mínima; ~ **for** *vt fus* cuidar de; (*like*) gostar de
career [kə'rɪə*] *n* carreira ♦ *vi* (*also*: ~ **along**) correr a toda velocidade
carefree ['kɛəfriː] *adj* despreocupado
careful ['kɛəful] *adj* (*thorough*) cuidadoso; (*cautious*) cauteloso; (**be**) ~! tenha cuidado!; ~**ly** *adv* cuidadosamente; cautelosamente
careless ['kɛəlɪs] *adj* descuidado; (*heedless*) desatento
caress [kə'rɛs] *n* carícia ♦ *vt* acariciar
caretaker ['kɛəteɪkə*] *n* zelador(a) *m/f*
car-ferry *n* barca para carros (*BR*), barco de passagem (*PT*)
cargo ['kɑːgəʊ] (*pl* ~**es**) *n* carga
car hire (*BRIT*) *n* aluguel *m* (*BR*) ou aluguer *m* (*PT*) de carros
Caribbean [kærɪ'biːən] *n* the ~ (**Sea**) o Caribe
caring ['kɛərɪŋ] *adj* (*person*) bondoso; (*so-*

ciety) humanitário
carnage ['kɑːnɪdʒ] *n* carnificina, matança
carnation [kɑː'neɪʃən] *n* cravo
carnival ['kɑːnɪvl] *n* carnaval *m*; (*US*: *funfair*) parque *m* de diversões
carol ['kærəl] *n*: (**Christmas**) ~ cântico de Natal
carp [kɑːp] *n inv* (*fish*) carpa; ~ **at** *vt fus* criticar
car park (*BRIT*) *n* estacionamento
carpenter ['kɑːpɪntə*] *n* carpinteiro
carpet ['kɑːpɪt] *n* tapete *m* ♦ *vt* atapetar; ~ **slippers** *npl* chinelos *mpl*; ~ **sweeper** *n* limpador *m* de tapetes
car phone *n* telefone *m* de carro
carriage ['kærɪdʒ] *n* carruagem *f*; (*BRIT*: *RAIL*) vagão *m*; (*of goods*) transporte *m*; (: *cost*) porte *m*; ~ **return** *n* retorno do carro; ~**way** (*BRIT*) *n* (*part of road*) pista
carrier ['kærɪə*] *n* transportador(a) *m/f*; (*company*) empresa de transportes, transportadora; (*MED*) portador(a) *m/f*; ~ **bag** (*BRIT*) *n* saco, sacola
carrot ['kærət] *n* cenoura
carry ['kærɪ] *vt* levar; (*transport*) transportar; (*involve*: *responsibilities etc*) implicar ♦ *vi* (*sound*) projetar-se; **to get carried away** (*fig*) exagerar; ~ **on** *vi* seguir, continuar ♦ *vt* prosseguir, continuar; ~ **out** *vt* (*orders*) cumprir; (*investigation*) levar a cabo, realizar; ~**cot** (*BRIT*) *n* moisés *m inv*; ~**-on** (*inf*) *n* alvoroço, rebuliço
cart [kɑːt] *n* carroça, carreta ♦ *vt* transportar (em carroça)
carton ['kɑːtən] *n* (*box*) caixa (de papelão); (*of yogurt*) pote *m*; (*of milk*) caixa; (*packet*) pacote *m*
cartoon [kɑː'tuːn] *n* (*drawing*) desenho; (*BRIT*: *comic strip*) história em quadrinhos (*BR*), banda desenhada (*PT*); (*film*) desenho animado
cartridge ['kɑːtrɪdʒ] *n* cartucho; (*of record player*) cápsula
carve [kɑːv] *vt* (*meat*) trinchar; (*wood, stone*) cinzelar, esculpir; (*initials, design*) gravar; ~ **up** dividir, repartir; **carving** *n* (*object*) escultura; (*design*) talha, entalhe *m*; **carving knife** (*irreg*) *n* trinchante *m*, faca de trinchar
cascade [kæs'keɪd] *n* cascata
case [keɪs] *n* caso; (*for spectacles etc*) estojo; (*LAW*) causa; (*BRIT*: *also*: **suit**~) mala; (*of wine etc*) caixa; **in** ~ (**of**) em caso (de); **in any** ~ em todo caso; **just in** ~ se por acaso ♦ *adv* por via das dúvidas
cash [kæʃ] *n* dinheiro (em espécie) ♦ *vt* descontar; **to pay** (**in**) ~ pagar em dinheiro; ~ **on delivery** pagamento contra entrega; ~**book** *n* livro-caixa *m*; ~ **card** (*BRIT*) *n* cartão *m* de saque; ~ **desk** (*BRIT*) *n* caixa; ~ **dispenser** *n* cai-

xa automática *or* eletrônica

cashew [kæˈʃuː] *n* (*also*: ~ **nut**) castanha de caju

cashier [kæˈʃɪə*] *n* caixa *m/f*

cash register *n* caixa registradora

casing [ˈkeɪsɪŋ] *n* invólucro

casino [kəˈsiːnəu] *n* cassino

cask [kɑːsk] *n* barril *m*

casket [ˈkɑːskɪt] *n* cofre *m*, porta-jóias *m inv*; (*US*: *coffin*) caixão *m*

casserole [ˈkæsərəul] *n* panela de ir ao forno; (*food*) ensopado (*BR*) no forno, guisado (*PT*) no forno

cassette [kæˈsɛt] *n* fita-cassete *f*; ~ **player** *n* toca-fitas *m inv*; ~ **recorder** *n* gravador *m*

cast [kɑːst] (*pt, pp* **cast**) *vt* (*throw*) lançar, atirar; (*THEATRE*) dar a alguém o papel de Hamlet ♦ *n* (*THEATRE*) elenco; (*also*: **plaster** ~) gesso; **to** ~ **one's vote** votar; ~ **off** *vi* (*NAUT*) soltar o cabo; (*KNITTING*) rematar os pontos; ~ **on** *vi* montar os pontos

castaway [ˈkɑːstəwəɪ] *n* náufrago/a

caster sugar [ˈkɑːstə*-] (*BRIT*) *n* açúcar *m* branco refinado

casting vote [ˈkɑːstɪŋ-] (*BRIT*) *n* voto decisivo, voto de minerva

cast iron *n* ferro fundido

castle [ˈkɑːsl] *n* castelo; (*CHESS*) torre *f*

castor [ˈkɑːstə*] *n* (*wheel*) rodízio; ~ **oil** *n* óleo de rícino

casual [ˈkæʒjul] *adj* (*by chance*) fortuito; (*work*) eventual; (*unconcerned*) despreocupado; (*clothes*) descontraído, informal; ~**ly** *adv* casualmente; (*dress*) informalmente

casualty [ˈkæʒjultɪ] *n* ferido/a; (*dead*) morto/a; (*of situation*) vítima; (*department*) pronto-socorro

cat [kæt] *n* gato

catalogue [ˈkætəlɔg] (*US* **catalog**) *n* catálogo ♦ *vt* catalogar

catalyst [ˈkætəlɪst] *n* catalisador *m*

catalytic convertor [kætəˈlɪtɪk kənˈvɜːtə*] *n* conversor *m* catalítico

catapult [ˈkætəpʌlt] (*BRIT*) *n* (*sling*) atiradeira

cataract [ˈkætərækt] *n* catarata

catarrh [kəˈtɑː*] *n* catarro

catastrophe [kəˈtæstrəfɪ] *n* catástrofe *f*

catch [kætʃ] (*pt, pp* **caught**) *vt* pegar (*BR*), apanhar (*PT*); (*fish*) pescar; (*arrest*) prender, deter; (*person: by surprise*) flagrar, surpreender; (*attention*) atrair; (*hear*) ouvir; (*also*: ~ **up**) alcançar ♦ *vi* (*fire*) pegar; (*in branches etc*) ficar preso, prender-se ♦ *n* (*fish*) pesca; (*game*) manha, armadilha; (*of lock*) trinco, língueta; **to** ~ **fire** pegar fogo; (*building*) incendiar-se; **to** ~ **sight of** avistar; ~ **on** *vi* (*understand*) entender (*BR*), perceber (*PT*); (*grow popular*) pegar; ~ **up** *vi* equiparar-se ♦ *vt* (*also*: ~ **up with**) alcançar; ~**ing** *adj* (*MED*) contagioso;

~**ment area** (*BRIT*) *n* área atendida por um hospital, uma escola *etc*; ~**phrase** *n* clichê *m*, slogan *m*; ~**y** *adj* que pega fácil, que gruda no ouvido

category [ˈkætɪgərɪ] *n* categoria

cater [ˈkeɪtə*] *vi* preparar comida; ~ **for** *vt fus* (*needs*) atender a; (*consumers*) satisfazer; ~**er** *n* (*service*) serviço de bufê; ~**ing** *n* serviço de bufê; (*trade*) abastecimento

caterpillar [ˈkætəpɪlə*] *n* lagarta; ~ **track** ® *n* lagarta

cathedral [kəˈθiːdrəl] *n* catedral *f*

catholic [ˈkæθəlɪk] *adj* eclético; **C**~ *adj*, *n* (*REL*) católico/a

cat's-eye (*BRIT*) *n* (*AUT*) catadióptrico

cattle [ˈkætl] *npl* gado

catty [ˈkætɪ] *adj* malicioso

caucus [ˈkɔːkəs] *n* (*POL*: *group*) panelinha (de políticos); (: *US*) comitê *m* eleitoral (para indicar candidatos)

caught [kɔːt] *pt, pp of* **catch**

cauliflower [ˈkɔlɪflauə*] *n* couve-flor *f*

cause [kɔːz] *n* causa; (*reason*) motivo, razão *f* ♦ *vt* causar, provocar

caustic [ˈkɔːstɪk] *adj* cáustico; (*fig*) mordaz

caution [ˈkɔːʃən] *n* cautela, prudência; (*warning*) aviso ♦ *vt* acautelar, avisar

cautious [ˈkɔːʃəs] *adj* cauteloso, prudente, precavido

cavalry [ˈkævəlrɪ] *n* cavalaria

cave [keɪv] *n* caverna, gruta; ~ **in** *vi* (*roof etc*) ceder; ~**man** (*irreg*) *n* troglodita *m*, homem *m* das cavernas

cavity [ˈkævɪtɪ] *n* cavidade *f*; (*in tooth*) cárie *f*

cavort [kəˈvɔːt] *vi* cabriolar

CB *n abbr* = **Citizens' Band (Radio)**

CBI *n abbr* (= *Confederation of British Industry*) federação de indústria

cc *abbr* (= *cubic centimetre*) cc; (*on letter etc*) = **carbon copy**

CD *n abbr* = **compact disc**; **compact disc player**; ~**-ROM** *n abbr* (=*compact disc read-only memory*) CD-ROM *m*

cease [siːs] *vt, vi* cessar; ~**fire** *n* cessar-fogo *m*; ~**less** *adj* contínuo, incessante

cedar [ˈsiːdə*] *n* cedro

ceiling [ˈsiːlɪŋ] *n* (*also fig*) teto

celebrate [ˈsɛlɪbreɪt] *vt* celebrar ♦ *vi* celebrar; (*birthday, anniversary etc*) festejar; (*REL*: *mass*) rezar; ~**d** *adj* célebre; **celebration** *n* (*party*) festa

celery [ˈsɛlərɪ] *n* aipo

cell [sɛl] *n* cela; (*BIO*) célula; (*ELEC*) pilha, elemento

cellar [ˈsɛlə*] *n* porão *m*; (*for wine*) adega

'cello [ˈtʃɛləu] *n* violoncelo

cellphone [ˈsɛlfəun] *n* telefone *m* celular

Celt [kɛlt, sɛlt] *n* celta *m/f*; ~**ic** *adj* celta

cement [səˈmɛnt] *n* cimento; ~ **mixer** *n* betoneira

cemetery [ˈsɛmɪtrɪ] *n* cemitério

censor [ˈsɛnsə*] *n* censor(a) *m/f* ♦ *vt*

censurar; ~**ship** n censura
censure ['sɛnʃə*] vt criticar
census ['sɛnsəs] n censo
cent [sɛnt] n cêntimo; see also **per**
centenary [sɛn'tiːnərɪ] n centenário
center ['sɛntə*] (US) = **centre**
centigrade ['sɛntɪgreɪd] adj centígrado
centimetre ['sɛntɪmiːtə*] (US **centimeter**)
n centímetro
centipede ['sɛntɪpiːd] n centopéia
central ['sɛntrəl] adj central; **C~** America n América Central; ~ **heating** n
aquecimento central; ~ **reservation**
(BRIT) n (AUT) canteiro divisor
centre ['sɛntə*] (US **center**) n centro; (of
room, circle etc) meio ♦ vt centrar; ~-
forward n centro-avante m, centro; ~-
half n centro médio
century ['sɛntjʊrɪ] n século; **20th** ~ século vinte
ceramic [sɪ'ræmɪk] adj cerâmico
ceremony ['sɛrɪmənɪ] n cerimônia; (ritual) rito; **to stand on** ~ fazer cerimônia
certain ['sɜːtən] adj (sure) seguro; (person): **a** ~ **Mr Smith** um certo Sr.
Smith; (particular): ~ **days/places** certos dias/lugares; (some): **a** ~ **coldness/
pleasure** uma certa frieza/um certo
prazer; **for** ~ com certeza; ~**ly** adv certamente, com certeza; ~**ty** n certeza
certificate [sə'tɪfɪkɪt] n certidão f
certified mail ['sɜːtɪfaɪd-] (US) n correio
registrado
certified public accountant
['sɜːtɪfaɪd-] (US) n perito-contador m
certify ['sɜːtɪfaɪ] vt certificar
cervical ['sɜːvɪkl] adj: ~ **cancer** câncer
m (BR) or cancro (PT) do colo do útero
cervix ['sɜːvɪks] n cérvice f
cesspit ['sɛspɪt] n fossa séptica
cf. abbr (= compare) cf.
CFC n abbr (= chlorofluorocarbon) CFC m
ch. abbr (= chapter) cap.
chafe [tʃeɪf] vt (rub) roçar
chagrin ['ʃægrɪn] n desgosto
chain [tʃeɪn] n corrente f; (of islands)
grupo; (of mountains) cordilheira; (of
shops) cadeia; (of events) série f ♦ vt
(also: ~ **up**) acorrentar; ~-**smoke** vi fumar um (cigarro) atrás do outro; ~-
store n magazine m (BR), grande armazém f (PT)
chair [tʃɛə*] n cadeira; (armchair) poltrona; (of university) cátedra; (of meeting)
presidência, mesa ♦ vt (meeting) presidir; ~**lift** n teleférico; ~**man** (irreg) n
presidente m
chalice ['tʃælɪs] n cálice m
chalk [tʃɔːk] n (GEO) greda; (for writing)
giz m
challenge ['tʃælɪndʒ] n desafio ♦ vt desafiar; (right) disputar, contestar; **challenging** adj desafiante; (tone) de desafio
chamber ['tʃeɪmbə*] n câmara; (BRIT:

LAW: gen pl) sala de audiências; ~ **of
commerce** câmara de comércio; ~**maid**
n arrumadeira (BR), empregada (PT); ~
music n música de câmara
chamois ['ʃæmwɑː] n camurça
champagne [ʃæm'peɪn] n champanhe m
or f
champion ['tʃæmpɪən] n campeão/peã
m/f; (of cause) defensor(a) m/f; ~**ship** n
campeonato
chance [tʃɑːns] n (opportunity) oportunidade, ocasião f; (likelihood) chance f;
(risk) risco ♦ vt arriscar ♦ adj fortuito,
casual; **to take a** ~ arriscar-se; **by** ~
por acaso; **to** ~ **it** arriscar-se
chancellor ['tʃɑːnsələ*] n chanceler m;
C~ of the Exchequer (BRIT) Ministro
da Economia (Fazenda e Planejamento)
chandelier [ʃændə'lɪə*] n lustre m
change [tʃeɪndʒ] vt (alter) mudar; (wheel,
money) trocar; (replace) substituir; (clothes, house) mudar de, trocar de; (nappy)
mudar, trocar; (transform): **to** ~ **sb
into** transformar alguém em ♦ vi
mudar(-se); (change clothes) trocar-se;
(trains) fazer baldeação (BR), mudar
(PT); (be transformed): **to** ~ **into**
transformar-se em ♦ n mudança; (exchange) troca; (difference) diferença; (of
clothes) muda; (coins) trocado; **to** ~
gear (AUT) trocar de marcha; **to** ~
one's mind mudar de idéia; **for a** ~
para variar; ~**able** adj (weather, mood)
instável; ~ **machine** n máquina que
fornece trocado; ~**over** n mudança
changing ['tʃeɪndʒɪŋ] adj variável; ~
room (BRIT) n (in shop) cabine f de provas
channel ['tʃænl] n canal m; (of river) leito; (groove) ranhura; (fig: medium) meio,
via ♦ vt canalizar; **the (English) C~** o
Canal da Mancha; **C~ Islands** npl: **the
C~ Islands** as ilhas Anglo-Normandas
chant [tʃɑːnt] n canto; (REL) cântico ♦ vt
cantar; (slogan) entoar
chaos ['keɪɒs] n caos m
chap [tʃæp] n (BRIT: inf: man) sujeito
(BR), tipo (PT)
chapel ['tʃæpəl] n capela
chaperon(e) ['ʃæpərəun] n mulher f
acompanhante ♦ vt acompanhar
chaplain ['tʃæplɪn] n capelão m
chapped [tʃæpt] adj ressecado
chapter ['tʃæptə*] n capítulo
char [tʃɑː*] vt (burn) tostar, queimar ♦ n
(BRIT) = **charlady**
character ['kærɪktə*] n caráter m; (in novel, film) personagem m/f; (letter) letra;
~**istic** adj característico
charcoal ['tʃɑːkəul] n carvão m de lenha; (ART) carvão m
charge [tʃɑːdʒ] n (LAW) encargo, acusação f; (fee) preço, custo; (responsibility)
encargo ♦ vt (battery) carregar; (MIL)
atacar; (customer) cobrar dinheiro de;

(LAW): **to ~ sb (with)** acusar alguém (de) ♦ vi precipitar-se; **~s** npl: **bank ~s** taxas fpl cobradas pelo banco; **to reverse the ~s** (BRIT: TEL) ligar a cobrar; **how much do you ~?** quanto você cobra?; **to ~ an expense (up) to sb's account** pôr a despesa na conta de alguém; **to take ~ of** encarregar-se de, tomar conta de; **to be in ~ of** estar a cargo de or encarregado de; **~ card** n cartão m de crédito (emitido por uma loja)

charitable ['tʃærɪtəbl] adj beneficente

charity ['tʃærɪtɪ] n caridade f; (organization) obra de caridade; (kindness) compaixão f; (money, gifts) donativo

charlady ['tʃɑːleɪdɪ] (BRIT) n diarista

charm [tʃɑːm] n (quality) charme m; (talisman) amuleto; (on bracelet) berloque m ♦ vt encantar, deliciar; **~ing** adj encantador(a)

chart [tʃɑːt] n (graph) gráfico m; (diagram) diagrama m; (map) carta de navegação ♦ vt traçar; **~s** npl (MUS) paradas fpl (de sucesso)

charter ['tʃɑːtə*] vt fretar ♦ n (document) carta, alvará m; **~ed accountant** (BRIT) n perito-contador m/perita-contadora f; **~ flight** n vôo charter or fretado

charwoman ['tʃɑːwumən] (irreg) n = **charlady**

chase [tʃeɪs] vt perseguir; (also: ~ away) enxotar ♦ n perseguição f, caça

chasm ['kæzəm] n abismo

chassis ['ʃæsɪ] n chassi m

chastity ['tʃæstɪtɪ] n castidade f

chat [tʃæt] vi (also: **have a ~**) conversar, bater papo (BR), cavaquear (PT) ♦ n conversa, bate-papo m (BR), cavaqueira (PT); **~ show** (BRIT) n programa m de entrevistas

chatter ['tʃætə*] vi (person) tagarelar; (animal) emitir sons; (teeth) tiritar ♦ n tagarelice f; emissão f de sons; (of birds) chilro; **~box** n tagarela m/f

chatty ['tʃætɪ] adj (style) informal; (person) conversador(a)

chauffeur ['ʃəufə*] n chofer m, motorista m/f

chauvinist ['ʃəuvɪnɪst] n (also: **male ~**) machista m; (nationalist) chauvinista m/f

cheap [tʃiːp] adj barato; (poor quality) barato, de pouca qualidade; (behaviour) vulgar; (joke) de mau gosto ♦ adv barato; **~ly** adv barato, por baixo preço

cheat [tʃiːt] vi trapacear; (at cards) roubar (BR), fazer batota (PT); (in exam) colar (BR), cabular (PT) ♦ vt: **to ~ sb (out of sth)** passar o conto do vigário em alguém ♦ n fraude f; (person) trapaceiro/a

check [tʃɛk] vt (examine) controlar; (facts) verificar; (halt) conter, impedir; (restrain) parar, refrear ♦ n controle m,

inspeção f; (curb) freio; (US: bill) conta; (pattern: gen pl) xadrez m; (US) = **cheque** ♦ adj (pattern, cloth) xadrez inv; **~ in** vi (in hotel) registrar-se; (in airport) apresentar-se ♦ vt (luggage) entregar; **~ out** vi pagar a conta e sair; **~ up** vi: **to ~ up on sth** verificar algo; **to ~ up on sb** investigar alguém; **~ered** (US) adj = **chequered**; **~ers** (US) n (jogo de) damas fpl; **~in (desk)** n check-in m; **~ing account** (US) n conta corrente; **~mate** n xeque-mate m; **~out** n caixa; **~point** n (ponto de) controle m; **~room** (US) n depósito de bagagem; **~up** n (MED) check-up m

cheek [tʃiːk] n bochecha; (impudence) folga, descaramento; **~bone** n maçã f do rosto; **~y** adj insolente, descarado

cheep [tʃiːp] vi piar

cheer [tʃɪə*] vt dar vivas a, aplaudir; (gladden) alegrar, animar ♦ vi gritar com entusiasmo ♦ n (gen pl) gritos mpl de entusiasmo; **~s** npl (of crowd) aplausos mpl; **~s!** saúde!; **~ up** vi animar-se, alegrar-se ♦ vt alegrar, animar; **~ful** adj alegre; **~io** (BRIT) excl tchau (BR), adeus (PT)

cheese [tʃiːz] n queijo; **~board** n (in restaurant) sortimento de queijos

cheetah ['tʃiːtə] n chitá m

chef [ʃɛf] n cozinheiro-chefe/cozinheira-chefe m/f

chemical ['kɛmɪkəl] adj químico ♦ n produto químico

chemist ['kɛmɪst] n (BRIT: pharmacist) farmacêutico/a; (scientist) químico/a; **~ry** n química; **~'s (shop)** (BRIT) n farmácia

cheque [tʃɛk] (BRIT) n cheque m; **~book** n talão m (BR) or livro (PT) de cheques; **~ card** (BRIT) n cartão m (de garantia) de cheques

chequered ['tʃɛkəd] (US **checkered**) adj (fig) variado, acidentado

cherish ['tʃɛrɪʃ] vt (person) tratar com carinho; (memory) lembrar (com prazer)

cherry ['tʃɛrɪ] n cereja; (also: ~ **tree**) cerejeira

chess [tʃɛs] n xadrez m; **~board** n tabuleiro de xadrez

chest [tʃɛst] n (ANAT) peito; (box) caixa, cofre m; **~ of drawers** cômoda

chestnut ['tʃɛsnʌt] n castanha

chew [tʃuː] vt mastigar; **~ing gum** n chiclete m (BR), pastilha elástica (PT)

chic [ʃɪk] adj elegante

chick [tʃɪk] n pinto; (inf: girl) broto

chicken ['tʃɪkɪn] n galinha; (food) galinha, frango; (inf: coward) covarde m/f, galinha; **~ out** (inf) vi agalinhar-se; **~pox** n catapora (BR), varicela (PT)

chief [tʃiːf] n (of tribe) cacique m, morubixaba m; (of organization) chefe m/f ♦ adj principal; **~ executive** (US ~ **executive officer**) n diretor(a) m/f; **~ly**

~**ly** adv principalmente

chiffon ['ʃɪfɔn] n gaze f

chilblain ['tʃɪlbleɪn] n frieira

child [tʃaɪld] (pl ~**ren**) n criança; (offspring) filho/a; ~**birth** n parto; ~**hood** n infância; ~**ish** adj infantil; ~**like** adj infantil, ingênuo; ~ **minder** (BRIT) n cuidadora de crianças

Chile ['tʃɪlɪ] n Chile m

chill [tʃɪl] n frio, friagem f; (MED) resfriamento ♦ vt (CULIN) semi-congelar; (person) congelar

chilli ['tʃɪlɪ] (US **chili**) n pimentão m picante

chilly ['tʃɪlɪ] adj frio; (person) friorento

chime [tʃaɪm] n (of bell) repique m; (of clock) soar m ♦ vi repicar; soar

chimney ['tʃɪmnɪ] n chaminé f; ~ **sweep** n limpador m de chaminés

chimpanzee [tʃɪmpæn'ziː] n chimpanzé m

chin [tʃɪn] n queixo

China ['tʃaɪnə] n China

china ['tʃaɪnə] n porcelana; (crockery) louça fina

Chinese [tʃaɪ'niːz] adj chinês/esa ♦ n inv chinês/esa m/f; (LING) chinês m

chink [tʃɪŋk] n (opening) fenda, fissura; (noise) tinir m

chip [tʃɪp] n (gen pl: CULIN) batata frita; (: US: also: **potato** ~) batatinha frita; (of wood) lasca; (of glass, stone) lasca, pedaço; (COMPUT: also: **micro**~) chip m ♦ vt (cup, plate) lascar; ~ **in** (inf) vi interromper; (contribute) compartilhar as despesas

chiropodist [kɪ'rɔpədɪst] (BRIT) n pedicuro/a

chirp [tʃəːp] vi chilrar, piar

chisel ['tʃɪzl] n (for wood) formão m; (for stone) cinzel m

chit [tʃɪt] n talão m

chitchat ['tʃɪtʃæt] n conversa fiada

chivalry ['ʃɪvəlrɪ] n cavalheirismo

chives [tʃaɪvz] npl cebolinha

chlorine ['klɔːriːn] n cloro

chock-a-block [tʃɔk-] adj abarrotado, apinhado

chock-full [tʃɔk-] adj = chock-a-block

chocolate ['tʃɔklɪt] n chocolate m

choice [tʃɔɪs] n (selection) seleção f; (option) escolha; (preference) preferência ♦ adj seleto, escolhido

choir ['kwaɪə*] n coro

choke [tʃəuk] vi sufocar-se; (on food) engasgar ♦ vt estrangular; (block) obstruir ♦ n (AUT) afogador m (BR), ar m (PT)

cholera ['kɔlərə] n cólera m

cholesterol [kə'lestərɔl] n colesterol m

choose [tʃuːz] (pt chose, pp chosen) vt escolher; **to** ~ **to do** optar por fazer; **choosy** adj exigente

chop [tʃɔp] vt (wood) cortar, talhar; (CULIN: also: ~ **up**) cortar em pedaços; (meat) picar ♦ n golpe m; (CULIN) coste-

leta; ~**s** npl (inf: jaws) beiços mpl

chopper ['tʃɔpə*] n helicóptero

choppy ['tʃɔpɪ] adj (sea) agitado

chopsticks ['tʃɔpstɪks] npl pauzinhos mpl, palitos mpl

choral ['kɔːrəl] adj coral

chord [kɔːd] n (MUS) acorde m

chore [tʃɔː*] n tarefa; (routine task) trabalho de rotina

choreographer [kɔrɪ'ɔgrəfə*] n coreógrafo/a

chortle ['tʃɔːtl] vi rir, gargalhar

chorus ['kɔːrəs] n (group) coro; (song) coral m; (refrain) estribilho

chose [tʃəuz] pt of choose; ~**n** pp of choose

Christ [kraɪst] n Cristo

christen ['krɪsn] vt batizar; (nickname) apelidar

Christian ['krɪstɪən] adj, n cristão/tã m/f; ~**ity** n cristianismo; ~ **name** n prenome m, nome m de batismo

Christmas ['krɪsməs] n Natal m; **Happy** or **Merry** ~! Feliz Natal!; ~ **card** n cartão m de Natal; ~ **Day** n dia m de Natal; ~ **Eve** n véspera de Natal; ~ **tree** n árvore f de Natal

chrome [krəum] n = chromium

chromium ['krəumɪəm] n cromo

chronic ['krɔnɪk] adj crônico; (fig: drunkenness) inveterado

chronicle ['krɔnɪkl] n crônica

chubby ['tʃʌbɪ] adj roliço, gorducho

chuck [tʃʌk] vt jogar (BR), deitar (PT); (BRIT: also: ~ **up**, ~ **in**: job) largar; (: person) acabar com; ~ **out** vt (thing) jogar (BR) or deitar (PT) fora; (person) expulsar

chuckle ['tʃʌkl] vi rir

chug [tʃʌg] vi mover-se fazendo ruído de descarga; (car, boat: also: ~ **along**) ir indo

chum [tʃʌm] n camarada m/f

chunk [tʃʌŋk] n pedaço, naco

church [tʃəːtʃ] n igreja; ~**yard** n adro, cemitério

churlish ['tʃəːlɪʃ] adj (silence) constrangedor(a); (behaviour) grosseiro, rude

churn [tʃəːn] n (for butter) batedeira; (also: **milk** ~) lata, vasilha; ~ **out** vt produzir em série

chute [ʃuːt] n rampa; (also: **rubbish** ~) despejador m

chutney ['tʃʌtnɪ] n conserva picante

CIA (US) n abbr (= Central Intelligence Agency) CIA f

CID (BRIT) n abbr = Criminal Investigation Department

cider ['saɪdə*] n sidra

cigar [sɪ'gɑː*] n charuto

cigarette [sɪgə'rɛt] n cigarro; ~ **case** n cigarreira; ~ **end** n ponta de cigarro, guimba (BR)

Cinderella [sɪndə'rɛlə] n Gata Borralheira

cinders ['sɪndəz] *npl* cinzas *fpl*

cine-camera ['sɪnɪ-] (*BRIT*) *n* câmera (cinematográfica)

cine-film ['sɪnɪ-] (*BRIT*) *n* filme *m* cinematográfico

cinema ['sɪnəmə] *n* cinema *m*

cinnamon ['sɪnəmən] *n* canela

cipher ['saɪfə*] *n* cifra

circle ['sə:kl] *n* círculo; (*in cinema*) balcão *m* ♦ *vi* dar voltas ♦ *vt* (*surround*) rodear, cercar; (*move round*) dar a volta de

circuit ['sə:kɪt] *n* circuito; (*lap*) volta; (*track*) pista; **~ous** *adj* tortuoso

circular ['sə:kjulə*] *adj* circular ♦ *n* (*carta*) circular *f*

circulate ['sə:kjuleɪt] *vt, vi* circular; **circulation** *n* circulação *f*; (*of newspaper, book etc*) tiragem *f*

circumcise ['sə:kəmsaɪz] *vt* circuncidar

circumflex ['sə:kəmfleks] *n* (*also*: ~ accent) (acento) circunflexo

circumspect ['sə:kəmspekt] *adj* prudente, cauteloso

circumstances ['sə:kəmstənsɪz] *npl* circunstâncias *fpl*; (*conditions*) condições *fpl*; (*financial condition*) situação *f* econômica

circumvent [sə:kəm'vent] *vt* (*rule etc*) driblar, burlar

circus ['sə:kəs] *n* circo

CIS *n abbr* (= *Commonwealth of Independent States*) CEI *f*

cistern ['sɪstən] *n* tanque *m*; (*in toilet*) caixa d'água

cite [saɪt] *vt* citar; (*LAW*) intimar

citizen ['sɪtɪzn] *n* (*of country*) cidadão/dã *m/f*; (*of town*) habitante *m/f*; **~ship** *n* cidadania

citrus fruit ['sɪtrəs-] *n* citrino

city ['sɪtɪ] *n* cidade *f*; **the C~** centro financeiro de Londres

civic ['sɪvɪk] *adj* cívico, municipal; **~ centre** (*BRIT*) *n* sede *f* do município

civil ['sɪvɪl] *adj* civil; (*polite*) delicado, cortês; **~ian** *adj, n* civil *m/f*

civilized ['sɪvɪlaɪzd] *adj* civilizado

civil: ~ **law** *n* direito civil; ~ **servant** *n* funcionário/a público/a; **C~ Service** *n* administração *f* pública; ~ **war** *n* guerra civil

clad [klæd] *adj*: ~ (**in**) vestido (de)

claim [kleɪm] *vt* exigir, reclamar; (*rights etc*) reivindicar; (*responsibility, credit*) assumir; (*assert*) **to** ~ **that**/**to be** afirmar que/ser ♦ *vi* (*for insurance*) reclamar ♦ *n* reclamação *f*; (*assertion*) afirmação *f*; (*wage* ~ *etc*) reivindicação *f*; **~ant** *n* (*ADMIN, LAW*) requerente *m/f*

clairvoyant [kleə'vɔɪənt] *n* clarividente *m/f*

clam [klæm] *n* molusco

clamber ['klæmbə*] *vi* subir; (*up hill etc*) escalar

clammy ['klæmɪ] *adj* (*hands, face*) úmido e pegajoso

clamour ['klæmə*] (*US* **clamor**) *vi*: **to** ~ **for** clamar

clamp [klæmp] *n* grampo ♦ *vt* (*two things together*) grampear; (*put: one thing on another*) prender; ~ **down on** *vt fus* suprimir, proibir

clan [klæn] *n* clã *m*

clang [klæŋ] *vi* retinir

clap [klæp] *vi* bater palmas, aplaudir; **~ping** *n* aplausos *mpl*, palmas *fpl*

clarify ['klærɪfaɪ] *vt* esclarecer

clarinet [klærɪ'net] *n* clarinete *m*

clarity ['klærɪtɪ] *n* clareza

clash [klæʃ] *n* (*fight*) confronto; (*disagreement*) desavença; (*of beliefs*) divergência; (*of colours, styles*) choque *m*; (*of dates*) coincidência; (*noise*) estrondo ♦ *vi* (*gangs, beliefs*) chocar-se; (*disagree*) entrar em conflito, ter uma desavença; (*colours*) não combinar; (*dates*) coincidir; (*weapons, cymbals etc*) estrefritar

clasp [klɑːsp] *n* fecho; (*embrace*) abraço ♦ *vt* prender; abraçar

class [klɑːs] *n* classe *f*; (*lesson*) aula; (*type*) tipo ♦ *vt* classificar

classic ['klæsɪk] *adj* clássico ♦ *n* clássico; **~al** *adj* clássico

classified ['klæsɪfaɪd] *adj* secreto; ~ **advertisement** *n* classificado

classmate ['klæsmeɪt] *n* colega *m/f* de aula

classroom ['klæsrum] *n* sala de aula

clatter ['klætə*] *n* ruído, barulho; (*of hooves*) tropel *m* ♦ *vi* fazer barulho *or* ruído

clause [klɔːz] *n* cláusula; (*LING*) oração *f*

claw [klɔː] *n* (*of animal*) pata; (*of bird of prey*) garra; (*of lobster*) pinça; ~ **at** *vt fus* arranhar; (*tear*) rasgar

clay [kleɪ] *n* argila

clean [kliːn] *adj* limpo; (*story*) inocente ♦ *vt* limpar; (*hands etc*) lavar; ~ **out** *vt* limpar; ~ **up** *vt* limpar, assear; **~-cut** *adj* alinhado; **~er** *n* faxineiro/a; (*product*) limpador *m*; **~er's** *n* (*also*: **dry ~er's**) tinturaria; **~ing** *n* limpeza; **~liness** *n* limpeza

cleanse [klenz] *vt* limpar; (*purify*) purificar; **~r** *n* (*for face*) creme *m* de limpeza

clean-shaven [-'ʃeɪvn] *adj* sem barba, de cara raspada

cleansing department ['klenzɪŋ-] (*BRIT*) *n* departamento de limpeza

clear [klɪə*] *adj* claro; (*footprint, photograph*) nítido; (*obvious*) evidente; (*glass, water*) transparente; (*road, way*) limpo, livre; (*conscience*) tranquilo; (*skin*) macio ♦ *vt* (*space*) abrir; (*room*) esvaziar; (*LAW: suspect*) absolver; (*fence*) saltar, transpor; (*cheque*) compensar ♦ *vi* (*weather*) abrir; (*sky*) clarear; (*fog etc*) dissipar-se ♦ *adv*: ~ **of** a salvo de; **to** ~ **the table** tirar a mesa; ~ **up** *vt* limpar; (*mystery*) resolver, esclarecer; **~ance** *n* remoção *f*;

her) abafado ♦ *adv* perto; ~ **to** perto
de; ~ **by** perto, pertinho; ~ **at hand** =
~ **by**; **to have a ~ shave** (*fig*) livrar-se
por um triz

close² [kləʊz] *vt* fechar; (*end*) encerrar ♦
vi fechar; (*end*) concluir-se, terminar-se
♦ *n* (*end*) fim *m*, conclusão *f*, terminação *f*; ~ **down** *vi* fechar definitivamente; ~**d shop** *n* estabelecimento industrial que só admite empregados sindicali-
zados

close-knit *adj* muito unido

closely [ˈkləʊslɪ] *adv* (*watch*) de perto;
(*connected, related*) intimamente; (*resemble*) muito

closet [ˈklɒzɪt] *n* (*cupboard*) armário

close-up [ˈkləʊs-] *n* close *m*, close-up *m*

closure [ˈkləʊʒə°] *n* fechamento

clot [klɒt] *n* (*gen: blood* ~) coágulo; (*inf:
idiot*) imbecil *m/f* ♦ *vi* coagular-se

cloth [klɒθ] *n* (*material*) tecido, fazenda *f*,
(*rag*) pano

clothe [kləʊð] *vt* vestir

clothes [kləʊðz] *npl* roupa; ~ **brush** *n*
escova (para a roupa); ~ **line** *n* corda
(para estender a roupa); ~ **peg** (*US* ~
pin) *n* pregador *m*

clothing [ˈkləʊðɪŋ] *n* = **clothes**

cloud [klaʊd] *n* nuvem *f*; ~**burst** *n* aguaceiro; ~**y** *adj* nublado; (*liquid*) turvo

clout [klaʊt] *vt* dar uma bofetada em

clove [kləʊv] *n* cravo; ~ **of garlic** dente
m de alho

clover [ˈkləʊvə°] *n* trevo

clown [klaʊn] *n* palhaço ♦ *vi* (*also:* ~
about; ~ **around**) fazer palhaçadas

cloying [ˈklɔɪɪŋ] *adj* (*taste, smell*) enjoativo, nauseabundo

club [klʌb] *n* (*society*) clube *m*; (*weapon*)
cacete *m*; (*also: golf* ~) taco ♦ *vt* esbor-
doar ♦ *vi*: **to** ~ **together** cotizar-se; ~**s**
npl (*CARDS*) paus *mpl*; ~ **car** (*US*) *n*
(*RAIL*) vagão-restaurante *m*; ~**house** *n*
sede *f* do clube

cluck [klʌk] *vi* cacarejar

clue [kluː] *n* indício, pista; (*in crossword*)
definição *f*; **I haven't a** ~ não faço
idéia

clump [klʌmp] *n* (*of trees etc*) grupo

clumsy [ˈklʌmzɪ] *adj* (*person*) desajeitado;
(*movement*) deselegante, mal-feito; (*attempt*) inábil

clung [klʌŋ] *pt, pp of* **cling**

cluster [ˈklʌstə°] *n* grupo; (*of flowers*)
ramo ♦ *vi* agrupar-se, apinhar-se

clutch [klʌtʃ] *n* (*grip, grasp*) garra; (*AUT*)
embreagem *f* (*BR*), embraiagem *f* (*PT*) ♦
vt empunhar, pegar em

clutter [ˈklʌtə°] *vt* (*also:* ~ **up**) abarrotar,
encher desordenadamente

cm *abbr* = *centimetre*) cm

CND *n abbr* = **Campaign for Nuclear
Disarmament**

Co. *abbr* = **county;** (= *company*) Cia.

c/o *abbr* (= *care of*) a/c

(*permission*) permissão *f*; ~-**cut** *adj* bem
definido, nítido; ~**ing** *n* (*in wood*) clareira; ~**ing bank** (*BRIT*) *n* câmara de
compensação; ~**ly** *adv* distintamente;
(*obviously*) claramente; (*coherently*) coe-
rentemente; ~**way** (*BRIT*) *n* estrada onde
não se pode estacionar

cleaver [ˈkliːvə°] *n* cutelo (de
açougueiro)

clef [klef] *n* (*MUS*) clave *f*

cleft [kleft] *n* (*in rock*) fissura

clench [klentʃ] *vt* apertar, cerrar; (*teeth*)
trincar

clergy [ˈklɜːdʒɪ] *n* clero; ~**man** (*irreg*) *n*
clérigo, pastor *m*

clerical [ˈklerɪkəl] *adj* de escritório; (*REL*)
clerical

clerk [klɑːk, (*US*) klɜːrk] *n* auxiliar *m/f*
de escritório; (*US: sales person*) balconista *m/f*

clever [ˈklevə°] *adj* inteligente; (*deft*) hábil; (*arrangement*) engenhoso

click [klɪk] *vt* (*tongue*) estalar; (*heels*) bater ♦ *vi* estalar

client [ˈklaɪənt] *n* cliente *m/f*

cliff [klɪf] *n* penhasco

climate [ˈklaɪmɪt] *n* clima *m*

climax [ˈklaɪmæks] *n* clímax *m*, ponto
culminante; (*sexual*) clímax

climb [klaɪm] *vi* subir; (*plant*) trepar;
(*plane*) ganhar altitude; (*prices etc*) escalar ♦ *vt* (*stairs*) subir; (*tree*) trepar em;
(*hill*) escalar ♦ *n* subida; (*of prices etc*)
escalada; ~-**down** *n* retração *f*; ~**er** *n*
alpinista *m/f*; (*plant*) trepadeira; ~**ing** *n*
alpinismo

clinch [klɪntʃ] *vt* (*deal*) fechar; (*argument*)
decidir, resolver

cling [klɪŋ] (*pt, pp* **clung**) *vi*: **to** ~ **to**
pegar-se a, aderir a; (*support, idea*)
agarrar-se a; (*clothes*) ajustar-se a

clinic [ˈklɪnɪk] *n* clínica; ~**al** *adj* clínico;
(*fig*) frio, impessoal

clink [klɪŋk] *vi* tinir

clip [klɪp] *n* (*for hair*) grampo (*BR*), gancho (*PT*); (*also:* **paper** ~) mola, clipe *m*;
(*TV, CINEMA*) clipe ♦ *vt* (*cut*) aparar; (*fasten*) grampear; ~**pers** *npl* (*for gardening*) podadeira; (*also:* **nail** ~**pers**) alicate *m* de unhas; ~**ping** *n* recorte *m*

clique [kliːk] *n* panelinha

cloak [kləʊk] *n* capa, manto ♦ *vt* (*fig*) encobrir; ~**room** *n* vestiário; (*BRIT: WC*)
sanitários *mpl* (*BR*), lavatórios *mpl* (*PT*)

clock [klɒk] *n* relógio; ~ **in** *or* **on** (*BRIT*)
vi assinar o ponto na entrada; ~ **off** *or*
out (*BRIT*) *vi* assinar o ponto na saída;
~**wise** *adv* em sentido horário; ~**work**
n mecanismo de relógio ♦ *adj* de corda

clog [klɒg] *n* tamanco ♦ *vt* entupir ♦ *vi*
(*also:* ~ **up**) entupir-se

cloister [ˈklɔɪstə°] *n* claustro

close¹ [kləʊs] *adj*: ~ (**to**) próximo (a);
(*friend*) íntimo; (*examination*) minucioso;
(*watch*) atento; (*contest*) apertado; (*weat-*

coach [kəutʃ] n (bus) ônibus m (BR), autocarro (PT); (horse-drawn) carruagem f, coche m; (of train) vagão m; (SPORT) treinador(a) m/f, instrutor(a) m/f; (tutor) professor(a) m/f particular ♦ vt (SPORT) treinar; (student) preparar, ensinar; ~ **trip** n passeio de ônibus (BR) or autocarro (PT)

coal [kəul] n carvão m; ~**field** n região f carbonífera

coalition [kəuə'lɪʃən] n (POL) coalizão f

coal: ~**man** (irreg) n carvoeiro; ~ **merchant** n = ~**man**; ~**mine** n mina de carvão

coarse [kɔːs] adj grosso, áspero; (vulgar) grosseiro, ordinário

coast [kəust] n costa, litoral m ♦ vi (AUT) ir em ponto morto; ~**al** adj costeiro; ~**guard** n (person) guarda m que policia a costa; (service) guarda costeira; ~**line** n litoral m

coat [kəut] n (overcoat) sobretudo; (of animal) pelo; (of paint) demão f, camada f ♦ vt cobrir, revestir; ~ **hanger** n cabide m; ~**ing** n camada; ~ **of arms** n brasão m

coax [kəuks] vt persuadir com meiguice

cob [kɔb] n see **corn**

cobbler ['kɔblə*] n sapateiro

cobbles ['kɔblz] npl pedras fpl arredondadas

cobblestones ['kɔblstəunz] npl = **cobbles**

cobweb ['kɔbwɛb] n teia de aranha

cocaine [kə'keɪn] n cocaína

cock [kɔk] n (rooster) galo; (male bird) macho ♦ vt (gun) engatilhar; ~**erel** n frango, galo pequeno; ~**-eyed** adj (fig: idea etc) absurdo

cockle ['kɔkl] n berbigão m

cockney ['kɔkni] n londrino/a (nativo dos bairros populares do leste de Londres)

cockpit ['kɔkpɪt] n (in aircraft) cabina; (in racing car) compartimento do piloto

cockroach ['kɔkrəutʃ] n barata

cocktail ['kɔkteɪl] n coquetel m (BR), cocktail m (PT); ~ **cabinet** n móvel-bar m; ~ **party** n coquetel (BR), cocktail (BR)

cocoa ['kəukəu] n cacau m; (drink) chocolate m

coconut ['kəukənʌt] n coco

cocoon [kə'kuːn] n casulo m

COD abbr = **cash** (BRIT) or (US) **collect on delivery**

cod [kɔd] n inv bacalhau m

code [kəud] n cifra; (dialling ~, post ~) código; ~ **of practice** deontologia

coercion [kəu'əːʃən] n coerção f

coffee ['kɔfi] n café m; ~ **bar** n (BRIT) n café m, lanchonete f; ~ **break** n hora do café; ~**pot** n cafeteira; ~ **table** n mesinha de centro

coffin ['kɔfɪn] n caixão m

cog [kɔg] n (tooth) dente m; (wheel) roda dentada

cogent ['kəudʒənt] adj convincente

coherent [kəu'hɪərənt] adj coerente

coil [kɔɪl] n rolo; (ELEC) bobina; (contraceptive) DIU m ♦ vt enrolar

coin [kɔɪn] n moeda ♦ vt (word) cunhar, criar; ~**age** n moeda, sistema m monetário; ~ **box** (BRIT) n telefone m público

coincide [kəuɪn'saɪd] vi coincidir; ~**nce** n coincidência

Coke [kəuk] ® n (drink) coca

coke [kəuk] n (coal) coque m

colander ['kɔləndə*] n coador m, passador m

cold [kəuld] adj frio ♦ n frio; (MED) resfriado (BR), constipação f (PT); **it's** ~ está frio; **to be** or **feel** ~ (person) estar com frio; (object) estar frio; **to catch** ~ resfriar-se (BR), apanhar constipação (PT); **to catch a** ~ apanhar um resfriado (BR) or uma constipação (PT); **in** ~ **blood** a sangue frio; ~**ly** adv friamente; ~**-shoulder** vt tratar com frieza; ~ **sore** n herpes m labial

coleslaw ['kəulslɔː] n salada de repolho cru

collapse [kə'læps] vi cair, tombar; (building) desabar; (resistance, government) sucumbir; (MED) desmaiar ♦ n desabamento, desmoronamento; (of government) queda; (MED) colapso; **collapsible** adj dobrável

collar ['kɔlə*] n (of shirt) colarinho; (of coat etc) gola; (for dog) coleira; (TECH) aro, colar m; ~**bone** n clavícula

collateral [kə'lætrəl] n garantia subsidiária or pignoratícia

colleague ['kɔliːg] n colega m/f

collect [kə'lɛkt] vt (as a hobby) colecionar; (gather) recolher; (wages, debts) cobrar; (donations, subscriptions) colher; (mail) coletar; (BRIT: call for) ir buscar, vir apanhar ♦ vi (people) reunir-se ♦ adv: **to call** ~ (US: TEL) ligar a cobrar; ~**ion** n coleção f; (of people) grupo; (of donations) arrecadação f; (of post, for charity) coleta; (of writings) coletânea; ~**or** n colecionador/a m/f; (of taxes etc) cobrador(a) m/f

college ['kɔlidʒ] n (of university) faculdade f; (of technology, agriculture) escola de nível superior

collide [kə'laɪd] vi: **to** ~ (**with**) colidir (com)

colliery ['kɔliəri] (BRIT) n mina de carvão

collision [kə'liʒən] n colisão f

Colombia [kə'lɔmbiə] n Colômbia

colon ['kəulən] n (sign) dois pontos; (MED) côlon m

colonel ['kəːnl] n coronel m

colony ['kɔləni] n colônia

colour ['kʌlə*] (US **color**) n cor f ♦ vt colorir; (with crayons) colorir, pintar; (dye) tingir; (fig: account) falsear ♦ vi (blush) corar; ~s npl (of party, club) cores fpl; in ~ (photograph etc) a cores; ~ in vt (drawing) colorir; ~ bar n discriminação f racial; ~-blind adj daltônico; ~ed adj colorido; (person) de cor; ~ film n filme m a cores; ~ful adj colorido; (account) vívido; (personality) vivo, animado; ~ing n colorido; (complexion) tez f; (in food) colorante m; ~ scheme n distribuição f de cores; ~ television n televisão f a cores

colt [kəult] n potro

column [ˈkɔləm] n coluna; (of smoke) faixa; (of people) fila; ~ist n cronista m/f

comb [kəum] n pente m; (ornamental) crista ♦ vt pentear; (area) vasculhar

combat [ˈkɔmbæt] n combate m ♦ vt combater

combination [kɔmbɪˈneɪʃən] n combinação f; (of safe) segredo

combine [vt, vi kəmˈbaɪn, n ˈkɔmbaɪn] vt combinar; (qualities) reunir ♦ vi combinar-se ♦ n (ECON) associação f; ~ (harvester) n ceifeira debulhadora

KEYWORD

come [kʌm] (pt came, pp come) vi 1 (movement towards) vir; ~ with me vem comigo; to ~ running vir correndo

2 (arrive) chegar; she's ~ here to work ela veio aqui para trabalhar; to ~ home chegar em casa

3 (reach): to ~ to chegar a; the bill came to £40 a conta deu £40; her hair came to her waist o cabelo dela batia na cintura

4 (occur): an idea came to me uma idéia me ocorreu

5 (be, become) ficar; to ~ loose/undone soltar-se/desfazer-se; I've ~ to like him passei a gostar dele

come about vi suceder, acontecer

come across vt fus (person) topar com; (thing) encontrar

come away vi (leave) ir-se embora; (become detached) desprender-se, soltar-se

come back vi (return) voltar

come by vt fus (acquire) conseguir

come down vi (price) baixar; (tree) cair; (building) desmoronar-se

come forward vi apresentar-se

come from vt fus (subj: person) ser de; (: thing) originar-se de

come in vi entrar; (on deal) participar; (be involved) estar envolvido

come in for vt fus (criticism) merecer

come into vt fus (money) herdar; (fashion) ser; (be involved) estar envolvido em

come off vi (button) desprender-se, soltar-se; (attempt) dar certo

come on vi (pupil, work, project) avan-

çar; (lights, electricity) ser ligado; ~ on! vamos!, vai!

come out vi (fact) vir à tona; (book) ser publicado; (stain, sun) sair

come round vi voltar a si

come to vi voltar a si

come up vi (sun) nascer; (in conversation) surgir; (event) acontecer

come up against vt fus (resistance, difficulties) tropeçar com, esbarrar em

come up with vt fus (idea) propor, sugerir; (money) contribuir

come upon vt fus encontrar, achar

comeback [ˈkʌmbæk] n volta

comedian [kəˈmiːdɪən] n cômico, humorista m

comedienne [kəmiːdɪˈen] n cômica, humorista

comedy [ˈkɔmɪdɪ] n comédia

comeuppance [kʌmˈʌpəns] n: to get one's ~ pagar

comfort [ˈkʌmfət] n (well-being) bem-estar m; (relief) alívio ♦ vt consolar, confortar; ~s npl (of home etc) conforto; ~able adj confortável; (financially) tranqüilo; (walk, climb etc) fácil; ~ably adv confortavelmente; ~ station (US) n banheiro (BR), lavatórios mpl (PT)

comic [ˈkɔmɪk] adj (also: ~al) cômico ♦ n (person) humorista m/f; (BRIT: magazine) revista em quadrinhos (BR), revista de banda desenhada (PT), gibi m (BR: inf); ~ strip n história em quadrinhos (BR), banda desenhada (PT)

coming [ˈkʌmɪŋ] n vinda, chegada ♦ adj que vem, vindouro; ~(s) and going(s) n(pl) vaivém m, azáfama

comma [ˈkɔmə] n vírgula

command [kəˈmɑːnd] n ordem f, mandado; (control) controle m; (MIL: authority) comando; (mastery) domínio ♦ vt mandar; ~eer vt requisitar; ~er n (MIL) comandante m/f; ~ment n (REL) mandamento; ~o n (group) comando; (soldier) soldado

commemorate [kəˈmeməreɪt] vt (with monument) comemorar; (with celebration) celebrar

commence [kəˈmens] vt, vi começar, iniciar

commend [kəˈmend] vt elogiar, louvar; (recommend) recomendar

commensurate [kəˈmenʃərɪt] adj: ~ with/to compatível com

comment [ˈkɔment] n comentário ♦ vi: to ~ (on) comentar (sobre); "no ~" "sem comentário"; ~ary n comentário; ~ator n comentarista m/f

commerce [ˈkɔmɔːs] n comércio

commercial [kəˈmɔːʃəl] adj comercial ♦ n anúncio, comercial m; ~ radio/television n rádio/televisão f comercial

commiserate [kəˈmɪzəreɪt] vi: to ~ with comiserar-se de, condoer-se de

commission [kə'mɪʃən] n comissão f; (order) empreitada, encomenda ♦ vt (work of art) encomendar; **out of** ~ com defeito; **~aire** (BRIT) n porteiro; **~er** n comissário/a

commit [kə'mɪt] vt cometer; (resources) alocar; (to sb's care) entregar; **to ~ o.s. (to do)** comprometer-se (a fazer); **to ~ suicide** suicidar-se; **~ment** n compromisso; (political etc) engajamento; (undertaking) promessa

committee [kə'mɪtɪ] n comitê m

commodity [kə'mɔdɪtɪ] n mercadoria

common ['kɔmən] adj comum; (vulgar) vulgar ♦ n área verde aberta ao público; **C~s** npl (BRIT: POL): **the (House of) C~s** a Câmara dos Comuns; **in ~** em comum; **~er** n plebeu/béia m/f; **~ law** n lei f consuetudinária; **~ly** adv geralmente; **C~ Market** n Mercado Comum; **~place** adj vulgar; **~ room** n (SCH) sala dos professores (or estudantes); **~ sense** n bom senso; **C~wealth** n: **the C~wealth** a Comunidade Britânica

commotion [kə'məuʃən] n tumulto, confusão f

communal ['kɔmjuːnl] adj comum

commune [n 'kɔmjuːn, vi kə'mjuːn] n (group) comuna ♦ vi: **to ~ with** comunicar-se com

communicate [kə'mjuːnɪkeɪt] vt comunicar ♦ vi: **to ~ (with)** comunicar-se (com); **communication** n comunicação f; (letter, call) mensagem f; **communication cord** (BRIT) n sinal m de alarme

communion [kə'mjuːnɪən] n (also: **Holy C~**) comunhão f

communiqué [kə'mjuːnɪkeɪ] n comunicado

communism ['kɔmjunɪzəm] n comunismo; **communist** adj, n comunista m/f

community [kə'mjuːnɪtɪ] n comunidade f; **~ centre** n centro social; **~ chest** (US) n fundo de assistência social; **~ home** (BRIT) n reformatório

commutation ticket [kɔmjuˈteɪʃən-] (US) n passe m, bilhete m de assinatura

commute [kə'mjuːt] vi viajar diariamente ♦ vt comutar; **~r** n viajante m/f habitual

compact [adj kəm'pækt, n 'kɔmpækt] adj compacto ♦ n (also: **powder ~**) estojo; **~ disc** n disco laser, CD m; **~ disc player** n som cd m

companion [kəm'pænɪən] n companheiro/a; **~ship** n companhia, companheirismo

company ['kʌmpənɪ] n companhia; (COMM) sociedade f, companhia; **to keep sb ~** fazer companhia a alguém; **~ secretary** (BRIT) n (COMM) secretário/a geral (de uma companhia)

comparative [kəm'pærətɪv] adj (study) comparativo; (peace, safety) relativo; (stranger) meio; **~ly** adv relativamente

compare [kəm'pɛə*] vt comparar ♦ vi: **to ~ with** comparar-se com; **comparison** n comparação f

compartment [kəm'pɑːtmənt] n compartimento; (of wallet) divisão f

compass ['kʌmpəs] n bússola; **~es** npl compasso

compassion [kəm'pæʃən] n compaixão f

compatible [kəm'pætɪbl] adj compatível

compel [kəm'pɛl] vt obrigar; **~ling** adj (fig: argument) convincente

compensate ['kɔmpənseɪt] vt indenizar ♦ vi: **to ~ for** compensar; **compensation** n compensação f; (damages) indenização f

compère ['kɔmpɛə*] n apresentador(a) m/f

compete [kəm'piːt] vi (take part) competir; (vie): **to ~ (with)** competir (com), fazer competição (com)

competent ['kɔmpɪtənt] adj competente

competition [kɔmpɪ'tɪʃən] n (contest) concurso; (ECON) concorrência; (rivalry) competição f

competitive [kəm'pɛtɪtɪv] adj competitivo; (person) competidor(a)

competitor [kəm'pɛtɪtə*] n (rival) competidor(a) m/f; (participant, ECON) concorrente m/f

complacency [kəm'pleɪsnsɪ] n satisfação f consigo mesmo

complain [kəm'pleɪn] vi queixar-se; **to ~ of** (pain) queixar-se de; **~t** n (objection) objeção f; (criticism) queixa; (MED) achaque m, doença

complement ['kɔmplɪmənt] n complemento; (esp ship's crew) tripulação f ♦ vt complementar; **~ary** adj complementar

complete [kəm'pliːt] adj completo; (finished) acabado ♦ vt (finish: building, task) acabar; (: set, group) completar; (a form) preencher; **~ly** adv completamente; **completion** n conclusão f, término; (of contract etc) realização f

complex ['kɔmplɛks] adj complexo ♦ n complexo; (of buildings) conjunto

complexion [kəm'plɛkʃən] n (of face) cor f, tez f

compliance [kəm'plaɪəns] n submissão f; (agreement) conformidade f; **in ~ with** de acordo com, conforme

complicate ['kɔmplɪkeɪt] vt complicar; **~d** adj complicado; **complication** n problema m; (MED) complicação f

compliment [n 'kɔmplɪmənt, 'kɔmplɪmɛnt] n (praise) elogio ♦ vt elogiar; **~s** npl (regards) cumprimentos mpl; **to pay sb a ~** elogiar alguém; **~ary** adj lisonjeiro; (free) gratuito

comply [kəm'plaɪ] vi: **to ~ with** cumprir com

component [kəm'pəunənt] adj componente ♦ n (part) peça

compose [kəm'pəuz] vt compor; **to be ~d of** compor-se de; **to ~ o.s.**

tranqüilizar-se; **~d** *adj* calmo; **~r** *n*
(*MUS*) compositor(a) *m/f*; **composition**
n composição *f*
compost ['kɔmpɔst] *n* adubo
composure [kəm'pəuʒə*] *n* serenidade *f*,
calma
compound [*n, adj* 'kɔmpaund] *n* (*CHEM,
LING*) composto; (*enclosure*) recinto ♦ *adj*
composto
comprehend [kɔmprɪ'hend] *vt* compreender
comprehensive [kɔmprɪ'hensɪv] *adj* abrangente; (*INSURANCE*) total; **~** (**school**)
(*BRIT*) *n* escola secundária de amplo programa
compress [*vt* kəm'pres, *n* 'kɔmpres] *vt*
comprimir; (*text, information etc*) reduzir
♦ *n* (*MED*) compressa
comprise [kəm'praɪz] *vt* (*also:* be **~d** of)
compreender, constar de; (*constitute*)
constituir
compromise ['kɔmprəmaɪz] *n* meio-
termo ♦ *vt* comprometer ♦ *vi* chegar a
um meio-termo
compulsion [kəm'pʌlʃən] *n* compulsão *f*;
(*force*) coação *f*, força
compulsive [kəm'pʌlsɪv] *adj* compulsório
compulsory [kəm'pʌlsərɪ] *adj* obrigatório; (*retirement*) compulsório
computer [kəm'pjuːtə*] *n* computador *m*;
~ game *n* video game *m*; **~ize** *vt* informatizar, computadorizar; **~ pro-
gra(m)mer** *n* programador(a) *m/f*; **~
program(m)ing** *n* programação *f*; **~
science** *n* informática; **computing** *n*
computação *f*; (*science*) informática
comrade ['kɔmrɪd] *n* camarada *m/f*;
~ship *n* camaradagem *f*
con [kɔn] *vt* enganar; (*cheat*) trapacear ♦
n vigarice *f*
conceal [kən'siːl] *vt* ocultar; (*information*) omitir
concede [kən'siːd] *vt* (*admit*) reconhecer,
admitir
conceit [kən'siːt] *n* presunção *f*; **~ed** *adj*
vaidoso
conceive [kən'siːv] *vt* conceber ♦ *vi* conceber, engravidar
concentrate ['kɔnsəntreɪt] *vi* concentrar-
se ♦ *vt* concentrar; **concentration** *n*
concentração *f*; **concentration camp** *n*
campo de concentração
concept ['kɔnsept] *n* conceito; **~ion** *n*
(*idea*) conceito, idéia; (*BIO*) concepção *f*
concern [kən'sɔːn] *n* (*COMM*) empresa;
(*anxiety*) preocupação *f* ♦ *vt* preocupar;
(*involve*) envolver; (*relate to*) dizer respeito a; **to be ~ed (about)** preocupar-
se (com); **~ing** *prep* sobre, a respeito
de, acerca de
concert ['kɔnsət] *n* concerto; **~ed** *adj*
(*joint*) conjunto; **~ hall** *n* sala de con-
certos
concertina [kɔnsə'tiːnə] *n* sanfona

concession [kən'seʃən] *n* concessão *f*;
tax ~ redução no imposto
conclude [kən'kluːd] *vt* (*finish*) acabar,
concluir; (*treaty etc*) firmar; (*agreement*)
chegar a; (*decide*) decidir; **conclusive**
adj conclusivo, decisivo
concoct [kən'kɔkt] *vt* (*excuse*) fabricar;
(*plot*) tramar; (*meal*) preparar; **~ion** *n*
(*mixture*) mistura
concourse ['kɔnkɔːs] *n* (*hall*) saguão *m*
concrete ['kɔnkriːt] *n* concreto (*BR*), betão *m* (*PT*) ♦ *adj* concreto
concur [kən'kɔː*] *vi* estar de acordo, concordar
concurrently [kən'kʌrntlɪ] *adv* ao mesmo tempo, simultaneamente
concussion [kən'kʌʃən] *n* (*MED*) concus-
são *f* cerebral
condemn [kən'dem] *vt* denunciar; (*prisoner, building*) condenar
condensation [kɔnden'seɪʃən] *n* condensação *f*
condense [kən'dens] *vi* condensar-se ♦
vt condensar; **~d milk** *n* leite *m* con-
densado
condition [kən'dɪʃən] *n* condição *f*;
(*MED: illness*) doença ♦ *vt* condicionar;
~s *npl* (*circumstances*) circunstâncias
fpl; **on ~ that** com a condição (de)
que; **~er** *n* (*for hair*) condicionador *m*;
(*for fabrics*) amaciante *m*
condolences [kən'dəulənsɪz] *npl*
pêsames *mpl*
condom ['kɔndɔm] *n* preservativo, camisinha, camisa-de-Venus *f*
condominium [kɔndə'mɪnɪəm] (*US*) *n*
(*building*) edifício
condone [kən'dəun] *vt* admitir, aceitar
conducive [kən'djuːsɪv] *adj*: **~ to** conducente para *or* a
conduct [*n* 'kɔndʌkt, *vt* kən'dʌkt] *n* conduta, comportamento ♦ *vt* (*research etc*)
fazer; (*heat, electricity*) conduzir; (*MUS*)
reger; **to ~ o.s.** comportar-se; **~ed tour**
n viagem *f* organizada; **~or** *n* (*of orchestra*) regente *m/f*; (*on bus*) cobra-
dor(a) *m/f*; (*US: RAIL*) revisor(a) *m/f*;
(*ELEC*) condutor *m*; **~ress** *n* cobradora
cone [kəun] *n* cone *m*; (*BOT*) pinha; (*for
ice-cream*) casquinha; (*on road*) cone colorido para sinalizar obras
confectioner [kən'fekʃənə*] *n*
confeiteiro/a (*BR*), pasteleiro/a (*PT*);
~'s (shop) *n* confeitaria (*BR*), pastelaria (*PT*); (*sweet shop*) confeitaria; **~y** *n*
(*sweetmeats*) doces *mpl*; (*sweets*) balas *fpl*
confer [kən'fɔː*] *vt*: **to ~ sth on** conferir algo a; (*advantage*) conceder algo a
♦ *vi* conferenciar
conference ['kɔnfərns] *n* congresso
confess [kən'fes] *vt* confessar ♦ *vi* (*admit*) admitir; **~ion** *n* admissão *f*; (*REL*)
confissão *f*
confetti [kən'fetɪ] *n* confete *m*
confide [kən'faɪd] *vi*: **to ~ in** confiar

em, fiar-se em

confidence ['kɒnfɪdns] *n* confiança; *(faith)* fé *f*; *(secret)* confidência; **in ~** em confidência; **~ trick** *n* conto do vigário; **confident** *adj* confiante, convicto; *(positive)* seguro; **confidential** *adj* confidencial

confine [kən'faɪn] *vt* *(shut up)* encarcerar; *(limit)*: **to ~ (to)** confinar (a); **~d** *adj* *(space)* reduzido; **~ment** *n* prisão *f*; **~s** *npl* confins *mpl*

confirm [kən'fɜːm] *vt* confirmar; **~ation** *n* confirmação *f*; *(REL)* crisma; **~ed** *adj* inveterado

confiscate ['kɒnfɪskeɪt] *vt* confiscar

conflict [*n* 'kɒnflɪkt, *vi* kən'flɪkt] *n* *(disagreement)* divergência; *(of interests, loyalties etc)* conflito; *(fighting)* combate *m* ♦ *vi* estar em conflito; *(opinions)* divergir; **~ing** *adj* *(reports)* divergente; *(interests)* oposto

conform [kən'fɔːm] *vi* conformar-se; **to ~** ajustar-se a, acomodar-se a

confound [kən'faʊnd] *vt* confundir

confront [kən'frʌnt] *vt* *(problems)* enfrentar; *(enemy, danger)* defrontar-se com; **~ation** *n* confrontação *f*

confuse [kən'fjuːz] *vt* *(perplex)* desconcertar; *(mix up)* confundir, misturar; *(complicate)* complicar; **~d** *adj* confuso; **confusing** *adj* confuso; **confusion** *(mix-up)* mal-entendido; *(perplexity)* perplexidade *f*; *(disorder)* confusão *f*

congeal [kən'dʒiːl] *vi* coagular-se

congenial [kən'dʒiːnɪəl] *adj* simpático, agradável

congestion [kən'dʒɛstʃən] *n* *(MED)* congestão *f*; *(traffic)* congestionamento

congratulate [kən'grætjuleɪt] *vt* parabenizar; **congratulations** *npl* parabéns *mpl*

congregate ['kɒŋgrɪgeɪt] *vi* reunir-se; **congregation** *n* *(in church)* fiéis *mpl*

congress ['kɒŋgrɛs] *n* congresso; *(US)*: **C~** Congresso; **~man** *(US: irreg)* *n* deputado

conjunctivitis [kəndʒʌŋktɪ'vaɪtɪs] *n* conjuntivite *f*

conjure ['kʌndʒə*] *vi* fazer truques; **~ up** *vt* *(ghost, spirit)* fazer aparecer, invocar; *(memories)* evocar; **~r** *n* mágico/a, prestidigitador/a

conk out [kɒŋk-] *(inf)* *vi* pifar

con man ['kɒn-] *(irreg)* *n* vigarista *m*

connect [kə'nɛkt] *vt* *(ELEC, TEL)* ligar; *(fig: associate)* associar; *(join)*: **to ~ sth (to)** juntar *or* unir algo (a) ♦ *vi*: **to ~ with** *(train)* conectar com; **to be ~ed with** estar relacionado com; **I'm trying to ~ you** *(TEL)* estou tentando completar a ligação; **~ion** *n* ligação *f*; *(ELEC, RAIL, fig)* conexão *f*; *(TEL)* ligação *f*

connive [kə'naɪv] *vi*: **to ~ at** ser conivente em

connoisseur [kɒnɪ'sə*] *n* conhecedor(a) *m/f*, apreciador(a) *m/f*

conquer ['kɒŋkə*] *vt* conquistar; *(enemy)* vencer; *(feelings)* superar; **conquest** *n* conquista

cons [kɒnz] *npl* *see* convenience

conscience ['kɒnʃəns] *n* consciência

conscientious [kɒnʃɪ'ɛnʃəs] *adj* consciencioso

conscious ['kɒnʃəs] *adj* consciente; *(deliberate)* intencional; **~ness** *n* consciência; *(MED)*: **to lose/regain ~ness** perder/recuperar os sentidos

conscript ['kɒnskrɪpt] *n* recruta *m/f*; **~ion** *n* serviço militar obrigatório

consent [kən'sɛnt] *n* consentimento ♦ *vi*: **to ~** to consentir em

consequence ['kɒnsɪkwəns] *n* consequência; *(significance)*: **of ~** de importância; **consequently** *adv* por conseguinte

conservation [kɒnsə'veɪʃən] *n* conservação *f*; *(of the environment)* preservação *f*

conservative [kən'sɜːvətɪv] *adj* conservador(a); *(cautious)* moderado; *(BRIT: POL)*: **C~** conservador(a) ♦ *n* *(BRIT: POL)* conservador(a) *m/f*

conservatory [kən'sɜːvətrɪ] *n* *(MUS)* conservatório; *(greenhouse)* estufa

conserve [kən'sɜːv] *vt* *(preserve)* preservar; *(supplies, energy)* poupar ♦ *n* conserva

consider [kən'sɪdə*] *vt* considerar; *(take into account)* levar em consideração; *(study)* estudar, examinar; **to ~ doing sth** pensar em fazer algo

considerable [kən'sɪdərəbl] *adj* considerável; *(sum)* importante

considerate [kən'sɪdərɪt] *adj* atencioso; **consideration** *n* consideração *f*; *(deliberation)* deliberação *f*; *(factor)* fator *m*

considering [kən'sɪdərɪŋ] *prep* em vista de

consign [kən'saɪn] *vt*: **to ~ to** *(place)* relegar para; *(care)* confiar a; **~ment** *n* consignação *f*

consist [kən'sɪst] *vi*: **to ~ of** *(comprise)* consistir em

consistency [kən'sɪstənsɪ] *n* coerência; *(thickness)* consistência

consistent [kən'sɪstənt] *adj* *(person)* coerente, estável; *(idea)* sólido

consolation [kɒnsə'leɪʃən] *n* conforto

console [*vt* kən'səʊl, *n* 'kɒnsəʊl] *vt* confortar ♦ *n* consolo

consommé [kən'sɒmeɪ] *n* consomê *m*, caldo

consonant ['kɒnsənənt] *n* consoante *f*

consortium [kən'sɔːtɪəm] *(pl* ~s *or* consortia) *n* consórcio

conspicuous [kən'spɪkjuəs] *adj* conspícuo

conspiracy [kən'spɪrəsɪ] *n* conspiração *f*, trama

constable ['kʌnstəbl] *(BRIT)* *n* policial *m/f* *(BR)*, polícia *m/f* *(PT)*; **chief ~** chefe *m/f* de polícia; **constabulary** *n* policia (distrital)

constant ['kɔnstənt] *adj* constante

constipated ['kɔnstɪpeɪtəd] *adj* com prisão de ventre

constipation [kɔnstɪ'peɪʃən] *n* prisão *f* de ventre

constituency [kən'stɪtjuənsɪ] *n* (POL) distrito eleitoral; (*people*) eleitorado; **constituent** *n* (POL) eleitor(a) *m/f*; (*component*) componente *m*

constitute ['kɔnstɪtjuːt] *vt* (*represent*: *challenge*) representar; (: *emergency*) constituir; (*make up*) constituir

constitution [kɔnstɪ'tjuːʃən] *n* constituição *f*; (*health*) compleição *f*

constraint [kən'streɪnt] *n* coação *f*, pressão *f*; (*restriction*) limitação *f*

construct [kən'strʌkt] *vt* construir; **~ion** *n* construção *f*; (*structure*) estrutura

construe [kən'struː] *vt* interpretar

consul ['kɔnsl] *n* cônsul *m/f*; **~ate** *n* consulado

consult [kən'sʌlt] *vt* consultar; **~ant** *n* (MED) (médico/a) especialista *m/f*; (*other specialist*) assessor(a) *m/f*, consultor(a) *m/f*; **~ation** *n* (MED) consulta; (*discussion*) discussão *f*; **~ing room** (BRIT) *n* consultório

consume [kən'sjuːm] *vt* (*eat*) comer; (*drink*) beber; (*fire etc, COMM*) consumir; **~r** *n* consumidor(a) *m/f*; **~r goods** *npl* bens *mpl* de consumo; **~r society** *n* sociedade *f* de consumo

consumption [kən'sʌmpʃən] *n* consumação *f*; (*buying, amount*) consumo

cont. *abbr* = **continued**

contact ['kɔntækt] *n* contato ♦ *vt* entrar or pôr-se em contato com; **~ lenses** *npl* lentes *fpl* de contato

contagious [kən'teɪdʒəs] *adj* contagioso; (*fig: laughter etc*) contagiante

contain [kən'teɪn] *vt* conter; to ~ o.s. conter-se; **~er** *n* recipiente *m*; (*for shipping etc*) container *m*, cofre *m* de carga

contaminate [kən'tæmɪneɪt] *vt* contaminar

cont'd *abbr* = **continued**

contemplate ['kɔntəmpleɪt] *vt* (*idea*) considerar; (*person etc*) contemplar

contemporary [kən'tɛmpərərɪ] *adj* (*account*) contemporâneo; (*design*) moderno ♦ *n* contemporâneo/a

contempt [kən'tɛmpt] *n* desprezo; ~ of court (LAW) desacato à autoridade do tribunal; **~ible** *adj* desprezível; **~uous** *adj* desdenhoso

contend [kən'tɛnd] *vt* (*assert*): to ~ that afirmar que ♦ *vi*: to ~ with (*struggle*) lutar com; (*difficulty*) enfrentar; (*compete*): to ~ for competir por; **~er** *n* contendor(a) *m/f*

content [*adj, vt* kən'tɛnt, *n* 'kɔntɛnt] *adj* (*happy*) contente; (*satisfied*) satisfeito ♦ *vt* contentar, satisfazer ♦ *n* conteúdo; (*fat* ~, *moisture* ~ *etc*) quantidade *f*; **~s**

npl (*of packet, book*) conteúdo; **~ed** *adj* contente, satisfeito

contention [kən'tɛnʃən] *n* (*assertion*) asserção *f*; (*disagreement*) contenda

contentment [kən'tɛntmənt] *n* contentamento

contest [*n* 'kɔntɛst, *vt* kən'tɛst] *n* contenda; (*competition*) concurso ♦ *vt* (*legal case*) defender; (POL) ser candidato a; (*competition*) disputar; (*statement*) contestar; **~ant** *n* competidor(a) *m/f*; (*in fight*) adversário/a

context ['kɔntɛkst] *n* contexto

continent ['kɔntɪnənt] *n* continente *m*; the C~ (BRIT) o continente europeu; **~al** *adj* continental; **~al quilt** (BRIT) *n* edredom *m*

contingency [kən'tɪndʒənsɪ] *n* contingência; **contingent** *n* contingente *m*

continual [kən'tɪnjuəl] *adj* contínuo; **~ly** *adv* constantemente

continuation [kəntɪnju'eɪʃən] *n* prolongamento

continue [kən'tɪnjuː] *vi* prosseguir, continuar ♦ *vt* continuar; (*start again*) recomeçar, retomar; **continuous** *adj* contínuo; **continuous stationery** (COMPUT) formulários *mpl* contínuos

contort [kən'tɔːt] *vt* contorcer

contour ['kɔntuə] *n* contorno; (*also: ~ line*) curva de nível

contraband ['kɔntrəbænd] *n* contrabando

contraceptive [kɔntrə'sɛptɪv] *adj* anticoncepcional ♦ *n* anticoncepcional *m*

contract [*n* 'kɔntrækt, *vt, vi* kən'trækt] *n* contrato ♦ *vi* (*become smaller*) contrair-se, encolher-se; (COMM): to ~ to do sth comprometer-se por contrato a fazer algo ♦ *vt* contrair; **~ion** *n* contração *f*; **~or** *n* contratante *m/f*

contradict [kɔntrə'dɪkt] *vt* contradizer, desmentir

contraption [kən'træpʃən] (*pej*) *n* engenhoca, geringonça

contrary[1] ['kɔntrərɪ] *adj* contrário ♦ *n* contrário; on the ~ muito pelo contrário; unless you hear to the ~ salvo aviso contrário

contrary[2] [kən'trɛərɪ] *adj* teimoso

contrast [*n* 'kɔntrɑːst, *vt* kən'trɑːst] *n* contraste *m* ♦ *vt* comparar; in ~ to em contraste com, ao contrário de

contravene [kɔntrə'viːn] *vt* infringir

contribute [kən'trɪbjuːt] *vt* contribuir ♦ *vi* dar; to ~ to (*charity*) contribuir para; (*newspaper*) escrever para; (*discussion*) participar de; **contribution** *n* (*donation*) doação *f*; (BRIT: *for social security*) contribuição *f*; (*to debate*) intervenção *f*; (*to journal*) colaboração *f*; **contributor** *n* (*to appeal*) contribuinte *m/f*; (*to newspaper*) colaborador(a) *m/f*

contrive [kən'traɪv] *vi*: to ~ to do chegar a fazer

control [kən'trəul] *vt* controlar; (*machi-*

nery) regular; (*temper*) dominar ♦ *n* controle *m*; (*of car*) direção *f* (*BR*), condução *f* (*PT*); (*check*) freio, controle; ~s *npl* (*of vehicle*) instrumentos *mpl* de controle; (*on radio, television etc*) controle; (*governmental*) medidas *fpl* de controle; **to be in ~ of** ter o controle de; (*in charge of*) ser responsável por; ~ **panel** *n* painel *m* de instrumentos; ~ **room** *n* sala de comando; ~ **tower** *n* (*AVIAT*) torre *f* de controle

controversial [kɔntrə'vəːʃl] *adj* controvertido, polêmico

controversy ['kɔntrəvəːsɪ] *n* controvérsia, polêmica

convalesce [kɔnvə'lɛs] *vi* convalescer

convector [kən'vɛktə*] *n* (*heater*) aquecedor *m* de convecção

convene [kən'viːn] *vt* convocar ♦ *vi* convocar-se

convenience [kən'viːnɪəns] *n* (*easiness*) facilidade *f*; (*suitability*) conveniência; (*advantage*) vantagem *f*, conveniência; **at your ~** quando lhe convier; **all modern ~s** (*also: BRIT: all mod cons*) com todos os confortos

convenient [kən'viːnɪənt] *adj* conveniente

convent ['kɔnvənt] *n* convento

convention [kən'vɛnʃən] *n* (*custom*) costume *m*; (*agreement*) convenção *f*; (*meeting*) assembléia; ~**al** *adj* convencional

conversant [kən'vəːsnt] *adj*: **to be ~ with** estar familiarizado com

conversation [kɔnvə'seɪʃən] *n* conversação *f*, conversa; ~**al** *adj* de conversa

converse [*n* 'kɔnvəːs, *vi* kən'vəːs] *n* inverso ♦ *vi* conversar; ~**ly** *adv* pelo contrário, inversamente

convert [*vt* kən'vəːt, *n* 'kɔnvəːt] *vt* converter ♦ *n* convertido/a; ~**ible** *n* conversível *m*

convey [kən'veɪ] *vt* transportar, levar; (*thanks*) expressar; (*information*) exprimir; ~**or belt** *n* correia transportadora

convict [*vt* kən'vɪkt, *n* 'kɔnvɪkt] *vt* condenar ♦ *n* presidiário/a; ~**ion** *n* condenação *f*; (*belief*) convicção *f*; (*certainty*) certeza

convince [kən'vɪns] *vt* (*assure*) assegurar; (*persuade*) convencer; **convincing** *adj* convincente

convoluted ['kɔnvəluːtɪd] *adj* (*argument*) complicado

convoy ['kɔnvɔɪ] *n* escolta

convulse [kən'vʌls] *vt*: **to be ~d with laughter/pain** morrer de rir/dor

coo [kuː] *vi* arrulhar; (*person*) falar suavemente

cook [kuk] *vt* cozinhar; (*meal*) preparar ♦ *vi* cozinhar ♦ *n* cozinheiro/a; ~**book** *n* livro de receitas; ~**er** *n* fogão *m*; ~**ery** *n* culinária; ~**ery book** (*BRIT*) *n* = ~**book**; ~**ie** (*US*) *n* bolacha, biscoito; ~**ing** *n* cozinha

cool [kuːl] *adj* fresco; (*calm*) calmo; (*unfriendly*) frio ♦ *vt* resfriar ♦ *vi* esfriar; ~**ness** *n* frescura

coop [kuːp] *n* (*for poultry*) galinheiro; (*for rabbits*) capoeira; ~ **up** *vt* (*fig*) confinar

cooperate [kəu'ɔpəreɪt] *vi* colaborar; (*assist*) ajudar; **cooperative** *adj* cooperativo ♦ *n* cooperativa

coordinate [*vt* kəu'ɔːdɪneɪt, *n* kəu'ɔːdɪnət] *vt* coordenar ♦ *n* (*MATH*) coordenada; ~**s** *npl* (*clothes*) coordenados *mpl*

co-ownership [kəu-] *n* co-propriedade *f*, condomínio

cop [kɔp] (*inf*) *n* polícia *m/f*, policial *m/f* (*BR*), tira *m* (*inf*)

cope [kəup] *vi*: **to ~ with** poder com, arcar com; (*problem*) estar à altura de

copper ['kɔpə*] *n* (*metal*) cobre *m*; (*BRIT: inf: policeman/woman*) polícia *m/f*, policial *m/f* (*BR*); ~**s** *npl* (*coins*) moedas *fpl* de pouco valor

coppice ['kɔpɪs] *n* bosquete *m*

copse [kɔps] *n* = **coppice**

copy ['kɔpɪ] *n* duplicata; (*of book etc*) exemplar *m* ♦ *vt* copiar; (*imitate*) imitar; ~**right** *n* direitos *mpl* autorais, copirraite *m*

coral ['kɔrəl] *n* coral *m*

cord [kɔːd] *n* corda; (*ELEC*) fio, cabo; (*fabric*) veludo cotelê

cordial ['kɔːdɪəl] *adj* cordial ♦ *n* (*BRIT: drink*) bebida à base de fruta

cordon ['kɔːdn] *n* cordão *m*; ~ **off** *vt* isolar

corduroy ['kɔːdərɔɪ] *n* veludo cotelê

core [kɔː*] *n* centro; (*of fruit*) caroço; (*of problem*) âmago ♦ *vt* descaroçar

coriander [kɔrɪ'ændə*] *n* coentro

cork [kɔːk] *n* rolha; (*tree*) cortiça; ~**screw** *n* saca-rolhas *m inv*

corn [kɔːn] *n* (*BRIT*) trigo; (*US: maize*) milho; (*on foot*) calo; ~ **on the cob** (*CULIN*) espiga de milho

corned beef ['kɔːnd-] *n* carne *f* de boi enlatada

corner ['kɔːnə*] *n* (*outside*) esquina; (*inside*) canto; (*in road*) curva; (*FOOTBALL, BOXING*) córner *m* ♦ *vt* (*trap*) encurralar; (*COMM*) açambarcar, monopolizar ♦ *vi* fazer uma curva; ~**stone** *n* (*fig*) base *f*, fundamento

cornet ['kɔːnɪt] *n* (*MUS*) cornetim *m*; (*BRIT: of ice-cream*) casquinha

cornflakes ['kɔːnfleɪks] *npl* flocos *mpl* de milho

cornflour ['kɔːnflauə*] (*BRIT*) *n* farinha de milho, maisena ®

cornstarch ['kɔːnstɑːtʃ] (*US*) *n* = **cornflour**

Cornwall ['kɔːnwɔl] *n* Cornualha

corny ['kɔːnɪ] (*inf*) *adj* (*joke*) gasto

coronary ['kɔrənərɪ] *n*: ~ (**thrombosis**) trombose *f* (coronária)

coronation [kɔrə'neɪʃən] *n* coroação *f*

coroner ['kɒrənə*] n magistrado que investiga mortes suspeitas

coronet ['kɒrənɪt] n coroa aberta, diadema m

corporal ['kɔ:pərl] n cabo ♦ adj: ~ punishment castigo corporal

corporate ['kɔ:pərɪt] adj coletivo; (finance) corporativo; (image) de empresa

corporation [kɔ:pə'reɪʃən] n (of town) município, junta; (COMM) sociedade f

corps [kɔ:*, pl kɔ:z] (pl corps) n (MIL) unidade f; (diplomatic) corpo; the press ~ a imprensa

corpse [kɔ:ps] n cadáver m

corral [kə'rɑ:l] n curral m

correct [kə'rɛkt] adj exato; (proper) correto ♦ vt corrigir

correspond [kɒrɪs'pɒnd] vi (write): to ~ (with) corresponder-se (com); (be equal to): to ~ to corresponder a; (be in accordance): to ~ (with) corresponder a; ~ence n correspondência; ~ent n correspondente m/f

corridor ['kɒrɪdɔ:*] n corredor m

corrode [kə'rəud] vt corroer ♦ vi corroer-se; **corrosion** n corrosão f

corrugated ['kɒrəgeɪtɪd] adj corrugado; ~ **iron** n chapa ondulada or corrugada

corrupt [kə'rʌpt] adj corrupto; (COMPUT) corrupto, danificado ♦ vt corromper; corromper, danificar; ~**ion** n corrupção f; corrupção, danificação f

corset ['kɔ:sɪt] n espartilho; (MED) colete m

Corsica ['kɔ:sɪkə] n Córsega

cosh [kɒʃ] (BRIT) n cassetete m

cosmetic [kɒz'mɛtɪk] n cosmético ♦ adj (fig) simbólico, artificial

cosmos ['kɒzmɒs] n cosmo

cosset ['kɒsɪt] vt paparicar

cost [kɒst] (pt, pp cost) n (price) preço ♦ vt custar; ~**s** npl (COMM: overheads) custos mpl; (LAW) custas fpl; **at all** ~**s** custe o que custar

co-star [kəu-] n co-estrela m/f

Costa Rica ['kɒstə'ri:kə] n Costa Rica

cost-effective adj rentável

costly ['kɒstlɪ] adj caro

cost-of-living adj: ~ **allowance** ajuda de custo; ~ **index** índice m de preços ao consumidor

costume ['kɒstju:m] n traje m; (BRIT: also: **swimming** ~: woman's) maiô m (BR), fato de banho (PT); (: man's) calção m (de banho) (BR), calções mpl de banho (PT); ~ **jewellery** n bijuteria

cosy ['kəuzɪ] (US cozy) adj aconchegante; (person) confortável

cot [kɒt] n (BRIT) cama (de criança), berço; (US) cama de lona

cottage ['kɒtɪdʒ] n casa de campo; ~ **cheese** n ricota (BR), queijo creme (PT)

cotton ['kɒtn] n algodão m; (thread) fio, linha; ~ **on** (inf) vi: to ~ **on** (to sth) sacar (algo); ~ **candy** (US) n algodão m doce; ~ **wool** (BRIT) n algodão m (hidrófilo)

couch [kautʃ] n sofá m; (doctor's) cama; (psychiatrist's) divã m

couchette [ku:'ʃɛt] n leito

cough [kɒf] vi tossir ♦ n tosse f; ~ **drop** n pastilha para a tosse

could [kud] pt, conditional of can²

couldn't ['kudnt] = could not

council ['kaunsl] n conselho; **city** or **town** ~ câmara municipal; ~ **estate** (BRIT) n conjunto habitacional; ~ **house** (BRIT) n casa popular; ~**lor** n vereador(a) m/f

counsel ['kaunsl] n (advice) conselho; (lawyer) advogado/a ♦ vt aconselhar; ~**lor** (US **counselor**) n conselheiro/a; (US: LAW) advogado/a

count [kaunt] vt contar; (include) incluir ♦ vi contar ♦ n (of votes etc) contagem f; (of pollen, alcohol) nível m; (nobleman) conde m; ~ **on** vt fus (expect) esperar; (depend on) contar com; ~**down** n contagem f regressiva

countenance ['kauntɪnəns] n expressão f ♦ vt tolerar

counter ['kauntə*] n (in shop) balcão m; (in post office etc) guichê m; (in games) ficha ♦ vt contrariar ♦ adv: ~ **to** ao contrário de; ~**act** vt neutralizar

counterfeit ['kauntəfɪt] n falsificação f ♦ vt falsificar ♦ adj falso, falsificado

counterfoil ['kauntəfɔɪl] n canhoto (BR), talão m (PT)

countermand ['kauntəmɑ:nd] vt revogar

counterpart ['kauntəpɑ:t] n (of person) homólogo/a; (of company etc) equivalente m/f

counterproductive ['kauntəprə'dʌktɪv] adj contraproducente

countersign ['kauntəsaɪn] vt autenticar

countess ['kauntɪs] n condessa

countless ['kauntlɪs] adj inumerável

country ['kʌntrɪ] n país m; (nation) nação f; (native land) terra; (as opposed to town) campo; (region) região f, terra; ~ **dancing** (BRIT) n dança regional; ~ **house** n casa de campo; ~**man** n (national) compatriota m; (rural) camponês m; ~**side** n campo

county ['kauntɪ] n condado

coup [ku:] n golpe de mestre; (also: ~ **d'état**) golpe (de estado)

couple ['kʌpl] n (of things, people) par m; (married ~) casal m; **a** ~ **of** um par de; (a few) alguns/algumas

coupon ['ku:pɒn] n cupom m (BR), cupão m (PT); (voucher) vale m

courage ['kʌrɪdʒ] n coragem f

courgette [kuə'ʒɛt] (BRIT) n abobrinha

courier ['kurɪə*] n correio; (for tourists) guia m/f, agente m/f de turismo

course [kɔ:s] n (direction) direção f; (process) desenvolvimento; (of river, SCH) curso; (of ship) rumo; (GOLF) campo;

(*part of meal*) prato; ~ **of treatment** tratamento; **of** ~ naturalmente; (*certainly*) certamente; **of** ~! claro!, lógico!

court [kɔːt] *n* (*royal*) corte *f*; (*LAW*) tribunal *m*; (*TENNIS etc*) quadra ♦ *vt* (*woman*) cortejar, namorar; **to take to** ~ demandar, levar a julgamento

courteous ['kɔːtɪəs] *adj* cortês/esa

courtesan [kɔːtɪˈzæn] *n* cortesã *f*

courtesy ['kɔːtɪsɪ] *n* cortesia; **(by)** ~ **of** com permissão de

court-house (*US*) *n* palácio de justiça

courtier ['kɔːtɪə*] *n* cortesão *m*

court martial (*pl* **courts martial**) *n* conselho de guerra

courtroom ['kɔːtrum] *n* sala de tribunal

courtyard ['kɔːtjɑːd] *n* pátio

cousin ['kʌzn] *n* primo/a *m/f*; **first** ~ primo/a irmão/mã

cove [kəuv] *n* angra, enseada

covenant ['kʌvənənt] *n* compromisso

cover ['kʌvə*] *vt* cobrir; (*with lid*) tapar; (*chairs etc*) revestir; (*distance*) percorrer; (*include*) abranger; (*protect*) abrigar; (*issues*) tratar ♦ *n* (*lid*) tampa; (*for chair etc*) capa; (*for bed*) cobertor *m*; (*of book, magazine*) capa; (*shelter*) abrigo; (*INSURANCE: also: of spy*) cobertura; **to take** ~ abrigar-se; **under** ~ (*indoors*) abrigado; **under separate** ~ (*COMM*) em separado; ~ **up** *vi*: **to** ~ **up for sb** cobrir alguém; ~**age** *n* cobertura; ~ **charge** *n* couvert *m*; ~**ing** *n* cobertura; (*of snow, dust etc*) camada; ~**ing letter** (*US* ~ **letter**) *n* carta de cobertura; ~ **note** *n* nota de cobertura

covert ['kʌvəːt] *adj* (*threat*) velado

cover-up *n* encobrimento (dos fatos)

covet ['kʌvɪt] *vt* cobiçar

cow [kau] *n* vaca ♦ *vt* intimidar

coward ['kauəd] *n* covarde *m/f*; ~**ice** *n* covardia; ~**ly** *adj* covarde

cowboy ['kaubɔɪ] *n* vaqueiro

cower ['kauə*] *vi* encolher-se (de medo)

coxswain ['kɔksn] *n* (*abbr*: **cox**) timoneiro/a

coy [kɔɪ] *adj* tímido

cozy ['kəuzɪ] (*US*) *adj* = **cosy**

CPA (*US*) *n abbr* = **certified public accountant**

crab [kræb] *n* caranguejo; ~ **apple** *n* maçã ácida

crack [kræk] *n* rachadura; (*gap*) brecha; (*noise*) estalo; (*drug*) crack *m* ♦ *vt* quebrar; (*nut*) partir, descascar; (*wall*) rachar; (*whip etc*) estalar; (*joke*) soltar; (*mystery*) resolver; (*code*) decifrar ♦ *adj* (*expert*) de primeira classe; ~ **down on** *vt fus* (*crime*) ser linha dura com; ~ **up** *vi* (*PSYCH*) sofrer um colapso nervoso; ~**er** *n* (*biscuit*) biscoito; (*Christmas* ~) busca-pé-surpresa *m*

crackle ['krækl] *vi* crepitar

cradle ['kreɪdl] *n* berço

craft [krɑːft] *n* (*skill*) arte *f*; (*trade*) ofício;

(*boat*: *pl inv*) barco; (*plane*: *pl inv*) avião; ~**sman** (*irreg*) *n* artífice *m*, artesão *m*; ~**smanship** *n* qualidade *f*; ~**y** *adj* astuto, esperto

crag [kræg] *n* penhasco

cram [kræm] *vt* (*fill*): **to** ~ **sth with** encher *or* abarrotar algo de; (*put*): **to** ~ **sth into** enfiar algo em ♦ *vi* (*for exams*) estudar na última hora

cramp [kræmp] *n* (*MED*) cãibra; ~**ed** *adj* apertado, confinado

crampon ['kræmpən] *n* gato de ferro

cranberry ['krænbərɪ] *n* oxicoco

crane [kreɪn] *n* (*TECH*) guindaste *m*; (*bird*) grou *m*

crank [kræŋk] *n* manivela; (*person*) excêntrico/a; ~**shaft** *n* virabrequim *m*

cranny ['krænɪ] *n see* **nook**

crash [kræʃ] *n* (*noise*) estrondo; (*of car*) batida; (*of plane*) desastre *m* de avião; (*COMM*) falência, quebra; (*STOCK EXCHANGE*) craque *m* ♦ *vt* (*car*) colidir; (*plane*) espatifar ♦ *vi* bater; cair, espatifar-se; (*cars*) colidir, bater; (*COMM*) falir, quebrar; ~ **course** *n* curso intensivo; ~ **helmet** *n* capacete *m*; ~ **landing** *n* aterrissagem *f* forçada (*BR*), aterragem *f* forçosa (*PT*)

crate [kreɪt] *n* caixote *m*; (*for bottles*) engradado

cravat [krəˈvæt] *n* gravata

crave [kreɪv] *vt*, *vi*: **to** ~ **for** ansiar por

crawl [krɔːl] *vi* arrastar-se; (*child*) engatinhar; (*insect*) andar; (*vehicle*) arrastar-se a passo de tartaruga ♦ *n* (*SWIMMING*) crawl *m*

crayfish ['kreɪfɪʃ] *n inv* (*freshwater*) camarão-d'água-doce *m*; (*saltwater*) lagostim *m*

crayon ['kreɪən] *n* lápis *m* de cera, crayon *m*

craze [kreɪz] *n* (*fashion*) moda

crazy ['kreɪzɪ] *adj* louco, maluco, doido; ~ **paving** (*BRIT*) *n* pavimento irregular

creak [kriːk] *vi* chiar, ranger

cream [kriːm] *n* (*of milk*) nata; (*artificial* ~, *cosmetic*) creme *m*; (*élite*): **the** ~ **of** a fina flor de ♦ *adj* (*colour*) creme *inv*; ~ **cake** *n* bolo de creme; ~ **cheese** *n* ricota (*BR*), queijo creme (*PT*); ~**y** *adj* (*colour*) creme *inv*; (*taste*) cremoso

crease [kriːs] *n* (*fold*) dobra, vinco; (*in trousers*) vinco; (*wrinkle*) ruga ♦ *vt* (*wrinkle*) amassar, amarrotar ♦ *vi* amassar-se, amarrotar-se

create [kriːˈeɪt] *vt* criar; (*produce*) produzir; **creator** *n* criador(a) *m/f*; (*inventor*) inventor(a) *m/f*

creature ['kriːtʃə*] *n* (*animal*) animal *m*, bicho; (*living thing*) criatura

credence ['kriːdns] *n*: **to lend** *or* **give** ~ **to** dar crédito a

credible ['kredɪbl] *adj* acreditável; (*trustworthy*) digno de crédito

credit ['kredɪt] *n* crédito; (*merit*) mérito ♦

vt (*also*: **give ~ to**) acreditar; (*COMM*) creditar; **~s** *npl* (*CINEMA, TV*) crédito; **to ~ sb with sth** (*fig*) atribuir algo a alguém; **to be in ~** ter fundos; **~ card** *n* cartão m de crédito; **~or** *n* credor(a) *m/f*

creed [kri:d] *n* credo

creek [kri:k] *n* enseada; (*US*) riacho

creep [kri:p] (*pt, pp* **crept**) *vi* (*animal*) rastejar; (*person*) deslizar(-se); **~er** *n* trepadeira; **~y** *adj* horripilante

cremate [krɪ'meɪt] *vt* cremar; **cremation** *n* cremação *f*; **crematoria** *npl* of **crematorium**; **crematorium** (*pl* **crematoria**) *n* crematório

crêpe [kreɪp] *n* (*fabric*) crepe m; (*rubber*) borracha; **~ bandage** (*BRIT*) *n* atadura de crepe

crept [krɛpt] *pt, pp of* **creep**

crescent ['krɛsnt] *n* meia-lua; (*street*) rua semicircular

cress [krɛs] *n* agrião m

crest [krɛst] *n* (*of bird*) crista; (*of hill*) cimo, topo; (*of coat of arms*) timbre m; **~fallen** *adj* abatido, cabisbaixo

Crete [kri:t] *n* Creta

crevice ['krɛvɪs] *n* fenda; (*gap*) greta

crew [kru:] *n* (*of ship*) tripulação *f*; (*CINEMA*) equipe *f*; **~-cut** *n* corte m à escovinha; **~-neck** *n* gola arredondada

crib [krɪb] *n* manjedoura, presépio; (*US: cot*) berço ♦ *vt* (*inf*) colar

crick [krɪk] *n* cãibra; **~ in the neck** torcicolo

cricket ['krɪkɪt] *n* (*insect*) grilo; (*game*) criquete m, cricket m

crime [kraɪm] *n* (*no pl: illegal activities*) crime m; (*offence*) delito; (*fig*) pecado, maldade *f*; **criminal** *n* criminoso ♦ *adj* criminal; (*morally wrong*) imoral

crimson ['krɪmzn] *adj* carmesim *inv*

cringe [krɪndʒ] *vi* encolher-se

crinkle ['krɪŋkl] *vt* amassar, enrugar

cripple ['krɪpl] *n* aleijado-a ♦ *vt* aleijar

crises ['kraɪsi:z] *npl of* **crisis**

crisis ['kraɪsɪs] (*pl* **crises**) *n* crise *f*

crisp [krɪsp] *adj* fresco; (*bacon etc*) torrado; (*manner*) seco; **~s** (*BRIT*) *npl* batatinhas *fpl* fritas

criss-cross [krɪs-] *adj* (*design*) entrecruzado; (*pattern*) em xadrez; **~ pattern** (*padrão m* em) xadrez m

criteria [kraɪ'tɪərɪə] *npl of* **criterion**

criterion [kraɪ'tɪərɪən] (*pl* **criteria**) *n* critério

critic ['krɪtɪk] *n* crítico/a; **~al** *adj* crítico; (*illness*) grave; **to be ~ of sth/sb** criticar algo/alguém; **~ally** *adv* (*examine*) criteriosamente; (*speak*) criticamente; (*ill*) gravemente; **~ism** *n* crítica; **~ize** *vt* criticar

croak [krəuk] *vi* (*frog*) coaxar; (*bird*) crocitar; (*person*) estar rouco

Croatia [krəu'eɪʃə] *n* Croácia

crochet ['krəuʃeɪ] *n* crochê m

crockery ['krɔkərɪ] *n* louça

crocodile ['krɔkədaɪl] *n* crocodilo

crocus ['krəukəs] *n* açafrão-da-primavera m

croft [krɔft] (*BRIT*) *n* pequena chácara

crony ['krəunɪ] (*inf: pej*) *n* camarada *m/f*, compadre m

crook [kruk] *n* (*inf: criminal*) vigarista *m/f*; (*of shepherd*) cajado; **~ed** *adj* torto; (*dishonest*) desonesto

crop [krɔp] *n* (*produce*) colheita; (*amount produced*) safra; (*riding ~*) chicotinho ♦ *vt* cortar; **~ up** *vi* surgir

cross [krɔs] *n* cruz *f*; (*hybrid*) cruzamento ♦ *vt* cruzar; (*street etc*) atravessar; (*thwart*) contrariar ♦ *adj* zangado, mal-humorado; **~ out** *vt* riscar; **~ over** *vi* atravessar; **~bar** *n* (*SPORT*) barra transversal; **~-country (race)** *n* corrida pelo campo; **~-examine** *vt* (*LAW*) reperguntar; **~-eyed** *adj* vesgo; **~fire** *n* fogo cruzado; **~ing** *n* (*sea passage*) travessia; (*also*: **pedestrian ~ing**) faixa (para pedestres) (*BR*), passadeira (*PT*); **~ing guard** (*US*) *n* guarda *m/f* para pedestres; **~-purposes** *npl*: **to be at ~purposes** não entender-se; **~-reference** *n* referência remissiva; **~roads** *n* cruzamento; **~ section** *n* (*of object*) corte m transversal; (*of population*) grupo representativo; **~walk** (*US*) *n* faixa (para pedestres) (*BR*), passadeira (*PT*); **~wind** *n* vento costal; **~word** *n* palavras *fpl* cruzadas

crotch [krɔtʃ] *n* (*ANAT*) local em que as pernas se destacam do tronco; (*of garment*) fundilho

crotchet ['krɔtʃɪt] *n* (*MUS*) semínima

crotchety ['krɔtʃɪtɪ] *adj* rabugento

crouch [krautʃ] *vi* agachar-se

crow [krəu] *n* (*bird*) corvo; (*of cock*) canto, cocoricó m ♦ *vi* (*cock*) cantar, cocoricar

crowbar ['krəuba:'] *n* pé-de-cabra m

crowd [kraud] *n* multidão *f* ♦ *vt* (*fill*) apinhar ♦ *vi* (*gather*): **to ~ round** reunir-se; (*cram*): **to ~ in** apinhar-se em; **~ed** *adj* (*full*) lotado; (*densely populated*) superlotado

crown [kraun] *n* coroa; (*of head, hill*) topo ♦ *vt* coroar; (*fig*) rematar; **~ jewels** *npl* jóias *fpl* reais; **~ prince** *n* príncipe m herdeiro

crow's-feet *n* pés-de-galinha *mpl*

crucial ['kru:ʃl] *adj* (*decision*) vital; (*vote*) decisivo

crucifix ['kru:sɪfɪks] *n* crucifixo; **~ion** *n* crucificação *f*

crude [kru:d] *adj* (*materials*) bruto; (*fig: basic*) tosco; (*: vulgar*) grosseiro; **~ (oil)** *n* petróleo em bruto

cruel ['kruəl] *adj* cruel

cruise [kru:z] *n* cruzeiro ♦ *vi* (*ship*) fazer um cruzeiro; (*car*): **to ~ at ... km/h** ir a ... km por hora; **~r** *n* (*motorboat*) barco a motor; (*warship*) cruzador *m*

crumb [krʌm] *n* (*of bread*) migalha; (*of cake*) farelo

crumble ['krʌmbl] *vt* esfarelar ♦ *vi* (*building*) desmoronar-se; (*plaster, earth*) esfacelar-se; (*fig*) desintegrar-se; **crumbly** *adj* farelento

crumpet ['krʌmpɪt] *n* bolo leve

crumple ['krʌmpl] *vt* (*paper*) amassar; (*material*) amarrotar

crunch [krʌntʃ] *vt* (*food etc*) mastigar; (*underfoot*) esmagar ♦ *n* (*fig*): **the ~ o** momento decisivo; **~y** *adj* crocante

crusade [kru:'seɪd] *n* (*campaign*) campanha

crush [krʌʃ] *n* (*crowd*) aglomeração *f*; (*love*): **to have a ~ on sb** ter um rabicho por alguém; (*drink*): **lemon ~** limonada ♦ *vt* (*press*) esmagar; (*squeeze*) espremer; (*paper*) amassar; (*cloth*) enrugar; (*army, opposition*) aniquilar; (*hopes*) destruir; (*person*) arrasar

crust [krʌst] *n* (*of bread*) casca; (*of snow*) crosta; (*of earth*) camada

crutch [krʌtʃ] *n* muleta

crux [krʌks] *n* ponto crucial

cry [kraɪ] *vi* chorar; (*shout: also: ~ out*) gritar ♦ *n* grito; (*of bird*) pio; (*of animal*) voz *f*; **~ off** *vi* desistir

cryptic ['krɪptɪk] *adj* enigmático

crystal ['krɪstl] *n* cristal *m*; **~-clear** *adj* cristalino, claro

cub [kʌb] *n* filhote *m*; (*also: ~ scout*) lobinho

Cuba ['kju:bə] *n* Cuba

cubbyhole ['kʌbɪhəʊl] *n* esconderijo

cube [kju:b] *n* cubo ♦ *vt* (*MATH*) elevar ao cubo; **~ root** *n* raiz *f* cúbica; **cubic** *adj* cúbico; **cubic capacity** *n* (*AUT*) cilindrada

cubicle ['kju:bɪkl] *n* cubículo

cuckoo ['kuku:] *n* cuco; **~ clock** *n* relógio de cuco

cucumber ['kju:kʌmbə*] *n* pepino

cuddle ['kʌdl] *vt* abraçar ♦ *vi* abraçar-se

cue [kju:] *n* (*SNOOKER*) taco; (*THEATRE etc*) deixa

cuff [kʌf] *n* (*of shirt, coat etc*) punho; (*US: on trousers*) bainha; (*blow*) bofetada; **off the ~** de improviso; **~ links** *npl* abotoaduras *fpl*

cuisine [kwɪ'zi:n] *n* cozinha

cul-de-sac ['kʌldəsæk] *n* beco sem saída

cull [kʌl] *vt* (*story, idea*) escolher, selecionar ♦ *n* matança seletiva

culminate ['kʌlmɪneɪt] *vi*: **to ~ in** terminar em; **culmination** *n* (*of career*) auge *m*; (*of process*) conclusão *f*

culottes [kju:'lɒts] *npl* saia-calça

culprit ['kʌlprɪt] *n* culpado/a

cult [kʌlt] *n* culto

cultivate ['kʌltɪveɪt] *vt* cultivar; **cultivation** *n* cultivo

culture ['kʌltʃə*] *n* cultura; **~d** *adj* culto

cumbersome ['kʌmbəsəm] *adj* pesado,

desajeitado; (*person*) lente, ineficiente

cunning ['kʌnɪŋ] *n* astúcia ♦ *adj* astuto, malandro; (*device, idea*) engenhoso

cup [kʌp] *n* xícara (*BR*), chávena (*PT*); (*prize, of bra*) taça

cupboard ['kʌbəd] *n* armário

cup tie (*BRIT*) *n* jogo eliminatório

curate ['kjuərɪt] *n* coadjutor *m*

curator [kjuə'reɪtə*] *n* diretor(a) *m/f*

curb [kə:b] *vt* refrear ♦ *n* freio; (*US: kerb*) meio-fio (*BR*), borda do passeio (*PT*)

curdle ['kə:dl] *vi* coalhar

cure [kjuə*] *vt* curar ♦ *n* (*MED*) tratamento, cura; (*solution*) remédio

curfew ['kə:fju:] *n* toque *m* de recolher

curio ['kjuərɪəʊ] *n* antiguidade *f*

curious ['kjuərɪəs] *adj* curioso; (*nosy*) abelhudo; (*unusual*) estranho

curl [kə:l] *n* (*of hair*) cacho ♦ *vt* (*loosely*) frisar; (: *tightly*) encrespar ♦ *vi* (*hair*) encaracolar; **~ up** *vi* encaracolar-se; **~er** *n* rolo, bobe *m*; **~y** *adj* cacheado, crespo

currant ['kʌrnt] *n* passa de corinto; (*black~, red~*) groselha

currency ['kʌrnsɪ] *n* moeda; **to gain ~** (*fig*) consagrar-se

current ['kʌrnt] *n* corrente *f* ♦ *adj* corrente; (*present*) atual; **~ account** (*BRIT*) *n* conta corrente; **~ affairs** *npl* atualidades *fpl*; **~ly** *adv* atualmente

curricula [kə'rɪkjulə] *npl of* **curriculum**

curriculum [kə'rɪkjuləm] (*pl* **~s** *or* **curricula**) *n* programa *m* de estudos; **~ vitae** *n* curriculum vitae *m*, currículo

curry ['kʌrɪ] *n* caril *m* ♦ *vt*: **to ~ favour with** captar simpatia de; **~ powder** *n* pós *mpl* de caril, curry *m*

curse [kə:s] *vi* xingar (*BR*), praguejar (*PT*) ♦ *vt* (*swear at*) xingar (*BR*); (*bemoan*) amaldiçoar ♦ *n* maldição *f*; (*swearword*) palavrão *m* (*BR*), baixo calão *m* (*PT*); (*problem*) castigo

cursor ['kə:sə*] *n* (*COMPUT*) cursor *m*

cursory ['kə:sərɪ] *adj* rápido, superficial

curt [kə:t] *adj* seco, brusco

curtail [kə:'teɪl] *vt* (*freedom, rights*) restringir; (*visit etc*) abreviar, encurtar; (*expenses etc*) reduzir

curtain ['kə:tn] *n* cortina; (*THEATRE*) pano

curts(e)y ['kə:tsɪ] *vi* fazer reverência

curve [kə:v] *n* curva ♦ *vi* encurvar-se, torcer-se; (*road*) fazer (uma) curva

cushion ['kuʃn] *n* almofada; (*of air*) colchão *m* ♦ *vt* amortecer

custard ['kʌstəd] *n* nata, creme *m*

custodian [kʌs'təʊdɪən] *n* guarda *m/f*

custody ['kʌstədɪ] *n* custódia; **to take into ~** deter

custom ['kʌstəm] *n* (*tradition*) tradição *f*; (*convention*) costume *m*; (*habit*) hábito; (*COMM*) clientela; **~ary** *adj* costumeiro; **~er** *n* cliente *m/f*; **~ized** *adj* (*car etc*) feito sob encomenda; ~-**made** adj (car) feito sob encomenda; (clothes) feito sob medida

customs ['kʌstəmz] npl alfândega; ~ **duty** n imposto alfandegário; ~ **officer** n inspetor(a) m/f da alfândega, aduaneiro/a

cut [kʌt] (pt, pp **cut**) vt cortar; (reduce) reduzir ♦ vi cortar ♦ n corte m; (in spending) redução f; (of garment) talho; ~ **down** vt (tree) derrubar; (consumption) reduzir; ~ **off** vt (piece, TEL) cortar; (person, village) isolar; (supply) suspender; ~ **out** vt (shape) recortar; (activity etc) suprimir; (remove) remover; ~ **up** vt cortar em pedaços; ~**back** n redução f, corte m

cute [kjuːt] adj bonitinho, gracinha

cuticle ['kjuːtɪkl] n cutícula

cutlery ['kʌtlərɪ] n talheres mpl

cutlet ['kʌtlɪt] n costeleta; (vegetable ~, nut ~) medalhão m

cut:~**out** n (shape) figura para recortar; (switch) interruptor m; ~**price** (US ~ **rate**) adj a preço reduzido; ~**throat** n assassino/a ♦ adj feroz; ~**ting** adj cortante ♦ n (BRIT: from newspaper) recorte m; (from plant) muda

CV n abbr = **curriculum vitae**

cwt abbr = **hundredweight**

cyanide ['saɪənaɪd] n cianeto

cybercafé ['saɪbəkæfeɪ] n cibercafé m

cyberspace ['saɪbəspeɪs] n ciberespaço

cycle ['saɪkl] n ciclo; (bicycle) bicicleta ♦ vi andar de bicicleta

cycling ['saɪklɪŋ] n ciclismo

cyclist ['saɪklɪst] n ciclista m/f

cygnet ['sɪgnɪt] n cisne m novo

cylinder ['sɪlɪndə*] n cilindro; (of gas) bujão m

cymbals ['sɪmblz] npl pratos mpl

cynic ['sɪnɪk] n cínico/a; ~**al** adj cínico; ~**ism** n cinismo

Cyprus ['saɪprəs] n Chipre f

cyst [sɪst] n cisto; ~**itis** n cistite f

czar [zɑː*] n czar m

Czech [tʃɛk] adj tcheco ♦ n tcheco/a; (LING) tcheco

Czechoslovakia [tʃɛkəsləˈvækɪə] n Tchecoslováquia, Tcheco-Eslováquia; ~**n** adj, n tchecoslovaco/a

D

D [diː] n (MUS) ré m

dab [dæb] vt (eyes, wound) tocar (de leve); (paint, cream) aplicar de leve

dabble ['dæbl] vi: to ~ **in** interessar-se por

dad [dæd], **daddy** ['dædɪ] (inf) n papai m

daffodil ['dæfədɪl] n narciso-dos-prados m

daft [dɑːft] adj bobo, besta

dagger ['dægə*] n punhal m, adaga

daily ['deɪlɪ] adj diário ♦ n (paper) jornal m, diário ♦ adv diariamente

dainty ['deɪntɪ] adj delicado

dairy ['dɛərɪ] n leiteria; ~ **farm** n fazenda de gado leiteiro; ~ **products** npl laticínios mpl; ~ **store** (US) n leiteria

dais ['deɪɪs] n estrado

daisy ['deɪzɪ] n margarida; ~ **wheel** n (on printer) margarida

dale [deɪl] (BRIT) n vale m

dam [dæm] n represa, barragem f ♦ vt represar

damage ['dæmɪdʒ] n (harm) prejuízo; (dents etc) avaria ♦ vt danificar; (harm) prejudicar; ~**s** npl (LAW) indenização f por perdas e danos

damn [dæm] vt condenar; (curse) maldizer ♦ n (inf): **I don't give a** ~ não dou a mínima, estou me lixando ♦ adj (inf: also: ~**ed**) danado, maldito; ~ **(it)!** (que) droga!; ~**ing** adj (evidence) prejudicial

damp [dæmp] adj úmido ♦ n umidade f ♦ vt (also: ~**en**: cloth, rag) umedecer; (: enthusiasm etc) jogar água fria em

damson ['dæmzən] n ameixa pequena

dance [dɑːns] n dança; (party etc) baile m ♦ vi dançar; ~ **hall** n salão m de baile; ~**r** n dançarino/a; (professional) bailarino/a; **dancing** n dança

dandelion ['dændɪlaɪən] n dente-de-leão m

dandruff ['dændrəf] n caspa

Dane [deɪn] n dinamarquês/esa m/f

danger ['deɪndʒə*] n perigo; (risk) risco; "~!" (on sign) "perigo!"; **to be in** ~ **of** correr o risco de; **in** ~ em perigo; ~**ous** adj perigoso

dangle ['dæŋgl] vt balançar ♦ vi pender balançando

Danish ['deɪnɪʃ] adj dinamarquês/esa ♦ n (LING) dinamarquês m

dapper ['dæpə*] adj garboso; (appearance) esmerado

dare [dɛə*] vt: **to** ~ **sb to do sth** desafiar alguém a fazer algo ♦ vi: **to** ~ **(to) do sth** atrever-se a fazer algo, ousar fazer algo; **I** ~ **say** (I suppose) acho provável que; ~**devil** n intrépido, atrevido; **daring** adj audacioso; (bold) ousado ♦ n coragem f, destemor m

dark [dɑːk] adj escuro; (complexion) moreno ♦ n escuro; **to be in the** ~ **about** (fig) estar no escuro sobre; **after** ~ depois de escurecer; ~**en** vt escurecer; (colour) fazer mais escuro ♦ vi escurecer(-se); ~ **glasses** npl óculos mpl escuros; ~**ness** n escuridão f; ~**room** n câmara escura

darling ['dɑːlɪŋ] adj, n querido/a

darn [dɑːn] vt cerzir

dart [dɑːt] n dardo; (in sewing) alinhavo ♦ vi precipitar-se, correr para; **to** ~ **away/along** ir-se/seguir precipitadamente; ~**board** n alvo (para jogo de dardos); **~s** n (game) jogo de dardos

dash [dæʃ] n (sign) hífen m; (: long) travessão m; (quantity) pontinha ♦ vt arremessar; (hopes) frustrar ♦ vi correr para, ir depressa; ~ **away** vi sair apressado; ~ **off** vi = ~ **away**

dashboard ['dæʃbɔːd] n painel m de instrumentos

dashing ['dæʃɪŋ] adj arrojado

data ['deɪtə] npl dados mpl; **~base** n banco de dados; ~ **processing** n processamento de dados

date [deɪt] n data; (with friend) encontro; (fruit) tâmara ♦ vt datar; (person) namorar; **to ~** até agora; **out of** ~ fora de moda; (expired) desatualizado; **up to** ~ moderno; **~d** adj antiquado

daub [dɔːb] vt borrar

daughter ['dɔːtə*] n filha; **~-in-law** (pl **~s-in-law**) n nora

daunting ['dɔːntɪŋ] adj desanimador(a)

dawdle ['dɔːdl] vi (go slow) vadiar

dawn [dɔːn] n alvorada, amanhecer m; (of period, situation) surgimento, início ♦ vi (day) amanhecer; (fig): it ~ed on him that ... começou a perceber que ...

day [deɪ] n dia m; (working ~) jornada, dia útil; (heyday) apogeu m; **the ~ before** a véspera; **the ~ before yesterday** anteontem; **the ~ after tomorrow** depois de amanhã; **by ~** de dia; **~break** n amanhecer m; **~dream** vi devanear; **~light** n luz f (do dia); **~ return** (BRIT) n bilhete m de ida e volta no mesmo dia; **~time** n dia m; **~-to-** adj cotidiano

daze [deɪz] vt (stun) aturdir ♦ n: **in a** ~ aturdido

dazzle ['dæzl] vt (bewitch) deslumbrar; (blind) ofuscar

DC abbr (ELEC) = direct current

D-day ['diːdeɪ] n o dia D

dead [dɛd] adj morto; (numb) dormente; (telephone) cortado; (ELEC) sem corrente ♦ adv completamente; (exactly) absolutamente; **~en** vt (blow, sound) amortecer; (pain) anestesiar; **~ end** n beco sem saída; ~ **heat** n (SPORT): **to finish in a** ~ **heat** ser empatado; **~line** n prazo final; **~lock** n impasse m; ~ **loss** (inf) n: **to be a** ~ **loss** não ser de nada; **~ly** adj mortal, fatal; (accuracy, insult) devastador(a); (weapon) mortífero; **~pan** adj sem expressão

deaf [dɛf] adj surdo; **~en** vt ensurdecer; **~ness** n surdez f

deal [diːl] (pt, pp dealt) n (agreement) acordo ♦ vt (cards, blows) dar; **a good** or **great** ~ (of) bastante, muito; ~ **in** vt fus (COMM) negociar em or com; ~ **with** vt fus (people) tratar com; (problem) ocupar-se de; (subject) tratar de;

~er n negociante m/f; **~ings** npl transações fpl; **~t** pt, pp of **deal**

dean [diːn] n (REL) decano; (SCH: BRIT) reitor(a) m/f; (: US) orientador(a) m/f de estudos

dear [dɪə*] adj querido, caro; (expensive) caro ♦ n: **my** ~ meu querido/minha querida ♦ excl: ~ **me!** ai, meu Deus!; **D~ Sir/Madam** (in letter) Ilmo. Senhor/Exma. Senhora (BR), Exmo. Senhor/Exma. Senhora (PT); **D~ Mr/Mrs X** Caro Sr./Cara Sra. X; **~ly** adv (love) ternamente; (pay) caro

death [dɛθ] n morte f; (ADMIN) óbito; ~ **certificate** n certidão f de óbito; **~ly** adj (colour) pálido; (silence) profundo; ~ **penalty** n pena de morte; ~ **rate** n (índice m de) mortalidade f; ~ **toll** n número de mortos (em acidentes)

debacle [deɪ'bɑːkl] n fracasso

debar [dɪ'bɑː*] vt: **to ~ sb from doing** proibir a alguém fazer or que faça

debase [dɪ'beɪs] vt degradar; (value) desvalorizar; (quality) piorar

debatable [dɪ'beɪtəbl] adj discutível

debate [dɪ'beɪt] n debate m ♦ vt debater

debauchery [dɪ'bɔːtʃərɪ] n decadência

debit ['dɛbɪt] n débito ♦ vt: **to ~ a sum to sb** or **to sb's account** lançar uma quantia ao débito de alguém or à conta de alguém; see also **direct**

debris ['dɛbriː] n escombros mpl

debt [dɛt] n dívida; (state) endividamento; **to be in** ~ ter dívidas, estar endividado; **~or** n devedor(a) m/f

debunk [diː'bʌŋk] vt desmascarar

début ['deɪbjuː] n estréia

decade ['dɛkeɪd] n década

decadence ['dɛkədəns] n decadência

decaffeinated [dɪ'kæfɪneɪtɪd] adj descafeinado

decanter [dɪ'kæntə*] n garrafa ornamental

decay [dɪ'keɪ] n ruína; (also: tooth ~) cárie f ♦ vi (rot) apodrecer-se

deceased [dɪ'siːst] n falecido/a

deceit [dɪ'siːt] n engano; (duplicity) fraude f; **~ful** adj enganador(a)

deceive [dɪ'siːv] vt enganar

December [dɪ'sɛmbə*] n dezembro

decent ['diːsənt] adj (proper) decente; (kind, honest) honesto, amável

deception [dɪ'sɛpʃən] n engano; (deceitful act) fraude f; **deceptive** adj enganador(a)

decide [dɪ'saɪd] vt (person) convencer; (question) resolver ♦ vi decidir; **to ~ on sth** decidir-se por algo; **~d** adj decidido; (definite) claro, definido; **~dly** adv claramente; (emphatically) decididamente

decimal ['dɛsɪməl] adj decimal ♦ n decimal m; ~ **point** n vírgula de decimais

decision [dɪ'sɪʒən] n (choice) escolha; (act of choosing) decisão f; (decisiveness) resolução f

decisive [dɪ'saɪsɪv] *adj* (*action*) decisivo; (*person*) decidido

deck [dɛk] *n* (*NAUT*) convés *m*; (*of bus*): top ~ andar *m* de cima; (*of cards*) baralho; **record** ~ toca-discos *m inv*; ~**chair** *n* cadeira de lona, espreguiçadeira

declaration [dɛklə'reɪʃən] *n* declaração *f*; (*public*) pronunciamento

declare [dɪ'klɛə*] *vt* (*intention*) revelar; (*result*) divulgar; (*income, at customs*) declarar

decline [dɪ'klaɪn] *n* declínio; (*lessening*) diminuição *f*, baixa *f* ♦ *vt* recusar ♦ *vi* diminuir

decode [di:'kəud] *vt* decifrar

decompose [di:kəm'pəuz] *vi* decompor-se

décor ['deɪkɔ:*] *n* decoração *f*; (*THEATRE*) cenário

decorate ['dɛkəreɪt] *vt* (*adorn*) adornar; (*paint*) pintar; (*paper*) decorar com papel; **decoration** *n* enfeite *m*; (*act*) decoração *f*; (*medal*) condecoração *f*; **decorative** *adj* decorativo; **decorator** *n* (*painter*) pintor(a) *m/f*

decorum [dɪ'kɔ:rəm] *n* decoro

decoy ['di:kɔɪ] *n* (*person*) armadilha; (*object*) engodo, chamariz *m*

decrease [*n* 'di:kri:s, *vt, vi* di:'kri:s] *n*: ~ (in) diminuição *f* (de) ♦ *vt* reduzir ♦ *vi* diminuir

decree [dɪ'kri:] *n* decreto; ~ **nisi** *n* ordem *f* provisória de divórcio

dedicate ['dɛdɪkeɪt] *vt* dedicar; **dedication** *n* dedicação *f*; (*in book*) dedicatória; (*on radio*) mensagem *f*

deduce [dɪ'dju:s] *vt* deduzir

deduct [dɪ'dʌkt] *vt* deduzir; ~**ion** *n* (*deducting*) redução *f*; (*amount*) subtração *f*; (*deducing*) dedução *f*

deed [di:d] *n* feito; (*LAW*) escritura, título

deem [di:m] *vt* julgar, estimar

deep [di:p] *adj* profundo; (*voice*) baixo, grave; (*breath*) fundo; (*colour*) forte, carregado ♦ *adv*: **the spectators stood 20** ~ os espectadores formaram-se em 20 fileiras; **to be 4 metres** ~ ter 4 metros de profundidade; ~**en** *vt* aprofundar ♦ *vi* aumentar; ~**freeze** *n* congelador *m*, freezer *m* (*BR*); ~**fry** *vt* fritar em recipiente fundo; ~**ly** *adv* fundo; (*moved*) profundamente; ~**sea** *cpd*: ~**sea diver** escafandrista *m/f*; ~**sea diving** mergulho com escafandro; ~**sea fishing** pesca de alto-mar; ~**seated** *adj* arraigado

deer [dɪə*] *n inv* veado, cervo; ~**skin** *n* camurça, pele *f* de cervo

deface [dɪ'feɪs] *vt* desfigurar

default [dɪ'fɔ:lt] *n* (*COMPUT*: *also*: ~ **value**) valor *m* de default; **by** ~ (*win*) por desistência

defeat [dɪ'fi:t] *n* derrota; (*failure*) malogro ♦ *vt* derrotar, vencer; ~**ist** *adj*, *n* derrotista *m/f*

defect [*n* 'di:fɛkt, *vi* dɪ'fɛkt] *n* defeito ♦

vi: **to** ~ **to the enemy** desertar para se juntar ao inimigo; ~**ive** *adj* defeituoso

defence [dɪ'fɛns] (*US* **defense**) *n* defesa, justificação *f*; ~**less** *adj* indefeso

defend [dɪ'fɛnd] *vt* defender; (*LAW*) contestar; ~**ant** *n* acusado/a; (*in civil case*) réu/ré *m/f*; ~**er** *n* defensor(a) *m/f*; (*SPORT*) defesa

defense [dɪ'fɛns] (*US*) *n* = **defence**

defensive [dɪ'fɛnsɪv] *adj* defensivo ♦ *n*: **on the** ~ na defensiva

defer [dɪ'fɜ:*] *vt* (*postpone*) adiar

defiance [dɪ'faɪəns] *n* desafio, rebeldia; **in** ~ **of** a despeito de

defiant [dɪ'faɪənt] *adj* desafiador(a)

deficiency [dɪ'fɪʃənsɪ] *n* (*lack*) deficiência, falta; (*defect*) defeito

deficit ['dɛfɪsɪt] *n* déficit *m*

defile [dɪ'faɪl] *vt* (*memory*) desonrar; (*statue etc*) profanar

define [dɪ'faɪn] *vt* definir

definite ['dɛfɪnɪt] *adj* (*fixed*) definitivo; (*clear, obvious*) claro, categórico; (*certain*) certo; **he was** ~ **about it** ele foi categórico; ~**ly** *adv* sem dúvida

definitive [dɪ'fɪnɪtɪv] *adj* conclusivo

deflate [di:'fleɪt] *vt* esvaziar

deflect [dɪ'flɛkt] *vt* desviar

defogger [dɪ'fɔgə*] (*US*) *n* = **demister**

deform [dɪ'fɔ:m] *vt* distorcer

defraud [dɪ'frɔ:d] *vt*: **to** ~ **sb (of sth)** trapacear alguém (por causa de algo)

defrost [di:'frɔst] *vt* descongelar

deft [dɛft] *adj* (*hands*) destro; (*movement*) hábil

defunct [dɪ'fʌŋkt] *adj* extinto

defuse [di:'fju:z] *vt* tirar o estopim *or* a espoleta de; (*situation*) neutralizar

defy [dɪ'faɪ] *vt* desafiar; (*resist*) opor-se a

degenerate [*vi* dɪ'dʒɛnəreɪt, *adj* dɪ'dʒɛnərɪt] *vi* degenerar ♦ *adj* degenerado

degree [dɪ'gri:] *n* grau *m*; (*SCH*) diploma *m*, título; ~ **in maths** formatura em matemática; **by** ~**s** (*gradually*) pouco a pouco; **to some** ~, **to a certain** ~ até certo ponto

dehydrated [di:haɪ'dreɪtɪd] *adj* desidratado; (*eggs, milk*) em pó

de-ice [di:'aɪs] *vt* (*windscreen*) descongelar

deign [deɪn] *vi*: **to** ~ **to do** dignar-se a fazer

deity ['di:ɪtɪ] *n* divindade *f*, deidade *f*

dejected [dɪ'dʒɛktɪd] *adj* deprimido

delay [dɪ'leɪ] *vt* (*decision etc*) retardar, atrasar; (*train, person*) atrasar ♦ *vi* hesitar ♦ *n* demora; (*postponement*) adiamento; **to be** ~**ed** estar atrasado; **without** ~ sem demora *or* atraso

delectable [dɪ'lɛktəbl] *adj* (*person*) gostoso; (*food*) delicioso

delegate [*n* 'dɛlɪgɪt, *vt* 'dɛlɪgeɪt] *n* delegado/a ♦ *vt* (*person*) autorizar; (*task*) delegar; **delegation** *n* (*group*) delegação *f*; (*by leader*) autorização *f*

delete [dɪ'liːt] *vt* eliminar, riscar; (*COMPUT*) deletar

deliberate [*adj* dɪ'lɪbərɪt, *vi* dɪ'lɪbəreɪt] *adj* (*intentional*) intencional; (*slow*) pausado, lento ♦ *vi* considerar; **~ly** *adv* (*on purpose*) de propósito

delicacy ['dɛlɪkəsɪ] *n* delicadeza; (*of problem*) dificuldade *f*; (*food*) iguaria

delicate ['dɛlɪkɪt] *adj* delicado; (*health*) frágil

delicatessen [dɛlɪkə'tɛsn] *n* delicatessen *m*

delicious [dɪ'lɪʃəs] *adj* delicioso; (*food*) saboroso

delight [dɪ'laɪt] *n* prazer *m*, deleite *m*; (*person*) encanto; (*experience*) delícia ♦ *vt* encantar, deleitar; **to take (a) ~ in** deleitar-se com; **~ed** *adj*: **~ed (at** *or* **with)** encantado (com); **~ful** *adj* encantador(a), delicioso

delinquent [dɪ'lɪŋkwənt] *adj, n* delinqüente *m/f*

delirious [dɪ'lɪrɪəs] *adj* delirante; **to be ~** delirar

deliver [dɪ'lɪvə*] *vt* (*distribute*) distribuir; (*hand over*) entregar; (*message*) comunicar; (*speech*) proferir; (*MED*) partejar; **~y** *n* distribuição *f*; (*of speaker*) enunciação *f*; (*MED*) parto; **to take ~y of** receber

delude [dɪ'luːd] *vt* iludir, enganar

deluge ['dɛljuːdʒ] *n* dilúvio; (*fig*) enxurrada

delusion [dɪ'luːʒən] *n* ilusão *f*

delve [dɛlv] *vi*: **to ~ into** (*subject*) investigar, pesquisar; (*cupboard etc*) vasculhar

demand [dɪ'maːnd] *vt* exigir; (*rights*) reivindicar, reclamar ♦ *n* exigência; (*claim*) reivindicação *f*; (*ECON*) procura; **to be in ~** estar em demanda; **on ~** à vista; **~ing** *adj* (*boss*) exigente; (*work*) absorvente

demean [dɪ'miːn] *vt*: **to ~ o.s.** rebaixar-se

demeanour [dɪ'miːnə*] (*US* **demeanor**) *n* conduta, comportamento

demented [dɪ'mɛntɪd] *adj* demente, doido

demise [dɪ'maɪz] *n* falecimento

demister [dɪ'mɪstə*] (*BRIT*) *n* (*AUT*) desembaçador *m* de pára-brisa

demo ['dɛməu] (*inf*) *n abbr* (= *demonstration*) passeata

democracy [dɪ'mɔkrəsɪ] *n* democracia; **democrat** *n* democrata *m/f*; **democratic** *adj* democrático

demolish [dɪ'mɔlɪʃ] *vt* demolir, derrubar; (*argument*) refutar, contestar

demonstrate ['dɛmənstreɪt] *vt* demonstrar ♦ *vi*: **to ~ (for/against)** manifestar-se (a favor de/contra); **demonstration** *n* (*POL*) manifestação *f*; (: *march*) passeata; (*proof*) demonstração *f*; (*exhibition*) exibição *f*; **demonstrator** *n* manifestante *m/f*

demote [dɪ'məut] *vt* rebaixar de posto

demure [dɪ'mjuə*] *adj* recatado

den [dɛn] *n* (*of animal*) covil *m*; (*of thieves*) antro, esconderijo; (*room*) aposento privado, cantinho

denatured alcohol [diː'neɪtʃəd-] *n* álcool *m* desnaturado

denial [dɪ'naɪəl] *n* refutação *f*; (*refusal*) negativa

denim ['dɛnɪm] *n* brim *m*, zuarte *m*; **~s** *npl* jeans *m* (*BR*), jeans *mpl* (*PT*)

Denmark ['dɛnmaːk] *n* Dinamarca

denomination [dɪnɔmɪ'neɪʃən] *n* valor *m*, denominação *f*; (*REL*) confissão *f*, seita

denounce [dɪ'nauns] *vt* denunciar

dense [dɛns] *adj* denso, espesso; (*inf*: *stupid*) estúpido, bronco; **~ly** *adv*: **~ly populated** com grande densidade de população

density ['dɛnsɪtɪ] *n* densidade *f*; **single/double ~ disk** (*COMPUT*) disco de densidade simples/dupla

dent [dɛnt] *n* amolgadura, depressão *f* ♦ *vt* amolgar, dentar

dental ['dɛntl] *adj* (*treatment*) dentário; (*hygiene*) dental; **~ surgeon** *n* cirurgião/giã *m/f* dentista

dentist ['dɛntɪst] *n* dentista *m/f*; **~ry** *n* odontologia

dentures ['dɛntʃəz] *npl* dentadura

deny [dɪ'naɪ] *vt* negar; (*refuse*) recusar

deodorant [diː'əudərənt] *n* desodorante *m* (*BR*), desodorizante *m* (*PT*)

depart [dɪ'paːt] *vi* ir-se, partir; (*train etc*) sair; **to ~ from** (*fig*: *differ from*) afastar-se de

department [dɪ'paːtmənt] *n* (*SCH*) departamento; (*COMM*) seção *f*; (*POL*) repartição *f*; **~ store** *n* magazine *m* (*BR*), grande armazém *m* (*PT*)

departure [dɪ'paːtʃə*] *n* partida, ida; (*of train etc*) saída; (*of employee*) saída; **a new ~** uma nova orientação; **~ lounge** *n* sala de embarque

depend [dɪ'pɛnd] *vi*: **to ~ (up)on** depender de; (*rely on*) contar com; **it ~s** depende; **~ing on the result ...** dependendo do resultado ...; **~able** *adj* (*person*) de confiança, seguro; (*car*) confiável; **~ant** *n* dependente *m/f*; **~ent** *adj*: **to be ~ent (on)** depender (de), ser dependente (de) ♦ *n* = **~ant**

depict [dɪ'pɪkt] *vt* (*in picture*) retratar, representar; (*describe*) descrever

depleted [dɪ'pliːtɪd] *adj* esgotado

deploy [dɪ'plɔɪ] *vt* dispor

depopulation ['diːpɔpju'leɪʃən] *n* despovoamento

deport [dɪ'pɔːt] *vt* deportar

deportment [dɪ'pɔːtmənt] *n* comportamento; (*way of walking*) (modo de) andar *m*

depose [dɪ'pəuz] *vt* depor

deposit [dɪ'pɔzɪt] *n* (*COMM, GEO*) depósito;

(*CHEM*) sedimento; (*of ore, oil*) jazida; (*down payment*) sinal *m* ♦ *vt* depositar; (*luggage*) guardar; ~ **account** *n* conta de depósito a prazo

depot ['dɛpəu] *n* (*storehouse*) depósito, armazém *m*; (*for vehicles*) garagem *f*, parque *m*; (*US*) estação *f*

depreciate [dɪ'priːʃɪeɪt] *vi* depreciar-se, desvalorizar-se

depress [dɪ'prɛs] *vt* deprimir; (*wages*) reduzir; (*press down*) apertar; ~**ed** *adj* deprimido; (*area*) em depressão; ~**ing** *adj* deprimente; ~**ion** *n* depressão *f*; (*hollow*) achatamento

deprivation [dɛprɪ'veɪʃən] *n* privação *f*

deprive [dɪ'praɪv] *vt*: **to** ~ **sb of** privar alguém de; ~**d** *adj* carente

depth [dɛpθ] *n* profundidade *f*; (*of feeling*) intensidade *f*; **in the** ~**s of despair** no auge do desespero; **to be out of one's** ~ (*BRIT: swimmer*) estar sem pé; (*fig*) estar voando

deputation [dɛpju'teɪʃən] *n* delegação *f*

deputize ['dɛpjutaɪz] *vi*: **to** ~ **for sb** substituir alguém

deputy ['dɛpjutɪ] *adj*: ~ **chairman** vice-presidente/a *m/f* ♦ *n* (*assistant*) adjunto/a; (*POL: MP*) deputado/a; ~ **head** (*BRIT: SCH*) diretor adjunto/ diretora adjunta *m/f*

derail [dɪ'reɪl] *vt*: **to be** ~**ed** descarrilhar; ~**ment** *n* descarrilhamento

deranged [dɪ'reɪndʒd] *adj* (*person*) louco, transtornado

derby ['dəːbɪ] (*US*) *n* chapéu-coco

derelict ['dɛrɪlɪkt] *adj* abandonado

deride [dɪ'raɪd] *vt* ridicularizar, zombar de; **derisory** *adj* (*sum*) irrisório; (*person, smile*) zombeteiro

derive [dɪ'raɪv] *vt*: **to** ~ (**from**) obter *or* tirar (de) ♦ *vi*: **to** ~ **from** derivar-se de

derogatory [dɪ'rɔgətərɪ] *adj* depreciativo

derv [dəːv] (*BRIT*) *n* gasóleo

descend [dɪ'sɛnd] *vt, vi* descer; **to** ~ **from** descer de; **to descambar em**; ~**ant** *n* descendente *m/f*; **descent** *n* descida; (*origin*) descendência

describe [dɪs'kraɪb] *vt* descrever; **description** *n* descrição *f*; (*sort*) classe *f*, espécie *f*; **descriptive** *adj* descritivo

desecrate ['dɛsɪkreɪt] *vt* profanar

desert [*n* 'dɛzət, *vt, vi* dɪ'zəːt] *n* deserto ♦ *vt* (*place*) desertar; (*partner, family*) abandonar ♦ *vi* (*MIL*) desertar; ~**er** *n* desertor *m*; ~**ion** (*MIL*) deserção *f*; (*LAW*) abandono do lar; ~ **island** *n* ilha deserta; ~ *npl*: **to get one's just** ~**s** receber o que merece

deserve [dɪ'zəːv] *vt* merecer; **deserving** *adj* (*person*) merecedor/a, digno; (*action, cause*) meritório

design [dɪ'zaɪn] *n* (*sketch*) desenho, esboço; (*layout, shape*) plano, projeto; (*pattern*) desenho, padrão *m*; (*art*) design *m*; (*intention*) propósito, intenção *f* ♦ *vt*

(*plan*) projetar

designate [*vt* 'dɛzɪgneɪt, *adj* 'dɛzɪgnɪt] *vt* (*appoint*) nomear ♦ *adj* designado

designer [dɪ'zaɪnə*] *n* (*ART*) artista *m/f* gráfico/a; (*TECH*) desenhista *m/f*, projetista *m/f*; (*fashion* ~) estilista *m/f*

desire [dɪ'zaɪə*] *n* anseio; (*sexual*) desejo ♦ *vt* querer, desejar, cobiçar

desk [dɛsk] *n* (*in office*) mesa, secretária; (*for pupil*) carteira *f*; (*at airport*) balcão *m*; (*in hotel*) recepção *f*; (*BRIT: in shop, restaurant*) caixa

desolate ['dɛsəlɪt] *adj* (*place*) deserto; (*person*) desolado

despair [dɪs'pɛə*] *n* desesperança ♦ *vi*: **to** ~ **of** desesperar-se de

despatch [dɪs'pætʃ] *n, vt* = **dispatch**

desperate ['dɛspərɪt] *adj* desesperado; (*situation*) desesperador(a); (*fugitive*) violento; **to be** ~ **for sth/to do** estar louco por algo/para fazer; ~**ly** *adv* desesperadamente; (*very: unhappy*) terrivelmente; (: *ill*) gravemente; **desperation** *n* desespero, desesperança; **in (sheer) desperation** desesperado

despise [dɪs'paɪz] *vt* desprezar

despite [dɪs'paɪt] *prep* apesar de, a despeito de

despondent [dɪs'pɔndənt] *adj* abatido, desanimado

dessert [dɪ'zəːt] *n* sobremesa

destination [dɛstɪ'neɪʃən] *n* destino

destined ['dɛstɪnd] *adj*: **to be** ~ **to do sth** estar destinado a fazer algo; ~ **for** com destino a

destiny ['dɛstɪnɪ] *n* destino

destitute ['dɛstɪtjuːt] *adj* indigente, necessitado

destroy [dɪs'trɔɪ] *vt* destruir; (*animal*) sacrificar; ~**er** *n* (*NAUT*) contratorpedeiro; **destruction** *n* destruição *f*

detach [dɪ'tætʃ] *vt* separar; (*unstick*) desprender; ~**ed** *adj* (*attitude*) imparcial, objetivo; (*house*) independente, isolado; ~**ment** *n* distanciamento; (*MIL*) destacamento

detail ['diːteɪl] *n* detalhe *m*; (*trifle*) bobagem *f* ♦ *vt* detalhar; **in** ~ pormenorizado, em detalhe

detain [dɪ'teɪn] *vt* deter; (*in captivity*) prender; (*in hospital*) hospitalizar

detect [dɪ'tɛkt] *vt* perceber; (*MED. POLICE*) identificar; (*MIL. RADAR, TECH*) detectar; ~**ion** *n* descoberta; ~**ive** *n* detetive *m/f*; ~**ive story** *n* romance *m* policial; ~**or** *n* detetor *m*

détente [deɪ'tɑːnt] *n* distensão *f* (de relações), détente *f*

detention [dɪ'tɛnʃən] *n* detenção *f*, prisão *f*; (*SCH*) castigo

deter [dɪ'təː*] *vt* (*discourage*) desanimar; (*dissuade*) dissuadir

detergent [dɪ'təːdʒənt] *n* detergente *m*

deteriorate [dɪ'tɪərɪəreɪt] *vi* deteriorar-se

determine [dɪ'təːmɪn] *vt* descobrir; (*li-*

mits) demarcar; **~d** _adj_ (_person_) resoluto; **~d to do** decidido a fazer

detour [ˈdiːtuəʳ] _n_ desvio

detract [dɪˈtrækt] _vi_: **to ~ from** diminuir

detriment [ˈdetrɪmənt] _n_: **to the ~ of**
em detrimento de; **~al** _adj_: **~al (to)**
prejudicial (a)

devalue [diːˈvæljuː] _vt_ desvalorizar

devastate [ˈdevəsteɪt] _vt_ devastar; (_fig_):
to be ~d by estar arrasado com

develop [dɪˈveləp] _vt_ desenvolver; (_PHOT_)
revelar; (_disease_) contrair; (_resources_) ex-
plotar ♦ _vi_ (_advance_) progredir; (_evolve_)
evoluir; (_appear_) aparecer; **~ing country** país _m_ em desenvolvimento; **~ment**
_n_ desenvolvimento; (_advance_) progresso;
(_of land_) urbanização _f_

device [dɪˈvaɪs] _n_ aparelho, dispositivo

devil [ˈdevl] _n_ diabo; **~ish** _adj_ diabólico

devious [ˈdiːvɪəs] _adj_ (_person_) malandro,
esperto

devise [dɪˈvaɪz] _vt_ (_plan_) criar; (_machine_)
inventar

devoid [dɪˈvɔɪd] _adj_: **~ of** destituído de

devolution [diːvəˈluːʃən] _n_ (_POL_) descen-
tralização _f_

devote [dɪˈvəut] _vt_: **to ~ sth to** dedicar
algo a; **~d** _adj_ (_friendship_) leal; (_part-
ner_) fiel; **to be ~d to** estar devotado a;
the book is ~d to politics o livro trata de política; **~e** _n_ adepto/a, entusiasta _m/f_; (_REL_) devoto/a; **devotion** _n_ devoção _f_; (_to duty_) dedicação _f_

devour [dɪˈvauəʳ] _vt_ devorar

devout [dɪˈvaut] _adj_ devoto

dew [djuː] _n_ orvalho

dexterity [deksˈterɪtɪ] _n_ (_manual_) destreza; (_mental_) habilidade _f_

diabetes [daɪəˈbiːtiːz] _n_ diabete _f_

diabolical [daɪəˈbɔlɪkl] (_inf_) _adj_ (_dreadful_)
horrível

diagnoses [daɪəgˈnəusiːz] _npl of_ **diagnosis**

diagnosis [daɪəgˈnəusɪs] (_pl_ **diagnoses**) _n_
diagnóstico

diagonal [daɪˈægənl] _adj_ diagonal ♦ _n_
diagonal _f_

diagram [ˈdaɪəgræm] _n_ diagrama _m_, esquema _m_

dial [ˈdaɪəl] _n_ disco ♦ _vt_ (_number_) discar
(_BR_), marcar (_PT_)

dialect [ˈdaɪəlekt] _n_ dialeto

dialling code [ˈdaɪəlɪŋ-] (_US_ **dial code**)
_n_ código de discagem

dialling tone [ˈdaɪəlɪŋ-] (_US_ **dial tone**) _n_
sinal _m_ de discagem (_BR_) or de marcar
(_PT_)

dialogue [ˈdaɪəlɔg] (_US_ **dialog**) _n_ diálogo;
(_conversation_) conversa

diameter [daɪˈæmɪtəʳ] _n_ diâmetro

diamond [ˈdaɪəmənd] _n_ diamante _m_;
(_shape_) losango, rombo; **~s** _npl_ (_CARDS_)
ouros _mpl_

diaper [ˈdaɪəpəʳ] (_US_) _n_ fralda

diaphragm [ˈdaɪəfræm] _n_ diafragma _m_

diarrhoea [daɪəˈriːə] (_US_ **diarrhea**) _n_
diarréia

diary [ˈdaɪərɪ] _n_ (_daily account_) diário;
(_engagements book_) agenda

dice [daɪs] _n inv_ dado ♦ _vt_ (_CULIN_) cortar
em cubos

Dictaphone [ˈdɪktəfəun] ® _n_ ditafone ®
_m_, máquina de ditar

dictate [dɪkˈteɪt] _vt_ ditar; **dictation** _n_ (_of
letter_) ditado; (_of orders_) ordem _f_

dictator [dɪkˈteɪtəʳ] _n_ ditador(a) _m/f_;
~ship _n_ ditadura

dictionary [ˈdɪkʃənrɪ] _n_ dicionário

did [dɪd] _pt of_ **do**

didn't [ˈdɪdnt] = **did not**

die [daɪ] _vi_ morrer; (_fig: fade_) murchar;
to be dying for sth/to do sth estar
louco por algo/para fazer algo; **~ away**
_vi_ (_sound, light_) extinguir-se lentamente;
~ down _vi_ (_fire_) apagar-se; (_wind_) abrandar; (_excitement_) diminuir; **~ out** _vi_
desaparecer; **~hard** _n_ reacionário/a,
reaça _m/f_ (_inf_)

diesel [ˈdiːzl] _n_ diesel _m_; (_also_: **~ oil**)
óleo diesel; **~ engine** [ˈdiːzəl-] _n_ motor
_m_ diesel

diet [ˈdaɪət] _n_ dieta; (_restricted food_) regime _m_ ♦ _vi_ (_also_: **be on a ~**) estar de
dieta, fazer regime

differ [ˈdɪfəʳ] _vi_ (_be different_): **to ~ from**
sth ser diferente de algo, diferenciar-se
de algo; (_disagree_): **to ~ (about)** discordar (sobre); **~ence** _n_ diferença; (_disa-
greement_) divergência; **~ent** _adj_ diferente; **~entiate** _vi_: **to ~entiate (between)**
distinguir (entre); **~ently** _adv_ de outro
modo, de forma diferente

difficult [ˈdɪfɪkəlt] _adj_ difícil; **~y** _n_ dificuldade _f_

diffident [ˈdɪfɪdənt] _adj_ tímido

diffuse [_adj_ dɪˈfjuːs, _vt_ dɪˈfjuːz] _adj_ difuso
♦ _vt_ difundir

dig [dɪg] (_pt, pp_ **dug**) _vt_ cavar ♦ _n_ (_prod_)
pontada; (_archaeological_) escavação _f_;
(_remark_) alfinetada; **to ~ one's nails
into sth** cravar as unhas em algo; **~
into** _vt fus_ (_savings_) gastar; **~ up** _vt_
(_plant_) arrancar; (_information_) trazer à
tona

digest [_vt_ daɪˈdʒest, _n_ ˈdaɪdʒest] _vt_ (_food_)
digerir; (_facts_) assimilar ♦ _n_ sumário;
~ion _n_ digestão _f_; **~ive** _adj_ digestivo

digit [ˈdɪdʒɪt] _n_ (_MATH_) dígito; (_finger_)
dedo; **~al** _adj_ digital; **~al TV** televisão
_f_ digital

dignified [ˈdɪgnɪfaɪd] _adj_ digno

dignity [ˈdɪgnɪtɪ] _n_ dignidade _f_

digress [daɪˈgres] _vi_: **to ~ from** afastar-
se de

digs [dɪgz] (_BRIT: inf_) _npl_ pensão _f_, alojamento

dike [daɪk] _n_ = **dyke**

dilapidated [dɪˈlæpɪdeɪtɪd] _adj_ arruinado

dilemma [daɪˈlemə] _n_ dilema _m_

diligent [ˈdɪlɪdʒənt] _adj_ (_worker_) diligente; (*research*) cuidadoso

dilute [daɪˈluːt] *vt* diluir

dim [dɪm] *adj* fraco; (*outline*) indistinto; (*room*) escuro; (*inf: person*) burro ♦ *vt* diminuir; (*US: AUT*) baixar

dime [daɪm] (*US*) *n* dez centavos

dimension [dɪˈmɛnʃən] *n* dimensão *f*; (*measurement*) medida; (*also*: ~s: *scale*, *size*) tamanho

diminish [dɪˈmɪnɪʃ] *vi* diminuir

diminutive [dɪˈmɪnjutɪv] *adj* diminuto ♦ *n* (*LING*) diminutivo

dimmers [ˈdɪməz] (*US*) *npl* (*AUT*: *headlights*) faróis *mpl* baixos

dimple [ˈdɪmpl] *n* covinha

din [dɪn] *n* zoeira

dine [daɪn] *vi* jantar; ~**r** *n* comensal *m/f*; (*US*: *eating place*) lanchonete *f*

dinghy [ˈdɪŋgɪ] *n* dingue *m*; (*also*: rubber ~) bote *m*; (: *sailing* ~) bote de borracha

dingy [ˈdɪndʒɪ] *adj* (*room*) sombrio, lúgubre; (*clothes, curtains etc*) sujo

dining car [ˈdaɪnɪŋ-] (*BRIT*) *n* (*RAIL*) vagão-restaurante *m*

dining room [ˈdaɪnɪŋ-] *n* sala de jantar

dinner [ˈdɪnə*] *n* (*evening meal*) jantar *m*; (*lunch*) almoço; (*banquet*) banquete *m*; ~ **jacket** *n* smoking *m*; ~ **party** *n* jantar *m*; ~ **time** *n* (*midday*) hora de almoçar; (*evening*) hora de jantar

dint [dɪnt] *n*: **by** ~ **of** à força de

dip [dɪp] *n* (*slope*) inclinação *f*; (*in sea*) mergulho; (*CULIN*) pasta para servir com salgadinhos ♦ *vt* (*in water*) mergulhar; (*ladle*) meter; (*BRIT: AUT: lights*) baixar ♦ *vi* descer subitamente

diphthong [ˈdɪfθɒŋ] *n* ditongo

diploma [dɪˈpləumə] *n* diploma *m*

diplomat [ˈdɪpləmæt] *n* diplomata *m/f*

dipstick [ˈdɪpstɪk] (*US* **diprod**) *n* (*AUT*) vareta medidora

dipswitch [ˈdɪpswɪtʃ] (*BRIT*) *n* (*AUT*) interruptor *m* de luz alta e baixa

dire [daɪə*] *adj* terrível

direct [daɪˈrɛkt] *adj* direto; (*route*) reto; (*manner*) franco, sincero ♦ *vt* dirigir; (*order*): **to** ~ **sb to do sth** ordenar alguém para fazer algo ♦ *vt* direto; **can you** ~ **me to ...?** pode me indicar o caminho a ...?; ~ **debit** (*BRIT*) *n* (*BANKING*) débito direto; ~**ion** *n* (*way*) indicação *f*; (*TV, RADIO, CINEMA*) direção *f*; ~**ions** *npl* (*instructions*) instruções *fpl*; ~**ions for use** modo de usar; ~**ly** *adv* diretamente; (*at once*) imediatamente; ~**or** *n* diretor(a) *m/f*

directory [dɪˈrɛktərɪ] *n* (*TEL*) lista (telefónica); (*also*: *COMM*) anuário comercial; (*COMPUT*) diretório

dirt [dəːt] *n* sujeira (*BR*), sujidade (*PT*); ~-**cheap** *adj* baratíssimo; ~**y** *adj* sujo; (*joke*) indecente ♦ *vt* sujar; ~**y trick** *n* golpe *m* baixo, sujeira

disability [dɪsəˈbɪlɪtɪ] *n* incapacidade *f*

disabled [dɪsˈeɪbld] *adj* deficiente ♦ *npl*: **the** ~ os deficientes

disadvantage [dɪsədˈvɑːntɪdʒ] *n* desvantagem *f*; (*prejudice*) inconveniente *m*

disaffection [dɪsəˈfɛkʃən] *n* descontentamento

disagree [dɪsəˈgriː] *vi* (*differ*) diferir; (*be against, think otherwise*): **to** ~ (**with**) não concordar (com), discordar (de); ~**able** *adj* desagradável; ~**ment** *n* desacordo; (*quarrel*) desavença

disallow [ˈdɪsəˈlau] *vt* (*LAW*) vetar, proibir

disappear [dɪsəˈpɪə*] *vi* desaparecer, sumir; (*custom etc*) acabar; ~**ance** *n* desaparecimento, desaparição *f*

disappoint [dɪsəˈpɔɪnt] *vt* decepcionar; ~**ment** *n* decepção *f*; (*cause*) desapontamento

disapproval [dɪsəˈpruːvəl] *n* desaprovação *f*

disapprove [dɪsəˈpruːv] *vi*: **to** ~ **of** desaprovar

disarm [dɪsˈɑːm] *vt* desarmar; ~**ament** *n* desarmamento

disarray [dɪsəˈreɪ] *n*: **in** ~ (*troops*) desbaratado; (*organization*) desorganizado, caótico; (*thoughts*) confuso; (*clothes*) em desalinho

disaster [dɪˈzɑːstə*] *n* (*accident*) desastre *m*; (*natural*) catástrofe *f*

disband [dɪsˈbænd] *vt* dispersar ♦ *vi* dispersar-se, debandar

disbelief [dɪsbəˈliːf] *n* incredulidade *f*

disc [dɪsk] *n* disco; (*COMPUT*) = **disk**

discard [dɪsˈkɑːd] *vt* (*old things*) desfazer-se de; (*fig*) descartar

discern [dɪˈsəːn] *vt* perceber; (*identify*) identificar; ~**ing** *adj* perspicaz

discharge [*vt* dɪsˈtʃɑːdʒ, *n* ˈdɪstʃɑːdʒ] *vt* (*duties*) cumprir, desempenhar; (*patient*) dar alta a; (*employee*) despedir; (*soldier*) dar baixa em, dispensar; (*defendant*) pôr em liberdade; (*waste etc*) descarregar, despejar ♦ *n* (*ELEC, CHEM*) descarga; (*dismissal*) despedida; (*of duty*) desempenho; (*of debt*) quitação *f*; (*from hospital*) alta; (*from army*) baixa; (*LAW*) absolvição *f*; (*MED*) secreção *f*

disciple [dɪˈsaɪpl] *n* discípulo/a

discipline [ˈdɪsɪplɪn] *n* disciplina ♦ *vt* disciplinar; (*punish*) punir

disc jockey *n* (*on radio*) radialista *m/f*; (*in disco*) discotecário/a

disclaim [dɪsˈkleɪm] *vt* negar

disclose [dɪsˈkləuz] *vt* revelar; **disclosure** *n* revelação *f*

disco [ˈdɪskəu] *n abbr* discoteca

discoloured [dɪsˈkʌləd] (*US* **discolored**) *adj* descolorado; (*teeth*) amarelado

discomfort [dɪsˈkʌmfət] *n* (*unease*) inquietação *f*; (*physical*) desconforto

disconcert [dɪskənˈsəːt] *vt* desconcertar

disconnect [dɪskəˈnɛkt] *vt* desligar; (*pipe, tap*) desmembrar

discontent [dɪskən'tɛnt] *n* descontentamento; **~ed** *adj* descontente

discontinue [dɪskən'tɪnjuː] *vt* interromper; (*payments*) suspender; **"~d"** (*COMM*) "fora de linha"

discord ['dɪskɔːd] *n* discórdia; (*MUS*) dissonância

discount [*n* 'dɪskaunt, *vt* dɪs'kaunt] *n* desconto ♦ *vt* descontar; (*idea*) ignorar

discourage [dɪs'kʌrɪdʒ] *vt* (*dishearten*) desanimar; (*advise against*): **to ~ sth/sb from doing** desaconselhar algo/alguém a fazer

discourteous [dɪs'kəːtɪəs] *adj* descortês

discover [dɪs'kʌvə*] *vt* descobrir; (*missing person*) encontrar; (*mistake*) achar; **~y** *n* descoberta

discredit [dɪs'krɛdɪt] *vt* desacreditar; (*claim*) desmerecer

discreet [dɪ'skriːt] *adj* discreto; (*careful*) cauteloso

discrepancy [dɪ'skrɛpənsɪ] *n* diferença

discretion [dɪ'skrɛʃən] *n* discrição *f*; **at the ~ of** ao arbítrio de

discriminate [dɪ'skrɪmɪneɪt] *vi*: **to ~ between** fazer distinção entre; **to ~ against** discriminar contra; **discriminating** *adj* criterioso; **discrimination** *n* (*discernment*) discernimento *m*; (*bias*) discriminação *f*

discuss [dɪ'skʌs] *vt* discutir; (*analyse*) analisar; **~ion** *n* discussão *f*; (*debate*) debate *m*

disdain [dɪs'deɪn] *n* desdém *m*

disease [dɪ'ziːz] *n* doença

disembark [dɪsɪm'baːk] *vt*, *vi* desembarcar

disengage [dɪsɪn'geɪdʒ] *vt* (*AUT*): **to ~ the clutch** desembrear

disentangle [dɪsɪn'tæŋgl] *vt* desvencilhar; (*wool, wire*) desembaraçar

disfigure [dɪs'fɪgə*] *vt* (*person*) desfigurar; (*object*) estragar, enfear

disgrace [dɪs'greɪs] *n* ignomínia; (*shame*) desonra ♦ *vt* (*family*) envergonhar; (*name, country*) desonrar; **~ful** *adj* vergonhoso; (*behaviour*) escandaloso

disgruntled [dɪs'grʌntld] *adj* descontente

disguise [dɪs'gaɪz] *n* disfarce *m* ♦ *vt*: **to ~ (as)** disfarçar (de); **in ~** disfarçado

disgust [dɪs'gʌst] *n* repugnância ♦ *vt* repugnar a, dar nojo em; **~ing** *adj* repugnante; (*unacceptable*) inaceitável

dish [dɪʃ] *n* prato; (*serving ~*) travessa; **to do** *or* **wash the ~es** lavar os pratos *or* a louça; **~ out** *vt* repartir; **~ up** *vt* servir; **~cloth** *n* pano de prato *or* de louça

dishearten [dɪs'haːtn] *vt* desanimar

dishevelled [dɪ'ʃɛvəld] (*US* **disheveled**) *adj* (*hair*) despenteado; (*clothes*) desalinhado

dishonest [dɪs'ɔnɪst] *adj* (*person*) desonesto; (*means*) fraudulento

dishonour [dɪs'ɔnə*] (*US* **dishonor**) *n* desonra; **~able** *adj* (*person*) desonesto, vil; (*behaviour*) desonroso

dishtowel ['dɪʃtauəl] (*US*) *n* pano de prato

dishwasher ['dɪʃwɔʃə*] *n* máquina de lavar louça *or* pratos

disillusion [dɪsɪ'luːʒən] *vt* desiludir

disinfectant [dɪsɪn'fɛktənt] *n* desinfetante *m*

disintegrate [dɪs'ɪntɪgreɪt] *vi* desintegrar-se

disjointed [dɪs'dʒɔɪntɪd] *adj* desconexo

disk [dɪsk] *n* (*COMPUT*) disco; **single-/double-sided ~** disquete de face simples/dupla; **~ drive** *n* unidade *f* de disco; **~ette** (*US*) *n* = **disk**

dislike [dɪs'laɪk] *n* (*feeling*) desagrado; (*gen pl*: *object of ~*) antipatia, aversão *f* ♦ *vt* antipatizar com, não gostar de

dislocate ['dɪsləkeɪt] *vt* deslocar

dislodge [dɪs'lɔdʒ] *vt* mover, deslocar

disloyal [dɪs'lɔɪəl] *adj* desleal

dismal ['dɪzml] *adj* (*depressing*) deprimente; (*very bad*) horrível

dismantle [dɪs'mæntl] *vt* desmontar, desmantelar

dismay [dɪs'meɪ] *n* consternação *f* ♦ *vt* consternar

dismiss [dɪs'mɪs] *vt* (*worker*) despedir; (*pupils*) dispensar; (*soldiers*) dar baixa a; (*LAW, possibility*) rejeitar; **~al** *n* demissão *f*

dismount [dɪs'maunt] *vi* (*from horse*) desmontar; (*from bicycle*) descer; **disobedient** *adj* desobediente

disobey [dɪsə'beɪ] *vt* desobedecer a; (*rules*) transgredir

disorder [dɪs'ɔːdə*] *n* desordem *f*; (*rioting*) distúrbios *mpl*, tumulto; (*MED*) distúrbio; **~ly** *adj* (*untidy*) desarrumado; (*meeting*) tumultuado; (*behaviour*) escandaloso

disown [dɪs'əun] *vt* repudiar; (*child*) rejeitar

disparaging [dɪs'pærɪdʒɪŋ] *adj* depreciativo

disparate ['dɪspərɪt] *adj* (*groups*) diverso; (*levels*) desigual

disparity [dɪs'pærɪtɪ] *n* desigualdade *f*

dispassionate [dɪs'pæʃənət] *adj* imparcial

dispatch [dɪs'pætʃ] *vt* (*send: parcel etc*) expedir; (: *messenger*) enviar ♦ *n* (*sending*) remessa, urgência; (*PRESS*) comunicado; (*MIL*) parte *f*

dispel [dɪs'pɛl] *vt* dissipar

dispense [dɪs'pɛns] *vt* (*medicine*) preparar (e vender); **~ with** *vt fus* prescindir de; **~r** *n* (*device*) distribuidor *m* automático; **dispensing chemist** (*BRIT*) *n* farmácia

disperse [dɪs'pəːs] *vt* espalhar; (*crowd*) dispersar ♦ *vi* dispersar-se

dispirited [dɪs'pɪrɪtɪd] *adj* desanimado

displace [dɪs'pleɪs] *vt* (*shift*) deslocar; **~d**

person *n* (POL) deslocado/a de guerra

display [dɪsˈpleɪ] *n* (*in shop*) mostra; (*exhibition*) exposição *f*; (COMPUT. TECH: *information*) apresentação *f* visual; (: *device*) display *m*; (*of feeling*) manifestação *f* ♦ *vt* mostrar; (*ostentatiously*) ostentar

displease [dɪsˈpliːz] *vt* (*offend*) ofender; (*annoy*) aborrecer; **~d** *adj*: **~d with** descontente com; (*disappointed*) aborrecido com; **displeasure** *n* desgosto

disposable [dɪsˈpəʊzəbl] *adj* descartável; (*income*) disponível

disposal [dɪsˈpəʊzl] *n* (*of rubbish*) destruição *f*; (*of property etc*) venda, traspasse *m*; **at sb's ~** à disposição de alguém

dispose of [dɪsˈpəʊz-] *vt fus* (*unwanted goods*) desfazer-se de; (*problem, task*) lidar

disposed [dɪsˈpəʊzd] *adj*: **to be ~ to do sth** estar disposto a fazer algo; **to do well ~ towards sb** estar predisposto a favor de alguém; **disposition** *n* disposição *f*; (*temperament*) índole *f*

disprove [dɪsˈpruːv] *vt* refutar

dispute [dɪsˈpjuːt] *n* (*domestic*) briga; (*also*: **industrial ~**) conflito, disputa ♦ *vt* (*fact, statement*) questionar; (*ownership*) contestar

disqualify [dɪsˈkwɒlɪfaɪ] *vt* (SPORT) desclassificar; **to ~ sb for sth/from doing sth** desqualificar alguém para algo/de fazer algo

disquiet [dɪsˈkwaɪət] *n* inquietação *f*

disregard [dɪsrɪˈɡɑːd] *vt* ignorar

disrepair [dɪsrɪˈpɛə*] *n*: **to fall into ~** ficar dilapidado

disreputable [dɪsˈrɛpjʊtəbl] *adj* (*person*) de má fama; (*behaviour*) vergonhoso

disrupt [dɪsˈrʌpt] *vt* (*plans*) desfazer; (*conversation*) perturbar, interromper; **~ion** *n* interrupção *f*; (*disturbance*) perturbação *f*

dissatisfaction [dɪssætɪsˈfækʃən] *n* descontentamento

dissect [dɪˈsɛkt] *vt* dissecar

dissent [dɪˈsɛnt] *n* dissensão *f*

dissertation [dɪsəˈteɪʃən] *n* (*also*: SCH) dissertação *f*, tese *f*

disservice [dɪsˈsɜːvɪs] *n*: **to do sb a ~** prejudicar alguém

dissimilar [dɪˈsɪmɪlə*] *adj*: **~ (to)** dessemelhante (de), diferente (de)

dissipate [ˈdɪsɪpeɪt] *vt* dissipar; (*money, effort*) desperdiçar

dissolve [dɪˈzɒlv] *vt* dissolver ♦ *vi* dissolver-se; **to ~ in(to) tears** debulhar-se em lágrimas

distance [ˈdɪstns] *n* distância; **in the ~** ao longe

distant [ˈdɪstnt] *adj* distante; (*manner*) afastado, reservado

distaste [dɪsˈteɪst] *n* repugnância; **~ful** *adj* repugnante

distended [dɪsˈtɛndɪd] *adj* inchado

distil [dɪsˈtɪl] (US **distill**) *vt* destilar; **~lery** *n* destilaria

distinct [dɪsˈtɪŋkt] *adj* distinto; (*clear*) claro; (*unmistakable*) nítido; **as ~ from** em oposição a; **~ion** *n* diferença; (*honour*) honra; (*in exam*) distinção *f*

distinguish [dɪsˈtɪŋɡwɪʃ] *vt* (*differentiate*) diferenciar; (*identify*) identificar; **to ~ o.s.** distinguir-se; **~ed** *adj* (*eminent*) eminente; (*in appearance*) distinto; **~ing** *adj* (*feature*) distintivo

distort [dɪsˈtɔːt] *vt* distorcer

distract [dɪsˈtrækt] *vt* distrair; (*attention*) desviar; **~ed** *adj* distraído; (*anxious*) aturdido; **~ion** *n* distração *f*; (*confusion*) aturdimento, perplexidade *f*; (*amusement*) divertimento

distraught [dɪsˈtrɔːt] *adj* desesperado

distress [dɪsˈtrɛs] *n* angústia ♦ *vt* afligir; **~ing** *adj* angustiante; **~ signal** *n* sinal *m* de socorro

distribute [dɪsˈtrɪbjuːt] *vt* distribuir; (*share out*) repartir, dividir; **distribution** *n* distribuição *f*; (*of profits*) repartição *f*; **distributor** *n* (AUT) distribuidor *m*; (COMM) distribuidor(a) *m/f*

district [ˈdɪstrɪkt] *n* (*of country*) região *f*; (*of town*) zona; (ADMIN) distrito; **~ attorney** (US) *n* promotor/a *m/f* público/a; **~ nurse** (BRIT) *n* enfermeiro/a do Serviço Nacional que visita os pacientes em casa

distrust [dɪsˈtrʌst] *n* desconfiança ♦ *vt* desconfiar de

disturb [dɪsˈtɜːb] *vt* (*disorganize*) perturbar; (*upset*) incomodar; (*interrupt*) atrapalhar; **~ance** *n* (*upheaval*) convulsão *f*; (*political, violent*) distúrbio; (*of mind*) transtorno; **~ed** *adj* perturbado; (*childhood*) infeliz; **to be emotionally ~ed** ter problemas emocionais; **~ing** *adj* perturbador(a)

disuse [dɪsˈjuːs] *n*: **to fall into ~** cair em desuso; **~d** *adj* abandonado

ditch [dɪtʃ] *n* fosso; (*irrigation ~*) rego ♦ *vt* (*inf: partner*) abandonar; (: *car, plan etc*) desfazer-se de

dither [ˈdɪðə*] *vi* vacilar

ditto [ˈdɪtəʊ] *adv* idem

divan [dɪˈvæn] *n* (*also*: **~ bed**) divã *m*

dive [daɪv] *n* (*from board*) salto; (*underwater*) mergulho ♦ *vi* mergulhar; **to ~ into** (*bag, drawer*) enfiar a mão em; (*shop, car*) enfiar-se em; **~r** *n* mergulhador(a) *m/f*

diverse [daɪˈvɜːs] *adj* diverso; **diversion** *n* (BRIT: AUT) desvio; (*distraction*) diversão *f*; (*of funds*) desvio

divert [daɪˈvɜːt] *vt* desviar

divide [dɪˈvaɪd] *vt* (MATH) dividir; (*separate*) separar; (*share out*) repartir ♦ *vi* dividir-se; (*road*) bifurcar-se; **~d highway** (US) *n* pista dupla

dividend [ˈdɪvɪdɛnd] *n* dividendo; (*fig*): **to pay ~s** valer a pena

divine [dɪ'vaɪn] *adj* (*also fig*) divino
diving ['daɪvɪŋ] *n* salto; (*underwater*) mergulho; ~ **board** *n* trampolim *m*
divinity [dɪ'vɪnɪtɪ] *n* divindade *f*; (*SCH*) teologia
division [dɪ'vɪʒən] *n* divisão *f*; (*sharing out*) repartição *f*; (*disagreement*) discórdia; (*FOOTBALL*) grupo
divorce [dɪ'vɔːs] *n* divórcio ♦ *vt* divorciar-se de; (*dissociate*) dissociar; ~**d** *adj* divorciado; ~**e** *n* divorciado/a
DIY *n abbr* = **do-it-yourself**
dizzy ['dɪzɪ] *adj* tonto
DJ *n abbr* = **disc jockey**

KEYWORD
---

do [duː] (*pt* **did**, *pp* **done**) *vb aux* **1** (*in negative constructions*): **I don't understand** eu não compreendo
2 (*to form questions*): **didn't you know?** você não sabia?; **what ~ you think?** o que você acha?
3 (*for emphasis, in polite expressions*) **she does seem rather late** ela está muito atrasada; ~ **sit down/help yourself** sente-se/sirva-se; ~ **take care!** tome cuidado!
4 (*used to avoid repeating vb*): **she swims better than I ~** ela nada melhor que eu; ~ **you agree? – yes, I ~/ no, I don't** você concorda? – sim, concordo/não, não concordo; **she lives in Glasgow – so ~ I** ela mora em Glasgow – eu também; **who broke it? – I did** quem quebrou isso? – (fui) eu
5 (*in question tags*): **you like him, don't you?** você gosta dele, não é?; **he laughed, didn't he?** ele riu, não foi?
♦ *vt* **1** (*gen: carry out, perform etc*) fazer; **what are you ~ing tonight?** o que você vai fazer hoje à noite?; **to ~ the washing-up/cooking** lavar a louça/cozinhar; **to ~ one's teeth/ nails** escovar os dentes/fazer as unhas; **to ~ one's hair** (*comb*) pentear-se; (*style*) fazer um penteado; **we're ~ing Othello at school** (*studying*) nós estamos estudando Otelo na escola; (*performing*) nós vamos encenar Otelo na escola
2 (*AUT etc*): **the car was ~ing 100** o carro estava a 100 por hora; **we've done 200 km already** nós já fizemos 200 km; **he can ~ 100 in that car** ele consegue dar 100 nesse carro
♦ *vi* **1** (*act, behave*) fazer; ~ **as I ~** faça como eu faço
2 (*get on, fare*) ir; **how ~ you ~?** como você está indo?
3 (*suit*) servir; **will it ~?** serve?
4 (*be sufficient*) bastar; **will £10 ~?** £10 dá?; **that'll ~** é suficiente; **that'll ~!** (*in annoyance*) basta!, chega!; **to make ~ (with)** contentar-se (com)
♦ *n* (*inf: party etc*) festa; **it was rather a ~** foi uma festança

do away with *vt fus* (*kill*) matar; (*law etc*) abolir; (*withdraw*) retirar
do up *vt* (*laces*) atar; (*zip*) fechar; (*dress, skirt*) abotoar; (*renovate: room, house*) arrumar, renovar
do with *vt fus* (*need*): **I could ~ with a drink/some help** eu bem que gostaria de tomar alguma coisa/eu bem que precisaria de uma ajuda; (*be connected*) ter a ver com; **what has it got to ~ with you?** o que é que isso tem a ver com você?
do without *vi*: **if you're late for tea then you'll ~ without** se você chegar atrasado ficará sem almoço ♦ *vt fus* passar sem

dock [dɔk] *n* (*NAUT*) doca; (*LAW*) banco (dos réus) ♦ *vi* (*NAUT: enter* ~) entrar no estaleiro; (*SPACE*) unir-se no espaço; ~**s** *npl* docas *fpl*; ~**er** *n* portuário, estivador *m*; ~**yard** *n* estaleiro
doctor ['dɔktə*] *n* médico/a; (*PhD etc*) doutor(a) *m/f* ♦ *vt* (*drink etc*) falsificar; **D~ of Philosophy** *n* (*degree*) doutorado; (*person*) doutor(a) *m/f*
doctrine ['dɔktrɪn] *n* doutrina
document ['dɔkjumənt] *n* documento; ~**ary** *adj* documental ♦ *n* documentário
dodge [dɔdʒ] *n* (*trick*) trapaça ♦ *vt* esquivar-se de, evitar; (*tax*) sonegar; (*blow*) furtar-se a
dodgems ['dɔdʒəmz] (*BRIT*) *npl* carros *mpl* de choque
doe [dəu] *n* (*deer*) corça; (*rabbit*) coelha
does [dʌz] *vb see* **do**; ~**n't** = **does not**
dog [dɔg] *n* cachorro, cão *m* ♦ *vt* (*subj: person*) seguir; (*: bad luck*) perseguir; ~ **collar** *n* coleira de cachorro; (*of priest*) gola de padre; ~**-eared** *adj* surrado
dogged ['dɔgɪd] *adj* tenaz, persistente
dogsbody ['dɔgzbɔdɪ] (*BRIT*: *inf*) *n* faz-tudo *m/f*
doings ['duɪŋz] *npl* atividades *fpl*
do-it-yourself *n* sistema *m* faça-você-mesmo
doldrums ['dɔldrəmz] *npl*: **to be in the ~** (*person*) estar abatido; (*business*) estar parado *or* estagnado
dole [dəul] (*BRIT*) *n* (*payment*) subsídio de desemprego; **on the ~** desempregado; ~ **out** *vt* distribuir
doleful ['dəulful] *adj* triste, lúgubre
doll [dɔl] *n* boneca; (*US: inf: woman*) mulher *f* jovem e bonita
dollar ['dɔlə*] *n* dólar *m*
dolled up [dɔld-] (*inf*) *adj* embonecado
dolphin ['dɔlfɪn] *n* golfinho
domain [də'meɪn] *n* domínio
dome [dəum] *n* (*ARCH*) cúpula
domestic [də'mɛstɪk] *adj* doméstico; (*national*) nacional; ~**ated** *adj* domesticado; (*home-loving*) prendado
dominate ['dɔmɪneɪt] *vt* dominar
domineering [dɔmɪ'nɪərɪŋ] *adj* dominan-

dominion [dəˈmɪnɪən] n domínio; (territory) império
domino [ˈdɒmɪnəu] (pl ~es) n peça de
dominó; ~es n (game) dominó m
don [dɒn] (BRIT) n professor(a) m/f
universitário/a
donate [dəˈneɪt] vt: to ~ (to) doar (para)
done [dʌn] pp of do
donkey [ˈdɒŋkɪ] n burro
donor [ˈdəunə°] n doador(a) m/f
don't [dəunt] = do not
doodle [ˈduːdl] vi rabiscar
doom [duːm] n (fate) destino ♦ vt: to be
~ed to failure estar destinado or fada-
do ao fracasso; ~sday n o Juízo Final
door [dɔː°] n porta; ~bell n campainha;
~ handle n maçaneta (BR), puxador m
(PT); (of car) maçaneta; ~man (irreg) n
porteiro; ~mat n capacho; ~step n degrau m da porta, soleira; ~way n vão
m da porta, entrada
dope [dəup] n (inf: person) imbecil m/f;
(: drug) maconha ♦ vt (horse etc) dopar;
~y (inf) adj (groggy) zonzo; (stupid) imbecil
dormant [ˈdɔːmənt] adj inativo
dormice [ˈdɔːmaɪs] npl of dormouse
dormitory [ˈdɔːmɪtrɪ] n dormitório; (US)
residência universitária
dormouse [ˈdɔːmaus] (pl dormice) n
rato (de campo)
dosage [ˈdəusɪdʒ] n dosagem, posologia
dose [dəus] n dose f
doss house [ˈdɒs-] (BRIT) n pensão f barata or de malta (PT)
dot [dɒt] n ponto; (speck) marca pequena
♦ vt: ~ted with salpicado de; on the ~
em ponto
dote [dəut]: to ~ on vt fus adorar, idolatrar
dot-matrix printer n impressora ma-
tricial
dotted line [ˈdɒtɪd-] n linha pontilhada
double [ˈdʌbl] adj duplo ♦ adv (twice):
to cost ~ (sth) custar o dobro (de algo) ♦ n (person) duplo/a ♦ vt dobrar ♦
vi dobrar; at the ~ (BRIT), on the ~
em passo acelerado; ~ bass n contrabaixo; ~ bed n cama de casal; ~-
breasted adj trespassado; ~cross vt
(trick) enganar; (betray) atraiçoar;
~decker n ônibus m (BR) or autocarro
(PT) de dois andares; ~ glazing (BRIT)
n (janelas fpl de) vidro duplo; ~ room
n quarto de casal; ~s n (TENNIS) dupla;
doubly adv duplamente
doubt [daut] n dúvida ♦ vt duvidar; (suspect) desconfiar de; to ~ if or whether
duvidar que; ~ful adj duvidoso; ~less
adv sem dúvida
dough [dəu] n massa; ~nut (US donut)
n sonho (BR), bola de Berlim (PT)
douse [dauz] vt (with water) encharcar

de; (flames) apagar
dove [dʌv] n pomba; ~tail vi (fig)
encaixar-se
dowdy [ˈdaudɪ] adj (clothes) desalinhado;
(person) deselegante, pouco elegante
down [daun] n (feathers) penugem f ♦
adv (~wards) para baixo; (on the
ground) por terra ♦ prep (towards lower
level) embaixo de; (movement along) ao
longo de ♦ vt (inf: drink) tomar de um
gole só; ~ with X! abaixo X!; ~-and-
out n (tramp) vagabundo/a; ~-at-heel
adj descuidado, desmazelado; (appearance) deselegante; ~cast adj abatido;
~fall n queda, ruína; ~hearted adj desanimado; ~hill adv: to go ~hill descer, ir morro abaixo; (fig: business) degringolar; ~ payment n entrada, sinal
m; ~pour n aguaceiro; ~right adj (lie)
patente; (refusal) categórico; ~stairs
adv (below) (lá) em baixo; (~wards)
para baixo; ~stream adv água or rio
abaixo; ~-to-earth adj prático, realista;
~town adv no centro da cidade; ~ under adv na Austrália (or Nova Zelândia); ~ward adj, adv para baixo;
~wards adv = ~ward
dowry [ˈdaurɪ] n dote m
doz. abbr (= dozen) dz.
doze [dəuz] vi dormitar; ~ off vi cochilar
dozen [ˈdʌzn] n dúzia; a ~ books uma
dúzia de livros; ~s of milhares de
Dr abbr (= doctor) Dr(a) m/f
drab [dræb] adj sombrio
draft [drɑːft] n (first copy) rascunho;
(POL: of bill) projeto de lei; (bank ~) saque m, letra; (US: call-up) recrutamento
♦ vt (plan) esboçar; (speech, letter) rascunhar; see also draught
draftsman [ˈdrɑːftsmən] (US) n =
draughtsman
drag [dræg] vt arrastar; (river) dragar ♦
vi arrastar-se ♦ n (inf) chatice f (BR),
maçada (PT); (women's clothing): in ~
em travesti; ~ on vi arrastar-se
dragon [ˈdrægən] n dragão m
dragonfly [ˈdrægənflaɪ] n libélula
drain [dreɪn] n bueiro; (source of loss)
sorvedouro ♦ vt (glass) esvaziar; (land,
marshes) drenar; (vegetables) coar ♦ vi
(water) escorrer, escoar-se; ~age n (act)
drenagem f; (system) esgoto; ~board
(US) n = ~ing board; ~ing board
(BRIT) n escorredor m; ~pipe n cano de
esgoto
drama [ˈdrɑːmə] n (art) teatro; (play) drama m; ~tic adj dramático; (theatrical)
teatral; ~tist n dramaturgo/a
drank [dræŋk] pt of drink
drape [dreɪp] vt ornar, cobrir; ~s (US)
npl cortinas fpl
drastic [ˈdræstɪk] adj drástico
draught [drɑːft] (US draft) n (of air) corrente f; (NAUT) calado; (beer) chope m;

on ~ (*beer*) de barril; **~board** (*BRIT*) *n* tabuleiro de damas; **~s** (*BRIT*) *n* (jogo de) damas *fpl*

draughtsman ['drɑːftsmən] (*US* **draftsman**) (*irreg*) *n* desenhista *m/f* industrial

draw [drɔː] (*pt* **drew**, *pp* **drawn**) *vt* desenhar; (*cart*) puxar; (*curtain*) fechar; (*gun*) sacar; (*attract*) atrair; (*money*) tirar; (: *from bank*) sacar ♦ *vi* empatar ♦ *n* empate *m*; (*lottery*) sorteio; **to ~ near** aproximar-se; **~ out** *vt* (*money*) sacar; **~ up** *vi* (*stop*) parar(-se) ♦ *vt* (*chair etc*) puxar; (*document*) redigir; **~back** *n* inconveniente *m*, desvantagem *f*; **~bridge** *n* ponte *f* levadiça; **~er** *n* gaveta; **~ing** *n* desenho; **~ing board** *n* prancheta; **~ing pin** (*BRIT*) *n* tachinha (*BR*), pionés *m* (*PT*); **~ing room** *n* sala de visitas

drawl [drɔːl] *n* fala arrastada

drawn [drɔːn] *pp of* **draw**

dread [drɛd] *n* medo, pavor *m* ♦ *vt* temer, recear, ter medo de; **~ful** *adj* terrível

dream [driːm] (*pt*, *pp* **~ed** *or* **~t**) *n* sonho ♦ *vt*, *vi* sonhar; **~t** *pt*, *pp of* **dream**; **~y** *adj* sonhador(a), distraído; (*music*) sentimental

dreary ['drɪərɪ] *adj* (*talk*, *time*) monótono; (*weather*) sombrio

dredge [drɛdʒ] *vt* dragar

dregs [drɛgz] *npl* lia; (*of humanity*) escória, ralé *f*

drench [drɛntʃ] *vt* encharcar

dress [drɛs] *n* vestido; (*no pl*: *clothing*) traje *m* ♦ *vt* vestir; (*wound*) fazer curativo em ♦ *vi* vestir-se; **to get ~ed** vestir-se; **~ up** *vi* vestir-se com elegância; (*in fancy dress*) fantasiar-se; **~ circle** (*BRIT*) *n* balcão *m* nobre; **~er** *n* (*BRIT*: *cupboard*) aparador *m*; (*US*: *chest of drawers*) cômoda de espelho; **~ing** *n* (*MED*) curativo; (*CULIN*) molho; **~ing gown** (*BRIT*) *n* roupão *m*; (*woman's*) peignoir *m*; **~ing room** *n* (*THEATRE*) camarim *m*; (*SPORT*) vestiário; **~ing table** *n* penteadeira (*BR*), toucador *m* (*PT*); **~maker** *n* costureiro/a; **~ rehearsal** *n* ensaio geral; **~y** (*inf*) *adj* (*clothes*) chique

drew [druː] *pt of* **draw**

dribble ['drɪbl] *vi* (*baby*) babar ♦ *vt* (*ball*) driblar

dried [draɪd] *adj* (*fruit*, *beans*) seco; (*eggs*, *milk*) em pó

drier ['draɪə*] *n* = **dryer**

drift [drɪft] *n* (*of current etc*) força; (*of snow*) monte *m*; (*meaning*) sentido ♦ *vi* (*boat*) derivar; (*sand*, *snow*) amontoar-se; **~wood** *n* madeira flutuante

drill [drɪl] *n* furadeira; (*of dentist*) broca; (*for mining etc*) broca, furadeira; (*MIL*) exercícios *mpl* militares ♦ *vt* furar, brocar; (*MIL*) exercitar ♦ *vi* (*for oil*) perfurar

drink [drɪŋk] (*pt* **drank**, *pp* **drunk**) *n* bebida; (*sip*) gole *m* ♦ *vt*, *vi* beber; **a ~ of water** um copo d'água; **~er** *n* bebedor(a) *m/f*; **~ing water** *n* água potável

drip [drɪp] *n* gotejar *m*; (*one ~*) gota, pingo; (*MED*) gota a gota *m* ♦ *vi* gotejar; (*tap*) pingar; **~-dry** *adj* de lavar e vestir; **~ping** *n* gordura

drive [draɪv] (*pt* **drove**, *pp* **driven**) *n* passeio (de automóvel); (*journey*) trajeto, percurso; (*also*: **~way**) entrada; (*energy*) energia, vigor *m*; (*campaign*) campanha; (*COMPUT*: *also*: **disk ~**) unidade *f* de disco ♦ *vt* (*car*) dirigir (*BR*), guiar (*PT*); (*push*) empurrar; (*TECH*: *motor*) acionar; (*nail etc*) cravar ♦ *vi* (*AUT*: *at controls*) dirigir (*BR*), guiar (*PT*); (: *travel*) ir de carro; **left-/right-hand ~** direção à esquerda/direita; **to ~ sb mad** deixar alguém louco

drivel ['drɪvl] (*inf*) *n* bobagem *f*, besteira

driven ['drɪvn] *pp of* **drive**

driver ['draɪvə*] *n* motorista *m/f*; (*RAIL*) maquinista *m*; **~'s license** (*US*) *n* carteira de motorista (*BR*), carta de condução (*PT*)

driveway ['draɪvweɪ] *n* entrada

driving ['draɪvɪŋ] *n* direção *f* (*BR*), condução *f* (*PT*); **~ instructor** *n* instrutor(a) *m/f* de auto-escola (*BR*) *or* de condução (*PT*); **~ lesson** *n* aula de direção (*BR*) *or* de condução (*PT*); **~ licence** (*BRIT*) *n* carteira de motorista (*BR*), carta de condução (*PT*); **~ mirror** (*BRIT*) *n* retrovisor *m*; **~ school** *n* auto-escola *f*; **~ test** *n* exame *m* de motorista

drizzle ['drɪzl] *n* chuvisco

drone [drəun] *n* (*sound*) zumbido; (*male bee*) zangão *m*

drool [druːl] *vi* babar(-se)

droop [druːp] *vi* pender

drop [drɔp] *n* (*of water*) gota; (*lessening*) diminuição *f*; (*fall*: *distance*) declive *m* ♦ *vt* (*allow to fall*) deixar cair; (*voice*, *eyes*, *price*) baixar; (*set down from car*) deixar (saltar/descer); (*omit*) omitir ♦ *vi* cair; (*wind*) parar; **~s** *npl* (*MED*) gotas *fpl*; **~ off** *vi* (*sleep*) cochilar ♦ *vt* (*passenger*) deixar (saltar); **~ out** *vi* (*withdraw*) retirar-se; **~-out** *n* pessoa que abandona o trabalho, os estudos *etc*; **~per** *n* conta-gotas *m inv*; **~pings** *npl* fezes *fpl* (de animal)

drought [draut] *n* seca

drove [drəuv] *pt of* **drive**

drown [draun] *vt* afogar; (*also*: **~ out**: *sound*) encobrir ♦ *vi* afogar-se

drowsy ['drauzɪ] *adj* sonolento

drudgery ['drʌdʒərɪ] *n* trabalho enfadonho

drug [drʌg] *n* remédio, medicamento; (*narcotic*) droga ♦ *vt* drogar; **to be on ~s** estar viciado em drogas; (*MED*) estar sob medicação; **~ addict** *n* toxicômano/a; **~gist** (*US*) *n* farmacêutico/a; **~store** (US) n drogaria

drum [drʌm] n tambor m; (for oil, petrol) tambor, barril m; **~s** npl (kit) bateria; **~mer** n baterista m/f

drunk [drʌŋk] pp of **drink** ♦ adj bêbado ♦ n (also: **~ard**) bêbado/a; **~en** adj (laughter) de bêbado; (party) cheio de bêbado; (person) bêbado

dry [draɪ] adj seco; (day) sem chuva; (humour) irônico ♦ vt secar, enxugar; (tears) limpar ♦ vi secar; **~ up** vi secar completamente; **~-cleaner's** n tinturaria; **~-cleaning** n lavagem f a seco; **~er** n secador m; (US: spin-~) secadora; **~ness** n secura; **~ rot** n putrefação f fungosa

DSS (BRIT) n abbr (= Department of Social Security) ≈ INAMPS m

dual ['djuəl] adj dual, duplo; **~ carriageway** (BRIT) n pista dupla; **~-purpose** adj de duplo uso

dubbed [dʌbd] adj (CINEMA) dublado

dubious ['dju:bɪəs] adj duvidoso; (reputation, company) suspeitoso

Dublin ['dʌblɪn] n Dublin

duchess ['dʌtʃɪs] n duquesa

duck [dʌk] n pato ♦ vi abaixar-se repentinamente; **~ling** n patinho

duct [dʌkt] n conduto, canal m; (ANAT) ducto

dud [dʌd] n (object, tool): **it's a ~** não presta ♦ adj (BRIT): **~ cheque** cheque m sem fundos, cheque m voador (inf)

due [dju:] adj (proper) devido; (expected) esperado ♦ n: **to give sb his (or her) ~** ser justo com alguém ♦ adv: **~ north** exatamente ao norte; **~s** npl (for club, union) quota; (in harbour) direitos mpl; **in ~ course** no devido tempo; (eventually) no final; **~ to** devido a

duet [dju:'ɛt] n dueto

duffel bag ['dʌfl-] n mochila

duffel coat ['dʌfl-] n casaco de baeta

dug [dʌg] pt, pp of **dig**

duke [dju:k] n duque m

dull [dʌl] adj (light) sombrio; (wit) lento; (boring) enfadonho; (sound, pain) surdo; (weather) nublado, carregado ♦ vt (pain) aliviar; (mind, senses) entorpecer

duly ['dju:lɪ] adv devidamente; (on time) no devido tempo

dumb [dʌm] adj mudo; (pej: stupid) estúpido; **~founded** adj pasmado

dummy ['dʌmɪ] n (tailor's model) manequim m; (mock-up) modelo; (BRIT: for baby) chupeta ♦ adj falso

dump [dʌmp] n (also: **rubbish ~**) depósito de lixo; (inf: place) chiqueiro ♦ vt (put down) depositar, descarregar; (get rid of) desfazer-se de

dumpling ['dʌmplɪŋ] n bolinho cozido

dumpy ['dʌmpɪ] adj gorducho

dunce [dʌns] n burro, ignorante m/f

dung [dʌŋ] n estrume m

dungarees [dʌŋgə'ri:z] npl macacão m

(BR), fato macaco (PT)

dungeon ['dʌndʒən] n calabouço

dupe [dju:p] n (victim) otário/a, trouxa m/f ♦ vt enganar

duplex ['dju:plɛks] (US) n casa geminada; (also: **~ apartment**) duplex m

duplicate [n 'dju:plɪkət, vt 'dju:plɪkeɪt] n (of document) duplicata; (of key) cópia ♦ vt duplicar; (photocopy) multigrafar; (repeat) reproduzir

duplicity [dju:'plɪsɪtɪ] n falsidade f

durable ['djuərəbl] adj durável; (clothes, metal) resistente

duress [djuə'rɛs] n: **under ~** sob coação

during ['djuərɪŋ] prep durante

dusk [dʌsk] n crepúsculo, anoitecer m

dust [dʌst] n pó m, poeira ♦ vt (furniture) tirar o pó de; (cake etc): **to ~ with** polvilhar com; **~bin** n (BRIT) lata de lixo; **~er** n pano de pó; **~man** (BRIT: irreg) n lixeiro, gari m (BR: inf); **~y** adj empoeirado

Dutch [dʌtʃ] adj holandês/esa ♦ n (LING) holandês m ♦ adv: **let's go ~** (inf) cada um paga o seu; **the ~** npl (people) os holandeses; **~man** (irreg) n holandês m; **~woman** (irreg) n holandesa

dutiful ['dju:tɪful] adj respeitoso

duty ['dju:tɪ] n dever m; (tax) taxa; **on ~** de serviço; **off ~** de folga; **~-free** adj livre de impostos

duvet ['du:veɪ] (BRIT) n edredom m (BR), edredão m (PT)

DVD n abbr (= digital versatile disc) DVD m

dwarf [dwɔ:f] (pl **dwarves**) n anão/anã m/f ♦ vt ananicar

dwell [dwɛl] (pt, pp **dwelt**) vi morar; **~ on** vt fus estender-se sobre; **~ing** n residência; **dwelt** pt, pp of **dwell**

dwindle ['dwɪndl] vi diminuir

dye [daɪ] n tintura, tinta ♦ vt tingir

dyke [daɪk] (BRIT) n (embankment) dique m, represa

dynamite ['daɪnəmaɪt] n dinamite f

dynamo ['daɪnəməu] n dínamo

E

E [i:] n (MUS) mi m

each [i:tʃ] adj cada inv ♦ pron cada um(a); **~ other** um ao outro; **they hate ~ other** (eles) se odeiam

eager ['i:gə] adj ávido; **to be ~ for/to do sth** ansiar por/por fazer algo

eagle ['i:gl] n águia

ear [ɪə] n (external) orelha; (inner, fig) ouvido; (of corn) espiga; **~ache** n dor f de ouvidos; **~drum** n tímpano

earl [ə:l] (BRIT) n conde m

earlier ['ə:lɪə] adj mais adiantado; (edition) anterior ♦ adv mais cedo

early ['ə:lɪ] adv cedo; (before time) com antecedência ♦ adj cedo; (sooner than *expected*) prematuro; (*reply*) pronto; (*Christians, settlers*) primeiro; (*man*) primitivo; (*life, work*) juvenil; **in the ~ or ~ in the spring/19th century** no princípio da primavera/do século dezenove; **~ retirement** *n* aposentadoria antecipada

earmark ['ɪəmɑːk] *vt*: **to ~ sth for** reservar *or* destinar algo para

earn *vt* ganhar; (*COMM: interest*) render; (*praise*) merecer

earnest ['ɜːnɪst] *adj* (*wish*) intenso; (*manner*) sério; **in ~ a sério**

earnings ['ɜːnɪŋz] *npl* (*personal*) vencimentos *mpl*, salário, ordenado; (*of company*) lucro

ear: **~phones** *npl* fones *mpl* de ouvido; **~ring** *n* brinco; **~shot** *n*: **within ~shot** ao alcance do ouvido *or* da voz

earth [ɜːθ] *n* (*BRIT: ELEC*) fio terra ♦ *vt* (*BRIT: ELEC*) ligar à terra; **~enware** *n* louça de barro ♦ *adj* de barro; **~quake** *n* terremoto (*BR*), terramoto (*PT*); **~y** *adj* grosseiro

ease [iːz] *n* facilidade *f*; (*relaxed state*) sossego; (*comfort*) conforto ♦ *vt* facilitar; (*pain, tension*) aliviar; (*help pass*): **to ~ sth in/out** meter/ tirar algo com cuidado; **at ~!** (*MIL*) descansar!; **~ off** *vi* acalmar-se; (*slow*) baixar; (*rain*) moderar-se; **~ up** *vi* = **~ off**

easel ['iːzl] *n* cavalete *m*

easily ['iːzɪlɪ] *adv* facilmente, fácil (*inf*)

east [iːst] *n* leste *m* ♦ *adj* (*region*) leste; (*wind*) do leste ♦ *adv* para o leste; **the E~ o** Oriente; (*POL*) o Leste

Easter ['iːstə*] *n* Páscoa; **~ egg** *n* ovo de Páscoa

easterly ['iːstəlɪ] *adj* (*to the east*) para o leste; (*from the east*) do leste

eastern ['iːstən] *adj* do leste, oriental

East Germany *n* Alemanha Oriental

eastward(s) ['iːstwəd(z)] *adv* ao leste

easy ['iːzɪ] *adj* fácil; (*comfortable*) folgado, cômodo; (*relaxed*) natural, complacente; (*victim, prey*) desprotegido ♦ *adv*: **to take it** *or* **things ~** (*not worry*) levar as coisas com calma; (*go slowly*) ir devagar; (*rest*) descansar; **~ chair** *n* poltrona; **~-going** *adj* pacato, fácil

eat [iːt] (*pt* **ate**, *pp* **eaten**) *vt, vi* comer; **~ away** *vt* corroer; **~ away at** *vt fus* corroer; **~ into** *vt fus* = **~ away**

eaves [iːvz] *npl* beira, beiral *m*

eavesdrop ['iːvzdrɒp] *vi*: **to ~ (on)** escutar às escondidas

ebb [ɛb] *n* refluxo ♦ *vi* baixar; (*fig: also*: **~ away**) declinar

ebony ['ɛbənɪ] *n* ébano

EC *n abbr* (= *European Community*) CE *f*

eccentric [ɪk'sɛntrɪk] *adj, n* excêntrico/a

echo ['ɛkəʊ] (*pl* **~es**) *n* eco ♦ *vt* ecoar, repetir ♦ *vi* ressoar, repetir

éclair [eɪ'klɛə*] *n* (*CULIN*) bomba

eclipse [ɪ'klɪps] *n* eclipse *m*

ecology [ɪ'kɒlədʒɪ] *n* ecologia

economic [iːkə'nɒmɪk] *adj* econômico; (*business etc*) rentável; **~al** *adj* econômico; **~s** *n* economia ♦ *npl* aspectos *mpl* econômicos

economize [ɪ'kɒnəmaɪz] *vi* economizar, fazer economias

economy [ɪ'kɒnəmɪ] *n* economia; **~ class** *n* (*AVIAT*) classe *f* econômica; **~ size** *n* tamanho econômico

ecstasy ['ɛkstəsɪ] *n* êxtase *m*; **ecstatic** *adj* extasiado

ECU [eɪ'kjuː] *n abbr* (= *European Currency Unit*) ECU *m*

Ecuador ['ɛkwədɔː*] *n* Equador *m*

edge [ɛdʒ] *n* (*of knife etc*) fio; (*of table, chair etc*) borda; (*of lake etc*) margem *f* ♦ *vt* (*trim*) embainhar; **on ~** (*fig*) = **edgy**; **to ~ away from** afastar-se pouco a pouco de; **~ways** *adv* lateralmente; **he couldn't get a word in ~ways** não pôde entrar na conversa; **edgy** *adj* nervoso, inquieto

edible ['ɛdɪbl] *adj* comestível

Edinburgh ['ɛdɪnbərə] *n* Edimburgo

edit ['ɛdɪt] *vt* editar; (*be editor of*) dirigir; (*cut*) cortar, redigir; (*COMPUT, TV*) editar; (*CINEMA*) montar; **~ion** *n* edição *f*; **~or** *n* redator(a) *m/f*; (*of newspaper*) diretor(a) *m/f*; (*of column*) editor(a) *m/f*; (*of book*) organizador(a) *m/f* da edição; **~orial** *adj* editorial

educate ['ɛdjukeɪt] *vt* educar

education [ɛdju'keɪʃən] *n* educação *f*; (*schooling*) ensino; (*teaching*) pedagogia; **~al** *adj* (*policy, experience*) educacional; (*toy etc*) educativo

EEC *n abbr* (= *European Economic Community*) CEE *f*

eel [iːl] *n* enguia

eerie ['ɪərɪ] *adj* (*strange*) estranho; (*mysterious*) misterioso

effect [ɪ'fɛkt] *n* efeito ♦ *vt* (*repairs*) fazer; (*savings*) efetuar; **to take ~** (*law*) entrar em vigor; (*drug*) fazer efeito; **in ~** na realidade; **~ive** *adj* eficaz; (*actual*) efetivo; **~iveness** *n* eficácia

effeminate [ɪ'fɛmɪnɪt] *adj* efeminado

efficiency [ɪ'fɪʃənsɪ] *n* eficiência

efficient [ɪ'fɪʃənt] *adj* eficiente; (*machine*) rentável

effort ['ɛfət] *n* esforço; **~less** *adj* fácil

effrontery [ɪ'frʌntərɪ] *n* descaramento

effusive [ɪ'fjuːsɪv] *adj* efusivo; (*welcome*) caloroso

e.g. *adv abbr* (= *exempli gratia*) p. ex.

egg [ɛg] *n* ovo; **hard-boiled/soft-boiled ~** ovo duro/mole; **~ on** *vt* incitar; **~cup** *n* oveiro; **~plant** (*esp US*) *n* beringela; **~shell** *n* casca de ovo

ego ['iːgəʊ] *n* ego; **~tism** *n* egotismo *m*

Egypt ['iːdʒɪpt] *n* Egito; **~ian** *adj, n* egípcio/a

eiderdown ['aɪdədaʊn] *n* edredom *m* (*BR*), edredão *m* (*PT*)

eight [eɪt] *num* oito; **~een** *num* dezoito; **~h** *num* oitavo; **~y** *num* oitenta

Eire [ˈɛərə] *n* (República da) Irlanda

either [ˈaɪðəˣ] *adj* (*one or other*) um ou outro; (*each*) cada; (*both*) ambos ♦ *pron*: **~ (of them)** qualquer (dos dois) ♦ *adv*: no, I don't **~** eu também não ♦ *conj*: **~** yes or no ou sim ou não

eject [ɪˈdʒɛkt] *vt* expulsar

eke [iːk]: **to ~ out** *vt* fazer durar, esticar; (*money*) economizar; (*food*) economizar em

elaborate [*adj* ɪˈlæbərɪt, *vt*, *vi* ɪˈlæbəreɪt] *adj* complicado ♦ *vt* (*expand*) expandir; (*refine*) aperfeiçoar ♦ *vi*: **to ~ on** acrescentar detalhes a

elapse [ɪˈlæps] *vi* transcorrer

elastic [ɪˈlæstɪk] *adj* elástico; (*adaptable*) flexível, adaptável ♦ *n* elástico; **~ band** (*BRIT*) *n* elástico

elated [ɪˈleɪtɪd] *adj*: **to be ~** rejubilar-se; **elation** *n* exaltação *f*

elbow [ˈɛlbəu] *n* cotovelo

elder [ˈɛldəˣ] *adj* mais velho ♦ *n* (*tree*) sabugueiro; (*person*) o/a mais velho/a; **~ly** *adj* idoso, de idade ♦ *npl*: **the ~ly** as pessoas de idade, os idosos

eldest [ˈɛldɪst] *adj* mais velho ♦ *n* o/a mais velho/a

elect [ɪˈlɛkt] *vt* eleger ♦ *adj*: **the president ~** o presidente eleito; **to ~ to do** (*choose*) optar por fazer; **~ion** *n* (*voting*) votação *f*; (*installation*) eleição *f*; **~ioneering** *n* campanha or propaganda eleitoral; **~or** *n* eleitor(a) *m/f*; **~orate** *n* eleitorado

electric [ɪˈlɛktrɪk] *adj* elétrico; **~al** *adj* elétrico; **~ blanket** *n* cobertor *m* elétrico; **~ fire** lareira elétrica

electrician [ɪlɛkˈtrɪʃən] *n* eletricista *m/f*

electricity [ɪlɛkˈtrɪsɪtɪ] *n* eletricidade *f*

electrify [ɪˈlɛktrɪfaɪ] *vt* (*fence*, *RAIL*) eletrificar; (*audience*) eletrizar

electrocute [ɪˈlɛktrəkjuːt] *vt* eletrocutar

electronic [ɪlɛkˈtrɒnɪk] *adj* eletrônico; **~ mail** *n* correio eletrônico; **~s** *n* eletrônica

elegant [ˈɛlɪɡənt] *adj* (*person*, *building*) elegante; (*idea*) refinado

element [ˈɛlɪmənt] *n* elemento; **~ary** *adj* (*gen*) elementar; (*primitive*) rudimentar; (*school*, *education*) primário

elephant [ˈɛlɪfənt] *n* elefante/a *m/f*

elevation [ɛlɪˈveɪʃən] *n* elevação *f*; (*height*) altura

elevator [ˈɛlɪveɪtəˣ] (*US*) *n* elevador *m*

eleven [ɪˈlɛvn] *num* onze; **~ses** (*BRIT*) *npl* refeição leve da manhã; **~th** *num* décimo-primeiro

elf [ɛlf] (*pl* **elves**) *n* elfo, duende *m*

elicit [ɪˈlɪsɪt] *vt*: **to ~ (from)** (*information*) extrair (de); (*response*, *reaction*) provocar (de)

eligible [ˈɛlɪdʒəbl] *adj* elegível, apto; **to be ~ for sth** (*job etc*) ter qualificações para algo

elm [ɛlm] *n* olmo

elongated [ˈiːlɔŋɡeɪtɪd] *adj* alongado

elope [ɪˈləup] *vi* fugir

eloquent [ˈɛləkwənt] *adj* eloquente

El Salvador [ɛlˈsælvədɔːˣ] *n* El Salvador

else [ɛls] *adv* outro, mais; **something ~** outra coisa; **nobody ~ spoke** ninguém mais falou; **~where** *adv* (*be*) em outro lugar (*BR*), noutro sítio (*PT*); (*go*) para outro lugar (*BR*), a outro sítio (*PT*)

elucidate [ɪˈluːsɪdeɪt] *vt* esclarecer, elucidar

elude [ɪˈluːd] *vt* escapar de, esquivar-se de; (*subj*: *idea*) evadir

elusive [ɪˈluːsɪv] *adj* esquivo; (*quality*) indescritível

elves [ɛlvz] *npl of* **elf**

emaciated [ɪˈmeɪsɪeɪtɪd] *adj* emaciado, macilento

e-mail [ˈiːmeɪl] *n abbr* (= *electronic mail*) correio eletrônico

emanate [ˈɛməneɪt] *vi*: **to ~ from** emanar de

emancipate [ɪˈmænsɪpeɪt] *vt* libertar; (*women*) emancipar

embankment [ɪmˈbæŋkmənt] *n* aterro; (*of river*) dique *m*

embargo [ɪmˈbɑːɡəu] (*pl* **~es**) *n* (*COMM*) proibição *f*

embark [ɪmˈbɑːk] *vi* embarcar ♦ *vt* barcar; **to ~ on** (*fig*) empreender, começar; **~ation** *n* embarque *m*

embarrass [ɪmˈbærəs] *vt* constranger; (*politician*) embaraçar; **~ed** *adj* desconfortável; **~ing** *adj* embaraçoso, constrangedor(a); **~ment** *n* embaraço, constrangimento

embassy [ˈɛmbəsɪ] *n* embaixada

embedded [ɪmˈbɛdɪd] *adj* encravado

embellish [ɪmˈbɛlɪʃ] *vt* embelezar; (*story*) florear

embers [ˈɛmbəz] *npl* brasa, borralho

embezzle [ɪmˈbɛzl] *vt* desviar

embitter [ɪmˈbɪtəˣ] *vt* (*person*) amargurar; (*relations*) azedar

embody [ɪmˈbɔdɪ] *vt* (*features*) incorporar; (*ideas*) expressar

embossed [ɪmˈbɔst] *adj* realçado

embrace [ɪmˈbreɪs] *vt* abraçar, dar um abraço em; (*include*) abarcar, abranger ♦ *vi* abraçar-se ♦ *n* abraço

embroider [ɪmˈbrɔɪdəˣ] *vt* bordar; **~y** *n* bordado

embryo [ˈɛmbrɪəu] *n* embrião *m*

emerald [ˈɛmərəld] *n* esmeralda

emerge [ɪˈməːdʒ] *vi* sair; (*from sleep*) acordar; (*fact*, *idea*) emergir

emergency [ɪˈməːdʒənsɪ] *n* emergência; **in an ~** em caso de urgência; **~ cord** (*US*) *n* sinal *m* de alarme; **~ exit** *n* saída de emergência; **~ landing** *n* aterrissagem *f* forçada (*BR*), aterragem *f* forçosa (*PT*)

emery board [ˈɛmərɪ-] *n* lixa de unhas

emigrate ['ɛmɪgreɪt] vi emigrar

eminent ['ɛmɪnənt] adj eminente

emissions [ɪ'mɪʃənz] npl emissão f

emit [ɪ'mɪt] vt (smoke) soltar; (smell) exalar; (sound) produzir

emotion [ɪ'məuʃən] n emoção f; ~**al** adj (needs) emocional; (person) sentimental, emotivo; (scene) comovente; (tone) emocionante

emperor ['ɛmpərə'] n imperador m

emphasis ['ɛmfəsɪs] (pl **emphases**) n ênfase f

emphasize ['ɛmfəsaɪz] vt (word, point) enfatizar, acentuar; (feature) salientar

emphatic [ɛm'fætɪk] adj (statement) vigoroso, expressivo; (person) convincente; (manner) enfático; ~**ally** adv com ênfase; (certainly) certamente

empire ['ɛmpaɪə'] n império

employ [ɪm'plɔɪ] vt empregar; (tool) utilizar; ~**ee** n empregado/a; ~**er** n empregador(a) m/f, patrão/troa m/f; ~**ment** n (gen) emprego; (work) trabalho; ~**ment agency** n agência de empregos

empower [ɪm'pauə'] vt: to ~ sb to do sth autorizar alguém para fazer algo

empress ['ɛmprɪs] n imperatriz f

emptiness ['ɛmptɪnɪs] n vazio, vácuo

empty ['ɛmptɪ] adj vazio; (place) deserto; (house) desocupado; (threat) vão/vã ♦ vt esvaziar; (place) evacuar ♦ vi esvaziar-se; (place) ficar deserto; ~-**handed** adj de mãos vazias

emulate ['ɛmjuleɪt] vt emular com

emulsion [ɪ'mʌlʃən] n emulsão f; (also: ~ paint) tinta plástica

enable [ɪ'neɪbl] vt: to ~ sb to do sth (allow) permitir que alguém faça algo; (make possible) tornar possível que alguém faça algo

enact [ɪn'ækt] vt (law) pôr em vigor, promulgar; (play) representar; (role) fazer

enamel [ɪ'næməl] n esmalte m

enamel paint n esmalte m

enamoured [ɪ'næməd] adj: to be ~ of (person) estar apaixonado por; (activity etc) ser louco por; (idea) encantar-se com

encased [ɪn'keɪst] adj: ~ in (enclosed) encaixado em; (covered: plaster, shell) revestido de

enchant [ɪn'tʃɑːnt] vt encantar; ~**ed** adj encantado; ~**ing** adj encantador(a)

encircle [ɪn'sɜːkl] vt cercar, circundar

enc(l). abbr (in letters etc) = **enclosed; enclosure**

enclave ['ɛnkleɪv] n encrave m

enclose [ɪn'kləuz] vt (land) cercar; (with letter) anexar (BR), enviar junto (PT); **please find** ~**d** segue junto

enclosure [ɪn'kləuʒə'] n cercado

encompass [ɪn'kʌmpəs] vt abranger, encerrar

encore [ɔŋ'kɔː'] excl bis!, outra! ♦ n bis m

encounter [ɪn'kauntə'] n encontro ♦ vt encontrar, topar com; (difficulty) enfrentar

encourage [ɪn'kʌrɪdʒ] vt (activity) encorajar; (growth) estimular; (person): to ~ sb to do sth animar alguém a fazer algo; ~**ment** n estímulo

encroach [ɪn'krəutʃ] vi: to ~ (up)on invadir; (time) ocupar

encumber [ɪn'kʌmbə'] vt: to be ~ed with (carry) estar carregado de; (debts) estar sobrecarregado de

encyclop(a)edia [ɛnsaɪkləu'piːdɪə] n enciclopédia

end [ɛnd] n fim m; (of table, rope etc) ponta; (of street, town) final m ♦ vt acabar, terminar; (also: **bring to an** ~, **put an** ~ **to**) acabar com, pôr fim a ♦ vi terminar, acabar; **in the** ~ ao fim, por fim, finalmente; **on** ~ na ponta; **to stand on** ~ (hair) arrepiar-se; **for hours on** ~ por horas a fio; ~ **up** vi: to ~ up in terminar em; (place) ir parar em

endanger [ɪn'deɪndʒə'] vt pôr em risco

endearing [ɪn'dɪərɪŋ] adj simpático, atrativo

endeavour [ɪn'dɛvə'] (US **endeavor**) n esforço; (attempt) tentativa ♦ vi: to ~ to do esforçar-se para fazer; (try) tentar fazer

ending ['ɛndɪŋ] n fim m, conclusão f; (of book) desenlace m; (LING) terminação f

endive ['ɛndaɪv] n (curly) endívia; (smooth) chicória

endless ['ɛndlɪs] adj interminável; (possibilities) infinito

endorse [ɪn'dɔːs] vt (cheque) endossar; (approve) aprovar; ~**ment** n (BRIT: on driving licence) descrição f das multas; (approval) aval m

endow [ɪn'dau] vt (provide with money) dotar; (: institution) fundar; **to be** ~**ed with** ser dotado de

endurance [ɪn'djuərəns] n resistência

endure [ɪn'djuə'] vt (bear) agüentar, suportar ♦ vi (last) durar

enemy ['ɛnəmɪ] adj, n inimigo/a

energy ['ɛnədʒɪ] n energia

enforce [ɪn'fɔːs] vt (LAW) fazer cumprir

engage [ɪn'geɪdʒ] vt (attention) chamar; (interest) atrair; (lawyer) contratar; (clutch) engrenar ♦ vi engrenar; to ~ in dedicar-se a, ocupar-se com; to ~ sb in conversation travar conversa com alguém; ~**d** adj (BRIT: phone) ocupado (BR), impedido (PT); (: toilet) ocupado; (betrothed) noivo; to get ~**d** ficar noivo; ~**d tone** (BRIT) n (TEL) sinal m de ocupado (BR) or de impedido (PT); ~**ment** n encontro; (booking) contrato; (to marry) noivado; ~**ment ring** n aliança de noivado

engaging [ɪn'geɪdʒɪŋ] adj atraente, simpático

engine ['ɛndʒɪn] n (AUT) motor m; (RAIL) locomotiva; ~ **driver** n maquinista m/f

engineer [ɛndʒɪ'nɪə*] n engenheiro/a; (US: RAIL) maquinista m/f; (BRIT: for repairs) técnico/a; (on ship) engenheiro/a naval; ~**ing** n engenharia

England ['ɪŋglənd] n Inglaterra

English ['ɪŋglɪʃ] adj inglês/esa ♦ n (LING) inglês m; **the** ~ npl (people) os ingleses; ~ **Channel** n: **the** ~ **Channel** o Canal da Mancha; ~**man/woman** (irreg) n inglês/inglesa m/f

engraving [ɪn'greɪvɪŋ] n gravura

engrossed [ɪn'grəust] adj: ~ **in** absorto em

engulf [ɪn'gʌlf] vt (subj: fire, water) engolfar, tragar; (: panic, fear) tomar conta de

enhance [ɪn'hɑːns] vt (gen) ressaltar, salientar; (enjoyment) aumentar; (beauty) realçar; (reputation) melhorar; (add to) aumentar

enjoy [ɪn'dʒɔɪ] vt gostar de; (health, privilege) desfrutar de; **to** ~ **o.s.** divertir-se; ~**able** adj agradável; ~**ment** n prazer m

enlarge [ɪn'lɑːdʒ] vt aumentar; (PHOT) ampliar ♦ vi: **to** ~ **on** (subject) desenvolver, estender-se sobre

enlighten [ɪn'laɪtn] vt (inform) informar, instruir; ~**ed** adj sábio; (cultured) culto; (knowledgeable) bem informado; (tolerant) compreensivo; ~**ment** n esclarecimento; (HISTORY): **the** E~**ment** o Século das Luzes

enlist [ɪn'lɪst] vt alistar; (support) conseguir, aliciar ♦ vi alistar-se

enmity ['ɛnmɪtɪ] n inimizade f

enormous [ɪ'nɔːməs] adj enorme

enough [ɪ'nʌf] adj: ~ **time/books** tempo suficiente/livros suficientes ♦ pron: **have you got** ~? você tem o suficiente? ♦ adv: **big** ~ suficientemente grande; ~! basta!, chega!; **that's** ~, **thanks** chega, obrigado; **I've had** ~ **of him** estou farto dele; **which**, **funnily** or **oddly** ~ ... o que, por estranho que pareça ...

enquire [ɪn'kwaɪə*] vt, vi = inquire

enrage [ɪn'reɪdʒ] vt enfurecer, enraivecer

enrich [ɪn'rɪtʃ] vt enriquecer

enrol [ɪn'rəul] (US **enroll**) vt inscrever; (SCH) matricular ♦ vi inscrever-se; matricular-se; ~**ment** n inscrição f; (SCH) matrícula

en route [ɔn-] adv no caminho

ensue [ɪn'sjuː] vi seguir-se

ensure [ɪn'ʃuə*] vt assegurar

entail [ɪn'teɪl] vt implicar

enter ['ɛntə*] vt entrar em; (club) ficar or fazer-se sócio de; (army) alistar-se em; (competition) inscrever-se em; (sb for a competition) inscrever; (write down) completar; (COMPUT) entrar com ♦ vi entrar; ~ **for** vt fus inscrever-se em;

~ **into** vt fus estabelecer; (plans) fazer parte de; (debate) entrar em; (agreement) chegar a, firmar

enterprise ['ɛntəpraɪz] n empresa; (undertaking) empreendimento; (initiative) iniciativa; **enterprising** adj empreendedor(a)

entertain [ɛntə'teɪn] vt divertir, entreter; (guest) receber (em casa); (idea) estudar; ~**er** n artista m/f; ~**ing** adj divertido; ~**ment** n (amusement) entretenimento, diversão f; (show) espetáculo

enthralled [ɪn'θrɔːld] adj encantado, cativado

enthusiasm [ɪn'θuːzɪæzəm] n entusiasmo

enthusiast [ɪn'θuːzɪæst] n entusiasta m/f; ~**ic** adj entusiasmado; **to be** ~**ic about** entusiasmar-se por

entice [ɪn'taɪs] vt atrair, tentar

entire [ɪn'taɪə*] adj inteiro; ~**ly** adv totalmente, completamente; ~**ty** n: **in its** ~**ty** na sua totalidade

entitle [ɪn'taɪtl] vt: **to** ~ **sb to sth** dar a alguém direito a algo; ~**d** adj (book etc) intitulado; **to be** ~**d to do** ter direito de fazer

entity ['ɛntɪtɪ] n ente m

entourage [ɔntuˈrɑːʒ] n séquito

entrails ['ɛntreɪlz] npl entranhas fpl

entrance [n 'ɛntrəns, vt ɪn'trɑːns] n entrada; (arrival) chegada ♦ vt encantar, fascinar; **to gain** ~ **to** (university etc) ser admitido em; ~ **examination** n exame m de admissão; ~ **fee** n jóia; ~ **ramp** (US) n (AUT) entrada (para a rodovia)

entrant ['ɛntrənt] n participante m/f; (BRIT: in exam) candidato/a

entreat [ɛn'triːt] vt: **to** ~ **sb to do** suplicar com alguém para fazer

entrenched [ɛn'trɛntʃd] adj (position) fortalecido; (idea) arraigado

entrepreneur [ɔntrəprəˈnəː*] n empresário/a

entrust [ɪn'trʌst] vt: **to** ~ **sth to sb** confiar algo a alguém

entry ['ɛntrɪ] n entrada; (in competition) participante m/f; (in register) registro, assentamento; (in account) lançamento; (in dictionary) verbete m; (arrival) chegada; **"no** ~**"** "entrada proibida"; (AUT) "contramão" (BR), "entrada proibida" (PT); ~ **form** n formulário de inscrição; ~ **phone** (BRIT) n interfone m (em apartamento)

envelop [ɪn'vɛləp] vt envolver

envelope ['ɛnvələup] n envelope m

envious ['ɛnvɪəs] adj invejoso; (look) de inveja

environment [ɪn'vaɪərənmənt] n meio ambiente m; ~**al** adj ambiental

envisage [ɪn'vɪzɪdʒ] vt prever

envoy ['ɛnvɔɪ] n enviado/a

envy ['ɛnvɪ] n inveja ♦ vt ter inveja de; **to** ~ **sb sth** invejar alguém por algo, cobiçar algo de alguém

epic ['ɛpɪk] *n* epopéia ♦ *adj* épico
epidemic [ɛpɪ'dɛmɪk] *n* epidemia
epilepsy ['ɛpɪlɛpsɪ] *n* epilepsia
episode ['ɛpɪsəud] *n* episódio
epistle [ɪ'pɪsl] *n* epístola
epitome [ɪ'pɪtəmɪ] *n* epítome *m*; **epitomize** *vt* epitomar, resumir
equable ['ɛkwəbl] *adj* (*climate*) uniforme; (*temper*, *reply*) equânime
equal ['iːkwl] *adj* igual; (*treatment*) equitativo, equivalente ♦ *n* igual *m/f* ♦ *vt* ser igual a; to be ~ to (*task*) estar à altura de; ~**ity** *n* igualdade *f*; ~**ize** *vi* igualar; (*SPORT*) empatar; ~**ly** *adv* igualmente; (*share etc*) por igual
equate [ɪ'kweɪt] *vt*: to ~ sth with equiparar algo com
equator [ɪ'kweɪtə*] *n* equador *m*
equilibrium [iːkwɪ'lɪbrɪəm] *n* equilíbrio
equip [ɪ'kwɪp] *vt* equipar; (*person*) prover, munir; to be well ~ped estar bem preparado *or* equipado; ~**ment** *n* equipamento; (*machines*) equipamentos *mpl*, aparelhagem *f*
equitable ['ɛkwɪtəbl] *adj* equitativo
equities ['ɛkwɪtɪz] (*BRIT*) *npl* (*COMM*) ações *fpl* ordinárias
equivalent [ɪ'kwɪvələnt] *adj*: ~ (to) equivalente (a) ♦ *n* equivalente *m*
equivocal [ɪ'kwɪvəkl] *adj* equívoco; (*open to suspicion*) ambíguo
era ['ɪərə] *n* era, época
eradicate [ɪ'rædɪkeɪt] *vt* erradicar, eliminar
erase [ɪ'reɪz] *vt* apagar; ~**r** *n* borracha (de apagar)
erect [ɪ'rɛkt] *adj* (*posture*) ereto; (*tail*, *ears*) levantado ♦ *vt* erigir, levantar; (*assemble*) montar; ~**ion** *n* construção *f*; (*of tent*, *PHYSIO*) ereção *f*; (*assembly*) montagem *f*
ERM *n abbr* (= *Exchange Rate Mechanism*) SME *m*
ermine ['əːmɪn] *n* arminho
erode [ɪ'rəud] *vt* (*GEO*) causar erosão em; (*confidence*) minar
erotic [ɪ'rɔtɪk] *adj* erótico
err [əː] *vi* errar, enganar-se
errand ['ɛrnd] *n* recado, mensagem *f*
erratic [ɪ'rætɪk] *adj* imprevisível
error ['ɛrə*] *n* erro
erupt [ɪ'rʌpt] *vi* entrar em erupção; (*fig*) explodir, estourar; ~**ion** *n* erupção *f*; explosão *f*
escalate ['ɛskəleɪt] *vi* intensificar-se
escalator ['ɛskəleɪtə*] *n* escada rolante
escapade [ɛskə'peɪd] *n* peripécia
escape [ɪ'skeɪp] *n* fuga; (*of gas*) escapatória ♦ *vi* escapar; (*flee*) fugir, evadir-se; (*leak*) vazar, escapar ♦ *vt* fugir de; (*elude*): his name ~s me o nome dele me foge a memória; to ~ from (*place*) escapar de; (*person*) escapulir de
escort [*n* 'ɛskɔːt, *vt* ɪ'skɔːt] *n* acompanhante *m/f*; (*MIL*) escolta ♦ *vt* acompa-

nhar
Eskimo ['ɛskɪməu] *n* esquimó *m/f*
especially [ɪ'spɛʃlɪ] *adv* (*above all*) sobretudo; (*particularly*) em particular
espionage ['ɛspɪənɑːʒ] *n* espionagem *f*
esplanade [ɛsplə'neɪd] *n* (*by sea*) avenida beira-mar, esplanada
Esquire [ɪ'skwaɪə*] *n* (*abbr Esq.*): J. Brown, ~ Sr. J. Brown
essay ['ɛseɪ] *n* ensaio
essence ['ɛsns] *n* essência
essential [ɪ'sɛnʃl] *adj* (*necessary*) indispensável; (*basic*) essencial ♦ *n* elemento essencial
establish [ɪ'stæblɪʃ] *vt* estabelecer; (*facts*) verificar; (*proof*) demonstrar; (*reputation*) firmar; ~**ed** *adj* consagrado; (*business*) estabelecido; ~**ment** *n* estabelecimento; the E~ment a classe dirigente
estate [ɪ'steɪt] *n* (*land*) fazenda (*BR*), propriedade *f* (*PT*); (*LAW*) herança; (*POL*) estado; (*BRIT*: *also*: **housing** ~) conjunto habitacional; ~ **agent** (*BRIT*) *n* corretor(a) *m/f* de imóveis (*BR*), agente *m/f* imobiliário/a (*PT*); ~ **car** (*BRIT*) *n* perua (*BR*), canadiana (*PT*)
esteem [ɪ'stiːm] *n*: to hold sb in high ~ estimar muito alguém
esthetic [ɪs'θɛtɪk] (*US*) *adj* = **aesthetic**
estimate [*n* 'ɛstɪmət, *vt*, *vi* 'ɛstɪmeɪt] *n* (*assessment*) avaliação *f*; (*calculation*) cálculo; (*COMM*) orçamento ♦ *vt* estimar, avaliar, calcular; **estimation** *n* opinião *f*; cálculo
estranged [ɪ'streɪndʒd] *adj* separado
etc. *abbr* (= *et cetera*) etc.
etching ['ɛtʃɪŋ] *n* água-forte *f*
eternal [ɪ'təːnl] *adj* eterno
eternity [ɪ'təːnɪtɪ] *n* eternidade *f*
ether ['iːθə*] *n* éter *m*
ethical ['ɛθɪkl] *adj* ético
ethics ['ɛθɪks] *n* ética ♦ *npl* moral *f*
Ethiopia [iːθɪ'əupɪə] *n* Etiópia
ethnic ['ɛθnɪk] *adj* étnico; (*culture*) folclórico
ethos ['iːθɔs] *n* sistema *m* de valores
etiquette ['ɛtɪkɛt] *n* etiqueta
euro ['juərəu] *n* (*currency*) euro
Eurocheque ['juərəutʃɛk] *n* eurocheque *m*
Europe ['juərəp] *n* Europa; ~**an** *adj*, *n* europeu/péia
evacuate [ɪ'vækjueɪt] *vt* evacuar
evade [ɪ'veɪd] *vt* (*person*) evitar; (*question*, *duties*) evadir; (*tax*) sonegar
evaluate [ɪ'væljueɪt] *vt* avaliar
evaporate [ɪ'væpəreɪt] *vi* evaporar-se
evasion [ɪ'veɪʒən] *n* fuga; (*of tax*) sonegação *f*; **evasive** *adj* evasivo
eve [iːv] *n*: on the ~ of na véspera de
even ['iːvn] *adj* (*level*) plano; (*smooth*) liso; (*equal*) igual; (*number*) par ♦ *adv* até, mesmo; (*showing surprise*) até (mesmo); (*introducing a comparison*) ainda; ~ if mesmo que; ~ though mesmo

que, embora; ~ **more** ainda mais; ~ **so** mesmo assim; **not** ~ nem; **to get** ~ **with sb** ficar quite com alguém; ~ **out** *vi* nivelar-se

evening ['i:vnɪŋ] *n* (*early*) tarde *f*; (*late*) noite *f*; (*event*) noitada; **in the** ~ à noite; ~ **class** *n* aula noturna; ~ **dress** *n* (*man's*) traje *m* de rigor (*BR*) *or* de cerimónia (*PT*); (*woman's*) vestido de noite

event [ɪ'vent] *n* acontecimento *m*; (*SPORT*) prova; **in the** ~ **of** no caso de; ~**ful** *adj* movimentado, cheio de acontecimentos; (*game etc*) cheio de emoção, agitado

eventual [ɪ'vɛntʃuəl] *adj* final; ~**ly** *adv* finalmente; (*in time*) por fim

ever ['ɛvə*] *adv* (*always*) sempre; (*at any time*) em qualquer momento; (*in question*): **why** ~ **not?** por que não?; **the best** ~ o melhor que já se viu; **have you** ~ **seen it?** você alguma vez já viu isto?; **better than** ~ melhor que nunca; ~ **since ♦** *adv* desde então **♦** *conj* depois que; ~**green** *n* sempre-verde *f*; ~**lasting** *adj* eterno, perpétuo

KEYWORD

every ['ɛvrɪ] *adj* **1** (*each*) cada; ~ **one of** them cada um deles; ~ **shop in the town was closed** todas as lojas da cidade estavam fechadas
2 (*all possible*) todo/a; **I have** ~ **confidence in her** tenho absoluta confiança nela; **we wish you** ~ **success** desejamo-lhe o maior sucesso; **he's** ~ **bit as clever as his brother** ele é tão inteligente quanto o irmão
3 (*showing recurrence*) todo/a; ~ **other car had been broken into** cada dois carros foram arrombados; **she visits me** ~ **other/third day** ele me visita cada dois/três dias; ~ **now and then** de vez em quando

everybody ['ɛvrɪbɔdɪ] *pron* todos, todo mundo (*BR*), toda a gente (*PT*)
everyday ['ɛvrɪdeɪ] *adj* (*daily*) diário; (*usual*) corrente; (*common*) comum
everyone ['ɛvrɪwʌn] *pron* = **everybody**
everything ['ɛvrɪθɪŋ] *pron* tudo
everywhere ['ɛvrɪwɛə*] *adv* (*be*) em todo lugar (*BR*), em toda a parte (*PT*); (*go*) a todo lugar (*BR*), a toda a parte (*PT*); (*wherever*): ~ **you go you meet ...** aonde quer que se vá, encontra-se ...
evict [ɪ'vɪkt] *vt* despejar
evidence ['ɛvɪdəns] *n* (*proof*) depoimento; (*indication*) sinal *m*; **to give** ~ testemunhar, prestar depoimento
evident ['ɛvɪdənt] *adj* evidente; ~**ly** *adv* evidentemente; (*apparently*) aparentemente
evil ['i:vl] *adj* mau/má **♦** *n* mal *m*, maldade *f*
evoke [ɪ'vəuk] *vt* evocar
evolution [i:və'lu:ʃən] *n* evolução *f*; (*de-*

velopment) desenvolvimento
evolve [ɪ'vɔlv] *vt* desenvolver **♦** *vi* desenvolver-se
ewe [ju:] *n* ovelha
ex- [ɛks] *prefix* ex-
exacerbate [ɛks'æsəbeɪt] *vt* agravar
exact [ɪg'zækt] *adj* exato; (*person*) meticuloso **♦** *vt*: **to** ~ **sth (from)** exigir algo (de); ~**ing** *adj* exigente; (*conditions*) difícil; ~**ly** *adv* exatamente; (*indicating agreement*) isso mesmo
exaggerate [ɪg'zædʒəreɪt] *vt, vi* exagerar; **exaggeration** *n* exagero
exam [ɪg'zæm] *n abbr* = **examination**
examination [ɪgzæmɪ'neɪʃən] *n* exame *m*; (*inquiry*) investigação *f*
examine [ɪg'zæmɪn] *vt* examinar; (*inspect*) inspecionar; ~**r** *n* examinador(a) *m/f*
example [ɪg'zɑ:mpl] *n* exemplo; **for** ~ por exemplo
exasperate [ɪg'zɑ:spəreɪt] *vt* exasperar, irritar; **exasperating** *adj* irritante
excavate ['ɛkskəveɪt] *vt* escavar
exceed [ɪk'si:d] *vt* exceder; (*number*) ser superior a; (*speed limit*) ultrapassar; (*limits*) ir além de; (*powers*) exceder-se em; (*hopes*) superar; ~**ingly** *adv* extremamente
excel [ɪk'sɛl] *vi*: **to** ~ **in** sobressair em, distinguir-se em
excellent ['ɛksələnt] *adj* excelente
except [ɪk'sɛpt] *prep* (*also*: ~ **for**, ~**ing**) exceto, a não ser **♦** *vt* excluir; ~ **if**/ **when** a menos que, a não ser que; ~**ion** *n* exceção *f*; **to take** ~**ion to** ressentir-se de
excerpt ['ɛksə:pt] *n* trecho
excess [ɪk'sɛs] *n* excesso; ~ **baggage** *n* excesso de bagagem; ~ **fare** (*BRIT*) *n* (*RAIL*) sobretaxa de excesso; ~**ive** *adj* excessivo
exchange [ɪks'tʃeɪndʒ] *n* troca; (*of teachers, students*) intercâmbio; (*also*: **telephone** ~) estação *f* telefónica (*BR*), central *f* telefónica (*PT*) **♦** *vt*: **to** ~ **(for)** trocar (por); ~ **rate** *n* (taxa de) câmbio
Exchequer [ɪks'tʃɛkə*] (*BRIT*) *n*: **the** ~ ≈ o Tesouro Nacional
excise ['ɛksaɪz] *n* imposto de consumo
excite [ɪk'saɪt] *vt* excitar; **to get** ~**d** entusiasmar-se; ~**ment** *n* emoções *fpl*; (*agitation*) agitação *f*; **exciting** *adj* emocionante, empolgante
exclaim [ɪk'skleɪm] *vi* exclamar; **exclamation** *n* exclamação *f*; **exclamation mark** *n* ponto de exclamação (*BR*) *or* de admiração (*PT*)
exclude [ɪk'sklu:d] *vt* excluir
exclusive [ɪk'sklu:sɪv] *adj* exclusivo; ~ **of tax** sem incluir os impostos
excommunicate [ɛkskə'mju:nɪkeɪt] *vt* excomungar
excruciating [ɪk'skru:ʃɪeɪtɪŋ] *adj* doloroso, martirizante

excursion [ɪk'skəːʃən] n excursão f
excuse [n ɪk'skjuːs, vt ɪk'skjuːz] n desculpa ♦ vt desculpar, perdoar; **to ~ sb from doing sth** dispensar alguém de fazer algo; **~ me!** desculpe!; **if you will ~ me ...** com a sua licença ...
ex-directory (BRIT) adj: ~ **(phone) number** número que não figura na lista telefônica
execute ['ɛksɪkjuːt] vt (plan) realizar; (order) cumprir; (person, movement) executar; **execution** n realização f; (killing) execução f; **executioner** n verdugo, carrasco
executive [ɪg'zɛkjutɪv] adj, n executivo/a
executor [ɪg'zɛkjutə*] n executor(a) m/f testamentário/a, testamenteiro/a
exempt [ɪg'zɛmpt] adj isento ♦ vt: **to ~ sb from** dispensar or isentar alguém de; **~ion** n (from taxes) isenção f; (from duty) dispensa
exercise ['ɛksəsaɪz] n exercício ♦ vt exercer; (right) valer-se de; (dog) levar para passear; (mind) ocupar ♦ vi (also: **to take ~**) fazer exercício; **~ bike** n bicicleta do exercício; **~ book** n caderno
exert [ɪg'zəːt] vt exercer; **to ~ o.s.** esforçar-se, empenhar-se; **~ion** n esforço
exhale [ɛks'heɪl] vt expirar; (air) exalar; (smoke) emitir ♦ vi expirar
exhaust [ɪg'zɔːst] n (AUTO: also: ~ **pipe**) escape m, exaustor m; (fumes) escapamento (de gás) ♦ vt esgotar; **~ion** n exaustão f
exhibit [ɪg'zɪbɪt] n (ART) obra exposta; (LAW) objeto exposto ♦ vt (courage) manifestar, mostrar; (quality, emotion) demonstrar; (paintings) expor; **~ion** n exposição f; (of talent etc) mostra f
exhilarating [ɪg'zɪləreɪtɪŋ] adj estimulante, tônico
exile ['ɛksaɪl] n exílio; (person) exilado/a ♦ vt desterrar, exilar
exist [ɪg'zɪst] vi existir; (live) viver; **~ence** n existência; vida; **~ing** adj atual
exit ['ɛksɪt] n saída ♦ vi (COMPUT, THEATRE) sair; ~ **ramp** (US) n (AUT) saída da rodovia
exodus ['ɛksədəs] n êxodo
exonerate [ɪg'zɔnəreɪt] vt: **to ~ from** desobrigar de; (guilt) isentar de
exotic [ɪg'zɔtɪk] adj exótico
expand [ɪk'spænd] vt aumentar ♦ vi aumentar; (gas etc) expandir-se; (metal) dilatar-se
expanse [ɪk'spæns] n extensão f
expansion [ɪk'spænʃən] n (of town) desenvolvimento; (of trade) expansão f; (of population) aumento
expect [ɪk'spɛkt] vt esperar; (suppose) supor; (require) exigir ♦ vi: **to be ~ing** estar grávida; **~ancy** n expectativa; **life ~ancy** expectativa de vida; **~ant**

mother n gestante f; **~ation** n esperança; (belief) expectativa
expedience [ɛk'spiːdɪəns] n = **expediency**
expediency [ɛk'spiːdɪənsɪ] n conveniência
expedient [ɛk'spiːdɪənt] adj conveniente, oportuno ♦ n expediente m, recurso
expedition [ɛkspə'dɪʃən] n expedição f
expel [ɪk'spɛl] vt expelir; (from place, school) expulsar
expend [ɪk'spɛnd] vt gastar; **~able** adj prescindível; **~iture** n gastos mpl; (of energy) consumo
expense [ɪk'spɛns] n gasto, despesa; (expenditure) despesas fpl; **~s** npl (costs) despesas fpl; **at the ~ of** à custa de; **~ account** n relatório de despesas
expensive [ɪk'spɛnsɪv] adj caro
experience [ɪk'spɪərɪəns] n experiência ♦ vt (situation) enfrentar; (feeling) sentir; **~d** adj experiente
experiment [ɪk'spɛrɪmənt] n experimento, experiência ♦ vi: **to ~ (with/on)** fazer experiências (com/em)
expert ['ɛkspəːt] adj hábil, perito ♦ n especialista m/f; **~ise** n perícia
expire [ɪk'spaɪə*] vi expirar; (run out) vencer; **expiry** n expiração f, vencimento
explain [ɪk'spleɪn] vt explicar; (clarify) esclarecer; **explanatory** adj explicativo
explicit [ɪk'splɪsɪt] adj explícito
explode [ɪk'spləud] vi estourar, explodir
exploit [n 'ɛksplɔɪt, vt ɪk'splɔɪt] n façanha ♦ vt explorar; **~ation** n exploração f
explore [ɪk'splɔː*] vt explorar; (fig) examinar, pesquisar; **~r** n explorador(a) m/f
explosion [ɪk'spləuʒən] n explosão f
explosive [ɪk'spləusɪv] adj explosivo ♦ n explosivo
exponent [ɪk'spəunənt] n (of theory etc) representante m/f, defensor(a) m/f; (of skill) expoente m/f
export [vt ɛk'spɔːt, n, cpd 'ɛkspɔːt] vt exportar ♦ n exportação f ♦ cpd de exportação; **~er** n exportador(a) m/f
expose [ɪk'spəuz] vt expor; (unmask) desmascarar; **~d** adj (house etc) desabrigado
exposure [ɪk'spəuʒə*] n exposição f; (publicity) publicidade f; (PHOT) revelação f; **to die from ~** (MED) morrer de frio; **~ meter** n fotômetro
expound [ɪk'spaund] vt expor, explicar
express [ɪk'sprɛs] adj expresso, explícito; (BRIT: letter etc) urgente ♦ n rápido ♦ vt exprimir, expressar; (quantity) representar; **~ion** n expressão f; **~ly** adv expressamente; **~way** (US) n rodovia (BR), auto-estrada (PT)
expulsion [ɪk'spʌlʃən] n expulsão f; (of gas, liquid) emissão f
expurgate ['ɛkspəgeɪt] vt expurgar

exquisite [ɛk'skwızıt] adj requintado

extend [ık'stɛnd] vt (visit, street) prolongar; (building) aumentar; (offer) fazer; (hand) estender

extension [ık'stɛnʃən] n (ELEC) extensão f; (building) acréscimo, expansão f; (of time) prorrogação f; (of rights) ampliação f; (TEL) ramal m (BR), extensão f (PT); (of deadline) prolongamento, prorrogação f

extensive [ık'stɛnsıv] adj extenso; (damage) considerável; (coverage) amplo; (broad) vasto, amplo; ~ly adv: he's travelled ~ly ele já viajou bastante

extent [ık'stɛnt] n (breadth) extensão f; (of damage etc) dimensão f; (scope) alcance m; to some ~ até certo ponto

extenuating [ık'tɛnjueıtıŋ] adj: ~ circumstances circunstâncias fpl atenuantes

exterior [ɛk'stıərıə*] adj externo ♦ n exterior m; (appearance) aspecto

external [ɛk'stə:nl] adj externo

extinct [ık'stıŋkt] adj extinto

extinguish [ık'stıŋgwıʃ] vt extinguir; ~er n (also: fire ~er) extintor m

extort [ık'stɔ:t] vt extorquir; ~ionate adj extorsivo, excessivo

extra ['ɛkstrə] adj adicional ♦ adv adicionalmente ♦ n (luxury) luxo; (surcharge) extra m, suplemento; (CINEMA, THEATRE) figurante m/f

extra [ɛkstrə] prefix extra...

extract [vt ık'stræk, n 'ɛkstrækt] vt tirar, extrair; (tooth) arrancar; (mineral) extrair; (money) extorquir; (promise) conseguir, obter ♦ n extrato

extradite ['ɛkstrədaıt] vt (from country) extraditar; (to country) obter a extradição de

extramarital [ɛkstrə'mærıtl] adj extramatrimonial

extramural [ɛkstrə'mjuərl] adj de extensão universitária

extraordinary [ık'strɔ:dnrı] adj extraordinário; (odd) estranho

extravagance [ık'strævəgəns] n extravagância; (no pl: spending) esbanjamento

extravagant [ık'strævəgənt] adj (lavish) extravagante; (wasteful) gastador(a), esbanjador(a)

extreme [ık'stri:m] adj extremo ♦ n extremo; ~ly adv muito, extremamente

extricate ['ɛkstrıkeıt] vt: to ~ sb/sth (from) (trap) libertar alguém/algo de; (situation) livrar alguém/algo de

extrovert ['ɛkstrəvə:t] n extrovertido/a

exude [ıg'zju:d] vt exsudar; (confidence) esbanjar

eye [aı] n olho; (of needle) buraco ♦ vt olhar, observar; to keep an ~ on vigiar, ficar de olho em; ~ball n globo ocular; ~bath n (BRIT) n copinho (para lavar o olho); ~brow n sobrancelha; ~brow pencil n lápis m de sobrance-

lha; ~drops npl gotas fpl para os olhos; ~lash n cílio; ~lid n pálpebra; ~liner n delineador m; ~opener n revelação f, grande surpresa; ~shadow n sombra de olhos; ~sight n vista, visão f; ~sore n monstruosidade f; ~ witness n testemunha m/f ocular

F

F [ɛf] n (MUS) fá m ♦ abbr = Fahrenheit

fable ['feıbl] n fábula

fabric ['fæbrık] n tecido, pano

fabrication [fæbrı'keıʃən] n invencionice f

façade [fə'sɑ:d] n fachada

face [feıs] n cara, rosto; (grimace) careta; (of clock) mostrador m; (side) superfície f; (of building) frente f, fachada ♦ vt (facts) enfrentar; (direction) dar para; ~ down de bruços; (card) virado para baixo; to lose ~ perder o prestígio; to save ~ salvar as aparências; to make or pull a ~ fazer careta; in the ~ of diante de, à vista de; on the ~ of it a julgar pelas aparências, à primeira vista; ~ up to vt fus enfrentar; ~ cloth (BRIT) n toalhinha de rosto; ~ cream n creme m facial; ~ lift n (operação f) plástica; (of façade) remodelamento; ~ powder n pó m de arroz; ~-saving adj para salvar as aparências

facetious [fə'si:ʃəs] adj jocoso

face value n (of coin, stamp) valor m nominal; to take sth at ~ (fig) tomar algo em sentido literal

facile ['fæsaıl] adj superficial

facilities [fə'sılıtız] npl facilidades fpl, instalações fpl; credit ~ crediário

facing ['feısıŋ] prep de frente para

facsimile [fæk'sımılı] n fac-símile m

fact [fækt] n fato; in ~ realmente, na verdade

factor ['fæktə*] n fator m

factory ['fæktərı] n fábrica

factual ['fæktjuəl] adj real, fatual

faculty ['fækəltı] n faculdade f; (US) corpo docente

fad [fæd] (inf) n mania, modismo

fade [feıd] vi desbotar; (sound, hope) desvanecer-se; (light) apagar-se; (flower) murchar

fag [fæg] (BRIT: inf) n cigarro

fail [feıl] vt (candidate) reprovar; (exam) não passar em, ser reprovado em; (subj: leader) fracassar; (: courage): his courage ~ed him faltou-lhe coragem; (: memory) falhar ♦ vi fracassar; (brakes) falhar; (health) deteriorar; (light) desaparecer; to ~ to do sth deixar de fazer algo; (be unable) não conseguir fazer algo; without ~ sem falta; ~ing n defeito ♦ prep na or à falta de; ~ing that senão; ~ure n fracasso; (mechanical) falha

faint [feɪnt] *adj* fraco; (*recollection*) vago; (*mark*) indistinto; (*smell*) leve ♦ *n* desmaio ♦ *vi* desmaiar; **to feel ~** sentir tonteira

fair [fɛə*] *adj* justo; (*hair*) louro; (*complexion*) branco; (*weather*) bom; (*good enough*) razoável; (*sizeable*) considerável ♦ *adv*: **to play ~** fazer jogo limpo ♦ *n* (*also*: **trade ~**) feira; (*BRIT*: *funfair*) parque *m* de diversões; **~ly** *adv* (*justly*) com justiça; (*quite*) bastante; **~ness** *n* justiça; (*impartiality*) imparcialidade *f*; **~ play** *n* jogo limpo

fairy [ˈfɛərɪ] *n* fada

faith [feɪθ] *n* fé *f*; (*trust*) confiança; (*denomination*) seita; **~ful** *adj* fiel; (*account*) exato; **~fully** *adv* fielmente; **yours ~fully** (*BRIT*: *in letters*) atenciosamente

fake [feɪk] *n* (*painting etc*) falsificação *f*; (*person*) impostor/a *m/f* ♦ *adj* falso ♦ *vt* fingir; (*painting etc*) falsificar

falcon [ˈfɔːlkən] *n* falcão *m*

fall [fɔːl] (*pt* fell, *pp* fallen) *n* queda; (*US*: *autumn*) outono ♦ *vi* cair; (*price*) baixar; (*country*) render-se; **~s** *npl* (*waterfall*) cascata, queda d'água; **to ~ flat** cair de cara no chão; (*plan*) falhar; (*joke*) não agradar; **~ back** *vi* retroceder; **~ back on** *vt fus* recorrer a; **~ behind** *vi* ficar para trás; **~ down** *vi* (*person*) cair; (*building*) desabar; **~ for** *vt fus* (*trick*) cair em; (*person*) enamorar-se de; **~ in** *vi* ruir; (*MIL*) alinhar-se; **~ off** *vi* cair; (*diminish*) declinar, diminuir; **~ out** *vi* cair; (*friends etc*) brigar; **~ through** *vi* furar

fallacy [ˈfæləsɪ] *n* erro; (*misconception*) falácia

fallen [ˈfɔːlən] *pp of* **fall**

fallout [ˈfɔːlaut] *n* chuva radioativa

fallow [ˈfæləu] *adj* alqueivado, de pousio

false [fɔːls] *adj* falso; **under ~ pretences** por meios fraudulentos; **~ teeth** (*BRIT*) *npl* dentadura postiça

falter [ˈfɔːltə*] *vi* (*engine*) falhar; (*person*) vacilar

fame [feɪm] *n* fama

familiar [fəˈmɪlɪə*] *adj* (*well-known*) conhecido; (*tone*) familiar, íntimo; **to be ~ with** (*subject*) estar familiarizado com; **~ize** *vt* to **~ize o.s. with** familiarizar-se com

family [ˈfæmɪlɪ] *n* família

famine [ˈfæmɪn] *n* fome *f*

famished [ˈfæmɪʃt] *adj* faminto

famous [ˈfeɪməs] *adj* famoso, célebre; **~ly** *adv* (*get on*) maravilhosamente

fan [fæn] *n* (*hand-held*) leque *m*; (*ELEC*) ventilador *m*; (*person*) fã *m/f* (*BR*), fan *m/f* (*PT*) ♦ *vt* abanar; (*fire, quarrel*) atiçar; **~ out** *vi* espalhar-se

fanatic [fəˈnætɪk] *n* fanático/a

fan belt *n* correia do ventilador (*BR*) or da ventoinha (*PT*)

fanciful [ˈfænsɪful] *adj* (*notion*) irreal; (*design*) extravagante

fancy [ˈfænsɪ] *n* capricho; (*imagination*) imaginação *f*; (*fantasy*) fantasia ♦ *adj* ornamental; (*clothes*) extravagante; (*food*) elaborado; (*luxury*) luxoso ♦ *vt* desejar, querer; (*imagine*) imaginar; (*think*) acreditar, achar; **to take a ~ to** tomar gosto por; **he fancies her** (*inf*) ele está a fim dela; **~ dress** *n* fantasia

fang [fæŋ] *n* presa

fantastic [fænˈtæstɪk] *adj* fantástico

fantasy [ˈfæntəsɪ] *n* (*dream*) sonho; (*unreality*) fantasia; (*imagination*) imaginação *f*

far [fɑː*] *adj* (*distant*) distante ♦ *adv* muito; (*also*: **~ away**, **~ off**) longe; **at the ~ side/end** do lado mais afastado/do extremo mais afastado; **~ better** muito melhor; **~ from** longe de; **by ~** de longe; **go as ~ as the farm** vá até a (*BR*) or à (*PT*) fazenda; **as ~ as I know** que eu saiba; **how ~?** até onde?; (*fig*) até que ponto?; **~away** *adj* remoto, distante

farce [fɑːs] *n* farsa; **farcical** *adj* ridículo

fare [fɛə*] *n* (*on trains, buses*) preço (da passagem); (*in taxi*: *cost*) tarifa; (*food*) comida; **half/full ~** meia/inteira passagem

Far East *n*: **the ~** o Extremo Oriente

farewell [fɛəˈwɛl] *excl* adeus ♦ *n* despedida

farm [fɑːm] *n* fazenda (*BR*), quinta (*PT*) ♦ *vt* cultivar; **~er** *n* fazendeiro/a, agricultor *m*; **~hand** *n* lavrador(a) *m/f*, trabalhador(a) *m/f* rural; **~house** *n* casa da fazenda (*BR*) or da quinta (*PT*); **~ing** *n* agricultura; (*tilling*) cultura; (*of animals*) criação *f*; **~land** *n* terra de cultivo; **~ worker** *n* = **~hand**; **~yard** *n* curral *m*

far-reaching [-ˈriːtʃɪŋ] *adj* de grande alcance, abrangente

fart [fɑːt] (*inf!*) *vi* soltar um peido (*!*), peidar (*!*)

farther [ˈfɑːðə*] *adv* mais longe ♦ *adj* mais distante, mais afastado

farthest [ˈfɑːðɪst] *superl of* **far**

fascinate [ˈfæsɪneɪt] *vt* fascinar; **fascination** *n* fascinação *f*, fascínio

fascism [ˈfæʃɪzəm] *n* fascismo

fashion [ˈfæʃən] *n* moda; (~ *industry*) indústria da moda; (*manner*) maneira ♦ *vt* modelar, dar feitio a; **in ~** na moda; **~able** *adj* da moda, elegante; **~ show** *n* desfile *m* de moda

fast [fɑːst] *adj* rápido; (*dye, colour*) firme, permanente; (*clock*): **to be ~** estar adiantado ♦ *adv* rápido, rapidamente, depressa; (*stuck, held*) firmemente ♦ *n* jejum *m* ♦ *vi* jejuar; **~ asleep** dormindo profundamente

fasten [ˈfɑːsn] *vt* fixar, prender; (*coat*) fechar; (*belt*) apertar ♦ *vi* prender-se, fixar-se; **~er** n presilha, fecho; **~ing** n = **~er**

fast food n fast food f

fastidious [fæsˈtɪdɪəs] adj meticuloso

fat [fæt] adj gordo; (book) grosso; (wallet) recheado; (profit) grande ♦ n gordura; (lard) banha, gordura

fatal [ˈfeɪtl] adj fatal; (injury) mortal; **~ity** n (death) vítima m/f; **~ly** adv fatalmente; (injured) mortalmente

fate [feɪt] n destino; (of person) sorte f; **~ful** adj fatídico

father [ˈfɑːðə*] n pai m; **~-in-law** n sogro; **~ly** adj paternal

fathom [ˈfæðəm] n braça ♦ vt compreender

fatigue [fəˈtiːg] n fadiga, cansaço

fatten [ˈfætn] vt, vi engordar

fatty [ˈfætɪ] adj (food) gorduroso ♦ n (inf) gorducho/a

fatuous [ˈfætjuəs] adj fátuo

faucet [ˈfɔːsɪt] (US) n torneira

fault [fɔːlt] n (blame) culpa; (defect) defeito; (GEO) falha; (TENNIS) falta, bola fora ♦ vt criticar; **to find ~ with** criticar, queixar-se de; **at ~** culpado; **~y** adj defeituoso

fauna [ˈfɔːnə] n fauna

faux pas [ˈfəuˈpɑː] n inv gafe f

favour [ˈfeɪvə*] (US **favor**) n favor m ♦ vt favorecer; (assist) auxiliar; **to do sb a ~** fazer favor a alguém; **to find ~ with** cair nas boas graças de; **in ~ of** em favor de; **~ite** adj predileto ♦ n favorito/a

fawn [fɔːn] n cervo novo, cervato ♦ adj (also: **~-coloured**) castanho-claro inv ♦ vi: **to ~ (up)on** bajular

fax [fæks] n fax m, fac-símile m ♦ vt enviar por fax or fac-símile

FBI n abbr (= Federal Bureau of Investigation) FBI m

fear [fɪə*] n medo ♦ vt ter medo de, temer; **for ~ of** com medo de; **~ful** adj medonho, temível; (cowardly) medroso; (awful) terrível

feasible [ˈfiːzəbl] adj viável

feast [fiːst] n banquete m; (REL: also: **~ day**) festa ♦ vi banquetear-se

feat [fiːt] n façanha, feito

feather [ˈfeðə*] n pena, pluma

feature [ˈfiːtʃə*] n característica; (article) reportagem f ♦ vt (subj: film) apresentar ♦ vi: **to ~ in** figurar em; **~s** npl (of face) feições fpl; **~ film** n longa-metragem m

February [ˈfebruərɪ] n fevereiro

fed [fed] pt, pp of **feed**

federal [ˈfedərəl] adj federal

fed up adj: **to be ~** estar (de saco) cheio (BR), estar farto (PT)

fee [fiː] n taxa (BR), propina (PT); (of school) matrícula; (of doctor, lawyer) honorários mpl

feeble [ˈfiːbl] adj fraco; (attempt) ineficaz

feed [fiːd] (pt, pp **fed**) n (of baby) alimento infantil; (of animal) ração f; (on printer) mecanismo alimentador ♦ vt alimentar; (baby) amamentar; (animal) dar de comer a; (data): **to ~ into** introduzir em; **~ on** vt fus alimentar-se de; **~back** n reação f; **~ing bottle** (BRIT) n mamadeira

feel [fiːl] (pt, pp **felt**) n sensação f; (sense) tato; (impression) impressão f ♦ vt tocar, apalpar; (anger, pain etc) sentir; (think) achar, acreditar; **to ~ hungry/cold** estar com fome/frio (BR), ter fome/frio (PT); **to ~ lonely/better** sentir-se só/melhor; **I don't ~ well** não estou me sentindo bem; **it ~s soft** é macio ao toque; **to ~ like** querer; **to ~ about** or **around** tatear; **~er** n (of insect) antena; **to put out ~ers** or **a ~er** (fig) sondar opiniões, lançar um balão-de-ensaio; **~ing** n sensação f; (emotion) sentimento; (impression) impressão f

feet [fiːt] npl of **foot**

feign [feɪn] vt fingir

fell [fel] pt of **fall** ♦ vt (tree) lançar por terra, derrubar

fellow [ˈfeləu] n camarada m/f; (inf: man) cara m (BR), tipo (PT); (of learned society) membro ♦ cpd: **~ students** colegas m/fpl de curso; **~ citizen** n concidadão/dã m/f; **~ countryman** (irreg) n compatriota m; **~ men** npl semelhantes mpl; **~ship** n amizade f; (grant) bolsa de estudo; (society) associação f

felony [ˈfelənɪ] n crime m

felt [felt] pt, pp of **feel** ♦ n feltro; **~-tip pen** n caneta pilot ® (BR) or de feltro (PT)

female [ˈfiːmeɪl] n (ZOOL) fêmea; (pej: woman) mulher f ♦ adj fêmeo/a; (sex, character) feminino; (vote) das mulheres; (child) do sexo feminino

feminine [ˈfemɪnɪn] adj feminino

feminist [ˈfemɪnɪst] n feminista m/f

fence [fens] n cerca ♦ vt (also: **~ in**) cercar ♦ vi esgrimir; **fencing** n (sport) esgrima

fend [fend] vi: **to ~ for o.s.** defender-se, virar-se; **~ off** vt defender-se de

fender [ˈfendə*] n (of fireplace) guardafogo m; (on boat) defesa de embarcação; (US: AUT) pára-lama m

ferment [vi fəˈment, n ˈfɔːment] vi fermentar ♦ n (fig) agitação f

fern [fɜːn] n samambaia (BR), feto (PT)

ferocious [fəˈrəuʃəs] adj feroz

ferret [ˈferɪt] n furão m; **~ out** vt (information) desenterrar, descobrir

ferry [ˈferɪ] n (small) barco (de travessia); (large: also: **~boat**) balsa ♦ vt transportar

fertile [ˈfɜːtaɪl] adj fértil; (BIO) fecundo; **fertilizer** n adubo, fertilizante m

fervent [ˈfɜːvənt] adj ardente

fester [ˈfestə*] vi inflamar-se

festival ['fɛstɪvəl] n (REL) festa; (ART, MUS) festival m

festive ['fɛstɪv] adj festivo; **the ~ season** (BRIT: Christmas) a época do Natal

festivities [fɛsˈtɪvɪtɪz] npl festas fpl, festividades fpl

festoon [fɛsˈtuːn] vt: **to ~ with** engrinaldar de or com

fetch [fɛtʃ] vt ir buscar, trazer; (sell for) alcançar

fetching ['fɛtʃɪŋ] adj atraente

fête [feɪt] n festa

fetish ['fɛtɪʃ] n fetiche m

fetus ['fiːtəs] (US) n = **foetus**

feud [fjuːd] n disputa, rixa

fever ['fiːvə*] n febre f; ~**ish** adj febril

few [fjuː] adj, pron poucos/as; **a ~** ... alguns/algumas ...; ~**er** adj menos; ~**est** adj o menor número de

fiancé(e) [fɪˈãːŋseɪ] n noivo/a

fib [fɪb] n lorota

fibre ['faɪbə*] (US **fiber**) n fibra; ~-**glass** n fibra de vidro

fickle ['fɪkl] adj inconstante; (weather) instável

fiction ['fɪkʃən] n ficção f; ~**al** adj de ficção; **fictitious** adj fictício

fiddle ['fɪdl] n (MUS) violino; (swindle) trapaça ♦ vt (BRIT: accounts) falsificar; ~ **with** vt fus brincar com

fidget ['fɪdʒɪt] vi estar irrequieto, mexer-se

field [fiːld] n campo; (fig) área, esfera, especialidade f; ~ **marshal** n marechal-de-campo; ~**work** n trabalho de campo

fiend [fiːnd] n demônio; ~**ish** adj diabólico

fierce [fɪəs] adj feroz; (wind) violento; (heat) intenso

fiery ['faɪərɪ] adj ardente; (temperament) fogoso

fifteen [fɪfˈtiːn] num quinze

fifth [fɪfθ] num quinto

fifty ['fɪftɪ] num cinqüenta; ~-~ adv: **to share** or **go** ~-~ **with sb** dividir meio a meio com alguém, rachar com alguém ♦ adj: **to have a** ~-~ **chance** ter 50% de chance

fig [fɪg] n figo

fight [faɪt] (pt, pp **fought**) n briga; (MIL) combate m; (struggle: against illness etc) luta ♦ vt lutar contra; (cancer, alcoholism) combater; (election) competir ♦ vi lutar, brigar, bater-se; ~**er** n combatente m/f; (plane) caça m; ~**ing** n batalha; (brawl) briga

figment ['fɪgmənt] n: **a ~ of the imagination** um produto da imaginação

figurative ['fɪgjurətɪv] adj (expression) figurado; (style) figurativo

figure ['fɪgə*] n (DRAWING, MATH) figura, desenho; (number) número, cifra; (outline) forma; (person) personagem m ♦ vt (esp US) imaginar ♦ vi figurar; ~ **out** vt compreender; ~**head** n (NAUT) carranca

de proa; (pej: leader) chefe m nominal; ~ **of speech** n figura de linguagem

filch [fɪltʃ] (inf) vt surripiar, afanar

file [faɪl] n (tool) lixa; (dossier) dossiê m, pasta; (folder) pasta; (COMPUT) arquivo; (row) fila, coluna ♦ vt (wood, nails) lixar; (papers) arquivar; (LAW: claim) apresentar, dar entrada em ♦ vi: **to ~ in/out** entrar/sair em fila

filing cabinet n fichário, arquivo

fill [fɪl] vt: **to ~ with** encher com; (vacancy) preencher; (need) satisfazer ♦ n: **to eat one's ~** encher-se or fartar-se de comer; ~ **in** vt (form) preencher; (hole) tapar; (time) encher; ~ **up** vt encher ♦ vi (AUT) abastecer o carro

fillet ['fɪlɪt] n filete m, filé m; ~ **steak** n filé m

filling ['fɪlɪŋ] n (CULIN) recheio; (for tooth) obturação f (BR), chumbo (PT); ~ **station** n posto de gasolina

film [fɪlm] n filme m; (of liquid) camada, veu m ♦ vt rodar, filmar ♦ vi filmar; ~ **star** n astro/estrela do cinema; ~ **strip** n diafilme m

filter ['fɪltə*] n filtro ♦ vt filtrar; ~ **lane** (BRIT) n (AUT) pista para se dobrar à esquerda (or à direita); ~-**tipped** adj filtrado

filth [fɪlθ] n sujeira (BR), sujidade f (PT); ~**y** adj sujo; (language) indecente, obsceno

fin [fɪn] n barbatana

final ['faɪnl] adj final, último; (ultimate) maior; (definitive) definitivo ♦ n (SPORT) final f; ~**s** npl (SCH) exames mpl finais; ~**e** n final m; ~**ize** vt concluir, completar; ~**ly** adv finalmente, por fim

finance [faɪˈnæns] n fundos mpl; (money management) finanças fpl ♦ vt financiar; ~**s** npl (personal ~s) finanças; **financial** adj financeiro; **financier** n financiador(a) m/f

find [faɪnd] (pt, pp **found**) vt encontrar, achar; (discover) descobrir ♦ n achado, descoberta; **to ~ sb guilty** (LAW) declarar alguém culpado; ~ **out** vt descobrir; (person) desmascarar ♦ vi: **to ~ out about** (by chance) saber de; ~**ings** npl (LAW) veredito, decisão f; (of report) constatações fpl

fine [faɪn] adj fino; (excellent) excelente; (subtle) sutil ♦ adv muito bem ♦ n (LAW) multa ♦ vt (LAW) multar; **to be ~** (person) estar bem; (weather) estar bom; ~ **arts** npl belas artes fpl

finery ['faɪnərɪ] n enfeites mpl

finesse [fɪˈnɛs] n sutileza

finger ['fɪŋgə*] n dedo ♦ vt manusear; ~**nail** n unha; ~**print** n impressão f digital; ~**tip** n ponta do dedo

finicky ['fɪnɪkɪ] adj fresco, cheio de coisas

finish ['fɪnɪʃ] n fim m; (SPORT) chegada; (on wood etc) acabamento ♦ vt, vi terminar, acabar; **to ~ doing sth** terminar de fazer algo; **to ~ third** chegar no terceiro lugar; **~ off** *vt* terminar; (*kill*) liquidar; **~ up** *vt* acabar ♦ *vi* ir parar; **~ing line** *n* linha de chegada, meta; **~ing school** *n* escola de aperfeiçoamento (para moças)

Finland ['fɪnlənd] *n* Finlândia

Finn [fɪn] *n* finlandês/esa *m/f*; **~ish** *adj* finlandês/esa ♦ *n* (*LING*) finlandês *m*

fir [fəː] *n* abeto

fire ['faɪə] *n* fogo; (*accidental*) incêndio; (*gas* ~, *electric* ~) aquecedor *m* ♦ *vt* (*gun*) disparar; (*arrow*) atirar; (*interest*) estimular; (*dismiss*) despedir ♦ *vi* disparar; **on ~** em chamas; **~ alarm** *n* alarme *m* de incêndio; **~arm** *n* arma de fogo; **~ brigade** (*US* ~ **department**) *n* (*corpo de*) bombeiros *mpl*; **~ engine** *n* carro de bombeiro; **~ escape** *n* escada de incêndio; **~ extinguisher** *n* extintor *m* de incêndio; **~man** (*irreg*) *n* bombeiro; **~place** *n* lareira; **~side** *n* lugar *m* junto à lareira; **~ station** *n* posto de bombeiros; **~wood** *n* lenha; **~works** *npl* fogos de artifício

firing squad *n* pelotão *m* de fuzilamento

firm [fəːm] *adj* firme ♦ *n* firma; **~ly** *adv* firmemente

first [fəːst] *adj* primeiro ♦ *adv* (*before others*) primeiro; (*listing reasons*) em primeiro lugar ♦ *n* (*in race*) primeiro/a; (*AUT*) primeira; (*BRIT: SCH*) menção *f* honrosa; **at ~** no início; **~ of all** antes de tudo, antes de mais nada; **~ aid** *n* primeiros socorros *mpl*; **~-aid kit** *n* estojo de primeiros socorros; **~-class** *adj* de primeira classe; **~-hand** *adj* de primeira mão; **~ lady** (*US*) *n* primeira dama; **~ly** *adv* primeiramente, em primeiro lugar; **~ name** *n* primeiro nome *m*; **~-rate** *adj* de primeira categoria

fish [fɪʃ] *n inv* peixe *m* ♦ *vt, vi* pescar; **to go ~ing** ir pescar; **~erman** (*irreg*) *n* pescador *m*; **~ farm** *n* viveiro (de piscicultura); **~ fingers** (*BRIT*) *npl* filezinhos *mpl* de peixe; **~ing boat** *n* barco de pesca; **~ing line** *n* linha de pesca; **~ing rod** *n* vara (de pesca); **~monger** *n* peixeiro/a; **~monger's (shop)** *n* peixaria; **~ sticks** (*US*) *npl* = **~ fingers**; **~y** (*inf*) *adj* (*tale*) suspeito

fist [fɪst] *n* punho

fit [fɪt] *adj* em (boa) forma; (*suitable*) adequado, apropriado ♦ *vt* (*subj: clothes*) caber em; (*put in*) colocar; (*equip*) equipar; (*suit*) assentar ♦ *vi* (*clothes*) servir; (*parts*) ajustar-se; (*in space*) caber ♦ *n* (*MED*) ataque *m*; (*of anger*) acesso; **~ to** bom para; **~ for** adequado para; **by ~s and starts** espasmodicamente; **~ in** *vi* encaixar-se; (*person*) dar-se bem (com todos); **~ful** *adj* espasmódico, intermitente; **~ment** *n* móvel *m*; **~ness** *n*

(*MED*) saúde *f*, boa forma; **~ted** *adj* (*BRIT: kitchen*) com armários embutidos; **~ted carpet** carpete *m*; **~ter** *n* ajustador(a) *m/f*, montador(a) *m/f*; **~ting** *adj* apropriado ♦ *n* (*of dress*) prova; **~tings** *npl* (*in building*) instalações *fpl*, acessórios *mpl*; **~ting room** *n* cabine *f* (para experimentar roupa)

five [faɪv] *num* cinco; **~r** (*inf*) *n* (*BRIT*) nota de cinco libras; (*US*) nota de cinco dólares

fix [fɪks] *vt* (*secure*) fixar, colocar; (*arrange*) arranjar; (*meal, drink*) preparar ♦ *n*: **to be in a ~** estar em apuros; **~ up** *vt* (*meeting*) marcar; **to ~ sb up with sth** arranjar algo para alguém; **~ation** *n* fixação *f*; **~ed** *adj* (*prices, smile*) fixo; **~ture** *n* (*furniture*) móvel *m* fixo; (*SPORT*) desafio, encontro

fizzle out ['fɪzl] *vi* fracassar; (*interest*) diminuir

fizzy ['fɪzɪ] *adj* com gás, gasoso

flabbergasted ['flæbəɡɑːstɪd] *adj* pasmado

flabby ['flæbɪ] *adj* flácido

flag [flæɡ] *n* bandeira; (*for signalling*) bandeirola; (~*stone*) laje *f* ♦ *vi* acabar-se, descair; **~ down** *vt*: **to ~ sb down** fazer sinais a alguém para que pare

flagpole ['flæɡpəul] *n* mastro de bandeira

flagship ['flæɡʃɪp] *n* nau *f* capitânia; (*fig*) carro-chefe *m*

flair [flɛə] *n* (*talent*) talento; (*style*) habilidade *f*

flak [flæk] *n* (*MIL*) fogo antiaéreo; (*inf: criticism*) críticas *fpl*

flake [fleɪk] *n* (*of rust, paint*) lasca; (*of snow, soap powder*) floco ♦ *vi* (*also*: ~ **off**) lascar, descamar-se

flamboyant [flæm'bɔɪənt] *adj* (*dress*) espalhafatoso; (*person*) extravagante

flame [fleɪm] *n* chama

flammable ['flæməbl] *adj* inflamável

flan [flæn] (*BRIT*) *n* torta

flank [flæŋk] *n* flanco ♦ *vt* ladear

flannel ['flænl] *n* (*BRIT: also: face* ~) toalhinha de rosto; (*fabric*) flanela; **~s** *npl* calça (*BR*) *or* calças *fpl* (*PT*) de flanela

flap [flæp] *n* (*of pocket*) aba; (*of envelope*) dobra ♦ *vt* (*arms*) oscilar; (*wings*) bater ♦ *vi* (*sail, flag*) ondular; (*inf: also*: **be in a ~**) estar atarantado

flare [flɛə] *n* fogacho, chama; (*MIL*) artifício de sinalização; (*in skirt etc*) folga; **~ up** *vi* chamejar; (*fig: person*) encolerizar-se; (*: violence*) irromper

flash [flæʃ] *n* (*of lightning*) clarão *m*; (*also*: **news** ~) notícias *fpl* de última hora; (*PHOT*) flash *m* ♦ *vt* piscar; (*news, etc*) transmitir; (*look, smile*) brilhar ♦ *vi* brilhar; (*light on ambulance, eyes etc*) piscar; **in a ~** num instante; **to ~ by** *or* **past** passar como um raio; **~bulb** *n* lâmpada de flash; ~**cube** n cubo de flash; ~**light** n lanterna de bolso

flashy ['flæʃɪ] (pej) adj espalhafatoso

flask [flɑːsk] n frasco; (also: **vacuum** ~) garrafa térmica (BR), termo (PT)

flat [flæt] adj plano; (battery) descarregado; (tyre) vazio; (beer) choco; (denial) categórico; (MUS) abemolado; (: voice) desafinado; (rate) único; (fee) fixo ♦ n (BRIT: apartment) apartamento; (MUS) bemol m; (AUT) pneu m furado; ~ **out** (work) a toque de caixa; ~**ly** adv terminantemente; ~**ten** vt (also: ~**ten out**) aplanar; (demolish) arrasar

flatter ['flætə*] vt lisonjear; ~**ing** adj lisonjeiro; (clothes etc) favorecedor(a); ~**y** n bajulação f

flaunt [flɔːnt] vt ostentar, pavonear

flavour ['fleɪvə*] (US **flavor**) n sabor m ♦ vt condimentar, aromatizar; **strawberry-~ed** com sabor de morango; ~**ing** n condimento; (synthetic) aromatizante m

flaw [flɔː] n defeito; (in character) falha; ~**less** adj impecável

flax [flæks] n linho; ~**en** adj da cor de linho

flea [fliː] n pulga

fleck [flɛk] n mancha, sinal m

flee [fliː] (pt, pp **fled**) vt fugir de ♦ vi fugir

fleece [fliːs] n tosão m; (wool) lã f; (coat) velo ♦ vt (inf) espoliar

fleet [fliːt] n (of lorries etc) frota; (of ships) esquadra

fleeting ['fliːtɪŋ] adj (glimpse, happiness) fugaz; (visit) passageiro

Flemish ['flɛmɪʃ] adj flamengo

flesh [flɛʃ] n carne f; (of fruit) polpa; ~ **wound** n ferimento de superfície

flew [fluː] pt of **fly**

flex [flɛks] n fio ♦ vt (muscles) flexionar; ~**ible** adj flexível

flick [flɪk] n pancada leve; (with finger) peteleco, piparote m; (with whip) chicotada ♦ vt dar um peteleco; (towel) dar uma lambada; (whip) dar uma chicotada; (switch) apertar; ~ **through** vt fus folhear

flicker ['flɪkə*] vi tremular; (eyelids) tremer

flier ['flaɪə*] n aviador(a) m/f

flight [flaɪt] n vôo m; (escape) fuga; (of steps) lance m; ~ **attendant** (US) n comissário/a de bordo; ~ **deck** n (AVIAT) cabine f do piloto; (NAUT) pista de aterrissagem (BR) or aterragem (PT)

flimsy ['flɪmzɪ] adj (thin) delgado, franzino; (shoes) ordinário; (clothes) de tecido fino; (building) barato; (weak) débil; (excuse) fraco

flinch [flɪntʃ] vi encolher-se; **to ~ from sth/from doing sth** vacilar diante de algo/em fazer algo

fling [flɪŋ] (pt, pp **flung**) vt lançar

flint [flɪnt] n pederneira; (in lighter) pedra

flip [flɪp] vt (turn over) dar a volta em; (throw) jogar; (switch) mover; **to ~ a coin** tirar cara ou coroa

flippant ['flɪpənt] adj petulante, irreverente

flipper ['flɪpə*] n (of animal) nadadeira; (for swimmer) pé-de-pato, nadadeira

flirt [fləːt] vi flertar ♦ n namorador(a) m/f, paquerador(a) m/f

flit [flɪt] vi esvoaçar

float [fləʊt] n bóia; (in procession) carro alegórico; (sum of money) caixa ♦ vi flutuar; (swimmer) boiar

flock [flɔk] n rebanho; (of birds) bando ♦ vi: **to ~ to** afluir a

flog [flɔg] vt açoitar

flood [flʌd] n enchente f, inundação f; (of letters, imports etc) enxurrada ♦ vt inundar, alagar ♦ vi (place) alagar; (people, goods): **to ~ into** inundar; ~**ing** n inundação f; ~**light** n refletor m, holofote m

floor [flɔː*] n chão m; (storey) andar m; (of sea) fundo ♦ vt (fig: confuse) confundir, pasmar; (subj: blow) derrubar; (: question, remark) aturdir; **ground ~** (BRIT) or **first ~** (US) andar térreo (BR), rés-do-chão (PT); **first ~** (BRIT) or **second ~** (US) primeiro andar; ~**board** n tábua de assoalho; ~ **show** n show m

flop [flɔp] n fracasso ♦ vi fracassar; (into chair) cair pesadamente

floppy ['flɔpɪ] adj frouxo, mole; ~ (**disk**) n disquete m

flora ['flɔːrə] n flora

florid ['flɔrɪd] adj (style) florido; (complexion) corado

florist ['flɔrɪst] n florista m/f; ~'**s** (**shop**) n floricultura

flounce [flaʊns] n babado, debrum m; ~ **out** vi sair indignado

flounder ['flaʊndə*] (pl ~ or ~**s**) n (ZOOL) linguado ♦ vi (swimmer) debater-se; (fig: speaker) atrapalhar-se; (: economy) flutuar

flour ['flaʊə*] n farinha

flourish ['flʌrɪʃ] vi florescer ♦ vt brandir, menear ♦ n gesto floreado; ~**ing** adj próspero

flout [flaʊt] vt (law) desrespeitar

flow [fləʊ] n fluxo; (of river, ELEC) corrente f; (of blood) circulação f ♦ vi correr; (traffic) fluir; (blood, ELEC) circular; (clothes, hair) ondular; ~ **chart** n fluxograma m

flower ['flaʊə*] n flor f ♦ vi florescer, florir; ~ **bed** n canteiro; ~**pot** n vaso; ~**y** adj (perfume) a base de flor; (pattern) florido; (speech) floreado

flown [fləʊn] pp of **fly**

flu [fluː] n gripe f

fluctuate ['flʌktjʊeɪt] vi flutuar; (tempera-

ture) variar

fluent ['flu:ənt] *adj* fluente; **he speaks ~ French, he's ~ in French** ele fala francês fluentemente

fluff [flʌf] *n* felpa, penugem *f*; **~y** *adj* macio, fofo; (*toy*) de pelúcia

fluid ['flu:ɪd] *adj* fluido ♦ *n* fluido

fluke [flu:k] (*inf*) *n* sorte *f*

flung [flʌŋ] *pt, pp of* **fling**

fluoride ['fluəraɪd] *n* fluoreto; **~ toothpaste** *n* creme *m* dental con fluór

flurry ['flʌrɪ] *n* (*of snow*) lufada; **~ of activity** muita atividade

flush [flʌʃ] *n* (*on face*) rubor *m*; (*fig*) resplendor *m* ♦ *vt* lavar com água ♦ *vi* ruborizar-se ♦ *adj*: **~ with** rente com; **to ~ the toilet** dar descarga; **~ out** *vt* levantar; **~ed** *adj* ruborizado, corado

flustered ['flʌstəd] *adj* atrapalhado

flute [flu:t] *n* flauta

flutter ['flʌtə*] *n* agitação *f*; (*of wings*) bater *m* ♦ *vi* esvoaçar

flux [flʌks] *n*: **in a state of ~** mudando continuamente

fly [flaɪ] (*pt* **flew**, *pp* **flown**) *n* mosca; (*on trousers*: also: **flies**) braguilha ♦ *vt* (*plane*) pilotar; (*passengers, cargo*) transportar (de avião); (*distances*) percorrer ♦ *vi* voar; (*passengers*) ir de avião; (*escape*) fugir; (*flag*) hastear-se; **~ away** *or* **off** *vi* voar; **~ing** *n* aviação *f* ♦ *adj*: **~ing visit** visita de médico; **with ~ing colours** brilhantemente; **~ing saucer** *n* disco voador; **~ing start** *n*: **to get off to a ~ing start** começar muito bem; **~over** (*BRIT*) *n* viaduto; **~sheet** *n* duplo teto

foal [fəʊl] *n* potro

foam [fəʊm] *n* espuma; (*also*: **~ rubber**) espuma de borracha ♦ *vi* espumar

fob [fɔb] *vt*: **to ~ sb off** despachar alguém

focal point ['fəʊkəl-] *n* foco

focus ['fəʊkəs] (*pl* **~es**) *n* foco ♦ *vt* enfocar ♦ *vi*: **to ~** on enfocar, focalizar; **in/out of ~** em foco/fora de foco

fodder ['fɔdə*] *n* forragem *f*

foe [fəʊ] *n* inimigo

foetus ['fi:təs] (*US* **fetus**) *n* feto

fog [fɔg] *n* nevoeiro; **~gy** *adj*: **it's ~gy** está nevoento; **~ lamp** (*US* **~ light**) *n* farol *m* de neblina

foil [fɔɪl] *vt* frustrar ♦ *n* folha metálica; (*also*: **kitchen ~**) folha *or* papel *m* de alumínio; (*complement*) contraste *m*, complemento; (*FENCING*) florete *m*

fold [fəʊld] *n* dobra, vinco, prega; (*of skin*) ruga; (*AGR*) redil *m*, curral *m* ♦ *vt* dobrar; (*arms*) cruzar; **~ up** *vi* dobrar; (*business*) abrir falência ♦ *vt* dobrar; **~er** *n* pasta; **~ing** *adj* dobrável

foliage ['fəʊlɪdʒ] *n* folhagem *f*

folk [fəʊk] *npl* gente *f* ♦ *cpd* popular, folclórico; **~s** *npl* (*family*) família, parentes *mpl*; (*parents*) pais *mpl*; **~lore** *n* folclo-

re *m*; **~ song** *n* canção *f* popular *or* folclórica

follow ['fɔləʊ] *vt* seguir; (*event, story*) acompanhar ♦ *vi* seguir; (*person, period of time*) acompanhar; (*result*) resultar; **to ~ suit** fazer o mesmo; **~ up** *vt* (*letter*) responder a; (*offer*) levar adiante; (*case*) acompanhar; **~er** *n* seguidor(a) *m/f*; **~ing** *adj* seguinte ♦ *n* adeptos *mpl*

folly ['fɔlɪ] *n* loucura

fond [fɔnd] *adj* carinhoso; (*hopes*) absurdo, descabido; **to be ~ of** gostar de

fondle ['fɔndl] *vt* acariciar

font [fɔnt] *n* (*REL*) pia batismal; (*TYP*) fonte *f*, família

food [fu:d] *n* comida; **~ mixer** *n* batedeira; **~ poisoning** *n* intoxicação *f* alimentar; **~ processor** *n* multiprocessador *m* de cozinha; **~stuffs** *npl* gêneros *mpl* alimentícios

fool [fu:l] *n* tolo/a; (*CULIN*) puré *m* de frutas com creme ♦ *vt* enganar ♦ *vi* (*gen*: **~ around**) brincar; **~hardy** *adj* temerário; **~ish** *adj* burro; (*careless*) imprudente; **~proof** *adj* infalível

foot [fut] (*pl* **feet**) *n* pé *m*; (*of animal*) pata; (*measure*) pé (*304 mm; 12 inches*) ♦ *vt* (*bill*) pagar; **on ~** a pé; **~age** *n* (*CINEMA*: *length*) ~ metragem *f*; (*: material*) seqüências *fpl*; **~ball** *n* bola; (*game*: *BRIT*) futebol *m*; (*: US*) futebol norteamericano; **~ball player** (*BRIT*: *also*: **~baller**) jogador *m* de futebol; **~brake** *n* freio (*BR*) *or* travão *m* (*PT*) de pé; **~bridge** *n* passarela; **~hills** *npl* contraforte *m*; **~hold** *n* apoio para o pé; **~ing** *n* (*fig*) posição *f*; **to lose one's ~ing** escorregar; **~lights** *npl* ribalta; **~man** (*irreg*) *n* lacaio; **~note** *n* nota ao pé da página, nota de rodapé; **~path** *n* caminho, atalho; **~print** *n* pegada; **~step** *n* passo; **~wear** *n* calçados *mpl*

KEYWORD

for [fɔ:*] *prep* **1** (*indicating destination, direction*) para; **he went ~ the paper** foi pegar o jornal; **is this ~ me?** é para mim?; **it's time ~ lunch** é hora de almoçar

2 (*indicating purpose*) para; **what's it ~?** para quê serve?; **to pray ~ peace** orar pela paz

3 (*on behalf of, representing*) por; **he works ~ the government/a local firm** ele trabalha para o governo/uma firma local; **G ~ George** G de George

4 (*because of*) por; **~ this reason** por esta razão; **~ fear of being criticised** com medo de ser criticado

5 (*with regard to*) para; **it's cold ~ July** está frio para julho

6 (*in exchange for*) por; **it was sold ~ £5** foi vendido por £5

7 (*in favour of*) a favor de; **are you ~ or against us?** você está a favor de ou contra nós?; **I'm all ~ it** concordo plenamente, tem todo o meu apoio; **vote ~ X** vote em X

8 *(referring to distance)*: **there are roadworks ~ 5 km** há obras na estrada por 5 quilômetros; **we walked ~ miles** andamos quilômetros

9 *(referring to time)* **she will be away ~ a month** ela ficará fora um mês; **I have known her ~ years** eu a conheço há anos; **can you do it ~ tomorrow?** você pode fazer isso para amanhã?

10 *(with infinite clause)*: **it is not ~ me to decide** não cabe a mim decidir; **it would be best ~ you to leave** seria melhor que você fosse embora; **there is still time ~ you to do it** ainda há tempo para você fazer isso; **~ this to be possible ...** para que isso seja possível ...

11 *(in spite of)* apesar de
♦ *conj (since, as: rather formal)* pois, porque

forage [ˈfɒrɪdʒ] *vi* ir à procura de alimentos

foray [ˈfɒreɪ] *n* incursão *f*

forbad(e) [fəˈbæd] *pt of* **forbid**

forbid [fəˈbɪd] *(pt* **forbad(e)***, pp* **forbidden)** *vt* proibir; **to ~ sb to do sth** proibir alguém de fazer algo; **~den** *pp of* **forbid**; **~ding** *adj (prospect)* sombrio; *(look)* severo

force [fɔːs] *n* força ♦ *vt* forçar; **the F~s** *npl (BRIT)* as Forças Armadas; **in ~** em vigor; **~-feed** *(irreg) vt* alimentar à força; **~ful** *adj* enérgico, vigoroso

forceps [ˈfɔːsɛps] *npl* fórceps *m inv*

forcibly [ˈfɔːsəblɪ] *adv* à força

ford [fɔːd] *n* vau *m*

fore [fɔː] *n*: **to come to the ~** salientar-se

forearm [ˈfɔːrɑːm] *n* antebraço

foreboding [fɔːˈbəʊdɪŋ] *n* mau presságio

forecast [ˈfɔːkɑːst] *(irreg: like* **cast)** *n* previsão *f; (also:* **weather ~**) previsão do tempo ♦ *vt* prognosticar, prever

forecourt [ˈfɔːkɔːt] *n (of garage)* área de estacionamento

forefathers [ˈfɔːfɑːðəz] *npl* antepassados *mpl*

forefinger [ˈfɔːfɪŋgə] *n* (dedo) indicador *m*

forefront [ˈfɔːfrʌnt] *n*: **in the ~ of** em primeiro plano em

forego *(irreg: like* **go)** *vt* renunciar a; *(go without)* abster-se de

foregone [ˈfɔːgɒn] *pp of* **forego** ♦ *adj*: **it's a ~ conclusion** é uma conclusão inevitável

foreground [ˈfɔːgraʊnd] *n* primeiro plano

forehead [ˈfɒrɪd] *n* testa

foreign [ˈfɒrɪn] *adj* estrangeiro; *(trade)*

exterior; *(object, matter)* estranho; **~er** *n* estrangeiro/a; **~ exchange** *n* câmbio; **F~ Office** *(BRIT) n* Ministério das Relações Exteriores; **F~ Secretary** *(BRIT) n* Ministro das Relações Exteriores

foreleg [ˈfɔːlɛg] *n* perna dianteira

foreman [ˈfɔːmən] *(irreg) n* capataz *m; (in construction)* contramestre *m*

foremost [ˈfɔːməʊst] *adj* principal ♦ *adv*: **first and ~** antes de mais nada

forensic [fəˈrɛnsɪk] *adj* forense; **~ medicine** medicina legal

forerunner [ˈfɔːrʌnə] *n* precursor(a) *m/f*

foresee [fɔːˈsiː] *(irreg: like* **see)** *vt* prever; **~able** *adj* previsível

foreshadow [fɔːˈʃædəʊ] *vt* prenunciar

foresight [ˈfɔːsaɪt] *n* previdência

forest [ˈfɒrɪst] *n* floresta

forestall [fɔːˈstɔːl] *vt* prevenir

forestry [ˈfɒrɪstrɪ] *n* silvicultura

foretaste [ˈfɔːteɪst] *n* amostra

foretell [fɔːˈtɛl] *(irreg: like* **tell)** *vt* predizer, profetizar; **foretold** *pt, pp of* **foretell**

forever [fəˈrɛvə] *adv* para sempre

forewent *pt of* **forego**

foreword [ˈfɔːwəːd] *n* prefácio

forfeit [ˈfɔːfɪt] *vt* perder (direito a)

forgave [fəˈgeɪv] *pt of* **forgive**

forge [fɔːdʒ] *n* ferraria ♦ *vt* falsificar; *(metal)* forjar; **~ ahead** *vi* avançar constantemente; **~r** *n* falsificador(a) *m/f*; **~ry** *n* falsificação *f*

forget [fəˈgɛt] *(pt* **forgot***, pp* **forgotten)** *vt, vi* esquecer; **~ful** *adj* esquecido; **~me-not** *n* miosótis *m*

forgive [fəˈgɪv] *(pt* **forgave***, pp* **~n)** *vt* perdoar; **to ~ sb for sth** perdoar algo a alguém, perdoar alguém de algo; **~ness** *n* perdão *m*

forgo [fɔːˈgəʊ] *(irreg) vt =* **forego**

forgot [fəˈgɒt] *pt of* **forget**

forgotten [fəˈgɒtn] *pp of* **forget**

fork [fɔːk] *n (for eating)* garfo; *(for gardening)* forquilha; *(of roads etc)* bifurcação *f* ♦ *vi* bifurcar-se; **~ out** *(inf) vt (pay)* desembolsar, morrer em; **~-lift truck** *n* empilhadeira

forlorn [fəˈlɔːn] *adj* desolado; *(attempt)* desesperado; *(hope)* último

form [fɔːm] *n* forma; *(type)* tipo; *(SCH)* série *f; (questionnaire)* formulário ♦ *vt* formar; *(organization)* criar; **to ~ a queue** *(BRIT)* fazer fila; **in top ~** em plena forma

formal [ˈfɔːməl] *adj (offer)* oficial; *(person)* cerimonioso; *(occasion, education)* formal; *(dress)* a rigor *(BR)*, de cerimônia *(PT); (garden)* simétrico; **~ities** *npl (procedures)* formalidades *fpl*; **~ity** *n* formalidade *f; (behaviour, education)* formalismo; *(garden)* simetria; *(ceremony)* cerimônia; **~ly** *adv* formalmente

format [ˈfɔːmæt] *n* formato ♦ *vt (COM-*

PUT) formatar

former ['fɔːmə*] *adj* anterior; (*earlier*) antigo; **the ~ ... the latter ...** aquele ... este ...; **~ly** *adv* anteriormente

formidable ['fɔːmɪdəbl] *adj* terrível, temível

formula ['fɔːmjulə] (*pl* **~s** *or* **~e**) *n* fôrmula

forsake [fə'seɪk] (*pt* **forsook**, *pp* **forsaken**) *vt* abandonar

fort [fɔːt] *n* forte *m*

forth [fɔːθ] *adv* para adiante; **back and ~** de cá para lá; **and so ~** e assim por diante; **~coming** *adj* próximo, que está para aparecer; (*help*) disponível; (*person*) comunicativo; **~right** *adj* franco; **~with** *adv* em seguida

fortify ['fɔːtɪfaɪ] *vt* (*city*) fortificar; (*person*) fortalecer

fortitude ['fɔːtɪtjuːd] *n* fortaleza

fortnight ['fɔːtnaɪt] (*BRIT*) *n* quinzena, quinze dias *mpl*; **~ly** *adj* quinzenal ♦ *adv* quinzenalmente

fortress ['fɔːtrɪs] *n* fortaleza

fortunate ['fɔːtʃənɪt] *adj* (*event*) feliz; (*person*): **to be ~** ter sorte; **it is ~ that ...** é uma sorte que ...; **~ly** *adv* felizmente

fortune ['fɔːtʃən] *n* sorte *f*; (*wealth*) fortuna; **~-teller** *n* adivinho/a

forty ['fɔːtɪ] *num* quarenta

forum ['fɔːrəm] *n* foro

forward ['fɔːwəd] *adj* (*movement*) para a frente; (*position*) avançado; (*in time*) futuro; (*not shy*) imodesto, presunçoso ♦ *n* (*SPORT*) atacante *m* ♦ *vt* (*letter*) remeter; (*goods, parcel*) expedir; (*career*) promover; (*plans*) ativar; **to move ~** avançar; **~(s)** *adv* para a frente

fossil ['fɔsl] *n* fóssil *m*

foster ['fɔstə*] *vt* adotar (por um tempo limitado); (*activity*) promover; **~ child** (*irreg*) *n* filho adotivo (por um tempo limitado)

fought [fɔːt] *pt*, *pp of* **fight**

foul [faul] *adj* horrível; (*language*) obsceno ♦ *n* (*SPORT*) falta ♦ *vt* sujar; **~ play** *n* (*LAW*) crime *m*

found [faund] *pt*, *pp of* **find** ♦ *vt* (*establish*) fundar; **~ation** *n* (*act, organization*) fundação *f*; (*base*) base *f*; (*also*: **~ation cream**) creme *m* base; **~ations** *npl* (*of building*) alicerces *mpl*

founder ['faundə*] *n* fundador(a) *m/f* ♦ *vi* naufragar

foundry ['faundrɪ] *n* fundição *f*

fountain ['fauntɪn] *n* chafariz *m*; **~ pen** *n* caneta-tinteiro *f*

four [fɔː*] *num* quatro; **on all ~s** de quatro; **~-poster** *n* (*also*: **~-poster bed**) dossel *m*; **~some** *n* grupo de quatro pessoas; **~teen** *num* catorze; **~th** *num* quarto

fowl [faul] *n* ave *f* (doméstica)

fox [fɔks] *n* raposa ♦ *vt* deixar perplexo

foyer ['fɔɪeɪ] *n* saguão *m*

fraction ['frækʃən] *n* fração *f*

fracture ['fræktʃə*] *n* fratura ♦ *vt* fraturar

fragile ['frædʒaɪl] *adj* frágil

fragment ['frægmənt] *n* fragmento

fragrant ['freɪgrənt] *adj* fragrante, perfumado

frail [freɪl] *adj* (*person*) fraco; (*structure*) frágil

frame [freɪm] *n* (*of building*) estrutura; (*body*) corpo; (*of picture, door*) moldura; (*of spectacles*: *also*: **~s**) armação *f*, aro ♦ *vt* (*picture*) emoldurar; **~ of mind** *n* estado de espírito; **~work** *n* armação *f*

France [frɑːns] *n* França

franchise ['fræntʃaɪz] *n* (*POL*) direito de voto; (*COMM*) concessão *f*

frank [fræŋk] *adj* franco ♦ *vt* (*letter*) franquear; **~ly** *adv* francamente; (*candidly*) abertamente; **~ness** *n* franqueza

frantic ['fræntɪk] *adj* frenético; (*person*) fora de si

fraternity [frə'tɜːnɪtɪ] *n* (*feeling*) fraternidade *f*; (*club*) confraria

fraternize ['frætənaɪz] *vi* confraternizar

fraud [frɔːd] *n* fraude *f*; (*person*) impostor(a) *m/f*

fraught [frɔːt] *adj* tenso; **~ with** repleto de

fray [freɪ] *n* guerra ♦ *vi* esfiapar-se; **tempers were ~ed** estavam com os nervos em frangalhos

freak [friːk] *n* (*person*) anormal *m/f*; (*event*) anomalia

freckle ['frekl] *n* sarda

free [friː] *adj* livre; (*seat*) desocupado; (*costing nothing*) grátis, gratuito ♦ *vt* pôr em liberdade; (*jammed object*) soltar; **~ (of charge)** grátis, de graça; **~dom** *n* liberdade *f*; **~-for-all** *n* quebra-quebra *m*; **~ gift** *n* brinde *m*; **~hold** *n* propriedade *f* livre e alodial; **~ kick** *n* (tiro) livre *m*; **~lance** *adj* autônomo; **~ly** *adv* livremente; **F~mason** *n* maçom *m*; **F~post** ® *n* porte *m* pago; **~-range** *n* (*egg*) caseiro; **~ trade** *n* livre comércio; **~way** (*US*) *n* auto-estrada; **~ will** *n* livre arbítrio; **of one's own ~ will** por sua própria vontade

freeze [friːz] (*pt* **froze**, *pp* **frozen**) *vi* gelar(-se), congelar-se ♦ *vt* congelar ♦ *n* geada; (*on arms, wages*) congelamento; **~-dried** *adj* liofilizado; **~r** *n* congelador *m*, freezer *m* (*BR*); **freezing** *adj*: **freezing (cold)** (*weather*) glacial; (*water*) gelado; **3 degrees below freezing** 3 graus abaixo de zero; **freezing point** *n* ponto de congelamento

freight [freɪt] *n* (*goods*) carga; (*money charged*) frete *m*; **~ train** (*US*) *n* trem *m* de carga

French [frentʃ] *adj* francês/esa ♦ *n* (*LING*) francês *m*; **the ~** *npl* (*people*) os

franceses; ~ **bean** (BRIT) n feijão m comum; ~ **fried potatoes** (US ~ fries)
npl batatas fpl fritas; ~**man** (irreg) n
francês m; ~ **window** n porta-janela,
janela de batente; ~**woman** (irreg) n
francesa

frenzy ['frɛnzɪ] n frenesi m

frequent [adj 'friːkwənt, vt frɪ'kwɛnt] adj
freqüente ♦ vt freqüentar; ~**ly** adv freqüentemente, a miúdo

fresh [frɛʃ] adj fresco; (new) novo;
(cheeky) atrevido; ~**en** vi (wind, air)
tornar-se mais forte; ~**en up** vi (person)
lavar-se, refrescar-se; ~**er** (BRIT: inf) n
(SCH) calouro/a; ~**ly** adv recentemente,
há pouco; ~**man** (US: irreg) n = ~**er**;
~**ness** n frescor m; ~**water** adj de
água doce

fret [frɛt] vi afligir-se

friar ['fraɪə*] n frade m

friction ['frɪkʃən] n fricção f; (between
people) atrito

Friday ['fraɪdɪ] n sexta-feira f

fridge [frɪdʒ] (BRIT) n geladeira (BR), frigorífico (PT)

fried [fraɪd] adj frito; ~ **egg** ovo estrelado or frito

friend [frɛnd] n amigo/a; ~**ly** adj simpático; (match) amistoso; ~**ship** n amizade
f

frieze [friːz] n friso

fright [fraɪt] n terror m; (scare) pavor m;
to take ~ assustar-se; ~**en** vt assustar;
~**ened** adj: to be ~**ened** of ter medo
de; ~**ening** adj assustador(a); ~**ful** adj
terrível, horrível

frigid ['frɪdʒɪd] adj frígido, frio

frill [frɪl] n babado

fringe [frɪndʒ] n franja; (on shawl etc)
beira, orla; (edge: of forest etc) margem
f; ~ **benefits** npl benefícios mpl adicio-
nais

frisk [frɪsk] vt revistar

frisky ['frɪskɪ] adj alegre, animado

fritter ['frɪtə*] n bolinho frito; ~ **away**
vt desperdiçar

frivolous ['frɪvələs] adj frívolo; (activity)
fútil

frizzy ['frɪzɪ] adj frisado

fro [frəu] adj see **to**

frock [frɔk] n vestido

frog [frɔg] n rã f; ~**man** (irreg) n
homem-rã m

frolic ['frɔlɪk] vi brincar

from [frɔm] prep **1** (indicating starting
place) de; **where do you come ~?** de
onde você é?; ~ **London to Glasgow**
de Londres para Glasgow; **to escape ~
sth/sb** escapar de algo/alguém
2 (indicating origin etc) de; **a letter/
telephone call ~ my sister** uma
carta/um telefonema da minha irmã;
tell him ~ me that ... diga a ele que

da minha parte ...; **to drink ~ the bottle** beber na garrafa
3 (indicating time): ~ **one o'clock** to or
until or till **two** da uma hora até às
duas; ~ **January (on)** a partir de janeiro
4 (indicating distance) de; **we're still a
long way ~ home** ainda estamos muito
longe de casa
5 (indicating price, number etc) de;
prices range ~ £10 to £50 os preços
vão de £10 a £50
6 (indicating difference) de; **he can't
tell red ~ green** ele não pode diferenciar vermelho do verde
7 (because of/on the basis of): ~ **what
he says** pelo que ele diz; **to act ~ conviction** agir por convicção; **weak ~
hunger** fraco de fome

front [frʌnt] n frente f; (of vehicle) parte f
dianteira; (of house, fig) fachada; (also:
sea ~) orla marítima ♦ adj da frente;
in ~ (of) em frente (de); ~**age** n fachada; ~ **door** n porta principal; ~**ier**
n fronteira; ~ **page** n primeira página;
~ **room** (BRIT) n salão m, sala de estar;
~**-wheel drive** n tração f dianteira

frost [frɔst] n geada; (also: hoar~) gelo;
~**bite** n ulceração f produzida pelo frio;
~**ed** adj (glass) fosco; ~**y** adj (window)
coberto de geada; (welcome) glacial

froth [frɔθ] n espuma

frown [fraun] vi franzir as sobrancelhas,
amarrar a cara

froze [frəuz] pt of **freeze**

frozen ['frəuzn] pp of **freeze**

fruit [fruːt] n inv fruta; (fig: pl ~s) fruto;
~**erer** n fruteiro/a; ~**ful** adj proveitoso;
~**ion** n: **to come to ~ion** realizar-se;
~ **juice** n suco (BR) or sumo (PT) de
frutas; ~ **machine** (BRIT) n caça-níqueis
m inv (BR), máquina de jogo (PT)

frustrate [frʌs'treɪt] vt frustrar

fry [fraɪ] (pt, pp **fried**) vt fritar; see also
small; ~**ing pan** n frigideira

ft. abbr = **foot**; **feet**

fuddy-duddy ['fʌdɪdʌdɪ] n careta m/f

fudge [fʌdʒ] n (CULIN) ~ doce m de leite

fuel [fjuəl] n (for heating) combustível m;
(for propelling) carburante m; ~ **oil** n
óleo combustível; ~ **tank** n depósito de
combustível

fugitive ['fjuːdʒɪtɪv] n fugitivo/a

fulfil [ful'fɪl] (US **fulfill**) vt (function) cumprir; (condition) satisfazer; (wish, desire)
realizar; ~**ment** n satisfação f; (of wish,
desire) realização f

full [ful] adj cheio; (use, volume) máximo;
(complete) completo; (information) detalhado; (price) integral; (skirt) folgado ♦
adv: ~ **well** perfeitamente; **I'm ~ (up)**
estou satisfeito; ~ **employment** pleno
emprego; **a ~ two hours** duas horas
completas; **at ~ speed** a toda a veloci-

dade; **in** ~ integralmente; **~-length** *adj*
(*novel*) de tamanho normal; (*portrait*) de
corpo inteiro; (*coat*) longo; **~-length**
(**feature**) **film** longa-metragem *m*; ~
moon *n* lua cheia; **~-scale** *adj* (*model*)
em tamanho natural; (*war*) em grande
escala; ~ **stop** *n* ponto (final); **~-time**
adj, adv (*work*) de tempo completo *or*
integral; **~y** *adv* completamente; (*at
least*) pelo menos; **~y-fledged** *adj* (*teacher etc*) diplomado

fulsome ['fulsəm] (*pej*) *adj* extravagante

fumble ['fʌmbl] *vi*: **to** ~ **with** ♦ *vt fus*
atrapalhar-se com

fume [fju:m] *vi* fumegar; (*be angry*) estar
com raiva; **~s** *npl* gases *mpl*

fun [fʌn] *n* divertimento; **to have** ~
divertir-se; **for** ~ de brincadeira; **to
make** ~ **of** fazer troça de, zombar de

function ['fʌŋkʃən] *n* função *f*; (*reception, dinner*) recepção *f* ♦ *vi* funcionar;
~al *adj* funcional; (*practical*) prático

fund [fʌnd] *n* fundo; (*source, store*) fonte
f; **~s** *npl* (*money*) fundos *mpl*

fundamental [fʌndə'mɛntl] *adj* fundamental; **~ist** *n* fundamentalista *m/f*

funeral ['fju:nərəl] *n* (*burial*) enterro; ~
parlour *n* casa funerária; ~ **service** *n*
missa fúnebre

funfair ['fʌnfɛə*] (*BRIT*) *n* parque *m* de
diversões

fungus ['fʌŋgəs] (*pl* **fungi**) *n* fungo;
(*mould*) bolor *m*, mofo

funnel ['fʌnl] *n* funil *m*; (*of ship*) chaminé *m*

funny ['fʌnɪ] *adj* engraçado, divertido;
(*strange*) esquisito, estranho

fur [fə:*] *n* pele *f*; (*BRIT: in kettle etc*) depósito, crosta; ~ **coat** *n* casaco de peles

furious ['fjuərɪəs] *adj* furioso; (*effort*) incrível

furlong ['fə:lɔŋ] *n* = 201.17m

furlough ['fə:ləu] *n* licença

furnace ['fə:nɪs] *n* forno

furnish ['fə:nɪʃ] *vt* mobiliar (*BR*), mobilar (*PT*); (*supply*): **to** ~ **sb with sth** fornecer algo a alguém; **~ings** *npl* mobília

furniture ['fə:nɪtʃə*] *n* mobília, móveis
mpl; **piece of** ~ móvel *m*

furrow ['fʌrəu] *n* (*in field*) rego; (*in skin*)
sulco

furry ['fə:rɪ] *adj* peludo

further ['fə:ðə*] *adj* novo, adicional ♦
adv mais longe; (*more*) mais; (*moreover*)
além disso ♦ *vt* promover; ~ **education**
(*BRIT*) *n* educação *f* superior; **~more**
adv além disso

furthest ['fə:ðɪst] *superl of* **far**

fury ['fjuərɪ] *n* fúria

fuse [fju:z] *n* fusível *m*; (*for bomb etc*) espoleta, mecha ♦ *vt* fundir; (*fig*) unir ♦ *vi*
(*metal*) fundir-se; unir-se; **to** ~ **the
lights** (*BRIT: ELEC*) queimar as luzes; ~
box *n* caixa de fusíveis

fuselage ['fju:zəlɑ:ʒ] *n* fuselagem *f*

fuss [fʌs] *n* estardalhaço; (*complaining*)
escândalo; **to make a** ~ criar caso; **to
make a** ~ **of sb** paparicar alguém; **~y**
adj (*person*) exigente; (*dress, style*) espalhafatoso

futile ['fju:taɪl] *adj* (*existence*) fútil; (*attempt*) inútil

future ['fju:tʃə*] *adj* futuro ♦ *n* futuro;
in ~ no futuro

fuze [fju:z] (*US*) = **fuse**

fuzzy ['fʌzɪ] *adj* (*PHOT*) indistinto; (*hair*)
frisado, encrespado

G

G [dʒi:] *n* (*MUS*) sol *m*

g *abbr* (= *gram(s)*) g

G7 *n abbr* (= *Group of 7*) G7

gabble ['gæbl] *vi* tagarelar

gable ['geɪbl] *n* cumeeira

gadget ['gædʒɪt] *n* aparelho, engenhoca

Gaelic ['geɪlɪk] *adj* gaélico/a ♦ *n* (*LING*)
gaélico

gag [gæg] *n* (*on mouth*) mordaça; (*joke*)
piada ♦ *vt* amordaçar

gaiety ['geɪtɪ] *n* alegria

gaily ['geɪlɪ] *adv* alegremente; (*coloured*)
vivamente

gain [geɪn] *n* ganho; (*profit*) lucro ♦ *vt*
ganhar ♦ *vi* (*watch*) adiantar-se; (*benefit*): **to** ~ **from sth** tirar proveito de
algo; **to** ~ **on sb** aproximar-se de alguém; **to** ~ **3lbs** (**in weight**) engordar
3 libras

gait [geɪt] *n* modo de andar

gal. *abbr* = **gallon**

gala ['gɑ:lə] *n* festa, gala

Galapagos (**Islands**) [gə'læpəgəs-] *npl*:
the ~ as ilhas Galápagos

galaxy ['gæləksɪ] *n* galáxia

gale [geɪl] *n* ventania; ~ **force 10** vento
de força 10

gallant ['gælənt] *adj* valente; (*polite*) galante; **~ry** *n* valentia; galanteria

gall bladder [gɔ:l-] *n* vesícula biliar

gallery ['gælərɪ] *n* (*in theatre etc*) galeria;
(*also*: **art** ~: *public*) museu *m*; (: *private*) galeria (de arte)

galley ['gælɪ] *n* (*ship's kitchen*) cozinha

gallon ['gælən] *n* galão *m* (= *8 pints*;
BRIT = *4.5l*; *US* = *3.8l*)

gallop ['gæləp] *n* galope *m* ♦ *vi* galopar

gallows ['gæləuz] *n* forca

gallstone ['gɔ:lstəun] *n* cálculo biliar

galore [gə'lɔ:*] *adv* à beça

galvanize ['gælvənaɪz] *vt* arrebatar

gambit ['gæmbɪt] *n* (*fig*): (**opening**) ~
início (de conversa)

gamble ['gæmbl] *n* risco ♦ *vt* apostar ♦
vi jogar, arriscar; **~r** *n* jogador(a) *m/f*;
gambling *n* jogo

game [geɪm] *n* jogo; (*match*) partida; (*esp
TENNIS*) jogada; (*strategy*) plano, esquema *m*; (*HUNTING*) caça ♦ *adj* (*willing*):

to be ~ for anything topar qualquer parada; **big ~** caça grossa; **~keeper** n guarda-caça m

gammon ['gæmən] n (bacon) toucinho (defumado); (ham) presunto

gamut ['gæmət] n gama

gang [gæŋ] n bando, grupo; (of criminals) gangue f; (of workmen) turma ♦ vi: **to ~ up on sb** conspirar contra alguém

gangster ['gæŋstə*] n gângster m, bandido

gangway ['gæŋweɪ] n (BRIT: in cinema, bus) corredor m; (on ship) passadiço

gaol [dʒeɪl] (BRIT) n, vt = **jail**

gap [gæp] n brecha, fenda; (in trees, traffic) abertura; (in time) intervalo; (difference) diferença

gape [geɪp] vi (person) estar or ficar boquiaberto; (hole) abrir-se; **gaping** adj (hole) muito aberto

garage ['gærɑ:ʒ] n garagem f; (for car repairs) oficina (mecánica)

garbage ['gɑ:bɪdʒ] n (US) lixo; (inf: nonsense) disparates mpl; **~ can** (US) n lata de lixo

garbled ['gɑ:bld] adj deturpado, destorcido

garden ['gɑ:dn] n jardim m; **~s** npl (public park) jardim público, parque m; **~er** n jardineiro/a; **~ing** n jardinagem f

gargle ['gɑ:gl] vi gargarejar

garish ['gɛərɪʃ] adj (colour) berrante; (light) brilhante

garland ['gɑ:lənd] n guirlanda

garlic ['gɑ:lɪk] n alho

garment ['gɑ:mənt] n peça de roupa

garnish ['gɑ:nɪʃ] vt (food) enfeitar

garrison ['gærɪsn] n guarnição f

garrulous ['gærjuləs] adj tagarela

garter ['gɑ:tə*] n liga

gas [gæs] n gás m; (US: gasoline) gasolina ♦ vt asfixiar com gás; **~ cooker** (BRIT) n fogão m a gás; **~ cylinder** n bujão m de gás; **~ fire** (BRIT) n aquecedor m a gás

gash [gæʃ] n talho; (tear) corte m ♦ vt talhar; cortar

gasket ['gæskɪt] n (AUT) junta, gaxeta

gas mask n máscara antigás

gas meter n medidor m de gás

gasoline ['gæsəliːn] (US) n gasolina

gasp [gɑ:sp] n arfada ♦ vi arfar; **~ out** vt dizer com voz entrecortada

gas station (US) n posto de gasolina

gassy ['gæsɪ] adj gasoso

gate [geɪt] n portão m; **~crash** (BRIT) vt entrar de penetra em; **~way** n portão m, passagem f

gather ['gæðə*] vt colher; (assemble) reunir; (SEWING) franzir; (understand) compreender ♦ vi reunir-se; **to ~ speed** acelerar(-se); **~ing** n reunião f, assembléia

gauche [gəuʃ] adj desajeitado

gaudy ['gɔːdɪ] adj chamativo

gauge [geɪdʒ] n (instrument) medidor m ♦ vt (fig: character) avaliar

gaunt [gɔːnt] adj descarnado; (bare, stark) desolado

gauntlet ['gɔːntlɪt] n luva; (fig): **to run the ~** expôr-se (à crítica); **to throw down the ~** lançar um desafio

gauze [gɔːz] n gaze f

gave [geɪv] pt of **give**

gay [geɪ] adj (homosexual) gay; (oldfashioned: cheerful) alegre; (colour) vistoso; (music) vivo

gaze [geɪz] n olhar m fixo ♦ vi: **to ~ at** sth fitar algo

gazetteer [gæzə'tɪə*] n dicionário geográfico

gazumping [gə'zʌmpɪŋ] (BRIT) n o fato de um vendedor quebrar uma promessa de venda para conseguir um preço mais alto

GB abbr = **Great Britain**

GCE (BRIT) n abbr = **General Certificate of Education**

GCSE (BRIT) n abbr = **General Certificate of Secondary Education**

gear [gɪə*] n equipamento; (TECH) engrenagem f; (AUT) velocidade f, marcha (BR), mudança (PT) ♦ vt (fig: adapt): **to ~ sth to** preparar algo para; **top** (BRIT) or **high** (US)/**low** ~ quarta/primeira (marcha); **in ~** engrenado; **~box** n caixa de mudanças (BR) or de velocidades (PT); **~ lever** (US ~ **shift**) n alavanca de mudança (BR) or mudanças (PT)

geese [giːs] pl of **goose**

gel [dʒel] n gel m

gem [dʒem] n jóia, gema

Gemini ['dʒemɪnaɪ] n Gêminis m, Gêmeos mpl

gender ['dʒendə*] n gênero

general ['dʒenərl] n general m ♦ adj geral; **in ~** em geral; **~ delivery** (US) n posta-restante f; **~ election** n eleições fpl gerais; **~ly** adv geralmente; **~ practitioner** n clínico/a geral

generate ['dʒenəreɪt] vt gerar

generator ['dʒenəreɪtə*] n gerador m

generous ['dʒenərəs] adj generoso; (measure etc) abundante

genetic engineering [dʒɪ'nɛtɪk-] n engenharia genética

Geneva [dʒɪ'niːvə] n Genebra

genial ['dʒiːnɪəl] adj cordial, simpático

genitals ['dʒenɪtlz] npl órgãos mpl genitais

genius ['dʒiːnɪəs] n gênio

genteel [dʒen'tiːl] adj fino

gentle ['dʒentl] adj (touch) leve, suave; (landscape) suave; (animal) manso

gentleman ['dʒentlmən] (irreg) n senhor m; (social position) fidalgo; (well-bred man) cavalheiro

gentleness ['dʒentlnɪs] n doçura, meiguice f; (of touch) suavidade f; (of ani-

mal) mansidão *f*
gently ['dʒɛntlɪ] *adv* suavemente
gentry ['dʒɛntrɪ] *n* pequena nobreza
gents [dʒɛnts] *n* banheiro de homens
(*BR*), casa de banho dos homens (*PT*)
genuine ['dʒɛnjuɪn] *adj* autêntico; (*person*) sincero
geography [dʒɪ'ɔgrəfɪ] *n* geografia
geology [dʒɪ'ɔlədʒɪ] *n* geologia
geometry [dʒɪ'ɔmɪtrɪ] *n* geometria
geranium [dʒɪ'reɪnjəm] *n* gerânio
geriatric [dʒɛrɪ'ætrɪk] *adj* geriátrico
germ [dʒɜːm] *n* micróbio, bacilo
German ['dʒɜːmən] *adj* alemão/mã ♦ *n* alemão/mã *m/f*; (*LING*) alemão *m*; ~ **measles** *n* rubéola
Germany ['dʒɜːmənɪ] *n* Alemanha
gesture ['dʒɛstjə*] *n* gesto

KEYWORD
---

get [gɛt] (*pt, pp* **got**) (*US*: *pp* **gotten**) *vi* **1**
(*become, be*) ficar, tornar-se; **to ~ old/tired/cold** envelhecer/cansar-se/resfriar-se; **to ~ annoyed/bored** aborrecer-se/amuar-se; **to ~ drunk** embebedar-se; **to ~ dirty** sujar-se; **to ~ killed/married** ser morto/casar-se; **when do I ~ paid?** quando eu recebo?, quando eu vou ser pago?; **it's ~ting late** está ficando tarde
2 (*go*): **to ~ to/from** ir para/de; **to ~ home** chegar em casa
3 (*begin*) começar a; **to ~ to know sb** começar a conhecer alguém; **let's ~ going** *or* **started** vamos lá!
♦ *modal aux vb*: **you've got to do it** você tem que fazê-lo
♦ *vt* **1**: **to ~ sth done** (*do*) fazer algo; (*have done*) mandar fazer algo; **to ~ one's hair cut** cortar o cabelo; **to ~ the car going** *or* **to go** fazer o carro andar; **to ~ sb to do sth** convencer alguém a fazer algo; **to ~ sth/sb ready** preparar algo/arrumar alguém
2 (*obtain*) ter; (*find*) achar; (*fetch*) buscar; **to ~ sth for sb** arranjar algo para alguém; (*fetch*) ir buscar algo para alguém; **~ me Mr Jones, please** (*TEL*) pode chamar o Sr Jones por favor; **can I ~ you a drink?** você está servido?
3 (*receive: present, letter*) receber; (*acquire: reputation, prize*) ganhar
4 (*catch*) agarrar; (*hit: target etc*) pegar; **to ~ sb by the arm/throat** agarrar alguém pelo braço/pela garganta; **~ him!** pega ele!
5 (*take, move*) levar; **to ~ sth to sb** levar algo para alguém; **I can't ~ it in/out/through** não consigo enfiá-lo/tirá-lo/passá-lo; **do you think we'll ~ it through the door?** você acha que conseguiremos passar isto na porta?
6 (*plane, bus etc*) pegar, tomar
7 (*understand*) entender; (*hear*) ouvir; **I've got it** entendi; **I don't ~ your**

meaning não entendo o que você quer dizer
8 (*have, possess*): **to have got** ter
get about *vi* (*news*) espalhar-se
get along *vi* (*agree*) entender-se; (*depart*) ir embora; (*manage*) = **get by**
get around = **get round**
get at *vt fus* (*attack, criticize*) atacar; (*reach*) alcançar; **what are you ~ting at?** o que você está querendo dizer?
get away *vi* (*leave*) partir; (*escape*) escapar
get away with *vt fus* conseguir fazer impunemente
get back *vi* (*return*) regressar, voltar ♦ *vt* receber de volta, recobrar
get by *vi* (*pass*) passar; (*manage*) virar-se
get down *vi* descer ♦ *vt fus* abaixar ♦ *vt* (*object*) abaixar, descer; (*depress: person*) deprimir
get down to *vt fus* (*work*) pôr-se a (fazer)
get in *vi* entrar; (*train*) chegar; (*arrive home*) voltar para casa
get into *vt fus* entrar em; (*vehicle*) subir em; (*clothes*) pôr, vestir, enfiar; **to ~ into bed/a rage** meter-se na cama/ficar com raiva
get off *vi* (*from train etc*) saltar (*BR*), descer (*PT*); (*depart*) sair; (*escape*) escapar ♦ *vt* (*remove: clothes, stain*) tirar; (*send off*) mandar ♦ *vt fus* (*train, bus*) saltar de (*BR*), sair de (*PT*)
get on *vi* (*at exam etc*): **how are you ~ting on?** como vai?; (*agree*): **to ~ on (with)** entender-se (com) ♦ *vt fus* (*train etc*) subir em (*BR*), subir para (*PT*); (*horse*) montar em
get out *vi* (*of place, vehicle*) sair ♦ *vt* (*take out*) tirar
get out of *vt fus* (*duty etc*) escapar de
get over *vt fus* (*illness*) restabelecer-se de
get round *vt fus* rodear; (*fig: person*) convencer
get through *vi* (*TEL*) completar a ligação
get through to *vt fus* (*TEL*) comunicar-se com
get together *vi* (*people*) reunir-se ♦ *vt* reunir
get up *vi* levantar-se ♦ *vt fus* levantar
get up to *vt fus* (*reach*) chegar a; (*BRIT: prank etc*) fazer

getaway ['gɛtəweɪ] *n* fuga, escape *m*
geyser ['giːzə*] *n* (*GEO*) gêiser *m*; (*BRIT*) aquecedor *m* de água
ghastly ['gɑːstlɪ] *adj* horrível; (*building*) medonho; (*appearance*) horripilante; (*pale*) pálido
gherkin ['gɜːkɪn] *n* pepino em vinagre
ghost [gəʊst] *n* fantasma *m*
giant ['dʒaɪənt] *n* gigante *m* ♦ *adj* gigan-

tesco, gigante

gibberish ['dʒɪbərɪʃ] n algaravia

gibe [dʒaɪb] n deboche m

giblets ['dʒɪblɪts] npl miúdos mpl

Gibraltar [dʒɪ'brɔːltəˀ] n Gibraltar m (no article)

giddy ['gɪdɪ] adj (dizzy): **to be** or **feel** ~ estar com vertigem

gift [gɪft] n presente m, dádiva; (ability) dom m, talento; ~**ed** adj bem-dotado; ~ **token** n vale m para presente; ~ **voucher** n = ~ **token**

gigantic [dʒaɪ'gæntɪk] adj gigantesco

giggle ['gɪgl] vi dar risadinha boba

gill [dʒɪl] n (measure) = 0.25 pints (BRIT = 0.148l, US = 0.118l)

gills [gɪlz] npl (of fish) guelras fpl, brânquias fpl

gilt [gɪlt] adj dourado ♦ n dourado; ~-**edged** adj (stocks, securities) do Estado, de toda confiança

gimmick ['gɪmɪk] n truque m or macete m (publicitário)

gin [dʒɪn] n gim m, genebra

ginger ['dʒɪndʒəˀ] n gengibre m; ~ **ale** n cerveja de gengibre; ~ **beer** n cerveja de gengibre; ~**bread** n (cake) pão m de gengibre; (biscuit) biscoito de gengibre

gingerly ['dʒɪndʒəlɪ] adv cuidadosamente

gipsy ['dʒɪpsɪ] n cigano

giraffe [dʒɪ'rɑːf] n girafa

girder ['gəːdəˀ] n viga, trave f

girdle ['gəːdl] n (corset) cinta

girl [gəːl] n (small) menina (BR), rapariga (PT); (young woman) jovem f, moça; (daughter) filha; ~**friend** n (of girl) amiga; (of boy) namorada; ~**ish** adj ameninado, de menina

giro ['dʒaɪrəʊ] n (bank) ~ transferência bancária; (post office ~) transferência postal; (BRIT: welfare cheque) cheque do governo destinado a desempregados

girth [gəːθ] n circunferência; (of horse) cilha

gist [dʒɪst] n essencial m

KEYWORD

give [gɪv] (pt gave, pp given) vt **1** (hand over) dar; **to** ~ **sb sth**, ~ **sth to sb** dar algo a alguém

2 (used with n to replace a vb): **to** ~ **a cry/sigh/push** etc dar um grito/suspiro/empurrão etc; **to** ~ **a speech/a lecture** fazer um discurso/uma palestra

3 (tell, deliver: news, advice, message etc) dar; **to** ~ **the right/wrong answer** dar a resposta certa/errada

4 (supply, provide: opportunity, job etc) dar; (bestow: title, right) conceder; **the sun** ~**s warmth and light** o sol fornece calor e luz

5 (dedicate: time, one's life/attention) dedicar; **she gave it all her attention** ela dedicou toda sua atenção a isto

6 (organize): **to** ~ **a party/dinner** etc

dar uma festa/jantar etc

♦ vi **1** (also: ~ **way**: break, collapse) dar folga; **his legs gave beneath him** suas pernas bambearam; **the roof/floor gave as I stepped on it** o telhado/chão desabou quando eu pisei nele

2 (stretch: fabric) dar de si

give away vt (money, opportunity) dar; (secret, information) revelar

give back vt devolver

give in vi (yield) ceder ♦ vt (essay etc) entregar

give off vt (heat, smoke) soltar

give out vt (distribute) distribuir; (make known) divulgar

give up vi (surrender) desistir, dar-se por vencido ♦ vt (job, boyfriend, habit) renunciar a; (idea, hope) abandonar; **to** ~ **up smoking** deixar de fumar; **to** ~ **o.s. up** entregar-se

give way vi (yield) ceder; (break, collapse: rope) arrebentar; (: ladder) quebrar; (BRIT: AUT) dar a preferência (BR), dar prioridade (PT)

---

glacier ['glæsɪəˀ] n glaciar m, geleira

glad [glæd] adj contente

gladly ['glædlɪ] adv com muito prazer

glamorous ['glæmərəs] adj encantador(a), glamouroso

glamour ['glæməˀ] n encanto, glamour m

glance [glɑːns] n relance m, vista de olhos ♦ vi: **to** ~ **at** olhar (de relance); ~ **off** vt fus (bullet) ricochetear de; **glancing** adj (blow) oblíquo

gland [glænd] n glândula

glare [glɛəˀ] n (of anger) olhar m furioso; (of light) luminosidade f; (of publicity) foco ♦ vi brilhar; **to** ~ **at** olhar furiosamente para; **glaring** adj (mistake) notório

glass [glɑːs] n vidro, cristal m; (for drinking) copo; ~**es** npl (spectacles) óculos mpl; ~**house** n estufa; ~**ware** n objetos mpl de cristal

glaze [gleɪz] vt (door) envidraçar; (pottery) vitrificar ♦ n verniz m; ~**d** adj (eye) vidrado; (pottery) vitrificado

glazier ['gleɪzɪəˀ] n vidraceiro/a

gleam [gliːm] vi brilhar

glean [gliːn] vt (information) colher

glee [gliː] n alegria, regozijo

glen [glɛn] n vale m

glib [glɪb] adj (answer) pronto; (person) labioso

glide [glaɪd] vi deslizar; (AVIAT, birds) planar; ~**r** n (AVIAT) planador m; **gliding** n (AVIAT) vôo sem motor

glimmer ['glɪməˀ] n luz f trêmula; (of interest, hope) lampejo

glimpse [glɪmps] n vista rápida, vislumbre m ♦ vt vislumbrar, ver de relance

glint [glɪnt] vi cintilar

glisten ['glɪsn] vi brilhar

glitter ['glɪtə*] *vi* reluzir, brilhar
gloat [gləut] *vi*: **to ~ (over)** exultar (com)
global ['gləubl] *adj* mundial
globe [gləub] *n* globo, esfera
gloom [glu:m] *n* escuridão *f*; (*sadness*) tristeza; **~y** *adj* escuro; triste
glorious ['glɔːrɪəs] *adj* (*weather*) magnífi-co; (*future*) glorioso
glory ['glɔːrɪ] *n* glória
gloss [glɔs] *n* (*shine*) brilho; (*also*: ~ **paint**) pintura brilhante, esmalte *m*; ~ **over** *vt fus* encobrir
glossary ['glɔsərɪ] *n* glossário
glossy ['glɔsɪ] *adj* lustroso
glove [glʌv] *n* luva; ~ **compartment** *n* (*AUT*) porta-luvas *m inv*
glow [gləu] *vi* (*shine*) brilhar; (*fire*) arder
glower ['glauə*] *vi*: **to ~ at** (sb) olhar (alguém) de modo ameaçador
glucose ['glu:kəus] *n* glicose *f*
glue [glu:] *n* cola ♦ *vt* colar
glum [glʌm] *adj* (*mood*) abatido; (*person, tone*) triste
glut [glʌt] *n* abundância, fartura
glutton ['glʌtn] *n* glutão/ona *m/f*; **a ~ for work** um(a) trabalhador(a) incansá-vel; **~y** *n* gula
GM *adj abbr* (= *genetically modified*) transgênico
gnarled [nɑːld] *adj* nodoso, retorcido
gnat [næt] *n* mosquito
gnaw [nɔː] *vt* roer

KEYWORD

go [gəu] (*pt* went, *pp* gone, *pl* ~es) *vi* **1** ir; (*travel, move*) viajar; **a car went by** um carro passou; **he has gone to Aberdeen** ele foi para Aberdeen
2 (*depart*) partir, ir-se
3 (*attend*): **she went to university in Rio** ela fez universidade no Rio; **he ~es to the local church** ele freqüenta a igreja local
4 (*take part in an activity*) ir; **to ~ for a walk** ir passear
5 (*work*) funcionar; **the bell went just then** a campainha acabou de tocar
6 (*become*): **to ~ pale/mouldy** ficar pálido/mofado
7 (*be sold*): **to ~ for £10** ser vendido por £10
8 (*fit, suit*): **to ~ with** acompanhar, combinar com
9 (*be about to, intend*): **he's ~ing to do it** ele vai fazê-lo; **are you ~ing to come?** você vem?
10 (*time*) passar
11 (*event, activity*) ser; **how did it ~?** como foi?
12 (*be given*): **the job is to ~ to someone else** o emprego vai ser dado para outra pessoa
13 (*break*) romper-se; **the fuse went** o fusível queimou; **the leg of the chair**

went a perna da cadeira quebrou
14 (*be placed*): **where does this cup ~?** onde é que põe esta xícara?; **the milk ~es in the fridge** pode guardar o leite na geladeira
♦ *n* **1** (*try*): **to have a ~ (at)** tentar a sorte (com)
2 (*turn*) vez *f*
3 (*move*): **to be on the ~** ter muito para fazer
go about *vi* (*also*: ~ **around**: *rumour*) espalhar-se ♦ *vt fus*: **how do I ~ about this?** como é que eu faço isto?
go ahead *vi* (*make progress*) progredir; (*get going*) ir em frente
go along *vi* ir ♦ *vt fus* ladear; **to ~ along with** concordar com
go away *vi* (*leave*) ir-se, ir embora
go back *vi* (*return*) voltar; (*go again*) ir de novo
go back on *vt fus* (*promise*) faltar com
go by *vi* (*years, time*) passar ♦ *vt fus* (*book, rule*) guiar-se por
go down *vi* (*descend*) descer, baixar; (*ship*) afundar; (*sun*) pôr-se ♦ *vt fus* (*stairs, ladder*) descer
go for *vt fus* (*fetch*) ir buscar; (*like*) gos-tar de; (*attack*) atacar
go in *vi* (*enter*) entrar
go in for *vt fus* (*competition*) inscrever-se em; (*like*) gostar de
go into *vt fus* (*enter*) entrar em; (*inves-tigate*) investigar; (*embark on*) embarcar em
go off *vi* (*leave*) ir-se; (*food*) estragar, apodrecer; (*bomb, gun*) explodir; (*event*) realizar-se ♦ *vt fus* (*person, food etc*) dei-xar de gostar de
go on *vi* (*continue*) seguir, continuar; (*happen*) acontecer, ocorrer
go out *vi* sair; (*for entertainment*): **are you ~ing out tonight?** você vai sair hoje à noite?; (*couple*): **they went out for 3 years** eles namoraram 3 anos; (*fire, light*) apagar-se
go over *vi* (*ship*) soçobrar ♦ *vt fus* (*check*) revisar
go round *vi* (*news, rumour*) circular
go through *vt fus* (*town etc*) atravessar; (*search through*) vasculhar; (*examine*) percorrer de cabo a rabo
go up *vi* subir; (*price*) aumentar
go without *vt fus* passar sem

---

goad [gəud] *vt* aguilhoar
go-ahead *adj* empreendedor(a) ♦ *n* luz *f* verde
goal [gəul] *n* meta, alvo; (*SPORT*) gol *m* (*BR*), golo (*PT*); ~**keeper** *n* goleiro/a (*BR*), guarda-redes *m/f inv* (*PT*); ~**post** *n* trave *f*
goat [gəut] *n* cabra
gobble ['gɔbl] *vt* (*also*: ~ **down**, ~ **up**) engolir rapidamente, devorar
go-between *n* intermediário/a

god [gɔd] n deus m; G~ Deus; ~**child** n afilhado/a; ~ **daughter** n afilhada; ~**dess** n deusa; ~**father** n padrinho; ~-**forsaken** adj abandonado; ~**mother** n madrinha; ~**send** n dádiva do céu; ~**son** n afilhado

goggles ['gɔglz] npl óculos mpl de proteção

going ['gəuɪŋ] n (conditions) estado do terreno ♦ adj: **the ~ rate** tarifa corrente

gold [gəuld] n ouro ♦ adj de ouro; ~**en** adj (made of ~) de ouro; (~ in colour) dourado; ~**fish** n inv peixe-dourado m; ~**mine** n mina de ouro; ~-**plated** adj plaquê inv; ~**smith** n ourives m/f inv

golf [gɔlf] n golfe m; ~ **ball** n bola de golfe; (on typewriter) esfera; ~ **club** n clube m de golfe; (stick) taco; ~ **course** n campo de golfe; ~**er** n jogador(a) m/f de golfe, golfista m/f

gone [gɔn] pp of go

gong [gɔŋ] n gongo

good [gud] adj bom/boa; (kind) bom, bondoso; (well-behaved) educado ♦ n bem m; ~**s** npl (COMM) mercadorias fpl; ~**!** bom!; **to be ~ at** ser bom em; **to be ~ for** servir para; **it's ~ for you** faz-lhe bem; **a ~ deal (of)** muito; **a ~ many** muitos; **to make ~** reparar; **it's no ~ complaining** não adianta se queixar; **for ~** para sempre, definitivamente; ~ **morning/afternoon/evening!** bom dia/boa tarde/boa noite!; ~ **night!** boa noite!; ~**bye** excl até logo (BR), adeus (PT); **to say ~bye** despedir-se; G~ **Friday** n Sexta-Feira Santa; ~-**looking** adj bonito; ~-**natured** adj (person) de bom gênio; (pet) de boa índole; ~**ness** n (of person) bondade f; **for ~ness sake!** pelo amor de Deus!; ~**ness gracious!** meu Deus do céu!, nossa (senhora)!; ~**s train** (BRIT) n trem m de carga; ~**will** n boa vontade f

goose [guːs] (pl **geese**) n ganso

gooseberry ['guzbərɪ] n groselha; **to play ~** (BRIT) ficar de vela

gooseflesh ['guːsfleʃ] n, **goose pimples** npl pele f arrepiada

gore [gɔːʳ] vt escornar ♦ n sangue m

gorge [gɔːdʒ] n desfiladeiro ♦ vt: **to ~ o.s. (on)** empanturrar-se (de)

gorgeous ['gɔːdʒəs] adj magnífico, maravilhoso; (person) lindo

gorilla [gə'rɪlə] n gorila m

gorse [gɔːs] n tojo

gory ['gɔːrɪ] adj sangrento

go-slow (BRIT) n greve f de trabalho lento, operação f tartaruga

gospel ['gɔspl] n evangelho

gossip ['gɔsɪp] n (scandal) fofocas fpl (BR), mexericos mpl (PT); (chat) conversa; (scandalmonger) fofoqueiro/a (BR), mexeriqueiro/a (PT) ♦ vi (chat) bater (um) papo (BR), cavaquear (PT)

got [gɔt] pt, pp of get

gotten ['gɔtn] (US) pp of get

gout [gaut] n gota

govern ['gʌvən] vt governar; (event) controlar

governess ['gʌvənɪs] n governanta

government ['gʌvnmənt] n governo

governor ['gʌvənəʳ] n governador(a) m/f; (of school, hospital, jail) diretor(a) m/f

gown [gaun] n vestido; (of teacher, judge) toga

GP n abbr (MED) = **general practitioner**

grab [græb] vt agarrar ♦ vi: **to ~ at** tentar agarrar

grace [greɪs] n (REL) graça; (gracefulness) elegância, fineza ♦ vt (honour) honrar; (adorn) adornar; **5 days' ~** um prazo de 5 dias; ~**ful** adj elegante, gracioso; **gracious** adj gracioso, afável

grade [greɪd] n (quality) classe f, qualidade f; (degree) grau m; (US: SCH) série f, classe ♦ vt classificar; ~ **crossing** (US) n passagem f de nível; ~ **school** (US) n escola primária

gradient ['greɪdɪənt] n declive m

gradual ['grædjuəl] adj gradual, gradativo; ~**ly** adv gradualmente, gradativamente, pouco a pouco

graduate [n 'grædjuɪt, vi 'grædjueɪt] n graduado, licenciado; (US) diplomado do colégio ♦ vi formar-se, licenciar-se; **graduation** n formatura

graffiti [grə'fiːtɪ] n, npl pichações fpl

graft [grɑːft] n (AGR, MED) enxerto; (BRIT: inf) trabalho pesado; (bribery) suborno ♦ vt enxertar

grain [greɪn] n grão m; (no pl: cereals) cereais mpl; (in wood) veia, fibra

gram [græm] n grama m

grammar ['græməʳ] n gramática; ~ **school** n (BRIT) ≈ liceo; **grammatical** adj gramatical

gramme [græm] n = **gram**

grand [grænd] adj esplêndido; (inf: wonderful) ótimo, formidável; ~**child** (irreg) n neto/a; ~**dad** n vovô m; ~**daughter** n neta; ~**eur** n grandeza, magnificência; ~**father** n avô m; ~**iose** adj grandioso; (pej) pomposo; (house) imponente; ~**ma** n avó f, vovó f; ~**mother** n avó f; ~**pa** n = ~**dad**; ~**parents** npl avós mpl; ~ **piano** n piano de cauda; ~**son** n neto; ~**stand** n (SPORT) tribuna principal

granite ['grænɪt] n granito

granny ['grænɪ] (inf) n avó f, vovó f

grant [grɑːnt] vt (concede) conceder; (a request etc) anuir a; (admit) admitir ♦ n (SCH) bolsa; (ADMIN) subvenção f, subsídio; **to take sth for ~ed** dar algo por certo

granulated sugar ['grænjuleɪtɪd-] n açúcar m granulado

granule ['grænjuːl] n grânulo

grape [greɪp] *n* uva

grapefruit ['greɪpfruːt] (*pl inv or* ~**s**) *n* toranja, grapefruit *m* (*BR*)

graph [grɑːf] *n* gráfico; ~**ic** *adj* gráfico; ~**ics** *n* (*art*) artes *fpl* gráficas ♦ *npl* (*drawings*) dessenhos *mpl*

grapple ['græpl] *vi*: **to** ~ **with sth** estar às voltas com algo

grasp [grɑːsp] *vt* agarrar, segurar; (*understand*) compreender, entender ♦ *n* aperto de mão; (*understanding*) compreensão *f*; ~**ing** *adj* avaro

grass [grɑːs] *n* grama (*BR*), relva (*PT*); ~**hopper** *n* gafanhoto; ~**roots** *adj* popular

grate [greɪt] *n* (*fireplace*) lareira ♦ *vi* ranger ♦ *vt* (*CULIN*) ralar

grateful ['greɪtful] *adj* agradecido, grato

grater ['greɪtə*] *n* ralador *m*

grating ['greɪtɪŋ] *n* (*iron bars*) grade *f* ♦ *adj* (*noise*) áspero

gratitude ['grætɪtjuːd] *n* agradecimento

gratuity [grə'tjuːɪtɪ] *n* gratificação *f*, gorjeta

grave [greɪv] *n* cova, sepultura ♦ *adj* sério; (*mistake*) grave

gravel ['grævl] *n* cascalho

gravestone ['greɪvstəun] *n* lápide *f*

graveyard ['greɪvjɑːd] *n* cemitério

gravity ['grævɪtɪ] *n* (*PHYS*) gravidade *f*; (*seriousness*) seriedade *f*, gravidade

gravy ['greɪvɪ] *n* molho (de carne)

gray [greɪ] (*US*) *adj* = **grey**

graze [greɪz] *vi* pastar ♦ *vt* (*touch lightly*) roçar; (*scrape*) raspar ♦ *n* (*MED*) esfoladura, arranhadura

grease [griːs] *n* (*fat*) gordura; (*lubricant*) graxa, lubrificante *m* ♦ *vt* untar, lubrificar, engraxar; ~**proof paper** (*BRIT*) *n* papel *m* de cera (vegetal); **greasy** *adj* gordurento, gorduroso; (*skin*, *hair*) oleoso

great [greɪt] *adj* grande; (*inf*) genial; (*pain*, *heat*) forte; (*important*) importante; **G~ Britain** *n* Grã-Bretanha; ~**grandfather** *n* bisavô *m*; ~**grandmother** *n* bisavó *f*; ~**ly** *adv* imensamente, muito; ~**ness** *n* grandeza

Greece [griːs] *n* Grécia

greed [griːd] *n* (*also*: ~**iness**) avidez *f*, cobiça; ~**y** *adj* avarento; (*for food*) guloso

Greek [griːk] *adj* grego ♦ *n* grego/a; (*LING*) grego

green [griːn] *adj* verde; (*inexperienced*) inexperiente, ingênuo ♦ *n* verde *m*; (*stretch of grass*) gramado (*BR*), relvado (*PT*); (*on golf course*) green *m*; ~**s** *npl* (*vegetables*) verduras *fpl*; ~ **belt** *n* (*round town*) cinturão *m* verde; ~ **card** *n* (*BRIT*: *AUT*) carta verde; (*US*) autorização *f* de residência; ~**ery** *n* verdura; ~**grocer** (*BRIT*) *n* verdureiro/a; ~**house** *n* estufa; ~**house effect** *n* efeito estufa; ~**house gas** *n* gás provocado pelo efeito estufa; ~**ish** *adj* esverdeado

Greenland ['griːnlənd] *n* Groenlândia

greet [griːt] *vt* (*welcome*) acolher; (*news*) receber; ~**ing** *n* acolhimento; ~**ing(s) card** *n* cartão *m* comemorativo

gregarious [grə'gɛərɪəs] *adj* gregário

grenade [grə'neɪd] *n* granada

grew [gruː] *pt of* **grow**

grey [greɪ] (*US* **gray**) *adj* cinzento; (*dismal*) sombrio; ~-**haired** *adj* grisalho; ~**hound** *n* galgo

grid [grɪd] *n* grade *f*; (*ELEC*) rede *f*

grief [griːf] *n* dor *f*, pesar *m*

grievance ['griːvəns] *n* motivo de queixa, agravo

grieve [griːv] *vi* sofrer ♦ *vt* dar pena a, afligir; **to** ~ **for** chorar por

grievous ['griːvəs] *adj*: ~ **bodily harm** (*LAW*) lesão *f* corporal (grave)

grill [grɪl] *n* (*on cooker*) grelha; (*also*: **mixed** ~) prato de grelhados ♦ *vt* (*BRIT*) grelhar; (*inf*: *question*) interrogar cerradamente

grille [grɪl] *n* grade *f*; (*AUT*) grelha

grim [grɪm] *adj* desagradável; (*unattractive*) feio; (*stern*) severo

grimace [grɪ'meɪs] *n* careta ♦ *vi* fazer caretas

grime [graɪm] *n* sujeira (*BR*), sujidade *f* (*PT*)

grin [grɪn] *n* sorriso largo ♦ *vi*: **to** ~ **(at)** dar um sorriso largo (para)

grind [graɪnd] (*pt*, *pp* **ground**) *vt* triturar; ?(*coffee etc*) moer; (*make sharp*) afiar; (*US*: *meat*) picar ♦ *n* (*work*) trabalho (repetitivo e maçante)

grip [grɪp] *n* (*of person*) aperto de mão; (*of animal*) força; (*handle*) punho; (*of tyre*, *shoe*) aderência; (*holdall*) valise *f* ♦ *vt* agarrar; (*attention*) prender; **to come to** ~**s with** arcar com

gripping ['grɪpɪŋ] *adj* absorvente, emocionante

grisly ['grɪzlɪ] *adj* horrendo, medonho

gristle ['grɪsl] *n* (*on meat*) nervo

grit [grɪt] *n* areia, grão *m* de areia; (*courage*) coragem *f* ♦ *vt* (*road*) pôr areia em; **to** ~ **one's teeth** cerrar os dentes

groan [grəun] *n* gemido ♦ *vi* gemer

grocer ['grəusə*] *n* dono/a de mercearia; ~**ies** *npl* comestíveis *mpl*; ~**'s (shop)** *n* mercearia

groggy ['grɔgɪ] *adj* grogue

groin [grɔɪn] *n* virilha

groom [gruːm] *n* cavariço; (*also*: **bride**~) noivo ♦ *vt* (*horse*) tratar; (*fig*): **to** ~ **sb for sth** preparar alguém para algo; **well-**~**ed** bem-posto

groove [gruːv] *n* ranhura, entalhe *m*

grope [grəup] *vi*: **to** ~ **for** procurar às cegas

gross [grəus] *adj* (*flagrant*) grave; (*vulgar*) vulgar; (: *building*) de mau-gosto; (*COMM*) bruto; ~**ly** *adv* (*greatly*) enormemente, gritantemente

grotesque [grə'tɛsk] *adj* grotesco

grotto ['grɒtəu] *n* gruta

grotty ['grɒtɪ] (*BRIT*: *inf*) *adj* vagabundo

ground [graund] *pt, pp of* **grind ♦** *n* terra, chão *m*; (*SPORT*) campo; (*land*) terreno; (*reason*: *gen pl*) motivo, razão *f*; (*US*: *also*: ~**wire**) (ligação *f* à) terra, fio-terra *m* ♦ *vt* (*plane*) manter em terra; (*US*: *ELEC*) ligar à terra; ~**s** *npl* (*of coffee etc*) borra; (*gardens etc*) jardins *mpl*, parque *m*; **on the** ~ no chão; **to the** ~ por terra; ~ **cloth** (*US*) *n* = ~**sheet**; ~**ing** *n* (*SCH*) conhecimentos *mpl* básicos; ~**less** *adj* infundado; ~**sheet** (*BRIT*) *n* capa impermeável; ~ **staff** *n* pessoal *m* de terra; ~**swell** *n* (*of opinion*) onda; ~**work** *n* base *f*, preparação *f*

group [gru:p] *n* grupo; (*also*: **pop** ~) conjunto ♦ *vt* (*also*: ~ **together**) agrupar ♦ *vi* (*also*: ~ **together**) agrupar-se

grouse [graus] *n inv* (*bird*) tetraz *m*, galo-silvestre *m* ♦ *vi* (*complain*) queixar-se, resmungar

grove [grəuv] *n* arvoredo

grovel ['grɒvl] *vi* (*fig*): **to** ~ (**before**) abaixar-se (diante de)

grow [grəu] (*pt* **grew**, *pp* **grown**) *vi* crescer; (*increase*) aumentar; (*develop*): **to** ~ (**out of/from**) originar-se; (*become*): **to** ~ **rich/weak** enriquecer(-se)/ enfraquecer-se ♦ *vt* plantar, cultivar; (*beard*) deixar crescer; ~ **up** *vi* crescer, fazer-se homem/mulher; ~**er** *n* cultivador(a) *m/f*, produtor(a) *m/f*; ~**ing** *adj* crescente

growl [graul] *vi* rosnar

grown [grəun] *pp of* **grow**

grown-up *n* adulto/a, pessoa mais velha

growth [grəuθ] *n* crescimento; (*increase*) aumento; (*MED*) abcesso, tumor *m*

grub [grʌb] *n* larva, lagarta; (*inf*: *food*) comida, rango (*BR*)

grubby ['grʌbɪ] *adj* encardido

grudge [grʌdʒ] *n* motivo de rancor ♦ *vt*: **to** ~ **sb sth** dar algo a alguém de má vontade, invejar algo a alguém; **to bear sb a** ~ **for sth** guardar rancor de alguém por algo

gruelling ['gruəlɪŋ] (*US* **grueling**) *adj* duro, árduo

gruesome ['gru:səm] *adj* horrível

gruff [grʌf] *adj* (*voice*) rouco; (*manner*) brusco

grumble ['grʌmbl] *vi* resmungar, bufar

grumpy ['grʌmpɪ] *adj* rabugento

grunt [grʌnt] *vi* grunhir

G-string *n* tapa-sexo *m*

guarantee [gærən'ti:] *n* garantia ♦ *vt* garantir

guard [gɑ:d] *n* guarda; (*one person*) guarda *m*; (*BRIT*: *RAIL*) guarda-freio; (*on machine*) dispositivo de segurança; (*also*: **fire**~) guarda-fogo ♦ *vt* (*protect*): **to** ~ (**against**) proteger (contra); (*prisoner*)

vigiar; **to be on one's** ~ estar prevenido; ~ **against** *vt fus* prevenir-se contra; ~**ed** *adj* (*statement*) cauteloso; ~**ian** *n* protetor(a) *m/f*; (*of minor*) tutor(a) *m/f*; ~**'s van** (*BRIT*) *n* (*RAIL*) vagão *m* de freio

Guatemala [gwɒtə'mɑːlə] *n* Guatemala

guerrilla [gə'rɪlə] *n* guerrilheiro/a

guess [gɛs] *vt, vi* (*estimate*) avaliar, conjeturar; (*answer*) adivinhar; (*US*) achar, supor ♦ *n* suposição *f*, conjetura; **to take** *or* **have a** ~ adivinhar, chutar (*inf*); ~**work** *n* conjeturas *fpl*

guest [gɛst] *n* convidado/a; (*in hotel*) hóspede *m/f*; ~**-house** *n* pensão *f*; ~**room** *n* quarto de hóspedes

guffaw [gʌ'fɔ:] *vi* dar gargalhadas

guidance ['gaɪdəns] *n* conselhos *mpl*

guide [gaɪd] *n* (*person*) guia *m/f*; (*book, fig*) guia *m*; (*BRIT*: *also*: **girl** ~) escoteira ♦ *vt* guiar; ~**book** *n* guia *m*; ~ **dog** *n* cão *m* de guia; ~**lines** *npl* (*advice*) orientação *f*

guild [gɪld] *n* grêmio

guile [gaɪl] *n* astúcia

guillotine ['gɪlətiːn] *n* guilhotina

guilt [gɪlt] *n* culpa; ~**y** *adj* culpado

guinea ['gɪnɪ] (*BRIT*) *n* guinéu *m* (*21 shillings*: antiga unidade monetária)

guinea pig *n* porquinho-da-Índia *m*, cobaia; (*fig*) cobaia

guise [gaɪz] *n*: **in** *or* **under the** ~ **of** sob a aparência de, sob o pretexto de

guitar [gɪ'tɑ:ʳ] *n* violão *m*

gulf [gʌlf] *n* golfo; (*abyss*: *also fig*) abismo

gull [gʌl] *n* gaivota

gullet ['gʌlɪt] *n* esôfago

gullible ['gʌlɪbl] *adj* crédulo

gully ['gʌlɪ] *n* barranco

gulp [gʌlp] *vi* engolir em seco ♦ *vt* (*also*: ~ **down**) engolir

gum [gʌm] *n* (*ANAT*) gengiva; (*glue*) goma; (*also*: ~ **drop**) bala de goma; (*also*: **chewing-**~) chiclete *m* (*BR*), pastilha elástica (*PT*) ♦ *vt* colar; ~**boots** (*BRIT*) *npl* botas *fpl* de borracha, galochas *fpl*

gumption ['gʌmpʃən] *n* juízo, bom senso

gun [gʌn] *n* (*gen*) arma (de fogo); (*revolver*) revólver *m*; (*small*) pistola; (*rifle*) espingarda; (*cannon*) canhão *m*; ~**boat** *n* canhoneira; ~**fire** *n* tiroteio; ~**man** (*irreg*) *n* pistoleiro; ~**point** *n*: **at** ~**point** sob a ameaça de uma arma; ~**powder** *n* pólvora; ~**shot** *n* tiro (de arma de fogo)

gurgle ['gə:gl] *vi* (*baby*) balbuciar; (*water*) gorgolejar

guru ['guru:] *n* guru *m*

gush [gʌʃ] *vi* jorrar; (*fig*) alvoroçar-se

gusset ['gʌsɪt] *n* nesga

gust [gʌst] *n* (*of wind*) rajada

gusto ['gʌstəu] *n*: **with** ~ com garra

gut [gʌt] n intestino, tripa; ~s npl (ANAT) entranhas fpl; (inf: courage) coragem f, raça (inf)
gutter ['gʌtə*] n (of roof) calha; (in street) sarjeta
guy [gaɪ] n (also: ~rope) corda; (inf: man) cara m (BR), tipo (PT)
Guyana [gaɪ'ænə] n Guiana
guzzle ['gʌzl] vt engolir com gula
gym [dʒɪm] n (also: gymnasium) ginásio; (also: gymnastics) ginástica
gymnast ['dʒɪmnæst] n ginasta m/f
gymnastics [dʒɪm'næstɪks] n ginástica
gym shoes npl tênis mpl
gym slip (BRIT) n uniforme m escolar
gynaecologist [gaɪnɪ'kɔlədʒɪst] (US **gynecologist**) n ginecologista m/f
gypsy ['dʒɪpsɪ] n = **gipsy**
gyrate [dʒaɪ'reɪt] vi girar

H

haberdashery ['hæbə'dæʃərɪ] (BRIT) n armarinho
habit ['hæbɪt] n hábito, costume m; (addiction) vício; (REL) hábito
habitual [hə'bɪtjuəl] adj habitual, costumeiro; (drinker, liar) inveterado
hack [hæk] vt (cut) cortar; (chop) talhar ♦ n (pej: writer) escrevinhador/a m/f; ~er n (COMPUT) pirata m (de dados de computador)
hackneyed ['hæknɪd] adj corriqueiro, batido
had [hæd] pt, pp of **have**
haddock ['hædək] (pl inv or ~s) n hadoque m (BR), eglefim m (PT)
hadn't ['hædnt] = **had not**
haemorrhage ['hɛmərɪdʒ] (US **hemorrhage**) n hemorragia
haemorrhoids ['hɛmərɔɪdz] (US **hemorrhoids**) npl hemorróidas fpl
haggard ['hægəd] adj emaciado, macilento
haggle ['hægl] vi pechinchar, regatear
Hague [heɪg] n: The ~ Haia
hail [heɪl] n granizo; (of objects) chuva; (of criticism) torrente f ♦ vt (greet) cumprimentar; (taxi) chamar; (person, event) saudar ♦ vi chover granizo; ~**stone** n pedra de granizo
hair [hɛə*] n (of human) cabelo; (of animal) pêlo; **to do one's ~** pentear-se; ~**brush** n escova de cabelo; ~**cut** n corte m de cabelo; ~**do** n penteado; ~**dresser** n cabeleireiro/a; ~**dresser's** n cabeleireiro; ~ **dryer** n secador m de cabelo; ~**grip** n grampo (BRIT), gancho (PT); ~**net** n rede f de cabelo; ~**pin** n grampo (BRIT), gancho (PT), pinça; ~**pin bend** (US ~**pin curve**) n curva fechada; ~**raising** adj horripilante, de arrepiar os cabelos; ~ **remover** n (creme m) depilatório; ~ **spray** n laquê m (BR), laca

(PT); ~**style** n penteado; ~**y** adj cabeludo, peludo; (inf: situation) perigoso
hake [heɪk] (pl inv or ~s) n abrótea
half [hɑːf] (pl **halves**) n metade f; (RAIL, bus, of beer etc) meia ♦ adj meio ♦ adv meio, pela metade; ~ **a pound** meia libra; **two and a** ~ dois e meio; ~ **a dozen** meia-dúzia; **to cut sth in** ~ cortar algo ao meio; ~ **asleep/empty/closed** meio adormecido/vazio/fechado; ~**baked** (inf) adj (idea, scheme) mal planejado; ~**caste** n mestiço/a; ~**hearted** adj irresoluto, indiferente; ~**hour** n meia hora; ~**mast**: **at** ~**mast** adv (flag) a meio-pau; ~**penny** n meio pêni m; ~**price** adj, adv pela metade do preço; ~ **term** (BRIT) n (SCH) dias de folga no meio do semestre; ~**time** n meio tempo; ~**way** adv a meio caminho; (in time) no meio
halibut ['hælɪbət] n inv hipoglosso
hall [hɔːl] n (for concerts) sala; (entrance way) hall m, entrada
hallmark ['hɔːlmɑːk] n (also fig) marca
hallo [hə'ləu] excl = **hello**
hall of residence (BRIT: pl **halls of residence**) n residência universitária
Hallowe'en ['hæləu'iːn] n Dia m das Bruxas (31 de outubro)
hallway ['hɔːlweɪ] n hall m, entrada
halo ['heɪləu] n (of saint etc) auréola
halt [hɔːlt] n parada (BR), paragem f (PT) ♦ vi parar ♦ vt deter; (process) interromper
halve [hɑːv] vt (divide) dividir ao meio; (reduce by half) reduzir à metade
halves [hɑːvz] npl of **half**
ham [hæm] n presunto, fiambre m (PT)
hamburger ['hæmbəːgə*] n hambúrguer m
hamlet ['hæmlɪt] n aldeola, lugarejo
hammer ['hæmə*] n martelo ♦ vt martelar ♦ vi (on door) bater insistentemente
hammock ['hæmək] n rede f
hamper ['hæmpə*] vt dificultar, atrapalhar ♦ n cesto
hamster ['hæmstə*] n hamster m
hand [hænd] n mão f; (of clock) ponteiro; (writing) letra; (of cards) cartas fpl; (worker) trabalhador m ♦ vt dar, passar; **to give** or **lend sb a** ~ dar uma mãozinha a alguém, dar uma ajuda a alguém; **at** ~ à mão, disponível; **in** ~ livre; (situation) sob controle; **to be on** ~ (person) estar disponível; (emergency services) estar num estado de prontidão; **on the one** ~ ..., **on the other** ~ ... por um lado ..., por outro (lado) ...; ~ **in** vt entregar; ~ **out** vt distribuir; ~ **over** vt entregar; (responsibility) transferir; ~**bag** n bolsa; ~**book** n manual m; ~**brake** n freio (BR) or travão m (PT) de mão; ~**cuffs** npl algemas fpl; ~**ful** n punhado; (of people) grupo
handicap ['hændɪkæp] n (MED) incapaci-

dade *f*; (*disadvantage*) desvantagem *f*;
(*SPORT*) handicap *m* ♦ *vt* prejudicar;
mentally/physically ~ped deficiente
mental/físico

handicraft ['hændɪkrɑːft] *n* artesanato,
trabalho manual

handiwork ['hændɪwəːk] *n* obra

handkerchief ['hæŋkətʃɪf] *n* lenço

handle ['hændl] *n* (*of door etc*) maçaneta;
(*of cup etc*) asa; (*of knife etc*) cabo; (*for
winding*) manivela ♦ *vt* manusear; (*deal
with*) tratar de; (*treat: people*) lidar com;
"~ with care" "cuidado - frágil"; **to
fly off the ~** perder as estribeiras;
~bar(s) *n(pl)* guidom *m* (*BR*), guidão
m (*PT*)

hand: ~-luggage *n* bagagem *f* de mão;
~made *adj* feito à mão; **~out** *n* (*money, food*) doação *f*; (*leaflet*) folheto; (*at
lecture*) apostila; **~rail** *n* corrimão *m*;
~shake *n* aperto de mão

handsome ['hænsəm] *adj* bonito, elegante; (*profit*) considerável

handwriting ['hændraɪtɪŋ] *n* letra, caligrafia

handy ['hændɪ] *adj* (*close at hand*) à
mão; (*useful*) útil; (*skilful*) habilidoso,
hábil; **~man** (*irreg*) *n* faz-tudo *m*; (*in
hotel etc*) biscateiro

hang [hæŋ] (*pt, pp* **hung**) *vt* pendurar;
(*criminal: pt, pp ~ed*) enforcar ♦ *vi* estar pendurado; (*hair, drapery*) cair ♦ *n*
(*inf*): **to get the ~ of sth** pegar o jeito
de algo; **~ about or around** *vi* vadiar,
vagabundear; **~ on** *vi* (*wait*) esperar; **~
up** *vt* (*coat*) pendurar ♦ *vi* (*TEL*) desligar; **to ~ up on sb** bater o telefone na
cara de alguém

hangar ['hæŋə*] *n* hangar *m*

hanger ['hæŋə*] *n* cabide *m*

hanger-on *n* parasita *m/f*, filão/lona
m/f

hang-gliding *n* vôo livre

hangover ['hæŋəuvə*] *n* ressaca

hang-up *n* grilo

hanker ['hæŋkə*] *vi*: **to ~ after** (*long
for*) ansiar por

hankie ['hæŋkɪ] *n abbr* = **handkerchief**

hanky ['hæŋkɪ] *n abbr* = **handkerchief**

haphazard [hæp'hæzəd] *adj* desorganizado

happen ['hæpən] *vi* acontecer; **to ~ to
do sth** fazer algo por acaso; **as it ~s**
... acontece que ...; **~ing** *n* acontecimento, ocorrência

happily ['hæpɪlɪ] *adv* (*luckily*) felizmente;
(*cheerfully*) alegremente

happiness ['hæpɪnɪs] *n* felicidade *f*

happy ['hæpɪ] *adj* feliz; (*cheerful*) contente; **to be ~ (with)** estar contente
(com); **to be ~ to do** (*willing*) estar disposto a fazer; **~ birthday!** feliz aniversário; **~-go-lucky** *adj* despreocupado

harangue [hə'ræŋ] *vt* arengar

harass ['hærəs] *vt* importunar; **~ment** *n*

perseguição *f*

harbour ['hɑːbə*] (*US* **harbor**) *n* porto ♦
vt (*hope etc*) abrigar; (*hide*) esconder

hard [hɑːd] *adj* duro; (*difficult*) difícil;
(*work*) árduo; (*person*) severo, cruel;
(*facts*) verdadeiro ♦ *adv* (*work*) muito,
diligentemente; (*think, try*) seriamente:
to look ~ at olhar firme *or* fixamente
para; **no ~ feelings!** sem ressentimen-
tos!; **to be ~ of hearing** ser surdo; **to
be ~ done by** ser tratado injustamente;
~back *n* livro de capa dura; **~ cash** *n*
dinheiro vivo *or* em espécie; **~ disk** *n*
(*COMPUT*) disco rígido; **~en** *vt* endurecer; (*steel*) temperar; (*fig*) tornar insensível ♦ *vi* endurecer-se; **~-headed** *adj*
prático; **~ labour** *n* trabalhos *mpl* for-
çados

hardly ['hɑːdlɪ] *adv* (*scarcely*) apenas; (*no
sooner*) mal; **~ ever/anywhere** quase
nunca/em lugar nenhum

hardship ['hɑːdʃɪp] *n* privação *f*

hard up (*inf*) *adj* duro (*BR*), liso (*PT*)

hardware ['hɑːdwɛə*] *n* ferragens *fpl*;
(*COMPUT*) hardware *m*; **~ shop** *n* loja
de ferragens

hard-wearing [-'wɛərɪŋ] *adj* resistente

hard-working *adj* trabalhador(a); (*student*) aplicado

hardy ['hɑːdɪ] *adj* forte; (*plant*) resistente

hare [hɛə*] *n* lebre *f*; **~-brained** *adj* maluco, absurdo

harm [hɑːm] *n* mal *m*; (*damage*) dano ♦
vt (*person*) fazer mal a, prejudicar;
(*thing*) danificar; **out of ~'s way** a salvo; **~ful** *adj* prejudicial, nocivo; **~less**
adj inofensivo

harmonica [hɑː'mɔnɪkə] *n* gaita de boca,
harmônica

harmonious [hɑː'məunɪəs] *adj* harmo-
nioso

harmony ['hɑːmənɪ] *n* harmonia

harness ['hɑːnɪs] *n* (*for horse*) arreios
mpl; (*for child*) correia; (*safety*) correia de segurança ♦ *vt* (*horse*) arrear,
pôr arreios em; (*resources*) aproveitar

harp [hɑːp] *n* harpa ♦ *vi*: **to ~ on about**
bater sempre na mesma tecla sobre

harpoon [hɑː'puːn] *n* arpão *m*

harrowing ['hærəuɪŋ] *adj* doloroso, pungente

harsh [hɑːʃ] *adj* (*life*) duro; (*sound*) de-
sarmonioso; (*light*) forte

harvest ['hɑːvɪst] *n* colheita ♦ *vt* colher

has [hæz] *vb see* **have**

hash [hæʃ] *n* (*CULIN*) picadinho; (*fig:
mess*) confusão *f*

hashish ['hæʃɪʃ] *n* haxixe *m*

hasn't ['hæznt] = **has not**

hassle ['hæsl] (*inf*) *n* complicação *f*

haste [heɪst] *n* pressa; **~n** *vt* acelerar ♦
vi: **to ~n to do sth** apressar-se em fazer algo; **hastily** *adv* depressa; **hasty**
adj apressado; (*rash*) precipitado

hat [hæt] *n* chapéu *m*

hatch [hætʃ] n (NAUT: also: ~**way**) escotilha; (also: **service** ~) comunicação f entre a cozinha e a sala de jantar ♦ vi
sair do ovo, chocar
hatchback ['hætʃbæk] n (AUT) camionete
f, hatch m
hatchet ['hætʃɪt] n machadinha
hate [heɪt] vt odiar, detestar ♦ n ódio;
~**ful** adj odioso; **hatred** n ódio
haughty ['hɔːtɪ] adj soberbo, arrogante
haul [hɔːl] vt puxar ♦ n (of fish) redada;
(of stolen goods etc) pilhagem f, presa;
~**age** n transporte m (rodoviário);
(costs) gasto com transporte; ~**ier** (BRIT)
n (firm) transportadora; (person) trans-
portador(a) m/f
haunch [hɔːntʃ] n anca, quadril m; (of
meat) quarto traseiro
haunt [hɔːnt] vt (subj: ghost) assombrar;
(: problem, memory) perseguir ♦ n redu-
to; (~ed house) casa mal-assombrada

KEYWORD

have [hæv] (pt, pp had) aux vb **1** (gen)
ter; to ~ **gone/eaten** ter ido/comido;
he has been kind/promoted ele foi
bondoso/promovido; **having finished** or
when he had finished, **he left** quando
ele terminou, foi embora
2 (in tag questions): **you've done it**,
~**n't you?** você fez isto, não foi?; **he**
hasn't done it, **has he?** ele não fez
isto, fez?
3 (in short questions and answers):
you've made a mistake – **no I** ~**n't/**
so I ~ você fez um erro – não, eu não
fiz/sim, eu fiz; **I've been there before**,
~ **you?** eu já estive lá, e você?
♦ modal aux vb (be obliged): to ~ (**got**)
to do sth ter que fazer algo; **I** ~**n't got**
or **I don't** ~ **to wear glasses** eu não
preciso usar óculos
♦ vt **1** (possess) ter; **he has (got) blue**
eyes/dark hair ele tem olhos azuis/
cabelo escuro
2 (referring to meals etc): to ~ **break-**
fast tomar café (BR), tomar o pequeno
almoço (PT); to ~ **lunch/dinner**
almoçar/jantar; to ~ **a drink/a ciga-**
rette tomar um drinque/fumar um cigarro
3 (receive, obtain etc): **may I** ~ **your**
address? pode me dar seu endereço?;
you can ~ **it for 5 pounds** você pode
levá-lo por 5 libras; to ~ **a baby** dar à
luz (BR), ter um nenê or bebê (PT)
4 (maintain, allow): **he will** ~ **it that**
he is right ele vai insistir que ele está
certo; **I won't** ~ **it/this nonsense!** não
vou agüentar isso/este absurdo!; **we**
can't ~ **that** não podemos permitir isto
5: to ~ **sth done** mandar fazer algo; to
~ **one's hair cut** ir cortar o cabelo; to
~ **sb do sth** mandar alguém fazer algo
6 (experience, suffer): to ~ **a cold/flu**

estar resfriado (BR) or constipado (PT)/
com gripe; **she had her bag stolen** ela
teve sua bolsa roubada; to ~ **an opera-**
tion fazer uma operação
7 (+ n: take, hold etc): to ~ **a swim/**
walk/bath/rest ir nadar/passear/tomar
um banho/descansar; **let's** ~ **a look** vamos dar uma olhada; to ~ **a party** fazer uma festa
8 (inf: dupe): **he's been had** ele comprou gato por lebre
have out vt: to ~ **it out with sb** (settle a problem) explicar-se com alguém

haven ['heɪvn] n porto; (fig) abrigo, refúgio
haven't ['hævnt] = **have not**
haversack ['hævəsæk] n mochila
havoc ['hævək] n destruição f; **to play**
~ **with** (fig) estragar
Hawaii [həˈwaɪiː] n Havaí m
hawk [hɔːk] n falcão m
hay [heɪ] n feno; ~ **fever** n febre f do
feno; ~**stack** n palheiro
haywire ['heɪwaɪə*] (inf) adj: **to go** ~
desorganizar-se, degringolar
hazard ['hæzəd] n perigo, risco ♦ vt
aventurar, arriscar; ~**ous** adj perigoso;
~ **warning lights** npl (AUT) pisca-alerta
m
haze [heɪz] n névoa
hazelnut ['heɪzlnʌt] n avelã f
hazy ['heɪzɪ] adj nublado; (idea) confuso
he [hiː] pron ele; ~ **who** ... quem ...,
aquele que ...
head [hɛd] n cabeça; (of table) cabeceira;
(of queue) frente f; (of organization) chefe m/f; (of school) diretor(a) m/f ♦ vt
(list) encabeçar; (group) liderar; (ball)
cabecear; ~**s or tails** cara ou coroa; ~
first de cabeça; ~ **over heels** de pernas para o ar; ~ **over heels in love**
apaixonadíssimo; ~ **for** vt fus dirigir-se
a; (disaster) estar procurando; ~**ache** n
dor f de cabeça; ~**dress** n cocar m;
~**ing** n título, cabeçalho; ~**lamp** (BRIT)
n = ~**light**; ~**land** n promontório;
~**light** n farol m; ~**line** n manchete f;
~**long** adv (fall) de cabeça; (rush) precipitadamente; ~**master** n diretor m (de
escola); ~**mistress** n diretora (de escola); ~ **office** n matriz f; ~**-on** adj (collision) de frente; (confrontation) direto;
~**phones** npl fones mpl de ouvido;
~**quarters** npl sede f; (MIL) quartel m
general; ~**rest** n apoio para a cabeça;
~**room** n (in car) espaço (para a cabeça); (under bridge) vão m livre; ~**scarf**
(irreg) n lenço de cabeça; ~**strong** adj
voluntarioso, teimoso; ~ **waiter** n mai-
tre m (BR), chefe m de mesa (PT);
~**way** n: to **make** ~**way** avançar;
~**wind** n vento contrário; ~**y** adj emocionante; (intoxicating) estonteante
heal [hiːl] vt curar ♦ vi cicatrizar

health [hɛlθ] n saúde f; good ~! saúde!; ~ **food(s)** n(pl) alimentos mpl naturais; H~ **Service** (BRIT) n: the H~ Service o Serviço Nacional da Saúde; ~y adj (person) saudável; (air, walk) sadio; (economy) próspero, forte

heap [hi:p] n pilha, montão m ♦ vt: to ~ sth with encher algo de; ~s (of) (inf) um monte (de); to ~ sth on empilhar algo em

hear [hɪə*] (pt, pp ~d [hɔ:d]) vt ouvir; (listen to) escutar; (news) saber; to ~ about ouvir falar de; to ~ from sb ter notícias de alguém; ~d pt, pp of hear; ~ing n (sense) audição f; (LAW) audiência; ~ing aid n aparelho para a surdez; ~say n boato, ouvir-dizer m

hearse [hə:s] n carro fúnebre

heart [ha:t] n coração m; (of problem, city) centro; ~s npl (CARDS) copas fpl; to lose/take ~ perder o ânimo/criar coragem; at ~ no fundo; by ~ (learn, know) de cor; ~ **attack** n ataque m de coração; ~**beat** n batida do coração; ~**breaking** adj desolador(a); ~**broken** adj: to be ~broken estar inconsolável; ~**burn** n azia; ~ **failure** n parada cardíaca; ~**felt** adj sincero

hearth [ha:θ] n lareira

heartland ['ha:tlænd] n coração m (do país)

heartless ['ha:tlɪs] adj cruel, sem coração

hearty ['ha:tɪ] adj (person) energético; (laugh) animado; (appetite) bom/boa; (welcome) sincero; (dislike) absoluto

heat [hi:t] n calor m; (excitement) ardor m; (SPORT: also: qualifying ~) (prova) eliminatória ♦ vt esquentar; (room, house) aquecer; ~ **up** vi aquecer-se, esquentar ♦ vt esquentar; (food, house) aquecer; ~**ed** adj aquecido; (fig) acalorado; ~**er** n aquecedor m

heath [hi:θ] (BRIT) n charneca

heathen ['hi:ðn] adj, n pagão/pagã m/f

heather ['hɛðə*] n urze f

heating ['hi:tɪŋ] n aquecimento, calefação f

heatstroke ['hi:tstrəuk] n insolação f

heatwave ['hi:tweɪv] n onda de calor

heave [hi:v] vt (pull) puxar; (push) empurrar (com esforço); (lift) levantar (com esforço) ♦ vi (chest) palpitar; (retch) ter ânsias de vómito ♦ n puxão m; empurrão m; to ~ a sigh soltar um suspiro

heaven ['hɛvn] n céu m, paraíso; ~**ly** adj celestial; (REL) divino

heavily ['hɛvɪlɪ] adv pesadamente; (drink, smoke) excessivamente; (sleep, depend) profundamente

heavy ['hɛvɪ] adj pesado; (work) duro; (responsibility) grande; (rain, meal) forte; (drinker, smoker) inveterado; (weather) carregado; ~ **goods vehicle** (BRIT) n caminhão m de carga pesada;

~**weight** n (SPORT) peso-pesado

Hebrew ['hi:bru:] adj hebreu/hebréia ♦ n (LING) hebraico

Hebrides ['hɛbrɪdi:z] npl: the ~ as (ilhas) Hébridas

heckle ['hɛkl] vt apartear

hectic ['hɛktɪk] adj agitado

he'd [hi:d] = he would; he had

hedge [hɛdʒ] n cerca viva, sebe f ♦ vi dar evasivas ♦ vt: to ~ one's bets (fig) resguardar-se

hedgehog ['hɛdʒhɔg] n ouriço

heed [hi:d] vt (also: take ~ of) prestar atenção a

heel [hi:l] n (of shoe) salto; (of foot) calcanhar m ♦ vt (shoe) pôr salto em

hefty ['hɛftɪ] adj (person) robusto; (parcel) pesado; (profit) alto

heifer ['hɛfə*] n novilha, bezerra

height [haɪt] n (of person) estatura; (of building, tree) altura; (altitude, of plane) altitude f; (high ground) monte m; (fig: of power) auge m; (: of luxury) máximo; (: of stupidity) cúmulo; ~**en** vt elevar; (fig) aumentar

heir [ɛə*] n herdeiro; ~**ess** n herdeira; ~**loom** n relíquia de família

held [hɛld] pt, pp of hold

helicopter ['hɛlɪkɔptə*] n helicóptero

heliport ['hɛlɪpɔ:t] n heliporto

helium ['hi:lɪəm] n hélio

hell [hɛl] n inferno; ~! (inf) droga!

he'll [hi:l] = he will; he shall

hellish ['hɛlɪʃ] (inf) adj terrível

hello [hə'ləu] excl oi! (BR), olá! (PT); (surprise) ora essa!

helm [hɛlm] n (NAUT) timão m, leme m

helmet ['hɛlmɪt] n capacete m

help [hɛlp] n ajuda; (charwoman) faxineira ♦ vt ajudar; ~! socorro!; ~ **yourself** sirva-se; he can't ~ it não tem culpa; ~**er** n ajudante m/f; ~**ful** adj prestativo; (advice) útil; ~**ing** n porção f; ~**less** adj (incapable) incapaz; (defenceless) indefeso

hem [hɛm] n bainha ♦ vt embainhar; ~ **in** vt cercar, encurralar

hemisphere ['hɛmɪsfɪə*] n hemisfério

hemorrhage ['hɛmərɪdʒ] (US) n = haemorrhage

hemorrhoids ['hɛmərɔɪdz] (US) npl = haemorrhoids

hen [hɛn] n galinha; (female bird) fêmea

hence [hɛns] adv daí, portanto; 2 **years** ~ daqui a 2 anos; ~**forth** adv de agora em diante, doravante

henchman ['hɛntʃmən] (pej: irreg) n jagunço, capanga m

henpecked ['hɛnpɛkt] adj dominado pela esposa

hepatitis [hɛpə'taɪtɪs] n hepatite f

her [hə:*] pron (direct) a; (indirect) lhe; (stressed, after prep) ela ♦ adj seu/sua, dela; see also me; my

herald ['hɛrəld] n precursor(a) m/f ♦ vt

anunciar

heraldry [ˈherəldrɪ] n heráldica

herb [hɜːb] n erva

herd [hɜːd] n rebanho

here [hɪə*] adv aqui; (at this point) nesse ponto; ~! (present) presente!; ~ **is/are** aqui está/estão; ~ **she is!** aqui está ela!; ~**after** adv daqui por diante; ~**by** adv (in letter) por este meio

heredity [hɪˈredɪtɪ] n hereditariedade f

heresy [ˈherəsɪ] n heresia

heretic [ˈherətɪk] n herege m/f

heritage [ˈherɪtɪdʒ] n património

hermetically [hɜːˈmetɪklɪ] adv: ~ **sealed** hermeticamente fechado

hermit [ˈhɜːmɪt] n eremita m/f

hernia [ˈhɜːnɪə] n hérnia

hero [ˈhɪərəʊ] (pl ~**es**) n herói m; (of book, film) protagonista m

heroin [ˈherəʊɪn] n heroína

heroine [ˈherəʊɪn] n heroína; (of book, film) protagonista

heron [ˈherən] n garça

herring [ˈherɪŋ] (pl inv or ~**s**) n arenque m

hers [hɜːz] pron (o) seu/(a) sua, (o/a) dela; see also **mine**[1]

herself [hɜːˈself] pron (reflexive) se; (emphatic) ela mesma; (after prep) si (mesma); see also **oneself**

he's [hiːz] = **he is**; **he has**

hesitant [ˈhezɪtənt] adj hesitante, indeciso

hesitate [ˈhezɪteɪt] vi hesitar; **hesitation** n hesitação f, indecisão f

heterosexual [ˈhetərəʊˈseksjʊəl] adj heterossexual

hew [hjuː] (pp ~**ed** or ~**n**) vt cortar (com machado)

heyday [ˈheɪdeɪ] n: **the** ~ **of** o auge or apogeu da

HGV (BRIT) n abbr = **heavy goods vehicle**

hi [haɪ] excl oi!

hiatus [haɪˈeɪtəs] n hiato

hibernate [ˈhaɪbəneɪt] vi hibernar

hiccough [ˈhɪkʌp] vi soluçar ♦ npl: ~**s**: **to have (the)** ~**s** estar com soluço

hiccup [ˈhɪkʌp] = **hiccough**

hid [hɪd] pt of **hide**; ~**den** pp of **hide**

hide [haɪd] (pt **hid**, pp **hidden**) n (skin) pele f ♦ vt esconder, ocultar; (view) obscurecer ♦ vi: **to** ~ **(from sb)** esconder-se or ocultar-se (de alguém); ~**and-seek** n esconde-esconde m; ~**away** n esconderijo

hideous [ˈhɪdɪəs] adj horrível

hiding [ˈhaɪdɪŋ] n (beating) surra; **to be in** ~ (concealed) estar escondido

hierarchy [ˈhaɪərɑːkɪ] n hierarquia

hi-fi [ˈhaɪfaɪ] n alta-fidelidade f; (system) som m ♦ adj de alta-fidelidade

high [haɪ] adj alto; (number) grande; (price) alto, elevado; (wind) forte; (voice) agudo; (opinion) ótimo; (principles) nobre ♦ adv alto, a grande altura; **it is 20 m** ~ tem 20 m de altura; ~ **in the air** nas alturas; ~**brow** adj intelectual, erudito; ~**chair** n cadeira alta (para criança); ~**er education** n ensino superior; ~**handed** adj despótico; ~**heeled** adj de salto alto; ~ **jump** n (SPORT) salto em altura; **the H**~**lands** npl a Alta Escócia; ~**light** n (fig) ponto alto; (in hair) mecha ♦ vt realçar, ressaltar; ~**ly** adv: ~**ly paid** muito bem pago; (a lot): **to speak/think** ~**ly of** falar elogiosamente de/pensar muito bem de; ~**ly strung** adj tenso, irritadiço; ~**ness** n: **Her** (or **His**) **H**~**ness** Sua Alteza; ~**pitched** adj agudo; ~**rise** adj alto; ~ **school** n (BRIT) escola secundária; (US) científico; ~ **season** (BRIT) n alta estação f; ~ **street** (BRIT) n rua principal; ~**way** (US) n estrada; (main road) rodovia; **H**~**way Code** (BRIT) n Código Nacional de Trânsito

hijack [ˈhaɪdʒæk] vt seqüestrar; ~**er** n seqüestrador(a) m/f (de avião)

hike [haɪk] vi caminhar ♦ n caminhada, excursão f a pé; ~**r** n caminhante m/f, andarilho/a

hilarious [hɪˈlɛərɪəs] adj hilariante

hill [hɪl] n colina; (high) montanha; (slope) ladeira, rampa; ~**side** n vertente f; ~**y** adj montanhoso

hilt [hɪlt] n (of sword) punho, guarda; **to the** ~ (fig: support) plenamente

him [hɪm] pron (direct) o; (indirect) lhe; (stressed, after prep) ele; see also **me**; ~**self** pron (reflexive) se; (emphatic) ele mesmo; (after prep) si (mesmo); see also **oneself**

hind [haɪnd] adj traseiro

hinder [ˈhɪndə*] vt retardar; **hindrance** n (nuisance) estorvo; (interruption) impedimento

hindsight [ˈhaɪndsaɪt] n: **with** ~ em retrospecto

Hindu [ˈhɪnduː] adj hindu

hinge [hɪndʒ] n dobradiça ♦ vi (fig): **to** ~ **on** depender de

hint [hɪnt] n (suggestion) insinuação f; (advice) palpite m, dica; (sign) sinal m ♦ vt: **to** ~ **that** insinuar que ♦ vi: **to** ~ **at** fazer alusão a

hip [hɪp] n quadril m

hippopotamus [hɪpəˈpɒtəməs] (pl ~**es** or **hippopotami**) n hipopótamo

hire [ˈhaɪə*] vt (BRIT: car, equipment) alugar; (worker) contratar ♦ n aluguel m (BR), aluguer m (PT); **for** ~ aluga-se; (taxi) livre; ~ **purchase** (BRIT) n compra a prazo

his [hɪz] pron (o) seu/(a) sua, (o/a) dele ♦ adj seu/sua, dele; see also **my**; **mine**[1]

hiss [hɪs] vi (snake, fat) assoviar; (gas) silvar; (boo) vaiar

historian [hɪˈstɔːrɪən] n historiador(a) m/f

historic(al) [hɪ'stɔrɪk(l)] *adj* histórico
history ['hɪstərɪ] *n* história
hit [hɪt] (*pt, pp* **hit**) *vt* bater em; (*target*) acertar, alcançar; (*car*) bater em, colidir com; (*fig: affect*) atingir ♦ *n* golpe *m*; (*success*) sucesso; **to ~ it off with sb** dar-se bem com alguém; **~-and-run driver** *n* motorista que atropela alguém e foge da cena do acidente
hitch [hɪtʃ] *vt* (*fasten*) atar, amarrar; (*also:* ~ **up**) levantar ♦ *n* (*difficulty*) dificuldade *f*; **to ~ a lift** pegar carona (*BR*), arranjar uma boleia (*PT*)
hitch-hike *vi* pegar carona (*BR*), andar à boleia (*PT*); **~r** *n* pessoa que pega carona (*BR*) or anda à boleia (*PT*)
hi-tech *adj* tecnologicamente avançado ♦ *n* alta tecnologia
hitherto [hɪðə'tuː] *adv* até agora
HIV *n* **~-negative/-positive** *adj* HIV negativo/positivo
hive [haɪv] *n* colméia; ~ **off** (*inf*) *vt* transferir
HMS (*BRIT*) *abbr* = His (or Her) Majesty's Ship
hoard [hɔːd] *n* provisão *f*; (*of money*) tesouro ♦ *vt* acumular; **~ing** (*BRIT*) *n* tapume *m*, outdoor *m*
hoarfrost ['hɔːfrɔst] *n* geada
hoarse [hɔːs] *adj* rouco
hoax [həʊks] *n* trote *m*
hob [hɔb] *n* parte de cima do fogão
hobble ['hɔbl] *vi* mancar
hobby ['hɔbɪ] *n* hobby *m*, passatempo predileto; **~-horse** *n* (*fig*) tema *m* favorito
hobo ['həʊbəʊ] (*US*) *n* vagabundo
hockey ['hɔkɪ] *n* hóquei *m*
hoe [həʊ] *n* enxada
hog [hɔg] *n* porco ♦ *vt* (*fig*) monopolizar; **to go the whole ~** ir até o fim
hoist [hɔɪst] *vt* içar
hold [həʊld] (*pt, pp* **held**) *vt* segurar; (*contain*) conter; (*have*) ter; (*record etc: meeting*) realizar; (*detain*) deter; (*consider*): **to ~ sb responsible (for sth)** responsabilizar alguém (por algo); (*keep in certain position*): **to ~ one's head up** manter a cabeça erigida ♦ *vi* (*withstand pressure*) resistir; (*be valid*) ser válido ♦ *n* (*grasp*) pressão *f*; (*: fig*) influência, domínio; (*of ship*) porão *m*; (*of plane*) compartimento para cargo; (*control*) controle *m*; ~ **the line!** (*TEL*) não desligue!; **to ~ one's own** (*fig*) virar-se, sair-se bem; **to catch or get (a) ~ of** agarrar, pegar; ~ **back** *vt* reter; (*secret*) manter, guardar; ~ **down** *vt* (*person*) segurar; (*job*) manter; ~ **off** *vt* (*enemy*) afastar, repelir; ~ **on** *vi* agarrar-se; (*wait*) esperar; ~ **on!** espera aí!; (*TEL*) não desligue!; ~ **on to** *vt fus* agarrar-se a; (*keep*) guardar, ficar com; ~ **out** *vt* (*hand*) estender; (*hope*) ter ♦ *vi* (*resist*) resistir; ~ **up** *vt* (*raise*) levantar; (*sup-*

port) apoiar; (*delay*) atrasar; (*rob*) assaltar; **~all** (*BRIT*) *n* bolsa de viagem; **~er** *n* (*container*) recipiente *m*; (*of ticket*) portador(a) *m/f*; (*of record*) detentor(a) *m/f*; (*of office, title*) titular *m/f*; **~ing** (*share*) participação *f*; (*small farm*) pequena fazenda; **~-up** *n* (*robbery*) assalto; (*delay*) demora; (*BRIT: in traffic*) engarrafamento
hole [həʊl] *n* buraco; (*small: in sock etc*) furo ♦ *vt* esburacar
holiday ['hɔlɪdɪ] *n* (*BRIT: vacation*) férias *fpl*; (*day off*) dia *m* de folga; (*public* ~) feriado; **on ~** de férias; ~ **camp** (*BRIT*) *n* colônia de férias; **~-maker** (*BRIT*) *n* pessoa (que está) de férias; ~ **resort** *n* local *m* de férias
holiness ['həʊlɪnɪs] *n* santidade *f*
Holland ['hɔlənd] *n* Holanda
hollow ['hɔləʊ] *adj* oco, vazio; (*cheeks*) côncavo; (*eyes*) fundo; (*sound*) surdo; (*laugh, claim*) falso ♦ *n* (*in ground*) cavidade *f*, depressão *f* ♦ *vt*: **to ~ out** escavar
holly ['hɔlɪ] *n* azevinho
holocaust ['hɔləkɔːst] *n* holocausto
holster ['həʊlstə*] *n* coldre *m*
holy ['həʊlɪ] *adj* sagrado; (*person*) santo, bento
homage ['hɔmɪdʒ] *n* homenagem *f*; **to pay ~ to** prestar homenagem a, homenagear
home [həʊm] *n* casa, lar *m*; (*country*) pátria; (*institution*) asilo ♦ *cpd* caseiro, doméstico; (*ECON, POL*) nacional, interno; (*SPORT: team*) de casa; (*: game*) no próprio campo ♦ *adv* (*direction*) para casa; (*right in: nail etc*) até o fundo; **at ~** em casa; **make yourself at ~** fique à vontade; ~ **address** *n* endereço residencial; ~ **computer** *n* computador *m* residencial; **~land** *n* terra (natal); **~less** *adj* sem casa, desabrigado; **~ly** *adj* (*simple*) simples *inv*; **~-made** *adj* caseiro; **H~ Office** (*BRIT*) *n* Ministério do Interior; ~ **page** *n* (*COMPUT*) home page *f*, página de abertura; ~ **rule** *n* autonomia; **H~ Secretary** (*BRIT*) *n* Ministro/a do Interior; **~sick** *adj*: **to be ~sick** estar com saudades (do lar); ~ **town** *n* cidade *f* natal; **~ward** *adj* para casa, para a terra natal; **~work** *n* dever *m* de casa
homogeneous [hɔmə'dʒiːnɪəs] *adj* homogêneo
homosexual [hɔməʊ'sɛksjʊəl] *adj, n* homossexual *m/f*
Honduras [hɔn'djʊərəs] *n* Honduras *f* (*no article*)
honest ['ɔnɪst] *adj* (*truthful*) franco; (*trustworthy*) honesto; (*sincere*) sincero; **~ly** *adv* honestamente; **~y** *n* honestidade *f*, sinceridade *f*
honey ['hʌnɪ] *n* mel *m*; **~comb** *n* favo de mel; **~moon** *n* lua-de-mel *f*; (*trip*)

viagem f de lua-de-mel; **~suckle** n madressilva

honk [hɔŋk] vi buzinar

honor [ˈɔnəˀ] (US) = honour

honorary [ˈɔnərəri] adj (unpaid) não remunerado; (duty, title) honorário

honour [ˈɔnəˀ] (US honor) vt honrar ♦ n honra; **~able** adj honrado; **~s degree** n (SCH) diploma m com distinção

hood [hud] n capuz m; (of cooker) tampa; (BRIT: AUT) capota; (US: AUT) capô m

hoodlum [ˈhuːdləm] n pinta-braba m

hoodwink [ˈhudwɪŋk] vt tapear

hoof [huːf] (pl hooves) n casco, pata

hook [huk] n gancho; (on dress) gancho, colchete m; (for fishing) anzol m ♦ vt prender com gancho (or colchete); (fish) fisgar

hooligan [ˈhuːlɪgən] n desordeiro/a, bagunceiro/a

hoop [huːp] n arco

hooray [huːˈreɪ] excl = hurrah

hoot [huːt] vi (AUT) buzinar; (siren) tocar; (owl) piar; **~er** n (BRIT: AUT) buzina; (NAUT, factory) sirena

hoover [ˈhuːvəˀ] ® (BRIT) n aspirador m (de pó) ♦ vt passar o aspirador em

hooves [huːvz] npl of hoof

hop [hɔp] vi saltar, pular; (on one foot) pular num pé só

hope [həup] vt, vi esperar ♦ n esperança; I ~ so/not espero que sim/não; **~ful** adj (person) otimista, esperançoso; (situation) promissor(a); **~fully** adv esperançosamente; **~fully, they'll come back** é de esperar or esperamos que voltem; **~less** adj desesperado, irremediável; (useless) inútil

hops [hɔps] npl lúpulo

horde [hɔːd] n multidão f

horizon [həˈraɪzn] n horizonte m; **~tal** adj horizontal

hormone [ˈhɔːməun] n hormônio

horn [hɔːn] n corno, chifre m; (material) chifre; (MUS) trompa; (AUT) buzina

hornet [ˈhɔːnɪt] n vespão m

horny [ˈhɔːnɪ] (inf) adj excitado (sexualmente), com tesão (BR: inf!)

horoscope [ˈhɔrəskəup] n horóscopo

horrendous [həˈrɛndəs] adj horrendo

horrible [ˈhɔrɪbl] adj horrível; (terrifying) terrível

horrid [ˈhɔrɪd] adj horrível

horrify [ˈhɔrɪfaɪ] vt horrorizar

horror [ˈhɔrəˀ] n horror m; **~ film** n filme m de terror

hors d'œuvre [ɔːˈdəːvrə] n entrada

horse [hɔːs] n cavalo; **~back: on ~back** adj, adv a cavalo; **~chestnut** n castanha-da-índia; **~man** (irreg) n cavaleiro; (skilled) ginete m; **~power** n cavalo-vapor m; **~racing** n corridas fpl de cavalo, turfe m; **~radish** n rábano-bastardo; **~shoe** n ferradura

horticulture [ˈhɔːtɪkʌltʃəˀ] n horticultura

hose [həuz] n (also: **~pipe**) mangueira

hosiery [ˈhəuzɪərɪ] n meias fpl e roupa de baixo

hospice [ˈhɔspɪs] n asilo

hospitable [ˈhɔspɪtəbl] adj hospitaleiro

hospital [ˈhɔspɪtl] n hospital m

hospitality [hɔspɪˈtælɪtɪ] n hospitalidade f

host [həust] n anfitrião m; (TV, RADIO) apresentador(a) m/f; (REL) hóstia; (large number): **a ~ of** uma multidão de

hostage [ˈhɔstɪdʒ] n refém m/f

hostel [ˈhɔstl] n albergue m, abrigo; (also: **youth ~**) albergue da juventude

hostess [ˈhəustɪs] n anfitriã f; (BRIT: air ~) aeromoça (BR), hospedeira de bordo (PT); (TV, RADIO) apresentadora

hostile [ˈhɔstaɪl] adj hostil

hostility [hɔˈstɪlɪtɪ] n hostilidade f

hot [hɔt] adj quente; (as opposed to only warm) muito quente; (spicy) picante; (fierce) ardente; **to be ~** (person) estar com calor; (thing, weather) estar quente; **~bed** n (fig) foco, ninho; **~ dog** n cachorro-quente m

hotel [həuˈtɛl] n hotel m; **~ier** n hoteleiro/a; (manager) gerente m/f (de hotel)

hot: ~headed adj impetuoso; **~house** n estufa; **~ line** n (POL) telefone m vermelho, linha direta; **~ly** adv ardentemente, apaixonadamente; **~plate** n (on cooker) chapa elétrica; **~water bottle** n bolsa de água quente

hound [haund] vt acossar, perseguir ♦ n cão m de caça, sabujo

hour [ˈauəˀ] n hora; **~ly** adj de hora em hora; (rate) por hora

house [n haus, pl ˈhauzɪz, vt hauz] n (gen, firm) casa; (POL) câmara; (THEATRE) assistência, lotação f ♦ vt (person) alojar; (collection) abrigar; **on the ~** (fig) por conta da casa; **~ arrest** n prisão f domiciliar; **~boat** n casa flutuante; **~bound** adj confinado em casa (por invalidez); **~breaking** n arrombamento de domicílio; **~coat** n roupão m; **~hold** n família; (house) casa; **~keeper** n governanta; **~keeping** n (work) economia doméstica; (money) economia doméstica; **~warming (party)** n festa de inauguração de uma casa; **~wife** (irreg) n dona de casa; **~work** n trabalhos mpl domésticos; **housing** n (provision) alojamento; (houses) residências fpl; **housing development** (BRIT housing estate) n conjunto residencial

hovel [ˈhɔvl] n casebre m

hover [ˈhɔvəˀ] vi pairar; **~craft** n aerobarco

KEYWORD

how [hau] adv **1** (in what way) como; **~ was the film?** que tal o filme?; **~ are you?** como vai?

2 (*to what degree*) quanto; ~ **much milk/many people?** quanto de leite/quantas pessoas?; ~ **long have you been here?** quanto tempo você está aqui?; ~ **old are you?** quantos anos você tem?; ~ **tall is he?** qual é a altura dele?; ~ **lovely/awful!** que ótimo/terrível!

however [hau'evə*] *adv* de qualquer modo; (+ *adj*) por mais ... que; (*in questions*) como ♦ *conj* no entanto, contudo

howl [haul] *vi* uivar

H.P. (*BRIT*) *n abbr* = **hire purchase**

h.p. *abbr* (*AUT*) (= *horsepower*) CV

HQ *n abbr* (= *headquarters*) QG *m*

hub [hʌb] *n* cubo; (*fig*) centro

hubbub ['hʌbʌb] *n* algazarra, vozerio

hubcap ['hʌbkæp] *n* (*AUT*) calota

huddle ['hʌdl] *vi*: **to** ~ **together** aconchegar-se

hue [hju:] *n* cor *f*, matiz *m*; ~ **and cry** *n* clamor *m* público

huff [hʌf] *n*: **in a** ~ com raiva

hug [hʌg] *vt* abraçar; (*thing*) agarrar, prender

huge [hju:dʒ] *adj* enorme, imenso

hulk [hʌlk] *n* (*wreck*) navio velho, carcaça; (*person*) brutamontes *m inv*; (*building*) trambolho

hull [hʌl] *n* (*of ship*) casco

hullo [hə'ləu] *excl* = **hello**

hum [hʌm] *vt* cantarolar ♦ *vi* cantarolar; (*insect, machine etc*) zumbir

human ['hju:mən] *adj* humano ♦ *n* (*also*: ~ **being**) ser *m* humano

humane [hju:'mein] *adj* humano

humanitarian [hju:mænɪ'tɛərɪən] *adj* humanitário

humanity [hju:'mænɪtɪ] *n* humanidade *f*

humble ['hʌmbl] *adj* humilde ♦ *vt* humilhar

humbug ['hʌmbʌg] *n* embuste *m*; (*BRIT*: *sweet*) bala de hortelã

humdrum ['hʌmdrʌm] *adj* monótono, enfadonho

humid ['hju:mɪd] *adj* úmido

humiliate [hju:'mɪlɪeɪt] *vt* humilhar

humility [hju:'mɪlɪtɪ] *n* humildade *f*

humor ['hju:mə*] (*US*) *n* = **humour**

humorous ['hju:mərəs] *adj* humorístico; (*person*) engraçado

humour ['hju:mə*] (*US* **humor**) *n* humorismo, senso de humor; (*mood*) humor *m* ♦ *vt* fazer a vontade de

hump [hʌmp] *n* (*in ground*) elevação *f*; (*camel's*) corcova, giba; (*deformity*) corcunda; ~**backed** *adj*: ~**backed bridge** ponte pequena e muito arqueada

hunch [hʌntʃ] *n* (*premonition*) pressentimento, palpite *m*; ~**back** *n* corcunda *m/f*; ~**ed** *adj* corcunda

hundred ['hʌndrəd] *num* cem; (*before lower numbers*) cento; ~**s of people** centenas de pessoas; ~**weight** *n* (*BRIT*)

50.8 kg; 112 lb; (*US*) = **45.3 kg; 100 lb**

hung [hʌŋ] *pt, pp of* **hang**

Hungarian [hʌŋ'gɛərɪən] *adj* húngaro ♦ *n* húngaro/a; (*LING*) húngaro

Hungary ['hʌŋgərɪ] *n* Hungria

hunger ['hʌŋgə*] *n* fome *f* ♦ *vi*: **to** ~ **for** (*desire*) desejar ardentemente; ~ **strike** *n* greve *f* de fome

hungry ['hʌŋgrɪ] *adj* faminto, esfomeado; (*keen*): ~ **for** (*fig*) ávido de, ansioso por; **to be** ~ estar com fome

hunk [hʌŋk] *n* naco

hunt [hʌnt] *vt* buscar; (*criminal, fugitive*) perseguir; (*SPORT, for food*) caçar ♦ *vi* caçar; (*search*) **to** ~ (**for**) procurar (por) ♦ *n* caça, caçada; ~**er** *n* caçador(a) *m/f*; ~**ing** *n* caça

hurdle ['hə:dl] *n* (*SPORT*) barreira; (*fig*) obstáculo

hurl [hə:l] *vt* arremessar, lançar; (*abuse*) gritar

hurrah [hu'rɑ:] *excl* oba!, viva!

hurray [hu'reɪ] *excl* = **hurrah**

hurricane ['hʌrɪkən] *n* furacão *m*

hurried ['hʌrɪd] *adj* apressado; (*rushed*) feito às pressas; ~**ly** *adv* depressa, apressadamente

hurry ['hʌrɪ] *n* pressa ♦ *vi* (*also*: ~ **up**) apressar-se ♦ *vt* (*also*: ~ **up**: *person*) apressar; (: *work*) acelerar; **to be in a** ~ estar com pressa

hurt [hə:t] (*pt, pp* **hurt**) *vt* machucar; (*injure*) ferir; (*fig*) magoar ♦ *vi* doer; ~**ful** *adj* (*remark*) que magoa, ofensivo

hurtle ['hə:tl] *vi*: **to** ~ **past/down** passar como um raio/cair com violência

husband ['hʌzbənd] *n* marido, esposo

hush [hʌʃ] *n* silêncio, quietude *f* ♦ *vt* silenciar, fazer calar; ~! silêncio!, psiu!; ~ **up** *vt* abafar, encobrir

husk [hʌsk] *n* (*of wheat*) casca; (*of maize*) palha

husky ['hʌskɪ] *adj* rouco ♦ *n* cão *m* esquimó

hustle ['hʌsl] *vt* apressar ♦ *n*: ~ **and bustle** grande movimento

hut [hʌt] *n* cabana, choupana; (*shed*) alpendre *m*

hutch [hʌtʃ] *n* coelheira

hyacinth ['haɪəsɪnθ] *n* jacinto

hybrid ['haɪbrɪd] *n* híbrido; (*mixture*) combinação *f*

hydrant ['haɪdrənt] *n* (*also*: **fire** ~) hidrante *m*

hydraulic [haɪ'drɔ:lɪk] *adj* hidráulico

hydroelectric [haɪdrəʊ'lɛktrɪk] *adj* hidroelétrico

hydrofoil ['haɪdrəfɔɪl] *n* hidrofoil *m*, aliscafo

hydrogen ['haɪdrədʒən] *n* hidrogênio

hyena [haɪ'i:nə] *n* hiena

hygiene ['haɪdʒi:n] *n* higiene *f*

hymn [hɪm] *n* hino

hype [haɪp] (*inf*) *n* titití *m*, falatório

hypermarket ['haɪpəmɑ:kɪt] (*BRIT*) *n* hipermercado

hyphen ['haɪfn] n hífen m

hypnosis [hɪp'nəʊsɪs] n hipnose f; **hypnotist** n hipnotizador(a) m/f; **hypnotize** vt hipnotizar

hypocrite ['hɪpəkrɪt] n hipócrita m/f; **hypocritical** adj hipócrita

hypothermia [haɪpəˈθəːmɪə] n hipotermia

hypothesis [haɪ'pɒθɪsɪs] (pl **hypotheses**) n hipótese f

hysterical [hɪ'stɪrɪkl] adj histérico; (funny) hilariante; **hysterics** npl (nervous) crise f histérica; (laughter) ataque m de riso; **to be in** or **have hysterics** (anger, panic) ter uma crise histérica; (laughter) ter um ataque de riso

I

I [aɪ] pron eu

ice [aɪs] n gelo; (~ cream) sorvete m ♦ vt (cake) cobrir com glacê ♦ vi (also: ~ over, ~ up) gelar; **~berg** n iceberg m; **~box** n (US) geladeira; (BRIT: in fridge) congelador m; (insulated box) geladeira portátil; ~ **cream** n sorvete m (BR), gelado (PT); ~ **cube** n pedra de gelo; **~d** adj (drink) gelado; (cake) glaçado; ~ **hockey** n hóquei m sobre o gelo

Iceland ['aɪslənd] n Islândia

ice: ~ **lolly** (BRIT) n picolé m; ~ **rink** n pista de gelo, rinque m; **~-skating** n patinação f no gelo

icicle ['aɪsɪkl] n pingente m de gelo

icing ['aɪsɪŋ] n (CULIN) glacê m; ~ **sugar** (BRIT) n açúcar m glacê

icy ['aɪsɪ] adj gelado

I'd [aɪd] = I would; I had

idea [aɪ'dɪə] n idéia

ideal [aɪ'dɪəl] n ideal m ♦ adj ideal

identical [aɪ'dɛntɪkl] adj idêntico

identification [aɪdɛntɪfɪ'keɪʃən] n identificação f; **means of** ~ documentos pessoais

identify [aɪ'dɛntɪfaɪ] vt identificar

Identikit [aɪ'dɛntɪkɪt] ® n: ~ **picture** retrato falado

identity [aɪ'dɛntɪtɪ] n identidade f; ~ **card** n carteira de identidade

idiom ['ɪdɪəm] n expressão f idiomática; (style) idioma m, linguagem f

idiosyncrasy [ɪdɪəʊ'sɪŋkrəsɪ] n idiossincrasia

idiot ['ɪdɪət] n idiota m/f; **~ic** adj idiota

idle ['aɪdl] adj ocioso; (lazy) preguiçoso; (unemployed) desempregado; (question, conversation) fútil; (pleasure) descontraído ♦ vi (machine) funcionar com a transmissão desligada; ~ **away** vt: **to** ~ **away the time** perder or desperdiçar tempo

idol ['aɪdl] n ídolo; **~ize** vt idolatrar

idyllic [ɪ'dɪlɪk] adj idílico

i.e. abbr (= id est: that is) i.e., isto é

if [ɪf] conj **1** (conditional use) se; ~ **necessary** se necessário; ~ **I were you** se eu fôsse você

2 (whenever) quando

3 (although): (even) ~ mesmo que

4 (whether) se

5: ~ **so/not** sendo assim/do contrário; ~ **only** se pelo menos; see also **as**

ignite [ɪg'naɪt] vt incendiar ♦ vi acender

ignition [ɪg'nɪʃən] n (AUT) ignição f; **to switch on/off the** ~ ligar/desligar o motor; ~ **key** n (AUT) chave f de ignição

ignorant ['ɪgnərənt] adj ignorante; **to be** ~ **of** ignorar

ignore [ɪg'nɔː] vt (person) não fazer caso de; (fact) não levar em consideração, ignorar

I'll [aɪl] = I will; I shall

ill [ɪl] adj doente; (harmful: effects) nocivo ♦ n mal m ♦ adv: **to speak/think** ~ **of sb** falar/pensar mal de alguém; **to be taken** ~ ficar doente; **~-advised** adj pouco recomendado; (person) imprudente; **~-at-ease** adj constrangido, pouco à vontade

illegal [ɪ'liːgl] adj ilegal

illegible [ɪ'lɛdʒɪbl] adj ilegível

illegitimate [ɪlɪ'dʒɪtɪmət] adj ilegítimo

ill-fated adj malfadado

ill feeling n má vontade f, rancor m

illiterate [ɪ'lɪtərət] adj analfabeto

ill-mannered [-'mænəd] adj mal-educado, grosseiro

illness ['ɪlnɪs] n doença

illogical [ɪ'lɒdʒɪkl] adj ilógico

ill-treat vt maltratar

illuminate [ɪ'luːmɪneɪt] vt iluminar, clarear; **illumination** n iluminação f; **illuminations** npl (decorative lights) luminárias fpl

illusion [ɪ'luːʒən] n ilusão f

illusory [ɪ'luːsərɪ] adj ilusório

illustrate ['ɪləstreɪt] vt ilustrar; (point) exemplificar; **illustration** n ilustração f; (example) exemplo; (explanation) esclarecimento

ill will n animosidade f

I'm [aɪm] = I am

image ['ɪmɪdʒ] n imagem f; **~ry** n imagens fpl

imaginary [ɪ'mædʒɪnərɪ] adj imaginário

imagination [ɪmædʒɪ'neɪʃən] n imaginação f; (inventiveness) inventividade f

imagine [ɪ'mædʒɪn] vt imaginar

imbalance [ɪm'bæləns] n desigualdade f

imbecile ['ɪmbəsiːl] n imbecil m/f

imbue [ɪm'bjuː] vt: **to** ~ **sb/sth with** imbuir alguém/algo de

imitate ['ɪmɪteɪt] vt imitar; **imitation** n imitação f; (copy) cópia; (mimicry) mímica

immaculate [ɪ'mækjulət] *adj* impecável; (*REL*) imaculado

immaterial [ɪmə'tɪərɪəl] *adj* irrelevante

immature [ɪmə'tjuə*] *adj* imaturo; (*fruit*) verde; (*cheese*) fresco

immediate [ɪ'miːdɪət] *adj* imediato; (*pressing*) urgente, premente; (*neighbourhood, family*) próximo; **~ly** *adv* imediatamente; (*directly*) diretamente; **~ly next to** bem junto a

immense [ɪ'mɛns] *adj* imenso; (*importance*) enorme

immerse [ɪ'məːs] *vt* submergir; **to be ~d in** (*fig*) estar absorto em

immersion heater [ɪ'məːʃn-] (*BRIT*) *n* aquecedor *m* de imersão

immigrant [ɪ'mɪɡrənt] *n* imigrante *m/f*

immigration [ɪmɪ'ɡreɪʃən] *n* imigração *f*

imminent [ɪmɪnənt] *adj* iminente

immobile [ɪ'məubaɪl] *adj* imóvel

immoral [ɪ'mɔrl] *adj* imoral

immortal [ɪ'mɔːtl] *adj* imortal

immune [ɪ'mjuːn] *adj*: **~ to** imune a, imunizado contra; **immunity** *n* imunidade *f*

immunize [ɪmjunaɪz] *vt* imunizar

imp [ɪmp] *n* (*small devil*) diabinho; (*child*) criança levada

impact [ɪmpækt] *n* impacto (*BR*), impacte *m* (*PT*)

impair [ɪm'pɛə*] *vt* prejudicar

impale [ɪm'peɪl] *vt* perfurar, empalar

impart [ɪm'pɑːt] *vt* (*make known*) comunicar; (*bestow*) dar

impartial [ɪm'pɑːʃl] *adj* imparcial

impassable [ɪm'pɑːsəbl] *adj* (*river*) intransponível; (*road*) intransitável

impassive [ɪm'pæsɪv] *adj* impassível

impatience [ɪm'peɪʃəns] *n* impaciência

impatient [ɪm'peɪʃənt] *adj* impaciente; **to get** *or* **grow ~** impacientar-se

impeccable [ɪm'pɛkəbl] *adj* impecável

impede [ɪm'piːd] *vt* impedir, estorvar

impediment [ɪm'pɛdɪmənt] *n* obstáculo; (*also*: **speech ~**) defeito (de fala)

impending [ɪm'pɛndɪŋ] *adj* iminente, próximo

impenetrable [ɪm'pɛnɪtrəbl] *adj* impenetrável; (*fig*) incompreensível

imperative [ɪm'pɛrətɪv] *adj* (*tone*) imperioso, obrigatório; (*need*) vital; (*necessary*) indispensável ♦ *n* (*LING*) imperativo

imperfect [ɪm'pəːfɪkt] *adj* imperfeito; (*goods etc*) defeituoso ♦ *n* (*LING*: *also*: **~ tense**) imperfeito

imperial [ɪm'pɪərɪəl] *adj* imperial

impersonal [ɪm'pəːsənl] *adj* impessoal

impersonate [ɪm'pəːsəneɪt] *vt* fazer-se passar por, personificar; (*THEATRE*) imitar

impertinent [ɪm'pəːtɪnənt] *adj* impertinente, insolente

impervious [ɪm'pəːvɪəs] *adj* (*fig*): **~ to**

insensível a

impetuous [ɪm'pɛtjuəs] *adj* impetuoso, precipitado

impetus [ɪmpətəs] *n* ímpeto; (*fig*) impulso

impinge [ɪm'pɪndʒ]: **to ~ on** *vt fus* impressionar, impingir em; (*affect*) afetar

implacable [ɪm'plækəbl] *adj* implacável, impiedoso

implement [*n* 'ɪmplɪmənt, *vt* 'ɪmplɪmɛnt] *n* instrumento, ferramenta; (*for cooking*) utensílio ♦ *vt* efetivar

implicate [ɪmplɪkeɪt] *vt* (*compromise*) comprometer; (*involve*) implicar, envolver; **implication** *n* implicação *f*, conseqüência; (*involvement*) involvimento

implicit [ɪm'plɪsɪt] *adj* implícito; (*complete*) absoluto

implore [ɪm'plɔː*] *vt* implorar, suplicar

imply [ɪm'plaɪ] *vt* (*mean*) significar; (*hint*) dar a entender que

impolite [ɪmpə'laɪt] *adj* indelicado, maleducado

import [*vt* ɪm'pɔːt, *n* 'ɪmpɔːt] *vt* importar ♦ *n* importação *f*; (*article*) mercadoria importada

importance [ɪm'pɔːtəns] *n* importância

important [ɪm'pɔːtənt] *adj* importante; **it's not ~** não tem importância, não importa

importer [ɪm'pɔːtə*] *n* importador(a) *m/f*

impose [ɪm'pəuz] *vt* impor ♦ *vi*: **to ~ on sb** abusar de alguém; **imposing** *adj* imponente; **imposition** *n* (*of tax etc*) imposição *f*; **to be an imposition on sb** (*person*) abusar de alguém

impossible [ɪm'pɔsɪbl] *adj* impossível; (*situation*) inviável; (*person*) insuportável

impotent [ɪmpətənt] *adj* impotente

impound [ɪm'paund] *vt* confiscar

impoverished [ɪm'pɔvərɪʃt] *adj* empobrecido; (*land*) esgotado

impracticable [ɪm'præktɪkəbl] *adj* impraticável, inexeqüível

impractical [ɪm'præktɪkl] *adj* pouco prático

imprecise [ɪmprɪ'saɪs] *adj* impreciso, inexato

impregnable [ɪm'prɛɡnəbl] *adj* (*castle*) inexpugnável

impregnate [ɪmprɛɡneɪt] *vt* embeber

impress [ɪm'prɛs] *vt* impressionar; (*mark*) imprimir; **to ~ sth on sb** inculcar algo em alguém

impression [ɪm'prɛʃən] *n* impressão *f*; (*imitation*) caricatura; **to be under the ~ that** estar com a impressão de que; **~ist** *n* (*ART*) impressionista *m/f*; (*entertainer*) caricaturista *m/f*

impressive [ɪm'prɛsɪv] *adj* impressionante

imprint ['ɪmprɪnt] *n* impressão *f*, marca; (*PUBLISHING*) nome *m* (da coleção)

imprison [ɪm'prɪzn] *vt* encarcerar;

~**ment** n prisão f

improbable [ɪmˈprɔbəbl] adj improvável; (story) inverossímil (BR), inverosímil (PT)

impromptu [ɪmˈprɔmptjuː] adj improvisado

improper [ɪmˈprɔpəʳ] adj (unsuitable) impróprio; (dishonest) desonesto

improve [ɪmˈpruːv] vt melhorar ♦ vi melhorar; (pupils) progredir; ~**ment** n melhora; progresso

improvise [ˈɪmprəvaɪz] vt, vi improvisar

imprudent [ɪmˈpruːdnt] adj imprudente

impudent [ˈɪmpjudnt] adj insolente, impudente

impulse [ˈɪmpʌls] n impulso; **on** ~ sem pensar, num impulso

impunity [ɪmˈpjuːnɪtɪ] n: **with** ~ impunemente

impure [ɪmˈpjuəʳ] adj impuro; (adulterated) adulterado

KEYWORD

in [ɪn] prep **1** (indicating place, position) em; ~ **the house/garden** na casa/no jardim; **I have it** ~ **my hand** eu estou assegurando isto; ~ **here/there** aqui dentro/lá dentro
2 (with place names: of town, country, region) em; ~ **London/Rio** em Londres/no Rio; ~ **England/Japan/the United States** na Inglaterra/no Japão/nos Estados Unidos
3 (indicating time: during) em; ~ **spring/autumn** na primavera/no outono; ~ **1988** em 1988; ~ **May** em maio; **I'll see you** ~ **July** até julho; ~ **the morning de manhã**; **at 4 o'clock** ~ **the afternoon** às 4 da tarde
4 (indicating time: in the space of) em; **I did it** ~ **3 hours/days** fiz isto em 3 horas/dias; ~ **2 weeks** or ~ **2 weeks' time** daqui a 2 semanas
5 (indicating manner etc): ~ **a loud/soft voice** em voz alta/numa voz suave; **written** ~ **pencil/ink** escrito a lápis/à caneta; ~ **English/Portuguese** em inglês/português; **the boy** ~ **the blue shirt** o menino de camisa azul
6 (indicating circumstances): ~ **the sun** ao or sob o sol; ~ **the rain** na chuva; **a rise** ~ **prices** um aumento nos preços
7 (indicating mood, state): ~ **tears** aos prantos; ~ **anger/despair** com raiva/desesperado; ~ **good condition** em boas condições
8 (with ratios, numbers): **1** ~ **10** 1 em 10, 1 em cada 10; **20 pence** ~ **the pound** vinte pênis numa libra; **they lined up** ~ **twos** eles se alinharam dois a dois
9 (referring to people, works) em
10 (indicating profession etc): **to be** ~ **teaching/publishing** ser professor/

trabalhar numa editora
11 (after superl): **the best pupil** ~ **the class** o melhor aluno da classe; **the biggest/smallest** ~ **Europe** o maior/menor na Europa
12 (with present participle): ~ **saying this** ao dizer isto
♦ adv: **to be** ~ (person: at home) estar em casa; (: at work) estar no trabalho; (fashion) estar na moda; (ship, plane, train): **it's** ~ chegou; **is he** ~? ele está?; **to ask sb** ~ convidar alguém para entrar; **to run/limp** etc ~ entrar correndo/mancando etc
♦ n: **the** ~**s and outs** (of proposal, situation etc) os cantos e recantos, os pormenores

in. abbr = **inch(es)**

inability [ɪnəˈbɪlɪtɪ] n: ~ **(to do)** incapacidade f (de fazer)

inaccurate [ɪnˈækjurət] adj inexato, impreciso

inadequate [ɪnˈædɪkwət] adj insuficiente; (person) impróprio

inadvertently [ɪnədˈvəːtntlɪ] adv inadvertidamente, sem querer

inadvisable [ɪnədˈvaɪzəbl] adj desaconselhável, inoportuno

inane [ɪˈneɪn] adj tolo

inanimate [ɪnˈænɪmət] adj inanimado

inappropriate [ɪnəˈprəuprɪət] adj inadequado; (word, expression) impróprio

inarticulate [ɪnɑːˈtɪkjulət] adj (person) incapaz de expressar-se (bem); (speech) inarticulado

inasmuch as [ɪnəzˈmʌtʃ-] adv na medida em que

inaudible [ɪnˈɔːdɪbl] adj inaudível

inauguration [ɪnɔːgjuˈreɪʃən] n inauguração f; (of president, official) posse f

in-between adj intermediário

inborn [ɪnˈbɔːn] adj inato

inbred [ɪnˈbred] adj inato; (family) de procriação consangüínea

Inc. (US) abbr = **incorporated**

incalculable [ɪnˈkælkjuləbl] adj incalculável

incapable [ɪnˈkeɪpəbl] adj incapaz

incapacitate [ɪnkəˈpæsɪteɪt] vt incapacitar

incense [n ˈɪnsɛns, vt ɪnˈsɛns] n incenso ♦ vt (anger) exasperar, enraivecer

incentive [ɪnˈsɛntɪv] n incentivo

incessant [ɪnˈsɛsnt] adj incessante, contínuo; ~**ly** adv constantemente

inch [ɪntʃ] n polegada (= 25 mm; 12 in a foot); **to be within an** ~ **of** estar a um passo de; **he didn't give an** ~ ele não cedeu nem um milímetro; ~ **forward** vi avançar palmo a palmo

incidence [ˈɪnsɪdns] n incidência

incident [ˈɪnsɪdnt] n incidente m, evento

incidental [ɪnsɪˈdɛntl] adj adicional; ~ **to** relacionado com; ~**ly** adv (by the *way*) a propósito

incite [ɪn'saɪt] *vt* (*rioters*) incitar; (*violence*) provocar

inclination [ɪnklɪ'neɪʃən] *n* (*tendency*) tendência; (*disposition*) inclinação *f*

incline [*n* 'ɪnklaɪn, *vt, vi* ɪn'klaɪn] *n* inclinação *f*, ladeira ♦ *vt* curvar, inclinar ♦ *vi* inclinar-se; **to be ~d** to tender a, ser propenso a

include [ɪn'kluːd] *vt* incluir

including [ɪn'kluːdɪŋ] *prep* inclusive

inclusive [ɪn'kluːsɪv] *adj* incluído, inclusivo; **~ of** incluindo

incoherent [ɪnkəu'hɪərənt] *adj* incoerente

income ['ɪŋkʌm] *n* (*earnings*) renda, rendimentos *mpl*; (*unearned*) renda; **~ tax** *n* imposto de renda (*BR*), imposto complementar (*PT*)

incoming ['ɪnkʌmɪŋ] *adj* (*flight*) de chegada; (*mail*) de entrada; (*government*) novo; (*tide*) enchente

incompetent [ɪn'kɔmpɪtənt] *adj* incompetente

incomplete [ɪnkəm'pliːt] *adj* incompleto; (*unfinished*) por terminar

incongruous [ɪn'kɔŋgruəs] *adj* incongruente; (*remark, act*) impróprio

inconsiderate [ɪnkən'sɪdərət] *adj* sem consideração

inconsistent [ɪnkən'sɪstnt] *adj* inconsistente; **~ with** incompatível com

inconspicuous [ɪnkən'spɪkjuəs] *adj* modesto, discreto

inconvenience [ɪnkən'viːnjəns] *n* (*quality*) inconveniência; (*problem*) inconveniente *m* ♦ *vt* incomodar

inconvenient [ɪnkən'viːnjənt] *adj* inconveniente, incômodo; (*time, place*) inoportuno

incorporate [ɪn'kɔːpəreɪt] *vt* incorporar; (*contain*) compreender; **~d company** (*US*) *n* ≈ sociedade *f* anônima

incorrect [ɪnkə'rɛkt] *adj* incorreto

incorruptible [ɪnkə'rʌptɪbl] *adj* (*not open to bribes*) insubornável

increase [*n* 'ɪnkriːs, *vi, vt* ɪn'kriːs] *n* aumento ♦ *vi, vt* aumentar; **increasing** *adj* crescente, em aumento; **increasingly** *adv* (*more intensely*) progressivamente; (*more often*) cada vez mais

incredible [ɪn'krɛdɪbl] *adj* inacreditável; (*enormous*) incrível

incredulous [ɪn'krɛdjuləs] *adj* incrédulo

increment ['ɪnkrɪmənt] *n* aumento, incremento

incriminate [ɪn'krɪmɪneɪt] *vt* incriminar

incubator ['ɪnkjubeɪtə³] *n* incubadora

incumbent [ɪn'kʌmbənt] *n* titular *m/f* ♦ *adj*: **it is ~ on him to ...** cabe a ele ...

incur [ɪn'kəː³] *vt* incorrer em; (*expenses*) contrair

indebted [ɪn'dɛtɪd] *adj*: **to be ~ to sb** estar em dívida com alguém, dever obrigação a alguém

indecent [ɪn'diːsnt] *adj* indecente; **~ assault** (*BRIT*) *n* atentado contra o pudor; **~ exposure** *n* exibição *f* obscena, exibicionismo

indecisive [ɪndɪ'saɪsɪv] *adj* indeciso

indeed [ɪn'diːd] *adv* de fato; (*certainly*) certamente; (*furthermore*) aliás; **yes ~!** claro que sim!

indefinite [ɪn'dɛfɪnɪt] *adj* indefinido; (*period, number*) indeterminado; **~ly** *adv* indefinidamente

indemnity [ɪn'dɛmnɪtɪ] *n* garantia, seguro; (*compensation*) indenização *f*

independence [ɪndɪ'pɛndns] *n* independência

independent [ɪndɪ'pɛndnt] *adj* independente; (*inquiry*) imparcial

index ['ɪndɛks] (*pl* **~es**) *n* (*in book*) índice *m*; (*in library etc*) catálogo; (*pl*: **indices**: *ratio, sign*) índice *m*, expoente *m*; **~ card** *n* ficha de arquivo; **~ finger** *n* dedo indicador; **~-linked** (*US* **~ed**) *adj* vinculado ao índice (do custo de vida)

India ['ɪndɪə] *n* Índia; **~n** *adj, n* (*from India*) indiano/a; (*American, Brazilian*) índio/a; **Red ~n** índio/a pele vermelha; **~n Ocean** *n*: **the ~n Ocean** o oceano Índico

indicate ['ɪndɪkeɪt] *vt* (*show*) sugerir; (*point to, mention*) indicar; **indication** *n* indício, sinal *m*; **indicative** *adj*: **indicative of** sintomático de ♦ *n* (*LING*) indicativo; **indicator** *n* indicador *m*; (*AUT*) pisca-pisca *m*

indices ['ɪndɪsiːz] *npl of* **index**

indictment [ɪn'daɪtmənt] *n* acusação *f*, denúncia; (*charge*) indiciação *f*

indifference [ɪn'dɪfrəns] *n* indiferença

indifferent [ɪn'dɪfrənt] *adj* indiferente; (*quality*) mediocre

indigenous [ɪn'dɪdʒɪnəs] *adj* indígena, nativo

indigestion [ɪndɪ'dʒɛstʃən] *n* indigestão *f*

indignant [ɪn'dɪgnənt] *adj*: **to be ~ about sth/with sb** estar indignado com algo/alguém, indignar-se de algo/alguém; **indignation** *n* indignação *f*

indignity [ɪn'dɪgnɪtɪ] *n* indignidade *f*

indigo ['ɪndɪgəu] *n* anil *m*

indirect [ɪndɪ'rɛkt] *adj* indireto

indiscreet [ɪndɪ'skriːt] *adj* indiscreto

indiscriminate [ɪndɪ'skrɪmɪnət] *adj* indiscriminado

indispensable [ɪndɪ'spɛnsəbl] *adj* indispensável, imprescindível

indisposed [ɪndɪ'spəuzd] *adj* (*unwell*) indisposto

indisputable [ɪndɪ'spjuːtəbl] *adj* incontestável

indistinct [ɪndɪ'stɪŋkt] *adj* indistinto; (*memory, noise*) confuso, vago

individual [ɪndɪ'vɪdjuəl] *n* indivíduo ♦ *adj* individual; (*personal*) pessoal; (*characteristic*) particular; **~ly** *adv* individualmente, particularmente

indoctrinate [ɪn'dɔktrɪneɪt] *vt* doutrinar

indolent ['ɪndələnt] adj indolente, preguiçoso

Indonesia [ɪndə'niːzɪə] n Indonésia

indoor ['ɪndɔː'] adj (inner) interno, interior; (inside) dentro de casa; (plant) para
dentro de casa; (swimming pool) coberto; (games, sport) de salão; ~s adv em
lugar fechado

induce [ɪn'djuːs] vt (MED) induzir; (bring
about) causar, produzir; ~ment n incentivo

indulge [ɪn'dʌldʒ] vt (desire) satisfazer;
(whim) condescender com; (person) comprazer; (child) fazer a vontade de ♦ vi:
to ~ in entregar-se a, satisfazer-se com;
~nce n (of desire) satisfação f; (leniency)
indulgência, tolerância; ~nt adj indulgente

industrial [ɪn'dʌstrɪəl] adj industrial; ~
action n greve f; ~ estate (BRIT) n
zona industrial; ~ist n industrial m/f;
~ park (US) n = ~ estate

industrious [ɪn'dʌstrɪəs] adj trabalha-
dor(a); (student) aplicado

industry ['ɪndəstrɪ] n indústria; (diligence) aplicação f, diligência

inebriated [ɪ'niːbrɪeɪtɪd] adj embriagado,
bêbado

inedible [ɪn'edɪbl] adj não-comestível

ineffective [ɪnɪ'fektɪv] adj ineficaz

ineffectual [ɪnɪ'fektʃuəl] adj = **ineffective**

inefficiency [ɪnɪ'fɪʃənsɪ] n ineficiência

inefficient [ɪnɪ'fɪʃənt] adj ineficiente

inept [ɪ'nept] adj inepto

inequality [ɪnɪ'kwɔlɪtɪ] n desigualdade f

inert [ɪ'nɜːt] adj inerte; (immobile) imóvel; ~ia n (laziness) lerdeza

inescapable [ɪnɪ'skeɪpəbl] adj inevitável

inevitable [ɪn'evɪtəbl] adj inevitável; in-
evitably adv inevitavelmente

inexcusable [ɪnɪks'kjuːzəbl] adj imperdoável, indesculpável

inexhaustible [ɪnɪg'zɔːstɪbl] adj inesgotável, inexaurível

inexpensive [ɪnɪk'spensɪv] adj barato,
econômico

inexperienced [ɪnɪk'spɪərɪənst] adj inexperiente

infallible [ɪn'fælɪbl] adj infalível

infamous ['ɪnfəməs] adj infame, abominável

infancy ['ɪnfənsɪ] n infância

infant ['ɪnfənt] n (baby) bebê m; (young
child) criança; ~ile adj infantil; (pej)
acriançado

infantry ['ɪnfəntrɪ] n infantaria

infant school (BRIT) n pré-escola

infatuated [ɪn'fætjueɪtɪd] adj: ~ with
apaixonado por

infatuation [ɪnfætju'eɪʃən] n gamação f,
paixão f louca

infect [ɪn'fekt] vt (person) contagiar;
(food) contaminar; ~ion n infecção f;
~ious adj contagioso, (fig) infeccioso

infer [ɪn'fɜː'] vt deduzir, inferir; ~ence
n dedução f, inferência

inferior [ɪn'fɪərɪə'] adj inferior; (goods)
de qualidade inferior ♦ n inferior m/f;
(in rank) subalterno/a; ~ity n inferioridade f; ~ity complex n complexo de
inferioridade

inferno [ɪn'fɜːnəu] n inferno

infertile [ɪn'fɜːtaɪl] adj infértil; (person,
animal) estéril

infested [ɪn'festɪd] adj: ~ (with) infesta-
do (de), assolado (por)

in-fighting n lutas fpl internas, conflitos
mpl internos

infiltrate ['ɪnfɪltreɪt] vt infiltrar-se em

infinite ['ɪnfɪnɪt] adj infinito

infinitive [ɪn'fɪnɪtɪv] n infinitivo

infinity [ɪn'fɪnɪtɪ] n (also MATH) infinito;
(an ~) infinidade f

infirm [ɪn'fɜːm] adj (ill) enfermo; (weak)
fraco; ~ary n enfermaria, hospital m;
~ity n fraqueza; (illness) enfermidade f,
achaque m

inflamed [ɪn'fleɪmd] adj inflamado

inflammable [ɪn'flæməbl] adj inflamável

inflammation [ɪnflə'meɪʃən] n inflamação f

inflatable [ɪn'fleɪtəbl] adj inflável

inflate [ɪn'fleɪt] vt (tyre, balloon) inflar,
encher; (price) inflar; **inflation** n (ECON)
inflação f

inflict [ɪn'flɪkt] vt: to ~ on infligir em

influence ['ɪnfluəns] n influência ♦ vt influir em, influenciar; **under the** ~ of
alcohol sob o efeito do álcool; **influential** adj influente

influenza [ɪnflu'enzə] n gripe f

influx ['ɪnflʌks] n (of refugees) afluxo; (of
funds) influxo

inform [ɪn'fɔːm] vt informar ♦ vi: to ~
on sb delatar alguém

informal [ɪn'fɔːml] adj informal; (visit,
discussion) extra-oficial; ~ity n informa-
lidade f

informant [ɪn'fɔːmənt] n informante m/f

information [ɪnfə'meɪʃən] n informação
f, informações fpl; (knowledge) conhecimento; **a piece of** ~ uma informação;
~ **office** n escritório de informações

informative [ɪn'fɔːmətɪv] adj informativo

informer [ɪn'fɔːmə'] n informante m/f

infringe [ɪn'frɪndʒ] vt infringir, transgredir ♦ vi: to ~ on violar; ~ment n
transgressão f; (of rights) violação f

infuriating [ɪn'fjuərɪeɪtɪŋ] adj de dar raiva, enfurecedor(a)

ingenious [ɪn'dʒiːnjəs] adj engenhoso;
ingenuity n engenho, habilidade f

ingenuous [ɪn'dʒenjuəs] adj ingênuo

ingot ['ɪŋgət] n lingote m

ingrained [ɪn'greɪnd] adj arraigado, en-
raizado

ingratiate [ɪn'greɪʃɪeɪt] vt: to ~ o.s.
with cair nas (boas) graças de

ingredient [ɪn'griːdɪənt] n ingrediente m; (of situation) fator m

inhabit [ɪn'hæbɪt] vt habitar; ~**ant** n habitante m/f

inhale [ɪn'heɪl] vt inalar ♦ vi (in smoking) tragar

inherent [ɪn'hɪərənt] adj: ~ **in** or **to** inerente a

inherit [ɪn'hɛrɪt] vt herdar; ~**ance** n herança

inhibit [ɪn'hɪbɪt] vt inibir; ~**ed** adj inibido; ~**ion** n inibição f

inhospitable [ɪnhɔs'pɪtəbl] adj (person) inospitaleiro; (place) inóspito

inhuman [ɪn'hjuːmən] adj inumano, desumano

iniquity [ɪ'nɪkwɪtɪ] n iniqüidade f; (injustice) injustiça

initial [ɪ'nɪʃl] adj inicial ♦ n inicial f ♦ vt marcar com iniciais; ~**s** npl (of name) iniciais fpl; ~**ly** adv inicialmente, no início

initiate [ɪ'nɪʃɪeɪt] vt (start) iniciar, começar; (person) iniciar; **to** ~ **sb into** a secret revelar um segredo a alguém

initiation [ɪnɪʃɪ'eɪʃən] n iniciação f; (beginning) começo, início

initiative [ɪ'nɪʃətɪv] n iniciativa

inject [ɪn'dʒɛkt] vt (liquid, fig: money) injetar; (person) dar uma injeção em; ~**ion** n injeção f

injunction [ɪn'dʒʌŋkʃən] n injunção f, ordem f

injure [ɪ'ndʒə*] vt ferir; (reputation etc) prejudicar; (feelings) ofender; ~**d** adj ferido; (feelings) ofendido, magoado; **injury** n ferida; **injury time** n (SPORT) desconto

injustice [ɪn'dʒʌstɪs] n injustiça

ink [ɪŋk] n tinta

inkling [ɪŋklɪŋ] n vaga idéia

inlaid [ɪ'nleɪd] adj (with gems) incrustado; (table etc) marchetado

inland [adj 'ɪnlənd, adv ɪn'lænd] adj interior, interno ♦ adv para o interior; **I~ Revenue** (BRIT) n ≈ fisco, ≈ receita federal (BR)

in-laws npl sogros mpl

inlet [ɪ'nlɛt] n (GEO) enseada, angra

inmate [ɪ'nmeɪt] n (in prison) presidiário/a; (in asylum) internado/a

inn [ɪn] n hospedaria, taberna

innate [ɪ'neɪt] adj inato

inner [ɪ'nə*] adj (place) interno; (feeling) interior; ~ **city** n aglomeração f urbana, metrópole f; ~ **tube** n (of tyre) câmara de ar

innings [ɪ'nɪŋz] n (SPORT) turno

innocence [ɪ'nəsns] n inocência

innocent [ɪ'nəsnt] adj inocente

innocuous [ɪ'nɔkjuəs] adj inócuo

innovation [ɪnəu'veɪʃən] n inovação f, novidade f

innuendo [ɪnjuː'ɛndəu] (pl ~**es**) n insinuação f, indireta

innumerable [ɪ'njuːmrəbl] adj incontável

inoculation [ɪnɔkju'leɪʃən] n inoculação f, vacinação f

inordinately [ɪ'nɔːdɪnɪtlɪ] adv desmedidamente, excessivamente

in-patient n paciente m/f interno/a

input [ɪ'nput] n entrada; (resources) investimento

inquest [ɪ'nkwɛst] n inquérito judicial

inquire [ɪn'kwaɪə*] vi pedir informação ♦ vt perguntar; ~ **about** vt fus pedir informações sobre; ~ **into** vt fus investigar, indagar; **inquiry** n pergunta; (LAW) investigação f, inquérito; **inquiry office** (BRIT) ~ seção f de informações

inquisitive [ɪn'kwɪzɪtɪv] adj curioso, perguntador(a)

inroads [ɪ'nrəudz] npl: **to make** ~ **into** consumir parte de

ins. abbr = **inches**

insane [ɪn'seɪn] adj louco, doido; (MED) demente, insano; **insanity** n loucura; insanidade f, demência

inscription [ɪn'skrɪpʃən] n inscrição f; (in book) dedicatória

inscrutable [ɪn'skruːtəbl] adj inescrutável, impenetrável

insect [ɪ'nsɛkt] n inseto; ~**icide** n inseticida m

insecure [ɪnsɪ'kjuə*] adj inseguro; **insecurity** n insegurança

insemination [ɪnsɛmɪ'neɪʃən] n: **artificial** ~ inseminação f artificial

insensible [ɪn'sɛnsɪbl] adj inconsciente

insensitive [ɪn'sɛnsɪtɪv] adj insensível

insert [ɪn'səːt] vt (between things) intercalar; (into sth) introduzir, inserir; ~**ion** n inserção f

in-service adj (training) contínuo; (course) de aperfeiçoamento, de reciclagem

inshore [ɪn'ʃɔː*] adj perto da costa, costeiro ♦ adv (be) perto da costa; (move) em direção à costa

inside [ɪ'nsaɪd] n interior m ♦ adj interior, interno ♦ adv (be) dentro; (go) para dentro ♦ prep dentro de; (of time): ~ **10 minutes** em menos de 10 minutos; ~**s** npl (inf) entranhas fpl; ~ **forward** n (SPORT) centro avante; ~ **information** n informação f privilegiada; ~ **lane** n (AUT: in Britain) pista da esquerda; (: in US, Europe etc) pista da direita; ~ **out** adv às avessas; (know) muito bem; **to turn sth** ~ **out** virar algo pelo avesso; ~**r dealing, ~r trading** n (STOCK EXCHANGE) uso de informação privilegiada, insider dealing m

insight [ɪ'nsaɪt] n insight m

insignia [ɪn'sɪgnɪə] n inv insígnias fpl

insignificant [ɪnsɪg'nɪfɪknt] adj insignificante

insincere [ɪnsɪn'sɪə*] adj insincero

insinuate [ɪn'sɪnjueɪt] vt insinuar

insipid [ɪn'sɪpɪd] adj insípido, insosso; (person) sem graça

insist [ɪn'sɪst] vi insistir; **to** ~ **on doing**

insistir em fazer; **to ~ that** insistir que; (*claim*) cismar que; **~ent** *adj* insistente, pertinaz; (*continual*) persistente

insole ['ɪnsəul] *n* palmilha

insolent ['ɪnsələnt] *adj* insolente, atrevido

insomnia [ɪn'sɒmnɪə] *n* insônia

inspect [ɪn'spɛkt] *vt* inspecionar; (*building*) vistoriar; (*BRIT: tickets*) fiscalizar; (*troops*) passar revista em; **~ion** *n* inspeção *f*; vistoria; fiscalização *f*; **~or** *n* inspetor(a) *m/f*; (*BRIT: on buses, trains*) fiscal *m*

inspire [ɪn'spaɪə*] *vt* inspirar

install [ɪn'stɔːl] *vt* instalar; (*official*) nomear; **~ation** *n* instalação *f*

instalment [ɪn'stɔːlmənt] (*US* **installment**) *n* (*of money*) prestação *f*; (*of story*) fascículo; (*of TV serial etc*) capítulo; **in ~s** (*pay*) a prestações; (*receive*) em várias vezes

instance ['ɪnstəns] *n* exemplo; **for ~** por exemplo; **in the first ~** em primeiro lugar

instant ['ɪnstənt] *n* instante *m*, momento ♦ *adj* imediato; (*coffee*) instantâneo; **~ly** *adv* imediatamente

instead [ɪn'stɛd] *adv* em vez disso; **~ of** em vez de, em lugar de

instep ['ɪnstɛp] *n* peito do pé; (*of shoe*) parte *f* de dentro

instigate ['ɪnstɪgeɪt] *vt* fomentar

instil [ɪn'stɪl] *vt*: **to ~ sth (into)** infundir *or* incutir algo (em)

instinct ['ɪnstɪŋkt] *n* instinto

institute ['ɪnstɪtjuːt] *n* instituto; (*professional body*) associação *f* ♦ *vt* (*inquiry*) começar, iniciar; (*proceedings*) instituir, estabelecer

institution [ɪnstɪ'tjuːʃən] *n* instituição *f*; (*organization*) instituto; (*MED: home*) asilo; (*asylum*) manicômio; (*custom*) costume *m*

instruct [ɪn'strʌkt] *vt*: **to ~ sb in sth** instruir alguém em *or* sobre algo; **to ~ sb to do sth** dar instruções a alguém para fazer algo; **~ion** *n* (*teaching*) instrução *f*; **~ions** *npl* (*orders*) ordens *fpl*; **~ions (for use)** modo de usar; **~ive** *adj* instrutivo; **~or** *n* instrutor(a) *m/f*

instrument ['ɪnstrumənt] *n* instrumento; **~al** *adj* (*MUS*) instrumental; **to be ~al in** contribuir para

insufferable [ɪn'sʌfrəbl] *adj* insuportável

insufficient [ɪnsə'fɪʃənt] *adj* insuficiente

insular ['ɪnsjulə*] *adj* (*outlook*) estreito; (*person*) de mente limitada

insulate ['ɪnsjuleɪt] *vt* isolar; (*protect*) segregar; **insulation** *n* isolamento

insulin ['ɪnsjulɪn] *n* insulina

insult [*n* 'ɪnsʌlt, *vt* ɪn'sʌlt] *n* ofensa ♦ *vt* insultar, ofender; **~ing** *adj* insultante, ofensivo

insuperable [ɪn'sjuːprəbl] *adj* insuperável

insurance [ɪn'ʃuərəns] *n* seguro; **fire/life ~** seguro contra incêndio/de vida; **~ policy** *n* apólice *f* de seguro

insure [ɪn'ʃuə*] *vt* segurar

intact [ɪn'tækt] *adj* intacto, íntegro; (*unharmed*) ileso, são e salvo

intake ['ɪnteɪk] *n* (*of food*) quantidade *f* ingerida; (*BRIT: SCH*) **an ~ of 200 a year** 200 matriculados por ano

integral ['ɪntɪgrəl] *adj* (*part*) integrante, essencial

integrate ['ɪntɪgreɪt] *vt* integrar ♦ *vi* integrar-se

integrity [ɪn'tɛgrɪtɪ] *n* integridade *f*

intellect ['ɪntəlɛkt] *n* intelecto; **~ual** *adj*, *n* intelectual *m/f*

intelligence [ɪn'tɛlɪdʒəns] *n* inteligência; (*MIL etc*) informações *fpl*

intelligent [ɪn'tɛlɪdʒənt] *adj* inteligente

intelligible [ɪn'tɛlɪdʒɪbl] *adj* inteligível, compreensível

intend [ɪn'tɛnd] *vt* (*gift etc*): **to ~ sth for** destinar algo a; **to ~ to do sth** tencionar *or* pretender fazer algo; (*plan*) planejar fazer algo; **~ed** *adj* (*effect*) desejado; (*insult*) intencional; (*victim*) intencionado

intense [ɪn'tɛns] *adj* intenso; (*person*) muito emotivo; **~ly** *adv* (*very*) extremamente

intensive [ɪn'tɛnsɪv] *adj* intensivo; **~ care unit** *n* unidade *f* de tratamento intensivo

intent [ɪn'tɛnt] *n* intenção *f* ♦ *adj*: **to be ~ on doing sth** estar resolvido a fazer algo; **to all ~s and purposes** para todos os efeitos

intention [ɪn'tɛnʃən] *n* intenção *f*, propósito; **~al** *adj* intencional, propositado; **~ally** *adv* de propósito

intently [ɪn'tɛntlɪ] *adv* atentamente

inter [ɪn'təː*] *vt* enterrar

interact [ɪntər'ækt] *vi* interagir; **~ion** *n* interação *f*, ação *f* recíproca; **~ive** *adj* (*COMPUT*) interactivo

intercept [ɪntə'sɛpt] *vt* interceptar; (*person*) deter

interchange ['ɪntətʃeɪndʒ] *n* intercâmbio; (*exchange*) troca, permuta; (*on motorway*) trevo; **~able** *adj* permutável

intercom ['ɪntəkɒm] *n* interfone *m*

intercourse ['ɪntəkɔːs] *n*: **sexual ~** relações *fpl* sexuais

interest ['ɪntrɪst] *n* interesse *m*; (*COMM: sum*) juros *mpl*; (: *in company*) participação *f* ♦ *vt* interessar; **to be ~ed in** interessar-se por, estar interessado em; **~ing** *adj* interessante; **~ rate** *n* taxa de juros

interface ['ɪntəfeɪs] *n* (*COMPUT*) interface *f*

interfere [ɪntə'fɪə*] *vi*: **to ~ in** interferir *or* intrometer-se em; **to ~ with** (*objects*) mexer em; (*hinder*) impedir; (*plans*) interferir em

interference [ɪntə'fɪərəns] *n* intromissão *f*; (*RADIO*, *TV*) interferência

interim ['ɪntərɪm] *adj* interino, provisório ♦ *n*: **in the ~** neste ínterim, nesse meio tempo

interior [ɪn'tɪərɪə*] *n* interior *m* ♦ *adj* interno; (*ministry*) do interior; **~ designer** *n* arquiteto/a de interiores

interjection [ɪntə'dʒɛkʃən] *n* interrupção *f*; (*LING*) interjeição *f*, exclamação *f*

interlock [ɪntə'lɔk] *vi* entrelaçar-se

interloper ['ɪntələupə*] *n* intruso/a

interlude ['ɪntəluːd] *n* interlúdio; (*rest*) descanso; (*THEATRE*) intervalo

intermarry [ɪntə'mærɪ] *vi* ligar-se por casamento

intermediate [ɪntə'miːdɪət] *adj* intermediário

interminable [ɪn'təːmɪnəbl] *adj* interminável

intermission [ɪntə'mɪʃən] *n* intervalo

intermittent [ɪntə'mɪtnt] *adj* intermitente; (*publication*) periódico

intern [*vt* ɪn'təːn, *n* 'ɪntəːn] *vt* internar ♦ *n* (*US*) médico-interno/médica-interna

internal [ɪn'təːnl] *adj* interno; **~ly** *adv*: **"not to be taken ~ly"** "uso externo"; **I~ Revenue (Service)** (*US*) *n* ≈ fisco, ≈ receita federal (*BR*)

international [ɪntə'næʃənl] *adj* internacional ♦ *n* (*BRIT: SPORT: game*) jogo internacional

Internet ['ɪntənɛt] *n* Internet *f*; **~ café** cibercafé *m*; **~ service provider** provedor *m* de acesso à Internet

interplay ['ɪntəpleɪ] *n* interação *f*

interpret [ɪn'təːprɪt] *vt* interpretar; (*translate*) traduzir ♦ *vi* interpretar; **~er** *n* intérprete *m/f*

interrelated [ɪntərɪ'leɪtɪd] *adj* inter-relacionado

interrogate [ɪn'tɛrəgeɪt] *vt* interrogar; **interrogation** *n* interrogatório; **interrogative** *adj* interrogativo

interrupt [ɪntə'rʌpt] *vt*, *vi* interromper; **~ion** *n* interrupção *f*

intersect [ɪntə'sɛkt] *vi* (*roads*) cruzar-se; **~ion** *n* cruzamento

intersperse [ɪntə'spəːs] *vt*: **to ~ with** entremear com *or* de

intertwine [ɪntə'twaɪn] *vi* entrelaçar-se

interval ['ɪntəvl] *n* intervalo

intervene [ɪntə'viːn] *vi* intervir; (*event*) ocorrer; (*time*) decorrer; **intervention** *n* intervenção *f*

interview ['ɪntəvjuː] *n* entrevista ♦ *vt* entrevistar; **~er** *n* entrevistador(a) *m/f*

intestine [ɪn'tɛstɪn] *n* intestino

intimacy ['ɪntɪməsɪ] *n* intimidade *f*

intimate [*adj* 'ɪntɪmət, *vt* 'ɪntɪmeɪt] *adj* íntimo; (*knowledge*) profundo ♦ *vt* insinuar, sugerir

into ['ɪntu] *prep* em; **she burst ~ tears** ela desatou a chorar; **come ~ the house** venha para dentro; **research ~** cancer pesquisa sobre o câncer; **he worked late ~ the night** ele trabalhou até altas horas; **he was shocked ~ silence** ele ficou mudo de choque; **~ 3 pieces/French** em 3 pedaços/para o francês

intolerable [ɪn'tɔlərəbl] *adj* intolerável, insuportável

intolerant [ɪn'tɔlərənt] *adj*: **~ (of)** intolerante (com *or* para com)

intonation [ɪntəu'neɪʃən] *n* entonação *f*, inflexão *f*

intoxicated [ɪn'tɔksɪkeɪtɪd] *adj* embriagado

intoxication [ɪntɔksɪ'keɪʃən] *n* intoxicação *f*, embriaguez *f*

intractable [ɪn'træktəbl] *adj* (*child*) intratável; (*problem*) espinhoso

intranet ['ɪntrənɛt] *n* intranet *f*

intransitive [ɪn'trænsɪtɪv] *adj* intransitivo

intravenous [ɪntrə'viːnəs] *adj* intravenoso

in-tray *n* cesta para correspondência de entrada

intricate ['ɪntrɪkət] *adj* complexo, complicado

intrigue [ɪn'triːg] *n* intriga ♦ *vt* intrigar; (*fascinate*) fascinar; **intriguing** *adj* curioso

intrinsic [ɪn'trɪnsɪk] *adj* intrínseco

introduce [ɪntrə'djuːs] *vt* introduzir; **to ~ sb (to sb)** apresentar alguém (a alguém); **to ~ sb to** (*pastime, technique*) iniciar alguém em; **introduction** *n* introdução *f*; (*of person*) apresentação *f*; **introductory** *adj* introdutório

introvert ['ɪntrəuvəːt] *n* introvertido/a ♦ *adj* (*also*: **~ed**) introvertido

intrude [ɪn'truːd] *vi*: **to ~ (on)** intrometer-se (em); **~r** *n* intruso/a

intuition [ɪntjuː'ɪʃən] *n* intuição *f*

inundate ['ɪnʌndeɪt] *vt*: **to ~ with** inundar de

invade [ɪn'veɪd] *vt* invadir

invalid [*n* 'ɪnvəlɪd, *adj* ɪn'vælɪd] *n* inválido/a ♦ *adj* inválido, nulo

invaluable [ɪn'væljuəbl] *adj* valioso, inestimável

invariably [ɪn'vɛərɪəblɪ] *adv* invariavelmente

invasion [ɪn'veɪʒən] *n* invasão *f*

invent [ɪn'vɛnt] *vt* inventar; **~ion** *n* invenção *f*; (*inventiveness*) engenho; (*lie*) ficção *f*, mentira; **~or** *n* inventor(a) *m/f*

inventory ['ɪnvəntrɪ] *n* inventário, relação *f*

invert [ɪn'vəːt] *vt* inverter; **~ed commas** (*BRIT*) *npl* aspas *fpl*

invest [ɪn'vɛst] *vt* investir ♦ *vi*: **to ~ in** investir em; (*acquire*) comprar

investigate [ɪn'vɛstɪgeɪt] *vt* investigar; **investigation** *n* investigação *f*

investment [ɪn'vɛstmənt] *n* investimento

investor [ɪn'vɛstə*] *n* investidor(a) *m/f*

invigilator [in'vidʒileitǝ*] n fiscal m/f (de exame)
invigorating [in'vigǝreitiŋ] adj revigorante
invisible [in'vizibl] adj invisível
invitation [invi'teiʃǝn] n convite m
invite [in'vait] vt convidar; (opinions etc) incitar; **inviting** adj convidativo
invoice ['invɔis] n fatura ♦ vt faturar
invoke [in'vǝuk] vt invocar; (law) apelar para
involuntary [in'vɔlǝntri] adj involuntário
involve [in'vɔlv] vt (entail) implicar; (require) exigir; (concern) envolver; **to ~ sb (in)** envolver alguém (em); **~d** adj (complex) complexo; **to be ~d in** estar envolvido em; **~ment** n envolvimento
inward ['inwǝd] adj (movement) interior, interno; (thought, feeling) íntimo; **~(s)** adv para dentro
iodine ['aiǝudi:n] n iodo
ion ['aiǝn] n íon m, ião m (PT)
iota [ai'ǝutǝ] n (fig) pouquinho, tiquinho
IOU n abbr (= I owe you) vale m
IQ n abbr (= intelligence quotient) QI m
IRA n abbr (= Irish Republican Army) IRA m
Iran [i'rɑ:n] n Irã m (BR), Irão m (PT); **~ian** adj, n iraniano/a
Iraq [i'rɑ:k] n Iraque m; **~i** adj, n iraquiano/a
irate [ai'reit] adj irado, enfurecido
Ireland ['aiǝlǝnd] n Irlanda
iris ['airis] (pl **~es**) n íris f
Irish ['airiʃ] adj irlandês/esa ♦ npl: **the ~** os irlandeses; **~man** (irreg) n irlandês m; **~ Sea** n: **the ~ Sea** o mar da Irlanda; **~woman** (irreg) n irlandesa
irksome ['ǝ:ksǝm] adj aborrecido
iron ['aiǝn] n ferro; (for clothes) ferro de passar roupa ♦ adj de ferro ♦ vt (clothes) passar; **~ out** vt (problem) resolver; **I~ Curtain** n: **the I~ Curtain** a cortina de ferro
ironic(al) [ai'rɔnik(l)] adj irônico
ironing ['aiǝniŋ] n (activity) passar m roupa; (clothes) roupa passada; **~ board** n tábua de passar roupa
ironmonger ['aiǝnmʌŋgǝ*] (BRIT) n ferreiro/a; **~'s (shop)** (BRIT) n loja de ferragens
irony ['airǝni] n ironia
irrational [i'ræʃǝnl] adj irracional
irreconcilable [irekǝn'sailǝbl] adj irreconciliável; (ideas) incompatível
irregular [i'regjulǝ*] adj irregular; (surface) desigual
irrelevant [i'relǝvǝnt] adj irrelevante
irreplaceable [iri'pleisǝbl] adj insubstituível
irrepressible [iri'presǝbl] adj irreprimível, irrefreável
irresistible [iri'zistibl] adj irresistível
irrespective [iri'spektiv]: **~ of** prep independente de, sem considerar

irresponsible [iri'spɔnsibl] adj irresponsável
irreverent [i'revǝrnt] adj irreverente
irrigate ['irigeit] vt irrigar; **irrigation** n irrigação f
irritable ['iritǝbl] adj irritável
irritate ['iriteit] vt irritar; **irritating** adj irritante; **irritation** n irritação f
IRS (US) n abbr = **Internal Revenue Service**
is [iz] vb see **be**
Islam ['izlɑ:m] n islamismo
island ['ailǝnd] n ilha; **~er** n ilhéu/ilhoa m/f
isle [ail] n ilhota, ilha
isn't ['iznt] = **is not**
isolate ['aisǝleit] vt isolar; **~d** adj isolado
isolation [aisǝ'leiʃǝn] n isolamento
ISP n abbr = **Internet Service Provider**
Israel ['izreil] n Israel m (no article); **~i** adj, n israelense m/f
issue ['isju:] n questão f, tema m; (of book) edição f; (of stamps) emissão f ♦ vt (statement) fazer; (rations, equipment) distribuir; (orders) dar; **at ~** em debate; **to take ~ with sb (over sth)** discordar de alguém (sobre algo); **to make an ~ of sth** criar caso com algo
isthmus ['ismǝs] n istmo

KEYWORD

---

it [it] pron **1** (specific: subject) ele/ela; (: direct object) o/a; (: indirect object) lhe; **~'s on the table** está em cima da mesa; **I can't find ~** não consigo achá-lo; **give ~ to me** dê-mo; **about/from ~** sobre/de isto; **did you go to ~?** (party, concert etc) você foi?
2 (impers) isto, isso; (after prep) ele, ela; **~'s raining** está chovendo (BR) or a chover (PT); **~'s six o'clock/the 10th of August** são seis horas/ hoje é (dia) 10 de agosto; **who is ~? – ~'s me** quem é? – sou eu

Italian [i'tæljǝn] adj italiano ♦ n italiano/a; (LING) italiano
italics [i'tæliks] npl itálico
Italy ['itǝli] n Itália
itch [itʃ] n comichão f, coceira ♦ vi (person) estar com or sentir comichão or coceira; (part of body) comichar, coçar; **I'm ~ing to do sth** estou louco para fazer algo; **~y** adj que coça; **to be ~y** = **to itch**
it'd ['itd] = **it would; it had**
item ['aitǝm] n item m; (on agenda) assunto; (in programme) número; (also: **news ~**) notícia; **~ize** vt detalhar, especificar
itinerant [i'tinǝrǝnt] adj itinerante
itinerary [ai'tinǝrǝri] n itinerário
it'll ['itl] = **it will; it shall**
its [its] adj seu/sua, dele/dela ♦ pron o

seu/a sua, o dele/a dela
it's [ɪts] = it is; it has
itself [ɪt'sɛlf] *pron (reflexive)* si mesmo/a; *(emphatic)* ele mesmo/ela mesma
ITV *(BRIT) n abbr (= Independent Television)* canal de televisão comercial
IUD *n abbr (= intra-uterine device)* DIU *m*
I've [aɪv] = I have
ivory ['aɪvərɪ] *n* marfim *m*
ivy ['aɪvɪ] *n* hera

J

jab [dʒæb] *vt* cutucar ♦ *n* cotovelada, murro; *(MED: inf)* injeção *f*; to ~ sth into sth cravar algo em algo
jack [dʒæk] *n (AUT)* macaco; *(CARDS)* valete *m*; ~ up *vt (AUT)* levantar com macaco
jackal ['dʒækl] *n* chacal *m*
jackdaw ['dʒækdɔː] *n* gralha
jacket ['dʒækɪt] *n* jaqueta, casaco curto, forro; *(of book)* sobrecapa
jack-knife *vi:* the lorry ~d o reboque do caminhão deu uma guinada
jack plug *n* pino
jackpot ['dʒækpɔt] *n* bolada, sorte *f* grande
jade [dʒeɪd] *n (stone)* jade *m*
jaded ['dʒeɪdɪd] *adj (tired)* cansado; *(fed-up)* aborrecido, amolado
jagged ['dʒægɪd] *adj* dentado, denteado
jail [dʒeɪl] *n* prisão *f*, cadeia ♦ *vt* encarcerar
jam [dʒæm] *n* geléia; *(also:* traffic ~) engarrafamento; *(inf)* apuro ♦ *vt* obstruir, atravancar; *(mechanism)* emperrar; *(RADIO)* bloquear, interferir ♦ *vi (mechanism, drawer etc)* emperrar; to ~ sth into sth forçar algo dentro de algo
Jamaica [dʒə'meɪkə] *n* Jamaica
jangle ['dʒæŋgl] *vi* soar estridentemente
janitor ['dʒænɪtə*] *n* zelador *m*
January ['dʒænjuərɪ] *n* janeiro
Japan [dʒə'pæn] *n* Japão *m*; ~ese *adj* japonês/esa ♦ *n inv* japonês/esa *m/f*; *(LING)* japonês *m*
jar [dʒɑː*] *n* jarro ♦ *vi (sound)* ranger, chiar; *(colours)* destoar
jargon ['dʒɑːgən] *n* jargão *m*
jasmin(e) ['dʒæzmɪn] *n* jasmim *m*
jaundice ['dʒɔːndɪs] *n* icterícia; ~d *adj (fig: unenthusiastic)* desanimado
jaunt [dʒɔːnt] *n* excursão *f*; ~y *adj* alegre, jovial; *(step)* lépido
javelin ['dʒævlɪn] *n* dardo de arremesso
jaw [dʒɔː] *n* mandíbula, maxilar *m*
jay [dʒeɪ] *n* gaio
jaywalker ['dʒeɪwɔːkə*] *n* pedestre *m/f* imprudente *(BR)*, peão *m* imprudente *(PT)*
jazz [dʒæz] *n* jazz *m*; ~ up *vt* animar, avivar
jealous ['dʒɛləs] *adj* ciumento; ~y *n*

ciúmes *mpl*
jeans [dʒiːnz] *npl* jeans *m(pl PT)*
jeep [dʒiːp] ® *n* jipe ® *m*
jeer [dʒɪə*] *vi:* to ~ (at) zombar (de)
jelly ['dʒɛlɪ] *n* gelatina; *(jam)* geléia; ~fish *n inv* água-viva
jeopardy ['dʒɛpədɪ] *n:* to be in ~ estar em perigo, estar correndo risco
jerk [dʒəːk] *n* solavanco, sacudida; *(wrench)* puxão *m*; *(inf: idiot)* babaca *m* ♦ *vt* sacudir ♦ *vi* dar um solavanco
jerkin ['dʒəːkɪn] *n* jaqueta
jersey ['dʒəːzɪ] *n* suéter *m or f (BR)*, camisola *(PT)*; *(fabric)* jérsei *m*, malha
jest [dʒɛst] *n* gracejo, brincadeira
Jesus ['dʒiːzəs] *n* Jesus *m*
jet [dʒɛt] *n (of gas, liquid)* jato; *(AVIAT)* (avião *m* a) jato; *(stone)* azeviche *m*; ~-**black** *adj* da cor do azeviche; ~ **engine** *n* motor *m* a jato; ~ **lag** *n* cansaço devido à diferença de fuso horário
jettison ['dʒɛtɪsn] *vt* alijar
jetty ['dʒɛtɪ] *n* quebra-mar *m*, cais *m*
Jew [dʒuː] *n* judeu/dia *m/f*
jewel ['dʒuːəl] *n* jóia; ~**ler** *(US* ~**er**) *n* joalheiro/a; ~**ler's** **(shop)** *n* joalheria; ~**lery** *(US* ~**ry**) *n* jóias *fpl*
Jewess ['dʒuːɪs] *n (offensive)* judia
Jewish ['dʒuːɪʃ] *adj* judeu/judia
jibe [dʒaɪb] *n* = gibe
jiffy ['dʒɪfɪ] *(inf) n:* in a ~ num instante
jig [dʒɪg] *n* jiga
jigsaw ['dʒɪgsɔː] *n (also:* ~ **puzzle)** quebra-cabeça *m*
jilt [dʒɪlt] *vt* dar o fora em
jingle ['dʒɪŋgl] *n (for advert)* música de propaganda ♦ *vi* tilintar, retinir
jinx [dʒɪŋks] *(inf) n* caipora, pé m frio
jitters ['dʒɪtəz] *(inf) npl:* to get the ~ ficar muito nervoso
job [dʒɔb] *n* trabalho; *(task)* tarefa; *(duty)* dever *m*; *(post)* emprego; it's not my ~ não faz parte das minhas funções; it's a good ~ that ... ainda bem que ...; just the ~! justo o que queria!; ~ **centre** *n* agência de emprego; ~**less** *adj* desempregado
jockey ['dʒɔkɪ] *n* jóquei *m* ♦ *vi:* to ~ for position manobrar para conseguir uma posição
jocular ['dʒɔkjulə*] *adj* jocoso
jog [dʒɔg] *vt* empurrar, sacudir ♦ *vi* fazer jogging *or* cooper; ~ **along** *vi* ir levando; ~**ging** *n* jogging *m*
join [dʒɔɪn] *vt (things)* juntar, unir; *(queue)* entrar em; *(become member of)* associar-se a; *(meet)* encontrar-se com; *(accompany)* juntar-se a ♦ *vi (roads, rivers)* confluir ♦ *n* junção *f*; ~ **in** *vi* participar ♦ *vt fus* participar em; ~ **up** *vi* unir-se; *(MIL)* alistar-se
joiner [dʒɔɪnə*] *(BRIT) n* marceneiro
joint [dʒɔɪnt] *n (TECH)* junta, união *f*; *(wood)* encaixe *m*; *(ANAT)* articulação *f*; *(BRIT: CULIN)* quarto; *(inf: place)* espelun-

ca; (: *of marijuana*) baseado ♦ *adj* comum; (*combined*) conjunto; (*committee*) misto; ~ **account** *n* conta conjunta

joist [dʒɔɪst] *n* barrote *m*

joke [dʒəuk] *n* piada; (*also:* **practical** ~) brincadeira, peça ♦ *vi* brincar; **to play a ~ on** pregar uma peça em; ~**r** *n* (*CARDS*) curingão *m*

jolly [ˈdʒɔlɪ] *adj* (*merry*) alegre; (*enjoyable*) divertido ♦ *adv* (*BRIT: inf*) muito, extremamente

jolt [dʒəult] *n* (*shake*) sacudida, solavanco; (*shock*) susto ♦ *vt* sacudir; (*emotionally*) abalar

Jordan [ˈdʒɔːdən] *n* Jordânia; (*river*) Jordão *m*

jostle [ˈdʒɔsl] *vt* acotovelar, empurrar

jot [dʒɔt] *n*: **not one** ~ nem um pouquinho; ~ **down** *vt* anotar; ~**ter** (*BRIT*) *n* bloco (de anotações)

journal [ˈdʒəːnl] *n* jornal *m*; (*magazine*) revista; (*diary*) diário; ~**ism** *n* jornalismo; ~**ist** *n* jornalista *m/f*

journey [ˈdʒəːnɪ] *n* viagem *f*; (*distance covered*) trajeto

jovial [ˈdʒəuvɪəl] *adj* jovial, alegre

joy [dʒɔɪ] *n* alegria; ~**ful** *adj* alegre; ~**ride** *n* passeio de carro; (*illegal*) passeio (*com veículo roubado*); ~**rider** *n* jovem que se diverte dirigindo carro roubado especificamente para este fim; ~**stick** *n* (*AVIAT*) manche *m*, alavanca de controle; (*COMPUT*) joystick *m*

JP *n abbr* = Justice of the Peace

Jr *abbr* = junior

jubilee [ˈdʒuːbɪliː] *n* jubileu *m*

judge [dʒʌdʒ] *n* juiz/juíza *m/f*; (*in competition*) árbitro; (*fig: expert*) especialista *m/f*, conhecedor(a) *m/f* ♦ *vt* julgar; (*competition*) arbitrar; (*estimate*) avaliar; (*consider*) considerar; **judg(e)ment** *n* juízo; (*opinion*) opinião *f*; (*discernment*) discernimento

judicial [dʒuːˈdɪʃl] *adj* judicial

judiciary [dʒuːˈdɪʃɪərɪ] *n* poder *m* judiciário

judo [ˈdʒuːdəu] *n* judô *m*

jug [dʒʌg] *n* jarro

juggernaut [ˈdʒʌgənɔːt] (*BRIT*) *n* (*huge truck*) jamanta

juggle [ˈdʒʌgl] *vi* fazer malabarismos; ~**r** *n* malabarista *m/f*

Jugoslav etc [ˈjuːgəuslɑːv] = Yugoslav etc

juice [dʒuːs] *n* suco (*BR*), sumo (*PT*); **juicy** *adj* suculento

jukebox [ˈdʒuːkbɔks] *n* juke-box *m*

July [dʒuːˈlaɪ] *n* julho

jumble [ˈdʒʌmbl] *n* confusão *f*, mixórdia ♦ *vt* (*also:* ~ **up**: *mix up*) misturar; ~ **sale** (*BRIT*) *n* venda de objetos usados, bazar *m*

jumbo (jet) [ˈdʒʌmbəu-] *n* avião *m* jumbo

jump [dʒʌmp] *vi* saltar, pular; (*start*)

sobressaltar-se; (*increase*) disparar ♦ *vt* pular, saltar ♦ *n* pulo, salto; (*increase*) alta; (*fence*) obstáculo; **to ~ the queue** (*BRIT*) furar a fila (*BR*), pôr-se à frente (*PT*)

jumper [ˈdʒʌmpə*] *n* (*BRIT: pullover*) suéter *m* (*BR*), camisola (*PT*); (*US: pinafore dress*) avental *m*; ~ **cables** (*US*) *npl* = jump leads

jump leads (*BRIT*) *npl* cabos *mpl* para ligar a bateria

jumpy [ˈdʒʌmpɪ] *adj* nervoso

Jun. *abbr* = junior

junction [ˈdʒʌŋkʃən] (*BRIT*) *n* (*of roads*) cruzamento; (*RAIL*) entroncamento

juncture [ˈdʒʌŋktʃə*] *n*: **at this** ~ neste momento, nesta conjuntura

June [dʒuːn] *n* junho

jungle [ˈdʒʌŋgl] *n* selva, mato

junior [ˈdʒuːnɪə*] *adj* (*in age*) mais novo or moço; (*position*) subalterno ♦ *n* jovem *m/f*; ~ **school** (*BRIT*) *n* escola primária

junk [dʒʌŋk] *n* (*cheap goods*) tranqueira, velharias *fpl*; (*rubbish*) lixo; ~ **food** *n* comida pronta de baixo valor nutritivo; ~**ie** (*inf*) *n* drogado/a; ~ **shop** *n* loja de objetos usados

Junr *abbr* = junior

juror [ˈdʒuərə*] *n* jurado/a

jury [ˈdʒuərɪ] *n* júri *m/f*

just [dʒʌst] *adj* justo ♦ *adv* (*exactly*) justamente, exatamente; (*only*) apenas, somente; **he's ~ done it/left** ele acabou (*BR*) *or* acaba (*PT*) de fazê-lo/ir; ~ **right** perfeito; ~ **two o'clock** duas (horas) em ponto; **she's ~ as clever as you** ela é tão inteligente como você; **it's ~ as well that ...** ainda bem que ...; ~ **as he was leaving** no momento em que ele saía; ~ **before/enough** justo antes/o suficiente; ~ **here** bem aqui; **he ~ missed** falhou por pouco; ~ **listen** escute aqui!

justice [ˈdʒʌstɪs] *n* justiça; (*US: judge*) juiz/juíza *m/f*; **to do ~ to** (*fig*) apreciar devidamente; **J~ of the Peace** *n* juiz/juíza *m/f* de paz

justification [dʒʌstɪfɪˈkeɪʃən] *n* (*reason*) justificativa

justify [ˈdʒʌstɪfaɪ] *vt* justificar

jut [dʒʌt] *vi* (*also:* ~ **out**) sobressair

juvenile [ˈdʒuːvənaɪl] *adj* juvenil; (*court*) de menores; (*books*) para adolescentes; (*humour, mentality*) infantil ♦ *n* menor *m/f* de idade

juxtapose [ˈdʒʌkstəpəuz] *vt* justapor

K

K *abbr* (= *kilobyte*) K ♦ *n abbr* (= *one thousand*) mil

Kampuchea [kæmpuˈtʃɪə] *n* Kampuchea *m*, Camboja *m*

kangaroo [kæŋgəˈruː] *n* canguru *m*

karate [kə'rɑ:ti] *n* karatê *m*

kebab [kə'bæb] *n* churrasquinho, espetinho

keel [ki:l] *n* quilha; **on an even ~** (*fig*) em equilíbrio

keen [ki:n] *adj* (*interest, desire*) grande, vivo; (*eye, intelligence*) penetrante; (*competition*) acirrado, intenso; (*edge*) afiado; (*eager*) entusiasmado; **to be ~ to do** *or* **on doing sth** sentir muita vontade de fazer algo; **to be ~ on sth/sb** gostar de algo/alguém

keep [ki:p] (*pt, pp* **kept**) *vt* guardar, ficar com; (*house etc*) cuidar; (*detain*) deter; (*shop etc*) tomar conta de; (*preserve*) conservar; (*accounts, family*) manter; (*promise*) cumprir; (*chickens, bees etc*) criar; (*prevent*): **to ~ sb from doing sth** impedir alguém de fazer algo ♦ *vi* (*food*) conservar-se; (*remain*) ficar ♦ *n* (*of castle*) torre *f* de menagem; (*food etc*): **to earn one's ~** ganhar a vida; (*inf*): **for ~s** para sempre; **to ~ doing sth** continuar fazendo algo; **to ~ sb happy** manter alguém satisfeito; **to ~ a place tidy** manter um lugar limpo; **~ on** *vi*: **to ~ on doing** continuar fazendo; **to ~ on (about sth)** falar sem parar (sobre algo); **~ out** *vt* impedir de entrar; **"~ out"** "entrada proibida"; **~ up** *vt* manter ♦ *vi* não atrasar-se, acompanhar; **to ~ up with** (*pace*) acompanhar; (*level*) manter-se ao nível de; **~er** *n* guarda *m*, guardião/diã *m/f*; **~ fit** *n* ginástica; **~ing** *n* (*care*) cuidado; **in ~ing with** de acordo com; **~sake** *n* lembrança

kennel ['kɛnl] *n* casa de cachorro; **~s** *n* (*establishment*) canil *m*

Kenya ['kɛnjə] *n* Quênia *m*

kept [kɛpt] *pt, pp* of **keep**

kerb [kə:b] (*BRIT*) *n* meio-fio (*BR*), borda do passeio (*PT*)

kernel ['kə:nl] *n* amêndoa; (*fig*) cerne *m*

ketchup ['kɛtʃəp] *n* molho de tomate, catsup *m*

kettle ['kɛtl] *n* chaleira; **~ drums** *npl* tímpanos *mpl*

key [ki:] *n* chave *f*; (*MUS*) clave *f*; (*of piano, typewriter*) tecla ♦ *cpd* (*issue etc*) chave ♦ *vt* (*also*: **~ in**) colocar; **~board** *n* teclado; **~ed up** *adj*: **to be (all) ~ed up** estar excitado *or* ligado (*inf*); **~hole** *n* buraco da fechadura; **~note** *n* (*MUS*) tônica; (*fig*) idéia fundamental; **~ring** *n* chaveiro

khaki ['kɑ:ki] *adj* cáqui

kick [kik] *vt* dar um pontapé em; (*ball*) chutar; (*inf: habit*) conseguir superar ♦ *vi* (*horse*) dar coices ♦ *n* (*from person*) pontapé *m*; (*from animal*) coice *m*, patada; (*to ball*) chute *m*; (*inf: thrill*): **he does it for ~s** faz isso para curtir; **~ off** *vi* (*SPORT*) dar o chute inicial

kid [kid] *n* (*inf: child*) criança; (*animal:*

cabrito; (*leather*) pelica ♦ *vi* (*inf*) brincar

kidnap ['kidnæp] *vt* seqüestrar; **~per** *n* seqüestrador(a) *m/f*; **~ping** *n* seqüestro

kidney ['kidni] *n* rim *m*

kill [kil] *vt* matar; (*murder*) assassinar ♦ *n* ato de matar; **~er** *n* assassino/a; **~ing** *n* assassinato; **to make a ~ing** (*inf*) faturar uma boa nota; **~joy** *n* desmancha-prazeres *m inv*

kiln [kiln] *n* forno

kilo ['ki:ləu] *n* quilo; **~byte** *n* quilobyte *m*; **~gram(me)** *n* quilograma *m*; **~metre** (*US* **~meter**) *n* quilômetro; **~watt** *n* quilowatt *m*

kilt [kilt] *n* saiote *m* escocês

kin [kin] *n see* **kith**; **next**

kind [kaind] *adj* (*friendly*) gentil; (*generous*) generoso; (*good*) bom/boa, bondoso, amável; (*voice*) suave ♦ *n* espécie *f*, classe *f*; (*species*) gênero; **in ~** (*COMM*) em espécie

kindergarten ['kindəgɑ:tn] *n* jardim *m* de infância

kind-hearted *adj* de bom coração, bondoso

kindle ['kindl] *vt* acender; (*emotion*) despertar

kindly ['kaindli] *adj* bom/boa, bondoso; (*gentle*) gentil, carinhoso ♦ *adv* bondosamente, amavelmente; **will you ~ ...** você pode fazer o favor de ...

kindness ['kaindnis] *n* bondade *f*, gentileza

kindred spirit ['kindrid-] *n* pessoa com os mesmos gostos

kinetic [ki'nɛtik] *adj* cinético

king [kiŋ] *n* rei *m*; **~dom** *n* reino; **~fisher** *n* martim-pescador *m*; **~size(d)** *adj* tamanho grande

kinky ['kiŋki] (*pej*) *adj* excêntrico, esquisito; (*sexually*) pervertido

kiosk ['ki:ɔsk] *n* banca (*BR*), quiosque *m* (*PT*); (*BRIT: TEL*) cabine *f*

kipper ['kipə*] *n* arenque defumado

kiss [kis] *n* beijo ♦ *vt* beijar; **to ~ (each other)** beijar-se; **~ of life** (*BRIT*) *n* respiração *f* artificial

kit [kit] *n* (*for sport etc*) kit *m*; (*equipment*) equipamento; (*tools*) caixa de ferramentas; (*for assembly*) kit *m* para montar

kitchen ['kitʃin] *n* cozinha; **~ sink** *n* pia (de cozinha)

kite [kait] *n* (*toy*) papagaio, pipa

kith [kiθ] *n*: **~ and kin** amigos e parentes *mpl*

kitten ['kitn] *n* gatinho

kitty ['kiti] *n* fundo comum, vaquinha

km *abbr* (= *kilometre*) km

knack [næk] *n* jeito

knapsack ['næpsæk] *n* mochila

knead [ni:d] *vt* amassar

knee [ni:] *n* joelho; **~cap** *n* rótula

kneel [ni:l] (*pt, pp* **knelt**) *vi* (*also*: **~ down**) ajoelhar-se

knelt [nɛlt] *pt, pp of* **kneel**

knew [nju:] *pt of* **know**

knickers ['nɪkəz] (*BRIT*) *npl* calcinha (*BR*), cuecas *fpl* (*PT*)

knife [naɪf] (*pl* **knives**) *n* faca ♦ *vt* esfaquear

knight [naɪt] *n* cavaleiro; (*CHESS*) cavalo; ~**hood** (*BRIT*) *n* (*title*): **to get a ~hood** receber o título de Sir

knit [nɪt] *vt* tricotar; (*brows*) franzir ♦ *vi* tricotar (*BR*), fazer malha (*PT*); (*bones*) consolidar-se; ~**ting** *n* tricô *m*; ~**ting machine** *n* máquina de tricotar; ~**ting needle** *n* agulha de tricô (*BR*) or de malha (*PT*); ~**wear** *n* roupa de malha

knives [naɪvz] *npl of* **knife**

knob [nɔb] *n* (*of door*) maçaneta; (*of stick*) castão *m*; (*on TV etc*) botão *m*

knock [nɔk] *vt* bater em; (*bump into*) colidir com; (*inf*) criticar, malhar ♦ *n* pancada, golpe *m*; (*on door*) batida ♦ *vi*: **to ~** *at or* **on the door** bater à porta; ~ **down** *vt* derrubar; (*pedestrian*) atropelar; ~ **off** *vi* (*inf*: *finish*) terminar ♦ *vt* (*inf*: *steal*) abafar; (*from price*): **to ~ off £10** fazer um desconto de £10; ~ **out** *vt* pôr nocaute, nocautear; (*defeat*) eliminar; ~ **over** *vt* derrubar; (*pedestrian*) atropelar; ~**er** *n* aldrava; ~**out** *n* nocaute *m* ♦ *cpd* com eliminatórias

knot [nɔt] *n* nó *m* ♦ *vt* dar nó em; ~**ty** *adj* (*fig*) cabeludo, espinhoso

know [nəu] (*pt* **knew**, *pp* **known**) *vt* saber; (*person, author, place*) conhecer; **to ~ how to swim** saber nadar; **to ~ about** *or* **of sth** saber de algo; ~**-all** (*BRIT*: *pej*) *n* sabichão/chona *m/f*; ~**-how** *n* know-how *m*, experiência; ~**ing** *adj* (*look*) de cumplicidade; ~**ingly** *adv* (*purposely*) de propósito; (*spitefully*) maliciosamente

knowledge ['nɔlɪdʒ] *n* conhecimento; (*learning*) saber *m*, conhecimentos *mpl*; ~**able** *adj* entendido, versado

known [nəun] *pp of* **know**

knuckle ['nʌkl] *n* nó *m*

K.O. *n abbr* = **knockout**

Koran [kɔ'rɑːn] *n*: **the ~** o Alcorão

Korea [kə'rɪə] *n* Coréia

kosher ['kəuʃə*] *adj* kosher *inv*

L

L (*BRIT*) *abbr* (*AUT*) *of* **learner**

l *abbr* (= *litre*) l

lab [læb] *n abbr* = **laboratory**

label ['leɪbl] *n* etiqueta, rótulo ♦ *vt* etiquetar, rotular

labor *etc* ['leɪbə*] (*US*) = **labour** *etc*

laboratory [lə'bɔrətəri] *n* laboratório

labour ['leɪbə*] (*US* **labor**) *n* trabalho; (*workforce*) mão-de-obra *f*; (*MED*): **to be in ~** estar em trabalho de parto ♦ *vi* trabalhar ♦ *vt* insistir em; **the L~ Par-**

ty (*BRIT*) o Partido Trabalhista; ~**ed** *adj* forçado; ~**er** *n* operário; **farm** ~**er** trabalhador *m* rural, peão *m*

lace [leɪs] *n* renda; (*of shoe etc*) cadarço ♦ *vt* (*shoe*) amarrar

lack [læk] *n* falta ♦ *vt* (*money, confidence*) faltar; (*intelligence*) carecer de; **through** *or* **for ~ of** por falta de; **to be ~ing** faltar; **to be ~ing in** carecer de

lackadaisical [lækə'deɪzɪkl] *adj* apático, indiferente

lacquer ['lækə*] *n* laca; (*hair ~*) fixador *m*

lad [læd] *n* menino, rapaz *m*, moço

ladder ['lædə*] *n* escada *f* de mão; (*BRIT*: *in tights*) defeito (em forma de escada)

laden ['leɪdn] *adj*: ~ (**with**) carregado (de)

ladle ['leɪdl] *n* concha (de sopa)

lady ['leɪdɪ] *n* senhora; (*distinguished, noble*) dama; (*in address*): **ladies and gentlemen** ... senhoras e senhores ...; **young ~** senhorita; **"ladies' (toilets)"** "senhoras"; ~**bird** (*US* ~**bug**) *n* joaninha; ~**like** *adj* elegante, refinado; ~**ship** *n*: **your** ~**ship** Sua Senhoria

lag [læg] *n* atraso, retardamento ♦ *vi* (*also*: ~ **behind**) ficar para trás ♦ *vt* (*pipes*) revestir com isolante térmico

lager ['lɑːgə*] *n* cerveja leve e clara

lagoon [lə'guːn] *n* lagoa

laid [leɪd] *pt, pp of* **lay**; ~-**back** (*inf*) *adj* descontraído; ~ **up** *adj*: **to be ~ up with flu** ficar de cama com gripe

lain [leɪn] *pp of* **lie**

lair [lɛə*] *n* covil *m*, toca

lake [leɪk] *n* lago

lamb [læm] *n* cordeiro

lame [leɪm] *adj* coxo, manco; (*excuse, argument*) pouco convincente, fraco

lament [lə'mɛnt] *n* lamento, queixa ♦ *vt* lamentar-se d'

laminated ['læmɪneɪtɪd] *adj* laminado

lamp [læmp] *n* lâmpada; ~**post** (*BRIT*) *n* poste *m*; ~**shade** *n* abajur *m*, quebra-luz *m*

lance [lɑːns] *n* lança ♦ *vt* (*MED*) lancetar

land [lænd] *n* terra; (*country*) país *m*; (*piece of ~*) terreno; (*estate*) terras *fpl*, propriedades *fpl* ♦ *vi* (*from ship*) desembarcar; (*AVIAT*) pousar, aterrissar (*BR*), aterrar (*PT*); (*fig*: *arrive*) cair, terminar ♦ *vt* desembarcar; **to ~ sb with sth** (*inf*) sobrecarregar alguém com algo; ~ **up** *vi* ir parar; ~**fill site** *n* local *m* de despejo de resíduos; ~**ing** *n* (*AVIAT*) pouso, aterrissagem *f* (*BR*), aterragem *f* (*PT*); (*of staircase*) patamar *m*; ~**ing gear** *n* trem *m* de aterrissagem (*BR*) or de aterragem (*PT*); ~**ing strip** *n* pista de aterrissagem (*BR*) or de aterragem (*PT*); ~**lady** *n* senhoria; (*of pub*) dona, proprietária; ~**locked** *adj* cercado de terra; ~**lord** *n* senhorio, locador *m*; (*of pub*) dono, proprietário; ~**mark** *n* lugar *m* conhecido; (*fig*) marco; ~**owner** *n* latifundiário/a

landscape ['lændskeɪp] *n* paisagem *f*; ~ **gardener** *n* paisagista *m/f*

landslide ['lændslaɪd] *n* (*GEO*) desmoronamento, desabamento; (*fig*: *POL*) vitória esmagadora

lane [leɪn] *n* caminho, estrada estreita; (*AUT*) pista; (*in race*) raia

language ['læŋgwɪdʒ] *n* língua; (*way one speaks*) linguagem *f*; **bad** ~ palavrões *mpl*; ~ **laboratory** *n* laboratório de línguas

languid ['læŋgwɪd] *adj* lânguido

languish ['læŋgwɪʃ] *vi* elanguescer, debilitar-se

lank [læŋk] *adj* (*hair*) liso

lanky ['læŋkɪ] *adj* magricela

lantern ['læntn] *n* lanterna

lap [læp] *n* (*of track*) volta; (*of person*) colo ♦ *vt* (*also*: ~ **up**) lamber ♦ *vi* (*waves*) marulhar; ~ **up** *vt* (*fig*) receber com sofreguidão

lapel [lə'pεl] *n* lapela

Lapland ['læplænd] *n* Lapónia

lapse [læps] *n* lapso; (*bad behaviour*) deslize *m* ♦ *vi* (*law*) prescrever; **to** ~ **into bad habits** adquirir maus hábitos

laptop (computer) ['læptɒp-] *n* laptop *m*

larceny ['lɑːsənɪ] *n* furto

larch [lɑːtʃ] *n* lariço

lard [lɑːd] *n* banha de porco

larder ['lɑːdə*] *n* despensa

large [lɑːdʒ] *adj* grande; **at** ~ (*free*) em liberdade; (*generally*: *as whole*) em geral; ~**ly** *adv* em grande parte; (*introducing reason*) principalmente; ~**scale** *adj* (*map*) em grande escala; (*fig*) importante, de grande alcance

largesse [lɑː'dʒεs] *n* generosidade *f*

lark [lɑːk] *n* (*bird*) cotovia; (*joke*) brincadeira, peça; ~ **about** *vi* divertir-se, brincar

laryngitis [lærɪn'dʒaɪtɪs] *n* laringite *f*

laser ['leɪzə*] *n* laser *m*; ~ **printer** *n* impressora a laser

lash [læʃ] *n* (*blow*) chicotada; (*also*: eye~) pestana, cílio ♦ *vt* chicotear, açoitar; (*subj*: *rain, wind*) castigar; (*tie*) atar; ~ **out** *vi*: **to** ~ **out at sb** atacar alguém violentamente; (*criticize*) atacar alguém verbalmente

lass [læs] (*BRIT*) *n* moça

lasso [læ'suː] *n* laço

last [lɑːst] *adj* último; (*final*) derradeiro ♦ *adv* em último lugar ♦ *vi* durar; (*continue*) continuar; ~ **night/week** ontem à noite/na semana passada; **at** ~ finalmente; ~ **but one** penúltimo; ~**ditch** *adj* desesperado, derradeiro; ~**ing** *adj* duradouro; ~**ly** *adv* por fim, por último; (*finally*) finalmente; ~**minute** *adj* de última hora

latch [lætʃ] *n* trinco, fecho, tranca

late [leɪt] *adj* (*not on time*) atrasado; (*far on in day etc*) tardio; (*former*) antigo, ex-, anterior; (*dead*) falecido ♦ *adv* tarde; (*behind time, schedule*) atrasado; **of** ~ recentemente; **in** ~ **May** no final de maio; ~**comer** *n* retardatário/a; ~**ly** *adv* ultimamente

later ['leɪtə*] *adj* (*date etc*) posterior; (*version etc*) mais recente ♦ *adv* mais tarde, depois; ~ **on** mais tarde

latest ['leɪtɪst] *adj* último; **at the** ~ no mais tardar

lathe [leɪð] *n* torno

lather ['lɑːðə*] *n* espuma (de sabão) ♦ *vt* ensaboar

Latin ['lætɪn] *n* (*LING*) latim *m* ♦ *adj* latino; ~ **America** *n* América Latina; ~ **American** *adj*, *n* latino-americano/a

latitude ['lætɪtjuːd] *n* latitude *f*

latter ['lætə*] *adj* último; (*of two*) segundo ♦ *n*: **the** ~ o último, este; ~**ly** *adv* ultimamente

lattice ['lætɪs] *n* treliça

laudable ['lɔːdəbl] *adj* louvável

laugh [lɑːf] *n* riso, risada ♦ *vi* rir, dar risada (*or* gargalhada); (**to do sth) for a** ~ (fazer algo) só de curtição; ~ **at** *vt fus* rir de; ~ **off** *vt* disfarçar sorrindo; ~**able** *adj* ridículo, absurdo; ~**ing stock** *n* alvo de riso; ~**ter** *n* riso, risada

launch [lɔːntʃ] *n* (*boat*) lancha; (*COMM, of rocket etc*) lançamento ♦ *vt* lançar; ~ **into** *vt fus* lançar-se a

launder ['lɔːndə*] *vt* lavar e passar; ~**ette** (*BRIT*) *n* lavanderia automática; **laundromat** ® (*US*) *n* = ~**ette**

laundry ['lɔːndrɪ] *n* lavanderia; (*clothes*) roupa para lavar

laureate ['lɔːrɪət] *adj* see **poet**

laurel ['lɔrl] *n* loureiro

lava ['lɑːvə] *n* lava

lavatory ['lævətərɪ] *n* privada (*BR*), casa de banho (*PT*)

lavender ['lævəndə*] *n* lavanda

lavish ['lævɪʃ] *adj* (*amount*) generoso; (*person*): ~ **with** pródigo em, generoso com ♦ *vt*: **to** ~ **sth on sb** encher *or* cobrir alguém de algo

law [lɔː] *n* lei *f*; (*rule*) regra; (*SCH*) direito; ~**abiding** *adj* obediente à lei; ~ **and order** *n* a ordem pública; ~ **court** *n* tribunal *m* de justiça; ~**ful** *adj* legal, lícito; ~**less** *adj* ilegal

lawn [lɔːn] *n* gramado (*BR*), relvado (*PT*); ~**mower** *n* cortador *m* de grama (*BR*) *or* de relva (*PT*); ~ **tennis** *n* tênis *m* de gramado (*BR*) *or* de relvado (*PT*)

law school (*US*) *n* faculdade *f* de direito

lawsuit ['lɔːsuːt] *n* ação *f* judicial, processo

lawyer ['lɔːjə*] *n* advogado/a; (*for sales, wills etc*) notário/a, tabelião/liã *m/f*

lax [læks] *adj* (*discipline*) relaxado; (*person*) negligente

laxative ['læksətɪv] n laxante m

lay [leɪ] (pt, pp **laid**) pt of **lie** ♦ adj leigo ♦ vt colocar; (eggs, table) pôr; ~ **aside** or **by** vt pôr de lado; ~ **down** vt depositar; (rules etc) impor, estabelecer; to ~ **down the law** (pej) impor regras; to ~ **down one's life** sacrificar voluntariamente a vida; ~ **off** vt (workers) demitir; ~ **on** vt (meal etc) prover; ~ **out** vt (spread out) dispor em ordem; ~**about** (inf) n vadio/a, preguiçoso/a; ~**by** (BRIT) n acostamento

layer ['leɪə*] n camada

layman ['leɪmən] (irreg) n leigo

layout ['leɪaʊt] n (of garden, building) desenho; (of writing) leiaute m

laze [leɪz] vi (also: ~ **about**) vadiar

lazy ['leɪzɪ] adj preguiçoso; (movement) lento

lb. abbr = **pound** (weight)

lead¹ [liːd] (pt, pp **led**) n (front position) dianteira; (SPORT) liderança; (fig) vantagem f; (clue) pista; (ELEC) fio; (for dog) correia; (in play, film) papel m principal ♦ vt levar; (be leader of) chefiar; (start, guide: activity) encabeçar ♦ vi encabeçar; to be in the ~ (SPORT: in race) estar na frente; (: in match) estar ganhando; to ~ the way assumir a direção; ~ **away** vt levar; ~ **back** vt levar de volta; ~ **on** vt (tease) provocar; ~ **to** vt fus levar a, conduzir a; ~ **up to** vt fus conduzir a

lead² [lɛd] n chumbo; (in pencil) grafite f; ~**en** adj (sky, sea) cor de chumbo, cinzento

leader ['liːdə*] n líder m/f; ~**ship** n liderança; (quality) poder m de liderança

lead-free [lɛd-] adj sem chumbo

leading ['liːdɪŋ] adj principal; (role) de destaque; (first, front) primeiro, dianteiro; ~ **lady** n (THEATRE) primeira atriz f; ~ **light** n (person) figura principal, destaque m; ~ **man** (irreg) n (THEATRE) ator m principal

lead singer n cantor(a) m/f

leaf [liːf] (pl **leaves**) n folha ♦ vi: to ~ **through** (book) folhear; to **turn over a new** ~ mudar de vida, partir para outra (inf)

leaflet ['liːflɪt] n folheto

league [liːg] n liga; **to be in** ~ **with** estar de comum acordo com

leak [liːk] n (of liquid, gas) escape m, vazamento; (hole) buraco, rombo; (in roof) goteira; (fig: of information) vazamento ♦ vi (ship) fazer água; (shoe) deixar entrar água; (roof) gotejar; (pipe, container, liquid) vazar; (gas) escapar ♦ vt (news) vazar

lean [liːn] (pt, pp ~**ed** or ~**t**) adj magro ♦ vt: to ~ **sth on** encostar or apoiar algo em ♦ vi inclinar-se; to ~ **against** encostar-se or apoiar-se contra; to ~ **on** encostar-se or apoiar-se em; ~

forward/back vi inclinar-se para frente/para trás; ~ **out** vi inclinar-se; ~ **over** vi debruçar-se ♦ vt fus debruçar-se sobre; ~**ing** n: ~**ing (towards)** inclinação f (para)

leap [liːp] (pt, pp ~**ed** or ~**t**) n salto, pulo ♦ vi saltar; ~**frog** n jogo de pular carniça; ~**t** pt, pp of **leap**; ~ **year** n ano bissexto

learn [ləːn] (pt, pp ~**ed** or ~**t**) vt aprender; (by heart) decorar ♦ vi aprender; to ~ **about sth** (SCH: hear, read) saber de algo; ~**ed** adj erudito; ~**er** n principiante m/f; (BRIT: also: ~**er driver**) aprendiz m/f de motorista; ~**ing** n (knowledge) saber m; ~**t** pt, pp of **learn**

lease [liːs] n arrendamento ♦ vt arrendar

leash [liːʃ] n correia

least [liːst] adj: the ~ + n o/a menor; (smallest amount of) a menor quantidade de ♦ adv: the ~ + adj o/a menos; at ~ pelo menos; not in the ~ de maneira nenhuma

leather ['lɛðə*] n couro

leave [liːv] (pt, pp **left**) vt deixar; (go away from) abandonar ♦ vi ir-se, sair; (train) sair ♦ n licença; to ~ **sth to sb** deixar algo para alguém; to **be left** sobrar; ~ **behind** vt deixar para trás; (forget) esquecer; ~ **out** vt omitir; ~ **of absence** n licença excepcional

leaves [liːvz] npl of **leaf**

Lebanon ['lɛbənən] n Líbano

lecherous ['lɛtʃərəs] (pej) adj lascivo

lecture ['lɛktʃə*] n conferência, palestra; (SCH) aula ♦ vi dar aulas, lecionar ♦ vt (scold) passar um sermão em; ~**r** (BRIT) n (at university) professor(a) m/f

led [lɛd] pt, pp of **lead¹**

ledge [lɛdʒ] n (of window) peitoril m; (of mountain) saliência, proeminência

ledger ['lɛdʒə*] n livro-razão m, razão m

lee [liː] n sotavento

leech [liːtʃ] n sanguessuga

leek [liːk] n alho-poró m

leer [lɪə*] vi: to ~ **at sb** olhar maliciosamente para alguém

leeway ['liːweɪ] n (fig): to **have some** ~ ter certa liberdade de ação

left [lɛft] pt, pp of **leave** ♦ adj esquerdo ♦ n esquerda ♦ adv à esquerda; **on the** ~ à esquerda; **to the** ~ para a esquerda; **the L~** (POL) a Esquerda; ~**-handed** adj canhoto; ~**-hand side** n lado esquerdo; ~**-luggage (office)** (BRIT) n depósito de bagagem; ~**overs** npl sobras fpl; ~**-wing** adj (POL) de esquerda, esquerdista

leg [lɛg] n (of animal) pata; (CULIN: of meat) perna; (of journey) etapa; **1st/2nd** ~ (SPORT) primeiro/segundo turno

legacy ['lɛgəsɪ] n legado; (fig) herança

legal ['liːgl] adj legal; ~ **holiday** (US) n feriado; ~**ly** adv legalmente; (in terms of law) de acordo com a lei; ~ **tender** n moeda corrente

legend ['lɛdʒənd] n lenda; (person) mito; ~**ary** adj legendário

legislation [lɛdʒɪs'leɪʃən] n legislação f

legislature ['lɛdʒɪslətʃə*] n legislatura

legitimate [lɪ'dʒɪtɪmət] adj legítimo

leg-room n espaço para as pernas

leisure ['lɛʒə*] n lazer m; **at ~** desocupado, livre; ~ **centre** n centro de lazer; ~**ly** adj calmo, vagaroso

lemon ['lɛmən] n limão(-galego) m; ~**ade** n limonada; ~ **tea** n chá m de limão

lend [lɛnd] (pt, pp lent) vt emprestar; ~**ing library** n biblioteca circulante

length [lɛŋθ] n comprimento, extensão f; (amount of time) duração f; **at ~** (at last) finalmente, afinal; (lengthily) por extenso; ~**en** vt encompridar, alongar ♦ vi encompridar-se; ~**ways** adv longitudinalmente, ao comprido; ~**y** adj comprido, longo; (meeting) prolongado

lenient ['li:nɪənt] adj indulgente

lens [lɛnz] n (of spectacles) lente f; (of camera) objetiva

Lent [lɛnt] n Quaresma

lent [lɛnt] pt, pp of **lend**

lentil ['lɛntl] n lentilha

Leo ['li:əu] n Leão m

leotard ['li:ətɑːd] n collant m

leprosy ['lɛprəsɪ] n lepra

lesbian ['lɛzbɪən] n lésbica

less [lɛs] adj, pron, adv menos ♦ prep: ~ **tax/10% discount** menos imposto/10% de desconto; ~ **than ever** menos do que nunca; ~ **and** ~ cada vez menos; **the** ~ **he works** ... quanto menos trabalha ...

lessen ['lɛsn] vi diminuir, minguar ♦ vt diminuir, reduzir

lesser ['lɛsə*] adj menor; **to a ~ extent** nem tanto

lesson ['lɛsn] n aula; (example, warning) lição f; **to teach sb a ~** (fig) dar uma lição em alguém

lest [lɛst] conj: ~ **it happen** para que não aconteça

let [lɛt] (pt, pp let) vt (allow) deixar; (BRIT: lease) alugar; **to ~ sb know sth** avisar alguém de algo; ~**'s go!** vamos!; **"to ~"** "aluga-se"; ~ **down** vt (tyre) esvaziar; (disappoint) desapontar; ~ **go** vt, vi soltar; ~ **in** vt deixar entrar; (visitor etc) fazer entrar; ~ **off** vt (culprit) perdoar; (firework etc) soltar; ~ **on** vi revelar; ~ **out** vt deixar sair; (scream) soltar; ~ **up** vi cessar, afrouxar

lethal ['li:θl] adj letal

lethargic [lɛ'θɑːdʒɪk] adj letárgico

letter ['lɛtə*] n (of alphabet) letra; (correspondence) carta; ~ **bomb** n cartabomba; ~**box** (BRIT) n caixa do correio; ~**ing** n letras fpl

lettuce ['lɛtɪs] n alface f

let-up n diminuição f, afrouxamento

leukaemia [lu:'ki:mɪə] (US **leukemia**) n leucemia

level ['lɛvl] adj (flat) plano ♦ adv: **to draw ~ with** alcançar ♦ n nível m; (height) altura ♦ vt aplanar; **"A" ~s** (BRIT) npl ≈ vestibular m; **"O" ~s** npl exames optativos feitos após o término do 10 Grau; **to be ~ with** estar no mesmo nível que; **on the ~** em nível; (fig: honest) sincero; ~ **off or out** vi (prices etc) estabilizar-se; ~ **crossing** (BRIT) n passagem f de nível; ~**-headed** adj sensato

lever ['li:və*] n alavanca; (fig) estratagema m; ~**age** n força de uma alavanca; (fig: influence) influência

levity ['lɛvɪtɪ] n leviandade f, frivolidade f

levy ['lɛvɪ] n imposto, tributo ♦ vt arrecadar, cobrar

lewd [lu:d] adj obsceno, lascivo

liability [laɪə'bɪlɪtɪ] n responsabilidade f; (handicap) desvantagem f; **liabilities** npl (COMM) exigibilidades fpl, obrigações fpl

liable ['laɪəbl] adj (subject): ~ **to** sujeito a; (responsible): ~ **for** responsável por; (likely): ~ **to do** capaz de fazer

liaise [li:'eɪz] vi: **to ~ (with)** cooperar (com)

liaison [li:'eɪzɒn] n (coordination) ligação f; (affair) relação f amorosa

liar ['laɪə*] n mentiroso/a

libel ['laɪbl] n difamação f ♦ vt caluniar, difamar

liberal ['lɪbərl] adj liberal; (generous) generoso

liberate ['lɪbəreɪt] vt libertar; **liberation** n liberação f, libertação f

liberty ['lɪbətɪ] n liberdade f; (criminal): **to be at ~** estar livre; **to be at ~ to do** ser livre de fazer

Libra ['li:brə] n Libra, Balança

librarian [laɪ'brɛərɪən] n bibliotecário/a

library ['laɪbrərɪ] n biblioteca

Libya ['lɪbɪə] n Líbia; ~**n** adj, n líbio/a

lice [laɪs] npl of **louse**

licence ['laɪsns] (US **license**) n (gen, COMM) licença; (AUT) carta de motorista (BR), carta de condução (PT)

license ['laɪsns] n (US) = **licence** ♦ vt autorizar, dar licença a; ~**d** adj (car) autorizado oficialmente; (for alcohol) autorizado para vender bebidas alcoólicas; ~ **plate** n (US) (AUT) placa (de identificação) (do carro)

lick [lɪk] vt lamber; (inf: defeat) arrasar, surrar; **to ~ one's lips** (also fig) lamber os beiços

licorice ['lɪkərɪs] (US) n = **liquorice**

lid [lɪd] n tampa; (eye~) pálpebra

lie [laɪ] (pt lay, pp lain) vi (act) deitar-se; (state) estar deitado; (object: be situated) estar, encontrar-se; (fig: problem, cause) residir; (*in race, league*) ocupar; (*tell ~s: pt, pp ~d*) mentir ♦ *n* mentira; **to ~ low** (*fig*) esconder-se; **~ about** *or* **around** *vi* (*things*) estar espalhado; (*people*) vadiar; **~-down** (*BRIT*) *n*: **to have a ~-down** descansar; **~-in** (*BRIT*) *n*: **to have a ~-in** dormir até tarde

lieu [luː]: **in ~ of** *prep* em vez de

lieutenant [lɛfˈtɛnənt, (*US*) luːˈtɛnənt] *n* (*MIL*) tenente *m*

life [laɪf] (*pl* **lives**) *n* vida; **to come to ~** animar-se; **~ assurance** (*BRIT*) *n* = **~ insurance**; **~belt** (*BRIT*) *n* cinto salva-vidas; **~boat** *n* barco salva-vidas; **~guard** *n* (guarda *m/f*) salva-vidas *m/f inv*; **~ imprisonment** *n* prisão *f* perpétua; **~ insurance** *n* seguro de vida; **~ jacket** *n* colete *m* salva-vidas; **~less** *adj* sem vida; **~like** *adj* natural; (*realistic*) realista; **~line** *n* corda salva-vidas; **~long** *adj* que dura toda a vida; **~ preserver** (*US*) *n* = **~belt**; **~ jacket**; **~ sentence** *n* pena de prisão perpétua; **~-size(d)** *adj* de tamanho natural; **~span** *n* vida, duração *f*; **~ style** *n* estilo de vida; **~ support system** *n* (*MED*) sistema *m* de respiração artificial; **~time** *n* vida

lift [lɪft] *vt* levantar ♦ *vi* (*fog*) dispersar-se, dissipar-se ♦ *n* (*BRIT: elevator*) elevador *m*; **to give sb a ~** (*BRIT*) dar uma carona para alguém (*BR*), dar uma boleia a alguém (*PT*); **~-off** *n* decolagem *f*

light [laɪt] (*pt, pp* **lit**) *n* luz *f*; (*AUT: headlight*) farol *m*; (: *rear ~*) luz traseira; (*for cigarette etc*) **have you got a ~?** tem fogo? ♦ *vt* acender; (*room*) iluminar ♦ *adj* (*colour, room*) claro; (*not heavy, fig*) leve; (*rain, traffic*) fraco; (*movement*) delicado; **~s** *npl* (*AUT*) sinal *m* de trânsito; **to come to ~** vir à tona; **in the ~ of** à luz de; **~ up** *vi* iluminar-se ♦ *vt* iluminar; **~ bulb** *n* lâmpada; **~en** *vt* tornar mais leve; **~er** *n* (*also:* **cigarette ~er**) isqueiro, acendedor *m*; **~-headed** *adj* (*dizzy*) aturdido, tonto; (*excited*) exaltado; **~-hearted** *adj* alegre, despreocupado; **~house** *n* farol *m*; **~ing** *n* iluminação *f*; **~ly** *adv* ligeiramente; **to get off ~ly** conseguir se safar, livrar a cara (*inf*); **~ness** *n* (*in weight*) leveza

lightning [ˈlaɪtnɪŋ] *n* relâmpago, raio; **~ conductor** *n* pára-raios *m inv*; **~ rod** (*US*) *n* = **~ conductor**

light: **~ pen** *n* caneta leitora; **~weight** *adj* (*suit*) leve; (*BOXING*) peso-leve; **~ year** *n* ano-luz *m*

like [laɪk] *vt* gostar de ♦ *prep* como; (*such as*) tal qual ♦ *adj* parecido, semelhante ♦ *n*: **the ~** coisas *fpl* parecidas; **his ~s and dislikes** seus gostos e aversões; **I would ~, I'd ~** (*inf*) gostaria de; **to be or look ~ sb/sth** parecer-se com alguém/algo, parecer alguém/algo; **do it ~ this** faça isso assim; **it is nothing ~**

... não se parece nada com ...; **~able** *adj* simpático, agradável

likelihood [ˈlaɪklɪhud] *n* probabilidade *f*

likely [ˈlaɪklɪ] *adj* provável; **he's ~ to leave** é provável que ele se vá; **not ~!** (*inf*) nem morto!

likeness [ˈlaɪknɪs] *n* semelhança; **that's a good ~** tem uma grande semelhança

likewise [ˈlaɪkwaɪz] *adv* igualmente; **to do ~** fazer o mesmo

liking [ˈlaɪkɪŋ] *n* afeição *f*, simpatia; **to be to sb's ~** ser ao gosto de alguém

lilac [ˈlaɪlək] *n* lilás *m*

lily [ˈlɪlɪ] *n* lírio, açucena; **~ of the valley** *n* lírio-do-vale *m*

limb [lɪm] *n* membro

limber up [ˈlɪmbə*-*] *vi* (*SPORT*) fazer aquecimento

limbo [ˈlɪmbəu] *n*: **to be in ~** (*fig*) viver na expectativa

lime [laɪm] *n* (*tree*) limeira; (*fruit*) limão *m*; (*also:* **~ juice**) suco (*BR*) *or* sumo (*PT*) de limão; (*GEO*) cal *f*

limelight [ˈlaɪmlaɪt] *n*: **to be in the ~** ser o centro das atenções

limerick [ˈlɪmərɪk] *n* quintilha humorística

limestone [ˈlaɪmstəun] *n* pedra calcária

limit [ˈlɪmɪt] *n* limite *m* ♦ *vt* limitar; **~ed** *adj* limitado; **to be ~ed to** limitar-se a; **~ed (liability) company** (*BRIT*) *n* ≈ sociedade *f* anônima

limp [lɪmp] *n*: **to have a ~** mancar, ser coxo ♦ *vi* mancar ♦ *adj* frouxo

limpet [ˈlɪmpɪt] *n* lapa

line [laɪn] *n* linha; (*rope*) corda; (*wire*) fio; (*row*) fila, fileira; (*on face*) ruga ♦ *vt* (*road, room*) encarreirar; (*container, clothing*) forrar; **to ~ the streets** ladear as ruas; **in ~ with** de acordo com; **~ up** *vi* enfileirar-se ♦ *vt* enfileirar; (*set up, have ready*) preparar, arranjar

lined [laɪnd] *adj* (*face*) enrugado; (*paper*) pautado

linen [ˈlɪnɪn] *n* artigos de cama e mesa; (*cloth*) linho

liner [ˈlaɪnə*-*] *n* navio de linha regular; (*also:* **bin ~**) saco para lata de lixo

linesman [ˈlaɪnzmən] (*irreg*) *n* (*SPORT*) juiz *m* de linha

line-up *n* formação *f* em linha, alinhamento; (*SPORT*) escalação *f*

linger [ˈlɪŋgə*-*] *vi* demorar-se, retardar-se; (*smell, tradition*) persistir

lingerie [ˈlænʒəriː] *n* lingerie *f*, roupa de baixo (de mulher)

lingo [ˈlɪŋgəu] (*inf*) (*pl* **~es**) *n* língua

linguistics [lɪŋˈgwɪstɪks] *n* lingüística

lining [ˈlaɪnɪŋ] *n* forro; (*ANAT*) parede *f*

link [lɪŋk] *n* (*of a chain*) elo; (*connection*) conexão *f* ♦ *vt* vincular, unir; (*associate*): **to ~ with** *or* **to unir a**; **~s** *npl* (*GOLF*) campo de golfe; **~ up** *vt* acoplar ♦ *vi* unir-se

lino [ˈlaɪnəu] *n* = **linoleum**

linoleum [lɪ'nəulɪəm] n linóleo

lion ['laɪən] n leão m; **~ess** n leoa

lip [lɪp] n lábio; **~read** (irreg) vi ler os lábios; **~ salve** n pomada para os lábios; **~ service** n: **to pay ~ service to sth** devotar-se a or elogiar algo falsamente; **~stick** n batom m

liqueur [lɪ'kjuə*] n licor m

liquid ['lɪkwɪd] adj líquido ♦ n líquido

liquidize ['lɪkwɪdaɪz] (BRIT) vt (CULIN) liqüidificar, passar no liqüidificador; **~r** (BRIT) n (CULIN) liqüidificador m

liquor ['lɪkə*] n licor m, bebida alcoólica

liquorice ['lɪkərɪs] (BRIT) n alcaçuz m

liquor store (US) n loja que vende bebidas alcoólicas

Lisbon ['lɪzbən] n Lisboa

lisp [lɪsp] n ceceio ♦ vi cecear, falar com a língua presa

list [lɪst] n lista ♦ vt (write down) fazer uma lista or relação de; (enumerate) enumerar; **~ed building** (BRIT) n prédio tombado

listen ['lɪsn] vi escutar, ouvir; **to ~ to** escutar; **~er** n ouvinte m/f

listless ['lɪstlɪs] adj apático, indiferente

lit [lɪt] pt, pp of **light**

liter ['liːtə*] (US) n = **litre**

literacy ['lɪtərəsɪ] n capacidade f de ler e escrever, alfabetização f

literal ['lɪtərl] adj literal

literary ['lɪtərərɪ] adj literário

literate ['lɪtərət] adj alfabetizado, instruído; (educated) culto, letrado

literature ['lɪtərɪtʃə*] n literatura; (brochures etc) folhetos mpl

lithe [laɪð] adj ágil

litigation [lɪtɪ'geɪʃən] n litígio

litre ['liːtə*] (US **liter**) n litro

litter ['lɪtə*] n (rubbish) lixo; (young animals) ninhada; **~ bin** (BRIT) n lata de lixo; **~ed** adj: **~ed with** semeado de

little ['lɪtl] adj (small) pequeno; (not much) pouco ♦ often translated by suffix: eg: **~ house** casinha ♦ adv pouco; **a ~** um pouco (de); **for a ~ while** por um instante; **as ~ as possible** o menos possível; **~ by ~** pouco a pouco; **~ finger** n dedo mindinho

live [vb lɪv, adj laɪv] vi viver; (reside) morar ♦ adj vivo; (wire) eletrizado; (broadcast) ao vivo; (shell) carregado; **~ ammunition** munição de guerra; **~ down** vt redimir; **~ on** vt fus viver de, alimentar-se de; **to ~ on £50 a week** viver com £50 por semana; **~ together** vi viver juntos; **~ up to** vt fus (fulfil) cumprir

livelihood ['laɪvlɪhud] n meio de vida, subsistência

lively ['laɪvlɪ] adj vivo

liven up ['laɪvn-] vt animar ♦ vi animar-se

liver ['lɪvə*] n fígado

livery ['lɪvərɪ] n libré f

lives [laɪvz] npl of **life**

livestock ['laɪvstɔk] n gado

livid ['lɪvɪd] adj lívido; (inf: furious) furioso

living ['lɪvɪŋ] adj vivo ♦ n: **to earn** or **make a ~** ganhar a vida; **~ conditions** npl condições fpl de vida; **~ room** n sala de estar; **~ standards** npl padrão m or nível m de vida; **~ wage** n salário de subsistência

lizard ['lɪzəd] n lagarto

load [ləud] n carga; (weight) peso ♦ vt (gen, COMPUT) carregar; **a ~ of**, **~s of** (fig) um monte de, uma porção de; **~ed** adj (vehicle): **to be ~ed with** estar carregado de; (question) intencionado; (inf: rich) cheio da nota

loaf [ləuf] (pl **loaves**) n pão-de-forma m

loan [ləun] n empréstimo ♦ vt emprestar; **on ~** emprestado

loath [ləuθ] adj: **to be ~ to do sth** estar pouco inclinado a fazer algo, relutar em fazer algo

loathe [ləuð] vt detestar, odiar

loaves [ləuvz] npl of **loaf**

lobby ['lɔbɪ] n vestíbulo, saguão m; (POL: pressure group) grupo de pressão, lobby m ♦ vt pressionar

lobe [ləub] n lóbulo

lobster ['lɔbstə*] n lagostim m; (large) lagosta

local ['ləukl] adj local ♦ n (pub) bar m (local); **the ~s** npl (~ inhabitants) os moradores locais; **~ authority** n município; **~ call** n (TEL) ligação f local; **~ government** n administração f municipal; **~ly** adv nos arredores, na vizinhança

locate [ləu'keɪt] vt (find) localizar, situar; (situate): **to be ~d in** estar localizado em

location [ləu'keɪʃən] n local m, posição f; **on ~** (CINEMA) em externas

loch [lɔx] n lago

lock [lɔk] n (of door, box) fechadura; (of canal) eclusa; (of hair) anel m, mecha ♦ vt (with key) trancar ♦ vi (door etc) fechar-se à chave; (wheels) travar-se; **~ in** vt trancar dentro; **~ out** vt trancar do lado de fora; **~ up** vt (criminal, mental patient) prender; (house) trancar ♦ vi fechar tudo

locker ['lɔkə*] n compartimento com chave

locket ['lɔkɪt] n medalhão m

locksmith ['lɔksmɪθ] n serralheiro/a

lockup ['lɔkʌp] (US) n prisão f

locomotive [ləukə'məutɪv] n locomotiva

locum ['ləukəm] n (MED) (médico/a) interino/a

locust ['ləukəst] n gafanhoto

lodge [lɔdʒ] n casa do guarda, guarita; (hunting ~) pavilhão m de caça ♦ vi (person): **to ~ (with)** alojar-se (na casa de) ♦ vt (complaint) apresentar; **~r** n inquilino/a, hóspede *m/f*

lodgings ['lɔdʒɪŋz] *npl* quarto (mobiliado)

loft [lɔft] *n* sótão *m*

lofty ['lɔftɪ] *adj* (*haughty*) altivo, arrogante; (*sentiments, aims*) nobre

log [lɔg] *n* (*of wood*) tora; (*book*) = **logbook** ♦ *vt* registrar

logbook ['lɔgbuk] *n* (*NAUT*) diário de bordo; (*AVIAT*) diário de vôo; (*of car*) documentação *f* (do carro)

loggerheads ['lɔgəhɛdz] *npl*: at ~ (with) às turras (com)

logic ['lɔdʒɪk] *n* lógica; ~**al** *adj* lógico

logo ['ləugəu] *n* logotipo

loin [lɔɪn] *n* (*CULIN*) (carne *f* de) lombo

loiter ['lɔɪtə*] *vi* perder tempo

loll [lɔl] *vi* (*also*: ~ **about**) refestelar-se, reclinar-se

lollipop ['lɔlɪpɔp] *n* pirulito (*BR*), chupachupa *m* (*PT*); ~ **lady** (*BRIT*) *n* guarda para pedestres; ~ **man** (*BRIT*: *irreg*) *n* guarda *m* para pedestres

London ['lʌndn] *n* Londres; ~**er** *n* londrino/a

lone [ləun] *adj* (*person*) solitário; (*thing*) único

loneliness ['ləunlɪnɪs] *n* solidão *f*, isolamento

lonely ['ləunlɪ] *adj* (*person*) só; (*place*) solitário, isolado

long [lɔŋ] *adj* longo; (*road, hair, table*) comprido ♦ *adv* muito tempo ♦ *vi*: to ~ for sth ansiar or suspirar por algo; how ~ is the street? qual é a extensão da rua?; how ~ is the lesson? quanto dura a lição?; all night ~ a noite inteira; he no ~er comes ele não vem mais; ~ before/after muito antes/ depois; before ~ (+ *future*) dentro de pouco; (+ *past*) pouco tempo depois; at ~ last por fim, no final; so or as ~ as contando que; ~-**distance** *adj* (*travel*) de longa distância; (*call*) interurbano; ~-**haired** *adj* cabeludo; (*animal*) peludo; ~**hand** *n* escrita usual; ~**ing** *n* desejo, anseio

longitude ['lɔŋgɪtjuːd] *n* longitude *f*

long: ~ **jump** *n* salto em distância; ~-**life** *adj* longa vida; ~-**lost** *adj* perdido há muito (tempo); ~-**playing record** *n* elepê *m* (*BR*), LP *m* (*PT*); ~-**range** *adj* de longo alcance; (*forecast*) a longo prazo; ~-**sighted** *adj* presbita; ~-**standing** *adj* de muito tempo; ~-**suffering** *adj* paciente, resignado; ~-**term** *adj* a longo prazo; ~ **wave** *n* (*RADIO*) onda longa; ~-**winded** *adj* prolixo, cansativo

loo [luː] (*BRIT*: *inf*) *n* banheiro (*BR*), casa de banho (*PT*)

look [luk] *vi* olhar; (*seem*) parecer; (*building etc*): to ~ **south**/(**out**) **onto the** **sea** dar para o sul/o mar ♦ *n* olhar *m*; (*glance*) olhada, vista de olhos; (*appearance*) aparência, aspecto; ~**s** *npl* (*good*

~s) físico, aparência; ~ (**here**)! (*annoyance*) escuta aqui!; ~! (*surprise*) olha!; ~ **after** *vt fus* cuidar de; (*deal with*) lidar com; ~ **at** *vt fus* olhar (para); (*read quickly*) ler rapidamente; (*consider*) considerar; ~ **back** *vi*: to ~ **back on** (*remember*) recordar, rever; ~ **down on** *vt fus* (*fig*) desdenhar, desprezar; ~ **for** *vt fus* procurar; ~ **forward to** *vt fus* aguardar com prazer, ansiar por; (*in letter*): **we** ~ **forward to hearing from** **you** no aguardo de suas notícias; ~ **into** *vt fus* investigar; ~ **on** *vi* assistir; ~ **out** *vi* (*beware*): to ~ **out** (**for**) tomar cuidado (com); ~ **out for** *vt fus* (*await*) esperar; ~ **round** *vi* virar a cabeça, voltar-se; ~ **through** *vt fus* (*papers, book*) examinar; ~ **to** *vt fus* (*rely on*) contar com; ~ **up** *vi* levantar os olhos; (*improve*) melhorar ♦ *vt* (*word*) procurar; ~**out** *n* (*tower etc*) posto de observação, guarita; (*person*) vigia *m*; **to** **be on the** ~**out for sth** estar na expectativa de algo

loom [luːm] *n* tear *m* ♦ *vi* (*also*: ~ **up**) agigantar-se; (*event*) aproximar-se

loony ['luːnɪ] (*inf*) *adj* meio doido ♦ *n* debil *m/f* mental

loop [luːp] *n* laço ♦ *vt*: to ~ **sth round** **sth** prender algo em torno de algo; ~**hole** *n* escapatória

loose [luːs] *adj* solto; (*not tight*) frouxo ♦ *n*: **to be on the** ~ estar solto; ~ **change** *n* trocado; ~ **chippings** *npl* (*on* *road*) pedrinhas *fpl* soltas; ~ **end** *n*: **to** **be at a** ~ **end** (*BRIT*) or **at** ~ **ends** (*US*) (*fig*) não ter o que fazer; ~**ly** *adv* frouxamente, folgadamente; ~**n** *vt* (*free*) soltar; (*slacken*) afrouxar

loot [luːt] *n* saque *m*, despojo ♦ *vt* saquear, pilhar

lop off [lɔp-] *vt* cortar; (*branches*) podar

lopsided [lɔp'saɪdɪd] *adj* torto

lord [lɔːd] *n* senhor *m*; **L**~ **Smith** Lord Smith; **the L**~ (*REL*) o Senhor; **good** **L**~! Deus meu!; **the** (**House of**) **L**~**s** (*BRIT*) a Câmara dos Lordes; ~**ship** (*BRIT*) *n*: **Your L**~**ship** Vossa senhoria

lore [lɔː*] *n* sabedoria popular, tradições *fpl*

lorry ['lɔrɪ] (*BRIT*) *n* caminhão *m* (*BR*), camião *m* (*PT*); ~ **driver** (*BRIT*) *n* caminhoneiro (*BR*), camionista *m/f* (*PT*)

lose [luːz] (*pt, pp* **lost**) *vt, vi* perder; **to** ~ (**time**) (*clock*) atrasar-se; ~**r** *n* perdedor(a) *m/f*; (*inf*: *failure*) derrotado/a, fracassado/a

loss [lɔs] *n* perda; (*COMM*): **to make a** ~ sair com prejuízo; **heavy** ~**es** (*MIL*) grandes perdas; **to be at a** ~ estar perplexo

lost [lɔst] *pt, pp of* **lose** ♦ *adj* perdido; ~ **and found** (*US*) (seção *f* de) perdidos e achados *mpl*; ~ **property** (*BRIT*) *n* (objetos *mpl*) perdidos e achados *mpl*

lot [lɔt] n (set of things) porção f; (at auctions) lote m; the ~ tudo, todos/as; a ~ muito, bastante; a ~ of, ~s of muito(s); I read a ~ leio bastante; to draw ~s tirar à sorte

lotion ['ləuʃən] n loção f

lottery ['lɔtəri] n loteria

loud [laud] adj (voice) alto; (shout) forte; (noise) barulhento; (support, condemnation) veemente; (gaudy) berrante ♦ adv alto; **out** ~ em voz alta; **~-hailer** (BRIT) n megafone m; **~ly** adv ruidosamente; (aloud) em voz alta; **~speaker** n altofalante m

lounge [laundʒ] n sala f de estar; (of airport) salão m; (BRIT: also: ~ **bar**) bar m social ♦ vi recostar-se, espreguiçar-se; ~ **about** vi ficar à-toa; ~ **around** vi = ~ **about**; ~ **suit** (BRIT) n terno (BR), fato (PT)

louse [laus] (pl **lice**) n piolho

lousy ['lauzi] (inf) adj ruim, péssimo; (ill): **to feel** ~ sentir-se mal

lout [laut] n rústico, grosseiro

lovable ['lʌvəbl] adj adorável, simpático

love [lʌv] n amor m ♦ vt amar; (care for) gostar; (activity): **to** ~ **to do** gostar (muito) de fazer; ~ **(from) Anne** (on letter) um abraço or um beijo, Anne; **I** ~ **coffee** adoro o café; "**15** ~" (TENNIS) "15 a zero"; **to be in** ~ **with** estar apaixonado por; **to fall in** ~ **with** apaixonar-se por; **to make** ~ fazer amor; ~ **affair** n aventura (amorosa), caso (de amor); ~ **letter** n carta de amor; ~ **life** n vida sentimental

lovely ['lʌvli] adj encantador(a), delicioso; (beautiful) lindo, belo; (holiday) muito agradável, maravilhoso

lover ['lʌvə*] n amante m/f

loving ['lʌviŋ] adj carinhoso, afetuoso; (actions) dedicado

low [ləu] adj baixo; (depressed) deprimido; (ill) doente ♦ adv baixo ♦ n (METEOROLOGY) área de baixa pressão; **to be** ~ **on** (supplies) ter pouco; **to reach a new** or **an all-time** ~ cair para o seu nível mais baixo; **~-alcohol** adj de baixo teor alcoólico; **~-cut** adj (dress) decotado; **~er** adj mais baixo; (less important) inferior ♦ vt abaixar; (reduce) reduzir, diminuir; **~-fat** adj magro; **~lands** npl planície f; **~ly** adj humilde

loyal ['lɔiəl] adj leal; **~ty** n lealdade f

lozenge ['lɔzindʒ] n (MED) pastilha

LP n abbr = **long-playing record**

L-plates ['elpleits] npl placas fpl de aprendiz de motorista

Ltd (BRIT) abbr (= **limited (liability) company**) SA

lubricate ['lu:brikeit] vt lubrificar

luck [lʌk] n sorte f; **bad** or **hard** ~ azar m; **good** ~! boa sorte!; **bad** or **hard** or **tough** ~! que azar!; **~ily** adv por sorte, felizmente; **~y** adj (person) sortudo; (situation) afortunado; (object) de sorte

ludicrous ['lu:dikrəs] adj ridículo

lug [lʌg] (inf) vt arrastar

luggage ['lʌgidʒ] n bagagem f; ~ **rack** n porta-bagagem m, bagageiro

lukewarm ['lu:kwɔːm] adj morno, tépido; (fig) indiferente

lull [lʌl] n pausa, interrupção f ♦ vt: **to** ~ **sb to sleep** acalentar alguém; **to** ~**ed into a false sense of security** ser acalmado com uma falsa sensação de segurança

lullaby ['lʌləbai] n canção f de ninar

lumber ['lʌmbə*] n (junk) trastes mpl velhos; (wood) madeira serrada, tábua f ♦ vt: **to** ~ **sb with sth/sb** empurrar algo/alguém para cima de alguém; **~jack** n madeireiro, lenhador m

luminous ['lu:minəs] adj luminoso

lump [lʌmp] n torrão m; (fragment) pedaço; (on body) galo, caroço; (also: **sugar** ~) cubo de açúcar ♦ vt: **to** ~ **together** amontoar; a ~ **sum** uma quantia global; **~y** adj encaroçado

lunatic ['lu:nətik] adj louco/a

lunch [lʌntʃ] n almoço

luncheon ['lʌntʃən] n almoço formal; ~ **meat** n bolo de carne; ~ **voucher** (BRIT) n vale m para refeição, ticket m restaurante

lunch time n hora do almoço

lung [lʌŋ] n pulmão m

lunge [lʌndʒ] vi (also: ~ **forward**) dar estocada or bote; **to** ~ **at** arremeter-se contra

lurch [lə:tʃ] vi balançar ♦ n solavanco; **to leave sb in the** ~ deixar alguém em apuros, deixar alguém na mão (inf)

lure [luə*] n isca ♦ vt atrair, seduzir

lurid ['luərid] adj horrível

lurk [lə:k] vi (hide) esconder-se; (wait) estar à espreita

luscious ['lʌʃəs] adj (person, thing) atraente; (food) delicioso

lush [lʌʃ] adj exuberante

lust [lʌst] n luxúria; (greed) cobiça; ~ **after** or **for** vt fus cobiçar

lustre ['lʌstə*] (US **luster**) n lustre m, brilho

lusty ['lʌsti] adj robusto, forte

Luxembourg ['lʌksəmbə:g] n Luxemburgo

luxuriant [lʌg'zjuəriənt] adj luxuriante, exuberante

luxurious [lʌg'zjuəriəs] adj luxuoso

luxury ['lʌkʃəri] n luxo ♦ cpd de luxo

lying ['laiiŋ] n mentira(s) f(pl) ♦ adj mentiroso, falso

lynch [lintʃ] vt linchar

lyrical ['lirikəl] adj lírico

lyrics ['liriks] npl (of song) letra

M

m abbr (= metre) m; (= mile) mil.; = million

M.A. abbr (SCH) = Master of Arts

mac [mæk] (BRIT) n capa impermeável

Macao [mə'kau] n Macau

macaroni [mækə'rəunɪ] n macarrão m

machine [mə'ʃiːn] n máquina ♦ vt (dress etc) costurar à máquina; (TECH) usinar; ~ **gun** n metralhadora; ~ **language** n (COMPUT) linguagem f de máquina; ~**ry** n maquinaria; (fig) máquina

macho ['mætʃəu] adj machista

mackerel ['mækrəl] n inv cavala

mackintosh ['mækɪntɔʃ] (BRIT) n capa impermeável

mad [mæd] adj louco; (foolish) tolo; (angry) furioso, brabo; (keen): **to be ~ about** ser louco por

madam ['mædəm] n senhora, madame f

madden ['mædn] vt exasperar

made [meɪd] pt, pp of **make**

Madeira [mə'dɪərə] n (GEO) Madeira; (wine) (vinho) Madeira m

made-to-measure (BRIT) adj feito sob medida

madly ['mædlɪ] adv loucamente; ~ **in love** louco de amor

madman ['mædmən] (irreg) n louco

madness ['mædnɪs] n loucura; (foolishness) tolice f

Madrid [mə'drɪd] n Madri (BR), Madrid (PT)

magazine [mægə'ziːn] n (PRESS) revista; (RADIO, TV) programa m de atualidades

maggot ['mægət] n larva de inseto

magic ['mædʒɪk] n magia, mágica ♦ adj mágico; ~**al** adj mágico; ~**ian** n mago/a; (entertainer) mágico/a

magistrate ['mædʒɪstreɪt] n magistrado/a, juiz/juíza m/f

magnet ['mægnɪt] n ímã m; ~**ic** adj magnético

magnificent [mæg'nɪfɪsnt] adj magnífico

magnify ['mægnɪfaɪ] vt aumentar; ~**ing glass** n lupa, lente f de aumento

magnitude ['mægnɪtjuːd] n magnitude f

magpie ['mægpaɪ] n pega

mahogany [mə'hɔgənɪ] n mogno, acaju m

maid [meɪd] n empregada; **old ~** (pej) solteirona

maiden ['meɪdn] n moça, donzela ♦ adj (aunt etc) solteirona; (speech, voyage) inaugural; ~ **name** n nome m de solteira

mail [meɪl] n correio; (letters) cartas fpl ♦ vt pôr no correio; ~**box** (US) n caixa do correio; ~**ing list** n lista de clientes, mailing list m; ~ **order** n pedido por reembolso postal

maim [meɪm] vt mutilar, aleijar

main [meɪn] adj principal ♦ n (pipe) cano or esgoto principal; **the ~s** npl (ELEC, gas, water) a rede; **in the ~** na maior parte; ~**frame** n (COMPUT) mainframe m; ~**land** n: **the ~land** o continente; ~**ly** adv principalmente; ~ **road** n estrada principal; ~**stay** n (fig) esteio; ~**stream** n corrente f principal

maintain [meɪn'teɪn] vt manter; (keep up) conservar (em bom estado); (affirm) sustentar, afirmar; **maintenance** n manutenção f; (alimony) alimentos mpl, pensão f alimentícia

maize [meɪz] n milho

majestic [mə'dʒɛstɪk] adj majestoso

majesty ['mædʒɪstɪ] n majestade f

major ['meɪdʒə*] n (MIL) major m ♦ adj (main) principal; (considerable) importante; (MUS) maior

Majorca [mə'jɔːkə] n Maiorca

majority [mə'dʒɔrɪtɪ] n maioria

make [meɪk] (pt, pp made) vt fazer; (manufacture) fabricar, produzir; (cause to be): **to ~ sb sad** entristecer alguém, fazer alguém ficar triste; (force): **to ~ sb do sth** fazer com que alguém faça algo; (equal): **2 and 2 ~ 4** dois e dois são quatro ♦ n marca; **to ~ a profit/loss** ter um lucro/uma perda; **to ~ it** (arrive) chegar; (succeed) ter sucesso; **what time do you ~ it?** que horas você tem?; **to ~ do with** contentar-se com; ~ **for** vt fus (place) dirigir-se a; ~ **out** vt (decipher) decifrar; (understand) compreender; (see) divisar, avistar; (cheque) preencher; ~ **up** vt (constitute) constituir; (invent) inventar; (parcel) embrulhar ♦ vi reconciliar-se; (with cosmetics) maquilar-se (BR), maquilhar-se (PT); ~ **up for** vt fus compensar; ~**believe** n: **a world of ~-believe** um mundo de faz-de-conta; ~**r** n (of film etc) criador m; (manufacturer) fabricante m/f; ~**shift** adj provisório; ~**-up** n maquilagem f (BR), maquilhagem f (PT); ~**-up remover** n removidor m de maquilagem

making ['meɪkɪŋ] n (fig): **in the ~** em vias de formação; **he has the ~s of an actor** ele tem tudo para ser ator

malaise [mæ'leɪz] n mal-estar m, indisposição f

malaria [mə'lɛərɪə] n malária

Malaysia [mə'leɪzɪə] n Malaísia (BR), Malásia (PT)

male [meɪl] n macho ♦ adj masculino; (child etc) do sexo masculino

malevolent [mə'lɛvələnt] adj malévolo

malfunction [mæl'fʌŋkʃən] n funcionamento defeituoso

malice ['mælɪs] n (ill will) malícia; (rancour) rancor m; **malicious** adj malevolente

malign [mə'laɪn] vt caluniar, difamar

malignant [mə'lɪgnənt] adj (MED) maligno

mall [mɔ:l] n (also: shopping ~) shopping m

mallet ['mælɪt] n maço, marreta

malnutrition [mælnju:'trɪʃən] n desnutrição f

malpractice [mæl'præktɪs] n falta profissional

malt [mɔ:lt] n malte m

Malta ['mɔ:ltə] n Malta

mammal ['mæml] n mamífero

mammoth ['mæməθ] n mamute m ♦ adj gigantesco, imenso

man [mæn] (pl men) n homem m ♦ vt (NAUT) tripular; (MIL) guarnecer; (machine) operar; an old ~ um velho; ~ and wife marido e mulher

manage ['mænɪdʒ] vi arranjar-se, virar-se ♦ vt (be in charge of) dirigir, administrar; (business) gerenciar; (ship, person) controlar; ~able adj manejável; (task etc) viável; ~ment n administração f, direção f, gerência f; ~r n gerente m/f; (SPORT) técnico/a; ~ress n gerente f; ~rial adj administrativo, gerencial; managing director n diretor(a) m/f geral, diretor-gerente/diretora-gerente m/f

mandarin ['mændərɪn] n (fruit) tangerina; (person) mandarim m

mandatory ['mændətərɪ] adj obrigatório

mane [meɪn] n (of horse) crina; (of lion) juba

maneuver [mə'nu:və*] (US) = manoeuvre

manfully ['mænfəlɪ] adv valentemente

mangle ['mæŋgl] vt mutilar, estropiar

mango ['mæŋgəu] (pl ~es) n manga

mangy ['meɪndʒɪ] adj sarnento, esfarrapado

manhandle ['mænhændl] vt maltratar

manhole ['mænhəul] n poço de inspeção

manhood ['mænhud] n (age) idade f adulta; (masculinity) virilidade f

man-hour n hora-homem f

manhunt ['mænhʌnt] n caça ao homem

mania ['meɪnɪə] n mania; ~c n maníaco/a; (fig) louco/a

manic ['mænɪk] adj maníaco

manicure ['mænɪkjuə*] n manicure f (BR), manicura (PT); ~ set n estojo de manicure (BR) or manicura (PT)

manifest ['mænɪfɛst] vt manifestar, mostrar ♦ adj manifesto, evidente; ~ation n manifestação f

manifesto [mænɪ'fɛstəu] (pl ~s or ~es) n manifesto

manipulate [mə'nɪpjuleɪt] vt manipular

mankind [mæn'kaɪnd] n humanidade f, raça humana

manly ['mænlɪ] adj másculo, viril

man-made adj sintético, artificial

manner ['mænə*] n modo, maneira; (behaviour) conduta, comportamento; (type): all ~ of things todos os tipos de coisa; ~s npl (conduct) boas maneiras fpl, educação f; bad ~s falta de educação; all ~ of todo tipo de; ~ism n maneirismo,

hábito

manoeuvre [mə'nu:və*] (US maneuver) vt manobrar; (manipulate) manipular ♦ vi manobrar ♦ n manobra

manor ['mænə*] n (also: ~ house) casa senhorial, solar m

manpower ['mænpauə*] n potencial m humano, mão-de-obra f

mansion ['mænʃən] n mansão f, palacete m

manslaughter ['mænslɔ:tə*] n homicídio involuntário

mantelpiece ['mæntlpi:s] n consolo da lareira

manual ['mænjuəl] adj manual ♦ n manual m

manufacture [mænju'fæktʃə*] vt manufaturar, fabricar ♦ n fabricação f; ~r n fabricante m/f

manure [mə'njuə*] n estrume m, adubo

manuscript ['mænjuskrɪpt] n manuscrito

many ['mɛnɪ] adj, pron muitos/as; a great ~ muitíssimos; ~ a time muitas vezes

map [mæp] n mapa m; ~ out vt traçar

maple ['meɪpl] n bordo

mar [mɑ:*] vt estragar

marathon ['mærəθən] n maratona

marauder [mə'rɔ:də*] n saqueador(a) m/f

marble ['mɑ:bl] n mármore m; (toy) bola de gude

March [mɑ:tʃ] n março

march [mɑ:tʃ] vi marchar; (demonstrators) desfilar ♦ n marcha; passeata

mare [mɛə*] n égua

margarine [mɑ:dʒə'ri:n] n margarina

margin ['mɑ:dʒɪn] n margem f; ~al adj marginal; ~al seat (POL) cadeira ganha por pequena maioria

marigold ['mærɪgəuld] n malmequer m

marijuana [mærɪ'wɑ:nə] n maconha

marinate ['mærɪneɪt] vt marinar, pôr em escabeche

marine [mə'ri:n] adj marinho; (engineer) naval ♦ n fuzileiro naval

marital ['mærɪtl] adj matrimonial, marital; ~ status estado civil

maritime ['mærɪtaɪm] adj marítimo

marjoram ['mɑ:dʒərəm] n manjerona

mark [mɑ:k] n marca, sinal m; (imprint) impressão f; (stain) mancha; (BRIT: SCH) nota; (currency) marco ♦ vt marcar; (stain) manchar; (indicate) indicar; (commemorate) comemorar; (BRIT: SCH) dar nota em; (: correct) corrigir; to ~ time marcar passo; ~ed adj acentuado; ~er n (sign) marcador m, marca; (bookmark) marcador

market ['mɑ:kɪt] n mercado ♦ vt (COMM) comercializar; ~ garden (BRIT) n horta; ~ing n marketing m; ~place n mercado; ~ research n pesquisa de mercado

marksman ['mɑ:ksmən] (irreg) n bom atirador m

marmalade ['mɑːməleɪd] n geléia de laranja

maroon [mə'ruːn] vt: **to be ~ed** ficar abandonado (numa ilha) ♦ adj de cor castanho-avermelhado, vinho inv

marquee [mɑː'kiː] n toldo, tenda

marquess ['mɑːkwɪs] n marquês m

marquis ['mɑːkwɪs] n = **marquess**

marriage ['mærɪdʒ] n casamento; ~ **bureau** n agência matrimonial; ~ **certificate** n certidão f de casamento

married ['mærɪd] adj casado; (life, love) conjugal

marrow ['mærəu] n medula; (vegetable) abóbora

marry ['mærɪ] vt casar(-se) com; (subj: father, priest etc) casar, unir ♦ vi (also: **get married**) casar(-se)

Mars [mɑːz] n Marte m

marsh [mɑːʃ] n pântano; (salt ~) marisma

marshal ['mɑːʃl] n (MIL: also: **field ~**) marechal m; (at sports meeting etc) oficial m ♦ vt (thoughts, support) organizar; (soldiers) formar

martyr ['mɑːtə] n mártir m/f; ~**dom** n martírio

marvel ['mɑːvl] n maravilha ♦ vi: **to ~ (at)** maravilhar-se (de or com); ~**lous** (US ~**ous**) adj maravilhoso

Marxist ['mɑːksɪst] adj, n marxista m/f

marzipan ['mɑːzɪpæn] n maçapão m

mascara [mæs'kɑːrə] n rímel ® m

masculine ['mæskjulɪn] adj masculino

mash [mæʃ] vt (CULIN) fazer um purê de; (crush) amassar; ~**ed potatoes** n purê m de batatas

mask [mɑːsk] n máscara ♦ vt (face) encobrir; (feelings) esconder, ocultar

mason ['meɪsn] n (also: **stone ~**) pedreiro/a; (also: **free~**) maçom m; ~**ry** n alvenaria

masquerade [mæskə'reɪd] vi: **to ~ as** disfarçar-se de, fazer-se passar por

mass [mæs] n quantidade f; (people) multidão f; (PHYS) massa; (REL) missa; (great quantity) montão m ♦ cpd de massa ♦ vi reunir-se; (MIL) concentrar-se; **the ~es** npl (ordinary people) as massas; ~**es of** (inf) montes de

massacre ['mæsəkə] n massacre m, carnificina

massage ['mæsɑːʒ] n massagem f

masseur [mæ'sɜː] n massagista m; **masseuse** n massagista f

massive ['mæsɪv] adj (large) enorme; (support) massivo

mass media npl meios mpl de comunicação de massa, mídia

mass production n produção f em massa, fabricação f em série

mast [mɑːst] n (NAUT) mastro; (RADIO etc) antena

master ['mɑːstə] n mestre m; (fig: of situation) dono; (in secondary school) pro-

fessor m; (title for boys): **M~ X** o menino X ♦ vt controlar; (learn) conhecer a fundo; ~ **key** n chave f mestra; ~**ly** adj magistral; ~**mind** n (fig) cabeça ♦ vt dirigir, planejar; **M~ of Arts/ Science** n (degree) mestrado; ~**piece** n obra-prima; ~**y** n domínio

masturbate ['mæstəbeɪt] vi masturbar-se; **masturbation** n masturbação f

mat [mæt] n esteira; (also: **door~**) capacho; (also: **table~**) descanso ♦ adj = **matt**

match [mætʃ] n fósforo; (game) jogo, partida; (equal) igual m/f ♦ vt (also: ~ **up**) casar, emparelhar; (go well with) combinar com; (equal) igualar; (correspond to) corresponder a ♦ vi combinar; (couple) formar um bom casal; ~**box** n caixa de fósforos; ~**ing** adj que combina (com)

mate [meɪt] n (inf) colega m/f; (assistant) ajudante m/f; (animal) macho/fêmea; (in merchant navy) imediato ♦ vi acasalar-se

material [mə'tɪərɪəl] n (substance) matéria; (equipment) material m; (cloth) pano, tecido; (data) dados mpl ♦ adj material; ~**s** npl (equipment) material; ~**istic** adj materialista; ~**ize** vi materializar-se, concretizar-se

maternal [mə'tɜːnl] adj maternal

maternity [mə'tɜːnɪtɪ] n maternidade f; ~ **dress** n vestido de gestante; ~ **hospital** n maternidade f

math [mæθ] (US) n = **maths**

mathematical [mæθə'mætɪkl] adj matemático

mathematics [mæθə'mætɪks] n matemática

maths [mæθs] (US **math**) n matemática

matinée ['mætɪneɪ] n matinê f

mating call ['meɪtɪŋ-] n chamado do macho

matrices ['meɪtrɪsiːz] npl of **matrix**

matriculation [mətrɪkju'leɪʃən] n matrícula

matrimony ['mætrɪmənɪ] n matrimônio, casamento

matrix ['meɪtrɪks] (pl **matrices**) n matriz f

matron ['meɪtrən] n (in hospital) enfermeira-chefe f; (in school) inspetora

matt [mæt] adj fosco, sem brilho

matted ['mætɪd] adj embaraçado

matter ['mætə] n questão f, assunto; (PHYS) matéria; (substance) substância; (reading ~ etc) material m; (MED: pus) pus m ♦ vi importar; ~**s** npl (affairs) questões fpl; **it doesn't ~** não importa; (I don't mind) tanto faz; **what's the ~?** o que (é que) há?, qual é o problema?; **no ~ what** aconteça o que acontecer; **as a ~ of course** por rotina; **as a ~ of fact** na realidade, de fato; ~**-of-fact** adj prosaico, prático

mattress ['mætrɪs] n colchão m

mature [mə'tjuə] adj maduro; (cheese,

wine) amadurecido ♦ *vi* amadurecer; **maturity** *n* maturidade *f*

maul [mɔːl] *vt* machucar, maltratar

mauve [məuv] *adj* cor de malva *inv*

maverick ['mævrɪk] *n* (*fig*) dissidente *m/f*

maxim ['mæksɪm] *n* máxima

maximum ['mæksɪməm] (*pl* **maxima** *or* ~**s**) *adj* máximo ♦ *n* máximo

May [meɪ] *n* maio

may [meɪ] (*pt, conditional* **might**) *aux vb* (*indicating possibility*): **he** ~ **come** pode ser que ele venha, é capaz de vir; (*be allowed to*): ~ **I smoke?** posso fumar?; (*wishes*): ~ **God bless you!** que Deus lhe abençoe

maybe ['meɪbiː] *adv* talvez; ~ **not** talvez não

May Day *n* dia *m* primeiro de maio

mayhem ['meɪhɛm] *n* caos *m*

mayonnaise [meɪə'neɪz] *n* maionese *f*

mayor [mɛə*] *n* prefeito (*BR*), presidente *m* do município (*PT*); ~**ess** *n* prefeita (*BR*), presidenta do município (*PT*)

maze [meɪz] *n* labirinto

MBChB (*BRIT*) *n abbr* (= *Bachelor of Medicine and Surgery*) grau universitário

MBE (*BRIT*) *n abbr* (= *Member of the Order of the British Empire*) título honorífico

me [miː] *pron* me; (*stressed, after prep*) mim; **he heard** ~ ele me ouviu; **it's** ~ sou eu; **he gave** ~ **the money** ele me deu o dinheiro para mim; **give it to** ~ dê-mo; **with** ~ comigo; **without** ~ sem mim

meadow ['mɛdəu] *n* prado, campina

meagre ['miːgə*] (*US* **meager**) *adj* escasso

meal [miːl] *n* refeição *f*; (*flour*) farinha; ~**time** *n* hora da refeição

mean [miːn] (*pt, pp* ~**t**) *adj* (*with money*) sovina, avarento, pão-duro *inv* (*BR*); (*unkind*) mesquinho; (*shabby*) malcuidado, dilapidado; (*average*) médio ♦ *vt* (*signify*) significar, querer dizer; (*refer to*): **I thought you** ~**t her** eu pensei que você estivesse se referindo a ela; (*intend*): **to** ~ **to do sth** pretender *or* tencionar fazer algo ♦ *n* meio, meio termo; ~**s** *npl* (*way, money*) meio; **by** ~**s of** por meio de, mediante; **by all** ~**s!** claro que sim!, pois não; **do you** ~ **it?** você está falando sério?

meander [mɪ'ændə*] *vi* serpentear

meaning ['miːnɪŋ] *n* sentido, significado; ~**ful** *adj* significativo; (*relationship*) sério; ~**less** *adj* sem sentido

meant [mɛnt] *pt, pp of* **mean**

meantime ['miːntaɪm] *adv* (*also*: **in the** ~) entretanto, enquanto isso

meanwhile ['miːnwaɪl] *adv* = **meantime**

measles ['miːzlz] *n* sarampo

measly ['miːzlɪ] (*inf*) *adj* miserável

measure ['mɛʒə*] *vt, vi* medir ♦ *n* medida; (*ruler: also*: **tape** ~) fita métrica;

~**d** *adj* medido, calculado; (*tone*) ponderado; ~**ments** *npl* (*size*) medidas *fpl*

meat [miːt] *n* carne *f*; **cold** ~**s** (*BRIT*) frios; ~**ball** *n* almôndega; ~ **pie** *n* bolo de carne

Mecca ['mɛkə] *n* Meca; (*fig*): **a** ~ (**for**) a meca (de)

mechanic [mɪ'kænɪk] *n* mecânico; ~**al** *adj* mecânico; ~**s** *n* mecânica ♦ *npl* mecanismo

mechanism ['mɛkənɪzəm] *n* mecanismo

medal ['mɛdl] *n* medalha; ~**lion** *n* medalhão *m*; ~**list** (*US* ~**ist**) *n* (*SPORT*) ganhador(a) *m/f* de medalha

meddle ['mɛdl] *vi*: **to** ~ **in** meter-se em, intrometer-se em; **to** ~ **with sth** mexer em algo

media ['miːdɪə] *npl* meios *mpl* de comunicação, mídia

mediaeval [mɛdɪ'iːvl] *adj* = **medieval**

median ['miːdɪən] (*US*) *n* (*also*: ~ **strip**) canteiro divisor

mediate ['miːdɪeɪt] *vi* mediar; **mediator** *n* mediador(a) *m/f*

Medicaid ['mɛdɪkeɪd] (*US*) *n programa de ajuda médica*

medical ['mɛdɪkl] *adj* médico ♦ *n* (*examination*) exame *m* médico

Medicare ['mɛdɪkɛə*] (*US*) *n sistema federal de seguro saúde*

medicated ['mɛdɪkeɪtɪd] *adj* medicinal, higienizado

medication [mɛdɪ'keɪʃən] *n* medicação *f*

medicine ['mɛdsɪn] *n* medicina; (*drug*) remédio, medicamento

medieval [mɛdɪ'iːvl] *adj* medieval

mediocre [miːdɪ'əukə*] *adj* medíocre

meditate ['mɛdɪteɪt] *vi* meditar

Mediterranean [mɛdɪtə'reɪnɪən] *adj* mediterrâneo; **the** ~ (**Sea**) o (mar) Mediterrâneo

medium ['miːdɪəm] (*pl* **media** *or* ~**s**) *adj* médio ♦ *n* (*means*) meio; (*pl* ~**s**: *person*) médium *m/f*; ~ **wave** *n* (*RADIO*) onda média

medley ['mɛdlɪ] *n* mistura; (*MUS*) potpourri *m*

meek [miːk] *adj* manso, dócil

meet [miːt] (*pt, pp* **met**) *vt* encontrar; (*accidentally*) topar com, dar de cara com; (*by arrangement*) encontrar-se com, ir ao encontro de; (*for the first time*) conhecer; (*go and fetch*) ir buscar; (*opponent, problem*) enfrentar; (*obligations*) cumprir; (*need*) satisfazer ♦ *vi* encontrar-se; (*for talks*) reunir-se; (*join*) unir-se; (*get to know*) conhecer-se; ~ **with** *vt fus* reunir-se com; (*difficulty*) encontrar; ~**ing** *n* encontro; (*session: of club etc*) reunião *f*; (*assembly*) assembléia; (*SPORT*) corrida

megabyte ['mɛgəbaɪt] *n* (*COMPUT*) megabyte *m*

megaphone ['mɛgəfəun] *n* megafone *m*

melancholy ['mɛlənkəlɪ] *n* melancolia ♦

adj melancólico

mellow ['mɛləʊ] *adj* (*sound*) melodioso, suave; (*colour, wine*) suave ♦ *vi* (*person*) amadurecer

melody ['mɛlədɪ] *n* melodia

melon ['mɛlən] *n* melão *m*

melt [mɛlt] *vi* (*metal*) fundir-se; (*snow*) derreter ♦ *vt* derreter; **~ down** *vt* fundir; **~down** *n* fusão *f*; **~ing pot** *n* (*fig*) mistura

member ['mɛmbə*] *n* membro/a; (*of club*) sócio/a; (*ANAT*) membro; **M~ of Parliament** (*BRIT*) deputado/a; **~ship** *n* (*state*) adesão *f*; (*members*) número de sócios; **~ship card** *n* carteira de sócio

memento [mə'mɛntəʊ] *n* lembrança

memo ['mɛməʊ] *n* memorando, nota

memoirs ['mɛmwɑːz] *npl* memórias *fpl*

memorandum [mɛmə'rændəm] (*pl* **memoranda**) *n* memorando

memorial [mɪ'mɔːrɪəl] *n* monumento comemorativo ♦ *adj* comemorativo

memorize ['mɛməraɪz] *vt* decorar, aprender de cor

memory ['mɛmərɪ] *n* memória; (*recollection*) lembrança

men [mɛn] *npl of* **man**

menace ['mɛnəs] *n* ameaça; (*nuisance*) droga ♦ *vt* ameaçar; **menacing** *adj* ameaçador(a)

mend [mɛnd] *vt* consertar, reparar; (*darn*) remendar ♦ *n*: **to be on the ~** estar melhorando; **~ing** *n* conserto, reparo; (*clothes*) roupas *fpl* por consertar

menial ['miːnɪəl] *adj* (*often pej*) humilde, subalterno

meningitis [mɛnɪn'dʒaɪtɪs] *n* meningite *f*

menopause ['mɛnəʊpɔːz] *n* menopausa

menstruation [mɛnstru'eɪʃən] *n* menstruação *f*

mental ['mɛntl] *adj* mental; **~ity** *n* mentalidade *f*

menthol ['mɛnθɒl] *n* mentol *m*

mention ['mɛnʃən] *n* menção *f* ♦ *vt* (*speak of*) falar de; **don't ~ it!** não tem de quê!, de nada!

menu ['mɛnjuː] *n* (*set ~*, COMPUT) menu *m*; (*printed*) cardápio (BR), ementa (PT)

MEP *n abbr* = **Member of the European Parliament**

mercenary ['mɜːsɪnərɪ] *adj* mercenário ♦ *n* mercenário

merchandise ['mɜːtʃəndaɪz] *n* mercadorias *fpl*

merchant ['mɜːtʃənt] *n* comerciante *m/f*; **~ bank** (*BRIT*) *n* banco mercantil; **~ navy** (US **~ marine**) *n* marinha mercante

merciful ['mɜːsɪful] *adj* (*person*) misericordioso, humano; (*release*) afortunado

merciless ['mɜːsɪlɪs] *adj* desumano, inclemente

mercury ['mɜːkjurɪ] *n* mercúrio

mercy ['mɜːsɪ] *n* piedade *f*; (REL) misericórdia; **at the ~ of** à mercê de

mere [mɪə*] *adj* mero, simples *inv*; **~ly** *adv* simplesmente, somente, apenas

merge [mɜːdʒ] *vt* unir ♦ *vi* unir-se; (*COMM*) fundir-se; **~r** *n* fusão *f*

meringue [mə'ræŋ] *n* suspiro, merengue *m*

merit ['mɛrɪt] *n* mérito; (*advantage*) vantagem *f* ♦ *vt* merecer

mermaid ['mɜːmeɪd] *n* sereia

merry ['mɛrɪ] *adj* alegre; **M~ Christmas!** Feliz Natal!; **~-go-round** *n* carrossel *m*

mesh [mɛʃ] *n* malha

mesmerize ['mɛzməraɪz] *vt* hipnotizar

mess [mɛs] *n* confusão *f*; (*in room*) bagunça; (MIL) rancho; **to be in a ~** ser uma bagunça, estar numa bagunça; **~ about** (*inf*) *vi* perder tempo; (*pass the time*) vadiar; **~ about with** (*inf*) *vt fus* mexer com; **~ around** (*inf*) *vi* = **~ about**; **~ around with** (*inf*) *vt fus* = **~ about with**; **~ up** *vt* (*spoil*) estragar; (*dirty*) sujar

message ['mɛsɪdʒ] *n* recado, mensagem *f*

messenger ['mɛsɪndʒə*] *n* mensageiro/a

Messrs ['mɛsəz] *abbr* (*on letters*: = *messieurs*) Srs

messy ['mɛsɪ] *adj* (*dirty*) sujo; (*untidy*) desarrumado

met [mɛt] *pt, pp of* **meet**

metal ['mɛtl] *n* metal *m*

metaphor ['mɛtəfə*] *n* metáfora

mete out [miːt-] *vt* infligir

meteorology [miːtɪə'rɒlədʒɪ] *n* meteorologia

meter ['miːtə*] *n* (*instrument*) medidor *m*; (*also*: **parking ~**) parcômetro; (*US*: *unit*) = **metre**

method ['mɛθəd] *n* método; **~ical** *adj* metódico

Methodist ['mɛθədɪst] *n* metodista *m/f*

meths [mɛθs] (*BRIT*) *n* = **methylated spirit**

methylated spirit ['mɛθɪleɪtɪd-] (*BRIT*) *n* álcool *m* metílico *or* desnaturado

meticulous [me'tɪkjuləs] *adj* meticuloso

metre ['miːtə*] (*US* **meter**) *n* metro

metric ['mɛtrɪk] *adj* métrico

metropolitan [mɛtrə'pɒlɪtən] *adj* metropolitano; **M~ Police** (*BRIT*) *n*: **the M~ Police** a polícia de Londres

mettle ['mɛtl] *n*: **to be on one's ~** meter-se em brios

mew [mjuː] *vi* miar

mews [mjuːz] (*BRIT*) *n*: **~ cottage** *pequena casa resultante de reforma de antigos estábulos*

Mexico ['mɛksɪkəʊ] *n* México

miaow [miː'aʊ] *vi* miar

mice [maɪs] *npl of* **mouse**

micro... [maɪkrəʊ] *prefix* micro...; **~chip** *n* microchip *m*; **~(computer)** *n* micro(computador) *m*; **~film** *n* microfilme *m*; **~phone** *n* microfone *m*; **~scope** *n* microscópio; **~wave** n (also: **~wave oven**) forno microoondas

mid [mɪd] adj: **~ May/afternoon** meados de maio/meio da tarde; **in ~ air** em pleno ar; **~day** n meio-dia m

middle ['mɪdl] n meio; (waist) cintura ♦ adj meio; (quantity, size) médio, mediano; **~-aged** adj de meia-idade; **M~ Ages** npl: **the M~ Ages** a Idade Média; **~ class** n: **the ~ class(es)** a classe média ♦ adj (also: **~-class**) de classe média; **M~ East** n: **the M~ East** o Oriente Médio; **~man** n intermediário; **~ name** n segundo nome m; **~-of-the-road** adj (policy) de meio-termo; (music) romântico; **~weight** n (BOXING) peso médio

middling ['mɪdlɪŋ] adj mediano

midge [mɪdʒ] n mosquito

midget ['mɪdʒɪt] n anão/anã m/f

Midlands ['mɪdləndz] npl região central da Inglaterra

midnight ['mɪdnaɪt] n meia-noite f

midriff ['mɪdrɪf] n barriga

midst [mɪdst] n: **in the ~ of** no meio de, entre

midsummer [mɪd'sʌmə*] n: **a ~ day** um dia em pleno verão

midway [mɪd'weɪ] adj, adv: **~ (between)** no meio do caminho (entre)

midweek [mɪd'wiːk] adv no meio da semana

midwife ['mɪdwaɪf] (pl **midwives**) n parteira

midwinter [mɪd'wɪntə*] n: **in ~** em pleno inverno

might [maɪt] see **may** ♦ n poder m, força; **~y** adj poderoso, forte

migraine ['miːgreɪn] n enxaqueca

migrant ['maɪgrənt] adj migratório; (worker) emigrante

migrate [maɪ'greɪt] vi emigrar; (birds) arribar

mike [maɪk] n abbr = **microphone**

mild [maɪld] adj (character) pacífico; (climate) temperado; (taste) suave; (illness) leve, benigno; (interest) pequeno

mildew ['mɪldjuː] n mofo

mildly ['maɪldlɪ] adv brandamente; (slightly) ligeiramente, um tanto; **to put it ~** (inf) para não dizer coisa pior

mile [maɪl] n milha (1609 m); **~age** n número de milhas; (AUT) ≈ quilometragem f

mileometer [maɪ'lɔmɪtə*] (BRIT) n ≈ conta-quilômetros m inv

milestone ['maɪlstəun] n marco miliário

milieu ['miːljə:] n meio, meio social

militant ['mɪlɪtnt] adj, n militante m/f

military ['mɪlɪtərɪ] adj militar

militate ['mɪlɪteɪt] vi: **to ~ against** militar contra

milk [mɪlk] n leite m ♦ vt (cow) ordenhar; (fig) explorar, chupar; **~ choco-late** n chocolate m de leite; **~man** (irreg) n leiteiro; **~ shake** n milk-shake m, leite m batido com sorvete; **~y** adj leitoso; **M~y Way** n Via Láctea

mill [mɪl] n (wind~ etc) moinho; (coffee ~) moedor m de café; (factory) moinho, engenho ♦ vt moer ♦ vi (also: **~ about**) aglomerar-se, remoinhar

miller ['mɪlə*] n moleiro/a

milli... ['mɪlɪ] prefix: **~gram(me)** n miligrama m; **~metre** (US **~meter**) n milímetro

millinery ['mɪlɪnərɪ] n chapelaria de senhoras

million ['mɪljən] n milhão m; **a ~ times** um milhão de vezes; **~aire** n milionário/a

milometer [maɪ'lɔmɪtə*] n = **mileometer**

mime [maɪm] n mimo; (actor) mímico/a, comediante m/f ♦ vt imitar ♦ vi fazer mímica

mimic ['mɪmɪk] n mímico/a, imitador(a) m/f ♦ vt imitar, parodiar

min. abbr (= minute, minimum) min

mince [mɪns] vt moer ♦ vi (in walking) andar com afetação ♦ n (BRIT: CULIN) carne f moída; **~meat** n recheio de sebo e frutas picadas; (US: meat) carne f moída; **~ pie** n pastel com recheio de sebo e frutas picadas; **~r** n moedor m de carne

mind [maɪnd] n mente f; (intellect) intelecto; (opinion): **to my ~** a meu ver; (sanity): **to be out of one's ~** estar fora de si ♦ vt (attend to, look after) tomar conta de, cuidar de; (be careful of) ter cuidado com; (object to): **I don't ~ the noise** o barulho não me incomoda; **it is on my ~** não me sai da cabeça; **to keep** or **bear sth in ~** levar algo em consideração, não esquecer-se de algo; **to make up one's ~** decidir-se; **I don't ~** (it doesn't worry me) eu nem ligo; (it's all the same to me) para mim tanto faz; **~ you, ...** se bem que ...; **never ~!** não faz mal, não importa!; (don't worry) não se preocupe!; **"~ the step"** "cuidado com o degrau"; **~er** n (child~er) pessoa que toma conta de crianças; (inf: bodyguard) guarda-costas m/f inv; **~ful** adj (**~ful of** consciente de, atento a; **~less** adj (violence) insensato; (job) monótono

mine¹ [maɪn] pron (o) meu m/(a) minha f; **a friend of ~** um amigo meu

mine² [maɪn] n mina ♦ vt (coal) extrair, explorar; (ship, beach) minar; **~field** n campo minado; (fig) área delicada

miner ['maɪnə*] n mineiro

mineral ['mɪnərəl] adj mineral ♦ n mineral m; **~s** npl (BRIT: soft drinks) refrigerantes mpl; **~ water** n água mineral

mingle ['mɪŋgl] vi: **to ~ with** misturar-se com

miniature ['mɪnətʃə*] adj em miniatura

♦ *n* miniatura

minibus ['mɪnɪbʌs] *n* microônibus *m*

minim ['mɪnɪm] *n* (*MUS*) mínima

minimal ['mɪnɪml] *adj* mínimo

minimum ['mɪnɪməm] (*pl* **minima**) *adj* mínimo ♦ *n* mínimo

mining ['maɪnɪŋ] *n* exploração *f* de minas

miniskirt ['mɪnɪskə:t] *n* minissaia

minister ['mɪnɪstə'] *n* (*BRIT: POL*) ministro/a; (*REL*) pastor *m* ♦ *vi*: **to ~ sb** prestar assistência a alguém; **to ~ to sb's needs** atender às necessidades de alguém

ministry ['mɪnɪstrɪ] *n* (*BRIT: POL*) ministério; (*REL*): **to go into the ~** ingressar no sacerdócio

mink [mɪŋk] *n* marta

minnow ['mɪnəu] *n* peixinho (de água doce)

minor ['maɪnə'] *adj* menor; (*unimportant*) de pouca importância; (*MUS*) menor ♦ *n* (*LAW*) menor *m/f* de idade

minority [maɪ'nɒrɪtɪ] *n* minoria

mint [mɪnt] *n* (*plant*) hortelã *f*; (*sweet*) bala de hortelã ♦ *vt* (*coins*) cunhar; **the (Royal) M~** (*BRIT*) *or* **the (US) M~** (*US*) ≈ a Casa da Moeda; **in ~ condition** em perfeito estado

minus ['maɪnəs] *n* (*also*: **~ sign**) sinal *m* de subtração ♦ *prep* menos

minute[1] [maɪ'njuːt] *adj* miúdo, diminuto; (*search*) minucioso

minute[2] ['mɪnɪt] *n* minuto; **~s** *npl* (*of meeting*) atas *fpl*; **at the last ~** no último momento

miracle ['mɪrəkl] *n* milagre *m*

mirage ['mɪrɑːʒ] *n* miragem *f*

mirror ['mɪrə'] *n* espelho; (*in car*) retrovisor *m*

mirth [mə:θ] *n* risada

misadventure [mɪsəd'vɛntʃə'] *n* desgraça, infortúnio

misapprehension [mɪsæprɪ'hɛnʃən] *n* mal-entendido, equívoco

misappropriate [mɪsə'prəuprɪeɪt] *vt* desviar

misbehave [mɪsbɪ'heɪv] *vi* comportar-se mal

miscarriage ['mɪskærɪdʒ] *n* (*MED*) aborto (espontâneo); (*failure*): **~ of justice** erro judicial

miscellaneous [mɪsɪ'leɪnɪəs] *adj* (*items, expenses*) diverso; (*selection*) variado

mischance [mɪs'tʃɑːns] *n* infelicidade *f*, azar *m*

mischief ['mɪstʃɪf] *n* (*naughtiness*) travessura; (*fun*) diabrura; (*maliciousness*) malícia; **mischievous** *adj* travesso; (*playful*) traquino

misconception [mɪskən'sɛpʃən] *n* concepção *f* errada, conceito errado

misconduct [mɪs'kɒndʌkt] *n* comportamento impróprio; **professional ~** má conduta profissional

misdemeanour [mɪsdɪ'miːnə'] (*US* **misdemeanor**) *n* má ação *f*, contravenção *f*

miser ['maɪzə'] *n* avaro/a, sovina *m/f*

miserable ['mɪzərəbl] *adj* triste; (*wretched*) miserável; (*weather, person*) deprimente; (*contemptible: offer*) desprezível; (: *failure*) humilhante

miserly ['maɪzəlɪ] *adj* avarento, mesquinho

misery ['mɪzərɪ] *n* (*unhappiness*) tristeza; (*wretchedness*) miséria

misfire [mɪs'faɪə'] *vi* falhar

misfit ['mɪsfɪt] *n* inadaptado/a, deslocado/a

misfortune [mɪs'fɔːtʃən] *n* desgraça, infortúnio

misgiving(s) [mɪs'gɪvɪŋ(z)] *n(pl)* mau pressentimento; **to have ~s about sth** ter desconfianças em relação a algo

misguided [mɪs'gaɪdɪd] *adj* enganado

mishandle [mɪs'hændl] *vt* manejar mal

mishap ['mɪshæp] *n* desgraça, contratempo

misinform [mɪsɪn'fɔːm] *vt* informar mal

misinterpret [mɪsɪn'tə:prɪt] *vt* interpretar mal

misjudge [mɪs'dʒʌdʒ] *vt* fazer um juízo errado de, julgar mal

mislay [mɪs'leɪ] (*irreg*) *vt* extraviar, perder

mislead [mɪs'liːd] (*irreg*) *vt* induzir em erro, enganar; **~ing** *adj* enganoso, errôneo

mismanage [mɪs'mænɪdʒ] *vt* administrar mal; (*situation*) tratar de modo ineficiente

misnomer [mɪs'nəumə'] *n* termo impróprio *or* errado

misplace [mɪs'pleɪs] *vt* extraviar, perder

misprint ['mɪsprɪnt] *n* erro tipográfico

Miss [mɪs] *n* Senhorita (*BR*), a menina (*PT*)

miss [mɪs] *vt* (*train, class, opportunity*) perder; (*fail to hit*) errar, não acertar em; (*fail to see*): **you can't ~ it** e impossível não ver; (*regret the absence of*): **I ~ him** sinto a falta dele ♦ *vi* falhar ♦ *n* (*shot*) tiro perdido *or* errado; **~ out** (*BRIT*) *vt* omitir

misshapen [mɪs'ʃeɪpən] *adj* disforme

missile ['mɪsaɪl] *n* míssil *m*; (*object thrown*) projétil *m*

missing ['mɪsɪŋ] *adj* (*pupil*) ausente; (*thing*) perdido; (*removed*) que está faltando; (*MIL*) desaparecido; **to be ~** estar desaparecido; **to go ~** desaparecer

mission ['mɪʃən] *n* missão *f*; (*official representatives*) delegação *f*; **~ary** *n* missionário/a

misspent [mɪs'spɛnt] *adj*: **his ~ youth** sua juventude desperdiçada

mist [mɪst] *n* (*light*) neblina; (*heavy*) névoa; (*at sea*) bruma ♦ *vi* (*eyes: also*: **~ over**) enevoar-se; (*BRIT: also*: **~ over**, **~ up**: *windows*) embaçar

mistake [mɪs'teɪk] (*irreg*) *n* erro, engano
♦ *vt* entender *or* interpretar mal; **by ~**
por engano; **to make a ~** fazer um
erro; **to ~ A for B** confundir A com B;
~n *pp* of **mistake** ♦ *adj* errado; **to be**
~n enganar-se, equivocar-se

mister ['mɪstə*] (*inf*) *n* senhor *m*; *see*
Mr

mistletoe ['mɪsltəu] *n* visco

mistook [mɪs'tuk] *pt* of **mistake**

mistress ['mɪstrɪs] *n* (*lover*) amante *f*; (*of*
house) dona (da casa); (*BRIT: in school*)
professora, mestra; (*of situation*) dona;
see **Mrs**

mistrust [mɪs'trʌst] *vt* desconfiar de

misty ['mɪstɪ] *adj* (*day*) nublado; (*glasses*
etc) embaçado

misunderstand [mɪsʌndə'stænd] (*irreg*)
vt, *vi* entender *or* interpretar mal; **~ing**
n mal-entendido; (*disagreement*) desentendimento

misuse [*n* mɪs'juːs, *vt* mɪs'juːz] *n* uso impróprio; (*of power*) abuso; (*of funds*) desvio ♦ *vt* abusar de; desviar

mitigate ['mɪtɪgeɪt] *vt* mitigar, atenuar

mitt(en) ['mɪt(n)] *n* mitene *f*

mix [mɪks] *vt* misturar; (*combine*) combinar ♦ *vi* (*people*) entrosar-se ♦ *n* mistura; (*combination*) combinação *f*; **~ up** *vt*
(*confuse: things*) misturar; (: *people*) confundir; **~ed** *adj* misto; **~ed-up** *adj*
confuso; **~er** *n* (*for food*) batedeira; (*person*) pessoa sociável; **~ture** *n* mistura;
(*MED*) preparado; **~-up** *n* trapalhada,
confusão *f*

mm *abbr* (= *millimetre*) mm

moan [məun] *n* gemido ♦ *vi* gemer; (*inf:*
complain) **to ~** (**about**) queixar-se
(de), bufar (sobre) (*inf*)

moat [məut] *n* fosso

mob [mɔb] *n* multidão *f* ♦ *vt* cercar

mobile ['məubaɪl] *adj* móvel ♦ *n* móvel
m; **~ home** *n* trailer *m*, casa móvel; **~**
phone *n* telefone *m* celular

mock [mɔk] *vt* ridicularizar; (*laugh at*)
zombar de, gozar de ♦ *adj* falso, fingido;
(*exam etc*) simulado; **~ery** *n* zombaria;
to make a ~ery of ridicularizar; **~-up**
n maqueta, modelo

mode [məud] *n* modo; (*of transport*) meio

model ['mɔdl] *n* modelo; (*ARCH*) maqueta; (*person: for fashion, ART*) modelo *m/f*
♦ *adj* exemplar ♦ *vt* modelar ♦ *vi* servir
de modelo; (*in fashion*) trabalhar como
modelo; **to ~ o.s. on** mirar-se em; **~**
railway *n* trenzinho de brinquedo

modem ['məudem] *n* modem *m*

moderate [*adj* 'mɔdərət, *vi*, *vt* 'mɔdəreɪt]
adj moderado ♦ *vi* moderar-se, acalmar-
se ♦ *vt* moderar

modern ['mɔdən] *adj* moderno; **~ize** *vt*
modernizar, atualizar

modest ['mɔdɪst] *adj* modesto; **~y** *n* modéstia

modicum ['mɔdɪkəm] *n*: **a ~ of** um mí-

nimo de

modify ['mɔdɪfaɪ] *vt* modificar

mogul ['məugl] *n* (*fig*) magnata *m*

mohair ['məuheə*] *n* mohair *m*, angorá
m

moist [mɔɪst] *adj* úmido (*BR*), húmido
(*PT*), molhado; **~en** *vt* umedecer (*BR*),
humedecer (*PT*); **~ure** *n* umidade *f*
(*BR*), humidade *f* (*PT*); **~urizer** *n* creme
m hidratante

molar ['məulə*] *n* molar *m*

mold [məuld] (*US*) *n*, *vt* = **mould**

mole [məul] *n* (*animal*) toupeira; (*spot*)
sinal *m*, lunar *m*; (*spy*) espião/piã *m/f*

molest [məu'lɛst] *vt* molestar; (*attack sexually*) atacar sexualmente

mollycoddle ['mɔlɪkɔdl] *vt* mimar

molt [məult] (*US*) *vi* = **moult**

molten ['məultən] *adj* fundido; (*lava*) li-
quefeito

mom [mɔm] (*US*) *n* = **mum**

moment ['məumənt] *n* momento; **at the**
~ neste momento; **~ary** *adj* momen-
tâneo; **~ous** *adj* importantíssimo

momentum [məu'mɛntəm] *n* momento;
(*fig*) ímpeto; **to gather ~** ganhar ímpeto

mommy ['mɔmɪ] (*US*) *n* = **mummy**

Monaco ['mɔnəkəu] *n* Mônaco (*no article*)

monarch ['mɔnək] *n* monarca *m/f*; **~y**
n monarquia

monastery ['mɔnəstərɪ] *n* mosteiro, convento

Monday ['mʌndɪ] *n* segunda-feira

monetary ['mʌnɪtərɪ] *adj* monetário

money ['mʌnɪ] *n* dinheiro; (*currency*)
moeda; **to make ~** ganhar dinheiro; **~**
order *n* vale *m* (postal); **~-spinner**
(*inf*) *n* mina

mongol ['mɔŋgəl] *adj*, *n* (*offensive*) mon-
golóide *m/f*

mongrel ['mʌŋgrəl] *n* (*dog*) vira-lata *m*

monitor ['mɔnɪtə*] *n* (*TV, COMPUT*) terminal *m* (de vídeo) ♦ *vt* (*heartbeat, pulse*)
controlar; (*broadcasts, progress*) monito-
rar

monk [mʌŋk] *n* monge *m*

monkey ['mʌŋkɪ] *n* macaco; **~ nut**
(*BRIT*) *n* amendoim *m*; **~ wrench** *n*
chave *f* inglesa

mono ['mɔnəu] *adj* mono *inv*

monopoly [mə'nɔpəlɪ] *n* monopólio

monotone ['mɔnətəun] *n*: **to speak in a**
~ falar sem tom monótono

monotonous [mə'nɔtənəs] *adj* monótono

monsoon [mɔn'suːn] *n* monção *f*

monster ['mɔnstə*] *n* monstro

monstrous ['mɔnstrəs] *adj* (*huge*) descomunal; (*atrocious*) monstruoso

month [mʌnθ] *n* mês *m*; **~ly** *adj* mensal
♦ *adv* mensalmente

monument ['mɔnjumənt] *n* monumento;
~al *adj* monumental; (*terrific*) terrível

moo [muː] *vi* mugir

mood [muːd] *n* humor *m*; (*of crowd*) atmosfera; **to be in a good/bad** ~ estar de bom/mau humor; **~y** adj (variable) caprichoso, de veneta; (sullen) rabugento

moon [muːn] n lua; **~light** n luar m ♦ vi ter dois empregos, ter um bico; **~lighting** n trabalho adicional, bico; **~lit** adj: **a ~lit night** uma noite de lua

moor [muə*] n charneca ♦ vt (ship) amarrar ♦ vi fundear, atracar

moorland ['muələnd] n charneca

moose [muːs] n inv alce m

mop [mɔp] n esfregão m; (for dishes) esponja com cabeça; (of hair) grenha ♦ vt esfregar; ~ **up** vt limpar

mope [məup] vi estar or andar deprimido or desanimado

moped ['məupɛd] n moto f pequena (BR), motorizada (PT)

moral ['mɔrl] adj moral ♦ n moral f; **~s** npl (principles) moralidade f, costumes mpl

morale [mɔ'rɑːl] n moral f, estado de espírito

morality [mə'rælɪtɪ] n moralidade f; (correctness) retidão f, probidade f

morass [mə'ræs] n pântano, brejo

morbid ['mɔːbɪd] adj mórbido

more [mɔː*] adj **1** (greater in number etc) mais; ~ **people/work/letters than we expected** mais pessoas/trabalho/cartas do que esperávamos
2 (additional) mais; **do you want (some)** ~ **tea?** você quer mais chá?; **I have no or I don't have any** ~ **money** não tenho mais dinheiro
♦ pron **1** (greater amount) mais; ~ **than 10** mais de 10; **it cost** ~ **than we expected** custou mais do que esperávamos
2 (further or additional amount) mais; **is there any** ~**?** tem ainda mais?; **there's no** ~ não tem mais
♦ adv mais; ~ **dangerous/difficult** etc **than** mais perigoso/difícil etc do que; ~ **easily (than)** mais fácil (do que); ~ **and** ~ cada vez mais; ~ **or less** mais ou menos; ~ **than ever** mais do que nunca

moreover [mɔː'rəuvə*] adv além do mais, além disso

morgue [mɔːg] n necrotério

moribund ['mɔrɪbʌnd] adj agonizante

Mormon ['mɔːmən] n mórmon m/f

morning ['mɔːnɪŋ] n manhã f; (early ~) madrugada ♦ cpd da manhã; **in the** ~ de manhã; **7 o'clock in the** ~ (as) 7 da manhã; ~ **sickness** n náusea matinal

Morocco [mə'rɔkəu] n Marrocos m

moron ['mɔːrɔn] (inf) n débil mental m/f, idiota m/f

morose [mə'rəus] adj taciturno, rabugento

Morse [mɔːs] n (also: ~ **code**) código Morse

morsel ['mɔːsl] n (of food) bocado

mortal ['mɔːtl] adj, n mortal m/f

mortar ['mɔːtə*] n (cannon) morteiro; (CONSTR) argamassa; (dish) pilão m, almofariz m

mortgage ['mɔːgɪdʒ] n hipoteca ♦ vt hipotecar; ~ **company** (US) n sociedade f de crédito imobiliário

mortuary ['mɔːtjuərɪ] n necrotério

mosaic [məu'zeɪɪk] n mosaico

Moscow ['mɔskəu] n Moscou (BR), Moscovo (PT)

Moslem ['mɔzləm] adj, n = **Muslim**

mosque [mɔsk] n mesquita

mosquito [mɔs'kiːtəu] (pl ~**es**) n mosquito

moss [mɔs] n musgo

most [məust] adj **1** (almost all: people, things etc) a maior parte de, a maioria de; ~ **people** a maioria das pessoas
2 (largest, greatest: interest) máximo; (money): **who has (the)** ~ **money?** quem é que tem mais dinheiro?; **he derived the** ~ **pleasure from her visit** ele teve o maior prazer em recebê-la
♦ pron (greatest quantity, number) a maior parte, a maioria; ~ **of it/them** a maioria dele/deles; ~ **of the money** a maior parte do dinheiro; **do the** ~ **you can** faça o máximo que você puder; **I saw the** ~ vi mais; **to make the** ~ **of sth** aproveitar algo ao máximo; **at the (very)** ~ quando muito, no máximo
♦ adv (+ vb) o mais; (+ adj): **the** ~ **intelligent/expensive** etc o mais inteligente/caro etc; (+ adv: carefully, easily etc) o mais; (very: polite, interesting etc) muito; **a** ~ **interesting book** um livro interessantíssimo

mostly ['məustlɪ] adv principalmente, na maior parte

MOT (BRIT) n abbr (= Ministry of Transport): **the** ~ **(test)** vistoria anual dos veículos automotores

motel [məu'tɛl] n motel m

moth [mɔθ] n mariposa; (clothes ~) traça; **~ball** n bola de naftalina

mother ['mʌðə*] n mãe f ♦ adj materno ♦ vt (care for) cuidar de (como uma mãe); **~hood** n maternidade f; **~in-law** n sogra; **~ly** adj maternal; **~-of-pearl** n madrepérola; **~-to-be** n futura mamãe f; ~ **tongue** n língua materna

motif [məu'tiːf] n motivo

motion ['məuʃən] n movimento; (gesture) gesto, sinal m; (at meeting) moção f ♦ vt, vi: **to** ~ **(to) sb to do sth** fazer sinal a alguém para que faça algo; **~less** adj imóvel; ~ **picture** n filme m (cinematográfico)

motivated ['məutɪveɪtɪd] *adj*: ~ **(by)** motivado (por)

motive ['məutɪv] *n* motivo

motley ['mɒtlɪ] *adj* variado, heterogêneo

motor ['məutə*] *n* motor *m*; (*BRIT: inf: vehicle*) carro, automóvel *m* ♦ *cpd* (*industry*) de automóvel; ~**bike** *n* moto(cicleta) *f*, motoca (*inf*); ~**boat** *n* barco a motor; ~**car** (*BRIT*) *n* carro, automóvel *m*; ~**cycle** *n* motocicleta; ~**cyclist** *n* motociclista *m/f*; ~**ing** (*BRIT*) *n* automobilismo; ~**ist** *n* motorista *m/f*; ~ **racing** (*BRIT*) *n* corrida de carros, automobilismo; ~ **vehicle** *n* automóvel *m*, veículo automotor; ~**way** (*BRIT*) *n* rodovia (*BR*), autoestrada (*PT*)

mottled ['mɒtld] *adj* mosqueado, em furta-cores

motto ['mɒtəu] (*pl* ~**es**) *n* lema *m*

mould [məuld] (*US* **mold**) *n* molde *m*; (*mildew*) mofo, bolor *m* ♦ *vt* moldar; (*fig*) moldar; ~**y** *adj* mofado

moult [məult] (*US* **molt**) *vi* mudar (de penas *etc*)

mound [maund] *n* (*of earth*) monte *m*; (*of blankets, leaves etc*) pilha, montanha

mount [maunt] *n* monte *m* ♦ *vt* (*horse etc*) montar em, subir a; (*stairs*) subir; (*exhibition*) montar; (*picture*) emoldurar ♦ *vi* (*increase*) aumentar; ~ **up** *vi* aumentar

mountain ['mauntɪn] *n* montanha ♦ *cpd* de montanha; ~ **bike** *n* mountain bike *f*; ~**eer** *n* alpinista *m/f*, montanhista *m/f*; ~**eering** *n* alpinismo; ~**ous** *adj* montanhoso; ~ **rescue team** *n* equipe *m* de socorro para alpinistas; ~**side** *n* lado da montanha

mourn [mɔːn] *vt* chorar, lamentar ♦ *vi*: **to ~ for** chorar *or* lamentar a morte de; ~**er** *n* parente *m/f* (*or* amigo/a) do defunto; ~**ful** *adj* desolado, triste; ~**ing** *n* luto; **in** ~**ing** de luto

mouse [maus] (*pl* **mice**) *n* camundongo (*BR*), rato (*PT*); ~**trap** *n* ratoeira

mousse [muːs] *n* musse *f*; (*for hair*) mousse *f*

moustache [məs'tɑːʃ] (*US* **mustache**) *n* bigode *m*

mousy ['mausɪ] *adj* pardacento

mouth [mauθ, *pl* mauðz] *n* boca; (*of cave, hole*) entrada; (*of river*) desembocadura; ~**ful** *n* bocado; ~ **organ** *n* gaita; ~**piece** *n* (*of musical instrument*) bocal *m*; (*representative*) porta-voz *m/f*; ~**wash** *n* colutório; ~**watering** *adj* de dar água na boca

movable ['muːvəbl] *adj* móvel

move [muːv] *n* movimento; (*in game*) lance *m*, jogada; (: *turn to play*) turno, vez *f*; (*of house, job*) mudança ♦ *vt* (*change position of*) mudar; (: *in game*) jogar; (*emotionally*) comover; (*POL: resolution etc*) propor ♦ *vi* mexer-se, mover-se; (*traffic*) circular; (*also*: ~ **house**)

mudar-se; (*develop*: *situation*) desenvolver; **to ~ sb to do sth** convencer alguém a fazer algo; **to get a ~ on** apressar-se; ~ **about** *or* **around** *vi* (*fidget*) mexer-se; (*travel*) deslocar-se; ~ **along** *vi* avançar; ~ **away** *vi* afastar-se; ~ **back** *vi* voltar; ~ **forward** *vi* avançar; ~ **in** *vi* (*to a house*) instalar-se (numa casa); ~ **on** *vi* ir andando; ~ **out** *vi* sair (de uma casa); ~ **over** *vi* afastar-se; ~ **up** *vi* ser promovido

moveable ['muːvəbl] *adj* = **movable**

movement ['muːvmənt] *n* movimento; (*gesture*) gesto; (*of goods*) transporte *m*; (*in attitude*) mudança

movie ['muːvɪ] *n* filme *m*; **to go to the ~s** ir ao cinema; ~ **camera** *n* câmara cinematográfica

moving ['muːvɪŋ] *adj* (*emotional*) comovente; (*that moves*) móvel

mow [məu] (*pt* ~**ed**, *pp* ~**ed** *or* ~**n**) *vt* (*grass*) cortar; (*corn*) ceifar; ~ **down** *vt* (*massacre*) chacinar; ~**er** *n* ceifeira; (*also*: **lawn~er**) cortador *m* de grama (*BR*) *or* de relva (*PT*)

Mozambique [məuzəm'biːk] *n* Moçambique *m* (*no article*)

MP *n abbr* = **Member of Parliament**

mph *abbr* = **miles per hour** (*60 mph* = *96 km/h*)

Mr ['mɪstə*] (*US* **Mr.**) *n*: ~ **Smith** (o) Sr. Smith

Mrs ['mɪsɪz] (*US* **Mrs.**) *n*: ~ **Smith** (a) Sra. Smith

Ms [mɪz] (*US* **Ms.**) *n* (= *Miss or Mrs*): ~ **X** (a) Sa X

MSc *n abbr* = **Master of Science**

much [mʌtʃ] *adj* muito; **how ~ money/ time do you need?** quanto dinheiro/ tempo você precisa?; **he's done so ~ work for the charity** ele trabalhou muito para a obra de caridade; **as ~ as** tanto como

♦ *pron* muito; ~ **has been gained from our discussions** nossas discussões foram muito proveitosas; **how ~ does it cost?** – **too ~** quanto custa isso? – caro demais

♦ *adv* **1** (*greatly*) muito; **thank you very ~** muito obrigado/a; **we are very ~ looking forward to your visit** estamos aguardando a sua visita com muito ansiedade; **he is very ~ the gentleman/politician** ele é muito cavalheiro/político; **as ~ as** tanto como; **as ~ as you** tanto quanto você

2 (*by far*) de longe; **I'm ~ better now** estou bem melhor agora

3 (*almost*) quase; **how are you feeling?** – ~ **the same** como você está (se sentindo)? – do mesmo jeito

muck [mʌk] *n* (*dirt*) sujeira (*BR*), sujidade f (PT); ~ **about** or **around** (inf) vi fazer besteiras; ~ **up** (inf) vt estragar

mucus ['mju:kəs] n muco

mud [mʌd] n lama

muddle ['mʌdl] n confusão f, bagunça; (mix-up) trapalhada ♦ vt (also: ~ **up**: person, story) confundir; (: things) misturar; ~ **through** vi virar-se

muddy ['mʌdɪ] adj (road) lamacento

mudguard ['mʌdgɑːd] n pára-lama m

muesli ['mju:zlɪ] muesli m

muffin ['mʌfɪn] n bolinho redondo e chato

muffle ['mʌfl] vt (sound) abafar; (against cold) agasalhar; ~**d** adj abafado, surdo; ~**r** (US) n (AUT) silencioso (BR), panela de escape (PT)

mug [mʌg] n (cup) caneca; (: for beer) caneco, canecão; (inf: face) careta; (: fool) bobo/a ♦ vt (assault) assaltar; ~**ging** n assalto

muggy ['mʌgɪ] adj abafado

mule [mju:l] n mula

mull over [mʌl-] vt meditar sobre

multi-level ['mʌltɪ-] (US) adj = **multistorey**

multiple ['mʌltɪpl] adj múltiplo ♦ n múltiplo; ~ **sclerosis** [-sklɪə'rəusɪs] n esclerose f múltipla

multiply ['mʌltɪplaɪ] vt multiplicar ♦ vi multiplicar-se

multistorey ['mʌltɪ'stɔːrɪ] (BRIT) adj de vários andares

multitude ['mʌltɪtjuːd] n multidão f; (large number): **a** ~ **of** um grande número de

mum [mʌm] n (BRIT: inf) mamãe f ♦ adj: **to keep** ~ ficar calado

mumble ['mʌmbl] vt, vi resmungar, murmurar

mummy ['mʌmɪ] n (BRIT: mother) mamãe f; (embalmed) múmia

mumps [mʌmps] n caxumba

munch [mʌntʃ] vt, vi mascar

mundane [mʌn'deɪn] adj banal, mundano

municipal [mjuː'nɪsɪpl] adj municipal

mural ['mjuərl] n mural m

murder ['mɜːdə*] n assassinato ♦ vt assassinar; ~**er** n assassino; ~**ous** adj homicida

murky ['mɜːkɪ] adj escuro; (water) turvo

murmur ['mɜːmə*] n murmúrio ♦ vt, vi murmurar

muscle ['mʌsl] n músculo; (fig: strength) força (muscular); ~ **in** vi imiscuir-se, impor-se; **muscular** adj muscular; (person) musculoso

muse [mjuːz] vi meditar ♦ n musa

museum [mjuː'zɪəm] n museu m

mushroom ['mʌʃrum] n cogumelo ♦ vi crescer da noite para o dia, pipocar

music ['mjuːzɪk] n música; ~**al** adj musical; (harmonious) melodioso ♦ n musical m; ~**al instrument** n instrumento

musical; ~ **hall** n teatro de variedades; ~**ian** n músico/a

musk [mʌsk] n almíscar m

Muslim ['mʌzlɪm] adj, n muçulmano/a

muslin ['mʌzlɪn] n musselina

mussel ['mʌsl] n mexilhão m

must [mʌst] aux vb (obligation): **I** ~ **do it** tenho que or devo fazer isso; (probability): **he** ~ **be there by now** ele já deve estar lá; (suggestion, invitation): **you** ~ **come and see me soon** você tem que vir me ver em breve; (indicating sth unwelcome): **why** ~ **he behave so badly?** por que ele tem que se comportar tão mal? ♦ n (necessity) necessidade f; **it's a** ~ é imprescindível

mustache ['mʌstæʃ] (US) n = **moustache**

mustard ['mʌstəd] n mostarda

muster ['mʌstə*] vt (support) reunir; (energy) juntar; (MIL) formar

mustn't ['mʌsnt] = **must not**

musty ['mʌstɪ] adj mofado, com cheiro de bolor

mute [mjuːt] adj mudo

muted ['mjuːtɪd] adj (colour) suave; (reaction) moderado

mutilate ['mjuːtɪleɪt] vt mutilar

mutiny ['mjuːtɪnɪ] n motim m, rebelião f

mutter ['mʌtə*] vt, vi resmungar, murmurar

mutton ['mʌtn] n carne f de carneiro

mutual ['mjuːtʃuəl] adj mútuo; (shared) comum; ~**ly** adv mutuamente, reciprocamente

muzzle ['mʌzl] n (of animal) focinho; (guard: for dog) focinheira; (of gun) boca ♦ vt pôr focinheira em

my [maɪ] adj meu/minha; **this is** ~ **house/car/brother** esta é a minha casa/meu carro/meu irmão; **I've washed** ~ **hair/cut** ~ **finger** lavei meu cabelo/cortei meu dedo

myself [maɪ'self] pron (reflexive) me; (emphatic) eu mesmo; (after prep) mim mesmo; see also **oneself**

mysterious [mɪs'tɪərɪəs] adj misterioso

mystery ['mɪstərɪ] n mistério

mystify ['mɪstɪfaɪ] vt mistificar

mystique [mɪs'tiːk] n mística

myth [mɪθ] n mito; ~**ology** n mitologia

N

n/a abbr = **not applicable**

nag [næg] vt ralhar, apoquentar; ~**ging** adj (doubt) persistente; (pain) contínuo

nail [neɪl] n (human) unha; (metal) prego ♦ vt pregar; **to** ~ **sb down to a date/ price** conseguir que alguém se defina sobre a data/o preço; ~**brush** n escova de unhas; ~**file** n lixa de unhas; ~**polish** n esmalte m (BR) or verniz m (PT) de unhas; ~ **polish remover** n removedor m de esmalte (BR) or verniz

(PT); ~ **scissors** npl tesourinha de
unhas; ~ **varnish** (BRIT) n = ~ polish
naïve [naɪˈiːv] adj ingênuo
naked [ˈneɪkɪd] adj nu(a)
name [neɪm] n nome m; (surname) sobrenome m; (reputation) reputação f, fama
♦ vt (child) pôr nome em; (criminal)
apontar; (price) fixar; (date) marcar;
what's your ~? qual é o seu nome?,
como (você) se chama?; **by ~** de nome;
in the ~ of em nome de; **~less** adj
(unknown) sem nome; (anonymous)
anônimo; **~ly** adv a saber, isto é;
~sake n xará m/f (BR), homónimo/a
(PT)
nanny [ˈnænɪ] n babá f
nap [næp] n (sleep) soneca ♦ vi: **to be
caught ~ping** ser pego de surpresa
nape [neɪp] n: ~ **of the neck** nuca
napkin [ˈnæpkɪn] n (also: **table ~**) guardanapo
nappy [ˈnæpɪ] (BRIT) n fralda; ~ **rash** n
assadura
narcissus [nɑːˈsɪsəs] (pl **narcissi**) n narci-
ciso
narcotic [nɑːˈkɔtɪk] adj narcótico ♦ n
narcótico
narrative [ˈnærətɪv] n narrativa
narrow [ˈnærəʊ] adj estreito; (fig: majority) pequeno; (: ideas) tacanho ♦ vi
(road) estreitar-se; (difference) diminuir;
to have a ~ escape escapar por um
triz; **to ~ sth down to** restringir or reduzir algo a; **~ly** adv (miss) por pouco;
~-minded adj de visão limitada, bitola-
do
nasty [ˈnɑːstɪ] adj (remark) desagradável;
(: person) mau, ruim; (malicious) maldoso; (rude) grosseiro, obsceno; (taste,
smell) repugnante, asqueroso; (wound
etc) grave, sério
nation [ˈneɪʃən] n nação f
national [ˈnæʃənl] adj, n nacional m/f;
~ **dress** n traje m nacional; **N~
Health Service** (BRIT) n ≈ Instituto Nacional de Assistência Médica e Previdência Social, ≈ INAMPS m; **N~ Insurance** (BRIT) n previdência social; **~ism**
n nacionalismo; **~ist** adj, n nacionalista
m/f; **~ity** n nacionalidade f; **~ization** n
nacionalização f; **~ize** vt nacionalizar;
~ly adv (nationwide) de âmbito nacional; (as a nation) nacionalmente, como
nação
nationwide [ˈneɪʃənwaɪd] adj de âmbito
or a nível nacional ♦ adv em todo o
país
native [ˈneɪtɪv] n natural m/f, nativo/a;
(in colonies) indígena m/f, nativo/a ♦
adj (indigenous) indígena; (of one's birth)
natal; (language) materno; (innate) inato,
natural; **a ~ speaker of Portuguese**
uma pessoa de língua (materna) portu-
guesa
Nativity [nəˈtɪvɪtɪ] n (REL): **the ~** a Nati-

vidade
NATO [ˈneɪtəʊ] n abbr (= North Atlantic
Treaty Organization) OTAN f
natural [ˈnætʃrəl] adj natural; **~ize** vt:
to become ~ized (person) naturalizar-
se; (plant) aclimatar-se; **~ly** adv naturalmente; (of course) claro, evidentemente
nature [ˈneɪtʃə*] n natureza; (character)
caráter m, índole f
naught [nɔːt] n = **nought**
naughty [ˈnɔːtɪ] adj travesso, levado
nausea [ˈnɔːsɪə] n náusea; **~te** vt dar
náuseas a; (fig) repugnar
nautical [ˈnɔːtɪkl] adj náutico
naval [ˈneɪvl] adj naval; ~ **officer** n oficial m de marinha
nave [neɪv] n nave f
navel [ˈneɪvl] n umbigo
navigate [ˈnævɪgeɪt] vi navegar; (AUT) ler
o mapa; **navigation** n (action) navegação f; (science) náutica; **navigator** n na-
vegador(a) m/f
navvy [ˈnævɪ] (BRIT) n trabalhador m
braçal, cavouqueiro
navy [ˈneɪvɪ] n marinha (de guerra); ~
(-blue) adj azul-marinho inv
Nazi [ˈnɑːtsɪ] n nazista m/f (BR), nazi
m/f (PT)
NB abbr (= nota bene) NB
near [nɪə*] adj (place) vizinho; (time) próximo; (relation) íntimo ♦ adv perto ♦
prep (also: ~ **to**: space) perto de; (: time)
perto de, quase ♦ vt aproximar-se de;
~by adj próximo, vizinho ♦ adv à mão,
perto; **~ly** adv quase; **I ~ly fell** quase
que caí; ~ **miss** n: **to have a ~ miss**
(narrow escape) escapar por pouco;
~side n (AUT: right-hand drive) lado esquerdo; (: left-hand drive) lado direito ♦
adj esquerdo; direito; **~-sighted** adj
míope
neat [niːt] adj (place) arrumado, em ordem; (person) asseado, arrumado; (work)
organizado; (plan) engenhoso, bem bola-
do; (spirits) puro; **~ly** adv caprichosa-
mente, com capricho; (skilfully) habilmente
necessarily [ˈnɛsɪsrɪlɪ] adv necessaria-
mente
necessary [ˈnɛsɪsrɪ] adj necessário
necessitate [nɪˈsɛsɪteɪt] vt exigir, tornar
necessário
necessity [nɪˈsɛsɪtɪ] n (thing needed) necessidade f, requisito; (compelling circumstances) necessidade; **necessities** npl
(essentials) artigos mpl de primeira necessidade
neck [nɛk] n (ANAT) pescoço; (of garment)
gola; (of bottle) gargalo ♦ vi (inf) ficar
de agarramento; ~ **and** ~ emparelhados
necklace [ˈnɛklɪs] n colar m
neckline [ˈnɛklaɪn] n decote m
necktie [ˈnɛktaɪ] (esp US) n gravata
née [neɪ] adj: ~ **Scott** em solteira Scott

need [niːd] n (lack) falta, carência; (necessity) necessidade f; (thing) requisito, necessidade ♦ vt precisar de; I ~ to do it preciso fazê-lo

needle ['niːdl] n agulha ♦ vt (inf) provocar, alfinetar

needless ['niːdlɪs] adj inútil, desnecessário; ~ to say ... desnecessário dizer que ...

needlework ['niːdlwəːk] n (item(s)) trabalho de agulha; (activity) costura

needn't ['niːdnt] = need not

needy ['niːdɪ] adj necessitado, carente

negative ['nɛgətɪv] adj negativo ♦ n (PHOT) negativo; (LING) negativa

neglect [nɪ'glɛkt] vt (one's duty) negligenciar, não cumprir com; (child) descuidar, esquecer-se de ♦ n (of child) descuido, desatenção f; (of house etc) abandono; (of duty) negligência

negligee ['nɛglɪʒeɪ] n négligé m

negligence ['nɛglɪdʒəns] n negligência, descuido

negligible ['nɛglɪdʒɪbl] adj insignificante, desprezível, ínfimo

negotiate [nɪ'gəʊʃɪeɪt] vi: to ~ (with) negociar (com) ♦ vt (treaty, transaction) negociar; (obstacle) contornar; (path in road) fazer; **negotiation** n negociação f

Negress ['niːgrɪs] n negra

Negro ['niːgrəʊ] (pl ~es) adj, n negro/a

neigh [neɪ] vi relinchar

neighbour ['neɪbə'] (US **neighbor**) n vizinho/a; ~**hood** n (place) vizinhança, bairro; (people) vizinhos mpl; ~**ing** adj vizinho; ~**ly** adj amistoso, prestativo

neither ['naɪðə'] conj: I didn't move and ~ did he não me movi nem ele ♦ adj, pron nenhum (dos dois), nem um nem outro ♦ adv: ~ **good nor bad** nem bom nem mau; ~ **story is true** nenhuma das estórias é verdade

neon ['niːɔn] n neônio, néon m; ~ **light** n luz f de neônio

nephew ['nɛvjuː] n sobrinho

nerve [nəːv] n (ANAT) nervo; (courage) coragem f; (impudence) descaramento, atrevimento; **to have a fit of** ~s ter uma crise nervosa; ~**-racking** adj angustiante

nervous ['nəːvəs] adj (ANAT) nervoso; (anxious) apreensivo; (timid) tímido, acanhado; ~ **breakdown** n crise f nervosa

nest [nɛst] n (of bird) ninho; (of wasp) vespeiro; ~ **egg** n (fig) pé-de-meia m

nestle ['nɛsl] vi: to ~ **up to sb** aconchegar-se a alguém

net [nɛt] n rede f; (fabric) filó m; (fig) sistema m ♦ adj (COMM) líquido ♦ vt pegar na rede; (money: subj: person) faturar; (: deal, sale) render; **the N~** (Internet) a Rede; ~**ball** n espécie de basquetebol; ~ **curtains** npl cortinas fpl de voile

Netherlands ['nɛðələndz] npl: **the** ~ os Países Baixos

nett [nɛt] adj = net

netting ['nɛtɪŋ] n rede(s) f(pl)

nettle ['nɛtl] n urtiga

network ['nɛtwəːk] n rede f

neurotic [njʊ'rɔtɪk] adj, n neurótico/a

neuter ['njuːtə'] adj neutro ♦ vt (cat etc) castrar, capar

neutral ['njuːtrəl] adj neutro ♦ n (AUT) ponto morto; ~**ize** vt neutralizar

never ['nɛvə'] adv nunca; see also mind; ~**-ending** adj sem fim, interminável; ~**theless** adv todavia, contudo

new [njuː] adj novo; ~**born** adj recém-nascido; ~**comer** n recém-chegado/a, novato/a; ~**-fangled** (pej) adj ultramoderno; ~**-found** adj (friend) novo; (enthusiasm) recente; ~**ly** adv recém, novamente; ~**ly-weds** npl recém-casados mpl; ~ **moon** n lua nova

news [njuːz] n notícias fpl; (RADIO, TV) noticiário; **a piece of** ~ uma notícia; ~ **agency** n agência de notícias; ~**agent** (BRIT) n jornaleiro/a; ~**caster** n locutor(a) m/f; ~**dealer** (US) n = ~**agent**; ~ **flash** n notícia de última hora; ~**letter** n boletim m informativo; ~**paper** n jornal m; ~**print** n papel m de jornal; ~**reader** n = ~**caster**; ~**reel** n jornal m cinematográfico, atualidades fpl; ~**stand** n banca de jornais

newt [njuːt] n tritão m

New Year n ano novo; ~'**s Day** n dia m de ano novo; ~'**s Eve** n véspera de ano novo

New York [-jɔːk] n Nova Iorque

New Zealand [-'ziːlənd] n Nova Zelândia; ~**er** n neozelandês/esa m/f

next [nɛkst] adj (in space) próximo, vizinho; (in time) seguinte, próximo ♦ adv depois; depois, logo; ~ **time** na próxima vez; ~ **year** o ano que vem; ~ **to** ao lado de; ~ **to nothing** quase nada; ~ **door** adv na casa do lado ♦ adj vizinho; ~**-of-kin** n parentes mpl mais próximos

NHS n abbr = National Health Service

nib [nɪb] n ponta or bico da pena

nibble ['nɪbl] vt mordiscar, beliscar

Nicaragua [nɪkə'rægjuə] n Nicarágua

nice [naɪs] adj (likeable) simpático; (kind) amável, atencioso; (pleasant) agradável; (attractive) bonito; ~**ly** adv agradavelmente, bem

niceties ['naɪsɪtɪz] npl sutilezas fpl

nick [nɪk] n (wound) corte m; (cut, indentation) entalhe m, incisão f ♦ vt (inf: steal) furtar, arrochar; **in the** ~ **of time** na hora H, no momento exato

nickel ['nɪkl] n níquel m; (US) moeda de 5 centavos

nickname ['nɪkneɪm] n apelido (BR), alcunha (PT) ♦ vt apelidar de (BR), alcunhar de (PT)

niece [niːs] n sobrinha
Nigeria [naɪˈdʒɪərɪə] n Nigéria
nigger [ˈnɪgə*] (inf!) n (highly offensive) crioulo/a, baiano/a
niggling [ˈnɪglɪŋ] adj (trifling) insignificante, mesquinho; (annoying) irritante
night [naɪt] n noite f; **at** or **by** ~ à or de noite; **the** ~ **before last** anteontem à noite; ~**cap** n bebida tomada antes de dormir; ~**club** n boate f; ~**dress** n camisola (BR), camisa de noite (PT); ~**fall** n anoitecer m; ~**gown** n = ~**dress**; ~**ie** n = ~**dress**
nightingale [ˈnaɪtɪŋgeɪl] n rouxinol m
nightlife [ˈnaɪtlaɪf] n vida noturna
nightly [ˈnaɪtlɪ] adj noturno, de noite ♦ adv todas as noites, cada noite
nightmare [ˈnaɪtmɛə*] n pesadelo
night: ~ **porter** n porteiro da noite; ~ **school** n escola noturna; ~ **shift** n turno da noite; ~**time** n noite f; ~ **watchman** (irreg) n vigia m, guarda-noturno m
nil [nɪl] n nada; (BRIT: SPORT) zero
Nile [naɪl] n: **the** ~ o Nilo
nimble [ˈnɪmbl] adj (agile) ágil, ligeiro; (skilful) hábil, esperto
nine [naɪn] num nove; ~**teen** num dezenove (BR), dezanove (PT); ~**ty** num noventa; **ninth** num nono
nip [nɪp] vt (pinch) beliscar; (bite) morder
nipple [ˈnɪpl] n (ANAT) bico do seio, mamilo
nitrogen [ˈnaɪtrədʒən] n nitrogênio

---KEYWORD---

no [nəu] (pl ~**es**) adv (opposite of "yes") não; **are you coming?** – ~ ~ **(I'm not)** você vem? – não (eu não)
♦ adj (not any) nenhum(a), não ... algum(a); **I have** ~ **more money/time/books** não tenho mais dinheiro/tempo/livros; "~ **entry**" "entrada proibida"; "~ **smoking**" "é proibido fumar"
♦ n não m, negativa

nobility [nəuˈbɪlɪtɪ] n nobreza
noble [ˈnəubl] adj (person) nobre; (title) de nobreza
nobody [ˈnəubədɪ] pron ninguém
nocturnal [nɔkˈtəːnəl] adj noturno
nod [nɔd] vi (greeting) cumprimentar com a cabeça; (in agreement) acenar (que sim) com a cabeça; (doze) cochilar, dormitar ♦ vt: **to** ~ **one's head** inclinar a cabeça ♦ n inclinação f da cabeça; ~ **off** vi cochilar
noise [nɔɪz] n barulho; **noisy** adj barulhento
nominate [ˈnɔmɪneɪt] vt (propose) propor; (appoint) nomear; **nomination** n proposta; nomeação f; **nominee** n pessoa nomeada, candidato/a
non... [nɔn] prefix não..., des..., in..., anti-...; ~**alcoholic** adj não-alcoólico;

~**aligned** adj não-alinhado
nonchalant [ˈnɔnʃələnt] adj despreocupado
non-committal [-kəˈmɪtl] adj evasivo
nondescript [ˈnɔndɪskrɪpt] adj qualquer; (pej) mediocre
none [nʌn] pron (person) ninguém; (thing) nenhum(a), nada; ~ **of you** nenhum de vocês; **I've** ~ **left** não tenho mais
nonentity [nɔˈnentɪtɪ] n nulidade f, zero à esquerda m
nonetheless [nʌnðəˈlɛs] adv no entanto, apesar disso, contudo
non-existent [-ɪgˈzɪstənt] adj inexistente
non-fiction n literatura de não-ficção
nonplussed [nɔnˈplʌst] adj perplexo, pasmado
nonsense [ˈnɔnsəns] n disparate m, besteira, absurdo; ~! bobagem!, quê nada!
non: ~**smoker** n não-fumante m/f; ~**stick** adj tefal ®, não-aderente; ~**stop** adj ininterrupto; (RAIL) direto; (AVIAT) sem escala ♦ adv sem parar
noodles [ˈnuːdlz] npl talharim m
nook [nuk] n: ~**s and crannies** esconderijos mpl
noon [nuːn] n meio-dia m
no-one pron = **nobody**
noose [nuːs] n laço corrediço; (hangman's) corda da forca
nor [nɔː*] conj = **neither** ♦ adv see **neither**
norm [nɔːm] n (convention) norma; (requirement) regra
normal [ˈnɔːml] adj normal
north [nɔːθ] n norte m ♦ adj do norte, setentrional ♦ adv ao or para o norte; **N~ America** n América do Norte; ~**east** n nordeste m; ~**erly** adj norte; ~**ern** adj do norte, setentrional; **N~ern Ireland** n Irlanda do Norte; **N~ Pole** n: **the N~ Pole** o Pólo Norte; **N~ Sea** n: **the N~ Sea** o Mar do Norte; ~**ward(s)** adv em direção norte; ~**west** n noroeste m
Norway [ˈnɔːweɪ] n Noruega; **Norwegian** adj norueguês/esa ♦ n norueguês/esa m/f; (LING) norueguês m
nose [nəuz] n (ANAT) nariz m; (ZOOL) focinho; (sense of smell: of person) olfato; (: of animal) faro; ~ **about** vi bisbilhotar; ~ **around** vi = ~ **about**; ~**bleed** n hemorragia nasal; ~**dive** n (deliberate) vôo picado; (involuntary) parafuso; ~**y** (inf) adj = **nosy**
nostalgia [nɔsˈtældʒɪə] n nostalgia
nostril [ˈnɔstrɪl] n narina
nosy [ˈnəuzɪ] (inf) adj intrometido, abelhudo
not [nɔt] adv não; **he is** ~ or **isn't here** ele não está aqui; **it's too late, isn't it?** é muito tarde, não?; **he asked me** ~ **to do it** ele me pediu para não fazer isto; ~ **yet/now** ainda/agora não; see

also all; only
notably ['nəʊtəblɪ] *adv* (*particularly*) particularmente; (*markedly*) notavelmente
notary ['nəʊtərɪ] *n* (*also*: ~ **public**) tabelião/tabelioa *m/f*, notário/a
notch [nɔtʃ] *n* (*in wood*) entalhe *m*; (*in blade*) corte *m*
note [nəʊt] *n* (*MUS, bank~*) nota; (*letter*) nota, bilhete *m*; (*record*) nota, anotação *f*; (*tone*) tom *m* ♦ *vt* (*observe*) observar, reparar em; (*also*: ~ **down**) anotar, tomar nota de; ~**book** *n* caderno; ~**d** *adj* célebre, conhecido; ~**pad** *n* bloco de anotações; ~**paper** *n* papel *m* de carta
nothing ['nʌθɪŋ] *n* nada; (*zero*) zero; he does ~ ele não faz nada; ~ **new/much** nada de novo/quase nada; **for** ~ de graça, grátis; (*in vain*) em vão, por nada
notice ['nəʊtɪs] *n* (*sign*) aviso, anúncio; (*warning*) aviso; (*dismissal*) demissão *f*; (*of leaving*) aviso prévio; (*period of time*) prazo ♦ *vt* reparar em, notar; **at short** ~ de repente, em cima da hora; **until further** ~ até nova ordem; **to hand in one's** ~ demitir, pedir a demissão; **to take** ~ **of** prestar atenção a, fazer caso de; **to bring sth to sb's** ~ levar algo ao conhecimento de alguém; ~**able** *adj* evidente, visível; ~ **board** (*BRIT*) *n* quadro de avisos
notify ['nəʊtɪfaɪ] *vt*: **to** ~ **sb of sth** avisar alguém de algo
notion ['nəʊʃən] *n* noção *f*, idéia
notwithstanding [nɔtwɪθ'stændɪŋ] *adv* no entanto, não obstante ♦ *prep*: ~ **this** apesar disto
nougat ['nuːgɑː] *n* torrone *m*, nugá *m*
nought [nɔːt] *n* zero
noun [naʊn] *n* substantivo
nourish ['nʌrɪʃ] *vt* nutrir, alimentar; (*fig*) fomentar, alentar; ~**ing** *adj* nutritivo, alimentício; ~**ment** *n* alimento, nutrimento
novel ['nɔvl] *n* romance *m* ♦ *adj* novo, recente; ~**ist** *n* romancista *m/f*; ~**ty** *n* novidade *f*
November [nəʊ'vɛmbə*] *n* novembro
novice ['nɔvɪs] *n* principiante *m/f*, novato/a; (*REL*) noviço/a
now [naʊ] *adv* agora; (*these days*) atualmente, hoje em dia ♦ *conj*: ~ (**that**) agora que; **right** ~ agora mesmo; **by** ~ já; **just** ~ atualmente; ~ **and then,** ~ **and again** de vez em quando; **from** ~ **on** de agora em diante; ~**adays** *adv* hoje em dia
nowhere ['nəʊwɛə*] *adv* (*go*) a lugar nenhum; (*be*) em nenhum lugar
nozzle ['nɔzl] *n* bocal *m*
nuance ['njuːɑːns] *n* nuança, matiz *m*
nubile ['njuːbaɪl] *adj* jovem e bela
nuclear ['njuːklɪə*] *adj* nuclear
nucleus ['njuːklɪəs] (*pl* **nuclei**) *n* núcleo

nude [njuːd] *adj* nu(a) ♦ *n* (*ART*) nu *m*; **in the** ~ nu, pelado
nudge [nʌdʒ] *vt* acotovelar, cutucar (*BR*)
nudist ['njuːdɪst] *n* nudista *m/f*
nuisance ['njuːsns] *n* amolação *f*, aborrecimento; (*person*) chato; **what a** ~! que saco! (*BR*), que chatice! (*PT*)
null [nʌl] *adj*: ~ **and void** írrito e nulo
numb [nʌm] *adj*: ~ **with cold** duro de frio; ~ **with fear** paralisado de medo
number ['nʌmbə*] *n* número; (*numeral*) algarismo ♦ *vt* (*pages etc*) numerar; (*amount to*) montar a; **a** ~ **of** vários, muitos; **to be** ~**ed among** figurar entre; **they were ten in** ~ eram em número de dez; ~ **plate** (*BRIT*) *n* placa (do carro)
numeral ['njuːmərəl] *n* algarismo
numerate ['njuːmərɪt] (*BRIT*) *adj*: **to be** ~ ter uma noção básica da aritmética
numerical [njuː'mɛrɪkl] *adj* numérico
numerous ['njuːmərəs] *adj* numeroso
nun [nʌn] *n* freira
nurse [nɔːs] *n* enfermeiro/a; (*also*: ~**maid**) ama-seca, babá *f* ♦ *vt* (*patient*) cuidar de, tratar de
nursery ['nɔːsərɪ] *n* (*institution*) creche *f*; (*room*) quarto das crianças; (*for plants*) viveiro; ~ **rhyme** *n* poesia infantil; ~ **school** *n* escola maternal; ~ **slope** (*BRIT*) *n* (*SKI*) rampa para principiantes
nursing ['nɔːsɪŋ] *n* (*profession*) enfermagem *f*; (*care*) cuidado, assistência; ~ **home** *n* sanatório, clínica de repouso; ~ **mother** *n* lactante *f*
nurture ['nɔːtʃə*] *vt* alimentar
nut [nʌt] *n* (*TECH*) porca; (*BOT*) noz *f*; ~**crackers** *npl* quebra-nozes *m inv*
nutmeg ['nʌtmɛg] *n* noz-moscada
nutrient ['njuːtrɪənt] *n* nutrimento
nutritious [njuː'trɪʃəs] *adj* nutritivo
nuts [nʌts] (*inf*) *adj*: **he's** ~ ele é doido
nutshell ['nʌtʃɛl] *n* casca de noz; **in a** ~ (*fig*) em poucas palavras
nylon ['naɪlɔn] *n* náilon *m* (*BR*), nylon *m* (*PT*) ♦ *adj* de náilon

O

oak [əʊk] *n* carvalho ♦ *adj* de carvalho
OAP (*BRIT*) *n abbr* = **old-age pensioner**
oar [ɔː*] *n* remo
oasis [əʊ'eɪsɪs] (*pl* **oases**) *n* oásis *m inv*
oath [əʊθ] *n* juramento; (*swear word*) palavrão *m*
oatmeal ['əʊtmiːl] *n* farinha *or* mingau *m* de aveia
oats [əʊts] *n* aveia
obedience [ə'biːdɪəns] *n* obediência
obedient [ə'biːdɪənt] *adj* obediente
obey [ə'beɪ] *vt* obedecer a; (*instructions, regulations*) cumprir
obituary [ə'bɪtjʊərɪ] *n* necrológio
object [*n* 'ɔbdʒɪkt, *vi* əb'dʒɛkt] *n* objeto;

(*purpose*) objetivo ♦ *vi*: **to ~ to** (*attitude*) desaprovar, objetar a; (*proposal*) opor-se a; **I ~!** protesto!; **he ~ed that ...** ele objetou que ...; **expense is no ~** o preço não é problema; **~ion** *n* objeção *f*; **I have no ~ion to ...** não tenho nada contra ...; **~ionable** *adj* desagradável; (*conduct*) censurável; **~ive** *n* objetivo

obligation [ɔblɪ'geɪʃən] *n* obrigação *f*; **without ~** sem compromisso

obligatory [ə'blɪgətərɪ] *adj* obrigatório

oblige [ə'blaɪdʒ] *vt* (*do a favour for*) obsequiar, fazer um favor a; (*force*) obrigar, forçar; **to be ~d to sb for doing sth** ficar agradecido por alguém fazer algo; **obliging** *adj* prestativo

oblique [ə'bliːk] *adj* oblíquo; (*allusion*) indireto

obliterate [ə'blɪtəreɪt] *vt* (*erase*) apagar; (*destroy*) destruir

oblivion [ə'blɪvɪən] *n* esquecimento; **oblivious** *adj*: **oblivious of** inconsciente de, esquecido de

oblong [ˈɔblɔŋ] *adj* oblongo, retangular ♦ *n* retângulo

obnoxious [əb'nɔkʃəs] *adj* odioso, detestável; (*smell*) enjoativo

oboe [ˈəubəu] *n* oboé *m*

obscene [əb'siːn] *adj* obsceno

obscure [əb'skjuə*] *adj* obscuro, desconhecido; (*difficult to understand*) pouco claro ♦ *vt* ocultar, escurecer; (*hide*: *sun etc*) esconder

obsequious [əb'siːkwɪəs] *adj* obsequioso, servil

observance [əb'zəːvns] *n* observância, cumprimento

observant [əb'zəːvnt] *adj* observador(a)

observation [ɔbzə'veɪʃən] *n* observação *f*; (*MED*) exame *m*

observatory [əb'zəːvətrɪ] *n* observatório

observe [əb'zəːv] *vt* observar; (*rule*) cumprir; **~r** *n* observador/a *m/f*

obsess [əb'sɛs] *vt* obsedar, obcecar; **~ion** *n* obsessão *f*, idéia fixa

obsolescence [ɔbsə'lɛsns] *n* obsolescência

obsolete [ˈɔbsəliːt] *adj* obsoleto

obstacle [ˈɔbstəkl] *n* obstáculo; (*hindrance*) estorvo, impedimento

obstinate [ˈɔbstɪnɪt] *adj* obstinado

obstruct [əb'strʌkt] *vt* obstruir; (*block*: *hinder*) estorvar; **~ion** *n* obstrução *f*; (*object*) obstáculo

obtain [əb'teɪn] *vt* obter; (*achieve*) conseguir; **~able** *adj* disponível

obvious [ˈɔbvɪəs] *adj* óbvio; **~ly** *adv* evidentemente; **~ly not!** (é) claro que não!

occasion [ə'keɪʒən] *n* ocasião *f*; (*event*) acontecimento; **~al** *adj* de vez em quando; **~ally** *adv* de vez em quando

occult [ɔ'kʌlt] *n*: **the ~** as ciências ocultas

occupant [ˈɔkjupənt] *n* (*of house*) inquilino/a; (*of car*) ocupante *m/f*

occupation [ɔkju'peɪʃən] *n* ocupação *f*; (*job*) profissão *f*; **~al hazard** *n* risco profissional

occupier [ˈɔkjupaɪə*] *n* inquilino/a

occupy [ˈɔkjupaɪ] *vt* ocupar; (*house*) morar em; **to ~ o.s. in doing** ocupar-se de fazer

occur [ə'kəː*] *vi* ocorrer; (*phenomenon*) acontecer; **to ~ to sb** ocorrer a alguém; **~rence** *n* ocorrência, acontecimento; (*existence*) existência

ocean [ˈəuʃən] *n* oceano; **~-going** *adj* de longo curso

ochre [ˈəukə*] (*US* **ocher**) *adj* cor de ocre *inv*

o'clock [ə'klɔk] *adv*: **it is 5 ~** são cinco horas

OCR *n abbr* = **optical character reader**; **optical character recognition**

octave [ˈɔktɪv] *n* oitava

October [ɔk'təubə*] *n* outubro

octopus [ˈɔktəpəs] *n* polvo

odd [ɔd] *adj* (*strange*) estranho, esquisito; (*number*) ímpar; (*sock etc*) desemparelhado; **60~** 60 e tantos; **at ~ times** às vezes, de vez em quando; **to be the ~ one out** ficar sobrando, ser a exceção; **~ity** *n* coisa estranha, esquisitice *f*; (*person*) excêntrico/a; **~-job man** (*irreg*) *n* faz-tudo *m*; **~ jobs** *npl* biscates *mpl*, bicos *mpl*; **~ly** *adv* curiosamente; *see also* **enough**; **~ments** (*BRIT*) *npl* (*COMM*) retalhos *mpl*; **~s** *npl* (*in betting*) pontos *mpl* de vantagem; **it makes no ~s** dá no mesmo; **at ~s** brigados/as, de mal; **~s and ends** *npl* miudezas *fpl*

odometer [ɔu'dɔmɪtə*] *n* conta-quilômetros *m inv*

odour [ˈəudə*] (*US* **odor**) *n* odor *m*, cheiro; (*unpleasant*) fedor *m*

KEYWORD

of [ɔv, əv] *prep* **1** (*gen*) de; **a friend ~ ours** um amigo nosso; **a boy ~ 10** um menino de 10 anos; **that was very kind ~ you** foi muito gentil da sua parte

2 (*expressing quantity, amount, dates etc*) de; **how much ~ this do you need?** de quanto você precisa; **3 ~ them** 3 deles; **3 ~ us went** 3 de nós foram; **the 5th ~ July** dia 5 de julho

3 (*from, out of*) de; **made ~ wood** feito de madeira

KEYWORD

off [ɔf] *adv* **1** (*distance, time*): **it's a long way ~** fica bem longe; **the game is 3 days ~** o jogo é daqui a 3 dias

2 (*departure*): **I'm ~** estou de partida; **to go ~ to Paris/Italy** ir para Paris/a Itália; **I must be ~** devo ir-me

3 (*removal*): **to take ~ one's hat/ coat/clothes** tirar o chapéu/o casaco/a roupa; **the button came ~** o botão caiu; **10% ~** (*COMM*) 10% de abatimento *or* desconto
4 (*not at work*): **to have a day ~** tirar um dia de folga; (: *sick*): **to be ~ sick** estar ausente por motivo de saúde
♦ *adj* **1** (*not turned on*: *machine, water, gas*) desligado; (: *light*) apagado; (: *tap*) fechado
2 (*cancelled*) cancelado
3 (*BRIT*: *not fresh*: *food*) passado; (: *milk*) talhado, anulado
4: **on the ~ chance** (*just in case*) ao acaso; **today I had an ~ day** (*not as good as usual*) hoje não foi o meu dia
♦ *prep* **1** (*indicating motion, removal, etc*) de; **the button came ~ my coat** o botão do meu casaco caiu
2 (*distant from*) de; **5 km ~ (the road)** a 5 km (da estrada); **~ the coast** em frente à costa
3: **to be ~ meat** (*no longer eat it*) não comer mais carne; (*no longer like it*) enjoar de carne

offal [ˈɔfl] *n* (*CULIN*) sobras *fpl*, restos *mpl*
off-colour (*BRIT*) *adj* (*ill*) indisposto
offence [əˈfɛns] (*US* **offense**) *n* (*crime*) delito; **to take ~ at** ofender-se com, melindrar-se com
offend [əˈfɛnd] *vt* ofender; **~er** *n* delinquente *m/f*
offensive [əˈfɛnsɪv] *adj* (*weapon, remark*) ofensivo; (*smell etc*) repugnante ♦ *n* (*MIL*) ofensiva
offer [ˈɔfə*] *n* oferta; (*proposal*) proposta ♦ *vt* oferecer; (*opportunity*) proporcionar; **"on ~"** (*COMM*) "em oferta"; **~ing** *n* oferenda
off-hand [ɔfˈhænd] *adj* informal ♦ *adv* de improviso
office [ˈɔfɪs] *n* (*place*) escritório; (*room*) gabinete *m*; (*position*) cargo, função *f*; **to take ~** tomar posse; **doctor's ~** (*US*) consultório; **~ automation** *n* automação *f* de escritórios; **~ block** (*US* ~ **building**) *n* conjunto de escritórios; **~ hours** *npl* (horas *fpl* de) expediente *m*; (*US*: *MED*) horas *fpl* de consulta
officer [ˈɔfɪsə*] *n* (*MIL etc*) oficial *m/f*; (*of organization*) diretor(a) *m/f*; (*also*: **police ~**) agente *m/f* policial *or* de polícia
office worker *n* empregado/a *or* funcionário/a de escritório
official [əˈfɪʃl] *adj* oficial ♦ *n* oficial *m/f*; (*civil servant*) funcionário/a (público/a); **~dom** (*pej*) *n* burocracia
officiate [əˈfɪʃɪeɪt] *vi* oficiar
officious [əˈfɪʃəs] *adj* intrometido
offing [ˈɔfɪŋ] *n*: **in the ~** (*fig*) em perspectiva
off: **~-licence** (*BRIT*) *n* loja que vende bebidas alcoólicas; **~ line** *adj, adv* (*COMPUT*) fora de linha; **~-peak** *adj* (*heating etc*) de período de pouco consumo; (*ticket, train*) de período de pouco movimento; **~-putting** (*BRIT*) *adj* desconcertante; **~-season** *adj, adv* fora de estação *or* temporada
offset [ˈɔfsɛt] (*irreg*) *vt* compensar, contrabalançar
offshoot [ˈɔfʃuːt] *n* (*fig*) desdobramento
offshore [ɔfˈʃɔː*] *adj* (*breeze*) de terra; (*fishing*) costeiro; **~ oilfield** campo petrolífero ao largo
offside [ˈɔfsaɪd] *adj* (*SPORT*) impedido; (*AUT*) do lado do motorista
offspring [ˈɔfsprɪŋ] *n* descendência, prole *f*
off: **~stage** *adv* nos bastidores; **~-the-peg** (*US* **~-the-rack**) *adj* pronto; **~white** *adj* quase branco
often [ˈɔfn] *adv* muitas vezes, freqüentemente; **how ~ do you go?** quantas vezes você vai?
ogle [ˈəʊgl] *vt* comer com os olhos
oh [əʊ] *excl* oh!, ó!, ah!
oil [ɔɪl] *n* (*CULIN*) azeite *m*; (*petroleum*) petróleo; (*for heating*) óleo ♦ *vt* (*machine*) lubrificar; **~can** *n* almotolia; **~field** *n* campo petrolífero; **~ filter** *n* (*AUT*) filtro de óleo; **~ painting** *n* pintura a óleo; **~ refinery** *n* refinaria de petróleo; **~ rig** *n* torre *f* de perfuração; **~skins** *npl* capa de oleado; **~ tanker** *n* (*ship*) petroleiro; (*truck*) carro-tanque *m* de petróleo; **~ well** *n* poço petrolífero; **~y** *adj* oleoso; (*food*) gorduroso
ointment [ˈɔɪntmənt] *n* pomada
O.K. [ˈəʊˈkeɪ] *excl* está bem, está bom, tá (bem *or* bom) (*inf*) ♦ *adj* bom; (*correct*) certo ♦ *vt* aprovar
okay [ˈəʊˈkeɪ] = **O.K.**
old [əʊld] *adj* velho; (*former*) antigo, anterior; **how ~ are you?** quantos anos você tem?; **he's 10 years ~** ele tem 10 anos; **~er brother** irmão mais velho; **~ age** *n* velhice *f*; **~ age pensioner** (*BRIT*) *n* aposentado/a (*BR*), reformado/a (*PT*); **~-fashioned** *adj* fora de moda; (*person*) antiquado; (*values*) absoleto, retrógrado
olive [ˈɔlɪv] *n* (*fruit*) azeitona; (*tree*) oliveira ♦ *adj* (*also*: **~-green**) verde-oliva *inv*; **~ oil** *n* azeite *m* de oliva
Olympic [əʊˈlɪmpɪk] *adj* olímpico
omelet(te) [ˈɔmlɪt] *n* omelete *f* (*BR*), omeleta (*PT*)
omen [ˈəʊmən] *n* presságio, agouro
ominous [ˈɔmɪnəs] *adj* preocupante
omit [əʊˈmɪt] *vt* omitir

KEYWORD

on [ɔn] *prep* **1** (*indicating position*) sobre, em (cima de); **~ the wall** na parede; **~ the left** à esquerda
2 (*indicating means, method, condition*

etc): ~ **foot** a pé; ~ **the train/plane** no trem/no avião; ~ **the telephone/radio** no telefone/rádio; ~ **television** na televisão; **to be ~ drugs** (*addicted*) ser viciado em drogas; (*MED*) estar sob medicação; **to be ~ holiday** estar de férias
3 (*referring to time*): ~ **Friday** na sexta-feira; **a week ~ Friday** sem ser esta sexta-feira, a outra; ~ **arrival** ao chegar; ~ **seeing this** ao ver isto
4 (*about, concerning*) sobre
♦ *adv* **1** (*referring to dress, covering*): **to have one's coat ~** estar de casaco; **what's she got ~?** o que ela está usando?; **she put her boots ~** ela calçou as botas; **he put his gloves/hat ~** ele colocou as luvas/o chapéu; **screw the lid ~ tightly** atarraxar bem a tampa
3 (*further, continuously*): **to walk/drive ~** continuar andando/dirigindo; **to go ~** continuar (em frente); **to read ~** continuar a ler
♦ *adj* **1** (*functioning, in operation: machine*) em funcionamento; (*light*) aceso; (*radio*) ligado; (*tap*) aberto; (*brakes: of car etc*) **to be ~** estar freado; (*meeting*): **is the meeting still ~?** (*in progress*) a reunião ainda está sendo realizada?; (*not cancelled*) ainda vai haver reunião?; **there's a good film ~ at the cinema** tem um bom filme passando no cinema
2: **that's not ~!** (*inf: of behaviour*) isso não se faz!

---

once [wʌns] *adv* uma vez; (*formerly*) outrora ♦ *conj* depois que; ~ **he had left/it was done** depois que ele saiu/foi feito; **at ~** imediatamente; (*simultaneously*) de uma vez, ao mesmo tempo; ~ **more** mais uma vez; ~ **and for all** uma vez por todas; ~ **upon a time** era uma vez

oncoming ['ɒnkʌmɪŋ] *adj* (*traffic*) que vem de frente

one [wʌn] *num* um(a); ~ **hundred and fifty** cento e cinqüenta; ~ **by** ~ um por um
♦ *adj* **1** (*sole*) único; **the ~ book which ...** o único livro que ...
2 (*same*) mesmo; **they came in the ~ car** eles vieram no mesmo carro
♦ *pron* **1** um(a); **this** ~ este/esta; **that** ~ esse/essa, aquele/aquela; **I've already got ~/a red ~** eu já tenho um/um vermelho
2: ~ **another** um ao outro; **do you two ever see** ~ **another?** vocês dois se vêem de vez em quando?
3 (*impers*): ~ **never knows** nunca se sabe; **to cut ~'s finger** cortar o dedo; ~ **needs to eat** é preciso comer

one: ~**-day excursion** (*US*) *n* bilhete *m* de ida e volta; ~**-man** *adj* (*business*) individual; ~**-man band** *n* homem-orquestra *m*; ~**-off** (*BRIT: inf*) *n* exemplar *m* único

oneself [wʌn'sɛlf] *pron* (*reflexive*) se; (*after prep, emphatic*) si (mesmo/a); **by ~** sozinho/a; **to hurt ~** ferir-se; **to keep sth for ~** guardar algo para si mesmo; **to talk to ~** falar consigo mesmo

one: ~**-sided** *adj* (*argument*) parcial; ~**-to-~** *adj* (*relationship*) individual; ~**-upmanship** *n*: **the art of ~-upmanship** a arte de aparentar ser melhor do que os outros; ~**-way** *adj* (*street, traffic*) de mão única (*BRA*), de sentido único (*PT*)

ongoing ['ɒngəʊɪŋ] *adj* (*project*) em andamento; (*situation*) existente

onion ['ʌnjən] *n* cebola

on line *adj* (*COMPUT*) on-line, em linha ♦ *adv* em linha

onlooker ['ɒnlʊkə*] *n* espectador(a) *m/f*

only ['əʊnlɪ] *adv* somente, apenas ♦ *adj* único, só ♦ *conj* só que, porém; **an ~ child** um filho único; **not ~ ... but also ...** não só ... mas também ...

onset ['ɒnsɛt] *n* começo

onshore ['ɒnʃɔ:*] *adj* (*wind*) do mar

onslaught ['ɒnslɔːt] *n* investida, arremetida

onto ['ɒntʊ] *prep* = **on to**

onus ['əʊnəs] *n* responsabilidade *f*

onward(s) ['ɒnwəd(z)] *adv* (*move*) para diante, para a frente; **from this time ~** de (ag)ora em diante

onyx ['ɒnɪks] *n* ônix *m*

ooze [u:z] *vi* ressumar, filtrar-se

opaque [əʊ'peɪk] *adj* opaco, fosco

OPEC ['əʊpɛk] *n abbr* (= *Organization of Petroleum-Exporting Countries*) OPEP *f*

open ['əʊpn] *adj* aberto; (*car*) descoberto; (*road*) livre; (*fig: frank*) franco; (*meeting*) aberto, sem restrições ♦ *vt* abrir ♦ *vi* abrir(-se); (*book etc*) começar; **in the ~ (air)** ao ar livre; ~ **on to** *vt fus* (*subj: room, door*) dar para; ~ **up** *vt* abrir; (*blocked road*) desobstruir ♦ *vi* (*COMM*) abrir; ~**ing** *adj* de abertura ♦ *n* abertura; (*start*) início; (*opportunity*) oportunidade *f*; ~**ly** *adv* abertamente; ~**-minded** *adj* aberto, imparcial; ~**-necked** *adj* aberto no colo; ~**-plan** *adj* sem paredes divisórias

opera ['ɒpərə] *n* ópera

operate ['ɒpəreɪt] *vt* fazer funcionar, pôr em funcionamento ♦ *vi* funcionar; (*MED*): **to ~ on sb** operar alguém

operatic [ɒpə'rætɪk] *adj* lírico, operístico

operating ['ɒpəreɪtɪŋ] *adj*: ~ **table** mesa de operações; ~ **theatre** sala de operações

operation [ɒpə'reɪʃən] *n* operação *f*; (*of machine*) funcionamento; **to be in ~** (*system*) estar em vigor; ~**al** *adj* operacional

operative ['ɔpərətɪv] *adj* em vigor

operator ['ɔpəreɪtə*] *n* (*of machine*) operador(a) *m/f*, manipulador(a) *m/f*; (*TEL*) telefonista *m/f*

opinion [ə'pɪnɪən] *n* opinião *f*; **in my ~** na minha opinião, a meu ver; **~ated** *adj* opinioso; **~ poll** *n* pesquisa, levantamento

opium ['əupɪəm] *n* ópio

opponent [ə'pəunənt] *n* oponente *m/f*; (*MIL, SPORT*) adversário/a

opportunist [ɔpə'tjuːnɪst] *n* (*pej*) oportunista *m/f*

opportunity [ɔpə'tjuːnɪtɪ] *n* oportunidade *f*; **to take the ~ of doing** aproveitar a oportunidade para fazer

oppose [ə'pəuz] *vt* opor-se a; **to be ~d to sth** opor-se a algo, estar contra algo; **as ~d to** em oposição a

opposing [ə'pəuzɪŋ] *adj* oposto, contrário

opposite ['ɔpəzɪt] *adj* oposto; (*house etc*) em frente ♦ *adv* (lá) em frente ♦ *prep* em frente de, defronte de ♦ *n* oposto, contrário

opposition [ɔpə'zɪʃən] *n* oposição *f*

oppress [ə'prɛs] *vt* oprimir

opt [ɔpt] *vi*: **to ~ for** optar por; **to ~ to do** optar por fazer; **~ out: to ~ out of doing sth** optar por não fazer algo

optical ['ɔptɪkl] *adj* ótico

optician [ɔp'tɪʃən] *n* oculista *m/f*

optimist ['ɔptɪmɪst] *n* otimista *m/f*; **~ic** *adj* otimista

optimum ['ɔptɪməm] *adj* ótimo

option ['ɔpʃən] *n* opção *f*; **~al** *adj* opcional, facultativo

or [ɔː*] *conj* ou; (*with negative*): **he hasn't seen ~ heard anything** ele não viu nem ouviu nada; **~ else** senão

oral ['ɔːrəl] *adj* oral ♦ *n* (exame *m*) oral *f*

orange ['ɔrɪndʒ] *n* (*fruit*) laranja ♦ *adj* cor de laranja *inv*, alaranjado

orator ['ɔrətə*] *n* orador(a) *m/f*

orbit ['ɔːbɪt] *n* órbita ♦ *vt* orbitar

orchard ['ɔːtʃəd] *n* pomar *m*

orchestra ['ɔːkɪstrə] *n* orquestra; (*US: seating*) platéia

orchid ['ɔːkɪd] *n* orquídea

ordain [ɔː'deɪn] *vt* ordenar, decretar

ordeal [ɔː'diːl] *n* experiência penosa, provação *f*

order ['ɔːdə*] *n* ordem *f*; (*COMM*) encomenda; (*good ~*) bom estado ♦ *vt* (*also*: **put in ~**) pôr em ordem, arrumar; (*in restaurant*) pedir; (*COMM*) encomendar; (*command*) mandar, ordenar; **in (working) ~** em bom estado; **in ~ to do/that** para fazer/que + *sub*; **on ~** (*COMM*) encomendado; **out of ~** com defeito, enguiçado; **~ form** *n* impresso para encomendas; **~ly** *n* (*MIL*) ordenança *m*; (*MED*) servente *m/f* ♦ *adj* (*room*) arrumado, ordenado; (*person*) me-

tódico

ordinary ['ɔːdnrɪ] *adj* comum, usual; (*pej*) ordinário, medíocre; **out of the ~** fora do comum, extraordinário

Ordnance Survey ['ɔːdnəns-] (*BRIT*) *n* serviço oficial de topografia e cartografia

ore [ɔː*] *n* minério

organ ['ɔːgən] *n* órgão *m*; **~ic** *adj* orgânico

organization [ɔːgənaɪ'zeɪʃən] *n* organização *f*

organize ['ɔːgənaɪz] *vt* organizar; **~r** *n* organizador(a) *m/f*

orgasm ['ɔːgæzəm] *n* orgasmo

orgy ['ɔːdʒɪ] *n* orgia

Orient ['ɔːrɪənt] *n*: **the ~** o Oriente; **o~al** *adj, n* oriental *m/f*

origin ['ɔrɪdʒɪn] *n* origem *f*

original [ə'rɪdʒɪnl] *adj* original ♦ *n* original *m*

originate [ə'rɪdʒɪneɪt] *vi*: **to ~ from** originar-se de, surgir de; **to ~ in** ter origem em

Orkneys ['ɔːknɪz] *npl*: **the ~** (*also*: **the Orkney Islands**) as ilhas Órcadas

ornament ['ɔːnəmənt] *n* ornamento; (*on dress*) enfeite *m*; **~al** *adj* decorativo, ornamental

ornate [ɔː'neɪt] *adj* enfeitado, requintado

orphan ['ɔːfn] *n* órfão/órfã *m/f*; **~age** *n* orfanato

orthodox ['ɔːθədɔks] *adj* ortodoxo

orthopaedic [ɔːθə'piːdɪk] (*US* **orthopedic**) *adj* ortopédico

oscillate ['ɔsɪleɪt] *vi* oscilar; (*person*) vacilar, hesitar

ostensibly [ɔs'tɛnsɪblɪ] *adv* aparentemente

ostentatious [ɔstɛn'teɪʃəs] *adj* pomposo, espalhafatoso; (*person*) ostentoso

ostracize ['ɔstrəsaɪz] *vt* condenar ao ostracismo

ostrich ['ɔstrɪtʃ] *n* avestruz *m/f*

other ['ʌðə*] *adj* outro ♦ *pron*: **the ~ (one)** o outro/a outra ♦ *adv* (*usually in negatives*): **~ than** (*apart from*) a não ser; (*anything but*) exceto; **~s** (**~ people**) outros; **~wise** *adv* (*in a different way*) de outra maneira; (*apart from that*) do contrário, caso contrário ♦ *conj* (*if not*) senão

otter ['ɔtə*] *n* lontra

ouch [autʃ] *excl* ai!

ought [ɔːt] (*pt* **ought**) *aux vb*: **I ~ to do it** eu deveria fazê-lo; **he ~ to win** (*probability*) ele deve ganhar

ounce [auns] *n* onça (= 28.35g; 16 in a pound)

our ['auə*] *adj* nosso; *see also* **my**; **~s** *pron* (o) nosso/(a) nossa *etc*; *see also* **mine**; **~selves** *pron pl* (*reflexive, after prep*) nós; (*emphatic*) nós mesmos/as; *see also* **oneself**

oust [aust] *vt* expulsar

npl despesas fpl

out [aut] adv 1 (not in) fora; **(to stand)**
~ in the rain/snow (estar em pé) na
chuva/neve; **~ loud** em voz alta
2 (not at home, absent) fora (de casa);
Mr Green is ~ at the moment Sr.
Green não está no momento; **to have a**
day/night ~ passar o dia fora/sair à
noite
3 (indicating distance): **the boat was 10**
km ~ o barco estava a 10 km da costa
4 (SPORT): **the ball is/has gone ~** a
bola caiu fora; **~!** (TENNIS etc) fora!
♦ adj 1: **to be ~** (unconscious) estar inconsciente; (~ of game) estar fora; (~ of
fashion) estar fora de moda
2 (have appeared: news, secret) do conhecimento público; (: flowers): **the flo-**
wers are ~ as flores desabrocham
3 (extinguished: light, fire) apagado; **be-**
fore the week was ~ (finished) antes
da semana acabar
4: **to be ~ to do sth** (intend) pretender
fazer algo; **to be ~ in one's calcula-**
tions (wrong) enganar-se nos cálculos
♦ prep: **~ of 1** (outside, beyond): **~ of**
fora de; **to go ~ of the house** sair da
casa; **to look ~ of the window** olhar
pela janela
2 (cause, motive) por
3 (origin): **to drink sth ~ of a cup** beber algo na xícara
4 (from among): **1 ~ of every 3** 1 entre
3
5 (without) sem; **to be ~ of milk/**
sugar/petrol etc não ter leite/açúcar/
gasolina etc

out-and-out adj (liar etc) completo, re-
matado
outback ['autbæk] n (in Australia): **the**
~ o interior
outboard ['autbɔːd] n (also: **~ motor**)
motor m de popa
outbreak ['autbreɪk] n (of war) deflagra-
ção f; (of disease) surto; (of violence etc)
explosão f
outburst ['autbɜːst] n explosão f
outcast ['autkɑːst] n pária m/f
outcome ['autkʌm] n resultado
outcrop ['autkrɔp] n afloramento
outcry ['autkraɪ] n clamor m (de protesto)
outdated ['aut'deɪtɪd] adj antiquado, fora
de moda
outdo [aut'duː] (irreg) vt ultrapassar, exceder
outdoor [aut'dɔː*] adj ao ar livre; (clothes) de sair; **~s** adv ao ar livre
outer ['autə*] adj exterior, externo; **~**
space n espaço (exterior)
outfit ['autfɪt] n roupa, traje m
outgoing ['autgəʊɪŋ] adj de saída; (character) extrovertido, sociável; **~s** (BRIT)

outgrow [aut'grəʊ] (irreg) vt: **he has ~n**
his clothes a roupa ficou pequena para
ele
outhouse ['authaus] n anexo
outing ['autɪŋ] n excursão f
outlaw ['autlɔː] n fora-da-lei m/f ♦ vt
(person) declarar fora da lei; (practice)
declarar ilegal
outlay ['autleɪ] n despesas fpl
outlet ['autlɛt] n saída, escape m; (of pipe) desagüe m, escoadouro; (US: ELEC)
tomada; (also: **retail ~**) posto de venda
outline ['autlaɪn] n (shape) contorno,
perfil m; (of plan) traçado; (sketch) esboço, linhas fpl gerais ♦ vt (theory, plan)
traçar, delinear
outlive [aut'lɪv] vt sobreviver a
outlook ['autluk] n (attitude) ponto de
vista; (fig: prospects) perspectiva; (: for
weather) previsão f
outlying ['autlaɪɪŋ] adj afastado, remoto
outmoded [aut'məʊdɪd] adj antiquado,
fora de moda, obsoleto
outnumber [aut'nʌmbə*] vt exceder em
número
out-of-date adj (passport, ticket) sem validade; (clothes) fora de moda
out-of-the-way adj remoto, afastado
outpatient ['autpeɪʃənt] n paciente m/f
externo/a or de ambulatório
outpost ['autpəust] n posto avançado
output ['autput] n (volume m de) produção f; (COMPUT) saída ♦ vt (COMPUT) liberar
outrage ['autreɪdʒ] n escândalo; (atrocity)
atrocidade f ♦ vt ultrajar; **~ous** adj ul-
trajante, escandaloso
outright [adv aut'raɪt, adj 'autraɪt] adv
(kill, win) completamente; (ask, refuse)
abertamente ♦ adj completo; franco
outset ['autsɛt] n início, princípio
outside [aut'saɪd] n exterior m ♦ adj exterior, externo ♦ adv (lá) fora ♦ prep
fora de; (beyond) além (dos limites) de;
at the ~ (fig) no máximo; **~ lane** n
(AUT: in Britain) pista da direita; (: in
US, Europe) pista da esquerda; **~ left** n
(FOOTBALL) extremo-esquerdo; **~ line** n
(TEL) linha de saída; **~r** n (stranger)
estranho/a, forasteiro/a
outsize ['autsaɪz] adj (clothes) de tamanho extra-grande or especial
outskirts ['autskɜːts] npl arredores mpl,
subúrbios mpl
outspoken [aut'spəʊkən] adj franco, sem
rodeios
outstanding [aut'stændɪŋ] adj excepcional; (work, debt) pendente
outstay [aut'steɪ] vt: **to ~ one's wel-**
come abusar da hospitalidade (demo-
rando mais tempo)
outstretched [aut'strɛtʃt] adj (hand) estendido
outstrip [aut'strɪp] vt ultrapassar

out tray n cesta de saída
outward ['autwəd] adj externo; (journey) de ida; ~**ly** adv para fora
outweigh [aut'weɪ] vt ter mais valor do que
outwit [aut'wɪt] vt passar a perna em
oval ['əuvl] adj ovalado ♦ n oval m
ovary ['əuvəri] n ovário
oven ['ʌvn] n forno; ~**proof** adj refratário

KEYWORD

over ['əuvə*] adv 1 (across: walk, jump, fly etc) por cima; **to cross ~ to the other side of the road** atravessar para o outro lado da rua; ~ **here** por aqui, cá; ~ **there** por ali, lá; **to ask sb ~** (to one's home) convidar alguém
2: **to fall ~** cair; **to knock ~** derrubar; **to turn ~** virar; **to bend ~** curvar-se, debruçar-se
3 (finished): **to be ~** estar acabado
4 (excessively: clever, rich, fat etc) muito, demais; **she's not ~ intelligent** ela não é superdotada
5 (remaining: money, food etc): **there are 3 ~** tem 3 sobrando/sobraram 3
6: **all ~** (everywhere) por todos os lados; ~ **and ~** (again) repetidamente
♦ prep 1 (on top of) sobre; (above) acima de
2 (on the other side of) no outro lado de; **he jumped ~ the wall** ele pulou o muro
3 (more than) mais de; ~ **and above** além de
4 (during) durante

overall [n, adj 'əuvərɔːl, adv əuvər'ɔːl] adj (length) total; (study) global ♦ adv (view) globalmente; (measure, paint) totalmente ♦ n (also: ~s) macacão m (BR), (fato) macaco (PT)
overawe [əuvər'ɔː] vt intimidar
overbalance [əuvə'bæləns] vi perder o equilíbrio, desequilibrar-se
overbearing [əuvə'bɛərɪŋ] adj autoritário, dominador(a)
overboard ['əuvəbɔːd] adv (NAUT) ao mar
overbook [əuvə'buk] vi reservar em excesso
overcast ['əuvəkɑːst] adj nublado, fechado
overcharge [əuvə'tʃɑːdʒ] vt: **to ~ sb** cobrar em excesso a alguém
overcoat ['əuvəkəut] n sobretudo
overcome [əuvə'kʌm] (irreg) vt vencer, dominar; (difficulty) superar
overcrowded [əuvə'kraudɪd] adj superlotado
overdo [əuvə'duː] (irreg) vt exagerar; (overcook) cozinhar demais; **to ~ it** (work too hard) exceder-se
overdose ['əuvədəus] n overdose f, dose

f excessiva
overdraft ['əuvədrɑːft] n saldo negativo
overdrawn [əuvə'drɔːn] adj (account) sem fundos, a descoberto
overdue [əuvə'djuː] adj atrasado; (change) tardio
overestimate [əuvər'ɛstɪmeɪt] vt sobrestimar
overflow [vi əuvə'fləu, n 'əuvəfləu] vi transbordar ♦ n (also: ~ **pipe**) tubo de descarga, ladrão m
overgrown [əuvə'grəun] adj (garden) coberto de vegetação
overhaul [vt əuvə'hɔːl, n 'əuvəhɔːl] vt revisar ♦ n revisão f
overhead [adv əuvə'hɛd, adj, n 'əuvəhɛd] adv por cima, em cima; (in the sky) no céu ♦ adj (lighting) superior; (railway) suspenso ♦ n (US) = ~**s**; ~**s** npl (expenses) despesas fpl gerais
overhear [əuvə'hɪə*] (irreg) vt ouvir por acaso
overheat [əuvə'hiːt] vi (engine) aquecer demais
overjoyed [əuvə'dʒɔɪd] adj: **to be ~ (at)** estar muito alegre (com)
overkill ['əuvəkɪl] n (fig): **it would be ~** seria exagero, seria matar mosquito com tiro de canhão
overland ['əuvəlænd] adj, adv por terra
overlap [əuvə'læp] vi (edges) sobrepor-se em parte; (fig) coincidir
overleaf [əuvə'liːf] adv no verso
overload [əuvə'ləud] vt sobrecarregar
overlook [əuvə'luk] vt (have view on) dar para; (miss) omitir; (forgive) fazer vista grossa a
overnight [adv əuvə'naɪt, adj 'əuvənaɪt] adv durante a noite; (fig) da noite para o dia ♦ adj de uma (or de) noite; **to stay ~** passar a noite, pernoitar
overpass ['əuvəpɑːs] (esp US) n viaduto
overpower [əuvə'pauə*] vt dominar, subjugar; (fig) assolar; ~**ing** adj (heat, stench) sufocante
overrate [əuvə'reɪt] vt sobrestimar, supervalorizar
override [əuvə'raɪd] (irreg) vt (order, objection) não fazer caso de, ignorar; **overriding** adj primordial
overrule [əuvə'ruːl] vt (decision) anular; (claim) indeferir
overrun [əuvə'rʌn] (irreg) vt (country etc) invadir; (time limit) ultrapassar, exceder
overseas [əuvə'siːz] adv (abroad) no estrangeiro, no exterior ♦ adj (trade) exterior; (visitor) estrangeiro
overshadow [əuvə'ʃædəu] vt ofuscar
overshoot [əuvə'ʃuːt] (irreg) vt ultrapassar
oversight ['əuvəsaɪt] n descuido
oversleep [əuvə'sliːp] (irreg) vi dormir além da hora
overstate [əuvə'steɪt] vt exagerar
overstep [əuvə'stɛp] vt: **to ~ the mark**

ultrapassar o limite

overt [əu'vɜːt] *adj* aberto, indissimulado

overtake [əuvə'teɪk] (*irreg*) *vt* ultrapassar

overthrow [əuvə'θrəu] (*irreg*) *vt* (*government*) derrubar

overtime ['əuvətaɪm] *n* horas *fpl* extras

overtone ['əuvətəun] *n* (*fig: also:* ~s) implicação *f*, tom *m*

overture ['əuvətʃuə*] *n* (*MUS*) abertura; (*fig*) proposta, oferta

overturn [əuvə'tɜːn] *vt* virar; (*system*) derrubar; (*decision*) anular ♦ *vi* (*car etc*) capotar

overweight [əuvə'weɪt] *adj* gordo demais, com excesso de peso

overwhelm [əuvə'wɛlm] *vt* esmagar, assolar; ~**ing** *adj* (*victory, defeat*) esmagador(a); (*heat*) sufocante; (*desire*) irresistível

overwork [əuvə'wɜːk] *n* excesso de trabalho

overwrought [əuvə'rɔːt] *adj* extenuado, superexcitado

owe [əu] *vt*: **to** ~ **sb sth, to** ~ **sth to sb** dever algo a alguém; **owing to** *prep* devido a, por causa de

owl [aul] *n* coruja

own [əun] *adj* próprio ♦ *vt* possuir, ter; **a room of my** ~ meu próprio quarto; **to get one's** ~ **back** ir à forra; **on one's** ~ sozinho; ~ **up** *vi*: **to** ~ **up to sth** confessar algo; ~**er** *n* dono/a, proprietário/a; ~**ership** *n* posse *f*

ox [ɔks] (*pl* ~**en**) *n* boi *m*

oxtail ['ɔksteɪl] *n*: ~ **soup** sopa de rabada

oxygen ['ɔksɪdʒən] *n* oxigênio; ~ **mask** *n* máscara de oxigênio

oyster ['ɔɪstə*] *n* ostra

oz. *abbr* = **ounce(s)**

ozone ['əuzəun] *n* ozônio; ~ **hole** *n* buraco (na camada) de ozônio; ~ **layer** *n* camada de ozônio

P

p [piː] *abbr* (= *page*) p; (*BRIT*) = **penny; pence**

PA *n abbr* = **personal assistant; public address system**

pa [pɑː] (*inf*) *n* papai *m*

p.a. *abbr* (= *per annum*) p.a.

pace [peɪs] *n* passo; (*speed*) velocidade *f* ♦ *vi*: **to** ~ **up and down** andar de um lado para o outro; **to keep** ~ **with** acompanhar o passo de; ~**maker** *n* (*MED*) marcapasso *m*

Pacific [pə'sɪfɪk] *n*: **the** ~ (**Ocean**) o (Oceano) Pacífico

pacify ['pæsɪfaɪ] *vt* acalmar, serenar

pack [pæk] *n* pacote *m*, embrulho; (*US: of cigarettes*) maço; (*of hounds*) matilha; (*of thieves*) bando, quadrilha; (*of cards*) baralho; (*back*~) mochila ♦ *vt* encher; (*in suitcase*) arrumar (na mala); (*cram*): **to** ~ **into** entupir de, enfiar com; **to** ~ (**one's**) **bags** fazer as malas; **to** ~ **sb off** despedir alguém; ~ **it in!** pára com isso!

package ['pækɪdʒ] *n* pacote *m*; (*bulky*) embrulho, fardo; (*also:* ~ **deal**) acordo global, pacote; ~ **holiday** (*BRIT*) *n* pacote *m* (de férias); ~ **tour** (*BRIT*) *n* excursão *f* organizada

packed lunch ['pækt-] (*BRIT*) *n* merenda

packet ['pækɪt] *n* pacote *m*; (*of cigarettes*) maço; (*of washing powder etc*) caixa

packing ['pækɪŋ] *n* embalagem *f*; (*act*) empacotamento

pad [pæd] *n* (*of paper*) bloco; (*to prevent friction*) acolchoado; (*inf: home*) casa ♦ *vt* acolchoar, enchumaçar; ~**ding** *n* enchimento

paddle ['pædl] *n* remo curto; (*US: for table tennis*) raquete *f* ♦ *vt* remar ♦ *vi* patinhar; ~ **steamer** *n* vapor *m* movido a rodas; **paddling pool** (*BRIT*) *n* lago de recreação

paddock ['pædək] *n* cercado; (*at race course*) paddock *m*

paddy field ['pædɪ-] *n* arrozal *m*

padlock ['pædlɔk] *n* cadeado

paediatrics [piːdɪ'ætrɪks] (*US* **pediatrics**) *n* pediatria

pagan ['peɪɡən] *adj, n* pagão/pagã *m/f*

page [peɪdʒ] *n* página; (*also:* ~ **boy**) mensageiro ♦ *vt* mandar chamar

pageant ['pædʒənt] *n* (*procession*) cortejo suntuoso; (*show*) desfile *m* alegórico; ~**ry** *n* pompa, fausto

pager ['peɪdʒə*], **paging device** ['peɪdʒɪŋ-] *n* bip *m*

paid [peɪd] *pt, pp of* **pay** ♦ *adj* (*work*) remunerado; (*holiday*) pago; (*official*) assalariado; **to put** ~ **to** (*BRIT*) acabar com

pail [peɪl] *n* balde *m*

pain [peɪn] *n* dor *f*; **to be in** ~ sofrer or sentir dor; **to take** ~**s to do sth** dar-se ao trabalho de fazer algo; ~**ed** *adj* magoado, aflito; ~**ful** *adj* doloroso; (*laborious*) penoso; (*unpleasant*) desagradável; ~**fully** *adv* (*fig*) terrivelmente; ~**killer** *n* analgésico; ~**less** *adj* sem dor, indolor; ~**staking** *adj* (*work*) esmerado; (*person*) meticuloso

paint [peɪnt] *n* pintura ♦ *vt* pintar; ~**brush** *n* (*artist's*) pincel *m*; (*decorator's*) broxa; ~**er** *n* (*artist*) pintor(a) *m/f*; (*decorator*) pintor(a) de paredes; ~**ing** *n* pintura; (*picture*) tela, quadro; ~**work** *n* pintura

pair [pɛə*] *n* par *m*; **a** ~ **of scissors** uma tesoura; **a** ~ **of trousers** uma calça (*BR*), umas calças (*PT*)

pajamas [pɪ'dʒɑːməz] (*US*) *npl* pijama *m*

Pakistan [pɑːkɪ'stɑːn] *n* Paquistão *m*; ~**i** *adj, n* paquistanês/esa *m/f*

pal [pæl] (*inf*) *n* camarada *m/f*, colega *m/f*

palace ['pæləs] *n* palácio

palatable ['pælɪtəbl] *adj* saboroso, apetitoso

palate ['pælɪt] *n* paladar *m*

palatial [pə'leɪʃəl] *adj* suntuoso, magnífico

palaver [pə'lɑ:və*] (*inf*) *n* confusão *f*

pale [peɪl] *adj* pálido; (*colour*) claro; (*light*) fraco ♦ *vi* empalidecer ♦ *n*: **to be beyond the ~** passar dos limites

Palestine ['pælɪstaɪn] *n* Palestina; **Palestinian** *adj, n* palestino/a

palette ['pælɪt] *n* palheta

palings ['peɪlɪŋz] *npl* (*fence*) cerca

pall [pɔːl] *n* (*of smoke*) manto ♦ *vi* perder a graça

pallid ['pælɪd] *adj* pálido, descorado

palm [pɑːm] *n* (*of hand*) palma; (*also: ~ tree*) palmeira ♦ *vt*: **to ~ sth off on sb** (*inf*) impingir algo a alguém; **P~ Sunday** *n* Domingo de Ramos

paltry ['pɔːltrɪ] *adj* irrisório

pamper ['pæmpə*] *vt* papariçar, mimar

pamphlet ['pæmflət] *n* panfleto

pan [pæn] *n* (*also*: **sauce~**) panela (*BR*), caçarola (*PT*); (*also*: **frying ~**) frigideira

panache [pə'næʃ] *n* desenvoltura

Panama ['pænəmɑː] *n* Panamá *m*

pancake ['pænkeɪk] *n* panqueca

panda ['pændə] *n* panda *m/f*; **~ car** (*BRIT*) *n* patrulhinha, carro policial

pander ['pændə*] *vi*: **to ~ to** favorecer

pane [peɪn] *n* vidraça, vidro

panel ['pænl] *n* (*of wood, RADIO, TV*) painel *m*; **~ling** (*US* **~ing**) *n* painéis *mpl*

pang [pæŋ] *n*: **a ~ of regret** uma sensação de pesar; **~s of hunger** fome aguda

panic ['pænɪk] *n* pânico ♦ *vi* entrar em pânico; **~ky** *adj* (*person*) assustadiço, apavorado; **~-stricken** *adj* tomado de pânico

pansy ['pænzɪ] *n* (*BOT*) amor-perfeito; (*inf*: *pej*) bicha (*BR*), maricas *m* (*PT*)

pant [pænt] *vi* arquejar, ofegar

panther ['pænθə*] *n* pantera

panties ['pæntɪz] *npl* calcinha (*BR*), cuecas *fpl* (*PT*)

pantihose ['pæntɪhəuz] (*US*) *n* meia-calça (*BR*), collants *mpl* (*PT*)

pantomime ['pæntəmaɪm] (*BRIT*) *n* pantomima, *revista musical montada na época de Natal, baseada em contos de fada*

pantry ['pæntrɪ] *n* despensa

pants [pænts] *npl* (*BRIT*: *underwear*: *woman's*) calcinha (*BR*), cuecas *fpl* (*PT*); (: *man's*) cueca (*BR*), cuecas (*PT*); (*US*: *trousers*) calças *fpl* (*PT*)

paper ['peɪpə*] *n* papel *m*; (*also*: **news~**) jornal *m*; (*also*: **wall~**) papel de parede; (*study, article*) artigo, dissertação *f*; (*exam*) exame *m*, prova ♦ *adj* de papel ♦ *vt* (*room*) revestir (com papel de parede); **~s** *npl* (*also*: **identity ~s**) documentos *mpl*; **~back** *n* livro de capa mole; **~ bag** *n* saco de papel; **~ clip** *n* clipe

m; **~ hankie** *n* lenço de papel; **~weight** *n* pesa-papéis *m* *inv*; **~work** *n* trabalho burocrático; (*pej*) papelada

papier-mâché ['pæpɪeɪ'mæʃeɪ] *n* papel *m* machê

paprika ['pæprɪkə] *n* páprica, pimentãodoce *m*

par [pɑː*] *n* paridade *f*, igualdade *f*; (*GOLF*) média *f*; **on a ~ with** em pé de igualdade com

parable ['pærəbl] *n* parábola

parachute ['pærəʃuːt] *n* pára-quedas *m* *inv*

parade [pə'reɪd] *n* desfile *m* ♦ *vt* (*show off*) exibir ♦ *vi* (*MIL*) passar revista

paradise ['pærədaɪs] *n* paraíso

paradox ['pærədɔks] *n* paradoxo; **~ically** *adv* paradoxalmente

paraffin ['pærəfɪn] (*BRIT*) *n*: **~ (oil)** querosene *m*

paragon ['pærəgən] *n* modelo

paragraph ['pærəgrɑːf] *n* parágrafo

Paraguay ['pærəgwaɪ] *n* Paraguai *m*

parallel ['pærəlel] *adj* (*lines etc*) paralelo; (*fig*) correspondente ♦ *n* paralela; correspondência

paralyse ['pærəlaɪz] (*BRIT*) *vt* paralisar

paralysis [pə'rælɪsɪs] (*pl* **paralyses**) *n* paralisia

paralyze ['pærəlaɪz] (*US*) *vt* = **paralyse**

paramount ['pærəmaunt] *adj* primordial; **of ~ importance** de suma importância

paranoid ['pærənɔɪd] *adj* paranóico

parapet ['pærəpɪt] *n* parapeito, balaustrada

parasol ['pærəsɔl] *n* guarda-sol *m*, sombrinha

paratrooper ['pærətruːpə*] *n* pára-quedista *m/f*

parcel ['pɑːsl] *n* pacote *m* ♦ *vt* (*also*: **~ up**) embrulhar, empacotar

parch [pɑːtʃ] *vt* secar, ressecar; **~ed** (*person*) morto de sede

parchment ['pɑːtʃmənt] *n* pergaminho

pardon ['pɑːdn] *n* (*LAW*) indulto ♦ *vt* perdoar; **~ me!, I beg your ~** (*apologizing*) desculpe(-me); **(I beg your) ~?** (*BRIT*), **~ me?** (*US*) (*not hearing*) como?, como disse?

parent ['pɛərənt] *n* (*father*) pai *m*; (*mother*) mãe *f*; **~s** *npl* (*mother and father*) pais *mpl*; **~al** *adj* paternal (*or* maternal), dos pais

parenthesis [pə'rɛnθɪsɪs] (*pl* **parentheses**) *n* parêntese *m*

Paris ['pærɪs] *n* Paris

parish ['pærɪʃ] *n* paróquia, freguesia

park [pɑːk] *n* parque *m* ♦ *vt, vi* estacionar

parking ['pɑːkɪŋ] *n* estacionamento; **"no ~"** "estacionamento proibido"; **~ lot** (*US*) *n* (parque *m* de) estacionamento; **~ meter** *n* parquímetro; **~ ticket** *n* multa por estacionamento proibido

parlance ['pɑːləns] *n* linguagem *f*

parliament ['pɑːləmənt] (*BRIT*) *n* parlamento; **~ary** *adj* parlamentar

parlour ['pɑːlə*] (*US* **parlor**) *n* sala de visitas, salão *m*, saleta

parochial [pə'rəukɪəl] (*pej*) *adj* provinciano

parole [pə'rəul] *n*: **on ~** em liberdade condicional, sob promessa

paroxysm ['pærəksɪzəm] *n* (*of anger, coughing*) acesso

parquet ['pɑːkeɪ] *n*: **~ floor(ing)** parquete *m*, assoalho de tacos

parrot ['pærət] *n* papagaio

parry ['pærɪ] *vt* aparar, desviar

parsley ['pɑːslɪ] *n* salsa

parsnip ['pɑːsnɪp] *n* cherivia, pastinaga

parson ['pɑːsn] *n* padre *m*, clérigo; (*in Church of England*) pastor *m*

part [pɑːt] *n* parte *f*; (*of machine*) peça; (*THEATRE etc*) papel *m*; (*of serial*) capítulo; (*US*: *in hair*) risca, repartido ♦ *adv* = **partly** ♦ *vt* dividir; (*hair*) repartir ♦ *vi* (*people*) separar-se; (*crowd*) dispersar-se; **to take ~ in** participar de, tomar parte em; **to take sb's ~** defender alguém; **for my ~** pela minha parte; **for the most ~** na maior parte; **to take sth in good ~** não se ofender com algo; **~ with** *vt fus* ceder, entregar; (*money*) pagar; **~ exchange** (*BRIT*) *n*: **in ~ exchange** como parte do pagamento

partial ['pɑːʃl] *adj* parcial; **to be ~ to** gostar de, ser apreciador(a) de

participate [pɑː'tɪsɪpeɪt] *vi*: **to ~ in** participar de; **participation** *n* participação *f*

participle ['pɑːtɪsɪpl] *n* particípio

particle ['pɑːtɪkl] *n* partícula; (*of dust*) grão *m*

particular [pə'tɪkjulə*] *adj* (*special*) especial; (*specific*) específico; (*fussy*) exigente, minucioso; **in ~** em particular; **~ly** *adv* em particular, especialmente; **~s** *npl* detalhes *mpl*; (*personal details*) dados *mpl* pessoais

parting ['pɑːtɪŋ] *n* (*act*) separação *f*; (*farewell*) despedida; (*BRIT*: *in hair*) risca, repartido ♦ *adj* de despedida

partisan [pɑːtɪ'zæn] *adj* partidário ♦ *n* partidário/a; (*in war*) guerrilheiro/a

partition [pɑː'tɪʃən] *n* (*POL*) divisão *f*; (*wall*) tabique *m*, divisória

partly ['pɑːtlɪ] *adv* em parte

partner ['pɑːtnə*] *n* (*COMM*) sócio/a; (*SPORT*) parceiro/a; (*at dance*) par *m*; (*spouse*) cônjuge *m/f*; **~ship** *n* associação *f*, parceria; (*COMM*) sociedade *f*

partridge ['pɑːtrɪdʒ] *n* perdiz *f*

part-time *adj, adv* de meio expediente

party ['pɑːtɪ] *n* (*POL*) partido; (*celebration*) festa; (*group*) grupo; (*LAW*) parte *f* interessada, litigante *m/f* ♦ *cpd* (*POL*) do partido, partidário; **~ dress** *n* vestido de gala; **~ line** *n* (*TEL*) linha compartilhada

pass [pɑːs] *vt* passar; (*exam*) passar em; (*place*) passar por; (*overtake*) ultrapassar; (*approve*) aprovar ♦ *vi* passar; (*SCH*) ser aprovado, passar ♦ *n* (*permit*) passe *m*; (*membership card*) carteira; (*in mountains*) desfiladeiro; (*SPORT*) passe *m*; (*SCH*): **to get a ~ in** ser aprovado em; **to make a ~ at sb** tomar liberdade com alguém; **~ away** *vi* falecer; **~ by** *vi* passar ♦ *vt* passar por cima de; **~ for** *vt fus* passar por; **~ on** *vt* (*news, illness*) transmitir; (*object*) passar para; **~ out** *vi* desmaiar; **~ up** *vt* deixar passar; **~able** *adj* (*road*) transitável; (*work*) aceitável

passage ['pæsɪdʒ] *n* (*also*: **~way**: *indoors*) corredor *m*; (: *outdoors*) passagem *f*; (*ANAT*) via; (*act of passing*) trânsito; (*in book*) passagem, trecho; (*by boat*) travessia

passbook ['pɑːsbuk] *n* caderneta

passenger ['pæsɪndʒə*] *n* passageiro/a

passer-by ['pɑːsə*-] (*pl* **passers-by**) *n* transeunte *m/f*

passing ['pɑːsɪŋ] *adj* (*fleeting*) passageiro, fugaz; *n*: **in ~** de passagem; **~ place** *n* trecho de ultrapassagem

passion ['pæʃən] *n* paixão *f*; **~ate** *adj* apaixonado

passive ['pæsɪv] *adj* passivo; **~ smoking** *n* fumo passivo

Passover ['pɑːsəuvə*] *n* Páscoa (dos judeus)

passport ['pɑːspɔːt] *n* passaporte *m*

password ['pɑːswɔːd] *n* senha, contra-senha

past [pɑːst] *prep* (*in front of*) por; (*beyond*) mais além de; (*later than*) depois de ♦ *adj* passado; (*president etc*) ex-, anterior ♦ *n* passado; **he's ~ forty** ele tem mais de quarenta anos; **ten/quarter ~ four** quatro e dez/quinze; **for the ~ few/3 days** nos últimos/3 dias

pasta ['pæstə] *n* massa

paste [peɪst] *n* pasta; (*glue*) grude *m*, cola ♦ *vt* grudar; **tomato ~** massa de tomate

pasteurized ['pæstəraɪzd] *adj* pasteurizado

pastille ['pæstɪl] *n* pastilha

pastime ['pɑːstaɪm] *n* passatempo

pastry ['peɪstrɪ] *n* massa; (*cake*) bolo

pasture ['pɑːstʃə*] *n* pasto

pasty [*n* 'pæstɪ, *adj* 'peɪstɪ] *n* empadão *m* de carne ♦ *adj* (*complexion*) pálido

pat [pæt] *vt* dar palmadinhas em; (*dog etc*) fazer festa em

patch [pætʃ] *n* retalho; (*eye* ~) tapa-olho *m*, tampão *m*; (*area*) área pequena; (*mend*) remendo ♦ *vt* remendar; (**to go through**) **a bad ~** (passar por) um mau pedaço; **~ up** *vt* consertar provisoriamente; (*quarrel*) resolver; **~work** *n* colcha de retalhos; **~y** *adj* (*colour*) desigual; (*information*) incompleto

pâté ['pætei] *n* patê *m*

patent ['peitnt] *n* patente *f* ♦ *vt* patentear ♦ *adj* patente, evidente; ~ **leather** *n* verniz *m*

paternal [pə'tə:nl] *adj* paternal; (*relation*) paterno

path [pɑ:θ] *n* caminho; (*trail, track*) trilha, senda; (*trajectory*) trajetória

pathetic [pə'θɛtik] *adj* (*pitiful*) patético, digno de pena; (*very bad*) péssimo

pathology [pə'θɔlədʒi] *n* patologia

pathos ['peiθɔs] *n* patos *m*, patético

pathway ['pɑ:θwei] *n* caminho, trilha

patience ['peiʃns] *n* paciência

patient ['peiʃnt] *adj, n* paciente *m/f*

patio ['pætiəu] *n* pátio

patriot ['peitriət] *n* patriota *m/f*

patrol [pə'trəul] *n* patrulha ♦ *vt* patrulhar; ~ **car** *n* carro de patrulha; ~**man** (*US: irreg*) guarda *m*, policial *m* (*BR*), polícia *m* (*PT*)

patron ['peitrən] *n* (*customer*) cliente *m/f*, freguês/esa *m/f*; (*of charity*) benfeitor(a) *m/f*; ~ **of the arts** mecenas *m*; ~**ize** *vt* (*pej*) tratar com ar de superioridade; (*shop*) ser cliente de; (*business, artist*) patrocinar; ~ **saint** *n* (santo/a) padroeiro/a

patter ['pætə*] *n* (*of rain*) tamborilada; (*of feet*) passos miúdos *mpl*; (*sales talk*) jargão *m* profissional ♦ *vi* correr dando passinhos; (*rain*) tamborilar

pattern ['pætən] *n* (*SEWING*) molde *m*; (*design*) desenho

paunch [pɔ:ntʃ] *n* pança, barriga

pauper ['pɔ:pə*] *n* pobre *m/f*

pause [pɔ:z] *n* pausa ♦ *vi* fazer uma pausa

pave [peiv] *vt* pavimentar; **to ~ the way for** preparar o terreno para

pavement ['peivmənt] (*BRIT*) *n* calçada (*BR*), passeio (*PT*)

pavilion [pə'viliən] *n* (*SPORT*) barraca

paving ['peiviŋ] *n* pavimento, calçamento; ~ **stone** *n* laje *f*, paralelepípedo

paw [pɔ:] *n* pata; (*of cat*) garra

pawn [pɔ:n] *n* (*CHESS*) peão *m*; (*fig*) títere *m* ♦ *vt* empenhar; ~**broker** *n* agiota *m/f*; ~**shop** *n* loja de penhores

pay [pei] (*pt, pp* **paid**) *n* salário; (*of manual worker*) paga ♦ *vt* pagar; (*debt*) liquidar, saldar; (*visit*) fazer ♦ *vi* valer a pena, render; **to ~ attention (to)** prestar atenção (a); **to ~ one's respects to sb** fazer uma visita de cortesia a alguém; ~ **back** *vt* (*money*) devolver; (*person*) pagar; ~ **for** *vt fus* pagar a; (*fig*) recompensar; ~ **in** *vt* depositar; ~ **off** *vt* (*debts*) saldar, liquidar; (*creditor*) pagar, reembolsar ♦ *vi* (*plan*) valer a pena; ~ **up** *vt* pagar; ~**able** *adj* pagável; (*cheque*): ~**able to** nominal em favor de; ~ **day** *n* dia *m* do pagamento;

~**ee** *n* beneficiário/a; ~ **envelope** (*US*) *n* = ~ **packet**; ~**ment** *n* pagamento; **monthly** ~**ment** pagamento mensal; ~ **packet** (*BRIT*) *n* envelope *m* de pagamento; ~ **phone** *n* telefone *m* público; ~**roll** *n* folha de pagamento; ~ **slip** (*BRIT*) *n* contracheque *m*

PC *n abbr* (= *personal computer*) PC *m*

pc *abbr* = **per cent**

pea [pi:] *n* ervilha

peace [pi:s] *n* paz *f*; (*calm*) tranqüilidade *f*, quietude *f*; ~**ful** *adj* (*person*) tranqüilo, pacífico; (*place, time*) tranqüilo, sossegado

peach [pi:tʃ] *n* pêssego

peacock ['pi:kɔk] *n* pavão *m*

peak [pi:k] *n* (*of mountain: top*) cume *m*; (*of cap*) pala, viseira; (*fig*) apogeu *m*; ~ **hours** *npl* horário de maior movimento; ~ **period** *n* período de pique

peal [pi:l] *n* (*of bells*) repique *m*, toque *m*; ~ **of laughter** gargalhada

peanut ['pi:nʌt] *n* amendoim *m*

pear [pɛə*] *n* pêra

pearl [pə:l] *n* pérola

peasant ['peznt] *n* camponês/esa *m/f*

peat [pi:t] *n* turfa

pebble ['pebl] *n* seixo, calhau *m*

peck [pɛk] *vt* (*also:* ~ **at**) bicar, dar bicadas em ♦ *n* bicada; (*kiss*) beijoca; ~**ing order** *n* ordem *f* de hierarquia; ~**ish** (*BRIT: inf*) *adj*: **I feel** ~**ish** estou a fim de comer alguma coisa

peculiar [pi'kju:liə*] *adj* (*strange*) estranho, esquisito; (*belonging to*): ~ **to** próprio de

pedal ['pedl] *n* pedal *m* ♦ *vi* pedalar

peddler ['pedlə*] *n* (*also:* **drugs** ~) mascate *m/f*, camelô *m*

pedestrian [pi'dɛstriən] *n* pedestre *m/f* (*BR*), peão *m* (*PT*) ♦ *adj* (*fig*) prosaico; ~ **crossing** (*BRIT*) *n* passagem *f* para pedestres (*BR*), passadeira (*PT*)

pediatrics [pi:di'ætriks] (*US*) *n* = **paediatrics**

pedigree ['pedigri:] *n* raça; (*fig*) genealogia ♦ *cpd* (*animal*) de raça

pee [pi:] (*inf*) *vi* fazer xixi, mijar

peek [pi:k] *vi*: **to ~ at** espiar, espreitar

peel [pi:l] *n* casca ♦ *vt* descascar ♦ *vi* (*paint, skin*) descascar; (*wallpaper*) desprender-se

peep [pi:p] *n* (*BRIT: look*) espiadela; (*sound*) pio ♦ *vi* espreitar; ~ **out** (*BRIT*) *vi* mostrar-se, surgir; ~**hole** *n* vigia, olho mágico

peer [piə*] *vi*: **to ~ at** perscrutar, fitar ♦ *n* (*noble*) par *m/f*; (*equal*) igual *m/f*; (*contemporary*) contemporâneo/a; ~**age** *n* pariato

peeved [pi:vd] *adj* irritado

peevish ['pi:viʃ] *adj* rabugento

peg [peg] *n* (*for coat etc*) cabide *m*; (*BRIT: also:* **clothes** ~) pregador *m*

Peking [pi:'kiŋ] *n* Pequim

pelican ['pɛlɪkən] n pelicano; ~ **cross-ing** (BRIT) n (AUT) passagem f sinalizada para pedestres (BR), passadeira para peões (PT)

pellet ['pɛlɪt] n bolinha; (for shotgun) pelota de chumbo

pelt [pɛlt] vt: **to ~ sb with sth** atirar algo em alguém ♦ vi (rain: also: ~ **down**) chover a cântaros; (inf: run) correr ♦ n pele f (não curtida)

pelvis ['pɛlvɪs] n pelvis f, bacia

pen [pɛn] n caneta; (for sheep etc) redil m, cercado

penal ['pi:nl] adj penal; ~**ize** vt impor penalidade a; (SPORT) penalizar

penalty ['pɛnltɪ] n pena, penalidade f; (fine) multa; (SPORT) punição f; ~ **kick** n (RUGBY) chute m de pênalti; (FOOTBALL) cobrança de pênalti

penance ['pɛnəns] n penitência

pence [pɛns] (BRIT) npl of **penny**

pencil ['pɛnsl] n lápis m; ~ **case** n lapiseira, porta-lápis m inv; ~ **sharpener** n apontador m (de lápis) (BR), apara-lápis m inv (PT)

pendant ['pɛndnt] n pingente m

pending ['pɛndɪŋ] prep, adj pendente

pendulum ['pɛndjuləm] n pêndulo

penetrate ['pɛnɪtreɪt] vt penetrar

penfriend ['pɛnfrɛnd] (BRIT) n amigo/a por correspondência, correspondente m/f

penguin ['pɛŋgwɪn] n pingüim m

peninsula [pə'nɪnsjulə] n península

penis ['pi:nɪs] n pênis m

penitent ['pɛnɪtnt] adj arrependido

penitentiary [pɛnɪ'tɛnʃərɪ] (US) n penitenciária, presídio

penknife ['pɛnnaɪf] (irreg) n canivete m

pen name n pseudônimo

penniless ['pɛnɪlɪs] adj sem dinheiro, sem um tostão

penny ['pɛnɪ] (pl **pennies** or (BRIT) **pence**) n pêni m; (US) cêntimo

penpal ['pɛnpæl] n amigo/a por correspondência, correspondente m/f

pension ['pɛnʃən] n pensão f; (old-age ~) aposentadoria, pensão do governo; ~**er** (BRIT) n aposentado/a (BR), reformado/a (PT)

pensive ['pɛnsɪv] adj pensativo

Pentecost ['pɛntɪkɔst] n Pentecostes m

penthouse ['pɛnthaus] n cobertura

pent-up [pɛnt-] adj reprimido

people ['pi:pl] npl gente f, pessoas fpl; (inhabitants) habitantes m/fpl; (citizens) povo; (POL): **the** ~ o povo ♦ n povo; **several** ~ **came** vieram várias pessoas; ~ **say that ...** dizem que ...

pep [pɛp] (inf) n pique m, energia, dinamismo; ~ **up** vt animar

pepper ['pɛpə*] n pimenta; (vegetable) pimentão m ♦ vt apimentar; (fig): **to ~ with** salpicar de; ~**mint** n (sweet) bala de hortelã

peptalk ['pɛptɔ:k] (inf) n conversa para levantar o espírito

per [pə:*] prep por; ~ **capita** adj, adv per capita, por pessoa

perceive [pə'si:v] vt perceber; (notice) notar; (realize) compreender

per cent n por cento

percentage [pə'sɛntɪdʒ] n porcentagem f, percentagem f

perceptive [pə'sɛptɪv] adj perceptivo

perch [pə:tʃ] (pl ~**es** n (for bird) poleiro; (pl: inv or ~**es**: fish) perca ♦ vi: **to ~ (on)** (bird) empoleirar-se (em); (person) encarapitar-se (em)

percolator ['pə:kəleɪtə*] n (also: **coffee** ~) cafeteira de filtro

peremptory [pə'rɛmptərɪ] adj peremptório; (imperious) autoritário

perennial [pə'rɛnɪəl] adj perene; (fig) constante

perfect [adj, n 'pə:fɪkt, vt pə'fɛkt] adj perfeito; (utter) completo ♦ n (also: ~ **tense**) perfeito ♦ vt aperfeiçoar; ~**ly** adv perfeitamente

perforate ['pə:fəreɪt] vt perfurar

perform [pə'fɔ:m] vt (carry out) realizar, fazer; (piece of music) interpretar ♦ vi (well, badly) interpretar; ~**ance** n desempenho; (of play, by artist) atuação f; (of car) performance f; ~**er** n (actor) artista m/f, ator/atriz m/f; (MUS) intérprete m/f

perfume ['pə:fju:m] n perfume m

perfunctory [pə'fʌŋktərɪ] adj superficial, negligente

perhaps [pə'hæps] adv talvez

peril ['pɛrɪl] n perigo, risco

perimeter [pə'rɪmɪtə*] n perímetro

period ['pɪərɪəd] n período; (SCH) aula; (full stop) ponto final; (MED) menstruação f, regra ♦ adj (costume, furniture) da época; ~**ic(al)** adj periódico; ~**ical** n periódico

peripheral [pə'rɪfərəl] adj periférico ♦ n (COMPUT) periférico

perish ['pɛrɪʃ] vi perecer; (decay) deteriorar-se; ~**able** adj perecível, deteriorável

perjury ['pə:dʒərɪ] n (LAW) perjúrio, falso testemunho

perk [pə:k] (inf) n mordomia, regalia; ~ **up** vi (cheer up) animar-se; ~**y** adj (cheerful) animado, alegre

perm [pə:m] n permanente f

permanent ['pə:mənənt] adj permanente

permeate ['pə:mɪeɪt] vi difundir-se ♦ vt penetrar; (subj: idea) difundir

permissible [pə'mɪsɪbl] adj permissível, lícito

permission [pə'mɪʃən] n permissão f; (authorization) autorização f

permit [n 'pə:mɪt, vt pə'mɪt] n licença; (to enter) passe m ♦ vt permitir; (authorize) autorizar

pernicious [pə:'nɪʃəs] adj nocivo; (MED)

pernicioso, maligno

perpetrate ['pə:pɪtreɪt] *vt* cometer

perpetual [pə'pɛtjuəl] *adj* perpétuo

perpetuate [pə'pɛtjueɪt] *vt* perpetuar

perplex [pə'plɛks] *vt* deixar perplexo

persecute [pə'sɪkju:t] *vt* importunar

persevere [pə:sɪ'vɪə] *vi* perseverar

Persian ['pə:ʃən] *adj* persa ♦ *n* (*LING*) persa *m*; the (~) Gulf o golfo Pérsico

persist [pə'sɪst] *vi*: to ~ (in) persistir (em); ~ent *adj* persistente; (*determined*) teimoso

person ['pə:sn] *n* pessoa; in ~ em pessoa; ~al *adj* pessoal; (*private*) particular; (*visit*) em pessoa, pessoal; ~al assistant *n* secretário/a particular; ~al call *n* (*TEL*) chamada pessoal; ~al column *n* anúncios *mpl* pessoais; ~al computer *n* computador *m* pessoal; ~ality *n* personalidade *f*; ~ally *adv* pessoalmente; to take sth ~ally ofender-se; ~al organizer *n* agenda

personnel [pə:sə'nɛl] *n* pessoal *m*

perspective [pə'spɛktɪv] *n* perspectiva

Perspex ['pə:spɛks] ® (*BRIT*) *n* Blindex ® *m*

perspiration [pə:spɪ'reɪʃən] *n* transpiração *f*

persuade [pə'sweɪd] *vt*: to ~ sb to do sth persuadir alguém a fazer algo

pertaining [pə'teɪnɪŋ]: ~ to *prep* relativo a

pertinent ['pə:tɪnənt] *adj* pertinente, a propósito

perturb [pə'tə:b] *vt* inquietar

Peru [pə'ru:] *n* Peru *m*

peruse [pə'ru:z] *vt* ler com atenção, examinar

pervade [pə'veɪd] *vt* impregnar, penetrar em

pervert [*n* 'pə:və:t, *vt* pə'və:t] *n* pervertido/a ♦ *vt* perverter, corromper; (*truth*) distorcer

pessimist ['pɛsɪmɪst] *n* pessimista *m/f*; **pessimistic** *adj* pessimista

pest [pɛst] *n* (*insect*) inseto nocivo; (*fig*) peste *f*

pester ['pɛstə] *vt* incomodar

pet [pɛt] *n* animal *m* de estimação ♦ *cpd* predileto ♦ *vt* acariciar ♦ *vi* (*inf*) acariciar-se; **teacher's** ~ (*favourite*) preferido/a do professor

petal ['pɛtl] *n* pétala

peter out ['pi:tə*] *vi* (*conversation*) esgotar-se; (*road etc*) acabar-se

petite [pə'ti:t] *adj* delicado, mignon

petition [pə'tɪʃən] *n* petição *f*; (*list of signatures*) abaixo-assinado

petrified ['pɛtrɪfaɪd] *adj* (*fig*) petrificado, paralisado

petrol ['pɛtrəl] (*BRIT*) *n* gasolina; **two/four-star** ~ gasolina de duas/quatro estrelas; ~ **can** *n* lata de gasolina

petroleum [pə'trəuliəm] *n* petróleo

petrol: ~ **pump** (*BRIT*) *n* bomba de gasolina; ~ **station** (*BRIT*) *n* posto (*BR*) *or* bomba (*PT*) de gasolina; ~ **tank** (*BRIT*) *n* tanque *m* de gasolina

petticoat ['pɛtɪkəut] *n* anágua

petty ['pɛtɪ] *adj* (*mean*) mesquinho; (*unimportant*) insignificante; ~ **cash** *n* fundo para despesas miúdas, caixa pequena, fundo de caixa; ~ **officer** *n* suboficial *m* da marinha

petulant ['pɛtjulənt] *adj* irascível

pew [pju:] *n* banco (de igreja)

pewter ['pju:tə*] *n* peltre *m*

phantom ['fæntəm] *n* fantasma *m*

pharmacist ['fɑ:məsɪst] *n* farmacêutico/a

pharmacy ['fɑ:məsɪ] *n* farmácia

phase [feɪz] *n* fase *f* ♦ *vt*: to ~ in/out introduzir/retirar por etapas

PhD *n abbr* = Doctor of Philosophy

pheasant ['fɛznt] *n* faisão *m*

phenomenon [fə'nɔmɪnən] (*pl* phenomena) *n* fenômeno

philanthropist [fɪ'lænθrəpɪst] *n* filantropo/a

Philippines ['fɪlɪpi:nz] *npl*: the ~ as Filipinas

philosophical [fɪlə'sɔfɪkl] *adj* filosófico; (*fig*) calmo, sereno

philosophy [fɪ'lɔsəfɪ] *n* filosofia

phlegm [flɛm] *n* fleuma

phobia ['fəubjə] *n* fobia

phone [fəun] *n* telefone *m* ♦ *vt* telefonar para, ligar para; **to be on the** ~ ter telefone; (*be calling*) estar no telefone; ~ **back** *vt, vi* ligar de volta; ~ **up** *vt* telefonar para ♦ *vi* telefonar; ~ **book** *n* lista telefônica; ~ **booth** *n* cabine *f* telefônica; ~ **box** (*BRIT*) *n* cabine *f* telefônica; ~ **call** *n* telefonema *m*, ligada; ~**card** *n* cartão para uso em telefone público; ~**-in** (*BRIT*) *n* (*RADIO*) programa com participação dos ouvintes; (*TV*) programa com participação dos espectadores

phonetics [fə'nɛtɪks] *n* fonética

phoney ['fəunɪ] *adj* falso; (*person*) fingido

phonograph ['fəunəgrɑ:f] (*US*) *n* vitrola

photo ['fəutəu] *n* foto *f*

photo... ['fəutəu] *prefix* foto...; ~**copier** *n* fotocopiadora *f*; ~**copy** *n* fotocópia, xerox *m* ® ♦ *vt* fotocopiar, xerocar

photograph ['fəutəgrɑ:f] *n* fotografia ♦ *vt* fotografar; ~**er** *n* fotógrafo/a; ~**ic** *adj* fotográfico; ~**y** *n* fotografia

phrase [freɪz] *n* frase *f* ♦ *vt* expressar; ~ **book** *n* livro de expressões idiomáticas (para turistas)

physical ['fɪzɪkl] *adj* físico; ~ **education** *n* educação *f* física

physician [fɪ'zɪʃən] *n* médico/a

physicist ['fɪzɪsɪst] *n* físico/a

physics ['fɪzɪks] *n* física

physique [fɪ'zi:k] *n* físico

pianist ['pi:ənɪst] *n* pianista *m/f*

piano [pɪ'ænəu] *n* piano

piccolo ['pɪkələu] n flautim m

pick [pɪk] n (tool: also: ~**axe**) picareta ♦ vt (select) escolher, selecionar; (gather) colher; (remove) tirar; (lock) forçar; **take your ~** escolha o que quiser; **the ~ of** o melhor de; **to ~ one's nose** colocar o dedo no nariz; **to ~ one's teeth** palitar os dentes; **to ~ a quarrel with sb** comprar uma briga com alguém; **~ at** vt fus (food) beliscar; **~ on** vt fus (person: criticize) criticar; (: treat badly) azucrinar, aporrinhar; **~ out** vt escolher; (distinguish) distinguir; **~ up** vi (improve) melhorar ♦ vt (from floor, AUT) apanhar; (POLICE) prender; (collect) buscar; (for sexual encounter) paquerar; (learn) aprender; (RADIO) pegar; **to ~ up speed** acelerar; **to ~ o.s. up** levantar-se

picket ['pɪkɪt] n (in strike) piquete m ♦ vt formar piquete em frente de

pickle ['pɪkl] n (also: ~**s**: as condiment) picles mpl; (fig: mess) apuro ♦ vt (in vinegar) conservar em vinagre; (in salt) conservar em sal e água

pickpocket ['pɪkpɔkɪt] n batedor(a) m/f de carteira (BR), carteirista m/f (PT)

pickup ['pɪkʌp] n (also: ~ **truck**, ~ **van**) camioneta, pick-up m

picnic ['pɪknɪk] n piquenique m

picture ['pɪktʃə*] n quadro; (painting) pintura; (drawing) desenho; (etching) água-forte f; (photograph) foto(grafia) f; (TV) imagem f; (film) filme m; (fig: description) descrição f; (: situation) conjuntura ♦ vt imaginar-se; **the ~s** npl (BRIT: inf) o cinema; **~ book** n livro de figuras

pie [paɪ] n (vegetable) pastelão m; (fruit) torta; (meat) empadão m

piece [piːs] n pedaço; (portion) fatia; (item): **a ~ of clothing/furniture/ advice** uma roupa/um móvel/um conselho ♦ vt: **to ~ together** juntar; **to take to ~s** desmontar; **~meal** adv pouco a pouco; **~work** n trabalho por empreitada or peça

pie chart n gráfico de setores

pier [pɪə*] n cais m; (jetty) embarcadouro, molhe m

pierce [pɪəs] vt furar, perfurar

piercing ['pɪəsɪŋ] adj (cry) penetrante, agudo; (stare) penetrante; (wind) cortante

pig [pɪg] n porco; (fig) porcalhão/lhona m/f; (pej: unkind person) grosseiro/a; (: greedy person) ganancioso/a

pigeon ['pɪdʒən] n pombo; **~hole** n escaninho

piggy bank ['pɪgɪ-] n cofre em forma de porquinho

pig-headed [-'hɛdɪd] (pej) adj teimoso, cabeçudo

piglet ['pɪglɪt] n porquinho, leitão m

pigskin ['pɪgskɪn] n couro de porco

pigsty ['pɪgstaɪ] n chiqueiro

pigtail ['pɪgteɪl] n rabo-de-cavalo, trança

pike [paɪk] n (pl inv or ~**s**) (fish) lúcio

pilchard ['pɪltʃəd] n sardinha

pile [paɪl] n (heap) monte m; (of carpet) pêlo; (of cloth) lado felpudo ♦ vt (also: ~ **up**) empilhar ♦ vi (also: ~ **up**: objects) empilhar-se; (: problems, work) acumular-se; **~ into** vt fus (car) apinhar-se

piles [paɪlz] npl hemorróidas fpl

pile-up n (AUT) engavetamento

pilfering ['pɪlfərɪŋ] n furto

pilgrim ['pɪlgrɪm] n peregrino/a; **~age** n peregrinação f, romaria

pill [pɪl] n pílula; **the ~** a pílula

pillage ['pɪlɪdʒ] vt pilhagem f

pillar ['pɪlə*] n pilar m; **~ box** (BRIT) n caixa coletora (do correio) (BR), marco do correio (PT)

pillion ['pɪljən] n: **to ride ~** andar na garupa

pillory ['pɪlərɪ] vt expor ao ridículo

pillow ['pɪləu] n travesseiro (BR), almofada (PT); **~case** n fronha

pilot ['paɪlət] n piloto/a ♦ cpd (scheme etc) piloto inv ♦ vt pilotar; **~ light** n piloto

pimp [pɪmp] n cafetão m (BR), cáften m (PT)

pimple ['pɪmpl] n espinha

pin [pɪn] n alfinete m ♦ vt alfinetar; **~s and needles** comichão f, sensação f de formigamento; **to ~ sth on sb** (fig) culpar alguém de algo; **~ down** vt (fig): **to ~ sb down** conseguir que alguém se defina or tome atitude

pinafore ['pɪnəfɔː*] n (also: ~ **dress**) avental m

pinball ['pɪnbɔːl] n fliper m, fliperama m

pincers ['pɪnsəz] npl pinça, tenaz f

pinch [pɪntʃ] n (of salt etc) pitada ♦ vt beliscar; (inf: steal) afanar; **at a ~** em último caso

pincushion ['pɪnkuʃən] n alfineteira

pine [paɪn] n pinho ♦ vi: **to ~ for** ansiar por; **~ away** vi consumir-se, definhar

pineapple ['paɪnæpl] n abacaxi m (BR), ananás m (PT)

ping [pɪŋ] n (noise) silvo, sibilo; **~-pong** ® n pingue-pongue m

pink [pɪŋk] adj cor de rosa inv ♦ n (colour) cor f de rosa; (BOT) cravo, cravina

pinnacle ['pɪnəkl] n cume m; (fig) auge m

pinpoint ['pɪnpɔɪnt] vt (discover) descobrir; (explain) identificar; (locate) localizar com precisão

pint [paɪnt] n quartilho (BRIT: = 568cc; US: = 473cc)

pin-up n pin-up f, retrato de mulher atraente

pioneer [paɪə'nɪə*] n pioneiro/a

pious ['paɪəs] adj pio, devoto

pip [pɪp] n (seed) caroço, semente f; **the ~s** npl (BRIT: time signal on radio) ≈ o toque de seis segundos

pipe [paɪp] n cano; (for smoking) cachimbo ♦ vt canalizar, encanar; ~s npl (also: **bag~s**) gaita de foles; ~ **down** (inf) vi calar o bico, meter a viola no saco; ~ **cleaner** n limpa-cachimbo; ~ **dream** n sonho impossível, castelo no ar; ~**line** n (for oil) oleoduto; (for gas) gaseoduto; ~**r** n (gen) flautista m/f; (of bagpipes) gaiteiro/a

piping [ˈpaɪpɪŋ] adv: ~ **hot** chiando de quente

pique [piːk] n ressentimento, melindre m

pirate [ˈpaɪərət] n pirata m ♦ vt piratear

Pisces [ˈpaɪsɪz] n Pisces m, Peixes mpl

piss [pɪs] (inf!) vi mijar; ~**ed** (inf!) adj (drunk) bêbado, de porre

pistol [ˈpɪstl] n pistola

piston [ˈpɪstən] n pistão m, êmbolo

pit [pɪt] n cova, fossa; (quarry, hole in surface of sth) buraco; (also: **coal** ~) mina de carvão ♦ vt: **to** ~ **one's wits against sb** competir em conhecimento or inteligência contra alguém; ~**s** npl (AUT) box m

pitch [pɪtʃ] n (MUS) tom m; (fig: degree) intensidade f; (BRIT: SPORT) campo; (tar) piche m, breu m ♦ vt (throw) arremessar, lançar; (tent) armar ♦ vi (fall forwards) cair (para frente); ~**-black** adj escuro como o breu; ~**ed battle** n batalha campal

pitchfork [ˈpɪtʃfɔːk] n forcado

piteous [ˈpɪtɪəs] adj lastimável

pitfall [ˈpɪtfɔːl] n perigo (imprevisto), armadilha

pith [pɪθ] n casca interna e branca

pithy [ˈpɪθɪ] adj substancial

pitiful [ˈpɪtɪful] adj comovente, tocante

pitiless [ˈpɪtɪlɪs] adj impiedoso

pittance [ˈpɪtns] n ninharia, miséria

pity [ˈpɪtɪ] n compaixão f, piedade f ♦ vt ter pena de, compadecer-se de

pivot [ˈpɪvət] n pino, eixo; (fig) pivô m

placard [ˈplækɑːd] n placar m; (in march etc) cartaz m

placate [pləˈkeɪt] vt apaziguar, aplacar

place [pleɪs] n lugar m; (position) posição f; (post) posto; (role) papel m; (home): **at/to his** ~ na/para a casa dele ♦ vt pôr, colocar; (identify) identificar, situar; **to take** ~ realizar-se; (occur) ocorrer; **out of** ~ (not suitable) fora de lugar, deslocado; **in the first** ~ em primeiro lugar; **to change** ~**s with sb** trocar de lugar con alguém; **to be** ~**d** (in race, exam) classificar-se

placid [ˈplæsɪd] adj plácido, sereno

plagiarism [ˈpleɪdʒərɪzm] n plágio

plague [pleɪg] n (MED) peste f; (fig) praga ♦ vt atormentar, importunar

plaice [pleɪs] n inv solha

plaid [plæd] n tecido de xadrez

plain [pleɪn] adj (unpatterned) liso; (clear) claro, evidente; (simple) simples inv,

despretensioso; (not handsome) sem atrativos ♦ adv claramente, com franqueza ♦ n planície f, campina; ~ **chocolate** n chocolate m amargo; ~**-clothes** adj (police officer) à paisana; ~**ly** adv claramente, obviamente; (hear, see) facilmente; (state) francamente

plaintiff [ˈpleɪntɪf] n querelante m/f, queixoso/a

plaintive [ˈpleɪntɪv] adj queixoso

plait [plæt] n trança, dobra

plan [plæn] n plano; (scheme) projeto; (schedule) programa m ♦ vt planejar (BR), planear (PT) ♦ vi fazer planos; **to** ~ **to do** pretender fazer

plane [pleɪn] n (AVIAT) avião m; (also: ~ **tree**) plátano; (fig: level) nível m; (tool) plaina; (MATH) plano

planet [ˈplænɪt] n planeta m

plank [plæŋk] n tábua

planner [ˈplænə*] n programador(a) m/f; (town ~) urbanista m/f

planning [ˈplænɪŋ] n planejamento (BR), planeamento (PT); **family** ~ planejamento or planeamento familiar; ~ **permission** (BRIT) n autorização f para construir

plant [plɑːnt] n planta; (machinery) maquinaria; (factory) usina, fábrica ♦ vt plantar; (field) semear; (bomb) colocar, pôr

plantation [plænˈteɪʃən] n plantação f; (area of trees) bosque m

plaque [plæk] n placa, insígnia; (also: **dental** ~) placa dental

plaster [ˈplɑːstə*] n (for walls) reboco; (also: ~ **of Paris**) gesso; (BRIT: also: **sticking** ~) esparadrapo, band-aid m ♦ vt rebocar; (cover): **to** ~ **with** encher or cobrir de; ~**ed** (inf) adj bêbado, de porre; ~**er** n rebocador(a) m/f, caiador(a) m/f

plastic [ˈplæstɪk] n plástico ♦ adj de plástico; ~ **bag** n sacola de plástico

Plasticine [ˈplæstɪsiːn] ® n plasticina ®

plastic surgery n cirurgia plástica

plate [pleɪt] n prato, chapa; (dental) chapa; (in book) gravura; **gold/silver** ~ placa de ouro/prata

plateau [ˈplætəu] (pl ~s or ~x) n planalto

plate glass n vidro laminado

platform [ˈplætfɔːm] n (RAIL) plataforma (BR), cais m (PT); (at meeting) tribuna; (raised structure: for landing etc) plataforma; (BRIT: of bus) plataforma; (POL) programa m partidário

platinum [ˈplætɪnəm] n platina

platitude [ˈplætɪtjuːd] n lugar m comum, chavão m

platoon [pləˈtuːn] n pelotão m

platter [ˈplætə*] n travessa

plausible [ˈplɔːzɪbl] adj plausível; (person) convincente

play [pleɪ] n (THEATRE) obra, peça ♦ vt jogar; (team) jogar contra; (music) tocar;

(*role*) fazer o papel de ♦ *vi* (*music*) tocar; (*frolic*) brincar; **to ~ safe** não se arriscar, não correr riscos; **~ down** *vt* minimizar; **~ up** *vi* (*person*) dar trabalho; (*TV*, *car*) estar com defeito; **~boy** *n* playboy *m*; **~er** *n* jogador(a) *m/f*; (*THEATRE*) ator/atriz *m/f*; (*MUS*) músico/a; **~ful** *adj* brincalhão/lhona; **~ground** *n* (*in park*) playground *m*; (*in school*) pátio de recreio; **~group** *n* espécie de jardim de infância; **~ing card** *n* carta de baralho; **~ing field** *n* campo de esportes (*BR*) or jogos (*PT*); **~mate** *n* colega *m/f*, camarada *m/f*; **~-off** *n* (*SPORT*) partida de desempate; **~pen** *n* cercado para crianças; **~thing** *n* brinquedo; (*fig*) joguete *m*; **~time** *n* (*SCH*) recreio; **~wright** *n* dramaturgo/a

plc *abbr* = **public limited company**

plea [pli:] *n* (*request*) apelo, petição *f*; (*LAW*) defesa

plead [pli:d] *vt* (*LAW*) defender, advogar; (*give as excuse*) alegar ♦ *vi* (*LAW*) declarar-se; (*beg*): **to ~ with sb** suplicar or rogar a alguém

pleasant [ˈplɛznt] *adj* agradável; (*person*) simpático; **~ries** *npl* amenidades *fpl* (na conversa)

please [pli:z] *excl* por favor ♦ *vt* agradar a, dar prazer a ♦ *vi* agradar, dar prazer; (*think fit*): **do as you ~** faça o que or como quiser; **~ yourself!** (*inf*) como você quiser!, você que sabe!; **~d** *adj* (*happy*): **~d (with)** satisfeito (com); **~d to meet you** prazer (em conhecê-lo); **pleasing** *adj* agradável

pleasure [ˈplɛʒəʳ] *n* prazer *m*; "**it's a ~**" "não tem de quê"; **~ boat** *n* barco de recreio

pleat [pli:t] *n* prega

pledge [plɛdʒ] *n* (*promise*) promessa ♦ *vt* prometer; **to ~ support for sb** empenhar-se a apoiar alguém

plentiful [ˈplɛntɪful] *adj* abundante

plenty [ˈplɛntɪ] *n*: **~ of** (*food*, *money*) bastante; (*jobs*, *people*) muitos/as

pliable [ˈplaɪəbl] *adj* flexível; (*fig*: *person*) adaptável, moldável

pliant [ˈplaɪənt] *adj* = **pliable**

pliers [ˈplaɪəz] *npl* alicate *m*

plight [plaɪt] *n* situação *f* difícil, apuro

plimsolls [ˈplɪmsɔlz] (*BRIT*) *npl* tênis *mpl*

plod [plɔd] *vi* caminhar pesadamente; (*fig*) trabalhar laboriosamente

plonk [plɔŋk] (*inf*) *n* (*BRIT*: *wine*) zurrapa ♦ *vt*: **to ~ sth down** deixar cair algo (pesadamente)

plot [plɔt] *n* (*scheme*) conspiração *f*, complô *m*; (*of story*, *play*) enredo, trama; (*of land*) lote *m* ♦ *vt* (*conspire*) tramar, planejar (*BR*), planear (*PT*); (*AVIAT*, *NAUT*, *MATH*) plotar ♦ *vi* conspirar; **a vegetable ~** (*BRIT*) uma horta; **~ter** *n* (*instrument*) plotadora

plough [plau] (*US* **plow**) *n* arado ♦ *vt*

arar; **to ~ money into** investir dinheiro em; **~ through** *vt fus* abrir caminho por; **~man's lunch** (*BRIT*) *n* lanche de pão, queijo e picles

ploy [plɔɪ] *n* estratagema *m*

pluck [plʌk] *vt* (*fruit*) colher; (*musical instrument*) dedilhar; (*bird*) depenar ♦ *n* coragem *f*, puxão *m*; **to ~ one's eyebrows** fazer as sobrancelhas; **to ~ up courage** criar coragem

plug [plʌg] *n* (*ELEC*) tomada (*BR*), ficha (*PT*); (*in sink*) tampa; (*AUT*: *also*: **spark(ing) ~**) vela (de ignição) ♦ *vt* (*hole*) tapar; (*inf*: *advertise*) fazer propaganda de; **~ in** *vt* (*ELEC*) ligar

plum [plʌm] *n* (*fruit*) ameixa ♦ *cpd* (*inf*): **a ~ job** um emprego jóia

plumb [plʌm] *vt*: **to ~ the depths** (*fig*) chegar ao extremo

plumber [ˈplʌməʳ] *n* bombeiro/a (*BR*), encanador(a) *m/f* (*BR*), canalizador(a) *m/f* (*PT*)

plumbing [ˈplʌmɪŋ] *n* (*trade*) ofício de encanador; (*piping*) encanamento

plume [plu:m] *n* pluma; (*on helmet*) penacho

plummet [ˈplʌmɪt] *vi*: **to ~ (down)** (*bird*, *aircraft*) cair rapidamente; (*price*) baixar rapidamente

plump [plʌmp] *adj* roliço, rechonchudo ♦ *vi*: **to ~ for** (*inf*: *choose*) escolher, optar por; **~ up** *vt* (*cushion*) afofar

plunder [ˈplʌndəʳ] *n* pilhagem *f*; (*loot*) despojo ♦ *vt* pilhar, espoliar

plunge [plʌndʒ] *n* (*dive*) salto; (*fig*) queda ♦ *vt* (*hand*, *knife*) enfiar, meter ♦ *vi* (*fall*, *fig*) cair; (*dive*) mergulhar; **to take the ~** topar a parada; **~r** *n* (*for blocked sink*) desentupidor *m*; **plunging** *adj* (*neckline*) decotado

pluperfect [plu:ˈpə:fɪkt] *n* mais-que-perfeito

plural [ˈpluərl] *adj* plural ♦ *n* plural *m*

plus [plʌs] *n* (*also*: **~ sign**) sinal *m* de adição ♦ *prep* mais; **ten/twenty ~** dez/vinte e tantos

plush [plʌʃ] *adj* suntuoso

ply [plaɪ] *n* (*of wool*) fio ♦ *vt* (*a trade*) exercer ♦ *vi* (*ship*) ir e vir; **to ~ sb with drink/questions** bombardear alguém com bebidas/perguntas; **~wood** *n* madeira compensada

PM (*BRIT*) *n abbr* = **Prime Minister**

p.m. *adv abbr* (= *post meridiem*) da tarde, da noite

pneumatic [njuːˈmætɪk] *adj* pneumático; **~ drill** *n* perfuratriz *f*

poach [pəutʃ] *vt* (*cook*: *fish*) escaldar; (: *eggs*) fazer poché (*BR*), escalfar (*PT*); (*steal*) furtar ♦ *vi* caçar (or pescar) em propriedade alheia; **~ed** *adj* (*egg*) poché (*BR*), escalfado (*PT*); **~er** *n* caçador *m* (*or* pescador *m*) furtivo

PO Box *n abbr* = **Post Office Box**

pocket [ˈpɔkɪt] *n* bolso; (*fig*: *small area*)

pedaço ♦ vt meter no bolso; (steal) embolsar; **to be out of** ~ (BRIT) perder, ter prejuízo; ~**book** (US) n carteira; ~ **knife** (irreg) n canivete m; ~ **money** n dinheiro para despesas miúdas; (for child) mesada

pod [pɔd] n vagem f

podgy ['pɔdʒɪ] (inf) adj gorducho, rechonchudo

podiatrist [pɔ'diːətrɪst] (US) n pedicuro/a

poem ['pəuɪm] n poema m

poet ['pəuɪt] n poeta/poetisa m/f; ~**ic** adj poético; ~ **laureate** n poeta m laureado; ~**ry** n poesia

poignant ['pɔɪnjənt] adj comovente

point [pɔɪnt] n ponto; (of needle etc) ponta; (purpose) finalidade f; (significant part) ponto principal; (position) lugar m, posição f; (moment) momento; (stage) estágio; (ELEC: also: **power** ~) tomada; (also: **decimal** ~): **2 ~ 3 (2.3)** dois vírgula três ♦ vt mostrar; (gun etc): **to ~ sth at sb** apontar algo para alguém ♦ vi: **to ~ at** apontar para; ~**s** npl (AUT) platinado, contato; (RAIL) agulhas fpl; **to be on the ~ of doing sth** estar prestes a or a ponto de fazer algo; **to make a ~ of** fazer questão de, insistir em; **to get the ~** perceber; **to miss the ~** não compreender mal; **to come to the ~** ir ao assunto; **there's no ~ (in doing)** não há razão (para fazer); ~ **out** vt (in debate etc) ressaltar; ~ **to** vt fus (fig) indicar; ~**blank** adv categoricamente; (also: **at** ~**-blank range**) à queima-roupa; ~**ed** adj (stick etc) pontudo; (remark) mordaz; ~**edly** adv sugestivamente; ~**er** n (on chart) indicador m; (on machine) ponteiro; (fig) dica; ~**less** adj (useless) inútil; (senseless) sem sentido; ~ **of view** n ponto de vista

poise [pɔɪz] n (composure) elegância; (calmness) serenidade f

poison ['pɔɪzn] n veneno ♦ vt envenenar; ~**ous** adj venenoso; (fumes etc) tóxico

poke [pəuk] vt cutucar; (put): **to ~ sth in(to)** enfiar or meter algo em; ~ **about** vi escarafunchar, espionar

poker ['pəukə*] n atiçador m (de brasas); (CARDS) pôquer m

poky ['pəukɪ] (pej) adj apertado

Poland ['pəulənd] n Polônia

polar ['pəulə*] adj polar; ~ **bear** n urso polar

Pole [pəul] n polonês/esa m/f

pole [pəul] n vara; (GEO) pólo; (telegraph ~) poste m; (flag~) mastro; ~ **bean** (US) n feijão-trepador; ~ **vault** n salto com vara

police [pə'liːs] n polícia ♦ vt policiar; ~ **car** n rádio-patrulha f; ~**man** (irreg) n policial m (BR), polícia m (PT); ~ **state** n estado policial; ~ **station** n delegacia (de polícia) (BR), esquadra (PT); ~ **wo-**

man (irreg) n policial f (feminina) (BR), mulher f polícia (PT)

policy ['pɔlɪsɪ] n política; (also: **insurance** ~) apólice f

polio ['pəulɪəu] n polio(mielite) f, polio f

Polish ['pəulɪʃ] adj polonês/esa ♦ n (LING) polonês m

polish ['pɔlɪʃ] n (for shoes) graxa; (for floor) cera (para encerar); (shine) brilho; (fig) refinamento, requinte m ♦ vt (shoes) engraxar; (make shiny) lustrar, dar brilho a; ~ **off** vt (work) dar os arremates a; (food) raspar; ~**ed** adj (person) culto; (manners) refinado

polite [pə'laɪt] adj educado; ~**ness** n gentileza, cortesia

political [pə'lɪtɪkl] adj político

politician [pɔlɪ'tɪʃən] n político/a

politics ['pɔlɪtɪks] n, npl política

poll [pəul] n (votes) votação f; (also: **opinion** ~) pesquisa, sondagem f ♦ vt (votes) receber, obter

pollen ['pɔlən] n pólen m

polling day ['pəulɪŋ-] (BRIT) n dia m de eleição

polling station ['pəulɪŋ-] (BRIT) n centro eleitoral

pollute [pə'luːt] vt poluir; **pollution** n poluição f

polo ['pəuləu] n (sport) pólo; ~**-necked** adj de gola rulê

poltergeist ['pɔltəgaɪst] n espírito perturbador (espécie de fantasma)

polyester [pɔlɪ'ɛstə*] n poliéster m

polystyrene [pɔlɪ'staɪriːn] n isopor ® m

polytechnic [pɔlɪ'tɛknɪk] n politécnico, escola politécnica

polythene ['pɔlɪθiːn] n politeno

pomegranate ['pɔmɪgrænɪt] n romã f

pomp [pɔmp] n pompa, fausto

pompom ['pɔmpɔm] n pompom m

pompon ['pɔmpɔn] n = **pompom**

pond [pɔnd] n (natural) lago pequeno; (artificial) tanque m

ponder ['pɔndə*] vt, vi ponderar, meditar (sobre); ~**ous** adj pesado

pong [pɔŋ] (BRIT: inf) n fedor m, fartum m (inf), catinga (inf)

pony ['pəunɪ] n pônei m; ~**tail** n rabo-de-cavalo; ~ **trekking** (BRIT) n excursão f em pônei

poodle ['puːdl] n cão-d'água m

pool [puːl] n (puddle) poça, charco; (pond) lago; (also: **swimming** ~) piscina; (fig: of light) feixe m; (: of liquid) poça; (SPORT) sinuca ♦ vt juntar; ~**s** npl (football ~s) loteria esportiva (BR), totobola (PT); **typing** or **secretary** (US) ~ seção f de datilografia

poor [puə*] adj pobre; (bad) inferior, mau ♦ npl: **the** ~ os pobres; ~ **in** (resources etc) deficiente em; ~**ly** adj adoentado, indisposto ♦ adv mal

pop [pɔp] n (sound) estalo, estouro; (MUS) pop m; (US: inf: father) papai m; (inf:

fizzy drink) bebida gasosa ♦ *vt*: to ~ sth into/onto *etc* (*put*) pôr em/sobre *etc* ♦ *vi* estourar; (*cork*) saltar; ~ **in** *vi* dar um pulo; ~ **out** *vi* dar uma saída; ~ **up** *vi* surgir, aparecer inesperadamente; ~**corn** *n* pipoca

pope [pəup] *n* papa *m*

poplar ['pɒplə*] *n* álamo, choupo

popper ['pɒpə*] (*BRIT*) *n* presilha

poppy ['pɒpɪ] *n* papoula

popsicle ['pɒpsɪkl] ® (*US*) *n* picolé *m*

populace ['pɒpjuləs] *n* povo

popular ['pɒpjulə*] *adj* popular; (*person*) querido; ~**ize** *vt* popularizar; (*science*) vulgarizar

population [pɒpju'leɪʃən] *n* população *f*

porcelain ['pɔːslɪn] *n* porcelana

porch [pɔːtʃ] *n* pórtico; (*US: verandah*) varanda

porcupine ['pɔːkjupaɪn] *n* porco-espinho

pore [pɔː*] *n* poro ♦ *vi*: to ~ **over** examinar minuciosamente

pork [pɔːk] *n* carne *f* de porco

pornography [pɔː'nɒgrəfɪ] *n* pornografia

porpoise ['pɔːpəs] *n* golfinho, boto

porridge ['pɒrɪdʒ] *n* mingau *m* (de aveia)

port [pɔːt] *n* (*harbour*) porto; (*NAUT: left side*) bombordo; (*wine*) vinho do Porto; ~ **of call** porto de escala

portable ['pɔːtəbl] *adj* portátil

porter ['pɔːtə*] *n* (*for luggage*) carregador *m*; (*doorkeeper*) porteiro

portfolio [pɔːt'fəuliəu] *n* (*case*) pasta; (*POL*) pasta ministerial; (*FINANCE*) carteira de ações ou títulos; (*of artist*) pasta, portfólio

porthole ['pɔːthəul] *n* vigia

portion ['pɔːʃən] *n* porção *f*, quinhão *m*; (*of food*) ração *f*

portly ['pɔːtlɪ] *adj* corpulento

portrait ['pɔːtreɪt] *n* retrato

portray [pɔː'treɪ] *vt* retratar; (*act*) interpretar; ~**al** *n* retrato; (*actor's*) interpretação *f*; (*in book, film*) representação *f*

Portugal ['pɔːtjugl] *n* Portugal *m* (*no article*)

Portuguese [pɔːtju'giːz] *adj* português/esa ♦ *n inv* português/esa *m/f*; (*LING*) português *m*

pose [pəuz] *n* postura, pose *f* ♦ *vi* (*pretend*): to ~ **as** fazer-se passar por ♦ *vt* (*question*) fazer; (*problem*) causar; to ~ **for** (*painting*) posar para

posh [pɒʃ] (*inf*) *adj* fino, chique; (*upper-class*) de classe alta

position [pə'zɪʃən] *n* posição *f*; (*job*) cargo; (*situation*) situação *f* ♦ *vt* colocar, situar

positive ['pɒzɪtɪv] *adj* positivo; (*certain*) certo; (*definite*) definitivo

posse ['pɒsɪ] (*US*) *n* pelotão *m* de civis armados

possess [pə'zɛs] *vt* possuir; ~**ion** *n* posse *f*, possessão *f*; ~**ions** *npl* (*belongings*)

pertences *mpl*; **to take ~ion of** sth tomar posse de algo

possibility [pɒsɪ'bɪlɪtɪ] *n* possibilidade *f*; (*of sth happening*) probabilidade *f*

possible ['pɒsɪbl] *adj* possível; **possibly** *adv* pode ser, talvez; (*surprise*): **what could they possibly want with me?** o que eles podem querer comigo?; (*emphasizing effort*): **they did everything they possibly could** eles fizeram tudo o que podiam; **I cannot possibly come** estou impossibilitado de vir

post [pəust] *n* (*BRIT: mail*) correio; (*job*) cargo, posto; (*pole*) poste *m*; (*MIL*) nomeação *f* ♦ *vt* (*BRIT: send by ~*) pôr no correio; (: *appoint*): **to ~ to** destinar a; ~**age** *n* porte *m*, franquia; ~**age stamp** *n* selo postal; ~**al** *adj* postal; ~**al order** *n* vale *m* postal; ~**box** (*BRIT*) *n* caixa de correio; ~**card** *n* cartão *m* postal; ~**code** (*BRIT*) *n* código postal, ≈ CEP *m* (*BR*)

poster ['pəustə*] *n* cartaz *m*; (*as decoration*) pôster *m*

posthumous ['pɒstjuməs] *adj* póstumo

postman ['pəustmən] (*irreg*) *n* carteiro

postmark ['pəustmɑːk] *n* carimbo do correio

postmortem [pəust'mɔːtəm] *n* autópsia

post office *n* (*building*) agência do correio, correio; (*organization*) ≈ Empresa Nacional dos Correios e Telégrafos (*BR*), ≈ Correios, Telégrafos e Telefones (*PT*); ~ **box** *n* caixa postal

postpone [pəs'pəun] *vt* adiar

postscript ['pəustskrɪpt] *n* pós-escrito

posture ['pɒstʃə*] *n* postura; (*fig*) atitude *f*

postwar [pəust'wɔː*] *adj* de após-guerra

posy ['pəuzɪ] *n* ramalhete *m*

pot [pɒt] *n* (*for cooking*) panela; (*for flowers*) vaso; (*container, tea~, coffee~*) pote *m*; (*inf: marijuana*) maconha ♦ *vt* (*plant*) plantar em vaso; **to go to ~** (*inf*) arruinar-se, degringolar

potato [pə'teɪtəu] (*pl* ~**es**) *n* batata; ~ **peeler** *n* descascador *m* de batatas

potent ['pəutnt] *adj* poderoso; (*drink*) forte; (*man*) potente

potential [pə'tɛnʃl] *adj* potencial ♦ *n* potencial *m*; ~**ly** *adv* potencialmente

pothole ['pɒthəul] *n* (*in road*) buraco; (*BRIT: underground*) caldeirão *m*, cova; **potholing** (*BRIT*) *n*: **to go potholing** dedicar-se à espeleologia

potluck [pɒt'lʌk] *n*: **to take ~** contentar-se com o que houver

potted ['pɒtɪd] *adj* (*food*) em conserva; (*plant*) de vaso; (*fig: shortened*) resumido

potter ['pɒtə*] *n* (*artistic*) ceramista *m/f*; (*artisan*) oleiro/a ♦ *vi* (*BRIT*): **to ~ around**, ~ **about** ocupar-se com pequenos trabalhos; ~**y** *n* cerâmica; (*factory*) olaria

potty ['pɔtɪ] *adj* (*inf*: *mad*) maluco, doido
♦ *n* penico
pouch [pautʃ] *n* (*ZOOL*) bolsa; (*for tobacco*) tabaqueira
poultry ['pəʊltrɪ] *n* aves *fpl* domésticas; (*meat*) carne *f* de aves domésticas
pounce [pauns] *vi*: **to ~ on** lançar-se sobre; (*person*) agarrar em; (*fig*: *mistake etc*) apontar
pound [paund] *n* libra (*weight = 453g, 16 ounces*; *money = 100 pence*) ♦ *vt* (*beat*) socar, esmurrar; (*crush*) triturar ♦ *vi* (*heart*) bater; **~ sterling** *n* libra esterlina
pour [pɔ:*] *vt* despejar; (*drink*) servir ♦ *vi* correr, jorrar; **~ away** *vt* esvaziar, decantar; **~ in** *vi* (*people*) entrar numa enxurrada; (*information*) chegar numa enxurrada; **~ off** *vt* esvaziar, decantar; **~ out** *vi* (*people*) sair aos borbotões ♦ *vt* (*drink*) servir; (*fig*) extravasar; **~ing** *adj*: **~ing rain** chuva torrencial
pout [paut] *vi* fazer beicinho *or* biquinho
poverty ['pɔvətɪ] *n* pobreza, miséria; **~-stricken** *adj* muito pobre, carente
powder ['paudə*] *n* pó *m*; (*face ~*) pó-de-arroz *m* ♦ *vt* (*face*) empoar, passar pó em; **~ compact** *n* estojo (de pó-de-arroz); **~ed milk** *n* leite *m* em pó; **~ puff** *n* esponja de pó-de-arroz; **~ room** *n* toucador *m*, banheiro de senhoras
power ['pauə*] *n* poder *m*; (*of explosion, engine*) força, potência; (*ability*) poder, poderio; (*electricity*) força; **to be in ~** estar no poder; **~ cut** (*BRIT*) *n* corte *m* de energia, blecaute *m* (*BR*); **~ed** *adj*: **~ed by** movido a; **~ failure** *n* corte *m* de energia; **~ful** *adj* poderoso; (*engine*) potente; (*body*) vigoroso; (*blow*) violento; (*argument*) convincente; (*emotion*) intenso; **~less** *adj* impotente; **~ point** (*BRIT*) *n* tomada; **~ station** *n* central *f* elétrica
pp *abbr* (= *per procurationem*) p.p.; = pages
PR *n abbr* = **public relations**
practicable ['præktɪkəbl] *adj* viável
practical ['præktɪkl] *adj* prático; **~ity** *n* (*of person*) índole *f* prática; **~ities** *npl* (*of situation*) aspectos *mpl* práticos; **~ joke** *n* brincadeira, peça
practice ['præktɪs] *n* (*habit*, *REL*) costume *m*, hábito; (*exercise*) prática; (*of profession*) exercício; (*training*) treinamento; (*MED*) consultório; (*LAW*) escritório ♦ *vt, vi* (*US*) = **practise**; **in ~** na prática; **out of ~** destreinado
practise ['præktɪs] (*US* **practice**) *vt* praticar; (*profession*) exercer; (*sport*) treinar ♦ *vi* (*doctor*) ter consultório; (*lawyer*) ter escritório; (*train*) treinar, praticar; **practising** *adj* (*Christian etc*) praticante; (*lawyer*) que exerce
practitioner [præk'tɪʃənə*] *n* (*MED*) médico/a

prairie ['prɛərɪ] *n* campina, pradaria
praise [preɪz] *n* louvor *m*; (*admiration*) elogio ♦ *vt* elogiar, louvar; **~worthy** *adj* louvável, digno de elogio
pram [præm] (*BRIT*) *n* carrinho de bebê
prance [prɑːns] *vi*: **to ~ about/up and down** *etc* (*horse*) curvetear, fazer cabriolas; (*person*) andar espalhafatosamente
prank [præŋk] *n* travessura, peça
prawn [prɔːn] *n* pitu *m*; (*small*) camarão *m*
pray [preɪ] *vi*: **to ~ for/that** rezar por/para que; **~er** *n* (*activity*) reza; (*words*) oração *f*, prece *f*
preach [priːtʃ] *vt* pregar ♦ *vi* pregar; (*pej*) catequizar
precede [prɪ'siːd] *vt* preceder
precedent ['prɛsɪdənt] *n* precedente *m*
preceding [prɪ'siːdɪŋ] *adj* anterior
precept ['priːsɛpt] *n* preceito
precinct ['priːsɪŋkt] *n* (*US*: *district*) distrito policial; **~s** *npl* (*of large building*) arredores *mpl*; **pedestrian ~** (*BRIT*) zona para pedestres (*BR*) *or* peões (*PT*); **shopping ~** (*BRIT*) zona comercial
precious ['prɛʃəs] *adj* precioso
precipitate [prɪ'sɪpɪteɪt] *vt* precipitar, acelerar
precise [prɪ'saɪs] *adj* exato, preciso; (*plans*) detalhado
preclude [prɪ'kluːd] *vt* excluir
precocious [prɪ'kəʊʃəs] *adj* precoce
precondition [priːkən'dɪʃən] *n* condição *f* prévia
predecessor ['priːdɪsɛsə*] *n* predecessor(a) *m/f*, antepassado/a
predicament [prɪ'dɪkəmənt] *n* situação *f* difícil, apuro
predict [prɪ'dɪkt] *vt* prever, predizer, prognosticar; **~able** *adj* previsível
predominantly [prɪ'dɔmɪnəntlɪ] *adv* predominantemente, na maioria
predominate [prɪ'dɔmɪneɪt] *vi* predominar
pre-empt [priː'ɛmt] (*BRIT*) *vt*: **to ~ sb/sth** antecipar-se a alguém/antecipar algo
preen [priːn] *vt*: **to ~ itself** (*bird*) limpar e alisar as penas (com o bico); **to ~ o.s.** enfeitar-se, envaidecer-se
prefab ['priːfæb] *n* casa pré-fabricada
preface ['prɛfəs] *n* prefácio
prefect ['priːfɛkt] *n* (*BRIT*: *SCH*) monitor(a) *m/f*, tutor(a) *m/f*; (*in Brazil*) prefeito/a
prefer [prɪ'fɜː*] *vt* preferir; **~ably** *adv* de preferência; **~ential** *adj*: **~ential treatment** preferência
prefix ['priːfɪks] *n* prefixo
pregnancy ['prɛgnənsɪ] *n* gravidez *f*; (*animal*) prenhez *f*
pregnant ['prɛgnənt] *adj* grávida; (*animal*) prenha
prehistoric [priːhɪs'tɔrɪk] *adj* pré-histórico

prejudice ['prɛdʒʊdɪs] n preconceito; ~**d** adj cheio de preconceitos; **to be** ~**d against sb/sth** estar com prevenção contra alguém/algo

preliminary [prɪ'lɪmɪnərɪ] adj preliminar, prévio

premarital [priː'mærɪtl] adj pré-nupcial

premature ['prɛmətʃʊə*] adj prematuro

premier ['prɛmɪə*] adj primeiro, principal ♦ n (POL) primeiro-ministro/primeira-ministra

première ['prɛmɪɛə*] n estréia

premise ['prɛmɪs] n premissa; ~**s** npl (of business, institution) local m

premium ['priːmɪəm] n prêmio; **to be at a** ~ ser caro; ~ **bond** (BRIT) n obrigação quê dá direito a prêmio mediante sorteio

premonition [prɛmə'nɪʃən] n presságio, pressentimento

preoccupied [priː'ɔkjʊpaɪd] adj preocupado

prep [prɛp] n (SCH: study) deveres mpl

prepaid [priː'peɪd] adj com porte pago

preparation [prɛpə'reɪʃən] n preparação f; ~**s** npl (arrangements) preparativos mpl

preparatory [prɪ'pærətərɪ] adj preparatório; ~ **school** n escola particular para crianças até 11 ou 13 anos de idade

prepare [prɪ'pɛə*] vt preparar ♦ vi: **to** ~ **for** preparar-se or aprontar-se para; ~**d to** disposto a; ~**d for** pronto para

preponderance [prɪ'pɔndərns] n predomínio

preposition [prɛpə'zɪʃən] n preposição f

preposterous [prɪ'pɔstərəs] adj absurdo, disparatado

prep school n = preparatory school

prerequisite [priː'rɛkwɪzɪt] n pré-requisito, condição f prévia

preschool [priː'skuːl] adj (education, age) pré-escolar; (child) de idade pré-escolar

prescribe [prɪ'skraɪb] vt prescrever; (MED) receitar

prescription [prɪ'skrɪpʃən] n receita

presence ['prɛzns] n presença; (spirit) espectro; ~ **of mind** n presença de espírito

present [adj, n 'prɛznt, vt prɪ'zɛnt] adj presente; (current) atual ♦ n presente m; (actuality): **the** ~ o presente ♦ vt (give): **to** ~ **sth to sb, to** ~ **sb with sth** entregar algo a alguém; (information, programme, threat) apresentar; (describe) descrever; **at** ~ no momento, agora; **to give sb a** ~ presentear alguém; ~**ation** n apresentação f; (ceremony) entrega; (of plan etc) exposição f; ~**-day** adj atual, de hoje; ~**er** n apresentador/a m/f; ~**ly** adv (after) logo após; (soon) logo, em breve; (now) atualmente

preservation [prɛzə'veɪʃən] n conservação f, preservação f

preserve [prɪ'zəːv] vt (situation) conservar, manter; (building, manuscript) preservar; (food) pôr em conserva ♦ n (often pl: jam) geléia; (: fruit) compota, conserva

preside [prɪ'zaɪd] vi: **to** ~ (**over**) presidir

presidency ['prɛzɪdənsɪ] n presidência

president ['prɛzɪdənt] n presidente/a m/f; ~**ial** adj presidencial

press [prɛs] n (printer's) imprensa, prelo; (newspapers) imprensa; (of switch) pressão f ♦ vt apertar; (clothes: iron) passar; (put pressure on: person) assediar; (insist): **to** ~ **sth on sb** insistir para que alguém aceite algo ♦ vi (squeeze) apertar; (pressurize): **to** ~ **for** pressionar por; **we are** ~**ed for time/money** estamos com pouco tempo/dinheiro; ~ **on** vi continuar; ~ **agency** n agência de informações; ~ **conference** n entrevista coletiva (para a imprensa); ~**ing** adj urgente; ~ **stud** (BRIT) n botão m de pressão; ~**-up** (BRIT) n flexão f

pressure ['prɛʃə*] n pressão f; **to put** ~ **on sb (to do sth)** pressionar alguém (a fazer algo); ~ **cooker** n panela de pressão; ~ **gauge** n manômetro

prestige [prɛs'tiːʒ] n prestígio

presume [prɪ'zjuːm] vt supor

presumption [prɪ'zʌmpʃən] n suposição f

pretence [prɪ'tɛns] (US **pretense**) n pretensão f; **under false** ~**s** por meios fraudulentos

pretend [prɪ'tɛnd] vt, vi fingir

pretense [prɪ'tɛns] (US US) n = **pretence**

pretentious [prɪ'tɛnʃəs] adj pretensioso, presunçoso

pretty ['prɪtɪ] adj bonito ♦ adv (quite) bastante

prevail [prɪ'veɪl] vi triunfar; (be current) imperar; ~**ing** adj (wind) dominante; (fashion) predominante

prevalent ['prɛvələnt] adj (common) predominante

prevent [prɪ'vɛnt] vt impedir; ~**ative** adj = ~**ive**; ~**ion** n prevenção f; ~**ive** adj preventivo

preview ['priːvjuː] n pré-estréia

previous ['priːvɪəs] adj (earlier) anterior; ~**ly** adv (before) previamente; (in the past) anteriormente

prewar [priː'wɔː*] adj anterior à guerra

prey [preɪ] n presa ♦ vi: **to** ~ **on** (feed on) alimentar-se de; **it was** ~**ing on his mind** preocupava-o, atormentava-o

price [praɪs] n preço ♦ vt fixar o preço de; ~**less** adj inestimável; (inf: amusing) impagável

prick [prɪk] n picada ♦ vt picar; (make hole in) furar; **to** ~ **up one's ears** aguçar os ouvidos

prickle ['prɪkl] n (sensation) comichão f, ardência; (BOT) espinho; **prickly** adj espinhoso; **prickly heat** n brotoeja

pride [praɪd] n orgulho; (pej) soberba ♦ vt: **to ~ o.s. on** orgulhar-se de

priest [priːst] n (Christian) padre m; (non-Christian) sacerdote m; **~ess** n sacerdotisa; **~hood** n sacerdócio

prig [prɪg] n esnobe m/f

prim [prɪm] (pej) adj (formal) empertigado; (affected) afetado; (easily shocked) pudico

primarily ['praɪmərɪlɪ] adv principalmente

primary ['praɪmərɪ] adj primário; (first in importance) principal ♦ n (US: election) eleição f primária; **~ school** (BRIT) n escola primária

prime [praɪm] adj primeiro, principal; (excellent) de primeira ♦ vt (wood) imprimir; (fig) aprontar, preparar ♦ n: **in the ~ of life** na primavera da vida; **~ example** exemplo típico; **~ minister** n primeiro-ministro/primeira-ministra

primeval [praɪ'miːvl] adj primitivo

primitive ['prɪmɪtɪv] adj primitivo; (crude) rudimentar

primrose ['prɪmrəuz] n prímula, primavera

primus (stove) ['praɪməs-] ® (BRIT) n fogão m portátil movido à parafina

prince [prɪns] n príncipe m

princess [prɪn'sɛs] n princesa

principal ['prɪnsɪpl] adj principal ♦ n (of school, college) diretor(a) m/f

principle ['prɪnsɪpl] n princípio; **in ~** em princípio; **on ~** por princípio

print [prɪnt] n (letters) letra de forma; (fabric) estampado; (ART) estampa, gravura; (PHOT) cópia; (foot~) pegada; (finger~) impressão f digital ♦ vt imprimir; (write in capitals) escrever em letra de imprensa; **out of ~** esgotado; **~ed matter** n impressos mpl; **~er** n (person) impressor(a) m/f; (firm) gráfica; (machine) impressora; **~ing** n (art) imprensa; (act) impressão f; **~out** n (COMPUT) cópia impressa

prior ['praɪə*] adj anterior, prévio; (more important) prioritário; **~ to doing** antes de fazer

priority [praɪ'ɔrɪtɪ] n prioridade f

prise [praɪz] vt: **to ~ open** arrombar

prison ['prɪzn] n prisão f ♦ cpd carcerário; **~er** n (in prison) preso/a, presidiário/a; (under arrest) detido/a

pristine ['prɪstiːn] adj imaculado

privacy ['prɪvəsɪ] n isolamento, solidão f, privacidade f

private ['praɪvɪt] adj privado; (personal) particular; (confidential) confidencial, reservado; (personal: belongings) pessoal; (: thoughts, plans) secreto, íntimo; (place) isolado; (quiet: person) reservado; (intimate) íntimo ♦ n soldado raso; **"~"** (on envelope) "confidencial"; (on door) "privativo"; **in ~** em particular; **~ en-**

terprise n iniciativa privada; **~ eye** n detetive m/f particular; **~ property** n propriedade f privada; **~ school** n escola particular; **privatize** vt privatizar

privet ['prɪvɪt] n alfena

privilege ['prɪvɪlɪdʒ] n privilégio

privy ['prɪvɪ] adj: **to be ~ to** estar inteirado de

prize [praɪz] n prêmio ♦ adj de primeira classe ♦ vt valorizar; **~-giving** n distribuição f dos prêmios; **~-winner** n premiado/a

pro [prəu] n (SPORT) profissional m/f ♦ prep a favor de; **the ~s and cons** os prós e os contras

probability [prɔbə'bɪlɪtɪ] n probabilidade f

probable ['prɔbəbl] adj provável; (plausible) verossímil

probation [prə'beɪʃən] n: **on ~** (employee) em estágio probatório; (LAW) em liberdade condicional

probe [prəub] n (MED, SPACE) sonda; (enquiry) pesquisa ♦ vt investigar, esquadrinhar

problem ['prɔbləm] n problema m

procedure [prə'siːdʒə*] n procedimento; (method) método, processo

proceed [prə'siːd] vi (do afterwards): **to ~ to do sth** passar a fazer algo; (continue): **to ~ (with)** continuar or prosseguir (com); (activity) continuar; (go) ir em direção a, dirigir-se a; **~ings** npl evento, acontecimento; (LAW) processo; **~s** npl produto, proventos mpl

process ['prəusɛs] n processo ♦ vt processar; **~ing** n processamento; **~ion** n desfile m, procissão f; **funeral ~ion** cortejo fúnebre

proclaim [prə'kleɪm] vt anunciar; **proclamation** n proclamação f; (written) promulgação f

procrastinate [prəu'kræstɪneɪt] vi protelar

procure [prə'kjuə*] vt obter

prod [prɔd] vt empurrar; (with finger, stick) cutucar ♦ n empurrão m; cotovelada; espetada

prodigal ['prɔdɪgl] adj pródigo

prodigious [prə'dɪdʒəs] adj colossal, extraordinário

prodigy ['prɔdɪdʒɪ] n prodígio

produce [n 'prɔdjuːs, vt prə'djuːs] n (AGR) produtos mpl agrícolas ♦ vt produzir; (cause) provocar; (evidence, argument) apresentar, mostrar; (show) apresentar, exibir; (THEATRE) pôr em cena or em cartaz; **~r** n (THEATRE) diretor(a) m/f; (AGR, CINEMA, of record) produtor(a) m/f; (country) produtor m

product ['prɔdʌkt] n produto

production [prə'dʌkʃən] n produção f; (of electricity) geração f; (THEATRE) encenação f; **~ line** n linha de produção or de montagem

profane [prə'feɪn] *adj* profano; *(language etc)* irreverente, sacrílego

profess [prə'fɛs] *vt* professar; *(feeling, opinion)* manifestar

profession [prə'fɛʃən] *n* profissão *f*; *(people)* classe *f*; **~al** *n* profissional *m/f* ♦ *adj* profissional; *(work)* de profissional

professor [prə'fɛsə*] *n* (BRIT) catedrático/a; (US, CANADA) professor(a) *m/f*

proficient [prə'fɪʃənt] *adj* competente, proficiente

profile ['prəufaɪl] *n* perfil *m*

profit ['prɒfɪt] *n* (COMM) lucro ♦ *vi*: **to ~ by** *or* **from** *(benefit)* aproveitar-se de, tirar proveito de; **~ability** *n* rentabilidade *f*; **~able** *adj* (ECON) lucrativo, rendoso

profound [prə'faund] *adj* profundo

profusion [prə'fjuːʒən] *n* profusão *f*, abundância

prognosis [prɒg'nəusɪs] *(pl* **prognoses**) *n* prognóstico

programme ['prəugræm] *(US* **program**) *n* programa *m* ♦ *vt* programar

progress [*n* 'prəugrɛs, *vi* prə'grɛs] *n* progresso ♦ *vi* progredir, avançar; **in ~** em andamento; **~ive** *adj* progressivo; *(person)* progressista

prohibit [prə'hɪbɪt] *vt* proibir; **~ion** *n* proibição *f*; (US): **P~ion** lei *f* seca

project [*n* 'prɒdʒɛkt, *vt*, *vi* prə'dʒɛkt] *n* projeto; (SCH: *research)* pesquisa ♦ *vt* projetar; *(figure)* estimar ♦ *vi* (stick out) ressaltar, sobressair

projectile [prə'dʒɛktaɪl] *n* projétil *m*

projection [prə'dʒɛkʃən] *n* projeção *f*; *(overhang)* saliência

projector [prə'dʒɛktə*] *n* projetor *m*

prolific [prə'lɪfɪk] *adj* prolífico

prolong [prə'lɒŋ] *vt* prolongar

prom [prɒm] *n abbr* = **promenade; promenade concert** (US: *ball)* baile *m* de estudantes

promenade [prɒmə'nɑːd] *n (by sea)* passeio (à orla marítima); **~ concert** (BRIT) *n* concerto (de música clássica)

prominent ['prɒmɪnənt] *adj* (standing out) proeminente; *(important)* eminente, notório

promise ['prɒmɪs] *n* promessa; *(hope)* esperança ♦ *vt, vi* prometer; **promising** *adj* promissor(a), promotedor(a)

promote [prə'məut] *vt* promover; *(product)* promover, fazer propaganda de; **~r** *n (of sporting event)* patrocinador(a) *m/f*; *(of cause etc)* partidário/a; **promotion** *n* promoção *f*

prompt [prɒmpt] *adj* pronto, rápido ♦ *adv (exactly)* em ponto, pontualmente ♦ *n* (COMPUT) sinal *m* de orientação, prompt *m* ♦ *vt (urge)* incitar, impelir; *(cause)* provocar, ocasionar; **to ~ sb to do sth** induzir alguém a fazer algo; **~ly**

adv imediatamente; *(exactly)* pontualmente

prone [prəun] *adj (lying)* de bruços; **~ to** propenso a, predisposto a

prong [prɒŋ] *n (of fork)* dente *m*

pronoun ['prəunaun] *n* pronome *m*

pronounce [prə'nauns] *vt* pronunciar; *(verdict, opinion)* declarar; **~d** *adj (marked)* pronunciado, marcado

pronunciation [prənʌnsɪ'eɪʃən] *n* pronúncia

proof [pruːf] *n* prova ♦ *adj*: **~ against** à prova de

prop [prɒp] *n* suporte *m*, escora; *(fig)* amparo, apoio ♦ *vt (also:* **~ up**) apoiar, escorar; *(lean)*: **to ~ sth against** apoiar algo contra

propaganda [prɒpə'gændə] *n* propaganda

propel [prə'pɛl] *vt* propelir, propulsionar; *(fig)* impelir; **~ler** *n* hélice *f*

proper ['prɒpə*] *adj (correct)* correto; *(socially acceptable)* respeitável, digno; *(authentic)* genuíno, autêntico; *(referring to place)*: **the village** ~ a cidadezinha propriamente dita; **~ly** *adv (eat, study)* bem; *(behave)* decentemente; **~ noun** *n* nome *m* próprio

property ['prɒpətɪ] *n* propriedade *f*; *(goods)* posses *fpl*, bens *mpl*; *(buildings)* imóveis *mpl*

prophesy ['prɒfɪsaɪ] *vt* profetizar

prophet ['prɒfɪt] *n* profeta *m/f*

proportion [prə'pɔːʃən] *n* proporção *f*; **~al** *adj* proporcional; **~al representation** *n* (POL) representação *f* proporcional; **~ate** *adj* proporcionado

proposal [prə'pəuzl] *n* proposta; *(of marriage)* pedido

propose [prə'pəuz] *vt* propor; *(toast)* erguer ♦ *vi* propor casamento; **to ~ to do** propor-se fazer

proposition [prɒpə'zɪʃən] *n* proposta, proposição *f*; *(offer)* oferta

proprietor [prə'praɪətə*] *n* proprietário/a, dono/a

propriety [prə'praɪətɪ] *n* propriedade *f*

pro rata [-'rɑːtə] *adv* pro rata, proporcionalmente

prose [prəuz] *n* prosa

prosecute ['prɒsɪkjuːt] *vt* processar; **prosecution** *n* acusação *f*; *(accusing side)* autor *m* da demanda; **prosecutor** *n* promotor(a) *m/f*; *(also:* **public prosecutor**) promotor(a) *m/f* público/a

prospect [*n* 'prɒspɛkt, *vi* prə'spɛkt] *n (chance)* probabilidade *f*; *(outlook)* perspectiva ♦ *vi*: **to ~ (for)** prospectar (por); **~s** *npl (for work etc)* perspectivas *fpl*; **~ive** *adj (possible)* provável; *(future)* futuro

prospectus [prə'spɛktəs] *n* prospecto, programa *m*

prosper ['prɒspə*] *vi* prosperar; **~ous** *adj* próspero

prostitute ['prɒstɪtjuːt] *n* prostituta;

male ~ prostituto

prostrate [prɔ'streɪt] *adj* prostrado

protect [prə'tɛkt] *vt* proteger; **~ion** *n* proteção *f*; **~ive** *adj* protetor(a)

protein ['prəutiːn] *n* proteína

protest [*n* 'prəutɛst, *vi, vt* prə'tɛst] *n* protesto ♦ *vi* protestar ♦ *vt* insistir

Protestant ['prɔtɪstənt] *adj, n* protestante *m/f*

protester [prə'tɛstə*] *n* manifestante *m/f*

protracted [prə'træktɪd] *adj* prolongado, demorado

protrude [prə'truːd] *vi* projetar-se

proud [praud] *adj* orgulhoso; (*pej*) vaidoso, soberbo

prove [pruːv] *vt* comprovar ♦ *vi*: to ~ (to be) correct *etc* vir a ser correto *etc*; to ~ o.s. pôr-se à prova

proverb ['prɔvəːb] *n* provérbio

provide [prə'vaɪd] *vt* fornecer, proporcionar; to ~ sb with sth fornecer alguém de algo, fornecer algo a alguém; ~ for *vt fus* (*person*) prover à subsistência de; ~d (that) *conj* contanto que + *sub*, sob condição de (que) + *sub*

providing [prə'vaɪdɪŋ] *conj*: ~ (that) contanto que + *sub*

province ['prɔvɪns] *n* província; (*fig*) esfera; **provincial** *adj* provincial; (*pej*) provinciano

provision [prə'vɪʒən] *n* (*supplying*) abastecimento; (*in contract*) cláusula, condição *f*; ~s *npl* (*food*) mantimentos *mpl*; ~al *adj* provisório, interino; (*agreement, licence*) provisório

proviso [prə'vaɪzəu] *n* condição *f*

provocative [prə'vɔkətɪv] *adj* provocante; (*sexually*) excitante

provoke [prə'vəuk] *vt* provocar; (*cause*) causar

prow [prau] *n* proa

prowess ['praus] *n* destreza, perícia

prowl [praul] *vi* (*also*: ~ about, ~ around) rondar, andar à espreita ♦ *n*: on the ~ de ronda, rondando; **~er** *n* tarado/a

proximity [prɔk'sɪmɪtɪ] *n* proximidade *f*

proxy ['prɔksɪ] *n*: by ~ por procuração

prude [pruːd] *n* pudico/a

prudent ['pruːdənt] *adj* prudente

prune [pruːn] *n* ameixa seca ♦ *vt* podar

pry [praɪ] *vi*: to ~ (into) intrometer-se (em)

PS *n abbr* (= *postscript*) PS *m*

psalm [sɑːm] *n* salmo

pseudo- [sjuːdəu] *prefix* pseudo-; **pseudonym** *n* pseudônimo

psyche ['saɪkɪ] *n* psiquismo

psychiatrist [saɪ'kaɪətrɪst] *n* psiquiatra *m/f*

psychiatry [saɪ'kaɪətrɪ] *n* psiquiatria

psychic ['saɪkɪk] *adj* psíquico; (*also*: **~al**: *person*) sensível a forças psíquicas

psychoanalyst [saɪkəu'ænəlɪst] *n* psicanalista *m/f*

psychologist [saɪ'kɔlədʒɪst] *n* psicólogo/a

psychology [saɪ'kɔlədʒɪ] *n* psicologia

psychopath ['saɪkəupæθ] *n* psicopata *m/f*

PTO *abbr* (= *please turn over*) v.v., vire

pub [pʌb] *n abbr* (= *public house*) pub *m*, bar *m*, botequim *m*

pubic ['pjuːbɪk] *adj* púbico, pubiano

public ['pʌblɪk] *adj* público ♦ *n* público; in ~ em público; to make ~ tornar público; ~ address system *n* sistema *m* (de reforço) de som

publican ['pʌblɪkən] *n* dono/a de pub

publication [pʌblɪ'keɪʃən] *n* publicação *f*

public: ~ **company** *n* sociedade *f* anônimaaberta; ~ **convenience** (*BRIT*) *n* banheiro público; ~ **holiday** *n* feriado; ~ **house** (*BRIT*) *n* pub *m*, bar *m*, taberna

publicity [pʌb'lɪsɪtɪ] *n* publicidade *f*

publicize ['pʌblɪsaɪz] *vt* divulgar

public: ~ **opinion** *n* opinião *f* pública; ~ **relations** *n* relações *fpl* públicas; ~ **school** *n* (*BRIT*) escola particular; (*US*) escola pública; **~-spirited** *adj* zeloso pelo bem-estar público; ~ **transport** (*US* ~ **transportation**) *n* transporte *m* coletivo

publish ['pʌblɪʃ] *vt* publicar; **~er** *n* editor(a) *m/f*; (*company*) editora; **~ing** *n* a indústria editorial

puce [pjuːs] *adj* roxo

pucker ['pʌkə*] *vt* (*fabric*) amarrotar; (*brow etc*) franzir

pudding ['pudɪŋ] *n* (*BRIT*: *dessert*) sobremesa; (*cake*) pudim *m*, doce *m*; **black** (*BRIT*) **or blood** (*US*) ~ morcela

puddle ['pʌdl] *n* poça

puff [pʌf] *n* sopro; (*of cigarette*) baforada; (*of air, smoke*) lufada ♦ *vt*: to ~ one's pipe tirar baforadas do cachimbo ♦ *vi* (*pant*) arquejar; ~ **out** *vt* (*cheeks*) encher; **~ed** (*inf*) *adj* (*out of breath*) sem fôlego; ~ **pastry** (*US* ~ **paste**) *n* massa folhada; **~y** *adj* inchado, entumecido

pull [pul] *n* (*tug*): to give sth a ~ dar um puxão em algo ♦ *vt* puxar; (*trigger*) apertar; (*curtain, blind*) fechar ♦ *vi* puxar, dar um puxão; to ~ to pieces picar em pedacinhos; to ~ one's punches não usar toda a força; to ~ one's weight fazer a sua parte; to ~ o.s. together recompor-se; to ~ sb's leg (*fig*) brincar com alguém, sacanear alguém (*inf*); ~ **apart** *vt* (*break*) romper; ~ **down** *vt* (*building*) demolir, derrubar; ~ **in** *vi* (*AUT*: *at the kerb*) encostar; (*RAIL*) chegar (na plataforma); ~ **off** *vt* tirar; (*fig*: *deal etc*) acertar; ~ **out** *vi* (*AUT*: *move from kerb*) sair; (*RAIL*) partir ♦ *vt* tirar, arrancar; ~ **over** *vi* (*AUT*) encostar; ~ **through** *vi* (*MED*) sobreviver; ~ **up** *vi* (*stop*) deter-se, parar ♦ *vt* levantar; (*uproot*) desarraigar, arrancar

pulley ['puli] n roldana
pullover ['puləuvə*] n pulôver m
pulp [pʌlp] n (of fruit) polpa
pulsate [pʌl'seit] vi pulsar, palpitar
pulse [pʌls] n (ANAT) pulso; (of music, engine) cadência; (BOT) legume m
pulverize ['pʌlvəraiz] vt pulverizar; (fig) esmagar, aniquilar
puma ['pju:mə] n puma, onça-parda
pummel ['pʌml] vt esmurrar, socar
pump [pʌmp] n bomba; (shoe) sapatilha (de dança) ♦ vt bombear; ~ **up** vt encher
pumpkin ['pʌmpkin] n abóbora
pun [pʌn] n jogo de palavras, trocadilho
punch [pʌntʃ] n (blow) soco, murro; (tool) punção m; (drink) ponche m ♦ vt (hit): **to ~ sb/sth** esmurrar or socar alguém/algo; ~**line** n remate m; ~**up** (BRIT: inf) n briga
punctual ['pʌŋktjuəl] adj pontual
puncture ['pʌŋktʃə*] n furo ♦ vt furar
pundit ['pʌndit] n entendedor(a) m/f
pungent ['pʌndʒənt] adj acre
punish ['pʌniʃ] vt punir, castigar; ~**ment** n castigo, punição f
punk [pʌŋk] n (also: ~ rocker) punk m/f; (also: ~ rock) punk m; (US: inf: hoodlum) pinta-brava m
punt [pʌnt] n (boat) chalana
punter ['pʌntə*] n (BRIT: gambler) jogador(a) m/f; (inf: client) cliente m/f
puny ['pju:ni] adj débil, fraco
pup [pʌp] n cachorro, cachorrinho (BR)
pupil ['pju:pl] n aluno/a; (of eye) pupila
puppet ['pʌpit] n marionete f, títere m; (fig) fantoche m
puppy ['pʌpi] n cachorro, cachorrinho (BR)
purchase ['pə:tʃis] n compra ♦ vt comprar; ~**r** n comprador(a) m/f
pure [pjuə*] adj puro
purée ['pjuərei] n purê m
purgatory ['pə:gətəri] n purgatório; (fig) inferno
purge [pə:dʒ] n (POL) expurgo
purify ['pjuərifai] vt purificar, depurar
puritan ['pjuəritən] n puritano/a
purity ['pjuəriti] n pureza
purple ['pə:pl] adj roxo, purpúreo
purport [pə:'pɔ:t] vi: **to ~ to be/do** dar a entender que é/faz
purpose ['pə:pəs] n propósito, objetivo; **on ~** de propósito; ~**ful** adj decidido, resoluto
purr [pə:*] vi ronronar
purse [pə:s] n (BRIT) carteira; (US) bolsa ♦ vt enrugar, franzir
purser ['pə:sə*] n (NAUT) comissário de bordo
pursue [pə'sju:] vt perseguir; (fig: activity) exercer; (: interest, plan) dedicarse a; (: result) lutar por
pursuit [pə'sju:t] n caça; (fig) busca; (pastime) passatempo

pus [pʌs] n pus m
push [puʃ] n empurrão m; (of button) aperto ♦ vt empurrar; (button) apertar; (promote) promover ♦ vi empurrar; (press) apertar; (fig): **to ~ for** reivindicar; ~ **aside** vt afastar com a mão; ~ **off** (inf) vi dar o fora; ~ **on** vi prosseguir; ~ **through** vi abrir caminho ♦ vt (measure) forçar a aceitação de; ~ **up** vt forçar a alta de; ~**chair** (BRIT) n carrinho; ~**er** n (also: **drug ~er**) traficante m/f or passador(a) m/f de drogas; ~**over** (inf) n: **it's a ~over** é sopa; ~**up** (US) n flexão f; ~**y** (pej) adj intrometido, agressivo
puss [pus] (inf) n gatinho
pussy(cat) ['pusi(kæt)] (inf) n gatinho
put [put] (pt, pp put) vt pôr, colocar; (~ into) meter; (person: in institution etc) internar; (say) dizer, expressar; (case) expor; (question) fazer; (estimate) avaliar, calcular; (write, type etc) colocar; ~ **about** vt (rumour) espalhar; ~ **across** vt (ideas) comunicar; ~ **away** vt guardar; ~ **back** vt (replace) repor; (postpone) adiar; (delay) atrasar; ~ **by** vt (money etc) poupar, pôr de lado; ~ **down** vt pôr em; (animal) sacrificar; (in writing) anotar, inscrever; (revolt etc) sufocar; (attribute: case, view): **to ~ sth down to** atribuir algo a; ~ **forward** vt apresentar, propor; ~ **in** vt (application, complaint) apresentar; (time, effort) investir, gastar; ~ **off** vt adiar, protelar; (discourage) desencorajar; ~ **on** vt (clothes, make-up, dinner) pôr; (light) acender; (play) encenar; (weight) ganhar; (brake) aplicar; (record, video, kettle) ligar; (accent, manner) assumir; ~ **out** vt (take out) colocar fora; (fire, cigarette, light) apagar; (one's hand) estender; (inf: person): **to be ~ out** estar aborrecido; ~ **through** vt (call) transferir; (plan) ser aprovado; ~ **up** vt (raise) levantar, erguer; (hang) prender; (build) construir, edificar; (tent) armar; (increase) aumentar; (accommodate) hospedar; ~ **up with** vt fus suportar, agüentar
putt [pʌt] n putt m, tacada leve; ~**ing green** n campo de golfe em miniatura
putty ['pʌti] n massa de vidraceiro, betume m
put-up adj: ~ **job** (BRIT) embuste m
puzzle ['pʌzl] n charada; (jigsaw) quebra-cabeça m; (also: **crossword ~**) palavras cruzadas fpl; (mystery) mistério ♦ vt desconcertar, confundir ♦ vi: **to ~ over** sth tentar entender algo; **puzzling** adj intrigante, confuso
pyjamas [pi'dʒɑ:məz] (US **pajamas**) npl pijama m or f
pylon ['pailən] n pilono, poste m, torre f
pyramid ['pirəmid] n pirâmide f
Pyrenees [pirə'ni:z] npl: **the ~** os Pirineus

python [ˈpaɪθən] n pitão m

Q

quack [kwæk] n grasnido; (pej: doctor) curandeiro/a, charlatão/tã m/f
quad [kwɔd] abbr = **quadrangle**; **quadruplet**
quadrangle [ˈkwɔdrængl] n pátio quadrangular
quadruplets [kwɔːˈdruːplɪts] npl quadrigêmeos mpl, quádruplos mpl
quagmire [ˈkwægmaɪə*] n lamaçal m, atoleiro
quail [kweɪl] n codorniz f, codorna (BR) ♦ vi acovardar-se
quaint [kweɪnt] adj (ideas) curioso, esquisito; (village etc) pitoresco
quake [kweɪk] vi (with fear) tremer ♦ n abbr = **earthquake**
Quaker [ˈkweɪkə*] n quacre m/f
qualification [kwɔlɪfɪˈkeɪʃən] n (skill, quality) qualificação f; (reservation) restrição f, ressalva; (modification) modificação f; (often pl: degree, training) título, qualificação
qualified [ˈkwɔlɪfaɪd] adj (trained) habilitado, qualificado; (professionally) diplomado; (fit): ~ **to** apto para, capaz de; (limited) limitado
qualify [ˈkwɔlɪfaɪ] vt (modify) modificar ♦ vi: **to** ~ **(as)** (pass examination(s)) formar-se or diplomar-se (em); **to** ~ **(for)** reunir os requisitos (para)
quality [ˈkwɔlɪtɪ] n qualidade f
qualm [kwɑːm] n (doubt) dúvida; (scruple) escrúpulo
quandary [ˈkwɔndrɪ] n: **to be in a** ~ estar num dilema
quantity [ˈkwɔntɪtɪ] n quantidade f; ~ **surveyor** n calculista m/f de obra
quarantine [ˈkwɔrntiːn] n quarentena
quarrel [ˈkwɔrl] n (argument) discussão f ♦ vi: **to** ~ **(with)** brigar (com); ~**some** adj brigão/gona
quarry [ˈkwɔrɪ] n (for stone) pedreira; (animal) presa, caça
quart [kwɔːt] n quarto de galão (1.136 l)
quarter [ˈkwɔːtə*] n quarto, quarta parte f; (of year) trimestre m; (district) bairro; (US: 25 cents) moeda de 25 centavos mpl de dólar ♦ vt dividir em quatro; (MIL: lodge) aquartelar; ~**s** npl (MIL) quartel m; (living ~s) alojamento; **a** ~ **of an hour** um quarto de hora; ~ **final** n quarta de final; ~**ly** adj trimestral ♦ adv trimestralmente
quartz [kwɔːts] n quartzo
quash [kwɔʃ] vt (verdict) anular
quasi- [ˈkweɪzaɪ] prefix quase-
quaver [ˈkweɪvə*] n (BRIT: MUS) colcheia ♦ vi tremer
quay [kiː] n (also: ~**side**) cais m
queasy [ˈkwiːzɪ] adj (sickly) enjoado

queen [kwiːn] n rainha; (also: ~ **bee**) abelha-mestra, rainha; (CARDS etc) dama; ~ **mother** n rainha-mãe f
queer [kwɪə*] adj (odd) esquisito, estranho ♦ n (inf: homosexual) bicha m (BR), maricas m inv (PT)
quell [kwɛl] vt (opposition) sufocar; (fears) abrandar, sufocar
quench [kwɛntʃ] vt: **to** ~ **one's thirst** matar a sede
querulous [ˈkwɛruləs] adj lamuriante
query [ˈkwɪərɪ] n pergunta ♦ vt questionar
quest [kwɛst] n busca
question [ˈkwɛstʃən] n pergunta; (doubt) dúvida; (issue) questão f; (in text) problema m ♦ vt (doubt) duvidar; (interrogate) interrogar, inquirir; **beyond** ~ sem dúvida; **out of the** ~ fora de cogitação, impossível; ~**able** adj discutível; (doubtful) duvidoso; ~ **mark** n ponto de interrogação
queue [kjuː] n (BRIT) n fila (BR), bicha (PT) ♦ vi (also: ~ **up**) fazer fila (BR) or bicha (PT)
quibble [ˈkwɪbl] vi: **to** ~ **about** or **over/with** tergiversar sobre/com
quick [kwɪk] adj rápido; (agile) ágil; (mind) sagaz, despachado ♦ n: **to cut sb to the** ~ ferir alguém; **be** ~! ande depressa!, vai rápido!; ~**en** vt apressar ♦ vi apressar-se; ~**ly** adv rapidamente, depressa; ~**sand** n areia movediça; ~**witted** adj perspicaz, vivo
quid [kwɪd] (BRIT: inf) n inv libra
quiet [ˈkwaɪət] adj (voice, music) baixo; (peaceful: place) tranqüilo; (person: calm) calmo; (not noisy: place) silencioso, (: person) calado; (silent) silencioso; (ceremony) discreto ♦ n (peacefulness) sossego; (silence) quietude f ♦ vt, vi (US) = ~**en**; ~**en** (also: ~**en down**) vi (grow calm) acalmar-se; (grow silent) calar-se ♦ vt tranqüilizar; fazer calar; ~**ly** adv silenciosamente; (talk) baixo
quilt [kwɪlt] n acolchoado, colcha; (continental) ~ (BRIT) edredom m (BR), edredão m (PT)
quin [kwɪn] n abbr = **quintuplet**
quintuplets [kwɪnˈtjuːplɪts] npl quíntuplos mpl
quip [kwɪp] n escárnio, dito espirituoso
quirk [kwəːk] n peculiaridade f
quit [kwɪt] (pt, pp quit or ~**ted**) vt (smoking etc) parar; (job) deixar; (premises) desocupar ♦ vi desistir; (resign) demitir-se, deixar o emprego
quite [kwaɪt] adv (rather) bastante; (entirely) completamente, totalmente; **that's not** ~ **big enough** não é suficientemente grande; ~ **a few of them** um bom número deles; ~ **(so)!** exatamente!, isso mesmo!
quits [kwɪts] adj: ~ **(with)** quite (com); **let's call it** ~ ficamos quites

quiver ['kwɪvə*] *vi* estremecer

quiz [kwɪz] *n* concurso (de cultura geral) ♦ *vt* interrogar; **~zical** *adj* zombeteiro

quota ['kwəutə] *n* cota, quota

quotation [kwəu'teɪʃən] *n* citação *f*; (*estimate*) orçamento; **~ marks** *npl* aspas *fpl*

quote [kwəut] *n* citação *f*; (*estimate*) orçamento ♦ *vt* citar; (*price*) propor; (*figure, example*) citar, dar; **~s** *npl* aspas *fpl*

R

rabbi ['ræbaɪ] *n* rabino

rabbit ['ræbɪt] *n* coelho; **~ hutch** *n* coelheira

rabble ['ræbl] (*pej*) *n* povinho, ralé *f*

rabies ['reɪbiːz] *n* raiva

RAC (*BRIT*) *n abbr* (= *Royal Automobile Club*) ≈ TCB *m* (*BR*), ≈ ACP *m* (*PT*)

raccoon [rə'kuːn] *n* mão-pelada *m*, guaxinim *m*

race [reɪs] *n* corrida *f*; (*species*) raça ♦ *vt* (*horse*) fazer correr ♦ *vi* (*compete*) competir; (*run*) correr; (*pulse*) bater rapidamente; **~ car** (*US*) *n* = **racing car**; **~ car driver** (*US*) *n* = **racing driver**; **~course** *n* hipódromo; **~horse** *n* cavalo de corridas; **~track** *n* pista de corridas; (*for cars*) autódromo

racing ['reɪsɪŋ] *n* corrida; **~ car** (*BRIT*) *n* carro de corrida; **~ driver** (*BRIT*) *n* piloto/a de corrida

racism ['reɪsɪzəm] *n* racismo; **racist** (*pej*) *adj, n* racista *m/f*

rack [ræk] *n* (*also*: **luggage ~**) bagageiro; (*shelf*) estante *f*; (*also*: **roof ~**) xalmas *fpl*, porta-bagagem *m*; (*dish* ~) secador *m* de prato ♦ *vt*: **~ed by** (*pain, anxiety*) tomado por; **to ~ one's brains** quebrar a cabeça

racket ['rækɪt] *n* (*for tennis*) raquete *f* (*BR*), raqueta (*PT*); (*noise*) barulheira, zoeira; (*swindle*) negócio ilegal, fraude *f*

racoon [rə'kuːn] *n* = **raccoon**

racquet ['rækɪt] *n* raquete *f* (*BR*), raqueta (*PT*)

racy ['reɪsɪ] *adj* ousado, picante

radiant ['reɪdɪənt] *adj* radiante, brilhante

radiate ['reɪdɪeɪt] *vt* irradiar ♦ *vi* difundir-se, estender-se

radiation [reɪdɪ'eɪʃən] *n* radiação *f*

radiator ['reɪdɪeɪtə*] *n* radiador *m*

radical ['rædɪkl] *adj* radical

radii ['reɪdɪaɪ] *npl of* **radius**

radio ['reɪdɪəu] *n* rádio ♦ *vt*: **to ~ sb** comunicar-se por rádio com alguém

radio... [reɪdɪəu] *prefix* radio...; **~active** *adj* radioativo; **~ station** *n* emissora, estação *f* de rádio

radish ['rædɪʃ] *n* rabanete *m*

radius ['reɪdɪəs] (*pl* **radii**) *n* raio

RAF (*BRIT*) *n abbr* = **Royal Air Force**

raffle ['ræfl] *n* rifa

raft [rɑːft] *n* balsa

rafter ['rɑːftə*] *n* viga, caibro

rag [ræg] *n* trapo; (*torn cloth*) farrapo; (*pej*: *newspaper*) jornaleco; (*UNIVERSITY*) atividades estudantis beneficentes; **~s** *npl* (*torn clothes*) trapos *mpl*, farrapos *mpl*; **~-and-bone man** (*BRIT*: *irreg*) *n* = **~man**; **~ doll** *n* boneca de trapo

rage [reɪdʒ] *n* (*fury*) raiva, furor *m* ♦ *vi* (*person*) estar furioso; (*storm*) assolar; (*debate*) continuar calorosamente; **it's all the ~** é a última moda

ragged ['rægɪd] *adj* (*edge*) irregular, desigual; (*clothes*) puído, gasto; (*appearance*) esfarrapado, andrajoso

ragman ['rægmæn] (*irreg*) *n* negociante *m* de trastes

raid [reɪd] *n* (*MIL*) incursão *f*; (*criminal*) assalto; (*attack*) ataque *m*; (*by police*) batida ♦ *vt* invadir, atacar; assaltar; atacar; fazer uma batida em

rail [reɪl] *n* (*on stair*) corrimão *m*; (*on bridge*) parapeito, anteparo; (*of ship*) amurada; **~s** *npl* (*for train*) trilhos *mpl*; **by ~** de trem (*BR*), por caminho de ferro (*PT*); **~ing(s)** *n(pl)* grade *f*; **~road** (*US*) *n* = **~way**; **~way** *n* estrada (*BR*) *or* caminho (*PT*) de ferro; **~way line** (*BRIT*) *n* linha de trem (*BR*) *or* de comboio (*PT*); **~wayman** (*BRIT*: *irreg*) *n* ferroviário; **~way station** (*BRIT*) *n* estação *f* ferroviária (*BR*) *or* de caminho de ferro (*PT*)

rain [reɪn] *n* chuva ♦ *vi* chover; **it's ~ing** está chovendo (*BR*), está a chover (*PT*); **~bow** *n* arco-íris *m inv*; **~coat** *n* impermeável *m*, capa de chuva; **~drop** *n* gota de chuva; **~fall** *n* chuva; (*measurement*) pluviosidade *f*; **~forest** *n* floresta tropical; **~y** *adj* chuvôso; **a ~y day** um dia de chuva

raise [reɪz] *n* aumento ♦ *vt* (*lift*) levantar; (*salary, production*) aumentar; (*morale, standards*) melhorar; (*doubts*) suscitar, despertar; (*cattle, family*) criar; (*crop*) cultivar, plantar; (*army*) recrutar, alistar; (*funds*) organizar-se; (*loan*) levantar, obter; **to ~ one's voice** levantar a voz

raisin ['reɪzn] *n* passa, uva seca

rake [reɪk] *n* ancinho ♦ *vt* (*garden*) revolver *or* limpar com o ancinho; (*with machine gun*) varrer

rally ['rælɪ] *n* (*POL etc*) comício; (*AUT*) rally *m*, rali *m*; (*TENNIS*) rebatida ♦ *vt* reunir ♦ *vi* reorganizar-se; (*sick person, Stock Exchange*) recuperar-se; **~ round** *vt fus* dar apoio a

RAM [ræm] *n abbr* (*COMPUT*) (= *random access memory*) RAM *f*

ram [ræm] *n* carneiro ♦ *vt* (*push*) cravar; (*crash into*) colidir com

ramble ['ræmbl] *n* caminhada, excursão *f* a pé ♦ *vi* caminhar; (*talk*: *also*: **~ on**) divagar; **~r** *n* caminhante *m/f*; (*BOT*) roseira trepadeira; **rambling** *adj* (*speech*) desconexo, incoerente; (*house*) cheio de recantos; (*plant*) rastejante

ramp [ræmp] *n* (*incline*) rampa; **on/off ~** (*US: AUT*) entrada (para a rodovia)/saída da rodovia

rampage [ræm'peɪdʒ] *n*: **to be on the ~** alvoroçar-se

rampant ['ræmpənt] *adj* (*disease etc*) violento, implacável

rampart ['ræmpɑːt] *n* baluarte *m*; (*wall*) muralha

ramshackle ['ræmʃækl] *adj* caindo aos pedaços

ran [ræn] *pt of* **run**

ranch [rɑːntʃ] *n* rancho, fazenda, estância; **~er** *n* rancheiro/a, fazendeiro/a

rancid ['rænsɪd] *adj* rançoso, rância

rancour ['ræŋkə*] (*US* **rancor**) *n* rancor *m*

random ['rændəm] *adj* ao acaso, casual, fortuito; (*COMPUT, MATH*) aleatório ♦ *n*: **at ~** a esmo, aleatoriamente; **~ access** *n* (*COMPUT*) acesso randômico *or* aleatório

randy ['rændɪ] (*BRIT*: *inf*) *adj* de fogo

rang [ræŋ] *pt of* **ring**

range [reɪndʒ] *n* (*of mountains*) cadeia, cordilheira; (*of missile*) alcance *m*; (*of voice*) extensão *f*; (*series*) série *f*; (*of products*) gama, sortimento; (*MIL*: *also*: **shooting ~**) estande *m*; (*also*: **kitchen ~**) fogão *m* ♦ *vt* (*place*) colocar; (*arrange*) arrumar, ordenar ♦ *vi*: **to ~ over** (*extend*) estender-se por; **to ~ from ... to ...** variar de ... a ..., oscilar entre ... e ...

ranger ['reɪndʒə*] *n* guarda-florestal *m/f*

rank [ræŋk] *n* (*row*) fila, fileira; (*MIL*) posto; (*status*) categoria, posição *f*; (*BRIT*: *also*: **taxi ~**) ponto de táxi ♦ *vi*: **to ~ among** figurar entre ♦ *adj* fétido, malcheiroso; **the ~ and file** (*fig*) a gente comum

rankle ['ræŋkl] *vi* doer, magoar

ransack ['rænsæk] *vt* (*search*) revistar; (*plunder*) saquear, pilhar

ransom ['rænsəm] *n* resgate *m*; **to hold sb to ~** (*fig*) encostar alguém contra a parede

rant [rænt] *vi* arengar

rap [ræp] *vt* bater de leve ♦ *n*: **~** (**music**) rap *m*

rape [reɪp] *n* estupro; (*BOT*) colza ♦ *vt* violentar, estuprar

rapid ['ræpɪd] *adj* rápido; **~s** *npl* (*GEO*) cachoeira

rapist ['reɪpɪst] *n* estuprador *m*

rapport [ræ'pɔː*] *n* harmonia, afinidade *f*

rapture ['ræptʃə*] *n* êxtase *m*, arrebatamento; **rapturous** *adj* (*applause*) entusiasta

rare [rɛə*] *adj* raro; (*CULIN*: *steak*) mal passado

raring ['rɛərɪŋ] *adj*: **to be ~ to go** (*inf*) estar louco para começar

rascal ['rɑːskl] *n* maroto, malandro

rash [ræʃ] *adj* impetuoso, precipitado ♦ *n* (*MED*) exantema *m*, erupção *f* cutânea; (*of events*) série *f*, torrente *f*

rasher ['ræʃə*] *n* fatia fina

raspberry ['rɑːzbərɪ] *n* framboesa

rasping ['rɑːspɪŋ] *adj*: **a ~ noise** um ruído áspero *or* irritante

rat [ræt] *n* rato (*BR*), ratazana (*PT*)

rate [reɪt] *n* (*ratio*) razão *f*; (*price*) preço, taxa; (: *of hotel*) diária; (*of interest, change*) taxa; (*speed*) velocidade *f* ♦ *vt* (*value*) taxar; (*estimate*) avaliar; **~s** *npl* (*BRIT*) imposto predial e territorial; (*fees*) pagamento; **to ~ sb/sth as** considerar alguém/algo como; **~able value** (*BRIT*) *n* valor *m* tributável (*de um imóvel*); **~payer** (*BRIT*) *n* contribuinte *m/f* de imposto predial

rather ['rɑːðə*] *adv* (*somewhat*) um tanto, meio; (*to some extent*) até certo ponto; (*more accurately*): **or ~** ou melhor; **it's ~ expensive** (*quite*) é meio caro; (*too*) é caro demais; **there's ~ a lot** há bastante *or* muito; **I would ~ go** preferiria *or* preferia ir

rating ['reɪtɪŋ] *n* (*assessment*) avaliação *f*; (*score*) classificação *f*; (*NAUT*: *BRIT*: *sailor*) marinheiro; **~s** *npl* (*RADIO, TV*) indice(s) *m(pl)* de audiência

ratio ['reɪʃɪəu] *n* razão *f*, proporção *f*

ration ['ræʃən] *n* ração *f* ♦ *vt* racionar; **~s** *npl* (*MIL*) mantimentos *mpl*, víveres *mpl*

rational ['ræʃənl] *adj* lógico; (*person*) sensato, razoável; **~e** *n* razão *f* fundamental

rat race *n*: **the ~** a competição acirrada na vida moderna

rattle ['rætl] *n* (*of door*) batida; (*of train etc*) chocalhada; (*of coins*) chocalhar *m*; (*object: for baby*) chocalho; ♦ *vi* (*small objects*) tamborilar; (*vehicle*): **to ~ along** mover-se ruidosamente ♦ *vt* sacudir, fazer bater; (*unnerve*) perturbar; **~snake** *n* cascavel *f*

raucous ['rɔːkəs] *adj* espalhafatoso, banelhento

ravage ['rævɪdʒ] *vt* devastar, estragar; **~s** *npl* estragos *mpl*

rave [reɪv] *vi* (*in anger*) encolerizar-se; (*MED*) delirar; (*with enthusiasm*): **to ~ about** vibrar com

raven ['reɪvən] *n* corvo

ravenous ['rævənəs] *adj* morto de fome, esfomeado

ravine [rə'viːn] *n* ravina, barranco

raving ['reɪvɪŋ] *adj*: **~ lunatic** doido/a varrido/a

ravishing ['rævɪʃɪŋ] *adj* encantador(a)

raw [rɔː] *adj* (*uncooked*) cru(a); (*not processed*) bruto; (*sore*) vivo; (*inexperienced*) inexperiente, novato; (*weather*) muito frio; **~ deal** (*inf*) *n*: **to get a ~ deal** levar a pior; **~ material** *n* matéria-prima

ray [reɪ] *n* raio; ~ **of hope** fio de esperança

rayon [ˈreɪɔn] *n* raiom *m*

raze [reɪz] *vt* arrasar, aniquilar

razor [ˈreɪzə*] *n* (*open*) navalha; (*safety* ~)
aparelho de barbear; (*electric*) aparelho
de barbear elétrico; ~ **blade** *n* gilete *m*
(*BR*), lâmina de barbear (*PT*)

Rd *abbr* = **road**

re [riː] *prep* referente a

reach [riːtʃ] *n* alcance *m*; (*of river etc*)
extensão *f* ♦ *vt* alcançar; (*arrive at: place*) chegar em; (: *agreement*) chegar a;
(*by telephone*) conseguir falar com ♦ *vi*
(*stretch out*) esticar-se; **within** ~ ao alcance (da mão); **out of** ~ fora de alcance; ~ **out** *vt* (*hand*) esticar ♦ *vi*: **to
** ~ **out for sth** estender *or* esticar a
mão para pegar (em) algo

react [riːˈækt] *vi* reagir; ~**ion** *n* reação *f*;
~**ions** *npl* (*reflexes*) reflexos *mpl*

reactor [riːˈæktə*] *n* (*also:* **nuclear** ~)
reator *m* nuclear

read [riːd, *pt, pp* red] (*pt, pp* **read**) *vi* ler
♦ *vt* ler; (*understand*) compreender;
(*study*) estudar; ~ **out** *vt* ler em voz
alta; ~**able** *adj* (*writing*) legível; (*book*)
que merece ser lido; ~**er** *n* leitor(a)
m/f; (*book*) livro de leituras; (*BRIT: at
university*) professor(a) *m/f* adjunto/a;
~**ership** *n* leitores mpl

readily [ˈrɛdɪlɪ] *adv* (*willingly*) de boa
vontade; (*easily*) facilmente; (*quickly*)
sem demora, prontamente

readiness [ˈrɛdɪnɪs] *n* (*willingness*) boa
vontade *f*; (*preparedness*) prontidão *f*; **in
** ~ (*prepared*) preparado, pronto

reading [ˈriːdɪŋ] *n* leitura; (*on instrument*) indicação *f*, registro (*BR*), registo
(*PT*)

readjust [riːəˈdʒʌst] *vt* reajustar ♦ *vi*
(*adapt*): **to** ~ **to** reorientar-se para

ready [ˈrɛdɪ] *adj* pronto, preparado; (*willing*) disposto; (*available*) disponível ♦ *n*:
at the ~ (*MIL*) pronto para atirar; **to
get** ~ *vi* preparar-se ♦ *vt* preparar; ~**-
made** *adj* (já) feito; (*clothes*) pronto; ~
money *n* dinheiro vivo *or* disponível;
~ **reckoner** (*BRIT*) *n* tabela de cálculos
feitos; ~**-to-wear** *adj* pronto, prêt à
porter *inv*

real [rɪəl] *adj* real; (*genuine*) verdadeiro,
autêntico; **in** ~ **terms** em termos reais;
~ **estate** *n* bens *mpl* imobiliários *or* de
raiz; ~**ist** *n* realista *m/f*; ~**istic** *adj*
realista

reality [riːˈælɪtɪ] *n* realidade *f*

realization [rɪəlaɪˈzeɪʃən] *n* (*fulfilment*)
realização *f*; (*understanding*) compreensão *f*; (*COMM*) conversão *f* em dinheiro,
realização

realize [ˈrɪəlaɪz] *vt* (*understand*) perceber;
(*fulfil, COMM*) realizar

really [ˈrɪəlɪ] *adv* (*for emphasis*) realmente; (*actually*): **what** ~ **happened?** o que

aconteceu na verdade?; ~**?** (*interest*) é
mesmo?; (*surprise*) verdade!; ~**!** (*annoyance*) realmente!

realm [rɛlm] *n* reino; (*fig*) esfera, domínio

realtor [ˈrɪəltə*] (*US*) *n* corretor(a) *m/f* de
imóveis (*BR*), agente *m/f* imobiliário/a
(*PT*)

reap [riːp] *vt* segar, ceifar; (*fig*) colher

reappear [riːəˈpɪə*] *vi* reaparecer

rear [rɪə*] *adj* traseiro, de trás ♦ *n* traseira ♦ *vt* criar ♦ *vi* (*also:* ~ **up**)
empinar-se

rearrange [riːəˈreɪndʒ] *vt* arrumar de
novo, reorganizar

rear-view mirror *n* (*AUT*) espelho retrovisor

reason [ˈriːzn] *n* (*cause*) razão *f*; (*ability*)
raciocínio; (*sense*) bom-senso ♦ *vi*: **to** ~
with sb argumentar com alguém, persuadir alguém; **it stands to** ~ **that** é
razoável *or* lógico que; ~**able** *adj* (*fair*)
razoável; (*sensible*) sensato; ~**ably** *adv*
razoavelmente; sensatamente; ~**ed** *adj*
fundamentado; ~**ing** *n* raciocínio

reassurance [riːəˈʃuərəns] *n* garantia

reassure [riːəˈʃuə*] *vt* tranqüilizar; **to** ~
sb of reafirmar a confiança de alguém
acerca de; **reassuring** *adj* animador(a),
tranqüilizador(a)

rebate [ˈriːbeɪt] *n* devolução *f*

rebel [*n* ˈrɛbl, *vi* rɪˈbɛl] *n* rebelde *m/f* ♦
vi rebelar-se; ~**lion** *n* rebelião *f*, revolta; ~**lious** *adj* insurreto; (*behaviour*) rebelde

rebound [*vi* rɪˈbaund, *n* ˈriːbaund] *vi* (*ball*)
ressaltar ♦ *n*: **on the** ~ ressalto; (*person*): **she married him on the** ~ ela
casou com ele logo após o rompimento
do casamento (*or* relacionamento) anterior

rebuff [rɪˈbʌf] *n* repulsa, recusa

rebuild [riːˈbɪld] (*irreg*) *vt* reconstruir;
(*economy, confidence*) recuperar

rebuke [rɪˈbjuːk] *vt* repreender

rebut [rɪˈbʌt] *vt* refutar

recall [rɪˈkɔːl] *vt* recordar, lembrar; (*parliament*) reunir de volta; (*ambassador*)
chamar de volta ♦ *n* (*memory*) recordação *f*, lembrança; (*of ambassador*) chamada (de volta)

recant [rɪˈkænt] *vi* retratar-se

recap [ˈriːkæp] *vt* sintetizar ♦ *vi* recapitular

recapitulate [riːkəˈpɪtjuleɪt] *vt, vi* = **recap**

recapture [riːˈkæptʃə*] *vt* (*town*) retomar,
recobrar; (*atmosphere*) recriar

recd. *abbr* = **received**

recede [rɪˈsiːd] *vi* (*tide*) baixar; (*lights*) diminuir; (*memory*) enfraquecer; (*hair*) escassear; **receding** *adj* (*chin*) metido *or*
puxado para dentro; (*hair*) que está es-
casseando nas têmporas

receipt [rɪˈsiːt] *n* recibo; (*act*) recebimento (BR), recepção f (PT); ~s npl (COMM) receitas fpl

receive [rɪˈsiːv] vt receber; (guest) acolher; (wound, criticism) sofrer; ~r n (TEL) fone m (BR), auscultador m (PT); (RADIO, TV) receptor m; (of stolen goods) receptador(a) m/f; (COMM) curador(a) m/f síndico/a de massa falida

recent [ˈriːsnt] adj recente; ~ly adv recentemente; (in recent times) ultimamente

receptacle [rɪˈsɛptɪkl] n receptáculo, recipiente m

reception [rɪˈsɛpʃən] n recepção f; (welcome) acolhida; ~ desk n (mesa de) recepção f; ~ist n recepcionista m/f

recess [rɪˈsɛs] n (in room) recesso, vão m; (secret place) esconderijo; (POL etc: holiday) férias fpl

recession [rɪˈsɛʃən] n recessão f

recharge [rɪˈtʃɑːdʒ] vt recarregar

recipe [ˈresɪpɪ] n receita

recipient [rɪˈsɪpɪənt] n recipiente m/f, recebedor(a) m/f; (of letter) destinatário/a

recite [rɪˈsaɪt] vt recitar

reckless [ˈrɛkləs] adj (driver) imprudente; (speed) imprudente, excessivo; (spending) irresponsável

reckon [ˈrɛkən] vt (calculate) calcular, contar; (think): I ~ that ... acho que ...; ~ on vt fus contar com; ~ing n (calculation) cálculo

reclaim [rɪˈkleɪm] vt (demand back) reivindicar; (land: from sea) aterrar; (waste materials) reaproveitar; **reclamation** n (of land) aterro

recline [rɪˈklaɪn] vi reclinar-se; **reclining** adj (seat) reclinável

recognition [rɛkəɡˈnɪʃən] n reconhecimento

recognize [ˈrɛkəɡnaɪz] vt reconhecer

recoil [vi rɪˈkɔɪl, n ˈriːkɔɪl] vi (person): to ~ from doing sth recusar-se a fazer algo ♦ n (of gun) coice m

recollect [rɛkəˈlɛkt] vt lembrar, recordar; ~ion n (memory) recordação f; (remembering) lembrança

recommend [rɛkəˈmɛnd] vt recomendar; ~ation n recomendação f

reconcile [ˈrɛkənsaɪl] vt reconciliar; (facts) conciliar, harmonizar; to ~ o.s. to sth resignar-se a or conformar-se com algo

reconnaissance [rɪˈkɔnɪsns] n (MIL) reconhecimento

reconnoitre [rɛkəˈnɔɪtə*] (US **reconnoiter**) vt (MIL) reconhecer

reconsider [riːkənˈsɪdə*] vt reconsiderar

reconstruct [riːkənˈstrʌkt] vt reconstruir; (event) reconstituir

record [n, adj ˈrɛkɔːd, vt rɪˈkɔːd] n (MUS) disco; (of meeting etc) ata, minuta; (COMPUT, of attendance) registro (BR), registo (PT); (written) história; (also: **criminal** ~) antecedentes mpl; (SPORT) recorde m ♦ vt (write down) anotar; (temperature, speed) registrar (BR), registar (PT); (MUS: song etc) gravar ♦ adj: in ~ time num tempo recorde; ~ off the ~ adj confidencial ♦ adv confidencialmente; ~ card n (in file) ficha; ~ed delivery letter (BRIT) n (POST) ≈ carta registrada (BR) or registada (PT); ~er n (MUS) flauta; ~ holder n (SPORT) detentor(a) m/f do recorde; ~ing n (MUS) gravação f; ~ player n toca-discos m inv (BR), gira-discos m inv (PT)

recount [rɪˈkaunt] vt relatar

re-count [n ˈriːkaunt, vt riːˈkaunt] n (POL: of votes) nova contagem f, recontagem f ♦ vt recontar

recoup [rɪˈkuːp] vt: to ~ one's losses recuperar-se dos prejuízos

recourse [rɪˈkɔːs] n: to have ~ to recorrer a

recover [rɪˈkʌvə*] vt recuperar ♦ vi (from illness) recuperar-se; (from shock) refazer-se; ~y n recuperação f; (MED) recuperação, melhora

recreation [rɛkrɪˈeɪʃən] n recreio; ~al adj recreativo

recruit [rɪˈkruːt] n recruta m/f; (in company) novato/a ♦ vt recrutar

rectangle [ˈrɛktæŋɡl] n retângulo

rector [ˈrɛktə*] n (REL) pároco; ~y n residência paroquial

recuperate [rɪˈkuːpəreɪt] vi recuperar-se

recur [rɪˈkəː*] vi repetir-se, ocorrer outra vez; (symptoms) reaparecer; ~rent adj repetido, periódico

recycle [riːˈsaɪkl] vt reciclar

red [rɛd] n vermelho; (POL: pej) vermelho/a ♦ adj vermelho; (hair) ruivo; (wine) tinto; to be in the ~ não ter fundos; ~ carpet treatment n: she was given the ~ carpet treatment ela foi recebida com todas as honras; R~ Cross n Cruz f Vermelha; ~currant n groselha; ~den vt avermelhar ♦ vi corar, ruborizar-se; ~dish adj avermelhado; (hair) arruivado

redeem [rɪˈdiːm] vt (REL) redimir; (sth in pawn) tirar do prego; (loan, fig: situation) salvar; ~ing adj: ~ing feature lado bom or que salva

redeploy [riːdɪˈplɔɪ] vt redistribuir

red: ~-haired adj ruivo; ~-handed adj: to be caught ~-handed ser apanhado em flagrante, ser flagrado; ~head n ruivo/a; ~ herring n (fig) pista falsa; ~-hot adj incandescente

redirect [riːdaɪˈrɛkt] vt (mail) endereçar de novo

red light n: to go through a ~ (AUT) avançar o sinal; **red-light district** n zona (de meretrício)

redo [riːˈduː] (irreg) vt refazer

redolent [ˈrɛdələnt] adj: ~ of que cheira a; (fig) que evoca

redouble [riːˈdʌbl] vt: to ~ one's ef-

forts redobrar os esforços
redress [rɪ'drɛs] n compensação f ♦ vt
retificar
Red Sea n: the ~ o mar Vermelho
redskin ['rɛdskɪn] n pele-vermelha m/f
red tape n (fig) papelada, burocracia
reduce [rɪ'djuːs] vt reduzir; (lower) rebaixar; "~ **speed now**" (AUT) "diminua a
velocidade"; **to ~ sb to** (silence, beg-
ging) levar alguém a; (tears) reduzir alguém a; **reduction** n redução f; (of price) abatimento
redundancy [rɪ'dʌndənsɪ] (BRIT) n (dismissal) demissão f; (unemployment) desemprego
redundant [rɪ'dʌndnt] adj (BRIT: worker)
desempregado; (detail, object) redundante, supérfluo; **to be made ~** ficar desempregado or sem trabalho
reed [riːd] n (BOT) junco; (MUS: of clarinet etc) palheta
reef [riːf] n (at sea) recife m
reek [riːk] vi: **to ~ (of)** cheirar (a), feder (a)
reel [riːl] n carretel m, bobina; (of film)
rolo, filme m; (on fishing-rod) carretilha;
(dance) dança típica da Escócia ♦ vi
(sway) cambalear, oscilar; **~ in** vt puxar enrolando a linha
ref [rɛf] (inf) n abbr = **referee**
refectory [rɪ'fɛktərɪ] n refeitório
refer [rɪ'fɜː*] vt (matter, problem): **to ~
sth to** submeter algo à apreciação de;
(person, patient): **to ~ sb to** encaminhar alguém a ♦ vi: **to ~ to** referir-se
or aludir a; (consult) recorrer a
referee [rɛfə'riː] n árbitro/a; (BRIT: for
job application) referência ♦ vt apitar
reference ['rɛfrəns] n referência; (mention) menção f; **with ~ to** com relação
a; (COMM: in letter) com referência a; ~
book n livro de consulta
referenda [rɛfə'rɛndə] npl of **referendum**
referendum [rɛfə'rɛndəm] (pl **referenda**)
n referendum m, plebiscito
refill [vt rɪ'fɪl, n 'riːfɪl] vt reencher; (lighter etc) reabastecer ♦ n (for pen) carga
nova
refine [rɪ'faɪn] vt refinar; **~d** adj refinado, culto
reflect [rɪ'flɛkt] vt refletir ♦ vi (think) refletir, meditar; **it ~s badly/well on
him** isso repercute mal/bem para ele;
~ion n reflexo; (thought, act) reflexão f;
(criticism): **~ion on** crítica de; **on ~ion**
pensando bem; **~or** n refletor m
reflex ['riːflɛks] adj reflexo ♦ n reflexo;
~ive adj (LING) reflexivo
reform [rɪ'fɔːm] n reforma ♦ vt reformar; **R~ation** n: the **R~ation** a Reforma; **~atory** (US) n reformatório
refrain [rɪ'freɪn] vi: **to ~ from doing**
abster-se de fazer ♦ n estribilho, refrão
m

refresh [rɪ'frɛʃ] vt refrescar; **~er
course** (BRIT) n curso de reciclagem; **~ing** adj
refrescante; (sleep) repousante; **~ments**
npl bebidas fpl (não-alcoólicas) e gulo-
seimas
refrigerator [rɪ'frɪdʒəreɪtə*] n refrigerador m, geladeira (BR), frigorífico (PT)
refuel [riː'fjuəl] vi reabastecer
refuge ['rɛfjuːdʒ] n refúgio; **to take ~
in** refugiar-se em
refugee [rɛfju'dʒiː] n refugiado/a
refund [n 'riːfʌnd, vt rɪ'fʌnd] n reembolso
♦ vt devolver, reembolsar
refurbish [riː'fɜːbɪʃ] vt renovar
refusal [rɪ'fjuːzl] n recusa, negativa;
first ~ primeira opção
refuse¹ [rɪ'fjuːz] vt recusar; (order)
recusar-se a ♦ vi recusar-se, negar-se;
(horse) recusar-se a pular a cerca
refuse² ['rɛfjuːs] n refugo, lixo; ~ **collection** n remoção f de lixo
regain [rɪ'geɪn] vt recuperar, recobrar
regal ['riːgl] adj real, régio; **~ia** n, npl
insígnias fpl reais
regard [rɪ'gɑːd] n (gaze) olhar m firme;
(attention) atenção f; (esteem) estima,
consideração f ♦ vt (consider) considerar; **to give one's ~s to** com as lembranças a; "**with kindest ~s**" "cordialmen-
te"; **as ~s, with ~ to** com relação a,
com respeito a, quanto a; **~ing** prep
com relação a; **~less** adv apesar de
tudo; **~less of** apesar de
régime [reɪ'ʒiːm] n regime m
regiment ['rɛdʒɪmənt] n regimento
region ['riːdʒən] n região f; **in the ~ of**
(fig) por volta de, ao redor de
register ['rɛdʒɪstə*] n registro (BR), registo (PT); (SCH) chamada ♦ vt registrar
(BR), registar (PT); (subj: instrument)
marcar, indicar ♦ vi (at hotel) registrar-
se (BR), registar-se (PT); (for work)
candidatar-se; (as student) inscrever-se;
(make impression) causar impressão;
~ed adj (letter, parcel) registrado (BR),
registado (PT); **~ed trademark** n marca registrada (BR) or registada (PT)
registrar ['rɛdʒɪstrɑː*] n oficial m/f de
registro (BR) or registo (PT), escrivão/
vã m/f; (in college) funcionário/a
administrativo/a sênior; (in hospital)
médico/a sênior
registration [rɛdʒɪs'treɪʃən] n (act) registro
(BR), registo (PT); (AUT: also: ~
number) número da placa
registry ['rɛdʒɪstrɪ] n registro (BR), registo (PT), cartório; ~ **office** (BRIT) n registro (BR) or registo (PT) civil, cartório; **to get married in a ~ office**
casar-se no civil
regret [rɪ'grɛt] n desgosto, pesar m ♦ vt
lamentar; (repent of) arrepender-se de;
~fully adv com pesar, pesarosamente;
~table adj deplorável
regular ['rɛgjulə*] adj regular; (frequent)

freqüente; (*usual*) habitual; (*soldier*) de linha ♦ *n* habitual *m/f*; ~**ly** *adv* regularmente; (*shaped*) simetricamente; (*often*) freqüentemente

regulate ['regjuleɪt] *vt* (*speed*) regular; (*spending*) controlar; (*TECH*) regular, ajustar; **regulation** *n* (*rule*) regra, regulamento; (*adjustment*) ajuste *m*

rehearsal [rɪ'hɜːsəl] *n* ensaio

rehearse [rɪ'hɜːs] *vt* ensaiar

reign [reɪn] *n* reinado; (*fig*) domínio ♦ *vi* reinar; imperar

reimburse [riːɪm'bɜːs] *vt* reembolsar

rein [reɪn] *n* (*for horse*) rédea

reindeer ['reɪndɪə*] *n inv* rena

reinforce [riːɪn'fɔːs] *vt* reforçar; ~**d** *adj* (*concrete*) armado; ~**ment** *n* reforço; ~**ments** *npl* (*MIL*) reforços *mpl*

reinstate [riːɪn'steɪt] *vt* (*worker*) readmitir; (*tax, law*) reintroduzir

reiterate [riː'ɪtəreɪt] *vt* reiterar, repetir

reject [*n* 'riːdʒekt, *vt* rɪ'dʒekt] *n* (*COMM*) artigo defeituoso ♦ *vt* rejeitar; (*offer of help*) recusar; (*goods*) refugar; ~**ion** *n* rejeição *f*; recusa

rejoice [rɪ'dʒɔɪs] *vi*: **to ~ at** *or* **over** regozijar-se *or* alegrar-se de

relapse [rɪ'læps] *n* (*MED*) recaída

relate [rɪ'leɪt] *vt* (*tell*) contar, relatar; (*connect*): **to ~ sth to** relacionar algo com ♦ *vi*: **to ~ to** relacionar-se com; ~**d** *adj* ligado a, relacionado a; **relating**: **relating to** *prep* relativo a, acerca de

relation [rɪ'leɪʃən] *n* (*person*) parente *m/f*; (*link*) relação *f*; ~**s** *npl* (*dealings*) relações *fpl*; (*relatives*) parentes *mpl*; ~**ship** *n* relacionamento; (*between two things*) relação *f*; (*also*: **family relationship**) parentesco

relative ['relətɪv] *n* parente *m/f* ♦ *adj* relativo; ~**ly** *adv* relativamente

relax [rɪ'læks] *vi* (*unwind*) descontrair-se; (*muscle*) relaxar-se ♦ *vt* (*grip*) afrouxar; (*control*) relaxar; (*mind, person*) descansar; ~**ation** *n* (*rest*) descanso; (*of muscle, control*) relaxamento; (*of grip*) afrouxamento; (*recreation*) lazer *m*; ~**ed** *adj* relaxado; (*tranquil*) descontraído

relay ['riːleɪ] *n* (*race*) (corrida de) revezamento ♦ *vt* (*message*) retransmitir

release [rɪ'liːs] *n* (*from prison*) libertação *f*; (*from obligation*) liberação *f*; (*of gas*) escape *m*; (*of water*) despejo; (*of film, book etc*) lançamento ♦ *vt* (*prisoner*) pôr em liberdade; (*book, film*) lançar; (*report, news*) publicar; (*gas etc*) soltar; (*free: from wreckage etc*) soltar; (*TECH: catch, spring etc*) desengatar, desapertar

relegate ['relɪgeɪt] *vt* relegar; (*SPORT*): **to be ~d** ser rebaixado

relent [rɪ'lent] *vi* (*yield*) ceder; ~**less** *adj* (*unceasing*) contínuo; (*determined*) implacável

relevant ['reləvənt] *adj* pertinente; ~ **to** relacionado com

reliability [rɪlaɪə'bɪlɪtɪ] *n* (*of person, firm*) confiabilidade *f*, seriedade *f*; (*of method, machine*) segurança; (*of news*) fidedignidade *f*

reliable [rɪ'laɪəbl] *adj* (*person, firm*: *digno*) de confiança, confiável, sério; (*method, machine*) seguro; (*news*) fidedigno; **reliably** *adv*: **to be reliably informed that ...** saber através de fonte segura que ...

reliance [rɪ'laɪəns] *n*: ~ (**on**) (*trust*) confiança (em), esperança (em); (*dependence*) dependência (de)

relic ['relɪk] *n* (*REL*) relíquia; (*of the past*) vestígio

relief [rɪ'liːf] *n* alívio; (*help, supplies*) ajuda, socorro; (*ART, GEO*) relevo

relieve [rɪ'liːv] *vt* (*pain, fear*) aliviar; (*bring help to*) ajudar, socorrer; (*take over from: gen*) substituir, revezar; (*: guard*) render; **to ~ sb of sth** (*load*) tirar algo de alguém; (*duties*) destituir alguém de algo; **to ~ o.s.** fazer as necessidades

religion [rɪ'lɪdʒən] *n* religião *f*; **religious** *adj* religioso

relinquish [rɪ'lɪŋkwɪʃ] *vt* abandonar; (*plan, habit*) renunciar a

relish ['relɪʃ] *n* (*CULIN*) condimento, tempero; (*enjoyment*) entusiasmo ♦ *vt* (*food etc*) saborear; (*thought*) ver com satisfação

relocate [riːləu'keɪt] *vt* deslocar ♦ *vi* deslocar-se

reluctant [rɪ'lʌktənt] *adj* relutante; ~**ly** *adv* relutantemente, de má vontade

rely on [rɪ'laɪ-] *vt fus* confiar em, contar com; (*be dependent on*) depender de

remain [rɪ'meɪn] *vi* (*survive*) sobreviver; (*stay*) ficar, permanecer; (*be left*) sobrar; (*continue*) continuar; ~**der** *n* resto, restante *m*; ~**ing** *adj* restante; ~**s** *npl* (*of body*) restos *mpl*; (*of meal*) sobras *fpl*; (*of building*) ruínas *fpl*

remand [rɪ'mɑːnd] *n*: **on ~** sob prisão preventiva ♦ *vt*: **to be ~ed in custody** continuar sob prisão preventiva, manter sob custódia; ~ **home** (*BRIT*) *n* instituição *f* do juizado de menores, reformatório

remark [rɪ'mɑːk] *n* observação *f*, comentário ♦ *vt* comentar; ~**able** *adj* (*outstanding*) extraordinário

remarry [riː'mærɪ] *vi* casar-se de novo

remedial [rɪ'miːdɪəl] *adj* de reforço; (*exercise*) terapêutico

remedy ['remədɪ] *n*: ~ (**for**) remédio (contra *or* a) ♦ *vt* remediar

remember [rɪ'membə*] *vt* lembrar-se de, lembrar; (*bear in mind*) ter em mente; (*send greetings*): ~ **me to her** dê lembranças a ela

remembrance [rɪ'membrəns] *n* (*memory*) memória; (*souvenir*) lembrança, recordação *f*

remind [rɪ'maɪnd] *vt*: **to ~ sb to do sth** lembrar a alguém que tem de fazer algo; **to ~ sb of sth** lembrar algo a alguém, lembrar alguém de algo; **~er** *n* lembrança; (*letter*) carta de advertência

reminisce [rɛmɪ'nɪs] *vi* relembrar velhas histórias; **~nt** *adj*: **to be ~nt of sth** lembrar algo

remiss [rɪ'mɪs] *adj* negligente, desleixado

remission [rɪ'mɪʃən] *n* remissão *f*; (*of sentence*) diminuição *f*

remit [rɪ'mɪt] *vt* remeter, enviar, mandar; **~tance** *n* remessa

remnant ['rɛmnənt] *n* resto; (*of cloth*) retalho; **~s** *npl* (*COMM*) retalhos *mpl*

remorse [rɪ'mɔːs] *n* remorso; **~ful** *adj* arrependido; **~less** *adj* (*fig*) implacável

remote [rɪ'məut] *adj* remoto; (*person*) reservado, afastado; **~ control** *n* controle *m* remoto; **~ly** *adv* remotamente; (*slightly*) levemente

remould ['riːməuld] (*BRIT*) *n* (*tyre*) pneu *m* recauchutado

removal [rɪ'muːvəl] *n* (*taking away*) remoção *f*; (*BRIT: from house*) mudança; (*from office: sacking*) afastamento, demissão *f*; (*MED*) extração *f*; **~ van** (*BRIT*) *n* caminhão *m* (*BR*) *or* camião *m* (*PT*) de mudanças

remove [rɪ'muːv] *vt* tirar, retirar; (*clothing*) tirar; (*stain*) remover; (*employee*) afastar, demitir; (*name from list, obstacle*) eliminar, remover; (*doubt, abuse*) afastar; (*MED*) extrair, extirpar; **~rs** (*BRIT*) *npl* (*company*) companhia de mudanças

Renaissance [rɪ'neɪsɔns] *n*: **the ~** a Renascença

render ['rɛndə*] *vt* (*thanks*) trazer; (*service*) prestar; (*make*) fazer, tornar; **~ing** *n* interpretação *f*

rendezvous ['rɔndɪvuː] *n* encontro; (*place*) ponto de encontro

renew [rɪ'njuː] retomar, recomeçar; (*loan etc*) prorrogar; (*negotiations*) reatar; **~able** *adj* (*energy*) renovável; **~al** *n* (*of contract*) renovação *f*; (*resumption*) retomada

renounce [rɪ'nauns] *vt* renunciar a

renovate ['rɛnəveɪt] *vt* renovar; (*house*) reformar

renown [rɪ'naun] *n* renome *m*; **~ed** *adj* renomado, famoso

rent [rɛnt] *n* aluguel *m* (*BR*), aluguer *m* (*PT*) ♦ *vt* (*also*: **~ out**) alugar; **~al** *n* (*for television, car*) aluguel *m* (*BR*), aluguer *m* (*PT*)

renunciation [rɪnʌnsɪ'eɪʃən] *n* renúncia

rep [rɛp] *n abbr* (*COMM*) = **representative**; (*THEATRE*) = **repertory**

repair [rɪ'pɛə*] *n* reparação *f*, conserto ♦ *vt* consertar; **in good/bad ~** em bom/mau estado; **~ kit** *n* caixa de ferramentas

repay [riː'peɪ] (*irreg*) *vt* (*money*) reembol-

sar, restituir; (*person*) pagar de volta; (*debt*) saldar, liquidar; (*sb's efforts*) corresponder, retribuir; (*favour*) retribuir; **~ment** *n* reembolso; (*of debt*) pagamento

repeal [rɪ'piːl] *n* (*of law*) revogação *f* ♦ *vt* revogar

repeat [rɪ'piːt] *n* (*RADIO, TV*) repetição *f* ♦ *vt* repetir; (*COMM: order*) renovar ♦ *vi* repetir-se

repel [rɪ'pɛl] *vt* repelir; (*disgust*) repugnar; **~lent** *adj* repugnante ♦ *n*: **insect ~lent** repelente *m* de insetos

repent [rɪ'pɛnt] *vi* arrepender-se; **~ance** *n* arrependimento

repertoire ['rɛpətwɑː*] *n* repertório

repertory ['rɛpətərɪ] *n* (*also*: **~ theatre**) teatro de repertório

repetitive [rɪ'pɛtɪtɪv] *adj* repetitivo

replace [rɪ'pleɪs] *vt* (*put back*) repor, devolver; (*take the place of*) substituir; **~ment** *n* (*substitution*) substituição *f*; (*substitute*) substituto/a

replay ['riːpleɪ] *n* (*of match*) partida decisiva; (*TV: also*: **action ~**) replay *m*

replenish [rɪ'plɛnɪʃ] *vt* (*glass*) reencher; (*stock etc*) completar, prover

replete [rɪ'pliːt] *adj* (*well-fed*) cheio, empanturrado

replica ['rɛplɪkə] *n* réplica, cópia, reprodução *f*

reply [rɪ'plaɪ] *n* resposta ♦ *vi* responder; **~ coupon** *n* cartão-resposta *m*

report [rɪ'pɔːt] *n* relatório; (*PRESS etc*) reportagem *f*; (*BRIT: also*: **school ~**) boletim *m* escolar; (*of gun*) estampido, detonação *f* ♦ *vt* informar sobre; (*PRESS etc*) fazer uma reportagem sobre; (*bring to notice*) comunicar, anunciar ♦ *vi* (*make a report*): **to ~ (on)** apresentar um relatório (sobre); (*present o.s.*): **to ~ (to sb)** apresentar-se (a alguém); (*be responsible to*): **to ~ to sb** obedecer as ordens de alguém; **~ card** (*US, SCOTTISH*) *n* boletim *m* escolar; **~edly** *adv*: **she is ~edly living in Spain** dizem que ela mora na Espanha; **~er** *n* repórter *m/f*

repose [rɪ'pəuz] *n*: **in ~** em repouso

reprehensible [rɛprɪ'hɛnsɪbl] *adj* repreensível, censurável, condenável

represent [rɛprɪ'zɛnt] *vt* representar; (*constitute*) constituir; (*COMM*) ser representante de; **~ation** *n* representação *f*; (*picture, statue*) representação, retrato; (*petition*) petição *f*; **~ations** *npl* (*protest*) reclamação *f*, protesto; **~ative** *n* representante *m/f*; (*US: POL*) deputado/a ♦ *adj*: **~ative of** representativo (de)

repress [rɪ'prɛs] *vt* reprimir; **~ion** *n* repressão *f*; **~ive** *adj* repressivo

reprieve [rɪ'priːv] *n* (*LAW*) suspensão *f* temporária; (*fig*) adiamento

reprimand ['rɛprɪmɑːnd] *n* reprimenda ♦ *vt* repreender, censurar

reprint [*n* 'riːprɪnt, *vt* riː'prɪnt] *n* reimpressão f ♦ vt reimprimir

reprisal [rɪ'praɪzl] n represália

reproach [rɪ'prəʊtʃ] n repreensão f, censura ♦ vt: to ~ sb for sth repreender alguém por algo; ~ful adj repreensivo, acusatório

reproduce [riːprə'djuːs] vt reproduzir ♦ vi reproduzir-se

reproof [rɪ'pruːf] n reprovação f, repreensão f

reprove [rɪ'pruːv] vt repreender

reptile ['rɛptaɪl] n réptil m

republic [rɪ'pʌblɪk] n república; ~an adj, n republicano/a; (US: POL): R~an membro/a do Partido Republicano

repudiate [rɪ'pjuːdɪeɪt] vt (accusation) rejeitar, negar; (violence) repudiar

repugnant [rɪ'pʌɡnənt] adj repugnante, repulsivo

repulse [rɪ'pʌls] vt repelir

reputable ['rɛpjutəbl] adj (make etc) bem conceituado, de confiança; (person) honrado, respeitável

reputation [rɛpju'teɪʃən] n reputação f

reputed [rɪ'pjuːtɪd] adj suposto, pretenso; ~ly adv segundo se diz, supostamente

request [rɪ'kwɛst] n pedido; (formal) petição f ♦ vt: to ~ sth of or from sb pedir algo a alguém; (formally) solicitar algo a alguém; ~ stop (BRIT) n (for bus) parada não obrigatória

require [rɪ'kwaɪə*] vt (need: subj: person) precisar de, necessitar; (: thing, situation) requerer, exigir; (want) pedir; (order): to ~ sb to do sth/sth of sb exigir que alguém faça algo/algo de alguém; ~ment n (need) necessidade f; (want) pedido

requisite ['rɛkwɪzɪt] n requisito ♦ adj necessário, indispensável

requisition [rɛkwɪ'zɪʃən] n: ~ (for) requerimento (para) ♦ vt (MIL) requisitar, confiscar

rescind [rɪ'sɪnd] vt (contract) rescindir; (law) revogar

rescue ['rɛskjuː] n salvamento, resgate m ♦ vt: to ~ (from) resgatar (de); (save, fig) salvar (de); ~ party n grupo or expedição f de resgate

research [rɪ'sɜːtʃ] n pesquisa ♦ vt pesquisar; ~er n pesquisador(a) m/f

resemblance [rɪ'zɛmbləns] n semelhança

resemble [rɪ'zɛmbl] vt parecer-se com

resent [rɪ'zɛnt] vt (attitude) ressentir-se de; (person) estar ressentido com; ~ful adj ressentido

reservation [rɛzə'veɪʃən] n reserva

reserve [rɪ'zɜːv] n reserva; (SPORT) suplente m/f, reserva m/f (BR) ♦ vt reservar; ~s npl (MIL) (tropas fpl da) reserva; (COMM) reserva; in ~ de reserva; ~d adj reservado

reservoir ['rɛzəvwɑː*] n represa

reshuffle [riː'ʃʌfl] n: Cabinet ~ (POL) reforma ministerial

reside [rɪ'zaɪd] vi residir

residence ['rɛzɪdəns] n residência; (formal: home) domicílio; ~ permit (BRIT) n autorização f de residência

resident ['rɛzɪdənt] n (of country, town) habitante m/f; (in hotel) hóspede m/f ♦ adj (population) permanente; (doctor) interno, residente; ~ial adj residencial

residue ['rɛzɪdjuː] n resto

resign [rɪ'zaɪn] vt renunciar a, demitir-se de ♦ vi: to ~ (from) demitir-se (de); to ~ o.s. to resignar-se a; ~ation f; (state of mind) resignação f; ~ed adj resignado

resilience [rɪ'zɪlɪəns] n (of material) elasticidade f; (of person) resistência

resilient [rɪ'zɪlɪənt] adj (person) forte; (material) resistente

resin ['rɛzɪn] n resina

resist [rɪ'zɪst] vt resistir a

resolute ['rɛzəluːt] adj resoluto, firme; (refusal) firme

resolution [rɛzə'luːʃən] n resolução f; (of problem) solução f

resolve [rɪ'zɔlv] n resolução f ♦ vt resolver ♦ vi: to ~ to do resolver-se a fazer; ~d adj decidido

resort [rɪ'zɔːt] n local m turístico, estação f de veraneio; (recourse) recurso ♦ vi: to ~ to recorrer a; in the last ~ em último caso, em última instância

resound [rɪ'zaund] vi ressoar; ~ing adj retumbante

resource [rɪ'sɔːs] n (raw material) recurso natural; ~s npl (coal, money, energy) recursos mpl; ~ful adj engenhoso, habilidoso

respect [rɪs'pɛkt] n respeito ♦ vt respeitar; ~s npl (greetings) cumprimentos mpl; ~able adj respeitável; (large) considerável; (result, player) razoável; ~ful adj respeitoso

respective [rɪs'pɛktɪv] adj respectivo

respite ['rɛspaɪt] n pausa, folga

resplendent [rɪs'plɛndənt] adj resplandecente

respond [rɪs'pɔnd] vi (answer) responder; (react) reagir; **response** n resposta; reação f

responsibility [rɪspɔnsɪ'bɪlɪtɪ] n responsabilidade f; (duty) dever m

responsible [rɪs'pɔnsɪbl] adj sério, responsável; (job) de responsabilidade; (liable): ~ (for) responsável (por)

responsive [rɪs'pɔnsɪv] adj receptivo

rest [rɛst] n descanso, repouso; (pause) pausa, intervalo; (support) apoio; (remainder) resto; (MUS) descansar; (stop) parar; (be supported): to ~ on apoiar-se em ♦ vt descansar; (lean): to ~ sth on/against apoiar algo em or sobre/contra; the ~ of them os outros; it ~s with him to do it cabe a ele fazê-lo

restaurant ['rɛstərɒŋ] n restaurante m;

~ **car** (*BRIT*) *n* vagão- restaurante *m*

restful ['rɛstful] *adj* tranqüilo, repousante

rest home *n* asilo, casa de repouso

restitution [rɛstɪ'tjuːʃən] *n*: **to make ~ to sb for sth** indenizar alguém por algo

restive ['rɛstɪv] *adj* inquieto, impaciente; (*horse*) rebelão/ona, teimoso

restless ['rɛstlɪs] *adj* desassossegado, irrequieto

restore [rɪ'stɔː*] *vt* (*building, order*) restaurar; (*sth stolen*) restituir; (*health*) restabelecer

restrain [rɪs'treɪn] *vt* (*feeling*) reprimir; (*growth, inflation*) refrear; (*person*): **to ~ (from doing)** impedir (de fazer); **~ed** *adj* (*style*) moderado, comedido; (*person*) comedido; **~t** *n* (*restriction*) restrição *f*; (*moderation*) moderação *f*, comedimento; (*of style*) sobriedade *f*

restrict [rɪs'trɪkt] *vt* restringir, limitar; (*people, animals*) confinar; (*activities*) limitar; **~ion** *n* restrição *f*, limitação *f*

rest room (*US*) *n* banheiro (*BR*), lavabo (*PT*)

result [rɪ'zʌlt] *n* resultado ♦ *vi*: **to ~ in** resultar em; **as a ~ of** como resultado *or* conseqüência de

resume [rɪ'zjuːm] *vt* (*work, journey*) retomar, recomeçar ♦ *vi* recomeçar

résumé ['reɪzjuːmeɪ] *n* (*summary*) resumo; (*US*: *curriculum vitae*) curriculum vitae *m*, currículo

resumption [rɪ'zʌmpʃən] *n* retomada

resurgence [rɪ'səːdʒəns] *n* ressurgimento

resurrection [rɛzə'rɛkʃən] *n* ressurreição *f*

resuscitate [rɪ'sʌsɪteɪt] *vt* (*MED*) ressuscitar, reanimar

retail ['riːteɪl] *adj* a varejo (*BR*), a retalho (*PT*) ♦ *adv* a varejo (*BR*), a retalho (*PT*); **~er** *n* varejista *m/f* (*BR*), retalhista *m/f* (*PT*); **~ price** *n* preço no varejo (*BR*) *or* de venda a retalho (*PT*)

retain [rɪ'teɪn] *vt* (*keep*) reter, conservar; **~er** *n* (*fee*) adiantamento

retaliate [rɪ'tælɪeɪt] *vi*: **to ~ (against)** revidar (contra); **retaliation** *n* represálias *fpl*, vingança

retch [rɛtʃ] *vi* fazer esforço para vomitar

retentive [rɪ'tɛntɪv] *adj* (*memory*) tenaz, de anjo

reticent ['rɛtɪsnt] *adj* reservado

retire [rɪ'taɪə*] *vi* aposentar-se; (*withdraw*) retirar-se; (*go to bed*) deitar-se; **~d** *adj* aposentado (*BR*), reformado (*PT*); **~ment** *n* aposentadoria (*BR*), reforma (*PT*); **retiring** *adj* de saída; (*shy*) acanhado, retraído

retort [rɪ'tɔːt] *vi* replicar, retrucar

retrace [riː'treɪs] *vt*: **to ~ one's steps** voltar sobre (os) seus passos, refazer o mesmo caminho

retract [rɪ'trækt] *vt* (*statement*) retirar, retratar; (*claws*) encolher; (*undercarriage*, *aerial*) recolher

retrain [riː'treɪn] *vt* reciclar; **~ing** *n* readaptação *f* profissional, reciclagem *f*

retread ['riːtrɛd] *n* pneu *m* recauchutado

retreat [rɪ'triːt] *n* (*place*) retiro; (*act*) retirada ♦ *vi* retirar-se

retribution [rɛtrɪ'bjuːʃən] *n* desforra, revide *m*, vingança

retrieval [rɪ'triːvəl] *n* recuperação *f*

retrieve [rɪ'triːv] *vt* (*sth lost*) reaver, recuperar; (*situation, honour*) salvar; (*error, loss*) reparar; **~r** *n* cão *m* de busca, perdigueiro

retrospect ['rɛtrəspɛkt] *n*: **in ~** retrospectivamente, em retrospecto; **~ive** *adj* retrospectivo; (*law*) retroativo

return [rɪ'təːn] *n* regresso, volta; (*of sth stolen etc*) devolução *f*; (*FINANCE*: *from land, shares*) rendimento ♦ *cpd* (*journey*) de volta; (*BRIT*: *ticket*) de ida e volta; (*match*) de revanche ♦ *vi* voltar, regressar; (*symptoms*) voltar; (*regain*): **to ~ to** (*consciousness*) recobrar; (*power*) retornar a ♦ *vt* devolver; (*favour etc*) retribuir; (*verdict*) proferir, anunciar; (*POL*: *candidate*) eleger; **~s** *npl* (*COMM*) receita; **in ~ (for)** em troca (de); **many happy ~s (of the day)!** parabéns!; **by ~ (of post)** por volta do correio

reunion [riː'juːnɪən] *n* (*family*) reunião *f*; (*two people, class*) reencontro

reunite [riːjuː'naɪt] *vt* reunir; (*reconcile*) reconciliar

rev [rɛv] *n abbr* (*AUT*: = *revolution*) revolução *f* ♦ *vt* (*also*: ~ **up**) aumentar a velocidade de

revamp ['riː'væmp] *vt* dar um jeito em

reveal [rɪ'viːl] *vt* revelar; (*make visible*) mostrar; **~ing** *adj* revelador(a)

reveille [rɪ'vælɪ] *n* (*MIL*) toque *m* de alvorada

revel ['rɛvl] *vi*: **to ~ in sth/in doing sth** deleitar-se com algo/em fazer algo

revelation [rɛvə'leɪʃən] *n* revelação *f*

revelry ['rɛvəlrɪ] *n* festança, folia

revenge [rɪ'vɛndʒ] *n* vingança, desforra; **to take ~ on** vingar-se de

revenue ['rɛvənjuː] *n* receita, renda

reverberate [rɪ'vəːbəreɪt] *vi* (*sound*) ressoar, repercutir, ecoar; (*fig*) repercutir

revere [rɪ'vɪə*] *vt* reverenciar, venerar

reverend ['rɛvərənd] *adj* (*in titles*) reverendo

reversal [rɪ'vəːsl] *n* (*of order*) reversão *f*; (*of direction*) mudança em sentido contrário; (*of decision*) revogação *f*; (*of roles*) inversão *f*

reverse [rɪ'vəːs] *n* (*opposite*) contrário; (*of cloth*) avesso; (*of coin*) reverso; (*of paper*) dorso; (*AUT*: *also*: ~ **gear**) marcha à ré (*BR*), marcha atrás (*PT*); (*setback*) revés *m*, derrota ♦ *adj* (*order*) inverso, oposto; (*direction*) contrário; (*process*) inverso ♦ *vt* inverter; (*position*) mudar; (*process, decision*) revogar; (*car*) dar marcha-re em ♦ *vi* (*BRIT: AUT*) dar (marcha à) ré (*BR*), fazer marcha atrás (*PT*); **~-charge call** (*BRIT*) *n* (*TEL*) ligação *f* a cobrar; **reversing lights** (*BRIT*) *npl* luzes *fpl* de ré (*BR*), luzes *fpl* de marcha atrás (*PT*)

revert [rɪ'vɜːt] *vi*: **to ~ to** voltar a; (*LAW*) reverter a

review [rɪ'vjuː] *n* (*magazine, MIL*) revista; (*of book, film*) crítica, resenha; (*examination*) recapitulação *f*, exame *m* ♦ *vt* rever, examinar; (*MIL*) passar em revista; (*book, film*) fazer a crítica *or* resenha de; **~er** *n* crítico/a

revile [rɪ'vaɪl] *vt* insultar

revise [rɪ'vaɪz] *vt* (*manuscript*) corrigir; (*opinion, procedure*) alterar; (*price*) revisar; **revision** *n* correção *f*; (*for exam*) revisão *f*

revitalize [riː'vaɪtəlaɪz] *vt* revitalizar, revivificar

revival [rɪ'vaɪvəl] *n* (*recovery*) restabelecimento; (*of interest*) renascença, renascimento; (*THEATRE*) reestréia; (*of faith*) despertar *m*

revive [rɪ'vaɪv] *vt* (*person*) reanimar, ressuscitar; (*economy*) recuperar; (*custom*) restabelecer, restaurar; (*hope, courage*) despertar; (*play*) reapresentar ♦ *vi* (*person: from faint*) voltar a si, recuperar os sentidos; (: *from ill-health*) recuperar-se; (*activity, economy*) reativar; (*hope, interest*) renascer

revolt [rɪ'vəult] *n* revolta, rebelião *f*, insurreição *f* ♦ *vi* revoltar-se ♦ *vt* causar aversão a, repugnar; **~ing** *adj* revoltante, repulsivo

revolution [revə'luːʃən] *n* revolução *f*; (*of wheel, earth*) rotação *f*

revolve [rɪ'vɔlv] *vi* girar

revolver [rɪ'vɔlvə*] *n* revólver *m*

revolving [rɪ'vɔlvɪŋ] *adj* giratório

revue [rɪ'vjuː] *n* (*THEATRE*) revista

revulsion [rɪ'vʌlʃən] *n* aversão *f*, repugnância

reward [rɪ'wɔːd] *n* recompensa ♦ *vt*: **to ~ (for)** recompensar *or* premiar (por); **~ing** *adj* (*fig*) gratificante, compensador(a)

rewind [riː'waɪnd] (*irreg*) *vt* (*tape*) voltar para trás

rewire [riː'waɪə*] *vt* (*house*) renovar a instalação elétrica de

rewrite [riː'raɪt] (*irreg*) *vt* reescrever, escrever de novo

rheumatism ['ruːmətɪzəm] *n* reumatismo

rhinoceros [raɪ'nɔsərəs] *n* rinoceronte *m*

rhubarb ['ruːbɑːb] *n* ruibarbo

rhyme [raɪm] *n* rima; (*verse*) verso(s) *m* (*pl*) rimado(s), poesia

rhythm ['rɪðm] *n* ritmo

rib [rɪb] *n* (*ANAT*) costela ♦ *vt* (*mock*) zombar de, encarnar em

ribbon ['rɪbən] *n* fita; **in ~s** (*torn*) em tirinhas, esfarrapado

rice [raɪs] *n* arroz *m*; **~ pudding** *n* arroz *m* doce

rich [rɪtʃ] *adj* rico; (*clothes*) valioso; (*soil*) fértil; (*food*) suculento, forte; (*colour*) intenso; (*voice*) suave, cheio ♦ *npl*: **the ~** os ricos; **~es** *npl* (*wealth*) riquezas *fpl*; **~ly** *adv* (*decorated*) ricamente; (*rewarded*) generosamente; (*deserved*) bem

rickets ['rɪkɪts] *n* raquitismo

rickety ['rɪkɪtɪ] *adj* fraco, sem firmeza

rickshaw ['rɪkʃɔː] *n* jinriquixá *m*

ricochet ['rɪkəʃeɪ] *vi* ricochetear

rid [rɪd] (*pt, pp* **rid**) *vt*: **to ~ sb of sth** livrar alguém de algo; **to get ~ of** livrar-se de; (*sth no longer required*) desfazer-se de

ridden ['rɪdn] *pp of* **ride**

riddle ['rɪdl] *n* (*conundrum*) adivinhação *f*; (*mystery*) enigma *m*, charada ♦ *vt*: **to be ~d with** estar cheio de

ride [raɪd] (*pt* **rode**, *pp* **ridden**) *n* (*gen*) passeio; (*on horse*) passeio a cavalo; (*distance covered*) percurso, trajeto ♦ *vi* (*as sport*) montar; (*go somewhere: on horse, bicycle*) ir (a cavalo, de bicicleta); (*journey: on bicycle, motorcycle, bus*) viajar ♦ *vt* (*a horse*) montar a; (*bicycle, motorcycle*) andar de; (*distance*) percorrer; **to ~ at anchor** (*NAUT*) estar ancorado; **to take sb for a ~** (*fig*) enganar alguém; **~r** *n* (*on horse: male*) cavaleiro; (: *female*) amazona; (*on bicycle*) ciclista *m/f*; (*on motorcycle*) motociclista *m/f*

ridge [rɪdʒ] *n* (*of hill*) cume *m*, topo; (*of roof*) cumeeira; (*wrinkle*) ruga

ridicule ['rɪdɪkjuːl] *n* escárnio, zombaria, mofa ♦ *vt* ridicularizar, zombar de; **ridiculous** *adj* ridículo

riding ['raɪdɪŋ] *n* equitação *f*

rife [raɪf] *adj*: **to be ~** ser comum; **to be ~ with** estar repleto de, abundar em

riffraff ['rɪfræf] *n* plebe *f*, ralé *f*, povinho

rifle ['raɪfl] *n* rifle *m*, fuzil *m* ♦ *vt* saquear; **~ through** *vt fus* vasculhar; **~ range** *n* campo de tiro; (*at fair*) tiro ao alvo

rift [rɪft] *n* fenda, fratura; (*in clouds*) brecha; (*fig: between friends*) desentendimento; (: *in party*) rompimento, divergência

rig [rɪg] *n* (*also*: **oil ~**) torre *f* de perfuração ♦ *vt* adulterar *or* falsificar os resultados de; **~ out** (*BRIT*) *vt*: **to ~ out as/in** ataviar *or* vestir como/com; **~ up** *vt* instalar, montar, improvisar; **~ging** *n* (*NAUT*) cordame *m*

right [raɪt] *adj* certo, correto; (*suitable*) adequado, conveniente; (: *decision*) certo; (*just*) justo; (*morally good*) bom; (*not left*) direito ♦ *n* direito; (*not left*) direita ♦ *adv* bem, corretamente; (*fairly*) adequadamente, justamente; (*not on the left*) à direita; (*exactly*): **~** now agora mesmo ♦ *vt* colocar em pé; (*correct*) corrigir, indireitar ♦ *excl* bom!; **to be ~**

(*person*) ter razão; (*answer, clock*) estar certo; **by ~s** por direito; **on the ~** à direita; **to be in the ~** ter razão; **~ away** imediatamente, logo, já; **~ in the middle** bem no meio; **~ angle** *n* ângulo reto; **~eous** *adj* justo, honrado; (*anger*) justificado; **~ful** *adj* (*heir*) legítimo; (*place*) justo, legítimo; **~-handed** *adj* destro; **~-hand man** *n* braço direito; **~-hand side** *n* lado direito; **~ly** *adv* (*with reason*) com razão; **~ of way** *n* prioridade *f* de passagem; (*AUT*) preferência; **~-wing** *adj* de direita

rigid ['rɪdʒɪd] *adj* rígido; (*principle*) inflexível

rigmarole ['rɪgmərəul] *n* processo

rile [raɪl] *vt* irritar, aborrecer

rim [rɪm] *n* borda, beira; (*of spectacles, wheel*) aro

rind [raɪnd] *n* (*of bacon*) pele *f*; (*of lemon etc*) casca; (*of cheese*) crosta, casca

ring [rɪŋ] (*pt* **rang**, *pp* **rung**) *n* (*of metal*) aro; (*on finger*) anel *m*; (*of people, objects*) círculo, grupo; (*for boxing*) ringue *m*; (*of circus*) pista, picadeiro; (*bull's*) picadeiro, arena; (*of light, smoke*) círculo; (*of small bell*) toque *m*; (*of large bell*) badalada, repique *m* ♦ *vi* (*on telephone*) telefonar; (*bell*) tocar; (*also:* **~ out**) soar; (*ears*) zumbir ♦ *vt* (*BRIT: TEL*) telefonar a, ligar para; (*bell etc*) badalar; (*doorbell*) tocar; **to give sb a ~** (*BRIT: TEL*) dar uma ligada *or* ligar para alguém; **~ back** (*BRIT*) *vi* (*TEL*) telefonar *or* ligar de volta ♦ *vt* telefonar *or* ligar de volta para; **~ off** (*BRIT*) *vi* (*TEL*) desligar; **~ up** (*BRIT*) *vt* (*TEL*) telefonar a, ligar para; **~ing** *n* (*of telephone*) toque *m*; (*of bell*) repicar *m*; (*in ears*) zumbido; **~ing tone** (*BRIT*) *n* (*TEL*) sinal *m* de chamada; **~leader** *n* cabeça *m/f*, cérebro

ringlets ['rɪŋlɪts] *npl* caracóis *mpl*, anéis *mpl*

ring road (*BRIT*) *n* estrada periférica *or* perimetral

rink [rɪŋk] *n* (*also:* **ice ~**) pista de patinação, rinque *m*

rinse [rɪns] *n* enxaguada ♦ *vt* enxaguar; (*also:* **~ out:** *mouth*) bochechar

riot ['raɪət] *n* distúrbio, motim *m*, desordem *f*; (*of colour*) festival *m*, profusão *f* ♦ *vi* provocar distúrbios, amotinar-se; **to run ~** desenfrear-se; **~ous** *adj* (*crowd*) desordeiro; (*behaviour*) turbulento; (*party*) tumultuado, barulhento

rip [rɪp] *n* rasgão *m* ♦ *vt* rasgar ♦ *vi* rasgar-se; **~cord** *n* corda de abertura (de pára-quedas)

ripe [raɪp] *adj* maduro; **~n** *vt, vi* amadurecer

ripple ['rɪpl] *n* ondulação *f*, encrespação *f*; (*of laughter etc*) onda ♦ *vi* encrespar-se

rise [raɪz] (*pt* **rose**, *pp* **risen**) *n* elevação *f*, ladeira; (*hill*) colina, rampa; (*in wa-*

ges: *BRIT*) aumento; (*in prices, temperature*) subida; (*to power etc*) ascensão *f* ♦ *vi* levantar-se, erguer-se; (*prices, waters*) subir; (*sun*) nascer; (*from bed etc*) levantar(-se); (*sound*) aumentar, erguer-se; (*also:* **~ up:** *building*) erguer-se; (: *rebel*) sublevar-se; (*in rank*) ascender, subir; **to give ~ to** ocasionar, dar origem a; **to ~ to the occasion** mostrar-se à altura da situação; **~n** *pp* of **rise**; **rising** *adj* (*prices*) em alta; (*number*) crescente, cada vez maior; (*tide*) montante; (*sun, moon*) nascente

risk [rɪsk] *n* risco, perigo; (*INSURANCE*) risco ♦ *vt* pôr em risco; (*chance*) arriscar, aventurar; **to take** *or* **run the ~ of doing** correr o risco de fazer; **at ~** em perigo; **at one's own ~** por sua própria conta e risco; **~y** *adj* perigoso

risqué ['ri:skeɪ] *adj* (*joke*) picante

rite [raɪt] *n* rito; **last ~s** últimos sacramentos

ritual ['rɪtjuəl] *adj* ritual ♦ *n* ritual *m*; (*of initiation*) rito

rival ['raɪvl] *adj, n* rival *m/f*; (*in business*) concorrente *m/f* ♦ *vt* competir com; **~ry** *n* rivalidade *f*

river ['rɪvə*] *n* rio ♦ *cpd* (*port, traffic*) fluvial; **up/down ~** rio acima/abaixo; **~bank** *n* margem *f* (do rio); **~bed** *n* leito (do rio)

rivet ['rɪvɪt] *n* rebite *m*, cravo ♦ *vt* (*fig*) fixar

road [rəud] *n* via; (*motorway etc*) estrada (de rodagem); (*in town*) rua ♦ *cpd* rodoviário; **~block** *n* barricada; **~hog** *n* dono da estrada; **~ map** *n* mapa *m* rodoviário; **~ safety** *n* segurança do trânsito; **~side** *n* beira da estrada; **~sign** *n* placa de sinalização; **~ user** *n* usuário/a da via pública; **~way** *n* pista, estrada; **~ works** *npl* obras *fpl* (na estrada); **~worthy** *adj* em bom estado de conservação e segurança

roam [rəum] *vi* vagar, perambular, errar

roar [rɔ:*] *n* (*of animal*) rugido, urro; (*of crowd*) bramido; (*of vehicle, storm*) estrondo; (*of laughter*) barulho ♦ *vi* (*animal, engine*) rugir; (*person, crowd*) bradar; **to ~ with laughter** dar gargalhadas; **~ing** *adj*: **to do a ~ing trade** fazer um bom negócio

roast [rəust] *n* carne *f* assada, assado ♦ *vt* assar; (*coffee*) torrar; **~ beef** *n* rosbife *m*

rob [rɔb] *vt* roubar; (*bank*) assaltar; **to ~ sb of sth** roubar algo de alguém; (*fig: deprive*) despojar alguém de algo; **~ber** *n* ladrão/ladra *m/f*; **~bery** *n* roubo

robe [rəub] *n* toga, beca; (*also:* **bath ~**) roupão *m* (de banho)

robin ['rɔbɪn] *n* pisco-de-peito-ruivo (*BR*), pintarroxo (*PT*)

robot ['rəubɔt] *n* robô *m*

robust [rəu'bʌst] *adj* robusto, forte; (*(...*

petite) sadio; (*economy*) forte

rock [rɔk] *n* rocha; (*boulder*) penhasco, rochedo; (*US*: *small stone*) cascalho; (*BRIT*: *sweet*) pirulito ♦ *vt* (*swing gently*: *cradle*) balançar, oscilar; (: *child*) embalar, acalentar; (*shake*) sacudir ♦ *vi* (*object*) balançar-se; (*person*) embalar-se; **on the ~s** (*drink*) com gelo; (*marriage etc*) arruinado, em dificuldades; **~ and roll** *n* rock-and-roll *m*; **~-bottom** *adj* (*fig*) mínimo, ínfimo; **~ery** *n jardim de plantas rasteiras entre pedras*

rocket ['rɔkɪt] *n* foguete *m*

rocking ['rɔkɪŋ]: **~ chair** *n* cadeira de balanço; **~ horse** *n* cavalo de balanço

rocky ['rɔkɪ] *adj* rochoso, bambo, instável; (*marriage*) instável

rod [rɔd] *n* vara, varinha; (*also*: **fishing ~**) vara de pescar

rode [rəud] *pt of* **ride**

rodent ['rəudnt] *n* roedor *m*

rodeo ['rəudɪəu] (*US*) *n* rodeio

roe [rəu] *n* (*also*: **~ deer**) corça, cerva; (*of fish*): **hard/soft ~** ova/esperma *m* de peixe

rogue [rəug] *n* velhaco, maroto

role [rəul] *n* papel *m*

roll [rəul] *n* rolo; (*of banknotes*) maço; (*also*: **bread ~**) pãozinho; (*register*) rol *m*, lista; (*of drums etc*) rufar *m* ♦ *vt* rolar; (*also*: **~ up**: *string*) enrolar; (: *sleeves*) arregaçar; (*cigarette*) enrolar; (*eyes*) virar; (*also*: **~ out**: *pastry*) esticar; (*lawn, road etc*) aplanar ♦ *vi* rolar; (*drum*) rufar; (*vehicle*: *also*: **~ along**) rodar; (*ship*) balançar, jogar; **~ about** *or* **around** *vi* ficar rolando; **~ by** *vi* (*time*) passar; **~ in** *vi* (*mail, cash*) chegar em grande quantidade; **~ over** *vi* dar uma volta; **~ up** *vi* (*inf*) pintar, chegar, aparecer ♦ *vt* enrolar; **~ call** *n* chamada, toque *m* de chamada; **~er** *n* (*in machine*) rolo, cilindro; (*wheel*) roda, roldana; (*for lawn, road*) rolo compressor; (*for hair*) rolo; **~er coaster** *n* montanharussa; **~er skates** *npl* patins *mpl* de roda

rolling ['rəulɪŋ] *adj* (*landscape*) ondulado; **~ pin** *n* rolo de pastel; **~ stock** *n* (*RAIL*) material *m* rodante

ROM [rɔm] *n abbr* (*COMPUT*: = *read-only memory*) ROM *m*

Roman ['rəumən] *adj*, *n* romano/a; **~ Catholic** *adj*, *n* católico/a (romano/a)

romance [rə'mæns] *n* aventura amorosa, romance *m*; (*book*) história de amor; (*charm*) romantismo

Romania [ru:'meɪnɪə] *n* Romênia; **~n** *adj* romeno *n* romeno/a; (*LING*) romeno

Roman numeral *n* número romano

romantic [rə'mæntɪk] *adj* romântico

~me [rəum] *n* Roma

~ [rɔmp] *n* brincadeira, travessura ♦ **~ about**) brincar ruidosamente

rompers ['rɔmpəz] *npl* macacão *m* de bebê

roof [ru:f, *pl* ru:fs *or* ru:vz] *n* (*of house*) telhado; (*of car*) capota, teto ♦ *vt* telhar, cobrir com telhas; **the ~ of the mouth** o céu da boca; **~ing** *n* cobertura; **~ rack** *n* (*AUT*) bagageiro

rook [ruk] *n* (*bird*) gralha; (*CHESS*) torre *f*

room [ru:m] *n* (*in house*) quarto, aposento; (*also*: **bed~**) quarto, dormitório; (*in school etc*) sala; (*scope*: *for improvement etc*) espaço; **~s** *npl* (*lodging*) alojamento; **"~s to let"** (*BRIT*), **"~s for rent"** (*US*) "alugam-se quartos *or* apartamentos"; **~ing house** (*US*) *n* casa de cômodos; **~mate** *n* companheiro/a de quarto; **~ service** *n* serviço de quarto; **~y** *adj* espaçoso; (*garment*) folgado

roost [ru:st] *vi* empoleirar-se, pernoitar

rooster ['ru:stə*] *n* galo

root [ru:t] *n* raiz *f*; (*fig*) origem *f* ♦ *vi* enraizar, arraigar; **~s** *npl* (*family origins*) raízes *fpl*; **~ about** *vi* (*fig*): **to ~ about in** (*drawer*) vasculhar; (*house*) esquadrinhar; **~ for** *vt fus* torcer por; **~ out** *vt* extirpar

rope [rəup] *n* corda; (*NAUT*) cabo ♦ *vt* (*tie*) amarrar; (*climbers*: *also*: **~ together**) amarrar *or* atar com uma corda; (*area*: *also*: **~ off**) isolar; **to know the ~s** (*fig*) estar por dentro (do assunto); **~ in** *vt* (*fig*): **to ~ sb in** persuadir alguém a tomar parte; **~ ladder** *n* escada de corda

rosary ['rəuzərɪ] *n* rosário

rose [rəuz] *pt of* **rise** ♦ *n* rosa; (*also*: **~bush**) roseira; (*on watering can*) crivo

rosé ['rəuzeɪ] *n* rosado, rosé *m*

rosebud ['rəuzbʌd] *n* botão *m* de rosa

rosebush ['rəuzbʌʃ] *n* roseira

rosemary ['rəuzmərɪ] *n* alecrim *m*

rosette [rəu'zɛt] *n* roseta

roster ['rɔstə*] *n*: **duty ~** lista de tarefas, escala de serviço

rostrum ['rɔstrəm] *n* tribuna

rosy ['rəuzɪ] *adj* rosado, rosáceo; (*cheeks*) rosado; (*situation*) cor-de-rosa *inv*; **a ~ future** um futuro promissor

rot [rɔt] *n* (*decay*) putrefação *f*, podridão *f*; (*fig*: *pej*) besteira ♦ *vt*, *vi* apodrecer

rota ['rəutə] *n* lista de tarefas, escala de serviço

rotary ['rəutərɪ] *adj* rotativo

rotate [rəu'teɪt] *vt* fazer girar, dar voltas em; (*jobs*) alternar, revezar ♦ *vi* girar, dar voltas; **rotating** *adj* rotativo

rote [rəut] *n*: **by ~** de cor

rotten ['rɔtn] *adj* podre; (*wood*) carcomido; (*fig*) corrupto; (*inf*: *bad*) péssimo; **to feel ~** (*ill*) sentir-se podre

rotund [rəu'tʌnd] *adj* rechonchudo

rouble ['ru:bl] (*US* **ruble**) *n* rublo

rouge [ru:ʒ] *n* rouge *m*, blush *m*, carmim *m*

rough [rʌf] *adj* (*skin, surface*) áspero; (*terrain*) acidentado; (*road*) desigual; (*voice*) áspero, rouco; (*person, manner: violent*) violento; (: *brusque*) ríspido; (*weather*) tempestuoso; (*treatment*) brutal, mau/má; (*sea*) agitado; (*district*) violento; (*plan*) preliminar; (*work*) grosseiro; (*guess*) aproximado ♦ *n* (*GOLF*): **in the** ~ na grama crescida; **to sleep** ~ (*BRIT*) dormir na rua; **~age** *n* fibras *fpl*; **~-and-ready** (*of policeman*) improvisado, feito às pressas; **~cast** *n* reboco; ~ **copy** *n* rascunho; ~ **draft** *n* rascunho; **~ly** *adv* bruscamente; (*make*) toscamente; (*approximately*) aproximadamente; **~ness** *n* aspereza; (*rudeness*) grosseria

roulette [ruː'lɛt] *n* roleta

Roumania *etc* [ruː'meɪnɪə] *n* = **Romania** *etc*

round [raund] *adj* redondo ♦ *n* (*BRIT: of toast*) rodela; (*of milkman*) trajeto; (*of doctor*) visitas *fpl*; (*game: of cards etc*) partida; (*of ammunition*) cartucho; (*BOXING*) rounde *m*, assalto; (*of talks*) ciclo ♦ *vt* virar, dobrar ♦ *prep* (*surrounding*): ~ **his neck/the table** em volta do seu pescoço/ao redor da mesa; (*in a circular movement*): **to move** ~ **the room/**~ **the world** mover-se pelo quarto/dar a volta ao mundo; (*in various directions*) por; (*approximately*): ~ **about** aproximadamente ♦ *adv*: **all** ~ por todos os lados; **the long way** ~ o caminho mais comprido; **all the year** ~ durante todo o ano; **it's just** ~ **the corner** (*fig*) está pertinho; ~ **the clock** ininterrupto; **to go** ~ **the back** passar por detrás; **to go** ~ **a house** visitar uma casa; **enough to go** ~ suficiente para todos; **a** ~ **of applause** uma salva de palmas; **a** ~ **of drinks** uma rodada de bebidas; ~ **of sandwiches** sanduíche *m* (*BR*), sandes *f inv* (*PT*); ~ **off** *vt* terminar, completar; ~ **up** *vt* (*cattle*) encurralar; (*people*) reunir; (*price, figure*) arredondar; **~about** *n* (*BRIT: AUT*) rotatória; (: *at fair*) carrossel *m* ♦ *adj* indireto; **~ers** *npl* (*game*) jogo semelhante ao beisebol; **~ly** *adv* (*fig*) energicamente, totalmente; **~-shouldered** *adj* encurvado; ~ **trip** *n* viagem *f* de ida e volta; **~up** *n* (*of news*) resumo; (*of animals*) rodeio; (*of criminals*) batida

rouse [rauz] *vt* (*wake up*) despertar, acordar; (*stir up*) suscitar; **rousing** *adj* emocionante, vibrante

rout [raut] *n* (*MIL*) derrota ♦ *vt* derrotar

route [ruːt] *n* caminho, rota; (*of bus*) trajeto; (*of shipping*) rumo, rota; (*of procession*) rota; ~ **map** (*BRIT*) *n* (*for journey*) mapa *m* rodoviário

routine [ruː'tiːn] *adj* (*work*) rotineiro; (*procedure*) de rotina ♦ *n* rotina; (*THEATRE*) número

rove [rəuv] *vt* vagar por, perambular por

row¹ [rəu] *n* (*line*) fila, fileira; (*in theatre, boat*) fileira; (*KNITTING*) carreira, fileira ♦ *vi, vt* remar; **in a** ~ (*fig*) a fio, seguido

row² [rau] *n* barulho, balbúrdia; (*dispute*) discussão *f*, briga; (*scolding*) repreensão *f* ♦ *vi* brigar

rowboat ['rəubəut] (*US*) *n* barco a remo

rowdy ['raudɪ] *adj* (*person: noisy*) barulhento; (*occasion*) tumultuado

rowing ['rəuɪŋ] *n* remo; ~ **boat** (*BRIT*) *n* barco a remo

royal ['rɔɪəl] *adj* real; **R~ Air Force** (*BRIT*) *n* força aérea britânica; **~ty** *n* família real, realeza; (*payment: to author*) direitos *mpl* autorais

rpm *abbr* (= *revolutions per minute*) rpm

RSVP *abbr* (= *répondez s'il vous plaît*) ER

Rt Hon. (*BRIT*) *abbr* (= *Right Honourable*) título honorífico de conselheiro do estado ou juiz

rub [rʌb] *vt* friccionar; (*part of body*) esfregar ♦ *n*: **to give sth a** ~ dar uma esfregada em algo; **to** ~ **sb up** (*BRIT*) **or** ~ **sb** (*US*) **the wrong way** irritar alguém; ~ **off** *vi* sair esfregando; ~ **off on** *vt fus* transmitir-se para, influir sobre; ~ **out** *vt* apagar

rubber ['rʌbə*] *n* borracha; (*BRIT: eraser*) borracha; ~ **band** *n* elástico, tira elástica; ~ **plant** *n* figueira; **~y** *adj* elástico; (*food*) sem gosto

rubbish ['rʌbɪʃ] *n* (*waste*) refugo; (*from household, in street*) lixo; (*junk*) coisas *fpl* sem valor; (*fig: pej: nonsense*) disparates *mpl*, asneiras *fpl*; ~ **bin** (*BRIT*) *n* lata de lixo; ~ **dump** *n* (*in town*) depósito (de lixo)

rubble ['rʌbl] *n* (*debris*) entulho; (*CONSTR*) escombros *mpl*

ruble ['ruːbl] (*US*) *n* = **rouble**

ruby ['ruːbɪ] *n* rubi *m*

rucksack ['rʌksæk] *n* mochila

rudder ['rʌdə*] *n* leme *m*; (*of plane*) leme de direção

ruddy ['rʌdɪ] *adj* corado, avermelhado; (*inf*) maldito, desgraçado

rude [ruːd] *adj* (*person*) grosso, mal-educado; (*word, manners*) grosseiro; (*shocking*) obsceno, chocante; **~ness** *n* falta de educação

rudiments ['ruːdɪmənts] *npl* primeiras noções *fpl*

rueful ['ruːful] *adj* arrependido

ruffian ['rʌfɪən] *n* brigão *m*, desordeiro

ruffle ['rʌfl] *vt* (*hair*) despentear, desmanchar; (*clothes*) enrugar, amarrotar; (*fig*) perturbar, irritar

rug [rʌg] *n* tapete *m*; (*BRIT: for knees*) manta (de viagem)

rugby ['rʌgbɪ] *n* (*also*: ~ **football**) rúgbi *m* (*BR*), râguebi *m* (*PT*)

rugged ['rʌgɪd] *adj* (*landscape*) acidentado, irregular; (features) marcado; (character) severo, austero

rugger ['rʌgə*] (BRIT: inf) n rúgbi m (BR), râguebi m (PT)

ruin ['ru:ɪn] n ruína; (of plans) destruição f; (downfall) queda; (bankruptcy) bancarrota ♦ vt destruir; (future, person) arruinar; (spoil) estragar; ~s npl (of building) ruínas fpl; ~ous adj desastroso

rule [ru:l] n (norm) regra; (regulation) regulamento; (government) governo, domínio; (ruler) régua ♦ vt governar ♦ vi governar; (monarch) reger; (LAW): to ~ in favour of/against decidir oficialmente a favor de/contra; as a ~ por via de regra, geralmente; ~ out vt excluir; ~d adj pautado; ~r n (sovereign) soberano/a; (for measuring) régua; **ruling** adj (party) dominante; (class) dirigente ♦ n (LAW) parecer m, decisão f

rum [rʌm] n rum m

Rumania etc [ru:'meɪnɪə] n = **Romania** etc

rumble ['rʌmbl] n ruído surdo, barulho; (of thunder) estrondo, ribombo ♦ vi ribombar, ressoar; (stomach) roncar; (pipe) fazer barulho; (thunder) ribombar

rummage ['rʌmɪdʒ] vi vasculhar

rumour ['ru:mə*] (US rumor) n rumor m, boato ♦ vt: it is ~ed that ... corre o boato de que ...

rump [rʌmp] n (of animal) anca, garupa; ~ steak n alcatra

rumpus ['rʌmpəs] n barulho, confusão f, zorra

run [rʌn] (pt ran, pp run) n corrida; (in car) passeio (de carro); (distance travelled) trajeto, percurso; (journey) viagem f; (series) série f; (THEATRE) temporada; (SKI) pista; (in stockings) fio puxado ♦ vt (race) correr; (operate: business) dirigir; (: competition, course) organizar; (: hotel, house) administrar; (water) deixar correr; (bath) encher; (PRESS: feature) publicar; (COMPUT) rodar; (hand, finger) passar ♦ vi correr; (work: machine) funcionar; (bus, train: operate) circular; (: travel) ir; (continue: play) continuar em cartaz; (: contract) ser válido; (river, bath) fluir, correr; (colours) desbotar; (in election) candidatar-se; (nose) escorrer; there was a ~ on houve muita procura de; in the long ~ no final das contas, mais cedo ou mais tarde; on the ~ em fuga, foragido; ~ about or around vi correr por todos os lados; ~ across vt fus encontrar por acaso, topar com, dar com; ~ away vi fugir; ~ down vt (AUT) atropelar; (production) reduzir; (criticize) criticar; to be ~ down estar enfraquecido or exausto; ~ in (BRIT) vt (car) rodar; ~ into vt fus (meet: person) dar com, topar com; (: trouble) esbarrar em; (collide with) bater em; ~ off vi fugir; ~ out vi (person) sair correndo; (li-

quid) escorrer, esgotar-se; (lease, passport) caducar, vencer; (money) acabar; ~ out of vt fus ficar sem; ~ over vt (AUT) atropelar ♦ vt fus (revise) recapitular; ~ through vt fus (instructions, play) recapitular; ~ up vt (debt) acumular ♦ vi: to ~ up against esbarrar em; ~away adj (horse) desembestado; (truck) desgovernado; (person) fugitivo

rung [rʌŋ] pp of **ring** ♦ n (of ladder) degrau m

runner ['rʌnə*] n (in race) corredor(a) m/f; (horse) corredor m; (on sledge) patim m, lâmina; (for drawer) corrediça; ~ bean (BRIT) n (BOT) vagem f (BR), feijão m verde (PT); ~-up n segundo/a colocado/a

running ['rʌnɪŋ] n (sport) corrida; (of business) direção f ♦ adj (water) corrente; (commentary) contínuo, seguido; **6 days** ~ 6 dias seguidos or consecutivos; to be in/out of the ~ for sth disputar algo/estar fora da disputa por algo; ~ costs npl (of business) despesas fpl operacionais; (of car) custos mpl de manutenção

runny ['rʌnɪ] adj aguado; (egg) mole; to have a ~ nose estar com coriza, estar com o nariz escorrendo

run-of-the-mill ['rʌnəvðə'mɪl] adj mediocre, ordinário

runt [rʌnt] n (animal) nanico; (pej: person) anão/anã m/f

run-up n: ~ to sth (election etc) período que antecede algo

runway ['rʌnweɪ] n (AVIAT) pista (de decolagem or de pouso)

rupee [ru:'pi:] n rupia

rupture ['rʌptʃə*] n (MED) hérnia

rural ['ruərl] adj rural

ruse [ru:z] n ardil m, manha

rush [rʌʃ] n (hurry) pressa; (COMM) grande de procura or demanda; (BOT) junco; (current) torrente f; (of emotion) ímpeto ♦ vt apressar ♦ vi apressar-se, precipitar-se; ~ hour n rush m (BR), hora de ponta (PT)

rusk [rʌsk] n rosca

Russia ['rʌʃə] n Rússia; ~n adj russo ♦ n russo/a; (LING) russo

rust [rʌst] n ferrugem f ♦ vi enferrujar

rustle ['rʌsl] vi sussurrar ♦ vt (paper) farfalhar; (US: cattle) roubar, afanar

rustproof ['rʌstpru:f] adj inoxidável, à prova de ferrugem

rusty ['rʌstɪ] adj enferrujado

rut [rʌt] n sulco; (ZOOL) cio; to be in a ~ ser escravo da rotina

ruthless ['ru:θlɪs] adj implacável, sem piedade

rye [raɪ] n centeio

S

Sabbath ['sæbəθ] n (Christian) domingo; (Jewish) sábado

sabotage ['sæbətɑːʒ] n sabotagem f ♦ vt sabotar

saccharin(e) ['sækərın] n sacarina

sachet ['sæʃeɪ] n sachê m

sack [sæk] n (bag) saco, saca ♦ vt (dismiss) despedir; (plunder) saquear; **to get the ~** ser demitido; **~ing** n (dismissal) demissão f; (material) aniagem f

sacred ['seɪkrɪd] adj sagrado

sacrifice ['sækrɪfaɪs] n sacrifício ♦ vt sacrificar

sacrilege ['sækrɪlɪdʒ] n sacrilégio

sad [sæd] adj triste; (deplorable) deplorável, triste

saddle ['sædl] n sela; (of cycle) selim m ♦ vt selar; **to ~ sb with sth** (inf: task, bill) pôr algo nas costas de alguém; (: responsibility) sobrecarregar alguém com algo; **~bag** n alforje m

sadistic [sə'dɪstɪk] adj sádico

sadly ['sædlɪ] adv tristemente; (regrettably) infelizmente; (mistaken, neglected) gravemente; **~ lacking (in)** muito carente (de)

sadness ['sædnɪs] n tristeza

sae abbr = **stamped addressed envelope**

safe [seɪf] adj seguro; (out of danger) fora de perigo; (unharmed) ileso, incólume ♦ n cofre m, caixa-forte f; **~ from** protegido de; **~ and sound** são e salvo; **(just) to be on the ~ side** por via das dúvidas; **~-conduct** n salvo-conduto; **~-deposit** n (vault) cofre m de segurança; (box) caixa-forte f; **~guard** n salvaguarda, proteção f ♦ vt proteger, defender; **~keeping** n custódia, proteção f; **~ly** adv com segurança, a salvo; (without mishap) sem perigo; **~ sex** n sexo com segurança

safety ['seɪftɪ] n segurança; **~ belt** n cinto de segurança; **~ pin** n alfinete m de segurança; **~ valve** n válvula de segurança

saffron ['sæfrən] n açafrão m

sag [sæg] vi (breasts) cair; (roof) afundar; (hem) desmanchar

saga ['sɑːgə] n saga; (fig) novela

sage [seɪdʒ] n salva; (man) sábio

Sagittarius [sædʒɪ'tɛərɪəs] n Sagitário

Sahara [sə'hɑːrə] n: **the ~ (Desert)** o Saara

said [sɛd] pt, pp of **say**

sail [seɪl] n (on boat) vela; (trip): **to go for a ~** dar um passeio de barco a vela ♦ vt (boat) governar ♦ vi (travel: ship) navegar, velejar; (: passenger) ir de barco; (SPORT) velejar; (set off) zarpar; **they ~ed into Rio de Janeiro** entraram no porto do Rio de Janeiro; **~ through** vt fus (fig) fazer com facilidade; **~boat** (US) n barco a vela; **~ing** n (SPORT) navegação f a vela, vela; **to go ~ing** ir velejar; **~ing boat** n barco a vela; **~ing ship** n veleiro

sailor ['seɪlə*] n marinheiro, marujo

saint [seɪnt] n santo/a; **~ly** adj santo

sake [seɪk] n: **for the ~ of** por (causa de), em consideração a; **for sb's/sth's ~** pelo bem de alguém/algo

salad ['sæləd] n salada; **~ bowl** n saladeira; **~ cream** (BRIT) n maionese f; **~ dressing** n tempero or molho da salada

salami [sə'lɑːmɪ] n salame m

salary ['sælərɪ] n salário

sale [seɪl] n venda; (at reduced prices) liquidação f, saldo; (auction) leilão m; **~s** npl (total amount sold) vendas fpl; **"for ~"** "vende-se"; **on ~** à venda; **on ~ or return** em consignação; **~room** n sala de vendas; **~s assistant** (US **~s clerk**) n vendedor(a) m/f; **~sman/swoman** (irreg) n vendedor(a) m/f; (representative) vendedor(a) m/f viajante

salient ['seɪlɪənt] adj saliente

sallow ['sæləu] adj amarelado

salmon ['sæmən] n inv salmão m

salon ['sælɔn] n (hairdressing ~) salão m (de cabeleireiro); (beauty ~) salão (de beleza)

saloon [sə'luːn] n (US) bar m, botequim m; (BRIT: AUT) sedã m; (ship's lounge) salão m

salt [sɔːlt] n sal m ♦ vt salgar; **~ cellar** n saleiro; **~water** adj de água salgada; **~y** adj salgado

salute [sə'luːt] n (greeting) saudação f; (of guns) salva; (MIL) continência ♦ vt saudar; (MIL) fazer continência a

salvage ['sælvɪdʒ] n (saving) salvamento, recuperação f; (things saved) salvados mpl ♦ vt salvar

salvation [sæl'veɪʃən] n salvação f; **S~ Army** n Exército da Salvação

same [seɪm] adj mesmo ♦ pron: **the ~** o mesmo/a mesma; **the ~ book as** o mesmo livro que; **all** or **just the ~** apesar de tudo, mesmo assim; **the ~ to you!** igualmente!

sample ['sɑːmpl] n amostra ♦ vt (food, wine) provar, experimentar

sanctimonious [sæŋktɪ'məunɪəs] adj carola, beato

sanction ['sæŋkʃən] n sanção f ♦ vt sancionar

sanctity ['sæŋktɪtɪ] n santidade f

sanctuary ['sæŋktjuərɪ] n (holy place) santuário; (refuge) refúgio, asilo; (for animals) reserva

sand [sænd] n areia; (beach: also: **~s**) praia ♦ vt (also: **~ down**) lixar

sandal ['sændl] n sandália

sand: **~box** (US) n caixa de areia; **~castle** n castelo de areia; **~ dune** n duna (de areia); **~paper** n lixa; **~pit** n (for children) caixa de areia; **~stone** n arenito, grés m

sandwich ['sændwɪtʃ] n sanduíche m (BR), sandes f inv (PT) ♦ vt: **~ed between** encaixado entre; **~ course** (BRIT) n curso profissionalizante de teoria e prática alternadas

sandy ['sændɪ] adj arenoso; (colour) vermelho amarelado

sane [seɪn] adj são/sã do juízo; (sensible) ajuizado, sensato

sang [sæŋ] pt of **sing**

sanitary ['sænɪtərɪ] adj (system, arrangements) sanitário; (clean) higiênico; **~ towel** (US **~ napkin**) n toalha higiênica or absorvente

sanitation [sænɪ'teɪʃən] n (in house) instalações fpl sanitárias; (in town) saneamento; **~ department** (US) n comissão f de limpeza urbana

sanity ['sænɪtɪ] n sanidade f, equilíbrio mental; (common sense) juízo, sensatez f

sank [sæŋk] pt of **sink**

Santa Claus [sæntə'klɔːz] n Papai Noel m

sap [sæp] n (of plants) seiva ♦ vt (strength) esgotar, minar

sapling ['sæplɪŋ] n árvore f nova

sapphire ['sæfaɪə*] n safira

sarcasm ['sɑːkæzm] n sarcasmo

sardine [sɑː'diːn] n sardinha

Sardinia [sɑː'dɪnɪə] n Sardenha

sash [sæʃ] n faixa, banda

sat [sæt] pt, pp of **sit**

Satan ['seɪtn] n Satanás m, Satã m

satchel ['sætʃl] n sacola

satellite ['sætəlaɪt] n satélite m; **~ dish** n antena parabólica; **~ television** n televisão f via satélite

satin ['sætɪn] n cetim m ♦ adj acetinado

satire ['sætaɪə*] n sátira

satisfaction [sætɪs'fækʃən] n satisfação f; (refund, apology etc) compensação f; **satisfactory** adj satisfatório

satisfy ['sætɪsfaɪ] vt satisfazer; (convince) convencer, persuadir; **satisfying** adj satisfatório

saturate ['sætʃəreɪt] vt: **to ~ (with)** saturar or embeber (de)

Saturday ['sætədɪ] n sábado

sauce [sɔːs] n molho; (sweet) calda; **~pan** n panela (BR), caçarola (PT)

saucer ['sɔːsə*] n pires m inv

saucy ['sɔːsɪ] adj atrevido, descarado

Saudi ['saudɪ]: **~ Arabia** n Arábia Saudita; **~ (Arabian)** adj saudita

sauna ['sɔːnə] n sauna

saunter ['sɔːntə*] vi: **to ~ over/along** andar devagar para/por; **to ~ into** entrar devagar em

sausage ['sɔsɪdʒ] n salsicha, lingüiça; (cold meat) frios mpl; **~ roll** n folheado de salsicha

sauté ['səuteɪ] adj (CULIN) sauté

savage ['sævɪdʒ] adj (cruel, fierce) cruel, feroz; (primitive) selvagem ♦ n selvagem m/f

save [seɪv] vt (rescue, COMPUT) salvar; (money) poupar, economizar; (time) ganhar; (SPORT) impedir; (avoid: trouble) evitar; (keep: seat) guardar ♦ vi (also: ~ up) poupar ♦ n (SPORT) salvamento ♦ prep salvo, exceto

saving ['seɪvɪŋ] n (on price etc) economia ♦ adj: **the ~ grace of** o único mérito de; **~s** npl (money) economias fpl; **~s account** n (caderneta de) poupança; **~s bank** n caixa econômica, caderneta de poupança

saviour ['seɪvjə*] (US **savior**) n salvador(a) m/f

savour ['seɪvə*] (US **savor**) vt saborear; (experience) apreciar; **~y** adj (dish: not sweet) salgado

saw [sɔː] (pt **~ed**, pp **~ed** or **~n**) pt of **see** ♦ n (tool) serra ♦ vt serrar; **~dust** n serragem f, pó m de serra; **~ed-off shotgun** (US) n = **~n-off shotgun**; **~mill** n serraria; **~n** pp of **saw**; **~n-off shotgun** (BRIT) n espingarda de cano serrado

saxophone ['sæksəfəun] n saxofone m

say [seɪ] (pt, pp **said**) n: **to have one's ~** exprimir sua opinião, vender seu peixe (inf) ♦ vt dizer, falar; **to have a ~ or some ~ in sth** opinar sobre algo, ter que ver com algo; **could you ~ that again?** poderia repetir?; **that is to ~** ou seja; **~ing** n ditado, provérbio

scab [skæb] n casca, crosta (de ferida); (pej) fura-greve m/f inv

scaffold ['skæfəuld] n (for execution) cadafalso, patíbulo; **~ing** n andaime m

scald [skɔːld] n escaldadura ♦ vt escaldar, queimar

scale [skeɪl] n escala; (of fish) escama; (of salaries, fees etc) tabela ♦ vt (mountain) escalar; **~s** npl (for weighing) balança; **~ of charges** tarifa, lista de preços; **~ down** vt reduzir

scallop ['skɔləp] n (ZOOL) vieira, venera; (SEWING) barra, arremate m

scalp [skælp] n couro cabeludo ♦ vt escalpar

scalpel ['skælpl] n bisturi m

scamper ['skæmpə*] vi: **to ~ away** or **off** sair correndo

scampi ['skæmpɪ] npl camarões mpl fritos

scan [skæn] vt (examine) esquadrinhar, perscrutar; (glance at quickly) passar uma vista de olhos por; (TV, RADAR) explorar ♦ n (MED) exame m

scandal ['skændl] n escândalo; (gossip) fofocas fpl; (fig: disgrace) vergonha; **~ous** adj vergonhoso

Scandinavian [skændɪ'neɪvɪən] adj escandinavo

scant [skænt] adj escasso, insuficiente;

~y *adj* (*meal*) insuficiente, pobre; (*underwear*) sumário
scapegoat ['skeɪpgəut] *n* bode *m* expiatório
scar [skɑ:*] *n* cicatriz *f* ♦ *vt* marcar (com uma cicatriz)
scarce [skɛəs] *adj* escasso, raro; **to make o.s.** ~ (*inf*) dar o fora, cair fora; ~**ly** *adv* mal, quase não; (*barely*) apenas; **scarcity** *n* escassez *f*
scare [skɛə*] *n* susto; (*panic*) pânico ♦ *vt* assustar; **to ~ sb stiff** deixar alguém morrendo de medo; **bomb** ~ alarme de bomba; ~ **away** *vt* espantar; ~ **off** *vt* = ~ **away**; ~**crow** *n* espantalho; ~**d** *adj*: **to be ~d** estar assustado *or* com medo
scarf [skɑ:f] (*pl* ~**s** *or* **scarves**) *n* cachecol *m*; (*square*) lenço (de cabeça)
scarlet ['skɑ:lɪt] *adj* escarlate; ~ **fever** *n* escarlatina
scarves [skɑ:vz] *npl of* **scarf**
scary ['skɛərɪ] (*inf*) *adj* assustador(a)
scathing ['skeɪðɪŋ] *adj* mordaz
scatter ['skætə*] *vt* espalhar; (*put to flight*) dispersar ♦ *vi* espalhar-se; ~**brained** (*inf*) *adj* esquecido
scavenger ['skævəndʒə*] *n pessoa que procura comida no lixo*
scenario [sɪ'nɑ:rɪəu] *n* (*THEATRE, CINEMA*) roteiro; (*fig*) quadro
scene [si:n] *n* (*THEATRE, fig*) cena; (*of crime, accident*) cenário; (*sight*) vista, panorama *m*; (*fuss*) escândalo; ~**ry** *n* (*THEATRE*) cenário; (*landscape*) paisagem *f*; **scenic** *adj* pitoresco
scent [sɛnt] *n* perfume *m*; (*smell*) aroma; (*track, fig*) pista, rastro
sceptic ['skɛptɪk] (*US* **skeptic**) *n* cético/a
sceptre ['sɛptə*] (*US* **scepter**) *n* cetro
schedule ['ʃɛdju:l, (*US*) 'skɛdju:l] *n* (*of trains*) horário; (*of events*) programa *m*; (*list*) lista ♦ *vt* (*timetable*) planejar; (*visit*) marcar (a hora de); **on** ~ na hora, sem atraso; **to be ahead of/behind** ~ estar adiantado/atrasado; ~**d** *adj* (*flight*) de linha
scheme [ski:m] *n* (*plan*) maquinação *f*; (*pension* ~) projeto; (*arrangement*) arranjo ♦ *vi* conspirar; **scheming** *adj* intrigante ♦ *n* intrigas *fpl*
schism ['skɪzəm] *n* cisma *m*
scholar ['skɔlə*] *n* aluno/a, estudante *m/f*; (*learned person*) sábio/a, erudito/a; ~**ly** *adj* erudito; ~**ship** *n* erudição *f*; (*grant*) bolsa de estudos
school [sku:l] *n* escola; (*secondary* ~) colégio; (*US*: *university*) universidade *f* ♦ *cpd* escolar; ~ **age** *n* idade *f* escolar; ~**boy** *n* aluno; ~**children** *npl* alunos *mpl*; ~**days** *npl* anos *mpl* escolares; ~**girl** *n* aluna; ~**ing** *n* educação *f*, ensino; ~**master** *n* professor *m*; ~**mistress** *n* professora; ~**teacher** *n* professor(a) *m/f*
schooner ['sku:nə*] *n* escuna
science ['saɪəns] *n* ciência; ~ **fiction** *n* ficção *f* científica; **scientific** *adj* científico; **scientist** *n* cientista *m/f*
scintillating ['sɪntɪleɪtɪŋ] *adj* (*wit etc*) brilhante
scissors ['sɪzəz] *npl* tesoura; **a pair of** ~ uma tesoura
scoff [skɔf] *vt* (*BRIT*: *inf*: *eat*) engolir ♦ *vi*: **to ~ (at)** (*mock*) zombar (de)
scold [skəuld] *vt* ralhar
scone [skɔn] *n bolinho de trigo*
scoop [sku:p] *n* colherona; (*for flour etc*) pá *f*; (*PRESS*) furo (jornalístico); ~ **out** *vt* escavar; ~ **up** *vt* recolher
scooter ['sku:tə*] *n* (*also*: **motor** ~) lambreta; (*toy*) patinete *m*
scope [skəup] *n* liberdade *f* de ação; (*of undertaking*) âmbito; (*of person*) competência; (*opportunity*) oportunidade *f*
scorch [skɔ:tʃ] *vt* (*clothes*) chamuscar; (*earth, grass*) secar, queimar
score [skɔ:*] *n* (*points etc*) escore *m*, contagem *f*; (*MUS*) partitura; (*twenty*) vintena ♦ *vt* (*goal, point*) fazer; (*mark*) marcar, entalhar; (*success*) alcançar ♦ *vi* (*in game*) marcar; (*FOOTBALL*) marcar *or* fazer um gol; (*keep score*) marcar o escore; **on that** ~ a esse respeito, por esse motivo; ~**s of** (*fig*) um monte de; **to ~ 6 out of 10** conseguir um escore de 6 num total de 10; ~ **out** *vt* riscar; ~**board** *n* marcador *m*, placar *m*
scorn [skɔ:n] *n* desprezo ♦ *vt* desprezar, rejeitar; ~**ful** *adj* desdenhoso, zombador(a)
Scorpio ['skɔ:pɪəu] *n* Escorpião *m*
scorpion ['skɔ:pɪən] *n* escorpião *m*
Scot [skɔt] *n* escocês/esa *m/f*
Scotch [skɔtʃ] *n* uísque *m* (*BR*) *or* whisky *m* (*PT*) escocês
scotch [skɔtʃ] *vt* (*rumour*) desmentir; (*plan*) estragar
scot-free *adj*: **to get off** ~ (*unpunished*) sair impune
Scotland ['skɔtlənd] *n* Escócia; **Scots** *adj* escocês/esa; **Scotsman** (*irreg*) *n* escocês *m*; **Scotswoman** (*irreg*) *n* escocesa; **Scottish** *adj* escocês/esa
scoundrel ['skaundrəl] *n* canalha *m/f*, patife *m*
scour ['skauə*] *vt* (*search*) esquadrinhar, procurar em
scourge [skə:dʒ] *n* flagelo, tormento
scout [skaut] *n* (*MIL*) explorador *m*, batedor *m*; (*also*: **boy** ~) escoteiro; **girl** ~ (*US*) escoteira; ~ **around** *vi* explorar
scowl [skaul] *vi* franzir a testa; **to ~ at sb** olhar de cara feia para alguém
scrabble ['skræbl] *vi* (*claw*): **to ~ at** arranhar ♦ *n*: **S**~ ® mexe-mexe *m*; **to ~ (around) for sth** (*search*) tatear procurando algo
scraggy ['skrægɪ] *adj* magricela, descarnado

scram [skræm] (*inf*) *vi* dar o fora, safar-se

scramble ['skræmbl] *n* (*climb*) escalada (difícil); (*struggle*) luta ♦ *vi*: **to ~ out/through** conseguir sair com dificuldade; **to ~ for** lutar por; **~d eggs** *npl* ovos *mpl* mexidos

scrap [skræp] *n* (*of paper*) pedacinho; (*of material*) fragmento; (*fig: of truth*) mínimo; (*fight*) rixa, luta; (*also*: ~ **iron**) ferro velho, sucata ♦ *vt* sucatar, jogar no ferro velho; (*fig*) descartar, abolir ♦ *vi* brigar; **~s** *npl* (*leftovers*) sobras *fpl*, restos *mpl*; **~book** *n* álbum *m* de recortes; **~ dealer** *n* ferro-velho *m*, sucateiro/a

scrape [skreip] *n* (*fig*): **to get into a ~** meter-se numa enrascada ♦ *vt* raspar; (~ *against: hand, car*) arranhar, roçar ♦ *vi*: **to ~ through** (*in exam*) passar raspando; **~ together** *vt* (*money*) juntar com dificuldade

scrap: **~ heap** *n* (*fig*): **on the ~heap** rejeitado, jogado fora; **~ merchant** (*BRIT*) *n* sucateiro/a; **~ paper** *n* papel *m* de rascunho; **~py** *adj* (*piece of work*) desconexo

scratch [skrætʃ] *n* arranhão *m*; (*from claw*) arranhadura ♦ *cpd*: **~ team** time *m* improvisado, escrete *m* ♦ *vt* (*rub*) coçar; (*with claw, nail*) arranhar, unhar; (*damage*) arranhar ♦ *vi* coçar(-se); **to start from ~** partir do zero; **to be up to ~** estar à altura (das circunstâncias)

scrawl [skrɔ:l] *n* garrancho, garatujas *fpl* ♦ *vi* garatujar, rabiscar

scrawny ['skrɔ:nɪ] *adj* magricela

scream [skri:m] *n* grito ♦ *vi* gritar

scree [skri:] *n* seixos *mpl*

screech [skri:tʃ] *vi* guinchar

screen [skri:n] *n* (*CINEMA, TV, COMPUT*) tela (*BR*), écran *m* (*PT*); (*movable*) biombo; (*fig*) cortina ♦ *vt* (*conceal*) esconder, tapar; (*from the wind etc*) proteger; (*film*) projetar; (*candidates etc*) examinar; **~ing** *n* (*MED*) exame *m* médico; **~play** *n* roteiro

screw [skru:] *n* parafuso ♦ *vt* aparafusar; (*also*: ~ **in**) apertar, atarraxar; **to ~ up one's eyes** franzir os olhos; **~ up** *vt* (*paper etc*) amassar; **~driver** *n* chave *f* de fenda *or* de parafuso

scribble ['skrɪbl] *n* garrancho ♦ *vt* escrevinhar ♦ *vi* rabiscar

script [skrɪpt] *n* (*CINEMA etc*) roteiro, script *m*; (*writing*) escrita, caligrafia

Scripture(s) ['skrɪptʃə(z)] *n(pl)* Sagrada Escritura

scroll [skrəul] *n* rolo de pergaminho

scrounge [skraundʒ] (*inf*) *vt* filar ♦ *n*: **to be on the ~** viver às custas de alguém (*or* dos outros *etc*)

scrub [skrʌb] *n* mato, cerrado ♦ *vt* esfregar; (*inf*) cancelar, eliminar

scruff [skrʌf] *n*: **by the ~ of the neck** pelo cangote

scruffy ['skrʌfɪ] *adj* desmazelado

scrum(mage) ['skrʌm(ɪdʒ)] *n* rolo

scruple ['skru:pl] *n* escrúpulo

scrutinize ['skru:tɪnaɪz] *vt* examinar minuciosamente; (*votes*) escrutinar

scrutiny ['skru:tɪnɪ] *n* escrutínio, exame *m* cuidadoso

scuff [skʌf] *vt* desgastar

scuffle ['skʌfl] *n* tumulto

sculptor ['skʌlptə*] *n* escultor(a) *m/f*

sculpture ['skʌlptʃə*] *n* escultura

scum [skʌm] *n* (*on liquid*) espuma; (*pej: people*) ralé *f*, gentinha

scupper ['skʌpə*] (*BRIT*: *inf*) *vt* (*plans*) estragar

scurrilous ['skʌrɪləs] *adj* calunioso

scurry ['skʌrɪ] *vi* sair correndo; **~ off** *vi* sair correndo, dar no pé

scuttle ['skʌtl] *n* (*also*: **coal ~**) balde *m* para carvão ♦ *vt* (*ship*) afundar voluntariamente, fazer ir a pique ♦ *vi*: **to ~ away** *or* **off** sair em disparada

scythe [saɪð] *n* segadeira, foice *f* grande

SDP (*BRIT*) *n abbr* = **Social Democratic Party**

sea [si:] *n* mar *m* ♦ *cpd* do mar, marino; **on the ~** (*boat*) no mar; (*town*) junto ao mar; **to go by ~** viajar por mar; **out to** *or* **at ~** em alto mar; **to be all at ~** (*fig*) estar confuso *or* desorientado; **~board** *n* costa, litoral *m*; **~food** *n* mariscos *mpl*; **~front** *n* orla marítima; **~going** *adj* (*ship*) de longo curso; **~gull** *n* gaivota

seal [si:l] *n* (*animal*) foca; (*stamp*) selo ♦ *vt* fechar; **~ off** *vt* fechar

sea level *n* nível *m* do mar

sea lion *n* leão-marinho *m*

seam [si:m] *n* costura; (*where edges meet*) junta; (*of coal*) veio, filão *m*

seaman ['si:mən] (*irreg*) *n* marinheiro

seamy ['si:mɪ] *adj* sórdido

seance ['seɪɔns] *n* sessão *f* espírita

seaplane ['si:pleɪn] *n* hidroavião *m*

seaport ['si:pɔ:t] *n* porto de mar

search [sə:tʃ] *n* busca, procura; (*COMPUT*) procura; (*inspection*) exame *m*, investigação *f* ♦ *vt* (*look in*) procurar em; (*examine*) examinar; (*person*) revistar ♦ *vi*: **to ~ for** procurar; **in ~ of** à procura de; **~ through** *vt fus* dar busca em; **~ing** *adj* penetrante, perscrutador(a); **~light** *n* holofote *m*; **~ party** *n* equipe *f* de salvamento; **~ warrant** *n* mandado de busca

sea: **~shore** *n* praia, beira-mar *f*, litoral *m*; **~sick** *adj*: **to be ~sick** enjoar; **~side** *n* praia; **~side resort** *n* balneário

season ['si:zn] *n* (*of year*) estação *f*; (*sporting etc*) temporada; (*of films etc*) série *f* ♦ *vt* (*food*) temperar; **to be in/out of ~** (*fruit*) estar na época/fora de época; **~al** *adj* sazonal; **~ed** *adj* (*fig: traveller*) experiente; **~ing** *n* tempero; **~**

ticket n bilhete m de temporada
seat [siːt] n (in bus, train: place) assento; (chair) cadeira; (POL) lugar m, cadeira; (buttocks) traseiro, nádegas fpl; (of trousers) fundilhos mpl ♦ vt sentar; (have room for) ter capacidade para; **to be ~ed** estar sentado; **~ belt** n cinto de segurança

sea: **~ water** n água do mar; **~weed** n alga marinha; **~worthy** adj em condições de navegar, resistente

sec. abbr (= second) seg

secluded [sɪˈkluːdɪd] adj (place) afastado; (life) solitário

seclusion [sɪˈkluːʒən] n reclusão f, isolamento

second¹ [sɪˈkɔnd] (BRIT) vt (employee) transferir temporariamente

second² [ˈsɛkənd] adj segundo ♦ adv (in race etc) em segundo lugar ♦ n segundo; (AUT: also: ~ **gear**) segunda f; (COMM) artigo defeituoso; (BRIT: SCH: degree) qualificação boa mas sem distinção ♦ vt (motion) apoiar, secundar; **~ary** adj secundário; **~ary school** n escola secundária, colégio; **~class** adj em segunda classe; **~hand** adj de (BR) or em (PT) segunda mão, usado; **~ hand** n (on clock) ponteiro de segundos; **~ly** adv em segundo lugar; **~rate** adj de segunda categoria; **~ thoughts** (US **~ thought**) npl: **to have ~ thoughts (about doing sth)** pensar duas vezes (antes de fazer algo); **on ~ thoughts** pensando bem

secrecy [ˈsiːkrəsɪ] n sigilo
secret [ˈsiːkrɪt] adj secreto ♦ n segredo
secretarial [sɛkrɪˈtɛərɪəl] adj de secretário/a, secretarial
secretariat [sɛkrɪˈtɛərɪət] n secretaria, secretariado
secretary [ˈsɛkrətərɪ] n secretário/a; (BRIT: POL): **S~ of State** Ministro/a de Estado
secretive [ˈsiːkrətɪv] adj sigiloso, reservado
sect [sɛkt] n seita
section [ˈsɛkʃən] n seção f; (part) parte f, porção f; (of document) parágrafo, artigo; (of opinion) setor m; **cross-~** corte m transversal
sector [ˈsɛktə*] n setor m
secular [ˈsɛkjulə*] adj (priest) secular; (music, society) leigo
secure [sɪˈkjuə*] adj (safe) seguro; (firmly fixed) firme, rígido ♦ vt (fix) prender; (get) conseguir, obter; **security** n segurança; (for loan) fiança, garantia
sedan [sɪˈdæn] (US) n (AUT) sedã m
sedate [sɪˈdeɪt] adj calmo ♦ vt sedar, tratar com calmantes; **sedative** n calmante m, sedativo
seduce [sɪˈdjuːs] vt seduzir; **seduction** n sedução f; **seductive** adj sedutor/a
see [siː] (pt saw, pp ~n) vt ver; (understand) entender; (accompany): **to ~ sb to**

the door acompanhar or levar alguém até a porta ♦ vi ver; (find out) achar ♦ n sé f, sede f; **to ~ that** (ensure) assegurar que; **~ you soon!** até logo!; **~ about** vt fus tratar de; **~ off** vt despedir-se de; **~ through** vt fus enxergar através de ♦ vt levar a cabo; **~ to** vt fus providenciar

seed [siːd] n semente f; (sperm) esperma m; (fig: gen pl) germe m; (TENNIS) pré-selecionado/a; **to go to ~** produzir sementes; (fig) deteriorar-se; **~ling** n planta brotada da semente, muda; **~y** adj (shabby: place) mal-cuidado; (: person) maltrapilho

seeing [ˈsiːɪŋ] conj: **~ (that)** visto (que), considerando (que)

seek [siːk] (pt, pp **sought**) vt procurar; (post) solicitar

seem [siːm] vi parecer; **there ~s to be ...** parece que há ...; **~ingly** adv aparentemente, pelo que aparenta

seen [siːn] pp of **see**

seep [siːp] vi filtrar-se, penetrar

seesaw [ˈsiːsɔː] n gangorra, balanço

seethe [siːð] vi ferver; **to ~ with anger** estar danado (da vida)

see-through adj transparente

segment [ˈsɛgmənt] n segmento; (of orange) gomo

seize [siːz] vt agarrar, pegar; (power, hostage) apoderar-se de, confiscar; (territory) tomar posse de; (opportunity) aproveitar; **~ up** vi (TECH) gripar; **~ (up)on** vt fus valer-se de; **seizure** (MED) ataque m, acesso; (LAW, of power) confisco, embargo

seldom [ˈsɛldəm] adv raramente

select [sɪˈlɛkt] adj seleto, fino ♦ vt escolher, selecionar; (SPORT) selecionar, escalar; **~ion** n seleção f, escolha; (COMM) sortimento

self [sɛlf] (pl **selves**) pron see **herself**; **himself**; **itself**; **myself**; **oneself**; **ourselves**; **themselves**; **yourself** ♦ n: **the ~** o eu

self... [sɛlf] prefix auto...; **~-assured** adj seguro de si; **~-catering** (BRIT) adj (flat) com cozinha; (holiday) em casa alugada; **~-centred** (US **~-centered**) adj egocêntrico; **~-coloured** (US **~-colored**) adj de cor natural; (of one colour) de uma só cor; **~-confidence** n autoconfiança, confiança em si; **~-conscious** adj inibido, constrangido; **~-contained** (BRIT) adj (flat) completo, autônomo; **~-control** n autocontrole m, autodomínio; **~-defence** (US **~-defense**) n legítima defesa, autodefesa; **in ~-defence** em legítima defesa; **~-discipline** n autodisciplina; **~-employed** adj autônomo; **~-evident** adj patente; **~-governing** adj autônomo; **~-indulgent** adj que se permite excessos; **~-interest** n egoísmo; **~-ish** adj egoísta; **~-less** adj desinteressado; ~-**made** n: ~-**made man** homem m que se fez por conta própria; ~-**pity** n pena de si mesmo; ~-**portrait** n auto-retrato; ~-**possessed** adj calmo, senhor(a) de si; ~-**respect** n amor m próprio; ~-**righteous** adj farisaico, santarrão/rona; ~-**sacrifice** n abnegação f, altruísmo; ~-**satisfied** adj satisfeito consigo mesmo; ~-**service** adj de auto-serviço; ~-**sufficient** adj auto-suficiente; ~-**taught** adj autodidata

sell [sɛl] (pt, pp **sold**) vt vender; (fig): to ~ **sb an idea** convencer alguém de uma idéia ♦ vi vender-se; to ~ **at** or **for** £10 vender a or por £10; ~ **off** vt liquidar; ~ **out** vi vender todo o estoque ♦ vt: the tickets are all sold out todos os ingressos já foram vendidos; ~-**by date** n vencimento; ~**er** n vendedor(a) m/f; ~**ing price** n preço de venda

sellotape ['sɛləʊteɪp] ® (BRIT) n fita adesiva, durex ® m (BR)

selves [sɛlvz] pl of **self**

semblance ['sɛmbləns] n aparência

semi... [sɛmɪ] prefix semi..., meio...; ~**circle** n semicírculo; ~**colon** n ponto e vírgula; ~**conductor** n semicondutor m; ~**detached (house)** (BRIT) n (casa) geminada; ~**final** n semifinal f

seminar ['sɛmɪnɑː'] n seminário

seminary ['sɛmɪnərɪ] n seminário

semiskilled [sɛmɪ'skɪld] adj (work, worker) semi-especializado

senate ['sɛnɪt] n senado; **senator** n senador(a) m/f

send [sɛnd] (pt, pp **sent**) vt mandar, enviar; (dispatch) expedir, remeter; (transmit) transmitir; ~ **away** vt (letter, goods) expedir, mandar; (unwelcome visitor) mandar embora; ~ **away for** vt fus encomendar, pedir pelo correio; ~ **back** vt devolver, mandar de volta; ~ **for** vt fus mandar buscar; (by post) encomendar, pedir pelo correio; ~ **off** vt (goods) despachar, expedir; (BRIT: SPORT: player) expulsar; ~ **out** vt (invitation) distribuir; (signal) emitir; ~ **up** vt (person, price) fazer subir; (BRIT: parody) parodiar; ~**er** n remetente m/f; ~-**off** n: a good ~-**off** uma boa despedida

senior ['siːnɪə'] adj (older) mais velho or idoso; (on staff) mais antigo; (of higher rank) superior; ~ **citizen** n idoso/a; ~**ity** n (in service) status m

sensation [sɛn'seɪʃən] n sensação f; ~**al** adj sensacional; (headlines, result) sensacionalista

sense [sɛns] n sentido; (feeling) sensação f; (good ~) bom senso ♦ vt sentir, perceber; ~**less** adj insensato, estúpido; (unconscious) sem sentidos, inconsciente; **sensible** adj sensato, de bom senso; (reasonable: price) razoável; (: advice, decision) sensato

sensitive ['sɛnsɪtɪv] adj sensível; (fig: touchy) suscetível

sensual ['sɛnsjuəl] adj sensual

sensuous ['sɛnsjuəs] adj sensual

sent [sɛnt] pt, pp of **send**

sentence ['sɛntəns] n (LING) frase f, oração f; (LAW) sentença ♦ vt: to ~ **sb to death/ to 5 years** condenar alguém à morte/a 5 anos de prisão

sentiment ['sɛntɪmənt] n sentimento; (opinion: also pl) opinião f; ~**al** adj sentimental

sentry ['sɛntrɪ] n sentinela f

separate [adj 'sɛprɪt, vt, vi 'sɛpəreɪt] adj separado; (distinct) diferente ♦ vt separar; (part) dividir ♦ vi separar-se; ~**ly** adv separadamente; ~**s** npl (clothes) roupas fpl que fazem jogo

September [sɛp'tɛmbə'] n setembro

septic ['sɛptɪk] adj sético; (wound) infeccionado; ~ **tank** n fossa sética

sequel ['siːkwl] n conseqüência, resultado; (of film, story) continuação f

sequence ['siːkwəns] n série f, seqüência; (CINEMA) série

sequin ['siːkwɪn] n lantejoula, paetê m

serene [sɪ'riːn] adj sereno, tranqüilo

sergeant ['sɑːdʒənt] n sargento

serial ['sɪərɪəl] n seriado; ~**ize** vt (book) publicar em folhetim; ~ **number** n número de série

series ['sɪərɪːz] n inv série f

serious ['sɪərɪəs] adj sério; (matter) importante; (illness) grave; ~**ly** adv a sério, com seriedade; (hurt) gravemente

sermon ['sɜːmən] n sermão m

serrated [sɪ'reɪtɪd] adj serrado, dentado

serum ['sɪərəm] n soro

servant ['sɜːvənt] n empregado/a; (fig) servidor(a) m/f

serve [sɜːv] vt servir; (customer) atender; (subj: train) passar por; (apprenticeship) fazer; (prison term) cumprir ♦ vi (at table) servir-se; (TENNIS) sacar; (be useful): to ~ **as/for/to do** servir como/para/para fazer ♦ n (TENNIS) saque m; it ~s him right é bem feito para ele; ~ **out** vt (food) servir; ~ **up** vt = ~ **out**

service ['sɜːvɪs] n serviço; (REL) culto; (AUT) revisão f; (TENNIS) saque m; (also: dinner ~) aparelho de jantar ♦ vt (car, washing machine) fazer a revisão de, revisar; the S~s npl (army, navy etc) as Forças Armadas; to be of ~ to sb ser útil a alguém; ~**able** adj aproveitável, prático, durável; ~ **area** n (on motorway) posto de gasolina com bar, restaurante etc; ~ **charge** (BRIT) n serviço; ~**man** (irreg) n militar m; ~ **station** n posto de gasolina (BR), estação f de serviço (PT)

serviette [sɜːvɪ'ɛt] (BRIT) n guardanapo

session ['sɛʃən] n sessão f; to be in ~ estar reunido em sessão

set [sɛt] (pt, pp **set**) n (of things) jogo;

(radio ~, TV ~) aparelho; *(of utensils)* bateria de cozinha; *(of cutlery)* talher *m*; *(of books)* coleção *f*; *(of people)* grupo; *(TENNIS)* set *m*; *(THEATRE, CINEMA)* cenário; *(HAIRDRESSING)* penteado; *(MATH)* conjunto ♦ *adj* fixo; *(ready)* pronto ♦ *vt* pôr, colocar; *(table)* pôr; *(price)* fixar; *(rules etc)* estabelecer, decidir; *(record)* estabelecer; *(time)* marcar; *(adjust)* ajustar; *(task, exam)* passar ♦ *vi (sun)* pôr-se; *(jam, jelly, concrete)* endurecer, solidificar-se; **to be ~ on doing sth** estar decidido a fazer algo; **to ~ to music** musicar, pôr música em; **to ~ on fire** botar fogo em, incendiar; **to ~ free** libertar; **to ~ sth going** pôr algo em movimento; **~ about** *vt fus* começar com; **~ aside** *vt* deixar de lado; **~ back** *vt (cost)*: **it ~ me back £5** me deu um prejuízo de £5; *(in time)*: **to ~ sb back (by)** atrasar alguém (em); **~ off** *vi* partir, ir indo ♦ *vt (bomb)* fazer explodir; *(alarm)* disparar; *(chain of events)* iniciar; *(show up well)* ressaltar; **~ out** *vi* partir ♦ *vt (arrange)* colocar, dispor; *(state)* expor, explicar; **to ~ out to do sth** pretender fazer algo; **~ up** *vt* fundar, estabelecer; **~back** *n* revés *m*, contratempo; **~ menu** *n* refeição *f* a preço fixo

settee [sɛ'tiː] *n* sofá *m*

setting ['sɛtɪŋ] *n (background)* cenário; *(position)* posição *f*; *(of sun)* pôr-(do-sol) *m*; *(of jewel)* engaste *m*

settle ['sɛtl] *vt (argument, matter)* resolver, esclarecer; *(accounts)* ajustar, liquidar; *(MED: calm)* acalmar, tranqüilizar ♦ *vi (dust etc)* assentar; *(calm down: children)* acalmar-se; *(also: ~ down)* instalar-se, estabilizar-se; **to ~ for sth** concordar em aceitar algo; **to ~ on sth** optar por algo; **~ in** *vi* instalar-se; **~ up** *vi*: **to ~ up with sb** ajustar as contas com alguém; **~ment** *n (payment)* liquidação *f*; *(agreement)* acordo, convênio; *(village etc)* povoado, povoação *f*; **~r** *n* colono/a, colonizador(a) *m/f*

setup ['sɛtʌp] *n (organization)* organização *f*; *(situation)* situação *f*

seven ['sɛvn] *num* sete; **~teen** *num* dezessete; **~th** *num* sétimo; **~ty** *num* setenta

sever ['sɛvə*] *vt* cortar; *(relations)* romper

several ['sɛvərl] *adj, pron* vários/as; **~ of us** vários de nós

severance ['sɛvərəns] *n (of relations)* rompimento; **~ pay** *n* indenização *f* pela demissão

severe [sɪ'vɪə*] *adj* severo; *(serious)* grave; *(hard)* duro; *(pain)* intenso; *(dress)* austero

sew [səu] *(pt ~ed, pp sewn)* *vt* coser, costurar; **~ up** *vt* coser, costurar

sewage ['suːɪdʒ] *n* detritos *mpl*

sewer ['suːə*] *n* (cano do) esgoto, bueiro

sewing ['səuɪŋ] *n* costura; **~ machine** *n* máquina de costura

sewn [səun] *pp of* **sew**

sex [sɛks] *n* sexo; **~ist** *adj* sexista

sexual ['sɛksjuəl] *adj* sexual

sexy ['sɛksɪ] *adj* sexy

shabby ['ʃæbɪ] *adj (person)* esfarrapado, maltrapilho; *(clothes)* usado, surrado; *(behaviour)* indigno

shack [ʃæk] *n* choupana, barraca

shackles ['ʃæklz] *npl* algemas *fpl*, grilhões *mpl*

shade [ʃeɪd] *n* sombra; *(for lamp)* quebra-luz *m*; *(of colour)* tom *m*, tonalidade *f*; *(small quantity)*: **a ~ (more/too large)** um pouquinho (mais/grande) ♦ *vt* dar sombra a; *(eyes)* sombrear; **in the ~** à sombra

shadow ['ʃædəu] *n* sombra ♦ *vt (follow)* seguir de perto (sem ser visto); **~ cabinet** *(BRIT) n (POL)* gabinete paralelo formado pelo partido da oposição; **~y** *adj* escuro; *(dim)* vago, indistinto

shady ['ʃeɪdɪ] *adj* à sombra; *(fig: dishonest: person)* suspeito, duvidoso; *(: deal)* desonesto

shaft [ʃɑːft] *n (of arrow, spear)* haste *f*; *(AUT, TECH)* eixo, manivela; *(of mine, of lift)* poço; *(of light)* raio

shaggy ['ʃægɪ] *adj* desgrenhado

shake [ʃeɪk] *(pt shook, pp shaken)* *vt* sacudir; *(building, confidence)* abalar; *(surprise)* surpreender ♦ *vi* tremer; **to ~ hands with sb** apertar a mão de alguém; **to ~ one's head** *(in refusal etc)* dizer não com a cabeça; *(in dismay)* sacudir a cabeça; **~ off** *vt* sacudir; *(fig)* livrar-se de; **~ up** *vt* sacudir; *(fig)* reorganizar; **shaky** *adj (hand, voice)* trêmulo; *(table)* instável; *(building)* abalado

shall [ʃæl] *aux vb*: **I ~ go** irei; **~ I open the door?** posso abrir a porta?; **I'll get some, ~ I?** eu vou pegar algum, está bem?

shallow ['ʃæləu] *adj* raso; *(breathing)* fraco; *(fig)* superficial

sham [ʃæm] *n* fraude *f*, fingimento ♦ *vt* fingir, simular

shambles ['ʃæmblz] *n* confusão *f*

shame [ʃeɪm] *n* vergonha ♦ *vt* envergonhar; **it is a ~ (that/to do)** é (uma) pena (que/fazer); **what a ~!** que pena!; **~faced** *adj* envergonhado; **~ful** *adj* vergonhoso; **~less** *adj* sem vergonha, descarado

shampoo [ʃæm'puː] *n* xampu *m (BR)*, champô *m (PT)* ♦ *vt* lavar o cabelo (com xampu *or* champô); **~ and set** *n* lavagem *f* e penteado

shamrock ['ʃæmrɔk] *n* trevo

shandy ['ʃændɪ] *n* mistura de cerveja com refresco gaseificado

shan't [ʃɑːnt] = **shall not**

shanty town [ˈʃæntɪ-] *n* favela

shape [ʃeɪp] *n* forma ♦ *vt* (*form*) moldar; (*sb's ideas*) formar; (*sb's life*) definir, determinar; **to take ~** tomar forma; **~ up** *vi* (*events*) desenrolar-se; (*person*) tomar jeito; **~-d** *suffix*: **heart~d** em forma de coração; **~less** *adj* informe, sem forma definida; **~ly** *adj* escultural

share [ʃɛə*] *n* parte *f*; (*contribution*) cota; (*COMM*) ação *f* ♦ *vt* dividir; (*have in common*) compartilhar; **~ out** *vi* distribuir; **~holder** *n* acionista *m/f*

shark [ʃɑːk] *n* tubarão *m*

sharp [ʃɑːp] *adj* (*razor, knife*) afiado; (*point, features*) pontiagudo; (*outline*) definido, bem marcado; (*pain, voice*) agudo; (*taste*) acre; (*MUS*) desafinado; (*contrast*) marcado; (*quick-witted*) perspicaz; (*dishonest*) desonesto ♦ *n* (*MUS*) sustenido ♦ *adv*: **at 2 o'clock ~** às 2 (horas) em ponto; **~en** *vt* afiar; (*pencil*) apontar, fazer a ponta de; (*fig*) aguçar; **~ener** *n* (*also*: **pencil ~ener**) apontador *m* (*BR*), apara-lápis *m inv* (*PT*); **~-eyed** *adj* de vista aguda; **~ly** *adv* (*abruptly*) bruscamente; (*clearly*) claramente; (*harshly*) severamente

shatter [ˈʃætə*] *vt* despedaçar, estilhaçar; (*fig: ruin*) destruir, acabar com; (: *upset*) arrasar ♦ *vi* despedaçar-se, estilhaçar-se

shave [ʃeɪv] *vt* barbear, fazer a barba de ♦ *vi* fazer a barba, barbear-se ♦ *n*: **to have a ~** fazer a barba; **~r** *n* (*also*: **electric ~r**) barbeador *m* elétrico; **shaving** *n* (*action*) barbeação *f*; **shavings** *npl* (*of wood*) aparas *fpl*; **shaving brush** *n* pincel *m* de barba; **shaving cream** *n* creme *m* de barbear; **shaving foam** *n* espuma de barbear

shawl [ʃɔːl] *n* xale *m*

she [ʃiː] *pron* ela ♦ *prefix*: **~-elephant** *etc* elefante *etc* fêmea

sheaf [ʃiːf] (*pl* **sheaves**) *n* (*of corn*) gavela; (*of papers*) maço

shear [ʃɪə*] (*pt* **~ed**, *pp* **shorn**) *vt* (*sheep*) tosquiar, tosar; **~ off** *vi* cisalhar; **~s** *npl* (*for hedge*) tesoura de jardim

sheath [ʃiːθ] *n* bainha; (*contraceptive*) camisa-de-vênus *f*, camisinha

sheaves [ʃiːvz] *npl of* **sheaf**

shed [ʃed] (*pt, pp* **shed**) *n* alpendre *m*, galpão *m* ♦ *vt* (*skin*) mudar; (*load*) perder; (*tears, blood*) derramar; (*workers*) despedir

she'd [ʃiːd] **= she had; she would**

sheen [ʃiːn] *n* brilho

sheep [ʃiːp] *n inv* ovelha; **~dog** *n* cão *m* pastor; **~ish** *adj* tímido, acanhado; **~skin** *n* pele *f* de carneiro, pelego

sheer [ʃɪə*] *adj* (*utter*) puro, completo; (*steep*) íngreme, empinado; (*almost transparent*) fino, translúcido ♦ *adv* a pique

sheet [ʃiːt] *n* (*on bed*) lençol *m*; (*of paper*) folha; (*of glass, metal*) lâmina, chapa; (*of ice*) camada

sheik(h) [ʃeɪk] *n* xeque *m*

shelf [ʃelf] (*pl* **shelves**) *n* prateleira

shell [ʃel] *n* (*on beach*) concha; (*of egg, nut etc*) casca; (*explosive*) obus *m*; (*of building*) armação *f*, esqueleto *m* ♦ *vt* (*peas*) descascar; (*MIL*) bombardear

she'll [ʃiːl] **= she will; she shall**

shellfish [ˈʃelfɪʃ] *n inv* crustáceo; (*pl: as food*) frutos *mpl* do mar, mariscos *mpl*

shell suit *n* conjunto de náilon para jogging

shelter [ˈʃeltə*] *n* (*building*) abrigo; (*protection*) refúgio ♦ *vt* (*protect*) proteger; (*give lodging to*) abrigar ♦ *vi* abrigar-se, refugiar-se; **~ed** *adj* (*life*) protegido; (*spot*) abrigado, protegido; **~ed housing** *n* acomodação para idosos e defeituosos

shelve [ʃelv] *vt* (*fig*) pôr de lado, engavetar; **~s** *npl of* **shelf**

shepherd [ˈʃepəd] *n* pastor *m* ♦ *vt* guiar, conduzir; **~'s pie** (*BRIT*) *n* empadão *m* de carne e batata

sheriff [ˈʃerɪf] (*US*) *n* xerife *m*

sherry [ˈʃerɪ] *n* (*vinho de*) Xerez *m*

she's [ʃiːz] **= she is; she has**

Shetland [ˈʃetlənd] *n* (*also*: **the ~s, the ~ Isles**) as ilhas Shetland

shield [ʃiːld] *n* escudo; (*SPORT*) escudo, brasão *m*; (*protection*) proteção *f* ♦ *vt*: **to ~ (from)** proteger (contra)

shift [ʃɪft] *n* mudança; (*of work*) turno; (*of workers*) turma ♦ *vt* transferir; (*remove*) tirar ♦ *vi* mudar; **~less** *adj* indolente; **~ work** *n* trabalho em turnos; **~y** *adj* esperto, trapaceiro; (*eyes*) velhaco, maroto

shilling [ˈʃɪlɪŋ] (*BRIT*) *n* xelim *m* (= 12 *old pence; 20 in a pound*)

shilly-shally [ˈʃɪlɪʃælɪ] *vi* vacilar

shimmer [ˈʃɪmə*] *vi* cintilar, tremeluzir

shin [ʃɪn] *n* canela (da perna)

shine [ʃaɪn] (*pt, pp* **shone**) *n* brilho, lustre *m* ♦ *vi* brilhar ♦ *vt* (*glasses*) polir; (*shoes: pt, pp* **~d**) lustrar; **to ~ a torch on sth** apontar uma lanterna para algo

shingle [ˈʃɪŋgl] *n* (*on beach*) pedrinhas *fpl*, seixinhos *mpl*; **~s** *n* (*MED*) herpeszoster *m*

shiny [ˈʃaɪnɪ] *adj* brilhante, lustroso

ship [ʃɪp] *n* barco ♦ *vt* (*of goods*) embarcar; (*send*) transportar *or* mandar (*por via marítima*); **~ment** *n* carregamento; **~per** *n* exportador(a) *m/f*, expedidor(a) *m/f*; **~ping** *n* (*ships*) navios *mpl*; (*cargo*) transporte *m* de mercadorias (*por via marítima*); (*traffic*) navegação *f*; **~shape** *adj* em ordem; **~wreck** *n* (*event*) malogro; (*ship*) naufrágio ♦ *vt*: **to be ~wrecked** naufragar; **~yard** *n* estaleiro

shire [ʃaɪə*] (*BRIT*) *n* condado

shirk [ʃɜːk] *vt* (*work*) esquivar-se de; (*obligations*) não cumprir, faltar a

shirt [ʃɜːt] *n* (*man's*) camisa; (*woman's*) blusa; **in ~ sleeves** em manga de cami-

sa
shit [ʃɪt] (*inf!*) *excl* merda (!)
shiver ['ʃɪvə*] *n* tremor *m*, arrepio ♦ *vi* tremer, estremecer, tiritar
shoal [ʃəul] *n* (*of fish*) cardume *m*; (*fig: also:* ~s) bando, multidão *f*
shock [ʃɔk] *n* (*impact*) choque *m*; (*ELEC*) descarga; (*emotional*) comoção *f*, abalo; (*start*) susto, sobressalto; (*MED*) trauma *m* ♦ *vt* dar um susto em, chocar; (*offend*) escandalizar; ~ **absorber** *n* amortecedor *m*; ~**ing** *adj* chocante, lamentável; (*outrageous*) revoltante, chocante
shod [ʃɔd] *pt, pp of* **shoe**
shoddy ['ʃɔdɪ] *adj* de má qualidade
shoe [ʃu:] (*pt, pp* **shod**) *n* sapato; (*for horse*) ferradura ♦ *vt* (*horse*) ferrar; ~**brush** *n* escova de sapato; ~**lace** *n* cadarço, cordão *m* (de sapato); ~ **polish** *n* graxa de sapato; ~**shop** *n* sapataria; ~**string** *n* (*fig*): **on a** ~**string** com muito pouco dinheiro
shone [ʃɔn] *pt, pp of* **shine**
shoo [ʃu:] *excl* xô!
shook [ʃuk] *pt of* **shake**
shoot [ʃu:t] (*pt, pp* **shot**) *n* (*on branch, seedling*) broto ♦ *vt* disparar; (*kill*) matar à bala, balear; (*wound*) ferir à bala, balear; (*execute*) fuzilar; (*film*) filmar, rodar ♦ *vi*: ~ (**at**) atirar (em); (*FOOTBALL*) chutar; ~ **down** *vt* (*plane*) derrubar, abater; ~ **in/out** *vi* entrar/sair correndo; ~ **up** *vi* (*fig*) subir vertiginosamente; ~**ing** *n* tiros *mpl*, tiroteio; (*HUNTING*) caçada (com espingarda); ~**ing star** *n* estrela cadente
shop [ʃɔp] *n* loja; (*workshop*) oficina ♦ *vi* (*also: go* ~**ping**) ir fazer compras; ~ **assistant** (*BRIT*) *n* vendedor(a) *m/f*; ~ **floor** (*BRIT*) *n* operários *mpl*; ~**keeper** *n* lojista *m/f*; ~**lifting** *n* furto (em lojas); ~**per** *n* comprador(a) *f*; ~**ping** *n* (*goods*) compras *fpl*; ~**ping bag** *n* bolsa (de compras); ~**ping centre** (*US* ~**ping center**) *n* shopping (center) *m*; ~**soiled** *adj* danificado (*pelo tempo ou manuseio*); ~ **steward** (*BRIT*) *n* (*INDUSTRY*) representante *m/f* sindical; ~ **window** *n* vitrine *f* (*BR*), montra (*PT*)
shore [ʃɔ:*] *n* (*of sea*) costa, praia; (*of lake*) margem *f* ♦ *vt*: **to** ~ (**up**) reforçar, escorar; **on** ~ em terra
shorn [ʃɔ:n] *pp of* **shear**
short [ʃɔt] *adj* curto; (*in time*) breve, de curta duração; (*person*) baixo; (*curt*) seco, brusco; (*insufficient*) insuficiente, em falta; **to be** ~ **of sth** estar em falta de algo; **in** ~ em resumo; ~ **of doing ...** a não ser fazer ...; **everything** ~ **of ...** tudo a não ser ...; **it is** ~ **for é** a abreviatura de; **to cut** ~ (*speech, visit*) encurtar; **to fall** ~ **of** não ser à altura de; **to run** ~ **of sth** ficar sem algo; **to stop** ~ parar de repente; **to stop** ~ **of** chegar quase a; ~**age** *n* escassez *f*, fal-

ta; ~**bread** *n* biscoito amanteigado; ~**change** *vt*: **to** ~**change sb** roubar alguém no troco; ~ **circuit** *n* curto-circuito ♦ *vt* provocar um curto-circuito ♦ *vi* entrar em curto-circuito; ~**coming** *n* defeito, imperfeição *f*, falha; ~**(crust) pastry** (*BRIT*) *n* massa amanteigada; ~**cut** *n* atalho; ~**en** *vt* encurtar; (*visit*) abreviar; ~**fall** *n* déficit *m*; ~**hand** (*BRIT*) *n* estenografia; ~**hand typist** (*BRIT*) *n* estenodatilógrafo/a; ~ **list** (*BRIT*) *n* lista dos candidatos escolhidos; ~**lived** *adj* de curta duração; ~**ly** *adv* em breve, dentro em pouco; ~**s** *npl*: (**a pair of**) ~**s** um calção (*BR*), um short (*BR*), uns calções (*PT*); ~**sighted** (*BRIT*) *adj* míope; (*fig*) imprevidente; ~**staffed** *adj* com falta de pessoal; ~**story** *n* conto; ~**tempered** *adj* irritadiço; ~**term** *adj* a curto prazo; ~ **wave** *n* (*RADIO*) onda curta
shot [ʃɔt] *pt, pp of* **shoot** ♦ *n* (*of gun*) tiro; (*pellets*) chumbo; (*try, FOOTBALL*) tentativa; (*injection*) injeção *f*; (*PHOT*) fotografia; **to be a good/bad** ~ (*person*) ter boa/má pontaria; **like a** ~ como um relâmpago, de repente; ~**gun** *n* espingarda
should [ʃud] *aux vb*: **I** ~ **go now** devo ir embora agora; **he** ~ **be there now** ele já deve ter chegado; **I** ~ **go if I were you** se eu fosse você eu iria; **I** ~ **like to** eu gostaria de
shoulder ['ʃəuldə*] *n* ombro ♦ *vt* (*fig*) arcar com; ~ **bag** *n* sacola a tiracolo; ~ **blade** *n* omoplata *m*; ~ **strap** *n* alça
shouldn't ['ʃudnt] = **should not**
shout [ʃaut] *n* grito ♦ *vt* gritar ♦ *vi* (*also:* ~ **out**) gritar, berrar; ~ **down** *vt* fazer calar com gritos; ~**ing** *n* gritaria, berreiro
shove [ʃʌv] *vt* empurrar; (*inf: put*): **to** ~ **sth in** botar algo em; ~ **off** (*inf*) *vi* dar o fora
shovel ['ʃʌvl] *n* pá *f*; (*mechanical*) escavadeira ♦ *vt* cavar com pá
show [ʃəu] (*pt* ~**ed**, *pp* ~**n**) *n* (*of emotion*) demonstração *f*; (*semblance*) aparência; (*exhibition*) exibição *f*; (*THEATRE*) espetáculo, representação *f*; (*CINEMA*) sessão *f* ♦ *vt* mostrar; (*courage etc*) demonstrar, dar prova de; (*exhibit*) expor; (*depict*) ilustrar; (*film*) exibir ♦ *vi* mostrar-se; (*appear*) aparecer; **to be on** ~ estar em exposição; ~ **in** *vt* mandar entrar; ~ **off** *vi* (*pej*) mostrar-se, exibir-se ♦ *vt* (*display*) exibir, mostrar; ~ **out** *vt* levar até a porta; ~ **up** *vi* (*stand out*) destacar-se; (*inf: turn up*) aparecer, pintar ♦ *vt* descobrir; ~ **business** *n* o mundo do espetáculo; ~**down** *n* confrontação *f*
shower ['ʃauə*] *n* (*rain*) pancada de chuva; (*of stones etc*) chuva, enxurrada; (*also:* ~ **bath**) chuveiro ♦ *vi* tomar ba-

nho (de chuveiro) ♦ vt: to ~ sb with (gifts etc) cumular alguém de; to have or take a ~ tomar banho (de chuveiro); ~proof adj impermeável

showing ['ʃəʊɪŋ] n (of film) projeção f, exibição f

show jumping [-'dʒʌmpɪŋ] n hipismo

shown [ʃəʊn] pp of show

show: ~-off (inf) n (person) exibicionista m/f, faroleiro/a; ~piece n (of exhibition etc) obra mais importante; ~room n sala de exposição

shrank [ʃræŋk] pt of shrink

shrapnel ['ʃræpnl] n estilhaços mpl

shred [ʃred] n (gen pl) tira, pedaço ♦ vt rasgar em tiras, retalhar; (CULIN) desfiar, picar; ~der n (for vegetables) ralador m; (for documents) fragmentadora

shrewd [ʃruːd] adj perspicaz

shriek [ʃriːk] n grito ♦ vi gritar, berrar

shrill [ʃrɪl] adj agudo, estridente

shrimp [ʃrɪmp] n camarão m

shrine [ʃraɪn] n santuário

shrink [ʃrɪŋk] (pt shrank, pp shrunk) vi encolher; (be reduced) reduzir-se; (also: ~ away) encolher-se ♦ vt (cloth) fazer encolher ♦ n (inf: pej) psicanalista m/f; to ~ from doing sth não se atrever a fazer algo; ~age n encolhimento, redução f; ~wrap vt embalar a vácuo

shrivel ['ʃrɪvl] vt (also: ~ up: dry) secar; (: crease) enrugar ♦ vi secar-se; enrugar-se, murchar

shroud [ʃraʊd] n mortalha ♦ vt: ~ed in mystery envolto em mistério

Shrove Tuesday [ʃrəʊv-] n terça-feira gorda

shrub [ʃrʌb] n arbusto; ~bery n arbustos mpl

shrug [ʃrʌg] n encolhimento dos ombros ♦ vt, vi: to ~ (one's shoulders) encolher os ombros, dar de ombros (BR); ~ off vt negar a importância de

shrunk [ʃrʌŋk] pp of shrink

shudder ['ʃʌdə*] n estremecimento, tremor m ♦ vi estremecer, tremer de medo

shuffle ['ʃʌfl] vt (cards) embaralhar ♦ vi: to ~ (one's feet) arrastar os pés

shun [ʃʌn] vt evitar, afastar-se de

shunt [ʃʌnt] vt (RAIL) manobrar, desviar; (object) desviar

shut [ʃʌt] (pt, pp shut) vt fechar ♦ vi fechar(-se); ~ down vt, vi fechar; ~ off vt cortar, interromper; ~ up vi (inf: keep quiet) calar-se, calar a boca ♦ vt (close) fechar; (silence) calar; ~ter n veneziana; (PHOT) obturador m

shuttle ['ʃʌtl] n (plane: also: ~ service) ponte f aérea; (space ~) ônibus m espacial

shuttlecock ['ʃʌtlkɔk] n peteca

shy [ʃaɪ] adj tímido; (reserved) reservado; ~ness n timidez f

sibling ['sɪblɪŋ] n irmão/irmã m/f

sick [sɪk] adj (ill) doente; (nauseated) en-

joado; (humour) negro; (vomiting): to be ~ vomitar; to feel ~ estar enjoado; to be ~ of (fig) estar cheio or farto de; ~bay n enfermaria; ~en vt (disgust) enojar, repugnar; ~ening adj (fig) repugnante

sickle ['sɪkl] n foice f

sick: ~ leave n licença por doença; ~ly adj doentio; (causing nausea) nauseante; ~ness n doença, indisposição f; (vomiting) náusea, enjôo; ~ pay n salário pago em período de doença

side [saɪd] n lado; (of body) flanco; (of lake) margem f; (aspect) aspecto; (team) time m (BR), equipa (PT); (of hill) declive m ♦ cpd (door, entrance) lateral ♦ vi: to ~ with sb tomar o partido de alguém; by the ~ of ao lado de; ~ by ~ lado a lado, juntos; from ~ to ~ para lá e para cá; to take ~s with pôr-se ao lado de; ~board n aparador m; ~boards npl (BRIT) = ~burns; ~burns npl suíças fpl, costeletas fpl; ~ drum n caixa clara; ~ effect n efeito colateral; ~light n (AUT) luz f lateral; ~line n (SPORT) linha lateral; (fig: job) emprego suplementar; ~long adj de soslaio; ~saddle adv de silhão; ~show n (stall) barraca; ~step vt evitar; ~track vt (fig) desviar (do seu propósito); ~walk (US) n calçada; ~ways adv de lado; siding n (RAIL) desvio, ramal m

sidle ['saɪdl] vi: to ~ up (to) aproximar-se furtivamente de

siege [siːdʒ] n sítio, assédio

sieve [sɪv] n peneira ♦ vt peneirar

sift [sɪft] vt peneirar; (fig) esquadrinhar, analisar minuciosamente

sigh [saɪ] n suspiro ♦ vi suspirar

sight [saɪt] n (faculty) vista, visão f; (spectacle) espetáculo; (on gun) mira ♦ vt avistar; in ~ à vista; on ~ (shoot) no local; out of ~ longe dos olhos; ~seeing n turismo; to go ~seeing fazer turismo, passear

sign [saɪn] n (with hand) sinal m, aceno; (indication) indício; (notice) letreiro, tabuleta; (written) signo ♦ vt assinar; to ~ sth over to sb assinar a transferência de algo para alguém; ~ on vi (MIL) alistar-se; (BRIT: as unemployed) cadastrar-se para receber auxílio-desemprego; (for course) inscrever-se ♦ vt (MIL) alistar; (employee) efetivar; ~ up vi (MIL) alistar-se; (for course) inscrever-se ♦ vt recrutar

signal ['sɪgnl] n sinal m, aviso ♦ vi (also: AUT) sinalizar, dar sinal ♦ vt (person) fazer sinais para; (message) transmitir; ~man (irreg) n sinaleiro

signature ['sɪgnətʃə*] n assinatura; ~ tune n tema m (de abertura)

signet ring ['sɪgnət-] n anel m com o sinete or a chancela

significance [sɪg'nɪfɪkəns] n importância; **significant** adj significativo; (importante) importante

sign language n mímica, linguagem f através de sinais

sign post n indicador m

silence ['saɪləns] n silêncio ♦ vt silenciar, impor silêncio a; ~r n (on gun) silenciador m; (BRIT: AUT) silencioso

silent ['saɪlənt] adj silencioso; (not speaking) calado; (film) mudo; **to remain ~** manter-se em silêncio; **~ partner** n (COMM) sócio/a comanditário/a

silhouette [sɪluː'ɛt] n silhueta

silicon chip ['sɪlɪkən-] n placa or chip m de silício

silk [sɪlk] n seda ♦ adj de seda; **~y** adj sedoso

silly ['sɪlɪ] adj (person) bobo, idiota, imbecil; (idea) absurdo, ridículo

silt [sɪlt] n sedimento, aluvião m

silver ['sɪlvə*] n prata; (money) moedas fpl; (also: ~ware) prataria ♦ adj de prata; **~-plated** adj prateado, banhado a prata; **~smith** n prateiro/a; **~y** adj prateado

similar ['sɪmɪlə*] adj: **~ to** parecido com, semelhante a; **~ity** n semelhança; **~ly** adv da mesma maneira

simmer ['sɪmə*] vi cozer em fogo lento, ferver lentamente

simpering ['sɪmpərɪŋ] adj idiota

simple ['sɪmpl] adj simples inv; (foolish) ingênuo; **~ interest** n juros mpl simples; **simply** adv de maneira simples; (merely) simplesmente

simultaneous [sɪməl'teɪnɪəs] adj simultâneo; **~ly** adv simultaneamente

sin [sɪn] n pecado ♦ vi pecar

since [sɪns] adv desde então, depois ♦ prep desde ♦ conj (time) desde que; (because) porque, visto que, já que; **~ then** desde então; (ever) **~** desde que

sincere [sɪn'sɪə*] adj sincero; **~ly** adv: **yours ~ly** (at end of letter) atenciosamente; **sincerity** n sinceridade f

sinew ['sɪnjuː] n tendão m

sinful ['sɪnful] adj (thought) pecaminoso; (person) pecador(a)

sing [sɪŋ] (pt **sang**, pp **sung**) vt, vi cantar

Singapore [sɪŋgə'pɔː*] n Cingapura (no article)

singe [sɪndʒ] vt chamuscar

singer ['sɪŋə*] n cantor(a) m/f

singing ['sɪŋɪŋ] n canto; (songs) canções fpl

single ['sɪŋgl] adj único, só; (unmarried) solteiro; (not double) simples inv ♦ n (BRIT: also: **~ ticket**) passagem f de ida; (record) compacto; **~ out** vt (choose) escolher; (distinguish) distinguir; **~-breasted** adj não trespassado; **~ file** n: **in ~ file** em fila indiana; **~-handed** adv sem ajuda, sozinho; **~-minded** adj determinado; **~ room** n quarto indivi-

dual; **~s** n (TENNIS) partida simples; **singly** adv separadamente

singular ['sɪŋgjulə*] adj (odd) esquisito; (outstanding) extraordinário, excepcional; (LING) singular ♦ n (LING) singular m

sinister ['sɪnɪstə*] adj sinistro

sink [sɪŋk] (pt **sank**, pp **sunk**) n pia ♦ vt (ship) afundar; (foundations) escavar ♦ vi afundar-se; (heart) partir; (spirits) ficar deprimido; (also: ~ **back**, ~ **down**) cair or mergulhar gradativamente; **to ~ sth into** enterrar algo em; **~ in** vi (fig) penetrar

sinner ['sɪnə*] n pecador(a) m/f

sinus ['saɪnəs] n (ANAT) seio paranasal

sip [sɪp] n gole m ♦ vt sorver, bebericar

siphon ['saɪfən] n sifão m; **~ off** vt extrair com sifão; (funds) desviar

sir [sə*] n senhor m; **S~ John Smith** Sir John Smith; **yes, ~** sim, senhor

siren ['saɪən] n sirena

sirloin ['səːlɔɪn] n lombo de vaca

sissy ['sɪsɪ] (inf) n fresco

sister ['sɪstə*] n irmã f; (BRIT: nurse) enfermeira-chefe f; (nun) freira; **~-in-law** n cunhada

sit [sɪt] (pt, pp **sat**) vi sentar-se; (be sitting) estar sentado; (assembly) reunir-se; (for painter) posar ♦ vt (exam) prestar; **~ down** vi sentar-se; **~ in on** vt fus assistir a; **~ up** vi (after lying) levantar-se; (straight) endireitar-se; (not go to bed) aguardar acordado, velar

sitcom ['sɪtkɔm] n abbr (= situation comedy) comédia de costumes

site [saɪt] n local m, sítio; (also: **building ~**) lote m (de terreno) ♦ vt situar, localizar

sit-in n (demonstration) ocupação de um local como forma de protesto, manifestação f pacífica

sitting ['sɪtɪŋ] n (in canteen) turno; **~ room** n sala de estar

situation [sɪtju'eɪʃən] n situação f; (job) posição f; (location) local m; **"~s vacant"** (BRIT) "empregos oferecem-se"

six [sɪks] num seis; **~teen** num dezesseis; **~th** num sexto; **~ty** num sessenta

size [saɪz] n tamanho; (extent) extensão f; (of clothing) tamanho; (of shoes) número; **~ up** vt avaliar, formar uma opinião sobre; **~able** adj considerável, importante

sizzle ['sɪzl] vi chiar

skate [skeɪt] n patim m; (fish: pl inv) arraia ♦ vi patinar; **~board** n skate m, patim-tábua m; **~r** n patinador(a) m/f; **skating** n patinação f; **skating rink** n rinque m de patinação

skeleton ['skɛlɪtn] n esqueleto; (TECH) armação f; (outline) esquema m, esboço; **~ staff** n pessoal m reduzido (ao mínimo)

skeptic ['skɛptɪk] (US) n = **sceptic**

sketch [skɛtʃ] n (drawing) desenho; (ou-

tline) esboço, croqui *m*; (*THEATRE*) quadro, esquete *m* ♦ *vt* desenhar, esboçar; (*ideas: also*: ~ **out**) esboçar; ~**book** *n* caderno de rascunho; ~**y** *adj* incompleto, superficial

skewer ['skjuːə*] *n* espetinho

ski [skiː] *n* esqui *m* ♦ *vi* esquiar; ~ **boot** *n* bota de esquiar

skid [skɪd] *n* derrapagem *f* ♦ *vi* deslizar; (*AUT*) derrapar

ski: ~**er** *n* esquiador(a) *m/f*; ~**ing** *n* esqui *m*; ~ **jump** *n* pista para saltos de esqui; (*event*) salto de esqui

skilful ['skɪlful] (*US* **skillful**) *adj* habilidoso, jeitoso

ski lift *n* ski lift *m*

skill [skɪl] *n* habilidade *f*, perícia; (*for work*) técnica; ~**ed** *adj* hábil, perito; (*worker*) especializado, qualificado; ~**ful** (*US*) *adj* = **skilful**

skim [skɪm] *vt* (*milk*) desnatar; (*glide over*) roçar ♦ *vi*: **to** ~ **through** (*book*) folhear; ~**med milk** *n* leite *m* desnatado

skimp [skɪmp] *vt* (*work: also*: ~ **on**) atamancar; (*cloth etc*) economizar, regatear; ~**y** *adj* (*meagre*) escasso, insuficiente; (*skirt*) sumário

skin [skɪn] *n* pele *f*; (*of fruit, vegetable*) casca ♦ *vt* (*fruit etc*) descascar; (*animal*) tirar a pele de; ~ **cancer** *n* câncer *m* (*BR*) or cancro (*PT*) de pele; ~-**deep** *adj* superficial; ~ **diving** *n* caça-submarina; ~**ny** *adj* magro, descarnado; ~**tight** *adj* justo, grudado (no corpo)

skip [skɪp] *n* salto, pulo; (*BRIT: container*) balde *m* ♦ *vi* saltar; (*with rope*) pular corda ♦ *vt* (*pass over*) omitir, saltar; (*miss*) deixar de

ski pants *npl* calça (*BR*) or calças *fpl* (*PT*) de esquiar

ski pole *n* vara de esqui

skipper ['skɪpə*] *n* capitão *m*

skipping rope ['skɪpɪŋ-] (*BRIT*) *n* corda (de pular)

skirmish ['skəːmɪʃ] *n* escaramuça

skirt [skəːt] *n* saia ♦ *vt* orlar, circundar; ~**ing board** (*BRIT*) *n* rodapé *m*

ski slope *n* pista de esqui

ski suit *n* traje *m* de esqui

skit [skɪt] *n* paródia, sátira

skittle ['skɪtl] *n* pau *m*; ~**s** *n* (*game*) (jogo de) boliche *m* (*BR*), jogo da bola (*PT*)

skive [skaɪv] (*BRIT: inf*) *vi* evitar trabalhar

skulk [skʌlk] *vi* esconder-se

skull [skʌl] *n* caveira *f*; (*ANAT*) crânio

skunk [skʌŋk] *n* gambá *m*

sky [skaɪ] *n* céu *m*; ~**light** *n* clarabóia, escotilha; ~**scraper** *n* arranha-céu *m*

slab [slæb] *n* (*stone*) bloco; (*flat*) laje *f*; (*of cake*) fatia grossa

slack [slæk] *adj* (*loose*) frouxo; (*slow*) lerdo; (*careless*) descuidoso, desmazelado;

~**s** *npl* (*trousers*) calça (*BR*), calças *fpl* (*PT*); ~**en** *vi* (*also*: ~**en off**) afrouxar-se ♦ *vt* afrouxar; (*speed*) diminuir

slag heap [slæg-] *n* monte *m* de escória *or* de escombros

slag off [slæg-] (*BRIT: inf*) *vt* malhar

slain [sleɪn] *pp of* **slay**

slam [slæm] *vt* (*door*) bater *or* fechar (com violência); (*throw*) atirar violentamente; (*criticize*) malhar, criticar ♦ *vi* fechar-se (com violência)

slander ['slɑːndə*] *n* calúnia, difamação *f*

slang [slæŋ] *n* gíria; (*jargon*) jargão *m*

slant [slɑːnt] *n* declive *m*, inclinação *f*; (*fig*) ponto de vista; ~**ed**, ~**ing** *adj* inclinado; (*eyes*) puxado

slap [slæp] *n* tapa *m or f* ♦ *vt* dar um(a) tapa em; (*paint etc*): **to** ~ **sth on sth** passar algo em algo descuidadamente ♦ *adv* diretamente, exatamente; ~**dash** *adj* impetuoso; (*work*) descuidado; ~**stick** *n* (comédia-)pastelão *m*; ~-**up** (*BRIT*) *adj*: **a** ~-**up meal** uma refeição suntuosa

slash [slæʃ] *vt* cortar, talhar; (*fig: prices*) cortar

slat [slæt] *n* (*of wood*) ripa; (*of plastic*) tira

slate [sleɪt] *n* ardósia ♦ *vt* (*fig: criticize*) criticar duramente, arrasar

slaughter ['slɔːtə*] *n* (*of animals*) matança; (*of people*) carnificina ♦ *vt* abater; matar, massacrar; ~**house** *n* matadouro

slave [sleɪv] *n* escravo/a ♦ *vi* (*also*: ~ **away**) trabalhar como escravo; ~**ry** *n* escravidão *f*; **slavish** *adj* servil; (*copy*) descarado

slay [sleɪ] (*pt* **slew**, *pp* **slain**) *vt* (*literary*) matar

sleazy ['sliːzɪ] *adj* sórdido

sledge [sledʒ] *n* trenó *m*; ~**hammer** *n* marreta, malho

sleek [sliːk] *adj* (*hair, fur*) macio, lustroso; (*car, boat*) aerodinâmico

sleep [sliːp] (*pt, pp* **slept**) *n* sono ♦ *vi* dormir; **to go to** ~ dormir, adormecer; ~ **around** *vi* ser promíscuo sexualmente; ~ **in** *vi* (*oversleep*) dormir demais; ~**er** *n* (*RAIL: train*) vagão-leitos *m* (*BR*), carruagem-camas *f* (*PT*); ~**ing bag** *n* saco de dormir; ~**ing car** *n* vagão-leitos *m* (*BR*), carruagem-camas *f* (*PT*); ~**ing partner** (*BRIT*) *n* (*COMM*) sócio comanditário; ~**ing pill** *n* pílula para dormir; ~**less** *adj*: **a** ~**less night** uma noite em claro; ~**walker** *n* sonâmbulo; ~**y** *adj* sonolento; (*fig*) morto

sleet [sliːt] *n* chuva com neve *or* granizo

sleeve [sliːv] *n* manga; (*of record*) capa; ~**less** *adj* sem manga

sleigh [sleɪ] *n* trenó *m*

sleight [slaɪt] *n*: ~ **of hand** prestidigitação *f*

slender ['slɛndə*] *adj* esbelto, delgado; (*means*) escasso, insuficiente

slept [slɛpt] *pt, pp of* **sleep**
slew [slu:] *pt of* **slay** ♦ *vi* (BRIT: *also:* ~ **round**) virar
slice [slaɪs] *n* (*of meat, bread*) fatia; (*of lemon*) rodela; (*utensil*) pá *f or* espátula de bolo ♦ *vt* cortar em fatias
slick [slɪk] *adj* (*skilful*) jeitoso, ágil, engenhoso; (*clever*) esperto, astuto ♦ *n* (*also:* **oil** ~) mancha de óleo
slid [slɪd] *pt, pp of* **slide**
slide [slaɪd] (*pt, pp* **slid**) *n* deslizamento, escorregão *m*; (*in playground*) escorregador *m*; (*PHOT*) slide *m*; (BRIT: *also:* **hair** ~) passador *m* ♦ *vt* deslizar ♦ *vi* escorregar; ~ **rule** *n* régua de cálculo; **sliding** (*door*) corrediço; **sliding scale** *n* escala móvel
slight [slaɪt] *adj* (*slim*) fraco, franzino; (*frail*) delicado; (*small*) pequeno; (*trivial*) insignificante ♦ *n* desfeita, desconsideração *f*; **not in the** ~**est** em absoluto, de maneira alguma; ~**ly** *adv* ligeiramente, um pouco
slim [slɪm] *adj* esbelto, delgado; (*chance*) pequeno ♦ *vi* emagrecer
slime [slaɪm] *n* lodo, limo, lama
slimming ['slɪmɪŋ] *n* emagrecimento
sling [slɪŋ] (*pt, pp* **slung**) *n* (*MED*) tipóia; (*for baby*) bebêbag *m*; (*weapon*) estilingue•*m*, funda ♦ *vt* atirar, arremessar, lançar
slip [slɪp] *n* (*fall*) escorregão *m*; (*mistake*) erro, lapso; (*underskirt*) combinação *f*; (*of paper*) tira ♦ *vt* deslizar ♦ *vi* (*slide*) deslizar; (*lose balance*) escorregar; (*decline*) decair; (*move smoothly*): **to** ~ **into/ out of** entrar furtivamente em/sair furtivamente de; **to** ~ **sth on/off** enfiar/ tirar algo; **to give sb the** ~ esgueirar-se de alguém; **a** ~ **of the tongue** um lapso da língua; ~ **away** *vi* escapulir; ~ **in** *vt* meter ♦ *vi* (*errors*) surgir; ~ **out** *vi* (*go out*) sair (um momento); ~ **up** *vi* cometer um erro; ~**ped disc** *n* disco deslocado
slipper ['slɪpə'] *n* chinelo
slippery ['slɪpərɪ] *adj* escorregadio
slip road (BRIT) *n* (*to motorway*) entrada para a rodovia
slipshod ['slɪpʃɒd] *adj* descuidoso, desmazelado
slip-up *n* equívoco, mancada
slipway ['slɪpweɪ] *n* carreira
slit [slɪt] (*pt, pp* **slit**) *n* fenda; (*cut*) corte *m* ♦ *vt* (*cut*) rachar, cortar; (*open*) abrir
slither ['slɪðə'] *vi* escorregar, deslizar
sliver ['slɪvə'] *n* (*of glass, wood*) lasca; (*of cheese etc*) fatia fina
slob [slɒb] (*inf*) *n* (*in manners*) porco/a; (*in appearance*) maltrapilho/a
slog [slɒg] (BRIT) *vi* mourejar ♦ *n*: **it was a** ~ deu um trabalho louco
slogan ['sləugən] *n* lema *m*, slogan *m*
slop [slɒp] *vi* (*also:* ~ **over**) transbordar, derramar ♦ *vt* transbordar, entornar

slope [sləup] *n* ladeira; (*side of mountain*) encosta, vertente *f*; (*ski* ~) pista; (*slant*) inclinação *f*, declive *m* ♦ *vi*: **to** ~ **down** estar em declive; **to** ~ **up** inclinar-se; **sloping** *adj* inclinado, em declive; (*handwriting*) torto
sloppy ['slɒpɪ] *adj* (*work*) descuidado; (*appearance*) relaxado
slot [slɒt] *n* (*in machine*) fenda ♦ *vt*: **to** ~ **into** encaixar em
sloth [sləuθ] *n* (*vice*) preguiça
slot machine *n* (*for gambling*) caça-níqueis *m inv*; (BRIT: *vending machine*) distribuidora automática
slouch [slautʃ] *vi* ter má postura
slovenly ['slʌvənlɪ] *adj* (*dirty*) desalinhado, sujo; (*careless*) desmazelado
slow [sləu] *adj* (*not clever*) bronco, de raciocínio lento; (*watch*): **to be** ~ atrasar ♦ *adv* lentamente, devagar ♦ *vt, vi* (*ir* (mais) devagar; "~" (*road sign*) "devagar"; ~**ly** *adv* lentamente, devagar; ~ **motion** *n*: **in** ~ **motion** em câmara lenta
sludge [slʌdʒ] *n* lama, lodo
slue [slu:] (US) *vi* = **slew**
slug [slʌg] *n* lesma; ~**gish** *adj* vagaroso; (*business*) lento
sluice [slu:s] *n* (*gate*) comporta, eclusa; (*channel*) canal *m*
slum [slʌm] *n* (*area*) favela; (*house*) cortiço, barraco
slump [slʌmp] *n* (*economic*) depressão *f*; (*COMM*) baixa, queda ♦ *vi* (*person*) cair; (*prices*) baixar repentinamente
slung [slʌŋ] *pt, pp of* **sling**
slur [slə:'] *n* calúnia ♦ *vt* pronunciar indistintamente
slush [slʌʃ] *n* neve *f* meio derretida; ~ **fund** *n* verba para suborno
slut [slʌt] (*pej*) *n* mulher *f* desmazelada
sly [slaɪ] *adj* (*person*) astuto; (*smile, remark*) malicioso, velhaco
smack [smæk] *n* palmada ♦ *vt* bater; (*child*) dar uma palmada em; (*on face*) dar um tabefe em ♦ *vi*: **to** ~ **of** cheirar a, saber a
small [smɔ:l] *adj* pequeno; ~ **ads** (BRIT) *npl* classificados *mpl*; ~ **change** *n* trocado; ~ **fry** *npl* gente *f* sem importância; ~**holder** (BRIT) *n* pequeno/a proprietário/a; ~ **hours** *npl*: **in the** ~ **hours** na madrugada, lá pelas tantas (*inf*); ~**pox** *n* varíola; ~ **talk** *n* conversa fiada
smart [smɑːt] *adj* elegante; (*clever*) inteligente, astuto; (*quick*) vivo, esperto ♦ *vi* sofrer; ~**en up** *vi* arrumar-se ♦ *vt* arrumar
smash [smæʃ] *n* (*also:* ~**-up**) colisão *f*, choque *m*; (~ *hit*) sucesso de bilheteria ♦ *vt* (*break*) escangalhar, despedaçar; (*car etc*) bater com; (*SPORT: record*) quebrar ♦ *vi* despedaçar-se; (*against wall etc*) espatifar-se; ~**ing** (*inf*) *adj* excelente

smattering ['smætərɪŋ] *n*: **a ~ of** um conhecimento superficial de

smear [smɪə*] *n* mancha, nódoa; (*MED*) esfregaço ♦ *vt* untar; (*to make dirty*) lambuzar; **~ campaign** *n* campanha de desmoralização

smell [smɛl] (*pt, pp* **smelt** *or* **~ed**) *n* cheiro; (*sense*) olfato ♦ *vt* cheirar ♦ *vi* (*food etc*) cheirar; (*pej*) cheirar mal; **to ~ of** cheirar a; **~y** (*pej*) *adj* fedorento, malcheiroso

smile [smaɪl] *n* sorriso ♦ *vi* sorrir

smirk [smə:k] (*pej*) *n* sorriso falso *or* afetado

smithy ['smɪðɪ] *n* forja, oficina de ferreiro

smock [smɔk] *n* guarda-pó *m*; (*children's*) avental *m*

smog [smɔg] *n* nevoeiro com fumaça (*BR*) *or* fumo (*PT*)

smoke [sməuk] *n* fumaça (*BR*), fumo (*PT*) ♦ *vi* fumar; (*chimney*) fumegar ♦ *vt* (*cigarettes*) fumar; **~d** *adj* (*bacon*) defumado; (*glass*) fumée; **~r** *n* (*person*) fumante *m/f*; (*RAIL*) vagão *m* para fumantes; **~screen** *n* cortina de fumaça; **smoking** *n*: **"no smoking"** (*sign*) "proibido fumar"; **smoky** *adj* enfumaçado; (*taste*) defumado

smolder ['sməuldə*] (*US*) *vi* = **smoulder**

smooth [smu:ð] *adj* liso, macio; (*sauce*) cremoso; (*sea*) tranqüilo, calmo; (*flavour, movement*) suave; (*person: pej*) meloso ♦ *vt* (*also:* **~ out**) alisar; (*: difficulties*) aplainar

smother ['smʌðə*] *vt* (*fire*) abafar; (*person*) sufocar; (*emotions*) reprimir

smoulder ['sməuldə*] (*US* **smolder**) *vi* arder sem chamas; (*fig*) estar latente

smudge [smʌdʒ] *n* mancha ♦ *vt* manchar, sujar

smug [smʌg] (*pej*) *adj* convencido

smuggle ['smʌgl] *vt* contrabandear; **~r** *n* contrabandista *m/f*; **smuggling** *n* contrabando

smutty ['smʌtɪ] *adj* (*fig*) obsceno, indecente

snack [snæk] *n* lanche *m* (*BR*), merenda (*PT*); **~ bar** *n* lanchonete *f* (*BR*), snackbar *m* (*PT*)

snag [snæg] *n* dificuldade *f*, obstáculo *m*

snail [sneɪl] *n* caracol *m*

snake [sneɪk] *n* cobra

snap [snæp] *n* (*sound*) estalo; (*photograph*) foto *f* ♦ *adj* repentino ♦ *vt* quebrar; (*fingers*) estalar ♦ *vi* quebrar; (*fig: person*) retrucar asperamente; **to ~ shut** fechar com um estalo; **~ at** *vt fus* (*subj: dog*) tentar morder; **~ off** *vt* (*break*) partir; **~ up** *vt* arrebatar, comprar rapidamente; **~py** (*inf*) *adj* rápido; (*slogan*) vigoroso; **make it ~py!** faça rápido!; **~shot** *n* foto *f* (instantânea)

snare [snɛə*] *n* armadilha, laço

snarl [sna:l] *vi* grunhir

snatch [snætʃ] *n* (*small piece*) trecho ♦ *vt* agarrar; (*fig: look*) roubar

sneak [sni:k] (*pt* **~ed** *or* (*US*) **snuck**) *vi*: **to ~ in/out** entrar/sair furtivamente ♦ *n* (*inf*) dedo-duro; **to ~ up on sb** chegar de mausinho perto de alguém; **~ers** *npl* tênis *m* (*BR*), sapatos *mpl* de treino (*PT*)

sneer [snɪə*] *vi* rir-se com desdém; (*mock*): **to ~ at** zombar de, desprezar

sneeze [sni:z] *n* espirro ♦ *vi* espirrar

sniff [snɪf] *n* fungada; (*of dog*) farejada; (*of person*) fungadela ♦ *vi* fungar ♦ *vt* fungar, farejar; (*glue, drug*) cheirar

snigger ['snɪgə*] *vi* rir-se com dissimulação

snip [snɪp] *n* tesourada; (*BRIT: inf*) pechincha ♦ *vt* cortar com tesoura

sniper ['snaɪpə*] *n* franco-atirador(a) *m/f*

snippet ['snɪpɪt] *n* fragmento, trecho

snivelling ['snɪvlɪŋ] *adj* chorão/rona, lamuriento

snob [snɔb] *n* esnobe *m/f*; **~bery** *n* esnobismo; **~bish** *adj* esnobe

snooker ['snu:kə*] *n* sinuca

snoop [snu:p] *vi*: **to ~ about** bisbilhotar

snooty ['snu:tɪ] *adj* arrogante

snooze [snu:z] *n* soneca ♦ *vi* tirar uma soneca, dormitar

snore [snɔ:*] *vi* roncar ♦ *n* ronco

snorkel ['snɔ:kl] *n* tubo snorkel

snort [snɔ:t] *n* bufo, bufido ♦ *vi* bufar

snout [snaut] *n* focinho

snow [snəu] *n* neve *f* ♦ *vi* nevar; **~ball** *n* bola de neve ♦ *vi* (*fig*) aumentar (como bola de neve); **~bound** *adj* bloqueado pela neve; **~drift** *n* monte *m* de neve (formado pelo vento); **~drop** *n* campainha branca; **~fall** *n* nevada; **~flake** *n* floco de neve; **~man** (*irreg*) *n* boneco de neve; **~plough** (*US* **~plow**) *n* máquina limpa-neve, removedor *m* de neve; **~shoe** *n* raquete *f* de neve; **~storm** *n* nevasca, tempestade *f* de neve

snub [snʌb] *vt* desdenhar, menosprezar ♦ *n* repulsa; **~-nosed** *adj* de nariz arrebitado

snuff [snʌf] *n* rapé *m*

snug [snʌg] *adj* (*sheltered*) abrigado, protegido; (*fitted*) justo, cômodo

snuggle ['snʌgl] *vi*: **to ~ up to sb** aconchegar-se *or* aninhar-se a alguém

┌─────────────┐
│ KEYWORD │
└─────────────┘

so [səu] *adv* **1** (*thus, likewise*) assim, deste modo; **~ saying he walked away** falou isto e foi embora; **if ~** se for assim, se assim é; **I didn't do it – you did** – não fiz isso – você fez!; **~ do I, ~ am I** *etc* eu também; **~ it is!** é verdade!; **I hope/think ~** espero/acho que sim; **~ far** até aqui

2 (*in comparisons etc: to such a degree*) tão; **~ big/quickly (that)** tão grande/

rápido (que)

3: ~ **much** adj, adv tanto; **I've got ~ much work** tenho tanto trabalho; ~ **many** tantos/as; **there are ~ many people to see** tem tanta gente para ver **4** (phrases): **10 or** ~ 10 mais ou menos; ~ **long!** (inf: goodbye) tchau!

♦ conj **1** (expressing purpose): ~ **as to do** para fazer; **we hurried ~ as not to be late** nós apressamos para não chegarmos atrasados; ~ **(that)** para que, a fim de que

2 (result: so that): **he didn't arrive ~ I left** como ele não chegou, eu fui embora; ~ **I was right after all** então eu estava certo no final das contas

soak [səuk] vt embeber, ensopar; (put in water) pôr de molho ♦ vi estar de molho, impregnar-se; ~ **in** vi infiltrar; ~ **up** vt absorver

soap [səup] n sabão m; ~**flakes** npl flocos mpl de sabão; ~ **opera** n novela; ~ **powder** n sabão m em pó; ~**y** adj ensaboado

soar [sɔː*] vi (on wings) elevar-se em vôo; (rocket, temperature) subir; (building etc) levantar-se; (price, production) disparar

sob [sɔb] n soluço ♦ vi soluçar

sober [ˈsəubə*] adj (serious) sério; (not drunk) sóbrio; (colour, style) discreto; ~ **up** vi ficar sóbrio

so-called [-kɔːld] adj chamado

soccer [ˈsɔkə*] n futebol m

sociable [ˈsəuʃəbl] adj sociável

social [ˈsəuʃl] adj social ♦ n reunião f social; ~ **club** n clube m; ~**ism** n socialismo; ~**ist** adj, n socialista m/f; ~**ize** vi: to ~**ize (with)** socializar (com); ~**ly** adv socialmente; ~ **security** (BRIT) n previdência social; ~ **work** n assistência social, serviço social; ~ **worker** n assistente m/f social

society [səˈsaɪətɪ] n sociedade f; (club) associação f; (also: **high ~**) alta sociedade

sociology [səusɪˈɔlədʒɪ] n sociologia

sock [sɔk] n meia (BR), peúga (PT)

socket [ˈsɔkɪt] n bocal m, encaixe m; (BRIT: ELEC) tomada

sod [sɔd] n (of earth) gramado, torrão m; (BRIT: inf!) imbecil m/f

soda [ˈsəudə] n (CHEM) soda; (also: ~ **water**) água com gás; (US: also: ~ **pop**) soda

sodden [ˈsɔdn] adj encharcado

sodium [ˈsəudɪəm] n sódio

sofa [ˈsəufə] n sofá m

soft [sɔft] adj mole; (voice, music, light) suave; (kind) meigo, bondoso; ~ **drink** n refrigerante m; ~**en** vt amolecer, amaciar; (effect) abrandar; (expression) suavizar ♦ vi amolecer-se; (voice, expres-

sion) suavizar-se; ~**ly** adv suavemente; (gently) delicadamente; ~**ness** n maciez f; (gentleness) suavidade f; ~ **spot** n: **to have a ~ spot for sb** ter xodó por alguém; ~**ware** n (COMPUT) software m

soggy [ˈsɔgɪ] adj ensopado, encharcado

soil [sɔɪl] n terra, solo; (territory) território ♦ vt sujar, manchar

solace [ˈsɔlɪs] n consolo

solar [ˈsəulə*] adj solar; ~ **energy** n energia solar; ~ **panel** n painel m solar

sold [səuld] pt, pp of **sell** ♦ adj: ~ **out** (COMM) esgotado

solder [ˈsəuldə*] vt soldar ♦ n solda

soldier [ˈsəuldʒə*] n soldado; (army man) militar m

sole [səul] n (of foot, shoe) sola; (fish: pl inv) solha, linguado ♦ adj único; ~**ly** adv somente, unicamente

solemn [ˈsɔləm] adj solene

sole trader n (COMM) comerciante m/f independente

solicit [səˈlɪsɪt] vt (request) solicitar ♦ vi (prostitute) aliciar fregueses

solicitor [səˈlɪsɪtə*] n (BRIT) n (for wills etc) tabelião/lioa m/f; (in court) ~ advogado/a

solid [ˈsɔlɪd] adj sólido; (gold etc) maciço; (person) sério ♦ n sólido; ~**s** npl (food) comida sólida

solitaire [sɔlɪˈtɛə*] n solitário

solitary [ˈsɔlɪtərɪ] adj solitário, só; (walk) só; (isolated) isolado, retirado; (single) único; ~ **confinement** n prisão f celular, solitária

solo [ˈsəuləu] n, adv solo; ~**ist** n solista m/f

solution [səˈluːʃən] n solução f

solve [sɔlv] vt resolver, solucionar

solvent [ˈsɔlvənt] adj (COMM) solvente ♦ n (CHEM) solvente m

sombre [ˈsɔmbə*] (US **somber**) adj sombrio, lúgubre

KEYWORD

---

some [sʌm] adj **1** (a certain number or amount): ~ **tea/water/biscuits** um pouco de chá/água/uns biscoitos; ~ **children came** algumas crianças vieram

2 (certain: in contrasts) algum(a); ~ **people say that ...** algumas pessoas dizem que ...

3 (unspecified) um pouco de; ~ **woman was asking for you** uma mulher estava perguntando por você; ~ **day** um dia

♦ pron **1** (a certain number) alguns/algumas; **I've got ~** (books etc) tenho alguns; ~ **went for a taxi and ~ walked** alguns foram pegar um táxi e outros foram andando

2 (a certain amount) um pouco; **I've got**

~ (*milk etc*) tenho um pouco

♦ *adv*: ~ **10 people** umas 10 pessoas

some: ~**body** *pron* = **someone**; ~**how** *adv* de alguma maneira; (*for some reason*) por uma razão ou outra; ~**one** *pron* alguém; ~**place** (*US*) *adv* = **somewhere**

somersault ['sʌmǝsɔːlt] *n* (*deliberate*) salto-mortal; (*accidental*) cambalhota ♦ *vi* dar um salto-mortal (*or* uma cambalhota)

something ['sʌmθɪŋ] *pron* alguma coisa, algo (*BR*)

sometime ['sʌmtaɪm] *adv* (*in future*) algum dia, em outra oportunidade; (*in past*): ~ **last month** durante o mês passado

sometimes ['sʌmtaɪmz] *adv* às vezes, de vez em quando

somewhat ['sʌmwɔt] *adv* um tanto

somewhere ['sʌmwɛǝ*] *adv* (*be*) em algum lugar; (*go*) para algum lugar; ~ **else** em outro lugar; para outro lugar

son [sʌn] *n* filho

sonar ['sǝunɑː*] *n* sonar *m*

song [sɔŋ] *n* canção *f*; (*of bird*) canto

son-in-law ['sʌnɪnlɔː] *n* genro

sonny ['sʌnɪ] (*inf*) *n* meu filho

soon [suːn] *adv* logo, brevemente; (*a short time after*) logo após; (*early*) cedo; ~ **afterwards** pouco depois; *see also* **as**; ~**er** *adv* antes, mais cedo; (*preference*): **I would** ~**er do** that preferia fazer isso; ~**er or later** mais cedo ou mais tarde

soot [sut] *n* fuligem *f*

soothe [suːð] *vt* acalmar, sossegar; (*pain*) aliviar, suavizar

sophomore ['sɔfǝmɔː*] (*US*) *n* segunda-nista *m/f*

sopping ['sɔpɪŋ] *adj*: ~ (**wet**) encharcado

soppy ['sɔpɪ] (*pej*) *adj* piegas *inv*

soprano [sǝ'prɑːnǝu] *n* soprano *m/f*

sorcerer ['sɔːsǝrǝ*] *n* feiticeiro

sordid ['sɔːdɪd] *adj* (*dirty*) imundo, sórdido; (*wretched*) miserável

sore [sɔː*] *adj* dolorido ♦ *n* chaga, ferida; ~**ly** *adv*: **I am** ~**ly tempted (to)** estou muito tentado (a)

sorrow ['sɔrǝu] *n* tristeza, mágoa, dor *f*; ~**s** *npl* (*causes of grief*) tristezas *fpl*; ~**ful** *adj* (*day*) triste; (*smile*) aflito, magoado

sorry ['sɔrɪ] *adj* (*regretful*) arrependido; (*condition, excuse*) lamentável; ~! desculpe!, perdão!, sinto muito!; **to feel** ~ **for sb** sentir pena de alguém

sort [sɔːt] *n* tipo ♦ *vt* (*also*: ~ **out**: *papers*) classificar; (: *problems*) solucionar, resolver; ~**ing office** *n* departamento de distribuição

SOS *n abbr* (= *save our souls*) S.O.S. *m*

so-so *adv* mais ou menos, regular

sought [sɔːt] *pt, pp* of **seek**

soul [sǝul] *n* alma; (*person*) criatura; ~-

destroying *adj* desalentador(a); ~**ful** *adj* emocional, sentimental

sound [saund] *adj* (*healthy*) saudável, sadio; (*safe, not damaged*) sólido, completo; (*secure*) seguro; (*reliable*) confiável; (*sensible*) sensato ♦ *adv*: ~ **asleep** dormindo profundamente ♦ *n* (*noise*) som *m*, ruído, barulho; (*volume: on TV etc*) volume *m*; (*GEO*) estreito, braço (de mar) ♦ *vt* (*alarm*) soar ♦ *vi* soar, tocar; (*fig: seem*) parecer; **to** ~ **like** parecer; ~ **out** *vi* sondar; ~ **barrier** *n* barreira do som; ~ **effects** *npl* efeitos *mpl* sonoros; ~**ly** *adv* (*sleep*) profundamente; (*beat*) completamente; ~**proof** *adj* à prova de som; ~**track** *n* trilha sonora

soup [suːp] *n* sopa; **in the** ~ (*fig*) numa encrenca; ~ **plate** *n* prato fundo (para sopa); ~**spoon** *n* colher *f* de sopa

sour [sauǝ*] *adj* azedo, ácido; (*milk*) talhado; (*fig*) mal-humorado, rabugento; **it's** ~ **grapes!** (*fig*) é despeito!

source [sɔːs] *n* fonte *f*

south [sauθ] *n* sul *m* ♦ *adj* do sul, meridional ♦ *adv* ao or para o sul; **S~ Africa** *n* África do Sul; **S~ African** *adj, n* sul-africano/a; **S~ America** *n* América do Sul; **S~ American** *adj, n* sul-americano/a; ~**east** *n* sudeste *m*; ~**erly** *adj* para o sul; (*from the* ~) do sul; ~**ern** *adj* (*to the* ~) para o sul, em direção do sul; (*from the* ~) do sul, sulista; **the** ~ **hemisphere** o Hemisfério Sul; **S~ Pole** *n* Pólo Sul; ~**ward(s)** *adv* para o sul; ~**west** *n* sudoeste *m*

souvenir [suːvǝ'nɪǝ*] *n* lembrança

sovereign ['sɔvrɪn] *n* soberano/a

soviet ['sǝuvɪǝt] *adj* soviético; **the S~ Union** a União Soviética

sow¹ [sau] *n* porca

sow² [sǝu] (*pt* ~**ed**, *pp* ~**n**) *vt* semear; (*fig: spread*) disseminar, espalhar

soya ['sɔɪǝ] (*US* **soy**) *n*: ~ **bean** semente *f* de soja; ~ **sauce** molho de soja

spa [spɑː] *n* (*town*) estância hidromineral; (*US: also*: **health** ~) estância balnear

space [speɪs] *n* (*gen*) espaço; (*room*) lugar *m*; (*cpd*) espacial ♦ *vt* (*also*: ~ **out**) espaçar; ~**craft** *n* nave *f* espacial; ~**man** (*irreg*) *n* astronauta *m*, cosmonauta *m*; ~**ship** *n* = ~**craft**; ~**woman** (*irreg*) *n* astronauta, cosmonauta; ~ **spacing** *n* espaçejamento, espaçamento; ~**spacious** *adj* espaçoso

spade [speɪd] *n* pá *f*; ~**s** *npl* (*CARDS*) espadas *fpl*

spaghetti [spǝ'gɛtɪ] *n* espaguete *m*

Spain [speɪn] *n* Espanha

span [spæn] *n* (*also*: **wing**~) envergadura; (*of arch*) vão *m*; (*in time*) lapso, espaço ♦ *vt* estender-se sobre, atravessar; (*fig*) abarcar

Spaniard ['spænjǝd] *n* espanhol(a) *m/f*

Spanish ['spænɪʃ] *adj* espanhol(a) ♦ *n*

(LING) espanhol m, castelhano; **the ~** npl os espanhóis

spank [spæŋk] vt bater, dar palmadas em

spanner ['spænə'] (BRIT) n chave f inglesa

spar [spɑː'] n mastro, verga ♦ vi (BOXING) treinar

spare [spɛə'] adj vago, desocupado; (surplus) de sobra, a mais ♦ n = ~ **part** ♦ vt dispensar, passar sem; (make available) dispor de; (refrain from hurting) perdoar, poupar; **to ~** de sobra; **~ part** n peça sobressalente; **~ wheel** n estepe m; **sparing** adj: **to be sparing with** ser econômico com; **sparingly** adv frugalmente, com moderação

spark [spɑːk] n chispa, faísca; (fig) centelha; **~(ing) plug** n vela (de ignição)

sparkle ['spɑːkl] n cintilação f, brilho ♦ vi (shine) brilhar, faiscar; **sparkling** adj (mineral water) gasoso; (wine) espumante; (conversation) animado; (performance) brilhante

sparrow ['spærəu] n pardal m

sparse [spɑːs] adj escasso; (hair) ralo

spartan ['spɑːtən] adj (fig) espartano

spasm ['spæzəm] n (MED) espasmo

spastic ['spæstɪk] n espástico/a

spat [spæt] pt, pp of **spit**

spate [speɪt] n (fig): **a ~ of** uma enxurrada de

spatter ['spætə'] vt borrifar, salpicar

spatula ['spætjulə] n espátula

spawn [spɔːn] vi desovar, procriar ♦ n ovas fpl

speak [spiːk] (pt spoke, pp spoken) vt (language) falar; (truth) dizer ♦ vi falar; (make a speech) discursar; **~ up!** fale alto!; **~er** n (in public) orador(a) m/f; (also: loud~er) alto-falante m; (POL): **the S~er** o Presidente da Câmara

spear [spɪə'] n lança ♦ vt lancear, arpoar; **~head** vt (attack) encabeçar

spec [spek] (inf) n: **on ~** por acaso

special ['spɛʃl] adj especial; (edition etc) extra; (delivery) rápido; **~ist** n especialista m/f; **~ity** n especialidade f; **~ize** vi: **to ~ize (in)** especializar-se (em); **~ly** adv especialmente; **~ty** (esp US) n = **~ity**

species ['spiːʃiːz] n inv espécie f

specific [spə'sɪfɪk] adj específico; **~ation** n especificação f; (requirement) requinto; **~ations** npl (TECH) ficha técnica

specimen ['spɛsɪmən] n espécime m, amostra; (for testing, MED) espécime

speck [spɛk] n mancha, pinta

speckled ['spɛkld] adj pintado

specs [spɛks] (inf) npl óculos mpl

spectacle ['spɛktəkl] n espetáculo; **~s** npl (glasses) óculos mpl; **spectacular** adj espetacular ♦ n (CINEMA etc) superprodução f

spectator [spɛk'teɪtə'] n espectador(a) m/f

spectra ['spɛktrə] npl of **spectrum**

spectre ['spɛktə'] (US **specter**) n espectro, aparição f

spectrum ['spɛktrəm] (pl **spectra**) n espectro

speculate ['spɛkjuleɪt] vi especular

speech [spiːtʃ] n (faculty, THEATRE) fala; (formal talk) discurso; **~less** adj estupefato, emudecido

speed [spiːd] (pt, pp **sped**) n velocidade f; (rate) rapidez f; (haste) pressa; (promptness) prontidão f; **at full or top ~** a toda a velocidade; **~ up** (pt, pp **~ed up**) vt, vi acelerar; **~boat** n lancha; **~ily** adv depressa, rapidamente; **~ing** n (AUT) excesso de velocidade; **~limit** n limite m de velocidade, velocidade f máxima; **~ometer** n velocímetro; **~way** n (SPORT: also: **~way racing**) corrida de motocicleta; **~y** adj veloz, rápido; (prompt) pronto, imediato

spell [spɛl] (pt, pp **~ed**, (BRIT) **spelt**) n (also: **magic ~**) encanto, feitiço; (period of time) período, temporada ♦ vt (also: **~ out**) soletrar; (fig) pressagiar, ser sinal de; **to cast a ~ on sb** enfeitiçar alguém; **he can't ~** não sabe escrever bem, comete erros de ortografia; **~bound** adj enfeitiçado, fascinado; **~ing** n ortografia

spend [spɛnd] (pt, pp **spent**) vt (money) gastar; (time) passar; **~thrift** n esbanjador(a) m/f, perdulário/a

spent [spɛnt] pt, pp of **spend**

sperm [spɔːm] n esperma

spew [spjuː] vt vomitar, lançar

sphere [sfɪə'] n esfera

sphinx [sfɪŋks] n esfinge f

spice [spaɪs] n especiaria ♦ vt condimentar

spick-and-span [spɪk-] adj tudo arrumado

spicy ['spaɪsɪ] adj condimentado

spider ['spaɪdə'] n aranha

spike [spaɪk] n (point) ponta, espigão m; (BOT) espiga

spill [spɪl] (pt, pp **spilt** or **~ed**) vt entornar, derramar ♦ vi derramar-se; **~ over** vi transbordar

spin [spɪn] (pt **spun** or **span**, pp **spun**) n (AVIAT) parafuso; (trip in car) volta or passeio de carro; (ball): **to put ~ on** fazer rolar ♦ vt (wool etc) fiar, tecer ♦ vi girar, rodar; (make thread) tecer; **~ out** vt prolongar; (money) fazer render

spinach ['spɪnɪtʃ] n espinafre m

spinal ['spaɪnl] adj espinhal; **~ cord** n espinha dorsal

spindly ['spɪndlɪ] adj longo e espigado

spin-dryer (BRIT) n secadora

spine [spaɪn] n espinha dorsal; (thorn) espinho; **~less** adj (fig) fraco, covarde

spinning ['spɪnɪŋ] n fiação f; **~ top** n pião m; **~ wheel** n roca de fiar

spin-off n subproduto

spinster ['spinstə*] n solteira

spiral ['spaiərl] n espiral f ♦ vi (prices) disparar; ~ **staircase** n escada em caracol

spire ['spaiə*] n flecha, agulha

spirit ['spirit] n (soul) alma; (ghost) fantasma m; (courage) coragem f, ânimo; (frame of mind) estado de espírito; (sense) sentido; ~s npl (drink) álcool m; **in good ~s** alegre, de bom humor; ~**ed** adj animado, espirituoso; ~ **level** n nível m de bolha; ~**ual** adj espiritual ♦ n (also: **Negro ~ual**) canto religioso dos negros

spit [spit] (pt, pp **spat**) n (for roasting) espeto; (saliva) saliva ♦ vi cuspir; (sound) escarrar; (rain) chuviscar

spite [spait] n rancor m, ressentimento ♦ vt contrariar; **in ~ of** apesar de, a despeito de; ~**ful** adj maldoso, malévolo

spittle ['spitl] n cuspe m

splash [splæʃ] n (sound) borrifo, respingo; (of colour) mancha ♦ vt: **to ~ (with)** salpicar (de) ♦ vi (also: ~ **about**) borrifar, respingar

spleen [spli:n] n (ANAT) baço

splendid ['splendid] adj esplêndido; (impressive) impressionante

splint [splint] n tala

splinter ['splintə*] n (of wood, glass) lasca; (in finger) farpa ♦ vi lascar-se, estilhaçar-se, despedaçar-se

split [split] (pt, pp **split**) n fenda, brecha; (fig: division) rompimento; (: difference) diferença; (POL) divisão f ♦ vt partir, fender; (party, work) dividir; (profits) repartir ♦ vi (divide) dividir-se, repartir-se; ~ **up** vi (couple) separar-se, acabar; (meeting) terminar

splutter ['splʌtə*] vi crepitar; (person) balbuciar, gaguejar

spoil [spɔil] (pt, pp ~**t** or ~**ed**) vt (damage) danificar; (mar) estragar, arruinar; (child) mimar; ~**s** npl desojo, saque m; ~**sport** (pej) n desmancha-prazeres m/f inv

spoke [spəuk] pt of **speak** ♦ n raio

spoken ['spəukn] pp of **speak**

spokesman ['spəuksmən] (irreg) n porta-voz m

spokeswoman ['spəukswumən] (irreg) n porta-voz f

sponge [spʌndʒ] n esponja; (cake) pão-de-ló m ♦ vt lavar com esponja ♦ vi: **to ~ on sb** viver às custas de alguém; ~ **bag** (BRIT) n bolsa de toalete

sponsor ['sponsə*] n patrocinador(a) m/f ♦ vt patrocinar; apadrinhar; fiar; (applicant, proposal) apoiar, defender; ~**ship** n patrocínio

spontaneous [spɔn'teiniəs] adj espontâneo

spooky ['spu:ki] (inf) adj arrepiante

spool [spu:l] n carretel m; (of film) rolo; (for tape) bobina

spoon [spu:n] n colher f; ~**-feed** (irreg) vt dar de comer com colher; (fig) dar tudo mastigado a; ~**ful** n colherada

sporadic [spə'rædik] adj esporádico

sport [spɔ:t] n esporte m (BR), desporto (PT); (person) bom perdedor/boa perdedora m/f ♦ vt (wear) exibir; ~**ing** adj esportivo (BR), desportivo (PT); (generous) nobre; **to give sb a ~ing chance** dar uma grande chance a alguém; ~ **jacket** (US) n = ~**s jacket**; ~**s car** n carro esporte (BR), carro de sport (PT); ~**s jacket** (BRIT) n casaco esportivo (BR) or desportivo (PT); ~**sman** (irreg) n esportista m (BR), desportista m (PT); ~**smanship** n espírito esportivo (BR) or desportivo (PT); ~**swear** n roupa esportiva (BR) or desportiva (PT) or esporte; ~**swoman** (irreg) n esportista (BR), desportista (PT); ~**y** adj esportivo (BR), desportivo (PT)

spot [spɔt] n (mark) marca; (place) lugar m, local m; (dot: on pattern) mancha, ponto; (on skin) espinha; (RADIO, TV) hora; (small amount): **a ~ of** um pouquinho de ♦ vt notar; **on the ~** na hora; (there) ali mesmo; (in difficulty) em apuros; ~ **check** n fiscalização f de surpresa; ~**less** adj sem mancha, imaculado; ~**light** n holofote m, refletor m; ~**ted** adj com bolinhas; ~**ty** adj cheio de espinhas

spouse [spauz] n cônjuge m/f

spout [spaut] n (of jug) bico; (of pipe) cano ♦ vi jorrar

sprain [sprein] n distensão f, torcedura ♦ vt torcer

sprang [spræŋ] pt of **spring**

sprawl [sprɔ:l] vi esparramar-se

spray [sprei] n borrifo; (container) spray m, atomizador m; (garden ~) vaporizador m; (of flowers) ramalhete m ♦ vt pulverizar; (crops) borrifar, regar

spread [spred] (pt, pp **spread**) n extensão f; (distribution) expansão f, difusão f; (CULIN) pasta; (inf: food) banquete m ♦ vt espalhar; (butter) untar, passar; (wings, sails) abrir, desdobrar; (workload, wealth) distribuir; (scatter) disseminar ♦ vi (news, stain) espalhar-se; (disease) alastrar-se; ~ **out** vi dispersar-se; ~**-eagled** adj estirado; ~**sheet** n (COMPUT) planilha

spree [spri:] n: **to go on a ~** cair na farra

sprightly ['spraitli] adj ativo, ágil

spring [spriŋ] (pt **sprang**, pp **sprung**) n salto, pulo; (coiled metal) mola; (season) primavera; (of water) fonte f; ~ **up** vi aparecer de repente; ~**board** n trampolim m; ~**-cleaning** n limpeza total, faxina (geral); ~**time** n primavera

sprinkle ['spriŋkl] vt (liquid) salpicar; (salt, sugar) borrifar; **to ~ water on, ~ with water** salpicar de água; ~**r** n (for *lawn etc*) regador *m*; (*to put out fire*) sprinkler *m*

sprint [sprɪnt] *n* corrida de pequena distância ♦ *vi* correr a toda velocidade; ~**er** *n* corredor(a) *m/f*

sprout [spraut] *vi* brotar, germinar; ~**s** *npl* (*also*: **Brussels** ~**s**) couves-de-Bruxelas *fpl*

spruce [spru:s] *n inv* (*BOT*) abeto ♦ *adj* arrumado, limpo, elegante

sprung [sprʌŋ] *pp of* **spring**

spry [spraɪ] *adj* ativo, ágil

spun [spʌn] *pt, pp of* **spin**

spur [spə:*] *n* espora; (*fig*) estímulo ♦ *vt* (*also*: ~ **on**) incitar, estimular; **on the** ~ **of the moment** de improviso, de repente

spurious ['spjuərɪəs] *adj* espúrio, falso

spurn [spə:n] *vt* desdenhar, desprezar

spurt [spə:t] *n* (*of energy*) acesso; (*of blood etc*) jorro ♦ *vi* jorrar

spy [spaɪ] *n* espião/espiã *m/f* ♦ *vi*: **to** ~ **on** espiar, espionar ♦ *vt* enxergar, avistar; ~**ing** *n* espionagem *f*

sq. *abbr* (*MATH etc*) = **square**

squabble ['skwɔbl] *vi* brigar, discutir

squad [skwɔd] *n* (*MIL, POLICE*) pelotão *m*, esquadra; (*FOOTBALL*) seleção *f*

squadron ['skwɔdrən] *n* (*MIL*) esquadrão *m*; (*AVIAT*) esquadrilha; (*NAUT*) esquadra

squalid ['skwɔlɪd] *adj* (*conditions*) esquálido; (*story etc*) sórdido

squall [skwɔ:l] *n* (*storm*) tempestade *f*; (*wind*) pé *m* (de vento), rajada

squalor ['skwɔlə*] *n* sordidez *f*

squander ['skwɔndə*] *vt* esbanjar, dissipar; (*chances*) desperdiçar

square [skwɛə*] *n* quadrado; (*in town*) praça; (*inf*: *person*) quadrado/a, careta *m/f* ♦ *adj* quadrado; (*inf*: *ideas, tastes*) careta, antiquado ♦ *vt* (*arrange*) ajustar, acertar; (*MATH*) elevar ao quadrado; (*reconcile*) conciliar; **all** ~ igual, quite; **a** ~ **meal** uma refeição substancial; **2 metres** ~ um quadrado de dois metros de lado; **2** ~ **metres** 2 metros quadrados; ~**ly** *adv* diretamente; (*fully*) em cheio

squash [skwɔʃ] *n* (*BRIT*: *drink*): **lemon/orange** ~ limonada/laranjada concentrada; (*SPORT*) squash *m*; (*US*: *vegetable*) abóbora ♦ *vt* esmagar

squat [skwɔt] *adj* atarracado ♦ *vi* (*also*: ~ **down**) agachar-se, acocorar-se; ~**ter** *n* posseiro/a

squawk [skwɔ:k] *vi* grasnar

squeak [skwi:k] *vi* (*door*) ranger; (*mouse*) guinchar

squeal [skwi:l] *vi* guinchar, gritar agudamente

squeamish ['skwi:mɪʃ] *adj* melindroso, delicado

squeeze [skwi:z] *n* (*gen, of hand*) aperto; (*ECON*) arrocho ♦ *vt* comprimir, socar; (*hand, arm*) apertar; ~ **out** *vt* espre-

mer; (*fig*) extorquir

squelch [skwɛltʃ] *vi* fazer ruído de passos na lama

squid [skwɪd] *n* (*pl inv or* ~**s**) *n* lula

squiggle ['skwɪgl] *n* garatuja

squint [skwɪnt] *vi* olhar *or* ser vesgo ♦ *n* (*MED*) estrabismo

squire ['skwaɪə*] (*BRIT*) *n* proprietário rural

squirm [skwə:m] *vi* retorcer-se

squirrel ['skwɪrəl] *n* esquilo

squirt [skwə:t] *vi, vt* jorrar, esguichar

Sr *abbr* = **senior**

St *abbr* (= *saint*) S.; = *street*

stab [stæb] *n* (*with knife etc*) punhalada; (*of pain*) pontada; (*inf*: *try*): **to have a** ~ **at (doing) sth** tentar (fazer) algo ♦ *vt* apunhalar

stable ['steɪbl] *adj* estável ♦ *n* estábulo, cavalariça

stack [stæk] *n* montão *m*, pilha ♦ *vt* amontoar, empilhar

stadium ['steɪdɪəm] (*pl* **stadia** *or* ~**s**) *n* estádio

staff [sta:f] *n* (*work force*) pessoal *m*, quadro; (*BRIT*: *SCH*: *also*: **teaching** ~) corpo docente ♦ *vt* prover de pessoal

stag [stæg] *n* veado, cervo

stage [steɪdʒ] *n* palco, cena; (*point*) etapa, fase *f*; (*platform*) plataforma, estrado; (*profession*): **the** ~ o palco, o teatro ♦ *vt* pôr em cena, representar; (*demonstration*) montar, organizar; **in** ~**s** por etapas; ~**coach** *n* diligência; ~ **manager** *n* diretor(a) *m/f* de cena

stagger ['stægə*] *vi* cambalear ♦ *vt* (*amaze*) surpreender, chocar; (*hours, holidays*) escalonar; ~**ing** *adj* (*amazing*) surpreendente, chocante

stagnant ['stægnənt] *adj* estagnado

stag party *n* despedida de solteiro

staid [steɪd] *adj* sério, sóbrio

stain [steɪn] *n* mancha; (*colouring*) tinta, tintura ♦ *vt* manchar; (*wood*) tingir; ~**ed glass window** *n* janela com vitral; ~**less** *adj* (*steel*) inoxidável; ~ **remover** *n* tira-manchas *m*

stair [stɛə*] *n* (*step*) degrau *m*; ~**s** *npl* (*flight of steps*) escada; ~**case** *n* escadaria, escada; ~**way** *n* = ~**case**

stake [steɪk] *n* estaca, poste *m*; (*COMM*: *interest*) interesse *m*, participação *f*; (*BETTING*: *gen pl*) aposta ♦ *vt* apostar; (*claim*) reivindicar; **to be at** ~ estar em jogo

stale [steɪl] *adj* (*bread*) dormido; (*food*) estragado; (*air*) viciado; (*smell*) mofado; (*beer*) velho

stalemate ['steɪlmeɪt] *n* empate *m*; (*fig*) impasse *m*, beco sem saída

stalk [stɔ:k] *n* talo, haste *f* ♦ *vt* caçar de tocaia; **to** ~ **in/out** entrar/sair silenciosamente; **to** ~ **off** andar com arrogância

stall [stɔ:l] *n* (*BRIT*: *in market*) barraca,

(in stable) baia ♦ *vt (AUT)* fazer morrer; *(fig: delay)* impedir, atrasar ♦ *vi* morrer; esquivar-se, ganhar tempo; **~s** *npl (BRIT: in cinema, theatre)* platéia

stallion ['stælɪən] *n* garanhão *m*

stalwart ['stɔːlwət] *adj* leal

stamina ['stæmɪnə] *n* resistência

stammer ['stæmə*] *n* gagueira ♦ *vi* gaguejar, balbuciar

stamp [stæmp] *n* selo; *(rubber ~)* carimbo, timbre *m*; *(mark, also fig)* marca, impressão *f* ♦ *vi (also: ~ one's foot)* bater com o pé ♦ *vt (letter)* selar; *(mark)* marcar; *(with rubber ~)* carimbar; **~ album** *n* álbum *m* de selos; **~ collecting** *n* filatelia

stampede [stæm'piːd] *n* debandada, estouro (da boiada)

stance [stæns] *n* postura, posição *f*

stand [stænd] *(pt, pp stood)* *n* posição *f*, postura; *(for taxis)* ponto; *(also: hall ~)* pedestal *m*; *(also: music ~)* estante *f*; *(SPORT)* tribuna, palanque *m*; *(stall)* barraca ♦ *vi (be)* estar, encontrar-se; *(be on foot)* estar em pé; *(rise)* levantar-se; *(remain: decision, offer)* estar de pé; *(in election)* candidatar-se ♦ *vt (place)* pôr, colocar; *(tolerate)* agüentar, suportar; *(cost)* pagar; **to make a ~** resistir; *(fig)* ater-se a um princípio; **to ~ for parliament** *(BRIT)* apresentar-se como candidato ao parlamento; **~ by** *vi* estar a postos ♦ *vt fus (opinion)* aferrar-se a; *(person)* ficar ao lado de; **~ down** *vi* retirar-se; **~ for** *vt fus (signify)* significar; *(represent)* representar; *(tolerate)* tolerar, permitir; **~ in for** *vt fus* substituir; **~ out** *vi (be prominent)* destacar-se; **~ up** *vi* levantar-se; **~ up for** *vt fus* defender; **~ up to** *vt fus* enfrentar

standard ['stændəd] *n* padrão *m*, critério; *(flag)* estandarte *m*; *(level)* nível *m* ♦ *adj* padronizado, regular, normal; **~s** *npl (morals)* valores *mpl* morais; **~ lamp** *(BRIT)* *n* abajur *m* de pé

stand-by *adj* de reserva ♦ *n*: **to be on ~** estar de sobreaviso *or* de prontidão; **~ ticket** *n* bilhete *m* de stand-by

stand-in *n* suplente *m/f*

standing ['stændɪŋ] *adj (on foot)* em pé; *(permanent)* permanente ♦ *n* posição *f*, reputação *f*; **of many years' ~** de muitos anos; **~ joke** *n* piada conhecida; **~ order** *(BRIT)* *n* instrução *f* permanente; **~ room** *n* lugar *m* em pé

stand-offish [-'ɔfɪʃ] *adj* incomunicativo, reservado

standpoint ['stændpɔɪnt] *n* ponto de vista

standstill ['stændstɪl] *n*: **at a ~** paralisado, parado; **to come to a ~** *(car)* parar; *(factory, ship)* ficar paralisado

stank [stæŋk] *pt of* **stink**

staple ['steɪpl] *n (for papers)* grampo ♦ *adj (food etc)* básico ♦ *vt* grampear; **~r**

n grampeador *m*

star [stɑː*] *n* estrela; *(celebrity)* astro/ estrela ♦ *vi*: **to ~ in** ser a estrela em, estrelar ♦ *vt (CINEMA)* ser estrelado por; **the ~s** *npl (horoscope)* o horóscopo

starboard ['stɑːbəd] *n* estibordo

starch [stɑːtʃ] *n (in food)* amido, fécula; *(for clothes)* goma

stardom ['stɑːdəm] *n* estrelato

stare [stɛə*] *n* olhar *m* fixo ♦ *vi*: **to ~ at** olhar fixamente, fitar

starfish ['stɑːfɪʃ] *n inv* estrela-do-mar *f*

stark [stɑːk] *adj* severo, áspero ♦ *adv*: **~ naked** completamente nu, em pêlo

starling ['stɑːlɪŋ] *n* estorninho

starry ['stɑːrɪ] *adj* estrelado; **~-eyed** *adj (innocent)* deslumbrado

start [stɑːt] *n* princípio, começo; *(departure)* partida; *(sudden movement)* sobressalto, susto; *(advantage)* vantagem *f* ♦ *vt* começar, iniciar; *(cause)* causar; *(found)* fundar; *(engine)* ligar ♦ *vi* começar, iniciar; *(with fright)* sobressaltar-se, assustar-se; *(train etc)* sair; **~ off** *vi* começar, principiar; *(leave)* sair, pôr-se a caminho; **~ up** *vi* começar; *(car)* pegar, pôr-se em marcha ♦ *vt* começar; *(car)* ligar; **~er** *n (AUT)* arranque *m*; *(SPORT: official)* juiz/juíza *m/f* da partida; *(BRIT: CULIN)* entrada; **~ing point** *n* ponto de partida

startle ['stɑːtl] *vt* assustar, aterrar; **startling** *adj* surpreendente

starvation [stɑː'veɪʃən] *n* fome *f*

starve [stɑːv] *vi* passar fome; *(to death)* morrer de fome ♦ *vt* fazer passar fome; *(fig)* privar

state [steɪt] *n* estado ♦ *vt* afirmar, declarar; **the S~s** *npl (GEO)* os Estados Unidos; **to be in a ~** estar agitado; **~ly** *adj* majestoso, imponente; **~ment** *n* declaração *f*; **~sman** *(irreg)* *n* estadista *m*

static ['stætɪk] *n (RADIO, TV)* interferência ♦ *adj* estático

station ['steɪʃən] *n* estação *f*; *(POLICE)* delegacia; *(RADIO)* emissora ♦ *vt* colocar

stationary ['steɪʃnərɪ] *adj* estacionário

stationer ['steɪʃənə*] *n* dono de papelaria; **~'s (shop)** *n* papelaria; **~y** *n* artigos *mpl* de papelaria

station master *n (RAIL)* chefe *m* da estação

station wagon *(US)* *n* perua *(BR)*, canadiana *(PT)*

statistic [stə'tɪstɪk] *n* estatística; **~al** *adj* estatístico; **~s** *n (science)* estatística

statue ['stætjuː] *n* estátua

stature ['stætʃə*] *n* estatura, altura

status ['steɪtəs] *n* posição *f*; *(classification)* categoria; *(importance)* status *m*; **~ symbol** *n* símbolo de prestígio

statute ['stætjuːt] *n* estatuto, lei *f*

staunch [stɔːntʃ] *adj* fiel

stave off [steɪv-] *vt (attack)* repelir; *(threat)* evitar, protelar

stay [steɪ] n estadia, estada ♦ vi ficar; (as guest) hospedar-se; (spend some time) demorar-se; **to ~ put** não se mexer; **to ~ the night** pernoitar; **~ behind** vi ficar atrás; **~ in** vi ficar em casa; **~ on** vi ficar; **~ out** vi ficar fora de casa; **~ up** vi (at night) velar, ficar acordado; **~ing power** n resistência, raça

stead [stɛd] n: **in sb's ~** em lugar de alguém; **to stand sb in good ~** prestar bons serviços a alguém

steadfast ['stɛdfɑːst] adj firme, estável, resoluto

steadily ['stɛdɪlɪ] adv (firmly) firmemente; (unceasingly) sem parar, constantemente; (walk) regularmente

steady ['stɛdɪ] adj (job, boyfriend) constante; (speed) fixo; (regular) regular; (person, character) sensato; (calm) calmo, sereno ♦ vt (stabilize) estabilizar; (nerves) acalmar

steak [steɪk] n filé m; (beef) bife m

steal [stiːl] (pt stole, pp stolen) vt roubar ♦ vi mover-se furtivamente

stealth [stɛlθ] n: **by ~** furtivamente, às escondidas; **~y** adj furtivo

steam [stiːm] n vapor m ♦ vt (CULIN) cozinhar no vapor ♦ vi fumegar; **~ engine** n máquina a vapor; **~er** n vapor m, navio (a vapor); **~roller** n rolo compressor (a vapor); **~y** adj vaporoso; (room) cheio de vapor, úmido (BR), húmido (PT); (heat, atmosphere) vaporoso

steel [stiːl] n aço ♦ adj de aço; **~works** n (usina) siderúrgica

steep [stiːp] adj íngreme; (increase) acentuado; (price) exorbitante ♦ vt (food) colocar de molho; (cloth) ensopar, encharcar

steeple ['stiːpl] n campanário, torre f; **~chase** n corrida de obstáculos

steer [stɪə*] vt (person) guiar; (vehicle) dirigir ♦ vi conduzir; **~ing** n (AUT) direção f; **~ing wheel** n volante m

stem [stɛm] n (of plant) caule m, haste f; (of glass) pé m ♦ vt deter, reter; (blood) estancar; **~ from** vt fus originar-se de

stench [stɛntʃ] (pej) n fedor m

stencil ['stɛnsl] n (pattern, design) estêncil m; (lettering) gabarito de letra ♦ vt imprimir com estêncil

stenographer [stɛˈnɔgrəfə*] (US) n estenógrafo/a

step [stɛp] n passo m; (stair) degrau m ♦ vi: **to ~ forward** dar um passo a frente/atrás; **~s** npl (BRIT) = **ladder**; **to be in ~ (with)** (fig) manter a paridade (com); **to be out of ~ (with)** (fig) estar em disparidade (com); **~ down** vi (fig) renunciar; **~ on** vt fus pisar; **~ up** vt aumentar; **~brother** n meio-irmão m; **~daughter** n enteada; **~father** n padrasto; **~ladder** (BRIT) n escada portátil or de abrir; **~mother** n madrasta; **~ping stone** n pedra utilizada em passarelas; (fig) trampolim m; **~sister** n meia-irmã f; **~son** n enteado

stereo ['stɛrɪəu] n estéreo; (record player) (aparelho de) som m ♦ adj (also: **~phonic**) estereofônico

sterile ['stɛraɪl] adj esterelizado; (barren) estéril; **sterilize** vt esterilizar

sterling ['stəːlɪŋ] adj esterlino; (silver) de lei ♦ n (currency) libra esterlina; **one pound ~** uma libra esterlina

stern [stəːn] adj severo, austero ♦ n (NAUT) popa, ré f

stew [stjuː] n guisado, ensopado ♦ vt guisar, ensopar; (fruit) cozinhar

steward ['stjuːəd] n (AVIAT) comissário de bordo; **~ess** n aeromoça (BR), hospedeira de bordo (PT)

stick [stɪk] (pt, pp stuck) n pau m; (as weapon) cacete m; (walking ~) bengala, cajado ♦ vt (glue) colar; (thrust): **to ~ sth into** cravar or enfiar algo em; (inf: put) meter; (: tolerate) agüentar, suportar ♦ vi (become attached) colar-se; (be unmoveable) emperrar; (in mind etc) gravar-se; **~ out** vi estar saliente, projetar-se; **~ up** vi estar saliente, projetar-se; **~ up for** vt fus defender; **~er** n adesivo; **~ing plaster** n esparadrapo

stickler ['stɪklə*] n: **to be a ~ for** insistir em, exigir

stick-up (inf) n assalto a mão armada

sticky ['stɪkɪ] adj pegajoso; (label) adesivo; (fig) delicado

stiff [stɪf] adj (strong) forte; (hard) duro; (difficult) difícil; (moving with difficulty: person) teso; (: door, zip) empenado; (formal) formal ♦ adv (bored, worried) extremamente; **~en** vi enrijecer-se; (grow stronger) fortalecer-se; **~ neck** n torcicolo

stifle ['staɪfl] vt sufocar, abafar; (opposition) sufocar; **stifling** adj (heat) sufocante, abafado

stigma ['stɪgmə] n estigma m

stile [staɪl] n degraus para passar por uma cerca ou muro

stiletto [stɪˈlɛtəu] (BRIT) n (also: **~ heel**) salto alto e fino

still [stɪl] adj parado ♦ adv (up to this time) ainda; (even, yet) ainda; (nonetheless) entretanto, contudo; **~born** adj nascido morto, natimorto; **~ life** n natureza morta

stilt [stɪlt] n perna de pau; (pile) estaca, suporte m

stilted ['stɪltɪd] adj afetado

stimulate ['stɪmjuleɪt] vt estimular

stimuli ['stɪmjulaɪ] npl of **stimulus**

stimulus ['stɪmjuləs] (pl stimuli) n estímulo, incentivo

sting [stɪŋ] (pt, pp stung) n (wound) picada; (pain) ardência; (of insect) ferrão m ♦ vt arguilhar ♦ vi (insect, animal) picar; (*eyes, ointment*) queimar

stingy ['stɪndʒɪ] (*pej*) *adj* pão-duro, sovina

stink [stɪŋk] (*pt* stank, *pp* stunk) *n* fedor *m*, catinga ♦ *vi* feder, cheirar mal; ~**ing** (*inf*) *adj* (*fig*) maldito

stint [stɪnt] *n* tarefa, parte *f* ♦ *vi*: **to ~ on** ser parco com

stipulate ['stɪpjuleɪt] *vt* estipular

stir [stə:*] *n* (*fig*) comoção *f*, rebuliço ♦ *vt* mexer; (*fig*) comover ♦ *vi* mover-se, remexer-se; ~ **up** *vt* excitar; (*trouble*) provocar

stirrup ['stɪrəp] *n* estribo

stitch [stɪtʃ] *n* (*SEWING, KNITTING, MED*) ponto; (*pain*) pontada ♦ *vt* costurar; (*MED*) dar pontos em, suturar

stoat [stəut] *n* arminho

stock [stɔk] *n* suprimento; (*COMM: reserves*) estoque *m*, provisão *f*; (: *selection*) sortimento; (*AGR*) gado; (*CULIN*) caldo; (*lineage*) estirpe *f*, linhagem *f*; (*FINANCE*) valores *mpl*, títulos *mpl* ♦ *adj* (*reply etc*) de sempre, costumeiro ♦ *vt* ter em estoque, estocar; **in/out of ~** em estoque/esgotado; **to take ~ of** (*fig*) fazer um balanço de; ~**s and shares** valores e títulos mobiliários; ~ **up** *vi*: **to ~ up (with)** abastecer-se (de); ~**broker** *n* corretor(a) *m/f* de valores *or* da Bolsa; ~ **cube** (*BRIT*) *n* cubo de caldo; ~ **exchange** *n* Bolsa de Valores

stocking ['stɔkɪŋ] *n* meia

stockist ['stɔkɪst] (*BRIT*) *n* estoquista *m/f*

stock: ~ **market** (*BRIT*) *n* Bolsa, mercado de valores; ~ **phrase** *n* frase *f* feita; ~**pile** *n* reservas *fpl*, estocagem *f* ♦ *vt* acumular reservas de, estocar; ~**taking** (*BRIT*) *n* (*COMM*) inventário

stocky ['stɔkɪ] *adj* (*strong*) robusto; (*short*) atarracado

stodgy ['stɔdʒɪ] *adj* pesado

stoke [stəuk] *vt* atiçar, alimentar

stole [stəul] *pt of* **steal** ♦ *n* estola

stolen ['stəuln] *pp of* **steal**

stolid ['stɔlɪd] *adj* fleumático

stomach ['stʌmək] *n* (*ANAT*) estômago; (*belly*) barriga, ventre *m* ♦ *vt* suportar, tolerar; ~ **ache** *n* dor *f* de estômago

stone [stəun] *n* pedra; (*pebble*) pedrinha; (*in fruit*) caroço; (*MED*) pedra, cálculo; (*BRIT: weight*) = 6.348kg; *14 pounds* ♦ *adj* de pedra ♦ *vt* apedrejar; (*fruit*) tirar o(s) caroço(s) de; ~-**cold** *adj* gelado; ~-**deaf** *adj* surdo como uma porta; ~**work** *n* cantaria; **stony** *adj* pedregoso; (*fig*) glacial

stood [stud] *pt, pp of* **stand**

stool [stu:l] *n* tamborete *m*, banco

stoop [stu:p] *vi* (*also*: **have a ~**) ser corcunda; (*also*: ~ **down**) debruçar-se, curvar-se

stop [stɔp] *n* parada, interrupção *f*; (*for bus etc*) parada (*BR*), ponto (*BR*), paragem *f* (*PT*); (*also*: **full ~**) ponto ♦ *vt* pa-

rar, deter; (*break off*) interromper; (*cheque*) sustar, suspender; (*also*: **put a ~ to**) impedir ♦ *vi* parar, deter-se; (*watch, noise*) parar; (*end*) acabar; **to ~ doing sth** deixar de fazer algo; ~ **dead** *vi* parar de repente; ~ **off** *vi* dar uma parada; ~ **up** *vt* tapar; ~**gap** *n* (*person*) tapa-buraco *m*; (*measure*) paliativo; ~**over** *n* parada rápida; (*AVIAT*) escala; ~**page** *n* (*strike*) greve *f*; (*blockage*) obstrução *f*; ~**per** *n* tampa, rolha; ~ **press** *n* notícia de última hora; ~**watch** *n* cronômetro

storage ['stɔːrɪdʒ] *n* armazenagem *f*; ~ **heater** (*BRIT*) *n* tipo de aquecimento que armazena calor durante a noite emitindo-o durante o dia

store [stɔː*] *n* (*stock*) suprimento; (*depot*) armazém *m*; (*reserve*) estoque *m*; (*BRIT: large shop*) loja de departamentos; (*US: shop*) loja ♦ *vt* armazenar; ~**s** *npl* (*provisions*) víveres *mpl*, provisões *fpl*; **who knows what is in ~ for us?** quem sabe o que nos espera?; ~ **up** *vt* acumular; ~**room** *n* depósito, almoxarifado

storey ['stɔːrɪ] (*US* **story**) *n* andar *m*

stork [stɔːk] *n* cegonha

storm [stɔːm] *n* tempestade *f*; (*fig*) tumulto ♦ *vi* (*fig*) enfurecer-se ♦ *vt* tomar de assalto, assaltar; ~**y** *adj* tempestuoso

story ['stɔːrɪ] *n* história, estória; (*lie*) mentira; (*US*) = **storey**; ~**book** *n* livro de contos

stout [staut] *adj* sólido, forte; (*fat*) gordo, corpulento; (*resolute*) decidido, resoluto ♦ *n* cerveja preta

stove [stəuv] *n* (*for cooking*) fogão *m*; (*for heating*) estufa, fogareiro

stow [stəu] *vt* guardar; ~**away** *n* passageiro/a clandestino/a

straddle ['strædl] *vt* cavalgar

straggle ['strægl] *vi* (*houses*) espalhar-se desordenadamente; (*people*) vagar, perambular; **straggly** *adj* (*hair*) rebelde, emaranhado

straight [streɪt] *adj* reto; (*back*) esticado; (*hair*) liso; (*honest*) honesto; (*simple*) simples *inv* ♦ *adv* reto; (*drink*) puro; **to put** *or* **get sth ~** esclarecer algo; ~ **away**, ~ **off** imediatamente; ~**en** *vt* arrumar; ~**en out** *vt* endireitar; (*fig*) esclarecer; **to ~en things out** arrumar as coisas; ~-**faced** *adj* impassível; ~**forward** *adj* (*simple*) simples *inv*, direto; (*honest*) honesto, franco

strain [streɪn] *n* tensão *f*; (*TECH*) esforço; (*MED: back* ~) distensão *f*; (: *tension*) luxação *f*; (*breed*) raça, estirpe *f* ♦ *vt* forçar, torcer, distender; (*stretch*) puxar, estirar; (*CULIN*) coar; ~**s** *npl* (*MUS*) acordes *mpl*; ~**ed** *adj* distendido; (*laugh*) forçado; (*relations*) tenso; ~**er** *n* coador *m*; (*sieve*) peneira

strait [streɪt] *n* estreito; ~**s** *npl* (*fig*): **to be in dire ~s** estar em apuros; ~**jack-**

et n camisa-de-força; **~-laced** adj puritano, austero

strand [strænd] n (of thread, hair) fio; (of rope) tira; **~ed** adj preso

strange [streɪndʒ] adj (not known) desconhecido; (odd) estranho, esquisito; **~ly** adv estranhamente; **~r** n desconhecido/a; (from another area) forasteiro/a

strangle ['stræŋgl] vt estrangular; (fig) sufocar; **~hold** n (fig) domínio total

strap [stræp] n correia; (of slip, dress) alça

strapping ['stræpɪŋ] adj corpulento, robusto, forte

strata ['strɑːtə] npl of **stratum**

strategic [strə'tiːdʒɪk] adj estratégico

strategy ['strætɪdʒɪ] n estratégia

stratum ['strɑːtəm] (pl **strata**) n camada

straw [strɔː] n palha; (drinking ~) canudo; **that's the last ~!** essa foi a última gota!

strawberry ['strɔːbərɪ] n morango

stray [streɪ] adj (animal) extraviado; (bullet) perdido; (scattered) espalhado ♦ vi perder-se

streak [striːk] n listra, traço; (in hair) mecha ♦ vt listrar ♦ vi: **to ~ past** passar como um raio

stream [striːm] n riacho, córrego; (of people, vehicles) fluxo; (of smoke) rastro; (of questions etc) torrente f ♦ vt (SCH) classificar ♦ vi correr, fluir; **to ~ in/out** entrar/sair em massa

streamer ['striːmə*] n serpentina; (pennant) flâmula

streamlined ['striːmlaɪnd] adj aerodinâmico

street [striːt] n rua; **~car** (US) n bonde m (BR), eléctrico (PT); **~ lamp** n poste m de iluminação; **~ plan** n mapa m; **~wise** (inf) adj malandro

strength [strɛŋθ] n força; (of girder etc) firmeza, resistência; (fig) poder m; **~en** vt fortificar; (fig) fortalecer

strenuous ['strɛnjuəs] adj enérgico; (determined) tenaz

stress [strɛs] n pressão f; (mental strain) tensão f, stress m; (emphasis) ênfase f; (TECH) tensão ♦ vt realçar, dar ênfase a; (syllable) acentuar

stretch [strɛtʃ] n (of sand etc) trecho, extensão f ♦ vi espreguiçar-se; (extend): **to ~ to or as far as** estender-se até ♦ vt estirar, esticar; (fig: subj: job, task) exigir o máximo de; **~ out** vi esticar-se ♦ vt (arm etc) esticar; (spread) estirar

stretcher ['strɛtʃə*] n maca, padiola

strewn [struːn] adj: **~ with** coberto or cheio de

stricken ['strɪkən] adj (wounded) ferido; (devastated) arrasado; (ill) acometido; **~ with** tomado por

strict [strɪkt] adj (person) severo, rigoroso; (meaning) exato, estrito; **~ly** adv severamente; estritamente

stridden ['strɪdn] pp of **stride**

stride [straɪd] (pt **strode**, pp **stridden**) n passo largo ♦ vi andar a passos largos

strife [straɪf] n conflito

strike [straɪk] (pt, pp **struck**) n greve f; (of oil etc) descoberta; (attack) ataque m ♦ vt bater em; (fig): **the thought or it ~s me that ...** me ocorre que ...; (oil etc) descobrir; (deal) fechar, acertar ♦ vi estar em greve; (attack: soldiers, illness) atacar; (: disaster) assolar; (clock) bater; **on ~** em greve; **to ~ a match** acender um fósforo; **~ down** vt derrubar; **~ up** vt (MUS) começar a tocar; (conversation, friendship) travar; **~r** n grevista m/f; (SPORT) atacante m/f; **striking** adj impressionante

string [strɪŋ] (pt, pp **strung**) n (cord) barbante m (BR), cordel m (PT); (of beads) cordão m; (of onions) réstia; (MUS) corda ♦ vt: **to ~ out** esticar; **the ~s** npl (MUS) os instrumentos de corda; **to ~ together** (words) unir; (ideas) concatenar; **to get a job by pulling ~s** (fig) usar pistolão; **~ bean** n vagem f; **~(ed) instrument** n (MUS) instrumento de corda

stringent ['strɪndʒənt] adj rigoroso

strip [strɪp] n tira; (of land) faixa; (of metal) lâmina, tira ♦ vt despir; (also: **~ down**: machine) desmontar ♦ vi despir-se; **~ cartoon** n história em quadrinhos (BR), banda desenhada (PT)

stripe [straɪp] n listra; (MIL) galão m; **~d** adj listrado, com listras

strip lighting (BRIT) n iluminação f fluorescente

stripper ['strɪpə*] n artista m/f de striptease

strive [straɪv] (pt **strove**, pp **~n**) vi: **to ~ for sth/to do sth** esforçar-se por or batalhar para algo/para fazer algo

striven ['strɪvn] pp of **strive**

strode [strəud] pt of **stride**

stroke [strəuk] n (blow) golpe m; (MED) derrame m cerebral; (of paintbrush) pincelada; (SWIMMING: style) nado ♦ vt acariciar, afagar; **at a ~** de repente, de golpe

stroll [strəul] n volta, passeio ♦ vi passear, dar uma volta; **~er** (US) n carrinho (de criança)

strong [strɔŋ] adj forte; (imagination) fértil; (personality) forte, dominante; (nerves) de aço; **they are 50 ~** são 50; **~hold** n fortaleza; (fig) baluarte m; **~ly** adv firmemente; (defend) vigorosamente; (believe) profundamente; **~room** n casa-forte f

strove [strəuv] pt of **strive**

struck [strʌk] pt, pp of **strike**

structure ['strʌktʃə*] n estrutura; (building) construção f

struggle ['strʌgl] n luta, contenda ♦ vi (fight) lutar; (try hard) batalhar

strum [strʌm] vt (guitar) dedilhar

strung [strʌŋ] pt, pp of **string**

strut [strʌt] n escora, suporte m ♦ vi pavonear-se, empertigar-se

stub [stʌb] n (of ticket etc) canhoto; (of cigarette) toco, ponta; **to ~ one's toe** dar uma topada; **~ out** vt apagar

stubble ['stʌbl] n restolho; (on chin) barba por fazer

stubborn ['stʌbən] adj teimoso, cabeçudo, obstinado

stuck [stʌk] pt, pp of **stick** ♦ adj (jammed) emperrado; **~-up** adj convencido, metido, esnobe

stud [stʌd] n (shirt ~) botão m; (earring) tarraxa, rosca; (of boot) cravo; (also: ~ farm) fazenda de cavalos; (also: ~ horse) garanhão m ♦ vt (fig): **~ded with** salpicado de

student ['stjuːdənt] n estudante m/f ♦ adj estudantil; **~ driver** (US) n aprendiz m/f

studio ['stjuːdɪəʊ] n estúdio, (sculptor's) ateliê m; **~ flat** (US **~ apartment**) n apartamento conjugado

studious ['stjuːdɪəs] adj estudioso, aplicado; (careful) cuidadoso; **~ly** adv (carefully) com esmero

study ['stʌdɪ] n estudo; (room) sala de leitura or estudo ♦ vt estudar; (examine) examinar, investigar ♦ vi estudar; **studies** npl (subjects) estudos mpl, matérias fpl

stuff [stʌf] n (substance) troço; (things) troços mpl, coisas fpl ♦ vt (CULIN) rechear; (animals) empalhar; (inf: push) enfiar; **~ed toy** brinquedo de pelúcia; **~ing** n recheio; **~y** adj (room) abafado, mal ventilado; (person) rabujento, melindroso

stumble ['stʌmbl] vi tropeçar; **to ~ across** or **on** (fig) topar com; **stumbling block** n pedra no caminho

stump [stʌmp] n (of tree) toco; (of limb) coto ♦ vt: **to be ~ed** ficar perplexo

stun [stʌn] vt (subj: blow) aturdir; (: news) pasmar

stung [stʌŋ] pt, pp of **sting**

stunk [stʌŋk] pp of **stink**

stunning ['stʌnɪŋ] adj (news) atordoante; (appearance) maravilhoso

stunt [stʌnt] n façanha sensacional; (publicity ~) truque m publicitário; **~ed** adj atrofiado, retardado; **~man** (irreg) n dublê m

stupefy ['stjuːpɪfaɪ] vt deixar estupefato

stupendous [stjuː'pɛndəs] adj monumental

stupid ['stjuːpɪd] adj estúpido, idiota

sturdy ['stəːdɪ] adj (person) robusto, firme; (thing) sólido

stutter ['stʌtə*] n gagueira, gaguez f ♦ vi gaguejar

sty [staɪ] n (for pigs) chiqueiro

stye [staɪ] n (MED) terçol m

style [staɪl] n estilo; (elegance) elegância; **stylish** adj elegante, chique

stylus ['staɪləs] (pl styli or **~es**) n (of record player) agulha

suave [swɑːv] adj suave, melifluo

sub... [sʌb]. prefix sub...; **~conscious** adj do subconsciente; **~contract** vt subcontratar; **~divide** vt subdividir

subdue [səb'djuː] vt subjugar; (passions) dominar; **~d** adj (light) tênue; (person) desanimado

subject [n 'sʌbdʒɪkt, vt səb'dʒɛkt] n (of king) súdito/a; (theme) assunto; (SCH) matéria; (LING) sujeito ♦ vt: **to ~ sb to sth** submeter alguém a algo; **to be ~ to** estar sujeito a; **~ive** adj subjetivo; **~ matter** n assunto; (content) conteúdo

sublet [sʌb'lɛt] vt sublocar, subalugar

submachine gun [sʌbmə'ʃiːn-] n metralhadora de mão

submarine ['sʌbməriːn] n submarino

submerge [səb'məːdʒ] vt submergir ♦ vi submergir-se

submission [səb'mɪʃən] n submissão f; (to committee) petição f; (of plan) apresentação f; proposição f; **submissive** adj submisso

submit [səb'mɪt] vt submeter ♦ vi submeter-se

subnormal [sʌb'nɔːməl] adj (temperature) abaixo do normal

subordinate [sə'bɔːdɪnət] adj, n subordinado/a

subpoena [səb'piːnə] n (LAW) intimação f, citação f judicial

subscribe [səb'skraɪb] vi subscrever; **to ~ to** (opinion) concordar com; (fund) contribuir para; (newspaper) assinar; **~r** n assinante m/f; **subscription** n assinatura

subsequent ['sʌbsɪkwənt] adj subseqüente, posterior; **~ly** adv posteriormente, depois

subside [səb'saɪd] vi (feeling, wind) acalmar-se; (flood) baixar; **~nce** n (in road etc) afundamento da superfície

subsidiary [səb'sɪdɪərɪ] adj secundário ♦ n (also: ~ **company**) subsidiária

subsidize ['sʌbsɪdaɪz] vt subsidiar

subsidy ['sʌbsɪdɪ] n subsídio

subsistence [səb'sɪstəns] n subsistência; **~ allowance** n diária

substance ['sʌbstəns] n substância

substantial [səb'stænʃl] adj (solid) sólido; (reward, meal) substancial; **~ly** adv consideravelmente; (in essence) substancialmente

substantiate [səb'stænʃɪeɪt] vt comprovar, justificar

substitute ['sʌbstɪtjuːt] n substituto/a; (person) suplente m/f ♦ vt: **to ~ A for B** substituir B por A

subterranean [sʌbtə'reɪnɪən] adj subterrâneo

subtitle ['sʌbtaɪtl] n (CINEMA) legenda

subtle ['sʌtl] *adj* sutil; **~ty** *n* sutileza

subtotal [sʌb'təutl] *n* total *m* parcial, subtotal *m*

subtract [səb'trækt] *vt* subtrair, deduzir

suburb ['sʌbə:b] *n* subúrbio; **~an** *adj* suburbano; (*train etc*) de subúrbio; **~ia** *n* os subúrbios

subway ['sʌbweɪ] *n* (*BRIT*) passagem *f* subterrânea; (*US*) metrô *m* (*BR*), metro(-politano) (*PT*)

succeed [sək'si:d] *vi* (*person*) ser bem sucedido, ter êxito; (*plan*) sair bem ♦ *vt* suceder a; **to ~ in doing** conseguir fazer; **~ing** *adj* sucessivo, posterior

success [sək'sɛs] *n* êxito (*hit, person*) sucesso; **~ful** *adj* (*venture*) bem sucedido; (*writer*) de sucesso, bem sucedido; **to be ~ful (in doing)** conseguir (fazer); **~fully** *adv* com sucesso, com êxito

succession [sək'sɛʃən] *n* sucessão *f*, série *f*; (*to throne*) sucessão

such [sʌtʃ] *adj* tal, semelhante; (*of that kind: sg*): **~ a book** um livro parecido, tal livro; (*: pl*): **~ books** tais livros (*so much*): **~ courage** tanta coragem ♦ *adv* tão; **~ a long trip** uma viagem tão longa; **~ a lot of** tanto; **~ as** tal como; **~** como tal; **~-and-~** *adj* tal e qual

suck [sʌk] *vt* chupar; (*breast*) mamar; **~er** *n* (*ZOOL*) ventosa; (*inf*) trouxa *m/f*, otário/a

Sudan [su'dɑ:n] *n* Sudão *m*

sudden ['sʌdn] *adj* (*rapid*) repentino, súbito; (*unexpected*) imprevisto; **all of a ~** inesperadamente; **~ly** *adv* inesperadamente

suds [sʌdz] *npl* água de sabão

sue [su:] *vt* processar

suede [sweɪd] *n* camurça

suet ['suɪt] *n* sebo

suffer ['sʌfə*] *vt* sofrer; (*bear*) agüentar, suportar ♦ *vi* sofrer, padecer; **to ~ from** sofrer de, estar com; **~er** *n*: a **~er from** (*MED*) uma pessoa que sofre de; **~ing** *n* sofrimento

suffice [sə'faɪs] *vi* bastar, ser suficiente

sufficient [sə'fɪʃənt] *adj* suficiente, bastante; **~ly** *adv* suficientemente

suffix ['sʌfɪks] *n* sufixo

suffocate ['sʌfəkeɪt] *vi* sufocar(-se), asfixiar(-se); **suffocation** *n* sufocação *f*; (*MED*) asfixia

suffused [sə'fju:zd] *adj*: **~ with** banhado de

sugar ['ʃugə*] *n* açúcar *m* ♦ *vt* pôr açúcar em, açucarar; **~ beet** *n* beterraba (sacarina); **~ cane** *n* cana-de-açúcar *f*

suggest [sə'dʒɛst] *vt* sugerir; (*indicate*) indicar; **~ion** *n* sugestão *f*; indicação *f*; **~ive** (*pej*) *adj* indecente

suicide ['suɪsaɪd] *n* suicídio; (*person*) suicida *m/f*; *see also* **commit**

suit [su:t] *n* (*man's*) terno (*BR*), fato (*PT*); (*woman's*) conjunto; (*LAW*) processo;

(*CARDS*) naipe *m* ♦ *vt* convir a; (*clothes*) ficar bem a; (*adapt*): **to ~ sth to** adaptar *or* acomodar algo a; **they are well ~ed** fazem um bom par; **~able** *adj* conveniente; (*appropriate*) apropriado; **~ably** *adv* (*dressed*) apropriadamente; (*impressed*) bem

suitcase ['su:tkeɪs] *n* mala

suite [swi:t] *n* (*of rooms*) conjunto de salas; (*MUS*) suite *f*; (*furniture*) conjunto

suitor ['su:tə*] *n* pretendente *m*

sulfur ['sʌlfə*] (*US*) *n* = **sulphur**

sulk [sʌlk] *vi* ficar emburrado, fazer beicinho *or* biquinho (*inf*); **~y** *adj* emburrado

sullen ['sʌlən] *adj* rabugento; (*silence*) pesado

sulphur ['sʌlfə*] (*US* **sulfur**) *n* enxofre *m*

sultana [sʌl'tɑ:nə] *n* passa branca

sultry ['sʌltrɪ] *adj* abafado

sum [sʌm] *n* soma; (*calculation*) cálculo; **~ up** *vt, vi* resumir

summarize ['sʌməraɪz] *vt* resumir

summary ['sʌmərɪ] *n* resumo

summer ['sʌmə*] *n* verão *m* ♦ *adj* de verão; **in ~** no verão; **~house** *n* pavilhão *m*; **~time** *n* (*season*) verão *m*; **~ time** *n* (*by clock*) horário de verão

summit ['sʌmɪt] *n* topo, cume *m*; (*also*: **~ conference**) (conferência de) cúpula

summon ['sʌmən] *vt* (*person*) mandar chamar; (*meeting*) convocar; (*LAW: witness*) convocar; **~ up** *vt* concentrar; **~s** *n* (*JUR*) citação *f*, intimação *f*; (*fig*) chamada ♦ *vt* citar, intimar

sump [sʌmp] (*BRIT*) *n* (*AUT*) cárter *m*

sumptuous ['sʌmptjuəs] *adj* suntuoso

sun [sʌn] *n* sol *m*; **~bathe** *vi* tomar sol; **~burn** *n* queimadura do sol; **~burned** *adj* = **~burnt**; **~burnt** *adj* bronzeado; (*painfully*) queimado

Sunday ['sʌndɪ] *n* domingo; **~ school** *n* escola dominical

sundial ['sʌndaɪəl] *n* relógio de sol

sundown ['sʌndaun] *n* pôr *m* do sol

sundries ['sʌndrɪz] *npl* gêneros *mpl* diversos

sundry ['sʌndrɪ] *adj* vários, diversos; **all and ~** todos

sunflower ['sʌnflauə*] *n* girassol *m*

sung [sʌŋ] *pp of* **sing**

sunglasses ['sʌnglɑ:sɪz] *npl* óculos *mpl* de sol

sunk [sʌŋk] *pp of* **sink**

sun: **~light** *n* (luz *f* do) sol *m*; **~lit** *adj* ensolarado, iluminado pelo sol; **~ny** *adj* cheio de sol; (*day*) ensolarado, de sol; **~rise** *n* nascer *m* do sol; **~ roof** *n* (*AUT*) teto solar; **~set** *n* pôr *m* do sol; **~shade** *n* pára-sol *m*; **~shine** *n* (luz *f* do) sol *m*; **~stroke** *n* insolação *f*; **~tan** *n* bronzeado; **~tan lotion** *n* loção *f* de bronzear; **~tan oil** *n* óleo de bronzear, bronzeador *m*

super ['su:pə*] (*inf*) *adj* bacana (*BR*),

muito giro (PT)

superannuation [su:pərænju'eɪʃən] n pensão f de aposentadoria

superb [su:'pɔ:b] adj excelente

supercilious [su:pə'sɪliəs] adj arrogante, desdenhoso; (haughty) altivo

superfluous [su:'pɔ:fluəs] adj supérfluo, desnecessário

superhuman [su:pə'hju:mən] adj sobre-humano

superimpose [su:pərɪm'pəuz] vt: **to ~ (on/with)** sobrepor (a)

superintendent [su:pərɪn'tɛndənt] n superintendente m/f; (POLICE) chefe m/f de polícia

superior [su'pɪərɪə*] adj superior; (smug) desdenhoso ♦ n superior m

superlative [su'pɔ:lətɪv] n superlativo

superman ['su:pəmæn] (irreg) n super-homem m

supermarket ['su:pəmɑ:kɪt] n supermercado

supernatural [su:pə'nætʃərəl] adj sobrenatural ♦ n: **the ~** o sobrenatural

superpower ['su:pəpauə*] n (POL) super-potência

supersede [su:pə'si:d] vt suplantar

superstitious [su:pə'stɪʃəs] adj supersticioso

supertanker ['su:pətæŋkə*] n superpetroleiro

supervise ['su:pəvaɪz] vt supervisar, supervisionar; **supervision** n supervisão f; **supervisor** n supervisor(a) m/f; (academic) orientador(a) m/f

supine ['su:paɪn] adj em supinação

supper ['sʌpə*] n jantar m; (late evening) ceia

supple ['sʌpl] adj flexível

supplement [n 'sʌplɪmənt, vt sʌplɪ'mɛnt] n suplemento ♦ vt suprir, completar; **~ary** adj suplementar; **~ary benefit** (BRIT) n auxílio suplementar pago aos de renda baixa

supplier [sə'plaɪə*] n abastecedor(a) m/f, fornecedor(a) m/f

supply [sə'plaɪ] vt (provide): **to ~ sth (to sb)** fornecer algo (para alguém); (equip): **to ~ (with)** suprir (de) ♦ n fornecimento, provisão f; (stock) estoque m; (supplying) abastecimento; **supplies** npl (food) víveres mpl; (MIL) apetrechos mpl; **~ teacher** (BRIT) n professor(a) m/f suplente

support [sə'pɔ:t] n (moral, financial etc) apoio; (TECH) suporte m ♦ vt apoiar; (financially) manter; (TECH: hold up) sustentar; (theory etc) defender; **~er** n (POL etc) partidário/a; (SPORT) torcedor(a) m/f

suppose [sə'pəuz] vt supor; (imagine) imaginar; (duty): **to be ~d to do sth** dever fazer algo; **~dly** adv supostamente, pretensamente; **supposing** conj caso, supondo-se que

suppress [sə'prɛs] vt (information) suprimir; (feelings, revolt) reprimir; (yawn) conter; **suppression** n (of information) supressão f; (of feelings, revolt) repressão f; (of yawn) controle m; (of scandal) abafamento

supreme [su'pri:m] adj supremo

surcharge ['sɔ:tʃɑ:dʒ] n sobretaxa

sure [ʃuə*] adj seguro; (definite) certo; (aim) certeiro; **to make ~ of sth/that** assegurar-se de algo/que; **~!** claro que sim!; **~ enough** efetivamente; **~-footed** adj de andar seguro; **~ly** adv (certainly; US: also: **sure**) certamente; **~ty** n garantia, fiança

surf [sɔ:f] n (waves) ondas fpl, arrebentação f

surface ['sɔ:fɪs] n superfície f ♦ vt (road) revestir ♦ vi vir à superfície or à tona; (fig: news, feeling) vir à tona; **~ mail** n correio comum

surfboard ['sɔ:fbɔ:d] n prancha de surfe

surfeit ['sɔ:fɪt] n: **a ~ of** um excesso de

surfing ['sɔ:fɪŋ] n surfe m

surge [sɔ:dʒ] n onda ♦ vi (sea) encapelar-se; (people, vehicles) precipitar-se; (feeling) aumentar repentinamente

surgeon ['sɔ:dʒən] n cirurgião/giã m/f

surgery ['sɔ:dʒərɪ] n cirurgia; (BRIT: room) consultório; (: also: **~ hours**) horas fpl de consulta

surgical ['sɔ:dʒɪkl] adj cirúrgico; **~ spirit** (BRIT) n álcool m

surly ['sɔ:lɪ] adj malcriado, rude

surmount [sə'maunt] vt superar, sobrepujar, vencer

surname ['sɔ:neɪm] n sobrenome m (BR), apelido (PT)

surpass [sɔ:'pɑ:s] vt superar

surplus ['sɔ:pləs] n excedente m; (COMM) superávit m ♦ adj excedente, de sobra

surprise [sə'praɪz] n surpresa ♦ vt surpreender

surrender [sə'rɛndə*] n rendição f, entrega ♦ vi render-se, entregar-se

surreptitious [sʌrəp'tɪʃəs] adj clandestino, furtivo

surrogate ['sʌrəgɪt] n (BRIT) substituto/a; **~ mother** n mãe f portadora

surround [sə'raund] vt circundar, rodear; (MIL etc) cercar; **~ing** adj circundante, adjacente; **~ings** npl arredores mpl, cercanias fpl

surveillance [sɔ:'veɪləns] n vigilância

survey [n 'sɔ:veɪ, vt sɔ:'veɪ] n inspeção f; (of habits etc) pesquisa; (of land) levantamento; (of house) inspeção f ♦ vt observar, contemplar; (land) fazer um levantamento de; **~or** n (of land) agrimensor(a) m/f; (of building) inspetor(a) m/f

survival [sə'vaɪvl] n sobrevivência; (relic) remanescente m

survive [sə'vaɪv] vi sobreviver; (custom

etc) perdurar ♦ *vt* sobreviver a; **survivor** *n* sobrevivente *m/f*

susceptible [sə'sɛptəbl] *adj*: ~ **(to)** (*injury*) suscetível *or* sensível (a); (*flattery, pressure*) vulnerável (a)

suspect [*adj, n* 'sʌspɛkt, *vt* səs'pɛkt] *adj, n* suspeito/a ♦ *vt* suspeitar, desconfiar

suspend [səs'pɛnd] *vt* suspender; **~ed sentence** *n* condenação *f* condicional; **~er belt** *n* cinta-liga; **~ers** *npl* (*BRIT*) ligas *fpl*; (*US*) suspensórios *mpl*

suspense [səs'pɛns] *n* incerteza, ansiedade *f*; (*in film etc*) suspense *m*; **to keep sb in ~** manter alguém em suspense *or* na expectativa

suspension [səs'pɛnʃən] *n* suspensão *f*; (*of driving licence*) cassação *f*; **~ bridge** *n* ponte *f* pênsil

suspicion [səs'pɪʃən] *n* suspeita; **suspicious** *adj* (*suspecting*) suspeitoso; (*causing suspicion*) suspeito

sustain [səs'teɪn] *vt* sustentar; (*suffer*) sofrer; **~able** *adj* (*development*) sustentável; **~ed** *adj* (*effort*) contínuo; **sustenance** *n* sustento

swab [swɔb] *n* (*MED*) mecha de algodão

swagger ['swægə*] *vi* andar com ar de superioridade

swallow ['swɔləu] *n* (*bird*) andorinha ♦ *vt* engolir, tragar; (*fig: story*) engolir; (*pride*) pôr de lado; (*one's words*) retirar; **~ up** *vt* (*savings etc*) consumir

swam [swæm] *pt of* **swim**

swamp [swɔmp] *n* pântano, brejo ♦ *vt* atolar, inundar; (*fig*) assoberbar

swan [swɔn] *n* cisne *m*

swap [swɔp] *n* troca, permuta ♦ *vt*: **to ~ (for)** trocar (por); (*replace (with)*) substituir (por)

swarm [swɔːm] *n* (*of bees*) enxame *m*; (*of people*) multidão *f* ♦ *vi* enxamear; aglomerar-se; (*place*): **to be ~ing with** estar apinhado de

swarthy ['swɔːðɪ] *adj* moreno

swastika ['swɔstɪkə] *n* suástica

swat [swɔt] *vt* esmagar

sway [sweɪ] *vi* balançar-se, oscilar ♦ *vt* (*influence*) influenciar

swear [swɛə*] (*pt* **swore**, *pp* **sworn**) *vi* (*curse*) xingar ♦ *vt* (*promise*) jurar; **~word** *n* palavrão *m*

sweat [swɛt] *n* suor *m* ♦ *vi* suar; **~er** *n* suéter *m or f* (*BR*), camisola (*PT*); **~shirt** *n* suéter *m* de malha de algodão; **~y** *adj* suado

Swede [swiːd] *n* sueco/a

swede [swiːd] *n* tipo de nabo

Sweden ['swiːdən] *n* Suécia; **Swedish** *adj* sueco ♦ *n* (*LING*) sueco

sweep [swiːp] (*pt, pp* **swept**) *n* (*act*) varredura; (*also*: **chimney ~**) limpador *m* de chaminés ♦ *vt* varrer; (*with arm*) empurrar; (*subj: current*) arrastar; (: *fashion, craze*) espalhar-se por ♦ *vi* varrer; **~ away** *vt* varrer; **~ past** *vi* passar

rapidamente; **~ up** *vi* varrer; **~ing** *adj* (*gesture*) dramático; (*statement*) generalizado

sweet [swiːt] *n* (*candy*) bala (*BR*), rebuçado (*PT*); (*BRIT: pudding*) sobremesa ♦ *adj* doce; (*fig: air*) fresco; (: *water, smell*) doce; (: *sound*) suave; (: *kind*) meigo; (*baby, kitten*) bonitinho; **~corn** *n* milho; **~en** *vt* pôr açúcar em; (*temper*) abrandar; **~heart** *n* namorado/a; **~ness** *n* doçura; **~ pea** *n* ervilha-de-cheiro *f*

swell [swɛl] (*pt* **~ed**, *pp* **swollen** *or* **~ed**) *n* (*of sea*) vaga, onda ♦ *adj* (*US: inf: excellent*) bacana ♦ *vi* (*increase*) aumentar; (*get stronger*) intensificar-se; (*also*: **~ up**) inchar-se; **~ing** *n* (*MED*) inchação *f*

sweltering ['swɛltərɪŋ] *adj* (*heat*) sufocante; (*day*) mormacento

swept [swɛpt] *pt, pp of* **sweep**

swerve [swəːv] *vi* desviar-se

swift [swɪft] *n* (*bird*) andorinhão *m* ♦ *adj* rápido

swig [swɪg] (*inf*) *n* trago, gole *m*

swill [swɪl] *vt* (*also*: **~ out**, **~ down**) lavar, limpar com água

swim [swɪm] (*pt* **swam**, *pp* **swum**) *n*: **to go for a ~** ir nadar ♦ *vi* nadar; (*head, room*) rodar ♦ *vt* atravessar a nado; (*distance*) percorrer (a nado); **~mer** *n* nadador(a) *m/f*; **~ming** *n* natação *f*; **~ming cap** *n* touca de natação; **~ming costume** (*BRIT*) *n* (*woman's*) maiô *m* (*BR*), fato de banho (*PT*); (*man's*) calção *m* de banho (*BR*), calções *mpl* de banho (*PT*); **~ming pool** *n* piscina; **~ming trunks** *npl* sunga (*BR*), calções *mpl* de banho (*PT*); **~suit** *n* maiô *m* (*BR*), fato de banho (*PT*)

swindle ['swɪndl] *n* fraude *f* ♦ *vt* defraudar

swine [swaɪn] (*inf!*) *n* canalha *m*, calhorda *m*

swing [swɪŋ] (*pt, pp* **swung**) *n* (*in playground*) balanço; (*movement*) balanceio, oscilação *f*; (*in opinion*) mudança, virada; (*rhythm*) ritmo ♦ *vt* balançar; (*also*: **~ round**) girar, rodar ♦ *vi* oscilar; (*on swing*) balançar; (*also*: **~ round**) voltar-se bruscamente; **to be in full ~** estar a todo vapor; **~ bridge** *n* ponte *f* giratória; **~ door** (*US* **~ing door**) *n* porta de vaivém

swingeing ['swɪndʒɪŋ] (*BRIT*) *adj* esmagador(a); (*cuts*) devastador(a)

swipe [swaɪp] (*inf*) *n* (*steal*) afanar, roubar

swirl [swəːl] *vi* redemoinhar

swish [swɪʃ] *vi* (*tail*) abanar; (*clothes*) fazer ruge-ruge

Swiss [swɪs] *adj, n inv* suíço/a

switch [swɪtʃ] *n* (*for light, radio etc*) interruptor *m*; (*change*) mudança ♦ *vt* (*change*) trocar; **~ off** *vt* apagar; (*engine*) desligar; **~ on** *vt* acender; ligar;

~**board** n (TEL) mesa telefônica

Switzerland ['switsələnd] n Suiça

swivel ['swivl] vi (also: ~ **round**) girar (sobre um eixo), fazer pião

swollen ['swəulən] pp of **swell**

swoon [swu:n] vi desmaiar

swoop [swu:p] n (by police etc) batida ♦ vi (also: ~ **down**) precipitar-se, cair

swop [swɔp] n, vt = **swap**

sword [sɔ:d] n espada; ~**fish** n inv peixe-espada m

swore [swɔ:ˈ] pt of **swear**

sworn [swɔ:n] pp of **swear** ♦ adj (statement) sob juramento; (enemy) declarado

swum [swʌm] pp of **swim**

swung [swʌŋ] pt, pp of **swing**

syllable ['sɪləbl] n sílaba

syllabus ['sɪləbəs] n programa m de estudos

symbol ['sɪmbl] n símbolo

symmetry ['sɪmɪtrɪ] n simetria

sympathetic [sɪmpə'θetɪk] adj (understanding) compreensivo; (likeable) agradável; (supportive): ~ **to(wards)** solidário com

sympathize ['sɪmpəθaɪz] vi: ~ **with** (person) compadecer-se de; (sb's feelings) compreender; (cause) simpatizar com; ~**r** n (POL) simpatizante m/f

sympathy ['sɪmpəθɪ] n compaixão f; sympathies npl (tendencies) simpatia; in ~ em acordo; (strike) em ·solidariedade; with our deepest ~ com nossos mais profundos pêsames

symphony ['sɪmfənɪ] n sinfonia

symptom ['sɪmptəm] n sintoma m; (sign) indício

synagogue ['sɪnəgɔg] n sinagoga

syndicate ['sɪndɪkɪt] n sindicato; (of newspapers) cadeia

syndrome ['sɪndrəum] n síndrome f

synopsis [sɪ'nɔpsɪs] (pl synopses) n sinopse f, resumo

syntax ['sɪntæks] n sintaxe f

synthetic [sɪn'θetɪk] adj sintético

syphon ['saɪfən] = **siphon**

Syria ['sɪrɪə] n Síria; ~**n** adj sírio/a

syringe [sɪ'rɪndʒ] n seringa

syrup ['sɪrəp] n xarope m; (also: golden ~) melaço

system ['sɪstəm] n sistema m; (method) método; (ANAT) organismo m; ~**atic** adj sistemático; ~ **disk** n (COMPUT) disco do sistema; ~**s analyst** n analista m/f de sistemas

T

ta [tɑ:] (BRIT: inf) excl obrigado/a

tab [tæb] n lingüeta, aba; (label) etiqueta; to keep ~s on (fig) vigiar

tabby ['tæbɪ] n (also: ~ cat) gato malhado or listrado

table ['teɪbl] n mesa ♦ vt (motion etc)

apresentar; to lay or set the ~ pôr a mesa; ~ of contents índice m, sumário; ~**cloth** n toalha de mesa; ~ **d'hôte** n refeição f comercial; ~ **lamp** n abajur m (BR), candeeiro (PT); ~**mat** n descanso; ~**spoon** n colher f de sopa; (also: ~**spoonful**: as measurement) colherada

tablet ['tæblɪt] n (MED) comprimido; (of stone) lápide f

table tennis n pingue-pongue m, tênis m de mesa

table wine n vinho de mesa

tabloid ['tæblɔɪd] n tablóide m

tabulate ['tæbjuleɪt] vt (data, figures) dispor em forma de tabela

tacit ['tæsɪt] adj tácito, implícito

tack [tæk] n (nail) tachinha, percevejo ♦ vt prender com tachinha; (stitch) alinhavar ♦ vi virar de bordo

tackle ['tækl] n (gear) equipamento; (also: fishing ~) apetrechos mpl; (for lifting) guincho; (FOOTBALL) ato de tirar a bola de adversário ♦ vt (difficulty) atacar; (challenge: person) desafiar; (grapple with) atracar-se com; (FOOTBALL) tirar a bola de

tacky ['tækɪ] adj pegajoso, grudento; (inf: tasteless) cafona

tact [tækt] n tato, diplomacia; ~**ful** adj diplomático

tactics ['tæktɪks] n, npl tática

tactless ['tæktlɪs] adj sem diplomacia

tadpole ['tædpəul] n girino

taffy ['tæfɪ] (US) n puxa-puxa m (BR), caramelo (PT)

tag [tæg] n (label) etiqueta; ~ **along** vi seguir

tail [teɪl] n rabo; (of comet, plane) cauda; (of shirt, coat) aba ♦ vt (follow) seguir bem de perto; ~ **away** or **off** vi diminuir gradualmente; ~**back** (BRIT) n fila (de carros); ~ **end** n (of train) cauda; (of procession) parte f final; ~**gate** n (AUT) porta traseira

tailor ['teɪlə'] n alfaiate m; ~**ing** n (cut) feitio; (craft) ofício de alfaiate; ~**-made** adj feito sob medida; (fig) especial

tailwind ['teɪlwɪnd] n vento de popa or de cauda

tainted ['teɪntɪd] adj (food) estragado, passado; (water, air) poluído; (fig) manchado

take [teɪk] (pt took, pp taken) vt tomar; (photo, holiday) tirar; (grab) pegar (em); (prize) ganhar; (effort, courage) requerer, exigir; (tolerate) agüentar; (accompany, bring: person) acompanhar, trazer; (: thing) trazer, carregar; (exam) fazer; (passengers etc): it ~s 50 people cabem 50 pessoas; to ~ sth from (drawer etc) tirar algo de; (person) pegar algo de; I ~ it that ... suponho que ...; ~ **after** vt fus parecer-se com; ~ **apart** vt desmontar; ~ **away** vt (extract) tirar; (carry *off*) levar; (*subtract*) subtrair; ~ **back** *vt* (*return*) devolver; (*one's words*) retirar; ~ **down** *vt* (*building*) demolir; (*dismantle*) desmontar; (*letter etc*) tomar por escrito; ~ **in** *vt* (*deceive*) enganar; (*understand*) compreender; (*include*) abranger; (*lodger*) receber; ~ **off** *vi* (*AVIAT*) decolar; (*go away*) ir-se ♦ *vt* (*remove*) tirar; ~ **on** *vt* (*work*) empreender; (*employee*) empregar; (*opponent*) desafiar; ~ **out** *vt* tirar; (*extract*) extrair; (*invite*) acompanhar; ~ **over** *vt* (*business*) assumir; (*country*) tomar posse de ♦ *vi*: to ~ **over from sb** suceder a alguém; ~ **to** *vt fus* (*person*) simpatizar com; (*activity*) afeiçoar-se a; to ~ **to doing sth** criar o hábito de fazer algo; ~ **up** *vt* (*dress*) encurtar; (*time, space*) ocupar; (*hobby etc*) dedicar-se a; (*offer*) aceitar; to ~ **sb up on a suggestion/offer** aceitar a oferta/ sugestão de alguém sobre algo; ~**away** (*BRIT*) *adj* (*food*) para levar; ~**off** (*AVIAT*) decolagem *f*; ~**out** (*US*) *adj* = ~**away**; ~**over** *n* (*COMM*) aquisição *f* de controle; **takings** *npl* (*COMM*) receita, renda

talc [tælk] *n* (*also*: ~**um powder**) talco
tale [teɪl] *n* (*story*) conto; (*account*) narrativa; to **tell** ~**s** (*fig*: *lie*) dizer mentiras
talent [ˈtælənt] *n* talento; ~**ed** *adj* talentoso
talk [tɔːk] *n* conversa, fala; (*gossip*) mexerico, fofocas *fpl*; (*conversation*) conversa, conversação *f* ♦ *vi* falar; ~**s** *npl* (*POL etc*) negociações *fpl*; to ~ **about** falar sobre; to ~ **sb into/out of doing sth** convencer alguém a fazer algo/dissuadir alguém de fazer algo; to ~ **shop** falar sobre negócios/questões profissionais; ~ **over** *vt* discutir; ~**ative** *adj* loquaz, tagarela; ~ **show** *n* programa *m* de entrevistas
tall [tɔːl] *adj* alto; to **be 6 feet** ~ medir 6 pés, ter 6 pés de altura; ~ **story** *n* estória inverossímil
tally [ˈtælɪ] *n* conta ♦ *vi*: to ~ (**with**) conferir (com)
talon [ˈtælən] *n* garra
tambourine [tæmbəˈriːn] *n* tamborim *m*, pandeiro
tame [teɪm] *adj* domesticado; (*fig*: *story, style*) sem graça, insípido
tamper [ˈtæmpə*] *vi*: to ~ **with** mexer em
tampon [ˈtæmpɔn] *n* tampão *m*
tan [tæn] *n* (*also*: **sun**~) bronzeado ♦ *vi* bronzear-se ♦ *adj* (*colour*) bronzeado, marrom claro
tandem [ˈtændəm] *n*: **in** ~ junto
tang [tæŋ] *n* sabor *m* forte
tangent [ˈtændʒənt] *n* (*MATH*) tangente *f*; to **go off at a** ~ (*fig*) sair pela tangente
tangerine [tændʒəˈriːn] *n* tangerina, mexerica
tangle [ˈtæŋgl] *n* emaranhado; to **get**

in(to) a ~ meter-se num rolo
tank [tæŋk] *n* depósito, tanque *m*; (*for fish*) aquário; (*MIL*) tanque
tanker [ˈtæŋkə*] *n* (*ship*) navio-tanque *m*; (*truck*) caminhão-tanque *m*
tanned [tænd] *adj* (*skin*) moreno, bronzeado
tantalizing [ˈtæntəlaɪzɪŋ] *adj* tentador(a)
tantamount [ˈtæntəmaunt] *adj*: ~ **to** equivalente a
tantrum [ˈtæntrəm] *n* chilique *m*, acesso (de raiva)
tap [tæp] *n* (*on sink etc*) torneira; (*gentle blow*) palmadinha; (*gas* ~) chave *f* ♦ *vt* dar palmadinha em, bater de leve; (*resources*) utilizar, explorar; (*telephone*) grampear; **on** ~ disponível; ~**-dancing** *n* sapateado
tape [teɪp] *n* fita; (*also*: **magnetic** ~) fita magnética; (*sticky* ~) fita adesiva ♦ *vt* (*record*) gravar (em fita); (*stick with tape*) colar; ~ **deck** *n* gravador *m*, toca-fitas *m inv*; ~ **measure** *n* fita métrica, trena
taper [ˈteɪpə*] *n* círio ♦ *vi* afilar-se, estreitar-se
tape recorder *n* gravador *m*
tapestry [ˈtæpɪstrɪ] *n* (*object*) tapete *m* de parede; (*art*) tapeçaria
tar [tɑː*] *n* alcatrão *m*
target [ˈtɑːgɪt] *n* alvo
tariff [ˈtærɪf] *n* tarifa
tarmac [ˈtɑːmæk] *n* (*BRIT*: *on road*) macadame *m*; (*AVIAT*) pista
tarnish [ˈtɑːnɪʃ] *vt* empanar o brilho de
tarpaulin [tɑːˈpɔːlɪn] *n* lona alcatroada
tarragon [ˈtærəgən] *n* estragão *m*
tart [tɑːt] *n* (*CULIN*) torta; (*BRIT*: *inf*: *pej*: *woman*) piranha ♦ *adj* (*flavour*) ácido, azedo; ~ **up** (*inf*) *vt* arrumar, dar um jeito em; to ~ **o.s. up** arrumar-se; (*pej*) empetecar-se
tartan [ˈtɑːtn] *n* tartan *m* (*pano escocês axadrezado*) ♦ *adj* axadrezado
tartar [ˈtɑːtə*] *n* (*on teeth*) tártaro; ~(**e**) **sauce** *n* molho tártaro
task [tɑːsk] *n* tarefa; to **take to** ~ repreender; ~ **force** *n* (*MIL, POLICE*) força-tarefa
tassel [ˈtæsl] *n* borla, pendão *m*
taste [teɪst] *n* gosto; (*also*: **after**~) gosto residual; (*sample, fig*) amostra, idéia ♦ *vt* provar; (*test*) experimentar ♦ *vi*: to ~ **of** or **like** ter gosto or sabor de; **you can** ~ **the garlic (in it)** sente-se o gosto de alho; **in good/bad** ~ de bom/ mau gosto; ~**ful** *adj* de bom gosto; ~**less** *adj* insípido, insosso; (*remark*) de mau gosto; **tasty** *adj* saboroso, delicioso
tatters [ˈtætəz] *npl*: **in** ~ (*clothes*) em farrapos; (*papers etc*) em pedaços
tattoo [təˈtuː] *n* tatuagem *f*; (*spectacle*) espetáculo militar ♦ *vt* tatuar
tatty [ˈtætɪ] (*BRIT*: *inf*) *adj* (*clothes*) surrado; (*shop, area*) mal-cuidado

taught [tɔːt] *pt, pp of* **teach**

taunt [tɔːnt] *n* zombaria, escárnio ♦ *vt* zombar de, mofar de

Taurus ['tɔːrəs] *n* Touro

taut [tɔːt] *adj* esticado

tavern ['tævən] *n* taverna

tax [tæks] *n* imposto ♦ *vt* tributar; *(fig: test)* sobrecarregar; (: *patience*) esgotar; ~**able** *adj (income)* tributável; ~**ation** *n (system)* tributação *f*; *(money paid)* imposto; ~ **avoidance** *n* evasão *f* de impostos; ~ **disc** *(BRIT) n (AUT)* ≈ plaqueta; ~ **evasion** *n* sonegação *f* fiscal; ~-**free** *adj* isento de impostos

taxi ['tæksɪ] *n* táxi *m* ♦ *vi (AVIAT)* taxiar; ~ **driver** *n* motorista *m/f* de táxi; ~-**rank** *(BRIT) n* ponto de táxi; ~ **stand** *n* = ~ **rank**

tax: ~ **payer** *n* contribuinte *m/f*; ~ **relief** *n* isenção *f* de imposto; ~ **return** *n* declaração *f* de rendimentos

TB *abbr of* tuberculosis

tea [tiː] *n* chá *m*; *(BRIT: meal)* refeição *f* à noite; **high** ~ *(BRIT)* ajantarado; ~ **bag** *n* saquinho *(BR) or* carteira *(PT)* de chá; ~ **break** *(BRIT) n* pausa (para o chá)

teach [tiːtʃ] *(pt, pp* taught) *vt:* **to** ~ **sb sth,** ~ **sth to sb** ensinar algo a alguém; *(in school)* lecionar ♦ *vi* ensinar; *(be a teacher)* lecionar; ~**er** *n* professor(a) *m/f*; ~**ing** *n* ensino; *(as profession)* magistério

tea cosy *n* coberta do bule, abafador *m*

teacup ['tiːkʌp] *n* xícara *(BR) or* chávena *(PT)* de chá

teak [tiːk] *n* madeira de teca

tea leaves *npl* folhas *fpl* de chá

team [tiːm] *n (SPORT)* time *m (BR)*, equipa *(PT)*; *(group)* equipe *f (BR)*, equipa *(PT)*; *(of animals)* parelha; ~**work** *n* trabalho de equipe

teapot ['tiːpɔt] *n* bule *m* de chá

tear[1] [tɛəˈ] *(pt* tore, *pp* torn) *n* rasgão *m* ♦ *vt* rasgar ♦ *vi* rasgar-se; ~ **along** *vi (rush)* precipitar-se; ~ **up** *vt* rasgar

tear[2] [tiəˈ] *n* lágrima; **in** ~**s** chorando, em lágrimas; ~-**ful** *adj* choroso; ~ **gas** *n* gás *m* lacrimogênio

tearoom ['tiːruːm] *n* salão *m* de chá

tease [tiːz] *vt* implicar com

tea set *n* aparelho de chá

teaspoon ['tiːspuːn] *n* colher *f* de chá; *(also:* ~**ful:** *as measurement)* (conteúdo de) colher de chá

teat [tiːt] *n* bico (de mamadeira)

teatime ['tiːtaɪm] *n* hora do chá

tea towel *(BRIT) n* pano de prato

technical ['tɛknɪkl] *adj* técnico; ~ **college** *(BRIT) n* escola técnica; ~**ity** *n* detalhe *m* técnico; *(point of law)* particularidade *f*

technician [tɛk'nɪʃn] *n* técnico/a

technique [tɛk'niːk] *n* técnica

technology [tɛk'nɔlədʒɪ] *n* tecnologia

teddy (bear) ['tɛdɪ-] *n* ursinho de pelúcia

tedious ['tiːdɪəs] *adj* maçante, chato

tee [tiː] *n (GOLF)* tee *m*

teem [tiːm] *vi* abundar, pulular; **to** ~ **with** abundar em; **it is** ~**ing (with rain)** está chovendo a cântaros

teenage ['tiːneɪdʒ] *adj (fashions etc)* de *or* para adolescentes; ~**r** *n* adolescente *m/f*, jovem *m/f*

teens [tiːnz] *npl:* **to be in one's** ~ estar entre os 13 e 19 anos, estar na adolescência

tee-shirt *n* = T-shirt

teeter ['tiːtəˈ] *vi* balançar-se

teeth [tiːθ] *npl of* tooth; **to** ~ *vi* começar a ter dentes; ~**ing ring** *n* mastigador *m* para a dentição; ~**ing troubles** *npl (fig)* dificuldades *fpl* iniciais

teetotal ['tiː'təutl] *adj* abstêmio

telegram ['tɛlɪgræm] *n* telegrama *m*

telegraph ['tɛlɪgrɑːf] *n* telégrafo

telepathy [tə'lɛpəθɪ] *n* telepatia

telephone ['tɛlɪfəun] *n* telefone *m* ♦ *vt (person)* telefonar para; *(message)* telefonar; **to be on the** ~ *(BRIT)*, **to have a** ~ *(subscriber)* ter telefone; **to be on the** ~ *(be speaking)* estar falando no telefone; ~ **booth** *(BRIT* ~ **box)** *n* cabine *f* telefônica; ~ **call** *n* telefonema *m*; ~ **directory** *n* lista telefônica, catálogo *(BR)*; ~ **number** *n* (número de) telefone *m*; **telephonist** *(BRIT) n* telefonista *m/f*

telescope ['tɛlɪskəup] *n* telescópio; **telescopic** *adj* telescópico; *(legs, aerial)* desmontável

television ['tɛlɪvɪʒən] *n* televisão *f*; **on** ~ na televisão; ~ **set** *n* (aparelho de) televisão *f*, televisor *m*

telex ['tɛlɛks] *n* telex *m* ♦ *vt (message)* enviar por telex, telexar; *(person)* mandar um telex para

tell [tɛl] *(pt, pp* told) *vt* dizer; *(relate: story)* contar; *(distinguish):* **to** ~ **sth from** distinguir algo de ♦ *vi (have effect)* ter efeito; *(talk):* **to** ~ **(of)** falar (de *or* em); **to** ~ **sb to do sth** dizer para alguém fazer algo; ~ **off** *vt* repreender; ~**er** *n (in bank)* caixa *m/f*; ~**ing** *adj* revelador(a); ~**tale** *adj (sign)* revelador(a)

telly ['tɛlɪ] *(BRIT: inf) n abbr* = television

temp [tɛmp] *(BRIT: inf) abbr (*= *temporary)* ♦ *n* temporário/a ♦ *vi* trabalhar como temporário/a

temper ['tɛmpəˈ] *n (nature)* temperamento; *(mood)* humor *m*; *(fit of anger)* cólera ♦ *vt (moderate)* moderar; **to be in a** ~ estar de mau humor; **to lose one's** ~ perder a paciência *or* a calma, ficar zangado

temperament ['tɛmprəmənt] *n* temperamento; ~**al** *adj* temperamental

temperate ['tɛmprət] *adj* moderado; *(climate)* temperado
temperature ['tɛmprətʃə*] *n* temperatura; **to have** *or* **run a ~** ter febre
tempest ['tɛmpɪst] *n* tempestade *f*
tempi ['tɛmpi] *npl of* **tempo**
temple ['tɛmpl] *n (building)* templo; *(ANAT)* têmpora
tempo ['tɛmpəu] *(pl* ~s *or* **tempi** *) n* tempo; *(fig: of life etc)* ritmo
temporarily ['tɛmpərərɪlɪ] *adv* temporariamente; *(closed)* provisoriamente
temporary ['tɛmpərərɪ] *adj* temporário; *(passing)* transitório
tempt [tɛmpt] *vt* tentar; ~**ing** *adj* tentador(a)
ten [tɛn] *num* dez
tenancy ['tɛnənsɪ] *n* aluguel *m*
tenant ['tɛnənt] *n* inquilino/a, locatário/a
tend [tɛnd] *vt (sick etc)* cuidar de ♦ *vi:* **to ~ to do sth** tender a fazer algo
tendency ['tɛndənsɪ] *n* tendência
tender ['tɛndə*] *adj* terno; *(age)* tenro; *(sore)* sensível, dolorido; *(meat)* macio ♦ *n (COMM: offer)* oferta, proposta; *(money):* **legal ~** moeda corrente *or* legal ♦ *vt* oferecer; **to ~ one's resignation** pedir demissão; ~**ness** *n* ternura; *(of meat)* maciez *f*
tendon ['tɛndən] *n* tendão *m*
tenement ['tɛnəmənt] *n* conjunto habitacional
tenet ['tɛnət] *n* princípio
tennis ['tɛnɪs] *n* tênis *m;* ~ **ball** *n* bola de tênis; ~ **court** *n* quadra de tênis; ~ **player** *n* jogador(a) *m/f* de tênis; ~ **racket** *n* raquete *f* de tênis; ~ **shoes** *npl* tênis *m*
tenor ['tɛnə*] *n (MUS)* tenor *m*
tenpin bowling ['tɛnpɪn-] *(BRIT) n* boliche *m* com 10 paus
tense [tɛns] *adj* tenso; *(muscle)* rígido, teso ♦ *n (LING)* tempo
tension ['tɛnʃən] *n* tensão *f*
tent [tɛnt] *n* tenda, barraca
tentative ['tɛntətɪv] *adj* provisório, tentativo; *(person)* hesitante, indeciso
tenterhooks ['tɛntəhuks] *npl:* **on ~** em suspense
tenth [tɛnθ] *num* décimo
tent peg *n* estaca
tent pole *n* pau *m*
tenuous ['tɛnjuəs] *adj* tênue
tenure ['tɛnjuə*] *n (of property)* posse *f; (of job)* estabilidade *f*
tepid ['tɛpɪd] *adj* tépido, morno
term [tə:m] *n (expression)* termo, expressão *f; (period)* período; *(SCH)* trimestre *m* ♦ *vt* denominar; ~**s** *npl (conditions)* condições *fpl; (COMM)* cláusulas *fpl*, termos *mpl;* **in the short/long ~** a curto/longo prazo; **to be on good ~s with sb** dar-se bem com alguém; **to come to ~s with** aceitar

terminal ['tə:mɪnl] *adj* incurável ♦ *n (ELEC)* borne *m; (BRIT: also:* **air ~)** terminal *m; (also COMPUT)* terminal *m; (BRIT: also:* **coach ~)** estação *f* rodoviária
terminate ['tə:mɪneɪt] *vt* terminar; **to ~ a pregnancy** fazer um aborto
terminus ['tə:mɪnəs] *(pl* **termini***) n* terminal *m*
terrace ['tɛrəs] *n* terraço; *(BRIT: houses)* lance *m* de casas; **the ~s** *npl (BRIT: SPORT)* a arquibancada *(BR)*, a geral *(PT);* ~**d** *adj (house)* ladeado por outras casas; *(garden)* em dois níveis
terrain [tɛ'reɪn] *n* terreno
terrible ['tɛrɪbl] *adj* terrível, horroroso; *(conditions)* precário; *(inf: awful)* terrível; **terribly** *adv* terrivelmente; *(very badly)* pessimamente
terrific [tə'rɪfɪk] *adj* terrível, magnífico; *(wonderful)* maravilhoso, sensacional
terrify ['tɛrɪfaɪ] *vt* apavorar
territory ['tɛrɪtərɪ] *n* território
terror ['tɛrə*] *n* terror *m;* ~**ist** *n* terrorista *m/f;* ~**ize** *vt* aterrorizar
terse [tə:s] *adj (style)* conciso
Terylene ['tɛrɪli:n] ® *n* tergal ® *m*
test [tɛst] *n (trial, check)* prova, ensaio; *(of courage etc, CHEM)* prova; *(MED)* exame *m; (exam)* teste *m*, prova; *(also:* **driving ~)** exame de motorista ♦ *vt* testar, pôr à prova
testament ['tɛstəmənt] *n* testamento; **the Old/New T~** o Velho/Novo Testamento
testicle ['tɛstɪkl] *n* testículo
testify ['tɛstɪfaɪ] *vi (LAW)* depor, testemunhar; **to ~ to sth** atestar algo, testemunhar algo
testimony ['tɛstɪmənɪ] *n (LAW)* testemunho, depoimento; **to be (a) ~ to** ser uma prova de
test: ~ **match** *n (CRICKET, RUGBY)* jogo internacional; ~ **pilot** *n* piloto de prova; ~ **tube** *n* proveta, tubo de ensaio
tetanus ['tɛtənəs] *n* tétano
tether ['tɛðə*] *vt* amarrar ♦ *n:* **at the end of one's ~** a ponto de perder a paciência *or* as estribeiras
text [tɛkst] *n* texto; ~**book** *n* livro didático; *(SCH)* livro escolar
textiles ['tɛkstaɪlz] *npl* têxteis *mpl; (industry)* indústria têxtil
texture ['tɛkstʃə*] *n* textura
Thailand ['taɪlænd] *n* Tailândia
Thames [tɛmz] *n:* **the ~** o Tâmisa *(BR),* o Tamisa *(PT)*
than [ðæn, ðən] *conj (in comparisons)* do que; **more ~ 10** mais de 10; **I have more/less ~ you** tenho mais/menos do que você; **she has more apples ~ pears** ela tem mais maçãs do que peras; **she is older ~ you think** ela é mais velha do que você pensa
thank [θæŋk] *vt* agradecer; ~ **you (very**

much) muito obrigado/a; **~ful** adj: ~
ful (for) agradecido (por); **~ful that**
aliviado que; **~less** adj ingrato; **~s** npl
agradecimentos mpl ♦ excl obrigado/a!;
T~sgiving (Day) n Dia m de Ação de
Graças

KEYWORD

that [ðæt, ðət] (pl **those**) adj (demonstrative) esse/essa; (more remote) aquele/
aquela; ~ **man/woman/book** aquele
homem/aquela mulher/aquele livro; ~
one esse/essa

♦ pron **1** (demonstrative) esse/essa,
aquele/aquela; (neuter) isso, aquilo;
who's/what's ~? quem é?/o que é
isso?; **is ~ you?** é você?; **I prefer this
to ~** eu prefiro isto a aquilo; **~'s what
he said** foi isso o que ele disse; **~ is
(to say)** isto é, quer dizer

2 (relative: direct: thing, person) que; (:
person) quem; (relative: indirect: thing,
person) o/a qual sg, os/as quais pl; (:
person) quem; **the book (~) I read** o
livro que eu li; **the box (~) I put it
in** a caixa na qual eu botei-o; **the man
(~) I spoke to** o homem com quem or
o qual falei

3 (relative: of time): **on the day ~ he
came** no dia em que ele veio

♦ conj que; **she suggested ~ I phone
you** ela sugeriu que eu telefonasse para
você

♦ adv (demonstrative): **I can't work ~
much** não posso trabalhar tanto; **I
didn't realize it was ~ bad** não pensei
que fôsse tão ruim; **~ high** dessa altura, até essa altura

thatched [θætʃt] adj (roof) de sapê; ~
cottage chalé m com telhado de sapê or
de colmo

thaw [θɔː] n degelo ♦ vi (ice) derreter-se;
(food) descongelar-se ♦ vt (food) descongelar

KEYWORD

the [ðiː, ðə] def art **1** (gen: sg) o/a; (:
pl) os/as; ~ **books/children** os livros/
as crianças; **she put it on ~ table** ela
colocou-o na mesa; **he took it from ~
drawer** ele tirou isto da gaveta; **to
play ~ piano/violin** tocar piano/
violino; **I'm going to ~ cinema** vou ao
cinema

2 (+ adj to form n): ~ **rich and ~
poor** os ricos e os pobres; **to attempt
~ impossible** tentar o impossível

3 (in titles): **Richard ~ Second** Ricardo
II; **Peter ~ Great** Pedro o Grande

4 (in comparisons: + adv): ~ **more he
works ~ more he earns** quanto mais
ele trabalha, mais ele ganha

theatre ['θɪətə*] (US **theater**) n teatro;

(MED): also: **operating ~**) sala de operação; **~-goer** n freqüentador(a) m/f de
teatro; **theatrical** adj teatral

theft [θeft] n roubo

their [ðɛə*] adj seu/sua, deles/delas; **~s**
pron (o) seu/(a) sua; see also **mine²**

them [ðɛm, ðəm] pron (direct) os/as; (indirect) lhes; (stressed, after prep) a eles/a
elas

theme [θiːm] n tema m; ~ **park** n parque de diversões em torno de um único
tema; ~ **song** n tema m musical

themselves [ðəm'sɛlvz] pron eles
mesmos/elas mesmas, se; (after prep) si
(mesmos/as)

then [ðɛn] adv (at that time) então; (next)
em seguida; (later) logo, depois; (and also) além disso ♦ conj (therefore) então,
nesse caso, portanto ♦ adj: **the ~ president** o então presidente; **by ~** (past) até
então; (future) até lá; **from ~ on** a partir de então

theology [θɪˈɒlədʒɪ] n teologia

theoretical [θɪəˈrɛtɪkl] adj teórico

theorize ['θɪəraɪz] vi teorizar, elaborar
uma teoria

theory ['θɪərɪ] n teoria; **in ~** em teoria,
teoricamente

therapist ['θɛrəpɪst] n terapeuta m/f

therapy ['θɛrəpɪ] n terapia

KEYWORD

there [ðɛə*] adv **1** ~ **is**, ~ **are** há, tem;
~ **are 3 of them** há 3 deles; ~ **is no-
one here/no bread left** não tem ninguém aqui/não tem mais pão; ~ **has
been an accident** houve um acidente

2 (referring to place) aí, ali, lá; **put it
in/on/up/down ~** põe isto lá dentro/
cima/em cima/embaixo; **I want that
book ~** quero aquele livro lá; ~ **he is!**
lá está ele!

3: ~, ~! (esp to child) calma!

thereabouts ['ðɛərəbauts] adv por aí;
(amount) aproximadamente

thereafter [ðɛərˈɑːftə*] adv depois disso

thereby ['ðɛəbaɪ] adv assim, deste modo

therefore ['ðɛəfɔː] adv portanto

there's [ðɛəz] = **there is**; **there has**

thermal ['θəːml] adj térmico

thermometer [θəˈmɒmɪtə*] n termômetro

Thermos ['θəːməs] ® n (also: ~ **flask**)
garrafa térmica (BR), termo (PT)

thermostat ['θəːməstæt] n termostato

thesaurus [θɪˈsɔːrəs] n tesouro, dicionário de sinônimos

these [ðiːz] pl adj, pron estes/estas

theses ['θiːsiːz] npl of **thesis**

thesis ['θiːsɪs] (pl **theses**) n tese f

they [ðeɪ] pl pron eles/elas; ~ **say that
...** (it is said that) diz-se que ..., dizem
que ...; **~'d** = **they had**; **they would**;
~'ll = **they shall**; **they will**; **~'ve** =

they have

thick [θɪk] *adj* espesso; (*mud, fog, forest*) denso; (*sauce*) grosso; (*stupid*) burro ♦ *n*: **in the ~ of the battle** em plena batalha; **it's 20 cm ~** tem 20 cm de espessura; **~en** *vi* (*fog*) adensar-se; (*plot etc*) complicar-se ♦ *vt* engrossar; **~ness** *n* espessura, grossura; **~set** *adj* troncudo; **~-skinned** *adj* insensível, indiferente

thief [θiːf] (*pl* **thieves**) *n* ladrão/ladra *m/f*

thigh [θaɪ] *n* coxa

thimble [ˈθɪmbl] *n* dedal *m*

thin [θɪn] *adj* magro; (*slice*) fino; (*light*) leve; (*hair*) ralo; (*crowd*) pequeno; (*soup, sauce*) aguado ♦ *vt* (*also*: **~ down**) diluir

thing [θɪŋ] *n* coisa; (*object*) negócio; (*matter*) assunto, negócio; (*mania*) mania; **~s** *npl* (*belongings*) pertences *mpl*; **to have a ~ about sb/sth** ser vidrado em alguém/algo; **the best ~ would be to ...** o melhor seria ...; **how are ~s?** como vai?, tudo bem?; **she's got a ~ about ...** ela detesta ...; **poor ~!** coitadinho/a!

think [θɪŋk] (*pt, pp* **thought**) *vi* pensar; (*believe*) achar ♦ *vt* pensar, achar; (*imagine*) imaginar; **what did you ~ of them?** o que você achou deles?; **to ~ about sb/sth** pensar em algo/alguém; **I'll ~ about it** vou pensar sobre isso; **to ~ of doing sth** pensar em fazer algo; **I ~ so/not** acho que sim/não; **to ~ well of sb** fazer bom juízo de alguém; **~ over** *vt* refletir sobre, meditar sobre; **~ up** *vt* inventar, bolar; **~ tank** *n* comissão *f* de peritos

thinly [ˈθɪnlɪ] *adv* (*cut*) em fatias finas; (*spread*) numa camada fina

third [θɜːd] *adj* terceiro ♦ *n* terceiro/a; (*fraction*) terço; (*AUT*) terceira; (*SCH: degree*) terceira categoria; **~ly** *adv* em terceiro lugar; **~ party insurance** *n* seguro contra terceiros; **~-rate** *adj* medíocre; **T~ World** *n*: **the T~ World** o Terceiro Mundo

thirst [θɜːst] *n* sede *f*; **~y** *adj* (*person*) sedento, com sede; (*work*) que dá sede; **to be ~y** estar com sede

thirteen [ˈθɜːˈtiːn] *num* treze

thirty [ˈθɜːtɪ] *num* trinta

KEYWORD

this [ðɪs] (*pl* **these**) *adj* (*demonstrative*) este/esta; **~ man/woman/book** este homem/esta mulher/este livro; **these people/children/records** estas pessoas/crianças/estes discos; **~ one** este aqui
♦ *pron* (*demonstrative*) este/esta; (*neuter*) isto; **who/what is ~?** quem é esse?/o que é isso?; **~ is where I live** é aqui que eu moro; **~ is Mr Brown** este é o Sr Brown; (*on phone*) aqui é o Sr

Brown
♦ *adv* (*demonstrative*): **~ high/long** desta altura/deste comprimento; **we can't stop now we've gone ~ far** não podemos parar agora que fomos tão longe

thistle [ˈθɪsl] *n* cardo

thong [θɒŋ] *n* correia, tira de couro

thorn [θɔːn] *n* espinho

thorough [ˈθʌrə] *adj* (*search*) minucioso; (*knowledge, research, person*) metódico, profundo; **~bred** *adj* (*horse*) de puro sangue; **~fare** *n* via, passagem *f*; **"no ~fare"** "passagem proibida"; **~ly** *adv* minuciosamente; (*search*) profundamente; (*wash*) completamente; (*very*) muito

those [ðəʊz] *pl pron, adj* esses/essas

though [ðəʊ] *conj* embora, se bem que ♦ *adv* no entanto

thought [θɔːt] *pt, pp of* **think** ♦ *n* pensamento; (*idea*) idéia; (*opinion*) opinião *f*; (*reflection*) reflexão *f*; **~ful** *adj* pensativo; (*serious*) sério; (*considerate*) atencioso; **~less** *adj* desatencioso; (*words*) inconseqüente

thousand [ˈθaʊzənd] *num* mil; **two ~** dois mil; **~s (of)** milhares *mpl* (de); **~th** *num* milésimo

thrash [θræʃ] *vt* surrar, malhar; (*defeat*) derrotar; **~ about** *vi* debater-se; **~ out** *vt* discutir exaustivamente

thread [θrɛd] *n* fio, linha; (*of screw*) rosca ♦ *vt* (*needle*) enfiar; **~bare** *adj* surrado, puído

threat [θrɛt] *n* ameaça; **~en** *vi* ameaçar ♦ *vt*: **to ~en sb with sth/to do** ameaçar alguém com algo/de fazer

three [θriː] *num* três; **~-dimensional** *adj* tridimensional, em três dimensões; **~-piece suit** *n* terno (3 peças) (*BR*), fato de 3 peças (*PT*); **~-piece suite** *n* conjunto de sofá e duas poltronas; **~-ply** *adj* (*wool*) triple, com três fios

thresh [θrɛʃ] *vt* (*AGR*) debulhar

threshold [ˈθrɛʃhəʊld] *n* limiar *m*

threw [θruː] *pt of* **throw**

thrift [θrɪft] *n* economia, poupança; **~y** *adj* econômico, frugal

thrill [θrɪl] *n* emoção *f*; (*shudder*) estremecimento ♦ *vt* emocionar, vibrar; **to be ~ed** (*with gift etc*) estar emocionado; **~er** *n* romance *m* (*ou filme m*) de suspense; **~ing** *adj* emocionante

thrive [θraɪv] (*pt* **~d** *or* **throve**, *pp* **~d** *or* **thriven**) *vi* (*grow*) vicejar; (*do well*) **to ~ on sth** realizar-se ao fazer algo; **thriving** *adj* próspero

throat [θrəʊt] *n* garganta; **to have a sore ~** estar com dor de garganta

throb [θrɒb] *n* (*of heart*) batida; (*of engine*) vibração *f*; (*of pain*) latejo ♦ *vi* (*heart*) bater, palpitar; (*pain*) dar pontadas; (*engine*) vibrar

throes [θrəʊz] *npl*: **in the ~ of** no meio de

thrombosis [θrɔmˈbəusɪs] n trombose f

throne [θrəun] n trono

throng [θrɔŋ] n multidão f ♦ vt apinhar, apinhar-se em

throttle [ˈθrɔtl] n (AUT) acelerador m ♦ vt estrangular

through [θru:] prep por, através de; (time) durante; (by means of) por meio de, por intermédio de; (owing to) devido a ♦ adj (ticket, train) direto ♦ adv através; **to put sb ~ to sb** (TEL) ligar alguém com alguém; **to be ~** (TEL) estar na linha; (have finished) acabar; **"no ~ road"** "rua sem saída"; **I'm halfway ~ the book** estou na metade do livro; **~out** prep (place) por todo/a o/a ♦ (time) durante todo/a o/a ♦ adv por or em todas as partes

throve [θrəuv] pt of **thrive**

throw [θrəu] (pt **threw**, pp **thrown**) n arremesso, tiro; (SPORT) lançamento ♦ vt jogar, atirar; lançar; (rider) derrubar; (fig) desconcertar; **to ~ a party** dar uma festa; **~ away** vt (dispose of) jogar fora; (waste) desperdiçar; **~ off** vt desfazer-se de; (habit, cold) livrar-se; **~ out** vt expulsar; (rubbish) jogar fora; (idea) rejeitar; **~ up** vi vomitar, botar para fora; **~away** adj descartável; (remark) gratuito; **~-in** n (SPORT) lance m

thru [θru:] (US) prep, adj, adv = **through**

thrush [θrʌʃ] n (ZOOL) tordo

thrust [θrʌst] (pt, pp **thrust**) n impulso; (TECH) empuxo ♦ vt empurrar

thud [θʌd] n baque m, som m surdo

thug [θʌg] n facínora m/f

thumb [θʌm] n (ANAT) polegar m; **to ~ a lift** pegar carona (BR), arranjar uma boléia (PT); **~ through** vt fus folhear; **~tack** (US) n percevejo, tachinha

thump [θʌmp] n murro, pancada; (sound) baque m ♦ vt dar um murro em ♦ vi bater

thunder [ˈθʌndə*] n trovão m ♦ vi trovejar; (train etc) **to ~ past** passar como um raio; **~bolt** n raio; **~clap** n estampido do trovão; **~storm** n tempestade f com trovoada, temporal m; **~y** adj tempestuoso

Thursday [ˈθə:zdɪ] n quinta-feira

thus [ðʌs] adv assim, desta maneira; (consequently) conseqüentemente

thwart [θwɔ:t] vt frustrar

thyme [taɪm] n tomilho

tiara [tɪˈɑ:rə] n tiara, diadema m

Tibet [tɪˈbet] n Tibete m

tic [tɪk] n tique m

tick [tɪk] n (of clock) tique-taque m; (mark) tique m, marca; (ZOOL) carrapato; (BRIT: inf): **in a ~** num instante ♦ vi fazer tique-taque ♦ vt marcar, ticar; **~ off** vt assinalar, ticar; (person) dar uma bronca em; **~ over** (BRIT) vi (engine) funcionar em marcha lenta; (fig) ir indo

ticket [ˈtɪkɪt] n (for bus, plane) passagem f; (for theatre, raffle) bilhete m; (for cinema) entrada; (in shop: on goods) etiqueta; (parking ~: fine) multa; (for library) cartão m; **to get a (parking)** ~ (AUT) ganhar uma multa por estacionamento ilegal); **~ collector** n revisor(a) m/f; **~ office** n bilheteria (BR), bilheteira (PT)

tickle [ˈtɪkl] vt fazer cócegas em ♦ vi fazer cócegas; **ticklish** adj coceguento; (problem) delicado

tidal [ˈtaɪdl] adj de maré; **~ wave** n maréu m, onda gigantesca

tidbit [ˈtɪdbɪt] (esp US) n = **titbit**

tiddlywinks [ˈtɪdlɪwɪŋks] n jogo de fichas

tide [taɪd] n maré f; (fig) curso; **high/low ~** maré alta/baixa; **the ~ of public opinion** a corrente da opinião pública; **~ over** vt ajudar num período difícil

tidy [ˈtaɪdɪ] adj (room) arrumado; (dress, work) limpo; (person) bem arrumado ♦ vt (also: **~ up**) pôr em ordem, arrumar

tie [taɪ] n (string etc) fita, corda; (BRIT: also: **neck~**) gravata; (fig: link) vínculo, laço; (SPORT: draw) empate m ♦ vt amarrar ♦ vi (SPORT) empatar; **to ~ in a bow** dar um laço em; **to ~ a knot in sth** dar um nó em algo; **~ down** vt amarrar; (fig: restrict) limitar, restringir; (to date, price etc) obrigar; **~ up** vt embrulhar; (dog) prender; (boat, prisoner) amarrar; (arrangements) concluir; **to be ~d up** estar ocupado

tier [tɪə*] n fileira; (of cake) camada

tiger [ˈtaɪgə*] n tigre m

tight [taɪt] adj (rope) esticado, firme; (money) escasso; (clothes, shoes) justo; (bend) fechado; (budget, programme) rigoroso; (inf: drunk) bêbado ♦ adv (squeeze) bem forte; (shut) hermeticamente; **~en** vt (rope) esticar; (screw, grip) apertar; (security) aumentar ♦ vi esticar-se; apertar-se; **~-fisted** adj pão-duro; **~ly** adv firmemente; **~-rope** n corda (bamba)

tights [taɪts] (BRIT) npl collant m

tile [taɪl] n (on roof) telha; (on floor) ladrilho; (on wall) azulejo, ladrilho; **~d** adj ladrilhado; (roof) de telhas

till [tɪl] n caixa (registradora) ♦ vt (land) cultivar ♦ prep, conj = **until**

tiller [ˈtɪlə*] n (NAUT) cana do leme

tilt [tɪlt] vt inclinar ♦ vi inclinar-se

timber [ˈtɪmbə*] n (material) madeira f; (trees) mata, floresta

time [taɪm] n tempo; (epoch: often pl) época; (by clock) hora; (moment) momento; (occasion) vez f; (MUS) compasso ♦ vt calcular or medir o tempo de; (visit etc) escolher o momento para; **a long ~** muito tempo; **4 at a ~** quatro de uma vez; **for the ~ being** por enquanto; **from ~ to ~** de vez em quando; **at ~s** às vezes; **in ~** (soon enough) a tempo;

(*after some time*) com o tempo; (*MUS*) no compasso; **in a week's** ~ dentro de uma semana; **in no** ~ num abrir e fechar de olhos; **any** ~ a qualquer hora; **on** ~ na hora; **5** ~**s 5 is 25** 5 vezes 5 são 25; **what** ~ **is it?** que horas são?; **to have a good** ~ divertir-se; ~ **bomb** *n* bomba-relógio *f*; ~ **lag** (*BRIT*) *n* defasagem *f*; ~**less** *adj* eterno; ~**ly** *adj* oportuno; ~ **off** *n* tempo livre; ~**r** *n* (*in kitchen*) cronômetro; (*switch*) timer *m*; ~ **scale** *n* prazos *mpl*; ~ **switch** (*BRIT*) *n* interruptor *m* horário; ~**table** *n* horário; ~ **zone** *n* fuso horário

timid ['tɪmɪd] *adj* tímido

timing ['taɪmɪŋ] *n* escolha do momento; (*SPORT*) cronometragem *f*; **the** ~ **of his resignation** o momento que escolheu para se demitir

timpani ['tɪmpənɪ] *npl* tímbales *mpl*

tin [tɪn] *n* estanho; (*also*: ~ **plate**) folha-de-flandres *f*; (*BRIT*: **can**) lata; ~ **foil** *n* papel *m* de estanho

tinge [tɪndʒ] *n* matiz *m*; (*of feeling*) toque *m* ♦ *vt*: ~**d with** tingido de

tingle ['tɪŋgl] *vi* formigar

tinker ['tɪŋkə*] *n* funileiro/a; (*gipsy*) cigano/a; ~ **with** *vt* mexer com

tinned [tɪnd] (*BRIT*) *adj* (*food*) em lata, em conserva

tin opener (*BRIT*) *n* abridor *m* de latas (*BR*), abre-latas *m inv* (*PT*)

tinsel ['tɪnsl] *n* ouropel *m*

tint [tɪnt] *n* matiz *m*; (*for hair*) tintura, tinta; ~**ed** *adj* (*hair*) pintado; (*spectacles, glass*) fumê *inv*

tiny ['taɪnɪ] *adj* pequenininho, minúsculo

tip [tɪp] *n* ponta; (*gratuity*) gorjeta; (*BRIT*: *for rubbish*) depósito; (*advice*) dica ♦ *vt* dar uma gorjeta a; (*tilt*) inclinar; (*overturn*: *also*: ~ **over**) virar, emborcar; (*empty*: *also*: ~ **out**) esvaziar, entornar; ~**-off** *n* aviso, dica; ~**ped** (*BRIT*) *adj* (*cigarette*) com filtro

Tipp-Ex ['tɪpeks] ® (*BRIT*) *n* líquido corretor

tipsy ['tɪpsɪ] *adj* embriagado, tocado

tiptoe ['tɪptəu] *n*: **on** ~ na ponta dos pés

tiptop ['tɪp'tɔp] *adj*: **in** ~ **condition** em perfeitas condições

tire ['taɪə*] *n* (*US*) = **tyre** ♦ *vt* cansar ♦ *vi* cansar-se; (*become bored*) chatear-se; ~**d** *adj* cansado; **to be** ~**d of sth** estar farto *or* cheio de algo; ~**less** *adj* incansável; ~**some** *adj* enfadonho, chato; **tiring** *adj* cansativo

tissue ['tɪʃu:] *n* tecido; (*paper handkerchief*) lenço de papel; ~ **paper** *n* papel *m* de seda

tit [tɪt] *n* (*bird*) passarinho; **to give** ~ **for tat** pagar na mesma moeda

titbit ['tɪtbɪt] *n* (*food*) guloseima; (*news*) boato, rumor *m*

title ['taɪtl] *n* título; ~ **deed** *n* (*LAW*) título de propriedade; ~ **role** *n* papel *m*

principal

titter ['tɪtə*] *vi* rir-se com riso sufocado

TM *n abbr* = **trademark**

KEYWORD

to [tu:, tə] *prep* **1** (*direction*) a, para; (*towards*) para; **to go** ~ **France/London/ school/the station** ir à França/a Londres/ao colégio/à estação; **to go** ~ **Lígia's/the doctor's** ir à casa de Lígia/ao médico; **the road** ~ **Edinburgh** a estrada para Edinburgo; ~ **the left/right** à esquerda/direita

2 (*as far as*) até; **to count** ~ **10** contar até 10; **from 40** ~ **50 people** de 40 a 50 pessoas

3 (*with expressions of time*): **a quarter** ~ **5** quinze para as 5 (*BR*), 5 menos um quarto (*PT*)

4 (*for*) de, para; **the key** ~ **the front door** a chave da porta da frente; **a letter** ~ **his wife** uma carta para a sua mulher

5 (*expressing indirect object*): **to give sth** ~ **sb** dar algo a alguém; **to talk** ~ **sb** falar com alguém; **I sold it** ~ **a friend** vendi isto para um amigo; **to cause damage** ~ **sth** causar danos em algo

6 (*in relation to*) para; **3 goals** ~ **2** 3 a 2; **8 apples** ~ **the kilo** 8 maçãs por quilo

7 (*purpose, result*) para; **to come** ~ **sb's aid** prestar ajuda a alguém; **to sentence sb** ~ **death** condenar alguém à morte; ~ **my surprise** para minha surpresa

♦ + *vb* **1** (+ *infin*): ~ **go/eat** ir/comer

2 (*following another vb*): ~ **want/try** ~ **do** querer/tentar fazer; ~ **start** ~ **do** começar a fazer

3 (*without vb*): **I don't want** ~ eu não quero; **you ought** ~ você deve

4 (*purpose, result*) para

5 (*equivalent to relative clause*) para, a; **I have things** ~ **do** eu tenho coisas para fazer; **the main thing is** ~ **try** o principal é tentar

6 (*after adj etc*) para; **ready** ~ **go** pronto para ir; **too old/young** ~ ... muito velho/jovem para ...

♦ *adv*: **pull/push the door** ~ puxar/ empurrar a porta

---

toad [təud] *n* sapo

toadstool ['təudstu:l] *n* chapéu-de-cobra *m*, cogumelo venenoso

toast [təust] *n* (*CULIN*) torradas *fpl*; (*drink, speech*) brinde *m* ♦ *vt* torrar; brindar; ~**er** *n* torradeira

tobacco [tə'bækəu] *n* tabaco, fumo (*BR*); ~**nist** *n* vendedor(a) *m/f* de tabaco; ~**nist's (shop)** tabacaria, charutaria (*BR*)

toboggan [tə'bɔgən] *n* tobogã *m*

today [tə'deɪ] *adv*, *n* hoje *m*
toddler ['tɔdlə*] *n* criança que começa a andar
to-do *n* (*fuss*) rebuliço, alvoroço
toe [təʊ] *n* dedo do pé; (*of shoe*) bico ♦ *vt*: **to ~ the line** (*fig*) conformar-se, cumprir as obrigações
toffee ['tɔfɪ] *n* puxa-puxa *m* (*BR*), caramelo (*PT*); ~ **apple** (*BRIT*) *n* maçã *f* do amor
together [tə'gɛðə*] *adv* juntos; (*at same time*) ao mesmo tempo; ~ **with** junto com
toil [tɔɪl] *n* faina, labuta ♦ *vi* labutar, trabalhar arduamente
toilet ['tɔɪlət] *n* privada, vaso sanitário; (*BRIT: lavatory*) banheiro (*BR*), casa de banho (*PT*) ♦ *cpd* de toalete; ~ **paper** *n* papel *m* higiénico; ~**ries** *npl* artigos *mpl* de toalete; ~ **roll** *n* rolo de papel higiénico; ~ **water** *n* água de colónia
token ['təʊkən] *n* (*sign*) sinal *m*, símbolo, prova; (*souvenir*) lembrança; (*substitute coin*) ficha ♦ *adj* simbólico; **book/record** ~ (*BRIT*) vale para comprar livros/discos
Tokyo ['təʊkjəʊ] *n* Tóquio
told [təʊld] *pt*, *pp* of tell
tolerable ['tɔlərəbl] *adj* (*bearable*) suportável; (*fairly good*) passável
tolerant ['tɔlərnt] *adj*: ~ **of** tolerante com
tolerate ['tɔləreɪt] *vt*• suportar; (*MED, TECH*) tolerar
toll [təʊl] *n* (*of casualties*) número de baixas; (*charge*) pedágio (*BR*), portagem *f* (*PT*) ♦ *vi* dobrar, tanger
tomato [tə'mɑːtəʊ] (*pl* ~**es**) *n* tomate *m*
tomb [tuːm] *n* tumba
tomboy ['tɔmbɔɪ] *n* menina moleque
tombstone ['tuːmstəʊn] *n* lápide *f*
tomcat ['tɔmkæt] *n* gato
tomorrow [tə'mɔrəʊ] *adv*, *n* amanhã *m*; **the day after** ~ depois de amanhã; ~ **morning** amanhã de manhã
ton [tʌn] *n* tonelada (*BRIT = 1016kg; US = 907kg*); ~**s of** (*inf*) um monte de
tone [təʊn] *n* tom *m* ♦ *vi* harmonizar; ~ **down** *vt* (*colour, criticism*) suavizar; (*sound*) baixar; (*MUS*) entoar; ~ **up** *vt* (*muscles*) tonificar; ~-**deaf** *adj* que não tem ouvido
tongs [tɔŋz] *npl* (*for coal*) tenaz *f*; (*for hair*) ferros *mpl* de frisar cabelo
tongue [tʌŋ] *n* língua; ~ **in cheek** ironicamente; ~-**tied** *adj* (*fig*) calado; ~-**twister** *n* trava-língua *m*
tonic ['tɔnɪk] *n* (*MED*) tónico; (*also*: ~ **water**) (água) tónica
tonight [tə'naɪt] *adv*, *n* esta noite, hoje à noite
tonnage ['tʌnɪdʒ] *n* (*NAUT*) tonelagem *f*
tonsil ['tɔnsəl] *n* amígdala; ~**litis** *n* amigdalite *f*
too [tuː] *adv* (*excessively*) demais, muito;

(*also*) também; ~ **much** (*adv*) demais; (*adj*) demasiado; ~ **many** demasiados/as
took [tʊk] *pt* of take
tool [tuːl] *n* ferramenta
toot [tuːt] *n* (*of horn*) buzinada; (*of whistle*) apito ♦ *vi* buzinar
tooth [tuːθ] (*pl* **teeth**) *n* (*ANAT, TECH*) dente *m*; (*molar*) molar *m*; ~**ache** *n* dor *f* de dente; **to have** ~ estar com dor de dente; ~**brush** *n* escova de dentes; ~**paste** *n* pasta de dentes, creme *m* dental; ~**pick** *n* palito
top [tɔp] *n* (*of mountain*) cume *m*, cimo; (*of tree*) topo; (*of head*) cocuruto; (*of cupboard, table*) superfície *f*, topo; (*of box, jar, bottle*) tampa; (*of ladder, page*) topo; (*toy*) pião *m*; (*blouse etc*) top *m*, blusa ♦ *adj* (*shelf, step*) mais alto; (*marks*) máximo; (*in rank*) principal, superior ♦ *vt* exceder; (*be first in*) estar à cabeça de; **on** ~ **of** sobre, em cima de; (*in addition to*) além de; **from** ~ **to toe** (*BRIT*) da cabeça aos pés; **from** ~ **to bottom** de cima a baixo; ~ **up** (*US* = **off**) *vt* completar; ~ **floor** *n* último andar *m*; ~ **hat** *n* cartola; ~-**heavy** *adj* desequilibrado
topic ['tɔpɪk] *n* tópico, assunto; ~**al** *adj* atual
top: ~**less** *adj* (*bather etc*) topless *inv*, sem a parte superior do biquíni; ~-**level** *adj* (*talks*) de alto nível; ~**most** *adj* o mais alto
topple ['tɔpl] *vt* derrubar ♦ *vi* cair para frente
top-secret *adj* ultra-secreto, supersecreto
topsy-turvy ['tɔpsɪ'tɜːvɪ] *adj*, *adv* de pernas para o ar, confuso, às avessas
tore [tɔː*] *pt* of tear
torment [*n* 'tɔːment, *vt* tɔː'ment] *n* tormento, suplício ♦ *vt* atormentar; (*fig: annoy*) chatear, aborrecer
torn [tɔːn] *pp* of tear
torrent ['tɔrnt] *n* torrente *f*
torrid ['tɔrɪd] *adj* tórrido; (*fig*) abrasador(a)
tortoise ['tɔːtəs] *n* tartaruga; ~**shell** *cpd* de tartaruga
tortuous ['tɔːtjuəs] *adj* tortuoso; (*argument, mind*) confuso
torture ['tɔːtʃə*] *n* tortura ♦ *vt* torturar; (*fig*) atormentar
Tory ['tɔːrɪ] (*BRIT*) *adj*, *n* (*POL*) conservador(a) *m/f*
toss [tɔs] *vt* atirar, arremessar; (*head*) lançar para trás ♦ *vi*: **to ~ and turn in bed** virar de um lado para o outro na cama; **to ~ a coin** tirar cara ou coroa; **to ~ up for sth** (*BRIT*) jogar cara ou coroa por algo
tot [tɔt] *n* (*BRIT: drink*) copinho, golinho; (*child*) criancinha
total ['təʊtl] *adj* total ♦ *n* total *m*, soma

♦ *vt* (*add up*) somar; (*amount to*) montar a

totter ['tɔtə*] *vi* cambalear

touch [tʌtʃ] *n* (*sense*) toque *m*; (*contact*) contato ♦ *vt* tocar (em); (*tamper with*) mexer com; (*make contact with*) fazer contato com; (*emotionally*) comover; a ~ of (*fig*) um traço de; **to get in ~ with** sb entrar em contato com alguém; **to lose** ~ perder o contato; ~ **on** *vt fus* (*topic*) tocar em, fazer menção de; ~ **up** *vt* (*paint*) retocar; ~**and-go** *adj* arriscado; ~**down** *n* aterrissagem *f* (*BR*), aterragem *f* (*PT*); (*on sea*) amerissagem *f* (*BR*), amaragem *f* (*PT*); (*US: FOOTBALL*) touchdown *m*; ~**ed** *adj* comovido; (*inf*) tocado, muito louco; ~**ing** *adj* comovedor(a); ~**line** *n* (*SPORT*) linha de fundo; ~**y** *adj* suscetível, sensível

tough [tʌf] *adj* duro; (*difficult*) difícil; (*resistant*) resistente; (*person: physically*) forte; (: *mentally*) tenaz; (*firm*) firme, inflexível; ~**en** *vt* (*sb's character*) fortalecer; (*glass etc*) tornar mais resistente

toupee ['tu:peɪ] *n* peruca

tour ['tuə*] *n* viagem *f*, excursão *f*; (*also:* **package** ~) excursão organizada; (*of town, museum*) visita; (*by artist*) turnê *f* ♦ *vt* (*country, city*) excursionar por; (*factory*) visitar

tourism ['tuərɪzm] *n* turismo

tourist ['tuərɪst] *n* turista *m/f* ♦ *cpd* turístico; ~ **office** *n* (*in country*) escritório de turismo; (*in embassy etc*) departamento de turismo

tournament ['tuənəmənt] *n* torneio

tousled ['tauzld] *adj* (*hair*) despenteado

tout [taut] *vi*: **to** ~ **for** angariar clientes para ♦ *n* (*BRIT*: *ticket* ~) cambista *m/f*

tow [təu] *vt* rebocar; "**on** (*BRIT*) **or in** (*US*) ~" (*AUT*) "rebocado"

toward(s) [tə'wɔːd(z)] *prep* em direção a; (*of attitude*) para com; (*of purpose*) para; ~ **noon/the end of the year** perto do meio-dia/do fim do ano

towel ['tauəl] *n* toalha; ~**ling** *n* (*fabric*) tecido para toalhas; ~ **rail** (*US* ~ **rack**) *n* toalheiro

tower ['tauə*] *n* torre *f*; ~ **block** (*BRIT*) *n* prédio alto, espigão *m*, cortiço (*BR*); ~**ing** *adj* elevado; (*figure*) eminente

town [taun] *n* cidade *f*; **to go to** ~ ir à cidade; (*fig*) fazer com entusiasmo, mandar brasa (*BR*); ~ **centre** *n* centro (da cidade); ~ **council** *n* câmara municipal; ~ **hall** *n* prefeitura (*BR*), concelho (*PT*); ~ **plan** *n* mapa *m* da cidade; ~ **planning** *n* urbanismo

towrope ['təurəup] *n* cabo de reboque

tow truck (*US*) *n* reboque *m* (*BR*), pronto socorro (*PT*)

toxic ['tɔksɪk] *adj* tóxico

toy [tɔɪ] *n* brinquedo; ~ **with** *vt fus* brincar com; (*idea*) contemplar; ~**shop** *n* loja de brinquedos

trace [treɪs] *n* (*sign*) sinal *m*; (*small amount*) traço ♦ *vt* (*draw*) traçar, esboçar; (*follow*) seguir a pista de; (*locate*) encontrar; **tracing paper** papel *m* de decalque

track [træk] *n* (*mark*) pegada, vestígio; (*path: gen*) caminho, vereda; (: *of bullet etc*) trajetória; (: *of suspect, animal*) pista, rasto; (*RAIL*) trilhos (*BR*), carris *mpl* (*PT*); (*on tape*) trilha; (*SPORT*) pista; (*on record*) faixa ♦ *vt* seguir a pista de; **to keep** ~ **of** não perder de vista; (*fig*) manter-se informado sobre; ~ **down** *vt* (*prey*) seguir a pista de; (*sth lost*) procurar e encontrar; ~ **suit** *n* roupa de jogging

tract [trækt] *n* (*GEO*) região *f*; (*pamphlet*) folheto

tractor ['træktə*] *n* trator *m*

trade [treɪd] *n* comércio; (*skill, job*) ofício ♦ *vi* negociar, comerciar ♦ *vt*: **to** ~ **sth (for sth)** trocar algo (por algo); ~ **in** *vt* dar como parte do pagamento; ~ **fair** *n* feira industrial; ~**mark** *n* marca registrada; ~ **name** *n* marca *or* nome comercial de um produto; (*of company*) razão *f* social; ~**r** *n* comerciante *m/f*; ~**sman** (*irreg*) *n* lojista *m*; ~ **union** *n* sindicato; ~ **unionist** *n* sindicalista *m/f*

tradition [trə'dɪʃən] *n* tradição *f*; ~**al** *adj* tradicional

traffic ['træfɪk] *n* trânsito; (*air* ~ *etc*) tráfego; (*illegal*) tráfico ♦ *vi*: **to** ~ **in** (*pej*: *liquor, drugs*) traficar com, fazer tráfico com; ~ **circle** (*US*) *n* rotatória; ~ **jam** *n* engarrafamento, congestionamento; ~ **lights** *npl* sinal *m* luminoso; ~ **warden** *n* guarda *m/f* de trânsito

tragedy ['trædʒədɪ] *n* tragédia

tragic ['trædʒɪk] *adj* trágico

trail [treɪl] *n* (*tracks*) rasto, pista; (*path*) caminho, trilha; (*of smoke, dust*) rasto ♦ *vt* (*drag*) arrastar; (*follow*) seguir a pista de ♦ *vi* arrastar-se; (*hang loosely*) pender; (*in game, contest*) ficar para trás; ~ **behind** *vi* atrasar-se; ~**er** *n* (*AUT*) reboque *m*; (*US: caravan*) trailer *m* (*BR*), rulote *f* (*PT*); (*CINEMA*) trailer; ~**er truck** (*US*) *n* caminhão-reboque *m*

train [treɪn] *n* trem *m* (*BR*), comboio (*PT*); (*of dress*) cauda ♦ *vt* formar; (*teach skills to*) instruir; (*SPORT*) treinar; (*dog*) adestrar, amestrar; (*point: gun etc*): **to** ~ **on** apontar para ♦ *vi* (*learn a skill*) instruir; (*SPORT*) treinar; (*be educated*) ser treinado; **to lose one's** ~ **of thought** perder o fio; ~**ed** *adj* especializado; (*teacher*) formado; (*animal*) adestrado; ~**ee** *n* estagiário/a; ~**er** *n* (*SPORT*) treinador(a) *m/f*; (*of animals*) adestrador(a) *m/f*; ~**s** *npl* (*shoes*) tênis *m*; ~**ing** *n* instrução *f*; (*SPORT, for occupation*) treinamento; (*professional*) formação *f*; ~**ing college** *n* (*for teachers*) ≈ escola normal; ~**ing shoes** *npl* tênis *m*

traipse [treɪps] *vi* perambular

trait [treɪt] *n* traço

traitor ['treɪtə*] *n* traidor(a) *m/f*

tram [træm] (BRIT) *n* (also: ~car) bonde *m* (BR), eléctrico (PT)

tramp [træmp] *n* (person) vagabundo/a; (inf: pej: woman) piranha ♦ *vi* caminhar pesadamente

trample ['træmpl] *vt*: **to ~ (underfoot)** calcar aos pés

trampoline ['træmpəliːn] *n* trampolim *m*

trance [trɑːns] *n* estupor *m*

tranquil ['træŋkwɪl] *adj* tranqüilo; **~lizer** *n* (MED) tranqüilizante *m*

transact [træn'zækt] *vt* (business) negociar; **~ion** *n* transação *f*, negócio

transcend [træn'sɛnd] *vt* transcender, exceder

transcript ['trænskrɪpt] *n* cópia, traslado

transfer [*n* 'trænsfə*, *vt* træns'fəː*] *n* transferência; (picture, design) decalcomania ♦ *vt* transferir; **to ~ the charges** (BRIT: TEL) ligar a cobrar

transform [træns'fɔːm] *vt* transformar

transfusion [træns'fjuːʒən] *n* (also: **blood ~**) transfusão *f* (de sangue)

transient ['trænzɪənt] *adj* transitório

transistor [træn'zɪstə*] *n* (ELEC: also: ~ radio) transistor *m*

transit ['trænzɪt] *n*: **in ~** em trânsito, de passagem

transitive ['trænzɪtɪv] *adj* (LING) transitivo

translate [trænz'leɪt] *vt* traduzir; **translator** *n* tradutor(a) *m/f*

transmission [trænz'mɪʃən] *n* transmissão *f*

transmit [trænz'mɪt] *vt* transmitir; **~ter** *n* transmissor *m*

transparency [træns'pɛərnsɪ] *n* transparência; (BRIT: PHOT) diapositivo

transparent [træns'pærnt] *adj* transparente

transpire [træns'paɪə*] *vi* (turn out) tornar sabido; (happen) ocorrer, acontecer

transplant [*vt* træns'plɑːnt, *n* 'trænsplɑːnt] *vt* transplantar ♦ *n* (MED) transplante *m*

transport [*n* 'trænspɔːt, *vt* træns'pɔːt] *n* transporte *m* ♦ *vt* transportar; (carry) acarretar; **~ation** *n* transporte *m*; **~ café** (BRIT) *n* lanchonete *f* de estrada

transvestite [trænz'vɛstaɪt] *n* travesti *m/f*

trap [træp] *n* (snare) armadilha, cilada; (trick) cilada; (carriage) aranha, charrete *f* ♦ *vt* pegar em armadilha; (person: trick) armar; (: in bad marriage) prender; (: in fire): **to be ~ped** ficar preso; (immobilize) bloquear; **~ door** *n* alçapão *m*

trapeze [trə'piːz] *n* trapézio

trappings ['træpɪŋz] *npl* adornos *mpl*, enfeites *mpl*

trash [træʃ] *n* (pej: nonsense) besteiras

fpl; (US: rubbish) lixo; **~ can** (US) *n* lata de lixo

trauma ['trɔːmə] *n* trauma *m*

travel ['trævl] *n* viagem *f* ♦ *vi* viajar; (sound) propagar-se; (news) levar; (wine): **this wine ~s well** este vinho não sofre alteração ao ser transportado ♦ *vt* percorrer; **~s** *npl* (journeys) viagens *fpl*; **~ agent** *n* agente *m/f* de viagens; **~ler** (US **~er**) *n* viajante *m/f*; (COMM) caixeiro/a viajante; **~ler's cheque** (US **~er's check**) *n* cheque *m* de viagem; **~ling** (US **~ing**) *n* as viagens, viajar *m* ♦ *adj* (circus, exhibition) itinerante; (salesman) viajante ♦ *cpd* de viagem; **~ sickness** *n* enjôo

travesty ['trævəstɪ] *n* paródia

trawler ['trɔːlə*] *n* traineira

tray [treɪ] *n* bandeja; (on desk) cesta

treacherous ['trɛtʃərəs] *adj* traiçoeiro; (ground, tide) perigoso

treachery ['trɛtʃərɪ] *n* traição *f*

treacle ['triːkl] *n* melado

tread [trɛd] (pt **trod**, pp **trodden**) *n* (step) passo, pisada; (sound) passada; (of stair) piso; (of tyre) banda de rodagem ♦ *vi* pisar; **~ on** *vt fus* pisar (em)

treason ['triːzn] *n* traição *f*

treasure ['trɛʒə*] *n* tesouro; (person) jóia ♦ *vt* (value) apreciar, estimar; **~s** *npl* (art ~s etc) preciosidades *fpl*

treasurer ['trɛʒərə*] *n* tesoureiro/a

treasury ['trɛʒərɪ] *n* tesouraria

treat [triːt] *n* regalo, deleite *m* ♦ *vt* tratar; **to ~ sb to sth** convidar alguém para algo

treatment ['triːtmənt] *n* tratamento

treaty ['triːtɪ] *n* tratado, acordo

treble ['trɛbl] *adj* tríplice ♦ *vt* triplicar ♦ *vi* triplicar(-se); **~ clef** *n* clave *f* de sol

tree [triː] *n* árvore *f*

trek [trɛk] *n* (long journey) jornada; (walk) caminhada

trellis ['trɛlɪs] *n* grade *f* de ripas, latada

tremble ['trɛmbl] *vi* tremer

tremendous [trɪ'mɛndəs] *adj* tremendo; (enormous) enorme; (excellent) sensacional, fantástico

tremor ['trɛmə*] *n* tremor *m*; (also: **earth ~**) tremor de terra

trench [trɛntʃ] *n* trincheira

trend [trɛnd] *n* (tendency) tendência; (of events) curso; (fashion) modismo, tendência; **~y** *adj* (idea) de acordo com a tendência atual; (clothes) da última moda

trespass ['trɛspəs] *vi*: **to ~ on** invadir; **"no ~ing"** "entrada proibida"

trestle ['trɛsl] *n* cavalete *m*

trial ['traɪəl] *n* (LAW) processo; (test: of machine etc) prova, teste *m*; **~s** *npl* (unpleasant experiences) dissabores *mpl*; **by ~ and error** por tentativas; **to be on ~** ser julgado; **~ period** *n* período de experiência

triangle ['traɪæŋgl] n (MATH, MUS) triângulo

tribe [traɪb] n tribo f; ~**sman** (irreg) n membro de tribo

tribunal [traɪ'bju:nl] n tribunal m

tributary ['trɪbjʊtərɪ] n afluente m

tribute ['trɪbju:t] n homenagem f; **to pay** ~ **to** prestar homenagem a, homenagear

trice [traɪs] n: **in a** ~ num instante

trick [trɪk] n truque m; (joke) peça, brincadeira; (skill, knack) habilidade f; (CARDS) vaza ♦ vt enganar; **to play a** ~ **on sb** pregar uma peça em alguém; **that should do the** ~ (inf) isso deveria dar resultado; ~**ery** n trapaça, astúcia ·

trickle ['trɪkl] n (of water etc) fio (de água) ♦ vi gotejar, pingar

tricky ['trɪkɪ] adj difícil, complicado

tricycle ['traɪsɪkl] n triciclo

trifle ['traɪfl] n bagatela f, besteira; (CULIN) tipo de bolo com fruta e creme ♦ adv: **a** ~ **long** um pouquinho longo; **trifling** adj insignificante

trigger ['trɪgə*] n (of gun) gatilho; ~ **off** vt desencadear

trill [trɪl] vi trilar, gorjear

trim [trɪm] adj (figure) elegante; (house) arrumado; (garden) bem cuidado ♦ n (haircut) aparada; (on car) estofamento ♦ vt aparar, cortar; (decorate): **to** ~ (**with**) enfeitar (com); (NAUT: sail) ajustar; ~**mings** npl decoração f; (CULIN) acompanhamentos mpl

trinket ['trɪŋkɪt] n bugiganga; (piece of jewellery) berloque m, bijuteria

trip [trɪp] n viagem f; (outing) excursão f; (stumble) tropeção m ♦ vi tropeçar; (go lightly) andar com passos ligeiros; **on a** ~ de viagem; ~ **up** vi tropeçar ♦ vt passar uma rasteira em

tripe [traɪp] n (CULIN) bucho, tripa; (pej: rubbish) bobagem f

triple ['trɪpl] adj triplo, tríplice; ~**ts** npl trigêmeos/as m/fpl; **triplicate** n: **in triplicate** em triplicata, em três vias

tripod ['traɪpɒd] n tripé m

trite [traɪt] adj gasto, banal

triumph ['traɪʌmf] n (satisfaction) satisfação f; (great achievement) triunfo ♦ vi: **to** ~ (**over**) triunfar (sobre)

trivia ['trɪvɪə] npl trivialidades fpl

trivial ['trɪvɪəl] adj insignificante; (commonplace) trivial

trod [trɒd] pt of **tread**; ~**den** pp of **tread**

trolley ['trɒlɪ] n carrinho; (table on wheels) mesa volante; ~ **bus** n ônibus m elétrico (BR), trólei m (PT)

trombone [trɒm'bəʊn] n trombone m

troop [tru:p] n bando, grupo ♦ vi: **to** ~ **in/out** entrar/sair em bando; ~**s** npl (MIL) tropas fpl; ~**ing the colour** (BRIT) saudação da bandeira

trophy ['trəʊfɪ] n troféu m

tropic ['trɒpɪk] n trópico; ~**al** adj tropical

trot [trɒt] n trote m; (fast pace) passo rápido ♦ vi trotar; (person) andar rapidamente; **on the** ~ (fig: inf) a fio

trouble ['trʌbl] n problema(s) m(pl), dificuldade(s) f(pl); (worry) preocupação f; (effort) incômodo, trabalho; (POL) distúrbios mpl; (MED): **stomach** etc ~ problemas mpl gástricos etc ♦ vt perturbar; (worry) preocupar, incomodar ♦ vi: **to** ~ **to do sth** incomodar-se or preocupar-se de fazer algo; ~**s** npl (POL etc) distúrbios mpl; **to be in** ~ estar num aperto; (ship, climber etc) estar em dificuldade; **what's the** ~? qual é o problema?; ~**d** adj preocupado; (epoch, life) agitado; ~**maker** n criador(a)-de-casos m/f; (child) encrenqueiro/a; ~**shooter** n conciliador(a) m/f; ~**some** adj importuno; (child, cough) incômodo

trough [trɒf] n (also: **drinking** ~) bebedouro, cocho; (also: **feeding** ~) gamela; (depression) depressão f

troupe [tru:p] n companhia teatral

trousers ['traʊzəz] npl calça (BR), calças fpl (PT)

trousseau ['tru:səʊ] (pl ~**x** or ~**s**) n enxoval m

trout [traʊt] n inv truta

trowel ['traʊəl] n colher f

truant ['trʊənt] (BRIT) n: **to play** ~ matar aula (BR), fazer gazeta (PT)

truce [tru:s] n trégua, armistício

truck [trʌk] n caminhão m (BR), camião m (PT); (RAIL) vagão m; ~ **driver** n caminhoneiro/a (BR), camionista m/f (PT); ~ **farm** (US) n horta

trudge [trʌdʒ] vi andar com dificuldade, arrastar-se

true [tru:] adj verdadeiro; (accurate) exato; (genuine) autêntico; (faithful) fiel, leal; **to come** ~ realizar-se, tornar-se realidade

truffle ['trʌfl] n trufa; (sweet) docinho de chocolate or rum

truly ['tru:lɪ] adv realmente; (truthfully) verdadeiramente; (faithfully) fielmente; **yours** ~ (in letter) atenciosamente

trump [trʌmp] n trunfo; ~**ed-up** adj inventado, forjado

trumpet ['trʌmpɪt] n trombeta

truncheon ['trʌntʃən] n cassetete m

trundle ['trʌndl] vt empurrar lentamente ♦ vi: **to** ~ **along** rolar or rodar fazendo ruído

trunk [trʌŋk] n tronco; (of elephant) tromba; (case) baú m; (US: AUT) mala (BR), porta-bagagens m (PT); ~**s** npl (also: **swimming** ~**s**) sunga (BR), calções mpl de banho (PT)

truss [trʌs] n (MED) funda ♦ vt: **to** ~ (**up**) atar, amarrar

trust [trʌst] n confiança; (responsibility) responsabilidade f; (LAW) fideicomisso ♦ vt (rely on) confiar em; (entrust): **to** ~

sth to sb confiar algo a alguém; (*hope*): to ~ (that) esperar que; to take sth on ~ aceitar algo sem verificação prévia; ~ed *adj* de confiança; ~ee *n* (*LAW*) fideicomissário/a, depositário/a; (*of school etc*) administrador(a) *m/f*; ~ful *adj* confiante; ~ing *adj* confiante; ~worthy *adj* digno de confiança

truth [truːθ, *pl* truːðz] *n* verdade *f*; ~ful *adj* (*person*) sincero, honesto

try [traɪ] *n* tentativa; (*RUGBY*) ensaio ♦ *vt* (*LAW*) julgar; (*test: sth new*) provar, pôr à prova; (*strain*) cansar ♦ *vi* tentar; to have a ~ fazer uma tentativa; to ~ to do sth tentar fazer algo; ~ on *vt* (*clothes*) experimentar, provar; ~ing *adj* exasperante

tsar [zaːʳ] *n* czar *m*

T-shirt *n* camiseta (*BR*), T-shirt *f* (*PT*)

T-square *n* régua em T

tub [tʌb] *n* tina; (*bath*) banheira

tuba [ˈtjuːbə] *n* tuba

tubby [ˈtʌbɪ] *adj* gorducho

tube [tjuːb] *n* tubo; (*pipe*) cano; (*BRIT: underground*) metrô *m* (*BR*), metro(politano) (*PT*); (*for tyre*) câmara-de-ar *f*; ~ station (*BRIT*) *n* estação *f* de metrô

tubular [ˈtjuːbjuləʳ] *adj* tubular; (*furniture*) tubiforme

TUC *n abbr* (= *Trades Union Congress*) ≈ CUT *f*

tuck [tʌk] *vt* (*put*) enfiar, meter; ~ away *vt* esconder; to be ~ed away estar escondido; ~ in *vt* enfiar para dentro; (*child*) aconchegar ♦ *vi* (*eat*) comer com apetite; ~ up *vt* (*child*) aconchegar; ~ shop *n* loja de balas

Tuesday [ˈtjuːzdɪ] *n* terça-feira

tuft [tʌft] *n* penacho; (*of grass etc*) tufo

tug [tʌg] *n* (*ship*) rebocador *m* ♦ *vt* puxar; ~-of-war *n* cabo-de-guerra *m*; (*fig*) disputa

tuition [tjuːˈɪʃən] *n* ensino; (*private* ~) aulas *fpl* particulares; (*US: fees*) taxas *fpl* escolares

tumble [ˈtʌmbl] *n* (*fall*) queda ♦ *vi* cair, tombar; to ~ to sth (*inf*) sacar algo; ~down *adj* em ruínas; ~ dryer (*BRIT*) *n* máquina de secar roupa

tumbler [ˈtʌmbləʳ] *n* copo

tummy [ˈtʌmɪ] (*inf*) *n* (*belly*) barriga; (*stomach*) estômago

tumour [ˈtjuːməʳ] (*US* **tumor**) *n* tumor *m*

tuna [ˈtjuːnə] *n inv* (*also*: ~ **fish**) atum *m*

tune [tjuːn] *n* melodia ♦ *vt* (*MUS*) afinar; (*RADIO, TV*) sintonizar; (*AUT*) regular; to be in/out of ~ (*instrument*) estar afinado/desafinado; (*singer*) cantar afinado/desafinar; to be in/out of ~ with (*fig*) harmonizar-se com/destoar de; ~ in *vi* (*RADIO, TV*): to ~ in (to) sintonizar (com); ~ up *vi* (*musician*) afinar (seu instrumento); ~ful *adj* melodioso; ~r *n*: piano ~r afinador(a) *m/f* de pianos

tunic [ˈtjuːnɪk] *n* túnica

Tunisia [tjuːˈnɪzɪə] *n* Tunísia

tunnel [ˈtʌnl] *n* túnel *m*; (*in mine*) galeria ♦ *vi* abrir um túnel (*or* uma galeria)

turban [ˈtəːbən] *n* turbante *m*

turbulence [ˈtəːbjuləns] *n* (*AVIAT*) turbulência; **turbulent** *adj* turbulento

tureen [təˈriːn] *n* terrina

turf [təːf] *n* torrão *m* ♦ *vt* relvar, gramar; ~ out (*inf*) *vt* (*person*) pôr no olho da rua

turgid [ˈtəːdʒɪd] *adj* (*speech*) pomposo

Turk [təːk] *n* turco/a

Turkey [ˈtəːkɪ] *n* Turquia

turkey [ˈtəːkɪ] *n* peru(a) *m/f*

Turkish [ˈtəːkɪʃ] *adj* turco/a ♦ *n* (*LING*) turco; ~ **bath** *n* banho turco

turmoil [ˈtəːmɔɪl] *n* tumulto, distúrbio, agitação *f*; in ~ agitado, tumultuado

turn [təːn] *n* volta, turno; (*in road*) curva; (*of mind, events*) propensão *f*, tendência; (*THEATRE*) número; (*MED*) choque *m* ♦ *vt* dar volta a, fazer girar; (*collar*) virar; (*change*): to ~ sth into converter algo em ♦ *vi* virar; (*person: look back*) voltar-se; (*reverse direction*) mudar de direção; (*milk*) azedar; (*become*) tornar-se, virar; to ~ nasty engrossar; to ~ forty fazer quarenta anos; a good ~ um favor; it gave me quite a ~ me deu um susto enorme; "no left ~" (*AUT*) "proibido virar à esquerda"; it's your ~ é a sua vez; in ~ por sua vez; to take ~s (at) revezar (em); ~ away *vi* virar a cabeça ♦ *vt* recusar; ~ back *vi* voltar atrás ♦ *vt* voltar para trás; (*clock*) atrasar; ~ down *vt* (*refuse*) recusar; (*reduce*) baixar; (*fold*) dobrar, virar para baixo; ~ in *vi* (*inf: go to bed*) ir dormir ♦ *vt* (*fold*) dobrar para dentro; ~ off *vi* (*from road*) virar, sair do caminho ♦ *vt* (*light, radio etc*) apagar; (*engine*) desligar; ~ on *vt* (*light*) acender; (*engine, radio*) ligar; (*tap*) abrir; ~ out *vt* (*light, gas*) apagar; (*produce*) produzir ♦ *vi* (*troops*) ser mobilizado; to ~ out to be ... revelar-se (ser) ..., resultar (ser) ..., ir a ser ...; ~ over *vi* (*person*) virar-se ♦ *vt* (*object*) virar; ~ round *vi* voltar-se, virar-se; ~ up *vi* (*person*) aparecer, pintar; (*lost object*) aparecer ♦ *vt* (*collar*) subir; (*radio etc*) aumentar; ~ing *n* (*in road*) via lateral; ~ing point *n* (*fig*) momento decisivo, virada

turnip [ˈtəːnɪp] *n* nabo

turnout [ˈtəːnaut] *n* assistência; (*in election*) comparecimento às urnas

turnover [ˈtəːnəuvəʳ] *n* (*COMM: amount of money*) volume *m* de negócios; (: *of goods*) movimento; (*of staff*) rotatividade *f*

turnpike [ˈtəːnpaɪk] (*US*) *n* estrada *or* rodovia com pedágio (*BR*) *or* portagem (*PT*)

turnstile ['tə:nstail] n borboleta (BR), torniquete m (PT)

turntable ['tə:nteibl] n (on record player) prato

turn-up (BRIT) n (on trousers) volta, dobra

turpentine ['tə:pəntain] n (also: turps) aguarrás f

turquoise ['tə:kwɔiz] n (stone) turquesa ♦ adj azul-turquesa inv

turret ['tʌrit] n torrinha

turtle ['tə:tl] n tartaruga, cágado; ~neck (sweater) n pulôver m (BR) or camisola (PT) de gola alta

tusk [tʌsk] n defesa (de elefante)

tussle ['tʌsl] n (fight) luta; (scuffle) contenda, rixa

tutor ['tju:tə*] n professor(a) m/f; (private =) professor(a) m/f particular; ~ial n (SCH) seminário

tuxedo [tʌk'si:dəu] (US) n smoking m

TV n abbr (= television) TV f

twang [twæŋ] n (of instrument) dedilhado; (of voice) timbre m nasal

tweed [twi:d] n tweed m, pano grosso de lã

tweezers ['twi:zəz] npl pinça (pequena)

twelfth [twelfθ] num décimo segundo

twelve [twelv] num doze; at ~ (o'clock) (midday) ao meio-dia; (midnight) à meia-noite

twentieth ['twentiiθ] num vigésimo

twenty ['twenti] num vinte

twice [twais] adv duas vezes; ~ as much duas vezes mais

twiddle ['twidl] vt, vi: to ~ (with) sth mexer em algo; to ~ one's thumbs (fig) chupar o dedo

twig [twig] n graveto, varinha ♦ vi (inf) sacar

twilight ['twailait] n crepúsculo, meia-luz f

twin [twin] adj gêmeo; (beds) separado ♦ n gêmeo ♦ vt irmanar; ~(-bedded) room n quarto com duas camas

twine [twain] n barbante m (BR), cordel m (PT) ♦ vi enroscar-se, enrolar-se

twinge [twindʒ] n (of pain) pontada; (of conscience) remorso

twinkle ['twiŋkl] vi cintilar; (eyes) pestanejar

twirl [twə:l] vt fazer girar ♦ vi girar rapidamente

twist [twist] n torção f; (in road, coil) curva; (in flex) virada; (in story) mudança imprevista ♦ vt torcer, retorcer; (ankle) torcer; (weave) entrelaçar; (roll around) enrolar; (fig) deturpar ♦ vi serpentear

twit [twit] (inf) n idiota m/f, bobo/a

twitch [twitʃ] n puxão m; (nervous) tique m nervoso ♦ vi contrair-se

two [tu:] num dois; to put ~ and ~ together (fig) tirar conclusões; ~-door adj (AUT) de duas portas; ~-faced (pej)

adj (person) falso; ~fold adv: to increase ~fold duplicar ♦ adj (increase) em cem por cento; (reply) duplo; ~-piece n (also: ~-piece suit) traje m de duas peças; (also: ~-piece swimsuit) maiô m de duas peças, biquíni m; ~some n (people) casal m; ~-way adj: ~-way traffic trânsito em mão dupla

tycoon [tai'ku:n] n: (business) ~ magnata m

type [taip] n (category) tipo, espécie f; (model) modelo; (TYP) tipo, letra ♦ vt (letter etc) datilografar, bater (à máquina); ~cast adj que representa sempre o mesmo papel; ~face n tipo, letra; ~script n texto datilografado; ~writer n máquina de escrever; ~written adj datilografado

typhoid ['taifɔid] n febre f tifóide

typhoon [tai'fu:n] n tufão m

typical ['tipikl] adj típico

typify ['tipifai] vt tipificar, simbolizar

typing ['taipiŋ] n datilografia

typist ['taipist] n datilógrafo/a m/f

tyrant ['taiərənt] n tirano/a

tyre ['taiə*] (US tire) n pneu m; ~ pressure n pressão f dos pneus

tzar [zɑ:*] n = tsar

U

U-bend n (in pipe) curva em U

ubiquitous [ju:'bikwitəs] adj ubíquo, onipresente

udder ['ʌdə*] n ubre f

UFO ['ju:fəu] n abbr (= unidentified flying object) óvni m

Uganda [ju:'gændə] n Uganda (no article)

ugh [ə:h] excl uh!

ugliness ['ʌglinis] n feiúra

ugly ['ʌgli] adj feio; (dangerous) perigoso

UK n abbr = United Kingdom

ulcer ['ʌlsə*] n úlcera; mouth ~ afta

Ulster ['ʌlstə*] n Ulster m

ulterior [ʌl'tiəriə*] adj: ~ motive segundas intenções fpl

ultimate ['ʌltimət] adj último, final; (authority) máximo; ~ly adv (in the end) no final, por último; (fundamentally) no fundo

ultimatum [ʌlti'meitəm] (pl ~s or ultimata) n ultimato

ultrasound ['ʌltrəsaund] n (MED) ultra-som m

ultraviolet [ʌltrə'vaiəlit] adj ultravioleta

umbilical cord [ʌmbi'laikl-] n cordão m umbilical

umbrella [ʌm'brelə] n guarda-chuva m; (for sun) guarda-sol m, barraca (de praia)

umpire ['ʌmpaiə*] n árbitro ♦ vt arbitrar

umpteen [ʌmp'ti:n] adj inúmeros/as; ~th adj: for the ~th time pela enésima vez

UN *n abbr* (= *United Nations*) ONU *f*

unable [ʌn'eɪbl] *adj*: to be ~ to do sth não poder fazer algo

unaccompanied [ʌnə'kʌmpənɪd] *adj* desacompanhado; (*singing, song*) sem acompanhamento

unaccountably [ʌnə'kauntəblɪ] *adv* inexplicavelmente

unaccustomed [ʌnə'kʌstəmd] *adj*: to be ~ to não estar acostumado a

unanimous [juːˈnænɪməs] *adj* unânime

unarmed [ʌn'ɑːmd] *adj* (*without a weapon*) desarmado; (*defenceless*) indefeso

unashamed [ʌnə'ʃeɪmd] *adj* (*open*) desembaraçado; (*pleasure*) descarado

unassuming [ʌnə'sjuːmɪŋ] *adj* modesto, despretencioso

unattached [ʌnə'tætʃt] *adj* (*person*) livre; (*part etc*) solto, separado

unattended [ʌnə'tɛndɪd] *adj* (*car, luggage*) abandonado

unattractive [ʌnə'træktɪv] *adj* sem atrativos; (*building, appearance, idea*) pouco atraente

unauthorized [ʌn'ɔːθəraɪzd] *adj* não autorizado, sem autorização

unavoidable [ʌnə'vɔɪdəbl] *adj* inevitável

unaware [ʌnə'wɛə*] *adj*: to be ~ of ignorar, não perceber

unawares [ʌnə'wɛəz] *adv* improvisadamente, de surpresa

unbalanced [ʌn'bælənst] *adj* desequilibrado

unbearable [ʌn'bɛərəbl] *adj* insuportável

unbeatable [ʌn'biːtəbl] *adj* (*team*) invencível; (*price*) sem igual

unbeknown(st) [ʌnbɪ'nəun(st)] *adv*: ~ to me sem eu saber

unbelievable [ʌnbɪ'liːvəbl] *adj* inacreditável; (*amazing*) incrível

unbend [ʌn'bɛnd] (*irreg*) *vi* relaxar-se ♦ *vt* (*wire*) desentortar

unbiased [ʌn'baɪəst] *adj* imparcial

unborn [ʌn'bɔːn] *adj* por nascer

unbroken [ʌn'brəukən] *adj* (*seal*) intacto; (*line*) contínuo; (*silence, series*) ininterrupto; (*record*) mantido; (*spirit*) indômito

unbutton [ʌn'bʌtn] *vt* desabotoar

uncalled-for [ʌn'kɔːld-] *adj* desnecessário, gratuito

uncanny [ʌn'kænɪ] *adj* estranho; (*knack*) excepcional

unceasing [ʌn'siːsɪŋ] *adj* contínuo

unceremonious [ʌnsɛrɪ'məunɪəs] *adj* (*abrupt*) incerimonioso; (*rude*) rude

uncertain [ʌn'sɜːtn] *adj* incerto; (*character*) indeciso; (*unsure*): ~ about inseguro sobre; **in no ~ terms** em termos precisos; ~**ty** *n* incerteza; (*also*: **doubts**) dúvidas *fpl*

unchanged [ʌn'tʃeɪndʒd] *adj* inalterado

unchecked [ʌn'tʃɛkt] *adv* sem controle, descontrolado

uncivilized [ʌn'sɪvəlaɪzd] *adj* (*country,*

people) primitivo; (*fig: behaviour*) incivilizado; (: *hour*) de manhã bem cedo

uncle [ʌŋkl] *n* tio

uncomfortable [ʌn'kʌmfətəbl] *adj* incômodo; (*uneasy*) pouco à vontade; (*situation*) desagradável

uncommon [ʌn'kɔmən] *adj* raro, incomum, excepcional

uncompromising [ʌn'kɔmprəmaɪzɪŋ] *adj* intransigente, inflexível

unconcerned [ʌn'kənsɜːnd] *adj* indiferente, despreocupado

unconditional [ʌnkən'dɪʃənl] *adj* incondicional

unconscious [ʌn'kɔnʃəs] *adj* sem sentidos, desacordado; (*unaware*): ~ of inconsciente de ♦ *n*: the ~ o inconsciente

uncontrollable [ʌnkən'trəuləbl] *adj* (*temper*) ingovernável; (*child, animal, laughter*) incontrolável

unconventional [ʌnkən'vɛnʃənl] *adj* inconvencional

uncouth [ʌn'kuːθ] *adj* rude, grosseiro

uncover [ʌn'kʌvə*] *vt* descobrir; (*take lid off*) destapar, destampar

undecided [ʌndɪ'saɪdɪd] *adj* indeciso; (*question*) não respondido, pendente

under ['ʌndə*] *prep* embaixo de (*BR*), debaixo de (*PT*); (*fig*) sob; (*less than*) menos que; (*according to*) segundo, de acordo com ♦ *adv* embaixo; (*movement*) por baixo; ~ **there** ali embaixo; ~ **repair** em conserto

under... [ʌndə*] *prefix* sub-; ~**age** *adj* menor de idade; ~**carriage** (*BRIT*) *n* (*AVIAT*) trem *m* de aterrissagem; ~**charge** *vt* não cobrar o suficiente; ~**clothes** *npl* roupa de baixo, roupa íntima; ~**coat** *n* (*paint*) primeira mão *f*; ~**cover** *adj* secreto, clandestino; ~**current** *n* (*fig*) tendência; ~**cut** (*irreg*) *vt* (*person*) prejudicar; (*prices*) vender por menos que; ~**dog** *n* o mais fraco; ~**done** *adj* (*CULIN*) mal passado; ~**estimate** *vt* subestimar; ~**exposed** (*PHOT*) sem exposição suficiente; ~**fed** *adj* subnutrido; ~**foot** *adv* sob os pés; ~**go** (*irreg*) *vt* sofrer; (*test*) passar por; (*operation, treatment*) ser submetido a; ~**graduate** *n* universitário/a; ~**ground** *n* (*BRIT*) metrô *m* (*BR*), metro(-politano) (*PT*); (*POL*) organização *f* clandestina ♦ *adj* subterrâneo; (*fig*) clandestino ♦ *adv* (*work*) embaixo da terra; (*fig*) na clandestinidade; ~**growth** *n* vegetação *f* rasteira; ~**hand(ed)** *adj* (*fig*) secreto e desonesto; ~**lie** (*irreg*) *vt* (*fig*) ser a base de; ~**line** *vt* sublinhar; ~**ling** (*pej*) *n* subalterno/a; ~**mine** *vt* minar, solapar; ~**neath** *adv* embaixo, debaixo, por baixo ♦ *prep* embaixo de (*BR*), debaixo de (*PT*); ~**paid** *adj* mal pago; ~**pants** (*BRIT*) *npl* cueca(s) *f(pl)* (*BR*), cuecas *fpl* (*PT*); ~**pass** (*BRIT*) *n* passagem *f* inferior; ~**privileged** *adj* menos favorecido;

~**rate** vt depreciar, subestimar; ~**shirt** (US) n camiseta; ~**shorts** (US) npl cueca (BR), cuecas fpl (PT); ~**side** n parte f inferior; ~**skirt** (BRIT) n anágua

understand [Andə'stænd] (irreg) vt entender, compreender ♦ vi: **to ~ that** acreditar que; ~**able** adj compreensível; ~**ing** adj compreensivo ♦ n compreensão f; (knowledge) entendimento; (agreement) acordo

understatement [Andə'steɪtmənt] n (quality) subestimação f; (euphemism) eufemismo; **it's an ~ to say that ...** é uma subestimação dizer que ...

understood [Andə'stud] pt, pp of **understand** ♦ adj entendido; (implied) subentendido, implícito

understudy ['Andəstʌdɪ] n ator m substituto/atriz f substituta

undertake [Andə'teɪk] (irreg: like **take**) vt incumbir-se de, encarregar-se de; **to ~ to do sth** comprometer-se a fazer algo

undertaker ['Andəteɪkə*] n agente m/f funerário/a

undertaking ['Andəteɪkɪŋ] n empreendimento; (promise) promessa

undertone ['Andətəun] n: **in an ~** em meia voz

underwater [Andə'wɔːtə*] adv sob a água ♦ adj subaquático

underwear ['Andəwɛə*] n roupa de baixo, roupa íntima

underworld ['Andəwəːld] n (of crime) submundo

underwriter ['Andəraɪtə*] n (INSURANCE) subscritor(a) m/f (que faz resseguro)

undies ['Andɪz] (inf) npl roupa de baixo, roupa íntima

undisputed [Andɪ'spjuːtɪd] adj incontestável

undo [An'duː] (irreg: like **do**) vt (unfasten) desatar; (spoil) desmanchar

undoing [An'duːɪŋ] n ruína, desgraça

undoubted [An'dautɪd] adj indubitável

undress [An'drɛs] vi despir-se, tirar a roupa

undue [An'djuː] adj excessivo

undulating ['Andjuleɪtɪŋ] adj ondulante

unduly [An'djuːlɪ] adv excessivamente

unearth [An'əːθ] vt desenterrar; (fig) revelar

unearthly [An'əːθlɪ] adj: **at an ~ hour of the night** na calada da noite

uneasy [An'iːzɪ] adj (person) preocupado; (feeling) incômodo; (peace, truce) desconfortável

uneconomic(al) [Aniːkə'nɒmɪk(l)] adj antieconômico

uneducated [An'ɛdjukeɪtɪd] adj inculto, sem instrução, não escolarizado

unemployed [Anɪm'plɔɪd] adj desempregado ♦ npl: **the ~** os desempregados

unemployment [Anɪm'plɔɪmənt] n desemprego

unending [An'ɛndɪŋ] adj interminável

unerring [An'əːrɪŋ] adj infalível

uneven [An'iːvn] adj desigual; (road etc) irregular, acidentado

unexpected [Anɪk'spɛktɪd] adj inesperado; ~**ly** adv inesperadamente

unfailing [An'feɪlɪŋ] adj inexaurível

unfair [An'fɛə*] adj: ~ **(to)** injusto (com)

unfaithful [An'feɪθful] adj infiel

unfamiliar [Anfə'mɪlɪə*] adj pouco familiar, desconhecido; **to be ~ with sth** não estar familiarizado com algo

unfashionable [An'fæʃnəbl] adj fora da moda

unfasten [An'fɑːsn] vt desatar; (open) abrir

unfavourable [An'feɪvərəbl] (US **unfavorable**) adj desfavorável

unfeeling [An'fiːlɪŋ] adj insensível

unfinished [An'fɪnɪʃt] adj incompleto, inacabado

unfit [An'fɪt] adj sem preparo físico; (incompetent): ~ **(for)** incompetente (para), incapaz (de); ~ **for work** inapto para trabalhar

unfold [An'fəuld] vt desdobrar ♦ vi (situation) desdobrar-se

unforeseen [Anfɔː'siːn] adj imprevisto

unfortunate [An'fɔːtʃənət] adj infeliz; (event, remark) inoportuno

unfounded [An'faundɪd] adj infundado

unfriendly [An'frɛndlɪ] adj antipático

ungainly [An'geɪnlɪ] adj desalinhado

ungodly [An'gɒdlɪ] adj: **at an ~ hour** às altas horas da madrugada

ungrateful [An'greɪtful] adj mal agradecido, ingrato

unhappiness [An'hæpɪnɪs] n infelicidade f

unhappy [An'hæpɪ] adj triste; (unfortunate) desventurado; (childhood) infeliz; (dissatisfied): ~ **with** descontente com, insatisfeito com

unharmed [An'hɑːmd] adj ileso

unhealthy [An'hɛlθɪ] adj insalubre; (person) doentio; (fig) anormal

unheard-of [An'həːd-] adj insólito

unhurt [An'həːt] adj ileso

uniform ['juːnɪfɔːm] n uniforme m ♦ adj uniforme

unify ['juːnɪfaɪ] vt unificar, unir

uninhabited [Anɪn'hæbɪtɪd] adj inabitado

unintentional [Anɪn'tɛnʃənl] adj involuntário, não intencional

union ['juːnjən] n união f; (also: **trade ~**) sindicato (de trabalhadores) ♦ cpd sindical; **U~ Jack** n bandeira britânica

unique [juː'niːk] adj único, sem igual

unison ['juːnɪsn] n: **in ~** em harmonia, em uníssono

unit ['juːnɪt] n unidade f; (of furniture etc) seção f; (team, squad) equipe f; **kitchen ~** armário de cozinha

unite [juː'naɪt] vt unir ♦ vi unir-se; ~**d** adj unido; (effort) conjunto; **U~d King-**

dom n Reino Unido; **U~d Nations (Organization)** n (Organização f das) Nações fpl Unidas; **U~d States (of America)** n Estados Unidos mpl (da América)

unit trust (BRIT) n (COMM) fundo de investimento

unity ['ju:nɪtɪ] n unidade f

universal [ju:nɪ'vɜ:sl] adj universal

universe ['ju:nɪvɜ:s] n universo

university [ju:nɪ'vɜ:sɪtɪ] n universidade f

unjust [ʌn'dʒʌst] adj injusto

unkempt [ʌn'kempt] adj desleixado, descuidado; (hair) despenteado; (beard) mal tratado

unkind [ʌn'kaɪnd] adj maldoso; (comment etc) cruel

unknown [ʌn'nəʊn] adj desconhecido

unlawful [ʌn'lɔ:ful] adj ilegal

unleaded [ʌn'ledɪd] adj (petrol, fuel) sem chumbo

unleash [ʌn'li:ʃ] vt (fig) desencadear

unless [ʌn'les] conj a menos que, a não ser que; ~ **he comes** a menos que ele venha

unlike [ʌn'laɪk] adj diferente ♦ prep diferentemente de, ao contrário de

unlikely [ʌn'laɪklɪ] adj (not likely) improvável; (unexpected) inesperado

unlisted [ʌn'lɪstɪd] (US) adj (TEL) que não consta na lista telefônica

unload [ʌn'ləʊd] vt descarregar

unlock [ʌn'lɔk] vt destrancar

unlucky [ʌn'lʌkɪ] adj infeliz; (object, number) de mau agouro; **to be ~** ser azarado, ter azar

unmarried [ʌn'mærɪd] adj solteiro

unmistak(e)able [ʌnmɪs'teɪkəbl] adj inconfundível

unmitigated [ʌn'mɪtɪgeɪtɪd] adj não mitigado, absoluto

unnatural [ʌn'nætʃrəl] adj antinatural, artificial; (manner) afetado; (habit) depravado

unnecessary [ʌn'nesəsərɪ] adj desnecessário, inútil

unnoticed [ʌn'nəʊtɪst] adj: **(to go** or **pass ~** (passar) despercebido

UNO ['ju:nəʊ] n abbr (= United Nations Organization) ONU f

unobtainable [ʌnəb'teɪnəbl] adj inacessível; (TEL) ocupado

unobtrusive [ʌnəb'tru:sɪv] adj discreto

unofficial [ʌnə'fɪʃl] adj não-oficial, informal; (strike) desautorizado

unorthodox [ʌn'ɔ:θədɔks] adj pouco ortodoxo, heterodoxo

unpack [ʌn'pæk] vi desembrulhar ♦ vt desfazer

unpalatable [ʌn'pælətəbl] adj desagradável

unparalleled [ʌn'pærəleld] adj sem paralelo

unpleasant [ʌn'pleznt] adj desagradável; (person, manner) antipático

unplug [ʌn'plʌg] vt desligar

unpopular [ʌn'pɔpjulə*] adj impopular

unprecedented [ʌn'presɪdəntɪd] adj sem precedentes

unpredictable [ʌnprɪ'dɪktəbl] adj imprevisível

unprofessional [ʌnprə'feʃənl] adj (conduct) pouco profissional

unravel [ʌn'rævl] vt desemaranhar; (mystery) desvendar

unreal [ʌn'rɪəl] adj irreal, ilusório; (extraordinary) extraordinário

unrealistic [ʌnrɪə'lɪstɪk] adj pouco realista

unreasonable [ʌn'ri:znəbl] adj insensato; (demand) absurdo

unrelated [ʌnrɪ'leɪtɪd] adj sem relação; (family) sem parentesco

unrelenting [ʌnrɪ'lentɪŋ] adj implacável

unreliable [ʌnrɪ'laɪəbl] adj (person) indigno de confiança; (machine) incerto, perigoso

unremitting [ʌnrɪ'mɪtɪŋ] adj constante, incessante

unreservedly [ʌnrɪ'zɜ:vɪdlɪ] adv sem reserva, francamente

unrest [ʌn'rest] n inquietação f, desassossego; (POL) distúrbios mpl

unroll [ʌn'rəʊl] vt desenrolar

unruly [ʌn'ru:lɪ] adj indisciplinado; (hair) desalinhado

unsafe [ʌn'seɪf] adj perigoso

unsaid [ʌn'sed] adj: **to leave sth ~** deixar algo por dizer

unsatisfactory [ʌnsætɪs'fæktərɪ] adj insatisfatório

unsavoury [ʌn'seɪvərɪ] (US **unsavory**) adj (fig) repugnante, vil

unscathed [ʌn'skeɪðd] adj ileso

unscrew [ʌn'skru:] vt desparafusar

unscrupulous [ʌn'skru:pjuləs] adj inescrupuloso, imoral

unsettled [ʌn'setld] adj (weather) instável; (person) inquieto

unshaven [ʌn'ʃeɪvn] adj com a barba por fazer

unsightly [ʌn'saɪtlɪ] adj feio, disforme

unskilled [ʌn'skɪld] adj não-especializado

unspeakable [ʌn'spi:kəbl] adj indescritível; (awful) inqualificável

unstable [ʌn'steɪbl] adj em falso; (mentally) instável

unsteady [ʌn'stedɪ] adj trêmulo; (ladder) em falso

unstuck [ʌn'stʌk] adj: **to come ~** despegar-se; (fig) fracassar

unsuccessful [ʌnsək'sesful] adj (attempt) frustrado, vão/vã; (writer, proposal) sem êxito; **to be ~** (in attempting sth) ser mal sucedido, não conseguir; (application) ser recusado; **~ly** adv em vão, debalde

unsuitable [ʌn'su:təbl] adj inadequado; (time) inconveniente

unsure [ʌn'ʃuə*] adj inseguro, incerto;

to be ~ **of o.s.** não ser seguro de si

unsuspecting [ʌnsə'spɛktɪŋ] *adj* confiante, insuspeitado

unsympathetic [ʌnsɪmpə'θɛtɪk] *adj* insensível; (*unlikeable*) antipático

untapped [ʌn'tæpt] *adj* inexplorado

unthinkable [ʌn'θɪŋkəbl] *adj* impensável, inconcebível, incalculável

untidy [ʌn'taɪdɪ] *adj* (*room*) desarrumado, desleixado; (*appearance*) desmazelado, desalinhado

untie [ʌn'taɪ] *vt* desatar, desfazer; (*dog, prisoner*) soltar

until [ən'tɪl] *prep* até ♦ *conj* até que; ~ **he comes** até que ele venha; ~ **now** até agora; ~ **then** até então

untimely [ʌn'taɪmlɪ] *adj* inoportuno, intempestivo; (*death*) prematuro

untold [ʌn'təuld] *adj* (*story*) inédito; (*suffering*) incalculável; (*joy, wealth*) inestimável

untoward [ʌntə'wɔːd] *adj* desfavorável, inconveniente

unused[1] [ʌn'juːzd] *adj* novo, sem uso

unused[2] [ʌn'juːst] *adj*: **to be** ~ **to sth/ to doing sth** não estar acostumado com algo/a fazer algo

unusual [ʌn'juːʒuəl] *adj* (*strange*) estranho; (*rare*) incomum; (*exceptional*) extraordinário

unveil [ʌn'veɪl] *vt* desvelar, descobrir

unwanted [ʌn'wɒntɪd] *adj* não desejado, indesejável

unwavering [ʌn'weɪvərɪŋ] *adj* firme

unwelcome [ʌn'welkəm] *adj* (*guest*) inoportuno; (*news*) desagradável

unwell [ʌn'wel] *adj*: **to be** ~ estar doente; **to feel** ~ estar indisposto

unwieldy. [ʌn'wiːldɪ] *adj*: difícil de manejar, pesado

unwilling [ʌn'wɪlɪŋ] *adj*: **to be** ~ **to do sth** relutar em fazer algo, não querer fazer algo; ~**ly** *adv* de má vontade

unwind [ʌn'waɪnd] (*irreg*) *vt* desenrolar ♦ *vi* (*relax*) relaxar-se

unwise [ʌn'waɪz] *adj* imprudente

unwitting [ʌn'wɪtɪŋ] *adj* inconsciente, involuntário

unworkable [ʌn'wəːkəbl] *adj* (*plan etc*) inviável, inexequível

unworthy [ʌn'wəːðɪ] *adj* indigno

unwrap [ʌn'ræp] *vt* desembrulhar

unwritten [ʌn'rɪtən] *adj* (*agreement*) tácito

KEYWORD
---

up [ʌp] *prep*: **to go/be** ~ **sth** subir algo/estar em cima de algo; **we climbed/walked** ~ **the hill** nós subimos/andamos até em cima da colina; **they live further** ~ **the street** moram mais adiante nesta rua

♦ *adv* **1** (*upwards, higher*) em cima, para cima; ~ **in the sky/the moun-** tains lá no céu/nas montanhas; ~ **there** lá em cima; ~ **above** em cima

2: **to be** ~ (*out of bed*) estar de pé; (*prices, level*) estar elevado; (*building, tent*) estar erguido

3: ~ **to** (*as far as*) até; ~ **to now** até agora

4: **to be** ~ **to** (*depending on*): **it is** ~ **to you** você é quem sabe, você decide

5: **to be** ~ **to** (*equal to*) estar à altura de; **he's not** ~ **to it** (*job, task etc*) ele não é capaz de fazê-lo; **his work is not** ~ **to the required standard** seu trabalho não atende aos padrões exigidos

6: **to be** ~ **to** (*inf: be doing*) estar fazendo (*BR*) *or* a fazer (*PT*); ·**what is he** ~ **to**? o que é/ele está querendo?, o que ele está tramando?

♦ *n*: ~**s and downs** altos *mpl* e baixos *mpl*

---

upbringing ['ʌpbrɪŋɪŋ] *n* educação *f*, criação *f*

update [ʌp'deɪt] *vt* atualizar, pôr em dia

upgrade [ʌp'greɪd] *vt* (*person*) promover; (*job*) melhorar; (*house*) reformar

upheaval [ʌp'hiːvl] *n* transtorno; (*unrest*) convulsão *f*

uphill [ʌp'hɪl] *adj* ladeira acima; (*fig: task*) trabalhoso, árduo ♦ *adv*: **to go** ~ ir morro acima; (*face, look*) para cima

uphold [ʌp'həuld] (*irreg: like* **hold**) *vt* defender, preservar

upholstery [ʌp'həulstərɪ] *n* estofamento

upkeep ['ʌpkiːp] *n* manutenção *f*

upon [ə'pɒn] *prep* sobre

upper ['ʌpə*] *adj* superior, de cima ♦ *n* (*of shoe*) gáspea, parte *f* superior; ~ **class** *adj* de classe alta; ~ **hand** *n*: **to have the** ~ **hand** ter controle *or* domínio; ~**most** *adj* mais elevado; **what was** ~**most in my mind** o que me preocupava mais

upright ['ʌpraɪt] *adj* vertical; (*straight*) reto; (*fig*) honesto

uprising ['ʌpraɪzɪŋ] *n* revolta, rebelião *f*, sublevação *f*

uproar ['ʌprɔː*] *n* tumulto, algazarra

uproot [ʌp'ruːt] *vt* (*tree*) arrancar; (*fig*) desarraigar

upset [*n* 'ʌpsɛt, *vt, adj* ʌp'sɛt] (*irreg: like* **set**) *n* (*to plan etc*) revés *m*, reviravolta; (*stomach*) ~ indisposição *f* ♦ *vt* (*glass etc*) virar; (*plan*) perturbar; (*person: annoy*) aborrecer ♦ *adj* (*sad*) aflito; (*stomach*) indisposto

upshot ['ʌpʃɒt] *n* resultado, conclusão *f*

upside down ['ʌpsaɪd-] *adv* de cabeça para baixo; **to turn a place** ~ (*fig*) deixar um lugar de cabeça para baixo

upstairs [ʌp'stɛəz] *adv* (*be*) em cima; (*go*) lá em cima ♦ *adj* (*room*) de cima ♦ *n* andar *m* de cima

upstart ['ʌpstɑːt] (*pej*) *n* novo-rico, pessoa sem classe

upstream [ʌp'striːm] *adv* rio acima

uptake ['ʌpteɪk] *n*: **he is quick on the ~** ele vê longe; **he is slow on the ~** ele tem raciocínio lento

uptight [ʌp'taɪt] (*inf*) *adj* nervoso

up-to-date *adj* (*person*) moderno, atualizado; (*information*) atualizado

upturn ['ʌptɜːn] *n* (*in luck*) virada; (*in economy*) retomada

upward ['ʌpwəd] *adj* ascendente, para cima; ~(**s**) *adv* para cima; (*more than*): ~(**s**) **of** para cima de

urban ['ɜːbən] *adj* urbano, da cidade

urbane [ɜː'beɪn] *adj* gentil, urbano

urchin ['ɜːtʃɪn] (*pej*) *n* moleque *m*, criança maltrapilha

urge [ɜːdʒ] *n* desejo ♦ *vt*: **to ~ sb to do sth** incitar alguém a fazer algo

urgent ['ɜːdʒənt] *adj* urgente; (*tone, plea*) insistente

urinal ['juərɪnl] (*BRIT*) *n* (*vessel*) urinol *m*; (*building*) mictório

urinate ['juərɪneɪt] *vi* urinar, mijar

urine ['juərɪn] *n* urina

urn [ɜːn] *n* urna; (*also*: **tea ~**) samovar *m*

Uruguay ['juərəgwaɪ] *n* Uruguai *m*

us [ʌs] *pron* nos; (*after prep*) nós; *see also* **me**

US(A) *n abbr* (= *United States (of America)*) EUA *mpl*

usage ['juːzɪdʒ] *n* uso

use [*n* juːs, *vt* juːz] *n* uso, emprego; (*usefulness*) utilidade *f* ♦ *vt* usar, utilizar; (*phrase*) empregar; **in ~** em uso; **out of ~** fora de uso; **to be of ~** ser útil; **it's no ~** (*pointless*) é inútil; (*not useful*) não serve; **to be ~d to** estar acostumado a; **she ~d to do it** ela costumava fazê-lo; **~ up** *vt* esgotar, consumir; (*money*) gastar; **~d** *adj* usado; **~ful** *adj* útil; **~fulness** *n* utilidade *f*; **~less** *adj* inútil; (*person*) incapaz; **~r** *n* usuário/a (*BR*), utente *m/f* (*PT*); **~r-friendly** *adj* de fácil utilização

usher ['ʌʃə*] *n* (*at wedding*) oficial *m* de justiça; **~ette** *n* (*in cinema*) lanterninha (*BR*), arrumadora (*PT*)

USSR *n abbr* (= *Union of Soviet Socialist Republics*) URSS *f*

usual ['juːʒuəl] *adj* usual, habitual; **as ~** como de hábito, como sempre; **~ly** *adv* normalmente

utensil [juː'tɛnsl] *n* utensílio

utility [juː'tɪlɪtɪ] *n* utilidade *f*; (*public ~*) utilidade pública; **~ room** *n* área de serviço

utmost ['ʌtməʊst] *adj* maior ♦ *n*: **to do one's ~** fazer todo o possível

utter ['ʌtə*] *adj* total ♦ *vt* (*sounds*) emitir; (*words*) proferir, pronunciar; **~ance** *n* declaração *f*; **~ly** *adv* completamente, totalmente

U-turn *n* retorno

V

v *abbr* = **verse**; (= *vide: see*) vide; (= *versus*) x; (= *volt*) v

vacancy ['veɪkənsɪ] *n* (*BRIT*: *job*) vaga; (*room*) quarto livre

vacant ['veɪkənt] *adj* desocupado, livre; (*expression*) distraído; **~ lot** *n* terreno vago; (*uncultivated*) terreno baldio

vacate [və'keɪt] *vt* (*house*) desocupar; (*job*) deixar

vacation [və'keɪʃən] (*esp US*) *n* férias *fpl*

vaccinate ['væksɪneɪt] *vt* vacinar

vacuum ['vækjum] *n* vácuo *m*; **~ cleaner** *n* aspirador *m* de pó

vagina [və'dʒaɪnə] *n* vagina

vagrant ['veɪgrənt] *n* vagabundo/a, vadio/a

vague [veɪg] *adj* vago; (*blurred: memory*) fraco; **~ly** *adv* vagamente

vain [veɪn] *adj* vaidoso; (*useless*) vão/vã, inútil; **in ~** em vão

valentine ['væləntaɪn] *n* (*also*: **~ card**) cartão *m* do Dia dos Namorados; (*person*) namorado

valet ['væleɪ] *n* criado pessoal; (*in hotel*) camareiro

valiant ['væliənt] *adj* corajoso

valid ['vælɪd] *adj* válido

valley ['vælɪ] *n* vale *m*

valour ['vælə*] (*US* **valor**) *n* valor *m*, valentia

valuable ['væljuəbl] *adj* (*jewel*) de valor; (*time*) valioso; (*help*) precioso; **~s** *npl* objetos *mpl* de valor

valuation [vælju'eɪʃən] *n* avaliação *f*; (*of quality*) apreciação *f*

value ['væljuː] *n* valor *m*; (*importance*) importância ♦ *vt* (*fix price of*) avaliar; (*appreciate*) valorizar, estimar; **~s** *npl* (*principles*) valores *mpl*; **~ added tax** (*BRIT*) *n* imposto sobre a circulação de mercadorias (*BR*), imposto sobre valor acrescentado (*PT*); **~d** *adj* (*appreciated*) valorizado

valve [vælv] *n* válvula

van [væn] *n* (*AUT*) camionete *f* (*BR*), camioneta (*PT*)

vandal ['vændl] *n* vândalo/a; **~ize** *vt* destruir, depredar

vanguard ['vænguːd] *n*: **in the ~ of** na vanguarda da

vanilla [və'nɪlə] *n* baunilha

vanish ['vænɪʃ] *vi* desaparecer, sumir

vanity ['vænɪtɪ] *n* vaidade *f*

vantage point ['vɑːntɪdʒ-] *n* posição *f* estratégica

vapour ['veɪpə*] (*US* **vapor**) *n* vapor *m*

variance ['veərɪəns] *n*: **to be at ~ (with)** estar em desacordo (com)

variation [veərɪ'eɪʃən] *n* variação *f*; (*variant*) variante *f*

varicose ['værɪkəʊs] *adj*: **~ veins** varizes

fpl

variety [vəˈraɪətɪ] *n* variedade *f*, diversidade *f*; (*type, quantity*) variedade; ~ **show** *n* espetáculo de variedades

various [ˈvɛərɪəs] *adj* vários/as, diversos/as; (*several*) vários/as

varnish [ˈvɑːnɪʃ] *n* verniz *m*; (*nail* ~) esmalte *m* ♦ *vt* envernizar, pintar (com esmalte)

vary [ˈvɛərɪ] *vt* mudar ♦ *vi* variar; (*become different*): **to** ~ **with** variar de acordo com

vase [vɑːz] *n* vaso

vaseline [ˈvæsɪliːn] ® *n* vaselina ®

vast [vɑːst] *adj* enorme

VAT [væt] (*BRIT*) *n abbr* (= *value added tax*) ≈ ICM *m* (*BR*), IVA *m* (*PT*)

vat [væt] *n* tina, cuba

Vatican [ˈvætɪkən] *n*: **the** ~ o Vaticano

vault [vɔːlt] *n* (*of roof*) abóbada; (*tomb*) sepulcro; (*in bank*) caixa-forte *f* ♦ *vt* (*also*: ~ **over**) saltar (por cima de)

vaunted [ˈvɔːntɪd] *adj*: **much**-~ tão alardeado

VCR *n abbr* = **video cassette recorder**

VD *n abbr* = **venereal disease**

VDU *n abbr* = **visual display unit**

veal [viːl] *n* carne *f* de vitela

veer [vɪə*] *vi* virar

vegetable [ˈvɛdʒtəbl] *n* (*BOT*) vegetal *m*; (*edible plant*) legume *m*, hortaliça ♦ *adj* vegetal

vegetarian [vɛdʒɪˈtɛərɪən] *adj*, *n* vegetariano/a

vehement [ˈviːmənt] *adj* veemente; (*attack*) violento

vehicle [ˈviːɪkl] *n* veículo

veil [veɪl] *n* véu *m* ♦ *vt* velar

vein [veɪn] *n* veia; (*of ore etc*) filão *m*; (*on leaf*) nervura

velvet [ˈvɛlvɪt] *n* veludo ♦ *adj* aveludado

vending machine [ˈvɛndɪŋ-] *n* vendedor *m* automático

vendor [ˈvɛndɔ*] *n* vendedor(a) *m/f*

veneer [vəˈnɪə*] *n* (*wood*) compensado; (*fig*) aparência

venereal [vɪˈnɪərɪəl] *adj*: ~ **disease** doença venérea

Venetian blind [vɪˈniːʃən-] *n* persiana

Venezuela [vɛnɛˈzweɪlə] *n* Venezuela

vengeance [ˈvɛndʒəns] *n* vingança; **with a** ~ (*fig*) para valer

venison [ˈvɛnɪsn] *n* carne *f* de veado

venom [ˈvɛnəm] *n* veneno; (*bitterness*) malevolência; ~**ous** *adj* venenoso; (*look, stare*) malévolo

vent [vɛnt] *n*. (*in jacket*) abertura; (*also*: **air** ~) respiradouro ♦ *vt* (*fig: feelings*) desabafar, descarregar

ventilate [ˈvɛntɪleɪt] *vt* ventilar

ventriloquist [vɛnˈtrɪləkwɪst] *n* ventríloquo

venture [ˈvɛntʃə*] *n* empreendimento ♦ *vt* (*opinion*) arriscar ♦ *vi* arriscar-se; **business** ~ empreendimento comercial

venue [ˈvɛnjuː] *n* local *m*

verb [vɜːb] *n* verbo

verbatim [vɜːˈbeɪtɪm] *adj*, *adv* palavra por palavra

verbose [vɜːˈbəus] *adj* prolixo

verdict [ˈvɜːdɪkt] *n* veredicto, decisão *f*; (*fig*) opinião *f*, parecer *m*

verge [vɜːdʒ] *n* beira, margem *f*; (*on road*) acostamento (*BR*), berma (*PT*); **"soft** ~**s"** (*BRIT*: *AUT*) "acostamento mole"; **to be on the** ~ **of doing sth** estar a ponto *or* à beira de fazer algo; ~ **on** *vt fus* beirar em

veritable [ˈvɛrɪtəbl] *adj* verdadeiro

vermin [ˈvɜːmɪn] *npl* (*animals*) bichos *mpl*; (*insects*) insetos *mpl* nocivos

vermouth [ˈvɜːməθ] *n* vermute *m*

versatile [ˈvɜːsətaɪl] *adj* (*person*) versátil; (*machine, tool etc*) polivalente

verse [vɜːs] *n* verso, poesia; (*stanza*) estrofe *f*; (*in bible*) versículo

versed [vɜːst] *adj*: (**well**-)~ **in** versado em

version [ˈvɜːʃən] *n* versão *f*

versus [ˈvɜːsəs] *prep* contra, versus

vertical [ˈvɜːtɪkl] *adj* vertical

vertigo [ˈvɜːtɪɡəu] *n* vertigem *f*

verve [vɜːv] *n* garra, pique *m*

very [ˈvɛrɪ] *adv* muito ♦ *adj*: **the** ~ **book which** o mesmo livro que; **the** ~ **last** o último (de todos), bem o último; **at the** ~ **least** no mínimo; ~ **much** muitíssimo

vessel [ˈvɛsl] *n* (*NAUT*) navio, barco; (*container*) vaso, vasilha

vest [vɛst] *n* (*BRIT*) camiseta (*BR*), camisola interior (*PT*); (*US*: *waistcoat*) colete *m*

vested interests [ˈvɛstɪd-] *npl* (*COMM*) direitos *mpl* adquiridos

vet [vɛt] *n abbr* (= *veterinary surgeon*) veterinário/a ♦ *vt* examinar

veteran [ˈvɛtərn] *n* (*also*: **war** ~) veterano de guerra

veterinary [ˈvɛtrɪnərɪ] *adj* veterinário; ~ **surgeon** *n* veterinário/a

veto [ˈviːtəu] *n* (*pl* ~**es**) *n* veto ♦ *vt* vetar

vex [vɛks] *vt* irritar, apoquentar; ~**ed** *adj* (*question*) controvertido, discutido

via [ˈvaɪə] *prep* por, via

vibrant [ˈvaɪbrənt] *adj* (*lively*) entusiasmado; (*colour*) vibrante; (*voice*) ressonante

vibrate [vaɪˈbreɪt] *vi* vibrar

vicar [ˈvɪkə*] *n* vigário; ~**age** *n* vicariato

vicarious [vɪˈkɛərɪəs] *adj* indireto

vice [vaɪs] *n* (*evil*) vício; (*TECH*) torno mecânico

vice- [vaɪs] *prefix* vice-

vice squad *n* delegacia de costumes

vice versa [ˈvaɪsɪˈvɜːsə] *adv* vice-versa

vicinity [vɪˈsɪnɪtɪ] *n*: **in the** ~ **of** nas proximidades de

vicious [ˈvɪʃəs] *adj* violento; (*cruel*) cruel; ~ **circle** *n* círculo vicioso

victim ['vɪktɪm] *n* vítima *f*; ~**ize** *vt* fazer represália contra

victor ['vɪktə*] *n* vencedor(a) *m/f*

Victorian [vɪk'tɔːrɪən] *adj* vitoriano

victory ['vɪktərɪ] *n* vitória *f*

video ['vɪdɪəʊ] *n* (~ *film*) vídeo; (*also*: ~ **cassette**) videocassete *m*; (*also*: ~ **cassette recorder**) videocassete *m*; ~ **tape** *n* videoteipe *m*; (*cassette*) videocassete *m*

vie [vaɪ] *vi*: to ~ (**with sb**) (**for sth**) competir (com alguém) (por algo)

Vienna [vɪ'ɛnə] *n* Viena *f*

Vietnam ['vjɛt'næm] *n* Vietnã *m*; ~**ese** *adj* vietnamita *f* ♦ *n inv* vietnamita *m/f*; (*LING*) vietnamita *m*

view [vjuː] *n* vista; (*outlook*) perspectiva; (*opinion*) opinião *f*, parecer *m* ♦ *vt* olhar; **in full** ~ (**of**) à plena vista (de); **in my** ~ na minha opinião; **in** ~ **of the weather/the fact that** em vista do tempo/do fato de que; ~**er** *n* telespectador(a) *m/f*; ~**finder** *n* visor *m*; ~**point** *n* ponto de vista; (*place*) lugar *m*

vigil ['vɪdʒɪl] *n* vigília

vigorous ['vɪgərəs] *adj* vigoroso; (*plant*) vigoso

vigour ['vɪgə*] (*US* **vigor**) *n* energia, vigor *m*

vile [vaɪl] *adj* vil, infame; (*smell*) repugnante, repulsivo; (*temper*) violento

villa ['vɪlə] *n* (*country house*) casa de campo; (*suburban house*) vila, quinta

village ['vɪlɪdʒ] *n* aldeia, povoado; ~**r** *n* aldeão/aldeã *m/f*

villain ['vɪlən] *n* (*scoundrel*) patife *m*; (*in novel etc*) vilão *m*; (*BRIT*: *criminal*) marginal *m/f*

vindicate ['vɪndɪkeɪt] *vt* vingar; (*justify*) justificar

vindictive [vɪn'dɪktɪv] *adj* vingativo

vine [vaɪn] *n* planta trepadeira

vinegar ['vɪnɪgə*] *n* vinagre *m*

vineyard ['vɪnjɑːd] *n* vinha, vinhedo

vintage ['vɪntɪdʒ] *n* vindima; (*year*) safra, colheita ♦ *cpd* (*comedy*) de época; (*performance*) clássico; **the 1970** ~ a safra de 1970; ~ **car** *n* carro antigo; ~ **wine** *n* vinho velho

vinyl ['vaɪnl] *n* vinil *m*

viola [vɪ'əʊlə] *n* viola

violate ['vaɪəleɪt] *vt* violar

violence ['vaɪələns] *n* violência; (*strength*) força

violent ['vaɪələnt] *adj* violento; (*intense*) intenso

violet ['vaɪələt] *adj* violeta ♦ *n* violeta

violin [vaɪə'lɪn] *n* violino; ~**ist** *n* violinista *m/f*

VIP *n abbr* (= *very important person*) VIP *m/f*

viper ['vaɪpə*] *n* víbora

virgin ['vɜːdʒɪn] *n* virgem *m/f* ♦ *adj* virgem; ~**ity** *n* virgindade *f*

Virgo ['vɜːgəʊ] *n* Virgem *f*

virtually ['vɜːtjʊəlɪ] *adv* praticamente

virtue ['vɜːtjuː] *n* virtude *f*; (*advantage*) vantagem *f*; **by** ~ **of** em virtude de

virtuous ['vɜːtjuəs] *adj* virtuoso

virus ['vaɪərəs] *n* vírus *m*

visa ['viːzə] *n* visto

vis-à-vis [viːzə'viː] *prep* com relação a

visible ['vɪzəbl] *adj* visível

vision ['vɪʒən] *n* (*sight*) vista, visão *f*; (*foresight, in dream*) visão *f*

visit ['vɪzɪt] *n* visita ♦ *vt* (*person*: *US*: *also*: ~ **with**) visitar, fazer uma visita a; (*place*) ir a; ~**ing hours** *npl* horário de visita; ~**or** *n* visitante *m/f*; (*to one's house*) visita; (*tourist*) turista *m/f*

visor ['vaɪzə*] *n* viseira

visual ['vɪzjuəl] *adj* visual; ~ **aid** *n* recurso visual; ~ **display unit** *n* terminal *m* de vídeo; ~**ize** *vt* visualizar

vital [vaɪtl] *adj* essencial, indispensável; (*important*) de importância vital; (*crucial*) crucial; (*person*) vivo; (*of life*) vital; ~**ly** *adv*: ~**ly important de** importância vital; ~ **statistics** *npl* (*fig*) medidas *fpl*

vitamin ['vɪtəmɪn] *n* vitamina

vivacious [vɪ'veɪʃəs] *adj* vivaz, animado

vivid ['vɪvɪd] *adj* vívido; (*light*) claro, brilhante; (*imagination, colour*) vivo; ~**ly** *adv* vividamente; (*remember*) distintamente

V-neck *n*: ~ **jumper**, ~ **pullover** suéter *f* com decote em V

vocabulary [vəʊ'kæbjʊlərɪ] *n* vocabulário

vocal ['vəʊkl] *adj* vocal; (*noisy*) clamoroso; (*articulate*) claro, eloqüente; ~ **cords** *npl* cordas *fpl* vocais

vocation [vəʊ'keɪʃən] *n* vocação *f*; ~**al** *adj*: ~**al guidance/training** orientação *f* vocacional/ensino profissionalizante

vociferous [və'sɪfərəs] *adj* vociferante

vodka ['vɒdkə] *n* vodca

vogue [vəʊg] *n* voga, moda; **to be in** ~ estar na moda

voice [vɔɪs] *n* voz *f* ♦ *vt* expressar; ~ **mail** *n* correio de voz

void [vɔɪd] *n* vazio; (*hole*) oco ♦ *adj* nulo; (*empty*): ~ **of** destituído de

volatile ['vɒlətaɪl] *adj* volátil; (*situation, person*) imprevisível

volcano [vɒl'keɪnəʊ] (*pl* ~**es**) *n* vulcão *m*

volition [və'lɪʃən] *n*: **of one's own** ~ de livre vontade

volley ['vɒlɪ] *n* (*of gunfire*) descarga, salva; (*of stones etc*) chuva; (*of questions etc*) enxurrada, chuva; (*TENNIS etc*) voleio; ~**ball** *n* voleibol *m*, vôlei *m* (*BR*)

volt [vəʊlt] *n* volt *m*

voluble ['vɒljubl] *adj* (*person*) tagarela; (*speech*) loquaz

volume ['vɒljuːm] *n* volume *m*; (*of tank*) capacidade *f*

voluntarily ['vɒləntrɪlɪ] *adv* livremente, voluntariamente

voluntary ['vɒləntərɪ] *adj* voluntário; (*unpaid*) (a título) gratuito

volunteer [vɔlən'tɪə*] *n* voluntário/a ♦ *vt* oferecer voluntariamente ♦ *vi* (MIL) alistar-se voluntariamente; **to ~ to do** oferecer-se voluntariamente para fazer

vomit ['vɔmɪt] *n* vômito ♦ *vt, vi* vomitar

vote [vəut] *n* voto; (votes cast) votação *f*; (right to ~) direito de votar ♦ *vt*: **to be ~d chairman etc** ser eleito presidente etc; (propose): **to ~ that** propor que; (in election) votar ♦ *vi* votar; **~ of thanks** *n* agradecimento; **~r** *n* votante *m/f*, eleitor(a) *m/f*; **voting** *n* votação *f*

voucher ['vautʃə*] *n* (also: **luncheon ~**) vale-refeição *m*; (with petrol etc) vale *m*; (gift ~) vale *m* para presente

vouch for [vautʃ-] *vt fus* garantir, responder por

vow [vau] *n* voto ♦ *vt*: **to ~ to do/that** prometer solenemente fazer/que

vowel ['vauəl] *n* vogal *f*

voyage ['vɔɪdʒ] *n* viagem *f*

V-sign (BRIT) *n* gesto grosseiro; **to give a ~ to sb** ≈ dar uma banana para alguém

vulgar ['vʌlgə*] *adj* grosseiro, ordinário; (in bad taste) vulgar, baixo

vulture ['vʌltʃə*] *n* abutre *m*, urubu *m*

W

wad [wɔd] *n* (of cotton wool) chumaço; (of paper) bola; (of banknotes etc) maço

waddle ['wɔdl] *vi* andar gingando *or* bamboleando

wade [weɪd] *vi*: **to ~ through** andar em; (fig: a book) ler com dificuldade

wafer ['weɪfə*] *n* (biscuit) bolacha

waffle ['wɔfl] *n* (CULIN) waffle *m*; (empty talk) lengalenga ♦ *vi* encher linguiça

waft [wɔft] *vt* levar ♦ *vi* flutuar

wag [wæg] *vt* (tail) sacudir; (finger) menear ♦ *vi* abanar

wage [weɪdʒ] *n* (also: **~s**) salário, ordenado ♦ *vt*: **to ~ war** empreender *or* fazer guerra; **~ earner** *n* assalariado/a; **~ packet** (BRIT) *n* envelope *m* de pagamento

wager ['weɪdʒə*] *n* aposta, parada

waggle ['wægl] *vt* mover

wag(g)on ['wægən] *n* (horse-drawn) carroça; (BRIT: RAIL) vagão *m*

wail [weɪl] *n* lamento, gemido ♦ *vi* lamentar-se, gemer; (siren) tocar

waist [weɪst] *n* cintura; **~coat** *n* colete *m*; **~line** *n* cintura

wait [weɪt] *n* espera ♦ *vi* esperar; **I can't ~ to** (fig) estou morrendo de vontade de; **to ~ for sb/sth** esperar por alguém/algo; **~ behind** *vi* ficar para trás; **~ on** *vt fus* servir; **~er** *n* garçom *m* (BR), empregado (PT); **~ing** *n*: **"no ~ing"** (BRIT: AUT) "proibido estacionar"; **~ing list** *n* lista de espera; **~ing room** *n* sala de espera; **~ress** *n* garçonete *f*

(BR), empregada (PT)

waive [weɪv] *vt* abrir mão de

wake [weɪk] (pt woke *or* ~d, pp woken *or* ~d) *vt* (also: ~ up) acordar ♦ *vi* acordar ♦ *n* (for dead person) velório; (NAUT) esteira; **~n** *vt, vi* = **wake**

Wales [weɪlz] *n* País *m* de Gales

walk [wɔːk] *n* passeio; (hike) excursão *f* a pé, caminhada; (gait) passo, modo de andar; (in park etc) alameda, passeio ♦ *vi* andar; (for pleasure, exercise) passear ♦ *vt* (distance) percorrer a pé, andar; (dog) levar para passear; **it's 10 minutes' ~ from here** daqui são 10 minutos a pé; **people from all ~s of life** pessoas de todos os níveis; **~ out** *vi* sair; (audience) retirar-se (em protesto); (strike) entrar em greve; **~ out on** *vt fus* abandonar; **~er** *n* (person) caminhante *m/f*; **~ie-talkie** *n* transmissor-receptor *m* portátil, walkie-talkie *m*; **~ing** *n* o andar; **~ing shoes** *npl* sapatos *mpl* para caminhar; **~ing stick** *n* bengala; **~out** *n* (of workers) greve *f* branca; **~over** (inf) *n* barbada; **~way** *n* passeio, passadiço

wall [wɔːl] *n* parede *f*; (exterior) muro; (city ~ etc) muralha; **~ed** *adj* (city) cercado por muralhas; (garden) murado, cercado

wallet ['wɔlɪt] *n* carteira

wallflower ['wɔːlflauə*] *n* goivo-amarelo; **to be a ~** (fig) tomar chá de cadeira

wallop ['wɔləp] (BRIT: inf) *vt* surrar, espancar

wallow ['wɔləu] *vi* (in mud) chafurdar; (in water) rolar; (person: in guilt) regalar-se

wallpaper ['wɔːlpeɪpə*] *n* papel *m* de parede ♦ *vt* colocar papel de parede em

wally ['wɔlɪ] (inf) *n* mané *m*, boboca *m*

walnut ['wɔːlnʌt] *n* noz *f*; (tree, wood) nogueira

walrus ['wɔːlrəs] (pl inv *or* ~es) *n* morsa, vaca marinha

waltz [wɔːlts] *n* valsa ♦ *vi* valsar

wan [wɔn] *adj* pálido; (smile) amarelo

wand [wɔnd] *n* (also: **magic ~**) varinha de condão

wander ['wɔndə*] *vi* (person) vagar, perambular; (thoughts) divagar ♦ *vt* perambular

wane [weɪn] *vi* diminuir; (moon) minguar

wangle ['wæŋgl] (BRIT: inf) *vt*: **to ~ sth** conseguir algo através de pistolão

want [wɔnt] *vt* querer; (demand) exigir; (need) precisar de, necessitar; **~s** *npl* (needs) necessidades *fpl*; **to ~ sb to do sth** querer que alguém faça algo; **~ed** *adj* (criminal etc) procurado (pela polícia); **"cook ~ed"** (in advertisement) "precisa-se cozinheiro"; **~ing** *adj*: **to be found ~ing** não estar à altura da situação

wanton ['wɒntən] *adj* gratuito, irresponsável; (*licentious*) libertino, lascivo

war [wɔːʳ] *n* guerra; **to make ~ (on)** fazer guerra (contra)

ward [wɔːd] *n* (*in hospital*) ala; (*POL*) distrito eleitoral; (*LAW*: *child*) tutelado/a, pupilo/a; ~ **off** *vt* desviar, aparar; (*attack*) repelir

warden ['wɔːdn] *n* (*BRIT*: *of institution*) diretor(a) *m/f*; (*of park, youth hostel*) administrador(a) *m/f*; (*BRIT*: *also*: **traffic ~**) guarda *m/f*

warder ['wɔːdəʳ] (*BRIT*) *n* carcereiro/a

wardrobe ['wɔːdrəub] *n* guarda-roupa *m*; (*CINEMA, THEATRE*) figurinos *mpl*

warehouse ['wɛəhaus] *n* armazém *m*, depósito

wares [wɛəz] *npl* mercadorias *fpl*

warfare ['wɔːfɛəʳ] *n* guerra, combate *m*

warhead ['wɔːhɛd] *n* ogiva

warily ['wɛərɪlɪ] *adv* cautelosamente, com precaução

warlike ['wɔːlaɪk] *adj* (*nation*) guerreiro, bélico; (*appearance*) belicoso

warm [wɔːm] *adj* quente; (*thanks, welcome*) caloroso; **it's ~** está quente; **I'm ~** estou com calor; ~ **up** *vt, vi* esquentar; **~-hearted** *adj* afetuoso; **~ly** *adv* (*applaud, welcome*) calorosamente; (*dress*): **to dress ~ly** vestir-se com roupas de inverno; **~th** *n* calor *m*; (*friendliness*) calor humano

warn [wɔːn] *vt* prevenir, avisar; **to ~ sb that/of/(not) to do** prevenir alguém de que/de/para (não) fazer

warning ['wɔːnɪŋ] *n* advertência; (*in writing*) aviso; (*signal*) sinal *m*

warp [wɔːp] *vt* deformar ♦ *vi* empenar, deformar-se

warrant ['wɒrnt] *n* (*voucher*) comprovante *m*; (*LAW*: *to arrest*) mandado de prisão; (: *to search*) mandado de busca; **~y** *n* garantia

warren ['wɒrən] *n* (*of rabbits*) lura; (*fig*) labirinto

warrior ['wɒrɪəʳ] *n* guerreiro/a

Warsaw ['wɔːsɔː] *n* Varsóvia

warship ['wɔːʃɪp] *n* navio de guerra

wart [wɔːt] *n* verruga

wartime ['wɔːtaɪm] *n*: **in ~** em tempo de guerra

wary ['wɛərɪ] *adj* cauteloso, precavido

was [wɒz] *pt of* **be**

wash [wɒʃ] *vt* lavar ♦ *vi* lavar-se; (*subj*: ~*ing machine*) lavar; (*sea etc*): **to ~ over/against sth** bater contra/chocar-se contra algo; (*clothes*): **this shirt ~es well** esta camisa resiste bem à lavagem ♦ *n* (*clothes etc*) lavagem *f*; (~*ing programme*) programa *m* de lavagem; (*of ship*) esteira; **to have a ~** lavar-se; ~ **away** *vt* (*stain*) tirar ao lavar; (*subj*: *river etc*) levar, arrastar; ~ **off** *vt* tirar lavando ♦ *vi* sair ao lavar; ~ **up** *vi* (*BRIT*) lavar a louça; (*US*) lavar-se; **~ba-**

sin *n* pia (*BR*), lavatório (*PT*); **~cloth** (*US*) *n* toalhinha para lavar o rosto; **~er** *n* (*TECH*) arruela, anilha; **~ing** *n* (*dirty*) roupa suja; (*clean*) roupa lavada; **~ing machine** *n* máquina de lavar roupa, lavadora; **~ing powder** (*BRIT*) *n* sabão *m* em pó; **~ing-up** *n*: **to do the ~ing-up** lavar a louça; **~ing-up liquid** *n* detergente *m*; **~-out** (*inf*) *n* fracasso, fiasco; **~room** (*US*) *n* banheiro (*BR*), casa de banho (*PT*

wasn't ['wɒznt] = **was not**

wasp [wɒsp] *n* vespa

wastage ['weɪstɪdʒ] *n* desgaste *m*, desperdício; (*loss*) perda

waste [weɪst] *n* desperdício, esbanjamento; (*of time*) perda; (*also*: **household ~**) detritos *mpl* domésticos; (*rubbish*) lixo ♦ *adj* (*material*) de refugo; (*left over*) de sobra; (*land*) baldio ♦ *vt* (*squander*) esbanjar, desperdiçar; (*time, opportunity*) perder; ~**s** *npl* (*land*) ermos *mpl*; **to lay ~ devastar**; ~ **away** *vi* definhar; ~ **disposal (unit)** (*BRIT*) *n* triturador *m* de lixo; **~ful** *adj* esbanjador(a); (*process*) anti-econômico; ~ **ground** (*BRIT*) *n* terreno baldio; **~paper basket** *n* cesta de papéis; ~ **pipe** *n* cano de esgoto

watch [wɒtʃ] *n* (*clock*) relógio; (*also*: **wrist~**) relógio de pulso; (*act of* ~*ing*) vigia; (*guard*: *MIL*) sentinela; (*NAUT*: *spell of duty*) quarto ♦ *vt* (*look at*) observar, olhar; (*programme, match*) assistir a; (*television*) ver; (*spy on, guard*) vigiar; (*be careful of*) tomar cuidado com ♦ *vi* ver, olhar; (*keep guard*) montar guarda; ~ **out** *vi* ter cuidado; **~dog** *n* cão *m* de guarda; (*fig*) vigia *m/f*; **~ful** *adj* vigilante, atento; **~maker** *n* relojoeiro/a; **~man** (*irreg*) *n* *see* **night**; **~strap** *n* pulseira de relógio

water ['wɔːtəʳ] *n* água ♦ *vt* (*plant*) regar ♦ *vi* (*eyes*) lacrimejar; (*mouth*) salivar; **in British ~s** nas águas territoriais britânicas; ~ **down** *vt* (*milk*) aguar; (*fig*) diluir; ~ **cannon** *n* tanque de espirrar água para dispersar multidões; ~ **closet** (*BRIT*) *n* privada; **~colour** (*US* **~color**) *n* aquarela; **~cress** *n* agrião *m*; **~fall** *n* cascata, cachoeira; ~ **heater** *n* aquecedor *m* de água, boiler *m*; **~ing can** *n* regador *m*; ~ **level** *n* nível *m* d'água; ~ **lily** *n* nenúfar *m*; **~line** *n* (*NAUT*) linha d'água; **~logged** *adj* alagado; ~ **main** *n* adutora; **~melon** *n* melancia; **~proof** *adj* impermeável; **~shed** *n* (*GEO*) linha divisória das águas; (*fig*) momento crítico; **~-skiing** *n* esqui *m* aquático; **~tight** *adj* hermético, à prova d'água; **~way** *n* hidrovia; **~works** *npl* usina hidráulica; **~y** *adj* (*eyes*) úmido

watt [wɒt] *n* watt *m*

wave [weɪv] *n* (*of hand*) aceno, sinal *m*; (*in hair*) onda, ondulação *f* ♦ *vi* acenar com a mão; (flag, grass) tremular ♦ vt (hand) acenar; (handkerchief) acenar com; (weapon) brandir; ~**length** n comprimento de onda; **to be on the same ~length as** ter os mesmos gostos e atitudes que

waver ['weɪvə*] vi vacilar; (voice, eyes, love) hesitar

wavy ['weɪvɪ] adj (hair) ondulado; (line) ondulante

wax [wæks] n cera ♦ vt encerar; (car) polir ♦ vi (moon) crescer; ~**works** n museu m de cera ♦ npl (models) figuras fpl de cera

way [weɪ] n caminho; (distance) percurso; (direction) direção f, sentido; (manner) maneira, modo; (habit) costume m; **which ~? - this ~** por onde? - por aqui; **on the ~ (to)** a caminho (de); **to be on one's ~** estar a caminho; **to be in the ~** atrapalhar; **to go out of one's ~ to do sth** dar-se ao trabalho de fazer algo; **to lose one's ~** perder-se; **to be under ~** estar em andamento; **in a ~** de certo modo, até certo ponto; **in some ~s** a certos respeitos; **by the ~** a propósito; "**~ in**" (BRIT) "entrada"; "**~ out**" (BRIT) "saída"; **the ~ back** o caminho de volta; "**give ~**" (BRIT: AUT) "dê a preferência"; **no ~!** (inf) de jeito nenhum!; ~**lay** vt armar uma cilada para; ~**ward** adj caprichoso, voluntarioso

WC ['dʌblju'si:] n abbr (= water closet) privada

we [wi:] pl pron nós

weak [wi:k] adj fraco, débil; (morally, currency) fraco; (excuse) pouco convincente; (tea) aguado, ralo; ~**en** vi enfraquecer(-se); (give way) ceder; (influence, power) diminuir ♦ vt enfraquecer; ~**ling** n pessoa fraca or delicada; (morally) pessoa de personalidade fraca; ~**ness** n fraqueza; (fault) ponto fraco; **to have a ~ness for** ter uma queda por

wealth [wɛlθ] n riqueza; (of details) abundância; ~**y** adj rico, abastado; (country) rico

wean [wi:n] vt desmamar

weapon ['wɛpən] n arma

wear [wɛə*] (pt wore, pp worn) n (use) uso; (deterioration) desgaste m; (clothing): **baby/sports** ~ roupa infantil/de esporte ♦ vt (clothes) usar; (shoes) usar, calçar; (put on) vestir; (damage: through use) desgastar ♦ vi (last) durar; (rub through etc) gastar-se; **town/evening** ~ traje m de passeio/de noite; ~ **away** vt gastar ♦ vi desgastar-se; ~ **down** vt gastar; (strength) esgotar; ~ **off** vi (pain etc) passar; ~ **out** vt desgastar; (person, strength) esgotar; ~ **and tear** n desgaste m

weary ['wɪərɪ] adj cansado; (dispirited)

deprimido ♦ vi: **to ~ of** cansar-se de

weasel ['wi:zl] n (ZOOL) doninha

weather ['wɛðə*] n tempo ♦ vt (storm, crisis) resistir a; **under the ~** (fig: ill) doente; ~-**beaten** adj curtido; (building, stone) castigado, erodido; ~**cock** n cata-vento; ~ **forecast** n previsão f do tempo; ~**man** (irreg: inf) n meteorologista m; ~ **vane** n = ~**cock**

weave [wi:v] (pt wove, pp woven) vt tecer; ~**r** n tecelão/loa m/f; **weaving** n tecelagem f

web [wɛb] n (of spider) teia; (on foot) membrana; (network) rede f; **the (World Wide) W~** a Web

website ['wɛbsaɪt] n (COMPUT) site m

wed [wɛd] (pt, pp ~**ded**) vt casar ♦ vi casar-se

we'd [wi:d] = **we had; we would**

wedding ['wɛdɪŋ] n casamento, núpcias fpl; **silver/golden** ~ (anniversary) bodas fpl de prata/de ouro; ~ **day** n dia m de casamento; ~ **dress** n vestido de noiva; ~ **ring** n aliança

wedge [wɛdʒ] n (of wood etc) cunha, calço; (of cake) fatia ♦ vt (pack tightly) apinhar; (door) pôr calço em

Wednesday ['wɛnzdɪ] n quarta-feira

wee [wi:] (SCOTTISH) adj pequeno

weed [wi:d] n erva daninha ♦ vt capinar; ~**killer** n herbicida m; ~**y** adj (man) fraquinho

week [wi:k] n semana; **a ~ today** daqui a uma semana; **a ~ on Tuesday** sem ser essa terça-feira, a próxima; ~**day** n dia m de semana; (COMM) dia útil; ~**end** n fim m de semana; ~**ly** adv semanalmente ♦ adj semanal ♦ n semanário

weep [wi:p] (pt, pp wept) vi (person) chorar; ~**ing willow** n salgueiro chorão

weigh [weɪ] vt, vi pesar; **to ~ anchor** levantar ferro; ~ **down** vt sobrecarregar; (fig: with worry) deprimir, acabrunhar; ~ **up** vt ponderar, avaliar

weight [weɪt] n peso; **to lose/put on ~** emagrecer/engordar; ~**ing** n (allowance) indenização f de residência; ~**lifter** n levantador m de pesos; ~**y** adj pesado; (matters) importante

weir [wɪə*] n represa, açude m

weird [wɪəd] adj esquisito, estranho

welcome ['wɛlkəm] adj bem-vindo ♦ n acolhimento, recepção f ♦ vt dar as boas-vindas a; (be glad of) saudar; **you're ~** (after thanks) de nada

weld [wɛld] n solda ♦ vt soldar, unir

welfare ['wɛlfɛə*] n bem-estar m; (social aid) assistência social; ~ **state** n país auto-financiador da sua assistência social; ~ **work** n trabalho social

well [wɛl] n poço ♦ adv bem ♦ adj: **to be ~** estar bem (de saúde) ♦ excl bem!, então!; **as** ~ também; **as ~ as** assim como; ~ **done!** muito bem!; **get ~**

soon! melhoras!; **to do ~** ir *or* sair-se bem; (*business*) ir bem; **~ up** *vi* brotar

we'll [wiːl] = we will; we shall

well: **~-behaved** *adj* bem comportado; **~-being** *n* bem-estar *m*; **~-built** *adj* robusto; **~-deserved** *adj* bem merecido; **~-dressed** *adj* bem vestido; **~-heeled** (*inf*) *adj* rico

wellingtons ['wɛlɪŋtənz] *n* (*also:* **wellington boots**) botas de borracha até os joelhos

well: **~-known** *adj* conhecido; **~-mannered** *adj* bem educado; **~-meaning** *adj* bem intencionado; **~-off** *adj* próspero, rico; **~-read** *adj* lido, versado; **~-to-do** *adj* abastado; **~-wisher** *n* simpatizante *m/f*; (*admirer*) admirador(a) *m/f*

Welsh [wɛlʃ] *adj* galês/galesa ♦ *n* (*LING*) galês *m*; **the ~** *npl* (*people*) os galeses; **~man** (*irreg*) *n* galês *m*; **~ rarebit** *n* torradas com queijo derretido; **~woman** (*irreg*) *n* galesa

went [wɛnt] *pt of* go

wept [wɛpt] *pt, pp of* weep

were [wəː*] *pt of* be

we're [wɪə*] = we are

weren't [wəːnt] = were not

west [wɛst] *n* oeste *m* ♦ *adj* ocidental, do oeste ♦ *adv* para o oeste *or* ao oeste; **the W~** (*POL*) o Oeste, o Ocidente; **W~ Country** (*BRIT*) *n*: **the W~ Country** o sudoeste da Inglaterra; **~erly** *adj* (*situation*) ocidental; (*wind*) oeste; **~ern** *adj* ocidental ♦ *n* (*CINEMA*) western *m*, bangue-bangue (*BR*: *inf*); **W~ Germany** *n* Alemanha Ocidental; **W~ Indian** *adj*, *n* antilhano/a; **W~ Indies** *npl* Antilhas *fpl*; **~ward(s)** *adv* para o oeste

wet [wɛt] *adj* molhado; (*damp*) úmido; (*~ through*) encharcado; (*rainy*) chuvoso ♦ *n* (*BRIT*: *POL*) político de tendência moderada; **to get ~** molhar-se; **"~ paint"** "tinta fresca"; **~ blanket** (*pej*) *n* (*fig*) desmancha-prazeres *m/f inv*; **~suit** *n* roupa de mergulho

we've [wiːv] = we have

whack [wæk] *vt* bater

whale [weɪl] *n* (*ZOOL*) baleia

wharf [wɔːf] (*pl* **wharves**) *n* cais *m inv*

wharves [wɔːvz] *npl of* wharf

what [wɔt] *adj* **1** (*in direct/indirect questions*) que, qual; **~ size is it?** que tamanho é este?; **~ colour/shape is it?** qual é a cor/o formato?; **he asked me ~ books I needed** ele me perguntou de quais os livros eu precisava
2 (*in exclamations*) quê!, como!; **~ a mess!** que bagunça!
♦ *pron* **1** (*interrogative*) que, o que; **~ are you doing?** o que você está fazendo?; **~ is it called?** como se chama?; **~ about me?** e eu?; **~ about**

doing que tal fazer ...?
2 (*relative*) o que; **I saw ~ you did/was on the table** eu vi o que você fez/estava na mesa; **he asked me ~ she had said** ele me perguntou o que ela tinha dito
♦ *excl* (*disbelieving*): **~, no coffee!** o que, não tem café!

whatever [wɔtˈɛvə*] *adj*: **~ book** qualquer livro ♦ *pron*: **~ is necessary/you want** faça tudo o que for preciso/o que você quiser; **~ happens** aconteça o que acontecer; **no reason ~ or whatsoever** nenhuma razão seja qual for *or* em absoluto; **nothing ~** nada em absoluto

whatsoever [wɔtsəuˈɛvə*] *adj* = whatever

wheat [wiːt] *n* trigo

wheedle ['wiːdl] *vt*: **to ~ sb into doing sth** persuadir alguém a fazer algo; **to ~ sth out of sb** conseguir algo de alguém por meio de agrados

wheel [wiːl] *n* roda; (*also:* **steering ~**) volante *m*; (*NAUT*) roda do leme ♦ *vt* (*pram etc*) empurrar ♦ *vi* (*birds*) dar voltas; (*also:* **~ round**) girar, dar voltas, virar-se; **~barrow** *n* carrinho de mão; **~chair** *n* cadeira de rodas; **~ clamp** (*AUT*) grampo com que se imobiliza carros estacionados ilegalmente

wheeze [wiːz] *vi* respirar ruidosamente

when [wɛn] *adv* quando
♦ *conj* **1** (*at, during, after the time that*) quando; **~ you've read it, tell me what you think** depois que você tiver lido isto, diga-me o que acha; **that was ~ I needed you** foi quando eu precisei de você
2 (*on, at which*) quando, em que; **on the day ~ I met him** no dia em que o conheci; **one day ~ it was raining** um dia quando estava chovendo
3 (*whereas*) ao passo que; **you said I was wrong ~ in fact I was right** você disse que eu estava errado quando, na verdade, eu estava certo

whenever [wɛnˈɛvə*] *conj* quando, quando quer que; (*every time that*) sempre que ♦ *adv* quando você quiser

where [wɛə*] *adv* onde ♦ *conj* onde, onde; **this is ~ ...** aqui é onde ...; **~abouts** *adv* (por) onde ♦ *n*: **nobody knows his ~abouts** ninguém sabe o seu paradeiro; **~as** *conj* uma vez que, ao passo que; **~by** *adv* (*formal*) pelo qual (*or* pela qual *etc*); **~upon** *adv* depois do que; **~ver** *conj* onde quer que ♦ *adv* (*interrogative*) onde?; **~withal** *n* recursos *mpl*, meios *mpl*

whet [wɛt] *vt* afiar; (*appetite*) abrir

whether ['wɛðə*] *conj* se; **I don't know ~ to accept or not** não sei se aceito ou não; **~ you go or not** quer você vá quer não; **it's doubtful ~ ...** não é certo que ...

KEYWORD

which [wɪtʃ] *adj* **1** (*interrogative: direct, indirect*) que, qual; **~ picture do you want?** que quadro você quer?; **~ books are yours?** quais são os seus livros?; **~ one?** qual?

2: **in ~ case** em cujo caso; **by ~ time** momento em que

♦ *pron* **1** (*interrogative*) qual; **~ (of these) are yours?** quais (destes) são seus?

2 (*relative*) que, o que, o qual *etc*; **the apple ~ you ate** a maçã que você comeu; **the chair on ~ you are sitting** a cadeira na qual você está sentado; **he said he knew, ~ is true** ele disse que sabia, o que é verdade; **after ~** depois do que

---

whichever [wɪtʃ'ɛvə*] *adj*: **take ~ book you prefer** pegue o livro que preferir; **~ book you take** qualquer livro que você pegue

whiff [wɪf] *n* cheiro

while [waɪl] *n* tempo, momento ♦ *conj* enquanto, ao mesmo tempo que; (*as long as*) contanto que; (*although*) embora; **for a ~** durante algum tempo; **~ away** *vt* (*time*) encher

whim [wɪm] *n* capricho, veneta

whimper ['wɪmpə*] *n* (*moan*) lamúria ♦ *vi* choramingar, soluçar

whimsical ['wɪmzɪkl] *adj* (*person*) caprichoso, de veneta; (*look*) excêntrico

whine [waɪn] *n* (*of pain*) gemido; (*of engine, siren*) zunido ♦ *vi* gemer; zunir; (*fig*) lamuriar-se

whip [wɪp] *n* açoite *m*; (*for riding*) chicote *m*; (*POL*) líder *m/f* da bancada ♦ *vt* chicotear; (*snatch*) apanhar de repente; (*cream, eggs*) bater; (*move quickly*): **to ~ sth out/off/away** *etc* arrancar algo; **~ped cream** *n* (creme) chantilly *m*; **~round** (*BRIT*) *n* coleta, vaquinha

whirl [wɜːl] *vt* fazer girar ♦ *vi* (*dancers*) rodopiar; (*leaves, water etc*) redemoinhar; **~pool** *n* remoinho; **~wind** *n* furacão *m*, remoinho

whirr [wɜː*] *vi* zumbir

whisk [wɪsk] *n* (*CULIN*) batedeira ♦ *vt* bater; **to ~ sb away** *or* **off** levar alguém rapidamente

whiskers ['wɪskəz] *npl* (*of animal*) bigodes *mpl*; (*of man*) suíças *fpl*

whisky ['wɪskɪ] (*US, IRELAND* **whiskey**) *n* uísque *m* (*BR*), whisky *m* (*PT*)

whisper ['wɪspə*] *n* sussurro, murmúrio ♦ *vt, vi* sussurrar

whist [wɪst] (*BRIT*) *n* uíste *m* (*BR*), whist *m* (*PT*)

whistle ['wɪsl] *n* (*sound*) assobio; (*object*) apito ♦ *vt, vi* assobiar

white [waɪt] *adj* branco; (*pale*) pálido ♦ *n* branco; (*of egg*) clara; **~ coffee** *n* café *m* com leite; **~collar worker** *n* empregado/a de escritório; **~ elephant** *n* (*fig*) elefante *m* branco; **~ lie** *n* mentira inofensiva *or* social; **W~ Paper** *n* (*POL*) relatório oficial sobre determinado assunto; **~wash** *n* (*paint*) cal *f* ♦ *vt* caiar; (*fig*) encobrir

whiting ['waɪtɪŋ] *n inv* pescada

Whitsun ['wɪtsn] *n* Pentecostes *m*

whittle ['wɪtl] *vt*: **to ~ away, ~ down** reduzir gradualmente

whizz [wɪz] *vi*: **to ~ past** *or* **by** passar a toda velocidade; **~ kid** (*inf*) *n* prodígio

---

KEYWORD

who [huː] *pron* **1** (*interrogative*) quem?; **~ is it?** quem é?

2 (*relative*) que, o qual *etc*, quem; **my cousin, ~ lives in New York** meu primo que mora em Nova Iorque; **the man ~ spoke to me** o homem que falou comigo

---

whodunit [huː'dʌnɪt] (*inf*) *n* romance *m* (*or* filme *m*) policial

whole [həʊl] *adj* (*complete*) todo, inteiro; (*not broken*) intacto ♦ *n* (*all*): **the ~ of the time** o tempo todo; (*entire unit*) conjunto; **on the ~, as a ~** como um todo, no conjunto; **~foods** *n* comida integral; **~hearted** *adj* total; **~meal** (*BRIT*) *adj* integral; **~sale** *n* venda por atacado ♦ *adj* por atacado; (*destruction*) em grande escala ♦ *adv* por atacado; **~saler** *n* atacadista *m/f*; **~some** *adj* saudável, sadio; **~wheat** *adj* = **~meal**; **wholly** *adv* totalmente, completamente

---

KEYWORD

whom [huːm] *pron* **1** (*interrogative*) quem?; **to ~ did you give it?** para quem você deu isto?

2 (*relative*) que, quem; **the man ~ I saw/to ~ I spoke** o homem que eu vi/com quem eu falei

---

whooping cough ['huːpɪŋ-] *n* coqueluche *f*

whore [hɔː*] *n* (*inf: pej*) puta

KEYWORD

whose [huːz] *adj* **1** (*possessive: interrogative*): **~ book is this?**, **~ is this book?** de quem é este livro?; **I don't know ~ it is** eu não sei de quem é isto

2 (*possessive: relative*): **the man ~ son you rescued** o homem cujo filho você salvou; **the woman ~ car was stolen**

a mulher de quem o carro foi roubado
♦ *pron* de quem

---

why [waɪ] *adv* por que (*BR*), porque (*PT*); (*at end of sentence*) por quê (*BR*), porquê (*PT*)
♦ *conj* por que; that's not ~ I'm here não é por isso que estou aqui; the reason ~ a razão por que
♦ *excl* (*expressing surprise, shock, annoyance*) ora essa!; (*explaining*) bem!; ~, it's you! ora, é você!

---

wicked ['wɪkɪd] *adj* perverso; (*smile*) malicioso
wicker ['wɪkə*] *n* (trabalho de) vime *m*
♦ *adj* de vime
wicket ['wɪkɪt] *n* (*CRICKET*) arco
wide [waɪd] *adj* largo; (*area, publicity, knowledge*) amplo ♦ *adv*: to open ~ abrir totalmente; to shoot ~ atirar longe do alvo; ~-angle lens *n* lente *f* grande angular; ~-awake *adj* bem acordado; ~ly *adv* extremamente; (*travelled*) muito; (*believed, known*) ampliamente; ~n *vt* alargar; (*one's experience*) aumentar ♦ *vi* alargar-se; ~ open *adj* (*eyes*) arregalado; (*door*) escancarado; ~spread *adj* (*belief etc*) difundido, comum
widow ['wɪdəu] *n* viúva; ~ed *adj* viúvo; ~er *n* viúvo
width [wɪdθ] *n* largura
wield [wiːld] *vt* (*sword*) brandir, empunhar; (*power*) exercer
wife [waɪf] (*pl* wives) *n* mulher *f*, esposa
wig [wɪg] *n* peruca
wiggle ['wɪgl] *vt* menear, agitar
wild [waɪld] *adj* (*animal*) selvagem; (*plant*) silvestre; (*rough*) violento, furioso; (*idea*) disparatado, extravagante; (*person*) insensato; ~s *npl* (*remote area*) regiões *fpl* selvagens, terras *fpl* virgens; ~erness ['wɪldənəs] *n* ermo; ~-goose chase *n* (*fig*) busca inútil; ~life *n* animais *mpl* selvagens; ~ly *adv* (*behave*) freneticamente; (*hit, guess*) irrefletidamente; (*happy*) extremamente
wilful ['wɪlful] (*US* willful) *adj* (*person*) teimoso, voluntarioso; (*action*) deliberado, intencional

---

will [wɪl] (*vt*) (*pt, pp* ~ed) *aux vb* **1** (*forming future tense*): I ~ finish it tomorrow vou acabar isto amanhã; I ~ have finished it by tomorrow até amanhã eu terei terminado isto; ~ you do it? - yes I ~/no I won't você vai fazer isto? - sim, vou/não eu não vou
2 (*in conjectures, predictions*): he ~ come ele virá; he ~ or he'll be there by now nesta altura ele está lá; that ~ be the postman deve ser o carteiro;

this medicine ~/won't help you este remédio vai/não vai fazer efeito em você
3 (*in commands, requests, offers*): ~ you be quiet! fique quieto, por favor!; ~ you come? você vem?; ~ you help me? você pode me ajudar?; ~ you have a cup of tea? você vai querer uma xícara de chá *or* um chá?; I won't put up with it eu não vou tolerar isto
♦ *vt*: to ~ sb to do sth desejar que alguém faça algo; he ~ed himself to go on reuniu grande força de vontade para continuar
♦ *n* (*volition*) vontade *f*; (*testament*) testamento

---

willful ['wɪlful] (*US*) *adj* = wilful
willing ['wɪlɪŋ] *adj* disposto, pronto; (*enthusiastic*) entusiasmado; ~ly *adv* de bom grado, de boa vontade; ~ness *n* boa vontade *f*, disposição *f*
willow ['wɪləu] *n* salgueiro
willpower ['wɪlpauə*] *n* força de vontade
willy-nilly ['wɪlɪ'nɪlɪ] *adv* quer queira ou não
wilt [wɪlt] *vi* (*flower*) murchar; (*plant*) morrer
wily ['waɪlɪ] *adj* esperto, astuto
win [wɪn] (*pt, pp* won) *n* vitória ♦ *vt* ganhar, vencer; (*obtain*) conseguir, obter; (*support*) alcançar ♦ *vi* ganhar; ~ over *vt* conquistar; ~ round (*BRIT*) *vt* = ~ over
wince [wɪns] *vi* encolher-se, estremecer
winch [wɪntʃ] *n* guincho
wind¹ [wɪnd] *n* vento; (*MED*) gases *mpl*, flatulência; (*breath*) fôlego ♦ *vt* (*take breath away from*) deixar sem fôlego
wind² [waɪnd] (*pt, pp* wound) *vt* enrolar, bobinar; (*wrap*) envolver; (*clock, toy*) dar corda a ♦ *vi* (*road, river*) serpentear; ~ up *vt* (*clock*) dar corda em; (*debate*) rematar, concluir
windfall ['wɪndfɔːl] *n* golpe *m* de sorte
winding ['waɪndɪŋ] *adj* (*road*) sinuoso, tortuoso; (*staircase*) de caracol, em espiral
wind instrument *n* (*MUS*) instrumento de sopro
windmill ['wɪndmɪl] *n* moinho de vento
window ['wɪndəu] *n* janela; (*in shop etc*) vitrine *f* (*BR*), montra (*PT*); ~ box *n* jardineira (no peitoril da janela); ~ cleaner *n* limpador(a) *m/f* de janelas; ~ envelope *n* envelope *m* de janela; ~ ledge *n* peitoril m da janela; ~ pane *n* vidraça, vidro; ~-shopping *n*: to go ~-shopping ir ver vitrines; ~sill *n* (*inside*) peitoril *m*; (*outside*) soleira
windpipe ['wɪndpaɪp] *n* traquéia
wind power *n* energia eólica
windscreen ['wɪndskriːn] (*BRIT*) *n* pára-brisa *m*; ~ washer (*BRIT*) *n* lavador *m*

de pára-brisa; ~ **wiper** (BRIT) n limpador m de pára-brisa

windshield etc ['wɪndʃiːld] (US) n = **windscreen** etc

windswept ['wɪndswɛpt] adj varrido pelo vento

windy ['wɪndɪ] adj com muito vento, batido pelo vento; **it's** ~ está ventando (BR), faz vento (PT)

wine [waɪn] n vinho; ~ **bar** n bar m (para degustação de vinhos); ~ **cellar** n adega; ~ **glass** n cálice m (de vinho); ~ **list** n lista de vinhos; ~ **merchant** n negociante m/f de vinhos; ~ **waiter** n garção m dos vinhos

wing [wɪŋ] n asa; (of building) ala; (AUT) aleta, pára-lamas m inv; ~**s** npl (THEATRE) bastidores mpl; ~**er** n (SPORT) ponta, extremo

wink [wɪŋk] n piscadela ♦ vi piscar o olho; (light etc) piscar

winner ['wɪnə*] n vencedor(a) m/f

winning ['wɪnɪŋ] adj (team) vencedor(a); (goal) decisivo; (smile) sedutor(a); ~**s** npl ganhos mpl

winter ['wɪntə*] n inverno; ~ **sports** npl esportes mpl (BR) or desportos mpl (PT) de inverno; **wintry** adj glacial, invernal

wipe [waɪp] n: **to give sth a** ~ limpar algo com um pano ♦ vt limpar; (rub) esfregar; (erase: tape) apagar; ~ **off** vt remover esfregando; ~ **out** vt (debt) liquidar; (memory) apagar; (destroy) exterminar; ~ **up** vt limpar

wire ['waɪə*] n arame m; (ELEC) fio (elétrico); (telegram) telegrama m ♦ vt (house) instalar a rede elétrica em; (also: ~ up) conectar; (telegram) telegrafar para

wireless ['waɪəlɪs] n rádio

wiring ['waɪərɪŋ] n instalação f elétrica

wiry ['waɪərɪ] adj nervoso; (hair) grosso

wisdom ['wɪzdəm] n prudência; (of action, remark) bom-senso, sabedoria; ~ **tooth** (irreg) n dente m do siso

wise [waɪz] adj prudente; (action, remark) sensato

...wise [waɪz] suffix: **time**~ etc com relação ao tempo etc

wisecrack ['waɪzkræk] n piada

wish [wɪʃ] n desejo ♦ vt (want) querer; **best** ~**es** (on birthday etc) parabéns mpl, felicidades fpl; **with best** ~**es** (in letter) cumprimentos; **to** ~ **sb goodbye** despedir-se de alguém; **he** ~**ed me well** me desejou boa sorte; **to** ~ **to do/sb to do sth** querer fazer/que alguém faça algo; **to** ~ **for** desejar; ~**ful** adj: **it's** ~**ful thinking** é doce ilusão

wishy-washy ['wɪʃɪ'wɒʃɪ] (inf) adj (colour) indefinido; (person) sem caráter; (ideas) aguado

wisp [wɪsp] n mecha, tufo; (of smoke) fio

wistful ['wɪstful] adj melancólico

wit [wɪt] n (wittiness) presença de espírito, engenho; (intelligence: also: ~**s**) entendimento; (person) espirituoso/a

witch [wɪtʃ] n bruxa

KEYWORD

with [wɪð, wɪθ] prep **1** (accompanying, in the company of) com; **I was** ~ **him** eu estava com ele; **to stay overnight** ~ **friends** dormir na casa de amigos; **we'll take the children** ~ **us** vamos levar as crianças conosco; **I'll be** ~ **you in a minute** vou te ter um minuto; **I'm** ~ **you** (I understand) compreendo; **to be** ~ **it** (inf) estar por dentro; (aware) estar a par da situação; (: up-to-date) estar atualizado com

2 (descriptive) com, de; **a room** ~ **a view** um quarto com vista; **the man** ~ **the grey hat/blue eyes** o homem do chapéu cinza/de olhos azuis

3 (indicating manner, means, cause) com, de; ~ **tears in her eyes** com os olhos cheios de lágrimas; **to fill sth** ~ **water** encher algo de água

withdraw [wɪð'drɔː] (irreg) vt tirar, remover; (offer) retirar ♦ vi retirar-se; **to** ~ **money (from the bank)** retirar dinheiro (do banco); ~**al** n retirada; ~**al symptoms** npl síndrome f de abstinência; ~**n** adj (person) reservado, introvertido

wither ['wɪðə*] vi murchar

withhold [wɪð'həʊld] (irreg: like hold) vt (money) reter; (permission) negar; (information)

within [wɪð'ɪn] prep dentro de ♦ adv dentro; ~ **reach (of)** ao alcance (de); ~ **sight (of)** à vista (de); ~ **the week** antes do fim da semana; ~ **a mile of** a uma milha de

without [wɪð'aʊt] prep sem; ~ **anybody knowing** sem ninguém saber; **to go** ~ **sth** passar sem algo

withstand [wɪð'stænd] (irreg: like stand) vt resistir a

witness ['wɪtnɪs] n testemunha ♦ vt testemunhar, presenciar; (document) legalizar; **to bear** ~ **to sth** (fig) testemunhar algo; ~ **box** (US **witness stand**) n banco das testemunhas

witticism ['wɪtɪsɪzm] n observação f espirituosa, chiste m

witty ['wɪtɪ] adj espirituoso

wives [waɪvz] npl of **wife**

wizard ['wɪzəd] n feiticeiro, mago

wk abbr = **week**

wobble ['wɒbl] vi oscilar; (chair) balançar

woe [wəʊ] n dor f, mágoa

woke [wəʊk] pt of **wake**; ~**n** pp of **wake**

wolf [wulf] (pl **wolves**) n lobo

woman ['wʊmən] (pl **women**) n mulher f; ~ **doctor** médica; ~**ly** adj feminino

womb [wuːm] n (ANAT) matriz f, útero

women ['wɪmɪn] *npl of* **woman**

won [wʌn] *pt, pp of* **win**

wonder ['wʌndə*] *n* maravilha, prodígio; *(feeling)* espanto ♦ *vi* perguntar-se a si mesmo; **to ~ at** admirar-se de; **to ~ about** pensar sobre *or* em; **it's no ~ that** não é de admirar que; **~ful** *adj* maravilhoso; *(miraculous)* impressionante

won't [wəunt] = **will not**

woo [wuː] *vt (woman)* namorar, cortejar; *(audience)* atrair

wood [wud] *n (timber)* madeira; *(forest)* floresta, bosque *m*; **~ carving** *n (act)* escultura em madeira; *(object)* entalhe *m*; **~ed** *adj* arborizado; **~en** *adj* de madeira; *(fig)* inexpressivo; **~pecker** *n* pica-pau *m*; **~wind** *n (MUS)* instrumentos *mpl* de sopro de madeira; **~work** *n* carpintaria; **~worm** *n* carcoma, caruncho

wool [wul] *n* lã *f*; **to pull the ~ over sb's eyes** *(fig)* enganar alguém, vender a alguém gato por lebre; **~len** *adj* de lã; **~lens** *npl* artigos *mpl* de lã; **~ly** *(US ~y) adj* de lã; *(fig)* confuso

word [wəːd] *n* palavra; *(news)* notícia ♦ *vt* redigir; **in other ~s** em outras palavras, ou seja; **to break/keep one's ~** faltar à palavra/cumprir a promessa; **to have ~s with sb** discutir com alguém; **~ing** *n* fraseado; **~ processing** *n* processamento de textos; **~ processor** *n* processador *m* de textos

wore [wɔː*] *pt of* **wear**

work [wəːk] *n* trabalho; *(job)* emprego, trabalho; *(ART, LITERATURE)* obra ♦ *vi* trabalhar; *(mechanism)* funcionar; *(medicine etc)* surtir efeito, ser eficaz ♦ *vt (clay)* moldar; *(wood)* talhar; *(mine etc)* explorar; *(machine)* fazer trabalhar, manejar; *(effect, miracle)* causar; **to ~ loose** *(part)* soltar-se; *(knot)* afrouxar-se; **~ on** *vt fus* trabalhar em, dedicar-se a; *(person: influence)* tentar convencer; *(principle)* basear-se em; **~ out** *vi* dar certo, surtir efeito ♦ *vt (problem)* resolver; *(plan)* elaborar, formular; **it ~s out at £100** monta *or* soma a £100; **~able** *adj (solution)* viável; **~aholic** *n* burro de carga; **~er** *n* trabalhador(a) *m/f*, operário/a; **~ force** *n* força de trabalho; **~ing class** *n* proletariado, classe *f* operária ♦ *adj:* **~ing-class** do proletariado, da classe operária; **~ing order** *n:* **in ~ing order** em perfeito estado; **~man** *(irreg) n* operário, trabalhador *m*; **~manship** *n (skill)* habilidade *f*; **~s** *n (BRIT: factory)* fábrica, usina ♦ *npl (of clock, machine)* mecanismo; **~sheet** *n* registro das horas de trabalho; **~shop** *n* oficina; *(practical session)* aula prática; **~ station** *n* estação *f* de trabalho; **~-to-rule** *(BRIT) n* paralisação *f* de trabalho extraordinário *(forma de protesto)*

world [wəːld] *n* mundo ♦ *cpd* mundial; **to think the ~ of sb** *(fig)* ter alguém em alto conceito; **~ly** *adj* mundano; *(knowledgeable)* experiente; **~wide** *adj* mundial, universal

worm [wəːm] *n (also: earth~)* minhoca, lombriga

worn [wɔːn] *pp of* **wear** ♦ *adj* gasto; **~-out** *adj (object)* gasto; *(person)* esgotado, exausto

worry ['wʌrɪ] *n* preocupação *f* ♦ *vt* preocupar, inquietar ♦ *vi* preocupar-se, afligir-se

worse [wəːs] *adj, adv* pior ♦ *n* o pior; **a change for the ~** uma mudança para pior, uma piora; **~n** *vt, vi* piorar; **~ off** *adj* com menos dinheiro; *(fig):* **you'll be ~ off this way** assim você ficará pior que nunca

worship ['wəːʃɪp] *n* adoração *f* ♦ *vt* adorar, venerar; *(person, thing)* adorar; **Your W~** *(BRIT: to mayor)* vossa Excelência; *(: to judge)* senhor Juiz

worst [wəːst] *adj* (o/a) pior ♦ *adv* pior ♦ *n* o pior; **at ~** na pior das hipóteses

worth [wəːθ] *n* valor *m*, mérito ♦ *adj:* **to be ~** valer; **it's ~ it** vale a pena; **to be ~ one's while (to do)** valer a pena (fazer); **~less** *adj (person)* imprestável; *(thing)* inútil; **~while** *adj (activity)* que vale a pena; *(cause)* de mérito, louvável

worthy ['wəːðɪ] *adj (person)* merecedor(a), respeitável; *(motive)* justo; **~ of** digno de

KEYWORD

would [wud] *aux vb* **1** *(conditional tense):* **if you asked him, he ~ do it** se você pedisse, ele faria isto; **if you had asked him, he ~ have done it** se você tivesse pedido, ele teria feito isto

2 *(in offers, invitations, requests):* **~ you like a biscuit?** você quer um biscoito?; **~ you ask him to come in?** pode pedir a ele para entrar?; **~ you close the door, please?** quer fechar a porta por favor?

3 *(in indirect speech):* **I said I ~ do it** eu disse que eu faria isto

4 *(emphatic):* **you WOULD say that, ~n't you?** é lógico que você vai dizer isso

5 *(insistence):* **she ~n't behave** não houve feito dela se comportar

6 *(conjecture):* **it ~ have been midnight** devia ser meia-noite; **it ~ seem so** parece que sim

7 *(indicating habit):* **he ~ go on Mondays** costumava ir às segundas-feiras

would-be *adj* aspirante, que pretende ser

wouldn't ['wudnt] = **would not**

wound[1] [waund] *pt, pp of* **wind**[2]

wound[2] [wuːnd] *n* ferida ♦ *vt* ferir

wove [wəuv] *pt of* **weave**; ~**n** *pp of* **weave**

wrangle ['ræŋgl] *n* briga

wrap [ræp] *n (stole)* xale *m; (cape)* capa ♦ *vt (cover)* envolver; *(also:* ~ **up**) embrulhar; *(wind: tape etc)* amarrar; ~**per** *n* invólucro; *(BRIT: of book)* capa; ~**ping paper** *n* papel *m* de embrulho; *(fancy)* papel de presente

wrath [rɒθ] *n* cólera, ira

wreak [riːk] *vt:* **to** ~ **havoc (on)** causar estragos (em); **to** ~ **vengeance on** vingar-se em, tirar vingança de

wreath [riːθ, *pl* riːðz] *n* coroa

wreck [rɛk] *n (vehicle)* destroços *mpl; (ship)* restos *mpl* do naufrágio; *(pej: person)* ruína, caco ♦ *vt* destruir, danificar; *(fig)* arruinar, arrasar; ~**age** *n (of car, plane)* destroços *mpl; (of ship)* restos *mpl; (of building)* escombros *mpl*

wren [rɛn] *n (ZOOL)* carriça

wrench [rɛntʃ] *n (TECH)* chave *f* inglesa; *(tug)* puxão *m; (fig)* separação *f* penosa ♦ *vt* torcer com força; **to** ~ **sth from sb** arrancar algo de alguém

wrestle ['rɛsl] *vi:* **to** ~ **(with sb)** lutar (com *or* contra alguém); ~**r** *n* lutador *m;* **wrestling** *n* luta (livre)

wretched ['rɛtʃɪd] *adj* desventurado, infeliz; *(inf)* maldito

wriggle ['rɪgl] *vi (also:* ~ **about**) retorcer-se, contorcer-se

wring [rɪŋ] *(pt, pp* **wrung)** *vt (clothes, neck)* torcer; *(hands)* apertar; *(fig):* **to** ~ **sth out of sb** arrancar algo de alguém

wrinkle ['rɪŋkl] *n (on skin)* ruga; *(on paper)* prega ♦ *vt* franzir ♦ *vi* enrugar-se

wrist [rɪst] *n* pulso; ~**watch** *n* relógio *m* de pulso

writ [rɪt] *n* mandado judicial

write [raɪt] *(pt* **wrote,** *pp* **written)** *vt* escrever; *(cheque, prescription)* passar ♦ *vi* escrever; **to** ~ **to sb** escrever para alguém; ~ **down** *vt (note)* anotar; *(put on paper)* pôr no papel; ~ **off** *vt* cancelar; ~ **out** *vt* escrever por extenso; *(cheque etc)* passar; ~ **up** *vt* redigir; ~**-off** *n* perda total; ~**r** *n* escritor(a) *m/f*

writhe [raɪð] *vi* contorcer-se

writing ['raɪtɪŋ] *n* escrita; *(hand~)* caligrafia, letra; *(of author)* obra; **in** ~ por escrito

written ['rɪtn] *pp of* **write**

wrong [rɒŋ] *adj (bad)* errado, mau; *(unfair)* injusto; *(incorrect)* errado, equivocado; *(inappropriate)* impróprio ♦ *adv* mal, errado ♦ *n* injustiça ♦ *vt* ser injusto com; **you are** ~ **to do it** você se engana ao fazê-lo; **you are** ~ **about that, you've got it** ~ você está enganado sobre isso; **to be in the** ~ não ter razão; **what's** ~**?** o que é que há?; **to go** ~ *(person)* desencaminhar-se; *(plan)* dar errado; *(machine)* sofrer uma avaria; ~**ful** *adj* injusto; ~**ly** *adv* errado; ~ **side** *n*

(of cloth) avesso

wrote [rəut] *pt of* **write**

wrought [rɔːt] *adj:* ~ **iron** ferro forjado

wrung [rʌŋ] *pt, pp of* **wring**

wry [raɪ] *adj* irônico

wt. *abbr = weight*

WWW *n abbr (= World Wide Web)* WWW *f*

X

Xmas ['ɛksməs] *n abbr = Christmas*

X-ray [ɛks'reɪ] *n* radiografia ♦ *vt* radiografar, tirar uma chapa de

xylophone ['zaɪləfəun] *n* xilofone *m*

Y

yacht [jɒt] *n* iate *m;* ~**ing** *n* iatismo; ~**sman** *(irreg) n* iatista *m*

Yank [jæŋk] *(pej) n* ianque *m/f*

Yankee ['jæŋkɪ] *n =* **Yank**

yap [jæp] *vi (dog)* ganir

yard [jɑːd] *n* pátio, quintal *m; (measure)* jarda *(914 mm; 3 feet);* ~**stick** *n (fig)* critério, padrão *m*

yarn [jɑːn] *n* fio; *(tale)* longa história

yawn [jɔːn] *n* bocejo ♦ *vi* bocejar; ~**ing** *adj (gap)* enorme

yd *abbr = yard(s)*

yeah [jɛə] *(inf) adv* é

year [jɪə] *n* ano; **to be 8** ~**s old** ter 8 anos; **an eight-**~**-old child** uma criança de oito anos (de idade); ~**ly** *adj* anual ♦ *adv* anualmente

yearn [jɔːn] *vi:* **to** ~ **to do/for sth** ansiar fazer/por algo

yeast [jiːst] *n* levedura, fermento

yell [jɛl] *n* grito, berro ♦ *vi* gritar, berrar

yellow ['jɛləu] *adj* amarelo

yelp [jɛlp] *n* latido ♦ *vi* latir

yeoman ['jəumən] *(irreg) n:* **Y**~ **of the Guard** membro da guarda real

yes [jɛs] *adv, n* sim *m*

yesterday ['jɛstədɪ] *adv, n* ontem *m*

yet [jɛt] *adv* ainda ♦ *conj* porém, no entanto; **the best** ~ o melhor até agora; **as** ~ até agora, ainda

yew [juː] *n* teixo

Yiddish ['jɪdɪʃ] *n (i)*ídiche *m*

yield [jiːld] *n (AGR)* colheita; *(COMM)* rendimento ♦ *vt* produzir; *(profit)* render; *(surrender)* ceder ♦ *vi* render-se, ceder; *(US: AUT)* ceder

YMCA *n abbr (= Young Men's Christian Association) ≈* ACM *f*

yog(h)ourt ['jəugət] *n* iogurte *m*

yog(h)urt ['jəugət] *n =* **yog(h)ourt**

yoke [jəuk] *n (of oxen)* junta; *(fig)* jugo

yolk [jəuk] *n* gema (do ovo)

KEYWORD

you [juː] *pron* **1** (*subj: sg*) tu, você; (: *pl*) vós, vocês; ~ French enjoy your food vocês franceses gostam de comer; ~ and I will go nós iremos **2** (*direct object: sg*) te, o/a; (: *pl*) vos, os/as; (*indirect object: sg*) te, lhe; (: *pl*) vos, lhes; I know ~ eu lhe conheço; I gave it to ~ dei isto para você **3** (*stressed*) você; I told YOU to do it eu disse para você fazer isto **4** (*after prep, in comparisons: sg*) ti, você; (: *pl*) vós, vocês; (*polite form: sg*) o senhor/a senhora; (: *pl*) os senhores/as senhoras; **it's for** ~ é para você; **with** ~ contigo, com você; convosco, com vocês; com o senhor *etc* **5** (*impers: one*): ~ never know nunca se sabe; **apples do** ~ **good** as maçãs fazem bem à saúde

you'd [juːd] = **you had; you would**
you'll [juːl] = **you will; you shall**
young [jʌŋ] *adj* jovem ♦ *npl* (*of animal*) filhotes *mpl*, crias *fpl*; (*people*): **the** ~ a juventude, os jovens; **~er** *adj* mais novo; **~ster** *n* jovem *m/f*, moço/a
your [jɔː*] *adj* teu/tua, seu/sua; (*pl*) vosso, seu/sua; (*formal*) do senhor/da senhora; *see also* **my**
you're [juə*] = **you are**
yours [jɔːz] *pron* teu/tua, seu/sua; (*pl*) vosso, seu/sua; (*formal*) do senhor/da senhora; ~ **sincerely** *or* **faithfully** atenciosamente; *see also* **mine¹**
yourself [jɔːˈself] *pron* (*emphatic*) tu mesmo, você mesmo; (*object, reflexive*) te, se; (*after prep*) ti mesmo, si mesmo; (*formal*) o senhor mesmo/a senhora mesma; **yourselves** *pl, pron* vós mesmos, vocês mesmos; vos, se; vós mesmos, vóces mesmos; os senhores mesmos/as senhoras mesmas; *see also* **oneself**
youth [juːθ, *pl* juːðz] *n* mocidade *f*, ju-

ventude *f*; (*young man*) jovem *m*; ~ **club** *n* associação *f* de juventude; **~ful** *adj* juvenil; ~ **hostel** *n* albergue *m* da juventude
you've [juːv] = **you have**
YTS (*BRIT*) *n abbr* (= *Youth Training Scheme*) *programa de ensino profissionalizante*
Yugoslav [ˈjuːgəʊslɑːv] *adj, n* iugoslavo/a
Yugoslavia [juːgəʊˈslɑːvɪə] *n* Iugoslávia
yuppie [ˈjʌpɪ] (*inf*) *adj, n* yuppie *m/f*
YWCA *n abbr* (= *Young Women's Christian Association*) ≈ ACM *f*

Z

Zambia [ˈzæmbɪə] *n* Zâmbia
zany [ˈzeɪnɪ] *adj* tolo, bobo
zap [zæp] *vt* (*COMPUT*) apagar
zeal [ziːl] *n* entusiasmo; (*religious*) fervor *m*; **~ous** *adj* zeloso, entusiasta
zebra [ˈziːbrə] *n* zebra; ~ **crossing** (*BRIT*) *n* faixa (para pedestres) (*BR*), passadeira (*PT*)
zero [ˈzɪərəʊ] *n* zero
zest [zest] *n* vivacidade *f*, entusiasmo; (*of lemon etc*) zesto
zigzag [ˈzɪgzæg] *n* ziguezague *m* ♦ *vi* ziguezaguear
Zimbabwe [zɪmˈbɑːbwɪ] *n* Zimbábue *m*
zinc [zɪŋk] *n* zinco
zip [zɪp] *n* (*also:* ~ **fastener**) fecho ecler (*BR*) *or* éclair (*PT*) ♦ *vt* (*also:* ~ **up**) fechar o fecho ecler de, subir o fecho ecler de; ~ **code** (*US*) *n* código postal; **~per** (*US*) *n* = **zip**
zodiac [ˈzəʊdɪæk] *n* zodíaco
zombie [ˈzɒmbɪ] *n* (*fig*): **like a** ~ como um zumbi
zone [zəʊn] *n* zona
zoo [zuː] *n* (jardim *m*) zoológico
zoology [zuːˈɒlədʒɪ] *n* zoologia
zoom [zuːm] *vi*: **to** ~ **past** passar zunindo; ~ **lens** *n* zoom *m*, zum *m*
zucchini [zuːˈkiːnɪ] (*US*) *n(pl)* abobrinha

PORTUGUESE VERB FORMS

1 Gerund. **2** Imperative. **3** Present. **4** Imperfect. **5** Preterite. **6** Future. **7** Present subjunctive. **8** Imperfect subjunctive. **9** Future subjunctive. **10** Past participle. **11** Pluperfect. **12** Personal infinitive.

Etc indicates that the irregular root is used for all persons of the tense, e.g. **ouvir 7** ouça, ouças, ouça, ouçamos, ouçais, ouçam.

abrir 10 aberto
acudir 2 acode **3** acudo, acodes, acode, acodem
aderir 3 adiro **7** adira
advertir 3 advirto **7** advirta *etc*
agir 3 ajo **7** aja *etc*
agradecer 3 agradeço **7** agradeça *etc*
agredir 2 agride **3** agrido, agrides, agride, agridem **7** agrida *etc*
AMAR 1 amando **2** ama, amai **3** amo, amas, ama, amamos, amais, amam **4** amava, amavas, amava, amávamos, amáveis, amavam **5** amei, amaste, amou, amamos (*PT*: amá-), amastes, amaram **6** amarei, amarás, amará, amaremos, amareis, amarão **7** ame, ames, ame, amemos, ameis, amem **8** amasse, amasses, amasse, amássemos, amásseis, amassem **9** amar, amares, amar, ámarmos, amardes, amarem **10** amado **11** amara, amaras, amara, amáramos, amáreis, amaram **12** amar, amares, amar, amarmos, amardes, amarem
ansiar 2 anseia **3** anseio, anseias, anseia, anseiam **7** anseie *etc*
apreçar 7 aprece *etc*
arrancar 7 arranque *etc*
arruinar 2 arruína **3** arruíno, arruínas, arruína, arruínam **7** arruíne, arruínes, arruíne, arruí-nem
aspergir 3 aspirjo **7** aspirja *etc*
atribuir 3 atribuo, atribuis, atribui, atribuímos, atribuís, atribuem
averiguar 7 averigúe, avergúes, averigúe, averigúem
boiar 2 bóia, bóias, bóia, bóiam **7** bóie, bóies, bóie, bóiem
bulir 2 bole **3** bulo, boles, bole, bolem
caber 3 caibo **5** coube *etc* **7** caiba *etc* **8** coubesse *etc* **9** couber *etc*
cair 2 cai **3** caio, cais, cai, caímos, cais, caem **4** caía *etc* **5** caí, caíste **7** caia *etc* **8** caísse *etc*
cobrir 3 cubro **7** cubra *etc* **10** coberto
colorir 3 coluro **7** colura *etc*
compelir 3 compilo **7** compila *etc*
crer 2 crê **3** creio, crês, crê, cremos, credes, crêem **5** cri, creste, creu, cremos, crestes, creram **7** creia *etc*
cuspir 2 cospe **3** cuspo, cospes, cospe, cospem
dar 2 dá **3** dou, dás, dá, damos, dais, dão **5** dei, deste, deu, demos, destes, deram **7** dê, dês, dê, demos, deis, dêem **8** desse *etc* **9** der *etc* **11** dera *etc*
deduzir 2 deduz **3** deduzo, deduzes, deduz
denegrir 2 denigre **3** denigro, denigres, denigre, denigrem **7** denigra *etc*
despir 3 dispo **7** dispa *etc*

223

dizer 2 diz (dize) **3** digo, dizes, diz, dizemos, dizeis, dizem **5** disse *etc* **6** direi *etc* **7** diga *etc* **8** dissesse *etc* **9** disser *etc* **10** dito

doer 2 dói **3** dôo (*BR*), doo (*PT*), dóis, dói

dormir 3 durmo **7** durma *etc*

escrever 10 escrito

ESTAR 2 está **3** estou, estás, está, estamos, estais, estão **4** estava *etc* **5** estive, estiveste, esteve, estivemos, estivestes, estiveram **7** esteja *etc* **8** estivesse *etc* **9** estiver *etc* **11** estivera *etc*

extorquir 3 exturco **7** exturca *etc*

FAZER 3 faço **5** fiz, fizeste, fez, fizemos, fizestes, fizeram **6** farei *etc* **7** faça *etc* **8** fizesse *etc* **9** fizer *etc* **10** feito **11** fizera *etc*

ferir 3 firo **7** fira *etc*

fluir 3 fluo, fluis, flui, fluímos, fluís, fluem

fugir 2 foge **3** fujo, foges, foge, fogem, fogem **7** fuja *etc*

ganhar 10 ganho

gastar 10 gasto

gerir 3 giro **7** gira *etc*

haver 2 há **3** hei, hás, há, havemos, haveis, hão **4** havia *etc* **5** houve, houveste, houve, houvemos, houvestes, houveram **7** haja *etc* **8** houvesse *etc* **9** houver *etc* **11** houvera *etc*

ir 1 indo **2** vai **3** vou, vais, vai, vamos, ides, vão **4** ia *etc* **5** fui, foste, foi, fomos, fostes, foram **7** vá, vás, vá, vamos, vades, vão **8** fosse, fosses, fosse, fôssemos, fôsseis, fossem **9** for *etc* **10** ido **11** fora *etc*

ler 2 lê **3** leio, lês, lê, lemos, ledes, lêem **5** li, leste, leu, lemos, lestes, leram **7** leia *etc*

medir 3 meço **7** meça *etc*

mentir 3 minto **7** minta *etc*

ouvir 3 ouço **7** ouça *etc*

pagar 10 pago

parar 2 pára **3** paro, paras, pára

parir 3 pairo **7** paira *etc*

pecar 7 peque *etc*

pedir 3 peço **7** peça *etc*

perder 3 perco **7** perca *etc*

poder 3 posso **5** pude, pudeste, pôde, pudemos, pudestes, puderam **7** possa *etc* **8** pudesse *etc* **9** puder *etc* **11** pudera *etc*

polir 2 pule **3** pulo, pules, pule, pulem **7** pula *etc*

pôr 1 pondo **2** põe **3** ponho, pões, põe, pomos, pondes, põem **4** punha *etc* **5** pus, puseste, pôs, pusemos, pusestes, puseram **6** porei *etc* **7** ponha *etc* **8** pusesse *etc* **9** puser *etc* **10** posto **11** pusera *etc*

preferir 3 prefiro **7** prefire *etc*

prevenir 2 previne **3** previno, prevines, previne, previnem **7** previna *etc*

prover 2 provê **3** provejo, provês, provê, provemos, provedes, provêem **5** provi, proveste, proveu, provemos, provestes, proveram **7** proveja *etc* **8** provesse *etc* **9** prover *etc*

querer 3 quero, queres, quer **5** quis, quiseste, quis, quisemos, quisestes, quiseram **7** queira *etc* **8** quisesse *etc* **9** quiser *etc* **11** quisera *etc*

refletir 3 reflito **7** reflita *etc*

repetir 3 repito **7** repita *etc*

requerer 3 requeiro, requeres, requer **7** requeira *etc*

reunir 2 reúne **3** reúno, reúnes, reúne, reúnem **7** reúna *etc*

rir 2 ri **3** rio, ris, ri, rimos, rides, riem **5** ri, riste, riu, rimos, ristes, riram **7** ria *etc*

saber 3 sei, sabes, sabe, sabemos, sabeis, sabem **5** soube, soubeste, soube, soubemos, soubestes, souberam **7** saiba *etc* **8** soubesse *etc* **9** souber *etc* **11** soubera *etc*

seguir 3 sigo **7** siga *etc*

sentir 3 sinto **7** sinta *etc*

ser 2 sê **3** sou, és, é, somos, sois, são **4** era *etc* **5** fui, foste, foi, fomos, fostes, foram **7** seja *etc* **8** fosse *etc* **9** for *etc* **11** fora *etc*

servir 3 sirvo **7** sirva *etc*

subir 2 sobe **3** subo, sobes, sobe, sobem

suster 2 sustém **3** sustenho, sustens, sustém, sustendes, sustêm **5** sustive, sustiveste, susteve, sustivemos, sustivestes, sustiveram **7** sustenha *etc*

ter 2 tem **3** tenho, tens, tem, temos, tendes, têm **4** tinha *etc* **5** tive, tiveste, teve, tivemos, tivestes, tiveram **6** terei *etc* **7** tenha *etc* **8** tivesse *etc* **9** tiver *etc* **11** tivera *etc*

torcer 3 torço **7** torça *etc*

tossir 3 tusso **7** tussa *etc*

trair 2 trai **3** traio, trais, trai, traímos, traís, traem **7** traia *etc*

trazer 2 (traze) traz **3** trago, trazes, traz **5** trouxe, trouxeste, trouxe, trouxemos, trouxestes, trouxeram **6** trarei *etc* **7** traga *etc* **8** trouxesse *etc* **9** trouxer *etc* **11** trouxera *etc*

UNIR 1 unindo **2** une, uni **3** uno, unes, une, unimos, unis, unem **4** unia, unias, unia, uníamos, uníeis, uniam **5** uni, uniste, uniu, unimos, unistes,

uniram **6** unirei, unirás, unirá, uniremos, unireis, unirão **7** una, unas, una, unamos, unais, unam **8** unisse, unisses, unisse, uníssemos, unísseis, unissem **9** unir, unires, unir, unirmos, unirdes, unirem **10** unido **11** unira, uniras, unira, uníramos, uníreis, uniram **12** unir, unires, unir, unirmos, unirdes, unirem

valer 3 valho **7** valha *etc*

ver 2 vê **3** vejo, vês, vê, vemos, vedes, vêem **4** via *etc* **5** vi, viste, viu, vimos, vistes, viram **7** veja *etc* **8** visse *etc* **9** vir *etc* **10** visto **11** vira

vir 1 vindo **2** vem **3** venho, vens, vem, vimos, vindes, vêm **4** vinha *etc* **5** vim, vieste, veio, viemos, viestes, vieram **7** venha *etc* **8** viesse *etc* **9** vier *etc* **10** vindo **11** viera *etc*

VIVER 1 vivendo **2** vive, vivei **3** vivo, vives, vive, vivemos, viveis, vivem **4** vivia, vivias, vivia, vivíamos, vivíeis, viviam **5** vivi, viveste, viveu, vivemos, vivestes, viveram **6** viverei, viverás, viverá, viveremos, vivereis, viverão **7** viva, vivas, viva, vivamos, vivais, vivam **8** vivesse, vivesses, vivesse, vivêssemos, vivêsseis, vivessem **9** vi ver, viveres, viver, vivermos, viverdes, viverem **10** vivido **11** vivera, viveras, vivera, vivêramos, vivêreis, viveram **12** viver, viveres, viver, vivermos, viverdes, viverem

VERBOS INGLESES

present	pt	pp	present	pt	pp
arise	arose	arisen	feed	fed	fed
awake	awoke	awaked	feel	felt	felt
be (am, is, are, being)	was, were	been	fight	fought	fought
			find	found	found
bear	bore	born(e)	flee	fled	fled
beat	beat	beaten	fling	flung	flung
become	became	become	fly (flies)	flew	flown
befall	befell	befallen	forbid	forbade	forbidden
begin	began	begun	forecast	forecast	forecast
behold	beheld	beheld	forego	forewent	foregone
bend	bent	bent	foresee	foresaw	foreseen
beseech	besought	besought	foretell	foretold	foretold
beset	beset	beset	forget	forgot	forgotten
bet	bet, betted	bet, betted	forgive	forgave	forgiven
bid	bid, bade	bid, bidden	forsake	forsook	forsaken
bind	bound	bound	freeze	froze	frozen
bite	bit	bitten	get	got	got, (US) gotten
bleed	bled	bled			
blow	blew	blown	give	gave	given
break	broke	broken	go (goes)	went	gone
breed	bred	bred	grind	ground	ground
bring	brought	brought	grow	grew	grown
build	built	built	hang	hung, hanged	hung, hanged
burn	burnt, burned	burnt, burned	have (has; having)	had	had
burst	burst	burst	.		
buy	bought	bought	hear	heard	heard
can	could	(been able)	hide	hid	hidden
cast	cast	cast	hit	hit	hit
catch	caught	caught	hold	held	held
choose	chose	chosen	hurt	hurt	hurt
cling	clung	clung	keep	kept	kept
come	came	come	kneel	knelt, kneeled	knelt, kneeled
cost	cost	cost			
creep	crept	crept	know	knew	known
cut	cut	cut	lay	laid	laid
deal	dealt	dealt	lead	led	led
dig	dug	dug	lean	leant, leaned	leant, leaned
do (3rd person: he/she/ it/does)	did	done	leap	leapt, leaped	leapt, leaped
			learn	learnt, learned	learnt, learned
draw	drew	drawn	leave	left	left
dream	dreamed, dreamt	dreamed, dreamt	lend	lent	lent
drink	drank	drunk	let	let	let
drive	drove	driven	lie	lay	lain
dwell	dwelt	dwelt	light	lit, lighted	lit, lighted
eat	ate	eaten	lose	lost	lost
fall	fell	fallen	make	made	made

present	pt	pp	present	pt	pp
may	might	—	spell	spelt,	spelt,
mean	meant	meant		spelled	spelled
meet	met	met	spend	spent	spent
mistake	mistook	mistaken	spill	spilt,	spilt,
mow	mowed	mown,		spilled	spilled
		mowed	spin	spun	spun
must	(had to)	(had to)	spit	spat	spat
pay	paid	paid	split	split	split
put	put	put	spoil	spoiled,	spoiled,
quit	quit,	quit,		spoilt	spoilt
	quitted	quitted	spread	spread	spread
read	read	read	spring	sprang	sprung
rend	rent	rent	stand	stood	stood
rid	rid	rid	steal	stole	stolen
ride	rode	ridden	stick	stuck	stuck
ring	rang	rung	sting	stung	stung
rise	rose	risen	stink	stank	stunk
run	ran	run	stride	strode	stridden
saw	sawed	sawn	strike	struck	struck,
say	said	said			stricken
see	saw	seen	strive	strove	striven
seek	sought	sought	swear	swore	sworn
sell	sold	sold	sweep	swept	swept
send	sent	sent	swell	swelled	swollen,
set	set	set			swelled
shake	shook	shaken	swim	swam	swum
shall	should	—	swing	swung	swung
shear	sheared	shorn,	take	took	taken
		sheared	teach	taught	taught
shed	shed	shed	tear	tore	torn
shine	shone	shone	tell	told	told
shoot	shot	shot	think	thought	thought
show	showed	shown	throw	threw	thrown
shrink	shrank	shrunk	thrust	thrust	thrust
shut	shut	shut	tread	trod	trodden
sing	sang	sung	wake	woke,	woken,
sink	sank	sunk		waked	waked
sit	sat	sat	waylay	waylaid	waylaid
slay	slew	slain	wear	wore	worn
sleep	slept	slept	weave	wove,	woven,
slide	slid	slid		weaved	weaved
sling	slung	slung	wed	wedded,	wedded,
slit	slit	slit		wed	wed
smell	smelled,	smelled,	weep	wept	wept
	smelt	smelt	win	won	won
sow	sowed	sown,	wind	wound	wound
		sowed	withdraw	withdrew	withdrawn
speak	spoke	spoken	withhold	withheld	withheld
speed	sped,	sped,	withstand	withstood	withstood
	speeded	speeded	wring	wrung	wrung
			write	wrote	written

NÚMEROS

NUMBERS

um (uma)*	1	one
dois (duas)*	2	two
três	3	three
quatro	4	four
cinco	5	five
seis	6	six
sete	7	seven
oito	8	eight
nove	9	nine
dez	10	ten
onze	11	eleven
doze	12	twelve
treze	13	thirteen
catorze	14	fourteen
quinze	15	fifteen
dezesseis (BR), dezasseis (PT)	16	sixteen
dezessete (BR), dezassete (PT)	17	seventeen
dezoito	18	eighteen
dezenove (BR), dezanove (PT)	19	nineteen
vinte	20	twenty
vinte e um (uma)*	21	twenty-one
trinta	30	thirty
quarenta	40	forty
cinqüenta (BR), cinquenta (PT)	50	fifty
sessenta	60	sixty
setenta	70	seventy
oitenta	80	eighty
noventa	90	ninety
cem (cento)**	100	a hundred
cento e um (uma)*	101	a hundred and one
duzentos/as*	200	two hundred
trezentos/as*	300	three hundred
quinhentos/as*	500	five hundred
mil	1 000	a thousand
un milhão	1 000 000	a million

* "um" etc, "dois" etc and the hundreds (duzentos etc) agree in gender with their noun: trinta e uma pessoas. NB: 2 000 is **duas** mil before a feminine noun.

** "cem" is used when not followed by a lower number: cem mil, cem mulheres etc; "cento e" is used when a lower number follows: cento e vinte dias.

NÚMEROS

primeiro/a, 1º/1ª	
segundo/a, 2º/2ª	
terceiro/a, 3º/3ª	
quarto/a, 4º/4ª	
quinto/a	
sexto/a	
sétimo/a	
oitavo/a	
nono/a	
décimo/a	
décimo primeiro/a	
vigésimo/a	
trigésimo/a	
quadragésimo/a	
qüinquagésimo/a (*BR*), quinquagésimo/a (*PT*)	
sexagésimo/a	
setuagésimo/a (*BR*), septuagésimo/a (*PT*)	
octagésimo/a	
nonagésimo/a	
centésimo/a	
milésimo/a	

NUMBERS

first, 1st
second, 2nd
third, 3rd
fourth, 4th
fifth
sixth
seventh
eighth
ninth
tenth
eleventh
twentieth
thirtieth
fortieth
fiftieth

sixtieth
seventieth

eightieth
ninetieth
hundredth
thousandth

As Frações etc

um meio
um terço
dois terços
um quarto
um quinto
zero vírgula cinco, 0,5
três vírgula quatro, 3,4
dez por cento
cem por cento

Fractions etc

a half
a third
two thirds
a quarter
a fifth
(nought) point five, 0.5
three point four, 3.4
ten per cent
a hundred per cent

Exemplos

ele vai chegar no dia 7 (de maio)
ele mora no número dez
está *or* é no capítulo sete
ele mora no sétimo (andar)
ele chegou no sétimo (lugar)
uma parte de um sétimo
escala um para vinte e cinco mil

Examples

he's arriving on the 7th (of May)
he lives at number 10
it's in chapter 7
he lives on the 7th floor
he came in 7th
a share of one seventh
scale one to twenty-five thousand

AS HORAS

que horas são?	*what time is it?*
é ... *(midnight, noon, one o'clock)*	it's ...
são ... *(other times)*	
meia-noite	midnight, twelve p.m.
uma hora (da madrugada) (BR), uma hora (da noite) (PT)	one o'clock (in the morning), one (a.m.)
uma e dez	ten past one
uma e quinze (BR), uma e um quarto (PT)	a quarter past one, one fifteen
uma e meia	half past one, one thirty
quinze para as duas (BR), duas menos um quarto (PT)	a quarter to two, one forty-five
dez para as duas (BR), duas menos um quarto (PT)	ten to two, one fifty
meio-dia	twelve o'clock, midday, noon
uma (hora) (da tarde), treze horas	one o'clock (in the afternoon), one p.m.
seis (horas) (da tarde), dezoito horas	six o'clock (in the evening), six p.m.
dez e meia (da noite *or* da manhã), vinte e duas horas e trinta	half past ten (at night), ten thirty (p.m.)

THE TIME

a que horas?	*at what time?*
à uma hora	at one
às duas e quinze (BR), às duas e um quarto (PT)	at a quarter past two, at two fifteen
às três e pouco	just after three (o'clock)
por volta das quatro e meia	at about half past four
às quatro em ponto	at four sharp
das seis às oito	from six to eight
são quase nove horas	it's nearly nine o'clock
em vinte minutos	in twenty minutes
há quinze minutos	fifteen minutes ago

DATAS

DATES

The days of the week and the months start with a capital letter in Portugal and a small letter in Brazil.

hoje	today
todo dia	every day
ontem	yesterday
hoje de manhã	this morning
amanhã à noite	tomorrow night
anteontem à noite	the night before last
anteontem	the day before yesterday
noite passada/ontem à noite	last night
há dois dias/seis anos atrás	two days/six years ago
amanhã à tarde	tomorrow afternoon
depois de amanhã	the day after tomorrow
toda quatra-feira, na quarta	every Wednesday, on Wednesday
ele vai às quartas	he goes on Wednesdays
"Fecha às sextas"	"closed on Fridays"
de segunda a sexta-feira	from Monday to Friday
até quinta-feira	by Thursday
um sábado em março	one Saturday in March
daqui a uma semana	in a week's time
na outra terça	a week next/on Tuesday/Tuesday week
no domingo retrasado	a week last Sunday
nesta/na próxima/na última semana	this/next/last week
em duas semanas *ou* em una quinzena	in two weeks *or* a fortnight
duas semanas na segunda-feira	two weeks on Monday
na primeira/última sexta-feira do mês	the first/last Friday of the month
mês que vem	next month
ano passado	last year
o primeiro dia de janeiro, primeiro de janeiro	the 1st of January, January 1st
o segundo dia de maio, dois de maio	the 2nd of May, May 2nd
eu nasci em 1967	I was born in 1967
o aniversário dele é no dia cinco de junho	his birthday is on June 5th (*BRIT*) *or* 5th June (*US*)
no dia 18 de agosto de 1992	on 18th August (*BRIT*) *or* August 18th
em 89	in '89
a primavera de 87	in the Spring of '87
do dia 19 até o dia três	from the 19th to the 3rd
qual é a data?/que dia é hoje?	what's the date?, what date is it today?
a data de hoje é 28, hoje é 28	today's date is the 28th, today is the 28th
1965 – mil e novecentos e sessenta e cinco	1965 – nineteen (hundred and) sixty-five
exatamente seis anos atrás	6 years to the day
no fim do mês	at the end of the month
em fim do mês	at the month end (*ACCOUNTS*)
semana que acaba em 30/7	week ending 30/7
diariamente/semanalmente/mensalmente	daily/weekly/monthly
anualmente	annually
duaz vezes por semana/mês/ano	twice a week/month/year
bimensalmente	bi-monthly
no ano 2006	in the year 2006
4 a.C.	4 B.C., B.C. 4
70 d.C.	70 A.D., A.D. 70
no século XIII	in the 13th century
nos *ou* durante os anos 30	in *or* during the 1930s
em 1940 e poucos	in 1940 something

CABECALHO DE CARTAS

HEADING OF LETTERS

nove de julho de 1993	9th July 1993 or 9 July 1993
(veja também o texto principal do dicionário)	(see also the main text of the dictionary)